Venice

Fragile City

Margaret Plant

Venice
Fragile City

1797–1997

Yale University Press
New Haven and London

Designed by Gillian Malpass

Printed in China

Library of Congress Cataloging-in-Publication Data

Plant, Margaret.
 Venice : fragile city 1797-1997 / Margaret Plant.
   p. cm.
Includes bibliographical references and index.
 1. Architecture–Italy–Venice. 2. Venice (Italy)–Civilization.
3. Venice (Italy)–History. I. Title.
 NA1121.V4 P59 2002
 945'.31–dc21

                                    2002014452

A catalogue record for this book is available from
The British Library

Frontispiece   Giorgio Lotti, 'Basilica di San Marco in Acqua Alta'
(detail), from *Venice is Dying*, 1970.

Endpapers   Francesco Guardi, *Grey Lagoon* (detail),
Milan, Museo Poldi Pezzoli.

Contents

Acknowledgements

The initial research, made possible by a grant from the Australian Research Council was crucial to the gestation of this book. The work was begun in the Department of Visual Arts, Monash University, Melbourne. I thank my colleagues for their support: John Gregory, Conrad Hamann, Leigh Astbury and Ann Marsh; and for facilitating visual material: Jennie Durran, Kenneth Pleban and Terry Bourke. For interest sustained during Monash years and after, I am particularly indebted to Marion Wells. I was aided by students in my course 'The Idea of Venice'. Their interest and their concern for the fate of the city was of no little importance in prompting the publication of articles that brought our focus on historic Venice into the nineteenth and twentieth centuries. I thank *Transition*, and the then editor, Harriet Edquist, and *Art + Text* for prompting me to write on the issues that were later to contribute to this book.

For help in the early stages of the project I am grateful to Professor William Kent, Professor Julian Gardner, Louise Sweetland, then of Oxford University Press, Melbourne, Professor Jaynie Anderson and Emeritus Professor Bernard Smith.

There were two periods in Venice, before this book was contemplated, that were guided by Professor Bernard Hickey, then at the University of Ca' Foscari. I thank him for his generosity in so many ways, not least for his reading of the text in draft stages.

I am indebted to the research assistance of Andrew Hopkins and Lutz Presser. In Venice, I thank Sally Spector and Gianfranco Tosi for their invaluable contribution over some years. In Venice, I thank Professor Donatella Calabi, and the Rossi family, especially Marta. Claudio Ambrosini broadened my knowledge of contemporary Venetian music. I thank Margaret McGuire in Melbourne for her critical reading, and Susan Haskins in London. I thank also Pat Simons and Deborah Howard.

I am indebted to Hugh Honour for an early reading that corrected far more than my knowledge of Canova, and to Jeffrey Smart for his help, and for his Phidian encouragement that dates back to at least 1950.

The libraries I have used in person and, so often, via the internet, have made this study possible. In Melbourne, the Monash University library, and the dedication and interest of the librarians responsible for interlibrary loans, particularly Claudia De Salvo; the collection of the State Library of Victoria, with its invaluable holdings of nineteenth century material; the libraries of the University of Melbourne and La Trobe University (with an exemplary collection of more recent Italian material) have enabled my study to progress in my home town.

The British Library has been a focal point for my research over some years and I thank that institution for its unfailing courtesy to its 'readers'. The libraries in Venice to which I am indebted include the Biblioteca Marciana, the library of the Fondazione Querini Stampalia, the library of the IUAV, and the Archive library of the Biennale d'Arte. I have savoured my hours in the perfect setting of the library of the Fondazione Giorgio Cini in range of the bells of San Giorgio Maggiore, and I thank those unassuming librarians. I acknowledge the help of the Consorzio Venezia Nuova and the Istituto Veneto Accademia di Scienze, Lettere ed Arti. I am indebted to the Videoteca Pasinetti for its courtesy in screening films for me. In the difficult task of accessing certain films, I acknowledge the British Film Institute and the Österreichisches Filmarchiv, Vienna.

Gillian Malpass of Yale University Press has been supportive through the very many years of gestation and publication. During the process of publication, I was aided by Sandy Chapman, Celia Jones and Elain McAlpine.

I owe a particular debt to Dr Ruth Zubans for her meticulous readings and her linguistic skills. Udo Sellbach patiently read many of the German texts with me. I remember, with sadness, the late Michael Lloyd of the National Gallery of Australia for the stimulus of his J. M. W. Turner exhibition. Friends became Venice-watchers as well as providers of sustenance, mental and physical: I thank Alexandra Alderson, Bernice Murphy, Leon Paroissien, Peter Clarke, Colleen Morris, Jane Shepherd, Andy and the Burke family of Winter Street, the Plant family and the original staff of the Arts Bookshop in Armadale – in particular Elly Fink, Sandro Beggio, Nancy Underhill, Robert Owen, Lyndal Jones, Narelle Jubelin and Susan Norrie for various speculations on the Venice question. Juliana Engberg has been supportive over many years.

This study is indebted in many ways to the late John Hueston. In Italy and in London, for unbounded hospitality and support, I thank Hardy Jones, and for many special voyagings, over many years, I thank Brian Thompson.

Introduction

Most histories of Venice end where this one begins: with the Republic's fall after its defeat by Napoleon in 1797. After almost fourteen centuries it was a humiliating termination, as the Republic of the Serenissima had been independent since its foundation in 421 AD. There seemed to be no recovery: run-down, impoverished in trade, it passed to Austria in 1798, to France again in 1806 and to Austria again in 1814. Then, with a brief and brave interregnum in 1848–9, it remained under imperial Austrian rule until united with Italy in 1866. Yet Venice survives today as one of the great historic cities of the past. However fragile, it also represents a triumph of the present, and it still offers a spectacle of time and place that feeds the imagination.

This study attempts a wide-ranging cultural history of the anomalous creation of a modern city that has kept its relevance, and even enhanced it. The focus is upon the changes that have occurred since the late eighteenth century, but in particular from 12 May 1797, when the Republic ended, to 12 May 1997, when an occupation of the Campanile of San Marco took place with the intention of restoring the Republic.

Venice is a reference point for many urban histories because so much of its built fabric has remained. As a city raised up in water, it has a unique transit system lauded by Le Corbusier. We are so used to the sign of the gondola as the virtual emblem of Venice that its extraordinary survival is no longer questioned: but that, too, has a recent history. There have been attempts to bring trains, carriages and cars into the heart of the city. The complex of buildings that constitutes the Piazza San Marco – central as a symbol, stunning as a space and community meeting point – is regularly cited in the literature on town planning. Taking a cue from the pioneering work of Henri Lefebvre in *The Production of Space*, Venice may be approached as 'a space just as highly expressive and significant, just as unique and unified as a painting or a sculpture'. At the same time, and like so many, Lefebvre believes that the moment of Venice has passed; he has missed the continuing vitality of the very exemplum he so tellingly describes.[1]

Over the past two hundred years Venice has altered significantly, both at its centre and at its margins. From the coming of Napoleon in 1797, changes to the buildings in the Piazza San Marco have altered that precious space in a way that can be little understood if the focus stays with the Republic. Important buildings may present the face of the past to the casual visitor, but in many ways they are facsimiles, or heavily face-lifted. Looking at the Campanile of San Marco, few may realise that it collapsed in 1902 and was rebuilt faithfully, despite the opposition of those who thought it should be in modern style. The capitals of the Palazzo Ducale and the famed golden horses on the porch of the church of San Marco are copies. The opera house, La Fenice, burned for the second time in 1996, is to be reconstructed as a facsimile: as it was – *com'era*. Yet areas of Venice are in fact new creations: the public gardens – the Giardini Pubblici – at one end of the main island represent one such area, built on the sites of churches demolished after the advent of Napoleon, and now furnished at the eastern end with foreign pavilions constructed from the beginning of the twentieth century in honour of the Biennale d'Arte. The island cemetery of San Michele, now full and being extended, seems an inevitable and long-standing part of Venice's island culture, but it has existed only since 1812.

The Lido is an entirely modern creation. At the end of the eighteenth century it was a deserted sandbar, a Jewish cemetery and the site of the marble Murazzi, the sea wall at Pellestrina. In the early nineteenth century Byron rode his horses there, and until 1866 it was a fortress area for the French and the Austrians. With the advent of sea bathing the Lido became one of the most sophisticated pleasure grounds in Europe, with two grand hotels. The Hotel des Bains had been open only a few years when Thomas Mann visited in 1911 and made it the site for the death of Gustav von Aschenbach.

There have, in fact, been many changes to the outline of the islands: infills, new *fondamente*, canals covered over or filled in, islands joined, new islands created. A momentous change occurred in the mid-nineteenth century with the joining of the city to the mainland. When the rail bridge opened in 1846 after years of gestation, Venice's fabled maritime isolation ended. Soon after, the Rialto Bridge was challenged as the single crossing point over the Grand Canal. A bridge in cast iron was built at the Accademia, and another at the new railway station, in front of the church of the Scalzi. Both were demolished and rebuilt in traditional style, in tune with public opinion, in the 1930s. That forceful public opinion, resistance – or inertia – in the face of the new, is a theme of this study. It comes from within Venice itself, but has been amply endorsed by foreigners who would have Venice remain forever the same.

The most notable change in the twentieth century was the development of the port of Marghera on the mainland, established at the end of the First World War on the edge of the lagoon. The creation of this industrial site was seen as the way to preserve Venice by restoring her economy and her maritime leadership, by removing industry from the historic islands. It was hoped that improved conditions for both industry and housing would result, relieving overcrowding and insanitary conditions in the *centro storico*. Together with Mestre, Marghera has developed as an unattractive industrial city. Nevertheless, modern facilities have drawn away much of the population of old Venice. At the beginning of the twenty-first century Venice negotiates with difficulty its relationship with the larger and richer region of the Veneto.

The controversy that now attends Marghera and the consternation caused by environmental pollution and high water are essential considerations in this study. The flood of 3 November 1966 was the most threatening day of Venetian history, and the remedies to prevent its recurrence are not yet in place. Tourism is arguably as great a danger, stripping the city of its indigenous life and culture. 'The barbarians' were already in full possession in 1882, according to Henry James, and how much greater is their volume now.[2] Venice may appear to attract the most superficial of tourists, or be an extended convention centre or, less kindly, a propped-up stage set, or theme park. The Venetians, a dramatically declining population, themselves refer to their city overtaken by commercial carnival, bereft of supermarkets and facilities, as 'Disneyland'. Yet beyond the industrial age, Venice is, without question, a rare example of gratuitous beauty: that is the reason for its plight.

Venice is so well known, and its high tides and flooding so familiar as a recurrent threat, that it has become a metaphor for survival of the old, the delicate and the exotic. One of the few historians to tackle the historical entity of the lagoon was the late Manfredo Tafuri, whose sense of the Bacino di San Marco and the regulation of the waters of the lagoon had an ecological dimension.[3] In the later twentieth century, looking to Venice in the medieval period, Elizabeth Crouzet-Pavan studied the environmental fragility that the city has always had to negotiate and diagnosed the 'anxiety' that has always attended the city in water.[4] Another of the famous associations of Venice, its sexuality, has also been studied by modern-day writers; the bicentenary of Casanova's death was not forgotten.[5] The present state of the city and its lagoon sets the agenda for current-day historians.

After the demise of the Republic the Venetians were ardent custodians of their own tradition, performing amazing feats of celebration and bibliography, and endeavouring to keep the historical fabric alive within the unstable environment of the lagoon. The rich mid-nineteenth-century bibliography put together by Emmanuele Cicogna as an act of love for his city on the eve of the uprising of 1848 has been under-used by English-speaking writers.[6] The creative talent that flourished under foreign rule is under-appreciated: not only the eminent sculptor Antonio Canova, nurtured and patronised within Venice, but Ugo Foscolo, Isabella Teotochi Albrizzi, Giustina Renier Michiel, Luigi Carrer; the poets writing in dialect; the presses – Alvisopoli, Antonelli, Naratovich, Il Gondoliere, Ongania's press in the late nineteenth century, as well as the reprints and new titles from the later Filippi press. Ippolito Nievo's mid-century novel, *Confessioni d'un Italiano*, which spans the years from the late Republic to the 1860s, is one of the most sustained in that genre in the nineteenth century, and the most elegiac in recording the Republic's demise. It was born of a passion for achieving a Risorgimento Venice within a unified Italy, and it was first published within a united Italy, the cause for which its author died. Among painters (in the world's most painted city) there came Turner, Whistler, Sargent and Monet: but local painters Ippolito Caffi, Guglielmo Ciardi, Giacomo Favretto, Luigi Nono and Alessandro Milesi, painting in the late nineteenth century, uncovered their own layers of the city, imaging its residents and its waters. Brought up in Venice, Camillo Boito wrote of Venice in his short stories (*Senso* is the best known), in restoration projects and in journal reviews, and used it as an exemplar in his recommendations for a national scheme to preserve historic cities. There is more to Venetian restoration than Ruskin; Academy presidents Leopold Cicognara and Pietro Selvatico, and the scholar and conservator Pompeo Molmenti are just some of the Venetian voices that spoke with passion in their time, and effected lasting conservations inherited by a later century.

In the twentieth century the recovery of the great history of Venetian music, particularly of the work of Andrea and Giovanni Gabrieli, Claudio Monteverdi and Antonio Vivaldi, was due in large part to the devotion of Gian Francesco Malipiero, himself a formidable composer of symphonies, songs and theatrical works. He trained the young musicians Bruno Maderna and Luigi Nono, who likewise devoted themselves to the recovery of manuscripts in the Biblioteca Marciana. The tradition of the Venetian past informs their own musical works.

Venice has a material existence: but Venice is not simply materially based, for it exists also in the imaginations of both visitors and residents. This Venice is ongoing: it is best known, but incompletely, as the Venice of Byron, Turner, Ruskin and Thomas Mann, whose eloquent conceptions are familiar (and re-rehearsed in what follows, but within the culture of the Venice of their time). As far as possible in these pages they are presented as visitors carrying the histories of their own countries, speaking in part with pre-inscribed voices. Thus, Byron emanates from aristocratic England, while Chateaubriand and Stendhal as Frenchmen wrestle with their admiration for Napoleon while confronted by the devastation he wrought in Venice. It is not until Marcel Proust visited in 1900 that the 'desire' of Venice could be experienced *à la touriste*, freed from political speculation. At the turn of the century the French were full of ardour in their regard for Venice, as Barrès, De Régnier and others show, following Alfred de Musset and George Sand in the 1830s. George Sand wrote no less than six novels with Venetian settings, and she was just one of those who acclaimed Venice as a city of music – as Stendhal did some years before, paying tribute to Rossini's premieres in Venice, and the status of the opera house, La Fenice. It was a Frenchman who called for the end of Venice in 1995, declaring a surfeit.[7]

For Ruskin, having so much to say about Venice and its condition past and present, the fall of Venice was mediated through comparisons with England as a maritime power. He knew full well that he inherited the dying fall of Byron, not to mention the sunsets of his beloved Turner. For German visitors the work ethic of the Arsenale (still alive in Venice for Rilke), and the state of hygiene and the fight against cholera (at the centre of Thomas Mann's *Der Tod in Venedig*), were likewise preconditioned concerns. The mediation of place by the visitor's origin is thus a theme of the work, as indeed is the address to the bourgeois art of travel. Venice was always a highlight of the aristocratic grand tour, but bourgeois tourism compelled the city's modernisation, even while the visitors were coming to see what was old. From Florian's and Quadri's in the Piazza San Marco in the nineteenth century, to Harry's Bar and the Cipriani in the twentieth century, a special sense of the civilised has been retained.

The power of Venice over the imagination has been attested countless times, but perhaps there is room for another study accentuating the continuing dialectics that Venice keeps alive. Among them is the debate between the old and the new that has caused many Venices to be planned on paper with no less zeal and invention than that shown by Guardi and Canaletto in the eighteenth century. One has in mind the projects of the 'School of Venice': the Istituto Universitario di Architettura di Venezia, and, not least, its re-readings of the history of Venice (by Tafuri, Concina, Bellavitis, et al.). A Venice on paper has long existed as a utopian site, built and rebuilt in the imagination: Canaletto's *capricci* are but one response. A stream of international architects has interrogated the city, participating in competitions for such prime areas as Guidecca housing, the Accademia Bridge, and the Piazzale Roma. The Venice Biennale has now survived for over one hundred years as an antidote to the city's own abundance of traditional art. It is still arguably the most important forum for contemporary international art, and the Lion of Venice awarded by the Biennale del Cinema remains as prestigious as it was at its inauguration in the 1930s.

The Venice of intrigue is also still alive, even though the machinations of the Republic are no more. The very geography suggests hide and seek, flight and following, which keep the ghosts of the Council of Ten and the bravo alive in movies such as *Don't Look Now*, *The Comfort of Strangers* and the James Bond films. The intricacy of pathway and canal permits many archetypal notions of evil and pursuit to be played out, sometimes in a setting of consummate beauty, sometimes in back stretches of obvious decay. We have inherited pre-established genres – the intrigue of the bravo and the horror novella – from Monk Lewis, Jacques Cazotte, E. T. A. Hoffmann and Wilkie Collins.

The prevalence of death in Venice is well recognised, readily connected with plague and modern cholera, and traditional thanksgivings for survival, but also – and again archetypically – death and love, *thanatos* and *eros*, have remained persistent preoccupations. Not just the fabled affair of Sand and Musset, but Wagner's composition of part of *Tristan and Isolde* in Venice and his later death in the city compound the necrophilia. Luchino Visconti put Venice under scrutiny in two of the twentieth-century's best-known films: *Senso* and *Death in Venice*, both of which hover in that utopian space between condemnation and fascination and rewrite the scenarios of life and death. Visconti's Venices are at once seductive and catastrophic – explorations in the city's heady legacy, in short. Before Visconti, Gabriele D'Annunzio found fire and water emblematic of Venice. The art of glass, that molten material created from sand and fire, so long the speciality of Venice, has often been seen as the very emblem of the sinuous city.

The range of visual references – to buildings, gondolas, canals (advertising plays with them regularly) – the abundance of stories and images, is no longer confined to painting, Venice's traditional great art, but is the stockpile of the international medium of film, the detective novel, even Madonna's video *Like a Virgin*. The place is thick with texts. It is obvious that Venice is the world's most recognisable city: why it has become so still fascinates. It is not necessary to remain in the nineteenth century, although renegotiations of that time are still abundant, as in *Venice Desired*, Tony Tanner's bewitching, but old-fashioned work with its dense studies of the writers and its acute insights into their debts, the one to the other (Byron to Ann Radcliffe, Ruskin to Byron, Proust to Ruskin).[8] So many have responded to the pull of Venice. This study seeks to enlarge the canvas and a find a wider expression of recent opinion.

It seeks a cultural contour for contemporary Venice, a site for it that is more than the contamination of tourists. Foreign and local opinions both take their shape against the changes in the city and against the reality of existence for the Venetians. Venetian preoccupations under foreign rule and changing modern demands do not always accord with foreign expressions of a city where there are bridges to be built and floods to be controlled, yet Venice is under international surveillance, and has been so for over a century. The history of that surveillance is important in what follows.

The two Venices traced in these chapters, then, are the existing – and mutable – urban fabric, and the Venice of the Imaginary. The one sparks off the other in another of the profound dialectics that Venice inspires. Neither is static, for Venice is not of the past; if it were, it could not be encountered in so many telling ways. Still they came in the late twentieth century: Joseph Brodsky from the Soviet Union, Englishman Joseph Losey to shoot *Don Giovanni*, American Robert Coover, re-animating the *commedia dell'arte* in his novel *Pinocchio in Venice*, Australian Robert Dessaix inscribing his *Night Thoughts*. And they have their famous funerals, crossing the water to the Isola di San Michele: Diaghilev and Stravinsky, Ezra Pound and Joseph Brodsky. Edward Said has said that Venice 'is a place where one finds a quite special finality'.[9]

The chapters that follow move in sequence from the eighteenth century, but they cannot of course follow that elusive thing called 'history' in any detail, even if that story is only now beginning to be told.[10] Many of the 'events' in the life of Venice between 1797 and 1997 have been imposed from outside: the conquests by France and Austria, the unification of Italy, the two world wars, the Fascist regime when, arguably, Venice was at the peak of its fortunes, the flood of 1966. But there are pre-occupations and movements of taste that may not have originated in Venice, but which find particular resonance, concentration and imaginative life there: the metaphors of ruin and fall after the Republic, the patriotism of the Risorgimento that Nievo wrote about, as did Verdi in *Attila*. The ubiquitous barcarolle sounded across the nineteenth century. The water-crossing and cholera epidemics have spawned a whole host of deathly *fin-de-siècle* treatments, and that lineage before and after Thomas Mann. Carnival has its expression: not only in mask and fancy dress, but in architecture and scenography, and novels such as Coover's *Pinocchio in Venice*.

This study seeks, impossibly, to be complete and overarching, to be less than tokenistic as it travels its two centuries. Although the eloquence of foreigners is surely greater in relation to Venice than to any other place on earth, I have endeavoured to listen to *Venetian* voices also, if imperfectly dwelling, as I do, not only in a different continent but in a different hemisphere.

Rather than succumbing to the emotional charge that has been so well recorded, one must also engage with a Venice that is *rational*, the Venice of one-time traders and financiers, the Venice that participated in the Enlightenment even while its time-honoured government became moribund. As a living city it is still romantic *and* rational, and must be to survive. Its history was not in fact arrested in 1797, although both its physical and its psychical life altered. For some it is Eastern; the Basilica of San Marco its emblem. For many it is a Gothic city; for them the Palazzo Ducale stands as the supreme building, as it did for Viollet-le-Duc and Ruskin. Others cherish a classical or Neoclassical Venice in which Palladio built, Canaletto painted and Canova became the world's most famous sculptor. And there is a modern city where Carlo Scarpa built, if only modestly, and a host of international architects have dreamed. All these Venices were present and exploited in the twentieth century.

Beyond the work of conservation and renewal, the debate on the modern and the contemporary in the face of the old and traditional is nowhere more dramatically in evidence. The very singularity of the past, the seeming totality of its physical and mental grip on 'the idea of Venice', has been the cause of fascinating debates and frustration – but of creativity also. In the twentieth century one had only to encounter the musician Luigi Nono, the architect Carlo Scarpa, the painter Emilio Vedova, the film-maker Francesco Pasinetti, the writer P. M. Pasinetti, and the continuation of the Biennale, to realise the eminence of Venetian culture in our own time. That suave cartoonist Hugo Pratt, inventor of the adventurer Corto Maltese, one feels could only be Venetian. And one need think only of the wide-ranging scrutiny of the philosopher Massimo Cacciari: his cogitations on the philosophy of the metropolis, of the culture of Vienna, its architecture, writers and philosophers, and on Nietzsche.[11]

The mesh of tradition in serious and profound contemplation, together with the energy of will to live on, to harmonise with the elements and preserve the fragile and the beautiful (and the banal and the witty), to fulfil Nietzsche's prophecy of a post-humous city is the point of this study. The phoenix keeps rising from the semblance of ashes.

Part 1

Chapter 1

'THE LION OF VENICE WILL LIFT HIS PAWS FROM THE EARTH AND LEAVE THEM BUT LITTLE ON THE OCEAN': THE END OF THE REPUBLIC

Founded, as legend has it, on 25 April 421, by the eighteenth century the once splendid Republic of Venice had fallen victim to its myth of greatness. The golden basilica dedicated to St Mark, the four golden horses, the golden altar – the Pala d'Oro – were still in place, but the Golden Age was in the past. Once seen as the possessor of a model government and as a state of commanding economic power, it was now broadcast that Venice preferred carnival to trade, its government was effete and its policy of neutrality made the Serenissima irrelevant in the politics of Europe.

On 12 May 1797 the Venetian Republic was conquered by Napoleon, virtually without opposition. It was but a stage in the French campaign in Italy, which had begun in 1796 with the ceding of Savoy and Nice to France. The French attack on the Austrians in Lombardy extended across northern Italy through Milan, to the cities held by the Venetian Republic: Bergamo, Brescia and Verona.[1] Venice was offered an alliance to facilitate French passage through the Veneto; the alternative was war. Diplomatic missions apprised the Venetians of the terms, but after a stalemate in the negotiations, and a minor incident on the lagoon, French troops entered Venice.[2] The 'incident' involved the French vessel, provocatively named *Libérateur d'Italie*, under the command of Jean-Baptiste Laugier, which was fired on by order of the Venetian commander Domenico Pizzamano after entering the Venetian lagoon on 30 April 1797.[3] The French commander and four others were killed. Bonaparte considered the death of Laugier to be murder and an act of provocation: the attack on the *Libérateur d'Italie* was 'the most atrocious event of the century'.[4] His communications with the Directory made it clear that there could be no reprieve for the Venetian Republic: 'the example of Venice must be terrible; we must have blood; the most noble Venetian admiral who presided over the assassination must be publicly executed.'[5]

Napoleon's threats in response to declarations of Venetian neutrality were infamous, and emblematically pungent: 'as he had clipped the wings of the Imperial Eagle [of Austria] he would compel the lion [of Venice] to lift his paws from the earth and leave them but little on the ocean.'[6] Brazenly Napoleon styled himself the new Attila, and thus a potent danger to Venetians, who prided themselves on their conquest of the original Attila in the fifth century. An account of the 'revolution', *Rivoluzione della Repubblica Veneta* (circulated in English translation in 1804 as *An Accurate Account of the Republic of Venice and the True Character of Bonaparte*), took up Napoleon's self-reference: 'the panic spread by the eruption of barbarians under Attila gave birth to the Republic, the panic spread by the invasion of barbarians under Bonaparte destroyed it.'[7]

Later, Napoleon vindicated himself in writing, allegedly by his own dictation on St Helena, claiming that the invasion of Venice was the inevitable result of its refusal to accept French offers of armistice; he attacked only after provocation.[8] The element

Detail of fig. 11.

9

of Austrian partisanship within the governing council of Venice was reason for suspicion in the face of Venetian neutrality, which was seen as perfidious, tantamount to a declaration of war against France.[9] The Easter uprising in Verona, in the territory of the Venetian Republic in which Napoleonic troops were attacked, was interpreted as a massacre of the French to which the Venetians were party.[10]

A Venetian Enlightenment?

In view of the Republic's reputation for decadence, participation in the Enlightenment might appear contradictory, yet in its last decades the Republic could boast a tranquil state and compatriots famous throughout Europe. Among these were Giambattista Tiepolo and his sons in Würzburg and Madrid; Canaletto in London; Antonio Canova in Rome; Baldassare Galuppi at the Haymarket Theatre in London;[11] writer and adventurer Giacomo Casanova in Paris, St Petersburg and Dux; Mozart's librettist, Lorenzo Da Ponte, in Vienna; playwright Carlo Goldoni in Paris; man of letters and dealer Francesco Algarotti moving around Europe. The circle of Francesco Lodoli, 'famous as a teacher of philosophy, a scientific polymath, and a formidably caustic wit', was a potent cultural nexus with international connections.[12] Long after he had left Venice for Rome, Giovanni Battista Piranesi continued to sign himself 'Architectus venetianus'.[13] At the end of the century the sculptor Antonio Canova, the most famous artist in Europe, still signed himself 'Canova di Venezia'.

The embellishment of the city persisted in these years. Churches were built; some patricians – the Pisani, the Labia – continued to build palaces and called on Tiepolo to decorate them.[14] The monumental art of architecture showed no abeyance, or neglect, of its great Palladian legacy, and indeed the continuity of the Palladian tradition attested to the rationalism and classicism of Venetian architecture. On the Grand Canal there arose imposing new structures, beginning with Giovanni Scalfarotto's church of San Simeone Piccolo at the western end, in counterbalance to Baldassare Longhena's Santa Maria della Salute at the Bacino entrance to the east.[15] Giorgio Massari was the architect of the Palazzo Grassi, positioned mid-way on the Grand Canal, as well as of the Gesuati on the Zattere and the Pietà on the Riva degli Schiavoni: he carried on the Palladian tradition of siting churches on the water, and Giovanni Battista Piazzetta and Tiepolo adorned them with frescoes.[16] The painted embellishment of walls and ceilings, one of the great traditions of the Republic, continued. The music room of the Ospedaletto di Santa Maria dei Derelitti is one of the most perfect eighteenth-century interiors: an oval space in which the children gave their famous concerts, overseen by a painted orchestra of female players conducted by Apollo amid fictive arcades.[17]

The particular vigilance of the Republic, vulnerably sited within its lagoon, was registered in mathematician Bernardino Zendrini's project for the Murazzi, the vast walls of marble built to keep back the sea at Pellestrina.[18] Johann Wolfgang Goethe, among the most eminent visitors in the Republic's last years, visited the Murazzi in 1786 and remarked on the diligence with which the Venetians both past and present had preserved their lands amid the water.[19]

The public face of the Serenissima, its festivals and celebrations, continued in unabated splendour, perpetuating the state's fame – and perfidy. Venetian carnival in the eighteenth century had a reputation for lasting for a full six months.[20] Masks – the white *bautta*, covering the brow, eyes and nose – and the black cape and tricorne hat were worn, facilitating intrigue. Women with their male escorts, the *cicisbei*, took their pleasure in gondolas, sipped hot chocolate, gambled at the *ridotto* (gaming house), spent evenings at the theatre or opera. The life of the Venetian was seen as a continuous diversion. Carnival had its epicentre in the Piazza San Marco and the Piazzetta, where acrobatic feats and open-air theatre were witnessed by the doge from the loggia of the Palazzo Ducale. Carnival was a phenomenon that visitors were eager to witness, testing both the fabled licentiousness and the safety of the crowd. Venice during carnival was 'an enchanted city, a wonderful, mad city of masks and serenades, of amusements and pretence', as Philippe Monnier described it in his widely read *Venice in the Eighteenth Century*, published in 1907.[21] Writing about the Venice of 1760 some fifty years later, Stendhal called it that 'voluptuous paradise of sensuality'.[22]

A contributor to that reputation, the poet Giorgio Baffo, circulated erotic verses among like-minded sceptics and libertines in the *botteghe del caffè*. Casanova, a connoisseur in the field, called him

> a sublime genius, a poet in the most lascivious of all genres . . . great and unrivalled . . . his poems, though indecent, will never let his name perish. The State Inquisitors of Venice have contributed to his fame by their piety. By persecuting his works in manuscript, they made him sought after . . .[23]

Baffo was a patrician, and a member of the governing group, the Quarantia, and thus centrally implicated in the affairs of the Republic.[24] He might well address sonnets to eroticised body parts – praising buttocks, for example, in 'Lode al Culo' – but his writings were also politically engaged, addressing the issues of his times. He inhabited the adventurous circle that included Lodoli, Algarotti and Andrea Memmo – he praised Lodoli in a sonnet on his death, noting the flagellation of the nobility by this 'architect of the new and imaginative'.[25] Baffo wrote in anti-clerical vein, attacking the Venetian-born Pope Clement VIII of the house of Rezzonico, and addressed a sonnet to the suppression of the Jesuits (against papal enthusiasm for the Order).[26] At the time of his friend Angelo Querini's imprisonment, Baffo penned satirical verses, but it is his erotic poetry in dialect, published posthumously in 1771, that is now the treasured evidence of his libertine spirit.[27]

An unusual intimacy pervades Venetian life in the eighteenth century – in Goldoni's plays, Baffo's sonnets and Longhi's boudoir paintings. The trafficking between classes was material for satire and comedy; the habit of carnival, the ubiquitous mask and the covered gondola facilitated exchange. This ease is impossible to conceive in contemporaneous court culture – in France, Austria or in cities of geographical spread lacking a central space such as the Piazza San Marco or the water boulevard that is the Grand Canal. Seduction is a prevalent theme in Venetian art, geographically facilitated by the ease of assignations on land or water. The elisions fostered by carnival permitted expressions at once witty, vindictive and poignant, and gave the opening to Lorenzo da Ponte, well-experienced in amorous transactions, for a *Marriage of Figaro* or a *Don Giovanni*.[28] A celebrated testimony is the song written by the satirical vernacular poet, Antonio Lamberti, about the noblewoman Marina Querini Benzon: 'La Biondina in Gondoleta', the blonde in the gondola.[29] Slipping into sleep as she reclines in her gondola, she is ready for the act of love, or slumbers after it: the verses are both witty and affectionate, and were sung incessantly on the Grand Canal in the reaches of her palace in a captivating musical setting that is still heard today.[30] The composer Simon Mayr was a Bavarian musician who had come to train in Venice: responding to the water music and the barcarolle, he was among the first to make Venetian vernacular songs accessible to the salon, and indeed to much of Europe.[31]

Yet Venetian enticements brought moral censure: where once liberty had reigned, now came the rule of the libertine. Carnival and Casanova (the lover, rather than the disputer of Voltaire and de la Houssaie) are all too often taken as emblematic of the late Republic.[32] Played to the strains of Vivaldi endlessly circulating through the seasons, Settecento Venice was later interpreted virtually as a caricature of life lived in sensual gratification, cancelling all responsibility, all intellectuality, all seriousness of mien. The sheer wish-fulfilment that such a state invokes has led to many a later recreation of a mythical eighteenth century: Philippe Monnier's study is just one example of the classic treatment of the city-as-rococo, relishing its own decadence.

Yet Venetian culture in its public aspect, so pre-eminently visual, so self-conscious in recording its primary public moments, was not above taking hard-headed advantage of its stream of visitors. This society of spectacle kept collective memory both active and cumulative; it also instructed its guests, the *forestieri*, in the history of the Republic, while ensuring all were entertained.[33] As a centre of the Grand Tour second only to Rome, Venice was aware, then as now, of visitor potential.[34] The well-circulated guidebook first issued in 1740, *Forestiere illuminato*, listed the feasts and public *divertissements*, liturgical and state occasions, month by month.[35]

The Republic's re-enactments of anniversaries were recorded in paintings and albums by Luca Carlevaris, Michele Marieschi, Canaletto and Francesco Guardi, presenting the city and its people in a genre in which the Serenissima excelled: the ceremonial *veduta*.[36] Early in the century Carlevaris gave scale, ambition and sheer beauty to the representation of state visits and ceremonial welcomes, for example the regatta in honour of Frederick IV of Denmark in 1709 (fig. 1).[37] Canaletto and Guardi painted full cycles of dogal visits and feast days, attesting to the antiquity of both state and religious ceremonial and their contemporary vigour.[38] Folios of engravings popularised the images – their production constituted a virtual industry. In 1742 Antonio Visentini engraved Canaletto's representations of the principal ceremonies for the famous publishing house of Pasquali.[39]

Both Venetians and visitors thronged the cherished public spaces in front of San Marco and the Palazzo Ducale. To make the *passeggiata* – to promenade in the Piazza San Marco – was obligatory for the Grand Tourist. The ceremonies that were celebrated in the decorations of the Palazzo Ducale, in renderings of Venice and Venus, Venice and the Madonna, and the mythologies of homage and union with Neptune, god of the sea, still resonated in the festival of the Sensa, the annual ceremony in which the doge married the sea.[40] Even if the great days of the marine empire, the *stato da mar*, were well over, the Grand Tour was complete only if the Sensa was experienced, even if that realist Casanova called it 'the great and ridiculous ceremony', the 'burlesque wedding which even the Venetians regard with superstition'.[41] In case of accident (if, for example, the doge was drowned), the whole of Europe 'would not fail to say that the Doge of Venice had gone at last to consummate his marriage'.[42]

1 Luca Carlevaris, *The Bucintoro departing from San Marco*, 1710. Oil on canvas, 134.7 × 259.3 cm. Malibu, Ca., J. Paul Getty Museum.

2 Canaletto, *View of the Piazza looking West towards San Geminiano*, c.1726. Oil on canvas, 133.5 × 170 cm. London, Royal Collection.

In 1786 Goethe visited the Arsenale and saw the Bucintoro, the gilded state barge used for the ceremony: he viewed it affectionately for its day had passed, but he considered it akin to a family heirloom.[43]

The city in its full range of activities – from ordinary life to high festival – was painted with a conviction and originality that soared above mere genre to express the ideology of a tranquil metropolis, with measured spaces and a harmony of estates. Much of this art was for export, or for foreign residents.[44] View painters were attentive not only to the festivals but increasingly to the extent and detail of their city and the lagoon. Canaletto, with his clarity and sobriety, is appropriately seen as a painter of the Enlightenment, creating a view of a city state in all its lucidity and rationality; admiring of the legacy of Palladio in his classical *capricci*, but also respecting an earlier Gothic and Byzantine past, and painting the total fabric of his city with even hand (fig. 2). Algarotti's 1759 commission to Canaletto for an invention that included the architecture of Palladio, recharged the classical manner at the onset of Neoclassical taste.[45] Canaletto's capacity to conjure in paint from Palladio's plan a fully authentic-appearing Rialto Bridge as if it were actually on the canal and subject to Venetian light, and his ability to move Palladio's buildings from Vicenza to the banks of the Grand Canal and give them full authenticity are some measure of a formidable architectural imagination, as well as lessons in the absorbency of the Venetian environment.[46] At the same time, these 'inventions' of Canaletto working through the mind of Palladio offer Venice a way out of building: they permit the reinvention of the city on canvas or paper, but they also defy realisation. They confer liberty; even the most venerable icons of the Piazza San Marco can be shifted: the four golden horses can be removed from their Byzantine porch at San Marco to take up new positions on different podiums. By extension, with such defiance Venice itself can be rebuilt, as indeed it has been, anywhere in the world.

But not only classical architecture appears in Canaletto's Venice, or the architecture of the mind. The rich layers of actual Venice find homogeneity in his work, in a response to a given landscape as well as a belief in the integrity of all the elements that constitute that view, including people of all classes. Canaletto was the first to paint a comprehensive Venice with the peripheral areas that form a *Venezia minore*. The city of his pictures belongs to the working people and quotidian life: laundry is strung between buildings and a blind man feels his away along the wall in *Rio dei Mendicanti* (Venice, Ca' Rezzonico) ; people ply their trades and a mother chases her child in *The Stonemason's Yard* (London, National Gallery). In the central public spaces citizens are at ease in their environment: birdsellers share space with senators.[47]

The greatest painter of the lagoon, Francesco Guardi, turned his gaze from Venice as defined by its architecture and canals to the Venice of the lagoon and the periphery. Increasingly he painted the distances between sky and water, and the low-lying land.[48] Following Canaletto, he recorded the city's ceremonial, but the last triumphs of the doge are painted from above, and at a distance, as if they were already receding. Unlike Canaletto's steady, regal, planned passage for the Bucintoro setting out on the day of the fair of the Sensa, Guardi's is a frenetic affair with foam around the gondola oars, a lowering sky and a Campanile that seems spindly and vulnerable to high winds.[49]

Increasingly in Guardi's paintings the lagoon becomes the focus, its water, sky and low land quietly vying with the city's famous landmarks. Guardi's fascination with the lagoon view may owe something to the site of his studio on 'the other side' of Venice, on the northern Fondamenta Nuove, looking across to the islands of San Cristoforo and Murano. He first painted them in the 1750s, with an accurate and clear sense of appropriate distances and shipping, but later the waters take over as the predominant motif. Guardi circuits the lagoon from Marghera to the Giudecca, to the northern side in the vicinity of Murano and the Isola di Certosa, opposite the Lido. The *Grey Lagoon* (fig. 3) is an essay in delicate tonalities, in anticipation of

3   Francesco Guardi, *Grey Lagoon*. Oil on canvas. Milan, Museo Poldi Pezzoli.

Whistler and the virtual disappearance of Venice as an architectural city. That architecture is but a fringe viewed in golden retrospective light, pushed to the perimeter of a lagoon that is nearly empty of shipping, and is deep-toned, flat, even murky; a single gondolier leans on the oar as the prow of his vessel catches the last of the light. The lagoon has become a subject for visual contemplation, a site for invention, a space for the repose of the imagination. Guardi's *capricci* include many ruins from the antique, but they also ruin the present: they target the *sottoportico* of the Palazzo Ducale, they find waste and rubble along canals and allow weeds to grow in bridges. Turning from the well-celebrated architecture, Guardi may seem elegiac, prophetic of the city's decline.

There is no dissent with respect to the stature of Giambattista Tiepolo, the most acclaimed painter in Settecento Venice.[50] Equally at home in commissions both sacred and secular, Tiepolo's classical erudition, his supreme talent as a decorative painter, his *invenzione*, his consummate *grazia*, assured commissions beyond Venice. From the wall-paintings for the Palazzo Labia dedicated to Cleopatra's banqueting, the glorification of the Pisani family borne heavenwards on the ceiling of its palazzo at Strà, to the new decorations for the churches of the Pietà and the Gesuati and the Scuola Grande del Carmini, he was acknowledged as Venice's major talent. Tiepolo kept the insignia of Venice lightly aloft: Venus still acknowledged the homage of Neptune on one of the last decorations for the Palazzo Ducale.[51] Nevertheless, his was a talent in the service of the aristocracy, falling short of the democratic instincts of a Canaletto or a Longhi, producing an art that could be seen as inspired display, but located in the *trompe-l'oeil* realms of the heavens rather than the paving stones of the Piazza.

Eighteenth-century Venice was certainly not a hymn to itself only. Whatever the weight of conservatism, its cultural life was not limited, parochial or retardataire. Nor was it a culture with aristocratic address only. Pietro Longhi's paintings – his *vedutismo domestico* – and Carlo Goldoni's plays and libretti show the acute sense with which the *opera buffa* of daily life was appreciated; indeed the acuity of his observation of manners made Pietro Longhi inspirational for Goldoni (fig. 4).[52]

Gabriel Bella, whose naive style nevertheless found a patron in the patrician Andrea Querini, painted scenes of Venetian public life, including the communal games performed in the *campi* and around the canals: the bull fights and ball games, the ladies' regatta (they lean vigorously on their oars), and the traditional fist fights on the bridge over the Canale di San Barnaba (from which the defeated were dispatched to the waters).[53] While the music of Baldassare Galuppi and Antonio Vivaldi was known throughout Europe, so, too, was the song of the gondolier.[54]

The educated subjects of the Serenissima were not ignorant of Enlightenment thought, nor of the need for reform, whether in theatre, agriculture or politics. Ideas circulated through the many journals and newspapers for which Venice was noted. With other cities of the Veneto, Venice played an important role in the development of modern journalism – begining in the first decade of the century, with the *Giornale dei litterati d'Italia*, edited by Apostolo Zeno and Scipione Maffei.[55] Gasparo Gozzi published *L'Osservatore Veneto* and *La Gazzetta Veneta*, reporting the gossip of Venice, reviewing the plays of Goldoni and the ideas of Voltaire.[56] It was not only literature that was served by Veneto journalism: under the auspices of Francesco Griselini, the *Giornale d'Italia* covered the natural sciences and agriculture.[57] Alberto Fortis and Elisabetta and Domenico Caminer wrote for the *L'Europa letteratura* – on Rousseau, Paolo Sarpi and (against) Carlo Gozzi; the *Giornale enciclopedia* carried reports and polemic on matters pertaining to Venetian history and contemporary European figures.[58] Yet even such an eminent man of journalism as Gasparo Gozzi has been regarded as only 'halfway between the old and the new', and indeed this was the Venetian condition of many literati before the fall.[59] While many could discourse on the matters of the Enlightenment – as Casanova did, famously, throughout Europe – they were gifted spectators: conversationalists, not activists.

A distinctive Neoclassical taste is evident in late Settecento Venice, in line with advanced taste in Europe, and France in particular. Canova's formative years were decisively shaped by his experiences in Venice, particularly through the Farsetti collection of casts, which he studied with diligence, and the patronage of Venetian patricians who responded enthusiastically to the young artist, notably Giovanni Falier, Marco Antonio Grimani, Girolamo Zulian, Pietro Vettor Pisani and Giuseppe Albrizzi.[60] Canova's talent was first recognised in Venice and the surety and elegance of his style was established well before his journey to Rome and his subsequent international fame. In Rome he was aided by the protection of the Venetian ambassador, Girolamo Zulian, and he remained in contact with Venetians throughout his life: with his close friend the architect Giannantonio Selva, with the *saloniste* Isabella Teotochi Abrizzi and with Count Leopoldo Cicognara, president of the Academy of Venice and a notable figure during the Napoleonic domination.[61] In the years just before the end of the Republic, Canova planned important works intended to embellish Venice: the first, the pyramidal tomb intended for Titian that went through many permutations, became – poignantly – Canova's own memorial.[62]

Canova's affection for and gratitude to his first patrons in Venice remained with him. On his own initiative he prepared a stele for Giovanni Falier who gave him his first commissions, for *Orfeo* and *Euridice* (Venice, Museo Correr). Before being installed in Falier's garden at his palazzo near Asolo, *Orfeo* was shown in the Piazza San Marco on the occasion of the fair of the Sensa in 1775, at which time the artist first came to public attention – Canova himself remembered 'an immense and admiring crowd'.[63] He had prepared these works for Falier in his first Venetian studio in the cloister of the church of Santo Stefano, and his stele in Falier's memory was finally installed in the sacristy of the same church.

In June 1792 the Venetian Senate sought a commission from Canova to honour their last naval hero, Angelo Emo, who had died that year after an eminent career commanding sea battles and defeating the Algerians off the North African coast.[64] Canova's tribute (fig. 5) takes the form of Grecian stele with a bust of the hero, eyes

closed in death, raised up on a column in the midst of the sea.[65] Two Victories are in attendance: one – of consummate elegance – winged and hovering to crown him; the other kneeling at the foot of the stele, about to spell out the victorious name.

All the marks of Canova's sensuality in the handling of marble are present in the stele: in the Victories, whose drapery folds around genitals and, while covering, enhances; in fingers that arch before they touch with relish, and precision; in backs that are flexible – that of the girl curved as she bends toward her work of inscription, the boy's arched as he hovers to bestow the wreath. Amid the scrolls of the wondrously worked waves, the female Victory kneels on one of the special instruments of Emo's fame: his invention of the floating battery made of spars and casks lashed together to carry cannon close to enemy ships.[66] The mid-ocean cenotaph is embellished with the jutting prows of ships bearing the lion of St Mark, the still-proud sign of the Republic. For the Venetians Canova's tribute was a sublime work, and they extolled it, awarding him a pension for life.[67] To satisfy public curiosity the work was first exhibited at the Gesuati before being sited at the Arsenale.[68]

Canova's influence on interior design in the Neoclassical taste was also of some importance, especially through his friendship with Giannantonio Selva. There was ample evidence of the up-to-date nature of Venetian decoration, established in the last decades of the Republic by Selva's interiors for Doge Manin in the renovations to Palazzo Dolfin-Manin (originally owned by Joseph Smith, the British consul and then passed to Giuseppe Mangilli, the Pisani and others).[69] Selva's 1784 decoration has been called 'the first example of elegant adornment', and in 1800 Canova declared that the Palazzo Dolfin-Manin renovations showed that Selva was not only 'a true artist in architecture, but also in ornament, and knowledgeable in the other arts'.[70]

In 1796 the apartments of the new Procurator, Antonio Cappello, were opened in the Procuratie Nuove on an occasion of cultural celebration.[71] The so-called Canova Room, designed by Selva, was lined with bas-reliefs by the sculptor depicting subjects taken from Homer, *The Aeneid* and the life of Socrates. Canova had been inspired by the various projects to translate the classical authors undertaken by such scholars of the Veneto as Andrea Mustoxidi and Melchior Cesarotti, and had written enthusiastically to Cesarotti after reading his eight books of Homeric translation.[72]

Beyond Canova, the evidence of Neoclassical culture in Venice was considerable, pointing to a vigour and contemporaneity in taste and patronage.[73] The Masonic movement, emanating from France, had its adherents and fostered the principles of the Enlightenment.[74] The major Venetian architect of the last decades of the Republic, Tommaso Temanza, had the hallmarks of an Enlightenment architect.[75] One of the most distinctive Neoclassical monuments in the city is his church of the Maddalena (fig. 6): centralised in plan with a rotunda inspired by the Pantheon in Rome, it had a Venetian element in its references to Palladio's domed structures and the more recent San Simeone Piccolo. It became a model 'Temple moderne' in J. N. L. Durand's handbook for architects, first published in Paris in 1800 and then in a Venetian edition in 1857.[76] The oratory is at once austere and intimate, exemplary in its adaptation to a modest site closely surrounded by other buildings. Masonic emblems are displayed on the portal.

Temanza continued the pragmatic Venetian tradition of the architect-engineer in his design of bridges and hydraulic engineering: he worked on the water regulation schemes for the Brenta and, in the 1750s, on the great Murazzi project.[77] Concerned with the practice and theory of architecture in its widest applications, he was also an architectural historian, a custodian of the Republic's cultural tradition, writing the lives of celebrated architects and sculptors.[78] In the last years of his life he published an antique map of the settlement in the lagoon, one of the first representations of the emergent city.[79]

Canova's Emo stele was the Republic's last sculptural commission. A new opera house offering the best accommodation in terms of sightlines and acoustics would be its last building project. Theatre, and the new art of opera in particular, had become a Venetian speciality since the Tron family had presented *Andromeda* at their Teatro San Cassiano in 1637.[80] Venice's reputation as a centre for music and opera was unchallenged; from the seventeenth century and the advent of Monteverdi it led the world in the cultivation of opera.[81] At the end of the Republic there were no less than seven principal theatres; to these was added La Fenice – a public theatre of a new kind, since previously theatres had been owned by members of the nobility.[82]

The musical brilliance of Benedetto Marcello, Baldassare Galuppi and Antonio Vivaldi, and the vast output of drama, opera and vocal and instrumental music in the eighteenth century were measures of Venetian creativity and active patronage.[83] Discussion of theatre was lively: Francesco Algarotti wrote a *Saggio sopra l'opera* in 1755 in which he discussed the integration of music and text and recommended attention to acoustics and sightlines in theatres.[84] Francesco Milizia made the unusual recommendation of a semicircular auditorium without boxes in his *Trattato del teatro* of 1777, anticipating a more democratic layout.[85] The plays of Carlo Goldoni and Carlo Gozzi, author of *The Love of Three Oranges* and *Turandot*, attest to a specifically Venetian vitality – one not afraid of controversy in pitting the claims of the improvised *commedia dell'arte* against scripted theatre. Goldoni's vital sense of Venetian life entertained Venetians and Goethe alike.[86] Drawing on the *campiello*, the coffee-house, and everyday life, Goldoni's plays, of which there are some two hundred, are perhaps the most endearing works of the eighteenth century ('Oh', says Fabrizio to Mirandolina, 'Go away! Let me do my ironing!').[87]

Beset by controversy, born out of fire and twice destined to be returned to fire, the creation of La Fenice was a splendid episode in the last years of the Republic: a counterbalance to conservatism and inertia, not only in its construction, but also in its productions.[88] Debate on the format of theatres had been lively throughout the century, and in the 1750s two architects, Temanza and Pietro Bianchi, had each proposed designs for a public opera theatre to be sited on the Grand Canal.[89] Algarotti had praised Temanza's design for the dignity of its classical façade and the spacious amenities of ballroom, conversation area and *ridotto*, traditional in Venetian Settecento theatres.[90] Temanza probably created his scheme in response to a commission from Andrea Memmo, the noted dilettante and disciple of Lodoli.[91] Bianchi was ambitious as a theatre designer, and in 1787, the year in which the decision to build La Fenice was finally made, he dedicated elaborate plans to Doge Lodovico Manin.[92] Francesco Guardi was already lined up to design a theatre curtain.[93]

Following a fire at the Teatro San Benedetto plans were drawn up for a public theatre in the area of San Fantin. Approval by the Council of Ten was swift, an indication of the interest the governing class had in promoting theatre, one of the principal attractions at carnival time. The eminence of La Scala at Milan, built between 1776 and 1778 by Giuseppe Piermarini, was doubtless a competitive spur. The management of La Fenice, under the presidency of Girolamo Ascanio Giustinian, was to be drawn from the bourgeoisie as well as, more traditionally, from the nobility.[94]

After a competition the architect appointed in 1792 was Giannantonio Selva, a pupil of Temanza (fig. 7). Selva won the contract amid controversy after the prize was initially awarded to Pietro Bianchi, who appealed to the Academy of Bologna to support his design.[95] Selva, however, had made crucial contacts in his formative years: with Algarotti, whose art collection he had catalogued; with Canova, with whom he had visited Rome, Pompeii and Paestum; with the Venetian ambassador in Rome, Girolamo Zulian – Canova's patron whose apartment was one of Selva's first com-

7   Giannantonio Selva,
façade of Teatro La Fenice,
Campo San Fantin,
1790–92.

8 (*below*) Giannantonio
Selva, Teatro La Fenice,
auditorium (after the
Meduna reconstruction,
1854).

missions; and with Doge Lodovico Manin, the last doge, whose palace on the Grand Canal Selva was renovating when the Republic fell.[96] Selva's first commissions in Venice, in 1782, had been for decorations to mark the visit of Paul and Maria Feodorovna, the so-called Count and Countess of the North, on which occasion he had designed also the festive box for the Teatro San Benedetto.[97] For the regatta held in honour of the visit of Pope Pius VI in the same year, he had designed a triumphal arch, an early essay in Neoclassical style.[98]

The interior of La Fenice was a felicitous but traditional space in horseshoe formation, with five tiers of 174 equal boxes (fig. 8). The auditorium was ornate and gilded, but Selva's exterior was Neoclassical to the point of severity: the façade gave a dignified public face to the theatre. There could be no doubt that it served *opera seria* and the most elevated forms of music. A colonnaded loggia was surmounted by niche figures of Tragedy and Comedy, who were in turn surmounted by the emblematic phoenix turning towards the sun. The theatre and its ballrooms and salons was cleverly skewed on the uneven site, maximising the space. A water entrance, distinctively rusticated and in contrast to the land façade, was opened on a small *bacino* formed from the diversion of canals.

The opening spectacle, *I Giuochi d'Agrigento* (The Agrigento Games), was classical in theme, in line with advanced taste, with a ballet intermezzo by Onorato Vignanò, the leading choreographer of the time. The principal voice was that of the famed castrato Gasparo Pacchierotti, a favourite in Venice and adored as 'the divine'. He had been principal soloist at San Marco in the 1760s and 'primo uomo' at Teatro San Benedetto in the 1780s. The premiere of *I Giuochi* was his final stage appearance.[99] The composer was the acclaimed Neapolitan Giovanni Paisiello, brought to Venice at considerable expense to set to music a libretto commissioned from the Venetian Count Alessandro Pepoli.[100] Far from serving the establishment, Pepoli was known for his advanced Jacobin sentiments, which caused him to leave Venice in 1795 to join revolutionary groups in Milan and Bergamo.[101] He was a friend of Antonio Simone Sografi, who was to become the most eager of the dramatists writing for the municipal theatre after the fall of the Republic. Classical taste infused with republican values implied at least a degree of cultural association with revolutionary France. Sografi's *Morte di Semiramide*, an operatic treatment of Voltaire's play translated into Italian by the Paduan scholar Melchior Cesarotti, was a distinguished precedent to Rossini's better-known tragedy, which had its first performance at La Fenice in 1823.[102] In the late eighteenth century French classical taste was most in evidence in the many Venetian theatres, indeed more so, it is claimed, than in any other city in Italy.[103] In these last years of the Republic the stage was a seedbed for the municipal theatre that played after the fall when tyranny was regularly exposed, and vanquished.

The Foreign View

Part of the fascination of Venice came from its status as the longest-lasting republic and the challenge it posed to some of the key issues of political theory with respect to non-monarchical societies, their freedom and constraints. Although deemed to be decadent, the established reputation and ancient standing of the Republic brought it forcefully to the agenda of the French Enlightenment.[104] Leading French thinkers such as Montesquieu, Rousseau and Voltaire made fundamental observations on the aristocratic republic; their very disagreements were a measure of the vitality of the example.[105] The Abbé Marc-Antoine Laugier's interest was evident in his history of Venice published in Paris between 1759 and 1768 – a work consulted by Byron. Laugier's Venetian experience doubtless contributed to his famous *Essai en architecture*, a seminal text in Enlightenment aesthetics.[106] Laugier's acquaintance with Algarotti further confirmed the intellectual links between Venice and Paris.[107]

Well before the Enlightenment, however, Venice had been a target for criticism. It was wounded by the French long before Napoleon. In 1676 Amelot de la Houssaie published his *Histoire du gouvernement de Venise* following his years of experience as secretary to the French ambassador.[108] A basic source for the fashionable view that Venice was decadent, it was to be quoted and re-quoted throughout the nineteenth century. That Casanova saw fit to write a treatise against de la Houssaie is some evidence of the impact of the *Histoire* in the eighteenth century.[109] A modest pocket-sized edition circulated immediately after the fall of the Republic.[110]

In de la Houssaie's seventeenth-century view, it was more than evident that Venice was in decline by virtue of its policy of neutrality and the cumbersome motions of its government. He pointed to four failings: unwise policies of expansion on the Terraferma; the slowness of Council deliberations; too great a number of senators; and the propensity for taking 'the middle way which is commonly the worst'.[111]

The reputation for government by fear was increasingly noted with relation to the notoriety of the Council of Ten. De la Houssaie wrote: 'This dreadful council was at first only a Chamber of Justice erected for finding out the accomplices of the famous conspiracy of Bajamonte Tiepolo.'[112] He was referring to an incident that had occurred in 1310 and that had exposed the tensions within the ruling class, vigilant of treason within its own ranks. The Tiepolo conspiracy was invoked many times after the fall of the Republic.[113]

Yet for de la Houssaie the Republic had its semblance of majesty, and its appeal was still powerful:

> Though the state of Venice is at this day in its declension, yet in the condition it is, it retains something of majesty. Famous for the Form of its Government, which is a Masterpiece of Policy; and famous for its ancient Allegiance with the Crown of France, which has had it sometimes for its companion both in arms and victory.[114]

In 1797, after Venice had fallen to the French, an anonymous Venetian writer declared that it was Rousseau's *Social Contract* that was the most formidable of the writings to issue from the Enlightenment. An Italian translation was published in Venice in that very year.[115] Venice was a footnote to the discussion of republics in Rousseau's volume, in which he observed bluntly that '[it] has long since fallen into decay'.[116] Rousseau's experience of Venice was first hand: his biographical work *The Confessions* gives an account of his year in Venice as secretary to the French ambassador from late 1743 to 1744.[117] Devoted to duty, he nevertheless permitted himself a word on the 'famous amusements' which were, for him, music and restrained access to prostitution. The opera had the power to transport him to paradise: the choirs of young women from the *scuole* were exquisitely moving; he never missed vespers at the Mendicanti. It was Rousseau who made the barcarolle internationally famous: the singing of verses from Tasso echoing from gondolier to gondolier across the water became legendary following his account in his *Dictionnaire de musique*.[118] Some decades later Goethe was no less moved by the echoes of Tasso.[119]

In the Venice entry in his *Dictionnaire philosophique*, Voltaire, whose following in Italy was also sizeable, associated Venice forthrightly with a tradition of liberty, claiming that the rulers of Venice had the lagoon and its islands by right, as God is Lord of the Earth.[120] Here he expressed a historical view, whereas in *Candide*, that most popular of Enlightenment fables, he referred to a Venice inexorably in decline. Candide spends some months in Venice searching in vain for his beloved Cunégonde. Cast into despair, he eschews both opera and carnival. Given to observations at once platitudinous and acute, he offers a comparison between the perpetually singing gondoliers and the doge: 'The Doge has his troubles and the gondoliers have theirs. I admit that on the whole the gondolier's lot is preferable to the Doge's, but the difference seems to me so small that it is not worth examining.'[121] Visited by Candide's party in his palace on the Brenta, the host Pococurante reveals the excesses of pleasure offered by Venice and its Terraferma: too many women, too much art, music and literature, even an excess of gardens.

The episode towards the end of *Candide* that tells of the six dispossessed kings who came to Venice for carnival furnished the basis for an opera popular in Vienna in 1784, Paisiello's *Il Re Teodoro in Venezia*, with a libretto by Giambattista Casti.[122] The plot follows Teodoro's efforts to raise subsidies in order to assume the throne of Corsica. He lodges near the Rialto, within earshot of barcarolles (the first in opera), party to all the comings and goings across the bridge and to the spectacle of gondolas and other water traffic. The opera satirises dreams of kingship and illusions of power, and, with hindsight, was prophetic of the end of the Republic. A sprightly final chorus indulges the metaphor of the wheel of fortune which carries some to the top, some to the bottom: 'But let your wheel turn as you may, happy is he whose whole peace of mind is not affected by revolutions.'[123] The opera was playing in London and Paris when the Republic fell.

Montesquieu's scepticism with regard to the state of Venice is well known ('My eyes are very pleased by Venice; my mind and heart are not'), although in his travel writings he claimed at the same time that the Venetians were 'the best people in the world', and he was clearly enamoured of many aspects of the city, declaring he knew no other 'where one loves better being the first day . . . for the novelty of the spectacles and the pleasures'.[124] Nevertheless, his professional verdict was stern: Venice had 'No more strength, commerce, riches, law; only debauchery there has the name of liberty'.[125] Before him, his compatriot Alexandre Limojohn de Saint-Didier had resolutely associated the vacuity of carnival, as he saw it, with the government's laxity.[126]

The distinction that Montesquieu drew between aristocratic and democratic republics was a crucial one, and detrimental to an aristocratic republic. Yet, like Voltaire, he kept alive the reputation of the Republic's one-time liberty, conceding that the Venetians, in devising checks to power, 'have in many respects conducted themselves very wisely'.[127]

Montesquieu was read and quoted in Venice, but not heeded. Endeavouring to introduce reform into the governing body, the patrician Angelo Querini was arrested in 1761 for questioning the powers of the Inquisition: it was this that occasioned Baffo's poems in support of Querini.[128] The debate on the defence of the values of the Republic that Querini initiated in 1762 led to a citation from Montesquieu's denunciation of the 'Ten' in the Maggior Consiglio (Great Council), and the dismissal of his *L'Esprit des lois* as 'holiday reading' by patrician Malipiero.[129]

Nevertheless it was the French view of the Most Serene Republic – once a stronghold of liberty, but now decayed – that dominated popular opinion in the years before the fall. From the interrogations of the Enlightenment came the history that was told during the period of French occupation. The 'Municipality', which lasted but briefly, through summer to autumn, from May to October in 1797, by necessity challenged some of the dominant myths of the aristocratic Republic. One of the consequences of Napoleonic rule was that Venetian history was rewritten to discredit the Serenissima: the first new history of Republican Venice up to the time of its demise was written from Paris by one of Napoleon's generals, Pierre Darù.[130] By the time Darù published his first volume in 1817, the sack of Venice and its commercial decay were well known throughout Europe. The *Historie de la République de Venise* had as its subtext a defence of the French invasion of Venice on the grounds that its rule was sustained by inquisition and punishment. Outside Venice Darù's history became the most influential of the last days of the Republic, but in Venice itself the work was evidence of French calumny.[131]

Other visitors to the Republic in its closing years registered if not calumny, then intrigue, intimations of evil and strange effects: Venice was *unheimlich*. On ambassadorial service to Venice Rousseau became enamoured of the courtesan Giulietta; at first most eager in physical response, he was then unnerved at the sight of her malformed nipple.[132] The sexuality with which Venice was associated, particularly during its extended season of carnival, played havoc with a reputation for sobriety and rationality: at the same time it was, and has remained, one of the main sources of fascination. Visitors were impressed by the numerous cast of prostitutes and courtesans, by wives with their *cicisbeo*, by the circuit of masked balls, theatres and gambling houses, by the gondola, a water carriage for *amours* (Saint-Didier described it as 'una dolce dimora de delizie' – a sweet dwelling-place of delights).[133] The singing girls of the Ospedali and the Mendicanti were famous, and it seemed to the nineteenth-century Venetian historian Giorgio Tasini that Venice was filled with *una turba di giovanotti* – a multitude of young people.[134]

In his second visit to Venice, in 1790, Goethe succumbed to the libertine spirit in his *Venetianische Epigramme*, which engage frankly with sexual pursuit. Venice is a *locus classicus*, and not all the epigrams are particular to the place, but there is no avoiding the pretty girls who dart like lizards to and fro across the Piazza, and prompt liaisons in 'the holes and corners . . . little alleys and stairways', who inveigle one to take coffee, sing lewd songs, take the initiative in the sexual act. . . .[135] Venice was *die Neptunische Stadt*: Goethe's days in the city 'fled away like the hours in the city of Neptune'.[136]

Both the prison system and carnival, the one restraining, the other lifting restraints, may be perceived as running counter to rational systems. The mask was a powerful agent of deception and escape for resident and visitor. Escape from the prisons under 'the leads' of the Palazzo Ducale was made famous by Casanova in his account published in French in Leipzig in 1785: it gave notoriety to the prisons on the one hand, and created the adventurer type associated with the *esprit* of Venice on the other.[137] Casanova's account was the sensation of the salons of Paris, and beyond, in advance of his famous memoir, which was published two decades after his death in exile in Dux in 1798.[138] Love and escape: Casanova treated both with élan.[139]

More serious debate was sparked by the Milanese intellectual Cesare Beccaria, who indicted the Venetian justice system by implication in his famous treatise on crime and punishment, *Dei Delitti e delle pene*, published in 1764.[140] Beccaria was an associate of Il Caffè group in Milan, which included the Verri brothers, Pietro and Alessandro, noted for their Enlightenment views. No production was more far-reaching than Beccaria's *Dei Delitti e delle pene*.[141] The Venetian inquisitors took umbrage at the section 'Secret Accusations', although Beccaria had been careful to note that he was not discussing any specific government. Yet the lion's mouths set up expressly to receive anonymous accusations were a conspicuous feature of Venice, and Beccaria had spelt out his view that weakness of constitution went with 'tyrannical' government in the use of such practices: secrecy is 'tyranny's strongest shield', he declared.[142]

Beccaria's treatise was prohibited in Venice, and copies recalled from the distinguished bookseller and publisher Giambattista Pasquali.[143] One among a number of enlightened bookmen, Pasquali has been described as 'the most open and enterprising bookseller and publisher at the time': he published Canaletto and Goldoni, for example.[144] Since Beccaria's treatise followed closely on Angelo Querini's imprisonment by the Inquisition – Pasquali was a known friend – it was thought that the work had close Venetian connections. A defence of Venice quickly appeared, written by a monk, Ferdinand Facchinei, refuting Beccaria's fundamental principle of freedom and equality for all men.[145] But in effect Venice was further immured in its reputation for secrecy and weak constitutional practice; and the critique came from close by, from Milan, before it was circulated in France. The Verri brothers in their letters reveal little but contempt for the state of Venice – apart from Pietro Verri's respect for Goldoni.[146]

There is no literal link with Piranesi's suite of prison interiors, the *Carceri*, published between 1745 and 1761, and the actual Venetian prisons, but a connection is inevitably made. An account of Piranesi's 'dark brain' at work feverishly creating these sombre fantasies, with masonry and equipment for torture so specifically realised, owes more to Roman spaces, but the flavour of Venetian incarceration lingers.[147] At least one traveller made the connection. William Beckford crossed the Ponte dei Sospiri and was filled with foreboding:

> Horrors and dismal prospects haunted my fancy upon my return. I could not dine in peace, so strongly was my imagination affected: but snatching my pencil, I drew chasms and subterraneous hollows, the domain of fear and torture, with chains, rocks, wheels, and dreadful engines, in the style of Piranesi.[148]

The infamous Comte de Calgiostro's visits to Venice were enough to associate the city with alchemy and black magic: two foreign writers revealed the connections of love with the devil, or sorcery, and destabilising forces.[149] Both Jacques Cazotte in his *The Devil in Love*, and Friedrich Schiller in *The Ghost-Seer* mask their characters and set their works during carnival, so the interchange between the quotidian and the bizarre is intensified.[150]

In Cazotte's *The Devil in Love*, first published in 1772, Spanish-born Alvaro, the narrator, is enticed to Venice from his position as a guard in Naples by the command of Beelzebub. He is served by a beautiful page, who is transformed from a camel in to a fawning spaniel and finally in to Biondetta, a comely female whose beauties are swiftly unveiled. Venice during carnival is the appropriate venue for the display of satanic seduction: gambling, visits to a courtesan whose jealousy is aroused, a stabbing. Alvaro is in the grip of Biondetta's love which is, of course, the love of the devil. A summer sojourn in a palace on the Brenta only enforces her charms. In Venice, a visit to the church of the Frari gives rise to a maternal vision that does something to diminish the devilish powers, which are finally quelled after the narrator leaves Venice and returns to his native Spain, and to his mother. At the heart of the novella, Venice is the appropriate site for necromancy, prostitution, gambling – for all devilish wiles, in short.

Schiller's *The Ghost-Seer* was left incomplete – it was begun in 1786 and published in episodes in Schiller's own journal *Thalia*. But its effect as a fragment was still powerful. Byron said it took 'great hold' of him when he was boy and he never walked in St Mark's by moonlight without thinking of it and of the phrase 'at nine o'clock he died!'[151] Happenings are mysteriously announced in advance by a masked Armenian: thus a northern prince travelling incognito is accosted in the Piazza San Marco and told that a death will occur; the key to a casket and a ring are mysteriously recovered in line with his prophecy. A cabbalistic event is witnessed, then uncovered as sheer apparition and sorcery. Time wastes away in the pursuit of a woman first glimpsed from a window. The characters are held in some kind of Venetian spell from which it seems impossible to escape: both Cazotte's Spanish captain and Schiller's prince are visitors to Venice and fall victim to gambling and fraud and the enticements made famous by Count Cagliostro.[152]

Whether in fact or fiction, in the rationality of Goethe's sensible *Italienische Reise* or in his lewd epigrams describing the *calli* of Venice as sexual orifices, the state of the Republic and the city of Venice, for both good or ill, consumed the minds and imaginations of some of the foremost talents of the eighteenth century.[153]

The End of the Republic

In the decades before the Republic's demise attempts at political reform from within continued to be rigorously quashed; conservative policies were fatefully re-endorsed and the paralysing policy of neutrality kept in place. Far into the subsequent century, the Republic's reputation for repression and secrecy was the inspiration for plots for plays, painting and opera, most of them distorting or ignorant of the mechanisms for justice and protection that also existed in the Republic until 1797.[154]

As early as June 1796, as Napoleon moved his army through the mainland territories of the Republic, he made clear his intent to exploit those lands, instructing his general to 'draw as much as you can from Venetian territory, paying for nothing'.[155] Early in 1797 French ambassadors brought pressure to bear on the doge and his Council in order to force the Republic to its close. Pressure within the Venetian ranks led by Francesco Pesaro to seek an alliance with Austria were ignored. In March 1797 the French ambassador in Venice, Jean-Battiste Lallement, presented democratic reforms on behalf of Napoleon: the abolition of the Inquisitori di Stato and the reform of the administration, the release of political prisoners. The recommendations received only five votes at an extraordinary meeting of the Maggior Consiglio on 24 March 1797.[156] The two episodes that Napoleon could exploit as anti-French occurred close together: on 9 April French soldiers were killed in the Easter rising in Verona; then Captain Laugier of the *Libérateur d'Italie* was killed when the ship entered the Venetian lagoon on 20 April. Lallement was recalled by Bonaparte and reminded that 'French blood has flowed in Venice . . . I myself have refused to hear the deputies from the Senate because they are dripping with the blood of Laugier'.[157] A more ruthless secretary, Joseph Villetard, took up the negotiations in order to accelerate revolution against the ruling class. Rumours of French attack by land and sea, conspiracy among the Jacobins in Venice, sedition in the ranks of the Slavonian army that served Venice: these were some of the undermining measures.

For the last doge, Lodovico Manin, recipient of Napoleon's wrathful missives and the many concerned dispatches of his subjects, the fall of the Republic was predetermined.[158] He witnessed the events that he saw as inevitable 'with tears in his eyes', 'but things were already decided'.[159] He laid aside the *cornù* with dignity and no resistance. He never went again to the Palazzo Ducale or San Marco or the Piazza or the Merceria in daytime.[160] For his Venetian subjects there was no doubt of his weakness in the face of events, but at the same time it was understood that the collapse of the Republic could not be avoided.[161]

Simple fear of meeting the fate of the French aristocracy contributed to the panic at the last Council meeting in 1797 when its members fled from the people shouting 'Viva San Marco'.[162] It was not the patriciate but the working people of the Arsenale, the *arsenalotti*, who made what show of protest there was at the destruction of the Republic. But the 'Revolution' was an event of virtually one day, 12 May, when Venetians of French sympathy were targeted and attempts were made to destroy them or their property. The ex-patrician Bernardo Renier took discreet control of public order: the Rialto Bridge was armed with cannon, and orders to fire were given. Some twenty-four people were injured or killed and there were two hundred arrests, but the plea for calm and order and the return of looted property was obeyed the next day.[163]

The transferral of power to the Municipality was remarkably smooth and had the effect of preserving patrician property and ensuring rational and continuous mechanisms for governance.[164] There was care to moderate extreme views expressed against the aristocracy.[165] The very fact that ideas of democracy had so freely pervaded Venetian society aided the transition, which was virtually complete in three days.[166] On 16 May the sixty members of the Municipality were advertised to the public: among them were former patricians, which in itself assured some continuity of procedure. The new governing body proceeded to sit as the Maggior Consiglio had done in the appropriate chambers in the Palazzo Ducale. On behalf of the Municipality, Tommaso Gallino spoke to the people in the Piazza San Marco, asking for order and obedience to the new law. By 17 May 'the sovereignty of the people' was complete. General Baraguay d'Hilliers entered the city peaceably with some seven thousand French troops.

The process of indoctrination into the new order began. Municipalist Francesco Mengotti explained the meaning of the 'Revolution' to 'the free people of Venice':

> The Revolution of Venice does not signify the destruction of the Republic; nor the subversion of religion, justice, property, honour or public faith, but rather the reform of the government, which with time became defective, to make it more active, more vigorous and more responsible.[167]

Thus reassurance of continuity, and the discreet protection of property, ensured the Municipality's safe passage. It was not a matter of death and mourning, at least not publically, but of continuity and reform.

French propaganda against Venice circulated freely after May 1797. The Republic's fatal weakness was crisply conveyed by the noted journalist Jacques Mallet-du-Pan, who saw Venice as virtually redundant before the French invasion, since it was an impotent government grounded in fear – fear of the people, of the landed nobility on the Terraferma, of the clergy given over to vice and of the nobles and members of its own government.[168] Many Venetians acknowledged decadence – or impotence – in their government; but fear, beyond the customary operations of the Inquisition, no. The peaceable state of Venice in the Settecento was noted for its virtue as well as its weakness. For Vittorio Barzoni, attacking the late Republic's inertia and its failure to mount an active resistance to the French, Venice was nevertheless 'one of the most humane, good and honest governments that ever existed'.[169] The Venetians must have recognised the truth of the closing lines of one of Goldoni's most popular comedies, *La Bottega del Caffè*: the Spaniard Don Marzio prepares to leave saying, 'I'll give up a city where all live well, all have freedom, peace, and joy as long as they know how to be cautious, careful and honorable . . .'[170]

But caution had not saved the Republic; and there was clear evidence that certain Venetians were keen to embrace new democratic ideals and were eloquent in explanation.[171] Jacobin sentiment had strengthened in the 1790s, and a Masonic organisation had grown despite the Council of Ten. The Masonic lodge in Rio Marin was discovered in 1785, but Masonic culture was much more pervasive – ensconced in the circle of Canaletto's patron, the English consul Joseph Smith, for instance, and embraced by Casanova.[172] Certain citizens were more than ready to welcome French rule immediately after Napoleon defeated the Republic. Writing on 2 June 1797, on the occasion when the Tree of Liberty was set up in the Piazza San Marco, 'Cittadino' Vincenzo Dandolo – one of the most eager new Municipalists – described 'the day of exaltation, blessed for future generations . . . which had ended a government 'monstrous and terrible . . . This is the day of regeneration . . .'[173]

The Piazza San Marco continued to be the principal public forum for the new government, as it had been for the centuries of the now vanquished Republic. But to cry 'Viva San Marco' was now punishable by death. In the vicinity of the Piazza, symbols that had perpetuated 'the myth of Venice' were ordered to be smashed – notably the winged lions of St Mark, and this by order not of the French but the Municipalists.[174] Conspicuous among that pride of lions were those to whom doges Francesco Foscari and Andrea Gritti had knelt in the reliefs on the Palazzo Ducale.

With censorship lifted there was a proliferation of pamphlets explaining aristocracy, tyranny and despotism – the old constraints – and those expressing the new hopes for democracy and liberty within a just and reasonable state.[175] Some made public announcements at length: Cittadino Melchior Cesarotti in Padua felt it appropriate to explain 'enlightened patriotism' (*il patriotismo illuminato*), and held forth on the virtues of democracy now that 'our happiness has commenced'.[176] The new democratic age would strengthen *patria*: it was this sentiment rather than the French occupation that dominated the first heady days. Cesarotti also called for compassion towards the old order, underlining the civil nature of the government's change, for 'hatred felt towards an entire class can never be human, nor just'.

11 (*above*) Gaetano Zancon, *The Lion of San Marco transported from Venice*, 1797. Etching, 220 × 180 cm. Venice, Museo Correr.

12 (*right*) *The Republican Rooster killing the Venetian Lion*, 1797. Milan, Civica Raccolta delle Stampa Achille Bertarelli.

At the same time satirical images were unleashed in the popular press. The aristocracy was shown being cleansed by unsavoury enemas; lions were carted off to burial; harlequins and *pantaloni* – the last survivors of the *carnevale* – flitted around the *campi* proffering advice to a medley of classes, both dispossessed patricians and newly enfranchised citizens (figs 9–11). Under instruction, the *commedia dell'arte* led compulsory dances watched by French soldiers with bayonets. The crowing Gallic cock everywhere triumphed over the moribund Venetian lion (fig. 12).[177]

*   *   *

The Municipality

The first sitting of the sixty members of the Municipality took place on 23 May; every fifteen days the president was to change.[178] Various ranks and interests were represented: the patriciate, citizens who had been functionaries in the Republic, Jews, Dalmations, Greeks, representatives from the Terraferma, representatives of the professions, commerce, the military and the Church. A committee structure was set up to divide responsibility for finance and the Mint, military negotiations, the Arsenal and navy, sustenance, public safety, health, public instruction, and so on. While many of these areas obviously followed provisions already in place in the Republic, the Comitato di Pubblica Istruzioni was especially empowered to inculcate new democratic values in the population. The first meetings moved to stabilise prices of basic foods – wheat, meat and wine – to adopt the French revolutionary calendar and to announce the inaugural Festa della Libertà on 4 June.[179] The Venetian prisons were among the earliest subjects up for discussion, in an echo of the historic place assumed by the storming of the Bastille on 14 July 1789 before the French Revolution. The notorious *piombi* and *piozzi* – the prisons under the lead roofs of the Palazzo Ducale and the dungeons below water level, respectively – were seen as the instruments of a tyrannical state. The Municipality resolved to demolish them in 'the first year of Italian liberty'.[180] An album of aquatints, designed and printed by Francesco Gallimberti and Giovanni de Pian, illustrated the terrors of Venetian imprisonment – caverns lit by tiny barred windows housing prisoners unable to stand and threatened by torturers (fig. 13).[181] Doubtless aided by these grim images, the reputation of the prisons as evil was mercilessly exploited in the following century.[182]

A forceful woman took charge of the feminist cause for the Municipality. In the spirit of the French feminist Olympe de Gouges (who went to the guillotine), Annette Vadori published a *Discorso sulla causa delle donne*, calling for the presence of women in the reforms of Italy and nicely declaring as the first article that 'women by nature are equal, and therefore they are superior to men'.[183] The superiority of women lay in their ability to give birth, and in their creation after Adam, which meant they were advantageously distanced from the animals to which men were closer.

The centrepiece for the Fair of Liberty held in the Piazza San Marco was a Tree of Liberty, the first symbol of democratic revolution in France (fig. 14).[184] Scenographer Neumann Rizzi, who had previously designed *feste* for the Republic, created a U-shaped loggia decorated with revolutionary texts and bas-reliefs dedicated to Liberty, Justice and Truth. Four orchestras formed a triangle, with a choir of over three hundred voices singing patriotic choruses composed for the occasion. The procession

14 Anonymous, *The Tree of Liberty erected in Piazza San Marco, 4 June 1797.* Oil on canvas, 85 × 65 cm. Venice, Museo del Risorgimento.

passed by the Tree of Liberty: young girls kissed the leaves, old people laid agricultural tools at its feet, and the members of the Municipality threw earth and water on to the tree's roots to nourish the new liberty. After the requisite Te Deum in San Marco, a young couple was joined in matrimony. In the Piazza there were patriotic speeches from cleric Natale Talier, president of the Municipality, and Vincenzo Dandolo. Antonio Collalto praised Baiamonte Tiepolo, the thirteenth-century conspirator, as the opponent of the aristocracy.[185]

There followed 'the great holocaust', as *Il Monitore* – the leading journal of the Municipality – termed it. The symbols of aristocracy were incinerated: the book of gold (a copy) in which the aristocratic families were inscribed, and the dogal insignia – although there was some reluctance to consign the doge's gold robes to the flames. The ashes were thrown to the winds and dancing to the Carmagnola followed, headed by the general Baraguay d'Hilliers and his soldiers, who were rarely absent from 'festivities'. The young writer Ugo Foscolo had returned in haste from Bologna to Venice on the announcement of the new government, and he danced around the Tree of Liberty with Marina Querini Benzon, the blonde in the gondola, who on this occasion was daringly dressed in a Greek tunic.[186] Yet it was claimed that the general population did not participate in large numbers. A Venetian who jeered at the ceremony was arrested and measures were taken against sailors who refused to wear the cockade in the revolutionary colours of red, green and white.[187]

On 15 June the Municipality voted to terminate benefits paid to the clergy. On 17 June perhaps the most symbolic of the new government's gestures took place: the ceremony to recognise the historic figure of Baiamonte Tiepolo as an exemplary leader representing democratic values in opposition to the aristocracy (fig. 15).[188] A related ceremony took place on the island of Murano on 18 June: a Tree of Liberty was raised in the presence of Baraguay d'Hilliers, a consignment of French troops, the National Guard and the members of the Municipality. The most significant ceremony, indicative of the historical perception of the conquerors and the Venetian municipalists, was the exhumation of the ashes of Doge Pietro Grandenigo, the doge held responsible

for the definition of the ruling nobility and its assumption of power in 1297. Grandenigo's remains were taken from the church of San Cipriano in Murano and scattered to the winds.[189]

Freedom granted to the Jewish community was one of the early and humanitarian actions. In the name of civil rights – but also to ensure taxes payable to Napoleon – the Jewish ghetto was opened, with the effect that the Jewish population was no longer separated from other citizenry.[190] On 7 July the Guardia Civica formed in a circle in the centre of the Ghetto Nuovo: the gates of the Ghetto were burned and the Tree of Liberty was raised. Raffael Vivante hosted a democratic dinner and made an eloquent speech praising the French and 'the light of Philosophy'.[191]

In the spirit of rationalism at the service of democracy, Antonio Collalto presented a new map dividing Venice into six major areas of activity – beyond class – devoted to commerce, fishing and marine interests and *viveri* (spectacle).[192] His project, impractical but possessed of an undeniable originality and rigour, has been called the most singular and revolutionary fact in the revolutionary agenda.[193] It was 'democratic, wise and philosophical', to cite Collalto's own presentational title.

The idealism that ran high in these early weeks was evident in the adaptation of the French calendar and the renaming of key features of the city – the Piazza San Marco became the Piazza Grande – and the ideals of democracy were to be expressed by wearing the cockade – in the 'Italian' colours. Important to the success of the Municipality, however that may be adjudged, was the invocation of a unity beyond Venice in the name of Italy, in effect, the initiation of the Risorgimento. On 2 July ceremonies were held to celebrate 'the union of cities and territories of the Veneto nation with other free people and the regeneration of Italy'.[194] For some, the extinction of the Republic was seen to be from the beginning preliminary to the achievement of an 'Italian' state.

* * *

16   *Public Festival at the Teatro La Fenice, 28 May 1797.* Coloured etching, 30 × 41.5 cm. Venice, Museo del Risorgimento.

The Work of Public Instruction

As it had been for revolutionary France, public instruction was a serious responsibility for the new order, compelled to educate the citizens to fraternal duty. A civic theatre was announced; it was to be the chief organ of democratic education. Since it could draw upon dramatists of well-established republican persuasion, it was the most creative outcome of the short Municipal rule.[195] A range of Venetian theatres became venues for works of propaganda and entertainment, caught up in the enthusiasm that reigned, at least for a brief time. La Fenice, still new, prepared to adapt: its impressario Alberto Cavos promptly arranged a ball and a *festa pubblica* (fig. 16). The experienced librettist Antonio Simone Sografi was ready to pen patriotic lines. He had worked in the Venetian theatre regularly (his *Argonauti* was given at San Samuele in 1790); he was a member of the Società Filodrammatica and the librettist of the well-known opera by Domenico Cimarosa given at La Fenice in 1796, *Gli Orazi e i Curiazi*, based on Corneille.[196] That production appeared as a work of some portent, with a marked republican orientation. Jacques-Louis David's famous painting of 1785, *The Oath of the Horatii*, must have made the theme current and hardly innocent; and Cimarosa's republican sentiments could not have been unknown. On stage, the women are faced with the alternatives of death of their brother or death of the *patria*.

Beyond demonstrating considerable comic genius (in the plays of Goldoni and the *opera buffa*), Venice had a definite taste for *opera seria*. It has been remarked that 'nowhere on the peninsula was *opera seria* more assiduously cultivated than at Venice, both before and after the fall of the Republic in 1797'.[197] Audiences were well-accustomed to allegorical tragedy with a classical republican cast. The presence of murder, suicide and death in general had been taboo on the stage for much of the eighteenth century, but in Venice the conventions were challenged and altered, even before 1797. In the culminating act of Cimarosa's *Gli Orazi e i Curiazi*, Orazia is killed on stage and thrown down the stairs. In Alessandro Pepoli's *Virginia*, staged in 1794, a father murders his daughter by order of a tyrant.

Tragic endings, and the theme of tyranny's challenge through death, were further in evidence after the fall of the Republic. The nineteen-year-old Ugo Foscolo's first play *Tieste*, which concerned the clash between King Atreus and his brother Thyestes, is a case in point.[198] It was written and presented in January 1797 at the Teatro Sant'Angelo, and successful again on the stage of the Municipal theatre.

Ugo Foscolo was born at Zante, at that time still a possession of the Venetian Republic. He was of a new generation of writers that included the formidable literary figures born in the last years of the eighteenth century, Alessandro Manzoni and Giacomo Leopardi.[199] He received his first education in Spalato in Dalmatia, before moving with his widowed mother to Venice in 1792, when he was sixteen. Venice was the crucial stage for Foscolo's education.[200] He was educated at the Collegio San Cipriano on Murano: the historian Giovan Battista Galliccioli was his early master; he knew Jacopo Morelli, the esteemed librarian of the Marciana.[201] But the decisive contact was the *saloniste* Isabella Teotochi Albrizzi, Greek-born as was Foscolo and one of the number of brilliant Venetian women in these years.[202] Her cultural circle included Ippolito Pindemonte and Melchior Cesarotti, whom Foscolo called 'Padre'. He may also have met Canova – whom Albrizzi herself was later to write about – as he dedicated some sonnets to the sculptor and wrote a poem inspired by his work.[203]

Isabella's salon was by no means simply pro-French, for it included the opponent of Napoleon, Vittorio Barzoni, who ran a hostile periodical called *L'Equatore* in the first months of the Municipality and had the distinction of threatening Villetard with a pistol.[204] A close friend whom Albrizzi had known in the early 1790s was Vivant Denon, returned to Paris from Napoleonic campaigns and destined to establish the Musée Napoleon after taking custodianship of sequestered works of Venetian art.[205] The circle included also Doctor Francesco Aglietti, editor of the works of Algarotti and firmly anti-Austrian in opinion.[206]

In this circle Foscolo developed as a classical scholar and a political radical. His passionate Jacobin sentiments were soon known: he was only nineteen when he penned the uncompromising sonnet to Venice, 'A Venezia', at a decisive point in negotiations with the French, presumably around 27 September 1796, when the French had offered an alliance, which Venice repudiated.[207] The poem charged the state with a thousand tyrannies, *mille tiranni*, and pictured it ruined and crumbling, whereas the French offered 'the sublime example':

> Ma verrà il giorno, e gallico lo affretta
> Sublime esempio, ch'ei de' suoi tiranni,
> Farà vol loro scettro alta vendetta.

Pungent, if juvenile, Foscolo's epigram against the government – 'Contro i governanti di Venezia' – attacked patricians with big wigs and small brains.[208] He could not anticipate the defence he would make of the Venetian Republic later in life, in exile in England after Napoleon's fall.[209]

Foscolo was the most fiery member of the Municipality – he was appointed secretary and was ever ready to make speeches and interjections. Early on he challenged citizens to abandon Venice for the Cisalpine Republic.[210] He took a high moral tone, calling for the closing of casinos, gathering places for aristocrats who fermented the spirit of discord.[211]

Shortly after the establishment of the Municipality, the dramatist Sografi produced a manifesto of democratic values which announced the project to rewrite Venetian history. He was among the first of many to write republican accounts alleging that Venice had been genuinely democratic in its first eight centuries, until the time of the Serrata, which gave aristocratic families political control:

> Citizens, the pulpit of the brave French has always been the theatre . . . liberty has its miracles . . . the fusion of two epochs can be of no little instruction to the people:

I speak of the closing of the Maggior Consiglio in 1296 and the conspiracy of Baia-monte in 1310. The union of these two facts would form an action for democratic theatre.[212]

The first presentation of this new 'democratic theatre' was given at Teatro San Cassiano on 28 June with an anonymous allegorical farce, *La Fiera della Libertà* (The Fair of Liberty) – peopled by Merit, Beneficence and Justice, the enemies of the tyrannically ruled state. The evening climaxed in a eulogy to Napoleon.[213]

On 10 July at the Teatro San Giovanni Grisostomo, Vittorio Alfieri's *Brutus the First* was performed with a new prologue written for the occasion by the Venetian lawyer Mattia Butturini.[214] The highly esteemed Alfieri, resident in Florence, had an unimpeachable reputation, enhanced during the Municipality, as his work was devoted to the definition and repudiation of tyranny. Alfieri was the inspiration for Foscolo's *Tieste*.[215] In the session of the Municipality of 22 September Foscolo made an impassioned speech in praise of Alfieri's republican tragedies and their 'truth, passion, energy'.[216] Their author, he claimed, was deserving of the highest praise as 'the first man of the Revolution', and indeed that reputation was sustained long after the Municipality. After his death in 1803 Alfieri's tomb, destined for the national shrine of Santa Croce in Florence, was designed by Canova as a memorial to the writer who was seen as one of the prophetic voices for a unified Italy.[217] Some twenty years later Byron was to write his plays on Venetian themes with Alfieri as a model.

In lighter vein, on the stage of the Municipal theatre there were performances of Goldoni's *La Locandiera*, that established favourite of the local stage. As well as the classical themes that Sografi had absorbed during his students days with Melchior Cesarotti in Padua, he was sympathetic to the comic tradition of Goldoni and Gozzi and, indeed, his double interest in the comedy of ordinary life and the high tragedy of the classic theatre placed him in a pre-eminent position with respect to the new theatre.[218] Sografi had his first democratic success with *Il matrimonio democratico ossia il flagello de' feudatori* (Marriage of Democracy or the Scourge of Feudatory) – his first composition for the patriotic theatre. On opening night La Fenice was turned into a 'civic theatre': gondoliers and workmen were admitted free, and many of them danced on the stage to revolutionary songs and hymns. Some thought democracy had gone too far.[219] *Il matrimonio democratico* was presented to Napoleon in Padua. Other plays that targeted the aristocratic class followed on the Municipal stage: *L'ex-marchese della Tomboletta a Parigi*, and two of Voltaire's tragedies in Cesarotti's translations.

Giovanni Pindemonte, originally from Verona, was among the notable contemporary writers close to the Venetian circle.[220] He was already established as a playwright: his *I Baccanali* had been eagerly received only months before the Republic's termination.[221] More presciently, he was an outspoken opponent of the old order and the author of *Reflections on the Decadence of the Venetian Government*, published in 1796, before the fall, declaring the weaknesses of a government that had become an oligarchy, which, in the opinion of many, was the worst kind of government.[222] *Orso Ipato* was written specifically for the Municipal theatre: the subject was the third doge, who pressed for universal suffrage against mounting claims for aristocratic privilege.[223] The work underlined the exemplary liberty of early Venice as a genuine republic, open to all classes. It recast history, lauding the early centuries before aristocratic rule.

Sografi wrote two other plays recasting Venetian history: *La Rivoluzione a Venezia* and *La Giornata di San Michele sia La Serrata del Gran Consiglio Veneziano* (The Day of San Michele or the Serrata of the Great Council of Venice). Both were concerned with the early 'democratic' days and the loss of democracy to oligarchy when the nobility 'closed' its ranks and established hereditary rule through the Serrata.[224] Gondoliers on stage debated the merits of the new French regime against the old aristocratic government. The focus was on the years now seen as fateful, in which the aristocratic rulers, established in the Maggior Consiglio, became vulnerable to conspiracy and dissent. Baiamonte Tiepolo was the central figure again, turned from traitor to hero. Sografi declared his historical sources: the Venetian diarist Marin Sanudo, and Amelot de la Houssaie, who had highlighted the Tiepolo episode in 1674 in his discussion of the Council of Ten.[225] Venetian history was being rewritten in accordance with French history.

Sografi's last Municipal play, *Venzel*, was presented at the Teatro Sant'Angelo in October 1797. The Venzel of the title was a senator with republican sympathies. Venzel's town was neutral, as Venice had been, but it was located between Austrian and French fire. Venzel opposes the Austrians as does his daughter, in love with a French officer.[226] In the play the French liberated the city and released Venzel from his death sentence – but in actual fact the French were trading the real Venice to Austria.

The End of the Municipality

Although the preliminaries for the transferral to Austria were well in place and France was about to vacate Venice, the Empress Josephine and General Berthier made an official visit from 12 to 16 September, entering by gondola to the strains of 'La Biondina in Gondoleta'.[227] The city produced a traditional welcome with a regatta and illuminations at the head of the Grand Canal, and a performance of Sografi's *Matrimonio democratica*.

Increasingly the Municipality needed vigilance in the face of internal enemies, especially if they were ex-patricians. One such ex-patrician, Nicolò Morisino, was named 'an atrocious enemy of the people', and 'an infamous conspirator', as the result of his efforts to arm a ship, liberate the city and reinstate the confiscated territories of Istria and Dalmatia.[228] A wax effigy of him was burnt in traditional style on a platform in full public display between the columns on the Piazzetta – a space traditionally reserved for the display of felons and deviants. Emotions often ran high: at one point ex-patrician Pietro Bembo (a nevertheless committed member of the Municipality) had to be rebuked for tearful nostalgia towards the lost Republic during procedures on 1 September when the dissolution of ancient public institutions was under discussion.[229] As early as July the circulation of literature critical of the Municipality had provoked the threat of the death sentence; in other words, the democratic right of a free press was revoked.[230] One of the most extreme members of the new government, Giuseppe Giuliani, recommended a project similar to the French 'Terror', drawing up a list of ex-patricians and leading citizens to be elminated in order to cast the Municipality in a more positive light with regard to France.[231] The new French general in Venice, Balland, who had replaced Baraguay d'Hilliers, alleged a conspiracy by a certain Cercato, and took action, arming the city at strategic points and taking hostages.[232] It was yet another rumour suggesting that an army was being raised to secure Venice for Austria. Ironically, this had already happened.

The deterioration of the Municipality, its growing fiscal difficulties and the need for increasing vigilance and punitive measures was transparent by October. A crisis point was reached when the Treaty of Campoformio was confirmed.[233] Giovanni Spada and Alvise Pisani, delegates to Passariano (ironically the site of negotiations was the palace of the last doge, Manin), reported on the failure of negotiations. Dandolo, still passionate in the Jacobin cause, offered Napoleon troops and money and, in a diplomatic mission to Milan (with Giuliani), even moved Napoleon with his declarations in the name of liberty, although finally without effect.[234]

The Treaty of Campoformio of 18 October 1797 was the most decisive act for Venetian history after the fall of the Republic. Jacobin Venetians and the critics of the old Republic lamented that it meant that Venice was excluded from the Napoleonic confederation of Italian states, which was still seen to offer the hope of democratic government. For conservatives of the ex-Republic it signalled the preferable domination of Habsburg Austria.

Sérurier took control of the French evacuation. Decrees of 8 November compelled non-residents to leave, the civic guard was suspended, censorship established, the pro-democracy *Il Monitore* suppressed and the Society for Public Instruction ceased. A wave of immigration to the mainland occurred, one of many such episodes that was to halve the population over the next two centuries. Guiliani was arrested for disturbing the public peace, inviting the people to resist the incoming Austrians.[235] Foscolo threatened to set fire to principal sites, leaving the city in ashes for Austria.[236]

Isolated and reduced to being a city-state, Venice had been endeavouring to come to terms with the loss of the former territories of Istria and Dalmatia, occupied by Austrian forces since June. The creation of an Adriatic state reconciling these territories remained a dream. On 9 September Canova wrote to Selva lamenting the maltreatment of the poor that accompanied war and praying for the restitution of Istria and Dalmatia. Venice, he hoped, could still be 'the capital of a good Republic'.[237]

Rather than take the oath of loyalty to the French who had entered Rome in 1798, Canova returned to the Veneto, to his native Possagno, where he painted the *Mourning of the Dead Christ*, now above the main altar in the Tempio.[238] This singular religious work has visionary power: an almost surreal sense of alternative spheres. A God figure, dramatically foreshortened, erupts out of a sun and an aureole of angels. The relief-like Christ figure and his traditional mourners are below; the Christ figure glows in the unreal light. That this is a work of intercession is made explicit by an inscription: 'In the name of his attachment to his homeland Canova painted Possagno 1799'.[239] Closely connected with the *pietà* was a sculptural group of separate figures, almost like a medieval lamentation, despite its classical theme. *Hercules in Madness killing his Children* is an allegory of the contemporary state of war that pits the brute strength of a Hercules against helpless pleading figures, including a mother and child, desperate of gesture, among inert bodies on the ground.

Spoliation

The most controversial French action followed the order given through the French minister Giovanni Battista Lallement to assemble twenty paintings, notable examples of the Venetian school, and five hundred manuscripts which were to be shipped to Paris.[240] Not only Venice was depleted in this aftermath to the Treaty of Campoformio: Rome and other Italian cities were required to contribute to what became Napoleon's public parade of booty in Paris before its installation in the Louvre museum, known from 1800 as the Musée Napoléon.[241] Napoleon's action, and the later campaigns for restitution following the Congress of Vienna in 1815, were to give new international definition to the notion of patrimony.

The first target was the quadriga of antique bronze horses which had adorned the central porch of San Marco since the late thirteenth century, now destined to crown Napoleon's Arc du Carrousel in Paris.[242] So identified with Venice were these golden horses that a play performed in Paris some decades later, in 1839, by Messieurs Paul Fouché and Alboise, still made much of the event, giving it mythological status. *The Horses of the Carrousel, the Last Day of Venice*, had Bonaparte make an appearance at the end (with some historical licence) to the sound of the Marseillaise and, amid the cries of his soldiers, to extend his hand towards the horses and pronounce – 'To France – to the Carrousel!'[243] The removal of the horses on 13 December 1797, an elaborate manoeuvre – which was not made in Napoleon's presence – was accomplished with a military parade in front of the Basilica and recorded in a number of

17 Jean Duplessi-Berteaux, *The French in Venice* (*Removal of the Horses of San Marco*), 1797. Engraving, 28 × 40 cm. Venice, Museo del Risorgimento.

LES FRANÇAIS À VENISE.

engravings (fig. 17). On arrival in Paris the horses were put on display with a caption that cunningly implicated the Venetians themselves in their removal from their place of origin: 'brought from Corinth to Rome and from Rome to Constantinople, from Constantinople to Venice, from Venice to France: they are at last in a free country!'[244]

Venice's second most precious symbol, the bronze winged lion of St Mark resident on a column on the Piazzetta since the thirteenth century, was also dispatched to Paris. The diary of Venetian Emmanuele Antonio Cicogna reported that 'our lion was set on a pillar . . . in front of the Hôpital des Invalides and its tail was lowered and placed between its legs as an affront to Venetian grandeur'.[245] So potent was the lion as a local symbol that upon the fall of the Municipality a replacement in wood covered with copper was made by the master sculptor of the Arsenale, Giambattista Pelosa.[246] But it was the Municipality itself, the 'new' democratic Venetians, who had wanted the insignia of the aristocracy suppressed in the first days of the new order, and it was the Municipality who appointed a stonemason to remove the lions. In line with the revisionist iconography of the revolution, it was suggested in the Municipality that Canova be commissioned to produce a statue of Liberty as a substitute for the deposed Marcian lion on the column of the Piazzetta.[247]

The important task of supervising the shipment of works of art to France was given to Pietro Edwards: he had established himself in the days of the Republic as a restorer and dealer with a specialised knowledge of Venetian art.[248] He performed his new task with no little sadness, aware of the loss of patrimony – although proud that he had himself restored many of the works. Indeed, he managed to 'save' some – notably Tintoretto's *Last Judgement* in the Madonna dell'Orto – by emphasising the difficulties of removal and shipment, .

As residents of conquered territory, the Venetians were required to pay war levies, and the Municipality itself had to find funding in a period of dire economic contraction. Beyond individual taxes, the treasury of San Marco was plundered – increasingly so in the last days of the Municipality, as the public purse was emptied. The great repository of items in gold, silver and precious stones accumulated since the

Republic's Byzantine period was ordered to be transferred to the Mint, a task undertaken by Giovanni Jujovich in his capacity as President of the Finance Committee.[249] Some works were disassembled, others melted down. The losses included roses in gold and silver, candelabra, golden umbrellas and the cross of the Duke of Savoy, although the Pala d'Oro, San Marco's Byzantine altarpiece of gold and precious stones, remained unharmed.

The requisition of wealth in ships and silver was followed by a final bitter 'ceremony' in which the state barge of the Republic, the famous Bucintoro from which the doge performed the ceremony of the Sensa, wedding Venice to the sea, was towed to a site near the island of San Giorgio Maggiore, in full view of the Piazzetta, and set on fire. The 'family heirloom', as Goethe had termed it sympathetically, burnt for three days.[250]

After the Treaty of Campoformio the French had a last act of degradation to perform, this time attacking the shipbuilding centre of the Republic, the Arsenale. Its demise had a particular poignancy, given that it was at one time the most celebrated emblem of the Republic's power; its fame had made it a magnet for visitors. As the heart of the one-time maritime empire, its shell – a vast space and ghostly internal waters – retains the aura of its one-time power. During the Settecento the Arsenale had revised practices in line with the Galilean principles applied to naval architecture developed at the Studio di Padova.[251] Giovanni Scalfarotto contributed one of the major buildings to the complex around 1750: the Squadratori is a monumental modular building following the harmonics of Palladio in its ratio of thirteen arches in proportion with columns and vast roof height.[252] It has a simplicity in design appropriate to the reforms of Lodoli, evidence of the Venetian capacity for contextualisation: for reusing foundations, for resiting with respect for existing walls, for building for the present with reference to the respected past.

Beyond its importance to the economy, the Venetians had a keen curatorial interest in the establishment, as shown in 1772 when an artillery museum had been established. In 1779, in his capacity as General Inspector Superintendent of the Artillery – Sovrintendente Ispettore Generale delle Artiglieri – Domenico Gasperoni executed a set of illustrations for archival records.[253] The Arsenale's cultural legacy as well as its tourist interest were well understood.

The French spoliation of the Arsenale was not so much directed at the Venetians as at their new governors, in order to inhibit the naval power of the Austrians and to salvage whatever could be used by the French fleet.[254] The place was virtually stripped. Ships were removed, usable materials – canvas, wood and cannon – were taken. The traditional Venetian workers, the *arsenalotti*, were dismissed on 25 December 1797 with pay until 1 January; French soldiers were installed as guards in

18 (*below left*)
G. M. Maffioletti, scenographic projection of the Arsenale before the French despoliation, 1798. Pen and watercolour, 115 × 155 cm. Venice, Museo Storico Navale.

19 (*below right*)
G. M. Maffioletti, scenographic projection of the Arsenale after the French despoliation, 1798. Pen and watercolour, 1150 × 1550 cm. Venice, Museo Storico Navale.

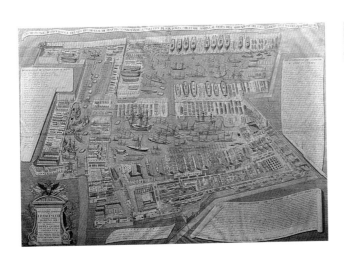

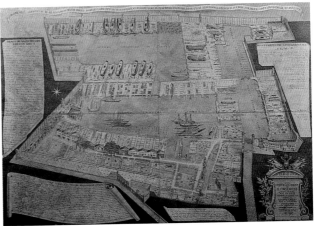

order to complete the destruction. Presentation drawings in birds'-eye view executed by Giammaria Maffioletti for Francis II of Austria on his assumption of power in Venice in the following year made the point explicitly, showing the Arsenale before and after the coming of the French (figs 18 and 19):[255] before, the French, the poly-hedrons of enclosed water known as the *darsene* are lined with rows of moored boats and docked ships in process of construction or repair; afterwards, the spaces are empty but for ruined vessels, the docks are wrecked and the deposits of arms and materials are stripped. Ironically, on the return of Napoleon in 1806, the Arsenale was to be regarded as important to French naval campaigns in the Adriatic and partly reconstituted.[256]

Elegies for the Republic

In the wake of the fall of the Republic, Venetians, both conservative and democratic, felt the iniquity of Campoformio. Their voices still sound sadly after two hundred years. In his urbane and ironical *Useless Memoirs*, Carlo Gozzi reaches the end of the account of his life and the point where, in 1798, 'the vast undulation', 'the awful typhoon' of the French Revolution that had caught up Venice and the Municipality had come and gone. Gozzi offered his 'useless' Cassandran warnings, referring to the dance around the Tree of Liberty as a Dance of Death:

> The sweet delusive dream of a democracy . . . made men howl and laugh and dance and weep together. The ululations of the dreamers, yelling out Liberty, Equality, Fraternity, deafened our ears; and those of us who still remained awake were forced to feign ourselves dreamers, in order to protect their honour, their property, their lives . . .[257]

In 1799 Lorenzo da Ponte returned to Venice after many years, and wrote of the plight of his city:

> I arrived in Venice at a time when the Germans were in possession, and I was obliged to drain two goblets bitter to the heart of any good citizen. The first concerned my wretched country, the second myself. . .
>
> I had heard much talk about pitiful conditions in the city, but what I had heard was child's play compared to what I saw in one night and one day. I thought I should like to see the Piazza of St Mark, which I had not visited for more than twenty years . . .[258]

Bemoaning the absence of people in the Piazza San Marco, and the sufferings that he heard about, he quoted another view, a further-reaching diagnosis of decline:

> We are surrounded . . . by hordes of people who through fear and through hatred have destroyed all commerce and annihilated manufactures, redoubling needs without limit, cutting off all means of earning, creating a thousand opinions, a thousand interests, a thousand bickering parties, bringing on rivalries between citizens, rancours, enmities, bad faith, and the miserable necessity of doing anything in order to live.[259]

In Ippolito Nievo's great novel-biography, *Confessioni d'un italiano*, written in 1858 at the high tide of the Risorgimento, the narrator, a patrician member of the last Council of the Republic, is present at the final meeting of the Republic when the doge rises to his feet, 'pale and trembling' to confirm the end. On 11 May there died 'a great queen of fourteen centuries, without tears, without dignity, without funeral'.[260] In this most important account of the death of the Republic by the next generation, the very stones of the Palazzo Ducale were wished away as the embodiment of such an undignified retreat. No Venetian spoke loudly in defence of the Republic. Nievo's discussion of the last decades of the Republic are suffused with a great sadness, not just for Venice, but for its Terraferma, for the Friuli where the narrator spent his boyhood, where French soldiers ultimately cause the death of a beloved grandmother. But in the loss of the Republic is the hope for a rebirth within a modern state.

There is no doubt of the Venetian love of *patria*, for the evidence is abundant in the eighteenth century, from Mario Foscarini's *Della letteratura veneziana* on which Gasparo Gozzi collaborated for fourteen years, and Foscarini's defence of a peaceful Venice, *Della perfezione della Repubblica veneziana* of 1722.[261] Gozzi himself wrote patriotic plays about Marco Polo and Enrico Dandolo.[262] So much of the art of the Venetian Settecento is urban-centred, not least the comedies of Goldoni and the painters of *veduti* and *fasti*. The vitality of vernacular Venetian was alive in the poetry of Giorgio Baffo, Francesco Gritti and Antonio Lamberti.[263] Love of *patria* was the mark of the sincere if ineffectual grief with which Doge Manin resigned his *cornù*.

At his Villa di Zianigo Giandomenico Tiepolo was remote from the business of the new Municipality and the transfer of Venice from France to Austria, but his last works appear, at least obliquely, to reflect conditions in the final years of the century. His *Divertimenti per li regazzi*, executed in pen and sepia wash in a fluent wistful style between 1797 and his death in 1804, refer to the Napoleonic invasions of the Veneto in scenes of military execution and hanging.[264] The central character is the Venetian figure of Pulcinello from the *commedia dell'arte*, who embodies an allegorical condition: this is already so in the fresco cycle that Tiepolo painted in his Zianigo villa in 1797 (now transferred to the Museo Ca' Rezzonico).[265] A work from that cycle, *Mondo Novo*, depicts the enticements of the New World, but indirectly: spectators glue their eyes to a hidden diorama, but they remain spectators rather than being participants, as Tiepolo well understood, showing them turning their backs to the viewer to watch the spectacle on offer in the tent. Beyond is the sea, the passage to the New World, folding into the sky. Pulcinello no longer plays in his swing or lies comatose with wine, as in other scenes. He is a haggard, silvery figure, turned mournfully away from the audience, absorbed in a novel new vision.

Imitating the human tragi-comedy in his ironic 'Diversion' drawings, Tiepolo has the *pulcinelle* participating in the rituals of ordinary humans, experiencing birth, growth, love, imprisonment, self-destruction and death. He drew upon the *commedia* and carnival traditions of the Veneto, in itself a comment on the interest that attended the plays of Goldoni and Gozzi and the transition from the *commedia* played by traditional masked figures, to the unmasked comedy of the modern style.[266] Thus Tiepolo uncovers the profound meaning of the carnival, referring to the very cycle of life – as well as spiritualisation and transgression.[267] The prison scene in the *Divertimenti* is explicitly Venetian, in accordance with the notoriety of the prisons – the infamous *piombi* and *pozzi*. Visitors crowd over a bridge with a gondola prow visible and the scene of the release from prison gives a view across to San Giorgio Maggiore (fig. 20). Events terminate in the death of Pulcinello himself, in his last journey in a funeral gondola, and, ultimately, his burial.[268] The lyricism of the drawings is elegiac, haunting, ambivalent; they do not have the biting stylus of Tiepolo's contemporary, Goya, whose work the Venetian knew. It is nevertheless evident that the *carnevale* and the *commedia*, so famous in the Venice of the eighteenth century, have run their course.

Beyond residents, evidence of the decline and sadness in Venice was immediately apparent to visitors. Johann Gottfried Seume was one of the first foreigners to visit during Austrian rule. In his *Journey to Syracuse*, written in 1802, he commented on the abandoned 'Palazzo della Repubblica', the cannons positioned by San Marco and the Rialto, the widespread poverty and begging in the central city, even more apparent on the Giudecca where he went to visit Palladio's church of the Redentore.[269]

William Wordsworth was one the first visitors to react to the fall in his *Poems Dedicated to National Independence and Liberty*. 'On the Extinction of the Venetian

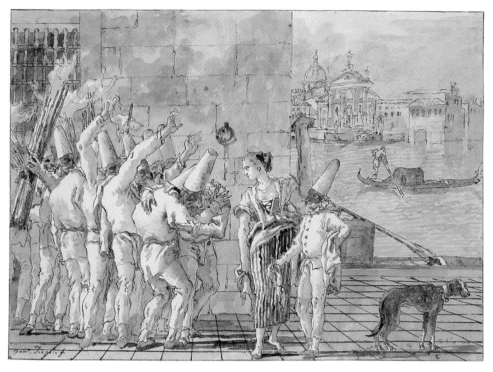

20 Giandomenico Tiepolo, *Pulcinello's Farewell to Venice*, from *Divertimenti per li regazzi*, 1798. Pen and brown ink with brown wash over black chalk on laid paper, 34.6 × 46.3 cm. Washington, National Gallery of Art. Gift of Robert H. and Clarice Smith.

Republic', written in 1802 and published in 1807,[270] is a dirge in the form of a sonnet, lamenting the passing of the Republic and its subjugation to Habsburg rule. Wordsworth recalls its former role as 'the safeguard of the West', the pathway to 'the gorgeous East', the springboard for the campaign against the Turks. Married to the sea, until that point Venice had never been ravished.

'On the Extinction of the Venetian Republic' is the first English reaction to the end of the Republic, written at the time of the naval clashes between Wordsworth's own country and France. He was led to speculate on the loss of the sea empire as the precipitant of Venetian decline: a point of view later endorsed by John Ruskin in the famous first pages of *The Stones of Venice*. For Wordsworth the fall of the Republic was the fall of the sixteenth-century government once lauded as perfect by Gasparo Contarini. It was this Republic that still had claim to the defence of liberty that interested him, and not a dissolute Venice of the eighteenth century. In the suite of sonnets that came to comprise the *Poems Dedicated to National Independence and Liberty*, he concerned himself with a number of European states – Switzerland, Poland, Sweden, for example – that currently had aspirations to liberty.[271] Venice was a still potent historical example; for Wordsworth it was due 'some tribute of regret'.

'On the Extinction of the Venetian Republic' was written when Byron was just fourteen and Venice was in a relatively stable position in Austrian hands, but still new to the loss of its freedom. In the next decade and a half blockades and isolation led to more obvious commercial contraction, and the decline of Venice became physical and material for all to see.[272] The tragedy and the recriminations thus deepened over the next twenty years.

In the sad, sweet tone of Wordsworth's sonnet there is little sensationalism, little of the almost salacious delight that so many later writers would bring to Venice – not to lament the loss of liberty but to take pleasure in the fall from grace of a once-powerful city. Venice, the tyrannical state brought to its knees, made dramatic copy. Nevertheless, new operas by Rossini were to have their first performance on the Venetian stage, and the barcarolle still sounded, despite rumours that it had been silenced.

Chapter 2

CAGED LION:
AUSTRIAN AND FRENCH RULE,
1798–1814

Austrian Rule, 1798–1806

The Treaty of Campoformio was seen as a betrayal. Criticism of Napoleon's treatment of Venice was widespread in Europe: in 1803 the Austrian representative in Milan accused him of ruining, sacrificing and betraying the Venetians, using Venice to make peace with the Austrians after giving them false hopes for a new democracy.[1] After the fall of the Municipality its two most passionate members, Ugo Foscolo and Vincenzo Dandolo, left Venice in anticipation of retaliation from the Austrians.[2] For Ugo Foscolo, deeply committed to the new democracy, Napoleon's action provoked the famous opening lines of his novel in letters *Ultime lettere di Jacopo Ortis*: 'The sacrifice of our country is consummated; all is lost.'[3] Foscolo wrote in the romantic manner that Goethe famously established in *The Sorrows of Young Werther*, but his Jacopo suffered not only the loss of his Teresa, but his *patria*. His grief was personal, urgent, exemplary. Set in 1798, immediately after Campoformio, when Jacopo leaves Venice for the Euganean Hills outside Padua, the book ends with Jacopo's suicide. A life unfulfilled politically cannot be sustained when human love is also lost.[4] The ode that Foscolo had written to Napoleon in the first heady days of the Municipality in May 1797 was now prefaced with a harsh dedication to the Napoleon who destroyed republics; but Foscolo still actively supported the confederation of Italian states under France, the Cisalpine Republic.[5]

On 18 January 1798 the Austrian general, Olviero von Wallis, entered Venice down the Grand Canal, initiating the first period of Austrian domination (fig. 21).[6] The ruling house of Habsburg was no stranger to northern Italy, nor Vienna to Venice. Cultural contacts between Venice and the imperial capital had been lively in the eighteenth century: Antonio Pellegrini frescoed churches in Vienna; Rosalba Carriera was called to the Habsburg court: Prince Joseph Wenzel von Lichenstein acquired thirteen Canalettos; Bernardo Bellotto, skilled follower of Canaletto, endowed his thirteen vistas of Vienna, painted at the behest of Empress Maria Theresa, with clarity, veracity and grace;[7] publisher Albrizzi dedicated his celebrated edition of *Gerusalemme liberata* with illustrations by Giambattista Piazzetta to the empress.[8]

Musical contacts were even stronger. Apostolo Zeno, who introduced the reforms that shaped *opera seria*, was imperial poet at the Habsburg court fom 1718 to 1729.[9] Mozart's sojourn in Venice at carnival in 1776 is well known, and Da Ponte's collaboration with him in Vienna created the most famous of the operas, *Cosi fan tutte*, *The Marriage of Figaro* and *Don Giovanni*.[10] The belief that *Don Giovanni* is in fact a version of the life of Da Ponte's friend Casanova, and that Casanova may have had an actual hand in the opera is suggested by Casanova's presence at the first performance, in Prague, and by a sketch found in his papers for one of Leporello's arias.[11] But Da Ponte's own life was not lacking in incident, or a libertine spirit: he brought

Detail of fig. 26.

his personal experience to the elaboration of plots for Mozart, as his memoirs so eloquently demonstrate.[12]

The interchange of musicians and productions between Venice and Vienna confirmed a shared love of music, particularly opera, which continued throughout the period of Austrian domination, and beyond.[13] Indeed, the mutual fascination between the cities gave them a bilateral reputation centred on the Rococo aspects of their cultures, and the dissolution of their long-standing empires – Venice in 1797, Vienna in 1918 – would be perceived to have much in common: *finis Venetiae* came to be regarded as a rehearsal for *finis Austriae*. Well into the early twentieth century Venice provided a wealth of themes that inspired the Austrian fascination with decadence.[14]

On 31 March 1798, in the first months of Habsburg domination, General Wallis promulgated eighty-nine articles for the organisation of Venice, reinstating the law of the Republic as it stood on 1 January 1796. The Habsburg empire represented the continuity of monarchical and aristocratic values and could expect allegiance from a conservative flank of the old patriciate. All subjects were required to take an oath of allegiance to the Emperor Francis II, organised for ordinary citizens through their parishes (in conjunction with an appropriate Mass), and for the nobility at a ceremony held in the Palazzo Ducale on 25 February 1798. However, upon assuming governance, the Austrians did not restore titles to the patriciate, who became merely *nobili* in the new regime.[15]

Most eminent among Venetians favoured by the Austrians was Francesco Pesaro, who had exiled himself in the early days of the Municipality after long opposing his Republic's policy of neutrality with respect to the French.[16] Appointed to high office when the Austrians gained power, he was made responsible for finance, the Arsenale and the Tribunale di Sanità, but died two months after his return.

There was minimum activity in the first years of Austrian rule until 1806. Structures for civic departments were put in place for the maintenance of streets and canals, lighting and the internal police.[17] The mechanisms of government were established and a *catasto*, a register of landed property, was set up. A bureaucracy was established by appointments drawn mainly from the nobility. Censorship protected the new rule, prohibiting affronts to religion, and works that could be seen to abuse authority or inspire democracy and those that might exhibit undue nostalgia towards the old Venetian government, either by criticism or commemoration.[18] As one visitor remarked, 'The Austrians seem to have shut up the mouths of the people, as well as those of the lions'.[19]

The theatre was one of the principal casualties of the first period of Austrian domination. A number of the private patriciate establishments closed permanently and only San Moisè was open regularly for musical performances.[20] There were restrictions on bringing republican themes to the stage; Alfieri's work was limited to four tragedies; and Goldoni was judged 'too libertine' and was banned. Restrictions on the use of the mask, seen to encourage intrigue at carnival, remained until 1802, when it was allowed, although only within theatres.[21] An academy of letters was permitted, however: the Nuova Accademia Veneta Letteraria was founded and became the Accademia Veneta in 1805, laying the foundation for the Ateneo Veneto in 1812.[22] Among the founding members were Carlo Gozzi, Jacopo Morelli, Ippolito Pindemonte and Melchior Cesarotti, names that recalled the lively culture of the Republic, and also the Municipality.

Some cultural continuity was maintained with an older generation: Carlo Gozzi was still living – he died in 1806 – Cimarosa was in Venice before his death in 1801 (Canova sculpted his bust to be placed in the Pantheon in Rome), and Melchior Cesarotti continued to hold court in his native Padua.[23] Older figures were conspicuous in the salons of Venice, which continued to play a crucial part in the visits of such noted foreigners as Byron, Stendhal and Chateaubriand. The Venice they experienced was filtered through the circles of the ex-patriciate in the salons of such distinguished women as Isabella Teotochi Albrizzi, Giustina Renier Michiel (niece of the penultimate doge), Chiaretta Contarini and Marina Querini Benzon – and would be for the next twenty to thirty years. In these circles the chameleon political loyalties of Melchior Cesarotti and the silence under Austrian rule of Foscolo's old friends Isabella Teotochi Albrizzi and Marina Benzon can be observed.[24] Most Venetians adapted to the new rule, although some patricians removed themselves from the city. The household of Isabella Teotochi Albrizzi retired to the Albrizzi villa on the Terraferma at San Trovaso near Treviso, to return only in 1806 when the French again took power.[25] But most adjusted, first to French rule, then to Austrian, then to French again, and finally to Austrian again in 1815. The leading architect, Giannantonio Selva, served all masters. In 1797 he was engaged on the renovations for ex-doge Manin's palace, but the order for Istrian stone was suspended and construction ceased.[26] After the cessation of the Municipality, whether by design or lack of patronage, Selva did not work in Venice. His major commission in 1798 was the theatre in Trieste, a commission earnt by his prominence as the architect of La Fenice.[27]

Such was the fame of Selva's friend Canova, that he was quickly involved in a project for the new rulers, receiving a commission for a memorial to the Archduchess Maria Cristina, who had died on 23 June 1798. Canova was in Vienna to negotiate his Venetian pension from his new masters.[28] The first maquette for the tomb was developed in Possagno and adapted his earlier design for the pyramidal Titian tomb: it must have seemed to Canova that a Venetian commission to honour Titian was now unlikely.[29] The new monument, destined for the Augustinerkirche in Vienna, recast the allegorical figures who mount the steps to the tomb door. On the left side, a figure of Charity leads a blind man towards the door of the tomb, linked to him by a floral garland. The conceit coincided with the wish of Duke Albert to celebrate the elevated qualities of his departed duchess, but it must also have expressed Canova's hope for the new Austrian rule in his home territory, which he had so poignantly observed to be devastated by war.[30] 'I pray to Heaven', Canova had written, 'that things can work out for poor humanity, because in war it is always the poor that are the worse treated'.[31] The recumbent lion at the face of the tomb fulfilled the duke's intention to represent Fortitude, but it must also have stirred memories of the Marcian lion. An angel, whose elegant leg is draped across the steps of the tomb ('languidly abandoned', in Canova's own words), rests his head on the lion's mane in sorrow.[32]

Some of the self-exiled patriciate returned with the change of government and took the new oaths of allegiance, even praising the incoming state. In the days of the Republic Girolamo Ascanio Molin, for example, held posts in the Council of Ten and the Inquisition, and was anti-French and anti-democratic. He had spent the months of the Municipality in Bassano writing a long poem called *Venezia tradita*, enthusing over Habsburg rule – most of the copies were destroyed when the French returned in 1806.[33] Melchior Cesarotti had welcomed Napoleon and advised citizens on the new fraternity, but he could equally celebrate the Austrians in the libretto *L'Adria consolata*, performed with music by Ferdinando Bertoni at La Fenice on the occasion of the Austrian emperor's birthday.[34] Adria, the personification of Venice, was consoled by the Genius of Austria amid choruses of dancing virtues and the genii of all the nations willingly subjected to the House of Habsburg.[35] A 'limpid' and 'vivacious' dawn awaited everyone.

Ex-patricians were appointed as censors in the new regime. Doubtless Grazioso Butta Calice had little trouble in condemning the French writers Mirabeau and Rousseau; the work of Venice's own sixteenth-century patriot and virulent critic of the Roman church, Paolo Sarpi, was prohibited. In his position as censor, the librarian of the Marciana, Jacopo Morelli, confiscated two copies of the complete works of Montesquieu, the old enemy of the conservative patriciate.[36]

The Austrians were not as patently cavalier in their public confiscation of Venetian art works as the French had been. However, much material was transferred to Vienna, and the requisition of material from the archives amounted to spoliation.[37] From 1802 'exchanges' favourable to the Austrians were conducted in a highly informed manner by the Viennese court librarian, Francesco Sebastiano Gassler. His recommendations included the multi-volumed diary of Marin Sanudo written between 1496 and 1533.[38] Because of the dire financial circumstances of many of the old patriciate, whole libraries came on to the market.[39] The fine collection of the Foscarini family in Santa Formosa (descendants of Marco Foscarini, the mid-eighteenth-century doge who had written a history of Venetian literature) was purchased by the Austrian government for Vienna's imperial library.[40] Governor Bissingen was interested in acquiring also the distinguished Farsetti collection of casts that Canova had studied, but the return of the French interrupted the transaction, and the material remained in Venetian collections.[41]

In these eight years the degradation of Venice overall was increasingly felt, not as a consequence of inherent corruption or decline, but through lack of commercial initiatives and the use of Trieste rather than Venice as the main port for the Austro-Hungarian empire.[42] There was little cultivation of new values or fostering of public spirit.

Following the change in status of the patriciate, there was considerable movement in real estate. Wealthy merchants acquired palaces, and renovation and redecoration followed. The retired castrato Gasparo Pacchierotti bought the Palazzo Farsetti in 1801. Ex-doge Manin continued the interior decoration of his palace. In 1804 the merchant Antonio Capovilla remodelled the Palazzo Belloni at Santa Stae.[43] It demonstrated the new 'rational' style, with reduced ceiling heights and rooms frescoed in *trompe-l'oeil* architecture with Neoclassical figures.[44] In 1805 the entrepreneur Giacomo Berti purchased the Palazzo Loredan.

After the death of Francesco Pesaro in 1799, so soon after his return from Vienna, the old patriciate headed by Giuseppe Priuli rallied to raise subscriptions for a tomb in Pesaro's honour, destined for no less a site than San Marco.[45] Canova was the obvious choice: his maquette not only conveys the sorrow felt for the departed patri-

cian, but the very loss of the Republic, which the artist himself felt keenly (fig. 22). It was less than two decades since Canova had been commissioned by the Republic to celebrate the marine strength of the state in his monument to Angelo Emo. Now a figure with wreath in hand grieves by the Pesaro sarcophagus; a pair of lions – a reference to both faith and the deposed Marcian lion – are also grieving. The Neoclassical bier carries reliefs of bowed Venetians imploring the Fates not to cut the thread of life held by one of their number. In the most poignant detail, a putto kneels before the tomb and nurses the ducal crown that Pesaro had anticipated but that now, as Canova well knew, was withheld forever. Canova was to say that the end of the Republic would grieve him all his life.[46]

Whatever the restrictions imposed by the new Austrian rule, a French visitor to Venice in 1805 could find that they did not weigh unduly heavily on the Venetians: their social habits seemed largely unchanged. Opera continued to be a key topic of discussion, and although there was great interest in the arrival of the newspapers at the *caffès*, political profundity was not in evidence.[47] At midday, wrote Sergent-Marceau, 'the beautiful Venetians are still in bed, or engaged in toilet preparations for their afternoon rounds of visits'.[48]

French rule, re-established in 1806 in Venice at the high point of Napoleon's career, following the victories of Austerlitz and Jena, lasted until his defeat in 1814.[49] The Treaty of Pressburg, concluded with the Austrian emperor in December 1805, ceded Venetia to France together with the old Venetian territories of Istria and Dalmatia, which had been Austrian since the treaties of Campoformio and Lunéville. They became the French territories of the Royaume d'Italie grafted onto the Cisalpine Republic which had been formed in 1802.[50] Napoleon had had himself crowned King of Italy in Milan cathedral in 1804. In 1806 he was the strongest man in Europe, with naval ambitions in the Adriatic to further his eastern drive through the Mediterranean.[51]

The French return to Venice did not, however, renew the former rhetoric of liberty and fraternity. The most ardent of the Municipalists had been vanquished by the Austrians or were self-exiled; the most conspicuous supporter of the Habsburg rule, Francesco Pesaro, was dead, and the city was substantially run by senior patricians, the new nobles.

After a brief period of relative optimism the further decline of Venice became apparent in the period of the blockades against Napoleonic territories from 1809 – from the English at sea, and then the Austrians on land – which caused the isolation of the island city and deprivation, not merely of commerce, but of the most fundamental foodstuffs and building materials.[52] In the first decade and a half of the new century Venice went from a state adjusting to the shift from its old Republican government long associated with stable, internal rule, to a city ruled from outside and unambiguously in decline.

In 1815, by the time of Waterloo, Venice was the place of ruin that would soon be recognisable in the poetry of Byron: it was a fallen city that had passed through three periods of foreign rule, with depletion of population and personal losses to its subjects and minimal commercial viability. Its patrimony was diminished, buildings had been demolished and works of art and manuscripts dispersed.[53] Venice's long history was now harshly interpreted not as a tradition of liberty, but of servitude and inquisition. Neither the Evangelist's lion nor the gilded Bucintoro, but the prisons, the *piombi* and *pozzi*, were its best-known symbols. Wordsworth's memory of the perfect republic was all but forgotten.

Yet the balance sheet under French rule does not read only in the negative. A local administration was consolidated and urban change was dramatic. Napoleon's view of cities, both Paris and those he had conquered, involved the designation of urban space as public and secular. This determined many changes for Venice: the city was altered more swiftly than at any point in the modern era. Public access to space determined many changes, as did the ambition to house the new government in high style in the Piazza San Marco.[54] A post-aristocratic government needed to be consolidated, and a new organisation of city services introduced: this was the legacy of French rule.[55]

French Governance: Prince Eugène de Beauharnais

Napoleon's viceroy in Italy, his stepson Prince Eugène de Beauharnais, was in Padua when the Treaty of Pressburg was signed on 26 December 1805. Four days later, on the evening of 31 December 1805, Beauharnais ordered sixty shots of cannon to be fired before he attended the theatre and announced French rule, which was formally reinstated on 19 January 1806.[56]

On 4 February 1806 Beauharnais entered Venice triumphantly, according to the account he gave to Napoleon, and lodged with the ex-patrician Alvise Pisani, Venetian ambassador to France at the time of the French Revolution. Pisani, a member of the wealthiest and best-known of the Venetian patriciate, had also been the Republic's delegate to Napoleon in Milan in the last days of the Republic, a member of the Municipality and, after Campoformio, one of the five appointed to steer the Municipality towards Austrian rule.[57] Thus continuity between patriciate and the post-patriciate ruling class was early established.

Beauharnais was careful to demonstrate his efficiency to his stepfather: he assured Napoleon of the odium in which the Venetians had held the Austrians and of the significant welcome that Napoleon himself could anticipate.[58] In the same month of February Napoleon underlined his right of conquest to Venice and made his priorities clear: 'It is not question of making roads and canals, it is first necessary to feed my army.' He added: 'I have without doubt treated Venice as a country of conquest. How have I obtained it other than by victory? The right of victory established, I will treat it as a good sovereign if they are good subjects . . .'[59] On 1 May 1806 Beauharnais informed Napoleon of the reaction to the official proclamation, hedging his bets by saying that it was received with pleasure, if not with enthusiasm, and that there was more enthusiasm for the new regime in Venice than in Milan.[60]

By 5 February 1806 Beauharnais had re-established local government in a decree establishing a *podestà* – Daniele Renier – and nine advisers, or *savi* (the traditional term), who formed the municipal authority. A *camera di commercio* was formed with Francesco Revedin as president, with nine Venetian members and six representatives from the provinces.[61] The Camera was to become a vital organ of economic survival and a future source of support for Daniele Manin's brief Republic of 1848–9. Under French rule the Napoleonic Code became mandatory, as did the French monetary system and the accord between Napoleon and the Pope.[62] The previous states of Venice became departments of the realm: Venice became the Adriatico, one of twenty-four departments in the larger area of Venetia.[63]

In July the Palazzo Ducale was decreed crown property, and the Prefect took up residence in March 1807.[64] The decree was reversed six months later with an allocation to transform the Procuratie Nuove into a new palace, perhaps the most decisive, conspicuous and controversial of the Napoleonic projects, for it involved changes to the very heart of the city.[65]

Once again the Venetians were called upon to subsidise the war effort by providing one thousand conscripts and by levies on 'rich' families. The Commissioner-General of Police, Pierre Lagarde, estimated that there were some twenty-five to thirty eligible families, some of whom brought diamonds in lieu of money.[66] Indeed, Lagarde showed some sympathy for the reduction in available private funds in these years.[67] It could not have been easy for Alvise Pisani to sell Napoleon the great family villa on the Brenta at Strà, as he did in 1806, but the parlous state of patriciate fortunes compelled such sales.[68] Built at the height of Pisani fortunes in the previous century, Strà had welcomed distinguished French visitors and, now a state building, was soon to be redecorated in Empire style.[69]

Almost immediately upon coming to power Lagarde addressed a dispatch to Daniele Renier with requests for urgent maintenance work, particularly canal dredging (said to have been neglected under Austrian rule), relief in the face of extensive begging in the city and measures to reactivate commerce.[70] Renier belonged to one of the oldest patrician families; from 1802 he had been a member of the Austrian advisory council, and his appointment as Podestà ensured continuity with the experienced ruling class. The agenda of items for urgent attention is of interest for it reveals that the Venetians were prepared to exaggerate the 'neglect' of the city under the Austrians in the hope of improved French involvement: the canals in fact had been systematically dredged during Austrian rule.[71] Renier followed with an address to the Minister of the Interior, Lodovico de Breme, protesting at the high level of taxation.

Evidence from Lagarde indicated that the welcome given to the French had quickly dissipated. Writing from Milan in June 1806, he claimed that each day showed a further alienation.[72] His sympathy with 'cette magnifique Venise' and the 'ancienne reine de l'Adriatique' was obvious, and his view quite clearly expressed: the city would perish if it became a city of the second order, subjugated to Milan within the Royaume d'Italie.

In June 1806 three Venetian deputies journeyed to Paris to take the oath of fealty to Napoleon, but also to petition directly for specific needs. Alvise Pisani was accompanied by Leonardo Giustinian and the banker Francesco Revedin, whom Lagarde regarded as the strongest among them. They were all Francophiles and had been original members of the Municipality.[73] Their demands, amounting to a considered programme of city maintenance, commercial and public benefits, covered the areas of public instruction and schooling from elementary school to the University of Padua (including education for girls); streets and waterways, with a general plan for water maintenance arguing the special needs of Venice; public benefits and pensions for poor patricians (who had been promised support in 1797) and the unemployed and needy; the establishment of a pawn-shop using Jewish capital, and control of the public debts; the facilitation of road and water communication, including a road to Ferrara; and the establishment of a bourse in the gallery of the Palazzo Ducale.[74] Napoleon's response is not known, but the mission appears decisive for modernisation and urban planning, indicating the degree to which an agenda was actively formulated by the Venetians.

Urban Change: The Decrees of 1806

On 28 July 1806 a viceregal decree ordered a concentration of monastic communities which effected the closure of fifteen monasteries and nineteen nunneries.[75] Nine churches were closed in the same year, and significant numbers of closures occurred each year until 1810.[76] There was no co-ordinated plan for redeployment of buildings or dispersal of contents – paintings, sculpture, inscriptions, church objects – all material was sequestered by the crown. The fact that artworks of quality could be requisitioned for the Brera in Milan as capital of the Regno Italico caused resentment, as it relegated Venice further to the status of a provincial city.[77] In June 1806 a meeting took place between the State Departmental Director, Osvaldo Gerosa and Pietro Edwards, who had earlier been responsible for the transfer of works of art to Paris. Of particular concern was the fate of works from the Scuola dei Mercanti at the Madonna dell'Orto and the paintings from the former Scuola di San Marco. One of the worst fates for a building was for it to become barracks for soldiers, as in the case of the Scuola dei Mercanti, for damage to works of art was inevitable.

Twelve establishments were requisitioned by order in October 1806. Some were used for new purposes: the State Archive was transferred to the Scuole Grande di San Teodoro (today it is an art gallery), and the Scuola di San Marco was used for a hospital (as it still is).[78] In 1806 much of the content of San Pietro di Castello, the cathedral of Venice throughout the Republic, was transferred to San Marco, now designated the city's cathedral. Although it occasioned little comment, this was a profound shift in the ecclesiastical focus of the city. Conventual buildings adjoining San Pietro di Castello, including the Sala Maggiore, decorated with portraits of the patriarchs and the site of an ancient baptism, were abandoned.[79]

The French construed public opinion to be fickle. The correspondence of Beauharnais with Napoleon suggests continuing caution with respect to potential disturbances. Napoleon was advised that a circle of nobles, with Correr said to be the main agitator, wanted an independent state, and there was correspondence between Venice and Paris to this effect.[80] But there was little visible opposition. In August 1806 the Milanese Marco Serbelloni was named Prefect, further underlining Venice's subsidiary relationship to Milan. Since it exacerbated long-standing rivalry between the two city states, this enforced link was not without consequences in kindling republican aspirations.[81] Serbelloni made a plea for Venetian support of the *Italian* nature of the Milanese alliance, and for he himself to be construed as *Italian*.

The Arsenale and the Port

Conscious of English maritime dominance after France's defeat at Trafalgar, Napoleon was ambitious to regenerate his fleet from Venice and to that end appointed Charles-Henri Bertin Commissioner-General of the Franco-Italian fleet in the Adriatic.[82] In 1805 representatives of the French Ponts et Chaussées division were already investigating the Adriatic ports.[83] On 16 August 1806, following the official celebrations for

Napoleon's birthday, Eugène de Beauharnais unveiled a bust of Napoleon in the Arsenale – a clear sign of the anticipated revival of Venice's sea power as a consequence of Napoleon's decision.[84] In 1806 Bertin had been advised to contact Beauharnais, who gave the instruction for regeneration of the shipyards, initiating the construction of twenty cannon-ships.[85] The Arsenale was visited by the French Inspector-General and the director of the Ecole Impériale aux Ponts et Chaussées between 1806 and 1807. In that capacity Gaspard-François-Claire-Marie le Roche de Prony was present in Venice and may well have been responsible for the *catasto* that was introduced in 1807 and completed in 1809, since he had been the director of the land registry process in Paris in 1791.[86] The recommendations of the enquiry into the Arsenale included the construction of new entrances and the dredging of a channel to the port of Malamocco, on the Lido.[87] Between 1809 and 1811 all the canals within the Arsenale were detailed in a new survey, an indication of the strategic importance of the outlet from the Arsenale to the Adriatic.[88] Malamocco was to become an issue for the future in view of its importance as the primary outlet from the lagoon to the sea.[89]

Andrea Savini was appointed Director of Hydraulics and Civic Building. A Venetian, whose career spanned the last years of the Republic through both the French and the Austrian changes of government, Savini had been trained in the Arsenale School and appointed by the Austrian regime as Director of Naval Construction in 1802.[90] He was sent on a study tour to Paris and to Dutch and French ports, and was subsequently responsible for the building programmes and double dykes constructed to protect the port of Malamocco from sandbars.[91]

The renovations to the Arsenale included a new gate, the Porta Nuova, on the north side, thus shifting the centuries' old defensive aspect from the south of the city directly into the lagoon.[92] In sympathy with the ancient walls and turrets that surrounded the Arsenale, the Porta Nuova was built in Gothic style, well in advance of the Gothic revival (fig. 23). But it was the defence of the Adriatic and not the preservation of Venice that was at issue. The ship construction priority was for ships fitted with cannon. A sizeable number of war vessels was built in these years, but however diligent the *arsenalotti*, goodwill was forestalled by the enforcement of naval conscription and the taboo on command for Venetians.[93] The lack of merchant naval activity contributed further to economic decline. An immediate effect of Napoleon's blockade of Britain in the Adriatic was felt in Venice: in 1805 nine British ships had visited, but there was none in 1806.[94]

The Venetians were acutely aware of the decline of their trade and their separation from the hinterland. They petitioned for the port to have free-trade status, which was granted in 1808, when the military authority was removed from the island of San Giorgio Maggiore where the port was sited.[95] The survival of Venet-

23 Porta Nuova Tower, Arsenale, 1810.

ian commerce at this time was of crucial concern, for it had in fact to be renegotiated after the demise of the guild system and the termination of Venice as a power with mainland territories supplying and receiving goods. Increasingly it had to bear the consequences of Napoleon's blockades. The lagoon, with its access to the Adriatic and also to the Terraferma, was now a military zone. Eventually new harbour facilities and a pair of lighthouses were constructed in 1813 to designs by Giuseppe Mezzani, who had been director of the first stages of construction of the Piazza Reale under Giovanni Antolini and had worked with Selva.[96] Built in Istrian stone with lanterns raised on Ionic columns and a rusticated base, the lighthouses add discreet Neoclassical accents to the area beside Palladio's church (fig. 24). The influence of Selva shows in their low-relief rustication and clarity of line.

The Chamber of Commerce – the Camera di Commercio – and its president Giuseppe Treves expressed their gratitude for the free port in a direct tribute to the emperor.[97] It was agreed to place a giant statue of Napoleon in one of the prime sites, on the Piazzetta in front of the Palazzo Ducale, an act that in itself symbolised the condition of Venice as a foreign-governed state, since it ran counter to a long-standing Venetian prohibition of personal tombs and memorials in the Basilica San Marco, the Piazza and the Piazzetta (fig. 25).[98] The statue was made by the Milanese Angelo Pizzi with the participation of Domenico Banti and erected in the Piazzetta in 1811.[99] Selva, to his credit, seems to have been the only one to oppose its location, but nevertheless he undertook the design of the pedestal.[100] The statue was not lacking in presence: Napoleon was portrayed carrying the orb, raising his arm in imperious gesture; the upper torso was bare, but the lower body was artfully draped. When it was unveiled on 15 August 1811 on Napoleon's official birthday, Giuseppe Treves

25   Domenico Banti,
Teodoro Matteini and Felice
Zuliani, *Statue of
Napoleon I*, 1811. Etching,
96.5 × 70.1 cm. Venice,
Mueso del Risorgimento.

delivered an oration and fireworks were set off in the evening. With the demise of Napoleonic rule, the statue was the first item to be removed.

The French priority was defence, not the salvation of Venetian commerce. To this end in 1810 Captain Auguste Denaix prepared a topographical map of the lagoon and undertook tidal measurements and related astronomical observations: like the authoritative *catasto* drawn up earlier for the city, Denaix's map was the model for all subsequent lagoon cartography.[101] At the same time a number of historical accounts of the lagoon were published by the Venetians, including Jacopo Filiasi,[102] and the early eighteenth-century architect of the Murazzi, Bernardo Zendramin, was published for the first time.[103] The Venetians were well aware of the shift in the status of their lagoon, once a thriving port, now the military zone of a foreign power.

French Writers

Cultural relations with Paris were not improved when the celebrated author Chateaubriand passed through Venice in August 1806 on his way to the Levant and published a letter about his visit in the Paris newspaper *Mercure de France*.[104] He described Venice as 'a city against nature' and detailed his complaints – and his ignorance:

> One cannot go there without taking a boat, or one is obliged to turn in narrow passages which seem more like corridors than streets. Only the Piazza San Marco has beauty in its ensemble of buildings and is remarkable and merits its renown.

The architecture is by Palladio and too varied! There are always two or three palaces built adjacent to each other. The famous gondolas are black and have the air of hearses. I took the first that I saw to be ferrying a dead person. The sky is not what it is beyond the Appenines . . .[105]

Distanced from familiar skies, he yet found something to admire in the many island churches, which he deemed 'picturesque and touching', particularly at night. And there were 'some good pictures' by Veronese, Tintoretto, Bassano and Titian.

Quite clearly Chateaubriand had a limited understanding of the growth of Venice as a canal city built in the lagoon with land at a premium. Venetians rushed to the defence of the city, among them the redoubtable Giustina Renier Michiel.[106] Well known for her salon and her friendship with literary figures in Venice and Padua, she was a woman of letters who never forgot that she was the niece of the penultimate doge, Paolo Renier. Her literary zeal led her, in the year after the fall of the Republic, to undertake translations of Shakespeare, beginning with *Othello, The Moor of Venice*, with its obvious local reference, its evidence of the pride of the Republic embodied in its military commander in the historic days of the *stato dal mar*.[107] The translation was one of the few in Italian, although it was not particularly well received, but the complexity of the text and its implicit tribute to Renier's *patria* should not be under-estimated.[108] Renier presented her work as a translation by a 'Venetian woman', taking the opportunity to commend Shakespeare for his 'tenderness and admiration' with regard to 'il bel sesso', as witnessed in Desdemona, Juliet, Rosalind. . . .[109] With a Venetian sensibility, she responded to that 'most theatrical and affecting of all the passions' revealed by Othello.[110] She was keen to offer wise counsel in the face of this passion.[111]

When Chateaubriand wrote she responded in French, accusing him of not having done his homework, and in particular of being ignorant of Venetian architecture.[112] She accused the French – 'others of your country' – of not departing from the early views of Amelot, not updating their knowledge of laws and political institutions or taking the trouble to examine them.[113] Chateaubriand had transformed Venice into a monster when it was, in fact, the most original of cities, constructed over many centuries, a miracle for the eyes, and evidence of human will: 'Venice is our creation [*notre ouvrage*] . . . each of our streets is a trophy of our endurance, and every step is taken on the soil of a monument of peaceful conquest.'[114] The Grand Canal, she admonished, should appeal to French taste as a great boulevard. The greatest monuments of modern Rome are the work of a Venetian, Canova.[115] Further, in response to the criticisms of the weather: 'We have neither the fog of London, the mud of Paris, nor the arduous heat of Sicily.'[116]

The outrage Chateaubriand occasioned prompted other literary figures in Venice to refute his accusations. Marchesa Orintia Romagnoli Sacrati asked how one could possibly respond to this man's delirium, and Lavinia Florio, daughter of a poet, wrote a poem in French informing the miscreant of the courageous creation of Venice in the fifth century as a defence against the sea and let him know the black gondola was the very evidence of Venetian egalitarianism.[117] Chateaubriand was to redeem himself later in his *Mémoires d'Outre Tombe* based on a more sympathetic and extended visit in 1833, but he hardly helped matters in 1806. However, the French had been critics of Venice before.

Shortly after Chateaubriand's visit the formidable Madame de Staël published a novel destined for fame, *Corinne ou l'Italie*, which added to the reputation of Venice as a melancholy city. Exiled from France by Napoleon in 1803, De Staël had been received cautiously by the Austrians in Venice when she arrived in 1805. She stopped first at Padua where she requested a meeting with Cesarotti – he spent a morning with her at her lodgings; then she requested a meeting with Giustina Renier Michiel.[118] Madame de Staël was in Venice for a mere five days, but she had obvious knowledge of the literary circles. That visit and her sense of the city inform her widely read novel *Corinne*, which she was working on at the time.

Corinne confirmed the reputation of Venice in decline.[119] Although the story is set in 1795, before the fall, Venice is already pervaded with melancholy which was no doubt the author's impression of it under Austrian rule: 'a feeling of sadness falls upon the spirits as you enter Venice.'[120] For Corinne, in some part surely the mouthpiece for her creator, Venetian architecture was 'grotesquely ornamented', and the city itself appeared almost submerged. The stillness was 'awful' and she felt the lack of 'nature, trees and vegetation'. The gondolas, sliding down the canals, were either 'coffins or cradles, the first and last resting place of man'. Corinne professed her 'profound melancholy' to Oswald, Lord Nevil, the Scottish aristocrat who brought her to Venice; the melancholy deepened when she heard the sound of three cannon shots fired to indicate a nun's taking of the veil in one of the island convents. However, Corinne and Oswald managed to tour in the conventional manner, visiting the Palazzo Ducale, admiring the *Last Judgement* and the representation of the humiliation of Frederick Barbarossa before the Senate of Venice. Lord Nevil was appreciative of the Arsenale's trophies of marine greatness, which reminded him of Britain. They ascended the Campanile and, like many before them, admired the extensive view over the Adriatic.

Madame de Staël's account was not uninformed; it had undeniable authenticity. At the same time, it repeated the predictable French view of the Republic and its tyranny, historical matter that Chateaubriand had bypassed. De Staël was explicit: 'The hatred of it was easily accounted for, because it had been dreaded, and could be easily altered now it was no longer feared. There was an aristocracy who sought popular favour, but sought it in a despotic manner by amusing the people without enlightening them.'[121] Rousseau finds his echo here: his *Letter to M. D. Alembert on the Theatre* recommended that the people be given amusements which make them 'like their stations and prevent them craving for a sweeter one'.[122] Once again Venice was beleaguered by its government, but the success of *Corinne* was its moody melancholy enhanced by the separation of Corinne and her escort, who returned to his masculine military duties while Corinne awaited him, marooned in Venice, chaste as the nun who had been celebrated by cannon fire when she took the veil. 'It is there [Venice] that I place the goodbyes in my book.'[123] Her account of Venice was an early announcement of the necrophilic Venice that so fascinated later visitors, and it was already the place where *affaires d'amour* could be atmospherically terminated.

Madame de Staël's influential portrait of the city came only some years after Madame de Krudener published *Valerie*.[124] A great success when it appeared in 1801, it took the fashionable epistolary form of lovers' letters, written mainly from Stockholm and Venice. Venice is still Republican, a city of art, but it is flawed, although not as morbidly as Madame de Staël presented it.[125] It is a Beccaria-style Venice, with frightful prisons that the sun never reaches, lions' mouths waiting for the letters of denunciation, a government quick to avenge, and a people under the shadow of despotism. And yet the people bathe in the canals, sing of their loves under a calm sky, the shops are luxurious, the opera plays and the Armenian silently smokes his cigar. It is still 'this magical place' – *ce lointain magique*.

Almost completely negative, Chateaubriand's views were remarkably similar to Madame de Staël's declaration that Venice was melancholy, silent and lacking in greenery. Neither De Staël nor Chateaubriand was original in likening the gondola to a coffin: Goethe had anticipated them – it was virtually a cliché.

* * *

Napoleon's Grand Tour and the Royal Decree, 1807

A famous writer's disdain must have seemed but another episode in the French betrayal of Venice. Yet the second period of Napoleonic rule began auspiciously enough and Napoleon consolidated his rule by visiting the city.[126] His state visit was treated with all the traditional ceremony of the old Republic. Neumann Rizzi, who had planned the decorations for the Municipality, created a Neptune float; naval forces were lined up in the Bacino. Architect Selva contrived a floating triumphal arch near the church of Santa Lucia on the Grand Canal – an echo of Palladio's arch of welcome for the French King Henry III, and his own earlier decorations for the visit of the Counts of the North, Paul and Maria Feodorovna of Russia in 1782.[127] The emperor was greeted as 'the hero of the century' – as indeed he was, in 1807 – and given two keys by Podestà Renier: one silver and one gold, carried by two Moors. Napoleon travelled in the ceremonial vessel, the *peata*, with Renier, accompanied by five *bissone* with a dozen rowers, and twenty-one private *bissone* (fig. 26). Like the regal visitors to the Republic, he disembarked at the Piazzetta, but he then proceeded, not to the Palazzo Ducale as of old, but to the Palazzo Reale in the Procuratie Nuove.

On 2 December, in ceremonial style, a regatta took place. Giuseppe Borsato designed a *macchina* with statues by the Venetian sculptors Luigi Zandomeneghi and Bartolomeo Ferrara to be placed at the conspicuous turn on the canal in front of the Palazzo Balbi. In contrast to the glossing over of Republican traditions during the Municipality, this was a traditional Venetian welcome. Carpets festooned balconies on the Grand Canal, festivals in traditional costumes took place, and renowned

26 Giuseppe Borsato, *Water Cortège for Napoleon passing in front of the Church of the Scalzi, 1807*. Pen, ink and watercolour, 50.8 × 72 cm. Venice, Museo del Risorgimento.

carnival feats reappeared, such as the pyramid of acrobats known as the Force of Hercules.[128] A banquet and ball were held at the Ridotto, a Te Deum was sung at San Marco, and the city was lit by 4,094 torches. La Fenice was redecorated. Abandoning the equally sized boxes – the Republic's expression of democratic principle – Selva designed a royal box for the centre of the theatre. Giuseppe Borsato was responsible for new decorations.[129] A performance of *Il Guidizio di Giove* was held, with Jupiter formed in the likeness of Napoleon. Obsequious verses were composed, imputing near-divinity to Napoleon.

A grand plan for Venice was announced on 7 December 1807, shortly after the official visit.[130] It must have appeared positive enough after the stagnation under Austrian rule.[131] A period of active – some would say over-active – intervention commenced with a decree proposing extensive changes, which opened a major new chapter in urban development.[132] Planning began for the establishment of a cemetery on the island of San Cristoforo; the continuation of the Riva degli Schiavoni – the main route along the Basin of St Mark's from the Palazzo Ducale eastwards to the Campo San Giuseppe; the formation of a public garden in the area beyond the Riva degli Schiavoni; and a piazza for military display with a grand *passeggiata* for the island of the Giudecca. This new piazza projected on the Giudecca island opposite the island of San Giorgio Maggiore was to be twice the size of San Marco. The official architect was Giannantonio Selva, recommended to the Minister for the Interior, Lodovico de Breme, by Beauharnais. With this appointment, Selva became the most influential Venetian architect, active from the last decades of the Republic to his death until 1819.

Certain aspects of the urban plan were similar to those Napoleon instigated for Paris, such as the regulations controlling symmetry and alignment of buildings, the provision of parklands, and arterial planning for improved transit. But the projects were persistently hampered by lack of finance; Napoleon's campaigns made greater budgetary demands: it was first necessary to feed his army.

Some initiatives had ongoing importance, notably the formation of a body to advise on aesthetic matters, the Commissione all'Ornato, which played a fundamental role in implementing planning regulations.[133] The commission was decreed in both Milan and Venice, and signed by Beauharnais in Milan on 9 January 1807.[134] Membership was honorary, consisting of five citizens with professed interest in aesthetic matters, and two architects. The founding members were the secretary of the Academy Antonio Diedo; the architect Giannantonio Selva; academician, architect and painter Davide Rossi; the engineer Pietro Lucchesi; and the architect and academician Giuseppe Mezzani.

Members of the Academy played a key role in the Commissione all'Ornato and, therefore, in the aesthetic decisions of the city with relation to buildings and the custodianship of artwork. In 1807 the Venice Academy had been given status comparable to those of Bologna and Milan, and its president was nominated for life by the government. In what was clearly a political appointment, Alvise Pisani was the first incumbent in the Napoleonic years. Following Pisani's death in 1808, Leopoldo Cicognara was given the post, acknowledging his involvement in the visual arts and a certain professionalism, as distinct from the general interest of other Venetians under consideration (they were the Podestà Daniele Renier, Ippolito Pindemonte and Francesco Gritti).[135] Pietro Edwards was appointed Keeper of Public Paintings.

The preliminary stage of operations for the Commission was a Regulatory Plan prepared in July 1807 by Selva, with Diedo's assistance.[136] This was the first of a long line of plans intended to impose modern urban principles on Venice. High on the agenda was the regulation of façades facing on to streets – the requirement that designs for all public façades be approved for the best maintenance of streets and that public safety be consulted in matters such as demolition. It was the beginning of official urban planning controls which would both facilitate and frustrate urban change over the next two hundred years.

However, while the Commission had an undeniable French charge under Napoleonic rule, such an organisational body was not unprecedented in the Venetian context. The concern for public utilities and for the canal system and its maintenance, and questions of regulation and aesthetics had traditionally been the province of the Giudici di Piovego di San Marco e Rialto, established in the thirteenth century. It had regulated public space, the canal system and maintenance, and controlled private building regulations.[137] Additionally, there had been a body with specific responsibility for the waters, the Savi alle Acque, whose key role in Venetian urban life had been maintained throughout the history of the Republic.

One of the Commission's early tasks was to approve removal of the fish-market from the area behind the Piazza so that the smells would not offend the inhabitants of the Palazzo Reale.[138] Other duties included the maintenance of bridges – always a priority in the days of the Republic. But the Commission's primary responsibility became the dispersal of the contents of demolished ecclesiastical buildings. The Commission was alert to the destruction of buildings that were 'the ornament' of the city (and thus properly the business of this commission 'all'Ornato') but nevertheless subjected to frequent and 'capricious demolition'.[139] For the first time on a significant scale, demolition had become the instrument of reform, freeing space for new building or enlarged streets. The attendant politics were to remain controversial through the modern history of Venice, giving rise to continuing debates between conservationists and those proposing renovation and clearance as answers to problems of housing and health.

The example of France itself was persuasive. Well before Haussmann's designs on Paris, Napoleon had issued demolition orders in order to create grand vistas terminating in squares or *places* and creating façades with regularity and symmetry. The rue de Rivoli, the result of a decree in October 1801, was his most grandiose project.[140] It has been called 'the first great enterprise in modern Parisian town planning'.[141] In the seventeenth century, under Henri IV, the principles of *alignement* and regulated street planning had been established.[142] As a consequence, the French saw the Piazza San Marco and the Procuratie buildings as a significant architectural ensemble – even Chateaubriand responded well; but their preference for regularised street architecture led them to deem Venice overall to be in need of straightening, widening and regulating. It was, after all, a city against nature.

It was also a city required to generate taxes for its masters, and to this end the French initiated a *catasto* decree on 12 January 1807 with a map of property drawn up between 17 August and 6 December under the direction of the engineer Pietro Toscani.[143] The Napoleonic projects appear in place on the map for the first time: the vast tract of cleared land awaiting Selva's gardens, and the adjacent thoroughfare, the Via Eugenia; the new designation of the Palazzo Reale and its staircase in the Piazza San Marco; and the cleared land on the waterside awaiting the royal gardens. The smallest holding in the city was marked as well as the extensive areas housing the military. Buildings were requisitioned for the royal marines in the vicinity of the Arsenale, as were buildings adjacent to San Francesco della Vigna and San Pietro di Castello – including the area designated for the storage of wood for use at the Arsenale. Where the map produced by Collalto presented to the Municipality had been a document of high idealism – an impossibility to realise, the *catasto* was prosaic, showing the city as it was, without idealism or symbolism of any kind: no lions of St Mark, personified winds or figures of Neptune – all the tokens of the one-time Serenissima were stripped away.[144] The *catasto* announced the modern configuration of Venice in which each parcel of land, to the smallest subdivision, is presumed taxable.

* * *

Public Spaces: Via Eugenia and the Public Gardens

After Napoleon's decree, planning for a new thoroughfare and for public gardens destined to offer ordinary Venetians access to 'the joys of verdure' began immediately.[145] In the area near the Arsenale a new street was to be created by covering over the Rio di Castello to make a thoroughfare three hundred metres long, much wider than the narrow pathways characteristic of old Venice. The Via Garibaldi, as it is now called, was first named the Via Eugenia in honour of Beauharnais, who supervised the plan. Giannantonio Selva was appointed as architect: he became the principal creator of Napoleonic Venice.

As in Paris, the new street was intended to open up the medieval heart of an old city to traffic, as well as conforming to the taste for vistas and regularity. Despite Venice's basic unsuitability for regularised streets that were, inevitably, in conflict with the network of canals, the practice of canal infill to discipline the topography persisted throughout the nineteenth century. The organisation in charge of water and land passages, the Commissione per lo Studio d'un Piano di Riforma delle Vie e Canali, was to have a life well beyond the period of French rule.[146] It was not a new practice, but under the Republic such infills had been relatively discreet and the original flow of water was maintained by building over underground arches.[147] Selva tried this practice on unprecedented scale in his new thoroughfare, which resulted in a number of calamitous collapses, embarrassing him and his engineer.[148]

The public garden, a familiar Napoleonic provision, was deemed particularly necessary in Venice, where public spaces, especially green ones, were limited. Montesquieu had earlier commented on the lack of greenery, as had Madame de Staël and Chateaubriand. The Castello area designated for the gardens was densely populated: in his classic guide Lorenzetti described it as '[a] spacious area – once the Motta di Sant'Antonio . . . the poor and picturesque area of fishermen, lace-makers, and *impirasse* [bead-threading women], the poor people described by Goldoni in his comedies'.[149] Arguably it was the most democratic, accessible site for the new gardens, commanding fine views of the Bacino, the Giudecca and San Giorgio Maggiore, the Lido and lagoon islands.

Selva's plan for the site, which combined two irregular and unequal tracts of land intercepted by a canal, was formal. The entrance opened off the new Via Eugenia in an imposing semicircle where a grand entrance gate was planned, to be surmounted by five sculptures. A formal walk then angled towards the bridge over the Rio di San Giuseppe, giving views of the lagoon. Selva was highly conscious of the potential of the vista, seeing the lagoon and islands as supplying a 'pleasant surprise' and a picturesque element that complemented his formal design.

Architect-designed gardens were a phenomenon of the time, and Selva's travels in England and France had acquainted him with such notable examples as Stowe, Versailles and Marly.[150] The buildings he planned for his gardens expressed his ambition for a public park rich in facilities as well as opportunities for the enjoyment of nature, including the provision of a botanical garden.[151] Close to the entrance on the Via Eugenia there were to be *caffès* and a *trattoria* accommodated in a two-storey building adorned with columns in Selva's favourite Ionic order (fig. 27). Provision was to be made for riding and the use of carriages, including a coachhouse and stables in neo-Palladian style. Another coffee-house, of simple, elegant design with a pedimented doorway and two lateral wings, was designed for the eastern extremity of the Motta Sant'Antonio. A small hill planted with evergreens was to have an eight-columned tempietto containing a statue of Napoleon. A major element in the initial plan, prophetic of the later development of sea bathing at the Lido, was Selva's proposal for public salt baths with an extended formal façade onto the lagoon, and an elevated portico with a pedimented porch, intended to take advantage of the views. However,

27a and b   Giannantonio
Selva and Giuseppe Rossi,
two views of the 'Trattoria,
Bottega di Caffè, etc' for the
Giardini Pubblici, 1809. Pen
and watercolour. Venice,
Museo Correr.

the limited budget meant that Selva's plans were compromised, and few of the build-ings were realised.

The Viceroy responded to the first plans on 3 June 1808, approving the Via Eugenia and the bridge in the gardens (which, unusually in Venice, was without steps). Beauharnais rejected the shop at the entrance, expressed reservations with respect to the pilasters and iron gate projected for the grand entrance (fig. 28), and said no to the tempietto and to the guardhouse and inspector's residence, which he deemed superfluous. He rejected also the baths.[152]

On 7 March 1808 Selva presented his revised plans, which included a stable and coachhouse (equestrian facilities were suitable for the area). A *caffè* and *trattoria* took the place of the baths. The placement of the stables and coachhouse was further modi-fied to take account of the view.[153] Obviously frustrated by the contraction of the budget, Selva made plans to use building materials from the demolished edifices – two bells from the old church of San Antonio were sold and the one building actually built (to be altered and eventually demolished when the gardens were used for the Bien-nale d'Arte in the late nineteenth century) made in wood on brick foundations. Given to illness and melancholy, Selva must have experienced some despondency in the creation of his garden, for his most splendid schemes came to nothing. The bridge he planned as an ornament to the Riva degli Schiavoni where the new street met the adjacent canal was first designed in stone, then more modestly in wood, but even that was not built in Selva's lifetime.[154]

The reaction to the gardens was generally negative, doubtless because of the per-ception that they were built on ruins, but also because informal garden design in the English manner had many adherents, and there was considerable reaction against Selva's formal style. The diarist Emmanuele Cicogna noted adverse opinions (he was generally hostile to Selva) and recorded what was obviously a popular view: that the entrance, with its enormous rusticated pillars, looked like a lion cage, or the gateway to a well-defended fortress.[155] It was clear that Selva was still associated with the con-troversy surrounding the competition for La Fenice – he was more popular with his patrons than the public. Further reaction can be gauged from a passionate letter written about the state of Venice at the end of French rule by Gaetano Pinali: he was an archaeologist, an amateur architect and a justice in the Court of Appeals. He praised the idea of the public garden, but condemned its location in an area so rich in churches.[156] He criticised the 'monotonous walks' and the obsolete preference for a formal garden, rather than one closer to nature.

Whatever the reservations, the gardens quickly featured in Venetian guidebooks. They were depicted on the frontispiece of the first comprehensive guides published in the nineteenth century, Moschini's 1815 *Guida per la Città di Venezia* and the

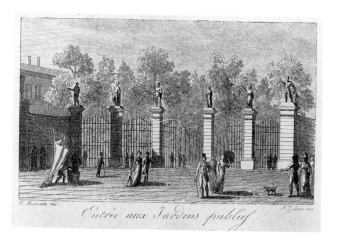

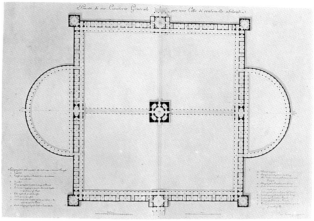

28 Giuseppe Borsato, *Entrance Gates of the Giardini Pubblici.* Engraving. Venice, Museo Correr.

29 Giannantonio Selva and Giuseppe Rossi, plan for the Cemetery of San Cristoforo della Pace, 1908. Pen and watercolour, 60.5 × 82.5 cm. Venice, Museo Correr.

Academy's folio volume compiled by Cicognara, Selva and Diedo on the best-known buildings in Venice, *Le Fabbriche più cospicue di Venezia.*[157] At the same time reactions continued to be critical, and the site was already in a state of some neglect only a decade or so later.[158] But later the gardens were well used and praised by those who did indeed seek greenery and the respite afforded by lagoon views.[159] Perhaps Franz Liszt, in Venice in 1838, made the point most aptly:

> Prince Eugene may well have done a fine thing for them [the Venetians] by planting a garden where they could go and enjoy the cool evening shadows, scented flowering shrubs, and a walk along the sandy paths with a fine view of the lagoon and the islands. But to be a Venetian is to prefer marble to foliage, a palace to a garden. The garden has been forsaken in favour of the piazza . . .[160]

After unification with Italy, the gardens accommodated monuments to the heroes of the Risorgimento, and busts of Verdi, Wagner and Carducci. From 1895 the eastern section, where once Selva had planned his tempietto to Napoleon and the bathing pavilion, became the venue for the internationally known Biennale d'Arte.

Selva's gardens may have been far from his original plan; but his grand project for the Passeggiata on the Giudecca was not even begun. The creation of a huge paradeground was doubtless suggested as much by military considerations as by public utility, since the grounds were adjacent to the new port on the island of San Giorgio and commanded access to the waters of the Bacino. The orientation, however, was towards the southern lagoon, opened up behind a row of buildings maintained on the Bacino side extending up to Palladio's Zitelle convent. Selva's love of formally centralised space – evident in the public gardens, and his plan for the cemetery (fig. 29) – is evident again in the rectangular central parade ground flanked on each side by double squares.[161] On the lagoon side there was to be a terrace and a brick building with a loggia adorned with four columns. But the contracted budget, the blockades and military impositions around 1813 cancelled the project.

Preservation and Patrimony

Many regarded the demolitions in the garden area as vandalism.[162] The churches destroyed included Sant'Antonio, San Nicolò, San Domenico and the Seminario of the Cappucine di Castello, as well as the Hospice for Retired Sailors. Emmanuele Cicogna confided his lament for lost columns and marble riches to his diary in 1810, noting particularly the destruction of the beautiful loggia of the church of Sant' Antonio.[163] The demolitions were publicly deplored by Giannantonio Moschini and

Jacopo Filiasi, anxious at least to convey appropriate artworks from the churches to the Accademia and make them available for public instruction. The genesis of public collections and the preservation of patrimony for all was now at issue. Moschini and Filiasi were two of the most ardent guardians of the lost Republic. The Abbot Moschini was a high-profile figure whose account of recent Venetian literature was one of the first responses to the need to connect Venetian culture with a new age.[164] In a further spirit of conservation, Moschini had begun the work for which he is best known, writing guides, with a study of his native island of Murano published in 1808 (extolling the glassmaking gifts that Murano had given the world).[165] Jacopo Filiasi was a historian of the ancient lagoon (following Tommaso Temanza in this respect). He published his compendium of writings on the early lagoon in 1811 and then continued his historical and critical research on lagoon history and geography.[166]

About this time Cicogna must have begun his vast labour recording the inscriptions in ecclesiastical buildings; they numbered well over a thousand. His eventual publication of 1824 was to be dedicated 'Alla Patria', a record of the illustrious Venetian names collected in a time when 'Venice seemed no longer ours'.[167] Each building listed by Cicogna was dedicated by him to a contemporary who had some particular connection with that church: thus the entry on the church and monastery of Santa Maria de' Servi, demolished in 1812, was addressed to Conte Nicolò Vendramin Calergi, for it had been the family church of the Vendramins and seventeen inscriptions to them were recorded.[168] The entry on the church and monastery of San Martino on the island of Murano was dedicated to Pietro Bigaglia, who sustained the industry manufacturing glass beads, a traditional art of the island; Cicogna noted that Bigaglia had won awards in Venice, Vienna and London.[169]

Selva himself was not ignorant of the value of the churches being demolished, since he had recommended that the Doric arch of the Lando chapel of Sant'Antonio, attributed to Sanmichele, and other important pieces should be incorporated into his Giardini.[170] The Lando arch still stands (fig. 30), the single reminder of the lost churches. At the same time Selva was certainly prepared to demolish, for this was the very premise for his new plans. In the first plan of 1808 he was careful to note that the Domenican convent, orchard and store that stood in the area to be the garden entrance was 'of no importance as an art monument', being already in use as a barracks.[171] On the worth of other buildings he was silent.

Pietro Edwards, who had been responsible for the dispatch of artworks to Paris during the Municipality, faced a colossal sorting task, with pictures from demolished buildings numbered in the thousands. Individual churches held an average of between fourteen and twenty items and some had many more, such as the Scuola di Sant' Orsola, with the famous suite by Carpaccio (later so loved by Ruskin) representing only a fraction of a total of 113 works.[172] Edwards was undoubtedly experienced, but he had frightening power. In 1807 he made a consignment to the vice-regal apartments through the architect Antolini: sixty-three paintings from the Palazzo Ducale and the convent of San Giorgio Maggiore were requisitioned.[173] With huge numbers of paintings, manuscripts and furnishings in state deposits, trading was rife, as was the extensive transferral of reliquaries. Little inventory or costing was involved; the Austrian crown bought five thousand paintings in a block.[174] In his magisterial study *Venezia scomparsa*, Alvise Zorzi recorded the history of works relocated or lost; he was particularly critical of Edwards's treatment of the church of Sant'Elena, its 102 paintings and its sculpture, including high-quality pieces by Antonio Rizzo and Matteo Raverti.[175]

At the same time it might be remembered that the dispersal of Venetian artworks was well established as a form of trading in the days of the Republic. The Venetians were adept at hawking their works around Europe and their artists were constantly employed outside Venice. Algarotti had been known as a collector and dealer: as a young man Selva had catalogued his collection. Consul Joseph Smith had assured sales

to his native England.[176] Clearly the brisk trading in Venetian works had alarmed the old Republic: a law of 1773 identified the problem of dispersal and led to the appointment of an official responsible for listing the works of notable artists *in situ* in *scuole*, monasteries, churches and public buildings, with indications of their conservation needs.[177]

However, the special preservation needs of central buildings was acknowledged. A commission appointed to oversee the Basilica of San Marco and the Palazzo Ducale, included Nicolò Vendramin, the secretary of the Accademia, Antonio Diedo, and Jacopo Filiasi, representing the Commissione all'Ornato.[178] In decades to come these two buildings were to be brought to international notice because of their restoration programmes, and the sentiment that they belonged to the world was more and more frequently expressed.

When, in early 1809, the demolitions required for the public gardens had taken place, opposition within Venice was hardened. Moschini and Filiasi made recommendations to Prefect Serbelloni concerning works of art and material of historical value that should be transferred to the Accademia, particularly the high-quality objects in Sant'Antonio di Castello. The need to petition for appropriate placement for these works became urgent, and on 21 December 1809 a conference was held with Podestà Renier and the most notable voices for conservation in the city: Diedo, Rossi, Selva, Borsato, Cicognara, Edwards, Morelli and Filiasi.[179] Both the Academy and the Commissione all'Ornato were prominent.

The body met again under Renier on 19 January 1810, when the President of the Academy, Cicognara, recommended a new position to oversee the relocation. Cicognara was a fortunate appointment to Venice: a count of Ferrara, he was totally loyal in his commitment to Venetian artistic patrimony and contemporary art practice. He was articulate, respected in Europe at large, devoted to Canova and possessed of a breadth of historical knowledge in his writings that made him a model for historiographers in his time.[180] In his early political career he had supported the French and held posts in Ferrara, Modena, Turin and Milan, but certain anti-French opinions led to his exile in 1803. He had then sought a non-political position, which led to his appointment at the Venetian Academy. In 1808 he dedicated his treatise on beauty to Napoleon – 'Emperor of the French and King of Italy'.[181]

While an amateur to some eyes, Cicognara was eminently qualified, with wide contacts.[182] His treatise on beauty, *Del Bello, Raggionamenti*, established the criteria of beauty in the 'Ancients', but Cicognara was also well versed in contemporary philosophy, reading Kant, Hogarth, Voltaire and Burke, and ready to find beauty and sublimity in personal vision.[183] He has been credited as one of the first Italian readers of Kant, and although an enthusiast rather than an analyst, his sense of the pertinence of the most recent literature was combined with his appreciation of tradition.[184]

Cicognara's leadership was fully apparent in August 1810 when, addressing the Academy, he followed a eulogy on Palladio – the 'Tasso of architecture', as he called him – with an attack on the 'sacrilegious hand' of Napoleon, who had defiled a tradition that had been the admiration of nations for centuries: 'Finally one cannot be silent for it would not be fitting in an age known for the splendour of its celebrations, for posterity one day to recognise the period as fatally damaging some of the great productions of human ingenuity.'[185] It was a brave summation. The remarks were received badly by the Viceroy and no action was taken to preserve the Venetian material.

By 1810 optimism with regard to the benefits of French rule was abating. Podestà Bartolomeo Gradenigo, Renier's successor, protested to the prefect of the Adriatico about the frequent demolition of well-known buildings, the secrecy of proceedings, reconstruction undertaken without licence and alterations made without approval.[186] Selva, as a member of the Commission, confirmed the many abuses, but his own position was equivocal. Early in his career he had encountered resistance when renovating the Manin palace – the Palazzo Dolfin, on the Grand Canal, built by Sansovino. He was obliged to preserve the façade and to limit his redesign to the interior.[187] The very fact that such a question arose is of interest, given the high regard in which Sansovino was held by Tommaso Temanza, Selva's master. Even before the demolition of San Geminiano, Selva accepted the commission to design a replacement church, San Maurizio.[188] The new project, an essay in Neoclassical manner – and important in this respect in Venice – was in gestation by 1806, although it was not finished in Selva's lifetime.

It appears that Selva was not strongly opposed to the demolition of San Geminiano. His last act of political compliance was the design of a monument to Napoleon's alpine crossing at Mont Cenis.[189] This was to be an unrepentantly Neoclassical building: a pyramid imposed over a circle inspired by the Pantheon, with a temple entrance approached by huge steps. At the same time Selva's dedication to historic Venetian architecture was evident during the blockade of 1813–14, when he wrote a study on the sixteenth-century Veronese architect Michele Sanmichele – perhaps his fortress architecture seemed particularly relevant – and a tract on his favourite Ionic volute.[190] Selva was also successful in overturning the demolition order on Temanza's church of the Maddalena, for that order must have been a threat to the very roots of his own training and practice.[191] Selva's ambivalent attitude to demolition may well have been influenced by his own current projects, but he was just one of many who adjusted to the shifts of governance and changing patrons and conditions.

To modernise, in short, implied demolition, and it continued to do so. In the period of French rule, elimination of some buildings on the one hand, the conservation of others and the appropriate custodianship of displaced works on the other, had become issues for government and appropriate committees of professionals.[192] These were new procedures, essential to shifting ideas of preservation and patrimony.

The Island Cemetery

Napoleon's urban reforms required the provision of cemeteries detached from local parishes and sited at a distance from the city centre: Père Lachaise in Paris was the most famous example.[193] To comply with the Edict of Saint-Cloud, Lagarde recommended to Podestà Renier that a cemetery be established outside the city in order to prevent contagion in hot weather.[194] The Commissione all'Ornato was to oversee the establishment; it would no longer be permissible to inter bodies in churches or cemeteries within the city. Discussions on the site led to the nomination of the island of San Cristoforo in the northern lagoon opposite Murano, adjacent to the island of San Michele.[195] The fifteenth-century church of San Cristoforo, a work by Pietro Lombardo, was demolished.[196]

Selva was the chosen architect. He planned squares in a formal disposition contained by a continuous brick wall at the edge of the water to be inset with domed chapels, but yet again his design was not fully executed.[197] The new cemetery opened in 1813, with a new small church, which, Emmanuele Cicogna noted in his diary, was entirely inferior to the original building.[198] Boats and sailors were appointed to service the cemetery, and the taxes on both interment and transport were fixed.[199] The island siting was no doubt pragmatic, quite in line with the Venetian tradition of isolating certain services on separate islands, but at the same time it appears inspired in its evocation of the classical journey across the River Lethe. The dead were rowed in full ceremony in a special gondola.

Napoleon's edict prompted musings on the geography of the dead, on graveyards and burial grounds, already a fashionable aesthetic subject at the turn of the century when poets brooded about sanctified ground and the resting places of the dead were a subject of contemplation. Among the most celebrated was Ugo Foscolo's poem *De' Sepolcri*, which he dedicated to Ippolito Pindemonte, so it has a connection with Venetian circles, and perhaps the local events that drove Jacopo Ortis to suicide. Foscolo protested against the Edict and the distancing of the dead from their parishes: 'sepulchral stones did not always serve as the floors of churches; nor did the stench of corpses surrounded with incense infect those who came to pray . . .'[200]

Yet the opening image of *De' Sepolcri* is a visual portent of the Venetian cemetery island that finds its poetry in the water setting and the shadow of cypresses: *all'ombra de' cypressi*. In time the cemetery came to represent the unavoidable necrophilia of Venice: it became a site of romantic yearnings and metaphysical journeys evoked throughout the nineteenth century by creative spirits who feasted, vampire-like, on the city's mortality. The ferrymen and their funeral boats were destined to enact the crossing of the River Lethe in many films in the following century. No doubt schooled by *De' Sepolcri*, Agostino Sagredo, visiting in 1832 on a cold February day, meditated on the vanity of human beings, some of them 'brought to their end before their time', and felt the place to be isolated from life – *an arido deserto*.[201] He lamented the loss of the 'great church of San Cristoforo'.[202]

The Royal Palace

It was in the very heart of Venice, in the Piazza San Marco, that the effects of French conquest were most dramatic. After their original conquest during the Municipality, the French had shipped out the golden horses of San Marco and destroyed the symbols of St Mark. Major public buildings had been disassociated from the names of aristocratic governance. With the more extreme imperial notions of his second period of rule, Napoleon recognised the Piazza San Marco as the site for a royal palace to be inhabited by Eugène Beauharnais: in the centre of Venice, the Piazza is remarkable for its spaciousness in a city where space is so restricted. Legend has it that it was

Napoleon who first described it in that felicitous and much-used metaphor as 'the finest drawing room in Europe', although the evidence is elusive. In a French guidebook of 1844 by Jules Lecomte – *Venise ou coup d'oeil, littérature, artistique, historique, poétique . . .* – Napoleon is quoted as saying 'The Piazza is a salon designed for the sky to serve as a canopy' (*La place Saint-Marc est un salon auquel le ciel est digne de servir de voûte).*[203] Lecomte added that it is 'like a huge, delicious salon'. Henry James echoed the words in 'The Aspern Papers' as he brought his characters from outer Venice to the Piazza, where 'the whole place . . . is an open-air salon dedicated to cooling drinks'.[204]

Whatever its origin, the trope of the living room of the world was in constant use during the nineteenth century as visitors and residents alike gravitated to the Piazza. Despite the presence of cannon and military, the orchestras played and the coffee-houses Quadri and Florian continued to attract clients. San Marco still glittered, and the phenomenal extension of arcading around the vast open space made it one of the great social and aesthetic sites of the nineteenth century. It was also the city nexus for the Venetians, not only a social but a political rallying point – as it would be in the time of uprising in 1848. One of the first acts of the new Napoleonic government was to make provision for full lighting in the Piazza.[205] Byron was still reacting to its novelty in 1816:

> 'Tis midnight – but it is not dark
> Within the spacious place, St Mark –
> The Lights within – the Lamps without –
> Shine above the revel rout.[206]

The Palazzo Reale was to occupy the entire wing of the Procuratie Nuove and the Sansovino library, and to extend on the western side of the Piazza as far as the Procuratie Vecchie on the northern side (fig. 31).[207] Interrupting this regal sweep was the venerable church of San Geminiano, completed by Jacopo Sansovino in 1557: it appears in all the western views of the Piazza painted before the nineteenth century.[208] San Geminiano was one of the oldest ecclesiastical sites in Venice, said to have been established in 552 on a canal, the Rio Balari, which was eventually interred below the paving; Sansovino's edifice dated from 1557. Because of its strategic position it had been requisitioned as barracks for soldiers in 1797. Now the instruction – the most controversial of all the demolition acts – was to raze it in order to accommodate a staircase to the new palace ballroom.

For some time after the ghost of San Geminiano troubled Venetians. Its status and sentimental significance is indicated by its retention in representations of the Piazza well after its destruction. An 1831 publication on the Piazza by Antonio Quadri, with engravings by Dionisio Moretti, showed the new Palazzo Reale, but it also represented San Geminiano 'as it was in the last century' (fig. 32).[209] The publication by Academicians Cicognara, Selva and Diedo on the best known works of Venetian architecture – *Le Fabbriche e i monumenti più cospicue di Venezia* – represented the church, noting that it was *demolità*.[210] The demolition was a subject of much discussion: indeed it became an international issue studied by the academies of Europe.[211]

The decision, however, represented some degree of compromise in the Venetian mind, since the site of San Geminiano at the western end of the Piazza was chosen in preference to the Biblioteca Marciana at the Piazzetta end of the Procuratie Nuove. This was generally agreed to be a better solution, since Sansovino's Marciana was of even greater value. The whole scheme was viewed as momentous because of the Piazza's centrality and prestige. Gaetano Pinali, an amateur architect deeply interested in the proceedings, recommended that since the buildings and the Piazza San Marco interested all Europe and the cultivated parts of the world, the best architects of all nations should be approached to present a model that could then be assessed for its suitability to the function, time and place.[212] Cicogna was so interested in the

31 Dionisio Moretti, 'New Building of the Royal Palace', from Antonio Quadri, *La Piazza di San Marco in Venezia considerate come monumenti*, 1831, pl. VII.

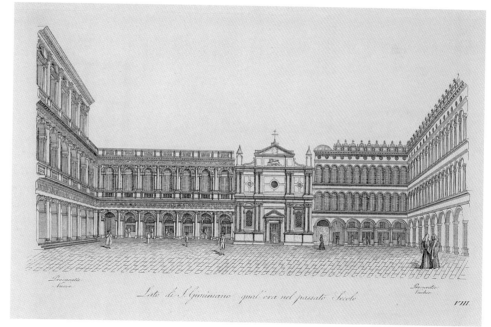

32 Dionisio Moretti, 'San Geminiano as it was in the Past Century', from Antonio Quadri, *La Piazza di San Marco in Venezia considerate come monumenti*, 1831, pl. VIII.

controversy and in Pinali's views – they were colleagues at the Court of Appeal – that he began the famous diary that would eventually record the cultural life of Venice up to the 1860s.[213]

Over and above the issue of demolition, Antolini's design for the palace provoked passionate debate. The first architect appointed to the contentious project, the Milanese Giovanni Antolini, had demonstrated his ambition in designing the Foro Bonaparto in Milan – a huge piazza in the area of the Castello Sforzesca planned in 1800 for the Cisalpine Republic, and the most ambitious and monumental scheme in Napoleonic Italy.[214] However, the controversy surrounding Antolini's designs for the new palace in Venice interrupted its construction and eventually caused the architect's dismissal. The building was left incomplete and its plans were confused for six years. Aesthetic correctness was of particular concern: critics attacked the heaviness of the architrave and its lack of sympathy with the surrounding Procuratie buildings. Such debate focusing on existing buildings and the harmony between them was not new in the Piazza: the controversy that attended Scamozzi's elevation of the Procuratie

Nuove, which added a storey to Sansovino's original design in the sixteenth century, had continued for four hundred years.[215]

Various proposals were made to counter the Antolini plan. The Venetians were even willing to incorporate an arch in Napoleon's honour in the vicinity of the demolished San Geminiano. Abbott Grazioso Butta Calice made such a proposal in a detailed submission.[216] At the height of the controversy, in 1808, Gaetano Pinali presented a design for the full façade incorporating a central triumphal arch dedicated to Napoleon (fig. 33). He attempted to reconcile the different treatments of the Procuratie buildings, old and new, to the right and left of the new wing by extending both and having different solutions on each side of a central arch. Thus, to the right the rounded arches on three levels would echo the Procuratie Vecchie with the skyline and the *merlatura* – the crenellation at roof line – topping extended to the arch. On the left the arches would mirror the arch scheme of the Procuratie Nuove and its original two storeys, keeping the proportionate arch structure. Pinali also planned an elaborate colonnade and pedimented façade above a rusticated base for the façade on the water, taking account of Sansovino's adjacent Zecca.[217] He was also intent on deflecting attention from the Biblioteca Marciana.

In 1810 a further furore effectively ended Antolini's control of the project. The Prefect of the Adriatic Department, Baron Galvagno, ordered the demolition of the western arches at the corner of the Procuratie Vecchie (previously reaching to the Sansovino church) because the variations that Sansovino had made to accommodate his building on an irregular façade line were proving problematic for the new building.[218]

Following Antolini's dismissal, Giuseppe Soli from Modena was appointed to the project and Lorenzo Santi, recommended by Canova, became responsible for the interior. A serviceable compromise was the result, but the debate continued until the Austrians came to power and established a commission to resolve the matter. Lorenzo Santi was appointed architect in charge and went on to contribute many buildings to Venice.[219]

The Napoleonic wing, the Ala Napoleonica (fig. 34), as it became known, was realised with a double order of Doric columns, surmounted by the Ionic order and an attic carrying statuary and low-reliefs. Stonecutters and sculptors began work in 1810: Antonio Bosa and Domenico Banti were responsible for the external decoration, completed in 1813.[220] The arches, decorated with leaning figures and heads positioned on the keystones, were in the manner of the adjacent Procuratie Nuove. A mythological frieze in low-relief was planned for the attic storey, intended to flank a representation of Napoleon enthroned as Jupiter, to be surmounted in turn by the imperial coat of arms. The triumphal arch was not built, so the arcade remained continuous, ensuring some measure of harmony around the three sides of the Piazza. There is no conspicuous point of entry; equilibrium is maintained with the old and new Procuratie buildings.[221] The lack of alignment of roof levels was accepted as inevitable.

On the water side of the Procuratie Nuove further demolition took place in order to create a palace garden. The area was cleared by demolition of the grain warehouse, the Granari di Terra Nova, by then in use as a barracks. Built in brick with a simple façade broken by regular doors and windows outlined with Istrian stone, with *merlatura* echoing the Palazzo Ducale, it was one of the most ancient structures in the city. The Fondaco del Megio, on the lower Grand Canal, now the only remaining example of this kind of warehouse, has a similar Gothic roofline.[222] It appears that the demolition of the Granari di Terra Nova, the oldest building in the San Marco complex, aroused little controversy, certainly in comparison with the furore over the Piazza.

The demolition of the granary effectively ended the commercial practice that had traditionally been situated in the Molo area, an area at one time as much commercial as it was political and ceremonial. The ambitious scale of the palace's planned

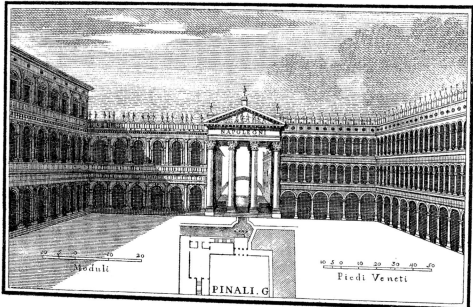

water façade is clear from Antolini's drawings prepared for the rear side of the Procuratie Nuove (fig. 35). He took his cue from Sansovino's Zecca, duplicating its rusticated structure quite literally in lavish extension. Because the architect was dismissed, the rear façade of the Procuratie Nuove remained unaffected. The gardens were eventually established, set up as a private precinct with a water entrance created by closing off bridges that had previously given public access to the area. The Ponte della Pescaria, an old bridge carrying five shops, was demolished and an iron gate with a belvedere was built to give a view of the garden.[223]

The Palazzo's interior decoration was less controversial; certainly it was less public. Unlike the exterior, it was the work of Venetian artists and artisans: notably Giuseppe Borsato, but also Carlo Bevilacqua, Paolo Guidolini, Davide Rossi, the older painter Giambattista Canal and, at the beginning of the new Austrian regime, the young Venetian-born painter Francesco Hayez, returned from Rome.[224] The decorative programmes attest to the remarkable Neoclassical poise at the time, which extended to the redecoration of the Palazzo Pisani at Strà, the royal residence on the Terraferma.[225] The surety of the Empire style, as the Neoclassical style had become, is seen to advantage in the new oval ballroom (fig. 36), the oval salon of audience and the various apartments for the emperor and empress in residence. Even if he were not in Venice, Canova kept Neoclassical taste current: in 1803 he had sent Selva studies of furniture from designs by Percier.[226]

As the principal artist among those at work on the royal palace, Giuseppe Borsato appears as a leading talent in the early nineteenth century.[227] He continued commissions well into the later period of Austrian rule. As well as designing floats for public events, Borsato recorded many of the most important cultural events in his time in modestly scaled history paintings. He painted the water pageant for Napoleon in 1807 (with Selva's triumphal arch in the background; fig. 26), and contributed to the official publication, the *Descrizione delle feste celebrate in Venezia*, with Albertolli.[228] Borsato worked on the embellishment of La Fenice for Napoleon's visit and, a little later, began what was to be a long career as a stage designer for the Fenice.[229] He recorded the Sala del Maggior Consiglio in the Palazzo Ducale, showing the book storage installed after Beauharnais's decree to transfer material from the Libreria

36 Lorenzo Santi,
Ala Napoleonica,
Oval Ballroom, *c.*1815.

Sansovino to make way for the royal residence.[230] For the baptism of Napoleon's son and his designation as the King of Rome in 1811, Borsato designed a column that was erected in the Piazza San Marco: illuminated from inside, it was in the form of a spiral, like Trajan's Column, with decorations painted on canvas.[231]

The fundamentals of Borsato's decorative work can be deduced from his *Opera ornamentale*, published by the Academy in 1831.[232] With sixty illustrations, it was contemporaneous with the collections of designs by Charles Percier and Pierre Fontaine, both esteemed by Napoleon. It confirmed the rapport between Venetian and French art, which lasted well into the century.

Canova and the Venetians

The most acclaimed sculptor of his time and admired by Napoleon, the expatriate Canova continued to inspire Venetian culture from afar. At first he resisted Napoleon's pressing invitation to have himself represented by the leading contemporary sculptor, accepting only after pressure from Pope Pius VII and Cardinal Consalvi, the Papal Secretary of State, who saw Canova not only as a great artist but also as a powerful emissary.[233] In the intriguing conversations that took place between Canova and Napoleon at Saint-Cloud in 1802 during a series of five sittings for a portrait bust, Canova reported the miseries of Rome and its despoliation, and a population affected by the restrictions of commerce and failure of credit.[234] He made a plea for peace, and indeed his depiction of Napoleon as Mars bringing peace appears evidence of Canova's sincerity. He also made it clear that he was still very much affected by the overthrow of Venice and specially mentioned the 'deportation' of the San Marco horses.[235]

Whatever his reservations, Canova presented Napoleon in heroic mode as a nude colossus, perfect of mien, turning his gaze on the globe surmounted by a golden victory. Eugène de Beauharnais immediately commissioned a bronze version for the Kingdom of Italy which, for the few remaining years of Napoleon's career, stood in the courtyard of the Brera Academy in Milan. Upon Napoleon's defeat the original commission was presented by the British Government to the Duke of Wellington; it still stands, a trophy at the base of the stairs of Wellington's Apsley House.[236]

Later, in Rome, Lucien Bonaparte, Napoleon's estranged brother, expressed surprise that Canova had consented to immortalise the image of someone who had destroyed his homeland. Canova insisted that Napoleon was portrayed as the bringer of peace, adding that 'Everything is in my signature Canova da Venezia'.[237]

In 1810 Canova was working in Florence on the monument to Alfieri when he was called to Paris to sculpt Napoleon's wife, the Empress Marie-Louise. In another of the fascinating exchanges between emperor and artist, Napoleon asked about the payment for the Alfieri monument, and discussed his own urban projects.[238] Canova took the opportunity to stress the importance of conservation for antique monuments and to inform Napoleon, yet again, of the lamentable state into which Rome had fallen.[239] In a discussion on architecture, the name of Guiseppe Soli, working at the new palace in Venice, was raised, and Canova spoke unflinchingly of the *bestialità* committed in the area of the Piazza San Marco. They discussed Selva, and Canova insisted that 'the Venetians are good, but they do not prosper'.[240] They spoke further of Venice and the Venetian edition of Machiavelli, who interested Napoleon, of course, and whom he quoted, saying that San Marco was painted with the sword. In Machiavelli's perception of San Marco as a deposit of war trophies Napoleon no doubt found his own justification for the removal of the horses.[241]

Canova's Venetian admirers followed his activities closely, and he himself was constantly in touch. In what must have been a true labour of love, in 1809 Selva planned a studio complex intended for a site on the Zattere in the hope that Canova could be induced to return (fig. 37). The position on the Ognissanti canal would have had a view across to Palladio's churches and been close to the new Academy. A grandiose combination of residence, personal studios, studios for young sculptors and a domed museum in the likeness of the Pantheon was planned to serve the several functions of studio, teaching area and display.[242] Three extended façades were envisaged in model classical manner. On the Zattere, facing the Giudecca canal, a structure in three blocks with a second storey behind was given a temple front with six Ionic columns. On the Ognissanti canal the order of a sequence of eight columns set against the wall was Doric, with blind arches between columns and three regularly positioned doors. An interior courtyard was surrounded by a Doric portico. The transverse section revealed the loggia and the museum modelled on the Pantheon, with coffered dome and two of Canova's sculptures sketched ready in position.

Selva's project was shown to the Accademia di Belle Arti in Milan in 1809 for recommendation to the minister of the interior, and in Rome, where it earned him election to the Accademia di San Lucca – but no actual building commission. Described as 'one of the highest moments in the neo-Classical architecture of Venice', the studio design had clarity, grace, a distinction of simple parts and measured, restrained ornamentation that would have made it an ornament indeed on the Zattere, in dialogue with Palladio's churches across the water.[243] Perhaps something of its potential quality can be felt in the Selva's church of the Nome di Gesù in Santa Chiara, sited in a peripheral area of Venice near today's Piazzale Roma.[244] This tiny church, one of the few ecclesiastical initiatives of the time, was begun in 1815 and completed faithfully by Antonio Diedo after Selva's death in 1822. It received the remains of San Geminiano, transferred from the demolished church that bore his name. Giant Ionic columns separate the nave from the apse, and above, a dome admits light that is felt as a palpitating presence. It illuminates the painted frieze by Borsato and the sculptural niches in Neoclassical style.

Selva's efforts to domicile Canova in Venice were unsuccessful. In 1822, in the last months of his life, the sculptor did return, and died in Venice, but he bequeathed his work to his native city of Possagno where, in his last years, he had planned his own Gipsoteca.[245]

37 Giannantonio Selva,
*Project for a Sculpture
Studio for Canova*, 1809.
Pen and watercolour, each
sheet: 42.4 × 88.5 cm.
Venice, Museo Correr.

Canova had other admirers in Venice. Isabella Teotochi Albrizzi produced a tract
on him in 1809, which became celebrated as an exemplary exercise in the literary evocation of the visual.[246] In the directness of the writing, the focus on the sculptures,
even the undue modesty with which it is presented, evoking each work in an era before
copious illustration, it is an exemplary text. Ungenerously, it was seen to have had a
ghost-writer – Albrizzi's close friend Ippolito Pindemonte. But Albrizzi's salon, as well
as her own Greek birth, gave her every opportunity to absorb the best in Greek scholarship and extend her interest to Canova's Neoclassical works. Certainly Pindemonte
was an habitué of the Albrizzi circle; he had written a poem on Canova's stele for
Emo, which was among the earliest literary evocations of Canova's work.[247] But
Albrizzi knew other Greek scholars closely: Melchior Cesarotti – Canova had been
inspired by his translations of Homer – Mustoxidi and Foscolo in his Venice years.
Foscolo had written a poem that initially was inspired by Canova's *Venus Italica* –
Le Grazie (Florence, Galleria Palatine) and had dedicated sonnets to Canova.[248]

Albrizzi's treatise was the product of the pen of a Venetian who regarded Canova
as 'our' artist: *il celebre nostro scultore*.[249] Thus she opens with the Emo stele and
likens the greatness of the subject to Domenico Michiel in Tyre, Enrico Dandolo at
Constantinople and Morosini in the Peloponnese – evidence indeed that the *stato da*

mar was still alive for the Serenissima's one-time subjects.[250] Albrizzi's essays on each work give a sense of their distinctive qualities – while avoiding, she modestly hoped, the repetition of epithets.[251] An ideal of beauty – the preoccupation of Cicognara at this time – was achieved: it involved imitation of the 'infinite variety of nature', 'to which was added the fortunate combination of ideal beauty'. The range of Canova's effects was dynamically conveyed: from *la dolcezza* and *la soavità* – the lyrical qualities of sweetness, gentleness – to *l'asprezza*, and *la severità* – harshness, severity.[252]

Albrizzi's fame and her special relationship to Canova were enhanced by his gift to her of the head of *Helen* in 1812 (fig. 38): surely intended as flattering acknowledgement to the authoress for her book on the artist.[253] Lord Byron in turn addressed a sonnet to 'this beloved marble', which he saw *in situ* in Isabella's palazzo in 1816 – exclaiming, 'Behold the *Helen* of the *heart*!'[254]

The most important written work on Canova was by Cicognara. In 1807, at the suggestion of Pietro Giordani, he began a grandiose history of sculpture that was to have Canova as its apogee: it is one of the most ambitious art-historical projects of its time.[255] The first volume, *Storia della scultura dal suo risorgimento fino in Italia sino al secolo di Napoleone*, which was dedicated to the Emperor Napoleon, appeared in 1813, with the claim that Canova 'had led modern art along the way of Greek sculpture'.[256] The history was fulsome and at its most detailed when it passed from Roman origins to the Pisani, Donatello, Michelangelo and Bernini, and thence Canova. Cicognara emphasised the national rise of sculpture, its *risorgimento*, in keeping with his patriotism.[257] The final volume brought the history to summation with Canova, and was dedicated to him. Cicognara's empathy for the sculptor's sensuous working of marble is more than evident: 'if statues could be made by stroking marble rather than by roughly cutting and chipping, I would say that this one had been formed by wearing down the surrounding marble by dint of kisses and caresses.'[258] For a time, at least, after his death in Venice in 1822, Canova continued to be inspirational for the circle of his friends who kept the cultural lights of Venice burning after the Republic's fall.

38 Antonio Canova, *Helen*, 1811. Marble, 64 × 32 cm. Venice, Palazzo Albrizzi.

The Ateneo and the Accademia

In tune with the principles of Enlightenment government, learned societies and academies were founded in the eighteenth century and played a conspicuous role in the following century in the areas of teaching, conservation and public exhibition. In an extension of cultural paternalism during Napoleon's rule (which went in tandem with demolition and taxation) the Accademia di Belle Arti and other societies were given prominence and housed in buildings redeployed after the closure of churches and *scuole*. The Accademia had been in existence in the Republic, but its public and political role was enhanced by the second president, Leopoldo Cicognara, as well as by Giannantonio Selva as professor of architecture.[259] Three buildings, dominated by the church of Santa Maria della Carità, were designated as the new premises.[260] Selva was responsible for initial designs for the rehousing, but again was hampered by budget limitations and the many other demands on his time; his pupil Francesco Lazzari was to be largely responsible for the renovation after Selva's death.[261] The Farsetti collection of plaster casts – studied by the young Canova – was at the time housed in the Accademia gallery, following its acquisition in 1805 during the Austrian rule.[262] The renovations that Selva initiated are now absorbed into other modifications, but he appears to have established the first gallery, the Sala Capitolare, preserving its fifteenth-century gilded coffered ceiling and acanthus-leaf cornice. It houses today the collection of Gothic altarpieces from the Venetian school, but in the early Ottocento it was the main public gallery, opened to the public in 1817 with the central painting – the Accademia's main attraction – Titian's *Assumption* from the church of the Frari. The *Assumption* remained in the Accademia until it was moved to the Frari after the First World War.[263] Under Cicognara the academy's teaching function was particularly prominent, with annual prizegivings and orations on great artists. He was eloquent in homage to specifically Venetian artists: Titian and Giorgione – 'equal to Raphael' – as well as Palladio.

Cicognara's public prominence did much to consolidate the reputation of the academy and preserve, under duress, the patrimony of his adopted city. His history of sculpture was illustrated by the pupils of the academy, as were the plates of the ambitious architectural study, *Le Fabbriche di Venezia*, written in collaboration with fellow-academicians Diedo and Selva.[264] While it drew on the tradition of Venetian writings on architecture, *Le Fabbriche* had the distinction of being entirely up-to-date, furnishing a history of *new* architecture, including the Palazzo Reale and the public gardens. In this work, as in the work on sculpture, Cicognara turned his attention to the arts that were not as well documented as Venetian painting, which had long been held as the supreme expression of the city. Both writing projects demonstrated his considerable breadth of taste, as well as his critical acumen and independence.

39   Francesco Hayez, *The Cicognara Family (with a Bust of Canova)*, 1816–17. Oil on canvas, 143 × 188 cm. Venice, private collection.

Cicognara was also president of the new Ateneo Veneto, founded in 1812 from a merging of other Venetian societies.[265] His cultural power was considerable, and was enhanced by his close friendship with Canova – a portrait of the Cicognara family by Francesco Hayez, the most talent Venetian painter of the new generation, shows the family beside a colossal bust of Canova (fig. 39): a comely son, Cicognara's second wife, dressed in fashionable French Empire-style and seated in an Empire-style chair, and Cicognara himself – husband and wife holding an engraving of Canova's projected sculpture of the Christian faith, *Religione Cattolica*.[266] Artist and academician were joined in friendship, ambition for the Christian realm of Italy, and art.

Rossini's Premieres

Venetian cultural life was further enhanced by the presence of a new star – the young composer Gioacchino Rossini. At the age of eighteen he came to Venice from his studies in Bologna, and from that point his brilliant professional career began. His first commissions were for the theatre of San Moisè, one-act operas for shared programmes. In November 1810 Rossini made his Venetian debut with the *opera buffa*, *La Cambiale di matrimonio*.[267] In Venice in 1812, again at the behest of the San Moisè, Rossini composed *L'Inganno felice* and *La Scala di seta*. He soon became known for the brilliance of his overtures – in *La Scala de seta*, for example – and for his sparkle and comic mastery. He was back at the end of the year for the carnival season with *L'Occasione fa il ladro* in November and *Il Signor Bruschino* in January 1813.

The early one-act operas are about marital preparations and contracts, manipulated and obfuscated, usually proving that true love or attraction can overcome obstacles in their way.[268] Scenes in the early operas are fast and farcical, with characters most often of the bourgeois class busily sorting out their destinies. In these intrigues, ingeniously and lightly orchestrated, Cimarosa was a notable precursor. Such plots can give rise to solo and duo singing between male and female voices with the mellifluous orchestral accompaniment for which Rossini became famous. The librettos were most often French-derived, beginning with *La Cambiale di matrimonio* (with Gaetano Rossi as librettist), but the capacity to set such plots to entertaining music was more Italian than French and had a venerable Venetian tradition from Goldoni to Cimarosa. The Venetian Rossi was highly experienced in that musical world and would provide the librettos for Rossini's triumphant productions of *Tancredi* in 1813 and, in 1823, *Semiramide*.[269]

In *La Cambiale di matrimonio*, the Canadian entrepreneur Slook is outwitted by Fanny and Edoardo, who clinch their own match. Giuseppe Foppa, another Venetian librettist adept at the *opera buffa* format, provided other early librettos. *L'Inganno felice* is concerned with the doubts of a husband (in this case a duke) as to the virtue of his missing wife and an action uncovering her true identity which reveals her love and his lack of faith, with a concluding chorus, 'Viva, viva, il vero amor', rousingly sung by all. Isabella's soprano floats above the male voices to attest to just retribution. In *Il Signor Bruschino* Sofia is united with Florville after various ploys to escape the son of Bruschino – Florville disguising himself as Bruschino's son to court Sofia before true identities are revealed.

Rossini's lasting fame came with *Tancredi*, which had its premier at La Fenice in February 1813, and *L'Italiana in Algeri* at the Teatro San Benedetto on 22 May 1813.[270] These were the theatres in which *opera serie* and *opera buffa* had flourished during the last years of the Republic, and for them Rossini produced full-length operas. *Tancredi*, with a libretto by Gaetano Rossi after Voltaire and sets by Giuseppe Borsato, was an ambitious 'heroic melodrama'.[271] With bravura fluency Borsato's designs evoked the grounds of palaces, a 'magnificent' Piazzale with a Gothic cathedral and equestrian statue, and a prison reminiscent of Piranesi's inventions.[272] At a time of mounting opposition to the French, patriotic sentiments were aroused with an opening chorus calling for 'Pace, onore, fede, amore', a white scarf to be worn as 'the emblem of harmony' between dissenting parties and the invocation to 'swear allegiance to our country in war and peace'.

L'Italiana in Algeri has remained one of the most popular of Rossini's operas, its comic élan undiminished after nearly two hundred years. On the simplest level, the title accentuates that this is an *Italian* plot about an *Italian* girl – rather than a French-derived comedy. Her worthwhile qualities are maintained throughout, as she has the ability to manage men of all nations. She is also responsible for the liberation of the Italian slaves, lauding their national identification. *L'Italiana in Algeri* is one of many Rossini plots involving former enemies of Italy, and of Venice in particular: the Turks, the Algerians, who were the pirates of the Barbary sea, and others.[273] Tancredi's final aria, for example, incites the Italians to think of their country, and prefigures the Verdi of the great patriotic choruses:

> Pensa alla patria, e intrepido
> Il tuo dover adempi;
> Vedi per tutta Italia
> Rinascere gli esempi
> Di ardere e di valor.[274]

Rossini is often taken to be apolitical (he appeared that way in later life), and possible political meanings in his operas have been disavowed. But his father was a staunch republican, at one time imprisoned by the Austrians, and the composition of *Tancredi* on the very eve of the blockade, as the anti-French forces concentrated around Venice itself, can hardly appear casual.[275] The French writer Stendhal, the most eloquent of Rossini's apologists, was well aware of the Risorgimento spirit of *L'Italiana in Algeri*; he saw the opera as remarkable for its historical content and implications.[276] 'You may rightly wonder exactly what "historical implications" are liable to be encountered in the finale of an *opera buffa*', he exclaimed, then quoted 'Pensa alla patria', attributing the new patriotism to Napoleon.[277]

Stendhal also made it apparent that there was a certain inevitability in Rossini's success in Venice, which was noted for its musicality and traditional comic sense. He wrote eloquently that 'the glittering reflection of the Venetian character falls across the texture of Venetian music':[278]

> of all the lands of Italy, Venetia stands supreme in the sureness of its taste and the keenness of its appreciation of music written for the human voice. Had the King Napoleon himself thought to honour Venice with his presence, the excitement of his arrival could have done nothing to tear people away from Rossini. Everyone, from the humblest gondolier to the proudest lord of the land, was singing, singing . . .[279]

In the new century, and despite foreign domination, Rossini sustained the Venetian reputation for musicality.

The Blockade (1813–1814) and the Fall of Napoleon

The blockade of 1813–14 silenced Rossini in Venice, at least for a time. Venice had experienced the repercussions from war fought in mainland Veneto in 1809, followed by the British blockade in the Adriatic in intervening years.[280] In 1809 Austrian forces had been as close as Mestre, just across the water. They left taking money, conscripts and supplies. But while there was marked discontent in the mainland, which had suffered most in the path of the armies, Venice remained quiet, although the Podestà warned against requisitioning one hundred sailors for fear of local discontent.[281]

As was customary, a *Te Deum* was sung for Napoleon's birthday on 10 August 1813. It fell shortly before the completion of the new wing of the palace, just then being adorned externally with Napoleon's initial and the heraldic eagle with lighting bolts in its claws.[282] By September volunteers were called to the army and navy as the French faced increasing threat from Austria. By early October the city was under siege, with provisions in hand for only six months. In his diary Emmanuele Cicogna recorded the high food prices and the difficulties facing state control and dispersal of food stocks. Conte Grandenigo wrote to the director of State Property (the *demanio*) asking for six buildings to be converted into mills, and Cicogna described a group of women petitioning for food in front of the palazzo of Governor Seras.[283] On 14 April 1814 Cicogna reported that sixteen people had died of starvation.[284] On 18 April, commenting on the English and German occupation, he noted that Venice was on the brink of a new destiny and that the Colossus Napoleon had fallen.[285] Even more tellingly, he recorded that some had hoped for a return to the Republic but – *povera Venezia* – 'we were bad enough under the rule of conceit, ignorance and weakness'. While there was sentiment abroad in favour of a united Italy, it is clear that the Republic was little mourned. Venice now felt its deprivation and isolation acutely.[286]

In the face of the city's plight, the poet Pietro Buratti, the leading satirical poet in Italy according to Stendhal, laid his customary wit aside to address the Prefect of Venice, Baron Francesco Galvagna, with a lamentation in dialect verse on the blockade of 1813.[287] 'With tears in his eyes', he described his city, the country of the one-time Queen of the Sea, now in ruins. The city had been halted in all its activities, its inns were empty, the *traghetti* stayed at their moorings:

> Co le lagreme su i ochi,
> E col cour tuto strazzà,
> Puzo in tera i mii zenochi,
> E domanda a vu pietà.

In Buratti's blunt view, Venice had been ruined by the 'democratic scum' of France; it was now in the process of passing in servitude to the Habsburg eagle:

> Per chi pensa che Francesco
> Gera za paron de nu,
> E che a un grosso osel tedesco
> Se ne dava in schiavitù.

Buratti recited the lamentation at an official dinner and was duly imprisoned. Under Austrian rule, the stanzas on the Habsburg occupation, with Venice 'in slavery' were censored.

The Austrian occupation was negotiated following the abdication of Napoleon and formalised on 20 April 1814 in the Treaty of Fontainebleau. Eugène de Beauharnais had accepted defeat, which was formalised at the Convention of Schiarino-Rizzino. The Austrians re-entered Venice.[288] Anti-French propaganda from Sicily, encouraged by the Englishmen Lord Bentinck, Vittorio Barzoni (now active for the English), August Bozzi Granville and secret societies such as the Carbonari, fuelled the Risorgimento spirit, but resistance was much less in evidence in Venice than in Milan.[289] With the establishment of a provisional government in Venice, Podestà Bartolomeo Gradenigo remained in power. By this stage the Venetians were bent on welcoming the Austrians; a flood of satirical writings and graphics attacked the French.[290] On their withdrawal in defeat in 1814, the statue of Napoleon was the first object to be removed – carted off to the island of San Giorgio Maggiore (the island of the free port) at five in the morning after an angry crowd had demonstrated in front of it the evening before (fig. 40). Thereafter the colossus was lampooned in satirical graphics celebrating Napoleon's fall.

On 15 May Prince Reuss-Plauen, Austrian governor of the Venetian territory, took formal possession of the city. Again Venice staged a splendid water-borne welcome.[291] Six days of Austrian-organised homage in San Marco were followed by a celebration in the Piazza. Even Foscolo in Milan, the young enthusiast of the first French days of the Municipality and one of the most ardent believers in a united Italy, praised the moderation of the Austrians, but he himself refused to take the oath of loyalty to the new power and again prepared himself for exile.[292]

Gaetano Pinali's eloquently bitter letter to Alvise Querini is a telling gauge of the reaction to French rule. Pinali reported on the disastrous state of the Arsenale with buildings irreparably damaged.[293] Trade was destroyed; the new procedures for customs and free port had failed to revive it. San Geminiano had been demolished. The library of San Marco had been transferred to the Palazzo Ducale to create space in the Palazzo Reale; the precious collections were inadequately housed. Churches, monasteries and convents had gone, and the public gardens were inadequate recompense. Houses and palaces were suffering from lack of maintenance and the contraction of the building industry. To Pinali all this amounted to 'So many excesses . . . much more than the ruin of vandals'.[294]

After Napoleon's final defeat, in terminal exile from the Cisalpine Republic and destined for London, Ugo Foscolo added a new letter to his novel *Ultime lettere di Jacopo Ortis*, sharpening all the criticism of the original text in a retrospective diatribe inserted as the letter of 17 March 1798.[295] Quoting from a Petrarch *canzona*, the narrator Jacopo succumbs to 'an overflow of tears' – 'che le lagrime mie si spargan sole'. With this brief quotation Foscolo recalls Petrarch's presence in the nearby Euganean Hills, and perhaps Petrarch's lament for Italy – *Italia mia* – and his famous praise of Venice as the city once famed for its liberty.[296] The letter of 17 March is a key document in the formative history of the Italian Risorgimento. The issues are larger than the trading of Venice, 'sold and betrayed' at Campoformio; its lack of defence and sinew is again lamented, and the charge of patricide renewed. But the tyranny of Napoleon is now revealed fully as 'base' and 'cruel'; the faith which had at one time nourished democratic hopes now filled Italy with conscripts, emigrants and exiles. It is the betrayal of Italy: it is possible for a land without people to exist, but never for people to exist without a land.[297]

The trading of Venetia to Austria for the second time was, for some of the French at least, a delicate matter. Stendhal was in Venice at the time of Waterloo, reading the newspapers at Florian's: 'I have read . . . of the capitulation of Paris; all is lost, even honour.'[298] He was hurt for Venice, but also, let it be said, for its loss to his own nation. The compassion articulated in his account of Italy in 1818 is among the last expressions for some time of sympathy for the achievements of the lost Republic – written at the very point when Stendhal's relative Pierre Darù was publishing a harsher, more influential historical picture. 'This poor Venice!' Stendhal wrote:

> If the circumstance of obeying its own laws, made and conserved by its own citizens, and during the long course of thirteen centuries of constantly preserving itself from conquest is a claim of nobility, no known city, not even ancient Rome, has

40 Anonymous, *The Fall of Napoleon*, 1814. Engraving. Venice, Museo Correr.

boasted a nobility equal to this poor Venice. The Venetians at no point acquired their land by usurpation or by the extermination of other men, but by belief in patient and wise industry as the sole means of building, extending their city by domination. There, amongst all the amiable Venetians, is the purest Italian blood, always defended against the armies of the earth by a sea of a depth of only two or three feet [*pieds*] and inaccessible to vessels. Finally it is still a glory for Venice to have succumbed only to the arms of Napoleon who will be celebrated in history for having terminated all the ancient monarchies of Europe and having changed their constitutional governments. This government was agreeable once, but it would be insupportable today. If Napoleon had not destroyed this charm, the progress of human affairs would have destroyed it. The government of Venice would be today worse than that of Berne, let us then be reconciled to its fall.[299]

In simple but telling terms – still seduced by those thirteen centuries of civilisation – Stendhal noted the isolation of the city from produce and trade, and the decline in population, correctly predicting that it would be even greater:

At the time of the coming of Attila, the fugitives of Padua went to form Venice. Today Venice, artificial city, is not sustained by anything. Venetian families have run en masse to Padua. In 1790 Venice had 180,000 inhabitants; miserable Venice has 84,000 in 1818 and it will be 30,000 in 1850.[300]

He still thought fit to call it 'la plus civilisée', but he underestimated its resilience: 'How I hate Bonaparte for having sacrificed Venice to the Austrians . . . it was further along the road to civilisation than London or Paris. Today it has 50,000 poor.'[301]

It is a telling statement from a Bonapartist who was to send a young Italian soldier in the passion of youth and commitment to join Napoleon's forces in *The Charterhouse of Parma*. But, even under duress after the exit of Napoleon and the Austrian reoccupation, Venice retained its fascination: after all it offered the grandest contemporary allegory of decline and fall. It affected its captors deeply: well into the twentieth century both nostalgia and mourning infuse the painting, the literature and the music of the two nations that conquered the Republic. And hedonism and love were still to be experienced through the Venetian example.

Chapter 3

VENICE IN THE THEATRE OF EUROPE: SECOND AUSTRIAN RULE, 1814–1848

The Return of the Horses

Another regatta and illuminations in the Piazza marked the Austrian return on 19 April 1814. In the following year the four golden horses of San Marco took up their pre-eminent positions in the heart of the city. It was the Austrians who took the initiative to return purloined artworks following the Congress of Vienna.[1]

The campaign for the restoration of Italian art sequestered by Napoleon began in 1800 through the initiative, not of Venice but of Rome, when Canova was persuaded to assume the position of Inspector General of Antiquities and Fine Arts for the Papal States. He undertook a crucial mission to Paris in 1815 after the defeat of Napoleon.[2] Canova had an international reputation, as well as a long-standing friendship with the French architect and theorist Quatremère de Quincy which dated back to their Roman days.[3] In the face of his own country's spoliations, Quatremère de Quincy had made one of the fullest and most articulate statements against confiscation of artworks. In his *Lettres sur le project d'enlever les monuments de l'Italie*, written at the beginning of the Napoleonic campaigns in 1796, when artworks were shipped from the Vatican to France, he had argued that Rome was a city-museum by virtue of the number and significance of its historical monuments.[4] The artists' pilgrimage to Rome must be respected: he argued this in his fifth letter.[5] The idea of liberty and its recent French associations was still sufficiently novel to be invoked in opposition to the spirit of conquest: 'l'esprit de conquête dans une république, est entièrement subversif de l'esprit de liberté'.[6] All the arts belong to Europe, Quatremère claimed in this important manifesto for modern conservation. They hold membership in a general republic of arts and sciences which is best served by them remaining in their countries of origin.

The Vatican approached the Austrian chancellor Prince Metternich and Lord Castelreagh, the British prime minister, for support in December 1813, when Talleyrand, the French negotiator, restated the territorial right of conquest by the French.[7] As a result of Metternich's intervention, the sequestered works were removed forcibly from the Louvre with the help of Austrian infantry, and among them were the four golden horses.[8]

The horses reached Venice on 7 December 1815, to be greeted at Fusina by a descendant of Doge Dandolo, who had first captured them in Constantinople. After repair, they were reinstated with full ceremony, raised up by engineer Salvini's machines onto the porch of San Marco on 13 December, the anniversary of their confiscation in 1797 (fig. 41).[9] Cicognara, as president of the Academy, made the address. The Habsburg emperor, Francis I, was in attendance, decreeing that a record be inscribed on the central arch of the Basilica marking the victorious restoration by Austria: 'Franc. I Imp. pacis orbi datae trophaeaum a. MDCCCXV victor reduxit.' But there were two responses: on the one hand celebration; on the other an awareness of hubris, with satires pointing out that the horses now symbolised two defunct powers.[10]

The bronze lion from the column on the Piazzetta was also returned, but, smashed during its removal in Paris, in eighty-four large fragments and needing intensive repair. Its restoration, the work of Bartolomeo Ferrari, was initiated under imperial patronage.[11] Emmanuele Cicogna reported the following year that 'at approximately ten-thirty on this seventeenth day of April, the lion returned from Paris and repaired to perfection, was raised upon its column'. A letter from Ferrari's son Luigi conveys something of the atmosphere, and the ardour:

> One morning in the year 1815, at the foundries of the Arsenal and in the presence of H. M. Francis I, the general staff of that establishment and the Emperor's entourage, Bartolomeo Ferrari personally assumed the task of repairing the lion; and about four months later he had completely fulfilled his undertaking. In addition to the response accorded the artist for his arduous work, it was His Majesty's pleasure to offer him a keepsake in the form of a diamond ring bearing the imperial initials.[12]

The ceremony with which the Austrians returned the city's most important monuments was a knowing exercise in political paternalism. The horses were returned to play their role on the façade of San Marco as 'the Quadriga of the Lord', but their re-siting had not been inevitable. Emperor Francis had asked Canova for his opinion on their location, and Canova had replied (intriguingly) 'that they would well be placed on the door of the Palazzo Ducale, two by two, facing San Giorgio'.[13]

Would they have better served the resurgence of Venice released from their ecclesiastical duties, one wonders. Tradition prevailed, of course. However the horses continued in the spotlight because of the interest in their provenance, in a period of great interest in all things Greek. Were they Greek or Roman? The question provoked intense debate in intellectual circles. The view that they were Greek had more support in a climate of enthusiasm for the Elgin marbles, which Canova had famously inspected by invitation in London after his 1815 mission to Paris.[14] Local Venetians and distinguished foreigners ventured their opinions: Cicognara maintained their origins were Roman, and thus Italian; Mustoxidi, the Greek scholar resident in Padua,

41   Vincenzo Chilone, *Return of the Horses of San Marco to Venice*, 1815. Oil on canvas, 60 × 85 cm. Venice, Baroness Elsa Treves de' Bonfili.

42 Sebastiano Santi, sketch for the *Triumph of Neptune* for the Palazzo Reale, *c.*1815. Venice, Museo Correr.

43 Lorenzo Santi, coffee house, Giardini Reale, San Marco, 1815–17.

argued for their Greek derivation; Friedrich Schlegel entered the controversy favouring the Greek, as did the Englishman Robert Benjamin Haydon, who compared one of the horse's heads with a head from the Elgin marbles, arguing for the superiority of the Elgin horse.[15]

On returning to Venice the Austrians continued the embellishment of the Palazzo Reale as the government residence. From 1810, under the French, the principal reception rooms newly designed by Lorenzo Santi had been frescoed (fig. 42).[16] Austrian decoration continued well into the 1830s, at first with the intention of eradicating references to Napoleon.[17] In revisionist vein, Giambattista Canal painted Jupiter as a sky god hurling thunderbolts at perjurers and Bevilacqua depicted *Victory guiding Peace to crown Europe* on the ceiling of the Council Room – his earlier Napoleonic works were destroyed.[18] Bevilacqua's *Feast of the Gods* decorated the dining room, in the company of Borsato's seahorses, urns and figures.[19]

Outside, the new garden on the water side of the palace, the site of the old granary, went ahead.[20] The area was isolated by a U-shaped canal, the Rio della Luna, called after the bridge that had once joined it to the old academy. The bridge adjacent to the granary had been demolished in 1807 in order to ensure the privacy of the palace and its water access: a new connecting bridge was not constructed until 1933 in the Fascist period.[21] The old Ponte della Pescaria was substantially changed, but not in accordance with architect Lorenzo Santi's project for a colonnade and statues.

But Santi's coffee-house was built at the corner of the gardens between 1815 and 1817 (fig. 43).[22] It is a high point in Neoclassical Venice, one of the most congenial of outdoor pavilions, intimate and gracious, a garden casino in the city – and, despite its realisation under Austrian rule, an essay in Empire taste. Of felicitous proportion in its three-part combination of domed spaces, it was built in characteristic Istrian stone with a Doric order and four turrets bearing sculpted vases and sea horses, legs and hooves daintily raised, swagged with garlands: Empire-style motifs with an aquatic Venetian flavour.[23]

Hardship, and the Death of Canova

However, while the regal accommodation was luxuriously refurbished, and the horses and the lion were returned in a cloud of imperial blessing, there was little to endear the Austrians to their Venetian subjects. The most important positions in the police, the Church and the bureaucracy were taken by Austrians, and there was active political suppression.[24] Outwardly the Venetians were compliant again: Cicogna observed in his diary on 1 January 1816 that the Milanese were not as accepting of Austrian rule as the Venetians. He saw Milan asserting its role as capital of the Regno d'Italia and less inclined to submit.[25] As the Risorgimento movement gained momentum and unrest was registered in Naples and Piedmont, Venice was accused of not having the Italian spirit. Cicogna noted that people were dissatisfied with their sovereigns across Europe and that the secret societies dedicated to the expulsion of foreign rulers – the Masons and the Carbonari – were strong.[26]

The consequences of French rule in the Veneto, and the considerable misery and impoverishment resulting from the naval blockade and poor harvests, caused a severe depression in the years from 1814 to 1818.[27] These years were probably the lowest point in Venetian history in terms of the welfare of its citizens. The cumbersome Austrian bureaucracy did little to facilitate recovery.[28] Riots against tax collection took place in the provinces, although there are records of efforts at relief in the face of starvation.[29] The population diminished as the result of epidemics, death and migration.[30] Diseases of malnutrition, such as pellagra, were widespread. In the final stages of pellagra its victims became mad and were isolated in the asylum on the island of San Servolo or in the hospital in the former Scuola di San Marco, which had been established in 1815.[31] Shelley wrote about the madmen of San Servolo in his 1818 poem *Julian and Maddalo*.[32] Economic collapse meant unemployment and conspicuous begging, and the workhouse, the Casa d'Industria, set up in 1812 under French rule in the old monastery of San Lorenzo, was for many crucial for their survival.[33] Visitors to Venice in those first post-Waterloo years of the new Austrian domination invariably commented adversely. Metternich, one of the official Austrian party visiting in 1815, wrote to his mother complaining about the wind he encountered on the Grand Canal and observing quite bluntly that Venice was a ruin – no doubt as a consequence of French rule.[34] Others laid the blame on Austria. An English tourist, James Galiffe, expounded on 'Causes of the Decay of Venice': 'It is utterly impossible, that a city built in the midst of the sea, can subsist by any other means than independence and commerce. The former has been destroyed; the latter is sacrificed to the prosperity of Trieste.'[35] William Stewart Rose (one of Foscolo's English friends) visited shortly after the Austrian restoration and commented on the 'ridiculous and vexatious conduct of the Austrians' and the neglect of the waterways: 'At present not even the canals of the town are cleaned, except where the immediate ill consequences of the neglect are felt by the government, as in the neighbourhood of the Arsenale.'[36]

It was the people who suffered most, and so acutely that the new Patriarch, a Hungarian appointed by the Austrians, Giovanni Ladislao Pyrker, addressed a petition to the Emperor Francis in 1825, reporting with some eloquence the low state into which the Venetians had been led by the contraction of resources under Napoleon. The report was presented after one full decade of Austrian rule, a period longer by then than the French occupation. Pyrker's document was considered courageous and had international circulation. It appeared in *The Times* in London and in the *Journal des*

Débâts in Paris, doubtless adding to the international conviction that Venice was ruined.[37]

Censorship did nothing to increase affection for the Austrians. Masonic orders were decreed illegal in September 1814: Venetians and Milanese regarded the decree as evidence of the suppression of liberty and the Austrians' fear of residual Jacobinism. A measure of agitation ensued when Napoleon escaped from Elba, and the fall of his general Murat, King of Naples, occasioned the scrutiny of Venetian residents who had served under him and might have remained loyal.[38] The imprisonment and trial of the writer Silvio Pellico brought the Austrian suppression into the open. Resident in Milan in these years, Pellico had written classical tragedies (notably *Francesco da Rimini*) and controversial material for the journal that launched Romanticism in Italy, *Il Conciliatore*. He was arrested in 1820 for his association with political groups, accused of spreading Carbonari propaganda in Venice during a visit of 1820 and tried in Venice with maximum publicity in 1821.[39] His imprisonment, first in the Palazzo Ducale and then in the prison for the Carbonari in the old convent of San Michele on the island, was followed by incarceration at Spielberg in Brno. Pellico's account of his imprisonment published in 1832, *I miei prigioni*, was one of the most widely read books of the time.[40] It damaged the Austrians' claim to be caring rulers.[41]

During the second period of Austrian rule from 1814 to the 1840s, the appearance of Venice changed profoundly, and no less significantly than it had under Napoleon. But there was no overall plan, no Napoleonic vision of city reform and sanitation, and no engagement of a local architect such as Selva. Funds were sought to swell the the public purse: from 1817 public land was made available for purchase.[42] Certainly churches, monasteries and *scuole* had been emptied during the Napoleonic period, but under Austrian rule demolition continued: Zorzi lists some hundreds of examples, including palaces that could not be maintained and buildings indiscriminately destroyed for the price of their materials.[43] Often these were of high quality and antiquity, and it was the Venetians themselves who were eager to transact sales. It was recognised that the cultural potential of the city merited maintenance of principal buildings, but the programmes were notoriously *ad hoc*.[44]

An early threat to the inner sanctum of the Basilica of San Marco came at the hands of the Patriarch Pyrker, who proposed the demolition of the iconostasis in order to improve visibility for the congregation. Surmounted by statues by Paolo and Jacobello dalle Masegne, the iconostasis was regarded as the sublime feature of San Marco's interior. It was described as 'an essential part and perhaps the most characteristic of this ancient and renowned temple' by Francesco Lazzari of the Academy when the issue was raised in December 1821; the matter was referred to Vienna by Governor d'Inzaghy.[45] In his capacity as president of the Academy, Cicognara invoked international support for the Academy's stand against Pyrker: a notable example of effective intervention into matters that might have been construed as being the Church's domain. Cicognara's appeal to save the iconostasis and to raise funds for a memorial to Canova set the precedent for the idea that Venice belonged, if not to the world, then at least to Europe.

Cicognara's partisan view of Venetian culture was evident in the proposed homage from the Veneto provinces addressed to the Empress Carolina Augusta for the imperial wedding in 1818 (the Emperor's fourth essay in matrimony). Cicognara proposed a presentation of works by Veneto artists in lieu of a gift of money. The centrepiece was Canova's seated sculpture of the Muse Polymnia (her drapery was 'sublime', according to Cicogna), together with other works in marble, vases with low reliefs, jewellery in the Neoclassical style and a presentation folio volume published by Alvisopoli.[46] Academy students engraved the works to be presented, producing images designed to flatter the imperial couple by alluding to great rulers. In plates by Francesco Hayez and Giovanni Demin the Queen of Sheba met Solomon, Ezekiel's piety was reconfirmed, and Moses was shown asking for the liberation of Israel. Plates

44 Giuseppe Borsato, *Leopoldo Cicognara giving the Funerary Oration before the Coffin of Canova at the Accademia di Venezia*, 1824. Oil on canvas, 61 × 78 cm. Venice, Galleria d'Arte Moderna, Ca' Pesaro.

specifically alluding to Venice under Habsburg rule showed the interior of San Marco during the oath of fidelity to the emperor from the provinces of the Veneto, taken from the detailed pen and watercolour record by Giuseppe Borsato, the return of the horses to San Marco, and the imperial party crossing the Rialto Bridge and viewing the royal gardens.[47]

Cicognara's attempts to elevate Canova to the status of the greatest Venetian master reached its apogee with Canova's death in Venice in 1822. The Austrians were wary of Venetian sentiment on the occasion, but after negotiation with Patriarch Pryker, who officiated at San Marco, Cicognara succeeded in having the funeral procession moved from there to the Academy where the coffin was placed in the main hall, in front of Titian's *Assunta*.[48] Borsato left a record of the occasion with the *Assunta* glowing behind the bier (fig. 44).[49] It was the second meeting of Canova and Titian: before the *Polymnia* was shipped to Vienna, Cicognara exhibited Canova's sculpture in the Academy in front of the *Assunta*.

The summation – the permanent union of the two Veneto artists in spirit at least – was realised across the interior of the church of the Frari, but not until 1852. The memorial to Canova preceded the Titian memorial by some decades.[50] Ironically, it was Canova who came to reside in the tomb he had intended for Titian. He had adapted his own original design of 1790 for Maria Cristina of Austria, and a group of Canova's followers – Bartolomeo Ferrari, Rinaldo Rinaldi, Luigi Zandomeneghi, Jacopo de' Martini and Antonio Bosa – would, in turn, adapt the same early design for him: the Muse of Sculpture leads her sister arts, Painting and Architecture, to the tomb door where a youthful genius reclines and the lion of St Mark grieves.[51] Canova's body, however, did not rest in Venice: he bequeathed it to his native Possagno, but his heart was preserved in a porphyry vase in the Frari, and a hand remained in the Accademia di Belle Arti.[52]

Cicognara's leadership, so crucial to Venice in the first twenty years of the nineteenth century – it was said that he had once enjoyed almost the popularity of Canova or Rossini – was already declining when he presided over the obsequies for Canova.

45   Giuseppe Borsato, *Discourse of Cicognara before the Tomb of Canova at the Frari*, 1828. Oil on canvas, 61 × 80 cm. Paris, Musée Marmottan.

Neoclassicism, for which he had been such an eloquent apologist, was about to succumb to the new order of Romanticism.[53] Nevertheless, in 1823 he published his appreciation of Canova and continued his European-wide plea for subscriptions for an appropriate tomb; Borsato was to paint Cicognara discoursing in front of the monument to an attentive crowd (fig. 45).[54] Jacopo Treves, one of Venice's conspicuous new entrepreneurs, showed his gigantic works by Canova to the admiring imperial party from Vienna in 1838: he had acquired the *Ajax* and *Hector* in 1827 and installed them in his palace on revolving stages in a room designed by Borsato. Borsato recorded the imperial visit in a painting.[55] But the fashion for Canova was passing; the new romantic taste was well suited to Venice, a city with stories and settings that would serve its expressive purposes particularly well.[56]

Calumny: Darù's History of the Republic

Perhaps no city provided more material for historical contemplation and exaggeration than did Venice at this time. The fallen Republic and its perceived hubris fascinated Europe and the New World and provoked operas, paintings, plays, poems and novels. In particular it was Pierre Darù, one-time general of Bonaparte, who gave currency to the notion of a flawed historical Venice in inexorable decline: his account, implicating the city in its own hubris, was the most successful of the century. In 1817, soon after the Austrian restoration, he published his multi-volume history, drawing for the first time on extensive Venetian archives, which had hitherto been closed. This is how he opened his history:

A republic famous, long powerful, remarkable for the singularity of its origin, of its site and institutions, has disappeared in our time, under our eyes, in a moment. Contemporary with the most ancient monarchies of Europe, isolated by its system and its position, it has perished in this great revolution that has overthrown many other states. A caprice of fortune has set up fallen thrones; Venice has disappeared with no possibility of returning; her people are effaced from the list of nations; and when, after the long storms, many of her ancient possessions will have regained their rights, the rich inheritance is no longer. Since her catastrophe, delivered up, exhausted, reconquered and enslaved for always, she has scarcely heard the weak voices beseeching pity for her, which is the last claim of the unfortunate.[57]

The work was swiftly translated, and as swiftly aroused Venetian ire.[58] On its publication in Italian, a Venetian ('A. B.'), wrote a vitriolic sonnet, condemning the 'malignant lies' that roused the Venetian lion to recall 'i gloriosi giorni' and inspired him to roar again as he had done for so many centuries.[59] Giannantonio Moschini planned a translation, and entered a sustained correspondence with Darù between 1820 and 1829 – nine letters of which are preserved in the Biblioteca Correr.[60] Moschini's tone was civil, even respectful, and Darù accepted his corrections and incorporated them into his revised edition. At the same time the French historian frequently felt called upon to stress his impartiality and to accuse the Venetian defence of bias amid evidence of 'the avarice of ambition, the corruption of customs'.[61]

The most sustained defence came from Count Domenico Tiepolo. Signing himself 'patrician', he published a two-volume rebuttal in 1828.[62] Such was the success of Tiepolo's critique that Darù worked through it carefully and listed significant points in the third French edition in 1853. Most of the criticisms concentrated on Darù's view that democracy had been suppressed when the aristocratic class took power and restricted participation in government to the nobility. In this, the famous Serrata, Darù saw the origins of the corruption of Venice and the commencement of the heinous powers of the Council of Ten, as de la Houssaie had done before him. A further dispute arose over the events of the 1620s concerning the Spanish ambassador Bedmar, Duke of Coeva, and the so-called Spanish conspiracy, an event that had inspired Thomas Otway's 1652 play, *Venice Preserv'd*.[63]

Tiepolo questioned not only Darù's accounts of events during the Republic, but those of the immediate past, relating to the last days of the Republic and the entry of the French into Venice. He queried Darù's account of the vessels in the Arsenale, his questioning of Venetian neutrality and his opinion that the demands of the Venetians were imperious and pre-empting.[64] Tiepolo was intent on exposing the falseness of the French: 'la falsità dell'imputazione.'[65] But Darù remained loyal to Napoleon's view of Venetian perfidy: 'What neutrality was that of Venice?'[66]

Another voice raised against Darù may seem surprising: that of Ugo Foscolo, in exile in England in 1827, impoverished, and near the end of his life.[67] No longer the wild boy of the Municipality, he wrote at length for the English journals the *Westminster Review* and the *Edinburgh Review*. His translator was Thomas Roscoe, who was himself the co-author of the fashionable *Legends of Venice*.[68] Foscolo was well aware of English reviews that condemned Venice as a result of Darù's researches and of his claim that 'the world is now first indebted for the full exposure of the principles of . . . tyranny': humanity had nothing to mourn with the loss of such a Republic.[69] Foscolo's first lengthy essay, 'History of the Democratical Constitution of Venice', was ostensibly a review of his old Greek professor in Venice, Giovanni Galliccioli, whose *Memorie venete* had recently been published; but Foscolo was more interested in Darù.[70] As he wrote to his publisher, John Murray: 'As to the details and particular intricacies of the Aristocratical Constitution and the Inquisition of State I know, I believe, by experience more than . . . [Darù] could have gathered from books.'[71]

In his essay Foscolo repeated the story of the city's amazing birth amid the lagoon, and its strength of conviction in the first centuries of the Republic – 'an extremely pure Democracy'; he wrote about the 'aversion of the Venetian people to foreign influence' and their 'inveterate hatred of monarchy', expressed in the checks to which the doge was subject.[72] He lauded the independence of the Republic against the Vatican ('What must have been the resources and the spirit of the Republic'); and if 'the encroachments of oligarchy' remained, nevertheless the Republic maintained 'a specious and imposing appearance of strength and dignity' up until the hour of its death.

Foscolo was provoked into further comments on what he called 'the apocryphal tradition relating to the Venetian inquisition' when he was reviewing the newly published *Memoirs of Casanova* in 1827.[73] It is one of the first of many critical writings on Casanova, whom Foscolo regarded as an inadequate representative of Venetian character. Casanova was not 'an ideal personage'; he was guilty of errors that were particularly heinous with regard to institutions, notably the Inquisition and the prisons, which he claimed to know first hand but could have known only by hearsay. Foscolo surmised that Casanova drew upon anecdotal material about Venice that was circulating in 1798 and from these overdrawn accounts had written a romance, rather than history. An inadequate son of the Republic, Casanova's voice is contradicted by the popularity of the Republic among its subjects over the centuries: 'They conceived their government to be the best that had ever been established, or ever could exist . . . their veneration for their government was the result of a long course of generations.'[74] Foscolo lamented that 'the people' had been debarred from government, but he recorded his general admiration for the regime. In dispute not only with Casanova, but also with Darù, Foscolo, the former Municipalist, came finally (near the end of his life) to defend the Republic, emphasising that 'the people accepted it as just', and it rarely compromised them.

The Theatre of Betrayal

Darù's account triumphed, however, at least for a time. He was consulted by another influential foreigner, Lord Byron, who was to write about Venice-past in terms that also showed its contemporary plight as inevitable. In 1816 Byron arrived in the place that was 'the greenest island of my imagination' (as he wrote to Thomas Moore).[75] He composed not only the famous Venice canto of *Childe Harold's Pilgrimage*, but, in a sustained period of residence in Venice and Ravenna, *Beppo*, *Don Juan* and the two plays devoted to notorious doges, Marino Faliero and Francesco Foscari.

The fourth canto of *Childe Harold* is the most famous and influential writing on Venice in modern times. Byron drafted it in the summer of 1817, dedicating it to his friend and fellow traveller John Cam Hobhouse, who produced a volume of elaborate notes.[76] Effectively the fourth canto did for Venice what Edward Gibbon's *Decline and Fall of the Roman Empire* had done for ancient Rome: the difference was that Venice's decline was a contemporary condition.[77] Byron gave life to the view of an iniquitous Venice, a great state in the past, but one that had built its fame and fortune on suppression and incarceration. 'A prison and a palace to one hand' was the oft-quoted juxtaposition in the first stanza. Thus Byron launched the popularity of the Bridge of Sighs as a symbol of the tragic link between government and suppression, for the bridge was the passage by which condemned prisoners passed from the civic world to incarceration in either the *pozzi* or the *piombi*.

Venice was at a low point when Byron first went there in 1816; if anything, he relished its physical decay and used vivid images to press home the nature of the fall: palaces were sinking to their waterlines, what was left of the Bucintoro was rotting and the golden horses were bridled. All these one-time marvels of the Venetian empire were now redolent of 'fallen states and buried greatness'. His preoccupation with a drowning Venice gave rise to spectacular watery images, as it did in the work of his friend the poet Shelley, who wrote of Venice as once 'ocean's nursling', now the ocean's prey, her palaces submerged so that they appeared like rocks draped in seaweed from the ocean itself.[78] The city's demise was, again, as much moral as physical. Venice was a perfect allegory of decline, which could be sustained as a personal as well as a national admonition: 'in the fall of Venice think of thine'.

Although a foreigner, Byron wrote with an inside knowledge of the cultural circles of Venice in which he himself participated. In the prefatory letter addressed to Hobhouse, he remarked – somewhat patronisingly – that 'Italy has great names still', and proceeded to list them. Most were Venetian, or had links with Venice: Canova came first (Byron had written his ode to the bust of Helen); then Vincenzo Monti (the dramatist who was present in Venice during the Municipality); Ugo Foscolo, now in London and a friend of Hobhouse as well as of Byron's publisher John Murray; Pindemonte; Morelli – Jacopo Morelli, the librarian of the Biblioteca Marciana; Cicognara, of course; Isabella Teotochi Albrizzi, whose salon Byron attended; and Mustoxidi, the Greek scholar in Padua. The list is a substantial tribute (and, even so, incomplete) to Venetian culture in the two decades after the city's fall.

For Byron, that culture – including the Armenian language, which he studied at the San Lazzaro degli Armeni – was still resplendent in the mind, even if the reputation and the forms of the Republic were past and now existed only as dreams. He might well have espoused the precious example of his compatriot William Beckford, who had visited in the last decades of the Republic, in the early 1780s, and found (he was among the first to do so) a dream world, a Venice dislocated from reality.[79] As the history of the Republic sank into the past, and was increasingly depicted as a tyranny, the view of the unreality of the city built on the water took hold.

For the English-speaking reader Byron appeared to be the creator of Venice as the conspiratorial state in his two plays focusing on the vulnerability of two doges, Faliero and Foscari. In 1354 Marino Faliero was appointed, at the age of seventy-six, to the office of doge, and was beheaded in 1355 when the Council of Ten found him guilty of treason.[80] His young wife provided a salacious contrast to the doge's advanced age: this had been the focus of one of the first nineteenth-century writings on Faliero, E. T. A. Hoffmann's *Doge and Dogaressa* published in 1818, before Byron's *Marino Faliero* (1820). In Hoffman's tale the young wife has a love affair with the man who had saved the doge from a storm on the lagoon. The doge is portrayed as a man of consummate pride, his reign beset from the outset with tempests, his jealousy of his young wife easily aroused.[81] In Hoffmann's tale, the youth who saved Faliero from drowning at the beginning meets his own death, together with the doge's widow. Death by drowning – the revenge of the sea, the spouse of Venice – makes a sinister leitmotiv.

Franceso Foscari was doge from 1453 until 1457 at the time the Condottiere Carmagnola from Piedmont was found guilty of betraying the Venetian state. This was the material for a play published in 1820 by the Milanese writer Alessandro Manzoni, whose novel *I Promessi sposi* later made him famous.[82] Manzoni's verse drama, *Il Conte de Carmagnola*, concerned the *condottiere* who came to the service of the Republic after he had fallen out with his previous employer, the Visconti lord of Milan. Manzoni's source was the recent historical work of his friend Francesco Lomanaco, who had published a study of notable military figures, *I Capitani*, in 1807.[83] From the Milanese point of view Carmagnola was innocent, falsely committed to prison for alleged treason against Venice.[84] The play debates the suspicion of Carmagnola's treason in favour of Milan as alleged by the Venetian government. Carmagnola is doubly betrayed, both by the state and by his friend Marco, a Venetian senator who acts against him. He is further tested in his loyalty to the state as he is forced to stand against the women who protect and nourish the family, and stand for peace against war. In the final act Carmagnola voices his innocence and the 'eternal infamy' of the Republic in front of the doge in the Sala del Consiglio dei Dieci: it is the first of a long series of plays, paintings and operas that bring victims of the Venetian state to face the doge and his tribunal in the chambers or the loggia of the

Palazzo Ducale. In Milan it must have recalled the writings of Beccaria and the Verri brothers, who deliberated some fifty years earlier on the secrecy and accusations of the Council of Ten.[85]

Written during the time of Napoleonic revisions of Venetian history and the Milanese sympathy for such views, it presented Carmagnola as a victim of the Venetian Republic. In Manzoni's account the count's probity was evident above all in his professionalism and his devotion to his soldiers and family. Contemporaries could hardly avoid making comparisons between Milan and Venice, or miss the nationalist import of the long chorus that follows the battle in the second act, which proclaims the unity of all subjects speaking the same language, while the earth is covered with bodies in a field of blood: 'I fratelli hanno ucciso i fratelli' – brothers have slain brothers.[86] Nor could the name Carmagnola be heard without invoking other associations, for it must have recalled the French revolutionary song performed wherever a Tree of Liberty had been raised. For Manzoni, the immediate context, when he began his play in 1815, was the Milanese uprising against the Austrians – the famous insurrection in which the Milanese demonstrated their refusal to submit passively to foreign rule.[87] In this they were in contrast with the compliant Venetians.

Ex-Venetian Foscolo responded to Manzoni in a review of his dramatic works, published in 1825 with a laudatory preface by Goethe.[88] For Foscolo the literary qualities were of less interest than Manzoni's representation of Venetian history, particularly the selective use of sources that cast Carmagnola as a hero and the Venetian patricians as representative of 'atrocious perfidy and inquisitions', and 'cruel out of cowardice'.[89]

At much the same time, in 1817, Byron conceived his project *Marino Faliero, Doge of Venice, An Historical Tragedy in Five Acts*.[90] As he wrote to John Murray, his inspiration was the blacked-out portrait of Faliero in the gallery of dogal portraits in the hall of the Maggior Consiglio in the Palazzo Ducale.[91] In his preparatory work Byron showed himself an exemplary historian, sifting through primary sources, and making speedy use of the new volumes by Darù.[92] Underlining Venetian hubris, he quoted Guingené's resonant prophecy: 'If thou does not change', he says to the proud republic, 'thy liberty, which is already on the wing, will not reckon a century more than the thousandth year', literally 'thy liberty will not last till 1797'.[93] History as melodrama was the legacy of Gibbon.

Byron's play and the theme of Venetian calumny inspired many other versions of Marino Faliero's fall. The distinguished French playwright Casimir Delavigne presented his tragedy at the Théâtre de la Port-Saint-Martin in Paris in 1829, maintaining that it was an independent work, *not* a translation of Byron; his version was recited in Italian translation in 1855.[94] Indeed, Delavigne appears to have taken his cue as much from Hoffmann as Byron, developing an illicit relationship between Faliero's young wife and a young patrician, which leads finally to an accusation of adultery. Like Byron, Delavigne presented his historical sources, based on Sanudo and Darù, in an appendix, as a 'critical evaluation'.[95] Meanwhile, the fashion for Faliero grew as Byron's play was translated into French in 1830, and into Italian by Buttafuoco in 1838.[96] Donizetti composed a three-act opera to a libretto by Bidera in 1837 – it was first performed in Théâtre-Italien, Paris, in 1835, and, following Delavigne, developed the adulterous relationship between the doge's wife and a younger man.[97] Giulio Pulle published a play in 1840;[98] Giusto Dall'Acqua published another in Padua in 1843.[99] A three-act tragedy by Antonio Spinelli was produced in Venice in April and May 1857.[100] These many performances and readings confirmed the phenomenal success of the theme of state punishment and retribution, taken up with relish in the age of Romanticism. One of the best-known visual representations was the 1826 painting by Eugène Delacroix, *The Execution of Doge Marino Faliero* (fig. 46), painted specifically for an exhibition for Greek relief in 1826 in response to Byron's death at

Missolonghi. Delacroix added a crisp note to his *Faliero*: 'Justice punishes traitors'. Beside the scene of decapitation is the lion of St Mark with the evangelical message written clearly.[101]

Byron's second historical play devoted to Venice, *The Two Foscari*, was written in 1821 at Ravenna, when Byron was an active member of the Carbonari, espousing the cause of Italian independence. Patriotism is an important theme and private and public loyalties are again tested as the old Doge Foscari is forced to accept the condemnation, torture and banishment of his last living child, Jacopo. The male patrician's fidelity to Venice is manifest in both father and son: in the father, in his stoic acceptance of the fate meted out to his son and, in Jacopo, who has already felt the acute pain of banishment but whose love of his city and youthful day-dreams prompt tender moments in the play. The doge's wife protests against the betrayal of the family demanded by the state: 'I tell thee, Doge, 'tis Venice is dishonoured; Her name shall be the foulest, worst reproach . . . Accursed be the city where the laws would stifle nature's!'[102]

Whatever the legends Byron helped to disseminate about Venice, his passion for the city was unbounded, even if it was subordinated to his larger historical concerns. In *Childe Harold* and in the Venetian plays he speaks of the richness of the Venetian past and its inspiration for those, like himself, who had 'loved it since his boyhood'. The tone is rhapsodic in *Childe Harold*, where he exhibits his love for history, symbol and the appearance and totality of a place that had few equals and was a continuing inspiration. In *The Two Foscari*, the son, the ardent patriot Jacopo Foscari, who prefers death to exile, speaks of Venice in 'a beautiful outburst':

> My beautiful, my own
> My only Venice, – *This is breath!*
>   Thy breeze
> Thine Adrian sea breeze, how it fans my face!
> The very winds feel native to my veins
> And cool them into calmness.[103]

Byron's life in Venice was notorious and probably at least as influential in associating Venice with sexual extravagance as was the varied literature on the decay of the Republic. It was possible to design a Byronic itinerary across Europe. *Finden's Landscape and Portrait Illustrations to the Life and Works of Lord Byron*, published in 1833, made the most of opportunities to present an illustrated text: Venice was shown in plates by J. D. Harding and Clarkson Stanfield. [104] Following Byron in Venice, travellers would linger outside the Palazzo Mocenigo, where he had lodgings, wonder at his marathon swim across the lagoon, visit the Lido, where he rode his horses with Shelley, and the Armenian monastery, where he studied with the monks. His sexual encounters seemed to be facilitated by residence in Venice, city of assignations. Thus while the bravos were lurking in the *calli* and political prisoners were purportedly dragged across the Bridge of Sighs, another Venice – the Venice of love – was in ascendancy, countering perfidy and hate. Byron, the Englishman, was the first post-Waterloo hero of romantic Venice, an aspect that appealed to the French, while the English lamented the dissoluteness of his life.[105] Where the English were denigratory – Thomas Moore described 'the irregularities of his private life' as 'an indelicate topic' – the French were admiring.[106]

The popularity of a Venice intriguing in its history and, at the same time, romantic as a *mise-en-scène*, is evident in the 1825 folio publication *Un Mois à Venise* by the Comte de Forbin, with illustrations by François-Louis Dejuinne (fig. 47).[107] It told the dramas of Venetian history in abbreviated form, casting them in the inevitable shadow of Darù. Offered as 'historical and explanatory' (*historique et explicatif*), the texts accompany the illustrations. Like Stendhal, this French author affirmed that Venice had contributed powerfully to the progress of civilisation in Europe, but

46 Eugène Delacroix, *The Execution of Doge Marino Faliero*, 1826. Oil on canvas, 145 × 113 cm. London, Wallace Collection.

sadness now affected an entire population, and the gondolier no longer sang his joyous barcarolles.[108] The judgement was simultaneously moral and economic: Venetian industry was once precocious, but it had stalled; no longer did it participate in the advances made by other nations.[109] For so long depicted as an enthroned queen, both Virgin and Venus, Venice now appeared lying sleeping with the sea lapping menacingly at her feet and her useless sceptre leaning against a column; beside her was a lethargic lion of St Mark. It was one of the early images of enervated Venice, and many were to follow.[110] The judgement, made so easily by foreigners, rolled sternly off the page: 'Venice is now in a state of agony . . . the lion of Saint Mark is effaced from the list of powerful nations to become a monument, an effigy covered by the waves, part of the ruined civilisations of Syria, Greece, Constantinople, Rome.' Thus citizens of buoyant nations recited the names of defunct empires, and included the Venice of their own time.

In other plates in the volume historic Venice was recreated in scenes depicting the Palazzo Ducale, erroneously claimed to have been begun by Marino Faliero, with the Staircase of the Giants now guarded by Austrians.[111] The staircase appears, anachronistically, as the site of the humiliation of the Emperor Barbarossa, the legendary event of 1177 in which Venice and the Papacy were reconciled against the northern leader. The external gallery looking over the Bacino is again the site; the Bocca del Leone is ready to receive letters of betrayal, invoking the inevitable presence of the Council of Ten. But the triumphant past is evoked in an illustration celebrating the doge's wedding with the sea and the high point of Franco-Venetian relations with an illustration of the reception of Henry III of France at the Palazzo Strà on the Brenta, now in Austrian hands.

As well as highlighting splendour and calumny, *Un Mois à Venise* staged an evocative return to the Venice that had been, in Byron's words, the 'masque of Italy', the Venice of his *Beppo*: this *città galante* was to be revisited many times over the next two hundred years. In anticipation, a carnival scene, the first after the fall, takes place in moonlight, with a dangerously laden gondola ferrying masked revellers along the Rio di Palazzo towards the Bridge of Sighs.[112] The use of the mask is explained in a lengthy quotation from Darù: the Bridge of Sighs (fig. 47) has begun to hear the sighs of lovers and honeymooners flocking to the watery city, rather than that of the prisoner.[113]

Un Mois à Venise was prophetic in its use of the new art of lithography, which would spread images of Venice around the world, and it was topical in associating the city with love, passion and dreaming – it consolidated that very reputation. It anticipated myriad picture books on Venice, such as the English *Legends of Venice* by J. R. Herbert and Thomas Roscoe in which the chosen narratives (assignations and balcony scenes) have a salacious edge.[114] An all-too-popular Venice was now on the international drawing boards.

The Bravo at Large

The fascination with early nineteenth-century Venice existed not only because it was in decline, but because it was pervaded with evil. This was not without paradox, given the city's fabled liberty and incontestable beauty which offered some evidence at least of largesse and public spirit. Long before the 1800s the tension between good and evil in the Serenissima had been rehearsed in foreign literature: in Shakespeare's *Merchant of Venice* and *Othello*, in Ben Jonson's *Volpone* and, pre-eminently, in Otway's *Venice Preserv'd*.[115] In the last years of the eighteenth century there were intimations of the supernatural and the sinister in Schiller and Jacques Cazotte: *The Devil in Love* and *The Ghost-Seer* are prophetic examples of a dangerous, destabilising effect. But in the early nineteenth century it was the bravo who embodied the evil and intrigue.

The bravo was a hired assassin, a kind of Venetian Robin Hood, who wreaked revenge upon the nobility and the rich but would defend *gondolieri* and *popolani*. He understood the betrayal system and the varying motifs, not always honest, that lead to denunciation by means of a letter posted in the lion's mouth. He had mastery of the *calli* and an enviable command of the sophisticated topography of the city, which could facilitate pursuit and flight. Later generations were thus alerted to the potential of a topography that could sustain murder and espionage – especially in film.

The bravo made his definitive appearance in a novel by Heinrich Zschokke, *Abällino*, of 1793, which was made into a play two years later. By 1815 bravos are everywhere in the novel by Mrs Catherine Smith, *Barozzi, or the Sorceress of Venice*, no doubt a result of the fame of Zschokke's work, which had become popular when translated into English 1805 by M. G. 'Monk' Lewis (this in turn was translated into Italian in 1834).[116] It was indeed timely; a powerful example of the new picture of evil in which both government and populace were implicated, despite the virtue exemplified by the bravo. All the motives of calumny were present: Venice has its character reaffirmed as sinister and evil, its people given over to indolence and gossip. There were the usual damning words about 'These hypocrites who govern the consciences of the bigotted [*sic*] Venetians, both man and woman, the noble and the mendicant, the Doge and the gondolier, bound fast in the chains of superstition. . . .'[117]

But the most potent treatment of the theme was James Fenimore Cooper's long novel, *The Bravo*, published in 1831, swiftly translated into Italian and made into a French play. It was also set in part as an opera, with music by Saverio Mercadante, which had its premiere at La Scala in Milan in 1839 – although the opera's plot attends more exclusively to the central love story.[118] Cooper had visited Venice during the late 1820s; his historical reading certainly included Darù, for he announced in his preface: 'For the justification of his likeness, after allowing for the defects of execution, he refers to the well-known work of M. Daru'.[119] Explanations were given for the benefit of the American reader to aid understanding of the singular history and strange customs of the Venetians. They were obviously intended to instruct the democratic American citizen in the devious ways of Venice. Thus:

> Distinctions in rank, as separated entirely from the will of the nation, formed the basis of Venetian polity. Authority, though divided, was no less a birthright than in those government in which it was openly avowed to be the dispensation of Providence. The patrician order had its high and exclusive privileges, which were guarded and maintained with a more selfish and engrossing spirit. He who was not born to govern, had little hope of ever entering into his natural rights; while he who was, by the intervention of chance, might yield a power of the most fearful and despotic character.[120]

There are many sprightly pages, full of intrigues and compelling evocations. The novel tells of secret assignations, subterfuge and espionage, and the great gondola regatta won by the old gondolier Antonio, who later meets his fate, drowned in the lagoon, at the hand of the state. The conclusion is unrelenting in its castigation of a flawed government, which forms a constant part of the author's reflections, reinforced by a conviction that America had inherited the mantle of democracy cast aside by Europe. The author is confident of the supremacy of his own state.[121]

Cooper's judgement was no more or less critical than most pronounced after the fall, but it particularly aroused the ire of the writer Luigi Carrer. He declared it to be a calumny: wilfully inaccurate in details of topography and custom, and exaggerated in its account of the numbers of denunciations committed to the lion's mouth – a vicious slander against the memory of the Venetian Republic.[122] Carrer accepted that liberties might be taken and tolerated in a work of fiction, but in the case of Cooper's *The Bravo*, 'the principal aim of the work is to render the government of Venice hateful and infamous, painting it in the blackest colours'.[123]

Even John Ruskin, whose own castigation of historical Venice was as forceful as was his love for its architecture, was moved to write to his father about the inaccuracies perpetrated in *The Bravo*:

> It is marvellous how ridiculous the common novel-sentiment about Venice appears to any one who really knows anything about it; but more marvellous still that a seaman like Cooper should never have found out that the lagoons were shallow – and should have represented the State inquisitors as drowning a criminal in the lagoons . . . The republicanism and abuse of the Venetian government are also so absurd that it may be worth while taking notice of them in a note, as I daresay this book is an authority with the Americans about Venice . . .[124]

But the fascination with the evil Republic grew, particularly in the 1830s. Victor Hugo made his contribution with two influential plays furthering the association of Venice with evil. *Lucrèce Borgia* begins in Venice, although the main action is in Ferrara and concerns the D'Este family.[125] Carnival, and the terrace of a palace in moonlight, the Giudecca canal afloat with revellers, masks concealing evil intent: these effects in the opening scenes assist in the unmasking of Lucrezia Borgia as a murderess. Hugo's 1835 play, *Angelo Tyran de Padou*, about Padua as a vassal of Venice, relished the evidence of evil everywhere, with the lions' mouths eager to receive denunciations, dark passageways *à la* Piranesi concealing miscreants and spies, and the notorious Canal Orfano ready to drown state victims by night, while the Signoria of Venice wields its brutal powers.[126] Venice was identified negatively by the Podestà of Padua with the pozzi, the piombi, and the Council of Ten: all these traits are exposed in early speeches. In a note accompanying the published play Hugo defended his melodramatic presentation against those critics who had found his work overdrawn by quoting his authorities, Amelot de la Houssaie and, of course, Darù; he also appended the statutes of the State Inquisition of 1454.[127] Hugo's plays were destined to be even more famous as operas – as the librettos for Donizetti's *Lucrezia Borgia* in 1833, and Ponchielli's *La Gioconda* in 1876.[128] Both were premiered in Milan, at La Scala.

The City in Water

While it inspired so many historical treatments, the Venice of the nineteenth century could also appear to postdate history, to occupy a neutral terrain where events and personalities of consequence no longer existed. Visual artists increasingly attentive to the scenery of Venice colluded in the disappearance of its history, and among them was J. M. W. Turner. Turner has often been linked with Byron – and certainly he himself appended Byron's verses to certain pictures – but his paintings seem rather to confirm the increasing recession of history, the redundancy of historical characters and the supremacy of the environment as a spectacle governed more by nature than by man.[129] In the 1836 painting *Juliet and her Nurse* (Argentina, private collection) Juliet is translated from Verona to Venice and found – almost absurdly – on the rooftops above the Piazzetta; but the view of the heart of Venice is dazzling. Juliet looks below to the golden space of the Piazza and beyond to the Bacino in the distance, ablaze with fireworks.

In its sheer incandescence, such a view hardly pertains to a Venice that is decayed or decaying, or visibly subjugated by Austrian rule. It is difficult to establish a Carbonari reading of Venice through Turner's eyes (inevitable, by contrast, for Byron, who was interested in the political and historical situation long before he succumbed to the Venetian phantasmagoria). Turner approached Venice for the first time in 1819 as a salaried agent of the picturesque view, making studies of monuments such as the Rialto Bridge and vignettes to illustrate the poems of Samuel Rogers. He also recorded the Grand Canal and the Bacino in a series of scenic watercolours.[130] The watercolours were to form a memory bank that Turner tapped in later decades.

It was only in 1833, some years after his first visit to Venice, that Turner exhibited his first *imaginative* painting of Venice at the Royal Academy. *The Bridge of Sighs, Ducal Palace and Custom-House, Venice: Canaletti Painting* (London, Tate Gallery) established that Turner's inspiration lay not so much in Byron as in earlier view painting. His subject is Canaletto, shown with his easel set up to look across the Bacino at the stretch of ceremonial water that fronted on to the great Piazzetta where the buildings appear suffused with gold.[131] Buildings and water are consumed and equalised in the light, losing much of the precision and certainty associated with Canaletto. The Bridge of Sighs lies behind a thick nest of shipping, masted boats and gondolas weighted down by gold brocades and tapestries, as if the Republic still cargoed in rich treasures from the East. Turner increasingly painted not the architecture in its historic accuracy, but the spectacle of Venice on the water (land views are rare): the effects of light, reflections, silhouettes, or the trajectory of a rocket. These scenographic attributes are discovered in a group of watercolours on dark paper executed some time between 1833 and 1835.[132] Rockets trace their paths against the night sky, lighting up the dome of Santa Maria della Salute, and the stars are out above the Bridge of Sighs.

English painters flocked to Venice from the 1820s – among them Richard Parkes Bonington, Samuel Prout and Clarkson Stanfield. It was William Etty, rather than Turner, who in 1830 translated Byron's conjunction of prison and palace into a compelling visual image in *The Bridge of Sighs* (fig. 48). The bridge is lit up in steely night

49 J. M. W. Turner,
*Morning, Returning from
the Ball San Martino*, 1845.
Oil on canvas,
61.6 × 92.4 cm. London,
Tate Britain.

light as a body is being transferred to the boat from a door at water level.[133] Shadows on palace and prison are razor-sharp. Turner, in contrast, appears uninterested in the prison as a prison, and more interested in the double bridge motif set up by the Bridge of Sighs and the lower Ponte deglia Paglia. Another work by him, a vignette of the Bridge of Sighs, shows the bridge from the land side looking out across the lagoon, with a female figure on a balcony and a male greeting her, a night scene certainly, but set up for love, not political intrigue.[134]

Turner's Venetian paintings executed towards the end of his life create, if not a dream Venice, then a place out of time or temporarily suspended. He anticipates the recession of history and the greater power and spectacle of visual Venice, sufficient in that reputation. *The Sun of Venice going to Sea* (London, Tate Gallery) of 1843 might well be intended as a comment on the railway then being built from the mainland, rather than a meditation on the loss of the Republic, for there is little real evidence that this exercised Turner's mind. In late works, architecture loses its prominence; revellers, going to balls and returning from them (fig. 49), weigh down their craft in the water, and are sucked into a mêlée of elements in which the famous architecture is a fringe on the horizon, relinquishing all precision. The crusts of paint make the very atmosphere palpable as it carries allegories of journeying – imprecise and dreamlike.

Custodians of the Republic

While foreigners were recasting the history and appearance of the city, the Venetians were not idle. The machine of memory was turning: it had begun with the rewriting of history during the Municipality, and accelerated with the changes effected during the first period of Austrian rule. Increasingly Venetians engaged with their long Republican history, although their work had less impact than foreign notions of conspiracy and decay. Filiasi, Moschini, Teotochi Albrizzi, Renier Michiel and Cicognara published distinguished work in the first decade of the century. A new generation was in

48 William Etty,
The Bridge of Sighs,
1833–5. Oil on canvas,
80 × 50.8 cm. York, City of
York Art Gallery.

the wings: Marina Querini Benzon's son, Vittore Benzon, was acclaimed as a poet for his long and involved saga *Nella*, about the early days of Venice.[135]

The Venetians had long been adept at the celebration and description of their city. Patrician procurators, responsible for the preservation of the fabric of San Marco and other prestigious buildings, were regarded highly among state appointees. Sansovino's *Venetia Città nobilissima et singolare* (1581) was the most famous instance of the celebratory genre of writing about the city's monuments.[136] Many others followed, such as the aquatic tour in verse form by Boschini, *La Carta nel navegar pitoresco* (1554), and the many *vite* of celebrated artists and architects, such as Carlo Ridolfi's *Maraviglie dell'arte, ovvero le vite degli illustri pittori veneti e dello stato* (1548). The strong sense of responsibility towards public artworks continued to the last days of the Republic, recorded in Tommaso Temanza's *Vite dei più celebri architetti e scultori veneziani* (1778) and Zanetti's *Della Pittura veneziana e delle opere pubbliche de veneziani maestri*, written in 1770 in his capacity as guardian of public works of art under the Republic.

The traditional format for these tracts was an enumeration of the monuments within monuments, both ecclesiastical and public, working through the six districts of Venice, the *sestiere*. The nineteenth-century guides abandoned that procedure in favour of a programme with a hierarchy of sights, or a compressed itinerary planned around what could feasibly be undertaken in the course of a single day or a number of days.[137] With these changes came mass tourism.

The first guide for the new century, the first after the fall of the Republic, was the work of Giannantonio Moschino, Abbot of San Cipriano in Murano, whom we have seen writing on recent literature and publishing a guide to his native Murano (spotlighting the glass industry, to which, 'the world owes the invention of crystal glass, *conterie* – glass beads, mirrors . . . et al.').[138] Moschini's guide to Venice, published in two volumes in 1815, was addressed to the 'friend of art' visiting Venice as an 'art city'.[139] The designation was prophetic. Moschini used the traditional format, treating each *sestiere* separately, beginning with the eastern end of the main island, at San Pietro di Castello. About halfway through the first volume we reach San Marco. Engravings were included: the frontispiece to the first volume was 'Il pubblico Palazzo sulla Piazzetta'; in deference to modern Venice the second volume featured the 'Giardini', the city's most recent civic embellishment. Moschini emphasised his own exemplary lineage back to Sabellico's *De Venetae urbis situ* of 1492, as well as his more immediate forbears and contemporaries, Temanza and Selva.

Thoroughly up-to-date, Moschini quoted Isabella Teotochi Albrizzi's description of the works of Canova, and Cicogna on the body of St Mark.[140] He referred to the royal box and imperial staircase installed at Teatro della Fenice for the visit of Napoleon, and praised his friend Selva for the public garden, and for his writings on Sanmichele and the Ionic volute.

The guide was received with some criticism, but with sufficient approbation for Moschini to produce a French edition in 1819: the *Itinéraire de Venise*.[141] It appeared in one compact volume, with tinted maps, just in advance of the fold-out maps that were soon to become a standard feature of guides. In tune with the times, the new edition was dedicated to the Podestà Calbo-Crotta – our 'legitimate successor', with words of praise for the Viceroy Ranieri ('bien-aimée'), who had allegedly given a considerable sum for the preservation of artworks. Moschini also included a letter from Bartolomeo Gamba, the librarian of the Biblioteca Marciana, giving a synopsis of Venetian architecture in four epochs for 'the enlightenment of the stranger', in the spirit of the art-historical essay that was to become standard in later guides.[142] Not uncharacteristically, Moschini praised his own work, underlining the excellence of his connections and the inspiration he had imparted to Selva and Diedo in their publication on eminent Venetian buildings, to Cicognara's history of sculpture, and to Selva's translation of Sabellico and Cicogna's work on inscriptions, *Veneto lapidario*.

Modesty aside, Moschini was the founder of nineteenth-century Venetian guide-writing, but it was Antonio Quadri who anticipated the format of the tourist guide for the modern traveller. He understood that time might be limited and brought that fact to bear upon his planning and group itineraries, arranged not in terms of art-works within the *sestiere*, but in daily tours: he favoured eight days spent in the delectation of the city (with a compressed four-day guide issued later, after his eight-day guides had run to many editions).[143] He chose a compact two-volume format with fold-out frontispiece maps. The first volume addressed questions of travel, of getting to A and B in the minimum time and marking tours that necessitated a gondola. Rather than besieging the reader with the totality of sights, Quadri offered a method of travel that was pre-selected. The visitor was assisted by that extraordinary topographical invention, the asterisk, which he used to identify principal sights ('cosi meritevoli di attenzione ed osservazioni'), with a P designating those that may be passed over. Rather than beginning at the eastern end of the main island at Castello, as was traditional, Day One begins at the Piazza di San Marco and its edifices – in other words, it goes straight to the central sights. Day Two takes in the eastern region of the Arsenale, the Pietà and the island of San Giorgio Maggiore; the third day is spent on the Grand Canal; the fourth at the Giudecca, and so on, until the eighth day in the lagoon islands: Murano for the glass, Burano for the lace, Torcello, and, finally, the Murazzi at Pellestrina, where 'the observer will find the clearest monument of the power and richness of the discontinued Republic'.[144]

The second volume, of nearly five hundred pages, gave a compendium of the history of Venice presented in brief essays covering the festivals, the principal periods of the Republic from its origin, and a list of doges who had headed government. History was divided into eight epochs from AD 421 to Epoch 8, the fall of the Republic. The diagnosis of the fall was telling in that it was the opinion of a Venetian: the government lacked the necessary energy to make resolutions in proportion to the grave difficulties that it faced; a false sense of tranquillity prevented engagement in war in 1796.[145] Nevertheless, the monuments remain, commanding universal admiration. Sure in this knowledge, the custodians of Venetian culture embarked on their programmes for cultural tourism.

Quadri understood the power of the image, working in tandem with the artist Dionisio Moretti to produce *Il Canal Grande di Venezia*, published in 1828, and *La Piazza San Marco in Venezia, considerata come monumento di arte e di storia* in 1831, with sixteen plates. While these volumes lacked the subtlety, density and originality of the great portfolios of the eighteenth century by Marieschi, Canaletto and others, they established a new standard for accessible printed volumes. Continuous plates laid out the most prestigious areas of the city, using a panoramic format joining one page to the next.[146] Brief descriptions addressed the traveller as if he or she were seeing the actual sight in the company of the author: 'you can see', 'now is the time to come back to the other side of the canal', 'the visitor crossing the canal by gondola or other boat, will be able to see how accurate the plates are, no one building is forgotten . . .'

The guides are evidence of the pride in the past and, at least to some degree, of confidence in the present. So, too, was the active cultivation of the vernacular. Pietro Buratti and Antonio Lamberti invariably used Venetian dialect for their poetry. On everyone's lips in 1817, apparently, was Buratti's poem *Elefanteide*, about the animal brought to the Riva degli Schiavoni for carnival, and its escape, taking sanctuary in a church, before capture and execution.[147] Bartolomeo Gamba brought together a collection of the best work in dialect for the Alvisopoli press in 1817. The press itself, founded by Alvise Mocenigo at his Veneto estate of Portogruaro soon after the fall of the Republic in 1801, and by 1817 directed in Venice by Bartolomeo Gamba, was brilliant evidence of cultural resilience. In 1825 Vincenzo Foscarini, one of the most patriotic of Venetian poets, published his *Soneti in dialeto veneziani*, and Alessandro

50 Luigi Zandomeneghi,
Giustina Renier Michiel,
1825. Gesso,
65 × 39 × 31 cm.
Venice, Museo Correr.

Zanchi his popular comedy in dialect, *La Regatta di Venezia*.[148] In 1827 the young Daniele Manin – destined to lead the revolution against the Austrians in 1848 – read a paper on the dialect at the Ateneo Veneto.[149]

One of Venice's great traditions, universally acknowledged, was its publishing. Undaunted by the fall, the publishing house of Alvisopoli continued the tradition. Between 1818 and 1852 Alvisopoli published 743 titles, including the Moschini guides, the work of the Ateneo Veneto, Michiel's *Origine delle feste veneziane*, Foscolo, and the first edition of *Le Fabbriche più cospicue* by Cicognara, Diedo and Selva in 1815.[150]

Giustina Renier Michiel, a venerable figure by then, was acclaimed for her historical *Origine delle feste veneziane*, published by Alvisopoli between 1817 and 1827 – a work, noted Cicogna, that one reads gladly because of its patriotic spirit.[151] In gestation from the first decade of the century, it made its first French edition appearance with a sad, revealing dedication: 'It was to the Countess of the North in 1782 that I dared to present myself as a small child of the Doge of Venice Paolo Renier, then reigning, the last of the Doges who finished his glorious days in dignity. How times have changed.'[152] The account of Venetian festivals proceeds like a laudatory history, celebrating the Church, Venetian saints, triumphs on the seas and survival from plague, from the earliest times to contemporary regattas. By the mid-1820s the author was a senior figure. A portrait bust made in 1825 by Luigi Zandomeneghi portrays her as an old women, slightly stooped, head decorously draped, but with curls protruding vigourously, and a smile at once shrewd and kindly (fig. 50).[153] Luigi Carrer included Michiel in his gallery of extraordinary Venetian women in his *Anello di sette gemme* (Ring with Seven Jewels) of 1838, in company with the historical figures Caterina Cornaro and Bianca Cappello.[154] Born in 1801, Luigi Carrer was representative of the new generation, who had never lived under Republican rule. He was a distinguished writer, one of the first scholars of Foscolo. The Gondoliere press which he founded (with Papadopoli's backing) was a forum for Venetian writing and published two of the important figures of the cultural Risorgimento, Ippolito Nievo and Niccolò Tommaseo.[15] In the years 1824 to 1825 Cicogna too published his collection of inscriptions, *Delle Iscrizioni veneziane raccolte ed illustrate*.[156] His significant library of Venetian material, eventually to be bequeathed to the city, was well established.[157]

A formidable contribution to the art and conservation of Venetian sculpture came from the modest Luigi Zandomeneghi, who was important for his custodianship of some central monuments. In 1822 he made a stele of Goldoni for the foyer of Teatro La Fenice and remade the copper angel that surmounted the Campanile of San Marco – it glittered there, waiting for the eye and eloquence of Marcel Proust to open his window onto it in 1900.[158] With Antonio Diedo, Zandomeneghi made an historical inventory of the city's sepulchral monuments with illustrations executed by students of the Academy – on the model of the architectural volume by Cicognara, Selva and Diedo. It was less renowned, but an important and timely record nevertheless.[159] In 1836 Zandomeneghi restored the ancient hunchback figure at the Rialto known as the Gobbo, a quietly characteristic Venetian monument.[160]

Among architectural publications, Antonelli published an Italian translation of J. N. L. Durand's famous collection of parallel examples, first issued in 1800, the *Recueil des édifices*, which illustrated the full history of architecture, in both the East and the West.[161] In the Italian edition of 1823, the Venetian edition, Venetian examples are conspicuous, with folio pages at the end that illustrate the 'modern arabesques' of Professor Borsato.[162] One is left in no doubt of the desire to embrace French taste, and excel in it.

Beyond individual initiatives, institutions were developed and consolidated in tandem with the zeal for protecting historic material. All Europe envied the vast state

51 Archivio di Stato di Venezia, Rio Terrà di San Toma.

archives of Venice, located in the former convent of the Frari and now at the disposal of scholars.[163] These were, in effect, the record of the Republic, made public for the first time. The archival holdings spanned centuries; every European country regarded its ambassadorial reports with fascination and access to them was one of the passions of the nineteenth century.[164] Lorenzo Santi was responsible for the adaptation of the building, providing a new monumental façade on the canal site of the Rio Terrà di San Toma (fig. 51).[165] The librarians and keepers of the archives were stalwart in defence of their collections, under threat first from French and then from Austrian interests. Leopold von Ranke came to use them in 1827, and it is well known that his influential historiography was grounded in the study of the ambassadorial accounts, the *relazioni*. His own collection was built up in the years when Venetian libraries and papers were being dispersed.[166] The Englishman Horatio Brown came to Venice in 1833 (in search of Thomas Mowbray, Duke of Norfolk, deceased in 1399 in Venice) and stayed to produce the calendar of Venetian state papers relating to England, which ran to six volumes.[167]

In 1836 the first civic museum opened. This marked the official début of Venice as a museum city, a status already accorded it in the guides to the city's churches and public buildings.[168] The benefactor Teodoro Correr had bequeathed his collections to his city in 1830, offering a range of material of all kinds – objects, textiles, books, manuscripts and so on, much of it acquired in the last years of the Republic. The museum was first housed in Correr's own house on the Grand Canal at San Zandegolà and then transferred to the Fondaco dei Turchi, opening there in 1887. Other collections were added to Correr's core collection, including Cicogna's huge library, received in 1868 after his death.[169] However, Correr's collection remained exemplary in its scope and thoroughness. The value attached to the arts of glass, ceramics, costume and woodwork and to libraries of manuscripts, books and maps augmented the Venetian reputation for greatness in the field of painting and was inspirational for later scholars, such as Pompeo Molmenti, whose history of the fine and applied arts, *Venezia nella vita privata*, was published in 1880.[170] During the 1920s Molmenti was a force in relocating the Correr Museum to its current site in the Procuratie Nuove.

Building memorials to famous Venetians was characteristic of the period, not only as a matter of pride and reaffirmation of Venetian greatness, but as a mark of Austrian paternalism and cultural conquest. The nineteenth century was passionate about Titian, and to a lesser extent Tintoretto. As the heroes of the Golden Age of Venice, the two painters inspired plays and paintings in Venice and elsewhere.[171] The interest of Ferdinand I (who became emperor in 1838) in Venetian themes was apparent in his commission of a major history painting on the familiar Doge Foscari subject. Michelangelo Grigoletti delivered his interpretation on a vast scale to Vienna in 1844, choosing the moment of the father's rejection of the son, hand raised, dome of San Marco visible through the window (fig. 52).[172] The Austro-Hungarian cultivation of Titian was further expressed in the grandiose commission given to Grigoletti to paint a version of Titian's *Assunta* for the cathedral of Esztergom.[173] There were other ambitious history paintings: in 1833 Alexandre-Jean-Baptiste Hesse painted *The Death of*

52 Michelangelo Grigoletti, *The Last Conversation of Doge Francesco Foscari and his Son Jacopo*, 1842. Oil on canvas, 336 × 475 cm. Vienna, Kunsthistorisches Museum.

Titian. At the height of the plague the funeral procession passes the Palazzo Ducale, and the body of Titian is carried upon a hooded catafalque above the fallen bodies of plague victims (fig. 53).[174] Titian was again the charismatic subject for the Piedmontese artist Antonio Zona, who in 1861 painted a young and dapper Veronese showing Titian a folio of drawings on the Ponte degli Paglia.[175] In the background are the columns of the lion of St Mark and St Theodore, and the Sansovino Libreria under construction. Foreign writers also took Titian as their subject, from Musset's

53 Alexandre-Jean-Baptiste Hesse, *Funerary Honours for Titian in Venice during the Plague of 1576*, 1833. Oil on canvas. Paris, Louvre.

54 Luigi and Pietro Zandomeneghi, monument to Titian, Santa Maria Gloriosa dei Frari, 1852.

short prose work about Titian's son, 'Le Fils du Titien', published in *Revue des deux mondes* in 1838, to the swansong, Hugo von Hofmannsthal's *Der Tod des Tizians* in 1892.[176]

It was in this climate that a memorial to Titian was built in the church of the Frari, following a commission from the Emperor Ferdinand during his visit to Venice in 1838. The work, by Luigi Zandomeneghi and his son Piero, is a conservative, cumbersome monument placed diagonally opposite the Canova memorial (fig. 54). The format is a triumphal arch, in type related to the Vendramin tomb (contemporary with Titian). The artist is seated like a patriarch in the centre, flanked by personifications of Painting, Drawing, Architecture and Sculpture. Behind him are bas-reliefs of his *Assunta* and other paintings.[177] The politics of the memorial were quite evident: the medallion Titian wears is inscribed with the Habsburg double eagle, and the patronage he received from the Habsburgs in his lifetime, and from their descendant Ferdinand, in 1838, is specifically commemorated on tablets carried by two men, one young and one old; one past, one present. The surmounting lion of St Mark also wears the Habsburg double eagle: in art, as in life.[178]

'Ammiglioramenti': The 'Improvements' in Venice

Despite the cultivation of the past, the modernisation of the city and the restoration of commerce was pressing; it ensured the very survival of the culture even while it might appear to conflict with it. In a city haunted by its one-time maritime greatness, no aspect of invasion had caused greater harm than the despoliation of the Arsenale and the blockades that restricted basic supplies of food and trade. The fabled isolation of Venice could be turned to the disadvantage of the city.

In 1829 the free-port status eagerly sought under Napoleon, but too limited by its restriction to San Giorgio Maggiore, was renegotiated and extended to the whole of Venice, an event received with jubilation by the populace, with services of thanksgiving and a special *omelia* read by the patriarch in San Marco.[179] The request to the Austrians had first been made in 1816, so its realisation was long-awaited. However as a solution it was incomplete: the effective location of a modern port in conjunction with the provision of modern docking and unloading facilities remained unresolved. The debates on the position of an entrepôt or a *stazione marittima* were to continue through the century. Just before the free-port contract, in 1828, James Fenimore Cooper remarked shrewdly on the port structures, indicating that the discussion was wide enough to be picked up by a visitor:

> The attempt to revive the importance of Venice by making of it a free port, is not likely to result in much benefit. It requires some peculiarly political combinations and a state of the world very different to that which exists today, to create a commercial supremacy for such places as Venice or Florence. Venice does not possess a single facility that is not equally enjoyed there [Trieste] . . .[180]

The greater use of Trieste caused resentment throughout the period of Austrian rule. Stripped of power, the Arsenale had no role to play in the debate. In 1825, by decree of Francis I, the Austrians had begun to restore the central garrison as an Austrian showcase. The refurbishment was complete by 1829 with a new portal, the Corpo di Guardia, designed with Doric portals by Giovanni Casoni, who published a guide celebrating the restoration.[181] The main gateway to the Arsenale, the Roman arch with its fabulous array of purloined sculptures – the winged lion, Neptune, Mars and the Virtues, and the other lions variously commandeered from Greece – featured in the new arts of lithography and photography, indicating that fashionable society enjoyed its leisure there before the Austrian sentry-boxes. But the renovations amounted to little more than a facelift.

However, the development of Malamocco on the Lido during Napoleon's rule established it as a major outlet to the Adriatic, and led to a further initiative in the mid-1830s with the construction of a breakwater system to protect the entrance from silting.[182] The project was developed by Pietro Paleocapa, a central figure in terms of his contribution to the governance of ports and hydraulic matters.[183] His reputation has expanded until he has become one of the most highly regarded Venetians of his age, not least because of his devotion to the cause of the Republic during 1848 and 1849. Yet it was Austrian patronage that was instrumental in renewing maritime trade: the first stones of the marble breakwater were laid by Emperor Ferdinand in 1838 during his first visit to Venice as Habsburg successor to Francis I.[184]

In reaction to restrictions on the Church and the religious orders imposed by Napoleon, and indicating their own religious preferences, the Austrians sought to conserve and expand the ecclesiastical presence. The clearest indicator was the construction of the Patriarchal Palace, adjacent to the north façade of the Basilica of San Marco on the Piazzetta dei Leoncini, intended to house the patriarch beside his church (fig. 55). The building was designed by Lorenzo Santi and work began in 1837. It was the last major intervention in the Piazza area, and the last essay in monumental Neoclassical architecture in Venice.[185]

The area had long been designated as ecclesiastical, as the site of the canonical houses – the Casa dei Canonica was linked by a corridor to the Palazzo Ducale. The Piazzetta dei Leoncini, formalised in the early eighteenth century when it was adorned with the pair of lions in Verona stone, was an area of intimacy and repose before the entry into the major Piazza. Santi ran through variants in a range of styles in the preliminary design stages.[186] The final façade appears Mannerist in style, because of Santi's use of six giant Corinthian pilasters projected through two storeys, yet these establish a rapport with the façade of the old church of San Basso to the north. The insistent verticality has the effect of compressing the building into itself, articulating it in a decisive and public way within its own parameters, emphatically separating it from the prestigious north façade of San Marco. The sculpted frieze adorned with patriarchal devices and instruments of the Mass links it visually with the Palazzo Reale frieze at the opposite end of the Piazza. The traditional tiled roof absorbs the building sympathetically into the area of rooftops behind San Marco.

In his discussion of the 'improvements' of Venice of 1843 Agostino Sagredo reflected on the preceding years, noting the reopening of churches and the signs of renewed and extended religious patronage under Austrian rule in the 1830s.[187] Insisting on the piety of the Venetians, Sagredo took the opportunity to remember the two hundred churches that functioned at the end of the Republic, finding it still pertinent to comment on

55 Lorenzo Santi, Palazzo Patriarchale, Piazzetta dei Leoncini, 1837–50.

those that were destroyed – for example the 'magnificent and vast church of Santa Maria dei Serviti, rich in precious monuments'.[188] But the list of reopened churches was substantial: Santa Sofia in Cannaregio was repurchased and reopened as a church in 1836.[189] Sant'Agnese on the Zattere was reopened by the Cavanis order after restoration by Gaspare Biondetti-Crovatto.[190] The completion of long-standing projects might also be noted: San Maurizio, which Selva began in 1806, was completed in 1828 with grisaille decorations painted by Giuseppe Borsato, and San Silvestro in San Polo was reconstructed in 1837 from Santi's designs.[191] The Patriarchal Palace was not mentioned, but it was the most conspicuous testimony to the consolidation of the Church under Austrian rule.

During the mid-1830s there was a prodigious display of rebuilding at La Fenice. When it burned down on 12 December 1836 (the principal bell of San Marco tolled in the Campanile) it was rebuilt with all alacrity under the direction of Tommaso and Giambattista Meduna. It reopened on 20 January 1837. With well-calculated modesty Tommaso Meduna wrote of their correction of the 'few defects' in the original building: the alignment of the entrance doors to the auditorium, for example, and the realignment of stairs and corridors.[192] Sagredo observed that Meduna 'generally followed Selva's design but much improved it'.[193] The rebuilding was a demonstration of a principle that was to become central to Venetian replicatory practice in the next century: where it was, as it was – *dov'era, com'era*. Selva's concept was changed only where convenience and modernisation demanded it.

During the 1830s, Sagredo noted, there had been an increase in public works. After the Napoleonic stasis, maintenance programmes peculiar to Venice were resumed, particularly the repair of bridges and, following Napoleonic precedents, the infill of canals, intended to improve movement through the city. Selva's pupil, Giuseppe Salvadori, was industrious in this respect, proposing filling in the Rio della Carità in 1817, to open up the area of the Dorsoduro between the Grand Canal and the Giudecca Canal.[194] Salvadori was working on bridges from 1818. The bridge for the Bacino end of the Via Eugenia near the Giardini Pubblici, not built in Selva's time, was completed in 1823; of Istrian stone, with an arch bearing the winged lion with dolphins playing on each side, it was a traditional bridge bearing the traditional insignia.[195] By 1833 the island cemetery of San Cristoforo was in need of enlargement. It was joined by a bridge to the adjacent San Michele in Isola as the first stage in a merging of the two islands. Salvadori made plans for the bridge and for new walls punctuated by octagonal sepulchres.[196]

A distinctive form of industrial architecture emerged in the 1830s, still sympathetic to Neoclassical principles and alert to modern notions of urban zoning.[197] The Venetian practice had long been a pragmatic one, siting utilitarian facilities in the vicinity of ceremonial public and ecclesiastical buildings, such as the old granary near the Piazzetta. The customs area of the Dogana, in the immediate region of the church of Santa Maria della Salute, was renewed in the 1830s. Giovanni Pigazzi designed new salt warehouses – the Magazzini del Sale – on the Giudecca side, building in traditional brick with round arch openings marked in Istrian stone. (Salt was a valuable commodity, highly taxed under Austrian rule.) Pigazzi's warehouse was, in fact, the last substantial building in the St Mark's basin area (fig. 56).

56a and b Giovanni Alvise Pigazzi, Magazzini del Sale, Zattere ai Saloni, c.1830.

The location of services on the peripheries of the main islands indicated the new zonal thinking. Following plans initiated in 1834 – and after the French modernised such practices as slaughtering animals – a communal abattoir was constructed in the San Giobbe area of Cannaregio by Salvadori and Giambattista Meduna; it remains today (although in process of redeployment). An extended one-storey building in felicitous Neoclassical mode, the abbatoir has a central pediment articulated in Istrian stone; elegant roundels mark the façade, which is surmounted by the carved head of an ox.[198] The site, near the wide Canale di Cannaregio facing on to the lagoon, was selected to facilitate deliveries from the mainland.

In the same period innovations characteristic of urban change everywhere were adopted by a Venice desirous of imitating the

modern metropolis. A gas company was founded in 1839, and in 1840 a commercial co-operative, the Società Veneta Commerciale, began operation. Illumination by gas came from gasworks established at Santa Marta from 1839, and then later at San Francesco della Vigna.[199] Extended further every day, the street-lighting project was one of the conspicuous signs of improvement noted by Agostino Sagredo, who kept the statistical records during these years and enthused where possible on such evidence of modernisation.[200] Ninety-eight lamps, one on each alternate arch, illuminated the Piazza San Marco. The establishment of the gasworks on the southern and northern boundaries of the central islands was the beginning of the development of the island outskirts for new industrial initiatives. It was further indication of the shift from the Bacino di San Marco and the upper Zattere and Giudecca, a shift that had been initiated with the demolition of the granary for the royal gardens. It would be another hundred years before the boat-building yards of the upper waters and the mercantile warehouses of the Giudecca and Zattere were closed, but the process had begun.

However, the principal change for the islands of Venice – and one of the most radical in its entire history – was the provision of a rail bridge to the mainland. Although completed only in 1846, it was in gestation for two decades. The acute sufferings during the blockade, when food supplies ran short, and the extended blockade of the Adriatic which stifled Venice's access to the Adriatic and trading, lay behind the increasing agitation for a bridge to the mainland and projects to link the main islands. More than any revolution, such a link was seen to terminate Venice's fabled virginal isolation and purity by joining it to the Terraferma. Chateaubriand, a remarkable witness to the discussion threatening the project, wrote to Madame Récamier during his last visit to Venice in 1845 declaring that the bridge should not be feared and it would not disfigure Venice, rather, 'it is an artery to lead more blood to the heart'.[201]

The land link was to be controversial, not only in its first stage as a railway, but later in the century, when plans were mooted for a carriageway – and then an automobile road – to the mainland. The controversy was to divide Venice into advocates of the bridge, the *pontisti*, and critics, the *anti-pontisti*.[202] That debate crystallised the need to conserve Venice and its picturesque qualities by keeping the marks of modernisation at bay. Appreciation of this picturesque Venice accelerated with passion later in the nineteenth century, after various debates and a growing focus on the city as a totality made up of its water and land, and of minor buildings as well as the famous landmarks.

In the 1820s the isolation of the islands and the slow passage between them obviously impeded easy transfer of both residents and visitors across town. The question of a link was raised in the wake of the famine of 1820, at a time of widespread poverty. Faith in bridges was at a high point in the early nineteenth century, the century of engineering. The crucial link was first with the mainland, and then between the main islands of the lagoon. There were many plans, and much debate.

Such projects were not new. Schemes to compensate for the water-bound nature of Venice and the separation of its islands had been considered under the Republic. In 1714 Vincenzo Coronelli proposed a bridge across the entrance of the Grand Canal from the Dogana to the area near the old granary, and another bridge on the southern side of the Dogana to link with the Giudecca.[203] Coronelli's bridges were solid affairs, with central drawbridges to admit shipping, with shops, ship-repair facilities, viewing areas and provision for the great processions that took place on temporary bridges to the votive churches of Santa Maria della Salute and Il Redentore.

The first nineteenth-century proposal for a mainland bridge was presented by Luigi Casarini in a lecture to the AteneoVeneto in 1822.[204] Emphasising the urgent need for growth of trade and the means by which a practical situation might be envisaged to prevent the threat of ruin, he proposed the 'radical remedy' of a bridge. The scheme became widely known. In a published report of over a hundred pages, Casarini emphasised the importance of facilitating links with trade fairs and markets on the mainland and positioned his bridge from Campalto on the mainland, entering the city at the northern point of Cannaregio. The bridge was then to pass along the filled-in Riva di Sant'Alvise and the Riva della Sensa to the Scuola della Misericordia, which was to be developed as the terminal.[205] In 1830, in a further development, Luigi Picotti presented a design for a project to pass across the lagoon to Cannaregio with a carriageway with two footpaths, rows of trees at the sides and a drawbridge at each end.[206] At the entrance to the island, the Rio di Sant'Alvise was to be filled in as far as the Sacca della Misericordia and the Rio della Sensa, about half way through the island where, at the Scuola di Misericordia, there would be a terminal. Halfway along the island there was to be a semicircular vantage-point planted with trees.[207] As a complementary aspect of opening up the northern area, Picotti recommended a link between the islands of Dorsoduro and San Marco, eventually to be realised with the Accademia bridge some two decades later. Detailed designs kept Casarini's project alive and firmly before the planning bodies, provoking local criticism, notably from Butta Calice, who claimed that Venice would lose its singularity.[208] It was a lament often sounded, but the isolationist cause was doomed.

In the end the 1836 proposal by Tommaso Meduna and Giovanni Milano was adopted and construction began between San Guiliana on the mainland and the western end of the main island: a watercolour by Meduna conveys a sense of the fragility of the new line of communication across the stretch of the lagoon.[209] Crucially linked with the plans for the lagoon bridge was the progress of the northern Italian railway, which involved leading figures in commerce who took the initiative, becoming shareholders of the Venice–Milan project, known as the Ferdin- andea.[210] The bridge was built, too slowly for the Venetians, between 1841 and 1846, and for some years afterwards was described by contemporary guidebooks as a miracle of modern engineering (fig. 57).[211] Not without controversy, the termination point and railway station necessitated substantial demolition at the western end of the Grand Canal, in the Sacca di Santa Chiara.[212] A variety of terminal points had been proposed – from Santa Chiara in the south west to Misericordia in the north, and there were projects that proposed taking the railway into the very heart of historic Venice. In 1835 Gaspare Biondetti-Crovato had published a panoramic view of the railway

57 Giovanni Pividor, *Railway Bridge*, 1850s. Lithograph. Venice, Museo Correr

58 Giuseppe Bertoja and Gaspare Biondetti-Crovato *Project for the Railroad to the Giudecca and San Giorgio Maggiore*, 1836. Lithograph. Venice, Biblioteca Marciana.

bridge with a steam-train charging purposefully along the Zattere past churches and houses, gondolas and merchant shipping, to terminate at Santa Maria della Salute (fig. 58); it became an classic representation of the industrial threat to Venice.[213]

Even if the railway did not in fact plunge into the heart of the city, it was clear that the fabled isolation of Venice was ended: the poet Jacopo Vincenzo Foscarini remarked in 1841 that the lagoon had become the Terraferma.[214]

The City in Love

The fall of the Republic altered the structure of real estate. Patrician fortunes declined and palaces fell empty. Some palaces were converted into apartments for local residents; they also became attractive to rich and aristocratic visitors.[215] The fame, high class, or notoriety of certain foreign residents and exiles, such as Byron, increased the charisma and social prestige of Venice. It was conspicuously evident that the palaces were being turned over to foreigners when the Archduke Frederick of Austria acquired the Palazzo Cavalli-Franchetti in 1830.[216] He was among the first of the influx. The Austrians were the closest Venice had come to a court, and, for some, their presence enhanced the cosmopolitan social world.

The conversion of palaces into hotels and the renting of apartments in palaces may have made them appealing to many travellers, but they represented the decline of the local aristocracy and resulted in the demolition of edifices that were not suitable for such conversions. Previously the most famous hotel establishments had been in the vicinity of the commercial area round the Rialto Bridge, in particular the Albergo del Leone Bianco, which disappeared in the mid-nineteenth century, but increasingly the area at the head of the Grand Canal and around Saint Mark's was given over to hotels. The new phase of residential tourism can be dated from 1816, following Waterloo, when Byron took rooms in the Palazzo Mocenigo; or, more widely, from 1822, when the Palazzo Dandolo on the Riva degli Schiavoni became the Hotel Danieli – soon to be the city's most prestigious hotel.

Chateaubriand was in town again in 1833. He, too, recalled Byron's presence and endeavoured to compensate for his own dismissive comments that had so enraged the Venetians in 1806. He approached Venice via the Brenta, beginning the visit that he recounts in *Memoires d'Outre Tombe*.[217] It is one of those journeys in which the French took distinguished compatriots as imaginary travelling companions. Thus Chateaubriand came quoting Philippe de Commines, Montaigne and Voltaire's *Candide* – that famous episode in which Candide and Martin take supper at the noble Pocurante's Brenta palace with six strangers who had come to Venice for carnival.[218]

Chateaubriand's visit appears to have taken place in perpetual anticipation of mail and a longing for contact with the Duchesse de Berri. She was to take up residence later in Venice, but at this point Chateaubriand met her at Ferrara. Arriving at the Hotel L'Europe in Venice, he looked out over the Bacino from his room and carefully identified the edifices, those passed over or confused in his infamous visit of 1806. Now their internal magic was equal to that of their exteriors and he could confirm his agreement with Philippe de Commines that Venice was the most triumphant city he had ever seen.[219] Here was restitution indeed. One of his best feats of revised assimilation occurred in a supplementary account in his *Memoires* in which he listed nine sites around the Piazza and the Piazzetta, across the centuries, from its earliest buildings to the new royal coffee-house.[220] Venice is characterised as the female city seated at the water's edge, like a beautiful woman about to be extinguished with the day; the wind ruffles her embalmed hair. She is dying surrounded by the grace and smiles of nature in the manner of *Un Mois à Venise*.

On his first visit it was the architecture that had so failed to impress Chateaubriand. This time he had the redoubtable and distinguished volumes by the Venetian academicians, *Le Fabbriche puì cospicue*, to hand, and he toured the notable buildings, the Frari, the Accademia and Santi Giovanni e Paolo, systematically. Generally, his observations were correct, his enthusiasm appropriately pitched and his itinerary not noticeably individual. However, his visit to the prison to see the cells that had been occupied by Silvio Pellico was a topical addition inspired by his reading of the French translation of *My Prisons*. He was even keen to find Pellico's gaoler.[221]

After his visit to the Arsenale Chateaubriand had to admit that no monarchy had ever managed a comparable nautical enterprise. After the tour of the rope-making factory – the Corderie – the foundries, the museum of antique armour and the gateway with the lions he was moved to observe that Venice had achieved an exemplary union of the arts with industry. But the artisans were virtually gone, prompting musings on the decline of such an industry, once described by Dante. (It was another cliché: to visit the Arsenale and quote Dante.) He visited the new cemetery opposite the Arsenale, finding it raw (democracy has taken over death, he observed), with five or six monuments in stone and little crosses of wood: very insignificant after the splendour of the mausoleums in the Frari and Santi Giovanni e Paolo. He was drawn to the island of San Michele, because Pellico had spent a period there in the prison for Carbonari. Shadowed by those past spirits who conferred authenticity and a sense of history on his visit, Chateaubriand reminisced about the women associated with Rousseau and Byron. He recalled the episode in Rousseau's *Confessions* that described the dinner with Captain Olivet of Marseilles and the meeting with the courtesan Zulietta. Similar salacious musings were offered on Byron, Shakespeare's Desdemona, and Otway's Belvidera in *Venice Preserv'd*: Venice still held its libidinous appeal.[222]

Chateaubriand visited the Lido because Byron rode his horses there. The salons were de rigueur for such a renowned literary figure, and he visited the 'belles Dames', Querini Benzon and Teotochi Albrizzi. He then retreated to meet the Duchesse de Berri, and to write up his account of this socio-literary visit.[223] In 1846 he returned to visit the Comte de Chambord in his palace on the Grand Canal.

The French gave currency to *la vie de Venise* by their very presence as visitors, recording it with no little self-consciousness in their memoirs and letters. They were amongst the most ardent mythologisers of a fallen Venice, but, as the years of Austrian rule distanced the memory of Campoformio, they were more inclined to express sympathy for it as an enslaved state. And more and more it was the city of *l'amour*.

Visitors could now come with up-to-date and compact guidebooks in their own language. The French guides were essayistic and interested in more than the well-known monuments. M. Valéry's widely read account, published in 1835, was a historical and literary study with an autobiographical slant, giving an account of Italy in the years 1826 to 1828.[224] His reaction to Venice in the 1820s was severe and (not surprisingly) very different to that of the Venetians. Buildings were in decay; it was 'a corpse of a city'.[225] Repairs to San Marco were costly; palaces were falling into ruin. Valéry registers the fall of Venice not metaphorically, but literally, and with urgency: 'No time ought to be lost in visiting Venice, to contemplate the works of Titian, the frescoes of Tintoretto . . . tottering on the very verge of destruction.'[226]

However overdrawn, the view that Venice was disappearing brought visitors: in 1900 Proust was still hurrying to get there before the inundation.[227] At the same time there were some interesting anti-Napoleonic reflections in Valéry, who maintained that the lion of St Mark should never have been removed for it was an act of humiliation; and the notorious prisons were probably not more horrible than others.[228] Valéry considered that Madame de Staël's *Corinne* exaggerated the 'stillness' of Venice and the absence of nature. On the positive side, he was interested in the learned institutions and collections, the Academy and the Archive, and took the trouble to peruse the correspondence of the French secretary of the legation, Villetard, on the negotiations with Napoleon in 1797. He described Napoleon's document as Venice's death warrant, a 'compound of contempt, banter and fury'.[229] Nevertheless, Venice still commenced with Attila and terminated with Napoleon: that was its life-span.

But it was love that was to dominate the fortunes of many French in Venice and help to create it as a city of modern romance. George Sand and Alfred de Musset became the most-publicised visitors. The story of Musset's illness and George Sand's affair with Dr Papallo were notorious: the episodes did much to consolidate the fame of both fever and love in Venice, as well as that of the Hotel Danieli.[230] The two writers published their experiences in the widely read *Revue des deux mondes*, which ran articles on Venice over a number of years.[231]

Musset saw himself as a new Casanova, no less. In 1851 he was among the first to write on Casanova's *Memoires*, following their publication in French between 1826 and 1838, some eighty years before their publication in English in 1894.[232] Both Musset's writings and his life were seen to resemble and allude to the adventurer, and to Byron, also regarded as a descendant of Casanova.[233] Love and an assignation on a Venetian balcony were the themes of Musset's early, wry little play of 1830, *La Nuit vénetienne*, in which a prince comes to meet his betrothed, a Venetian lady, whose current lover is waiting (stiletto hidden under the piano ready for the execution of the prince), but the lover is borne away by his friends who stand ready to protect him from murder or suicide.[234] He exits pleasantly in a gondola 'amid the sound of music'. The most successful of Musset's plays, *Lorenzaccio*, concerned the Medici and was set in Florence, but the death of Lorenzo, who has a price upon his head, occurs in Venice. He steps outside his door and is stabbed, and his body is thrown into the lagoon. Venice was the most appropriate venue for demise.

Yet both George Sand and Musset reclaimed the city's beauty and its capacity to serve love as much as death, and described its current vitality as much as its decline. In the opening lines of Musset's lyric poem written in 1842, *Venise*, the city is characterised as 'Venise rouge', a simple description that was to be quoted and requoted: it became virtually a epigraph for picturesque Venice. The poem evokes night, the inevitable gondola and the serenade; the gondola is 'the cradle of love' in which women lie languidly or don their black masks. But allusion to the Venice of the 1830s as an enslaved state was also made: the guards keep watch on the battlements of the Arsenale, and the final image of Venice, in a version written in 1865 for Gounod, refers to Venice enchained in its own beauty as it is in its political servitude:

Car Venise est si belle
Qu'une chaîne sur elle
Semble un collier jeté
Sur la beauté.[235]

Gounod's setting of part of *Venise* for voice and piano increased the poem's popularity as Venice entered international drawing rooms.[236]

Musset was prescient in his response to the work of the painter Léopold Robert, who had been in Venice during the 1830s, and who became legendary, not least because he died there, taking his life in 1835.[237] An instance of death in Venice. George Sand was fascinated, reporting that she had no doubt that 'the Venetian atmosphere, too exciting for certain constitutions, did much to augment the depression that took hold of him'.[238] Robert's monumental painting of the fisherfolk of Chioggia, the *Departure of the Adriatic Fishermen*, was exhibited in the Paris Salon of 1835 (fig. 59). 'People spoke of it as some mysterious marvel', George Sand wrote of its reputation in Venice.[239] Indeed, it was prophetic of the growing interest in local colour and the inhabitants of the lagoon islands, which were to become frequent subjects in painting and photography later in the century. Pathos and dignity merge in the range of noble figures assembled on the sea-shore in Robert's painting. They run the gamut of the ages of man in beauty and decline, with a mother and child, young boys and heroic fishermen. When he saw it in Paris Alfred de Musset described the painting as the high point of the Salon, sympathising with Robert's experience of the cold of a Venetian winter.[240]

Musset bequeathed 'Venise rouge' to common parlance, but George Sand's creative work on Venice reached further and had greater imaginative range. Sand's letters from Venice were sent back to the *Revue des deux mondes* in 1834, before being collected as the *Lettres d'un voyageur*.[241] Her Venice in springtime is blown with 'emerald dust' and suffused with songs echoing all night through the public places. The lagoon is 'overflowing' with fish and game. The city is still energised by the feuding parties of the Nicolotti and Castellani. In summer the 'marble city' is a

59   Léopold Robert,
Departure of the Adriatic Fishermen, 1834.
Oil on canvas,
186 × 247 cm. Neuchâtel,
Musée d'Art et Histoire.

'burning mirror'. Sand recognises Venice as a female city in which mobility, fluidity and fecundity predominate, despite a sometimes lugubrious climate (fostering Musset's typhoid) and the evidence of physical decay.[242] In *Lettres d'un voyageur*, she recounts a persistent dream, in which a boatload of friends, singing sweetly, approach and bear her away on the water; the dream becomes the reality of Venice in spring.

Sand did much to create the modern historical novel, and Venice was crucial in this regard.[243] Her Venice is manifestly original, not locked into the masculine themes of tyranny and conspiracy that prevailed in so much writing of the early nineteenth century. In *Leone Leoni*, she wrote of a 'bounder' who recalls the double figure of Casanova and Musset. *Les Maîtres mosaistes* is a penetrating study of the mosaic masters of San Marco, written at a time of some controversy over the making of modern mosaics for the Basilica. In the early pages Tintoretto eloquently defends the antiquity, artistry and longevity of Venetian mosaic-making.[244] Among her most popular works, *Consuelo, A Romance of Venice* tells the story of the rise to fame of a foundling singer in the choir of the Mendicanti who becomes a great Venetian soprano. Sand took her cue from Rousseau's account, acknowledging her source in the eighth book of the *Confessions*.[245] Consuelo was well endowed in both voice and temperament to benefit from her musical education in Venice: 'She was as calm as the waters of the lagunes [*sic*], and at the same time active as the light gondolas that skimmed along their surface.'[246]

But for her children, Sand declared, she would make her home in Venice, although her reaction to its occupation was a factor against residence: 'I would have loved all people and things in Venice, were it not for the odious and revolting Austrian occupation'.[247] Her autobiography records two such instances: after an Austrian soldier had urinated on her gondola she had to intervene to stop the gondolier being gaoled; when a play on the revenge of Pulcinello was given in a marionette theatre, the old *commedia* character spoke in Venetian dialect to abuse the Austrians who could not understand.[248] The 'Tedesco' came to Pulcinello to learn Italian and was then scorned for his many errors, to the delight of the audience.[249]

Wherever she was, George Sand exhibited a fierce egalitarianism; she responded to its manifestations in Venice as a distinguishing mark of the city. Her urban and social analysis was unaffected by her compatriot Darù:

> The principal charm of Venice, as I see it, which I have not formed anywhere else, is its egalitarian ways. Though an oligarchy, it has had the wisdom to simulate equality through its sumptuary laws; then, the misfortunes of defeat turned this appearance into reality. Moreover, the setting itself lends perfectly to the dissolution of the classes, in their work and leisure as in their feelings and interests. The lack of carriages and scarceness of land have made for the homogeneous population, who, though jostling one another on the sidewalk or crowding one another in the canals, show concern for the safety of each. All the walking and boating makes for heads on a level, where all eyes meet, where all mouths converse . . .'[250]

This is one of the most optimistic and sympathetic foreign responses to Venice at this time. Sand was closer to the ordinary people than most visitors, and she felt the loss of the Republic keenly. Thus, describing the 'common people' making fun of the aristocracy, she nevertheless felt that,

> Despite their cruel mockery, the people are still very fond of their old, those survivors from the last days of the Republic who were so rich, so prodigal and so credulous, so magnificent and so vain, so limited and so kind; those men who chose as their last Doge, Manin, who cried like a child when he was told that Napoleon was approaching, and then sent the keys of the city to the conqueror just as he was about to retreat, having decided that Venice was impregnable.[251]

If her historical facts are not quite accurate, her diagnosis of the 'survivors' was sympathetic.

The City of Music

Consuelo is but one story of the city of music. Venice had long been acclaimed as such and its reputation for music was extended in the nineteenth century, despite the disappearance of *castrati* and the closure of the *ospedali*, which deprived Venice of its celebrated choirs.[252] The fame of La Fenice grew to challenge the opera houses in Naples and Milan.[253] In 1818 La Fenice had been granted exclusive right to represent *opera seria* during carnival, the principal season.[254] With the premiere of Rossini's *Semiramide* in 1823 (another Venetian triumph for Rossini) and notable performances of operas by the rising stars Donizetti and Bellini, it was fulfilling a role not only as the official theatre in Venice, but as one of the major stages for grand opera in Italy, if not Europe.[255]

George Sand's musicality, cultivated since her adolescence, was delightfully in evidence in Venice.[256] She responded passionately to the local musical life and its spontaneity, painting a rare picture of a Venice not weighted down by its past, but filled with the songs of nightingales, as recounted in her *Lettres d'un voyageur*.[257] Of course Venice was noted for its opera, but its informal music of the water was equally famous and still heard throughout the city, despite Byron's melodramatic claim that 'Tasso's echoes were no more'. Sand was enchanted by the diffusion of operatic music through the city:

> A cavatina by Bellini is instantly transformed into a four-part chorus. A chorus is adapted for two voices in the middle of a duet by Mercadante; and the refrain of an old barcarolle by an unknown composer, adapted to the solemn tempo of a church anthem – the absence of carriages and horses and the sonority of the canals makes Venice the perfect city for unending songs and aubades, the choruses of facchini and gondoliers are superior to those of the Paris opera house.[258]

She loved the vernacular music of Venice, alerted to the particular 'simple and natural' pleasures of the boatmen's songs by Rousseau.[259] The barcarolle had already infiltrated opera by the late eighteenth century, in Paisiello's *Il Re di Venezia*. Venice did not even have to be the setting: there were barcarolles in Rossini's *Giullaume Tell* and Verdi's *Masked Ball*, which were not Venetian; in Donizetti's *Elisir d'Amore*, premiered in 1832, the barcarolle is 'the latest thing from Venice', is sung as a duet for male and female respectively in 'Io son ricci, e tu sei bella'. It sounded in operas set in Venice, often as a haunting off-stage refrain – in Verdi's *I due Foscari* and in the *Otello* settings by both Rossini and Verdi. It had a seemingly unstoppable vogue in the nineteenth century, assiduously cultivated by the French in opera, operetta, art-songs and piano pieces. It was a song of love, of serenade and seduction on the water, and appeared in piano music by Liszt, Chopin and Fauré. Later, in the central act of Offenbach's *Les Contes d'Hoffmann*, the barcarolle sounds as the ultimate cradle-song of love.[260]

Such music was not cultivated only by foreigners. Songs on the water were still highly favoured by the Venetians themselves and were a feature of the salons of Benzon, Albrizzi and Renier, where the European literati attended and learned something of the vernacular culture. The fame of Lamberti's 'La Biondina in Gondoleta' is reflected in the German poet Friedrich Rückert's version in German, the *Venezianisches Lied*, which he presented to Lamberti when he visited in 1819.[261] Musicians participated by setting characteristic song-types and new poetry in dialect. Antonio Buzzolla composed to words by Pietro Buratti and Antonio Lamberti over a number of years.[262] Franz Liszt increased the fame of 'La Biondina' by introducing it to the concert platform and the home pianoforte in his setting for *Années de pèlerinage*. He was in Venice in 1838, when he gave two concerts that had astounded the public with their virtuosity.[263] (Liszt's affection for Venice, and its water-music in particular, remained important for much later compositions, in celebration of Venice and

Wagner.) Equally famous as a song of the water was Pietro Buratti's 'La Barchetta,' in which the singer is eager to go with Nineta on the lagoon with the proper accompaniment of moonlight.[264] This time there was no vitriol in the pen of the satiric poet who had been imprisoned for his poem on the 1814 blockade.

Throughout the century the art-song gained in popularity and many Venetian poems were set to music. Franz Schubert and Robert Schumann set lieder from poetry with Venetian themes – as in Schubert's 'Gondolfahrer' as early as 1824 from a poem by Johann Mayrhofer, and Schumann's *Venezianisches Lied*, in March 1840 to poems by Thomas Moore.[265] Hector Berlioz has a soaring lament, half barcarolle – the 'Sur les Lagunes' in his *Nuits d'été*, which is a setting of poetry by another Frenchman enamoured of Venice, Théophile Gautier. It quotes a Venetian fishermen's lament:

> Ah! senza mare
> Andare sul mare,
> Col sposo del mare,
> Non suo consolare.[266]

It may well have brought to mind that topical painting, Léopold Robert's *Departure of the Adriatic Fishermen*.

Rossini's love of Venetian musical idioms and poetry in dialect was evident in the *Soirées musicales* composed in 1835 in Paris. Some of his songs return to venerable texts by Metastasio, but he also set Count Carlo Pepoli, whose verses have a folk-like simplicity and veracity. The regatta song, journeys by gondola and serenades anticipate the international drawing-room success of lilting rhythms and associated Venetian images. But Rossini's frivolity and humour was entirely his own: especially in *La regata*, in which a female audience cheers on the male rowers: 'Row up now, dear old Tonio, push, push' ('Voga, o Tonio, benedeto, voga, voga, arranca, arranca . . .')

Rossini's Venetian songs embody that lightness of spirit that Stendhal found so beguiling in the Venetians. But most visitors after Waterloo expected a wounded city. The compelling allegory of the Republic's fall was readily embraced. The Venetians defended themselves against the loss of their civilisation, the ignorance of Chateaubriand, and the calumnies of Darù and James Fenimore Cooper. Against the flood of foreign eloquence the battle was a losing one, but they were gathering ammunition and pride, and would find a patriotic outlet in the uprising of 1848.

Panoramic City

By the 1830s there had been some respite for the winged lion: a noticeable lift in the fortunes of Venice, some indication of a restoration of trade and evidence of new public works.[267] The bridge project displayed the city's zeal to strike out across the lagoon and unite the city with the Terraferma, but this decade and the next also saw the inception of the 'Venice-as-modern' crisis that was to accelerate at the close of the nineteenth century, and frustrate the twentieth.

Venetians pressed for modernisation against the strictures of Habsburg rule. On the one hand there was nostalgia, but on the other a new generation was responding to modern advances and increasingly noticed Austrian attempts to frustrate or delay. The Moschini tourist guide and the books of Cicognara and his team were addressed to the past *and* the present; and more so than most foreign guides. A formidable tourist industry was developing, and was fostered locally, even if it was increasingly at odds with the pursuit of change. In some senses a modern spirit ran counter to the survival of the city, and change ran counter to those who had a vested interest in the past (an increasing number of whom were foreign). Pressure might be brought to bear against alteration. Tourist par excellence, John Ruskin was to be most articulate detractor of change while he was, at the same time, one of the most perceptive analysts of the past. As a result of Ruskin's zeal, changing the 'stones' of the Basilica of San Marco in the interests of restoration was to become a matter for international debate.

Old Venice and New Venice were being drawn into further conflict. Writers wrote of the Venice of their dreams, or as a dream state, as evidence of its power. We know it from our childhood, Byron claimed; 'No one enters Venice as a stranger' Palgrave declared.[268] In one of the most quoted of August von Platen's suite of sonnets written in Venice: 'Venedig liegt nur noch im Land der Träume' (Venice now exists only in the land of dreams).[269] One enters, floating in as if in a dream, in an almost hallucinogenic state, as Charles Dickens described it in his *Pictures from Italy*, published in 1846. Some years earlier, Samuel Rogers had published *Italy*, with lines destined to be many times repeated:

> There is a glorious City in the Sea,
> The Sea is in the broad, the narrow streets,
> Ebbing and flowing; and the salt sea-weed
> Clings to the marble of her palaces.
> No track of man, no footsteps to and fro
> Lead to her gates. The path o'er the Sea,
> Invisible; and from the land we went
> As to a floating city – steering in,
> And gliding up her streets as in a dream,
> So smoothly, silently . . .[270]

Such a journey suggests the crossing of Lethe or that to the island of Cythera and the dream journeys familiar to psychoanalyis that uncover no less than the unconscious mind.[271]

Dickens called his 1844 journey 'an Italian Dream' as he floated into some 'unnamed' place, gliding past a cemetery, entering a 'phantom' street with houses on both sides rising out of water, advancing into a 'ghostly' city, passing under bridges that 'perplexed the Dream' and, in sleep, feeling as if still upon the water. Even the Piazza, in all 'its absorbing loveliness', felt as if afloat. So dream-like was the experience that certainty was suspended. San Marco confounded the dreaming. The Palazzo Ducale presented its lion's mouth and memories of its 'old wicked Council'; the dungeons hosted 'Hope's extinguisher, and Murder's herald', and on the Giants' Staircase came recollections of the last descent of Faliero and the bells tolling for his successor. In the Arsenale, a tiny model of the Bucintoro and a Turkish standard 'caged in dull air' were vestiges of lost greatness. The dream took him past rich altars in churches, decayed apartments, 'open doors, decayed and rotting', past Shylock and Desdemona, as time loses its precision and the Venetian cues assemble beyond it, out of time. The water, creeping and coiling, was always in waiting as he floated out, away to the Terraferma, wondering if the place was called 'Venice'.

With new theatrical lighting and the taste for visual sensation the journey could be taken at home. From the late eighteenth century the invention of the Eidophusikon brought peepshows to many European cities. The later fashion for the panorama contributed still further to the sense of the city as real and yet not real.[272] The vogue was ideal for depicting Venice, and its familiar features were unfolded before the eyes of dwellers in London, Paris and Berlin.[273] In London, one of the rivals of Turner, Clarkson Stanfield, developed his professional career as a *vedutisto*, working at panoramas and pantomimes. A new and splendid diorama, a panorama in movement, was part of a Christmas pantomime in Drury Lane in 1831.[274] Special effects with gas lighting enlivened the 'Lagoon at Night' and the 'Bridge of Sighs at Moonlight', now the quintessential romantic subjects. The effects changed throughout; gondolas passed across the foreground, as they would do in many later simulations on stage, in panoramas and in pleasure parks.

The seductive spread of the panorama was swiftly emulated by local artists and lithographers, for it was *the* fashionable view. The process of visualisation was aided and abetted by new technologies, not only the panorama and the diorama, but the lithograph and, increasingly, the photograph. In imitation of the famous map of Venice produced as a woodcut by Jacopo de' Barbari around 1500, the bird's-eye view became fashionable again, offering a view of the compact major islands networked with canals – even more extensive than the panorama could show. In the late 1820s Dionisio Moretti had anticipated such generous lateral spreads in his continuous, page to page views of the Grand Canal following a boat-ride along both sides of the canal, but in the format of a book.[275]

The Bacino di San Marco still inspired the greatest number of views: it offered its mirror of water encircled by architectural riches and all the variety of shipping. The gondola was the inevitable foreground accent, but the growing mixture of vessels was evidence of the renewed commercial face of Venice, and steam shipping was increasingly represented. Sails began to appear picturesque and old fashioned, as in Turner's painting of *The Sun of Venice going out to Sea* (London, Tate Gallery). This was not the first – or last – time that Venice was associated with old values and seen to bypass the industrial revolution: indeed, it was a thrill for the visitor to experience the time-warp and the weight of history. Yet Giovanni Pividor, the most important and genial of the local lithographic artists devoted to the depiction of Venice, permitted a steamer to belch smoke in front of the Palazzo Ducale in a depiction of the mixed water traffic, emphasising the modernity of his view – which takes in 200 degrees.[276] However, the most accomplished Venetian *vedute* painter of mid-century, Ippolito Caffi, shut his eyes to the modernity and unrolled the traditional panorama seen from the Campanile of San Giorgio Maggiore – looking towards the Dogana and Santa Maria della Salute, from the Zecca to the Giardini.[277]

Caffi brought the moonlight to Venice, becoming a specialist in nocturnal festivals with their fireworks and dramatic light effects.[278] Predictably he was called 'Canaletto moderno' – but more appropriately his *plein-air* work has been likened to that of Corot, who painted in Rome, and also, in 1828 and 1834, in Venice.[279] Caffi had trained at the Venetian Academy, but produced his first important work in Rome: indeed it was vistas of Rome that he painted in the upper rooms of the Caffè Pedrocchi in Padua in 1841.[280] In various visits to Venice he painted views that circumvented the clear light of classical Canaletto, favouring winter and snow – he may well have followed Borsato who had painted a commissioned view in 1833 – *Riva degli Schiavoni con la Neve* (Brescia, Pinacoteca Tosio Martinengo), but Caffi's scenographic flair went well beyond the even-handed Borsato (fig. 60).[281] He was, at the same time, less given to the fantastical lighting effects that Turner produced in the 1830s, or the night narrative of Etty's *Bridge of Sighs*, or the strong *Moonlight over the Piazzetta* (Bremen, Kunsthalle) that Friedrich Nerly painted in 1837.[282] Caffi showed buildings in dramatic partial light, making well-known sites and predictable views strange and uncanny, having lost the security of Canaletto's sunlight.[283] In one of his views looking across the Bacino snow lies on gondolas' prows and on the volutes of Santa Maria della Salute, and partially covers the domes. The Piazza is seen in fog: the new gas lamps glow poetically; the pinnacle of the Campanile is veiled. The originality of these views and the discovery of a new face of Venice is well in advance of Whistler's fogs on the Thames and his photographic albums of Venice in November.[284] The new angles reveal a city in which the centre is politically dissolved, relinquished to the picturesque.

More tragically, and in echo of the fashion for panoramas of contemporary wars and battles, Caffi, an ardent patriot, recorded the Austrian assault on Venice and, in particular, the night bombardment by the Austrians positioned at Fort Marghera on 2 May 1849.[285] This was a new panorama, beyond entertainment: a unique episode in Venetian history and another test for the Venetian people. In the years after the second arrival of the Austrians in 1814 – when Caffi was five years old – until the

1840s, Venice made restitution, reorganised its ruling class as far as was possible within the Austrian hegemony, and recovered its economy to some purposeful degree.[286] A modern Venice was on the rise – to be castigated by some, but also to be acknowledged as a post-aristocratic state of increasing viability. The decadence of Venice appeared in abeyance in the 1840s, although there were some who continued to believe in it and condemn its existence. But historians have become wary of 'the Napoleonic cliché' of a decrepit city, a living corpse whose death was certified at Campoformio.[287] Others heard the music on the water, and cultivated the poetry. After Waterloo at least three Venices were created, serving those who had battled in Adriatic waters or marched as victors in the Veneto: there was a British Venice, a French Venice, an Austrian Venice – and the Venetians were themselves forging a Risorgimento Venice.

Chapter 4

'VENICE WILL RESIST THE AUSTRIANS AT ANY COST': MODERNISATION, REVOLUTION, RESISTANCE

Venice gained new confidence in the years before the Revolution of 1848–9, expanding commercially and becoming increasingly critical of restrictions to free enterprise and free expression. The translagoon bridge was under construction after long years of gestation. Members of the Chamber of Commerce were identified as a group with wealth and leadership, both commercial and intellectual. There were emerging leaders of conspicuous eloquence and learning, notably the lawyer Daniele Manin and Niccolò Tommaseo.[1]

But the old Republic continued to taint the present and play out its perfidious role in the European imagination. Within Italy itself the reputation of Venice was at best ambivalent, or equally criticised. The Milanese, superior in view of their greater energy and reforms, took a stern view of the Venetian past, and by extension, its present. That ambivalence could affect even a native-born Venetian such as the painter Francesco Hayez who established his career in Milan.

Hayez understood the relevance and emotional power of certain episodes of Italian history within a climate of embryonic nationalism. As a child he had been taken by an attentive uncle, an antiquarian, to the Venetian churches: he grew up admiring Tiepolo, Piazzetta and Lazzarini, the masters of his youth. He was a friend of Canova and, like him, spent time drawing the Farsetti collection.[2] In his memoir, he recalled the fall of Venice in 1797: some were jubilant, others, like his uncle, wept. He remembered well the departure of the French and the first entry of the Austrians in 1798.[3]

As a young painter in Rome in 1816 Hayez was responsible for decorations in the Vatican that commemorated the return of Italian artworks from France to Italy. He painted briefly in Venice and Padua, decorating palaces, before his mature painting career developed in Milan, where he settled in 1822 after success at the Accademia di Brera.[4] From the markedly Neoclassical style of his early painting influenced by Canova and Cicognara, Hayez shifted to a new form of history painting.[5] Between 1818 and 1820 he worked on a Venetian historical subject from the 1330s, depicting Pietro Rossi, a *condottiere* who had been appointed by the Venetians to lead their army against the Scaligeri of Verona.[6] In what was to become a stock theme of romantic painting (and opera), the man of action must bid farewell to his family and the women express their sorrow and foreboding at his departure.[7]

Venice was uninterested in the Pietro Rossi painting and its historical content; Milan acclaimed it, and Hayez moved there and became involved with the circle around Alessandro Manzoni and the Milanese patriots. As his memoir makes clear, Hayez was well aware that he had joined the new ranks of Romantic artists associated with the journal *Il Conciliatore*. It is clear from the early Milanese paintings that Hayez soon took what might be termed the Milanese view of Venice.[8] He moved from classical literary themes and Neoclassical decorations (his *Three Graces* in the Palazzo Reale in Venice is both tribute and farewell to Canova), to historical subjects in which patriotic deeds or testing examples of loyalty were uppermost.[9] In an echo of the words of Tommaseo and the new commitment to Italian history, the paintings ask 'What need of Myth, when we have History?'[10]

Like Byron, Hayez read Sismondi's account of the Italian states, and his library contained Darù's history of Venice as well as the classical Venetian histories by Sabellico and Sanudo.[11] Over his long career he depicted a range of Venetian historical and literary subjects that were virtually an iconographic index for his time. In 1821 he painted the final scene from Manzoni's drama *Il Conte di Carmagnola*, in which the count, en route to prison, commends his family to his friend Gonzaga.[12] Manzoni's play was among the earliest contemporary works to reflect on tyranny and treason in Republican Venice, or by analogy on the power of the state against individuals. Hayez's painting was for a Milanese patron, Count Arese, who had been a political prisoner of the Austrians in 1823: the choice of a subject from the past could allude to the contemporary situation but skirt censorship. Such subjects held intense interest because of the then current trial of Silvio Pellico for subversive activity.

Other historical subjects were cultivated in the growing climate of the Risorgimento. The fourteenth-century general Vittore Pisani had relevance in the climate of Austrian repression and the growth of nationalist sentiment. Pisani had been imprisoned by the government of Venice, but was freed by pressure of the people to command the Venetian navy against Genoa in the 1380s. He was the subject for artists in Venice and elsewhere. Cicogna cites a three-part canon from 1844 and a song for a festive regatta in 1846. An opera by Achille Peri on Pisani was written by Verdi's librettist Francesco Maria Piave, who published a melodrama in 1857.[13] Hayez painted *Vittor Pisani liberated from Prison* (Tremezzo, Villa Carlotta) in 1840, choosing the moment that Pisani was carried in triumph into the doge's presence to resume his command.[14] Thus the will of the people was affirmed.

61   Francesco Hayez, *The Rival's Vendetta*, 1853. Oil on canvas, 54 × 39. Milan, Accademia di Brera.

Hayez also painted scenes of female dalliance and masquerade, exploiting the myths concerning the liberties afforded to Venetian women for assignations within marriage and the power of the denunciation system through the notorious Bocca del Leone (lion's mouth), through which defamatory notes were passed to the Council of Ten. Intrigues and mini-dramas have narrow *calli*, with glimpses of palaces and Gothic windows, as their setting. Such locations anticipate many a filmic *mise-en-scène* and many a plot that revolves around intrigue and betrayal (fig. 61). A gowned senator walks, letter in hand, in *The Venetian Woman* (Tremezzo, Villa Carlotta); a masked woman hands him a letter, the woman accompanying him recoils. *Secret Accusation* (Pavia, Galleria d'Arte Moderna) plays out a similar theme in the open loggia of the Palazzo Ducale, where a woman is about to commit a letter of denunciation to the lion's mouth.

The highly popular subject of Bianca Cappello was another excavation from the repository of themes of treachery in Venetian history, with additional erotic interest. Bianca Cappello, a noblewoman, had lived in the late sixteenth century at the time of the dogeship of Nicolò da Ponte.[15] After she eloped from her father's house with her low-born Florentine lover, her father pressed charges; the couple were declared *banditi*. Bianca turned to the son of Grand Duke Cosimo de' Medici who, as Grand Duke of Tuscany, married Bianca when she was widowed. She successfully petitioned the Republic of Venice to reinstate her, but died, as did her husband, within a few days. There were allegations of poisoning and all honours accorded to her by Venice were cancelled.

The Bianca Cappello story had everything: class-conflict, elopement and exile, a change of partners, restitution to the governing nobility and the homeland, then death and ignominy. Cicogna's bibliography indicates that the Bianca story was already a popular subject in the eighteenth century, but from the 1840s its popularity was phenomenal: a drama by Camillo Giuliani was set to music by Antonio Buzzi in 1842; Giovanni Sabbatini produced a 'dramatic picture of the sixteenth century' in 1844; there was a Florentine version by Gaetano Vestri in 1851; a drama by Francesco dall'Ongaro in 1851; another by Carlo Witen in 1854; and, in 1857, 'historical scenes' by Luigi Carrer.[16] Hayez's painting, *Bianca Cappello* (fig. 62), followed the vertical format of his Venetian courtyard paintings, which he particularly liked for shadowy scenes of intrigue. He favoured the first episode of elopement, when Bianca left her father's house with her lover to begin the drama of renunciation, reconciliation and the gain and loss of her native land. Again, the patriotic sub-plot was symptomatic of the times, and the growing Risorgimento spirit.

Hayez paid due attention to key Venetian historical plots circulating in the 1840s, neglecting only one or two. He did not depict the tragedy of Antonio Foscarini, for example: Foscarini had been denounced to the Council of Ten, allegedly for selling state secrets, imprisoned for three years, then released.[17] The presence in Venice during the 1620s of the English Countess of Arundel had led to allegations that he had committed treason during meetings in her residence. He was convicted and sentenced to death. The countess sought an audience with the Pope to clear her own name and subsequently Foscarini's conviction was declared posthumously to be erroneous; his body was exhumed, and he was given a state funeral. Soranzo lists a four-volume French version of this story, in the manner of Darù, published in 1826, *Antonio Foscarini: ou le Patricien de Venise*. Giovan Battista Niccolini published a popular tragedy in 1827; Filippo Cicognani produced another in 1831. Luigi Carrer also tackled the theme.[18]

Niccolini's play was seen as another instance of calumny with regard to the Venetian Republic. In the last act, the son addressed the 'superb city' and prophesies that its 'cruel lion disarmed in the years will be derided – you will be buried without sending out a roar'.[19] Niccolini had absorbed the fashionable sources, citing Darù, Byron, de la Houssaie and Saint-Réal, and yet again the scene was set in the Sala del Consiglio for a confrontation between the inquisitorial state and the individual under trial.[20] Giustina Renier Michiel, by now elderly but no less redoubtable, came to the defence of Venice for the last time. She wrote to Cicognara urging him to the defence.[21] From Paris, her uncle Bernardo Renier wrote sympathetically – such an 'ignorant insult to the dead lion' would not survive long.[22]

More optimistic in Venetian terms, and redolent of patriotic sentiments, was the life of the Queen of Cyprus, Caterina Cornaro, who sacrificed her

62 Francesco Hayez, *Bianca Cappello Leaving her Father's House*, 1870. Oil on canvas, 208 × 159 cm. Berlin, Staatliche Museen.

right to the throne of Cyprus for the good of Venice.[23] She made a triumphant return to her home city and set up her distinctive humanist court in nearby Asolo. An attractive subject in her own time, Cornaro had been painted kneeling devoutly with her ladies in the large work by Gentile Bellini and in ceremonial disembarkation by Antonio Visentini.[24] In her nineteenth-century reincarnation, Eugène Scribe, a highly popular French playwright whose plays were often performed in translation in Venice, wrote a libretto, *La Reine de Chypre*, for a Halèvy opera.[25] Donizetti also wrote a Caterina Cornaro opera to a libretto by Giacomo Sacchero.[26] Hayez painted Cornaro making the decision to leave Cyprus for the benefit of Venice (Bergamo, Accademia Carrara).

At the age of seventy, Hayez painted Marino Faliero; a subject he depicted at least five times.[27] In *The Last Moments of Doge Marino Faliero on the Staircase known as the Piombo* (Milan, Pinacoteca di Brera) painted in 1867, the old doge is about to place his head on the execution block. Also in *The Last Farewell of the Son of Doge Foscari to his Family*, likewise in a number of versions, the crucial moment in which the state takes action is shown. In the symbolic *veduta*, the first-floor loggia of the Palazzo Ducale frames, significantly, the state insignia behind: the columns of the lion of St Mark and of San Teodoro, and beyond, the islands of San Giorgio and the Giudecca. As Jacopo in chains kneels before the doge, his father turns to the granddaughter – beauty confronts old age, an enduring dialectic in Venice.

Increasingly it was opera that carried the full force of passion, history and love to large audiences, challenging censorship with tales of patriotism and fortitude that were taken as rousing messages for the Risorgimento.[28] In terms of Venetian plots, the most important was Verdi's version of the Foscari story, *I due Foscari*, with a libretto by the Venetian Francesco Maria Piave based primarily on Byron: it was the most frequently performed and lasting version of the Foscari theme. The premiere took place in 1844, not in Venice, but at the Teatro Agrigento in Rome, since the Society of La Fenice had rejected Verdi's idea for the opera because of its possible offence to Venetian members of the family.[29] They might well have been sensitive to yet another indictment of the unjust republic. Carmagnola is recalled when Jacopo Foscari, incarcerated in the state dungeon, has a nightmare vision of him condemned to death by the Council of Ten and haunting Foscari's prison. For contemporaries it would have been an instantly recognisable reference with a clear implication: that a man's first loyalty is to the state, and that the state of Venice carried a treacherous history.[30]

The stage settings for *I due Foscari* were those that had by this time been established as standard for Republican plots, highlighting early in the work the symbolic lion in the Piazzetta: 'Qui veglia costante, la notte ed il giorno sul veneto fato di Marco il Leon' (Here night and day, the Lion of St Mark keeps constant watch over Venice's fate).[31] Again, the sentiments of families torn apart are central to the action, as are the moving expressions of patriotism:

> Ecco la mia Venezia! . . . ecco il suo mare!
> Regina dell'onde, io ti saluto!
> Sebben meco crudele,
> io ti son pur de' figli il più fedele.[32]

Finally the weight of office and the exhortations of the Council of Ten are too great a weight for Doge Foscari, who dies as the bells ring for his successor.

'No One Enters Venice as a Stranger'

The perfidy of historic Venice did not discourage the contemporary tourist; rather the reverse, and the city adapted more and more to the tourist presence. A range of hotels was available for new patrons.[33] On the Riva degli Schiavoni, the new Londra and

63   Ludovico Cadorin,
Caffè Florian, Procuratie
Nuove, Piazza San Marco,
1858.

Beau Rivage opened, built by Carlo Ruffini and Giovanni Fuin in Neo-Lombard
style.[34] Not only the new hotels with their employees, but *caffès*, such as the Orientale on the Riva degli Schiavoni, served the expanding tourist market. The famous
establishments Quadri and Florian on the Piazza San Marco, were refurbished in 1858
(fig. 63).[35] Before the new rail bridge between Venice and the mainland was opened,
gondoliers waited at Fusina to ferry new clients across the lagoon to their hotels.
Venice also had its omnibus, reported as one of the city's 'improvements': it was not
drawn by horses of course, but was a commodious boat with four rowers and a
conductor, operated by Giovanni Busetto, known as Fisola. Passengers were picked
up from the Ferdinandea railway – the new track between Milan and Venice – and
transported to various stops on the main islands.[36]

   By 1845 the population of Venice was restored to 122,496, just a little over the
112,644 tourists that had visited in the previous year.[37] The phenomenon that would
see tourists equal to residents, and then numerically superior many times over, began
in the 1840s. Since 1833 Dr Rima's bathing establishment had been moored off the
Punta della Dogana (fig. 64), and others had followed at San Samuele and San
Benedetto. The craze for salt-water bathing was to become a major attraction by the
late century.[38] 'Signor Benevenuti' was the first to offer bathing facilities in a hotel,
the Regina d'Inghilterra.[39]

   Tourism was not merely a bourgeois phenomenon: Venice attracted increasing
numbers of aristocrats and celebrities pleased with the prospect of a palace on the
Grand Canal. It was particularly apposite for French nobles escaping from their own
Republic. In 1845 Chateaubriand had returned to visit the Duchesse de Berri, who
had created her own style in Venice after acquiring the Palazzo Vendramin-Calergi,

64 Dr Rima's floating baths, Punta della Dogana, c.1880.

by Mauro Codussi, on the Grand Canal at San Marcuola.[40] Henri, Comte de Chambord, acquired the Palazzo Cavalli at San Vidal, but his residence was interrupted by the 1848 Revolution, during which he left for Austrian-held Gorizia: Giambattista Meduna began renovations to the palace in 1849 (fig. 65).[41] The ballet dancer Taglioni acquired the Ca' d'Oro from her lover Prince Trubezkoi in 1847 and hired Meduna to undertake renovations.[42] Between 1840 and 1857 the Ca' Rezzonico, Longhena's great palace which is now the Museum of the Eighteenth Century, housed the daughter of the Duke of Modena and her husband, the Infante of Spain, Don Juan, and their son Don Carlos, before it was acquired by the son of Robert Browning.[43]

65 Palazzo Cavalli-Franchetti, fifteenth century, renovated 1849–82.

Large numbers of trades served the tourist market: there were luxury shops selling silk goods and antiques, and glassmaking and hairdressing establishments (numerous, too, in the days of the Republic).[44] Glassmaking, an art long associated with Venice, had been inhibited by Napoleon's dissolution of the guilds in 1806 and adversely affected by the competition from mirror-makers in France and crystal manufacturers in England and Bohemia.[45] But a revival of Murano's glass industry was in the offing, prompted by the renewed attention given to the great achievements of the Republic, the tourist market and the international cultivation of the industrial arts. Lorenzo Radi was one of the innovative glassmakers interested in new techniques for traditional materials, such as chalcedony, an opaque glass swirling with deeper marks giving it the appearance of agate (a technique used by sixteenth-century Venetian glassmakers). Domenico Bussolin also contributed to the revival and modernisation of the industry, creating works with spiral and mosaic effects. Lattimo work, with filigrees fused in stripes and net patterns resembling the historic *façon de Venise*, survives from the

66   Pietro Bigalia, filigree vases, *c.*1845. Murano, Museo Vetrario.

1840s.[46] Pietro Bigaglia was a prominent entrepreneur who promoted the revival of the local glass industry: as a businessman he was also involved in the negotiations to set up the Milan–Venice railway. He had white and red lead factories, and a number of glassmaking ventures, including mosaic-making and bead-making. Under his aegis vases with a mottled effect, known as 'granite' glass were blown using the traditional method known as aventurine. His blowers created multicoloured filigree vessels in blue, red and yellow that anticipate twentieth-century taste in their clear primary colours (fig. 66).[47] The initiatives were historically based, but such glass production has remained in the tourist repertoire.

One of the methods of inducing the modern traveller, and a fresdh medium for recording the journey, was the daguerreotype. The new art was in gestation in the 1840s and within a decade a corpus of Venetian views had been put together by pioneer traveller photographers: L. P. Lerebours's *Excursions daguerriennes* and

Alexander John Ellis's sixteen Venetian daguerreotypes taken in July 1841 were among the first.[48] Some of the most fascinating archival photographs are the architectural studies made by John Hobbes for Ruskin during his visit of 1848 – Ruskin soon grasped the potential of photography for art scholars. The photography of peasants of the Italian regions was a genre in which Antonio Sorgato worked from 1847, producing portfolios of *popolani* that anticipated the interest of painters and photographers in local figures in the later decades of the century.[49]

Exponents of the new art opened their studios on the Riva degli Schiavoni and the Piazza San Marco.[50] Two eminent photographers set up business in Venice – Carlo Ponti and Carlo Naya were to introduce the ever-popular photography of the 'classic' sites, lodging the city more deeply in the universal subconscious. The Paduan-born painter Domenico Bresolin saw architecture in a new way through the lens of the early camera, appreciating its potential for details and new angles on monuments – the horses of San Marco from balcony level, sections of the Basilica's façade, one particular door, or the base of one of the famous Piazza flagpoles.[51] With the other exponents of the new art, these images ensured that the Rialto Bridge, the view of the Piazzetta from the water, the Bridge of Sighs and the Piazza and San Marco were among the world's most instantly recognised sights.[52]

Carlo Ponti was another early master of architectural photography. His sense of light and use of ingenious angles gave a mobility of viewpoint to well-known images. He photographed the monument to Canova in the Frari at an acute angle so that the angel seated on the steps is in dramatic light and the marble of the pyramidal tomb swirls behind (fig. 67). The mourning figures filing towards the tomb's door, and the shadow and light on sculptures, columns and rafters behind make a dramatic, moody picture. Ponti systematically photographed the palaces of the Grand Canal, adapting the portfolio approach used by lithographers and engravers.

Thus photography became art, the instrument of archaeology and historical archive, and a popular means of record for tourists. The photographer mimicked and then virtually ousted the panorama painter. Photographs were grouped into albums that were to become accessories in every drawing room; and that most ubiquitous of tourist souvenirs, the postcard, was soon to appear.

Guidebooks proliferated in the 1840s, addressing their respective national travellers. The most stylish and wide-ranging guide to Venice in all its aspects – literary, artistic, historical, poetic, picturesque and social – was published by Jules Lecomte in 1842–4. Everything Venetian is assessed by comparing it with things Parisian: the Procuratie building in the Piazza San Marco with the Palais Royale; the Scalzi church with Notre-Dame-le-Lorette.[53] Lecomte knew the attractions concentrated in the Piazza, long before the advent of many a treatise on town-planning: 'C'est le Forum, le Longchamp, l'arène, le jardin, le cirque, et aussi, le salon de la ville dogale.'[54] 'The Piazza San Marco is the heart of Venice, everyone passes through it, as blood to the heart.'[55] The *caffès* satisfied national temperaments and patronage: thus 'Florian est calm et posé . . . Quadri est turbulent et tapageur . . . Quadri est Veneto-Germain – Florian est Franco-Vénetien, voilà toute la différence'.[56]

The mid-century guides inevitably reacted to the recent history and status of the city as the vassal of Austria. Lecomte avoids reference to the French conquest as far as possible – the end of the Republic was an 'end' favourable to the French, but they did not actively engineer it: it was 'the people' who proposed to plant the Tree of Liberty in the middle of the 'Place Saint-Marc', and to burn the insignia of the old government.[57]

The accommodation of the sophisticated 'étranger' is the guide's first obligation, so hotels were considered early in the volume: Chez Daniele, for example, was now distinguished by the predictable presence of George Sand.[58] And in keeping with the urbanity and the sense of sophistication that the French regard as pre-eminently their own, Lecomte devoted a chapter to the salons of the rich and the culturally distin-

67 Carlo Ponti, church of Santa Maria dei Frari, monument to Canova, *c.*1860. Albumen photograph, 33 × 27.2 cm.

guished.[59] A chapter on the biographies of Venetians who had contributed to the glory of their country included the distinguished *salonistes* Isabella Teotochi Albrizzi, Madame Giustina Renier Michiel and Marina Querini Benzon, and a *biographie moderne* acquainted the visitor with appropriate intellectual contacts.[60] Of course, visitors to romantic Venice should seek out 'la lune dans la colonnade du palais royal' and contemplate 'l'ombre mysterieuse'.[61]

The English equivalent of Lecomte, Murray's 1842 *Hand-book for Travellers in Northern Italy*, was written by Sir Francis Palgrave, father of the famous author of the *Golden Treasury*. He was Deputy Keeper of the Queen's Records, and a well-known historian and antiquarian who moved in the circles of Southey, Samuel Rogers, Macaulay and Sir Walter Scott.[62] Less social than Lecomte, Palgrave was unashamedly passionate and personalising in his treatment of Venice, and concerned with its condition under Austrian rule.

Like Lecomte's guide for the French, Murray familiarised patrons with a Venice that could be compared with England. Thus the lagoon had 'the complex character of the Sussex shores', the Lido presented 'the appearance of meadows bordering the South-hampton River', and fresco painting was linked to the new works in the Houses of Parliament. The appetite for Venice was naturally kindled by English eloquence, by the oft-quoted Rogers, in particular, invoking the 'glorious city in the sea'.

Palgrave's attitude was rousingly didactic, he aimed to describe 'not what may be seen, but what ought to be seen', and cited appropriate background reading, such as the *Letters of William Stewart Rose*, Byron (particularly *Marino Faliero*) and Rogers's *Italy*. Darù was 'entertaining and clear', but politically prejudiced.[63] The destruction of San Geminiano was a 'Gallic Vandalism . . . which has inflicted such irreparable injury upon the fine arts'.[64] The Giardino Publico [*sic*] prompted the sarcastic comment that it 'afforded an excuse for pulling down a few churches which in itself was a sufficient recommendation for the French . . . straight walks and stunted trees are all the garden offers, and all that it is possible it would offer'.[65] The bias against the French was uncompromising, and rang with Victorian authority: they 'absolutely *hated* Venice; they pillaged Venice, they crushed Venice.'[66]

However, the main function of the *Hand-book* was to indicate what treasures should be seen and how they should be approached, and here Palgrave was philosophical, and original. The city is construed as an 'idea' expressed primarily in landmarks. The markers in the Piazzetta, the St Theodore and the lion of St Mark, were given distinctive treatment as objects beyond mere history and geography, having additional psychological weight:

> at the extremity of the Piazzetta are the two granite columns, the one surmounted by the lion of St Mark, the other by St Theodore executed by Pietro Guilombardo (1329): these columns so completely formed a part of the IDEA of Venice, that they were copied in most of the cities subject to their domestication.[67]

Again, the opportunity to attack the French is not missed: the lion was 'the first victim of the revolution . . . removed to the Invalides at Paris . . . restored after the Fall of Paris'.[68]

The 'idea of Venice' is realised through buildings and through the sense of the city's continuity – it has survived for 'more than seven centuries'. Its centre is 'concentrated in the Piazza of San Marco in which the great element of the beauty of Venice, COLOUR, is seen with unexampled splendour'.[69] This comment predates the publication of Ruskin's second volume of *The Stones of Venice*, which famously treats the colour of San Marco. Palgrave comments that it is 'on its value as a piece of perfect and unchangeable colouring, that the claims of the edifice to our respect are finally rested'.[70]

Palgrave was unusual in his response to a range of architectural styles and his sense of the city as not merely the sum of its historical buildings, but an environment in which the very contrasts interact and enrich. Across the Bacino 'the byzantine cupolas [*sic*] group with the lofty campanile and the mosque-like arches of the old palace of the doge are balanced by the rich luxuriance of Palladian Art'.[71] A simplified schema presented Venetian churches in four styles: 'a very peculiar Gothic', and then the Lombard, the classical and the modern Italian.[72] The vexed question of dominant style is raised in relation to San Marco; its dating permits it to be a Byzantine work of art and its positive Byzantine nature is accepted. Palgrave had catholicity of taste, a virtue in a guide. Edward Gibbon's earlier view was that the Piazza San Marco was 'a large square decorated by the worst architecture I ever saw'; Franz Grillparzer thought the Palazzo Ducale looked like a 'crocodile', and Ruskin wrote of the Palladian church of San Giorgio Maggiore: 'It is impossible to conceive a design more gross, more barbarous, more childish in conception, more servile in plagiarism, more insipid in result, more contemptible under every point of rational regard.'[73]

Palgrave's elevated tone in the 1840s edition surely finds its echo in Ruskin's inflections in *The Stones of Venice* and Ruskin's later guide, *St Mark's Rest* (written, as he put it, 'for the Help of the Few Travellers who still care for her Monuments'), which follows an itinerary and addresses the reader as if to accompany him or her around the monuments.[74] (Proust insisted that Ruskin be read out loud to him as he toured San Marco.) Palgrave wrote atmospherically of Torcello and with a full sense of its history in a way that anticipates Ruskin: he found it 'almost deserted; its splendid and most singular fabrics rising out of the green and marshy fields, amidst the cabins of the few fisherman and cultivators who linger upon the site of this ancient city, which was settled and flourishing before the Hunnish invasion'. In the memorable first lines of *The Stones of Venice*, Ruskin rushed on to anticipate, through Torcello, the decline of Venice: 'Mother and daughter, you behold them both in their widowhood – Torcello and Venice.'[75]

Ruskin's Stones

Ruskin was destined to be one of Venice's most influential visitors. He had made his first visit without his parents in 1845 and, as always, he wrote diligently to his father: impassioned letters that give an acute sense of the appearance of Venice a few years before the 1848 uprising. He was hit by the full force of Veneto-Austrian modernisation, with the industrial and engineering projects that were an attempt to make the city competitive in the modern world. He was among the earliest critics of the effects of industrialisation upon Venice. Bridges with gas pipes laid over them, or modernised by iron balustrades earned his scorn – and a sketch for father.[76]

Because of his very lack of sympathy for modern Venice Ruskin would become a major player in the preservation of its past. He inspired the Venetians themselves with a sense of the urgency needed to conserve their monuments, not only as stable structures that must remain standing, but as markers of the passage of time. He did much to swing Venice away from innovation and, indeed, to make her fearful of it. Of course Ruskin's emphasis represented a historic viewpoint like any other: he was imbued with a preference for the picturesque and for evident patina. His intoxication with the forms and procedures of Gothic art was already evident in *The Seven Lamps of Architecture*, published in 1849, and was to determine his account of the Gothic pinnacles of Venetian architecture in *The Stones of Venice*.[77] His moral bias was Gothic – the taste just then being reasserted in Venice by architects such as Giambattista Meduna. The Renaissance and, even more, the Baroque were anathema, and only confirmed the early decay of the Serenissima.

It was the cleaning programme and the policy of replacing original material in old buildings that were to become the major controversies of the century, and not only in Venice. The debate played an important role in confirming the museum status of the city of Venice, domestically and internationally. Conservation *was* happening, but it was *ad hoc* and lacked a theoretical base. Ruskin's first visit to the Piazza revealed the Palazzo Ducale being painted yellow and black, the Austrian colours, and whitewash applied everywhere as a mark of modernisation.[78] The Austrians took some responsibility for the upkeep of monuments, but their efforts were often misplaced. To finance early repairs to the roof, items from the San Marco treasury, already plundered by the French, were sold.[79] The inconsistency was evident in one of the most prominent aspects of the Basilica: the lunette mosaics, which date from the great period of consolidation and decoration of San Marco in the 1200s, under Doge Ziani.

The northern lunette is the only one to retain the original frescoes. The artist chosen was Lattanzio Querena, universally held to be of indifferent standing.[80]

But it was the flourishing local architect Giambattista Meduna who was singled out as the enemy. He was one of the most controversial Venetians of his century, responsible for the efficient rebuilding of La Fenice in 1837, the project of restoration of the north façade of San Marco, the restoration of the Ca' d'Oro in the 1840s and the remodelling of a number of palaces.[81] He had the patronage of some of the most important Venetians at mid-century, and did much to establish Gothic as the dominant taste. But he was eventually driven to defend himself in the British press against charges of negligence and destructiveness at San Marco.[82] To begin with this was Ruskin's achievement. 'Dear old St Mark's' (which he construed as male),

> They have ordered him to be *pulito*, and after whitewashing the Doges palace, and daubing it with the Austrian national distillation of coffins and jaundice, they are scraping St Mark's clean. Off go all the glorious old weather stains, the rich hues of the marble which nature, mighty as she is, has taken ten centuries to bestow . . .[83]

He was unable to draw it for the tears in his eyes.[84]

The 1845 visit was fundamental for Ruskin's ideas on restoration and the beginning of the detailed fieldwork that led to the first volume of *The Stones of Venice*, published in 1851.[85] The authority that Ruskin came to claim was considerable, and his writing has endured beyond that of the work of the considerable Venetian scholars, Cicognara, Selvatico, Molmenti, Tassini and Paoletti.

Part of Ruskin's very effectiveness was his propensity for over-statement combined with an authentic passion and detailed visual scrutiny of individual monuments. At the same time his view of Venetian history and the long-standing immorality of the Republic was no less unforgiving than was that of Darù: 'I date the commencement of the Fall of Venice from the death of Carlo Zeno, 8th May, 1418.'[86]

His view of the immorality of the Republic shaped the very stones from which it was built: they 'show how the rise and fall of the Venetian builders' art depended on the moral or immoral temper of the state'.[87] This perception of degeneration overrode Ruskin's view of Venetian achievement. Though indubitably wider, his scholarship is less acute and discriminating than was Byron's, since Ruskin read his texts with many preconceived ideas. His preparation had been comprehensive in the Victorian manner, consulting Sismondi, Alison and Darù and, facilitated by Rawdon Brown, using the State Archive.[88] Ruskin's view of Venetian academicians was typically ungenerous:

> Fontana's *Fabbriche di Venezia* is . . . historically valuable, but does not attempt to give architectural detail. Cicognara, as is now generally known, is so inaccurate as hardly to deserve a mention. The work of Marchese Selvatico . . . is to be distinguished with respect; it is clear in arrangement, and full of useful, though vague information: and I have founds its statements of the chronological succession of the arts of Venice generally trustworthy.[89]

Pietro Selvatico, president of the Academy, was given some credence then, but he was surely deserving of more recognition, for he was the scholar responsible for the modern interpretation of Venetian Gothic.[90]

Ruskin's enthusiasm for the Gothic is well known: it is less appreciated that Eugène Viollet-le-Duc preceded him in the admiration for Venetian Gothic. In 1837 Viollet-le-Duc was writing to *his* father that the Palazzo Ducale was beyond all architecture in giving the most living impression: 'Les Palais des Doges?! Jamais aucune architecture ne m'a fait une plus vivre impression.'[91] He undertook an ambitious drawing of the Palazzo (fig. 68).[92]

The clash between the principles of restoration and conservation in the thinking of Viollet-le-Duc and Ruskin is of key importance for conservation practice in

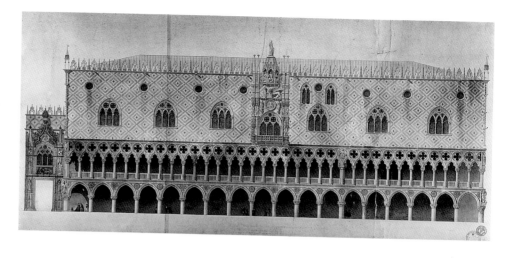

nineteenth-century Venice.[93] Viollet-le-Duc was an active practitioner working on French buildings, many of which had been partly destroyed during the Revolution. His practice was one of active post-Revolutionary intervention in order to complete and improve. Indeed he emphasised the *modernity* of restoration: 'Le mot et la chose sont modernes.' His edict was often-quoted, and controversial: 'To restore a building is not to preserve, to repair or rebuild it, it is to reconstitute it in a more complete state than it could have been at a given moment.'[94]

Both Le-Duc and Ruskin were ardent Gothicists, persuasive voices for their time, but a fundamental and unbridgeable point of difference concerned the degree to which restoration could be permitted to strip away the accretions of centuries. For Ruskin it was not so much a question of honesty of materials, it was rather his love of the picturesque, and, indeed, his positive concept of time in relation to buildings. He was opposed to the replacement of ancient materials by modern substitutes in order to 'restore'. For Viollet-le-Duc the evidence of time past, the weathering and changing effects on architectural fabrics, made a building a candidate for renewal and completion. For Ruskin the very distance from the new was a critical factor in his appreciation, and, equally, of his rejection of modern intrusions. The building is endowed with will, with its own inviolable patina that is the very token of its survival: 'the will of the old building asserted through all, stubbornly, though vainly, expressive.'[95]

Even more fundamental was Ruskin's opposition to the view that buildings should be 'finished'. Viollet-le-Duc relished modern engineering, its methods and materials; his attendant rationalism was in conflict with Ruskin's repudiation of iron bridges, gas lighting and the rail entry to Venice. To the advocate of the modern, cast iron was a wonder material. Ruskin scorned it, and not only in Venice.

In 1845 Ruskin extended his stay, reaching the desperate conclusion that 'Venice *itself* is now nothing', and 'Now, although there is no pleasure in being in Venice, I must stay a week more than I intended, to get a few of the more precious details before they are lost forever'.[96] 'You cannot imagine', he wrote to his father, 'what an unhappy day I spent yesterday before the Casa d'Oro, vainly attempting to draw it while the workmen were hammering it down before my face' (fig. 69).[97] And although his attention was focused almost exclusively on architecture (and some rowing for exercise), he noted other evidence of neglect, such as the level of mud in the lagoons.[98]

Apart from San Marco, his focus during the 1845 visit was on the Ca' d'Oro and the Palazzo Foscari: of the latter he wrote that 'the beauty of it is in the cracks and the stains'.[99] Ruskin made his drawings and measurements, but increasingly he became aware of the critical state of San Marco, and the Basilica became his main subject of concern in later visits.

69 John Ruskin, *The Ca'
d' Oro*, 1845. Pen and
watercolour, 33 × 47.6 cm.
University of Lancaster,
Ruskin Library.

Risorgimento

At much the same time as Ruskin was visiting the city, Antonio Sagredo was reporting on the improvements to be noted in Venice, improvements that Ruskin scorned.[100]
For Venetians, pride in the recovery of the present and insistence on the achievements
of the republican past marked the 1840s. Few visitors to Venice in the 1840s would
have had a perception of the shift so evident in retrospect: it was the first clear decade
of Risorgimento spirit that would lead in the short term to the thwarted Revolution
of 1848–9. In the longer term Venice would become part of Italy.

Certain Republican memories were fostered in order to celebrate an indomitable
spirit. The ambivalence of Verdi's first Venetian opera *I due Foscari* gave way to
the positive in his second Venetian opera, *Attila*, which opened at La Fenice in 1846,
two years before the Revolution. Ready for a Risorgimento, La Fenice, reborn after
the 1836 fire, now presented specific Venetian decorations on its curtains: the
Apotheosis of the Phoenix painted by Cosroe Dusi in honour of the theatre rising
again from ashes (fig. 70a), and – specifically historical in its charge – Giuseppe
Borsato's *Enrico Dandolo renouncing the Crown of Constantinople* – an episode from
a high point in the history of the Republic after the victory of the Fourth Crusade
(fig. 70b).[101]

Verdi's association with La Fenice, from the premiere of *Ernani* in 1843 – written
with the Venetian librettist Francesco Maria Piave, son of a glass-blower from Murano
– to *Simon Boccanegra* in 1857, was of some importance for the reputation of the
opera house as a leading venue, and a mid-century validation of Venice as the city of
music.[102] In the 1840s Verdi was increasingly associated with the Risorgimento cause
through his rousing choruses and librettos drawing upon episodes in Italian history.
Written specifically for Venetian audiences, Verdi's *Attila* made no secret of his shift
in the appreciation of Venetian history from the Republic of tyranny to the early centuries of fortitude, independence, developing patriotism, and resistance to the dominance of Attila. Attila himself recognises that in the lagoon islands he is in the terrain
of the gods: 'questo de' numi è il suol . . .'[103]

At the time of Attila, in the fifth century, Venice was in the process of formation,
still a village in the lagoon amid the flat marshy lands between earth and sky. The

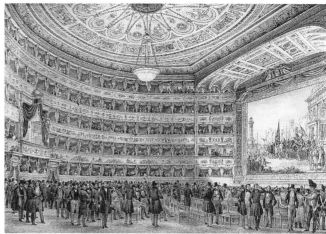

70a and b   Giovanni Pividor, 'Gran Teatro La Fenice in Venezia', lithographs showing the auditorium with drop curtains by Cosrue Dusi (*The Apotheosis of the Phoenix*) and Giovanni Busato (*Enrico Dandolo renouncing the Crown of Constantinople*), 1837. Venice, Museo Correr.

spectacle of the first primitive huts raised on piles above the water as protection against the elements and the enemy must have been stirring and patriotic for the Venetians. In the production of *Attila*, Verdi's set design was by the talented Giuseppe Bertoja, fluent in architectural set painting and ingenious in the use of platforms and balconies which activate the stage at various heights.[104] For *Attila*, Bertoja drew the emergent city still raised up on poles amid the water, as Prefect Cassiodorus famously described it in 523:

> For you live like seabirds, with your houses dispersed, like the Cyclades, across the surface of the water. The solidity of the earth on which they rest is secured only by osier and wattle; yet you do not hesitate to oppose so frail a bulwark to the wildness of the sea . . .[105]

Returning to this vision of a primordial Venice, the first audiences would have listened to the rousing chorus that ends the Prologue, making its double allusion to the phoenix that was the opera house, and the phoenix that they willed Venice to be, again 'the wonder of land and sea':

> Cara patria, già madre e regina
> Di possenti magnanimi figli,
> Or macerie, deserto, ruina,
> Su cui regna silenzio e equallor;
> Ma dall'alghe di questi marosi,
> Quel risorta fenice novella,
> Rivivra più superba, più bella
> Della terra, dell'onde stupor?[106]

Attila was the expression of a new defiance, characteristic of Verdi's thematics of resistance to oppression. The Italian women are to the fore, ranged against Attila. The overture evokes the sounds of mists and daybreak in the lagoon country, then Odabella the heroine makes her entry, dramatically calling for 'boundless love of Patria', with warriors 'rising to their swords like lions', and the Italian women, 'bosoms girt in steel', no longer standing by weeping at the departure of their men.

Venetians were also engaged in the work of preservation and interpretation of their own culture. Literary patriots spoke out in the 1840s: they were to play a major role in injecting passion into the uprising. Jacopo Vincenzo Foscarini, Luigi Carrer and Francesco dall'Ongaro were all directly involved in the Revolution.[107] Destined to play an active role, Jacopo Vincenzo Foscarini had been devoted to the preservation of the dialect since the 1820s, when he published his *Soneti in dialeto venezian*.[108] Signing himself 'the old boatman' (*el vechio baraciol*) he published a famous collection of the songs of the ordinary people in 1844, the *Canti del popolo veneziani*.[109] Dialogues between lovers, lullabies sung by mothers, an evocation of the Bucintoro, echoes of the feuding clans, the Nicolotti and Castellani, a comparison between Venice and Rome – Rome has Romulus and Remus ('Roma xe granda e xe Venezia bela'), Venice has love, songs of the ship's sail and the oar, songs against the Turks, regatta songs: the material is wide ranging. In the same volume Giulio Pullè provided commentaries with clarity and erudition, annotating the dialect and explaining Venetian customs. The *traghetto*, Pullè explains, is named from *tragittare*: to take a person across from one shore to another by boat, particularly across the Grand Canal, and he goes on to tell of the specific municipal laws and customs observed by the boatmen.[110] With evident pride, he notes that the regatta has been revived under Podestà Giovanni Correr: it was still splendid, an admirable spectacle such as Venice alone in the world could perform to advantage.[111]

Francesco dall'Ongaro was a well-known literary patriot, active in campaigns against the Austrians in the mountains of Friuli. His patriotic poems the *Stornello* – the 'Starling' – were well loved.[112] In 1845 at the Teatro Apollo, he premiered one of the most popular Venetian works ever: the drama *Il Fornaretto* – about a baker boy, falsely accused of the murder of a patrician, and vindicated; ever after, the state remembered with humility the example of the boy unjustly accused. The Venetian stage had retained its vitality and contributed to the growth of patriotism: the Teatro Apollo had been restored in the previous year, and gaslit even before La Fenice; with cheap ticket entry, it was to host a run of patriotic plays (including Goldoni's) and recitals.[113] In 1848–9 it was to have much the same role as the Municipal theatre had in 1797.[114]

As a writer and editor Luigi Carrer contributed to the new spirit of patriotism. As already seen, he united the famous Venetian women of the past and the present, including Giustina Renier Michiel, in his *Anello di sette gemme*. Between 1839 and 1841 he edited twenty-seven volumes of Italian classics and worked on a biography of Foscolo and an edition of his writings, as well as publishing *Il Gondoliere*.[115] He was active in the organisation of the science congress held in Venice in 1847, contributing the essay on literature and the Venetian dialect to the ambitious official volumes *Venezia e le sue lagune*.[116] In the Revolution his *Canto di Guerra* sounded (with no great subtlety) to drive out 'invidious Germans' – *tedesco infido*.[117]

The Scientific Congress, 1847

As patriotic feeling cohered, certain events were precipitous. In June 1847 the visit of the English champion of free trade and reform Richard Cobden culminated in a banquet on the Giudecca organised by Daniele Manin and Valentino Pasini, with Podestà Correr officiating.[118] It was interpreted as an act of defiance in the face of Austrian trade strictures. The Ninth Italian Scientific Congress held in September 1847 was an especial spur to local cohesion and expression of Venetian-ness.[119] One thousand delegates gathering in the Sala del Maggior Consiglio of the Palazzo Ducale made it a significant national event and a challenge to foreign rule.

Prominent commercial figures had readied themselves for the congress, undertaking elaborate programmes of decoration in their palaces. Conte Andrea Giovanelli, president of the congress, employed the Meduna brothers at his Gothic palace at Santa Fosca.[120] The topical emblems of science and art were introduced into the Sala d'Oro in a ceiling work by Giovanni Borsato showing Venice crowning the Sciences. Spiridione Papadopoli's palace at Tolentino was decorated with grisaille bands of frescoes depicting the great meetings of the Republic – the poet Gaspara Stampa with Henry III, and Veronica Franco with Collaltino di Collalto. The glass manufacturer Pietro

Bagaglia's Palazzo Bragadin at Santi Giovanni e Paolo was decorated in new luxurious manner.[121]

Like the Ateneo Veneto, the L'Istituto Veneto di Scienze, Lettere e Arte had considerable vitality in this period. Rehoused in historic premises on the second floor of the Palazzo Ducale in 1840, shortly before the congress it began to create a Pantheon of notable Veneto figures, commissioning busts to line the walls.[122] Andrea Memmo's Prato della Vale in Padua and Canova's scheme to introduce notable contemporaries into the Pantheon in Rome were distinguished precedents, but the Venetian project was fired with the mounting Risorgimento spirit inspired by the Congress. The first busts commissioned were of the scientist Giovanni Poleni and the writer Pietro Bembo.[123]

In this climate the congress became the opportunity for significant publishing ventures. In that year Samuele Romanin commenced his multi-volume *Storia documentata di Venezia*, the first comprehensive modern account of Venice by a Venetian.[124] In it he asserted that the beginning of the government of the Venetian republic was democratic.[125] In 1847 Cicogna published his great bibliographic essay, realised in conjunction with the congress and in tandem with the two large volumes issued for the congress: *Venezia e le sue lagune* under the editorship of Giovanni Correr.[126] Cicogna's compendium of Venice's culture, history and economics ran to 5,942 titles, brought together, 'per la diletta mia patria'.[127]

There were further extraordinary feats of local publishing, as if to confirm that Venice had been keeping an immense cultural stock in reserve for the event. In the year of the congress, Gianjacopo Fontana published his *Venezia monumentale* on the palaces, with atmospheric illustrations by Marco Moro (the palaces show little sign of dilapidation).[128] Pietro Selvatico, Cicognara's successor at the Academy, published his ambitious work on Venetian architecture and sculpture from the medieval period, *Sulla Architettura e sulla scultura in Venezia dal Medio Evo sino ai nostri giorni*.[129] Selvatico presented sculpture and architecture together, asserting that medieval and Quattrocento Venetian edifices were in large part works of statuary.[130] And while he never approximates to Ruskin's arching prose, nor indeed Ruskin's defining moral view of history, Selvatico attends to each artist and individual monument with an even hand, appreciative in particular of Byzantine and Arabic influence in the early centuries and, in the Quattrocento, of the Lombard School, which was just coming into favour as an historicist style at the time he was writing. At mid-century he pronounced that the great danger for the artist is imitation – this dictates the repudiation of sixteenth-century Venetian art bearing the mark of Rome, and, closer to Selvatico's own time, of Canova and the Neoclassical architects.[131] He 'does not love Canova, imitator of the Greeks'. The façade of La Fenice is 'a miserable distribution of the elements'; the straight lines of the *viale* in the Giardini are monotonous.[132] As well as being a modern index to the history of sculpture and architecture, Selvatico's *Sulla Architettura e sulla scultura* makes the shift in taste plain. It was the most significant Venetian study of the visual arts at mid-century; its repudiation of late eighteenth-century art has in large part kept its hold.

A further venture was a new map of the main islands, prepared by Bernardo and Gaetano Combatti (fig. 71). The first folios were dedicated to Podestà Correr and the congress. Noted for its lucidity, exactness and wealth of information, finely tabulated, map by map, it was a significant contribution to Venetian cartography.[133] The initial map – a view of the two major islands and the Giudecca – is the first cartographic presentation of the new railway line and station area, attesting to Venetian modernity and the desire to be united with the mainland. The second page gives a full description of the bridge with a transverse section. The cemetery island that now joined San Cristoforo with San Michele is also shown for the first time with the single name of the Isola di San Michele.

The Revolution of 1848–1849

One of the most important places for discussing Venetian matters, old and new, was
the Ateneo Veneto, founded under Napoleonic rule in 1812. It had already been the
forum for crucial proposals to change Venice. Casarini had presented his paper on
the lagoon bridge there in 1822. The Ateneo proved to be a volatile stage for the
future leaders of the Revolution. Daniele Manin addressed it in 1847 on the subject
of the need to revive commerce in Venice.[134] Throughout the 1840s he had been
involved with the Milan–Venice railway negotiations, a major initiative between the
two cities and their leading commercial and legal citizens. Manin had been the insti-
gator of a petition to the Austrian government asking for trade from India to favour
Venice rather than Trieste.[135] As a lawyer, Manin was determined to conduct a legal
battle with Austria, and persistently presented issues for action. Increasingly this 'local
middle class patriot', as Ginsborg style him, drew the confidence of a range of classes
in Venice, from his own professional and commercial colleagues to the *arsenalotti* and
the poor.[136] Indeed, Ginsborg's view was that 'Manin inspired in Venice a devotion to
his person unique among the Italian leaders of 1848, and only surpassed by Kossuth
in the rest of Europe'.[137]

Niccolò Tommaseo was closely associated with Manin, if less determined on a path
of action. But at the Ateneo he openly addressed that other burning issue: censorship.[138] Although Tommaseo had been born in Dalmatia he was passionate in his iden-
tificiation with Venice and its causes during his period of residence from 1839 until
1849. His criticism of Austrian procedures was the signal for his imprisonment, with
Daniele Manin, on 18 January 1848. The arrests in turn were the cue for the Venetians to demonstrate their intolerance of Austrian rule. The Venetians had already
begun a psychological war. The ancient clans of the Nicoletti and the Castellani ceased
their feuding, entwining their sashes on the altar steps of Santa Maria della Salute as
if to affirm that the honoured rivalries within Venice must be suspended and directed
to criticism of the foreigner.[139] The Bandieri brothers, Attilio and Emilio, killed in the
Risorgimento cause in Calabria as early as 1844, were celebrated as Venetian martyrs,
a tragic prelude to the sacrifices Venice was prepared to make for the cause.[140]

Carnival was banned, and smoking also, in order to frustrate the Austrian tax on tobacco; feathers, sashes and scarves in red, green and white were worn.[141] The opera houses, monitored by the Austrians over the decades, were now the occasion for rousing receptions of Verdi's *Macbeth* and *La Siciliana*, taken as political statements.[142] The Austrians closed La Fenice on 6 February 1848, when the playing of *La Siciliana* was received too enthusiastically.

When, on 17 March 1848, news of the Viennese revolution reached Venice, the people took it as their cue to invade the Palazzo Reale in the Piazza San Marco to demand that Manin and Tommaseo be released. Facing the prospect of insurrection, and well aware of the recent Viennese experience, the Austrian governor, Aloys Palffy, acquiesced.

Manin determined on action a few days after his release, when he and Tommaseo were born triumphantly into the Piazza (fig. 72). Power in Venice was still centred on a small area of the city, and the geography of the Revolution reveals how deeply entrenched was the city's ancient topography. The capture of the Arsenale in the traditional working-class area of the city, where the workers of Castello lived close to the Austrian military headquarters and the garrison area, was crucial in the early stages of 1848. It was there that Manin was able to establish essential rapport with the working class, and, from there, to enter the Piazza San Marco on 22 March 1848.[143] In his classic history of the Revolution, G. M. Trevelyan wrote graphically of the murder of Captain von Marivonich, the Austrian supervisor of the Arsenale, in the Porta Nuova, the tower built at the new opening of the Arsenale as part of Napoleon's project to facilitate access to the Adriatic.[144] Marivonich's murder precipitated a mass-movement of workers swiftly commanded by Manin to take the Arsenale and then to converge on the Riva degli Schiavoni, which, since the Napoleonic creation of the Giardini, linked the Piazza San Marco more directly with the Arsenale.[145] The Civic Guard, formed of Venetians, had meanwhile taken over the Austrian cannons in front of San Marco.[146] Flourishing the tricolour and accompanied by a vast crowd, Manin entered the Piazza from the Riva degli Schiavoni, shouting 'Viva la Repubblica! Viva San Marco! Viva la libertà!' The Revolution was

72 Napoleone Nani, *Daniele Manin and Niccolò Tommaseo freed from Prison and carried in Triumph to Piazza San Marco*, 1876. Oil on canvas, 252 × 357 cm. Venice, Fondazione Querini-Stampalia.

accomplished.[147] The Caffè Florian, where many revolutionary schemes had been planned, and the 'Austrian' Caffè Quadri, on the opposite side of the Piazza, were changed in name to 'Manin' and 'Tommaseo'.[148]

Implicit in Manin's ideology of revolution was the model of revolutionary France, but the local cry 'Viva San Marco' was associated with the aristocratic Republic. It had been raised when Venice fell to the French and became punishable by death. Fifty years had had to elapse before it could be heard again in a changed society. Like Napoleon and the Austrian conquerors before him, Manin had a *Te Deum* sung in San Marco when the new Republic was declared.[149] During the months of the Revolution radical preachers addressed the poor in Piazza San Marco which saw its age-old role as the forum of Venice revitalised, becoming meeting place, political nexus and the Revolution's centre of ceremony.[150]

The Revolution found its leader and its inspiration in Daniele Manin, and his hopes that a republican Venice could be achieved, not through the intervention of the monarchy of Piedmont, but with the help of France. As Manin wrote to Tommaseo: 'Venice has historical, legal and moral rights to its independence much more than have the Lombard cities – For the French have an immense debt to pay; they are obliged to repay the infamy of Campoformio.'[151] However, Manin's idea of French obligation to Venice was rather greater than that of the French. He was to be disappointed.

The politics of fusion (with existing Italian states) and the international and Italian reverberations of widespread revolution in 1848, were crucial for what happened in Venice, but the memory of the Republic was not entirely favourable. The university city of Padua was close by; among the crucial events in the first days of 1848 was an Austrian provocation of students at the Caffè Pedrocchi, Jappelli's new building that was already a noted academic meeting place; a forced entry by the army at bayonet point caused death and injury.[152] Yet the head of the Paduan administration, Andrea Meneghini, was cautious, writing to Manin: 'The way you have named your republic Venetian, and the crest of St Mark which you have adopted, arouse fears of a too restricted brotherhood, of the revivals of ancient and unworkable institutions . . .'[153]

Nevertheless, Manin's power was decisive in Venice and the first revolutionary months were charged with emotion and commitment. One of the first actions was the demolition of the imperial box in La Fenice,[154] where performances of such works as Rossini's *William Tell* (banned by the Austrians), were sung to the sound of cannon fire.[155] A benefit concert featured the seminal anthems of the Risorgimento: the chorus from Verdi's *Macbeth*, the sinfonia from *William Tell*, the finale of the second act of Verdi's *Attila* and the prayer from Rossini's *Mosè*.[156] Throughout the city patriotic hymns, cantata and barcarolles with Risorgimento sentiments were heard in which the lion's wings were renewed, Adria reborn, and praise given to Pope Pius IX, the liberal Pope, who was seen as an inspirational ally.[157]

As in the days of the Municipality, Venetian theatres played an active role in charging the patriotic atmosphere by playing works banned under Austrian rule.[158] On the anniversary of Manin's liberation from prison, the Teatro San Samuele was especially illuminated.[159] For carnival in 1848 a production called 'Venice enslaved by Austria and its prodigious rebirth' was performed.[160] Goldoni was staged at the Teatro Malibran, as were the tragedies of Alfieri, Pellico (and a 'musical', *Silvio Pellico allo Spielberg*) and Niccolini's *Antonio Foscarini*. Various contemporary dramas enacted the concurrent revolutions in Naples, Bologna, Milan and Vienna.[161]

The fervour aroused in these months was evident in a letter that Verdi wrote to his librettist 'Citizen Francesco Maria Piave, Venice', Murano-born, who was serving in the National Guard:

> You talk of music to me!! What are you thinking of? Do you imagine I want to occupy myself now with notes, with sounds? There is, and should be, only one kind of music pleasing to the ears of the Italians of 1848 – the music of the guns! I would

not write a note for all the gold in the world: I should feel immense remorse for using up paper, which is so good to make cartridges with. My brave Piave, and all brave Venetians, banish every petty municipal idea! Let us all reach out a fraternal hand, and Italy will become the first nation of the world.[162]

Austrian forces on the mainland soon mobilised in response to the Revolution. Ironically it was the new link to the mainland, the railway bridge, the point of access to Venice, that became a vital strategic point for controlling entry into the city. In support of the Venetians, Lieutenant-General Guglielmo Pepe's Neapolitan forces led the assault at Mestre which ended in the deliberate destruction of the Terraferma end of the bridge, dynamiting the last five arches.[163] Porto Marghera and other lagoon forts, developed earlier by both the French and the Austrians, were strategic defence points.[164] The lagoon became the theatre of war in sight of the city, within striking distance of Cannaregio which the Austrians were bombarding with incendiary cannon-balls dropped from balloons in a new form of aerial combat; gondoliers were praised for their courage in ferrying the wounded across the lagoon; and at the eastern end, cholera raged, exacerbated by the corpses around San Pietro di Castello. By all reports the city remained stoically calm, with 'hospitality and cordiality' everywhere as people were evacuated out of range of projectiles.[165] But the reputation of Venice as an undefiled city was ended with Venetian involvement in war in its immediate territory. With metaphorical flair, and sorrow, Tommaseo proclaimed 'the former queen of the seas . . . became a slave girl, and the winged lion no more than a water rat'.[166]

In response to the desperate state of the economy, the historic buildings at the heart of the Republic, the Palazzo Ducale and the Procuratie Nuove, were mortgaged to float an Italian loan of *moneta patriotica* – patriotic money. In an act reminiscent of the evacuation of works of art by the French and the Austrians, it was proposed to raise an international loan through a travelling exhibition of fifty-eight paintings, but the motion was defeated.[167] A group of concerned citizens made a sustained plea for the retention of the artworks on the grounds of climate changes, danger of travel, cost of shipping and so on, stressing the unique Venetian context of such works: for the 'singularity of site, uniqueness of form, splendour of memory, grandiloquence of monuments, the gentleness of the climate, the mildness of customs, variety of spectacle, diffusion of civilisation, facility for living, proverbial courtesy of the inhabitants, which made Venice the only appropriate place to study Venetian art in all its phases'.[168] The argument was not dissimilar to Quatremère de Quincy's plea on behalf of art sited in Rome some fifty years earlier. In Venice in 1848 patrimony proved more powerful than economics.

Statements of defiance became famous during the Revolution: 'A nation of 24 thousand cannot perish as long as it desires to fight.'[169] The historic assembly of 2 April 1849 decreed that 'Venice will resist the Austrians at any cost', and gave Manin full powers (fig. 73).[170] Half a century later, in 1915 in the midst of the First World War, the Venetian historian Professor Antonio Pilot was to re-present the history of the period with patriotic fervour, quoting local poetry to fuel the renewed opposition to Austria.[171] Much later, in 1993, P. M. Pasinetti's novel *Melodramma*, set in these times, was to use as the rallying cry throughout: 'Venice will resist the Austrian at any cost.'[172]

Historians have attributed the cohesion of the cause in 1848 and 1849 to Manin's leadership and his continued inspiration for the lower classes. His critics maintain that his fear of anarchy frustrated more radical action, which might have been more successful for the Risorgimento cause overall. Cicogna remarked tellingly in his diary that 'Manin although he holds the whip over the Venetian rich and poor alike, is nevertheless afraid when the people gather together'.[173]

In contrast to the diagnosis of decadence and inertia in 1797, there was only praise for the fortitude, resolution and zeal shown by the Venetians in 1848 and 1849 in the

face of attack, famine and cholera. General Pepe paid tribute: 'The people of Venice, surrounded by a Lagoon, and by internal canals, could not fight their assailers; they were compelled to endure patiently bombs, grenades, balls, cold and hot, cholera, and famine . . .'[174]

The solidarity of the ordinary people – and their identification of the Venetian Church with Austria – led to an attack by the people on the palace of the Patriarch, the Palazzo Querini-Stampalia, on 3 August 1849.[175] Furniture and pictures were thrown into the canal, prompting the Patriarch to escape by moonlight to the monastery island of San Lazzaro.[176]

Conditions in the city had deteriorated to such an extent that on 19 August the Republic surrendered. Gondoliers ferried white flags of surrender across the lagoon. On the same afternoon the forty most important leaders of the Revolution were dispatched to exile by the Austrians.[177] The white flag, the *bandiera bianca*, provided the sad refrain for the poem on these events written by another poet-patriot, Arnaldo Fusinato.[178] Isolated, returned to its island status, Venice could not hold out against famine and disease; the flag of surrender flew on the remains of the railway bridge:

> L'ira nemica
> la sua risuscita
> virtude antica;
> ma il morbo infuria,
> ma il pan le manca . . .
> Sul ponte sventolo
> bandiera bianca.[179]

Most would have sympathised with Pepe's compassion in the face of the city's final surrender: 'Thus fell Venice, not vanquished by a great empire, but because she had neither bread nor powder. She fell after sustaining a thousand misfortunes, and after sacrifices on the part of the population which were almost incredible . . .'[180]

Pepe was an active partisan and could be expected to speak for the revolutionaries, but it was evident that the Venetians had impressed much of Europe with their fortitude. Before the end of 1848 one of the most lucid accounts of events in Venice was published in the *Revue des deux mondes* by the Milanese patriot-in-exile in Paris, Christine de' Belgiojoso.[181] Her eloquence and clarity must have done much to inform and persuade an international public as she revealed the extent of deprivation and sacrifice affecting all classes: 'There is not a Venetian who possesses a bracelet or a gold chain . . . the costume of the grand dame is the same as a girl of the people.'[182]

The first of Belgiojoso's two articles for the *Revue* had focused on Milan, but she commended the Venetian cause as no less deserving of attention, setting Europe a great example. She dealt carefully with 'the wicked reputation of the Venetian people', and that of the old Republic and what must have been widespread misgivings that the newly declared Republic under Manin would return to the ways of tyranny and inquisition associated with the past. She reported the signs of cumulative decay under the Austrians: the palaces passing into the hands of strangers – bankers, Russian princes, even dancers (she had Taglioni at the Ca' d'Oro in mind), and the 'immense desert' of the Arsenale.[183]

Belgiojoso was informed in detail of the speeches given by Manin and Tommaseo at the Ateneo Veneto, the incendiary patriotism evident at the Scientific Congress the year before and the example set by the Bandieri brothers. Finally: 'After five months Venice was experiencing the stagnation of all commerce and industry but in the face of all the privations Venice displayed a constancy which borders on heroism.'[184] By publicising Venice's recent stoicism in the face of suffering, Belgiojoso helped to reverse international opinion. Darù's account, so pernicious in the first half of the nineteenth century, began to lose its hold. Venice was now seen as a tragically isolated city.

Venetian painters recorded the attacks on the city and lagoon during 1848 and 1849. Luigi Querena, twenty-four years old in 1848, was the most assiduous recorder of the conflict as the bombs fell on the city.[185] He was an active member of the distinguished Bandiera e Mora artillery. During the Austrian restoration, his war paintings were hidden in a garret; now they document the war in the Museo di Risorgimento. Eight small views of the action painted on cardboard commence with the bombardment of the fort at Marghera and the attack on Cannaregio launched from San Giuliano (figs 74 and 75). This airborne warfare had a ghastly similarity to the festive fireworks of the pageants Caffi painted. The evacuation of Cannaregio on the first night, 29 June 1849, when the refugees moved into the Piazza San Marco was a further episode; and the Scuola di San Geremia is shown under bombardment. The eighth scene moves to the Via Eugenia, Selva's thoroughfare in Castello, when the cholera epidemic was at its height. A more extensive series followed on the battle for the lagoon. A pair of tempera on canvas paintings of larger dimension show the explosion of a mine at San Giuliano, seen from a vantage point to the left of the lagoon bridge. *The Arrival of the Neapolitan Troops* records General Pepe's fleet waiting in the Bacino, in preparation for the defence of the lagoon. The traditional subject of the festival marking the arrival of a dignitary to the Piazzetta and the Palazzo Ducale, or the doge embarking in the Bucintoro, was here for the first time adapted to war.

Ippolito Caffi had returned from Rome to Venice to become a member of the Civic Guard after painting Risorgimento episodes associated with the popular figure of Pope Pius IX.[186] In Venice he painted the attack of the Austrians on Porta Marghera, during which the bridge was dynamited on 25 May 1849 to prevent the Austrian advance.[187] On the return of the Austrians Caffi was arrested, tried and exiled, to return later, acquitted, to paint the carnival and the Serenata in honour of visit of the Archduke Ferdinand Maximilan and his wife, Carlotta, on 2 August 1857 on the occasion of the inauguration of the new public thoroughfare on the Molo, when the Giardini Reale were opened to the public.[188]

74 Luigi Querena,
*Explosion of a Mine at San
Giuliano*, 1849.
Tempera on canvas,
104 × 166 cm. Venice,
Museo del Risorgimento.

75 Luigi Querena, *Fire at
the Scuola dei Monti at San
Geremia*, 1849.
Tempera on canvas,
104 × 165 cm. Venice,
Museo del Risorgimento.

Scenes of liberation and popular support for Manin entered the iconography of
Venetian painting over the next decades. Giambattista dalla Libera, a Paduan artist
and virtually the history painter of the Revolution, made a detailed historical record
of the meeting of 2 April 1849, when it was declared (as in the title) that *Venice will
resist the Austrians at any Cost* (fig. 73).[189] The scene is the highly charged meeting
in the Council Room of the Palazzo Ducale: the light illuminates Tintoretto's *Last
Judgement*, the shelves around the walls house the Biblioteca Marciana, and the faces
of Manin and his provisional government are depicted with portrait-like exactitude.

Although the painter Napoleone Nani was a child at the time of the Revolution, in
1876 he reconstructed the event that precipitated the revolution, the release of Manin
and Tommaseo from prison and their triumphal entry into the Piazza San Marco.
Nani's source was an *Album dell'Independenza*, patriotic material collected in

1848–9, but he also introduced his own contemporaries into the crowd, thus the heroes were honoured by a new generation.[190]

In exile in Corfu in 1851, Niccolò Tommaseo wrote poetry in homage to the Venice he had defended as still enslaved.[191] He wrote of a bridegroom seeing the virgin bride that is Venice waiting in her white veil, as a swimmer accosting the waves, as a mother nourishing her children. So the city is nourished by sacrifice.

The Austrians Return

General Radetzky entered Venice on 30 August 1849 with assurances that those who had been involved in the insurrection could leave safely and that lesser officials and soldiers would be pardoned. The Austrians reintroduced censorship and surveillance, amidst recriminations.[192]

One particular action demonstrated the power that the Austrians attributed to the published word and residual revolutionary feeling. Luigi Carrer, director of the Correr collection, and Jacopo Vincenzo Foscarini, his deputy, both of whom had served in the provisional government under Manin and were noted patriotic writers, were removed from their offices on the ground that they were unsuitable contacts for visitors and young people involved in the study of the fine arts.[193] Although defended by the Commune, they were dismissed and the museum closed.[194]

Other fields of employment were restricted. In the most crippling action, the privilege of free trade was confined to the island of San Giorgio Maggiore, effectively cancelling the benefits of the free port. It is clear from two letters written by Niccolò Priuli in 1850 that the Venetians themselves regarded the city as dead after the Revolution: it was 'exhausted on every front of activity'.[195] Priuli wrote to the Vice-Delegate, Barone Fini, on 30 May from Vienna pleading for compassion for Venice and the restoration of free trade, but on returning to Venice and finding no action, he addressed a second letter to the emperor. He was even more rhetorically explicit in stressing Venice's decline, appealing to the emperor's paternalistic feelings: 'Open your majestic heart in compassion towards our city which is faithful and sees clearly again after the fogs of the revolution. It is the third city of the empire, the second port and the first in its position with regard to monuments and history – it cannot survive financially in the century of progress.'[196]

A delegation comprising Priuli, Giovanni Correr and Giuseppe Giovanelli, with two representatives of the Camera di Commercio, Giacomo Treves de' Bonfili and Edoardo Becker, and the Patriarch, Cardinal Monaco, presented themselves in Vienna to argue for commercial and administrative reform, alluding to the promises made in Vienna to the rest of the Habsburg lands as the result of Austria's own experience of revolution in 1848.[197] The delegation appealed for relief from the public debt incurred by the revolutionary government and a halt to the depreciation of the currency. The reinstatement of the free port was pressed for, together with an appeal to reactivate the Arsenale and to develop the dyke system at Malamocco. The delegation pleaded for the military regime to be replaced by civilian rule, but they were more reprimanded than fêted.[198]

Soon after the Revolution visitors began to return and to mix freely with the Austrians. In 1849 John Ruskin, eager to proceed with his research for *The Stones of Venice*, brought his new bride, Effie, who declared herself 'much delighted with Radetzky and all I hear of him is to his credit'. She liked nothing better than to waltz off to an Austrian evening: 'I think it will be great fun to go to this Ball for once to get a glimpse of foreign manners.'[199] Compared to the Austrians, the Italians were 'very badly conducted'.[200]

Effie's friendship with the Austrian Charles Paulizza, who had master-minded the aerial bombardment of Venice, caused her no second thoughts: indeed she admired his ingenuity and seemingly gave little thought to the danger to the stones to which her husband was so devoted. Paulizza, she remarked with no little ingenuousness, 'did something against Venice very wonderful with balloons but I could not exactly understand what', and she reports most cheerfully of the expedition that they made to the island of San Giuliano – the nearest point to Venice – 'from which place he threw all the bombs into Venice . . . a most perfect picture of desolation everywhere, but still interesting'.[201] Her understanding of the dissolution of the churches and the famine of 1849 just before she arrived is revealed in her ignorant view that the Venetians have turned 'half their Churches into Mills because they can't be troubled to keep them in order'.[202]

Effie's happiness was even more complete during her second visit in 1851, when she was accepted into society. Socially speaking, these were increasingly international years; the displaced Bourbons were conspicuously renovating their palaces on the Grand Canal, Marie-Caroline, Duchesse de Berri and the Duc de Bordeaux, the Comte de Chambord, and Luisa Maria, the regent of the Duchy of Parma, were in residence. An elated Effie wrote that 'when the Duchesses of Angoulême and Berri return and the Duke of Bordeaux, I shall be presented to them and it will be interesting for me to make the acquaintance of the Daughter and Daughter-in-Law of Louis XVI and Marie Antoinette'.[203]

Her husband remained unrelenting in the face of modern Venice, attentive to his historical stones and the Venice of the past, noting that 'the Italians are suffering, partly for sins of past generations, partly for follies of their own', and that 'famine was written on all faces when we first arrived here, and hopelessness is on them still . . .' Damningly, with the full force of his Christian compassion, he found 'their miseries are their own causing and their church's, but they are pitiable enough still'.[204]

Modernisation

Despite Ruskin, projects of modernisation and maintenance were urgently needed to ensure Venice's survival. Basic necessities of life were at stake. Following European practice they built in iron and glass, opened up new traffic arteries and rebuilt housing on hygienic principles, but at the same time the demolition and slum clearance became increasingly controversial. In Paris the Haussmann plan brought the issue of full-scale city renovation to the forefront of public attention.[205] Many of the practices such as extensive demolition, planning of boulevards, parks and modernised sewerage systems seemed attractive to other European city dwellers, and not least Venice, anxious to open up its particularly tortuous city to straighter 'modern' paths.

In the period between 1848 and unification in 1866 the Austrians, with the participation of the Venetians, continued to implement modernisation projects and undertook the basic restoration of the city's principal buildings. New thoroughfares were created and bridges were built. The use of iron was a conspicuous feature of these developments, many of which were influenced by modernisation elsewhere. Underwater tunnels were designed to link the main islands, and the question of the development and relocation of the port continued to be a topic of debate. Nevertheless, most of the schemes remained on paper.

The principal programmes for improved communication involved linking the major island of San Marco with Dorsoduro on the opposite side of the Grand Canal, which was still bridged only at Rialto. Sagredo reported that residents in Dorsoduro had petitioned for a link to facilitate 'the life and prosperity which others enjoy' as early as 1834.[206] At first the bridge was proposed for the vicinity of Santa Maria della Salute. At the same time it was increasingly recognised that it would be intrusive to span the canal at its point of entry into the Bacino at that 'sublime juncture' where the Piazzetta and the Palazzo Ducale are revealed, where the Salute lifts its spirals and domes on the southern side, and the view opens across to Palladio's San Giorgio Maggiore. Increasingly the site favoured was further along the Grand Canal, in the vicinity of the Campo di San Stefano and the Academy opposite.

As early as 1838 the engineer Giuseppe Salvadori, who was engaged in an extraordinary number of projects in these years, drew up a plan for a bridge and an underground tunnel at the Accademia,[207] adjacent to the Palazzo Cavalli-Franchetti, in the early 1850s under restoration by Meduna.[208] The boatyards next to the palazzo had been demolished for the garden and the neighbouring site was appropriate for the approach to a bridge from the Campo San Stefano. There was considerable support for a drawbridge, which would not impede shipping, but Salvadori cautioned against the expense of hand-operated raising and lowering.[209] The committee assessing these projects was a descendent of the Napoleonic Commissione all'Ornato made up of the Secretary of the Academy, Selvatico; an engineer, Tommaso; an architect, Pigazzi; and the art historian, Francesco Zanotto.[210] In 1854 a design for an iron bridge submitted by an Englishman, A. E. Neville, was approved. Neville was a specialist in single-span bridge structures in cast iron and had constructed bridges on the Reading to Reigate railway line in England.[211] The Accademia bridge in Gothic style was to have a wide span of forty-eight metres without interrupting pylons (fig. 76).[212] It was cast in England and shipped to Venice, but such was Neville's success that he established a foundry in the San Rocco area and pursued a career of over two decades building bridges for Venice. Salvadori supported the Accademia design as a 'project that would give satisfaction that Venice in Italy was the first to possess a bridge constructed in a totally new system'.[213] Neville's bridge had a relatively brief existence: it was demolished in 1932 as it was increasingly felt that its design was out of sympathy with the environment.[214]

But it had the mark of modernity in the 1850s, and four years later Neville was again contracted to construct a bridge across the Grand Canal, this time at the western, station end, in the area of railway adjacent to the church of the Scalzi.[215] This was also destined to be controversial as the politics of the picturesque gained

76   A. E. Neville, Accademia Bridge, 1854.

momentum at the end of the century and hostility to industrial-age bridges grew. The Scalzi bridge was replaced by a traditional construction in Istrian stone in the 1920s.

Several small bridges were replaced in these years, many in iron – either entirely so, or with an iron balustrade above the traditional stone arch. Those permitted to remain still have a distinctive elegance, whatever the opinion that favoured traditionalism and Istrian stone. Many of the gracious designs of the 1850s came from the Collalto foundry at Mestre: in 1852 Collalto built the Ponte dei Conzafelzi; in 1843 the Ponte dell'Acquavita; the Ponte de la Malvasia Vecchia in 1858 and, from 1855 to 1859, the Ponte dei Ragusei in Dorsodoro.[216]

These projects were planned to facilitate movement across the two major islands, but they were also evidence of the recognition of the value of transit above the purity of the traditional spaces and views of Venice. Water was losing its status in Venice in an industrial age in favour of bridges and trains that would conquer distance and discipline water. And yet tourism depended on the very impediments that Venice offered, relishing its ambivalent Republican history and unique setting on the one hand, but endorsing those modern facilities that made tourism comfortable – hotels and bathing, railways and bridges – on the other.

Foreign and Venetian engineers contributed alike to the provision of the railway and bridges, the major agents of change. Among them were Giuseppe Salvadori, appointed to the main technical office by 1818, the brothers Giambattista and Tommaso Meduna, Pietro Paleocapa, Pietro Marsich and his son Francesco, the Parisian engineer Medail, and Neville. The culture of the industrial age was necessarily founded on engineering, but Venice itself had a venerable tradition of the engineer-architect.[217] Manfredo Tafuri and Ennio Concina are only two of the later historians who have emphasised the engineers' contribution to the humanist and political circles of Venice in the Renaissance, particularly in naval architecture.[218] In the latter days of the Republic Tommaso Temanza's projects for bridges and hydraulic systems indicate that the eighteenth century regarded the architect as an engineer within an inter-disciplinary tradition.[219]

The filling in of canals had continued under Austrian occupation and found support from at least some Venetians, who avoided those taxes levied for their excavation and maintenance.[220] Owner-occupiers often put forward requests for canals to be closed, and landlords hoped for increased rentals if access to properties was on dry land. The quaint Venice-on-water with its impediments to normal traffic, unique system of sewage disposal and special needs with respect to the maintenance of building foundations, did not have universal appeal for residents. But infill had become controversial by 1843.[221] The director of the Archive, Bartolomeo Cecchetti, was invited to report on the tradition, and, as a critic of the practice, Pietro Paleocapa gave crucial advice on the maintenance of the lagoon's circulation through the city canals, the maintenance of the sewerage system and, not least, the importance of the canals for the circulation of day-to-day water transport. He emphasised that 'the canals of Venice should be considered just like roads for vehicles in cities on the mainland'.[222]

The programme to widen certain *calli* and create arterial routes through the city was the most persistent 'improvement' of the later nineteenth century. In 1855 Giuseppe Bianco in his position as Chief Technician (Ufficio Tecnica del Comune), proposed a major programme of enlargements and improvements to streets, recommending thoroughfares of eight to ten metres.[223] New or widened bridges were part of the plan, as at the Ponte della Paglia by the Prigione, widened in 1842 to facilitate the *passeggiata* along the Riva degli Schiavoni.[224] The new areas for consideration were the passageways linking Piazza San Marco with the Rialto via the Merceria and the Frezzeria; the enlargement of the area around the Rialto bridge on the San Marco side in the vicinity of San Giovanni Grisostomo (near the post office and the Coin department store today); and the widening and raising of the area around the Scalzi church and the new bridge in the vicinity of the railway station.[225] Although the determined assault on narrow streets took place only after unification – endorsed by Venetians – the groundwork was laid, and something resembling an overall planning document was prepared under Austrian rule.

The question of the location of the port and its facilities was still unresolved at mid-century. A principal figure in the debate was the noted Paduan architect, Giuseppe Jappelli, a pupil of Selva and architect of Padua's celebrated Caffè Pedrocchi. In 1850 he presented the Camera di Commercio with his plan for an entrepôt – modern and ambitious, made with reference to the St Katherine docks in London – to be sited at the upper area of the Zattere near Santa Maria della Salute, and to be served by an extension of the railway.[226] The location was developed from earlier projects for moving rail traffic into the centre of Venice, even driving the railway as far the church of the Salute or, through the Giudecca, to San Giorgio Maggiore. Jappelli's project was highly regarded, but it was regressive. The railway terminal at the opposite end of the city was the logical gateway to the hinterland and it was there, rather than in the Bacino, that the port activity was eventually concentrated. But reluctance to vacate the ancient centre of Venice, or, more particularly, to accept the separation of commercial activity from the city's historical centre continued into the twentieth century, until the decision was taken to establish the industrial port of Marghera.

It was the Meduna brothers, Giambattista and Tommaso, who initiated the successful proposal to site the commercial maritime centre close to the railway station. Bridges were planned to connect it to the Giudecca and San Marco.[227] Now the provision of a connection with the Giudecca moved to the forefront of the discussion, since that area had become the new region for manufacture.

Tourism and the Fashion for Bathing

The accommodation of visitors and some measure of restoration of the sights they were to see were other preoccupations at mid-century. Realising tourism's import, in 1843 Podestà Giovanni Correr proposed a grand hotel complex with facilities for bathing, and engineer Benevenuti illustrated the proposal in Palladian style.[228] In the 1850s, in renewed response to the phenomenon of the bourgeois tourist, the grandest of projects for a hotel and tourist city was envisaged for the Riva degli Schiavoni. The chief entrepreneur was the prominent Giovanni Busetto-Fisola (later commemorated in the naming of the infill island, Sacca Fisola). Fisola was civic-minded: one of his gestures was to fund the repaving of the Piazza after the Revolution.[229] Working with architect Ludovico Cadorin, who was noted for the redecoration of the Caffè Florian, Fisola envisaged a huge development to include a grand hotel with a bathing facility, bazaar, reading room, exchange, coffee-houses and *birreria*. The collection of buildings was to run for 600 metres along the Riva degli Schiavoni from the Prisons, with various belvederes and turrets for observatories, a romantic garden with fountains and a piazza dedicated to Neptune. A full vocabulary of Venetian styles was to be quoted, predominantly the Lombard Codussian (the historical style was just then coming into favour), but with Neoclassical accents, as well as Gothic *merlatura*, turreting and the outdoor spiral staircase known in Venice as a *scala del bovolo*. In short, it was an essay in eclecticism, running the gamut of Venetian styles.

A folio of large coloured paintings in tempera was produced by Luigi Querina to advertise the project and to be used as a diorama for public display: it was a high point in architectural presentation. Seven renderings showed the project's detail, seductively realised, and washed through with blue-gold so the buildings glimmered in perpetual twilight (fig. 77). A *caffè ristorante*, a vast colonnaded vestibule with a double-storey glass façade, had prime views across the Bacino. A theatre, designed as a circular glass-enclosed hippodrome, could also be used for equestrian events. A view from the Ponte delle Veneta Marina back towards the Piazzetta showed the widened

77 Luigi Querena, *Project by Ludovico Cadorin for the Riva degli Schiavoni*, 1852. Pencil, pen and watercolour. Venice, Museo Correr.

riva and the huge block of a turreted hotel. Another block extended laterally towards the Prison. A frontal view showed the complete development, leading up to the Giardini; in the other direction the panorama took in the Palazzo Ducale and Sansovino's Libreria. Another view was as if from the Punta della Dogana, again blending the new buildings with the original buildings on the Piazzetta.

If realised, the project would have been the biggest complex ever constructed in Venice.[230] It remained elegantly and atmospherically on paper, opposed by the Commune for its incompatibility with the environment and the prestigious buildings that were its neighbours: it would have partly blocked and overwhelmed views of the Piazzetta.[231] It was also vetoed for reasons of military security, since the area lay between the Piazza San Marco and the Arsenale, the headquarters of the Austrian military. This had been the revolutionary path leading from the Arsenale back to San Marco on the not so distant 22 March 1848.

By this time bathing had become one of Venice's fashionable attractions. Since the unbuilt baths that Selva had planned for the Public Gardens, the Academy competition for a design in 1840 and the Municipality's competition of 1853 for 'un luogo di pubblici bagni' (a place for public bathing) interest had grown. Dr Camino's guide to bathing, *Venezia e i suoi bagni*, listed nine city establishments for the use of citizens and tourists alike, who would, he declared, discern an improvement in health at the same time as they were experiencing all the traditional beauties of Venice, *la stupenda città*.[232] Thus tourism was augmented by the benefits of swimming, either in canal establishments or at the Lido, where the double panorama of city and sea offered itself. Doctor Namias, a leading exponent of the health-giving properties of bathing, endorsed the practice, and a number of laws were passed by the Municipality: hours for swimming in the Grand Canal were restricted; security and decency prohibited swimming in front of sacred and educational premises and in front of the Piazzetta and the Riva degli Schiavoni.[233]

An episode in Camillo Boito's novello *Senso*, written in 1883, but set in the Risorgimento years of the 1860s, reflected the new vogue.[234] The novella revolves around the unattractive but compelling love affair between the Contessa Livia, who lives in Venice (where she was 'reborn', coming with a much older husband from Trento), and Lieutenant Remigio, of the occupying Austrian army. They meet at Rima's bathhouse; daringly he enters, diving below the partition. The contessa relates:

> I was in the habit of going to Rima's floating baths, situated between the Gardens of the Royal Palace and the Customs House Point. I had hired for one hour, from seven till eight, the Sirena, one of the two women's baths big enough to swim around in a little, and my maid came to dress and undress me. But since no one else could enter, I did not bother to put on bathing clothes. The bath was screened round with wooden panels and covered with a grey awning with red stripes. . . .
>
> A number of large openings just below the surface, let the water flow in and out freely, and if you put your eye to the gaps in the ill-fitted screens, you could see something of what was outside: the red campanile of San Giorgio, a stretch of the lagoon with boats swiftly sailing past, a thin strip of the military baths floating a little way off from my Sirena.
>
> I knew that Lieutenant Remigo went swimming there. . . .[235]

Lo and behold, he swims right in. The liaison prospers, in the last days of Austrian occupation, as Contessa Livia waits, keyed up for amorous adventure: 'The wicker chair that I sat on in the Piazza San Marco became a throne. I thought that the military band that played Strauss waltzes and Meyerbeer melodies in front of the Old Procurators' were performing their music solely for me, and the blue sky and ancient monuments seemed to rejoice in my happiness.'[236] Venice itself colludes in this treacherous affair.

However, the future of bathing and its fashionable home was to be on the sea-coast of the Lido, and here again Boito is a compelling witness. He wrote another short story, *Quattr'ore al Lido: Schizzo dal vero* (Four Hours at the Lido: A True Sketch), about the sheer exhilaration of sea bathing, half-floating, half-drowning, so far out at sea that the bathing establishment appears tiny on the beach.[237] In setting and one particular detail, Boito's story appears prophetic of Thomas Mann's *Death in Venice*, when an Englishwoman appears to the narrator like a Greek goddess on the beach – later she appears in Florian's, after the narrator has finished his swim and returned to the centre of Venice.

It was the frustration of Fisola's project on the Riva della Schiavoni that led to the outstanding development of the Lido: it was *the* change in Venice in the later nineteenth century. Fisola's initiative was perfectly timed, establishing a *stabilimento balneare* on the Adriatic beach in 1857.[238]

The Lido, the narrow neck of land that protects the lagoon from the Adriatic, was the city's outer limit. Its soil was sandy and unpropitious for farming, it had remained almost uninhabited, but it held its fascination within the geography of the lagoon, as various writers testified. The Sensa ceremony marrying Venice to the sea was performed near the church of San Nicolò in the days of the Republic; guests were welcomed there on entering the lagoon. Nearby, on deliberately separated ground, was the Jewish cemetery. Byron and Shelley rode their horses on the sand dunes; Shelley begins his poem *Julian and Maddalo* on the Lido:

> – a bare Strand
> Of hillocks, heaped from ever-shifting sand,
> Matted with thistles and amphibious weeds,
> Such as from earth's embrace the salt ooze breeds,
> Is this; – an uninhabited seaside,
> Which the lone fisher, when his nets are dried,

Abandons; and no other object breaks
The waste . . .[239]

In the early nineteenth century writers endowed the Lido with a special atmosphere. The melancholy novel *Jean Sbogar* by Charles Nodier had the character Lothario preferring the Lido to all that Venice offered because of its 'sadness and its solemnity', and the Jewish cemetery.[240] Chateaubriand 'dreamt' on the Lido, as he mentions in *Memoires d'Outre-Tombe*. In Cooper's *The Bravo* the hero lurks in the Jewish cemetery. William Dean Howells, American consul at mid-century, visited the cemetery and recorded that 'On a summer's day there the sun glares down upon the sand and flat gravestones (tombs of the Hebrews) and it seems the most desolate place where one's bones might be laid'.[241] It was also an important defence zone, heavily fortified under Austrian domination: 'the double headed eagle keeps watch and ward from a continuous line of forts along the shore', Howells remarked.[242]

Fisola's 1857 establishment was on the Adriatic coast at the end of the main boulevard, Santa Maria Elizabetta del Lido, which linked with the lagoon. It was the beginning of a propitious enterprise (fig. 78). By the turn of the century two luxury hotels would be on the drawing-board.[243]

78   Lido, bathing establishment, *c.*1890.

Passive Resistance

As the 1850s passed and the Risorgimento gathered momentum in Italy, so too did Austrian repression. Cicogna, no longer Austrian in bias, recorded the steady sequence of political arrests over many years, including those of his friends.[244] Covert manifestations of nationalist feeling were regularly triggered by significant events connected with the Revolution: the anniversary of Manin's assumption of power on 22 March 1848 was particularly volatile. In 1857 the white, green and red flag of Italy appeared on the flagpole in front of San Marco and it was concluded that only a sailor or a worker at the Arsenale could have tied the knot in such a way. An arrest was made and the alleged culprit sentenced. Lack of witnesses or proof of crime was no obstacle to arrest. Appeals to Vienna were constant.[245] On 22 March 1858 the Archduke Maximilian and his Duchess promenaded in the Piazza with the Austrian military band providing music. This was the cue for the Venetians to vacate the area. As a precaution that evening the archduke ordered theatres to be closed.[246]

In distinct contrast to the outsider Ruskin's claim that he had never seen the Austrians do anything provocative in Venice, Cicogna states that it seemed the Austrians adopted every means to make themselves hated. He documented many instances over a number of years.[247] The years from 1859 to the liberation of 1866 were rife with rumours of war, interruptions to communications and rumours of siege. In June 1859 it was said that the French and Sardinians were arriving and the Austrians were being evacuated: the population poured into San Marco with cries of 'Viva l'Italia'; arrests were made; and the Campanile was closed and guarded so that no one could view the Adriatic and spot incoming fleets.[248]

The Peace of Villafranca, which followed the Austrian defeat by the French and Piedmontese in Lombardy in 1859, promoted the false hope that Venetia would be ceded; bitterness against the occupiers intensified thereafter as 'the Venetian question' became a vital issue of European diplomacy from 1861 until 1866.[249] Should Venetia be sold, be exchanged for Candia (Crete), or for Egypt, or the Baltic States?[250] The British Prime Minister, Lord Palmerston, and his Foreign Secretary, Lord John Russell, favoured the outright sale of Venetia to Italy.[251] Sympathy for France and Napoleon III was based on the hope that the French would deliver Venetia from Austria. With the Austrian loss of Lombardy, the isolation of the Veneto was even more marked; the national cause appeared increasingly urgent. Cicogna recorded that Venetians were leaving for Milan and that many young people, including his nephew, had joined Garibaldi's army.[252] The archduke's presence in Venice brought a show of the Austrian colours of yellow and black in the Piazza. Rumours of war persisted.

On behalf of France, Napoleon III endeavoured to negotiate with Austria, requesting that Venetia be relinquished to the newly united Italian states under King Victor Emmanuel. The French effort may indeed have reflected some long-standing guilt with regard to Venice (recalling Manin's 'They are obliged to repay the infamy of Campoformio'), and continued sentimentality towards it. The Italian ambassador to Paris, Constantino Nigra, sought help by any means, to the extent of petitioning Empress Eugénie on the Fontainebleau lake with a barcarolle, pleading the cause of a Venice 'groaning and languishing', 'poor, rude and cadaverous'.[253] Empress Eugénie had contact with the Austrian ambassador in February 1863.[254]

Nigra also sought English and Prussian intervention. The 'Venetian Question' was pursued by the English, who claimed that even before the Revolution of 1848 'Austria backed by Russia, has been the great oppressor of thought and action in political life, in its own dominions and in its Italian states. Austria is unmovable, and weighs down the energies of the millions she rules, with a yoke of lead.'[255]

In Venice itself Cicogna noted further economic decline, increasingly affecting the poor. His comments were at all times matter-of-fact and unemotional. He was by no means a radical, but he had half a century of experience in recording public opinion. He described commerce as restricted because of the political uncertainty, the difficulties of communication and the disadvantageous state of the customs. No one wanted the vacant job of Podestà. The Venetians increasingly followed the Comitato Italiano, the clandestine organisers of resistance, whose directive was to stay away from the theatre and to cease their *passeggiati* in Piazza San Marco, particularly when the Austrian band played.[256] The Venetians would then transfer pointedly to the Giardini or the Zattere. Following voluntary restrictions on theatre attendance, the San Benedetto and the Apollo theatres were closed for lack of patrons. *Caffès* that took the Austrian newspaper *La Sferza* were avoided.

Foreign visitors noted the embargoes. During his first visit to Venice in 1858 Richard Wagner, whose association with Venice was to be emblematic of the deaths of artists there, commented on the 'oppressed and degenerate life of the Venetian populace'; he was acutely aware of the hostility towards the Austrians.[257] He himself found the Austrian military music of high standard and the acoustics of the Piazza 'truly superb' (especially when they played his own music, one surmises), but for the Venetians: 'no two hands ever forgot themselves to the extent of applauding, for any sign of approbation for an Austrian military band would have been looked on as treason to the Motherland.'[258] Wagner records taking his customary walk with a Venetian pianist at the time when Archduke Maximilian and his wife were visiting. The friend tried to divert Wagner from the crowd so that he did not to have to raise his hat to the archduke.[259]

Théophile Gautier was in Venice at the time of the Austrian emperor's birthday, an event celebrated ostentatiously by the Austrians, and ignored as far as possible by the Venetians:

> This people feigning death while their oppressors were exalting with joy, this city which was suppressing itself in order not to assist in this triumph, made a profound and peculiar impression on us . . . a general cry of malediction against the Emperor of Austria could not have been more energetic . . . In the evening there was not a single soul at the Café Florian.[260]

Almost every week Cicogna recorded the sermons preached in San Marco by the pro-Austrian Federico Maria Zanelli. After listening to Zanelli's rantings against the Italian movement, the moderate Cicogna was provoked to remark on the exaggeration and imprecision in his treatment of the burning question of the relationship between the sovereigns of Piedmont and France. During one such sermon, Zanelli's voice was drowned out by the congregation who left the church; this 'scandal' precipitated arrests under the heading of disturbing religion. Zanelli subsequently preached surrounded by police and spies.[261]

On another occasion Zanelli preached a sermon on the Book of Malachi, which he interpreted as an address to a disillusioned and confrontational people; God's curse should be put upon Italian causes and those involved should be excommunicated. He was finally appointed to a less controversial office in Treviso. Five priests were arrested in 1860 and there were increasing numbers of political arrests. The accused were detained on the islands of San Servolo and San Giorgio Maggiore. The Podestà newly in office, Pierluigi Bembo, had the continuing task of petitioning for their release.

In his diary Cicogna recorded that a pigeon was seen walking in the Piazza with a tricolour attached to its neck: it was finally killed, but not before the message was jubilantly noted.[262] The funeral of a flower-seller who had sold bouquets in Risorgimento colours and been imprisoned for his liberal sentiments became an anti-Austrian demonstration. The body was accompanied 'with great pomp' to the cemetery.[263]

When the 1861 lottery was held in Piazza San Marco – a major local event – the number sixty-one was drawn and it was said that it was to be the year of the withdrawal of the Austrians. The Italian parliament opened in Piedmont; it was taken as a momentous event in the Risorgimento. A large crowd gathered on the Riva degli Schiavoni. After the death of one of the leading architects of unification Camillo Cavour on 13 June 1861, Venetians were punished for attending his requiem Mass; San Marco was controlled by police and its doors guarded. The Venetians stayed away during the emperor's visit in October 1861. Following the proclamation of the Realm of Italy in June 1862, any show of the tricolour meant arrest.

Bombs exploded in the *caffès* and in San Marco in May and August 1864. The printer Naratovich was arrested and detained at San Servolo for publishing the patriotic poet Aleardo Aleardi – Manin's envoy to Paris to seek French aid during the rising. The Austrians allowed the Marcian lions, destroyed during the Napoleonic invasion, to be replaced on the Molo façade of the Palazzo Ducale and the Porta della

Carta, but at the same time military rule was installed, with General Allemann in charge. He was recalled in the city with terror and horror, although Cicogna presents him as favourable to the city he himself called 'povera Venezia'.[264] Many wounded were brought into the city after the battle between Austrian and Italian troops at Sommacampagna, near Verona.

Art for the Risorgimento

Whatever the economic gains under the Austrians, their occupation of the city was increasingly resented as the aims of the Risorgimento became more widespread. In 1859 an anonymous pamphlet entitled *Venezia e la libertà d'Italia* was published in Milan.[265] It was the work of a young writer Ippolito Nievo, whose reputation in literature was to be second only to that of Manzoni.[266] The pamphlet, a document of extreme, even overblown patriotism, begged for the liberation of Venice. It was 'the most Italian city after Rome', replete with the *spirito italico*, resounding with Verdi's chorus from *Attila*, waiting through the days of the Cisalpine Republic and the Austrian occupation, slowly augmenting its economy and showing its literary resurgence in the pages of the journal *Il Gondoliere* and the satires of Luigi Carrer. Union with Lombardy would not only be politically appropriate, but morally correct. Meantime the most splendid jewel of Italy was given over, Nievo wrote, to strangers.

An atmospheric account of the resistance at this time is found in a forgotten early novel by Giovanni Verga, covering events during the Venetian Risorgimento. Verga is celebrated for his stories of Sicily, but he published a short novel *Sulle Lagune*, in the Florentine journal *La Nuova Europa* in 1863.[267] It dealt at first hand with the Venetian situation in 1861, with family members accused, wounded, imprisoned or harassed by the Austrians in a way that no Venetian writer could have expressed under the restrictions of censorship. The prologue opens with a gathering in the Giardini to celebrate the entrance of Garibaldi into Naples – the campaign in which Nievo was involved. Within the beautiful setting of the lagoon, Austrian harassment of the Venetians continues; beauty and repression are in conflict.

Beyond Venice the unified states of the new Kingdom of Italy bemoaned Venice's continued occupation.[268] The 1861 Florence Esposizione was a showcase for a range of works depicting Venice in captivity in the climate that followed Villafranca.[269] Antonio Zona showed Venice weeping in the arms of liberated and protective Milan.[270] Andrea Appiani exhibited an image of *Venice who Hopes* (fig. 79): a glamorous figure, decolleté, a regal crown at her feet, her hand restraining the lion of St Mark.[271] In contrast to previous representations of an inert or slumbering state, Venice was now an is alert figure, intent of gaze and ready to rise.

Among Venetian artists in these years, the prolific Antonio Paoletti was inspired by 'le glorie nostra Republica', the love for which he declared to be 'ever burning in his most intimate heart'. Styling himself 'Pittore storico', he presented large history paintings on Venetian themes with emotional rhetorical orations delivered at the Municipal Offices at Ca' Farsetti, and subsequently published.[272] His themes were the high points of splendour and loyalty in the history of the Republic: the return of Antonio Grimani from exile after he was accused of failing in battles against the Turks; the entry of Henry III of France to 'our Grand Canal' with a list of the one hundred identifiable famous figures; and his meeting with the courtesan poet Veronica Franco.

The decades of the Risorgimento were a period of assiduous cultivation of Venetian tradition, particularly in architecture. Exercises in *venezianità* became more frequent, with Venetian Gothic dominating, but also with building in the Neo-Lombard and Byzantine styles. Giambattista Meduna's house in Campo Fantin and the Palazzo Giovanelli in Cannaregio were forthright essays in Venetian Neo-Gothic, as was the renovation of the Palazzo Cavalli-Franchetti, conspicuously sited on the

79 Andrea Appiano Jr, *Venice who Hopes*, 1861. Oil on canvas, 133 × 147.5 cm. Florence, private collection.

Grand Canal. After it was purchased by Baron Franchetti, work was undertaken in the 1880s by Camillo Boito and Carlo Matscheg (a master designer in the newly recognised field of the industrial arts), both displaying a rich decorative repertoire. They used panels in polychromatic marble on the exterior and intricate window traceries; inside there was extensive panelling and wrought-iron fittings, and the grand staircase designed as a new interior wing by Boito, his most important architectural work in Venice.[273]

After the Peace of Villafranca which isolated Venetia under Austrian rule, expression of local style – and *venezianità* – increased. In 1863 Nicola and Angelo Papadopoli established the Palazzo Papadopoli and garden at Santa Croce, near the church of the Tolentino.[274] History paintings on Venetian themes were commissioned, notably the *Death of Othello* by Pompeo Marino Molmenti, professor at the Academy.[275] Four episodes of the siege of Venice painted by Luigi Querena in 1848–9 hung in defiance of Austrian censorship (figs 74 and 75).[276] The sculptor, Bartolomeo Ferrari, who had restored the lion of St Mark when it returned from Paris, furnished six statues of illustratious Italians for Antonio Papadopoli: Machiavelli, Bembo, Sarpi, Campanella, Bruno and Galileo were gravely seated like Roman orators.[277] All were dissidents, brave enough to challenge bigotry and to provide models for a Risorgimento.

Among writers, Ippolito Nievo was the most gifted and the most passionate in his active devotion to the Risorgimento. He was the friend of the exiled poet Andrea Fusinato; both were committed to the project of liberation. Drowned at sea at the age of thirty, Nievo had served as one of Garibaldi's 'Thousand' and addressed a fervent suite of poems, *Gli Amori garibaldini*, to him.[278] From outside Venice, he made extravagant pleas for its freedom, with such declamations as: 'Venice is to me a divine thing. I pray to the heavens that I can live and die in a gondola.'[279] His vast novel-biography with the provocative title the *Confessioni d'un Italiano* although written in 1858 could only be published posthumously in 1867, after the Austrians had withdrawn from Venetia.[280]

The *Confessioni*, in the tradition of Manzoni's *I promessi sposi*, spans the period from the last years of the Republic to 1849 when the narrator's son is exiled from Italy, until his death in America.[281] An analysis of the fall of the Republic and the rise of the Risorgimento provides a crucial subtext, interpreting the events in which the narrator plays his part. In the famous first lines the narrator Carlino declares that he has been born a Venetian but will die an *Italian*. Reconciled with his aristocratic father in Venice, he is by right of birth a member of the Maggior Consiglio – and a witness to the last May sittings in 1797.[282] He both laments and accepts the decadence into which Venice had fallen, and, as noted, he writes poignantly of the loggia of the Palazzo Ducale filled with ghosts from the past mourning the passing of the Republic.[283] But a new order must take over: Carlino has the position of secretary to the new Municipality – Ugo Foscolo's position historically (and later, like Foscolo, Carlo lives in exile in London). Foscolo is a model for Nievo, a prophet of united Italy.[284]

In effect, Carlino gives a commentary on the events and attitudes that destroyed the Republic: Venice failed in administration (this is evident during the narrator's childhood, spent at the castle of Fratta in Friuli), in morality and in commerce. The loss of empire and commercial failure is understood through the writings of the narrator's uncle, the Conte Rinaldo di Fratta, based on Nievo's own uncle, the author of an account of the economy of Venice in the first years of its servitude from 1798 to 1806.[285] But that is the past: the novel runs with the Risorgimento cause and the hope that Venice will find a new destiny in united Italy. While the lament for the loss of Venice sounds throughout, *con dolore*, the narrator's sons, who are of Nievo's generation – members of the Giovane Italia – are dedicated to wider causes: one is killed at Missolonghi, inspired by Byron's fight for liberty in Greece; another fights, as had the author, for Garibaldi. Their lives are willingly sacrificed to the new democracies.

Nievo's interpretation of the Venetian past and his hope for the future are preoccupations of his earlier novel of 1856, *Angelo di Bontà* (The Angel of Goodness), which begins with events of 1749 and ends in 1768, a year before the birth of Bonaparte.[286] One of its chief characters is an inquisitor, Formiani, who is surrounded by women personifying both evil and goodness. On his deathbed Formiani prophesies that Venice will fall like the empires of Assyria, Babylon and Rome; but already the new generation is preparing the recovery.[287] The descendants of the good woman Morisina will create a better Italy: the beauty of Venice will compel a new society.

In 1866 unification was achieved – after intricate diplomatic exercises. Considering the occupation of Venice by the two countries since 1797, the treaty made between Austria and France appears ironic: Venetia was handed back to France, which in turn, after the formality of a plebiscite, passed it to the Italian states.[288] The Austrians left the Veneto on 19 October 1866. Earlier in that year the Venetians were still anticipating restrictions to the economy through a blockade and were protesting about the further imposition of taxes and reduction of industries.[289] In his diary entry of 8 July 1866, some three months before the final reconciliation with Italy, Cicogna set down the litany of servitude:

After the fall of the Republic on 12 May 1797, Venice fell to the French. With the treaty of Campoformio on 18 January 1798, it was conquered by the Austrians.

With the treaty of Pressburg, 26 December 1805, Austria ceded it to Napoleon, and the provinces of the Veneto were joined in the Kingdom of Italy.

With the overthrow of Napoleon, at the Battle of Leipzig in 1813, Venice was returned to Austria until 1848 at which time the people rose up against Austria . . .

With the convention of 22 August 1849 Venice was subjected anew to the Austrian empire, and thus it remains . . .[290]

But 3 October brought the peace of Vienna and the cession of Venetia to Napoleon III. On 4 November Venice became Italian and Italian troops entered on 19 October 1866. After liberation there were songs of jubilation and injunctions for Venice to 'Rise up, beautiful queen of the Waves, after the infamy of long servitude . . .' 'An ode written on the departure of the Austrians 19 October, 1866' declares the Venetians have been subjugated, but now the gondola sings his song again in gladness:

> Or che Italia i ceppi infranse
> He ti strinse lo straniero,
> Ti ritorna il gondoliero
> Col suo canto a rallegrar.[291]

Venice was a free city within Victor Emmanuel's new Italy.

Chapter 5

VENICE IN ITALY: AFTER 1866

The lion could roar again, but its voice was muted. Venice was liberated from Austria and annexed to Italy: the demise of the Republic was irreversible and the brief period of independence under Manin an interregnum now in the past. As a result, Venice was at risk of becoming merely scenic, a place of places, with old buildings that carried fulsome inscriptions of time, but which were, in large part, increasingly separated from active involvement in government – or from the execution of deeds either traitorous or virtuous.

The loss of history is evident in Countess Livia's reaction to Venice in Boito's *Senso*: 'One day the Lord-Lieutenant insisted on taking me to the Accademia Gallery: I understood next to nothing... In the presence of Titian's golden *Assumption*, Paolo Veronese's magnificent *Feast* or Bonifazio's fleshy, carnal, gleaming faces, I could be put in mind of the uninhibited songs I had heard the common people singing...'[1]

The liberation of Venice and its admission into Italy was *not* a particularly glorious affair. Garibaldi, fighting against the Austrians in the Veneto, was critical of the inertia of the Venetians, but they would have been hard pressed indeed to interfere in the dealings between France and Austria, which finally led to Austria's cession of Venice.[2]

The Austrians left an ambivalent legacy; again Venice needed to reconstitute itself as it had done after previous periods of foreign rule. With the establishment of the Kingdom of Italy, zeal to reform the city was immediately evident. An intense period of modernisation and industrialisation began, which, as a consequence, opened Venice to both local and international criticism.

The change-over from subjugation to celebration was not without setbacks; there was an exceptional *acqua alta* in 1867 and the spread of cholera made an urgent sanitary assessment of the city obligatory.[3] But the theatres reopened, carnival resumed, Victor Emmanuel II was given the classic water-borne welcome on 7 November 1866; the artist Girolamo Induno painted the occasion in the same format as the great welcomes to the Piazzetta in the days of the Republic (fig. 80).[4] At La Fenice Arrigo Boito conducted the orchestra in a performance dedicated to the king – a *canto popolare* composed by Antonio Buzzola, who had been Boito's first music master in the days of his Venetian youth.[5]

The creation of monuments and statues expressed public feeling with regard to the Manin revolution and unification. On 22 March 1868, the twentieth anniversary of the Revolution, the remains of Manin, who had died in Paris in 1859, were brought to Venice by rail. A great nighttime procession brought the body from the station along the Grand Canal to San Marco, where Manin was given a second funeral – an occasion of great importance for the city. At the stern of the barge bearing his body were huge imitation bronze statues of Italy consoling Venice: on the prow, the lion of St Mark. The sides were of stained glass and lit from within. Thousands of gondolas and boats followed, lit with torches and wax candles. The painter Giambattista dalla Libera who had recorded the faces of Manin's congress during the uprising, recorded the funeral in a series of paintings: the barge at dusk, like some ghostly Bucintoro, still moored near the church of the Scalzi at the station; the procession along the Grand Canal at night, with the boat lit by flares; the arrival at the Piazzetta, where

80 Girolamo Induno,
*Entry of Victor Emmanuel
II into Venice (7 November
1866)*. Oil on canvas,
152 × 252 cm. Milan,
Museo del Risorgimento.

the Italian flag was flying and the guard of honour was waiting; and the coffin lying in state on a special platform at the foot of the Campanile for the service on 22 March, anniversary of the uprising.[6] Manin's body was finally entombed in an external arcade on the northern façade of San Marco. The ancient decree restricting burial inside the church was upheld at the church's insistence, so the sarcophagus faced the Piazzetta dei Leoncini, sheltered by the walls of the Basilica only after great controversy.[7]

In 1875 a statue of Manin by Luigi Borro was erected in the Campo Paternian, where he had lived, and the campo, subjected to substantial demolition and remodelling, was renamed the Campo Manin.[8] (The demolition of the ancient Tower of San Paternian was not universally approved.[9]) Niccolò Tommaseo was honoured with a statue in Campo San Stefano.[10]

In 1885 a monument to Garibaldi was sited at the entrance of the Giardini Pubblici, with the hero seated on the top of a rocky mound, symbolic of his mountain campaigns; the lion of St Mark surmounts a goldfish pond at the base.[11] Two years later a monument to Victor Emmanuel by sculptor Ettore Ferrari was given a prominent position on the Riva degli Schiavoni, midway between the Arsenale and the Piazza San Marco (fig. 81). Although surmounted by the king on horseback (in the manner of Verrocchio's Colleoni monument), it is the figures of Venezia that dominate and energise the sculpture. On the one side is the enchained Venice with the broken standard of St Mark and her lion sleeping on the steps; on the other, Venice is in command again, with the lion with wings aloft, both freed from Austrian chains. The public homage to Venetian resistance and unification was in place.[12]

*   *   *

81 Ettore Ferrari, the figure of Venezia from the monument to Victor Emmanuel II, Riva degli Schiavoni, 1887.

Venice to Vienna

Quite apart from questions of censorship and economic structure, the relationship between Venice and Vienna in the third period of Austrian occupation had had its difficulties. In the last days of Austrian rule, on 21 July 1866, the Benedectine monk, Beda Düdek, came unannounced to the State Archives at the Frari, with an Austrian military escort, and demanded to see the catalogues in order to make a selection on behalf of the emperor. Despite the Austrians' appearance of willingness to support and preserve the city's patrimony, in the last days of Austrian rule Düdek collected twenty-six cases of codices and documents, which were dispatched to Vienna in a Lloyd-Austriaco steamship.[13] Venetian treasures were requisitioned quietly, without provoking the expressions of public loss occasioned by Napoleon's confiscations. In 1815 the Austrians had appeared generous and protective, recovering the horses of San Marco and reinstating the lion on the Piazzetta, but in their first period of occupation, in 1806, they had endeavoured to transfer one of the great documents of Venetian history, Sanudo's multi-volumed diary, to Vienna.[14] In 1816 forty-six works had been shipped out.[15] In 1838 a further collection of paintings and art objects from the storehouse of material in the Palazzo Ducale and the collections of the Arsenale, including historic instruments of torture allegedly in use by the Council of Ten and a model of the Bucintoro, were taken to the Belvedere Gallery in Vienna.

In 1867, after unification, an elaborate and impassioned report on this confiscation of artworks, books, manuscripts and vast tracts of the Venetian archive was made by Victor Cérésole, a member of the Swiss Society of Historians and the Ateneo in Venice, and the French translator of the monumental calendar of state papers and archives edited and published in England in 1864 by Rawdon Brown.[16] Using the polemical format of the published letter, Cérésole wrote to a fellow-historian in Paris, Armand

Baschet, author of a number of studies of the Venetian archive. Cérésole made a detailed inventory, including works from various Venetian collections which had remained in Paris after the French occupation, but his major concern was the backlog of material still retained by the Austrians in contradiction of Article VIII of the Treaty of Vienna, 3 October 1866. Cérésole reported the misinformation and exaggerated reports that had been circulated in both the Italian and French press, reminding Baschet that he himself had pronounced the documents taken to Vienna to be amongst the most precious and important in the whole archive.

The selection made by Düdek consisted of papers relating to diplomatic matters and pacts between Venetian states and European countries: a comprehensive brief indeed. The archive's Director, Count Girolamo Dandolo had tried to prevaricate, drawing attention to the assurance given by Emperor Franz Josef to his predecessor Fabio Mutinelli that the archive would be left intact,[17] Cérésole describes 'a veritable pillage' of 1,336 items. Bartolomeo Cecchetti, then an officer and later the distinguished director of the archive, protested, was detained on the island of San Giorgio Maggiore and then exiled for a time to Trieste.[18]

Preparation for the last confiscation was as thorough and professional as had been that of Düdek's predecessor, the archivist at the Court of Vienna, François-Bastien Gasller, who took a year to prepare the list of books and manuscripts removed in March 1805. The restitution of these confiscations prescribed under the terms of the Treaty of Pressburg had remained incomplete, and Vienna remains rich in Venetian material.

Cérésole's careful documentation and his involvement with Rawdon Brown and Armand Baschet, was a measure of the international interest in the archive, and the responsibility taken towards it. It was also evidence of the internationalisation of the Venetian heritage, but it registered another stage in the loss of Venice to the Venetians.

Austria and Venezianità

For Austria, nostalgia for the loss of Venice and expressions of mourning persisted for many decades. Indeed, desire for Venice deepened until it became a veritable topos of Austrian culture.[19] Not surprisingly, the Austrians presented themselves as paternalistic benefactors. The Viennese historian Heinrich Benedikt claimed that one of the major merits of Austrian rule was the constant care taken of maritime Venice; disregarding the many testimonies to the contrary, he declared Trieste was not a serious rival before the advent of steam.[20] The most important administrative work was the construction by Austria of roads involving the larger Veneto, and their major benefaction was the enlarging of the port entrance at Malamocco in 1864, and canal dredging.[21] With regard to trade, which the Venetians had always seen as constrained by Austria, Benedikt argued that Austria was hampered by being enmeshed in exclusions and difficulties among the pacts between Germany and England.[22] Venice was more than a material possession for Austria, and it had involved continuous financial sacrifice. Benedikt declared, probably rightly, that Austria held Venice forever in its heart: 'Gli austriaci avevano abbandonato Venezia nel 1866, ma là era rimasto il loro cuore.'[23]

The principal historian of the 1848–9 Revolution, Paul Ginsborg, found it 'difficult to see what Venetia gained economically from being part of the Austrian empire . . . apart from new road and public works'.[24] In the period of Austrian domination Venice looked to France, rather than to Vienna, for it was felt that the tradition of liberalism still existed there (Manin had always hoped for French support for the Venetian revolution); in addition, the splendour of the ancien régime still attracted adherents. Ensconced in their palaces on the Grand Canal, the ex-Bourbons were a reminder of old France.[25] In the arts and in city planning, French – or British – influence was far greater than Austrian. Jappelli's scheme for the entrepôt was influenced by British and French dock projects, and a residual Neoclassicism in the French manner. The Neo-Gothic renovations by Meduna and Cadorin had more in common with the Gothic Revival in France and England, which was alien to Habsburg interest in the late Baroque. The sympathy for the Lombard style was probably boosted by the residence of the Duchesse de Berri in the Calergi Vendramin palace (not to mention the residence of Wagner in the early 1880s). Whatever the sizeable achievements of urban planning in Vienna, Venice looked to Paris, to Les Halles and the arcades, in short to Haussmann's Paris, for the marks of progress. After all, Venice already had its watery Ringstrasse, and Vienna's modernisation projects were not introduced until 1857.[26] Indeed, the influence of Venice on Vienna was more notable. In the field of urban planning, Camillo Sitte's respect for Venice infuses his classic text *Der Städtebau*, in which Venice is cited as a seminal example for his influential urban aesthetic, much of which attacks Sitte's own Vienna and 'the prosaic and narrow spirit of the day'.[27]

Some of Sitte's most treasured and influential principles use Venice as exemplum. Chapter 2 of *The Birth of Modern City Planning*, 'That the Centre of Plazas be Kept Free', indicates that not only is the notion of a central meeting space fundamental to his aesthetic, but so also is the fusion of buildings, including churches flanked by buildings on two or three sides, like San Marco and the Procuratie buildings and the adjacent Palazzo Ducale.[28] With respect to the 'Size and Shape of Plazas', and 'Plaza Groupings', Sitte's extended discussion of the surroundings, shapes, access and size of public spaces in cities is illuminated by comparative comments on his own Vienna, but the pre-eminent example of a public space is Venice's combination of the Piazza San Marco and the Piazzetta (and Sitte could well have discussed the boulevard function of the Riva degli Schiavoni). His praise is abundant, even rhapsodic:

> So much beauty is united on this unique little patch of earth, that no painter has ever dreamt up anything surpassing it in architectural backgrounds; in no theater has there ever been seen anything more sense-beguiling than was able to arise here in reality. This is truly the sovereign set of a great power, a power of intellect, of art, and of industry, which assembled the riches of the world on her ships, and from here exercised dominion over the seas, relishing her acquired treasures, at this, the loveliest spot in the whole wide world.[29]

At the same time, Sitte found the street system visually unacceptable, as the organic growth or original topography of a place did not interest him, and neither did the style or individuality of any one building.[30] The streets of Venice frustrate any vistas: this was the very characteristic that would lead to opposition to street-widening projects in the later nineteenth century.

Of course Sitte recognised the special quality of water, an element of relief in the modern built-up city, and he was alert to the value of rivers and fountains. Venice again was pre-eminent in its water aspect.[31] In short, Sitte's praise was restricted to two aspects of the city: its Piazza, with all that implied, and the water setting. Yet his was a fundamental view of the importance of Venice for *modern* planning, and profoundly influential.[32]

Viennese painters also continued to be besotted with 'the loveliest spot in the whole wide world'. Hans Makart was perhaps the major perpetrator of Venice in Vienna. He was one of the best-known eclectic painters in the later nineteenth century, affecting a historicising Venetian style distinctive enough to be known as the Makartstil. In 1872, while in Vienna, Franz Liszt noted waspishly:

> Makart is finishing an immense and very sensational picture: the homage of the Senate of Venice to Catherine Cornaro. In it, Mme Dönhoff's hair is a burnished blond, à la Titian. It seems that Makart has a marked predilection for this tint to

the very point that his wife has had her hair dyed, and from brunette has become auburn-haired.[33]

Makart's historical pastiche drew in the crowds at the Vienna Exposition of 1873 held in honour of Franz Josef – an exhibition at which Venetian arts and crafts were well-represented and well-received. His vast *Homage to Queen Caterina Cornaro* (fig. 82) was a reworking of Veronese's *Marriage at Cana*, in an operatic style that recalled the variations on the Cornaro theme by Donizetti and others. Against a loggia that showed a streaky sky beyond, crowds of people push around the enthroned queen (dogs, plates of grapes held high, parasols, men carrying jugs of wine) who receives flowers from young children. Markart's pastiche is worlds away from Edouard Manet's modernisation of Titian's *Venus of Urbino* into the *Olympia*, or Giorgione, flattened into the Parisian woods of *Déjeuner sur l'Herbe*.[34]

82 Hans Makart, *Homage to Queen Caterina Cornaro*, 1873. Oil on canvas, 400 × 1060 cm. Vienna, Kunsthistorisches Museum.

Yet the Vienna of Sigmund Freud, Hugo von Hofmannsthal, Richard Strauss and Arthur Schnitzler was to generate many of the revolutions in art and thought of the earliest years of the twentieth century out of its acute diagnosis of a crisis of mind and spirit.[35] From the mid-nineteenth century the city had developed as a highly active urban centre. The vast building project of the Ringstrasse was substantially in place, encircling the inner city with neo-Baroque edifices dedicated to government and cultural enterprises.[36] While the exteriors may have aspired to the mass and authority of Rome, the interiors, rich in heavily veined marbles, suggested Venetian-based decorative programmes, as in the work of the young Gustav Klimt, who first came to prominence at the Burgtheater, painting with his brother Ernst and Fritz Matsch.[37] Klimt was at first seen as the heir to Makart, but Makart's blowzy Titian-style matrons soon became slimmer, younger, sexually enticing figures, dressed and coloured in a Quattrocento fashion inspired by Carpaccio and Bellini.[38] The decoration of the Kunsthistorisches Museum above the stairwell had been left incomplete at Makart's death: the main mural is the work of Michael Munkácsy in Tiepolo style. The Klimt brothers and Matsch worked on the spandrels around 1890 to 1891. Klimt's ornamental detail and gilding gives a new decorative bravura in the spandrels dedicated to the ages of art.[39] His Venetian tribute is an evocation of Bellini's portrait of Leonardo Loredan – reinvoking those exquisite white threads that hang from the skull cap the doge wears beneath the *cornù*. His spandrel dedicated to Melozzo da Forlì equally suggests Carpaccio in its patterning and gold: it heralds the Klimt who was to lead the painters of the Secession.

It was not a paradox but an inevitability that compelled Gustav Klimt in his youth to absorb Venetian decorative elements and colour, in preparation for the sensual erotic quality of so many of his painted woman. And Klimt was to become a major influence on the modern art of Venice, particularly after his exhibition at the Biennale of 1910.[40] He perfected a form of stylistic decoration, drawing on the outlines, the gold and the modules of mosaic: this was the enduring gift of Venetian art as Klimt realised it, and returned it to Venice.

The Austrians had little artistic interest in the contemporary city of Venice, but they held the Renaissance painters and the eighteenth century in high esteem: the latter was the period of Maria Theresa when their own fortunes ran high. The age of Casanova and perpetual carnival had obvious appeal to Biedermeier Vienna and increasingly it was inspiration and comfort in the later nineteenth century.[41] Johann Strauss's operetta *Eine Nacht in Venedig*, first performed in Berlin in 1883, is the epitome of the desire for the perpetual waltz mixed with the barcarolle and the masked ball, an amalgam of the froth of Venice and Vienna.[42] We know from Boito's *Senso* that the Austrian bands played Strauss waltzes in the Piazza San Marco. The waltz was the emblem of 'Gay Vienna'; its relentless rhythm could undermine the gentle barcarolle, imposing a resolute gaiety, endless circling, having potential for hysteria.[43] As a historian of operetta has observed, 'the waltz was the Austrian ingredient that transformed Viennese operetta'.[44] Perhaps it was also the rage rhythm that consoled Vienna after the loss of Venetia, as those famous Strauss waltzes the *Blue Danube* and *Tales from the Vienna Woods* sounded after the cession of 1866.[45]

In 1883 the theme of carnival in the eighteenth century had not yet become a cliché and the new operetta by Johann Strauss brought Venice and Vienna to Berlin, and then to Vienna. With relentless good-humour, *Eine Nacht in Venedig* plays out its unsubtle plot of class disguise under the aegis of masked carnival; with the gondola ready as the vessel of seduction ('Komm in die Gondel mit mir'). A tender *lied* is sung by the Duke of Urbino as a beguiling greeting to Venice; 'Sei mir gegrüsst, du holdes Venezia'; it is both barcarolle and waltz, while a version of the watercall of the gondolier signals the duke's sexual conquests. The city is given over to relentless dancing fuelled by wine; amid the inevitable confusion and partner swapping, the *popolani* vigorously repeat everything in an up-tempo mode, culminating in the carnival in Piazza San Marco. Cues to the well-recognised topography keep the scenes moving from the Piazza San Marco ('Ihr habt euren Markusplatz'), to the Rialto, the Merceria, the Ducal Palace and the Campanile. The pigeons of St Mark attend the finale as an untiring ensemble brings the work to a close. *Eine Nacht in Venedig* offers the lowest-common-denominator reaction to old Venice, put together in the last throes of the Habsburg Empire. Venice is associated with a lost hedonism that required that the past be relentlessly entertaining.

Late Betrayals

The wicked Republic did not instantly disappear, but it was in its last throes. Francesco Zanotto published his corrective study of the prisons, *I pozzi e i piombi*, in 1876 'to show the errors that were spread' including, of course, Darù's 'exaggerations'.[46] Lady Eastlake, writing in the prestigious *Edinburgh Review*, offered a revisionist opinion from abroad when she defended Venice against Darù and affirmed 'the suspicion that Venice has been painted much blacker than she deserves'.[47]

There is also incontrovertible evidence of the shift in French interpretations of the fall of the Republic in the later nineteenth century. In 1885 Edmondo Bonnal, on a mission to consult the Archive of the Regno d'Italia at the behest of the French Ministry of External Affairs, wrote an account of the fall of the Republic.[48] It was immediately translated into Italian by Giuseppe Ughi, who added a jubilant fore-

word drawing attention to the correction of Venetian history and the view that the Republic was justly conquered by Napoleon.[49] Darù's pernicious version which had so shaped foreign perceptions of Venice was countered by a compatriot who held an official position.

Nevertheless, in 1879 torture, the prisons and the Canale Orfano, the site for drowning the politically undesirable – all the myths, in short – were recharged in the opera by Ponchiello, *La Gioconda*, which had its first performance at La Scala, Milan (fig. 83).[50] The opera has remained in the repertoire by virtue if not of its setting, then of its passion. The libretto by 'Tobio Gorrio' was in fact the work of Arrigo Boito, who recast Victor Hugo's *Angelo, Tyran de Padou*, reactivating the inquisitorial Council of Ten together with abundant espionage, both political and personal: 'nel Canal Orfano ci son dei morti' – (there are bodies [again] in the Orfano Canal). All is heavy with pathos, good or evil (mostly evil) in design, accompanied by sinister swirling orchestral motifs and flashing daggers. Both the agent of the Inquisition, Barnaba, and the female lead, La Gioconda, are ballad singers, having a facility desirable in the medium of opera. In the course of the opera La Gioconda and her blind mother, who unwittingly incites superstitious crowds to violence, meet their deaths – the mother drowned, the daughter stabbing herself to escape the undesirable lover. Death, of course, will not leave Venice: in fact it is even more inevitable; but demise was no longer at the hand of an inquisitorial state.

The librettist Arrigo, brother of Camillo, was subsequently to become the most important of Verdi's librettists for his late operas. Arrigo's relationship with Venice, in which he had grown up and trained as a musician, had the ambivalence of many who later became residents of Milan. Yet Arrigo has his place in the history of Venetian poetry: he wrote some early librettos starring Harlequin and Colombine and Pantalone and Piero for the marionette theatre, drawing on the tradition of Carlo Gozzi.[51] But for Ponchiello, Arrigo re-staged all the old Venetian calumnies.

At much the same time Jacques Offenbach was composing *Les Contes d'Hoffmann* (left incomplete when the composer died in 1880, and performed some few months later in 1881).[52] This was at least the third Venetian reference in Offenbach's oeuvre. In 1861 he had composed an *opera buffa, Le Pont des Soupirs*, a farce involving a jealous doge husband (a Contarini) and a dogaressa and rival admirers, one of whom (named Malatromba) was a member of the Council of Ten, the other, the welcomed lover, was called Amoroso. There followed life sentences dispatched by Malatromba, disguised doges arrested and the requisite carnival with barcarolles ('Ah Venise c'est belle') and choirs of gondoliers, protesting their understanding of Venice, its joy and laughter, the farces of Pulcinello . . .[53] Arthur Sullivan had *Le Pont des Soupirs* in mind when he composed an English version, *The Gondoliers*, in 1889.[54] Offenbach mused at least indirectly on Venice the next year, composing *Le Voyage de Messieurs Dunanan, père et fils*, an *opera buffa* in which two provincial Frenchmen are persuaded they are in Venice when they are still, in fact, in France. Though mistaken, they have their share of barcarolles and a waltz dedicated to the Pearl of the Adriatic.[55] But only *Les Contes d'Hoffmann* has remained in the repertoire.[56]

83   Cover for the libretto of the first edition of Ponchiello, *La Gioconda*, 1879. Milan, Museo Teatrale alla Scala.

The absence of precise historical dimension evident in Offenbach's earlier works is also true of *Les Contes d'Hoffmann*, whose place in the repertoire is in large part owed to the celebrated barcarolle 'Belle nuit, O nuit d'amour'. The popularity of the song is proof of the indelible association of Venice and dangerous love, beyond calumny, or even particular associations of plot. Offenbach set a libretto developed from a French play by Michel Carré and Jules Barbier. This was based on E. T. A. Hoffmann's *Tales*, but in a shift from Hoffmann's original location the courtesan Giulietta is associated with Venice, rather than Florence. Love drives the action, of course; Giulietta is in league with the devil and is driven to capture men's souls. The move to Venice not only exploits the well-known association of Venice with courtesans, but also with the city of glassmaking and mirrors, for a mirror plays a major role.[57] Besotted with love, the narrator sells his reflection to Giulietta, uselessly of course. The devil is in love again. Cazotte haunts Venice once more.

For the English poet Robert Browning the myths of a dissipated Venetian state were still intact – and its fatal attraction. Venice is the place of music, where Galuppi plays, 'stately at the clavichord', albeit to a half-listening carnival audience ('Venice spent what Venice earned').[58] Assignations still occur in a gondola, under the *felza*, after a tryst upon the water with music and poetry ('He sings, She speaks'), which ends with the assassin's knife.[59] Don Juan, narrator in 'Fifine at the Fair', written in 1872, plays Schumann's *Carnival* and is transported, inevitably, to Venice, where he is 'in company with music', and in 'carnival-country proper'.[60] In the Piazza the masks talk of themselves and mill around in a crowd 'dumb as death'. Yet Browning's Venice has fatal ambivalence, since it is at the same time nothing less than 'the world', a telling microcosm:

> There went
> Conviction to my soul, that what I took of late
> For Venice was the world; its Carnival – the state
> Of mankind, masquerade in life-long permanence
> For all time, and no particular feast-day.[61]

And so Venice is a place where moral truths are revealed: 'What was all this except the lesson of a life?'[62]

Browning was a celebrated visitor to Venice in the 1880s, especially cultivated in the foreign palaces of Mrs Bronson, the Curtises, the Layards, and his own son Penn, who was resident at the Ca' Dario before he purchased the Palazzo Rezzonico.[63] Browning gave his celebrated readings in the palaces of his friends – reading himself of course.[64] He read, too, to Mrs Bronson in Asolo, perhaps from the poems in progress for his final volume: *Asolando: Fancies and Facts*, published in 1889. The narrator of 'Ponte dell'Angelo, Venice', Browning's last Venetian poem, stops on the bridge called 'The Angel', and, inevitably, hears of murder and blood on the table-cloth, and finds that the devil has more ease of passage than the angel. Victorian Browning, like Ruskin (but less passionately, and certainly not so visually), castigated the city he so loved.

The teasing of history and the cult of a kind of Venetian macabre continued to intrigue the Boito brothers, Camillo and Arrigo. This is evident in a number of Camillo Boito's stories (including *Senso*, written in 1883), which challenge the integrity of the Risorgimento effort in Venice. The affair between the Contessa Serpieri and her Austrian lover is both personally and politically demeaning.[65] The city itself has an essential role to play in heightening sensuality, a quality that Camillo Boito elsewhere refers to, as in the sordid story *Buddha's Collar*, which tells the tale of a naive and shabby customer who fears he will contract rabies after being bitten by a prostitute. At the end of one of the most twisted *calli* a canal glints in emerald hue – Giacomo, the smitten one, is 'momentarily calmed by the sight of that beautiful shimmering emerald'.[66] The snare of beauty in Venice and its particular sensuality, which Boito refers to often in his critical writings, anticipates a heavy *fin-de-siècle* sensuality, as in D'Annunzio's novel of 1900, *Il Fuoco*. That ambivalent beauty was to be visually intense almost one hundred years later in Visconti's film version of *Senso*.

The Urgency of Modernisation

After 1866 and emancipation from foreign rule came renewed zeal and civic energy. Thirteen citizens immediately petitioned for 'the future of the overall topography of the city'; asking for important buildings to be designated, identifying demolition areas for new housing and requesting an agenda for street and canal work with the aim of systematising circulation by targeting congested areas.[67] Submissions were to be invited and a final plan made available to the public: it was to be 'the first step to the Risorgimento of Venice'.[68] The chief gondoliers from Venezia, Murano and Mestre petitioned the new administration, interceding in retrospective terms that made reference to the status of customs and traditions in the old Republic.[69] They wanted the regattas to be confirmed as an annual event, to provide for the economic prosperity of gondoliers and for their competitive exercise. They also had an eye to the tourist market and the appeal to the new bathing public in summertime.[70]

Almost immediately, on 13 December 1866, Mayor Giobatta Giustinian set up a Commission for a 'Study of a Plan of Reform for the Streets and Canals of the City of Venice'.[71] A proposal by Piero Bianco was swiftly drawn up, with 131 interventions expanding on an 1855 proposal, and additional plans. Many were achieved over the next two decades: an aqueduct bringing water from the Terraferma opened amid jubilation in 1884, a fish, fruit and vegetable market opened at the Rialto and the cemetery was expanded.[72] Similar events occurred elsewhere in Europe as governments assumed responsibility for planning and public health.

The dependence of hygiene and health on sewerage, light and air and its circulation, was increasingly understood in a period of cholera epidemics to which Paris, as much as Venice, was prone.[73] In 1858 the Haussmann memorandum made proposals to modernise the Parisian sewerage system as well as create the arterial system of boulevards. The first part of the modern hygienic market project for Les Halles opened that year.[74] In the years between 1859 and 1866 Vienna was establishing its Ringstrasse.[75]

It was not until 1891 that Venice's Piano Regolatore was finalised, although in the years following unification a steady stream of projects was submitted to the Commune.[76] Many of them hold interest beyond the archival for they indicate the urgency of the need for sanitation, housing for the lower and middle classes, water supply through aqueducts and sewerage, as well as the continuation of the projects facilitating passage through the city and the concern of many citizens to modernise Venice and give it viability. Many of the schemes – for example, the Trevisanato plan to run a street from San Simeone Piccolo at the station end of the city along the Grand Canal to the church of the Salute, and Gaspare Biondetti-Crovato's continued interest in bringing the railway line into the heart of the city along the Zattere to a passenger station at the Abbey of San Gregorio – would now throw the international watchdogs into paroxysms because of their insensitivity to the classic views of Venice.[77] In their time, they were the product of a sense of urgency and the need to revitalise both culture and the economy. The circulation of air was seen as a priority in all cities where areas of housing had survived from medieval times. As was well known, these were razed in Paris. At least one eminent Venetian citizen asked if Venice had to go along with 'L'Haussmanismo'.[78]

Some proposals were particularly compassionate in their address to the immediate needs of ordinary Venetians. One year after unification, the engineer Pietro Marsich published a substantial pamphlet on the reordering of the city, raising the question of uneven concentration of population, and the inadequacy of housing and facilities outside the central area of San Marco.[79] Like so many of his contemporaries, he was preoccupied with decentralisation and the need for facilities beyond the area of San Marco, but linked to the central zone by improved arterials. Marsich was concerned not only with cutting through the land to facilitate access, but with water transport 'special to Venezia', always the quickest and most natural means of passage. He was among the first to recommend the introduction of small steamboats.[80]

Particular areas were to be linked to traditional practices, such as the Castello with the Arsenale, and the Giudecca with shipping and customs. Marsich's humanity was evident in his wish to provide markets and facilities equally over the areas of Venice, indicating his awareness of urban planning elsewhere in Europe.

Marsich planned for leisure facilities in Castello and Cannaregio, the areas beyond San Marco that did not have San Marco's concentration of ex-nobility and bourgeoisie.[81] A theatre with water access was proposed for the area by the Riva di Cannaregio, and a building with a *caffè*, a casino and a library with a reading room open to the public. A comprehensive market for vegetables, fish and meat was envisaged in colonnaded buildings with a piazza, as well as a zoological garden. A hospital, public baths and schools were on the drawing board.[82] The plans for Cannaregio are particularly interesting for they foreshadow the elaborate schemes by international architects in the 1980s: the *10 Immagini per Venezia* responded to the lack of facilities or 'centre of attraction' (in Marsich's words) in Cannaregio west. One hundred years later there was still the urge to facilitate access to the station and embellish that area which had lost so much in mid-century demolitions.[83]

In the 1860s the state of housing in the Castello area moved Marsich to sad eloquence and grief in the face of the vermin and pollution surrounding the Arsenale, once so famously praised by Dante,[84] and he urged radical reform of sewers and latrines.[85] The quality of water in Venice amid its salt lagoon had been a long-standing concern, more so once the dangers of contamination were better understood. Although various submissions had been made during Austrian rule, in 1881 the construction of an aqueduct to bring water from the Brenta river area became a priority in a period of cholera epidemics.[86] The public inauguration in 1884 was celebrated by the erection of a temporary fountain in front of San Marco (fig. 84).[87] Many *pozzi* – the old wellheads – were exported to the world's museums, or became objects of antiquarian interest.[88]

Among the most publicised of the unrealised plans after unification was Marsich's 1867 proposal for a Galleria Manin to run from San Marco to the Rialto, the central market area. In line with the *reordinamento* of that area, the *galleria* was intended to move traffic quickly from San Marco

84 Carlo Naya, inauguration of the aqueduct in Piazza San Marco, 1883. Gelatin photograph, 21 × 27 cm.

towards the station.[89] It was envisaged as an up-to-date construction in iron and glass based on the fashionable arcade prototype, but elevated above ground.

Various market proposals had been put forward earlier in the century, as the provision of markets and their regulation became one of the main areas of urban rationalisation in European cities. In 1838, as one of his many projects to commemorate the visit of the Austrian emperor, Giuseppe Salvadori had planned a Doric-fronted market with iron and glass warehouses – a characteristic combination of new technology in a Neoclassical format. In 1857 Neville had proposed a long narrow building with a central fountain and iron roofing, but Gothic-Renaissance details. Federico Berchet put forward a design for a huge iron construction in Lombard style in 1879.[90] Eventually, in 1884, Forcellini's relatively modest and unadorned iron-roofed building with open colonnades was built. Like Neville's bridges, its life as an example of modern technology was brief. Far from relishing modernism, the Venetians repudiated it as the conservation lobby gained momentum and the modern was expelled in favour of the traditional. In the early twentieth century the 1884 market building was demolished and, in a reversal of taste, a new Lombardesque structure was built in 1907.[91]

Also destined for notoriety was the plan put forward in 1871 by the Prefect Luigi Torelli.[92] Torelli had shown himself to be ambitious for Venice; he had a fresh perception of the city's needs, and his identification with the city was evident in his performance of the ceremonies at the reinterment of Manin's body at San Marco. In 1867 Torelli decreed that the city must 'either . . . accept and walk with progress which alone can give prosperity; or reject it and remain behind'.[93] Venice wrestled then with such advice, and has continued to do so. In Torelli's grandiose scheme a raised road wide enough to take carriages was to run along the Riva degli Schiavoni beyond the Public Gardens to Sant'Elena, which was to become a recreational area. An enclosed body of water, surrounded by seating for spectators, was to be a site for naval exercises as well as an economically viable oyster hatchery. The projected area was extensive enough to bear comparison with the Champs Elysées or Hyde Park; Torelli tabled comparative figures. The most contentious aspect of the project was the carriageway for horses, carriages, buses and pedestrians, to be supported on six hundred iron columns. The proposal revealed that the Venice of pedestrians and boats was by no means automatically accepted, especially in an age of expanding transport. Torelli's project was often referred to as the summit of absurdity in proposals for a new Venice.

The preoccupation with widening and altering passageways and filling in canals had been constantly on the agenda since the time of Napoleon. Following the principle of the Via Eugenia in the Castello, a major artery, the Via Vittorio Emanuele (now known as the Strada Nuova), was created from the church of Santi Apostoli, just below the Rialto, to Santa Fosca, giving access to the railway station via the Ponte delle Guglie and the Rio Terrà Lista di Spagna.[94] Opened in 1871, it was a swift response from the new planning committee and the first creation of the new municipality. It was not without controversy. Engineer Fano published a brochure opposing the mania for straightening operations in the area of Cannaregio, recommending that seven metres were adequate to facilitate through traffic without crowding.[95]

After unification plans were also submitted by the senior figure Giambattista Meduna, who proposed easing the congestion around the western area of the Piazza San Marco. As a result, the Via 22 Marzo, named after the first day of Manin's Republic, was completed in 1881. It opened up a more direct passage to the Accademia Bridge and the Campo Santo Stefano, giving access to the Dorsoduro. Developed over the next two decades, the elegant shop-fronts and commercial buildings in the Via 22 Marzo designed by Francesco Balduin in Lombard style enhanced the retail and commercial facilities behind the new hotels on the Grand Canal. The Via 2 Aprile, commemorating the day in 1849 when Venice had declared itself ready to 'resist the Austrians at any cost', opened in 1884, widening the area between the churches of

San Salvador and San Bartolomeo behind the Rialto Bridge, and facilitating the passage from San Marco to the Rialto.[96] Meduna also presented a scheme to systematise the canals behind the north side of the Piazza San Marco to form a 'bacino' and give rear access to the Procuratie Vecchie. This became the development known as the Bacino Orseolo: over the next three decades new commercial buildings and hotels were built around a large mooring area for gondolas.[97]

Despite the influence of Ruskin and Romantic architecture couched in the idiom of the Gothic, it was the Lombard style with Renaissance overtones that was most positively identified with commerce.[98] The Gothic style was seen to be appropriate for domestic and palazzo architecture. In the period of eclecticism, the classical style also had its adherents: an example that remained pertinent was Palladio's plan, described in the third of his *Quattri libri dell'architettura*, for a Rialto bridge in classical form; Canaletto's painting had given it currency and it remained a powerful image in Venice.[99] It was reinvoked in the 1880s, when the original Rialto project was revived by Venetian architects. In response to the hopes of increased commercial activity, Francesco Lazzari revived Guglielmo di Grandi's 1597 design with a double row of shops under cover and an upper terrace on each side, allowing a level shopping stretch and promenade.[100] Lazzari also wanted to rebuild the old wooden bridge of the Rialto when the plans for the Accademia bridge were discussed; in this he anticipated the wooden bridge preferred by Eugenio Miozzi, who replaced Neville's iron bridge in the 1930s.[101]

Bridges overcoming water and facilitating transit over land continued to be a priority, although the most ambitious remained on paper. Neville continued to supply cast-iron bridges in the 1860s, most notably the 1865 bridge for the Ghetto Nuovo in Cannaregio.[102] The question of facilitating travel on water seemed less important, but became controversial in the 1880s, when the introduction of steamboats within the city provoked debate and protest.[103] The primacy of the gondoliers had been challenged not only by the railway across the lagoon, but by Busetti's omnibus, which in 1842–3 began to collect passengers at Mestre and ferry them to stopping-off points along the Grand Canal.[104] But the steamboat offered an even more serious threat. The Compagnie des Bateaux Omnibus de Venise initiated the modern service, known today as the *vaporetti*, with the first journey of the *Regina Margherita*, which provoked the gondoliers to strike in 1881 (fig. 85).[105] The threat to the gondola was felt

85 Carlo Naya, the first vaporetto on the Grand Canal, *c*.1883. Gelatin photograph, 21 × 27 cm.

86 Alesandro Milesi, *The Gondolier's Lunch*, 1893. Oil on canvas, 72 × 105 cm. Rome, Galleria Nazionale d'Arte.

deeply and lastingly, as is indicated by the play in dialect by Giacinto Gallino, *Serenissima*, first performed in 1891.[106] It is set in 1876; Piero Grossi, the central character, is an old gondolier of the most traditional kind, so immersed in the life of city that he is known by its old name 'Serenissima'. Extolling the unique nature of Venice and the beauty of her waters, he must watch and eventually accept the inroads of the *vaporetti*. No longer able to make a living through his gondola, he is forced to seek work in the Arsenale.

The subject of the destitute gondolier lasted well beyond the immediate issue of the introduction of steamboats. In the many paintings of the 1880s depicting gondoliers and their families by emerging Venetian artists such as Alessandro Milesi and Luigi Nono – artists who practised a *verismo sociale* – poverty and begging were frequent subjects.[107] Milesi's *The Gondolier's Lunch* (fig. 86) of 1893 shows the gondolier eating, pitcher of wine in hand, while mother and child watch wistfully. In other paintings the gondolier's orphans beg by the waterside, or the fisherman's wife and children are shown destitute on the *fondamenta*, the mother, chin in hand, meagre possessions in a bundle at her feet.

Luigi Nono also painted orphans, and poor mothers and their children, extending the poverty of the gondolier to other mendicants.[108] Choosing Chioggia as a typical site, no doubt with Léopold Robert in mind, he depicted the sculpted Madonna on the *fondamenta* outside the cathedral – an outdoor devotional site accessible to all. The 1882 *Refugium peccatorum* (Rome, Galleria Nazionale d'Arte Moderna), and the 1892 *Ave Maria* (Trieste, Museo Civico Revoltella) both show a local Madonna, a mother holding her baby as she touches the statue of the Virgin. Her drooped head conveys her reverence, if not her desperation. A brother and sister huddle on a church porch in Nono's best-known painting, *Abandoned* (Venice, Museo d'Arte Moderna), empty begging cap on the pavement. The painting touched the heart of Queen Margherita, who acquired it at the 1903 Biennale and presented it to the city.[109]

* * *

Industrialisation

The 1880s were years of industrial growth and related building, particularly in the area of the Giudecca, once famous for humanist meetings and gardens as well as Palladio's Redentore and Il Zitelle churches.[110] The garden created by the Englishman Francis Eden, known felicitiously as 'The Eden Garden', enjoyed a special reputation at the end of the century as a kind of Symbolist retreat.[111] In the 1870s, at the western end of the island, industrial development accelerated with the founding of the Junghans clock-making factory by the Herron brothers in 1882, the presence of a manufacturer of rope and candles and traditional boat-building yards. The re-energising of the Giudecca was a consequence of its proximity across the canal to the railway area and Santa Marta, also being industrially developed.[112]

The debate on the port was continuous; in 1870 it was still maintained that the Bacino of San Marco was the true port.[113] The shift away from the Bacino, which began under Napoleon with the demolition of the granary in the centre of the city, had been compounded by the reduction in mixed trading along the Grand Canal. Substantial changes and relocations had taken place: the palaces on the Grand Canal had ceased to function commercially and trade gravitated towards the eastern end of the city to the vital link, the railway line. The famous *fondachi* of the Turks and the Germans had new post-mercantile functions; the great palaces near the Rialto, notably the Ca' Farsetti and the Ca' Loredan, had become the offices of local government.[114] Even small shipbuilding activity lessened, as is known from the closure of the boatyard next to the Palazzo Cavalli-Franchetti. Shipping round the Rialto largely concerned the delivery of food to the market, ferrying tourists to their hotel destinations and general cartage and passenger shipping along the canal. A 1867 commission headed by Pietro Paleocapa finally confirmed a location for the port in the vicinity of the railway, at Santa Chiara.[115]

A notable development at the station end of the city occurred during the period when the Cotonificio Veneziano was established at Santa Marta. It was seen by the conservationists to be insensitively sited in a picturesque area of Venice, further destroying local colour.[116] However, the ready access to the railway and the Giudecca meant that inevitably the Santa Marta area developed an industrial character. The construction of the cotton mill proceeded quietly in typical industrial style, built in brick with three floors, modest turrets, brick edging and discrete quoins of Istrian stone at the windows.[117]

The most prominent development, across the canal on the Giudecca, was the Stucky mill (fig. 87), which began operation in 1884. Its proprietor, Giovanni Stucky, was the son of a Swiss father and a Venetian mother, his family was involved in the pioneering industrialisation of the Veneto.[118] As a youth he had been apprenticed to Neville's iron foundry at San Rocco. The Stucky mill and silos were the most modern in Italy, and from 1896 they were housed in a vast multi-storey brick edifice, one of the most extraordinary exercises in industrial architecture. The first premises were built in 1882, on the site of the Convent of San Biagio and Cataldo, suppressed by Napoleon and converted into a hospital for typhoid patients in 1816. Stucky was ambitious for his site and thought in terms of monumental architecture. For the second phase of building he chose a German architect, Ernst Wullekopf, whose experience in industrial architecture in Hanover gave him excellent credentials.[119] The complex built for Stucky accorded with the local practice of brick construction, but it was embellished with blind arcades, castellations and turrets in a neo-Gothic mode developed from the architect's brewery in his native town. The new mill's dissonant appearance within Venice was immediately noted and plans were at first resisted by the Commissione all'Ornato – but the project went ahead in the face of Stucky's threat to dismiss employees if expansion was not approved.[120] The modern silos and the pasta factory became famous, and the modernity of the enterprise's techniques and facili-

ties was widely recognised. Stucky was eager to give his employees better access to the factory and supported an 1893 project for an iron bridge between the adjacent island and the Giudecca.[121] Despite considerable discussion it was never built, although Stucky replaced the stone bridge over the Rio di San Biagio with a modern iron bridge, and developed a shipping quay along the Giudecca canal.[122] His complex, which dominated the skyline, was the most conspicuous new architectural monument of the latter part of century.[123]

The Arsenale in United Italy

The Arsenale experienced something of a revival after 1866, when the new Italian kingdom looked to Venice for shipbuilding and defence in the Adriatic. Under the Austrians, shipbuilding activity had been restricted when the naval base was moved to Polo and the commercial base to Trieste. In 1867 a law for financing work on the Arsenale was passed, and one of the major changes in its history took place when the two large basins known as the Nuova and the Nuovissima were joined together to make an industrially scaled basin, the Darsena Grande.[124] In the 1880s two dry docks were constructed on the northern side, and the Arsenale was adapted for the construction of submarines. New wharves and workshops were built, following harmoniously in the tradition of brick construction, with arched windows outlined in Istrian stone.[125] Other workshops were built, again felicitously, in the contemporary neo-Gothic mode, sympathetic to the Gothic style of the Porta Nuova built during French rule. Two new Gothic turrets next to the Porta Nuova marked the eastern entrance to the complex.

On the northern perimeter of the Arsenale complex, the island known as the Isola delle Vergine was reclaimed and, after 1869, developed as dry docks. It was surrounded by the traditional wall with characteristic crenellation – a photograph from the Naya studio taken from an elevated position shows the process of reclamation

88 Giacomo Favretto, *Venice presenting the Baton of Command to Francesco Morosini*, 1879. Oil on canvas, 72 × 56 cm. Venice, Museo d'Arte Moderna, Ca' Pesaro.

89 Antonio Paoletti, *The Battle of Lepanto*, curtain for Teatro La Fenice, 1878.

and wall-building from the viewpoint of San Pietro di Castello.[126] Across the water lay the island of San Michele, the cemetery island, which after long delay was walled and given waterside chapels by engineer Annibale Forcellini, mixing neo-Gothic and Neoclassical modes, as did the Arsenale.

In the 1880s the Arsenale was supplied with new industrial cranes by Mitchel & Co. of Newcastle-upon-Tyne and the first major warships were launched: the *Amerigo Vespucci* in 1882, the Venetian-named *Francesco Morosini* in 1885 and the *Sicilia* in 1891.[127] The launching of the *Francesco Morosini* inspired the painting by Giacomo Favretto of 1879 (fig. 88). Morosini, the seventeenth-century soldier-doge noted for his conquests against the Turks, kneels at the feet of an enthroned Virgin who is also Venice, to receive the baton of command. Kneeling at the foot of the throne is a diligent secretary busily writing the name of Venice in the Book of History, for Venice had risen again – or the rhetoric, at least, was permissible once more. The Republic's ship of state, the Bucintoro, symbol of one-time sea-might, appears triumphantly on the seas behind.[128]

In a preliminary to this naval revival, the curtain of La Fenice was repainted with a scene of Venice's greatest naval triumph, the Battle of Lepanto, fought against the Turks in 1571 (fig. 89).[129] Antonio Paoletti, so patriotic in the last years before unification, represented Onfredo Giustiniani in the flagship *Angelo* returned with Turkish trophies to the Piazzetta, to the scene of the twin columns and the Palazzo Ducale, and a jubilant crowd. For contemporaries in the late nineteenth century the allegory would have been obvious.

* * *

Glass and Lace

The most important industries were not new; they were the revival of the city's traditional artisanship, particularly in the areas of glassmaking, luxury fabrics and lace-making, which have remained highly characteristic activities. These crafts have survived although the manufacturing areas of the historic city have become defunct, decimated by the industrially scaled activities of Marghera in the early twentieth century. The Stucky mill was to become derelict and the Arsenale virtually a ghost city, but the manufacture of glass and luxury fabrics continued.

The revival of Murano's glass industry owed much to the Abbot Vincenzo Zanetti and the support of the Murano mayor Antonio Colleoni. Zanetti's guide to Murano, which introduced contemporary furnaces as part of the island's tourist attractions, and his various *esposizioni* in Venice and abroad, established the modern industry as viable within the international market.[130] He founded an archive, including old handbooks and recipes, and the Museo Civico Vetrario in 1861, bringing together the history of glass from antiquity and some of the most distinctive examples of both past and current production, and he directed it until his death in 1883.[131] Classical examples from the past inspired many fine pieces, especially chalices and goblets with elaborate serpentine stems. The bead industry was reactivated, although its decline had never been absolute, given the continuing trading market for beads. The production of solid canes of glass worked into beads 'at the lamp' were the particular speciality of the *conterie*: the beads were slices of glass rods, multicoloured, like flowers or sweets.[132] The *millefiore* technique produced canes of wondrous colours, which were cut and embedded in paperweights (these were particularly fashionable in France, thanks to the initiatives of the entrepreneur Pietro Bigaglia).[133] Giacomo Franchini became a virtuoso creator of miniature images of pin-like precision and glowing colours, giving shape to tiny gondoliers, the Rialto Bridge, the Palazzo Ducale and portraits: Venetian subjects in a pre-eminently Venetian technique.[134]

Stringing glass beads to produce necklaces and decorative beading was a traditional cottage industry for Venetian women working outside the guild system. In the nineteenth century the *impiraresse*, together with the lacemakers of Burano, supplemented modest incomes with home work, sorting beads from a wooden box, often seated outside their houses, and catching the eye of visiting artists, who saw their occupation as picturesque.[135] Their products were traded round the world, valuable currency in an age of colonialism.[136]

Interest in glass and industrial crafts was stimulated internationally by the Crystal Palace exhibition in London in 1861 and the Paris expositions, which featured palaces for both the fine and the applied arts – a Palais de Beaux Arts and a Palais de l'Industrie.[137] In 1862 in Murano Zanetti founded a Scuola di Disegno Applicato all'Arte Vetraria to ensure future apprentices for the industry, and, as a further result of his zeal, the first specialised Murano glass exhibition took place in 1864. One of its most magnificent exhibits, displaying the virtuosity of the new glassblowers, was the chandelier by Giovanni Fuga and Lorenzo Graziati, which hangs today in the museum's first-floor salon (fig. 90).[138] This type of *lampadaria* can be an awe-inspiring glass architecture of arabesques, curlicues and multicoloured flowers; it attained great brilliance in the eighteenth century at the hand of Giuseppe Briati – an example of his work hangs in the Theatine library room in the Correr museum.[139] Such chandeliers, light-catching and reflecting, are a great Venetian tradition, animating the upper spaces of many vast rooms, in apparent defiance of gravity and in apparent competition with the sparkle of water outside. The traditional style has been no hindrance to its perpetuation, to the many fantasies on the theme as candles gave way to electric light globes and a basic type was adopted for the simplest of rooms.

Following the experiments of earlier nineteenth-century glassblowers, such as Domenico Bussolin and Pietro Bigaglia, the mechanisation of essential processes aided

the industry's modernisation, particularly the gas apparatus Bussolin invented in 1849, which made the use of candles for working obsolete.[140] In 1854 the firm of Toso brothers was founded and in 1859 the famous house of Antonio Salviati – lawyer turned glassmaker – was established in Murano in the twelfth-century Palazzo da Mula.[141] The Salviati firm became known world-wide. Initially the company was under the direction of Lorenzo Radi, who produced mosaics for the restoration of San Marco.[142] Blown glass was in production as early as 1862.[143] Salviati's partnership with the English archaeologist Sir Henry Austen Layard, the discoverer of Ninevah, resident in Venice from 1884, and the export of glass and commissions for external decorations abroad brought fame to the enterprise.[144] An important aspect of the activity was the production of mosaics, constantly in demand for San Marco, but increasingly popular as a decorative feature in the late nineteenth century. The showrooms in Venice, decorated with external mosaics, faced the main hotels at the opening of the Grand Canal.[145]

On the occasion of the second glass exhibition held at Murano in 1869, Zanetti declared that the promise hinted at only a few years earlier in 1864 had been realised, and Venetian glass, now assured of a future, was ready to make its contribution to the new state of Italy. Salviati was particularly successful in Vienna, London and Berlin. Emancipated from foreign rule, Zanetti continued, Venice must cast off economic slavery through its achievements in art, industry and commerce.[146]

90   Giovanni Fuga and Lorenzo Graziati, chandelier, c.1870. Murano, Museo Vetrario.

The Byzantine revival of the late nineteenth century, the vogue for mosaics not only from Venice, but also Ravenna, added to the appetite for luxury, gold and adornment that put mosaics on famous façades such as Liberty's of London and the South Kensington Museum, under the dome of St Paul's Cathedral, in Secessionist buildings in Vienna, and, in Venice itself, on palaces on the upper Grand Canal. The Art Nouveau taste for glass contributed to the international fame of the house of Salviati. Wherever there was a trade fair there was Salviati. In 1898 Baron Raimondi Franchetti took over the Società Veneziana per l'Industria del Conterie, some indication of the viability of the industry for an entrepreneur.[147]

The glass industry was not merely a revival of traditional skills; it had a sufficiently wide range of applications and number of gifted glassblowers for original and modern designs to be created. The eclectic approach encouraged creative variations on earlier themes, recreating the cage cup (a blown lattice overlay on a vase or goblet), the multicoloured enamels created by Salviati in the 1870s (fig. 92), and the Neo-

91 Salviati & Co., fruit stand with sea-horse and flower, 1895. Glass, 27 cm. Venice, Rossella Junck collection.

classical cameo glass bowls engraved by Attilo Spaccarelli.[148] The chalice and the stemmed goblet liberated inventive, almost sculptural creations by virtue of the attention lavished on elaborate silhouettes, on cup, handles, and – above all – stems. They could be a miracle of intricate lacings supporting a fragile bowl, as in the chalice owned by Michelangelo Guggenheim and known as the Guggenheim Cup. This was a tall ornamental vessel: a covered flask supported on an elaborate open stem entwined with crystal beads, and topped with a finial of crystal beads and chains (fig. 92).[149] It became a set piece for young virtuosi glassmakers when Isadoro Seguso and Giuseppe Barovier recreated it.[150]

The brothers Giovanni and Antonio Barovier – the Artisti Barovier (the name evokes the most revered tradition of Murano glassblowers) – were trained in the Salviati workshop before beginning their own company in 1896.[151] An early work by Barovier, made in the Salviati period and shown in the Paris Exposition of 1867, floats the bowl of the goblet on a fabulous stem – 'a small, twisted yellow and white glass rod' – entwined below the flat lobes of an elaborate lower support.[152] Motifs from nature, and the sea in particular, enjoyed a late nineteenth-century vogue in Venetian glassmaking (fig. 91). The metamorphosis of glass into translucent creature turned stems into dolphins balancing a vase on a curvaceous tail, or marine worms curling around a blue sea vessel.[153] Dragon-like sea horses sip from the lips of pitchers, or take up positions guarding the sides of a cup. Sea dragons are both stems and handles on elaborate Barovier vases from the last decades of the century.[154]

Not only glass, but Venetian luxury fabrics again became internationally famous. Best known at the turn of the century were to be Mariano Fortuny's hand-printed fabrics and couturier costumes, but the revival of traditional methods of production had taken place some thirty years before.[155] When Luigi Bevilacqua returned to old weaving techniques in 1876 and Lorenzo Rubelli began his workshop reproduction of brocades, damasks and velvets in 1880, the modern luxury trade was created.[156] The possibility of custom from the tourist industry and the resident foreign aristocracy must have influenced their decisions. As elsewhere in Europe, schools were set up to teach the revived crafts, and in 1872 Michelangelo Guggenheim founded the Scuola Veneta d'Arte Applicate alle Industrie.[157] Guggenheim was an important figure in the late nineteenth century for his support of education in the arts and industry, following the style of British teaching, and the international exhibitions that brought the arts and manufacture together. With the historical sense typical of the city fathers in the late nineteenth century, he collected a wide range of historical fabrics, which he eventually donated to the Museo Correr.[158]

Of course the revival of crafts was an international phenomenon; the Arts and Crafts movement in England, the Great Exhibition of 1851 and the foundation of what was to be the Victoria and Albert Museum had an impact well beyond Britain. The international exhibition displaying the productions of many nations was a further impetus. As art reviewer for the *Nuova Antologia*, Camillo Boito covered the industrial arts in the Esposizione di Milano of 1881, drawing approving attention to the revival of Venetian crafts.[159] 'What beauty there is in the glass of Murano, what variety and fragility', he exclaimed.[160] The art of glass had risen again in the factory of Salviati and in the Compagnia Venezia-Murano, and Boito responded to its vitality.[161] He also praised the lacework from the island of Burano, noting the revival of *punto in aria* (openwork lace, beautifully described in Italian as 'in the air'), and the arts about which Lo Zoppino wrote in 1530: Boito cited other historic texts on the lacemaking tradition. Like all the crafts it was in abeyance after the demise of the guild system under Napoleon, and a revival involved a conscious programme.

In 1882 Lady Layard translated a treatise on lacemaking into English, doubtless to make the excellence of the art known abroad. The many traditions were explained: the cutwork, net lace, open lace, flowered lace, pillow lace, the *punto di Burano* and the *punto di Venezia*, with their high points of fashion Europe-wide, especially in the seventeenth and eighteenth century.[162] An appendix explained the history of the foundation of the Burano lace school some eight years earlier when a particularly bitter winter had prevented the fishermen from obtaining an income. The school was started on the initiative of Paul Fambri with eight pupils who were given a daily payment to induce them to attend.[163] As it was women's work, it was under the patronage of Queen Margherita. By 1882 there were 320 participants, paid according to the work they performed; the parish priest had reported that the moral condition of the island had improved.[164]

The lace industry was well established by the 1870s. Michelangelo Jesurum, whose enterprise in lace and linen still flourishes, praised the new industry, claiming Venice had supremacy with Belgium and England, and the revival of which was particularly appropriate to women working at home. The moral implications were stressed: traditionally laceworkers were the wives and daughters of fisherman and sailors. Domestic conditions were preferable to factory work, and meant that women could maintain a virtuous proximity to their family and thus contribute to public morality.[165] The women workers themselves became tourist attractions, seated outside their Burano houses, and working with a pillow and a wooden cylinder on their knees. They reinforced the idea that the role of Venice in the new Italy was both vital and virtuous. That this view was not inevitably espoused by Venetian women is evident in Gallini's

92 Salviati & Co., covered chalice, 1866–70. London, Victoria and Albert Museum.

Serenissima – a play that documents these changes and their challenge to the old generation in the early 1890s: Gallini's main themes are the emancipation of women and the dilemma of the gondolier threatened by the *vaporetti*.[166] In *Serenissima* Cecilia wants to elope with her lover to Florence rather than be a Burano laceworker.

It could be argued that the new enterprises were in fact only revived cottage industries given a tourist application, or the result of a reactionary zeal to protect old Venice from iron, glass and passageways. Conservative thinking was widespread in the 1880s, at the time when the restoration of San Marco provoked international discussion and Venetians paid increasing attention to questions of conservation. Issues of conservation and regional expression were reinforced by the growing national sentiment aroused by the Risorgimento. Cultivation of the Venetian Gothic heritage affected both renovation and new building in the city. A revivalist and eclectic form of architecture was by no means exclusive there, but obviously the city was rich in views that might be deemed picturesque. At first preferences were put forward, favouring the custodianship of the old in the face of the new. Lines of division drawn between historic architecture, revivalist new building and renovation forced dilemma after dilemma in the 'modern' twentieth century, but the attitude was already evident around 1850s. The 1853 Cadorin project for the Riva degli Schiavoni was the first clear example of reaction against intrusion into a 'historic' area of the city. No such outspoken debate had attended Jappelli's project for the entrepôt just a few years before, around 1850, although the Zattere was an important panoramic stretch, adorned with Massari's Gesuati, and it faced the trio of Palladian churches across the Giudecca canal.

The Loss of History and the Visual Arts

With the popularisation of products made by hand came an interest in depiction of the *popolani*. The Realist, or Verismo movement was widespread, and had been foreshadowed in Venice by Robert's *Departure of the Fishermen*. In Venice, as elsewhere, history painting gave way to *veduta* painting *en plein air*. In recently united Italy there were *two* Italies comprising virtually two countries, the urban and the rural. In the later nineteenth century painters and writers identified both their subjects and values with one or other area and its people: Verga's novels are the classic case. In the Veneto, Nievo is an instance, writing on the peasants of Friuli and applauding their simple, forthright values, even while he observes their distance from a metropolis.[167]

The lagoon paintings by Guglielmo Ciardi return to the theatre of water and sky that was Guardi's focus, but in his interest in the Venetian who dwells apart from the city Ciardi follows a realist programme. His intention appears in the first instance to be the description of light, water, reflections and the geometry of the lagoon, but the people partake of the light: the peasant and the fishermen at work in the *barene* and the islanders are observed at their tasks with precision. The lagoon around them is at once empty, devoid of incidence, comfortless – or a lyrical site for the meeting of water, light and air. From 1869 Ciardi painted memorable canvases in the area of the lower Giudecca, closer to the heart of the city, but not yet a developed industrial area (fig. 93). It was grassy and still unpaved, a place for fishermen and modest shipping.

Ciardi had been a student of the painter-photographer Domenico Bresolin at the Accademia di Belle Arti. The Academy and its pupils had changed decisively at mid-century, as the commitment to Neoclassicism and the influence of Canova and Cicognara waned. The work of Venetian painters in the latter part of the century attest to the vigour and *sprezzatura* of their training and its stress on the local, but it was inevitably touched by the Macchiaioli movement in Florence: Ciardi's sense of light on the lagoon owes much to the Florentine example which he had experienced personally at the Caffè Michelangelo.[168] At the Academy Pietro Selvatico had made a

93 Guglielmo Ciardi, *Giudecca Canal*, 1869. Oil on canvas, 63 × 111 cm. Venice, Museo d'Arte Moderna, Ca' Pesaro.

plea for both the painting and photography of contemporary life, and painting specific to Venice.[169] Various changes in teaching practice – life-drawing from figures dressed in contemporary dress, active poses and natural lighting, for example – reflect the new studio practices[170] and are apparent in the work of a group of Ciardi's contemporaries who came to distinction in the 1860s and 1870s: Luigi Nono, Giacomo Favretto, Napoleone Nani, Ettore Tito and Alessandro Milesi.[171] Federico Zandomeneghi, who pursued his career in Paris, was another of that generation.[172]

In the last years of Austrian occupation the senior painter at the Academy, Michelangeli Grigoletti, had been considered too Germanic – attending the Munich Congress of German artists in 1858, working at Esztegom, and painting for Maria Carolina.[173] In contrast, Ciardi's peasant paintings depict local peasant-based values, and represent a way of life distanced from attempts to modernise and industrialise the city.

The peasant subject and the rural scene were also favoured by photographers in the late nineteenth century; indeed, their verism ran parallel to that of the painters. With the nineteenth-century urge to tabulate and classify, photographers grouped types of people together and took considerable interest in the *popolani*. These studies also gave an opportunity for figure-in-landscape compositions, such as Carlo Naya's fishermen from the islands of Pellestrina, Chioggia and Burano. Naya began his records with the poor people of Naples before making a systematic album of Venetian types entitled *L'Italie pittoresque: scènes et costumes pris d'après nature* (fig. 94).[174] Whether intentionally or not, mendicancy and poverty were bluntly on record; faces worn by hardship and exposure to the elements register expressions of tragic inertia, even in such subjects as fishermen mending their nets or a woman selling a roasted pumpkin. A multi-figured composition from Chioggia and the various photographs of urchins may sometimes show them playing cards or bathing, but often they are simply sitting in the shadow of buildings whose brickwork is stripped of stucco.[175] It is the squalor of Venice and its islands, and not the glamour, that these photographs record – perhaps the most authentic face of Venice.[176]

94 Carlo Naya, genre scene, from *L'Italie pittoresque: scènes et costumes pris d'après nature*. Albumen photograph, montage, 20.1 × 25.2 cm.

Tourism

For the tourist, however, Venice was an increasingly accessible destination, serviced by Cook's tours, Wagon-Lits railways and the Lloyd-Triestino shipping line. Baedeker's guidebooks put the mastery of cities within easy reach. Acknowledging a debt to Murray's guides, the Baedeker dealt in plainer facts, with no obtrusive value judgements, and little poetry. There is no bursting upon Venice, but, rather, a plain geographic explanation: 'Venice is situated in 45 24 N. Latitude, lies 2 and a half M. from the Mainland, in the Lagune, a shallow part of the Adriatic about 25 M. in length and 9 M. in width.'[177] Baedeker used the star system, indeed it is so associated with his guides that he is thought to have invented it. The Piazza San Marco has two stars, for example: its measurements are given together with the comment: 'On three sides it is enclosed by imposing structures which appear to form one vast marble palace, blackened by age and exposed to the weather.'[178] Only the entry on the Arsenale hints at a value judgement: 'the decline of Venice is nowhere more apparent than here.'[179]

History had blurred, becoming but a vague background to picturesque sights, gondola rides – more and more exotic in an age of steam – the ordinary people and their crafts, sea bathing, romance and even mystery. Wilkie Collins's tale *The Haunted Hotel*, published in 1879, is an early symptom of a new genre, among the first of an endless stream of books and films transporting foreigners to Venice for love and/or murder in hotel or *calle*.[180]

The conversion from palace to palace hotel is entirely up-to-date in *The Haunted Hotel* with its singular subtitle, *A Mystery of Modern Venice*. The characters are tourists living in their own hotel-world. They experience a destabilising and sinister Venice where murder takes place as if naturally, in a palace where chemical experiments are conducted in vaults below water level and a decapitated head is hidden in the chamber of a fireplace originally installed for escape from the Inquisition. The conversion of palace to hotel is described:

As the summer months advanced, the transformation of the Venetian palace into the modern hotel proceeded rapidly towards completion. The outside of the building with its fine Palladian front looking on the canal, was wisely left unaltered. Inside, as a matter of necessity, the rooms were almost rebuilt – so far at least as the size and the arrangement of them were concerned. The vast saloons were partitioned off into 'apartments' containing three or four rooms each. The broad corridors in the upper regions afforded spare space enough for rows of little bedchambers, devoted to servants and to travellers with limited means. Nothing was spared but the solid floors and the finely-carved ceiling. These last, in excellent preservation as to workmanship, merely required cleaning, and regilding here and there, to add greatly to the beauty and importance of the best rooms in the hotel.[181]

As the evil experienced when the hotel was a palace unnerves the residents, the good and pure Agnes feels its horror, and in answer to the question 'Am I right in believing that the sooner you get away from Venice the happier you will be?' replies 'You are more than right! No words can say how I long to be away from this horrible place'.[182] The possibility is a novel one. Now Venice, the Venice of tourists, could be 'a horrible place', unsafe and dangerous; it is readying itself for modern times when the tourist or the foreign resident might find the labyrinthine city threatening to the point of death.

Nevertheless, most visitors had no need to be on their guard; they came for art, leisure and honeymoons. After unification the Americans came in increasing numbers. Henry James, one of the more astute visitors, was aware of the paradoxes of the tourist trade.[183] His first visit in 1869 was 'an enchanted fortnight'. He arrived with the customary foreknowledge of the city, already possessed by the pulsating desire for Venice that marks writing up to the turn of the century – and beyond: 'of all the cities in the world [it] is the easiest to visit without going there.'[184] James admitted his ignorance of its history, although his love of Venetian painting was evident, even if in a generalised way. Perhaps his very lack of history helped him to see the water city more clearly as *contemporary*.

James had read Ruskin, indeed he had met him in 1869, but he was out of sympathy: he refers to the 'ill-humoured' late works, and the condensed edition of *The Stones of Venice* 'pitched in the nursery key ... might be supposed to emanate from an angry governess'.[185] James himself was clear and unsentimental in his perception of Venice as economically backward, but attractive by virtue of its picturesque poverty: 'The misery of Venice stands there for all the world to see; it is part of the spectacle – a thorough-going devotee of local colour might consistently say it is part of the pleasure.'[186]

In an 1882 essay James described the rampant tourism which, in fact, reflected upon the very success of the hotel programme, the railways, shipping and Baedekers that brought 'the barbarians in full possession', 'the horde of savage Germans encamped in the Piazza', then the English and the Americans. There are the 'long repasts' of the French in the Caffè Quadri (where they are out of the way), and guided tours of 'helpless captives' who 'treat the place as an orifice in a peep show'.[187]

At times, as was then fashionable, James wandered away from the asterisked sites, to 'a narrow canal in the heart of the city', where he admired 'a patch of green water and a surface of pink wall'.[188] Memorably, in his first essay of 1872, he pinpointed the scopophilia that Venice compels (taking hold as the great histories are being forgotten), a condition that comes from variety and light so that 'the mere use of one's eyes ... is happiness enough'.[189] Like the Impressionists and the Macchiaioli with their larger campaign of light, James was enamoured: 'light here is in fact a mighty magician.'[190]

After unification foreign painters, both amateur and professional, were increasingly in evidence. Edouard Manet visited in 1875 with James Tissot and painted his 'blue Venices' in the well-known areas, with a sunny, decorative, open tone.[191] He fixed on the motif of blue and white striped *pali* echoing the intense colour of summer sky and water, against the dark prows of gondolas, with the Salute in the background.

Auguste Renoir, arriving in November 1881, bestowed upon the conventional views more colour than they had seen till then, and more mobility of light, in keeping with his colour/light programme.[192] In *Piazza San Marco* (Minneapolis Institute of Arts), the Basilica almost levitates as blue-mauve shadows advance towards it, in preparation for the deepest mauve settling in the uppermost arch.

James McNeill Whistler came, bankrupted, in September 1879 with a modest commission, prepaid, to make a suite of twelve etchings. Wandering with his copperplate in hand as if it were a sketch pad, he attained one of the feats of foreign artistry in Venice in the late nineteenth century, producing etched views that are highly individual in their delicacy and shifting format. His painted nocturnes gave new mystery to the much-exposed subjects of San Marco and the Bacino.[193] Whistler's motifs seem just out of range, off-centred, distanced and somehow de-personalised, as if they had forfeited their individuality in the era of post-Romanticism. They were uniquely titled: *Upright Venice*, for example. Paintings and pastels appear under-scaled and intimate, anti-monumental, the fruits of a personal journey. The views are not so much views of architecture as of *ambiente*: the turns of the smaller canals, a worn window-ledge, or a staircase on the edge of the water. Whistler did paint some of the central views, but they too have a shifting focus, a casual quality that results from being unusually horizontal, or unusually vertical.

John Singer Sargent, born of American parents in Florence and schooled in Paris, came with the purpose of painting in autumn and winter 1880–81, and in summer 1882 – and many times afterwards.[194] In 1880 he began his distinctive paintings of Venetian figures in interior spaces, depicting the large cubic chasms of space characteristic of Venetian palaces, which he dramatised with black shadows and contrasts of light. The light makes its dramatic entrance through windows and balconies and in shafts through doors, as in the *Venetian Interior* (Pittsburg, Carnegie Institute), and the *Venetian Beadstringers* (Buffalo, Albright Knox Art Gallery). Sargent's women are at work stringing beads or threading onions, their black shawls worked into his abstraction of dark against light. Similar tonalities and angled light-effects are found in the *calli* or in the *campi*, where black-shawled women are again at work drawing water. Sargent's subjects were topical: the small *calli* and the women in the service of the tourist craft industry, or water-cartage, just before the coming of the aqueduct.

The influx of foreign artists was extraordinary: the Royal Academy in London and the Salon in Paris were flooded with Venetian views. Among Englishmen, there were the group around Frank Duveneck and Edward Poynter, painting the Salute in moonlight and the Ca' d'Oro, and Luke Fildes, who favoured folkloric figure compositions.[195] The German Ludwig Dills painted the canals, the Swede Oskar Björk favoured the market and Carl Skånberg observed the fishing boats in the Giudecca.[196] Among Americans, the Duveneck brothers were working in watercolour and etching, Robert Blum was painting the lacemakers and Charles Coleman was up on the balcony of San Marco with his eye trained on the four horses.[197]

This army of foreign painters sought its new visions of Venice and, it is true, they often found new angles and created new palettes. Essentially, they were the tourists of the picturesque, and their progeny would be many. Foreign writers also found new angles, among them, murder and mayhem and, increasingly, sickness and death as Venice was caught up in the fashions of Symbolism and became its most emblematic city.

* * *

The Restoration Debate

In these years extraordinary debates arose over issues of restoration, involving not only Venice, but an international public. If there were pressures to modernise, there were also increasingly greater pressures to preserve. It was not until the 1870s that the debits and credits of restoration and conservation were adequately theorised and debated. The Fondaco dei Turchi on the Grand Canal, restored in the 1860s, became recognised as a clear example of over-restoration; indeed, it focused the issue of inappropriate intervention for the first time. In the 1850s Ruskin had described the ancient Byzantine palace, once headquarters of the Turkish community and then a tobacco storehouse, as an 'unsightly heap . . . festering in its fall'.[198] The state of decay provoked inspired lines:

> It is a ghastly ruin; whatever is venerable or sad in its wreck being disguised by attempts to put it to present uses of the basest kind. It has been composed of arcades borne by marble shafts, and walls of brick faced with marble: but the covering stones have been torn away from it like the shroud from a corpse; and its walls, rent into a thousand chasms, are filled and refilled with fresh brickwork, and the seams and hollows are choked with clay and whitewash, oozing and trickling over the marble – itself balanced into dusty decay by the frost of the centuries. . . . [199]

The city acquired the property in 1858; it was destined to house the Correr Museum collection. The restoration undertaken between 1861 and 1869 by engineer Federico Berchet followed the principles of 'restoration' as described by Viollet-le-Duc, creating a building that never actually existed, defiantly symmetrical as the original had never been, with lateral towers and a form of triangular *merlatura* based on Turkish mosque prototypes.[200] A new set of circular Neo-Byzantine reliefs studded the façade, which was refaced with marbles, some of which had been originally part of the south façade of San Marco: all were rigorously cleaned by the 'scrape' pumicing method which was to become more and more controversial, particularly when used on San Marco. The entrance level, which had subsided virtually below water level, was raised up: a special commission was appointed to investigate this aspect.

Whenever the restoration was discussed two images were used to document the change: in the 1850s Jakob August Lorent photographed the building in an advanced state of ruin (fig. 95), and then later recorded Berchet's restoration, which makes it appear as if the building has been frozen at its point of restoration, its past obliterated and, as a consequence, its historical status virtually destroyed.[201] As Camillo Boito observed only a few years afterwards, it was 'too smooth', 'too polished', 'too complete and yet not complete', it was 'neither old, nor new' (fig. 96).[202]

95 (*below left*) Jakob August Lorent, *Fondaco dei Turchi*, 1853. Albumen photograph, 36.7 × 47 cm. Copenhagen, Kunstakademiets Bibliotek.

96 (*below right*) Fondaco dei Turchi after restoration.

It was Camillo Boito who brought together the divergent theories of restoration and took a leading position as a national expert, which he held well beyond the turn of the century.[203] He gained his first direct experience working on the church of Santa Maria e San Donato on the island of Murano in 1858. Interest in the origins of the tenth-century church, transitional between the ancient edifices of Torcello and San Marco, had been sparked by Boito's teacher, Piero Selvatico, as evidence of a new Venice growing in regional power and turned towards the East, and Arabic influence.[204] Selvatico's clear view of the admixture of styles that constituted the very originality of Venetian architecture was formed in advance of Ruskin, although both were observers of their time, particularly sensitive to the values of medieval art at the onset of a neo-Gothic revival. Santa Maria e San Donato was built in red and yellow brick, with elaborate bands of ornamentation in brick and inlaid marble, and a marble pavement that Ruskin held to be one of the miracles of Italy. In Boito's thinking, the church revealed architecture as living and organic, having a complexity of influence and expression, although in removing later accretions, including sundry chapels that had been added to the main body of the church, and Baroque overpainting and stucco work, he privileged the original medieval fabric.[205] But not with the sentimentality that Ruskin brought to the church, in Boito's view; the Englishman's passion for colour and patina risked reducing it to a curiosity shop: it falsified history; it misrepresented the monument which becomes no less than a lie.[206]

The distinction between conservation, favouring the original state, and restoration, which actually altered and completed a building, was to be the crucial issue that changed practice. In 1877 an essay destined to be of great importance in the history of conservation in *any* city was published by the Venetian Alvise Zorzi, with a preface by Ruskin that demonstrated the Englishman's importance in influencing ideas, particularly concerning San Marco.[207] Zorzi's *Osservazzioni intorno ai ristauri interni ed esterni della Basilica di San Marco* (Observations on the Internal and External Restoration of the Basilica of San Marco) was dedicated to Ruskin who had financed the project. Ruskin wrote an address to 'my dear friend', which was published as an introduction:

> I cannot enough thank you for the admirable care and completeness with which you have exposed the folly of this throwing away the priceless marbles of the original structure, and explained to your readers every point relating to the beauty and durability of such materials. Your analysis of the value of colours produced by age, is new in art and literature, and cannot possibly be better done.[208]

Zorzi called for an end to the practice of rebuilding old fabrics and the careless treatment of original materials. In line with the reactions against the theory and practice of Viollet-le-Duc, he argued for *conservare* against *ristorare* and invoked the training of the historian and archaeologist against the ignorant restorer, with specific quotation and refutation of Viollet-le-Duc's procedures.[209] A vital premise in the debate remained the sensitivity to original materials and the acceptance of time and age as active factors in the reception of architecture, in clear opposition to the Fondaco dei Turchi project. A further crucial distinction was made between an architectural monument and a museum of architecture, between a *monumento architettonico* and a *museo di architettura*.[210] Buildings designated as 'museum' architecture needed special attention.

The question of San Marco and its restoration did not remain a Venetian issue. In 1879 the English Society for the Protection of Ancient Buildings took up the issue, and William Morris drew attention in the British press to alterations proposed to the west façade of San Marco.[211] Morris added another element to the classification of key buildings when he described the Basilica as an ancient edifice that was not merely a work of art and a monument of a history, but 'a piece of nature': such monuments were at one time unnatural to the site, but over time they had become sacred, virtually removed from human manufacture. Morris wrote to Ruskin, to Robert Browning and to Gladstone, arousing the ire of the Ministry of Public Instruction in Italy, which accused the English of meddling.[212] Morris wrote to *The Times* to vindicate English interest in San Marco after his concern with the restoration of the pavement brought the charge of 'meddling'.[213]

Boito published a major article in the intellectual journal *Nuova Antologia*, accusing the English in particular of ignorance of the true state of the programme when they accused the Italians of being barbarians.[214] The love of patina and colour was certainly a great quality in Venetian architecture and painting; Boito had extolled it on many occasions. But what if the structure collapses? Ruskin's notions were preconceived, marred by sentimentality. So-called patina was often just dirt: Boito reminded his readers of the practices of the Venetian republic, which twice annually – for Christmas and Easter – had the interior mosaics of San Marco cleaned of the build-up of soot and oil. San Marco's chief restorer, Giambattista Meduna, appointed in 1857, tried to defend himself in the prestigious British *Building News* against 'the anathemas and censures which had been hurled against what had been done'.[215] Meduna's career in many respects had been a distinguished one, but he was, in effect, dismissed, and a new conservation project was put in place. In the meantime the view of Venetian architecture as art, history, archaeology *and* nature had been absorbed by the Venetians and polemicised in a pamphlet on the value of monuments and their future.[216] At the forefront of the discussion were the oppositional terms – *ristorare*, and *conservare*. But it was *repristino*, to restore in the sense of renewing and consolidating that was preferred practice. The pumice – or the means of over-cleaning surfaces, the process of *lucidatura*, was also central. And another term was heard increasingly: *sventramento* – demolition.

A test case arose in the late 1870s with the proposal to demolish the high Baroque church of San Moisè, the work of Alessandro Tremignon, completed in 1726. The façade was a complex sculpture, swathed in garlands with camels guarding the portal: it was the most ornate in Venice. Zorzi again intervened with an eloquent pamphlet against the demolition, protesting against the taste of the time that could condemn any architectural styles, since Venice had need for *both* the beautiful and the ugly.[217] Selvatico regarded San Moisè as 'the culmination of every architectural madness' – an *infelice costruzione* with 'detestable' external sculpture.[218] Predictably, Ruskin loathed San Moisè: 'one of the basest examples of the basest school of the Renaissance',[219] but it was the clergy, faced with the repair of the building, who had urged its demolition. It was also in the path of the proposed Via 22 Marzo.

Zorzi argued that the building was indeed the result of the 'mad fantasy of the epoch of decadent architecture', but that the ugly was of interest; that Venice demonstrated the full variety of architecture; and that no city was more *bizarre*.[220] It was, after all, a 'museum of the open air' (this phrase would be used repeatedly in subsequent years, but more and more for the purpose of excluding new building), and thus the beautiful and the ugly must be conserved equally. Zorzi listed the many styles in existence around the Piazza San Marco – a strategy that would be used for different purposes by many after him – from the *terrifico* prison and the *elegante* Ponte della Paglia, to the *gigantesco* of the Campanile. The opportunity to point out how much of the patrimony had been lost since 1800 was not lost.[221] In a notable victory running counter to prevailing taste, San Moisè was preserved by the intervention of the Commune.[222]

Next to San Marco, the most prized building in Venice was the Palazzo Ducale: for Ruskin it was the greatest building in the world. He had been appalled by the whitewashing in 1845; in 1852 he doubted that 'the Ducal Palace will stand 5 years more – its capitals are so rent and worn'.[223] For Camillo Boito, writing in 1882, the Palazzo Ducale was the most beautiful of palaces, having solemnity and sweetness in its extended harmony; being audacious in construction, but with elegance of detail;

exhibiting a taste for allegory, but also having a capricious spirit; having a heart that beats.[224] It was the blood and body of ancient Venice.

The restoration of the Palazzo Ducale never inspired the passion that San Marco aroused.[225] The principal restorer, Annibale Forcellini, was praised for his work from 1876 as he attended to the major problems of cracking and decay of the capitals – those on the ground-floor loggia that Ruskin had so fulsomely described in *The Stones of Venice*.[226] Using a buttressing wooden scaffold, the worn originals were removed and preserved, and substitute capitals put in place in one of the first instances of using facsimile casts *in situ*.[227] Forcellini argued discreetly for the practice, and aged the new intrusions so that they did not appear so.[228] The Porta della Carta, the elaborate Gothic gateway adjacent to San Marco, was renewed by sculptor Luigi Ferrari, with substitute figures of Doge Foscari and the lion of St Mark.

As the work at the Palazzo Ducale demonstrated, the practice of substituting originals by facsimiles proved acceptable: and so it has remained, in the face of collapse or fire in the later century, when the Campanile fell, for example, or La Fenice burned. The most controversial aspect of the Palazzo Ducale restoration lay in establishing the legitimacy of historic alterations, which in turn involved the acceptance of a pure form of the building in its earliest stages. The distinction was judged to be between his-torical value and antique value.[229] In particular, archaeological concerns arose with respect to three windows on the south side, which Forcellino wanted to brick in since they were not part of the original; he was opposed by Camillo Boito who wrote about the matter in detail in *La Nuova Antologia*, advocating the restoration of the tri-floreate windows evident in the painting of Gentile Bellini and in the Barbari map, then held to be the work of Dürer.[230] The wall built by Antonio da Ponte to stabilise the building after the fire of 1577 should also be removed in line with the policy of eliminating later excrescences.

The Polemics of Conservation

The issues of restoration were not of course exclusive to Venice: Rome had the Forum; Milan was at work on the completion of its cathedral; Florence was completing the façade of the Duomo, Santa Maria del Fiore and Santa Croce.[231] Around 1875 a national conservation organisation was established, creating the position of an inspec-tor of Excavations and Monuments and a Commission for Conservation for Monu-ments.[232] In 1883 the Congress of Architects and Engineers proposed a *Carta del Restauro*, largely the work of Camillo Boito.[233] It was he who effected the legislation, calling for national laws of preservation in the same spirit of developing authority that he had made his celebrated call for a national style of architecture for united Italy. He put forward his arguments in *Nuova Antologia* in 1885, using an easily accessible dialogue, as in one of his short stories – his protagonists chat and make comparative comments on how different governments handle their heritage.[234]

The recommendations were crucial for modern practice: consolidation and repair were endorsed as sound practice, with renovations or additions only if absolutely nec-essary, and then they must appear distinct. Existing work – marbles, mosaics, paint-ings – must be respected, and every stage of alteration and repair be documented by photographs, watercolours or other means, and copies lodged with the appropriate authorities and the Ministero della Pubblica Construzione. It was the debates on Venice, and San Marco in particular, that were very largely the impetus for such resolutions. The practice of documentation had a firm precedent in Carlo Naya's photographs of Giotto's Arena Chapel frescoes in Padua.[235] In Venice a flurry of diligent copyists descended on San Marco, inspired, or paid by Ruskin, attending to its delineation in detail before it changed.[236]

As polemics of preservation proliferated, the debate increasingly focused on demolition – *sventramento* – which was pitted against preservation – or *salvaguardi*. One year after Zorzi's *Osservazione*, Paolo Fambri wrote on the future of Venice, *L'Avvenire di Venezia*, a title to become almost as common in the next decades as *Il Problema di Venezia* after the flood of 1966.[237] Fambri sensibly contextualised the conservation debate within the concerns for the city's poor economic state. His essay was a call-to-arms, a reminder of recent perfidies balanced by a longer view of Venetian resilience and the slow history of environmental adaptation within the lagoon. That survival was both physical and mental. Fambri recalled the recent revisions of Venetian history by Lady Eastlake in the *Edinburgh Review*, when she defended Venice against Darù, James Fenimore Cooper and Victor Hugo (evidence that the Venetians did take note of these foreign views). He looked to the talented figures of the Republic's last century, recalling Angelo Querini, the friend of Voltaire, Marco Foscarini, one of the most illustrious doges, and Marco Barbaro, working to reform penal laws – as if to counter views of the decadence of the late Republic.[238]

Fambri's recommendations were radical and divided the reformists and the conservationists still further. He argued that part of the lagoon, the so-called *laguna morta*, should be filled in and cultivated, following Dutch models of reclamation.[239] An active policy of immigration should be pursued to aid commercial viability. The alternative to such initiatives was to watch the population of Venice shrink to that of ancient Torcello – a prophetic comment.[240] The lagoon could not be guaranteed forever.

At this point rumours that the Grand Canal was to become a boulevard had spread internationally. Camillo Sitte mentioned the canal scheme in *The Birth of Modern City Planning* – that seminal text in urban planning in which traditional Venice, and the Piazza in particular, had a paradigmatic role. Sitte asked: 'What would Venice be without water? If the barbaric project to fill in her canals had been carried out, the artistic and spiritually edifying splendour of Venice would have been buried with it.'[241]

Increasingly the condition and fate of ancient monuments took precedence over modernisation, and again it was not a subject confined to Venice. In 1893 a definitive account of the modern restorations of San Marco was presented in a monumental series, under the direction of Camillo Boito, published by Ferdinando Ongania in Italian, French and then English.[242] Ongania was the most important bookseller and publisher in Venice in the late nineteenth century. Issued in French and English, the San Marco volumes are one of the great publication projects of their time, revolutionary in their use of high-quality photography.[243] It was something of a public relations exercise also, intended to convince an audience that the patrimony was under protection. Federico Berchet detailed the vicissitudes and lack of historical understanding of restoration after the fall of the Republic, recalling the Austrian auction of jewels from the Basilica's treasury to fund repairs to the roof.[244] The account of the conservation of the mosaic work denounced the introduction of new materials and the banal efforts made to complete the portal lunettes of the *Last Judgement* in the fifth bay. Pietro Saccardo, who contributed the section on the mosaics, declared the new work by Lattanzio Querena to be 'void of effect and its execution quite unworthy of the place, as it was carried out with materials of all kinds'.[245] Even the ancient art of mosaics had been subjected to the vulgar interpolation of raw new materials. It was the Ruskin/Zorzi view of conservation that Ongania's publications promoted and consolidated.

Zorzi, in his 1877 publication, had petitioned for an authority to be established for San Marco and a committee had been appointed by the Minister for Public Instruction; two dedicated local conservationists, Federico Berchet and Pompeo Molmenti, were members. Heading the report was a declaration of the historical principle that 'Preservation ought to prevail over . . . reconstruction'.[246] In response to the primary criticism of new material in an old building, it was determined that 'the veneering of the walls shall be replaced with marble of the same kind as that taken down'.[247]

The focus on preservation led to growing criticism of new intrusions into Venice. Traditionalists won a victory in the matter of the base of the Campanile, traditionally a place of makeshift awnings and shops for traders, which were now ordered to be demolished. But the plans for a *caffè* in iron and glass were not approved.[248] For some, cast iron was the mark of progress and survival; for others, it was intrusive and destroyed the real Venice. The price of preserving the past was eventually to frustrate virtually any entrance of the present and to paralyse many plans for new building in the following century.

Past and Present, Molmenti and Favretto

No less than its parents, the generation born after the siege of Venice was notable for its patriotism. One of the most ardent conservationists and scholars of old Venice was Pompeo Molmenti (a nephew of the painter); his father had contributed to the defence of Venice in 1848–9, just a few years before Pompeo's birth in 1852. Molmenti was a contemporary and close friend of the painter Giacomo Favretto, born in 1849, conceived in the fighting months of the Revolution.[249]

The first new histories of nineteenth-century Venice were being written during the childhood years of Molmenti and Favretto. Unification with Italy meant liberation of the city from foreign domination, ending a recent chapter of its history. To celebrate and institutionalise the city and its history within unified Italy, the Deputazione Veneta di Storia Patria was founded in 1874. In 1878 it began publishing Sanudo's monumental diary (in fifty-eight volumes), under the guidance of Rinaldo Fulin (these were the volumes the Austrians had so coveted).[250] A conservatory of music named for Benedetto Marcello was founded, and a faculty of commerce, the Regia Scuola Superiore di Commercio, became the first department of the University of Venice at Ca' Foscari.[251]

In 1877, in this climate of renewal and local learning, the deputation organised a thematic competition for a written work on the 'Private life of Venice up to the fall of the Republic with special attention to the influence and interchange of the Government and the People'. This, the Querini-Stampalia prize, was organised by Rinaldo Fulin, a key intellectual in Venice during these years. The premise was of some interest in that it implied that the interchange of ruler and ruled was positive and not a feature of a despotic and inquisitional Venice. Pompeo Molmenti was awarded the prize for what was to be a widely translated three-volume study, *La storia nella vita privata dalle origini alla caduta della Repubblica* (The History of Venice in Private Life up to the Fall of the Republic).[252] The three volumes covered the foundations and medieval Venice, *La Grandezza*; the Renaissance, *Lo Splendore*; and the decline, *Il Decadimento*, from the early seventeenth century to 1797. Molmenti's use of a range of archives, both public and private, as well as modern photographic techniques to give a broad visual base to his study, were exemplary features of a historiography with a sociological thrust. Among his wide-ranging themes were the transformation of costume, the family, dwellings and furniture, economy, finance and money, warring armies and civic festivals, sanitary conditions, love and conversation, and, in line with his own times, the arts of industry.

Molmenti was writing about views of the city and its domestic and public life at the time when his close friend, the painter Giacomo Favretto, was painting canvases of such subjects in contemporary life. The *popolani* were already conspicuously featured in photographic studies: the verism of that new art preceded the painters' interest in the subject of everyday life, recommended some two decades earlier by Selvatico. Selvatico's influence in the Academy, espousing modern themes and techniques, inspired Favretto and the painter Pompeo Marino Molmenti, one of his most important teachers, who encouraged the painting of everyday life. Favretto's first subjects were drawn from the studios of the Academy, the subject closest to him, then extended to vendors *en plein air* – fruit and vegetable sellers, traders in antiques and sellers of birds who set up their booths in the *calli* and *campi*, spreading out their goods by doorways. One of Favretto's favourite themes, often repeated, shows well-wishers waiting for a wedding party to emerge from a parish church and be swept off in a gondola.[253]

With the same ease with which he attended to the working classes and the local wedding party, Favretto painted the Republic's last century, that aristocratic past, as though the street vendor of the 1870s and 1880s were to be associated with the exemplary figures of the old order. The return to Tiepolo and the aristocracy of painting was encouraged by Pompeo Molmenti, who in 1880 assembled a volume of essays called *Tiepolo: la Villa Valmarano*, illustrated by Favretto's line drawings.[254] An important shift in taste to values predating the Neoclassical occurs: Selvatico had already praised Tiepolo, which clearly had an impact on a generation of his students at the Academy: 'Many people will be surprised that I, who venerate the pure artists of the fourteenth century, should have given such abundant praise to the Baroque-infected [*imbarocchito*] Tiepolo', he lectured.[255] And in response to Molmenti, and doubtless Selvatico, Camillo Boito in 1881 praised Tiepolo's 'insolence of fantasy' and his 'feverish curiosity'.[256] One of Favretto's successful early pictures was painted at the time when the restoration of Venice was a subject of international interest – *Il Vandalismo: poveri antichi* (Vandalism: Poor Antiques; private collection) shows a painter restoring Tiepolo's *Madonna del Carmelo*. Favretto paints *alla macchia*, with heightened colour and bravura brushstrokes updating Tiepolo, rendering him a retrospective homage, like Manet before his historical models of Titian and Velázquez.

97 Antonio dal Zotto, monument to Carlo Goldoni, Campo San Bartolomeo, 1893.

Tiepolo blue is intensified. Division of labour in the male and female worlds is also the subject: a women in blue sits concentrating on her lacemaking, back turned to the male painter at his post-Tiepolo task.

Favretto's painting was not just a stylistic revival inevitable in a period of interest in the *macchia*; it was a return to eighteenth-century subject matter and the restitution of the Republic, glamorous again after a hundred years. It was inevitable that Favretto be linked to Goldoni, but in no sense does he alone effect a revival, for Goldoni had rarely left the boards of the Venetian theatre. Nevertheless, once again Goldoni infused Venice with local values, inspiring new plays in its vernacular.[257] The grandparents and parents of the actress Eleanora Duse played Goldoni, and she herself kept his plays at the forefront of her own repertoire.[258] Wagner in 1858 saw *Le Baruffe chiozziotte* at the Malibran theatre, and of course remembered that Goethe had enjoyed the same play at the same place.[259] At the time that Favretto was painting *Il primo passo di Goldoni* in 1887, Zotto's genial statue of the playwright had been positioned in busy Campo Bartolommeo for five years, striding out above the crowds, smiling (fig. 97).[260] And indeed Molmenti had written a small book to commemorate the statue, noting that in 1875 a committee was formed to erect a monument to the renewal of Italian theatre and they saw fit to propose Goldoni, 'an incomparable model of the painting of

98 Giacomo Favretto, *El Liston*, 1884. Oil on canvas, 81 × 155 cm. Rome, Galleria Nazionale d'Arte Moderna.

truth': 'no name was more popular, no glory more universally recognised'.[261] The Venetians were proud of his national status: Giosué Carducci, regarded virtually as the national poet, wrote a set of four sonnets that are almost a miniature biography of Goldoni, taking him on a journey through his life, to his exile in Paris in winter where he imagines the *dolce lume* smiling on San Marco, and the gilded canals, and he dies not knowing the fate of the Republic, ignorant of the completed tragedy involving the exit of the doge.[262]

Favretto painted eighteenth-century lovers meeting on the Ponte degli Paglia near the sculptures at the corner of the Ducal Palace, with figures appropriately costumed; the famous *passeggiata* in the Piazzetta appears in the painting called *El Liston* of 1884 (fig. 98). Its horizontal format accommodates an animated frieze of figures in the heart of Venice, graciously costumed, with Sansovino's Loggetta in the background. Favretto became one of Venice's most distinguished cultural exports, seen in national and international exhibitions in the 1880s in Milan, Rome, Turin, the Glaspalaste at Munich and the Paris exhibitions of 1879 and 1889. A *Liston Moderno* (private collection) was among his last paintings.[263] In this modern *passeggiata*, as charming and vivacious as its Republican counterpart, the portal of San Marco appears atmospherically in the background; the top hats of the bourgeois and the cap of the worker replace the eighteenth-century headgear, and modern nannies hold the baby fresh from a christening in the Basilica. Shortly after Favoretto's death King Umberto of Italy acquired the work for his collection of patriotic pictures. At the 1887 Venice international exhibition, the eighteenth-century *Liston* was shown with another of Favretto's panoramas, the *Traghetto della Maddalena* (private collection), painted from the window of Favretto's palazzetta on the Grand Canal, at the spot where the gondoliers ferried passengers across the Grand Canal. It was the decade of threat to the gondolier, who is shown going about his everyday work at the *traghetto* without undue glamour, not ferrying the tourist, but the local people. Favoretto's *esposizione* trilogy *alla venezianità* was completed with a vertical format canvas of the Easter Fair on the Rialto bridge (private collection), a subject popular in contemporary illustration.[264]

Favretto established the popularity of Venetian genre painting far beyond Venice, with his warm, palpable figures and informal subjects. His paintings were sensual and sexual: the easy-going meeting of vendors and their girlfriends in the *calle*, and narrative pictures that dwelt lightly on jealousy and rivalry among women for their men. For the Venetians who revered him, Favretto was the painter who saw the local people as vibrant and beautiful; he painted the past as if it were still graciously alive, still linked with contemporary Venice. He moved close to his subjects, away from the panorama, attending only to his city, its urbanity, its indigenous life where the tourist might be thought irrelevant. In 1887 Venice mourned his premature death at the age of thirty-eight.[265]

Disappearing Venice and the Custodians of the Past

Favretto's friend the scholar Pompeo Molmenti was also a delegate to the national parliament, and until his death in 1927 the fiercest defender of Venetian heritage.[266] Beyond the issue of single buildings, and San Marco in particular, he widened his reference to the whole city, which was frequently invoked at the discussion table and the subject of pamphlets and essays. Within the culture of modernisation through demolition, of *risanamento*, the danger of loss of the overall history of Venice was voiced increasingly. This attention paid to *Venezia scomparsa* came from local residents prepared to challenge the planned demolition for improved sanitation and communication. Pamphlets and articles argued for the retention of whole tracts of the city, and a stop to indiscriminate destruction. The polemics drew attention to a Venice beyond the well-known monuments, to a *Venezia minore*, a Venice that was *ambiente*. The architectural past was not held to be restricted to buildings of architectural merit, but increasingly identified as the city's overall fabric.

It was Camillo Boito who made one of the first sustained pleas for arresting the disappearance of old Venice in an essay published in the *Nuova Antologia* in 1872.[267] Boito's interests were wide-ranging, and embraced not only painting and architecture, but, in line with his principles, the crafts.[268] Thus his reviews for the *Nuova Antologia*, one of the most prestigious journals in united Italy, offered a range of articles to a varied readership, including international subscribers.[269] More than Ruskin, more than William Morris, it was Boito who laid the foundations of Italian restoration and preservation in Venice with the 1883 *Carta del Restaura*, the first such set of guidelines for restoration.[270] His fourth recommendation empowered the artist rather than the architectural historian as the arbiter of aesthetic matters, concerning 'beauty, singularity, the poetry of every aspect of the variety of marbles, mosaics, of painting, of aged colours . . .'[271] Although his aesthetic concern did not pertain only to Venice, it reflected the recent controversies surrounding San Marco.

After his first work in Venice, Boito's practice was largely in Milan.[272] His principal architectural work in Venice was the Gothic staircase in the renovated Palazzo Cavalli-Franchetti, completed in 1886, an extravagant historicist intervention making heavy use of marbled inlays (fig. 99).[273] But the staircase is not a specific exercise in *venezianità*: rather it suggests central European taste in the use of heavy grained marbles, four-part vaulted ceilings, elaborate bordering and inset sculptures of the liberal arts.[274] The use of wrought iron and the iron heraldic sculpture of the Franchetti griffin indicate a pride in industrial materials.

Boito was also an effective critic of changes to the Venetian environment: he helped to create a new poetics of the *ambiente*. In an 1872 article in the *Nuova Antologia*, he argued not just for the importance of historic buildings and sympathetic renewal through conservation, but for the totality of Venice as a landscape, always animated by its unique water. Its architecture was an architecture of gaiety, light-hearted and diverting. Modern intrusions were particularly inappropriate: Torelli's proposed carriageway along the Riva degli Schiavoni was 'an obscenity'.[275] Venice is categorically not suited to the new; it is the city for restoration and not for new building.[276] The

iron bridge built in 1869 at the Ponte del Paradiso, below a Gothic relief of the Madonna in a pointed arch spanning the *calle*, was deplored, and indeed it was demolished in 1901.[277] The Fondaco dei Turchi was criticised, but beside it came a nomination of an ideal restoration: the Scala del Bovolo, the external spiral staircase of the Palazzo Contarini.

In 1882, again in the *Nuova Antologia*, Boito wrote about two districts that had been particularly affected by industrial developments: the island of Sant'Elena at the east end of San Marco, and the area of Santa Marta in the opposite direction, in the vicinity of the railway and the new maritime port.[278] For Boito, modern intrusions challenged artistic sentiment, offended the picturesque, the poetic and the romantic, which constituted nothing less than the essence of the Venetian spirit. The cotton factory at Santa Marta and the factory for constructing railway carriages at Sant' Elena were the principal offenders, but the opportunity to attack Luigi Torelli was not lost either: he had been responsible for demolitions around the absidal area of Santi Giovanni e Paolo in the name of 'aeration of streets', and he had illuminated the crypt of San Marco with gaslight.

By the late 1880s, as foreign painters and writers extolled the Venetian picturesque, a need to 'defend Venice' had cohered. The city and its lagoon had become a battlefield where past and present were ranged as enemies, mutually destructive. With shifting degrees of intensity, the fight would continue through the next century; but the modern cause was largely lost.

Chapter 6

LOVE, ART AND DEATH IN
FIN-DE-SIECLE VENICE

Wagner's Death in Venice

Wagner first stayed in Venice in 1858 when he wrote the famous second act of *Tristan und Isolde*. It was his 'first conversation with death'.[1] He returned in 1882, and died on 13 February 1883 at the Palazzo Vendramin-Calergi.[2] That death was destined for literature: it became a theme for influential Symbolist writers: for Gabriele D'Annunzio, whose Venetian novel *Il Fuoco* (The Fire) was published in 1900; for Maurice Barrès, whose *La Mort de Venise* was published in 1903; and, at least indirectly, for Thomas Mann's 1911 *Death in Venice*, which tells of a musician meeting his death in the *Lagunenstadt*.[3] Friedrich Nietzsche declared that his *Thus Spake Zarathustra*, which 'might be reckoned as music', was completed 'precisely at that *sacred hour* [my italics] when Richard Wagner died in Venice'.[4]

As Wagner wrote to Liszt from Geneva on 24 August 1858, during his first residence, 'Venice is notoriously the quietest, i.e. most noiseless city in the world, which has decided me in its favour'.[5] Intimations from that visit played into the hands of mythologists when he recounted his first view of a gondola, associated unerringly and unoriginally with death in a climate of cholera: 'black on black, the actual sight of one was still a rude surprise. . . .' (fig. 100).[6] But it was the composition of the second act of *Tristan und Isolde* (his express purpose in seeking the quietness there), and its association with the song of the gondolier, that compounded the mythology. Wagner recorded a sleepless night when he heard the gondoliers echoing each other's calls in 'a strange, melancholy dialogue'; another time, as he was on the water in moonlight, he heard his own gondolier singing:

> Suddenly from his breast came a mournful sound not unlike the howl of an animal, swelling up from a deep, low note, and after a long-sustained 'Oh', it culminated in the simple musical phrase 'Venezia'. This was followed by some words I could not retain in my memory, being so greatly shaken by the emotion of the moment. Such were the impressions that seemed most characteristic of Venice to me during my stay, and they remained with me until the completion of the second act of Tristan, and perhaps even helped to inspire the long-drawn-out lament for the shepherd's horn at the beginning of the third act.[7]

Upon arriving for the final visit on 28 September 1882 Wagner wrote to Liszt assuring him that Venice 'has not disappointed my expectations'. The day after his return, Cosima Wagner (after her customary comment on the sort of night Wagner had passed) recorded: 'Following a good night, delight in Venice, our curious apartments pleases us, and a walk he takes to San Marco around Midday utterly enchants him; we are in no doubt that this is the loveliest place of all.'[8]

Visiting Wagner in those last months, Franz Liszt composed quintessential pieces of music in anticipation of Wagner's death. Two piano works, both having the title *Lugubrious Gondola*, were written when Liszt was staying at the Palazzo Vendramin-Calergi: he records seeing a gondola-hearse from the window.[9] The pieces are

prophetic of the fascination with Venice and death, Wagner's in particular.[10] After the event, and in similar mode with related rhythms and harmonies, Liszt composed *Richard Wagner, Venezia*. Long before, in 1839, Liszt had been one of the many to respond to the lilting song on the water 'La Biondina in Gondoleta', adapting it in his piano suite *Années de Pèlerinage*. Now the winter of old age had followed the springtime, as emblematically for Venice as for Liszt and Wagner. In Liszt's late works all is stripped away to leave but a glimmer of a rocking barcarolle, sunk to low bass notes and spare harmonies.

What followed from the death of Wagner in Venice (and continued well into the next century) was the urge to anthologise, to cite precedents and to proclaim the virtual inevitability of the composer's demise there rather than in any other city. It was a compelling theme for artists; the ultimate seal bestowed on Venice as an *art* city was an illustrious death.[11] Wagner's death was the first act in the plenitudinous *fin de siècle* that Venice would host, and the associated decadence that would make death in Venice a virtual expectation in the next century.[12]

As D'Annunzio tells it in *Il Fuoco*, Wagner is taken ill on the Lido in the area of San Nicolò. The young poet Stelio and his friend observe his difficulties and help him, carrying him to his gondola, but he dies later. The poet-hero Stelio hears as he is returning from the lagoon: 'The bells of St Mark's rang out the angelic Salutation, and their powerful tolling faded into drawn-out waves over the still crimson lagoon which they were leaving in the power of shadow and death.'[13] Stelio's friend awaits him to say that Richard Wagner is dead.

It was Maurice Barrès who most clearly associated Wagner and Venice with decadence and death, embellishing the conjunction that Wagner had made in the visit of 1858. Later in the century, as the fevers of the night rose up from the lagoon and Barrès was on the Grand Canal beneath the Palazzo Giustiniani, he savoured the post-Wagnerian emotion and experienced the mysterious nature of Wagner's genius.[14] Venice reveals itself as the night clouds are mirrored in the water and the church of the Salute appears like a phantom, breathing a sour anthem of aridity and nostalgia.[15] The exhumations were perceived more surely by Barrès than by Wagner; but Wagner's power to incite imaginative fantasies was undeniable. As one of the great decadent talents of his time, he had the effect of immuring the city further in decadence and necrophilia, compounding its reputation as a city of sexual excess and a place for artists. Beyond all places, it became the appropriate venue for the *fin de siècle*.[16]

*　　*　　*

After Wagner: The Lagunenstadt

For Nietzsche Venice was, quite simply, the city of music; he felt this through Peter Gast, his composer friend who left Munich for Venice in 1872 – the 'maestro' Nietzsche called him – and he made every effort to set up a performance of Gast's comic opera, *The Lion of Venice.*[17] Nietzsche visited Venice (and Gast) four times, and his utterances touched the city, and influenced other writers.[18] And of course he knew of Wagner's visits and grappled with the reputation of Wagner as Musician of the Future, as well as the pre-eminent talent of the present.[19] Nietzsche could write with total conviction: 'when I seek another word for music, I never find any other word than Venice.'[20]

In 1880, during his first visit, Nietzsche claimed that Venice had the best street paving, and 'shadows like a forest'; his room was '22 feet high and peaceful, like the end of the world'.[21] The city at its heart in Piazza San Marco seduced him, occasioning positive, lyrical thoughts, as in 'Mein Glück,' the first of his Venetian poems. In an ecstatic claim for personal happiness, he wrote that the Piazza San Marco was 'the handsomest study I ever had'.[22]

Nietzsche responded to the gondola's song with fresh wonder: 'Gondellied' was written in November or December 1889 from the Rialto bridge, from which he heard echoes of Tasso's famous songs:[23] 'Lately I stood on the bridge / In the brown night. / From afar there came a song . . .'[24] The intensity of the experience inevitably recalls Wagner's account of hearing the gondolier's song: it is not plaintive, rather it leaves him trembling 'with bright happiness'. The poem was included in *Ecce Homo* where it comes as a highly emotional point in a largely aphoristic text; the lagoon carries an imprecise but laden meaning; music is the transcendental expression. Venice is also clearly associated in Nietzsche's mind with artists of all types, as he writes in discussion of enthusiasts for Venice against Rome, listing Delacroix, Shakespeare, Byron, George Sand and Gautier – and Wagner of course.[25]

Yet beyond the Rialto bridge and the Piazza San Marco, Nietzsche's Venice is a strange almost surreal place at the end of the world, emptied out, beyond time, a place where Nietzsche, in deteriorating health, found solace and respite. Venice is liberated by virtue of its amphibious foundation, built amid marshes and stagnant water, but for Nietzche Venice was also the projection of human melancholy: 'all is now motionless, flat, dejected, gloomy, like the lagoon of Venice.'[26] The emphasis is contemporary, and important: the awareness of the outer waters in which Venice is set, the source of miasma, the immense, lonely beautiful stretches of flat water and barely emergent land that is still the setting for an immensely sophisticated and built-up city. The awareness of the lagoon, the exploitation of the lagoon as a poetic site: this is a condition of the late nineteenth century, in preparation for an ideology of conservation one hundred years later.

The lagoon distanced from humanity provoked Nietzsche's cleansing perception of the city, as if he penetrated to a primordial Venice: 'one hundred profound solitudes form together the city of Venice – that is its enchantment'.[27] There is little preoccupation with decay, with a Venice clogged and disintegrating. Melancholy, yes, but Nietzsche acknowledged the death of Venice by implication, passed over it, transcended it and discovered a posthumous city: the lagoon city living on, facing out to sea, released from history. The environment offered respite: an image for the 'man of the future'.[28] Venice was 'a solitary felicitous island'.[29] An obduracy born of the toughness that forged the city remained as a historic dimension, still part of the present. Thus it offered an example of the survival of human beings 'living together and thrown on their own resources': 'a type becomes fixed and strong, through protracted struggle against constant unfavourable conditions.'[30]

Nietzsche's relevance for Venice has remained. Some one hundred years later the philosopher Massimo Cacciari, mayor of the city of Venice from 1993 to 2000, gave a compelling interpretation. He uncovered in Nietzsche a resistance to the traditional face of a decadent city that released a kind of a utopia, a sense of a city forced into a renewal of itself.[31] Cacciari's views are among the most interesting and resonant, not least because Nietzsche appears as a determinant of Cacciari's own presence in Venice, compelled to seek renewal and serenity in the lagoon city. Perhaps the *Übermensch* visits the city, wills its resurgence, pushes it toward salvation, even more valid, more urgent for Cacciari, writing in the late twentieth century, than for Nietzsche.

Rather than utopia or posthumous life, Venice offered the spectacle of physical and moral decline to Maurice Barrès.[32] His writing became known in France in the 1880s, and like many members of his generation he entirely embraced the excesses of Wagner (in contrast, to Nietzsche's increasingly critical view), relishing his 'sentiments extrêmes'. His first visit to Venice was in part the matter of the autobiographical writing *Un Homme libre* of 1889: by his own admission, Barrès 'triumphed' in Venice on that visit, declaring his true self to be no less than Tiepolo.[33] But the most influential writing, *La Mort de Venise*, was published in 1903 in the work entitled *Amori et dolori sacrum*, a kind of journal of visits undertaken during the 1890s, in sentiment wholly of the *fin de siècle*.

For Barrès, Venice was not a seat of history, the fallen site of republicanism, nor a world centre for the new sports of bathing and tourism: it was *the* art city, fascinating in its cloying decadence. He basked in the aura of his artistic forerunners, listing his 'Pantheon' of great visitors, his 'Council of Ten', mostly French, of course, but he also admitted Goethe and Byron – with Chateaubriand, Musset and George Sand, the painter Léopold Robert, Gautier, Taine – and Wagner, evidence indeed that the nineteenth century had forged its own post-republic history.[34] (Marcel Proust remarked with some justification that Ruskin was conspicuously absent from Barrès's Venetian Pantheon.[35])

The geography of the lagoon and its outer islands separated from the cosmopolitan lights of the city becomes part of an itinerary of disease which Barrès followed in *La Mort de Venise*, bestowing such evocative titles as 'An Evening amid the silence and the winds of death', and 'Song of beauty moving towards death'.[36] Venice was both an erotic space and a literary space.[37] Like Chateaubriand before him, Barrès used his itinerary as the unabashed structure of his writing. After the cemetery island came Murano, where Barrès made one of his few comments on contemporary Venice, claiming that Murano was degraded by virtue of its industry. He proceeded to Mazzorbo, at that time dominated by a Benedictine convent and linked to Burano by a wooden bridge, as it is today, then to Torcello, which, by virtue of being deserted, he found 'wrapped in a wind more tragic than can be experienced in Ravenna'. He visited the outer islands – the Isola delle Donne – where bones from churchyards had been deposited; the site of Anania, the legendary submerged island; and San Francesco del Deserto, the island of the Franciscan monks, which appeared as 'the most sublime of desolations'.

Barrès's *paludisme* is an untranslatable notion referring to the stagnant waters and the malaria-infested islands of the lagoon, picking up the fatal miasmas associated with stagnancy and evening emissions productive of fever and hallucination. In his lugubrious pages, *paludisme* became topical by virtue of the admixture of the sublime and the desolate and the relevance of the environmental theory that linked disease with exhalations of foul air. Venice now had a contemporary itinerary of disease: we recall the 1830s when cholera was first experienced, when Alfred de Musset contracted typhoid and Léopold Robert died, according to George Sand, from being in a fever-begetting place. The poisons that arise appear inevitable and contagious, akin to the poisoned chalice of Tristan and Isolde (they may be Celtic, but their deaths are Venetian-inspired). And we await the arrival of Gustav Aschenbach.

* * *

Verdi and Otello

Passion, it need hardly be remarked, is the driving force behind Wagner's *Tristan und Isolde*: it was also the motivation in *Otello*, Verdi's penultimate opera, with a libretto by Arrigo Boito, which was first performed at La Scala, Milan, on 5 February 1887. Verdi's 'great dream' of setting a Shakespearian tragedy was finally realised: '*Otello* exists', he said after a protracted period of composition, 'The great dream has become reality'.[38] For Verdi, the Risorgimento was now in the past: as one essayist has commented:

> In earlier days he might have composed an Otello in which Desdemona sings of Venice 'O Patria mia', or Otello rallies a Venetian army to drive the Moslems from Cyprus. . . . Verdi dropped all the ephemera of politics and nationality to plumb the psychological truth of the human drama. The opera is art without topical allusion . . . he concentrated with more power than he had ever brought to an opera before on the two great mysteries of existence, love and death.[39]

Even if set in Cyprus, it is never in doubt that Otello was 'the Moor of Venice', that he was the triumphant hero acclaimed by the Venetian Republic who was felled by love. Whether in the form of play, opera or film, the story of Otello is inevitably performed with emblematic lions, prows of gondolas and Gothic fenestration (as in Orson Welles's film *Othello*, for instance). For Boito and Verdi the Venetian context could hardly be dismissed, and it appears implicitly if not directly.

The city, then, had a role vastly different to that of Verdi's earlier operas with Venetian settings, *Attila* and *I due Foscari*.[40] Yet Otello's crime of passion was easily associated with topical, overdrawn amorous states begotten by Venice, especially at the end of the nineteenth century. It is the setting for the dangerous consummation of love expressed early in the rhapsodic duet sung by Desdemona and Otello, 'Ancora un baccio', and then brought to destruction and inevitable tragedy by the machinations of Iago. The incriminating handkerchief, the *fazzoletto*, is the trivial token of jealousy, the instrument of tragedy.

Librettist Arrigo Boito had spent his formative years in Venice, and his brother Camillo had remained closely in touch with Venice; indeed, Camillo was head of a national committee for assessing Venetian urban programmes at the time of *Otello*'s composition. Arrigo's libretto was in part written in Venice (with the agony of a tooth abscess). After *La Gioconda*, it was Boito's second libretto with Venice as a setting. Shakespeare's *Othello* had had various treatments as novel and play throughout the century: Giustina Renier Michiel had translated it and so had Victor Hugo, and Boito again looked to Hugo for inspiration, referring to Hugo's French text. Boito's libretto has been judged ambivalently; for many it is a masterful and poetic work of condensation and operatic expression, having its own life and authenticity after Shakespeare.[41] The tribute to Shakespeare seems implicit in Boito's letter of 26 May 1887 addressed to Verdi as 'Caro Maestro': 'Otello triumphs also in his adoptive country, before the real lion of St Mark's, And he will continue his great flight in space and time . . .'[42]

Rossini's *Otello*, first performed in 1816, was an important precedent for Verdi. It had had an ambivalent critical reception – from Rossini's fan Stendhal, among others (Stendhal's ire was directed mainly at the 'fatuous imbecility' of Rossini's librettist, Francesco Mario Berio).[43] But certain of Rossini's effects are echoed in Verdi's work: notably the offshore barcarolle that recalls lines from Dante, hauntingly sung by a gondolier in the third act of Rossini's opera.[44] It has been observed that Rossini's Desdemona is a much more complete character than Verdi's female lead; nevertheless, the full-bodied orchestra of the late nineteenth century adds to the passionate *crescendi* that Verdi brought to his *Otello*, furthering that link with the mythology of Venice and passion. Nietzsche observed to Peter Gast with some sarcasm that after performances of *Otello*, Verdi had been acclaimed 'the lion of Venice'.[45]

We might wonder what was in Camillo Boito's mind some few years later with relation to Venice when he was writing his last *storiella*, published in *Nuova Antologia* in 1891.[46] 'Il Maestro di setticlavio, novella veneziana' (The Singing Master) is set in the 1850s when the Boito brothers lived in Venice and *Rigoletto* was premiered at La Fenice. Chisiola, the choirmaster of San Marco, an ancient figure from an earlier generation, and his pupil the bass singer Zen, likewise ancient, agree to reject the new music. The story ends amid delirium when a young soprano succumbs to hallucinations after a night of music and love at the festival of the Redentore (rowing in a *sandalo* with her lover under torpid skies, amid torpid, rat-infested waters), and the singing master is confined in madness to the island of San Servolo where he can be heard singing 'Do Re Do Mi Do Fa' . . . Camillo Boito was not immune to the miasmas rising from the lagoon – nor to the life-affirming nature of art in Venice.

The vapours, and seductiveness of music raised to a neurotic pitch by a phantom castrato from the eighteenth century; a flight from Wagnerian complexities and the wish to return to the compelling simplicity of the single voice, suggests the not dissimilar terrain of Vernon Lee's story of 1890, 'A Wicked Voice'.[47] Wagner's music of the future is countered by a desire for the music of the Venetian past, for the invisible male singer of 'La Biondina in Gondoleta'. Vernon Lee's Venice is at its most cloying, a sunken place of heated lagoons where the voice sounds disembodied on the Grand Canal. It has the power to kill and unnerve across the century. For Boito and Lee, Venetian vocal music in its particular Venetian setting has the power to render the sane mad.

Love/Death

Tristan und Isolde and *Otello* both tell of crimes of passion, and much is made of their association with Venice, increasingly sexualised in the literature of the 1890s. Venice as female, sacred and profane, Madonna and Venus, was a long-established historical association, to be recharged for modern times.[48] In the third decade of his visits to Venice, like many men before him, Henry James referred to the city as a woman, and one of whom you become 'tenderly fond'. The paradox, that 'style sits among ruins', as he put it in one of his essays, infuses his creative works that have Venice as a setting and have ruin, decadence, secrecy and tuberculosis as themes.[49] In 1892 he recognised 'decadence and ruin. . . . in Venice more brilliant than any prosperity'. On this insight into the enfeebling picturesque James built his reading of a prostituted Venice, engendered from a 'battered peep show and bazaar' with San Marco 'the biggest booth in Venice', and the whole city 'a vast mausoleum with a turnstile at its door'.[50] James exploited picturesque Venice in his creative writing, relishing the contradictions of pleasure and simultaneous pain. Thus Milly in *The Wings of a Dove* can only take flight in the midst of her illness to a place that is, like herself, both ill and beautiful.[51]

D'Annunzio's *Il Fuoco* fuses the female character, actress La Foscarina, with Venice, with the result that the poet's dying love for the woman – cloying, patronising, but at times exhilarating – is one with autumnal Venice sinking into its Stygian waters. But the city is still replete, and sexually charged. The Venetian poet of the Cinquecento, Gaspara Stampa, is invoked as a woman of fire, a precedent for La Foscarini, who is charismatic and tragic in *Il Fuoco*.[52] (Woman was never so clearly *other*.) As was well known, the character was based on Eleanora Duse, the actress adored by many, including Arrigo Boito in the 1880s when he had written a *Cleopatra* for her which she performed in Milan.[53]

Venice as siren, as queen of the sea, was pictured by Gustave Moreau, French painter of the *fin de siècle*, in full Symbolist mode; but in truth he abandoned lady Venice and her lion of the erect wings in the far lagoon, mooring her offshore with her city remote in the background (fig. 101).[54] As so many commentators remark, Ruskin had felt the sirenic power, consummating his marriage, not to Effie, but to

Venice.[55] In 1877, besotted with his departed love, the twelve-year-old Rose de la Touche, he made his final visit to try to capture her soul, which he hoped could be approached through the medium of Carpaccio.[56]

That this desire still ran conservatively and strongly after one hundred years was evident in the 1990s: Tony Tanner's study of literary Venice is incontestably in the tradition of desiring Venice, making the city a sexual quest via literature. Tanner's major protagonists are foreign writers of the nineteenth century.[57] In the 1890s famous lovers appeared anew before the public in a spate of publications. Casanova's *Memoirs* were translated into English for the first time and privately printed in 1894; the internationally known affair between Alfred de Musset and George Sand had a new lease of posthumous life with the publication of their letters.[58] In 1898 the Viennese writer Hugo von Hofmannsthal was reading Casanova in Venice.[59]

The Republic's history of prostitution was of renewed interest. G. B. Lorenzi not only assembled collections of documents relating to the Palazzo Ducale, but also recounted the history of prostitution, which was privately printed by the Earl of Oxford.[60] In 1883 the historical tariffs for Venetian prostitutes were published in France.[61] Distinguished journeys relating encounters with prostitution abounded in these years: those of Charles de Brosses were republished in 1885; Montaigne appeared in Italian translation in 1895; and the Baron de Montesquieu's *Voyages* were published between 1894 and 1896.[62] Pompeo Molmenti did not miss the opportunity to describe prostitution in *Venezia nella vita privata*. Giuseppe Tassini, a prolific writer of anecdotal local history, revived many of the fables of promiscuity in his *Il Libertinaggio in Venezia* – stories of doges (the wife of Marino Faliero, inevitably), of sodomy and rape, of the activities of the clergy, the extent of syphilis, the laws of the Republic.[63] It is acknowledged that many foreign observers have remarked on Venetian licentiousness: Didier is cited specifically, and, in the eighteenth century, Charles de Brosses.[64] As the Republic drew to its close, we are reminded, women sauntered with their *cavalieri serventi*, dancers and singers were part of the sexual climate, the casinos welcomed patrons, all licentiousness would appear to be escalating. Tassini is as accusatory as any foreigner.

'Decadence' carried a potent sexual charge at the *fin de siècle*. It was an international fashion, seductive and a stimulus to creativity for Marcel Proust, Oscar Wilde, Robert de Montesquiou, Whistler and many others. Venice provided intense

101 Gustave Moreau, *Venice*, 1880–85. Watercolour, 25.5 × 23.5 cm. Paris, Musée Gustave Moreau.

settings – interiors, as well as the predictable location of the city and lagoon. In anticipation of the *fin de siècle*, Edgar Allen Poe's thrilling story published in 1844, *The Assignation*, evoked a Venetian decor overdrawn in voluptuousness, the appropriate setting for a poisoning.[65] Thus:

> Rich draperies in every part of the room trembled to the vibration of low, melancholy music, whose origin was not to be discovered. The senses were oppressed by mingled and conflicting perfumes, reeking up from strange convoluted censers, together with multitudinous flaring and flickering tongues of emerald and violet fire.[66]

Homo-erotic consciousness was heightened in the climate of the trial of Oscar Wilde. Venice could be a haven for male love.[67] In the sixteenth century, in one of the classic documentary sources for Venetian history, Priuli spoke of

> the wicked and pernicious vice, which was practised and highly esteemed in this city ... openly practised in Venice without shame; indeed it had become so habitual that it was more highly regarded than having to do with one's own wife. Young Venetian nobles and citizens tricked themselves out with so many ornaments, and with garments that opened to show the chest, and with so many perfumes, that there was no indecency in the world to compare with the frippery and finery of Venetian youth and their provocative acts of luxury and venery.[68]

In the late eighteenth century William Beckford was an early and articulate advocate of sexual freedom (mornings idled away in a gondola, 'wrapped in furs', nights in cafés and at the opera made him 'more than ever effeminate'), a role appreciated by Lord Byron, who himself had a reputation for 'Greek love'.[69] There were eloquent echoes in Horatio Brown, Arthur Symons, John Addington Symonds, Proust and Montesquiou in the 1880s and 1890s. In the early years of the next century Baron Corvo and that emblematic fictional visitor Gustav von Aschenbach in Thomas Mann's *Death in Venice*, followed a male Eros. The gondolier could be an attractive specimen, as John Addington Symonds found when he went with Horatio Brown to one of their drinking places on the Lido and saw Angelo Fusinato for the first time:

> Angelo's eyes, as I met them, had the flame and vitreous intensity of opals, as though the quintessential colour of Venetian waters were vitalised in them and fed from inner founts of passion. This marvellous being had a rough hoarse voice which, to develop the simile of a sea-god, might have screamed in a storm or whispered raucous messages from crests of tossing waves. He fixed and fascinated me.[70]

This wonderful sea-god gave rise to a range of poems disguisedly published as if addressed to the female rather than the male sex in which the explicit 'theme' is the living god: 'he stands, / Flings back his hair; / Lifts his strong arms, and spreads his hands / To the warm air.'[71]

But love was paired as much with death as with life: the *Liebestod* was replayed many times. With its immense antiquity and battered beauty, Venice could hardly avoid becoming the epitome of the symbol of death: the cult of *passéisme* was in the ascendant. Furthermore, death had a highly visual aspect in Venice. The island cemetery of San Michele, to which dead bodies were rowed in special mourning vessels, was conspicuous, ideally situated, self-contained and movingly distant. Voyages both real and metaphorical increasingly dominated imaginative reactions to Venice: they still do so.

In the late nineteenth century even paintings with no historical link with Venice were seen to emanate from there, notably Arnold Böcklin's five versions of *The Isle of the Dead*, painted in 1880.[72] The connection between Böcklin and Venice was made specifically, but inaccurately, by Maurice Barrès during his pilgrimage through the lagoon islands as he made his first stop at San Michele.[73] Barrès described the island encircled by a red brick wall, its church with its heavy, marble flagstones, the Lombard poplars and cypresses – the scenario, he maintained, for Böcklin. The association between the paintings and Venice has remained powerful: a century later, in a beautiful treatise devoted to oblivion, the Venetian art historian Manlio Brusatin wrote of the Böcklin pictures and the Isola di San Michele as though the identifucation of the Venetian cemetery were a 'given' – it is, after all, *the* island cemetery and in one of the paintings it is fittingly evoked by a gondolier-rower using a single oar.[74]

Between 1872 and 1881 the engineer-architect Annibale Forcellini had undertaken further building at the cemetery, giving it its now familiar appearance.[75] Various schemes to link the Fondamenta Nuove with the Isola di San Michele were broached in these decades.[76] Each year on All Saints' Day the populace made its way to the cemetery across a temporary bridge built on boats, in the manner of the annual thanksgiving ceremonies associated with Santa Maria della Salute and the church of Il Redentore (fig. 102).[77]

102   Naya studio, *All Saints' Day, San Michele*, *c*.1900.

In March 1880 Nietzsche looked out from his lodgings on the Fondamenta Nuove, across to the islands of the lagoon to the nearest island, the cemetery island of San Michele – he called it the *Todeninsel*. Zarathustra's 'Funeral Song' invokes the island and, with it, the symbolic biography of the passage across life to death: 'Yonder is the grave-island, the silent island. Yonder, too, are the graves of my youth.'[78]

I am anticipating famous twentieth-century burials and cortèges of gondolas travelling across the water – those of Diaghilev and Stravinsky, Ezra Pound and Joseph Brodsky. At the turn of the century the island of San Michele was a highly visible symbol of a pervasive necrophilia that was savoured widely because it was perfectly attuned to the international Symbolist climate on the one hand, and was associated with the debate on the decay of the fabric and the *ambiente* on the other.

The Fortuny Phenomenon

One of Wagner's most devoted admirers in Venice was Mariano Fortuny – painter and etcher, photographer, theatre designer and, in the twentieth century, world famous textile designer and couturier.[79] Fortuny might be thought of as the emblematic Venetian of the *fin de siècle*, forward-looking on the one hand, in his interest in photography and electric light, passionately retrospective and traditional on the other. He was the son of the well-known painter Martigo y Fortuny, Spanish-born, but resident in Rome, where he died when Fortuny was three.[80] The Fortuny family, mother Doña Cecilia and her children, came to Venice in 1899 from Paris, to the Palazzo Martinengo on the Grand Canal.

In 1892, with his mother and sister, Mariano Fortuny made the pilgrimage to Bayreuth, meeting Cosima Wagner; thereafter the Valkyrie, Siegfried and Sieglinde were subjects of paintings and etchings in the 1890s.[81] Sigmund and Sieglinde embrace, the flower maidens intertwine in the company of Venetian subjects and styles drawn from Carpaccio and Tiepolo. Fortuny's etching style was particularly fine and dense, brilliantly exploited to create caverns past which Parsifal could make his essential journey, or the Rhine maidens cavort. His painting style owned something to the bravura of Venetian masters, but also the post-Empire revival style of such French painters as Jean Baudry and Benjamin Constant, and the Paris circle Fortuny knew during his teenage years. He retained close links with Paris, establishing a couturier outlet at 67 rue Pierre Charron in 1920.[82]

Drawn to current inventions, Fortuny used the new Kodak panorama camera from 1888 and built up a photographic oeuvre, carefully ordered and filed, testimony to the importance it held for him.[83] In photographs taken after 1889 he used the spread horizontal format so well-suited to Venice. Thus images stress the horizontality of Venice along the water, as buildings are stretched along extended shorelines lapped by canals whose surfaces appear to anticipate Fortuny's silks (fig. 103).[84]

103   Mariano Fortuny, panoramic view of the Bacino di San Marco, *c*.1902. Venice, Museo Fortuny.

The reforms for the stage were also resolutely modern.[85] His perception of the potential of electric light for the stage, in which white light replaced the yellowing distortions of gas, was revolutionary.[86] His association with the actress Eleonora Duse and the writer Gabriele D'Annunzio, born of their Venetian sojourns, was of crucial importance for the stage, for the production in Paris of *La Città di morte* (Mycenae in this case) in 1898, and then in 1898 the commission for Wagner's *Tristan und Isolde* at La Scala, Milan.[87] Staged in 1901, the production realised the ship's deck as a great boudoir, draped with curtain-sails, at once protective, erotic and symbolic of journeying. Further collaboration with D'Annunzio for his *Francesco da Rimini* led to Fortuny's undertaking costume design for the first time in 1901, and then to his celebrated career as couturier.[88]

We might surmise that, had Fortuny been in Venice rather earlier, Wagner would
have sought out his fabrics for the decoration of his chambers. During his first visit
to Venice in 1858, Wagner had taken rooms in the Giustiniani palace, moved in
his piano and had the room hung with cheap dark-red wallpaper and matching curtains to enhance the atmosphere for composition.[89] Responding later to Wagner's
talent for *mise-en-scène*, For-
tuny espoused the totality of
the arts, the *Gesamtkunstwerk*.
At the same time, Fortuny's
sense of the *mise-en-scène* must,
in part, have been an inheritance from his father, whose
proto-Symbolist studio, described as 'luxurious and
refined', had been well known
in Rome.[90] Madame de Fortuny
had brought her husband's
extensive collection of antiquities, precious fabrics, liturgical
vessels and artworks to Venice;
a visitor described her conducting her concert of fabrics with
the gestures of a magician.[91]
With the imprint of the familial
setting, Fortuny set up his own
dwelling, workshop and studio
in the Palazzo Orfei, which he
acquired in 1899 (fig. 104). His
sultry velvet drapes and rugs
were hung from the high
wooden rafters characteristic of

105 Mariano Fortuny,
fabric. Venice, Museo
Fortuny.

Venetian Gothic palaces and lit by the huge circles of the reflector lights he designed. In keeping with the theatrical ensemble, paintings were shown on easels amid cabinets full of curios and sculptures, and (later) mannequins wearing his couturier garments. The opulent decor has been preserved in the palace that has become the Museo Fortuny.

Venice had long been famous for fabrics and the import of luxury materials from the East.[92] Fortuny told of his discovery of ancient printed fabrics in Greece, but his sources range from the Far East to Persia and Turkey, to the Spain native to his family, and Morocco.[93] Although he did not restrict himself to Venetian precedents, nevertheless the luxury of gilt and silver prints, the silks and the velvets (as well as the printed cotton), are augmented by pictorial references to the fifteenth and sixteenth centuries, to Bellini, Carpaccio, the painted velvets of Titian and the brocades of Veronese and Tiepolo. Designs have a preponderance of symmetrical motifs, of flowers, vegetal motifs and birds (fig. 105). Pomegranates, palmettes and peacocks carry their precious burden of Venetian luxury.[94] Yet Fortuny's production of fabrics came well after the resuscitation of the fabric industry by Bevilacqua and Rubelli, and the collection of historical fabrics made by Michelangelo Guggenheim, part of a wider interest in luxury fabrics at the end of the century.[95] Nevertheless, the real fame of Fortuny's designs was created by their transposition into garments adored by international society: the Delphos gown, the Knossos scarf, the tunics of liturgical richness, all of which used to advantage the glowing colours of meticulous hand-worked materials in silk, velvet and cotton.

Fortuny fabrics glow, are incandescent by virtue of the irregularities and layers in their hand-dying and the process of hand-stencilling which compels the refraction of light. The shimmering pleated silks used for the Delphos shift are in calculated harmony and complication with richly figured cloths (lavender velvet stencilled with silver) and linings with Murano glass beads, detailing and weighting the fabrics.[96] Marcel Proust's narrator in *Remembrance of Things Past* saw the queen of Parisian society, Madame de Guermantes, in her Fortuny garment and knew of its provenance in the garments worn in Carpaccio and Titian: they are 'evocative of sunlight and turbans'; they are 'faithfully antique but markedly original', recalling a Venice 'saturated with oriental splendour'. Marcel Proust was to be an inspired spokesman for Fortuny's highly sensual quality, ensuring that his fabrics were indissolubly linked to the very essence of Venice, even if Proust could have known them only through Paris.[97]

D'Annunzio's City of Fire

Fortuny's friend Gabriel D'Annunzio was the leading exponent of decadence in Italy and one of the best-known Italians of his time; his association with Venice was vital in the 1890s.[98] As well as the unforgettable evocation of Wagner's last days, D'Annunzio's novel *Il Fuoco* offers the most sustained portrait of Venice in the late nineteenth century. It is the most significant work inspired by the city at that time. The last pages, which follow Wagner's funeral procession from the Palazzo Vendramin-Calergi to the railway station, activate all senses in response to the Wagnerian model: visually, as the cortège moves onto the water accompanied by the compelling figure of Cosima Wagner and the bier is heaped with laurels at the station; aurally, with the profound tribute of silence and the sound of the water lapping against the sides of the vessels making up the cortège; olfactorily, as the great wreaths of laurel scent the 'ashen' air.[99]

D'Annunzio's association with Venice dated from 1887 and the Esposizione Nazionale d'Arte.[100] He was in Venice again for the first Biennale of 1895, when the painting by Francesco Paolo Michetti, *La Figlia di Sorio*, based on his play of that name, was elected prizewinner. Announcing the elemental metaphors of fire and water with which D'Annunzio associated Venice, the first of his works with Venetian characters and settings was *Sogno d'un tramonto d'autunno* (Dream of an Autumn Sunset), a historical play revolving around the widow of the Doge Grandenigo, set in her villa on the Brenta.[101] Its last pages were incendiary, associating Venice with fire: the Bucintoro is consumed by flames and heaped with corpses, and millions of swords flash with fire and blood in an extravagantly imagined Venetian apocalypse.

Il Fuoco moves out of a strict time zone: a doge and dogaressa are in office, and yet the central characters, the poet Stelio and the actress Foscarina, are contemporary with Wagner. Venice is characterised as autumnal, but not in a destructive sense. It has experienced the full summer, rather than being an anticipation of winter. One particular image is brilliant, and persistent – the image of Venice in an underwater bier:

> There she lies, in her funeral barge, dressed in gold like the wife of a Doge, like a Loredana or a Morosina or a Soranza from the glorious past. The cortège sails out towards the island of Murano where a master of glass-making, a Lord of Fire, seals her into a crystal coffin, and then when her body sinks into the lagoon she will stare out through her diaphanous eyelids and watch the swirling play of seaweed and believe that it is her own richly flowing hair waving around her body as she waits for the time when she will be born again.[102]

Throughout *Il Fuoco*, even if still in its crystalline tomb, Venice is in perpetual process of gathering up its long, rich history, in anticipation of being born again. At the same time it yields up the full vigour and beauty of the lagoon to its characters, challenging them to lives that are charged with the recognition of art. There is a constant sense not only of the architectural city, but of the compelling natural setting of the lagoon, enjoyed through healthy rowing, which Stelio experiences with such overly-masculine vigour, of the kind D'Annunzio himself relished. The waters of the canal and the lagoon are constantly active, fluid agents bearing the lovers. The city is fused with the water, the church of the Salute is rebuilt out of the seaweed that swirls round its foundations. The purging metaphor of fire also transfuses the novel, giving it its title, setting up its literal presence in an evocative scene that follows a master forging Murano glass. La Foscarini asks the glassblower Seguso for a tribute of this inimitably Venetian art, a product of fire and molten liquid, for 'the shining vases, the slaves of the flame'.[103] The metamorphosis catches up the many faces of the city and unifies them: its waters, its glass, its boat-borne inhabitants.

The Venice of *Il Fuoco* is a city of poets and artists. From the first line it invigorates its inhabitants: 'Stelio isn't your heart beating fast for the first time?' Foscarina asks as they approach the Ducal Palace, under the shining angels of the campaniles of San Marco and San Giorgio. In the novel's early pages the poet is crowned at the Palazzo Ducale, but he must leave Venice in order to write, to return to another homeland. The Euganean Hills appear in the distance at one point, evoking Petrarch and his house at Arquà. Towards the end of the novel the two lovers go to the Brenta and the Villa Pisani at Strà; panic and fear erupt when Foscarina is ensnared in the labyrinth in the garden of Strà in a compelling scene of female entrapment. Is this the larger labyrinth of Venice? The undertow of autumn, age and death is always present, but the fluidity and energising waters of the canals and the lagoon, and the moment when Foscarina shatters the perfect glass from Murano, ensures that this Venice is never saccharine, never a resort city. At one point, in the distance, the madwomen incarcerated on the island of San Clemente are heard singing: 'From the island of La Follia, from that desolate, clear asylum, from the barred windows of the huge prison, rose a cheerful, yet lugubrious chorus.'[104]

D'Annunzio's commitment to the city led to his residence there in the First World War and to the bizarre events during which he founded the republic at Fiume.[105] For all its Wagnerian orientation, the inspiration of *Italian* art is held paramount. It was a period of revaluation of the composers of the seventeenth and early eighteenth century, and inspires Antimo della Bella, one of Stelio's friends, to declare that 'We should praise the greatest innovator of all, he who was consecrated a Venetian by his passion and his death, the man whose tomb is in the church of the Frari and is worthy of any pilgrimage – the divine Claudio Monteverdi. "Now there is the pure essence of a true Italian soul". . . .'[106] On the occasion of his oration at the Palazzo Ducale Stelio hears the *andante* of a work by Benedetto Marcello.[107] The response is rhapsodic, befitting Stelio's charged poetic soul.[108] The opposition between the Italian and the German schools is never directly discussed, but it is implicit. Benedetto Marcello is the musical flame; the painter Giorgione is the visual flame.

In less than two decades Venice was to be aligned on the edge of Italy, in the path of war. In 1909 D'Annunzio's play *La Nave* presented Venice with an allegory of renewal, which repositions it within the Adriatic as powerfully as in the days of the first Republic. In this double sense of an autumnal history and a future linked to the Adriatic, D'Annunzio is a creator on the cusp of two centuries. His Venice recognises death without succumbing to it; his Venice is not immured like that of Barrès in *paludisme*: while it negotiates its past it anticipates a future.

Venise le Rouge: *Safeguarding the Picturesque*

As Henry James made abundantly clear, the decadence of Venice was its very attraction. Even the most superficial visitor could gain a sense of history, readily dramatised in the opposites of beauty and decay, power and fall. Its history was signalled simply by the many works that were marked by asterisks in guide books: San Marco, the Palazzo Ducale, the Bridge of Sighs, the lion and the San Teodoro columns in the Piazzetta, the Prison, and the splendid concourse of the Grand Canal. But history was increasingly irrelevant to Symbolist perception, which extolled Venetian colour above all, making it a feature in the international imagination. In *The Picture of Dorian Gray*, Oscar Wilde has Dorian read a Venetian poem by Gautier which sends him, in imagination, floating on 'the green waters of the pink and pearly city', with 'sudden flashes' conjuring up 'opal-and-iris throated birds'.[109] Highly coloured, opalescent: Venice overall was now both exotic and picturesque, the sum of its most humble parts, of small turns in canals and *calli*, and buildings in which the disintegration and crumbling were desirable evidence of a patina and the play of time, delicious or destructive. Boito was not unique in extolling the *colore locale* born of the water and the sirocco, endowing San Marco and the humblest building and waterway with 'the unique virtue, the virtue most important to the artist: being picturesque'.[110]

An environment so ardently watched, locally and internationally, with faded traces of luxury, crumbling marbles and the evidence of one-time aristocratic grace, was in danger of becoming an overwrought scenario in which allegories of life, love and death were necessarily heightened and brought to crisis point. Following the polemics of the 1870s there was a spate of articles in the 1880s warning that demolition was at danger level, threatening change to extensive areas. These were local views, as distinct from those of such famous foreigners as Ruskin and William Morris.

Like all cities at that time, Venice was subject to epidemics of cholera. The ancient Republic's controls to guard against epidemics of the plague and its exemplary provisions for aspects of public health were well known; paradoxically, the very history of its vigilance worked to keep alive the symbiosis of Venice and disease.[111] Hospitals and quarantines situated on the lagoon islands bore witness to the efforts to contain and distance disease.[112] The churches of Il Redentore and Santa Maria della Salute, their rituals of deliverance re-enacted annually, stood as conspicuous memorials to survival, with the result that they consolidated association with plague.

Stringent laws had been passed in 1835 and 1836, when the first cholera epidemic raged.[113] The last period of Austrian rule and the first years of the Commune were a time of increased protest, as the coincidence between sanitation and disease was recognised and the housing situation worsened, drawing attention to the extent of poverty and disease.[114] In 1873 a general inspection of housing took place.[115] In 1887 a central plan for demolition was finalised, with the result that opposition mobilised, for it was felt by those unaffected by inferior housing that nothing less than the essence of Venice would be destroyed. It was a decisive point in Venetian history; repercussions from it would continue into the next century.

On 14 December 1886 the Mayor, Dante Serego degli Alghieri, released a plan for 'the sanitation of the city and the improvement of its viability'. It is an important document in the modern history of Venice.[116] Recommendations were intended, in the first instance, to counter epidemics and contagious diseases, to demolish low-grade housing for the poor and the working class and provide hygienic and comfortable housing in their place, to create space so that air might circulate, to provide a sewerage system that did not discharge into waterways and so reduce the unhygienic odours that impaired the air in streets and lower-floor dwellings.[117] The plan was aware that imposing radical innovations could alter the special character of the city, indicating that while planning initiatives after unification had created a climate for positive modern responses, the Alghieri administration anticipated widespread criticism.

The chief critic was Pompeo Molmenti. In 1883 his article 'Delendae Venetiae' published in the *Nuova Antologia*, protested to an audience beyond Venice that Venetian poetry was dying of hunger:

> We remember another Venice, picturesque, poetic, full of fascination and mystery that is destroyed, not for the utility and decorum of citizens, not for the exigencies of administration and new industries, but because of the desire to renovate . . . Who wants to reduce Venice to a boring monotonous modern city, with wide thoroughfares driven through areas of artistic delectation against which would come the protests of all who feel the cult of beauty . . . ?[118]

It was time the 'innovations' of recent years were reviewed, and castigated. In particular the new thoroughfares of Via Vittorio Emanuele, Via 22 Marzo and Via 2 Aprile were criticised as unnecessarily wide, they had no need to accommodate carriages. The new buildings lining them were held to be uniformly vulgar. Demolition (*sventramento*) was a highly charged word.

Some two months after publication of the Commune's plan, a pamphlet reprinted Molmenti's essay, with additional discussion an indication of the fervour that the issue aroused.[119] Three newspaper articles countering Molmenti were prepared to extol the poetry of Venice, but also to emphasise the need for new industries to feed the people, to move them along new arterials and in *vaporetti*. The danger, recognised well in advance of the Futurists, was the creation, in a telling phrase, of a dead city, 'una città morta'. Molmenti defended Venice against the charge that it was becoming 'a Pompeii'.

Academy architects responded cautiously to the debate, no doubt mindful of the opportunities demolition created. But painters and sculptors in large number – not only such local artists as Ciardi, Favretto and Nono, but non-Venetian artists also – signed a manifesto in support of the picturesque city.[120] Heading the artists' campaign, Favretto confirmed with Molmenti that 'certain projects which aim to destroy the most beautiful city in the world alarm everybody'.[121]

The *Delendae venetiae* issue still endures, atrophying processes of building and frustrating the introduction of new architecture. It began quite precisely in 1887, when the city was fetishized and its face was turned resolutely to the past. At that point zealously guarded Venice became a commodity city, a package of the total picturesque. The result was, in effect, to pre-empt 'Venice for the Venetians'; it became a virtual cliché to declaim that Venice had the world as its audience; its own citizens were confirmed as a lower order.

Some views were more tempered than those of Molmenti, but they had the effect, nevertheless, of endorsing the past. In the 1880s Giacomo Boni was eloquently attentive to the issue of preservation. At that time he was employed in the Forcellini workshop restoring the Palazzo Ducale; he was later to achieve fame for directing excavations at the Roman forum and, in the new century, for directing the rebuilding of the Campanile.[122] In 1887 he entitled an article 'Il cosidetto sventramento, appunti di un veneziano', emphasising the *Venetian* point of view.[123] With a further essay in the same year, 'Venezia imbellettata', he embraced a range of issues, sketching in a scenario that had the Grand Canal turned into a boulevard with rows of trees, two tramways and a carriageway, the Piazza glassed over, and the gondola a model in a museum.[124] He was critical of the exodus of works of art from Venice, the controversial restoration of the Fondaco dei Turchi, the danger of fire in the Palazzo Ducale, and so on.[125] At the same time, his views were notable for the range of urban reference and considerations that went beyond those of major renovation projects, raising larger questions. The indiscriminate widening of *calli* and the infill of canals were targets for criticism, but Boni was not a sentimental defender of the picturesque: the importance of sanitation was acknowledged, and he was by no means entirely opposed to street widening and the argument for demolition. Aware that he was in debate with hygienists as well as advocates for Venice's economic future based on road access, he covered the overall importance of issues affecting the health of the lagoon for Venice – every infill subtracted the water available for revivifying the lagoon – tidal flow was blocked as a result of closing off canals. These arguments would be advanced many times in the next century.

International interest was considerable, for now everyone owned Venice. In 1889 D'Annunzio spoke to Robert de Souzo in an interview for the Parisian newspaper *Figaro*, stating that in forty years the Grand Canal would be paved, and traversed by trams.[126] Within a decade Marinetti and the Futurists would be waiting in the wings, ready to promote a revivified lagoon city, freed from the stigmas of canals.[127]

In 1889 opponents of slum clearance had further mobilised, regarding the demolitions as destroying 'typical' houses. The Riccardo Selvatico administration, in power between 1890 and 1895, had to tread carefully in order to pass the 1891 Piano Regolatore. As well as seeking professionals in the area of public health, Commission members were chosen for their interest in art.[128] The Commissione per le Case Sane e Economiche e Popolari reported in 1893, and as a result some workers' housing was built, but only in the peripheral areas of Sant'Elena, San Giobbe and Dorsoduro.[129] Since then there have been regular debates on housing; opponents of change, defenders of the traditional city and developers have continued to distance themselves from the needs of the ordinary resident.

Towards the end of the century Molmenti was involved in a new phase of battle, as the leading figure in the movement dubbed the *anti-pontisti*, the faction opposing a new bridge to convey road traffic across the lagoon. The debate was sustained from the 1880s until a road bridge linked to the existing railway was approved in 1917.[130] According to Molmenti, not only the historic centre, but the entire *ambiente* to which people were increasingly attuned was under new threat. There were other schemes, such as Antonio Baffo's ambitious project to link Murano and San Michele with the Fondamenta Nuove (building an iron bridge, of course); the debate then concerned the linkage point with the mainland at Mestre. Further projects tried to come to grips with the cost involved, and directed the bridge from Mestre to San Giobbe in Cannaregio, in a more direct link with the mainland. In 1898 the architect Giuseppe Torres and the engineer Vendiaso proposed a termination point at Cannaregio, in front of the abattoirs facing the lagoon. With respect to the new bridge, Molmenti had responded in 1894 in his *Venezia calunniata*, arguing for the cheapness of water transport and suggesting that it would be necessary to supply clients with quinine to combat malaria at an island restaurant on the new bridge. Above all, the new bridge would be a constant menace to the unique aspect of Venice. Its terminal would necessitate demolition and widening projects and would further destroy Venice.[131]

In 1898, when four proposals for iron bridges across the lagoon were in circulation, Molmenti wrote for the *Nuova Antologia*, to proclaim the danger of Venice for the city that was 'patrimonio artistico di tutto il mondo'.[132] Many of Molmenti's arguments were anticipated by Boito and more prudently covered by Boni, but Molmenti repeated his list of Venetian sins against the environment again and again. His passion and commitment carried over the decades. In 1900 he wrote an article, 'Per Venezia e per l'arte', for the journal *Emporium*, and illustrated it with 'before' and 'after' photographs of places that had become centres of attention in the debate between *antichi* and *moderni*. The targets were the islands of Sant'Elena and Santa Maria della Grazia (both of which had been given over to factories), the iron warehouse on the Giudecca within sight of San Giorgio Maggiore, the old stone bridge of the Ponte del Paradiso beside a modernised iron bridge, and the iron bridge of the Accademia in front of the Grand Canal famously painted by Canaletto.[133] The appeal to an international audience was constant by this stage: 'Venice is not only an Italian glory, it is the artistic patrimony of the civilised world.'[134] Molmenti argued – as his second concern, after the destruction of beauty – for the health of the lagoon in terms that would not be unfamiliar one hundred years later.[135] The road bridge already interfered with the tidal system and further parapets would only exacerbate the problem. The rail bridge also obstructed the free movement of the winds, causing the lagoon to become muddy or slimy and, in turn, to silt up the canal system.

106 Frontispiece of *Calle e canali in Venezia*, published by Ferdinando Ongania, 1890–91. Venice, Archivio Tomasso Filippi.

The result of cultivating the *ambiente* was a new geography increasingly evident in literature and the visual arts in the age of the picturesque. In his 1888 novella, *The Aspern Papers*, Henry James located the sisters who are central to his story in a crumbling palace, well away from the centre of Venice.[136] One sister remarks: 'Our house is very far from the centre, but the little canal is very *comme il faut*.'[137] When the aged protagonists make their novel excursion to the Piazza San Marco it serves to highlight the hidden intricacies and contrasts of large tracts of Venice beyond the centre. Whistler claimed to have found a Venice that nobody else had discovered.[138] Paradoxically visitors were coming to see typical Venetian buildings in an artistic state of decay, but they were using the new train route and staying at the modern hotels in the most scenic and historic area of the Bacino.

Now the supremacy of the Grand Canal and the Piazza San Marco were challenged by the unmarked sites – a doorway, a turn in a small canal, the twist of a narrow passageway between modest buildings, or a *traghetto* cabin where the gondoliers rested. For Molmenti, no doubt with Favretto's paintings in mind, *traghetti* stops were 'the most Venetian thing that was in Venice, the dearest to the artist who loved local colour'.[139] In 1890–91 Ferdinando Ongania published *Calli e canali in Venezia* (fig. 106), a photographic album with a preface by Pompeo Molmenti and Dino Mantovani drawing attention to *Venezia minore* and the city of artists in which 'the aristocracy of birth' had given away to 'the aristocracy of genius'.[140] In 1898 an English version was prefaced by Ruskin, who decried the modernisations (for the last time before his death in

1900) and exhorted that 'the voice of poetry be sought in the gloomy canals and picturesque alleys': his association of gloom with poetry is telling.[141] Ongania wrote commending the 'new' sites distanced from the centre: a canal in the Giudecca, the *squero* at San Trovaso – the one remaining boatyard – which acquired a particular fame at the time (which has not been lost), a quay on the island of Chioggia where traditional fishing boats docked. These, he wrote, were appropriate subjects for painters, and thereafter they have been the amateur's paradise.

At the end of the century the city governors were calling for overall plans and distinctions to be made between the *grande* and the *minore*, in order to effect improvements to urban sanitation and cleanliness. The lobbying continued: in 1899 the mayor was addressed by a group calling themselves the Society for Public Art in Venice: Molmenti was president.[142] Other members were the painters Mariano Fortuny and Italo Brass; Luigi Nono; the designer-educator, Michelangelo Guggenheim; architect Domenico Rupolo; scholar Filippo Nani-Mocenigo; and Prince Frederik von Hohenlohe, who had recently published his *Notes vénétiennes* complaining about 'the vulgarity of [the] times', and 'the immense sadness of all this innovation'.[143] The mayor was asked as matter of urgency to safeguard 'the character of Venice', to protect it from the affronts it had suffered – the familiar complaints. The colour of Venice no longer existed amid the barbarisms; a dirty grey replaced the bright rose of traditional Venice, even municipal buildings were not exempt. Works of art were leaving the city, private collections were dispersing, few palaces remained intact. The use of cast iron was under attack, as was the removal of well-heads, the *pozzi*. Further, the steam boats on the Grand Canal were eroding the *fondamente* and becoming the curse of the *traghetti*: all this anticipated another century of protests.[144] The Commissione all'Ornato, that jurisdiction created during Napoleon's rule, was found inadequate to the task of controlling the vandalism, as witness the iron Ponte del Paradiso and the fish market at the Rialto, modernisations permitted at the expense of architecture and beauty. Annibale Forcellini was cited as a typical case: preserving the Palazzo Ducale on the one hand, building the fish market with an iron roof on the other. The power of the new lobby was evidenced by the demolition of the Ponte del Paradiso and the fish market early in the new century.[145]

Venezianità

The debate concerning picturesque Venice and the retention of its low-key, but characteristic areas went in tandem not only with conservation priorities, but with a cult of Venetianness in *over*-production, as if to forestall loss. With an over-mixing of elements from past local styles comes *venezianità*. The Fondaco dei Turchi was a classic instance, with more Byzantine arches and *merlatura*, more low-relief roundels, than the original. In the 1880s *venezianità* brought about the renovation of the Palazzo Cavalli-Franchetti with new industrial-age interpretations of traditional motifs, such as the Boito staircase in combination with a full repertoire of reliefs and ornamental motifs, Boito's interest in restoring the trifloriate windows of the Palazzo Ducale to reinstate the Gothic aspects of the building, and the revivalist aspects of the glass industry producing works more elaborate than the original models. In the 1890s Michelangelo Guggenheim's decoration for the Palazzo Papadopoli was an instance of heightened Venetian treatment particularly adapted to interior spaces, with an abundance of furnishings, velvet drapery and glass chandeliers, together with one of the first hydraulic lifts in Venice.[146] Like Boito, Guggenheim embraced the industrial arts and endorsed educational programmes, but the great examples of the past were still the determinants.[147] His decor ran the gamut of historical styles, including a Louis-Quattorze Hall, with throne-like drapery, a consonance of furniture and velvet-covered walls, neo-Baroque fresco decorations painted by Cesare Rotta, stucco dec-

orations repeatedly featuring the Papadopoli coat of arms, a Hall of Tapestries in Louis-Seize style, a Venetian-styled panelled library and a Chinoiserie room.[148]

The Ca' d'Oro on the Grand Canal was already the most ornate palace in Venice, yet its reputation as an extreme point in the realisation of Venetian decorated Gothic was pushed even further in the late nineteenth century. Meduna had been responsible for considerable restoration and remodelling at the behest of Prince Troubeskoy and Taglioni, taking little account of original materials in accordance with mid-century practices, and making 'improvements' to the windows and extending balconies.[149] In 1894, after a period in which the palazzo was converted into apartments (one of which Pompeo Molmenti occupied for a time), Baron Giorgio Franchetti acquired the palace and began its alteration in a spirit of *venezianità*. He rescued the Bartolomeo Bon well-head from a Paris antique dealer (a genuine act of restoration), constructed an external staircase with some interpolation of the original staircase which had been demolished, laid an elaborate mosaic floor *à la San Marco* on the water entrance level, and accommodated works from his important art collection in elaborate marble chapel-like settings.[150] The most famous of his paintings was the Mantegna *St Sebastian*, which D'Annunzio saw in the company of Angelo Conti at the Ca' d'Oro in 1896 (fig.

107 The Ca' d'Oro, *c.*1895, with Mantegna's *St Sebastian* (now in the Giorgio Franchetti Gallery, Venice). Photograph by Ugo Mulas, from Michelangelo Muraro, *Invitation to Venice*, London, 1963.

107). D'Annunzio reacted predictably, extolling the work in homo-erotic terms, in a flight of biographical aestheticism:

He was standing there, upright, inside this shrine . . . He was naked except for a plain cloth round the thighs; a shapely figure with chest squared. The arrows in his body were artfully placed, as hairpins are in a well-styled head of hair. His blood dripped sparingly as if the taut muscles were trying to hold it in. I did not recognise the song-bird of my youth in this figure that looked towards an Orient blood-steeped in mystery . . .[151]

The point at which dialect and local survival becomes embellished and compounded into *venezianità* is elusive. It is a knowingly self-conscious and indulgent pursuit, in which obsolescence or decadence are relished. Riccardo Selvatico, mayor of Venice between 1895 and 1900, gave a boost to *venezianità* through his artistic as well as political leadership, as a writer of plays and poetry in dialect in the 1870s.[152] Feelings of patriotism under foreign rule stirred writers to keep the dialect intact in the earlier part of the century; a proud regionalism anxious to foster and guard identity continued it in united Italy. The plays of Giacinto Gallina, concerned with local characters and topical issues, are a case in point for the later century. Gallina was performed by the Venetian company of Angelo Moro Lin, which also kept the plays of Goldoni to the forefront of their repertoire.[153] Selvatico's own poems and plays wear the writer's heart conspicuously on the sleeve, making little secret of his soaring, even cloying love of Venice.

But it was in architecture that the respect for the *ambiente*, and the Boitian programme of renewing Italian architecture through attention to medieval sources in particular, led to the most visible exercises in *venezianità*. Reaching beyond Gothic or Byzantine revival, it affected building projects in the 1890s, and well into the twentieth century. Here Giovanni Sardi is an outstanding figure, working with a heightened form of Gothicism in his various designs for small palaces into the twentieth century, and with more complicated and creative sources in his grand hotel project for the Lido.[154] Sardi was not merely working with the eclecticism that was common practice in the 1880s and 1890s; he was engaged with specifically Venetian sources. In 1890 he added a Gothic wing to the Bauer-Grünwald Hotel, prominently sited on

108 Giovanni Sardi, Hotel
Excelsior, Lido, 1908.
Venice, Archivio Tomasso
Filippi.

the upper Grand Canal. The façade was consonant with the adjacent Gothic palace;
the main wing of the hotel had pointed arches inset in marble, inset medallions, and
balconies, just over-stepping the match with original features.[155]

In 1898 Sardi's Hotel Excelsior Palace, to be built on the Lido seafront, was on the
drawing-board: the only comparison in scale was Wullekopf's Stucky mill, under construction in the 1890s. Industry and tourism represent the two largest building enterprises in *fin-de-siècle* Venice. The Excelsior was the most flamboyant and the most
linguistically intricate in its admixture of Moorish and Gothic elements, permissible
in a pleasure palace or a resort hotel (fig. 108). Turrets, domes and bold *merlatura*
give character to the varied skyline. Windows arched in the Moorish manner (the
blurring of sources contributing to the vitality of detail) open along the extensive
blocks and varied storey heights. In a period of eclecticism that favoured Gothic or
Lombard prototypes, Sardi effectively broadened the repertoire of sources, unerringly
seeking out the most exotic, and binding them to the orientalism inherent in earlier
Venetian architecture. The boldness of realising a luxury hotel project in this monumental exotic mode must owe something to Cadorin's unbuilt designs for the Riva
degli Schiavoni (which led the developer Fisola to turn his attention to the Lido). Now
there was the foundation for an exotic building which, with the Hotel des Bains (fig.
109), would capture a major share of international tourism within a decade.

* * *

City of Modern Art: The Cosmopolis

Given the historical weight it increasingly bore, and the increasing number of voices attuned to the defence of old Venice, it may have appeared an unlikely venue for modern art. Yet the ambitions of Venice as a city of art were confirmed with the creation of the Biennale d'Arte, which has now lasted over a hundred years, keeping its supremacy within the context of international exhibitions.[156]

The first opportunity to offer Venice as a showcase for art occurred when the Esposizione Artistica Nazionale for 1887 was assigned to Venice in 1883 by the Eighth Artistic Congress in Rome. Paolo Fambri, Venetian representative in the national parliament, was appointed president. Like other cities, Venice was keen to pursue the benefits familiar from the Great Exhibition in London in 1851 and the successful sequence of expositions in Paris. But the Venetian emphasis was on fine art, from the models of the salons and secessions of the later nineteenth century.[157] The key feature in its success was the cession of part of the Giardini Pubblici as the venue, the most decisive change for the area since Napoleon's original decree in 1807. Despite criticism, a lobby from supporters for building a hospital for contagious diseases and the claims of the existing riding school, the Commune conceded the site. Municipal architect Enrico Trevisanato and the young architect Raimondo d'Aronco (to become one of Italy's pre-eminent practitioners in the Stile Liberty), adapted the existing pavilion into a series of pagodas and kiosks arranged 'in bizarre form but with elegant line'.[158] Reviewing the Esposizione for the *Nuova Antologia*, Camillo Boito rhapsodised over

110 Ettore Tito, *The Old Fishmarket*, 1893. Oil on canvas, 131 × 200 cm. Rome, Galleria Nazionale d'Arte Moderna.

the great venue on the lagoon – and gave most space to Favretto.[159] On the occasion of the royal opening, Conte Serego discoursed to the king on the wonders of traditional Venetian painting.

The prize-winning painting was resolutely Venetian. Ettore Tito, trained at the Accademia, won with his *Old Fishmarket* (fig. 110) – which exists today in a larger, more famous version of 1893.[160] A comparison of the two versions is instructive, for the focus in the first painting is indicative of contemporary polemical views in the Venice of the day. A masterpiece of local colour, Tito's painting has the informal Rialto market of tarpaulins on poles as a setting, and not the new cast-iron fishmarket. The background has changed to give an enticing view of the Grand Canal with the Ca' d'Oro in the background. Amid the shoppers and vendors that represent all ages and stations, the figure of a gondolier stands out. It is the same model who appeared in the 1887 painting, but in 1893 he wears the striped shirt of the gondolier and he holds his plate with but a modest single fish upon it. In that market full of produce and elegant women buyers, his face is ruddy and unsmiling, his central position even more heightened as he is painted in front of the conspicuous Ca' d'Oro (fig. 111). Tito's illustrations for articles on the conservation of old Venice for such writers as Molmenti and Zorzi, suggest that this focus on old Venice and the plight of the gondolier threatened by the new *vaporetti* was deliberate, and pointed.[161]

In the wake of the success of the Esposizione, three Venetians met at Florian's (the venue is part of the mythology): Riccardo Selvatico, Antonio Fradeletto and the philosopher Giovanni Bordiga developed the concept of a permanent exhibition, to show international contemporary art (to be known as the Biennale only after the First World War).[162] After three years of gestation the Biennale came into being, in the first instance as a belated homage to King Umberto I and Queen Margherita of Savoy on the occasion of their silver wedding anniversary. On 30 March 1894 the Commune

approved the proposal from the commission set up to organise the event.[163] The secretary's task was to initiate the selection of foreign artists who were then reviewed by an international 'Committee of Patronage'. Antonio Fradeletto as first secretary was the key activist for the first exhibitions, and a central figure in the cultural and social life of Venice well into the next century.[164] The international emphasis was deliberate and productive, reflecting the ambition to make the exhibition an international event. In this way it diverged significantly from previous national expositions, although Italian and Venetian art were well represented.[165]

Mayor Riccardo Selvatico was the first president: from the beginning the conjunction of roles involved the city and its government at the highest level, which has contributed to the Biennale's survival. The support of the mayor and his own evident engagement with the arts carried the Commune with it; it was a factor in both the success of the first event and the recognition of Venice as an art city.[166] Despite Selvatico's dismissal from office in 1895 for opposing prayers in state schools, and the troughs and administrative crises that have occurred throughout its history, the Biennale has survived.[167] Supported by the next mayor, Filippo Grimani, 'the Golden Mayor', who was in office for twenty-five years, until the appearance of Fascism in 1920, the Biennale prospered, despite charges of conservatism.

The buildings for the first Esposizione, before the construction of national pavilions which began in 1907, comprised a central salon and nine smaller adjacent galleries constructed by Trevisanato. The artists Marius de Maria, recently arrived from Rome (soon to become one of Venice's most conspicuous Symbolist talents), and Bartolomeo Bezzi were responsible for the decoration of the façade in a neo-Greek manner generally regarded as unsuitable (fig. 112).[168] Interior settings were carefully considered, and included the use of draped velvet and furnishings from artists' studios. The idea of the galleries as special interiors was established from the outset.

In the first Biennale 285 artists showed a total of 516 works. The representation included the English Pre-Raphaelites Edward Burne-Jones, John Everett Millais and Holman Hunt, and Whistler; the French Symbolists Puvis de Chavannes and Odilon Redon; the Germans Franz von Stuck and Franz von Lenbach (again characterised as Symbolists); and a strong representation of Norwegian and Dutch artists.[169] Whistler's *Woman in White* is probably the exhibit best-known one hundred years later. Twelve prizes were awarded: the overall winner was Francesco Paolo Michetti's *Daughter of Jorio*, based on D'Annunzio's play and having a salacious appeal in its subject of a young girl walking past male spectators. (D'Annunzio was a useful proselytiser for Michetti.) Ettore Tito won the City of Venice's first prize for *Autumn*, a work on an Alpine theme showing a young girl leading a flock of cows and goats down a mountain slope.[170] A scandal was provoked by Giacomo Grosso's *The Last Gathering*, in which five female nudes in gay abandon romped around a funeral bier within a church (a minor incidence of death and Venice). The attack, headed by the patriarch of Venice, Giuseppe Sarto, later to become Pope Pius X, further contributed to the anti-clerical reputation of Mayor Selvatico.

Vittorio Pica, who held office in the Biennale of 1912, was an outstanding critic of the early expositions, increasing awareness through his writings on the international representation.[171] One of his articles had been among the first to characterise international Symbolist art – which Pica termed, in approbation, 'aristocratic art'.[172] In the context of the first Biennale, he wrote authoritatively about the under-representation of the School of Paris, of Courbet and Manet (long dead), and other Impressionists.[173] The breadth of his interests was important to the development of Biennales in the field of decorative and graphic arts.[174] At the Second Exposition, in 1897, prizes were instituted for criticism – Vittorio Pica was among the winners.[175]

In 1895, in an action of some initiative, the Commune of Murano contributed a prize in honour of the royal wedding anniversary and sponsored an exhibition of glass at the Museo Vetrario at the same time as the Biennale.[176] Later expositions were to have the effect of stimulating artists to produce special studio glass, but in 1895 the decision was taken to exclude 'arts applied to industry', which had been a category in the 1887 Esposizione.[177] The result was an exhibition at Murano with the title *Vetri artistici*, an important emphasis.[178] A creation of consummate elegance survives from that exhibition: a goblet blown by the Artisti Barovier, so thin and transparent it appears to hover at the very point of creation (fig. 113). Its shallow cup floats on the pinhead of a spiral that seems to spring from a base too light for the supporting task.

Although not the emphasis of the first exposition, the decorative arts were to assume a more and more important role. In 1897 an Eastern art collection, including Japanese Gaku and Kakemo, was shown and works acquired for the new museum collection.[179] In the third Biennale in 1899, the Glasgow Four – Frances and Margaret Macdonald, Herbert Macnair and, most eminently, Charles Rennie Mackinstosh – exhibited in what retrospectively must be regarded as a major avant-garde design event in Italy at that time.[180]

The second Esposizione in 1897 saw a further important stage in the patronage of the art city: the foundation of a city collection of modern art linked to the Biennale, stimulated in the first instance through the donation of Prince Alberto Giovanelli.[181] The following year, in a major bequest of great subsequent importance for modern art in Venice, Bevilacqua La Masa willed the Palazzo Pesaro to the Commune for the specific use of young artists. Inaugurated in 1902, the group associated with the Palazzo Pesaro was to develop in part in opposition to the perceived conservatism of the official Biennale.[182]

In Biennales to come, the one-man exhibition and the retrospective were to have increasing prominence. In 1899 Giacomo Favretto was given a posthumous retrospective, proving that he was by far the most popular Venetian painter of the second half of the nineteenth century. However resolutely international, the expositions did much to boost Venetian art and artists, and to prompt foreign artists to take up Venetian subjects. In 1899 the prize-winning work was Ettore Tito's *On the Lagoon* (Museo d'Arte Moderna, Ca' Pesaro), a composition of some élan depicting a gondolier rowing a young girl in one corner and wavelets reaching diagonally across the lagoon.[183] Mariano Fortuny showed a portrait of Princess von Hohenlohe in high Empire style.[184]

In 1895 the fringe events that Selvatico was so adept at handling were in place, spreading the effects of the exposition throughout the lagoon and giving it its specific Venetian edge which, arguably, it has never lost. Mayor Selvatico, who had read his own poetry at two regattas in 1891 and 1893, presided over serenades, fireworks, concerts, a *baccanale del Redentore* and theatrical spectacles.[185] The regatta made a comeback, enriched by its evocation of the past and maritime glory, now actively revived as celebration and tourist attraction.[186] It drew on all those traditions so beautifully mapped by Renier Michiel in her study of festivals written during the Austrian occupation.

By 1899 the existence of the exposition as a regular event was confirmed. For the third show, the local newspaper, *Il Gazzettino*, offered a general guide to Venice with sixty-two views of the city, taking the visitor to the periphery of the city, from Mestre to the Grand Canal, past the palaces and churches to the Giardini and hence

113 ?Giuseppe Barovier, Artisti Barovier, spiral stem goblet, 1895. Glass, 22 cm. Murano, Museo del Vetrario.

to the twenty rooms of the Biennale in a grand cultural progression. From the beginning Venetian insignia adorned the posters and catalogues in a form of local advertising (fig. 114). The winged lion graced the central Palazzo dell'Esposizione.[187] Interior decorations highlighted the lion. The poster for the first exposition bore the lion in one corner, and the programme for auxiliary attractions carried a schematic gondola prow. Thereafter, Venice was converted into a graphic parade of San Marcos, domes of Santa Maria delle Salute, Campaniles and Ducal Palaces for posters and programmes, all confirming the vitality of the present amid the riches of the past. When, in the 1930s, the Cinema Biennale was established with its now-famous award of the Golden Lion, the venue of the Lido was included in the circuit of cultural tourism.

The first Biennale was also impressive in the literary field; D'Annunzio gave a recital for the closing ceremony. His 'homage' was his 'Allegory to Autumn', produced at an intense lyrical level which in effect announced D'Annunzio's fascination with Venetian themes in rehearsal for his novel *Il Fuoco*.[188] Everything, he declared, shares 'a deep eloquence', as the 'city of shore and water' existed in 'a spirit of pure artifice'.

Activating the allegorical contrast between youth and age, D'Annunzio extolled the youth of Giorgione against the venerable old age of Titian: they shared opulence and goldenness; beside them was Carpaccio's Ursula, innocently virginal in her bed (the latter noted by Ruskin at much the same time). But pre-eminently it was Giorgione, beloved of the Symbolists, of Walter Pater and Angelo Conti, who best represented the Promethean 'epiphany of fire' celebrated by D'Annunzio at the close of the exposition of contemporary art.[189] His praise re-echoed in *Il Fuoco*, in which Giorgione is at the centre of the aesthetic which the novel proclaims, the supreme reason for its title: 'all the art of Venice is fired by his revelations. The great Vecellio apparently took from him the secret of giving his creations luminous blood in their veins. In fact, what Giorgione represents in painting is the Epiphany of Fire. Like Prometheus, he deserves the title of "Bearer of Fire".'[190]

Extolling 'Venezia, città trionfante', D'Annunzio's affirmatory rhetoric must have cheered the Venetians at a time when they were defensive about their city, both locally and internationally. Yet this Venice was also quite firmly of the past, although there was no doubt of how brightly its fires still burnt. D'Annunzio was confirmed as a spokesman for Venice, a role that he would embellish over the next twenty-five years.[191]

In effect, this first Esposizione, with D'Annunzio's brilliant intervention, increased the repertoire available to the visitor to Venice: on offer was the unique spectacle of a city built in a lagoon, the spectacle of history, equally singular, and benignly known in a simplified version throughout Europe, if not the world. The vast history of the Republic was on show, as well as the odd pleasure of witnessing its modern decline.

115 Giuseppe Primoli,
Eleonora Duse in a
Gondola on the Canale
della Giudecca, 1889.
Gelatin photograph. Rome,
Fondazione Primoli.

Since the survival of unique features was visibly under attack according to conservationists, there was an awareness of fragility, which brought an ever-increasing pathos.
Churches and galleries offered an unparalleled spread of Venetian painting, and many
were restored in the 1890s, no doubt in the expectation of art tourists. The Correr
collection was showing in the Fondaco dei Turchi, and the Accademia gallery, now
independent of the teaching establishment, had been replanned from 1895.[192] New
guides signalled the abundance of great buildings; the stones of Venice, especially
Gothic Venice, were formative for a taste much in vogue in international Gothic
revivals. Sea bathing was possible in a Mediterranean climate, and increasingly hotel
life was de luxe. New train services linked Venice to the exotic East; the city reas-
sumed something of its fairytale character as the hinge of Europe and with it, the lure
of a city interpreted as sexual and sensual: sensual in its water setting and art, and
for sexual licence, by no means extinct, but flourishing, particularly among males.

   Increasingly, too, it was the city of artists, not just the Giorgiones of the past, but
of the present. They had come in the early century – Madame de Staël, Byron,
Chateaubriand, Musset and Sand, but the guest list swelled in the later century.
Social and artistic nexes frequently overlapped. Paul Bourget, dedicating his 1892
Cosmopolis to Count Primoli of Rome, called it 'a novel of international life', which
begins in Italy, but travels to Florence, Venice, Nice, London, Paris and Constantinople, following the life of the artist who finds his subjects and artistic renewal in
travelling.[193] Count Primoli, a creature of the cosmopolis, was frequently in Venice
taking distinctive photographs, among them Eleanora Duse standing wistfully in a
gondola (fig. 115), and honeymooning couples in gondolas.

In the prime area at the top of the Grand Canal, many of the palaces were now foreign-owned, and sub-centres of the cosmopolis. The Russian painter Alexander Wolkof was in residence at Palazzo Barbaro; the spectacular Marchesa Casati was keeping leopards in the palace of the Venier dei Leoni – Fortuny photographed her with the poet Paul Helleu and the painter Giovanni Boldini.[194] Eleanora Duse's apartment was on the top floor of the Wolkof's Palazzo Barbaro; it remained a retreat for her for many years.[195] In 1894 Prince Edmond de Polignac and his wife, Winnaretta, who liked to collect artists and musicians around her, acquired the Palazzo Manzoni-Angaron on the Grand Canal (virtually opposite the Curtises), renaming it the Palazzo Polignac.[196] Keeping tradition alive after the death of the prince in 1901, the widowed princess had Siegfried's funeral music from *Götterdämmerung* performed in the courtyard of Wagner's last residence, the Palazzo Vendramin-Calergi.

In 1892, further along the Grand Canal on the opposite shore, the Americans Mr and Mrs Daniel Sargent Curtis had acquired the upper floors of the Palazzo Barbaro: Daniel Curtis was an amateur painter, offering views of ladies languid in scirocco conditions beside canals.[197] On the opposite side of the Canalazzo was the Casetta Rossa, where the Austrian Prince Frederick von Hohenlohe lived; born in Venice, he was a stout defender of the traditional city.[198] His sister was Maria von Thurn und Taxis, patron of the poet Rainer Maria Rilke, who lived at the Castello Duino near Gorizia. When the First World War broke out and Hohenlohe was required to leave Venice, D'Annunzio took over the Casetta Rossa.

National enclaves formed: the French came to the Polignacs, the Layards were in residence at Ca' Capello and the English gravitated there, and to Horatio Brown's Ca' Torresella.[199] The Americans came to the Curtises and Mrs Bronson. When the Curtises acquired part of the Palazzo Barbaro, Mrs Curtis was pleased with it 'as a good investment', 'there is a boom in Venetian palaces', she wrote hopefully, 'the price will rapidly rise, if rich foreigners begin to set the fashion of buying them'.[200] John Singer Sargent's painting of the Curtis family taking tea at home at the Palazzo Barbaro in 1899 (*An Interior in Venice*; London, Royal Academy), shows them disarmingly casual in formal dress beneath the vast authentic chandelier that lights the darkness (locale and dress are at some remove from Sargent's earlier Venetian paintings of women stringing beads and onions).[201] Among the Curtis's distinguished guests were Henry James and Mrs Isabella Stewart Gardner, patron of Sargent, who recalled the rooms of Palazzo Barbaro when she designed her 'Venetian' palace, Fenway Court in Boston.[202] Mrs Bronson was at the Casa Alvisi opposite Santa Maria della Salute, another fabled stop-over for Americans: 'the social *porto di mare*', Henry James called it.[203] Robert Browning was a close friend, and dedicated his last book of poetry, *Asolando: Fancies and Facts*, to Mrs Bronson whose hospitality he enjoyed, not only in Venice at the Casa Alvisi, but at her house, La Mura, in Asolo.[204] Browning's son Pen acquired the great Longhena palace, the Palazzo Rezzonico in 1889. Robert Browning died there in December 1899 and was taken across the water to the island of San Michele before his body was returned to England for burial in Westminster Abbey.[205]

Venice hosted high society, or offered the charged silence that aided the composition of *Tristan und Isolde*; or a simple motive such as the undulating pavement in San Marco which would later resound through Proust's *Remembrance of Things Past*. It was an exotic place of residence for the well off, and a repository of images and memories for some of the major artists of the time. By the end of the century Venice was saturated with the literature and poetics, the music and painting of a hundred-odd years. Over and beyond its lavish Republican past, it had inspired a vast modern body of work.

* * *

Nostalgia for the gaiety of a vanished age appeased Venetian and foreigner alike as they yearned for a Venice before the fall. It may well have been enhanced by the realisation that a full century had elapsed since 1797. Nostalgia for the old Serenissima had not abated, especially for its one-time custodians in Vienna. In the 1890s Hugo von Hofmannsthal began the first of his works with a focus on Venice, symptomatic of a fascination that was to reach well into the next century. Hofmannsthal gravitated to its Golden Age: in the first instance, to celebrate Titian again, as if the Frari memorial of recent Habsburg memory were still prominent. *Der Tod des Tizians* was the last essay on the artist in the century that had been so attentive to him, and his death.[206] This short play reflects on Titian's creative life overall, and the reputation of a great old painter registered by the young. Venice is again the art city, but seen from a vantage-point above, beyond the plague.

At the beginning, the Master demands his easel as his apprentices keep watch, wondering at the nearness of Titian's death, and the paradox of death for one who has created so much life. Giannino, Tizianello, Desiderio and Battista are young and beautiful; they speak for a new generation. Looking down on Venice, Giannino sees it in its glittering dress, appreciating its liquidity, its colour of red-blood and its shimmering phosphate poetry: the qualities we might think of in Titian's paintings.[207]

The inspiration for Hofmannsthal's second Venetian work came in 1898 when he read Casanova's memoirs in Venice, and wrote a short work on the adventurer's encounter with a famous contemporary soprano Thérèse.[208] Casanova's original account is shifted in venue from Florence to Venice, in deference no doubt to the ready association of Venice with opera. Casanova is transformed into the Baron Weidenstamm. *Der Abenteur und die Sängerin* suggests the beginning of a souring of Venice in Germanic literature that takes its cue from Casanova, finding him emblematic: erotic of course, but too mobile and deceitful. Indeed he becomes the prophet of *finis Venetiae*, exposing corrupt values in his culture as the Viennese writers in the 1890s were themselves seen to embody *finis Austriae*.[209]

The adventurer-type represented by Casanova is flawed; not a swashbuckler anti-hero like the bravo, he is altogether a more philosophical creature, who by compulsion must leave his native city, but remains tied to it and forever homesick (in itself the condition of Vienna with respect to Venice). The inner quest is as significant as the external adventures. Casanova is the adventurer-creator, in anticipation of the Decadence.

At the end of the century Hofmannsthal appears to be uncovering the layers of Venice, finding beauty still, but hearing a city singing its *Liebestod*. Beauty is shot through with ruin; the mask is the very condition of the dissembling citizen. In 1904 Hofmannsthal reworked the Otway play, *Venice Preserv'd*: his *Das gerettete Venedig* is a study of the flaws, political and personal, at work in the Republic, and by implication, in the present time.[210] Venice appears with Vienna as both partner and symptom in decadence: as it had been remarked in Boito's *Senso* in 1883 which explored the Risorgimento allegiance between a Venetian and an Austrian: 'Austria is nothing now'.[211] It was in 1883 that Johann Strauss premiered *Eine Nacht in Venedig* as cultural alliances between the two cities soured.

For Georg Simmel, writing only a decade later, the adventurer-type would signify nothing less than the psychology of an unanchored and unreliable Venice.[212] After the First World War, Arthur Schnitzler returned a decadent and aged Casanova to his home city in *Casanova's Homecoming*. The mutual cultivation of music in Vienna and Venice was investigated by Franz Werfel some two decades later, writing after the Second World War about Verdi and Wagner with even more protracted ambivalence with regard to beauty and decadence in Venice. On the other hand, the example of the Viennese Secession, its painters and architects, offered Venice its principal lesson in modern architecture.

Turn of the Century: Visitor Proust

For the French at the end of the century, Venice was chic (for the Polignacs), beguilingly miasmatic (for Barrès) and, from the turn of the century, a profound strand of personal memory (for Marcel Proust).

Proust was only briefly in Venice, but the profundity of the experience resonates through his vast literary work, *Remembrance of Things Past*.[213] His father, Dr Adrien Proust, was one of the most ardent campaigners for action against European-wide cholera, a disease in no way exclusive to Venice. Dr Proust worked at its alleviation throughout his life, after his first-hand experience of the devastation cholera wrought in France. He was a regular speaker at cholera summits held throughout Europe: Rome in 1885, Venice in 1882.[214] Yet the son Marcel was much more interested in Venice, the art city; unlike his compatriot Barrès, Venetian *paludisme* and fever were of little interest, despite his own notorious ill-health. The role that Venice city played in *Remembrance of Things Past* is well-known: it was a Venice of architecture and fashion, epitomised by San Marco, the golden angel on the Campanile and Fortuny's gowns.

Proust arrived in Venice in 1900. There is little evidence in *Jean Santeuil*, the extended sketch for *Remembrance of Things Past*, which he wrote from 1895 to 1900, that Venice had any thematic meaning for him before that visit.[215] But his circle of friends in Paris: notably the Polignacs, the poet Madame Anna de Noailles, whose poetry he admired, and his close friend the musician Reynaldo Hahn, who was related to the Fortunys, must have prepared him for a Venice with which they were linked by society, property and cultural love.[216] They revelled in its lyricism, its beauty, its effects of light, the grandeur of palace life on the Grand Canal, the musicality. At the Polignacs in Paris Proust had met Gabriel Fauré, a frequent visitor. Fauré's music for piano, his barcarolles and nocturnes were inspired by Venetian themes and rhythms, and the song-cycle *Cinq Mélodies de Venise*, setting poems by Verlaine, had been written in 1891 while visiting Winnaretta Polignac, who was making copies of Carpaccio's Saint Ursula ('comme tout le monde').[217]

But it was Ruskin who was Proust's declared mentor, and a major influence both on his style of writing, its cumulative clauses and sensuous detail, and his love of art and architecture. Proust perfectly understood that Ruskin's Venice was a Venice of the mind, of Ruskin's mind; 'a kind of urban autobiography of consciousness', it has been called.[218] Before Venice, Proust's passion for the cathedrals of France was stimulated by Ruskin and inspired a major translation project. (After bouts of insanity and, finally, influenza, Ruskin died on 20 January 1900.)

At the time of his first visit in 1900, Proust's work on Ruskin was at a high point, as he was in process of translating *The Bible of Amiens* into French.[219] Believing he was near death, and obviously picking up on the contemporary view that Venice was likewise, Proust wrote as if to confound the city's well-established reputation for mortality:

> I set off for Venice in order, before I died, to approach, to touch, to see embodied, in palaces that were decaying yet still upright, still pink, Ruskin's ideas on the domestic architecture of the Middle Ages. What importance, what reality can a town so special, so localized in time and so particularised in space as Venice have in the eyes of someone about to take leave of the earth. . . .[220]

Proust understood both the spatial and the temporal as hallmarks of the Venetian experience, of the special dimension in time, that area in which Proust was a connoisseur, and that geography peculiar to the island-city that could lodge itself in the mind forever. Proust's literary imagination was capable of leaping from Dante to Shakespeare to the Piazzetta, and he could transport the reader as if on lion's wings. For him 'certain days of reading' – the most inspiring occupation for Marcel Proust

– were comparable to 'days spent strolling in Venice', on the Piazzetta, for example, where the columns rose up in the imagination to take their positions high above the tourists: 'These two beautiful and slender foreigners came once from the East, across the sea that is breathing at their feet; uncomprehending of the remarks exchanged around them, they continue to leave out their twelfth-century days amidst the crowds of today.'[221]

In May 1900, finally arriving by train with his mother reading *The Stones of Venice* aloud as they crossed the lagoon, he met his English cousin, Mlle Marie Nordlinger and her aunt, and Reynoldo Hahn (who was to compose a suite of songs in the Venetian dialect the following year).[222] In October of the same year Proust made another visit to Venice alone, but almost nothing is known of it: we know only that he signed the visitors' book at the monastery of San Lazzaro.[223]

These brief visits ignited Proust's imagination. As Julia Kristeva has remarked, 'once Venice has infiltrated . . . the text partakes of sensation . . . Venice vibrates in the air that surrounds the book.'[224] In the novel the visit is long delayed because of the narrator's illness, which has increased the longing and contributed to the profound mixture of recognition and surprise experienced when at last he arrives. In truth, Proust's actual knowledge of Venice was a fictional creation, and retrospective, making it a fixture of his boyhood, powerful long before the narrator in *Remembrance* reaches adulthood. Upon arrival he sought out the architecture he knew through the mediation of Ruskin, and the fashionable taste for the Venice of the Bellini, Mantegna, Carpaccio, and nearby, in Padua, of the frescoes of Giotto, which he came to know during his boyhood through 'Swann'. When he wanders into 'labyrinthine' Venice, he comments that 'it was very seldom that, in the course of my wanderings, I did not come across some strange and spacious piazza of which no guide-book, no tourist had ever told me'. In making that very comment, he confirms himself as the tourist who sometimes abandons the mandatory itinerary and wanders off with little sense of direction, as James, Sargent and Whistler had done quite recently. Proust's visit took place before the grand hotels of the Lido had opened, so he stayed in the leading hotel on the Riva degli Schiavoni, the Daniele. He did not mix with Venetians, no local person impinges. As ever, his world is dominated by his mother, awaiting his return. When she leaves Venice, the city that is always the projection of this narrator, becomes 'a ruin'. Its reality, its history was unspecific, much less important than its immediate sensory impact. Darù might never have written. Its political state, or that of the country at large, is irrelevant. The moral weight of Ruskin's writing is of little importance: for Ruskin San Marco may well be a splendid Bible, but it is its artistic completeness rather than its theology which intoxicates.[225]

Venetian leitmotivs ripple through the many pages of *Remembrance*, as primary metaphors and as triggers of time and *personal* memory. These poetic reverberations are perhaps more complete and more life-enhancing in this respect than in any other writer. The uneven floor of the baptistery of San Marco is recalled when the narrator somewhere else stumbles over some cobblestones or worn paving; the golden angel on the Campanile, which he sees of a morning when he opens the shutters at the Hotel Daniele, is one of the long novel's most optimistic and splendid motifs. Time and space are fused, and profoundly so, in effect changing life.

Cardboard Cities

In the 1890s there was a multiplication of Venices beyond the city itself; the other Venices were made in plywood and canvas for the new pleasure gardens of Europe and America. More substantially, Mrs Isabella Stewart Gardner, a frequent visitor to Venice in the 1880s and 1890s, was busy amassing an art collection with the help of Bernhard Berenson, including Titian's *Rape of Europa*. She was also intent on repro-

ducing Venice in Boston. From 1899 she began constructing Fenway Court in imitation of a Venetian palace (with liberal admixtures of Romanesque, Spanish and Chinese), using architectural fragments purchased in Europe. On the occasion of the opening on New Year's Eve 1903 it was exclaimed that:

> From the eight balconies that once graced the Ca' D'Oro hung round flame-coloured lanterns, brilliant and yet soft globes of light in the lofty court, and through windows and arches came the flickering gleam of a myriad candles. The whole scene was indescribably beautiful, and as the rooms gradually filled with people it seemed as if the Venetian Renaissance had been reincarnated in twentieth century Boston. The thrill was beyond words.[226]

Professor William James considered it 'quite in line with a gospel miracle', no less.[227]

On the same side of the Atlantic, 1893 had been the year of the World Columbian Exposition in Chicago (fig. 116).[228] The opportunity for a site on the lake with a grand water entrance and the development of a natural lagoon was not lost, neither was its Venetian potential. A fleet of gondolas plied up and down the entrance waterway. Scenic views imitated the *vedute* traditional to Venice – showing the water in front of the Agricultural Building and the Arts Building on the Grand Basin, framing it with gondolas and casting it in crepuscular light with gondolas and ducks in the shadows.[229]

The gondola was a remarkable export: for some centuries it had been an aristocratic toy to be sailed on the artificial waters of Europe's palaces – at Fontainebleau, for example, and in the imitation Venices of Versailles and Nymphenburg.[230] In the 1890s it became an accessory of the bourgeois pleasure park, a feature, for instance, on the lake in Central Park, New York.

Venice was constructed internationally for popular taste. In 1891 in London, the entrepreneur Imre Kiralfy created a pageant named *Venice: The Bride of the Sea* (fig. 117), a medley of historical events played out in reconstructions of famous buildings that were housed in the new palace of exhibitions at Olympia.[231] An essential element was the provision of *faux*-canals with gondolas on hand for sixpenny trips. Individual exhibitions showed mosaic work, glass and toys, and in an annexe with a further sixpenny entry the indefatigable Salviati demonstrated glass production. A fine-art gallery exhibited Favretto, 'recently deceased'.

The 'historical' events reinforced an image of Venice by that time diffused: it was the benign domicile of Portia and the Merchant of Venice. On the occasion of the Sensa, the Bucintoro sailed out with auxiliary regatta. The fall of Chioggia was re-enacted, permitting marine ballets, while 'the great bell of the Campanile [tolled] notes of alarm', all mixed up with scenes from *The Merchant of Venice*. The Arsenale was in full production, *circa* 1378, turning out the ship the *Adriatica*. In his accompanying souvenir book Kiralfy presented himself overcoming all obstacles in the achievement of these Venetian splendours, emphasising the intrigue of his chosen period of 1378 to 1380, a time, in his own words, when, 'beset by powerful foes, Venice seemed doomed, but the spirit of patriotism was strong'. There lived three great heroes: Doge Andrea Contarini, Vettore Pisani, admiral of the fleet, and Carlo Zeno, general of the fleet. Thus Venice was still an exemplum of patriotism and sea power, appropriate to Victorian England. Ruskin's works were advertised in Kiralfy's souvenir.

Kiralfy's facsimile Venice must have had a familiar air to readers of the *Illustrated London News*, which, over the century, had reported the subjugation of Venice by Austria, the diplomatic intricacies of the Italian Question, the funeral of Manin and, increasingly after unification, a folksy, picturesque Venice where 'citizens' bought lanterns and decorations for festivals.[232] It was a telling comment on the state of Venice in popular history. In 1893 Kiralfy took his Venice to Paris, where he hoped that the cultivated French would recognise the exceptional quality of his artistry.

In 1895, on the site of the English Garden at the Vienna Prater, the park on the outskirts of the city, *Venedig in Wien* was created with navigable canals and forty imported gondolas, and with genuine gondoliers rowing past facsimiles of the Ca' d'Oro and the Palazzo Ducale. There was no doubt now that Venice was on the Danube, or close by. The architect of this *faux Venedig* realised as a semi-permanent attraction, Oskar Maromek, was a pupil of the Secessionist architect Otto Wagner; the painter was Ferdinand Moser, also a member of the Vienna Secession.[233]

References to Venice, at once exotic and familiar, were instantly recognised worldwide. At the Paris World Exposition of 1900 Carlo Ceppi erected the Italian pavilion on the banks of the Seine in hybrid Venetian style, a melange of San Marco and the Palazzo Ducale (fig. 118). Here was an exercise in exported *venezianità*, having cupolas, peaked portals embellished with sculpted friezes, floriate windows and *merlatura*.[234]

But the biggest crowds gathered in the New World to visit Coney Island off Manhattan where they could experience the ultimate honeymoon in Venice. Coney Island was ready for the film set, an incubator for the fantasies and deliriums of New York, as Rem Koolhaas has shown so brilliantly.[235] *The Canals of Venice* was part of the Coney Island extravaganza called Dreamland, touting its true-to-life effect as 'real gondolas carry the visitors through a Grand Canal reproduced with faithful regard for detail' with life in Venice – all the occupations of the original city – revealed on each side of the canals. Coney Island was a training ground for New York: for its skyscraper Gothic fantasies and its dreams of canals carrying cars on bridges built on the model of the Rialto. Dreamland burnt down in 1911, but analogies continued between water-bound Manhattan and Venice, the two island cities that have or have had economic power, both cherishing their reputation as world cities.[236]

* * *

117   Imre Kiralfy, cover of programme for *Venice: The Bride of the Sea*, Olympia, London, 1891/92. London, British Library.

118 Carlo Ceppi, 'Italian Pavilion', from Louis Rousselet, *L'Exposition Universelle de 1900*, 1901.

In 1897 a century had passed since the fall. The late years of the Republic were still regarded as decadent by the Venetians themselves. One hundred years later the eminent local historian Filippo Nani Mocenigo gave a sad account of the events that led to the termination of the Republic.[237] Molmenti had not hesitated to call the final part of his *Venezia, la vita privata* 'The Decadence' and to castigate the last doge for his 'cowardly resignation' that 'robbed the last hours of the Republic of that reverential pity which attends misfortune'.[238]

Yet by necessity, and with bouts of both high energy and inertia, Venice had turned its aristocratic Republic into a bourgeois government within the new nation of Italy. In the world's eyes, with the advent of Napoleon, it had lost the self-determining powers that had made it as great a nation as any on earth; its decadence had long been an accepted fact in Europe. Campoformio had receded into history. The 1848–9 resistance and Daniele Manin's leadership did much to restore the credibility of Venice and Venetians.

Over the century Venice had lost many churches and conventual buildings and many kilometres of canals had been interred. A railway to the mainland, new thoroughfares, cast-iron bridges, steam ferries on the canals, hotels and a bathing industry had altered appearances and procedures. At the end of the century, it concerned itself with sanitation and housing, war against disease, new industries, art and tourism. At some remove from the historic city, the Lido was being developed: in 1899 military lands had been acquired and the Excelsior Hotel and the Hotel des Bains were on the drawing board.[239] The Biennale had occured three times. The residency of Wagner and the rhetoric of D'Annunzio confirmed Venice's status as an art city. At the same time the marks of modernisation which had been driven by urgent need were increasingly forestalled by rising sentimentality with respect to old Venice.

During the 1890s the political parties in Venice factionalised in line with the division in conservation: certain moderates looked to the past and to conservation (Molmenti, elected to the national senate in 1890 was conspicuous), but a new preparedness to equate a conservative right position with more progressive social moves was also evident. The clerical influence in politics and the eminence of the patriarch Giuseppe Sarto were sufficient to end Selvatico's administration in 1895 and initiate the long reign of the Grimani administration, which lasted until 1919.[240] A socialist party was cohering in support of health and housing initiatives.

Local housing problems aside, what the world knew, and was repeatedly told, was the great repository of the past that Venice offered. The key monuments in the city, especially San Marco, had provoked international debate focused on patrimony and restoration. Even Venetians acknowledged that Venice belonged to the world; paradoxically, in protecting its patrimony that patrimony was forfeited. Molmenti was increasingly heard on a national scale. The city was visited increasingly for its picturesque qualities; it was felt to be sublimely pictorial. Foreigners were living in the palaces on the Grand Canal; foreign artists and writers might seem more conspicuous than the Venetian-born. The authority of historian Darù which had so shaped the creative agenda in the early part of the century, appeared diminished, absorbed into a *fin-de-siècle* cloud of nostalgia, guilt, love and death, as admonition or pity for Venice yielded to necrophilia and nocturnes sounded with barcarolles. Ponchielli's *La*

Gioconda and Hofmannstahl's reworking of Otway's *Venice Preserv'd* suggest that the interest in Venetian conspiracy was still alive; but the vapours of Barrès were more topical. The bravo appeared quite out of fashion; gondoliers had taken over the stage in Vienna and London and were plying the international *faux*-canals.

During the last years of the century there was a widespread return to the *mise-en-scène* of the late Republic, both in Venice and abroad. While Pompeo Molmenti wrote about Goldoni, the Villa Valmarano and the *Vita privata*, painter Giacomo Favretto was recreating the world of Tiepolo and Goldoni and painting nineteenth-century *popolani* with an eighteenth-century brush.

The Venetian eighteenth century fascinated Hofmannsthal and Markat; it sounded its faux-waltzes in Johann Strauss; devotees and critics of Casanova multiplied; Sitte lauded the town-planning of the old city. In France, the Goncourt brothers found their own eighteenth-century painters attentive to Venice, not only in lessons learnt from Tiepolo, but in an increasingly cultivated spirit of nostalgia. Watteau was reinvoked, for he had felt Venice not only through the *commedia dell'arte* and the motif of embarkation, but as a pervasive wistful spirit. As the brothers Goncourt wrote:

> It is indeed true that in the recesses of Watteau's art, beneath the laughter of its utterance, there murmurs an indefinable harmony, slow and ambiguous; throughout his *fêtes galantes* sadness; and, like the enchantment of Venice, there is audible an indefinable poetry, veiled and sighing, whose soft converse captivates our spirits.[241]

In 1901 Proust's friend Reynaldo Hahn caught the melancholy of the journey when he set to music a poem in dialect written by Pietro Pagello, George Sand's Venetian lover, replete with soft concourse, veiled and sighing:

> Coi penieri malinconici
> No te star a tormentar;
> Vien con mi, montemo
>   in gondola,
> Andaremo fora in mar.
> Passaremo i porti e l'isole
> Che circonda la città.
> El sol more senza nuvole
> E la luna spuntarà.[242]

The journeys to Venice, to the islands of the lagoon, the serenade and the coming of night, and the inevitable waft of melancholy mark the mood of the *fin de siècle*.

Within two years of Proust's second visit to Venice in September 1900, the collapse of the Campanile of St Mark's turned the angel on the summit to dust. When he began writing *Remembrance of Things Past* the process of rebuilding was only half finished; nevertheless, in 1909 Proust left the angel in its traditional, radiant position, never admitting its fall. He kept it intact in his own memory and vision, as he opened and re-opened the window of the Danieli hotel. Some ninety years after his visit, after the passing of nearly a century, the undulating floor of San Marco was worn to such an extent that it was covered with a special carpet.

Part 2

Chapter 7

THE HEAVY PAST:
FROM THE TURN OF THE CENTURY
TO THE FIRST WORLD WAR

Beyond Venice, at the turn of the century, the city's familiar icons were reproduced in international pleasure grounds, reaching audiences of thousands. The world abounded with Venetian glass and lace, exported gondolas, facsimiles of the Palazzo Ducale, the Bridge of Sighs and the Rialto Bridge. Ruskin's Gothic Venice was influential throughout the world, from Manchester to Melbourne. Venice in 'Dreamworld' was open to the crowds at Coney Island, and, from 1905, California was creating its Venice on the beach, building bridges and arcades, and importing gondolas and gondoliers.[1]

Familiar to almost everyone, Venice in the twentieth century became the world's most popular tourist destination. At the end of that century, threatened by flood and excessive numbers of visitors, it appeared no less vulnerable than it did to Byron, with his vision of the marble palaces sinking to the water-line. The *ruin* of Venice was a given for the Romantics, but it was the death of Venice that was perpetrated in the twentieth century. Venice had become the very allegory for history, decay and the threat of the elements, powerful still at the onset of the twenty-first century.

The century was punctuated by debates between the *anciens* and the *modernes*, with the *anciens* in ascendancy. For F. T. Marinetti and his Futurists, who attacked the city in 1910, Venice was the very embodiment of *passéisme* (the obsessive cult of the past), the disease of old Italy. In the first decade of the century, it was no longer blonde and beautiful as in the persistent metaphor of the lost Republic; 'she' was the old whore, the battered procuress. It was a city of epidemics and death for Thomas Mann. For others – pre-eminently Gabriele D'Annunzio, among the best-known Italians of his period – Venice was strategic still, the springboard to the renewal of Italy across the Adriatic. Venice produced a number of notable entrepreneurs in the first years of the new century, particularly Giuseppe Volpi, who was keen to expand business beyond the Veneto, and committed to the Irredentist project to free native-speaking Italians from foreign government.[2] Volpi was to become one of the best-known Italians during the period between the two World Wars. He had import and export interests in Hungary and in the Balkans, and a banking partnership with Giuseppe Toeplitz in Naples. He was the primary developer of electricity in the Veneto region. A steamship company and crucial interests in the luxury hotels under construction on the Lido extended his areas of influence, ensuring that both tourism and transport were in place in the portfolio.

The new century opened with the old argument concerning the construction of a carriageway to the mainland. Modernists, eager to admit modern life, to come to terms with the new motor car and develop an economic base wider than tourism, were ranged against those who wanted the city suspended in time, to be forever historic and picturesque. Those against the bridge – the *anti-pontisti* – were eloquently headed by Pompeo Molmenti, by then an elder statesman with ten years' experience in the national government.[3] He was an effective opponent of the project, at least until

Raimondo Zago, *The Fall of the Campanile, 14 July 1902.*

the end of the First World War.[4] By then, wartime isolation made the provision of a bridge inevitable, although it was not opened until 1934, when the momentous decision was taken to limit motor traffic to the station area.[5] The argument that was once so bitter is now forgotten. It is assumed that Venice was never able to accommodate motor traffic, that it lived in a time-warp of gondolas, with the *vaporetti* the only concession to the modern age. The *vaporetti* service had been extended in 1905 only after a positive plebiscite that led to the foundation of the ACNIL company, which is still in control of the inter-lagoon service.[6]

A proposal for a new port was also controversial. In the *Gazzetta di Venezia* of 3 August 1902, Luciano Petit launched 'the revolutionary idea' to site a new port on shores that could be reclaimed from marshland on the nearby Terraferma, passing by Venice via the channel along the Giudecca to the lagoon flats, near mainland Mestre at Marghera.[7] Marghera had been the site of a fort in the time of the Republic, and beyond; it had been a strategic centre during the revolution against the Austrians in 1848–9. Petit was supported by Piero Foscari, descendent of doges, a man of singular energy and authority, and close to the influential Giuseppe Volpi.[8] The 1902 idea was another and crucial stage in the debates on the location of the port that had begun in the Napoleonic era when a free-trade area was located on the island of San Giorgio Maggiore. In the 1920s Porto Marghera was established as the new industrial and economic hope of the old city; in the 1970s it was castigated as the cause of pollution and destructive high tides – *acque alte* – in the historic city. Yet in the early twentieth century the scheme was won with the argument that historic Venice would be protected by the removal of industry and the establishment of a separate port.

Because of the extent and quality of its remaining past, the city was driven, above all, to uphold the old, to make it available to tourists and to accept that economic viability lay in tourism. The development of the Lido was spectacular in the first decade of the century. From time to time there were endeavours to move beyond dependence on tourism, to create work for residents and new facilities within an old fabric, but there was little urge to confront the new, to uphold new life in the old centre, to engage with the life of the times, for it was so easily demonstrated that the new went against the interest of the old city. The new was an enemy; it was *contra* Venice. Modern traits were possible in the design of buildings that by and large stayed on paper. To accommodate the modern, Venice had the Esposizione d'Arte, an initiative that became known as the Biennale. For the duration of the events Venice appeared to embrace contemporary art.

The Fall of the Campanile

The considerable power of the past was demonstrated by the most dramatic event in the first years of the new century. On 14 July 1902 the Campanile of San Marco collapsed.[9] The disaster had been anticipated for at least a week, after repairs were made to the roof of the Loggetta: a crack opened up and in a few days it had reached the height of the fifth window. There had been warnings, but they went unheeded. The authority for the Loggia was not the same as the authority for San Marco and the Campanile, so nothing was done.[10] The weekend before the collapse visitors were still allowed to climb the Campanile although cracks were visibly rising; it was not until Sunday that the orchestras in the Piazza were silenced to avoid undue vibration. On Monday morning came the collapse: mercifully compact, killing no one, crushing Sansovino's Loggetta, but causing little damage to the adjacent Basilica or the Palazzo Ducale. A pyramid of rubble reached to the upper arches of San Marco, but only the north-east corner of Sansovino's Biblioteca and four shops along the Procuratie Nuove were damaged (fig. 119).

119 A. Zaghis, *The Fall of the Campanile, 9.52 a.m., 14 July 1902.*

The world watched aghast. Dramatic photographs showed the pile of rubble (fig. 120); reportage was awed:

> All about lie broken columns, bits of carving, pieces of hewn stone, huge twisted sheets of copper roofing (for the green sloping roof of the loggia on the top of the Campanile was copper); iron bars bent and broken, and shattered, splintered marbles everywhere – gleaming, too, here and there, all over the heaps were pieces of broken bronze bells that, hung high up in the loggia, had called the senators to the council hall, the worker to the arsenal and the people to prayer . . . [11]

The city immediately demonstrated its loyalty to its beloved monument. After a meeting of the Filippo Grimani administration, the decision to rebuild on the same site was taken unanimously, on the very day of the collapse. *Dov'era, com'era* became a slogan for the project in defiance of the modernists who would design it anew. Giacomo Boni was recalled from the excavations of the Forum in Rome to take charge of the rubble and the rebuilding endorsed by the Commune.[12] Boni's specialist knowledge had been established with his archaeological excavations of the building's foundations undertaken in 1885.[13] He was unhesitating in his advice to rebuild, supervising the transfer of precious fragments to the courtyard of the Palazzo Ducale, and conducting a funeral ceremony for the rubble which was taken by ship for 'burial' offshore from the church of San Nicolò on the Lido – in the seas where the doges cast St Mark's ring to the waters.[14]

The loss of their Campanile affected Venetians deeply. The great bell, the Marangona, would sound no more. Old Papa, 'El Papà dei Campanile', as the Campanile

120a and b   Naya studio, gelatin photographs showing the rubble from the fall of the Campanile, 14 July 1902. Venice, Archivio Osväldo Bohm.

was affectionately known, was gone. Pompeo Molmenti lamented the loss of the symbol of Venice's masculine vigour.[15] In Rome D'Annunzio wept, while in Milan Giosué Carducci told the socialist newspaper that the Campanile ought *not* to be rebuilt.[16] Serge Diaghilev, the creator of the Ballets Russes, who spent most of his summers on the Lido, liked to tell the story of the Venetian sea captain returning by sea on the day the Campanile fell, who saw it was no longer there, and went mad.[17]

With the commitment to rebuilding came the criticism that it was reactionary. Only three days after the collapse, on 17 July, the Trieste paper, *L'Adriatico*, published a telegraph from the leading Viennese architect Otto Wagner, headlined 'The eccentricities of a Viennese engineer'.[18] Wagner claimed that the whole city was destined to disappear because of the unstable foundations of the lagoon region, which caused continual movement. The collapse of the Campanile had been threatened for a long time, and, further, he considered rebuilding to be beyond the competence of his Italian colleagues. To add insult to injury, he recommended that the Campanile should be moved, since its position marred the aesthetic harmony of the Piazza. But the major contention was that a new Campanile should be built in modern style since it 'would be a falsification of the history of architecture to reconstruct it in the old style'.

But victory for preservationists and sentimentalists was assured. In wicked response to Wagner, a caricature of the tower as a Secessionist monument appeared in the Viennese weekly *Der Floh*, with San Marco tarted up as a Secessionist building, given gold-leaf domes, white-washed walls with motifs of peacock's tails, and a row of clipped trees in front. The Campanile itself became a giant candelabra (fig. 121).[19] A further malicious touch was a lion gnawing a bone, chained up in a kennel in front of San Marco. More serious reconstructions were offered, mainly in decorated Gothic, with the Campanile appearing like an over-extended version of London's Albert Memorial. Photomontages showed the supposedly improved effect of siting the Campanile on the opposite side of San Marco, on the Piazzetta dei Leoncini.[20]

Otto Wagner's commitment to a building in an appropriate contemporary style was not a whim of the moment. In 1911, when the work of rebuilding was virtually complete, he had more to say.[21] Writing on 'The Lay Opinion in Art', which opinion he took to be limited if not reactionary, he modified his views a little, misquoting himself as saying that the Campanile should indeed inhabit the same site and keep its original outline; the power of a familiar image was great, and art should respect and respond to the familiar.[22] His thoughts for a modern monument had taken further shape as he now advocated a new tower to replace the 'ugly bricks' with mosaics that would tell the history of Venice, using the thriving local mosaic industry. It was a beguiling volte-face in which the influence of the mosaics of Ravenna and Venice on Secessionist Vienna was commended, in turn, to Venice. In time, Wagner declared, the limitations of lay judgement are superseded, and taste readjusts. The mixture of building styles in the Piazza San Marco – from the Byzantine-Roman San Marco, through to the Gothic, Renaissance and Baroque buildings – had come to be recognised as *eine entzückende Symphonie*, 'a symphony of delight', entirely acceptable to lay opinion.[23] The city's decision to reconstruct the old merely created 'a waxworks' and the opportunity for creating a significant contemporary monument would be lost.

However, a Viennese compatriot, the art historian Alois Riegl, found a way of defending the replacement of an edifice as prominent as the Venice Campanile.[24] In 1903, at a time when the Austro-Hungarian empire was legislating for the protection of its own historic buildings, Riegl wrote a paper on the nature of monuments, declaring that an artefact should be of its own time, exemplifying its own *Kunstwollen*. The blurring of past and present was not recommended. The argument was against distinctions drawn between art monuments and historical monuments: since the historically sensitive nineteenth century, there had been 'a dramatically increased appreciation of historical value'.[25] Taking the Campanile as a topical case, Riegl accorded it obvious historical value, or 'age-value', as it represented a particular stage of human development.[26]

Following the collapse, a host of articles attested to the enchantment of the Piazza San Marco, waxing lyrical at such a concentration of marvels in one place.[27] The fall of the Campanile had brought the Piazza to world attention yet again. The full complement of paeans devoted to its power and profile were collected for an official volume in 1912 on the occasion of its dedication, and local worthies committed to preservation had an opportunity to employ all their eloquence.[28] Antonio Fradeletto, secretary of the Biennale, opened with a history of the reconstruction. With words like *superba*, Pompeo Molmenti followed the Campanile's long history and its many rebuildings, the lightning strikes, the festivals in the Piazza and the tightrope displays performed from the Campanile, all the forces of destiny of the 'gloriosa antenna' turned to rubble on 14 July 1902, but now raised up again. Giacomo Boni, among the most stalwart defenders of local colour, wrote on the collapse, the ruins and his own archaeological findings of 1885, which had confirmed the vast antiquity of the site.[29] Luca Beltrami, who had resigned from the project during early difficulties, wrote in detail on the first crucial stages of reconstruction from March to June 1903. The last stage was the painstaking reconstruction of the fragments of Sansovino's Loggetta.[30] Every stage was followed by photographs showing the miraculous re-erection of the tower, culminating in the lifting of the bells and the final re-positioning of the gilded angel on the summit.

The success of the forces of preservation, replication and civic self-congratulation was confirmed in the ceremony for the rededication on St Mark's Day, 25 April 1912. In the decade that had passed there had been a limited infiltration of modernism, but it was pushed to the periphery, held at bay on the Lido. The fall of the Campanile confirmed the value of the past; and world opinion condoned it.

The authors of the rebuilding were well versed in the issues of preservation in the last decades of the previous century: there was little real opposition to the replication. The dedication ceremonies reconfirmed the great history of Venice, the Piazza and its monuments. Alongside the photographers, many artists documented the rebuilding. Italico Brass added topical interest to his *vedute* of the Piazza over a number of years, following the tower as it rose again.[31] Ettore Tito painted the re-dedication ceremony in neo-Baroque mode with bell-ringers and choristers elevated above the crowd in almost angelic formation.[32] During the years of rebuilding the organisers of the Biennale took full advantage of the energy they saw confirmed by the Campanile's reconstruction and used the scaffolding-tower as a motif in their posters and the rising Campanile as a symbol of the modern and the progressive.[33] The phrase *dov'era, com'era* became local law, to be invoked by implication with every restoration, and in the face of every disaster. When the opera house La Fenice burnt in 1996 the Campanile's collapse was recalled: the phoenix must always be reborn, *dov'era, com'era*. And modernism must always be held at bay.

* * *

The Case of Modern Architecture: Gothic Victory

In effect, the reconstruction of the Campanile went against the interests of modern architecture in the heart of the city. No local architect came out specifically against the rebuilding. Reconstruction of the old triumphed over the advocacy of the new. The euphoric climate that saw the Campanile's regrowth made it almost impossible for a genuine appreciation of the modern to take root against the force of tradition and regional style.

In 1906, when the foundations of the new tower had been laid, the first of the city's Soprintendente ai Monumenti, Massimiliano Ongaro, addressed the Ateneo Veneto on 'Monuments and their Restoration'. As a spokesmen in public office, Ongaro expressed a view that must have had some adherents at that time in his professional circle.[34] Principally he was concerned with the relation of the present to the past, which he rightly identified as *the* crucial issue for Venice. He wanted to expose 'falseness' as the primary danger for current architecture.

Ongaro was direct in saying that shifts in taste inevitably involved condemnation of earlier work. Palladio's recommendation to demolish the Gothic Palazzo Ducale in order to modernise it by rebuilding in *classical* mode was an instance of an architect espousing values that ran counter to the preservation of the past.[35] Yet it was possible to reconcile appreciation of both Gothic and Baroque: his examples were the Ca' d'Oro and the Palazzo Pesaro, Carpaccio and Tiepolo, the Gothic Palazzo Ducale co-existing with a Renaissance courtyard, and the 'bizarre mixtures of form' that constituted San Marco: who would dare reduce it to a single style? The point may seem obvious, and close to Otto Wagner's, but it was not long since Ruskin had expressed his preference for the Gothic against the Renaissance and the Baroque. After all, the High Baroque church of San Moisè had only recently been threatened with demolition. Ongaro's main point was clear but hardly heeded: the desire to build in old styles was false. Current architects accomplished their deceits subtly; they added false gems to the authentic crown of Venice.[36]

Some six years later, in 1912, when the Campanile was only months from completion, Ongaro addressed the question of modern architecture in Venice more directly.[37] Again he invoked the principle of pluralism in artistic history. Revision and renewal were the very forces which had created a 'Venice . . . beautiful because she was always modern for that is her tradition and the essence of her life'.[38] The argument was clever in its appeal to the present in terms of the past – Ongaro's listeners were asked to imagine a city frozen in the ninth century, a primitive Byzantine Venice of reed huts and a San Marco made of unadorned brick.[39]

Yet Ongaro himself could not so easily relinquish the past. Despite his stated will-to-the-modern, he exhibited little understanding of the alternatives to historicism or eclecticism. He believed that modern architecture could find new life in old traditions, in *tradizione antica*, without indulging in obsessive searches for new styles. He commended the study of Venetian sources, but not what he called servile and spineless imitation: 'Venice should jealously guard the old art that remains, but should give space to the modern.'[40] Only the first principle was fully understood.

It was not only the conservation of monuments that was at stake, but the expanded and polemicised agenda for demolition, housing and the preservation of 'local colour'. The parameters of the problem had been decisively set in the 1870s. Issues had sharpened, but they had not basically changed after the turn of the century; indeed their tenacity was demonstrated even in those with a professed will-to-the-modern. Public bodies extended their jurisdiction beyond the major monuments to attend even to the *ambiente*. La Società per l'Arte Pubblica in Venezia had been formed to comment on any aspect of the city or the lagoonscape. As we have seen, in 1899 Carlo Emo had spoken on behalf of the wide range of Venetians who comprised the society, and found it unacceptable that 'ruins were evident in all parts of the city'.[41] Traditional colours were no longer used: among the worst offenders were the palaces belonging to the Municipality. The society's paper was one of the most extreme statements of the conservative position: among the signatories were the city's most prominent cultural figures, all determined that nothing new should mar the face of old Venice.

In an article published in the Turin architectural journal *L'Architettura Italiana* in 1909, its director, Giovanni Lavini, endorsed the prestige of the city as a museum yet again.[42] He wrote about Venice as if nothing had or would change: it was the kind of polemic that might have provoked the anti-Venice views from the Futurists. As the 'superb queen' conserved her aspect as a great city every attempt to modernise was mistaken and every transformation an anachronism. It was a matter for triumph that the iron roofs of the fish market on the Grand Canal had been demolished in 1902 and replaced with a loggia in classicising Lombard style by Cesare Laurenti and Domenico Rupolo.[43] This was an event of importance, indeed, it was prophetic: the first demolition of a 'modern' nineteenth-century structure now deemed intrusive. The modern must be banished to the peripheries and take refuge on the Lido or the Terraferma, where there was nothing to confront it. In Venice it was not only the architecture, but the water, and the reflections that appealed. Lavini's cloying and socially patronising view ran to praise of handsome gondoliers, beautiful working girls and *popolani* with languid glances inhabiting their indigenous housing while serenades sounded in perpetuum. Venice must not change or be transformed since its buildings and characteristic life were bound together. The city was a museum, but it was living, animated and festive.

Lavini considered that the fall of the Campanile was a disaster, but providential because it led to the inspection of other historic buildings. Falling pieces had been recorded from many famous monuments – the Scuola Grande di San Marco, the basilica of Santi Giovanni e Paolo and the Frari.[44] An inspection of the Procuratie Vecchie shortly after the collapse of the Campanile revealed dangerous weaknesses in its foundations.[45]

Against Lavin's sentimentality, Ongaro's cautious receptivity to something he imagined to be modern was brave indeed. Eclectic building, particularly in the Gothic mode, dominated in the first decades of the twentieth century.

The Venetian architect most alert to the modern movement, and to Viennese Secessionism in particular, was Giuseppe Torres, one of the most remarkable Venetian talents in the early century.[46] His Garage Marçon in Mestre, built in 1907 and now demolished, was a notable demonstration of his grasp of the Secessionist manner in the clarity of its curvilinear modern line.[47] His most radical designs, never built, were made in 1908 for a pair of free-standing villas: the House of Silence (fig. 122) in basic white cement, and the House of the Poet (fig. 123), both free from Gothic reference and manifestly sympathetic to Secessionism in their clean cubic forms, unadorned white walls with rounded edges and assymetrical styling.[48]

At the turn of the century Alfredo Melani and other critics had seen the influence of the Austrian Secession as an impediment to the realisation of a national style, particularly after the 1902 exhibition in Turin.[49] For some Venetian architects Viennese architecture was the main conduit to modernism, or at least *arte nuova*, and the counter to provincial modes. For Giuseppe Torres and his brother Duilio the Vienna school was the means of liberation from the repetitive eclecticism of local Gothic.[50] It promised a revision of ornament and a new geometry. Nor was it a stylistic fad; it was a profound and lasting line of influence that recognised the geographical link of Venice with *Mittel Europa* and the historic ties of the countries; the direct path of influence led to central Europe, rather than to Paris.[51] Ironically the influence seemed possible only after Vienna had moved into its last imperial phase, decades after the withdrawal of Vienna from Venice. The influence of Vienna went far beyond the interventions of Otto Wagner and Alois Riegl in the matter of the Campanile.

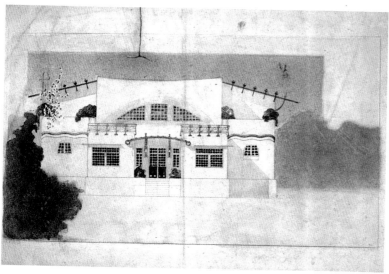

Modernism in architecture, in so far as it disturbed the conservatism of Venice, carried the imprint of the Secession. In particular, villa architecture – the novel projects for the Lido – took its cue from Viennese modernism. Later in the century Carlo Scarpa's oeuvre, the most important architecture in Venice in the twentieth century, is unthinkable without his understanding of the Viennese School. As he himself wrote: 'the tradition of my studies, by a sort of natural geographic affinity, has brought me close to a modernity which comes from Vienna . . . in the artist I most admired, Josef Hoffmann . . . there is a profound expression of the sense of decoration . . .'[52] The longevity of the influence of the Viennese School is evident in Massimo Cacciari's philosophical and theoretical enquiry into the thought and practice of Adolf Loos, Otto Wagner, Ludwig Wittgenstein and others.[53] Vienna was also a profound influence for Aldo Rossi, working out of the architectural 'School of Venice' in the 1980s.[54] In his early career he wrote carefully on the work of Adolf Loos.[55] The most radical readings of architecture and society in the early twentieth-century, those of the institute's architectural historian and theorist Manfredo Tafuri, centred on Germany and Vienna.[56]

In 1912, when Alfredo Melani was discussing new building in Venice in the journal *Italia*, he declared that Venice was opposed to modernity, and that construction should proceed only if it did not infringe local conditions.[57] Seen as 'Italy's most radical critic', Melani diagnosed an architectural condition that was to be dominant throughout the century, inhibiting the modern while at times appearing to support it. He himself felt strongly for the city, admiring not only the Basilica, but also the 'silent corners', 'the many magic places'.[58] At the same time he had some understanding of the gridlock created by the strength of the past and its inhibition about change, in order to keep the city as a museum for sentimental tourists. Venice is (yet again) a crowning jewel in the Italian artistic heritage: why does 'she' not want to add 'the gem of modernity' to her crown?[59]

Amid declarations of love for the city and comments on the renovating sequence of styles that had made Venetian architecture and painting distinctive in the past, Melani recommended that architects should *not* restrict themselves to past styles. Two architects, Giuseppe Torres and Giulio Alessandi, were acceptable because they embraced the new, and yet the illustrations of their work showed a Gothicising architecture. Torres's own house, sited on the small canal at Rio del Gaffaro, was built in the years 1905 to 1907, not in an overtly Secessionist style, but in the mellow mode

122 (*top*) Giuseppe Torres, *The House of Silence*, 1908. Pencil and watercolour, 48.3 × 33 cm. Venice, Collection Giulia Torres.

123 (*above*) Giuseppe Torres, *The House of the Poet*, 1908. Pencil and watercolour, 24.4 × 29.1 cm. Venice, Collection Giulia Torres.

of the Venetian Byzantine revival (fig. 124).[60] Constructed in brick with the overhanging eaves popular in adaptations of Alpine architecture, it was scaled adeptly to its small site. Yet Arabic pointed arches, Corinthian capitals in a four-light window, a round arch in decorative brick with Ravennate motifs of animals in low relief, an iconic figure set in a niche, an iron door worked in low relief, and 'Carpaccio' chimneys – these are hardly the elements of a modern vocabulary.[61] In so far as modernism intrudes, it does so in the untraditional cream and green of the geometrically edged shutters.

Melani illustrated the work of Ambrogio Nardizzi most fully, making connections back to local nineteenth-century Gothic and buildings including Meduna's Palazzo Giovannelli near the Strada Nova at Cannaregio, and the various projects undertaken on the Palazzo Cavalli-Franchetti. He regarded Cadorin's buildings as participants in the local tradition, notably his terracotta-decorated Palazzina Marioni on the Grand Canal near San Trovaso from the 1890s, and the Palazzo Giovanezza on the upper Grand Canal, near Santa Maria della Salute. His brick architecture featured Gothic windows in various arched formations, traditional balconies and sculptural roundels inset in the Byzantine-Venetian manner. The *altana* – the roof-top balcony made of wood – the traditional staircase with under-arches and the shaped chimney were predictable elements. This vocabulary confirmed the *venezianità* of the early twentieth century. It is ironic, then, that Melani considered himself to be a leading member of the Italian avant-garde, which had been recommending the purge of 'dead' styles as early as 1887.[62] However, the forces against such a purge were collective memory and the fraught question of Venetian identity. That identity was Gothic.[63]

The Gothic mode was the preferred style of building for turn-of-the-century Venice until the First World War, a period in which there was considerable construction, particularly in the Lido. The Gothicising work of Meduna and Boito in the previous century had given rise to projects that were opulent and conspicuous; and there were many more restrained essays in local Gothic. Sardi's Bauer Grünewald Hotel on the Grand Canal had its modernised Gothic wing; further down at San Barnaba, Giuseppe Berti, with the collaboration of painter and decorator Raffaele Mainella, had built the

Palazzetto Stern with Gothic balconies, Byzantine medallions, conspicuous asymmetry, a loggetta and a balustraded garden on the water.

The most distinctive façade built in the early twentieth century is on the Giudecca: the house known as Tre Ochi (Three Eyes) designed by the artist Mario de Maria, still emphatic and stylish across the Bacino (fig. 125).[64] Mario de Maria was a conservative painter, but this building was the most adventurous built at that time. Its distinction comes from a confident overstatement of local elements, which are taken into the curvilinear terrain of Stile Liberty architecture. The façade, dominated by three large, quaintly shuttered windows – the three eyes – is outlined in stucco in imitation of Istrian stone. Patterned brickwork in diamond formation quotes the Palazzo Ducale over the water, as does the over-scaled *merletura* that caps the building. The three windows bulge out beneath exaggeratedly peaked arches that have semicircular balconies with small iron balustrades. The central eye is crowned with a stucco cutout, an open quatrefoil in a pointed arch arrangement. Shaped 'Carpaccio' chimneys, an element in the architecture of the local picturesque, animate the roofline.

Mario de Maria signed himself 'Marius Pictor': trained in Bologna, and a friend of D'Annunzio in Rome, he came to Venice in 1892 and was the last of the Venetian history painters. Eschewing the bright lights of modernism, he favoured the crepuscular tones of Symbolism and themes of historical decadence. His paintings remained conservative, in historicist mode. The best-known is the *Fondaco dei Turchi in Venice* (fig. 126) of 1909: heavily shadowed, encrusted, re-creating the canal-side life of the old warehouse that had become notorious for of its over-restoration. De Maria restored it to the exotic time of Titian, showing the façade draped with striped awnings, and slaves disembarking from a boat. Titian is seated near the water's edge painting a naked woman.[65] Deep shadows, a feature of most of de Maria's tenebrous paintings, dramatise the façade.

In the 1912 Biennale Mario de Maria exhibited a grand painting (Venice, private collection) – itself made during an outbreak of cholera – of the epidemic that raged at the time of Manin's uprising of 1848. With a salacious edge, he created another lugubrious scene of a boat heaped with corpses, and receiving more – angled light falls upon a body draped over a window ledge.[66] Like other Venetians – or adopted Venetians such as Mariano Fortuny – de Maria was caught in the peculiarly Venetian condition of the new in collusion with the old. Yet his own house, the studio house with three 'eyes', is the most conspicuous Venetian essay in Stile Liberty.

Historicism was the norm in architectural practice at the turn of the century, and in this Venice was no different from many other places. Berti's Palazzetto Stern constructed from 1909 to 1912, the residence on the Zattere that he built from 1912 to 1914 and the architect Giuseppe Torres's house were characteristic examples of a modest, warm Gothic historicism, products of a local culture that was articulate and confident within the local picturesque tradition.[67] It was evident in the Gothic style of domestic building as well as the domestic comfort and luxury expressed in the revivals of traditional brocades and velvets inspired by Carpaccio paintings. The Byzantine style was an element in this quasi-modernism: gilt and mosaics were its features, particu-

125 Mario de Maria, Casa dei Tre Ochi, Giudecca, 1912.

larly evident in work by the Vienna Secessionists, who took the mosaics of Ravenna and Venice as a source. Mariano Fortuny was an increasingly famous exponent of the patterns of the past seemingly brought up-to-date and appealing to the couture world in the age of Worth and Poiret (fig. 127).[68] From 1906 he occupied the original Gothic Palazzo Orfei, now the Museo Fortuny, draping its interior with his own silks and velvets.[69] Moving in an aristocratic circle that included both foreigners and Venetians, he knew D'Annunzio and Eleanora Duse, the Marchesa Casati, the aristocrat Prince von Hohenlohe and the Comtesse de Noailles, all assiduous cultivators of *venezianità*. Fortuny's production of fabrics and his couturier activity began at much the same time, as an extension of his stage designs for D'Annunzio and Duse in *Francesca da Rimini*.[70] He readily acknowledged the inspiration of Carpaccio, but it was not only the painted costumes, but Gothic domestic architecture that gave undeniable warmth to turn-of-the-century Venice. Marcel Proust, equally enthused by Carpaccio and the fabrics of Fortuny, was acutely aware of their interconnection.[71] In *Remembrance of Things Past*, Albertine, dressed by Fortuny, becomes the very likeness of Venice at its most opulent and vibrant: 'The Fortuny gown which Albertine was wearing that evening seemed to me the tempting phantom of that invisible Venice. It was overrun, like Venice, with Arab ornamentation, like the Venetian palaces hidden like sultan's wives behind a screen of pierced stone . . .'[72] As the narrator looked at the fabric, it 'transformed itself into a malleable gold by virtue of those same transmutations which, before an advancing gondola, change into dazzling metal the azure of the Grand Canal'.[73] As he kisses Albertine, he virtually kisses Venice; he was in the act of 'pressing to my heart the shimmering azure of the Grand Canal', no less. Proust understood Fortuny's fabulous chromatic skills and their rich genealogy in Venetian art, describing the sleeves of the evening gown as 'lined with a cherry pink which is so peculiarly Venetian that it is called Tiepolo pink'.[74]

In the 1950s Peggy Guggenheim could still remark that her own modern style appeared strange in the midst of the old-fashioned interiors of Venice.[75] Yet photographed in her prized Fortuny gown, she too had her continuity with that past.

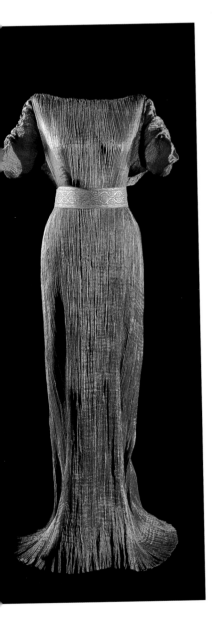

The Esposizione Internazionale d'Arte and Venetian Painters

The climate in which the Fortuny Delphos gown was created, around 1908, was one which cherished luxurious surfaces and inspiration of mosaics – from Ravenna, in vogue then, as much as Venice. The return to Byzantium pervaded all the arts.[76] Early Biennales have been seen as conservative and reactionary: they did not display modernist practice.[77] Symbolist art dominated. Work was selected by the sponsoring countries, who sent Secessionists and Symbolists, rather than emerging Fauvists and Expressionists. Nevertheless, the exhibitions were a register of the pluralist nature of the times, at that stage not regarded as dominated by the School of Paris, or German Expressionism. Major living artists were the focus of the important one-person exhibitions that gave a retrospective dimension to the Biennales, such as those of Rodin in 1901, and Renoir and Klimt in 1910.

But it was the appeal to countries to represent themselves permanently in Venice that was at the heart of the Biennale's success. Antonio Fradeletto's invitation to the *paesi* to contribute their own pavilions in the Giardini ensured the Biennale's longevity. The first, built by Belgium, opened in 1907. Designed by Léon Sneyers, the Belgian pavilion was in thoroughly up-to-date Secessionist style, with sculptural figures by George Minne, a decorative fountain in the foyer and paintings by the Symbolist Khnopff (fig. 128). Both Minne and Khnopff were well known from previous exhibitions.[78]

In 1909 Hungary, Britain and Germany opened pavilions, and national commissioners responsible for their country's art selection joined Venetian organisers.[79] The Hungarian pavilion, built in a rustic Hungarian style, was the first to be specifically national. It has remained substantially unchanged, preserving the generously arched doorway, the dramatic diagonal roofline and the elaborate ceramic work around the doorway from the workshop of Zsolnay di Pécs, who worked in Venice from 1907 to 1914.[80] France inaugurated a pavilion in 1912, the work of the Venetian architect Faust Finzi which was financed by the Esposizione.[81] The Swedish pavilion was built by Ferdinand Boberg in 1912 and used by The Netherlands until 1943.[82] It was a felicitous meld of flattened classical pilasters in a curved and stuccoed façade in anticipation of Art Deco. The Russian pavilion was opened by the Grand Duchess Vladimir on 29 April 1914.[83] The pavilion, the work of Aleksey Scusev, was also strongly regional in a Byzantine Gothic manner, raised on a rusticated base with a staircase leading to an ornamental portal.[84]

In terms of the exhibits of these pre-war years, it was Klimt's one-man exhibition of 1910 that appeared the most modern, especially to those familiar with the Vienna Secession. In 1910 Klimt was at the height of his golden manner, and the mosaic work of Ravenna and Venice, his acknowledged inspiration, prompted some Venetian artists to re-engage with their own tradition.[85] Klimt's work was shown in a white setting with an austerity foreign to Venice, at least before the practice of architect Carlo Scarpa, but it obviously had a fashionable following since the Excelsior Hotel held a *festa alla Klimt* (fig. 129).[86] Klimt's impact was particularly evident in the oeuvre of the Venetian Vittorio Zecchin. Murano-born, Zecchin interpreted the new Byzantine mode in glassmaking, becoming one of the first exponents of modernism in that fundamentally Venetian art.[87] Byzantinism was reinstated as part of *venezianità*.

The Biennales were more than individual works and artists; they created rooms that were ensembles, considered essays in display. The decorative schemes and commissions given specifically to painters, designers and architects were a distinctive

126 (*facing page top*) Mario de Maria, *Fondaco dei Turchi in Venice*, 1909. Oil on canvas, 49 × 70 cm. Rome, private collection.

127 (*facing page bottom*) Mariano Fortuny, Delphos garment, c.1908. Venice, Museo Fortuny.

128 (*above*) Léon Sneyers, Belgian Pavilion, Giardini di Biennale, 1907 (destroyed). Biennale di Venezia, Archivio Storico delle Arti Contemporanee.

part of the Biennale's early history.[88] Individual foreign artists were given responsibility for the design of pavilions: Frank Brangwyn, for instance, for the British Room in 1903.[89] Venetian themes, particularly of men at work, were constant in his oeuvre.[90] For the same Biennale, Cesare Laurenti executed a 'Frieze of Portraits' in painted majolica. In 1907 Sartorio formed 'a poem of human life' with inscriptions by D'Annunzio. 'The Art of Dream' was a composite room installation by Plionio Nomelli and Galileo Chini (a Florentine) – the most important artist of decorative schemes in the early decades of the Biennale – executed in tempera, pastel and gilt. In 1909 Chini unveiled his lavish decoration for the cupola of the entrance room – a work that was recovered and restored for the Biennale of 1986 (fig. 130).[91] The space itself invoked the famous Tribuna of the Palazzio Vecchio in Florence with decorations celebrating the contribution of Venice to art, and depicting the history of art from primitive and Egyptian art to the present.

130 (*above*) Galileo Chini, detail of central cupola, Italian Pavilion, Giardini di Biennale. 1909. Biennale di Venezia, Archivio Storico delle Arti Contemporanee.

St Mark's lion was present again, also Murano as the great centre of glass. In Chini's own words, his aim 'was to find an eminently decorative, colourful note, to feel the power of your St Mark's in my own way'. Encircling the dome, allegorical figures represent all stages of the arts in the company of the artists.[92] Following his success in Venice, where his work caught the eye of the King of Siam, Chini's fashionable orientalism found an exotic venue in the Eastern water city of Bangkok.[93]

Other decorative programmes allegorised the symbiosis of art and life, and Venice itself, emerging into a new age. In 1912 Pieretto Bianco contributed wall decorations dedicated to 'The Reawakening of Venice', with panels showing the Arsenale, the port and the topical rebuilding of the Campanile. The energy that the rebuilding symbolised is nowhere more clearly expressed.[94] This was indeed a remarkable scheme in terms of the optimism inherent in industry just before the First World War. In the last Biennale before the war, in 1914, Cirilli redecorated the main façade of the Pro Arte pavilion and Chini painted the central pavilion with a decoration dedicated to Spring.[95] Allusions to the mosaics of Ravenna and those of Venice's San Marco were mixed with fashionable allusions to Klimt, both in details of tesserae-like painting with motifs of birds pecking at grapes, and in the colour – an abundance of blue and gold.

The arts and crafts were cultivated together, most famously, in the Italian context, in the Turin Esposizione of 1902 dedicated to the decorative arts.[96] Venice took up the challenge in the following year in its Esposizione, giving space to the decorative arts and creating special galleries for the regions.[97] Lacework from the Jesurum company and glass from Murano were shown. In 1901 the prominent decorative artist Raffaele Mainella created a room in Stile Liberty for the press; the Sala del Giornale using hangings from the Jesurum firm and glass from the Compagnia Venezia-Murano. Jesurum hangings and light fittings by Tito and Toso were used in the regional gallery, the Sala Veneta.[98]

129 (*previous page bottom*) Gustav Klimt installation, Esposizione Internazionale d'Arte della Città di Venezia, 1910.

Every alternate year the Esposizione posters drew on well-known Venetian motifs: a view across the Bacino from the San Marco porch of the horses in 1901, the Moors on the clock tower in 1903; in 1905 a female figure pointing across the Bacino to the Palazzo Ducale and the still-intact Campanile; in 1909 a heroic poster of the Campanile rising from its scaffolding.[99] The traditional Venetian images were associated with the modernity of the Esposizione and the reputation of the city as a city of art.

Venetian artists were conspicuous not only as decorators in the pavilions, but as artists given retrospectives in their own right. Old Venice still inspired affectionate painting, as in the oeuvre of Italico Brass and his paintings of the Lido, the votive bridges that crossed to the cemetery island of San Michele on All Saints' Day, the ceremonies at Santa Maria della Salute and Il Redentore, and the Piazza, still an extraordinary social space.[100] Alessandro Milesi was working in his characteristic fluent mode developed from the Impressionist-Realist schools of the previous decades. Some years earlier he had painted the poor gondoliers and their families, but now his portrait sitters were among the most prominent of his time: in 1904 the writer Giosué Carducci glowering from beneath his eyebrows; Pope Pius X, the well-loved Venetian Cardinal Sarto, before his elevation to the papacy; Filippo Grimani, the 'Golden Mayor' at the midpoint of his Venetian power; the surgeon Davide Giordano, destined to follow Grimani as mayor, and the first to hold power under the Fascists.[101] Milesi's paintings followed stylishly in Favretto's path, with reinvocations in Settecento mode of concerts and meetings at the Caffè Florian, beside the daily life of the *popolani* on the bridges and in the markets, the local wedding ceremonies and the fishermen of Chioggia. In 1912 Milesi was given a substantial personal showing at the Biennale. As in other places, and not least Paris, avant-gardist and realist exhibited side by side.

The pre-war Biennales were a complex phenomenon in a number of ways: in the display of national cultures, in defining international connections and allegiances, in installation and display, and in the integration of the arts and crafts. As their intricacy has become better understood, accusations of conservatism have been modified. In part, the Biennale's reputation for conservatism was created by a group of young Venetian artists whose support, ironically, was in itself the result of the first Biennales and the benefaction set up by the late Duchessa Felicita Bevilacqua. Her Longhena palace, Ca' Pesaro on the Grand Canal, which she bequeathed to the city, housed a collection of modern art which, from 1902, included purchases from the Biennale. A foundation was formed to foster the work of young artists and to organise and administer regular exhibitions.[102]

In 1907 a young critic from Ferrara, Nino Barbantini, was appointed to oversee the Bevilacqua legacy. Under his dynamic leadership young artists – notably Ugo Valeri, Gino Rossi, Arturo Martini, Felice Casorati and Umberto Boccioni – challenged, and indeed polarised, the Venetian art world to the degree that *i morti* (the dead) were associated with the Biennale, and *i vivi* (the living) with Ca' Pesaro.[103]

Barbantini began a distinguished residence in Venice, notable for contributions over the next four decades not only to new young art, but also to traditional painting, in major exhibitions in the 1930s devoted to Titian and Tintoretto, and the art of his hometown Ferrara.[104] Barbantini regarded 'youth' as the force of the new art. His understanding of a vibrant local tradition was stimulated by the facilities he could offer young artists in studio space in the Ca' Pesaro – a floor was made available for them, as well as a regular programme of exhibitions. The warmth of his support for artists was expressed in letters to such artists as Gino Rossi and Arturo Martini, and is part of the social history of these years.[105] Martini called Barbantini a 'free strong spirit'.[106] A young journalist who was to be prominent in Venice over many decades, Gino Damerini, gave considerable space to sympathetic reviews of the Ca' Pesaro exhibitions. Marinetti, just then developing his Futurist agenda, asked to reprint a review of the artist Ugo Valeri (who died tragically in 1911).[107]

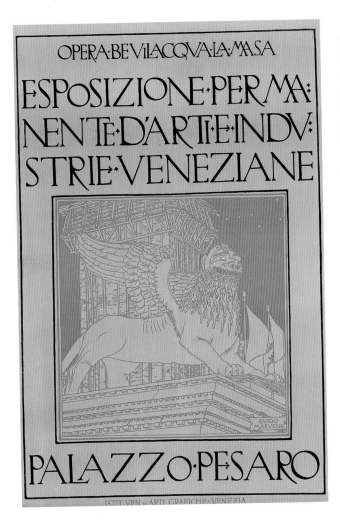

OPERA·BE·VILACQVA·LA·MASA

ESPOSIZIONE·PERMA·NENTE·D'ARTI·E·INDV·STRIE·VENEZIANE

PALAZZO·PESARO

ISTIT·VEN ʰ·ARTI·GRAFICHE·VENEZIA

131 Guido Marussig, poster for the first exhibition at Ca' Pesaro, 1908. Venice, Museo d'Arte di Moderna, Ca' Pesaro.

The first 1908 exhibition at Ca' Pesaro brought together a group of young artists, who remained in touch, even though not all of them lived in Venice.[108] It was an important event in the elderly Venice of the early twentieth century, rebuilding its Campanile and debating its road bridge to the mainland. Indeed, the poster for the first exhibition, designed by Guido Marussig, was an image of a virile lion of St Mark standing in front of the newly rising Campanile (fig. 131).[109] While noting that Futurism was Italy's most significant initiative in the early century, the art historian Guido Perocco regarded the Ca' Pesaro exhibitions from 1908 as its immediate precursor.[110]

The solidarity of the Ca' Pesaro artists was apparent from the time Barbantini came to Venice, but they produced few manifestos or 'programmes'. The artists were united in their opposition to naturalism, the Accademia and, increasingly, to the conservatism of the Biennale, although some of them were certainly represented, and their antagonism can be overplayed. Some of the Ca' Pesaro group were enrolled at the Accademia in the life class – Amedeo Modigliani was there in 1903 before he went to Montmartre,[111] and Umberto Boccioni worked there through the academic year 1907–8.[112]

The contemporary French school was almost unknown in Venice, although Gino Rossi, who had returned from a visit to Britanny in 1907, Umberto Moggioli and Luigi Scopinich found an environment akin to Gauguin's Brittany in the lagoon island of Burano, where they painted solid colours defined by line, in the manner of *cloissonisme*. Although in the manner of the Symbolist and Primitivist vision, their work was intensely localised, favouring the local costumes and the traditionally coloured houses along the canals (fig. 132). It was a creative alternative to the city views of Venice that dominated, locally and internationally, and still had a Settecento tinge in the work of such artists as Italico Brass and Alessandro Milesi. However conservative the Burano school may now appear in the context of Fauvism and Expressionism, it represented a radical point of artistic activity in Venice in the first decade of the twentieth century.[113]

The presence of Umberto Boccioni in Venice – eventually the most important Futurist painter and sculptor, who gave persuasive visual form to Marinetti's manifestos as well as his own – was further encouragement for anti-Establishment artists. Boccioni's association with Marinetti was crucial in cohering an avant-garde that went well beyond Venice. During the 1910 Biennale some forty paintings by Boccioni were shown at the Ca' Pesaro, and although the work was relatively conservative – conventional canal views, divisionist in style – Boccioni was already at work on *The City Rises*, one of the first important Futurist canvases.[114] For Boccioni himself, such continuity was decisive; he told Barbantini that he recalled their discussions at Florian's and arranged for Marinetti to meet Barbantini there.[115] Barbantini particularly relished the Futurist 'words of fire'.[116]

The Ca' Pesaro artists and Barbantini lost no opportunity to stress the conservatism of the Biennale, and Futurism was no doubt the subtext for the increased division between the parties. In 1913 Arturo Martini organised a counter-Biennale in the modern surroundings of the Excelsior Hotel on the Lido. Boccioni wrote to Marinetti

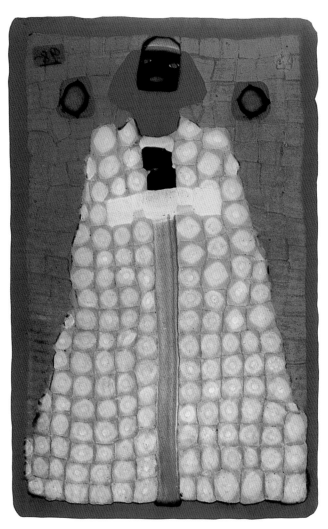

that the exhibition had 'great echoes' among young painters in Milan.[117] It was at this point that opposition to the conservatism of the Biennale was most marked.

Barbantini had a particular interest in the decorative arts, and the Ca' Pesaro exhibitions regularly included glass, tapestry, embroidery and other crafts. Murano glass was reinvigorated by emulating the boldness of modern painting, finding freedom of colour through an adaptation of the murrhine technique that produced mosaic glass by fusing coloured canes – an effect that was inspired by Klimt's painted tesserae. Glassmakers gained a new freedom of expression: glass no longer needed to be purely functional, it too could adopt the decorative expressionism of Arte Nuova.[118] This new freedom in Murano – prophetic for later artists such as Carlo Scarpa – was evident in the works made by Vittorio Zecchin and Teodoro Wolf-Ferrari for the Barovier firm.[119]

Zecchin, Murano-born, wrote poetry in dialect about the lagoon and the islands.[120] His partnership with Teodoro Wolf-Ferrari was productive, enriched by Wolf-Ferrari's sojourn in Munich and his interest in forming a secessionist group in Venice, called L'Aratro (The Plough), which had greater vitality than longevity.[121] Their paintings inspired their glassworks. Zecchin was a post-Symbolist, influenced in his early work by Jan Toorop and Klimt, and favouring wan and mysterious female subjects, hieratic inhabitants of flowery forests touched with gold. A glass slab made of fused mosaic pieces is an example of his new intense colour – *The*

249

Barbarian has a single figure, dark-faced, wearing a green-yellow cloak, against a background of brilliant blue that causes it to vibrate in its colour field (fig. 133).

Zecchin and Wolf-Ferrari showed at the Biennale in 1914, as well as in the Ca' Pesaro exhibitions. Their goblet-like vases with brazen flared feet were ornamented with incandescent glass mosaic designs of trees and flowers in a late flowering of Arte Nuova as it moves towards Art Deco, and close to their stylised painting.[122]

Forging a New Venice: D'Annunzio, Rilke and Baron Corvo

In the season, in the foreign-owned palaces on the Grand Canal and on the Lido, Venice was an international centre in the early twentieth century.[123] In 1910 the world watched agog as the Russian Countess Maria Tarnowska was accused of murder for inciting one of her lovers to kill her husband, Count Paul Kamarowsky, who was shot in his apartment on the Lido on 3 September 1907 by his friend Nicolas Navoff.[124] Tarnowska's subsequent trial in Venice, at which the countess was cast as a female temptress, a Circe who might seduce even her gaolers, was further evidence, if it were needed, of the wiles of Venice itself.[125]

The French and the English continued to inhabit their palazzi in the season and artists were frequently their guests. Edmond de Polignac's widow, Winnaretta, was in residence at the Palazzo Polignac with her various lesbian lovers.[126] In 1898 Madame Isabella de la Baume bought the Palazzo Dario, a masterpiece of Lombard style inlaid with coloured marbles, close to Santa Maria della Salute, where Henri de Régnier was a frequent visitor (a plaque at the rear commemorates him) as was the poet Anna de Noailles, whom Proust so admired. Prince von Hohenlohe was at the Casetta Rossa, and his daughter, the Princess Marie von Thurn und Taxis at the Palazzo Valmarana, where she frequently entertained the poet Rainer Maria Rilke.

For the English, the undisputed centre remained the Ca' Cappello, where Sir Henry Austen Layard's widow entertained assiduously (she also tended sick seamen at her Ospedale Cosmopolitana on the Giudecca and attending the English church that she helped found at San Vio).[127] On Mondays Horatio Brown held his famous men-only soirées at his Ca' Torresella on the Zattere. In the early years of the century the gondolier Antonio Salin was in attendance and Brown was translating Molmenti's *Venezia nella vita privata* and devoting himself to the papers of John Addington Symonds.[128]

Mrs Bronson at the Ca' Alvise had died in 1900, but the American Curtises were still at the Palazzo Barbaro – the setting for Henry James's *The Wings of a Dove* (he wrote it in England during 1901). He visited them again in 1908: it was his last visit and Venice had never seemed 'more lovable'.[129]

On every bridge and *fondamenta* one can imagine the foreign painters in front of their easels, exploiting every picturesque view. It was the high point for the colour sketch *en plein air*. Sargent came many times – less interested in the figure subject, he often painted around the Salute.[130] Frank Brangwyn was a regular visitor – painting the men. William Sickert, highly fashionable in England, came regularly after 1895 and painted Venice as if it were immersed in verdigris.[131] From Australia, Arthur Streeton, Emmanuel Phillips Fox and Hans Heysen painted the conventional views.

Amid all the foreigners, an Italian painter created a new pictorial Venice, though he is too little noticed. A fashionable portrait painter, regularly represented in the Biennales, Giovanni Boldini, originally from Ferrara, painted Venice over two decades, making speed both his technique and his subject – in anticipation of the Futurists.[132] His dynamic lines and angled views turned the gondola into an abstract creature: black prow sharp against dark water, its movement seen from water level defined by the angle of an oar. Well-known edifices angle up from the water line. A steamship painted in the Bacino confirms the modern age.

The Venices of the new century were multiple: parochial and international; conservative, yet at times keen host to the new. Simply positing the old against the new cannot do justice to the complex admixture of traditionalism and renovation, or to the new regionalism that would push Venice forward to the Adriatic and beyond. It yearned for its golden Byzantine past. One of the best-known cultural figures in Italy, if not Europe, Gabriele D'Annunzio was to renew and expand his contacts with Venice in the new century; his role was crucial, both in terms of his writing and the political messages he delivered to the city. Recognising its key position in the Adriatic, he desired to lift Venice from its lethargy, to charge it with allegorical energy and give new wings to the lion of St Mark. Certain right-wing Venetian industrialists – Volpi, Foscari, Nicola Spada – men who would drive Venice's fortunes into the fascist 1920s – were closely linked with D'Annunzio.[133]

The Irredentist issue of the control of the Adriatic and the Italian-speaking border cities of Trento and Trieste, as well as Dalmatia (a territory in the one-time republic), was the sub-text for an allegorical play that D'Annunzio began in 1905, La Nave, or The Ship.[134] Set in the sixth century, it returns to an embryonic Venice at the beginning of its greatness. The energy that would ultimately create the mature Republic is encapsulated in the Arsenale: not merely the arsenal for the building of ships, but the powerhouse of civic energy that drove the very foundation of the city. D'Annunzio claimed that his play was 'molded [sic] by the mud of the lagoon, the gold of Byzantium, and the life force of my most ardent passion for Italy'.[135] In La Nave Venice becomes again the city of enviable longevity and durability in which nature, art and history come forcibly together. The sixth-century citizens call for conquest of the world as the ship is armed and launched: Il Mondo! Il Mondo! arma la Nave grande ...' It was a modern cry-to-arms, a premonition of the steps that D'Annunzio was to take later at Fiume to restore Italy's lost power in the Adriatic.[136] Venice was again at the heart of the peninsula's access to the Adriatic.

D'Annunzio's presentation of the play was overtly political: first performed in January 1908 at the Compagnia Stabile Romana in Rome before King Umberto and Queen Margherita, only later was it produced in Venice.[137] The Austrians took it as inflammatory. The day chosen for the performance at La Fenice was St Mark's Day, 25 April 1909, under the auspices of the Lega Navale, whose president was D'Annunzio's friend Piero Foscari. Foscari encouraged D'Annunzio to donate the manuscript of the play to the city, amid hostility from the clergy concerned not only about its Irredentist ambitions but its representation of a history of Venice that undermined the religious nature of its foundation.[138] But the ceremony took place, and was followed by other congratulatory meetings on subsequent days of the production, including a presentation by the oarsmen of the Bucintoro rowing club, to which D'Annunzio gave the motto Senz'ali non può (without wings you can do nothing).[139]

La Nave offered Venice a vision of historic energy with contemporary relevance, revitalising a view of early democratic history so cultivated during the short term of the Municipality in 1797. Nevertheless, most people did not want to escape the romantic history of the lost Republic or challenge the pleasantries of social life, such as those described by the amiable Henri Régnier in his essays and novels about Venetian life and the smart set, as in La Peur d'Amour, published in 1912, the epitome of modern-day romance.[140]

In the first decade of the new century the German poet Rainer Maria Rilke was one of the few who distinguished between the romantic Venice, the chatter of high society and an obduracy seen to be characteristic of the Republic. At the same time Rilke cultivated an intense lyricism. In winter 1907 he wrote to his sister:

I think it was a good thing to come here in all this strangeness. Do you remember how great it is, how incalculable? This Venice seems to me almost hard to admire; it has to be learned over again from the beginning. Ashen its marble stands there, gray in the grayness, light as the ashy edge of a log that has just been aglow. And how unexplained in its selection is the red on walls, the green on window shutters; discreet and yet not to be surpassed; bygone, but with a fullness of transiency; pale, but as a person turns pale in excitement. And this not from a hotel: from a little house, with old things, two sisters and a maid; before which the water now lies, black and gleaming, a couple of sailboats in which the hawsers creak; and in an hour the full moon is bound to come across from the Riva. I am full of expectancy . . .[141]

There is little here of the clichéd view of Venice known in advance of a visit. It is a new city, able to shock and confront the visitor, as when Rilke was there in 1897: 'Venice! I gaze and gaze and am like a child. Am in accord with everything.'[142] He admired his own facility with the 'phantasm of Venice . . . strangers in the labyrinthine windings of the Calle had only to ask me if they wanted to reach their destination . . .'[143]

The wonder still flowers in Rilke's short poems of 1908 written in Paris, such as 'Venetianischer Morgen' (Venetian Morning): The city is born anew each morning, but it carries the past with it, for it wears the jewels of the previous day:

> Each new morning must first show her
> the opals she wore yesterday, and pull
> rows of reflections out of the canal . . .[144]

Rilke's associations with Venice and the Veneto were impeccably aristocratic, given his friendships with Anna de Noailles, and his patron Princess Marie von Thurn und Taxis. He had access to the best society – the very society of Bourget's 'Cosmopolis'. But, tellingly, in a prose work written in Paris between 1903 and 1910, *The Note-books of Malte Laurids Brigge*, the hero finds the seasonal crowd that oscillates between Venice and Paris to be superficial.[145] Laurids Brigge notes that 'It was at Venice, in autumn, in one of those salons where foreigners, passing, gather round the lady of the house who is as foreign as they are . . .'[146] He speculates with a sense of superiority on the triviality before him, and on the dispersal of the crowd as winter sets in and the real Venice, the Venice of winter, is in the ascendant. Winter will mean the absence of those foreigners who 'abandon themselves to the rewarding swoon of gondolas'.[147] The city in winter, divested of foreigners, is 'the real one, awake, brittle to the breaking point'.[148] In his poem 'San Marco', Rilke writes that 'the bright prospect is still intact'.[149] He enters 'the golden cobalt like a cave' and imagines the four golden horses on the portico – 'the proud enduring of the team-of-four'.

Venice is a city in positive mode, a place that is willed; it is an entire arsenal, worked into splendour from its meagre primary assets, salt and glass. This perception recalls Mallarmé's image in a prose-poem evoking winter, 'Frisson d'hiver', in which a Venetian mirror is lodged as 'deep as a cold spring in a shore of tarnished serpents'.[150] 'Who looked at themselves in it?' the poem asks.

Rilke reflected earlier on the limitations of tourists, using the self-satisfied German Mr Baum as his target in a sympathetic story published in 1900, 'A Scene from the Venice Ghetto'. Herr Baum had made the usual tourist round, and he describes it predictably, building by building.[151] In response, the narrator tells his story of the Ghetto, of the old Jew Melchisedech and his young grandaughter Esther, whose homes were built higher and higher on the scarce ground, growing more fragile with each additional level. Melchisedech is always the first to climb to the new level, and he does so again with his granddaughter, who has given birth to a blond child. The three generations emerge onto the roof of the new building: the old man opens his arms to the sky for he sees God and the light of the sea – 'a still silvery light' ('ein stilles, silbernes Licht: Das Meer'). For the first time the sea is visible to the Ghetto inhabitants, from the oldest to the youngest, who appear to be as high as the clouds.[152] Mr

Baum is embarrassed listening to this visionary story about a Venice beyond his comprehension.

For Rilke the Ghetto was a place of aspiration and spirituality. Venice is manmade and industrious, its survival is exemplary. His perception is a crucial one, bound up with the Venetian winter. Bereft of tourists, the city is thrown back on itself and its will to survive is a source of energy: here lies its resistance to romantic superficiality and its over-abundance of tourists. Doubtless Rilke was amplifying the positive autumnal mood so characteristic of D'Annunzio's writings on Venice as he moved to an appreciation of 'the vibrating stillness', 'the city overlaid with the grey, cold pallor of autumn'.

Rilke's fascination with Venetian energy found a focal point in Admiral Carlo Zeno, who defended Venice against the Genoese in the fourteenth century and served as a character study in Venetian determination.[153] Rilke arranged to study Zeno in the Archives, and although the exercise was not finally fruitful, the energy he admired in him touches other Venice poems. Autumn and the force of the Arsenale are united in his poem 'Spätherbst in Venedig', written in Paris in 1908, in which he charts the rise of volition:

> as if overnight
> The commander of the sea had to double
> The galleys in the sleepless arsenal,
> In order to tar the next morning breeze
> With a fleet . . .[154]

Another foreign visitor, among the most eccentric, responded to a Venice in the present tense: Frederick Rolfe, the self-styled Baron Corvo. His fiction appears inseparable from the eccentric life told in the biography by A. J. A. Symons, *The Quest for Corvo*, and in Rolfe's correspondence, *The Venetian Letters*, in which his homosexuality is unabashed.[155] More eloquent than any resident, Rolfe takes to the lagoon in his *pupperin*, rowing in the Venetian manner, and swimming. He was reduced to abject poverty, unable to show himself in Venice during the day, taken to hospital with pneumonia and heart disease brought on by exposure; and yet resilient. In 1910 he noted in a letter that he had trapped the fifty-fourth rat in his bedroom near the Piazza San Marco.[156]

Both habitué of the lagoon and foreigner, Rolfe could never be described as a tourist; he lived socially and economically beyond the city's pale. He caricatured the English in Venice, offending them in large numbers, particularly at the funeral of Lady Layard, to which he went to heckle dressed as a cardinal; and yet he flew the Union Flag ostentatiously from his barque.

As Rolfe's biographer, Arthur Symons takes a literary but nevertheless salacious delight in his subject's sexuality, quoting for the first time from the unpublished correspondence, which became known as 'the Venetian letters'. Symons purports amazement:

> What shocked me about these letters was not the confession they made of perverse sexual indulgence: that phenomenon surprises no historian. But that a man of education, ideas, something near genius, should have enjoyed without remorse the destruction of the innocence of youth, that he should have been willing for a price to traffic in his knowledge of the dark byways of that Italian city . . .[157]

'That Italian city' reveals itself yet again as sexually charged by virtue of its labyrinthine composition of canals and *calli* – as Goethe had found so much earlier the narrow streets could be equated with erotic pursuit and masked assignations.[158] The very morphology of the city appeared erotic. In the modern age of Frederick Rolfe – and with Thomas Mann's almost-contemporary Aschenbach in *Death in Venice* – the city's reputation for bisexuality was reconfirmed.

Notoriously autobiographical, Rolfe's *The Desire and Pursuit of the Whole*, describes the year 1908.[159] The narrator, Nicholas Crabbe, an eccentric Englishman in Venice without funds, is reduced to living in his *pupperin* and bemoaning his lack of royalties and the refusals that came from his requests for money. The androgynous fictive character of a girl is capable of inspiring platonic love as she has the appearance of a boy with a boy's skill at Venetian-style rowing. Crabbe finds her in the ruins of the 1908 earthquake at Messina and she stays to serve him. In his reduced circumstances, Crabbe sleeps in his boat or wanders the city, exposed to the elements which, in real life, eventually killed Rolfe.[160] In the novel, the boy-girl tends Crabbe and saves him. The book is suffused with a high optimism, despite the characters' lack of sustenance; it is charged with the great beauty of the lagoon and the wonder of the city. Even in Crabbe's terrible nocturnal wanderings when he is destitute, the lagoon, the city and its dawns remain magical.[161] No writer has found more beauty in the colour of the lagoon, elevated in Corvo's writings to a new prominence, more opalescent even than in Rilke: 'Imagine a twilight world of cloudless sky and smoothest sea, all made of violet and lavender, with bands of burnished copper set with emeralds, merging, on the other hand, into the fathomless blue of the eyes of the prides of peacocks, where the moon rose, rosy as mother-of-pearl.'[162] It might be the familiar clichéd 'jewels in the crown of Venice', but the eloquence springs from close and passionate observation, close to the water where Baron Corvo is afloat with his boys.

For Barrès the lagoon and its islands were the site of malaria and decay; for Rolfe the lagoon is for swimming in, and skimming over. He cannot leave it to return to his homeland. The poet W. H. Auden's prefatory remarks to *The Desire and Pursuit of the Whole* reveal as much about himself as about Rolfe: 'Venice was for him the Great Good Place, a city built by strong and passionate men in the image of their Mother, the perfect embodiment of everything he most craved and admired, beauty, tradition, grace and ease.'[163] Sweeping through canals in his *pupperin*, bathing in the lagoon for Rolfe, the environment is always rhapsodically beautiful beyond all material considerations. It is never sentimentalised; it stays crisp, braced with interpolations of Venetian dialect: 'On the distant bark of the wide canal of Zuecca, the lengthy lines of light along Spinalonga fluttered like little pale daffodils in a night-mist coloured like the bloom on the fruit of the vine . . .'

A devout convert, Rolfe attended mass and followed the religious calendar, observing the Armenian Mass at San Marco and All Saints' Day.[164] He died in penury in the city in 1913. It was Fernando Ongania, that rare connoisseur and scholar of his city, who eventually had the manuscript of *The Desire and Pursuit of the Whole: A Romance of Modern Venice* published. Its libellous nature, its ranting and the vilification of those who did not publish Rolfe's manuscripts, pay royalties or subsidise his life, held back its publication until 1934.[165]

The New Art of the Movies

If, for Corvo, Venice was the 'Great Good Place', a place of beauty, personal liberation and fulfilment, it was for many a place of evil, a setting for ill-starred lovers, gigolos, criminals and murderers. Increasingly, such characters came to inhabit Venice in the twentieth century, especially in the new celluloid world of film. Venice was never to sustain a movie industry of its own, but it attracted innumerable film directors and from 1932 it was to host one of the most illustrious of the world's film festivals.[166]

In 1896 scenic Venice featured in the first movies. Albert Promio, working as cinematographer for the Lumière brothers, has the reputation for shooting the *very* first moving film, from a gondola, following it with footage on the pigeons in Piazza San

Marco, and shots taken between the columns of St Theodore and St Mark.[167] In July, 1896 the Lumière brothers brought their equipment to Venice and gave a screening in the Teatro Minerva. Magically revealed in motion for the first time are a gondola approaching Santi Giovanni e Paolo, *vaporetti* at the Rialto and pigeons. The Teatro Rossini and the Teatro Malibran, those illustrious names in the history of Venetian stage, showed cinema in 1897, but it was the Minerva that claimed pride of place, screening 'from 8 to 11'.[168]

Venice soon had a number of movie houses, and some narrative films were created, mainly in a conservative stage and costume-drama tradition.[169] The most interesting productions of the pioneer years were the creations of Camillo Sebellin: he made a documentary of the removal of the reliquary of Sebastiano Venier from Murano to Venice.[170] In the first decade of moving pictures there was any number of new Merchants of Venice, Bianca Cappellos, Othellos and Casanovas. Mario Caserini was a prolific director of such dramas from 1907 to 1913.[171]

Some productions had specific local interest, such as those of the cinema proprietors Almerico and Luigi Roatto, who made *Biasio il luganegher* in 1907 with an accompanying recitation in dialect, and *L'Anima Santa*, which told the story of a young boatman.[172]

The most sustained and accomplished early film involving Venice was the work of the great Austrian director Max Reinhardt, *Eine venetianische Nacht*, of 1913. A visitor to Venice was its subject, but it was not the first film to dwell on the tourist – and many would follow, revealing beauty and pain, murder and love, pursuits in the labyrinth, and grand hotels. In 1910 *A Parisian's Day – Giornata di una Parigiana –* was shot by the brothers Pathé.[173] It ran for seven minutes, visiting the Piazza, lacemakers and glass-blowers, filming pigeons in San Marco, the grand hotels and so on. It was the beginning of an itinerary that was to become familiar.

Described as 'a quaint, macabre story', Reinhardt's *Eine venetianische Nacht* takes place in Venice in 1860, still under Austrian rule.[174] This most notable foreign production in the early years of the cinema was adapted from a play by Karl Vollmüller

134 Max Reinhardt, *Eine venetianische Nacht*, 1913. Film still. Vienna, Austrian Film Archive.

that had been staged in London at the Palace Theatre. The title itself evokes Johann Strauss and the glittering waltz-driven world of Venice and Vienna that Viennese artists liked to exploit. But this world is turned on its head in the film. Mood and plot are quite opposite; indeed, *Eine venetianische Nacht* is a skilful parody, using the silent movie language of rhetorical gesture to highlight foibles of character (fig. 134). The main character is a German student, guidebook – or perhaps Goethe's *Italienische Reise* – in hand. He arrives at the railway station – the entrance is interestingly industrial in its presentation – and is accosted by a witty beggar called Pipestrello, a pre-Chaplinesque comic, all exaggerated gestures, shuffles and occasional bursts of speed.[175] The gondola moves off with the German youth forcibly accompanied by Pipestrello, who at one point goes ashore and then leaps back on to the gondola's stern and, with considerable dexterity, manages to climb in. It is the wedding day of an English lady to a very fat oil baron from Mestre and she is passing in a gondola on her unhappy way to the wedding night, which, by strange coincidence, takes place in the inn where the visitor is staying. A flower she tosses to an Austrian cavalry officer is picked up by the student; it will disturb his dreams that night.

The bride leaves her husband carousing at the wedding breakfast and mounts to her chamber, and an assignation with the Austrian officer. Pipestrello enters from the window and stabs him. The bride implores the student to remove the body, which he does by sliding it down the balustrade and rowing it off to the lagoon where the body multiplies into a row of Austrian soldiers' corpses; they miraculously come alive, rise to their feet and chase the student, who flings himself into the canal. For the stage production Reinhardt used a revolving stage, as he did in his acclaimed 1905 production of *The Merchant of Venice* at the Deutsches Theater. He was noted for his Venetian evocations, that 'ever-singing, ever-buzzing Venice', as he styled it. He eschewed the waltzes and the eighteenth century, inventing a highly original Venice and a dream-fantasy that anticipated the Surrealists.

Reinhardt's film is distinctive in its comic response to Venetian 'types' and in its on-site filming, with footage showing the railway, the Grand Canal and the lagoon, in contrast to the cardboard sets of the earliest movies. Documentary films were creating a standard of veracity in early film that contributed to the subliminal recognition of Venice around the world, as filmgoers witnessed such popular events as the Feast of the Redentore, Venice in the Snow, and a Visit to the Esposizione.[176]

Among the writers who recognised the potential of film, none was more prescient than D'Annunzio. His Roman epic *Cabiria*, which was billed as 'a film of D'Annunzio',[177] enjoyed wide circulation. *La Nave* was first filmed in 1911, in highly declamatory style, by Arrigo Frusta.[178] At the end of the third episode, the ship *Totus Mundus* is ready to sail the Adriatic. Vignettes of the Basilica of San Marco rise up, with the golden horses, then the Palazzo Ducale. Trumpets are shown sounding; then comes the injunction for the ship to sail to Alexandria and bring back the body of the Evangelist to a great sepulchre. Only film could provide this flash-forward.

Housing, Health and the Lido

Venice before the First World War was given over increasingly to its visitors and foreign residents. For the most part it was the foreign artists who spoke for Venice and its history, or non-Venetians such as D'Annunzio. Conservative pressure kept vernacular architecture, which often meant sub-standard housing, as part of its 'ambience': the 'jewels of Venice' were part of the rhetoric of the time.

Protests against inadequate housing had been frequent during the last period of Austrian domination and the first years of the new Commune.[179] From the outset, the debate was linked with sanitation and epidemic control, particularly to epidemics of cholera. In 1873 there was a general inspection and a central plan for demolition was offered in 1887.[180] A commission to determine the exact condition of housing – the Commissione per le Case Sane e Economiche e Popolari – was finally established in 1893. Over the next decade some housing was constructed, away from central Venice in the areas of the Gesuiti, San Rocco, Madonna dell'Orto and San Leonardo.[181] Critics of demolition continued to write tracts on 'Disappearing Venice'.[182]

Responses to the problem of housing were judged to have been inadequate: in the first decade of the twentieth century that much is clear from a polemical tract published in 1910 by Angelo Fano.[183] He made a straightforward appeal to local self-interest by pointing out that crowded dwellings bred vice and alcoholism, as well as ill-health, and that the rich, too, could fall victim to epidemics. Fano quoted the findings of Professor Raffaele Vivante, the Medical Chief of Hygiene, who for forty years was untiring in exposing deficiencies in hygiene and housing and explaining the connection between sub-standard housing and disease – notably tuberculosis and cholera – and the necessity for street hygiene, the provision of water and sewerage, the collection of garbage and public conveniences.[184] He had begun to publish as early as 1900, claiming that improvement in housing was one of the recognised strategies for combatting tuberculosis. A detailed statistical study was circulated in 1910, the year of Fano's tract, listing the number of kitchens that had water closets in them, lacked access to running water and natural light, and so on.[185] The *sestiere* of Castello – the area in the vicinity of the Arsenale – was identified as one of the poorest housing areas. Vivante saw the problem as one of the most difficult facing local government, and one that certainly had not been ignored by the city of Venice. He gave a history of surveys from 1891, the time of the master plan's inauguration, offering the criterion that a dwelling be considered crowded when the number of inhabitants is more than twice the number of rooms: good hygiene requires that a kitchen is separate from other rooms.[186] Houses were to be declared uninhabitable only if their present defects were not eliminated or if they were not able to be adapted to the required hygienic standards. The greatest number of uninhabitable situations occurred in ground-floor dwellings affected by damp and lack of light.

The argument that there was insufficient land for housing gathered force, but Fano refuted it, pointing to the availability of areas of Sant'Elena, infill and parts of Cannaregio. In recognition of the burgeoning building projects on the Lido, he recommended workers' housing, improved water links between the Lido and the Giudecca, and he raised the question of the provision of housing on the Terraferma. His pamphlet was unyieldingly critical of a government alleged to be fearful of the large numbers of workers in the city and reluctant to engage in other capital works because of its preoccupation with rebuilding the Campanile.

But the policy was a cautious one; new housing was sited around the city's periphery, instead of on the Lido, which was being developed for a luxury clientele rather than for the badly housed residents of the old city. Holiday and luxury facilities were managed by a leading consortium of local entrepeneurs and communal government for private speculation.[187] Still sparsely populated and under military restrictions, the Lido had become part of the Commune of Venice in 1883, when the bathing 'industry' was being established.[188] Donkeys carried bathers along the Gran Viale Santa Maria Elisabetta from the lagoon to the sea, until the boulevard was enlarged and a horse-drawn tram service introduced. The bathing hut was the next stage, a boon to the resort; the individual cabin was then developed as a fashionable facility by the grand hotels. In 1899 Ettore Sorger, one of the main developers of the area, succeeded in effecting the transfer of military lands to the Commune. Electricity and an aqueduct for the water supply increased the potential of the area, and in 1905 an electric double track was laid from the lagoon to the beach. It was decided to co-ordinate the Commune's administration with the old Società dei Bagni. In 1905 Nicolò Spada

135 'La Plus Belle Plage du Monde', poster for the Hotel. Excelsior Palace, *c.*1909.

emerged as one of the major entrepreneurs, creating the Hotel Excelsior with the support of Ettore Sorger, who was responsible for the extension of the esplanade, the Lungo Mare, as far as the new hotel. The Excelsior was opened on 20 July 1908 watched by a crowd reported to be thirty-thousand strong; it was to be the centre of Venetian social life until the Second World War. Claims for low-cost housing on the Lido were subtly deflected, and villas rose up instead, most often in a blend of Florentine palazzo style, Alpine chalet and, predictably, local Gothic.[189]

The grand hotels dominated, and certain schemes for housing were curtailed by the First World War. The architect Duilio Torres designed a garden city, but individual villa housing for the well-to-do was responsible for most of the building boom, and socialist opposition to luxury developments had little real effect.[190] Spada's main initiative – one of the most significant for Venice in the century – was the formation of the hotel chain, the Compagnia Italiana dei Grandi Alberghi (CIGA), founded in March 1906 and still in existence.[191] Effectively, it controlled the Lido as a leisure centre. Some years earlier, an intriguing Futurist vision of Venice in 1930 had imagined a city of sailing regattas, a thoroughly international place: 'a place of events' linked by bridges to the mainland.[192] With its hotels, the casino and film Biennale, the Lido, as much as Venice, became the destination for leisure-seekers.

A full-blown advertising campaign accompanied the modern invention of the Lido, lauding its unique provision of the most modern facilities combined with a historical city across the water. The combination was seen many times in posters for the European railways, the *chemins de fer*, advertising 'La Plus Belle Plage du Monde' (fig. 135), the 'Station Climatherique et de Bains de Mer' and the Casino and the Kursaal at the Hotel Excelsior.[193] The creation of the Lido was the success story for Venice in the early twentieth century. It was a new prospect, a new face turned not only to the seaside, but to the smartest life in the grand hotel. Modernist buildings appeared in this space of comparative freedom, proof of the influence of Secessionism, of Olbrich's pioneering Darmstadt project and the diffusion of the Austrian style in the work of Italian architects such as Raimondo d'Aronco, seen at the influential Turin Esposizione of 1902.[194] The Villino Monplaisir, designed by Guido Sullam for a corner site on the Viale Santa Maria Elisabetta in 1905, bore the hallmarks of the modern style: emphatically arched windows, balconies, a cluster of columns carved with female heads, a mosaic band curling around the upper windows and an *altana* capped wildly by curvaceous ironwork.[195] Regrettably, a design by one of the major architects of the Viennese school was left on the drawing board: Adolf Loos's 1923 design for a Lido villa for the well-known actor Alexander Moissi was to be white and cubic in the modern manner of the 1920s.[196] A model was shown at the Salon d'Automne in Paris in 1923, but it was the first of a sequence of unbuilt projects by significant architects in the twentieth century.[197]

*   *   *

Dying on the Lido: Thomas Mann

The Lido in its early heyday was the setting for the most famous twentieth-century book on Venice: Thomas Mann's *Death in Venice*, published in 1912. Mortality is its central concern, affecting both place and character. Mann's novella was to inspire the film by Luchino Visconti and the opera by Benjamin Britten, as well as numberless ruminations on the inevitable conjunction of Venice and death.[198] The death of Venice is the city's most persistent modern theme. Mann's work is a *modern* fable, although the title recalls the tradition of plague and death, long-standing in Venetian mythologies.

The geography of *Death in Venice* (centred on the Lido) is a telling shift from the centre of Mann's earlier short story about Venice, *old* Venice 'Enttäuschung' (Disillusionment), which he wrote in 1896 after a visit.[199] 'Disillusionment' is suffused with *fin-de-siècle* decadence, as its name implies. The story takes place in the Piazza San Marco where the narrator encounters a man incapable of experiencing beauty, wonder or love, yet who is eloquently obsessed by his deficiency. For him, the Piazza with its 'great half-moon hung above the splendid spectacular façade of San Marco' fails in its famous effect.

The crisis Mann imputes to his main character in 'Enttäuschung' is not unlike the malaise described by Hofmannsthal in his 1903 *Letter of Lord Chandos*, in which Chandos confesses to a 'self-crisis', a failure of union with himself: it is a dilemma that appears to have affected many in the *fin de siècle*. Lord Chandos, writing from England, refers to the Piazza San Marco as a high point of world art. The famous site distances him from feelings of youth; Lord Chandos asks: 'Was it I who, at three-and-twenty, beneath the stone arcades of the Great Venetian piazza, found in myself that structure of Latin prose whose plan and order delighted me more than did the monuments of Palladio and Sansovino rising out of the sea?'[200]

For Thomas Mann's narrator in 'Enttäuschung', the Piazza offers one of the world's great experiences, but it has worn out its power to impress; the excesses of Venice have turned such experiences to clichés. For the central character in *Death in Venice*, exhaustion, lack of genuine inspiration and enervation are the characteristic traits of decadence.

Gustav von Aschenbach, the distinguished writer who is the central figure in *Death in Venice*, comes south from Munich for a recuperative holiday. He has overworked and driven himself to illness, and, after some unsatisfactory days spent on an island in the Adriatic, realises his destination is 'the incomparable, the fabulous, the like-nothing-else-in-the-world' Venice.[201] On his passage there, he meets an old man, foolish in the company of a band of youths: it is an omen for Aschenbach, although at first nothing detracts from the fairy-tale appearance of Venice – even though the gondola is coffin-black.

Aschenbach is destined not for the historic city, but for the new Lido: he is one of the many international guests seeking sun and elegance in the new grand hotels. He becomes more and more infatuated with a Polish boy Tadzio, holidaying with his family at the Hotel des Bains. Tadzio is the epitome of youth and beauty, of Greek perfection, in radiant contrast to his plain sisters. The infatuation Aschenbach soon feels for the boy keeps him in Venice despite his own discomfort and the danger of cholera.

Aschenbach's love is a new feeling; his emotional life has long been suppressed: his new love is homosexual, and unacknowledged. The years immediately before Mann wrote his story were ones of public debate and censure of homosexuality, particularly in relation to the male circle of Kaiser Wilhelm II in 1908 and 1909;[202] the Kaiser's association with Prince Philipp zu Eulenberg was particularly notorious.[203] Mann's *Death in Venice* has subsequently become the most forthright example of homosexual infatuation in Venice, even if that infatuation was unconsummated.[204]

Mann himself stayed at the Hotel des Bains with his wife and brother Heinrich in 1911.[205] He interrupted the writing of his comic novel *Felix Krull* to work on *Death in Venice*, having come, as he explained later, to a city familiar to him from his childhood in its resemblence to his native city of Lübeck.[206] Both were port cities, and although Venice was 'exotic as a fable' it was familiar as the source of oriental marzipan that Mann ate as a child.[207] As well has having the notable precedent of Wagner's demise in the city, *Death in Venice* was an expression of the avid German cultivation of Italy.[208] Thomas Mann was acutely aware of the connection between Wagner and Venice, and, by extension, with art and matters of the spirit. While he was at the Hotel des Bains he wrote an essay on Wagner – on the hotel notepaper – associating his encounter with Wagner with his own youth and romantic yearnings.[209] Venice is clearly a city of artists, and it is both *heimlich*, and *unheimlich*: 'Venice is still the most eccentric and most exotic place I know. And yet I regard it as mysteriously homelike: it is a Lübeck rendered into the oriental fantastic.'[210]

Of course literary scholars have mined the sources of *Death in Venice*, among them Schiller in his Venetian story *Der Geisterseher*, in which the noble prince is exposed to strange events, and is tested in the labyrinthine city.[211] Its likeness to Cazotte's *Le Diable amoureux*, in which the irrational and the sensual take over, has also been observed.[212] This is the tradition of the uncanny in Venice; it was far from exhausted in the early twentieth century.

But Mann's story is emphatically contemporary; its issues are topical. The sexual climate of Venice, and the notoriety of the Lido, had been highlighted by the trial of Marie Tarnowska the previous year. Although Mann could not have known the opera by Franz Schreker, *Der ferne Klang*, which was to have its first performance in Frankfurt in 1912, it is interesting to consider what the two had in common. The second Venetian act of Schreker's opera takes the central female character, Greta, to a famous bordello called La Casa di Maschere (The House of the Masks), on an island in the Venetian lagoon.[213] 'Venetian' sounds permeate the act in which Greta's lover repudiates her when he discovers she is a prostitute. The self-recognition forced upon visitors by a Venice that is much more than a backdrop recalls the middle act of Offenbach's *Tales of Hoffmann* – the mirror, the masks and the challenges to identity that Venice again effects. But while the analogies with Mann's Aschenbach are many, and Venice challenges him, it is the modern Lido that is the site for the self-discovery and the setting for his death.

To visit the Lido was to be entirely up to date. Never quite as exotic as the Excelsior, the neighbouring hotel, the Hotel des Bains, which turned its more classical façade towards the sea, was still a prominent destination, hardly a decade old. At several points in the book the combined services of the Hotel des Bains and the Excelsior are mentioned: for example, the shared facilities for transporting clients to the railway station. On the Lido the conversation is international: 'This was a broad and tolerant atmosphere of wide horizons. Subdued voices were speaking most of the principal European tongues.'[214]

Aschenbach is a serious artist, given to introspection. Venice is recognised as the ultimate destination, which will bring him recognition and fulfilment of desire. The awareness of mortality is suggested early on in the novella, during the gondola ride across to the Lido, but it is specifically generated from local conditions at the time of writing. Mann's declaration that *Death in Venice* contained nothing but truth, is evident in the references to cholera conditions in 1911.[215] Cholera was still *the* modern epidemic. The preoccupation with states of *Dekadenz*, death and epiphany, retain the flavour of the *fin de siècle*, but there is little reference to the Venetian past beyond the decay of the old city. When Aschenbach visits the *centro storico*, he comes from the new, clean, modern Venice of his Lido hotel in which he ascends to his room in a lift. In Visconti's famous film version made in 1971, the secrecy that attended the outbreak of cholera is specifically depicted as Aschenbach trails through the old centre of Venice, passing by the *pozzi*, the well-heads of Venice, the source of contaminated water, which are being doused with quicklime. The smell of carbolic penetrates even to the Lido. Cholera and contaminated water are eloquent testimony to the relevance of the polemics of Raffaele Vivante and Angelo Fano in the previous year.

Historic Venice is almost another country, visited from the distance of the Lido. Behind the Lido, Aschenbach cannot escape the putrid presence of the lagoon, the malodorous air, the Barrès-like miasmas: on the other side is the uncontaminated open sea where Tadzio bathes and Aschenbach himself succumbs to oceanic yearnings. The old city with its unrelenting commercialism revolts him: Aschenbach flees 'the huddled, narrow streets of the commercial city, [he] crossed many bridges, and came into the poor quarter of Venice. Beggars waylaid him, the canals sickened him with their evil exhalations.'[216] Trailing the Polish family and his love Tadzio, Aschenbach succumbs to the city's classic effect of disorientation.

The official secrecy – 'the city's evil secret' – which Aschenbach experiences in the midst of the epidemic, was actual city policy. The Commune and the tourist industry co-operated to control undue hysteria, which might adversely influence tourism and commerce.[217] Indeed, in the novella there are frequent comments on the commercial snares to which Aschenbach was subject and his concern at a city hiding its sickness for love of gain. The proprietor of the Excelsior, Nicolò Spada, was particularly anxious about the intervention of Dr Vivante and the Commune authorities and interested citizens who formed the organisation La Pro Venezia.[218] The year 1911 was viewed as a testing period, 'un periodo più delicato', and there was considerable relief that the epidemic had done little to damage the brilliance of the 1912 season. While Aschenbach is aware of the epidemic, other guests at the Hotel des Bains are not. Visconti's film, following the novella in this respect, makes the visual geography clear at the outset.[219] Aschenbach's initial entry to Venice by ship brings him to the classic Molo in front of the Palazzo Ducale; he is then disconcerted by the exploitation of tourists at the hands of gondoliers shipping visitors and baggage across to the Lido.

The tensions and the contradictions between old and new – disease and Aschenbach at the end of his life, versus youth, beauty, sea, sun and the boy Tadzio: these allegorical states are at the heart of the novella. It is as though Mann had written an allegory of the city itself, its yearning for a new youth, the desire for liberation from an old Venice to a new one located on the Lido. Despite the similarity of title to Barrès's *La Mort de Venise* and the presentation of a fairy-tale city marred by exploitation and disease, Barrès had pursued a very different geography, which referred to the old malarial sites of the lagoon islands, such as Torcello. Mann's *Death in Venice* reveals the entrepreneurial resilience that had recently created the international Lido and had its echo in other aspects of Venetian culture. The *Dekadenz* of recent decades was, in effect, brought up to date by an infusion of modernity and optimism. It had much to do with the circle of new capitalists in Venice – Nicolò Spada, Giuseppe Volpi, Piero Foscari and the bard who adopted the Irredentist cause, Gabriele D'Annunzio. It was the zeal of these men that carried Venice through the First World War to the industrial alliances of the 1920s.

The Futurists Attack

The putrescence of the old and its sometime undeniable beauty, beside the desire for the modern, remain at the heart of the Venetian agenda in the twentieth century. In *Il Fuoco* D'Annunzio had turned to the autumn of Venice, to both its abundance and its destructiveness. But it was the Futurists who levelled with the city and caricatured its pathetic will to the modern, highlighting the aura of decay, death and turpitude. In 1910 Marinetti launched the first attack from the Torre dell'Orologio in the Piazza San Marco with a drop of leaflets – a first essay in performance art.[220] Accompanied by a silver trumpet, reading through a megaphone, he delivered his diatribe against the obsolescence and overloading of the city.

The pamphlet, printed simultaneously in Italian, French and English, landed from above on 27 April 1910. It read:

> We repudiate Ancient Venice, exhausted and ravaged by centuries of pleasure, the Venice that we too have loved and possessed in a great nostalgic dream. We repudiate the Venice of the foreigners, market of antiquarians fakers, magnet of universal snobbishness and stupidity, bed worn out by her procession of lovers, jewelled hip-bath of cosmopolitan courtesans, great sewer of traditionalism.

> We want to heal this rotting city, magnificent sore of the past. We want to give new life and nobility to the Venetian people, fallen from their ancient grandeur, drugged by a nauseating cowardice and abused by the habit of dirty little business deals.

> We want to prepare the birth of an industrial and military Venice able to dominate the Adriatic, that great Italian lake. Let us fill the stinking little canals with the rubble of the tottering, infected old palaces. Let us burn the gondolas, rocking chairs for idiots, raise to the sky the majestic geometry of metal bridges and factories, abolishing the drooping curves of ancient buildings. Let the reign of divine Electric Light come at last, to free Venice from her venal hotel-room moonlight.

> F. T. Marinetti, U. Boccioni, C. Carrà and L. Russolo.[221]

This is a pungently overdrawn statement of the Venice that has sewerage problems, as well as a long-standing reputation for eroticism and licence. All these positions had been well rehearsed in the *fin de siècle*, but Marinetti's was a powerful re-imaging: to go against Venice like that! Yet the call for an re-energised Venice in 1910 showed a certain ignorance of the designs of Piero Foscari, Achille Gaggia and Giuseppe Volpi, whose initiatives had brought hydroelectricity to the Veneto through their SADE company, formed in 1905.[222] This was one venture at least that gave the Veneto industrial leadership in the period, bringing these men into industrial and civic prominence. Moonlight remained, of course, but electric light galvanised the Lido's night life and ran the trams. Shipping interests in Venice had endeavoured to challenge the Austrian Lloyd company by founding the Società Veneziana di Navigazione a Vapore.[223] And the Lido was linked to the new entrepreneurial activity that D'Annunzio had called *la città nuova*.

Marinetti had certainly read *La Nave*, but he preferred to cast D'Annunzio in the role of a Symbolist, tainted with *passéisme*.[224] With irony, and perhaps some grain of truth, Marinetti declared that he was almost forced to admire D'Annunzio as a distinguished seducer, 'ineffable descendant of Cagliostro and Casanova and of many other Italian adventurers'.[225]

Marinetti's criticism was, without doubt, one of the most astringent and well founded ever directed at Venice. His campaign came a short time before the completion of the rebuilt Campanile, and he fully understood its status as a fetish: it was a perfect example of the Venetian cult of the past and repudiation of the present. In remarks addressed to an English audience, Marinetti attacked 'the deplorable Ruskin', who 'would have wanted to reconstruct that absurd Campanile of San Marco, as if to give a little girl who had lost her grandmother a cardboard doll which resembled the dead one'.[226] Ruskin had endeared the English to 'a sickly dream of rustic and primitive life' and the cult of 'haunting the past'.[227] As a result, the English judgement of contemporary Italy was tainted.

The Futurist manifesto immediately inspired caricatures. In the journal *Commoedia*, André Warnod took up the call to war, turning the gondoliers into infantryman, arming a gondola with a machine gun, turning another into a submarine, showing Venice before and after Futurism with the tourists exterminated by smoke stacks and

136 André Warnod,
'Futurist Venice',
Commoedia, 1910.

air buses (fig. 136). Electric light conspires to wipe out the tired old moonlight.[228] Venice was the image of the old courtesan leering in front of the Piazzetta.

Marinetti followed the Manifesto with a performance at La Fenice, further abusing the Old Procuress and the seedy romantic profile of the City of Love imagined under her 'heavy mosaic mantilla'.[229] The Futurists had been intent on attacking the moon-light for some time; Venice of course had an ample supply, creating its fabled effects for foreigners, conducting 'the greatest bordello in history'. The Futurists called for the widening and dredging of the Grand Canal followed by an infusion of locomo-tives, trams and automobiles. The islands of Torcello, Burano and the cemetery island of San Michele were targeted as sites of putrefaction, of 'diseased literature and all that romantic embroidery draped over them by poets poisoned with the Venetian fever' – Barrès was probably their target here.[230] The Society of Grand Hotels, the consortium set up in 1907 as the Compagnia Italiana dei Grandi Alberghi, was a further example of grovelling before foreigners, a poor substitute for 'a great strong industrial, commercial, and military Venice on the Adriatic sea'.[231]

In 1911 Marinetti appeared at La Fenice with a troup of poets – Paolo Buzzi, Aldo Palazzeschi and Enrico Cavalchioli – who performed 'noises' and spoofs of D'Annunzio to an audience 'quick to clap and boo'. Later, after D'Annunzio's espou-sal of war and his connection with Mussolini, Marinetti was rather more supportive, but in 1911 Barrès and D'Annunzio were 'bards of putrefaction'. Futurist poetry cer-tainly exploited the imagery that Marinetti had used in the first pamphlet, but it was infused with energy and a wild range of similes that consolidated the division bet-ween the adherents of old and new.

In one of the first collections of futurist poetry, Corrado Govoni gave his version of Marinetti's *Contra Venezia passastisa* in his collection *Le poesie elettriche*.[232] The writer is seduced by the great procuress; he has Venice in his veins, the Venice whose canals are fetid and green with scum. Propped up in the midst of luxury, the sickened poet becomes an oozing anxiety-ridden torment of nerves. Gondolas are as flimsy as papier-mâché yet again, and harbingers of death. The abused moon is a 'pastille of quinine'.

Amando Mazza's *Venezia* opens with a declaration of love and hate for the canals that are sewers, the houses that are latrines and the palaces that are saccharine marble licked by the sickened sun.[233] The place is a sham parade of daggers and masks in an environment of seaweed, lichen, gondolas and harlots. The moon must be replaced by the chimneys and furnaces of industry.

Venice had a new generation of detractors. No longer was the old Republic the guilty treasonous state; it was the ancient physical face of the city that inspired devotion or contempt and marked the distance from the reality of the modern world. Marinetti's critique might appear highly original, and the first substantial attack on *passéisme*, but filling in the canals and the lagoon, boarding over the Grand Canal, providing carriageways, developing industry, opening up the Adriatic to Italian concerns, re-energising the city, all had been mooted and discussed by the Venetians themselves in the two previous decades. But in the new century the Campanile had fallen, and it was the old and not the new that was endorsed. The lobby for old Venice had staying power.

Foreign Custodians: Simmel, Hofmannsthal, Apollinaire, Monet and Ezra Pound

The old and the new clashed frequently, and were never to be reconciled in the twentieth century. Nor was Venice able to escape the vilification and ambivalence that appeared in the interpretations in the early century. But the old Serenissima was not yet dead: indeed there was renewed fascination with the eighteenth century. Venice still cherished the recent memory of its painter Giacomo Favretto and his recreations of a glamorous past. The Venetian-born composer Ernanno Wolf-Ferrari brought Goldoni to musical life in his *opera buffa* devoted to female shortcomings, *I quattri rusteghi*, first performed in Munich in 1906:[234] 'The period of the action: end of the eighteenth century. Place: Venice.'

A history written by a foreigner contributed to keep the past alive: Philippe Monnier's *Venise au dix-huitième siècle* gave new currency to the city of carnival, licence, disguise and endless play.[235] The book was enormously popular on the eve of the First World War, as Venice endeavoured to consolidate its image as a glamorous holiday destination for the international set. Venice is written about in the present tense, standing out conspicuously from the rest of Italy by virtue of its playwrights Goldini and Gozzi, and its printing presses. Little more than a century earlier 'Venice was neither more nor less than an enchanted city, a wonderful, mad city of masks and serenades, of amusement and pretence...'[236] But, of course, the end was nigh: 'Beneath the brilliance and charm of the surface, the corruption is deep-set... On the surface of the ancient organism, a thousand years old, dissolution is spreading in blotches....'[237] Thus Monnier enjoyed the *carnevale* that preceded the dissolution.

Hugo von Hofmannsthal read Monnier's book while on the Lido and found it inspirational for his projected novel *Andreas, oder die Vereinigten*, in which Andreas, the main character, is brought to Venice to play out the erotic adventures of youth and realise maturity.[238] Andreas seeks adventures and experiences in the straightforward manner of the prince of adventurers, Casanova, whom Hofmannsthal had read some years earlier. But Venice for Andreas is not an area only for adventure: at a self-consciously deeper level he experiences the dissembling nature of life that the city epitomises through its very topography.

Donning a mask, Andreas journeys to Venice chiefly because the people there are always masked and he himself is 'haunted by the difference between being and seeming'. Much has been made of the profundity of this distinction. Andreas reaches towards the insight that 'the whole world is so dreadfully puppet-like'. His condition approaches a nervous breakdown, not unlike the condition of Lord Chandos as he becomes 'two halves which gape asunder'.[239]

Venice kept its allure for Hofmannsthal as a place of deception. Schizophrenic on the eve of the war, it is beautiful and barbaric, a place of healthy and glamorous holidays on the Lido, but equally a source of divisiveness, cholera and death. Hofmannsthal had countenanced its betrayal in his version of *Venice Preserv'd*, reworked after Thomas Otway in 1904 with macabre overtones such as references to the odour of rotting fish and the presence of the eyes of the drowned in canals.[240] Venice is conspired against, but the conspirators are themselves betrayed. At first the city lies ripe for their taking: she is 'the Adrian harlot, resting on her islands as on a pillow'.[241] To conspirator Pierre, rehearsing his speech to the Inquisition before he is sentenced, he himself has failed, but Napoleon (by implication, he is not named) will succeed: 'Within one night he'll overthrow it.'[242] Hofmannsthal's new version of Otway challenges the city again and reactivates rumours of its death.

But that decayed Venice was almost immediately counter-balanced by the eighteenth-century Venice, indirectly evident in one of Hofmannsthal's best-known works, the libretto for the Richard Strauss opera *Der Rosenkavalier*, in which a Makart-like world of satins and brittle court life takes the stage. Habsburg Vienna lives again, and yields its allegories. The waltz, replete with its memories of the days of Johann Strauss, plays anachronistically in the Vienna of the eighteenth century, as it had done for Johann Strauss in his operetta about Venice in the eighteenth century.[243]

In the fragment *Cristinas Heimreise*, drafted in 1910, Hofmannsthal returned to the Venice of Goldoni's time with a Casanova-type central character, Signor Florindo. Yet again, Casanova exemplifies the genius of vitality – of *Lebens-geniale*.[244] Writing to his fellow-author Arthur Schnitzler, Hofmannsthal underlined Casanova's genius for play, his *Spielernatur* and – prophetically for Schnitzler's own later encounter with Casanova – 'his play with fate, [he] hazards audaciously and loses'.[245] After the Great War, the play is over. Schnitzler writes contemptuously of the weak Casanova, an aged and ugly representative of a crumbling city.

As if to counter his own absorption in conspiracy and the eighteenth-century, Hofmannsthal is unreservedly lyrical in his prose work of 1908, *Erinnerung schöner Tage* (A Memory of Beautiful Days).[246] It is Hofmannsthal's final work about Venice. Rilke had a perception of its future energy; Hofmannsthal was breathlessly retrospective. The narrator glides into the city by gondola in the company of a brother and sister. They penetrate the dark small canals, experiencing them inevitably as 'though in a dream'. The exoticism of palace architecture impresses, as does the ultimate radiance of the Bacino and the sight of the Campanile at its full height, though it was still being rebuilt when Hofmannsthal wrote. Gleaming jewels and silken flowers enhance the experience. Women resemble antique statues. Finally in his hotel, the narrator hears the sounds of lovemaking through the thin walls and he dreams of the unkissed mouth of his sister Katharine as he drops into sleep. It is the sleep of the unconscious that embraces death, life and imagined incest, the concerns at the heart of this piece of charged writing.

For the German sociologist Georg Simmel Venice was dangerous and unnerving as a result of its cult of appearances, its masquerade culture. In 1907 Simmel wrote comparative essays about Florence and Venice in which he cast Florence as the *male* city, strong and manly, with robust and 'sincere' palaces, and Venice as female, of course, severed from relationships, a shallow place of mere appearances.[247] Venice is the artificial city where the people walk, again, as if on a stage that lacks extension to right or left.[248] Nature is foreign to it, since greenery is absent and therefore the seasons make little impact.

Simmel admitted that Venice was 'a unique order of the form of world consciousness'. But it was a negative attribute: in fact it constituted 'the tragedy of Venice'.[249] He felt the proximity of the subconscious – and the irrational – and feared it, for it was compounded by the city's very appearance, its geography, material life, its lack of nature, and transport either by foot or by gondola. The tempo of the city of gondolas and pedestrians was akin to the monotony of walking, which made the experience close to dream and therefore unreal, without the jolts necessary to vitalise everyday life. A fateful ambiguity is born of the physical reality of canals and *calli*: it is neither land nor water. The water constantly moves, but goes nowhere. This is a life state, one of floating restlessness which dislodges the soul and makes it homeless, 'unsere Seele keine Heimat'.[250] While this disabling state creates 'the classic city of adventure', it is a condition of weakness, psychologically invalid, for it lacks forceful tension, and male willpower. Simmel's characterisation of Venice was potent, even if he ignored the energetic financial life that Venice surely represented as much as did Florence. Clearly he was himself a victim of Venice, deeply apprehensive in the face of that 'feminine' city.

The possibility of adventure was still current in the twentieth century, reconfirmed by Thomas Mann, Baron Corvo, Hofmannsthal and, not least, the rebellious Futurists. Guillaume Apollinaire, no stranger to the avant-garde, further stressed the Venetian erotic when he presented the work of the eighteenth-century poet Giorgio Baffo, called 'the Obscene', to French audiences.[251] Apollinaire demonstrated his knowledge of Venetian dialect literature in a preface to a French edition of the poems, in which it was clear he had mastered the dialect and developed an appreciation of the voluptuous nature of Venetian satire. He relates how Baffo's writing is preceded by the flavoursome comedies of Calmo and the songs of Maffeo Veniero. The brio and verve of the lagoons in the seventeenth century is also seen in the work of Bona, and, in the eighteenth century, in Goldoni and Casanova. Baffo, whose character was formed in the urbanity of Amnuirat III's seraglio, where he grew up, is the sublime key to the sexuality of the late Republic. The 'amphibious city', as Apollinaire famously styled it, is the 'cité humide, sexe femelle d'Europe'.[252] He imagined the young women of Baffo's time reading his salacious rhymes as they ate their sorbets. He enumerated the sites of the libertinous: the festivals, the *osterie*, the casinos and gambling houses, and the participating ballerinas and nuns. Among them, Baffo sings with his 'sublime obscenity'.

Another distinguished French artist accepted the challenge of Venice in the first decade of the twentieth century. Claude Monet's series of paintings devoted to the city were the fruit of a two-month stay in 1908. He was sixty-eight years old when he came with his wife Alice to the Palazzo Barbaro, later moving to the Hotel Britannia (now the Europa Hotel): Madame Monet found its plumbing and electricity were 'vraiment magique'.[253] Perhaps not surprisingly Monet did not move far from the upper Grand Canal and the Bacino for his painting trips. His geography was of the most conventional, but made exceptional because of his distinctive practice of concentrating on the single 'motif', dwelling on it at changing times and creating a suite of paintings of that motif which then swivels and angles as it succumbs to an intensified colour-light.[254] From the Palazzo Barbaro, Monet painted across the canal to the Palazzo Dario (fig. 137) and the Palazzo Contarini. In the area of the Bacino he painted the double view of the Palazzo Ducale from the island of San Giorgio Maggiore, and San Giorgio Maggiore from in front of the Palazzo Ducale.

These paintings are a late point in a *plein-air* tradition, the summation of the habit of looking now so intensively personalised they becomes expressionistic, reaching beyond ordinary specifics of colour and light. Monet chose motifs that were too well known, but he took ownership of his motifs, of the domes of Santa Maria della Salute,

137 Claude Monet, *Palazzo Dario*, 1908. Oil on canvas, 92 × 73 cm. Cardiff, National Museum and Gallery.

painting from the balcony of his hotel across the canal. Those domes swell into pink and mauve. The Palazzo Ducale in its different views hovers and shifts within webs of paint, at one with the texture of the band of water on which it floats. Atmosphere is palpable, never more tangible than in Monet's Venice, never more unifying of building and setting.

The writer Octave Mirbeau still saw Venice as lyrical but tainted when he wrote an influential review of Claude Monet's nineteen views of Venice, the product of the visit of 1908.[255] According to Mirbeau, whose eloquent essay appeared on the occasion of the exhibition at the Bernheim-Jeune gallery in Paris in 1912, up to that point Monet had resisted Venice, since to paint it was the measure of human stupidity. For Mirbeau himself it was a dead city, Europe's nuptial headquarters, sweetly sexual, a place for the bourgeoisie to marry – and part. It followed that Monet's scenic enterprise could be seen as an embarrassment. Indeed, people are excluded from Monet's views, and in their absence the motives become coloured-enriched, creating a sweet and roseate place. The buildings appear stripped of detail, dissolved into light and colour, blocks of paint; no longer functional buildings.

Perhaps Gustave Geffroy's words were the most apt, seeing in Monet's paintings 'a Venice not sculpted or constructed, but suspended in spray and in a distance of space which makes it a dream of a different time'.[256] Geffroy had a precise sense of Monet's time of visit when the city no longer had the precision it held for the old masters. Monet saw it, characteristically, with both ingenuousness and knowingness.[257]

In a variant of Simmel's critique – or the critique of the Futurists, Venice could only regurgitate motifs; it was a decor city, capsized by the weight of imbeciles. On the eve of the First World War its inspiration had been polarised: an unstable, plague city receiving the dead, city of the past with Casanova its famous hollow son, city of *passéisme*, of idiots in gondolas – or the greatest survival of the past and its beauty, roseate still, and precious beyond measure. There was no question of the devotion that the city could still inspire in the hearts of true believers – Rilke, Frederick Rolfe and also the young Ezra Pound. Pound came in 1908 during his first European visit and, with modest means, published a first volume of poetry with a title quoting Dante, *A lume spento* (With Tapers Quenched).[258] The poem 'Night Litany' is a prayer of thanks to the God who formed Venice: to the God of Waters who created something that could still be apprehended in all its loveliness. The sense of contemplation in the present is intense as the poet watches the night waves and the 'shadows of the waters'. This night Venice breathes softly through the poem and mortals have privileged entry. Pound's shadowy and private Venice, which he may have been seeing from the Punta della Dogana near his residence at San Vio, is a precious moment – not Symbolist, or decadent, or historic, uncorrupted by daytime, or by tourists. Beyond irony and decrepitude, it was a place that could still be beautiful. Here again is the city's phoenix-like capacity for renewal.

As the first decade of the new century closed, ideas and themes that would remain current for decades were in place. Venetian entrepreneurs wanted to develop the Lido, relocate the port, create an industrial site in the lagoon and support the Irredentist cause for expansion to the east. The painters were there, and the poets, architects, photographers and film-makers. The Campanile had collapsed, occasioning worldwide expressions of loss, as would the fire that destroyed the opera house La Fenice in 1994. Both were to be rebuilt 'where they were, as they were'; there was little challenge to the belief that the great Venetian icons must remain. Inhibiting modern architecture in the museum city adorned with the jewels of the past meant creating antagonistic positions that would reject grand projects by modern architects and lead Post Modernists to design Venices on paper. Yet the building of national pavilions in the Giardini was the guarantee of the life and the continuation of the Biennale through the century, confirming it as the world's most important art exhibition.

Venice never had the coherent intellectual circles that Florence formed in the early twentieth century with Giovanni Papini, Giuseppe Prezzolini, the painter Ardengo Soffici and the prominent avant-garde journals *Leonardo*, *La Voce* and *Lacerba*,[259] but as a meeting place, a melting-pot and a social nexus, it was unsurpassed. In the first years of the century the Lido was instantly successful as an extension of the already intense social season played out in the palaces along the Grand Canal. There was no more symbolic centre than the Hotel des Bains in the pre-war years. In 1911 Thomas Mann had meditated there on Wagner, and created Aschenbach. The following September Igor Stravinsky played to Serge Diaghilev on the ballroom piano – a first draft of the 'Danse des Adolescents' from *The Rite of Spring*.[260] During the war the Lido was a military zone again: an Austrian air attack destroyed one wing of the Hotel des Bains.[261] After the war the Lido recovered, and Diaghilev continued to spend his summers there, dying in a thunderstorm in 1929 at that same hotel.[262] In 1971 his friend Stravinsky, loyal to Venice for many decades, composer of music for San Marco, died in Venice. Death, and its obverse, life, had no more symbolic stage throughout the century, provoking writers, musicians and film-makers to variations that still seemed inexhaustible.

Chapter 8

THE YEARS OF THE WINGED LION:
1914–1940

The First World War: D'Annunzio's Nocturne

With the declaration of war, Venice needed no urging to protect her monuments, which were placed in the charge of the minister of war and the administration of fine arts under the directorship of Corrado Ricci.[1] The four horses of San Marco were removed to an undisclosed place (fig. 138); Titian's *Assunta* was taken to the mainland;[2] wood and sandbags protected the walls and windows of San Marco and the Palazzo Ducale; the Colleoni monument was encased in a padded house; seaweed from the lagoon was used to protect small statues and to stuff mattresses suspended above fragile items in the Palazzo Ducale.[3]

Austrian air attacks began on 24 May 1915, when nineteen bombs fell on the Castello area in the vicinity of the Arsenale.[4] Venetians at home waged war from their historic wooden roof terraces, the *altane*, where groups of gunmen trained anti-aircraft guns on the Austrian attackers. Over the period of the war various hits were recorded: the most serious caused the destruction of the Tiepolo ceiling in the church of the Scalzi in the strategic area of the railway, and shells fell on San Francesco della Vigna, Santa Maria Formosa and the civic hospital at the Scuola di San Marco.[5]

Gabriele D'Annunzio returned to Venice in July 1915 to make it his headquarters for war activity. Venice was centre stage for him in these years; he was fifty-two years old when he enlisted, and flew in some fifty missions.[6] He stayed at the Hotel Danieli initially, but in October he began his famous residence in Prince Hohenlohe Waldemberg's Casetta Rossa. D'Annunzio moved swiftly into a prominent position in the war effort, extolling the Venetian 'compagne d'arme e d'arte'.[7] He made notorious propaganda flights, dropping leaflets encouragingly over Trieste, and, insultingly, over Vienna. In January 1916 he lost the sight in his right eye in an air crash, which immobilised him. During his convalescence in the Casetta Rossa he wrote *Nocturne*.[8]

Nocturne is autobiographical, written, as the story tells, on strips of paper with a soft pencil which he could manage despite his bandaged eyes. It tells of contemporary Venice in war, a city of silence and emptiness to which the corpses of dead airmen are returned. There are flowers *in memoriam*, drenched in rain. Venice appears as a winter city, fog-bound; the Piazza is 'like a basin filled with opalescent water'; the Basilica San Marco 'like a rock in a misty sea'; the columns of San Marco and San Teodoro are 'columns of smoke'. It is night and the dead are abroad. Venice is muffled and ambiguous; the narrator feels himself in the presence of an absent comrade as he walks the city.

Returning home, he learns of the aircrash that has killed his aviator friends Giuseppe Miragha and Giorgio Fracassini, and he takes up vigil beside their bodies, which have been returned to Venice. Confined to bed, he transports himself in imagination from the Casetta Rossa to the opposite reaches of the Grand Canal, to Santa Maria della Salute, the Palazzo Dario and the palace now known as the Palazzo dei Leoni. At that time it was the residence of D'Annunzio's friend the extravagant

138 The removal of the horses from San Marco, 1915. Venice, Osväldo Bohm.

Marchesa Casati – and her leopards. In the story, a black boat carrying sulphur passes – it embodies the principle of male action which is, in *Nocturne*, associated with sacrifice in war. Despite its male heroics, *Nocturne* is the most distinctive work of art to emanate from the city in war, from a place of grey beauty and isolation.

The composer Gian Francesco Malipiero, on the threshold of a distinguished musical career, let the war sound in his music. The dead are abroad and the bells are tolling in his piano suite written in 1916, the *Poemi asolani*, which inhabits the zone of D'Annunzio's *Nocturne*.[9] The muffled, fog-bound terrain of war finds acoustic expression in the first movement of the Asolani poems, *La Notte dei Morti*. Later Malipiero was to embrace more acerbic harmonies, but here the music sounds submerged, like Debussy's music; the sonorities of the piano's bass strings are lugubrious and solemn against fragile snatches of melody in the high treble.[10] For Malipiero the likeness to D'Annunzio was not only a similarity of mood, for after long interest he had set D'Annunzio's melodramatic *Il Sogno d'Autunno* for voices on the eve of the war, in 1913.[11] Malipiero's melancholy had expressed itself earlier in a symphonic piece which suggests the *fin-de-siècle paludisme* of Barrès in the 1909–10 *Sinfonie del Silenzio e de la Morte*.[12]

During the war years Venice withdrew by necessity into a symbolic fog. It felt the tenuous nature of its link to the mainland and its vulnerability to the line of the Austrian advance. In the view of one Venetian, Camille Alberto Sebellin, writing in 1916, it was like a pack of cards that had collapsed swiftly with the declaration of war, brought to a commercial standstill as a result of over-dependence on tourism.[13] The connection with 1848 and the old Austrian enemy was quickly made. The Austrians governed the Adriatic, shipping lines were Austrian and American, Hungarian and Croat. The Italian administration did not favour Venice. The Arsenale was under-used. Sebellin asked whether a local people still existed, for it seemed that Venetians had forgotten to be Venetians; the Socialists were against the Catholic Democrats, content to be divided. Sebellin diagnosed the schism that would lead to the acceptance of Fascism.

In these years Venetian historians were at work studying parallel invasions from the past. Antonio Pilot and Nani Mocenigo published studies of Venice under Napoleon, and, even more relevantly, Venetian resistance to the Austrians in the previous century.[14] There was renewed relevance in the 1848 slogan 'Venice will defend itself against the Austrians at any cost'.

Writing between December 1915 and February 1916, Antonio Fradeletto, no longer active in Biennale duties, testified sadly to the low ebb of life in the city, which brought to mind the historic struggles against the Austrians. The port was closed to commerce again, visitors had left, workers were reduced to misery, the great glory of art was threatened with destruction. Venice was a martyr to the Italian war cause.[15]

The expression of Venice as autumnal had a historical ring for D'Annunzio, but for others it was a portent not just of imminent danger but of permanent decline. The debate on the future of Venice shifted in the climate of war. It was argued that bathing and hotels could not be the primary means of Venice's survival. It must be compelled to take up nautical engineering; a 'blocco Veneto' must represent interests in Rome; an industrial base was mandatory for recovery. This was the background to the foundation of the new industrial port of Marghera. With the defeat of Austria in the Adriatic and the liberation of Trento and Trieste, Venice was poised for recovery; its strategic position would certainly lead it to triumph with the return of Dalmatia achieving the dream of Irredentism – the old ambition to reintegrate the lost lands of the Republic.

Despite the stagnancy experienced during the war, it was possible to claim afterwards that Venice was one of the few victors.[16] It was vindicated in the face of its old master, Austria, and reconciled with France. As the first Italian city to suffer attack, it could be said to have constituted 'the front', and survived. The peace of Saint-

139 (*top left*) Giuseppe Torres, design for the Lido votive temple, *c.*1922. Pencil and watercolour, 49.5 × 57 cm. Venice, Collection Giulio Torres.

140a and b Napoleone Martinuzzi, monument to the Fallen, 1923–7. Murano.

Germain reversed the 1797 treaty of Campoformio: the historic centre was reunited with the border cities. Commemorations of the war dead were envisaged: Giuseppe Torres raised a votive temple on the Lido in 1924 (fig. 139). A domed building, elevated on a podium and surmounted by the figure of the Redeemer, the Torres temple is conspicuous across the water, but it is disappointingly mute: prominent, but unappealing. Its classical orientation would later result in its being labelled proto-fascist, but in fact it shows Torres's interest in the Viennese school of architecture and Otto Wagner's public buildings.[17] The cultural link between Venice and central Europe remained intact after the war.

A singular monument to the fallen was created between 1923 and 1927 by the sculptor and glassmaker Napoleone Martinuzzi for the island of Murano. It is Venice's most important public sculpture of these decades (fig. 140).[18] In the shadow of Murano's revered church Santa Maria e San Donato, the monument takes the form of a brick cloister set with sculptural reliefs, as if it were an annexe to the church beside it, recording recent Christian sacrifices. As is customary in First World War monuments, the central image glorifies male soldiers; the women mourn in the wings. The presentation is knowingly archaic, giving a timeless classicism to the figures, but with clear Venetian allusions, as it evokes the corner statues of the Palazzo Ducale, and the linearity of ancient sculptures at Torcello, San Marco and Murano.

In 1920, in the unstable climate following the war, D'Annunzio had set out illegally from Venice with troops to occupy Fiume, predominantly Italian-speaking, but retained by Austria after the Treaty of Versailles.[19] D'Annunzio had made it known

141 Guido Marussig,
Indented Prow, 1918. Oil
on canvas, 120 × 120 cm.
Museo d'Arte Moderna di
Ca' Pesaro.

to Mayor Grimani that his plane, *Serenissima*, had flown over enemy Vienna with the
lion of St Mark painted on its fuselage.[20] *La Nave* played again in Milan, with sets
designed by Guido Marussig who painted the powerful *Indented Prow* dramatising
the prows of gondolas which loom war-like out of darkness (fig. 141).[21] D'Annunzio's 'Letter to the Dalmations' published in the *Gazzetta di Venezia* in 1918, broadcast his frustrations with the war settlement, as did the spontaneous greeting from the
people in the Piazza San Marco on St Mark's Day, 25 April 1919, when he challenged
them in the spirit of the incomplete Irredentist cause, proclaiming himself 'a Venetian among Venetians'.[22] He delivered one of his classic orations, and, by his own
account, was acclaimed.[23] It was clear that he did not want the war to end, or his
own heroic reputation to be forgotten. Amid the ceremonies that unveiled the equestrian sculpture of Colleoni on its plinth in the Campo dei Santi Giovanni e Paolo,
D'Annunzio recalled the image of the *condottiere* setting out in triumph, a model for
new conquests: 'Not for me the Evviva, but for Colleoni.'[24]

Fuelled by a long-standing passion recorded in the first draft of *La Nave* in 1905,
D'Annunzio was to realise his Irredentist mission, if briefly. He took command of
Fiume and he kept Venice resonant in his rhetoric: 'When I took Fiume without
wounding anyone, silencing the armies and the allies, I believed that the shadow of
some proud Doge was before me . . .'[25] After Fiume, his Venetian life was behind him,
although Venetian artists befriended during the war years – Astolfo de Maria, Guido
Cadorin and Napoleone Martinuzzi – were the main contributors to the decoration
of D'Annunzio's last exotic residence at La Vittoriale a Gardone on the shores of Lake
Garda.[26] Here his living spaces were hung with damasks by Fortuny and with glass
candelabra by Martinuzzi (fig. 142), and set with flagpoles flying the pennant of San

142 Gabriele D'Annunzio's music room, with fabrics by Mariano Fortuny and glass lighting by Napoleone Martinuzzi, *c.*1925. Gardone Riviera, Fondazione Il Vittoriale degli Italiani.

143 Astolfo de Maria, *Dogaressa*, 1917–19. Tempera on cardboard, 59.4 × 55.5 cm. Gardone Riviera, Fondazione Il Vittoriale degli Italiani, Stanza della Leda.

Marco; the gardens were adorned with Martinuzzi's figure of Victory, the bedroom of 'pure dreams' was painted with panels by Guido Cadorin and in the dining room was Astolfo de Maria's razor-sharp portrait of a dogaressa. Here, in the most grandiose of D'Annunzio's dwellings, was the expression of his ingrained taste for *venezianità*. The Astolfo de Maria *Dogaressa*, painted between 1917 and 1919 in tempera, is one of the gems of Venetian neo-Realism and offers another twist on the famous dogal portrait by Gentile Bellini which has been turned from a right profile to a left and has been transformed from male into female (fig. 143).[27] The ancient dogaressa wears that inevitable skullcap with the delicate cords, and her frizzled grey hair protrudes as she sits implacable, her distinctive profile sharp against a Persian carpet and a distant Veneto mountain-scape. She is the alter ego of the proprietor of La Vittoriale.

The Creation of Porto Marghera, and Early Fascism

The war dramatised the plight of Venice. In 1917 the decision to create a new port on the margins of the lagoon at Bottenighi – to create Porto Marghera – was approved, almost two decades after Luciano Petit's original proposal to relocate the port inland. Piero Foscari, who had supported the project for more than ten years, published a pamphlet on the expansion of Venice and the establishment of a new port and sent it to all members of the government.[28] The result would remove heavy industry from the historic city and, at the same time, further develop the hydroelectric industry. Propitious relations with the Banca Commerciale and shipping companies already effectively managed by Venetians Giuseppe Volpi and Piero Foscari were in place. In the early years the prospect of construction work and workers' housing were claimed as great milestones in the progress of the economy and society. The enterprise boosted national production. The establishment of Porto Marghera and its industry was the biggest change to the modern city, and one of the most momentous in its history.[29]

In the period of its inception the coincidence of political and industrial interests was essential to the creation of Marghera. It was seen to serve nationalist interests, creating a productive area alongside Irredentist territories. The post-war rhetoric extolling 'Italia nuova', industrialisation and modernisation could only serve the Marghera cause, even if initially it polarised public opinion. *Il Gazzettino* published the contrary voices from the *antibottenighisti* with such headlines as 'Control il porto di Mestre'.[30] The small port of Chioggia – one of the historic ports of the ancient lagoon – protested, and the saying spread, 'in Mestre the roast, in Venice the smoke'.[31]

Nevertheless, in 1917 the creation of Marghera was handled at both regional and national levels with panache and speed over a matter of months. The activity has been described as frenetic.[32] Count Volpi – the most influential figure in the history of modern Venice – was the moving force. His presidency of the Società Adriatica di Electricità from 1904 was the foundation of his influence: backed by the Banca Commerciale Italiana, the society was a major partner in the Marghera cartel.[33] Volpi had also gained in national prestige as a result of his diplomatic negotiations for the Giolitti government in the treaties of 1912.[34] Inevitably he became president of the initiating body, the Società Porto Industriale.[35] Other interested parties, such as the steamship company, the Società Veneta per la Navigazione a Vapore, were quick to engage with the new operation; and such distinguished businessmen as Carlo Stucky, Alberto Treves and Nicolò Papadopoli were also involved in the foundation of naval shipyards.[36]

The project was accepted only three months after the formation of the syndicate, and five days after a submission by the engineer Coen, which was strongly supported by a government that endorsed the need for a 'Greater Venice' and new port.[37] Piero

Foscari's support was crucial throughout the project's long gestation; indeed his prominence and persistence kept the issue alive.[38] He claimed that the new site was of national import: it was to make Venice 'the eastern lung of the nation as Genoa was the western lung'.[39]

The nascent Fascist party readily identified with the creation of Marghera and its eminent directors. Nationalism and Fascism were in accord, the latter dependent on the former. Local figures with industrial significance, including Volpi and Foscari, supported D'Annunzio's occupation of Fiume for it was in the path of their eastern markets.[40] Introduced in 1919, during a period of local and national workers' strikes, Fascism gained ground swiftly in Venice. In the early years it was not greatly distinguished from the Social Democrat's party position.[41] Although the most militant Fascist was Pietro Marsich, a volunteer returned from Fiume, the key appointment to the position of mayor was a less extreme adherent: the eminent Venetian surgeon Davide Giordano was elected in 1920, indicating that Fascism was appropriate to the professional class.[42] Giordani's appointment opened the way to a straightforward alliance with Mussolini. Nevertheless, there were violent clashes with the Socialists in the Veneto region in the years from 1919 to 1922, and workers' strikes in the tobacco company and the Mulino Stucky.[43]

By the early 1920s the major components of the Marghera project were in place: the enlargement and deepening of the canal from the Stazione Marittima; the formation of the service area of the port with an internal canal providing two docks capable of servicing the largest naval vessels; the creation of a commercial area; an isolated port for receiving petrol and inflammable material; and the reclamation of an area of about five square kilometres for an industrial zone and a commercial port (fig. 144).[44] The Commune had the responsibility for urban implementation and the Società Porto Industriale for the railway network.

A new Venice was proclaimed with heightened rhetoric. Squalid marshy wastes were to be productive at last. As early as 1920 Gino Piva reported rhapsodically on the scale of excavations, dredging and reclamation, and the bosses and workers bronzed by the sun, working at full stretch.[45] Photographs documented the heroic event. The other Venice, historic Venice, was to be saved and glorified. The port of Marghera was to be recognised as one of the principal instruments of the new national economy.

144 Porto Marghera, 1920. Venice, Archivio Giacomelli.

Some twenty years later the rhetoric still continued. Count Volpi, now with the title Conte di Misurata bestowed during his service as governor in Tripoli, claimed Porto Marghera as no less than one of the great enterprises of the century and one of the great industrial ports of the world.[46] It was the product of a history he was proud to trace from the opposition to the League of Cambrai in the sixteenth century, the resistance to the Turks, and the challenge of new ocean routes that diminished Venetian trade, through to Marghera. As always the city triumphed. Italy under Mussolini had achieved a new imperial dignity to which Venice was contributing its own heroic example. A miracle had preserved Venice: the new terrestrial Venice, also born of the sea, had been resurrected by Venetians like Volpi himself, a self-styled man of poetry and action.[47] It was a high point of optimism in modern Venetian history.

Appropriate accommodation for workers near the site had been a feature of the original proposal, responding to the housing pressures on island Venice, and industry's need for a workforce. Yet the establishment of a housing development in Marghera, despite the claims for it as a solution to the housing crisis in historic Venice and the promise of a 'garden city', generated problems (fig. 145).[48] Barrack-like estates were increasingly seen as sub-standard. As the population grew in the industrial area the problems became more evident.[49] It had always been imperative to include the new area under the government of Venice, and thus Greater Venice was formed in 1926 to unite the historic islands of Venice, Marghera and Mestre on the Terraferma, as well as the islands of Murano and Burano, autonomous until then.[50] Under the mayor, Davide Giordano, it was clear that if Marghera were established on lands beyond Venice, then Venice must control the new site: 'where the port is is Venetian territory.'[51] Planning for Mestre, greatly expanded in population as a result of Marghera, was acknowledged as urgent in an era of legislated urbanism, the era of the Piano Regolatore.[52]

The movement of workers across the lagoon and from the central city to Mestre and Marghera posed additional problems. The problems of transit were not new, as Salvatori's pamphlet on 'A Greater Venice' made clear in 1911: he recommended tunnels to link the major islands (not a new solution), and a metropolitan railway system, radical for Venice, which would give the entire area new viability and arrest the population drain to Mestre.[53] Salvadori was among the first articulate critics of the project. All these projects, including a metropolitan transit system, were still being debated in the 1990s. Giacomo Trevissoi wrote on the problems of transit in 1925 and 1927, and, like Salvadori, attacked the aesthetic conservatism restraining the city.[54] These were no longer initiatives from individuals or even local governments: they awaited regulatory planning, particularly in view of the new conjunction of Venice and the mainland satellites. Legislation to protect historic cities was being introduced in the 1930s: Bergamo was the first to be protected by special legislation, Venice the second.[55] The passing of special laws was to haunt the city throughout subsequent decades; they were regarded more as impediment than protection.

Urban Planning, 1920s and 1930s

The state of the city in the 1920s and 1930s was constantly assessed in terms of the new discipline of urbanism. A major figure in the planning debates of these years, and one of the principal urban critics of Venice in the twentieth century, was Duilio Torres. In 1922–3 he was the architect of the heliotherapic hospital on the Lido, a pioneering example of Italian rationalist architecture, and testimony to the continued health industry on the Lido (fig. 146).[56] Together with the war memorial designed by his brother Giuseppe, it was the major public building in Venice in the early 1920s.

Torres was a passionate Venetian, who had learnt his conservation rules well and regarded the new 'science' of urbanisation as a crucial field for the architects' atten-

145 (*above left*) Porto
Marghera, urban quarter,
1928. Venice, Archivio
Giacomelli.

146 (*above right*) Duilio
Torres, Heliotherapic
Hospital, Lido, 1922–3.

tion. In late 1923 and early 1924 he published a series of articles for the *Gazzetta di Venezia* covering the future of building in the city and the areas available for housing.[57] Upholding the importance and relevance of those views, he republished them in 1941. He insisted on the preservation of gardens and greenery, and continued his advocacy of new housing on the Lido and Marghera, but with improvements in water transit to make such areas viable for their inhabitants. In 1924 he participated in the major competition staged for a master plan – a *piano regolatore* – the first of a sequence of such initiatives.[58]

Torres embraced the official line on Marghera, welcoming the creation of the port and praising its 'great industrial activities' as the salvation of monumental Venice by virtue of separating it from industry.[59] But in opposition to the fully conservationist position that would not touch old Venice, he favoured the sensitive interpolation of new buildings: it was a delicate problem, as already noted. Torres concurred with the view that the Lido was the place for new architecture, as was Porto Marghera, because the modern had no need to be camouflaged: 'If we have courage and daring it will be a superb spectacle to see the new city rising up in Marghera'. Venice could be saved.

In the 1920s Torres's building practice was chameleon, not uncharacteristic of the period. The Solarium was seen as prototypical Rationalism, but in 1926 he produced a textbook exercise in classical proto-Fascism for the 'Terme Littore' in Rome.[60] At the same time he was designing an elaborate hunting lodge on a remote lagoon island in an extravagant style influenced by Olbrich and the Vienna Secession.[61] A complex of buildings entirely occupies a small island, with steep-roofed edifices in chalet style having balconies opening from two or three windows in the Venetian manner, a central doorway with a splayed-out Istrian stone arch, and a tower with an winding outer staircase – a modern version of a *scala del bovolo*. Internally the construction was traditionally Venetian, with wooden rafters, but with widened scalloped arches over doorways echoing the exaggerated lines of the façade and roofline outside.

Torres summed up his urban views in 1933 in an address to the Ateneo Veneto on yet another occasion when the contemporary balance sheet was under scrutiny at that venue. The mood was buoyant; tourism was booming on the Lido, boosted by the new Biennale of Cinema, and Fascism was buoyant with the expectations of spiritual revolution and reconstruction in the aftermath of the war. A master plan was the very mark of a city's civilisation. Torres showed how totally he had absorbed the lesson of pluralism. Repeating the strategy used to save buildings in the late nineteenth century, he affirmed that all layers of Venetian architecture should be regarded as crucial to the archaeological richness of the city, valued evidence of their particular period: no doubt he had read Ongaro, Lavini and Melani in his early career. Using international modernism to argue for contextual change, he embraced the international style, noting the achievement of the Netherlands and Sweden in creating buildings in accordance with modern exigencies, using modern material and rational construction, and how America had found a way to maintain local character. Appropriate local materials were given considerable emphasis. Despite its use of imported marble, Venice reclaimed its local character by using materials consonant with its long existence in the lagoon.[62]

When Torres gave his lecture in 1933, the Fascist era had achieved its first decade. It was clear that Venice did not have a Roman legacy, but the sustained nature of Venetian history gave it a legitimate place in national imperial Italy. In the Fascist climate, Torres was prepared to argue for Roman qualities in Venice. Nationalist pre-occupations central to Fascism affected his comments: *romanità* and *latinità* were conjoined with *venezianità* to signal both strength and gentleness, embracing Venetian functionality in traditional housing.[63] Above all other cities, ancient Venice was fused with its environment.

Torres's view of urban particularity was attractive for it did something to counter emphasis on decadence and the cult of the picturesque that had dominated architectural discussion before the war. A year later, in 1934, in a further address to the Ateneo Veneto on local town planning, Alberto Magrini described Venice as a 'rational city', predicting that it would always be 'functional and aesthetic': it must be preserved, but without 'the bigotry and sentimentality of the decadents'.[64] Such revivals of rationalism in Venice have a cyclical life; new arguments for the functional city would reappear in the 1970s.

Later interpretations of so-called Rationalist architecture during the Fascist period elevate the cultivation of *latinità* with spiritual overtones above principles of design and the use of industrial materials.[65] The emphasis on the historic environment and the preservation of the values of 'ambience' served some vague but important terrain of the soul and imagination: this was so not only for Torres, but for such non-Venetian theorists of town planning as Gustavo Giovannoni, a leading figure in Italian architecture and urban design. He had written 'Vecchie città ed edilizia nuova' in the Roman context in 1913, calling for a rapport between the traditional and the modern.[66] For Torres, twenty years later, modernist architecture had to be grafted on to the established fabric of the city. A reassessment and critique of nineteenth-century eclecticism was involved: it was now regarded as an interruption to the 'divine' nature of Venetian building, dissipating spiritual force and producing building that was diligent, but deficient in 'character and living art'. The second half of the nineteenth century represented 'the dead period of every manifestation'. [67]

Apart from Torres's own hospital on the Lido, some modern buildings had been built, although they provoked little notice beyond the professional architectural journals. Brenno Del Guidice achieved a coherent body of built architecture between the wars.[68] In his early career he had worked with Giuseppe Torres and had been among the circle of the Ca' Pesaro.[69] In the 1920s he had built in the Stile Liberty on the Lido: the Villa Rossi, with Faust Finzi, in 1923–4, and the House of the Pharmacist in 1926–7, a notable example with a plain white façade topped with a bold curve echoed in the balconies of the three lower windows.[70]

Modernism was virtually limited to the Lido, but it was also permitted in the grounds of the Biennale. Del Guidice's architecture for the Biennale was a clear indication of its determinedly modern appearance of the Giardini between the wars.[71] In 1920 the Biennale still registered the aesthetic of the war and Fiume. The last of the Symbolist-style decorations was completed by Galileo Chini, who painted the central salon with scenes glorifying combat.[72] The horses of Phaeton rode for the last time against intense blue backgrounds and Prometheus hovered with a handful of flames, attended by females floating in cloud-like drapes, and by aviators, the new gods. The

147 (*above left*) Duilio Torres, Italian Pavilion, Giardini di Biennale, 1932. Venice, Biennale di Venezia, Archivio Storico delle Arti Contemporanee.

148 (*above right*) Brenno Del Guidice, Venetian Pavilion, Giardini di Biennale, 1932. Venice, Biennale di Venezia, Archivio Storico delle Arti Contemporanee.

renovations of 1928 exemplified a decisive shift in taste, when Gio Ponti covered over the Cirilli murals of the central pavilion with faux architectural motifs. The dome became an *architectural* space, no longer a ground for murals. In 1926 Del Guidice built new entrance kiosks in a forceful Deco style: open buildings, strongly cubic, contained niches with ceramic vases. He built terraces, a *caffè* and a salon in 1928. In 1932 Duilio Torres was responsible for the new Italian pavilion – *Italia* was lettered over the pediment of four unadorned columns in a simple but strong exercise in the imperial style (fig. 147).[73] The lion of St Mark, previously above the doorway, now shared the pediment with the eagle and fasces of Rome.[74] On the left, *The Queen of the Seas*, by Antonio Santagata, a variant on the pictorial tradition of Venice ruling the oceans, flanked Francesco Gentilini's *Birth of Rome*, depicting Romulus and Remus: Rome and Venice in obligatory partnership.

The creation of a special gallery to show local decorative arts represented an advance for the Venetian industry in the 1930s. Brenno Del Guidice built the new pavilion for the decorative arts in the area across the Sant'Elena canal in 1932, setting arched windows in emphatically flat walls articulated in modern style (fig. 148). A curved pergola gave a bold outline to the façade, and the walls inside were curved and inset with showcases for the glass and ceramics. The siting of Del Guidice's Venetian pavilion represented a major expansion of the Biennale grounds, together with the two new pavilions built to right and left of the wide lawn in front. To the right, a Greek pavilion was realised in brick Byzantine style .[75]

Del Guidice was the Venetian architect most in touch with the Art Deco manner in the 1920s and 1930s. His fire station on the Rio Nuova canal near Ca' Foscari was a notable infiltration into the historic city, constructed from 1928 to 1934 in an area that was largely original Gothic.[76] It is a rationalist building: emphatic arches opening on the water where the brigade boat docks are outlined in Istrian stone, but in an indisputably modern manner; at the same time the entrance was a variant on the Venetian *androne*, the traditional water entrance.

For the most part, however, modernism was compromised in Venice, and could hardly avoid being so, given the weight of sentimental and conservative opinion. In particular, Torres targeted the eclecticism of the new housing estate of Sant'Elena, that celebrated point at the eastern end of Old Venice, where Boito and Molmenti had lamented the intrusions of industrialisation in the closing decades of the nineteenth century.[77]

A programme for reclamation and the creation of housing had long been on the drawing board for Sant'Elena. In 1911 both Giuseppe and Duilio Torres had made a submission for the project, but it had lapsed during the war.[78] It was the most extensive housing built in the historic islands. The style was a mixture of Gothic buildings with pointed arches alongside Renaissance style with round arches.[79] As a project of the Istituto Autonomo per la Case Poplari, with the architects Gusso and Bertanza, it went ahead from 1923 to 1926, following the necessary infill to join up the islands. Torres was strongly critical of what he saw as external 'scenografia', in contrast to the 'sadness' inside.[80] He condemned the project as 'a melancholy reproduction from other times', an admixture of styles further confused by the mixed heights of the buildings.[81]

Sant'Elena was officially praised, of course, and Count Volpi was pleased to garner the honours, together with the Fascist government. Giovannoni cited Mestre and Marghera as ideal demonstrations of workers' housing anywhere: the estates were a felicitous solution, in tune with all that was best in contemporary urban planning.[82] The reality was otherwise. By 1925 philanthropic societies and charities such as the Opere Pie were already actively trying to do something about the barrack-like housing on the mainland.[83] In 1931 Alberto Magrini stated that Sant'Elena was 'openly condemned', and the census that year showed that one third of Venetians lived in substandard or over-crowded houses.[84] Raffaele Vivante, the vigilant head of the Ufficiale Sanitario del Comune, continued to demonstrate the connections between hygiene, epidemics and housing, drawing attention to deficiencies that were still as urgent in the 1930s as they had been in 1910.[85]

A Culture of Bridges

A consequence of the creation of Marghera was renewed agitation for a road link between the mainland and the old city in order to facilitate the movement of workers. The provision of this bridge was another significant event in Venetian history, and despite opposition, virtually inevitable. For over two decades Pompeo Molmenti had opposed it, dividing opinion between the *pontisti* and the *anti-pontisti*. His opposition culminated, just a few years before his death, in his collection of essays published in 1924 with the explicit title *I Nemici di Venezia* (The Enemies of Venice).[86] When Molmenti died in 1927 Volpi is alleged to have said, at the funeral, that now the bridge would go ahead.[87] As with the construction of the railway bridge in the previous century, the point of entry to historic Venice was controversial, and opinion was divided. There were the advocates of a link to the north of the city above the centre of San Marco – these were the *nordisti*. The *sudisti* advocated a link with the established port in the area of the Stazione Marittima and the railway station.[88]

Amid discussion about traffic flow and access, various extravagant schemes were proposed to link the Lido, the Giudecca and the principal islands of Murano and San Michele to the central area of San Marco and the Rialto, as well as to the Terraferma. A limited competition had been held in 1919, soon after the approval of Marghera. On 19 July 1921 Vittorio Umberto Fantucci's proposal was approved by the Consiglio Comunale, but the debate continued.[89] The least controversial solution, joining the new bridge with the existing railbridge, was finally approved. The Piazzale Roma became the single point of entry for mainland traffic.[90]

The main exponent of bridge building in Venice in those years was the Commune's chief engineer, Eugenio Miozzi.[91] Fascinated by bridges, and successful far beyond others in the projects he realised, Miozzi proposed a (still unrealised) scheme to encircle the entire lagoon with them, arched over shipping, nearly as high as the Campanile.[92] One related and significant victory was the exclusion of motor traffic from the historic centre. In 1932 artist (and cat-lover) Paul Klee had already written in amazement of a city 'without cars, cabs, horses, donkeys, trees, and not many dogs, and many cats . . .'[93] In 1933, as the new bridge neared completion, the Federazione Veneziana dei Fasci di Combattimento decreed that motor traffic be limited to it: 'Venetian fascism rejects all the fantasy projects of penetration into Venice by means

149 Aerial view of the rail and road bridge and arrival area.

of mainland transport beyond the limits already signalled by the construction of the new bridge.'⁹⁴ It was a momentous action. Projects that were vetoed when the decision to exclude cars was taken included links between the outer points of Venice at Tre Porti and Punta Sabbioni, and the introduction of vehicles on the Zattere and the Fondamenta Nuove. A year later Ernst Bloch likened Venice to a stone sailing-ship, with its decks made of bridges and *calli*, where the noise of cars, left behind on the Terraferma, never penetrated.⁹⁵ As a result 'the silence of Venice is deeper than an uninhabited landscape . . .' 'Silence puts life into Venice again and again.'

Amid predictable congratulations on the termination of Venice's millennium of isolation (in terms much the same as those that launched the rail bridge), the road bridge finally opened with the Fascist name of Ponte de Littorio, in reference to the Roman lictors who carried the fasces in imperial processions. 'In response to the exigencies of modern life and the providence of the Duce, the new bridge joins Venice with the mainland. It is a great and useful work.'⁹⁶

The establishment of the predictably named Piazzale Roma increased the concentration of water traffic at the termination point near the Grand Canal and raised the question of the dispersal of that traffic to the historic centre (fig. 149). At the terminal Miozzi had built a vast garage for incoming cars in uncompromising modern style. Described as early as 1941 by Duilio Torres as 'a blob of oil', the Piazzale Roma is now widely regarded as one of Venice's eyesores: 'a vast green and growing gangrene.'⁹⁷ The problem of traffic dispersal has remained, even though in the 1930s a radical solution was proposed: to create a new canal that would short-circuit the long S-bend of the Grand Canal and emerge at the turn of the Grand Canal at Ca' Foscari. Thus the 'Rio Nova' was established, but only after protests against proposals involving substantial demolition in the San Pantalon area, and the loss of precious public garden space in the Papadopoli area opposite the station. The disappearance of greenery was increasingly lamented in this period. Duilio Torres had drawn attention to the importance of such green areas a decade before, and, acutely aware of the threat, Gino Damerini had published a book on gardens in 1931.⁹⁸ But the Rio Nova, designed by Miozzi, went ahead, crossed by six bridges in Istrian stone on the model of the Ponte della Paglia.⁹⁹

Undoubtedly Miozzi was a key figure during these decades. Ambitious as he was to unite the world by bridges, in his actual designs he was conservative. His success

150 (*top*) Eugenio Miozzi, Accademia Bridge, 1932.

151 (*above*) Eugenio Miozzi, Ponte degli Scalzi with the Neville Bridge (1858), 1934. Venice, Archivio Giacomelli.

lay in this very blend of innovation and restraint. In the 1930s he was to effect some crucial restorative surgery on the Grand Canal, removing the 'Austrian' bridges at the Accademia and at the railway station in front of the church of the Scalzi. These iron bridges – the innovations of the previous century – were demolished by conservative taste in the period of modernism. However, the decision was not based wholly on aesthetic grounds, since the dangerous state of both bridges and their deficiencies in structural design were also at issue.[100] The inadequacies of the Accademia Bridge included its low height – insufficient at high tide for passenger boats to pass under – and the danger of collapse, especially when it was crowded for the popular festivals of Il Redentore and La Salute. A competition for a new bridge was announced in 1931, when Neville's iron bridge was demolished and a temporary wooden bridge built to Miozzi's design was substituted (fig. 150).[101] It is still in place, despite two competitions to replace it. It retains a certain elegance, triggering memories of an earlier Venice in which bridge-building in wood was habitual – as in the original Rialto Bridge.[102] Its success may well be owing to the fact that it is a 'soft' bridge, introduced with generous width in a premium area.

In 1933–4 Miozzi replaced the Neville Bridge at the Scalzi with a traditional form of masonry bridge designed to blend with the environment (fig. 151). He described it as 'a bridge in the Venetian manner', constructed with a single arch in Istrian stone peaked at forty metres, similar to the Rialto Bridge which he had studied closely, and with a parapet of maximum openness so as not to obscure the churches of the Scalzi and San Simeone.[103] The gradation of steps was modelled on the Ponte della Paglia.[104]

The controversies surrounding these bridges are all but forgotten. The 1931–2 competition made clear the preference for a conservative solution, stipulating that the bridge must harmonise with the environment and be distinctive in Venetian terms. Once again the city fathers were apprehensive in the face of radical intrusions. Distinguished local architects submitted designs, including Brenno Del Guidice, Guido Sullam and the young Carlo Scarpa. There were notable entries, but no victors. Duilio Torres's design was the nominal winner: single arched and balustraded – and also conservative, not unlike the bridges designed at the end of the Republic by Tomasso Temanza.[105]

A competition for the railway station was also destined to remain on paper. At much the same time the Florence railway station was under construction amid controversy provoked by its proximity to the historical church of Santa Maria Novella; later the station became 'one of the premier symbols of modernity in Italy'.[106] Venice committed itself to a new station only in the 1950s, and chose a singularly bland design.[107]

The City of Old Men

With the establishment of Marghera and Greater Venice, linked by bridges, the city of Venice appeared, at least to its leaders, vigorous and renewed, an Italian partner in modern Fascism. The world outside thought differently. Venice was diseased, aged to the point of death, a carrier of history that destroyed the viability of the present. In the eyes of Austria, one-time master and recent enemy, itself diagnosed as being in the throes of political disintegration, Venice was the site for replaying old allegories of decay with heightened relish. According to Hermann Broch, in diagnosis of his own city, Vienna itself was singing 'its spirit swan song', it was 'the metropolis of kitsch', 'the value vacuum of the epoch'.[108]

But it was the Venice of eighteenth-century carnival and decadence that a youthful Viennese generation wanted to recreate, in line with their own culture of discontent. For Hugo von Hofmannsthal, Arthur Schnitzler and the theatre director Max Reinhardt – young artists who must have walked together in the faux *Venedig* of the Prater – it was shot through with beauty, especially so for Hofmannsthal; but it was also clogged and decadent, the territory of old men, a setting capable of generating profound *ennui*. This Venice was of profound importance for Viennese writing, which, with that of Thomas Mann, Georg Simmel and Franz Werfel (originally from Prague) recreated a black legend for the twentieth century.[109] And it is said that Franz Kafka, writing in Prague at much the same time, drew on the prisons of the Republic for his novel *The Trial*.[110] If it is possible for Freudian metaphors of dream, desire, repression and illusion to take on the imprint of topography, then Venice achieved that in the early years of the century.

During the First World War the Viennese listened to the work of Erich Korngold, a new musical prodigy in their midst, who premiered his Venetian opera *Violanta* in 1916 when he was seventeen.[111] It was in traditional mode, set in the fifteenth century with an action involving crimes of passion, betrayal and revenge, leading to love with the enemy, then suicide, and taking place, inevitably, during carnival. The carnival song 'From their graves arise the dead to dance' sounds as a leitmotiv throughout, prophetic of the final outcome for Violanta, if not the very demise of the state of Venice.[112] It was an eerie refrain to be hearing in the years of the war.

The continued fascination of Venice for Vienna is evident in two novels about old age set in the city that was for so many unequivocally a metaphor for decay and ruin. In 1918 Arthur Schnitzler's *Casanova's Homecoming* returned the legendary lover-adventurer to his home city after his fabled escape from 'the leads' in 1757. Schnitzler set Casanova's return in 1774, after his first exile of eighteen years during which he had begged employment from the Republic. He comes back as a secret agent for the Inquisition; already a decadent figure, bankruptcy and scandal drive him away again. During the years in Venice he devotes himself to translating *The Iliad* and refuting Voltaire, projects to which Schnitzler frequently refers. Casanova's ambition is expressed in his desire to challenge Voltaire, who is a canker growing in his mind. In the beginning:

> Casanova was in his fifty-third year. Though no longer driven by the lust of adventure that had spurred him in his youth, he was still hunted athwart the world, hunted now by a restlessness due to the approach of old age. His yearning for Venice, the city of his birth, grew so intense that, like a wounded bird slowly circling downwards in its death flight, he began to move in ever-narrowing circles. Again and again, during the last ten years of his exile, he had implored the Supreme Council for leave to return home.[113]

The homecoming staged by Schnitzler is both obsessive and pathetic. Anxiety is compounded by nervousness as Casanova anticipates a secret mission that will stave off penury. Arriving from Mantua, ugly with age, the old hero appears corrupt and lewd, still bent on satisfying his sexual appetite. He meets a friend, reluctantly agrees to spend the night with him, but is soon enamoured of a woman whom he covets and must have, and does so through contrivance and disguise, submitting her to nothing short of rape, then killing her lover before setting off on the last leg of the carriage journey to Venice.

Casanova crawls home to a city that is itself presented as aged and decrepit. He comes to Mestre where he takes the boat and sees the city rising up, becoming more distinct. He takes sordid lodgings and puts on the second of his two remaining suits to visit his patron, Bragdino. In the evening he makes his way to the Piazza San Marco and the Caffè Quadri to identify the freethinkers and the revolutionaries, and finds his own great exploits all but forgotten. Walking back to his lodgings, it is evident that the one-time great adventurer is exhausted; a 'bitter aftertaste' is upon his lips as he falls asleep. Both he and the city of his birth show unattractive symptoms of old age.

The legend of the decadent city and Casanova persisted in Vienna in the 1920s. Stefan Zweig included Casanova in his series of portraits of 'great men' published in 1928: he was one of the 'adepts of self-portraiture'.[114] Near the end of his life, Casanova appears as if in fulfilment of Schnitzler's prophecy:

> We are in the years 1797 and 1798 . . . Here is a strange fellow, an old fellow rusticating in an out-of-the-way corner of Bohemia, who seems to have taken no note of the passing of time . . . His skin is like parchment; his great hooked nose projects formidably over his thin-lipped, slavering mouth . . .[115]

The libertine, now librarian at Dux, is unfashionably dressed, corpulent, rubicund. He has been obsequious in his dealings with the Venetian government, but still he struggles with his intellectual projects: he endeavours to refute De la Houssaie; he works on a new method of dyeing silk. Finally Zweig's verdict is as unyielding as Schnitzler's, and markedly similar: 'Lucky man that he is, he has only sensuality, and lacks the first beginnings of a soul . . . Casanova lives his three and seventy years in impudent self-satisfaction.'[116]

Fascination with Casanova was fascination with Venice in its erotic guise, with its reputation as the city of licentiousness and sensual adventurers – as Camillo Boito had interpreted it after Byron, George Sand and Musset. The French remained more besotted than critical. Illustrative presses took up Casanova's exploits in the 1920s, and the Marquis de Sade was given a voluptuous multi-sexual treatment with Venetian references in Couperyn's illustrations to *Le Bordel de Venise*.[117] Casanova was the subject of an ironic pleasure treatment by Apollinaire, who clearly recognised the eroticism of Venice, but whose work on the city is regrettably slight.[118] Just months before his untimely death, Apollinaire wrote his libretto *Casanova, comédie parodique* – a parody of love and of the *divertissements* devoted to it in the theatre, intended to be set to music. The conductor of Diaghilev's Ballets Russes, Henry Defosse, was the composer, but the work was never in repertoire.[119]

Apollinaire took up an episode that appears early in the Casanova *Memoirs*, at the beginning of Book 2, when he meets a family of travelling actors. In Apollinaire's version, they are performing the work of the Venetian playwright Carlo Gozzi. Casanova has access to the daughters (with the mother's permission), but remains teased by the beautiful Bellino, a castrato whom Casanova recognises, quite rightly, as a girl in disguise. Amid choruses declaring his madness, he continues by his own definition 'gay, tender and charming', living his life in 'a garden in which the women are flowers'. It is carnival of course, and masks abound, further confounding identity, while Casanova declares that love 'will rise like a phoenix'. Written in agile rhyming verse, Apollinaire's text springs from his being part of the Picasso and Diaghilev ballet circle, with its interest in the *commedia dell'arte*, but his scholarship in the Venetian Settecento is crucial. The good humour – the spirit of *opera buffa* – reinforces the difference between the positive reading maintained by French artists and the negativity

of the Austrian. Unfortunately, Apollinaire's early death stopped his projected work on Cazotte's *Le Diable Amoureux*.[120]

Casanova is voluptuous and the hero again some years later, in one of the most notable historical movies of the 1920s – Alexandre Volkoff's *Casanova* of 1927.[121] The film has Casanova in command of his exploits, duels and assignations at the Russian court of Catherine the Great, and in Venice of course, at carnival, conducting his liaisons in a covered gondola (fig. 152). Full of wit and balletic movement, a supreme master of eye-contact, Casanova, played by Mosjoukine, confounds his creditors and outwits cuckolded husbands. He is the consummate adventurer in the city that facilitates adventuring. The taut, thin mouth, the swooping nose, the commanding forehead and burning eyes make Mosjoukine the most memorable of a sequence of screen Casanovas: some decades later Donald Sutherland as Fellini's Casanova recalls the Mosjoukine facial type.[122]

Casanova's escape from the leads is played in the film's best balletic spirit. Carnival is in progress, and a guard of honour of pierrots is dancing around a circular sheet used as a trampoline to catch Casanova as he jumps from the balcony of the Palazzo Ducale after exhorting the citizens to 'love Venice, and love'. As Casanova escapes, the sheet traps the vengeful husband who caused his imprisonment. Amid the pierrots' sad farewells, Casanova leaves, catching a woman's eye as he mounts the gangplank of the waiting ship.

In terms of the film's originality and authenticity, the lighting was judged spectacular, the costumes by Bilkinsky rivalled those of Diaghilev, and Lochakoff's decor was combined with on-location shooting that was still a novelty at the time. This Venice was a magical city, and the final carnival scene was regarded as 'one of the masterpieces of set design in world film production'.[123] The filming must have been among the first of the many such spectacles that would fill the Grand Canal with crews and cameras.

Henri de Régnier wrote briefly about Casanova in 1927. His character remains genial and energetic in the face of the famous encounter with Voltaire at the philosopher's residence, Les Délices near Geneva.[124] De Régnier gives a version of the 1760 meeting when, amid sallies, the two men discussed Count Algarotti and Ariosto; Voltaire needles Casanova, challenging him to talk about the Venetian government. Far from bearing the Republic a grudge as the result of his exile, Casanova discourses on its freedom. And Casanova might well have the upper hand in the encounter, according to De Régnier, for Casanova sleeps well and Voltaire sleeps poorly.

Casanova was not the only historical figure introduced into fictional Venice by authors in Vienna. In 1924, at the time of his association with Alma Mahler and his residence with her in her Venetian palazzo, Franz Werfel published a novel that is one of the most sustained writings about Venice. It was written with the laudable intention of persuading Alma Mahler of the virtues of music other than the Wagnerian tradition. Werfel's interest in Verdi was long-standing, and included the publication of letters and the translation of librettos.[125] *Verdi: A Novel of the Opera* is inspired by the association of the city and music, giving an account of the composer Verdi in Venice.[126] Pitted against each other are the Italianate melodic virtues of Verdi and Wagner's vast music-dramas.

Many of the novel's motifs are devoted to Verdi's frustration later in life as he devotes himself unsuccessfully to an opera on the subject of King Lear, Shakespeare's late play of old age and madness. Yet again Venice is the setting for old age and, by implication, death. When the novel opens Giuseppe Verdi is making a one-day visit to the city in which his rival, Richard Wagner, is the famous resident in the last months of his life. The first scene is the opera house La Fenice, under 'a monstrous Christmas moon'.[127] 'It was the year 1882, not much more than a decade after the deliverance of Venice and the union of the Kingdom' – not much more, in other words, than a decade after the withdrawal of Austria from Venetia in 1866. Leaving the opera house, Verdi – not unlike Georg Simmel – finds himself ill-at-ease upon the ubiquitous water, which he feels as an abyss below him; he dreads every journey. Nevertheless, Verdi decides to take up residence.

Verdi is not the only old character, however. Among the novel's most compelling characters is an octogenarian, the Marchese Gritti, descendent of doges, born in 1781 and constantly warding off death as he goes every night to the opera, counting the performances, as he has done throughout a life that encompasses the fall of the Republic and the reign of Cimarosa, who had died in 1802. From Cimarosa to Verdi, the whole history of modern music is inscribed. As if to compound history, Monteverdi returns in another apotheosis. He is aged seventy-six, thin of blood and critical of a Venice diseased by an excess of 'stupid play activity'.[128] As so often, carnival is the very symbol of masking and falsity characteristic of the city. It is noted that this 'hollow sham' was revived after being suspended during the last years of Austrian rule.

Wagner's music goes against the native operatic tradition of 'the water-lapped, music-haunted city', the city of Monteverdi: 'Two hundred and forty years after Venice, the city of opera, had entombed the body of Monteverdi, she was harbouring Richard Wagner. He, the avenger of Monteverdi, had resurrected, unquestioned, the principle of the recitative music drama, and re-established it triumphantly.'[129] For Verdi, Venice is at first the enemy, but 'she' is 'chuckling softly to herself'. Verdi burns the manuscript of his opera of *King Lear* and turns to the composition of *Otello*, the masterpiece (with *Falstaff*) of his old age. It is the work that reconciles him with the city of water, love and death (recalling the last lines of *Otello*, which sound with the 'Evviva San Marco').

However, Werfel's Venice also turns the face of youth upon the city of the aged – of hospitals and illness, Wagner's death, and the ghost of the ancient Monteverdi, to focus on the beautiful young son of the dying musician. The geography of Werfel's Venice encompasses the Piazza in carnival time, the Riva degli Schiavoni, where Verdi lodges, and the Giudecca, where he visits the dying musician. He looks at Venice from the Campanile; it appears womanly and fluid: 'It was all feminine, this far-spreading creature – and grew ever fresher and more maidenly as it receded to the horizon . . . The chain of islands shimmered and swam like children at play.'[130] Yet the most forceful evocations of the city are negative, coming towards the end of the book, when Verdi is on the Fondamenta Nuove on the northern, shady side, in contrast to the main public face of Venice to the south. The area is desolate and poverty-stricken, the site of the gasworks and the hospital beside Santi Giovanni e Paolo. The waters of the northern lagoon are dark, soiled and polluted, looking onto 'a lagoon of corruption': 'Here Venice, like an aged Diva at midnight, where there is no longer eyes to admire her plumed and painted beauty, admits the truth and looks with disgust on her own grey and dismal ruin.'[131]

Visiting the hospital to see the musician, Verdi turns to face the cemetery island of San Michele, in the author's view, appropriately sited on that north side. It is All Saints' Day and the Venetians are crossing to the island by the boat bridge to visit their dead. Verdi hears the word *vendetta*: it acts as the release that directs him to the composition of *Otello*. The death face of Venice, illness, sickness, as well as the long musical history, fear of water and sordidness: all of Werfel's themes were well-rehearsed; he reworks them from the *fin de siècle*, from Nietzsche to Thomas Mann and Schnitzler. Yet unlike the impotent Aschenbach on the Lido, Verdi on the Fondamenta Nuove found a spur to creativity in the city of music.

Death and carnival, and the face of a dark brooding city, mark the Venice that appears in one of the most famous silent films of the 1920s: Fritz Lang's *Der müde Tod*, known in English as *Destiny*. A young girl begs Death, majestically played by Bernard Goetzske, to return her dead lover to her: weary Death will do so only if she can save one of three people destined soon to die. The girl is transported back into the past and to exotic places, to Baghdad, Venice and China, to enact the stories of the Three Lights, the three candles that Death will soon snuff out. The Venice sequence – the Story of the Second Light – is set in the Venice of the Renaissance, blending *Romeo and Juliet* and *Othello* in sequences that suggest the influence of Max Reinhardt. Fiametta, in love with Giorgfrancesco, plots to have her elderly fiancé killed and mistakenly stabs her own lover.[132] Here is another instance of the conjunction of Venice and death played out in part during carnival. The girl, dicing with Death, implores all manner of help to overcome the obstacles set in her path; finally she meets her end saving a baby from a burning house.

Siegfried Kracauer commended the originality of the Venice segment in terms of both technique and expression:

> The long-lived power of *Destiny*'s imagery is the more amazing as all had to be done with the immovable, hand-cranked camera, and night scenes were still impossible . . . 'A drawing brought to life', the Venetian episode resuscitates a genuine Renaissance spirit through such scenes as the carnival procession, silhouettes staggering over a bridge – and the splendid cockfight radiating bright and cruel southern passion . . . [133]

Destiny is dark, compelling, dignified and unpicturesque, and departs from the movie world of tourist sunshine and costume dramas.

Ezra Pound's Cantos

Two epic literary works came before the public in the 1920s. Proust's *Remembrance of Things Past*, and the first of Ezra Pound's *Cantos*. Both have a range that includes far more than Venice, but Venice has a central, even a symbolic role for both, although the writers are antithetical. Pound met Proust in Paris in 1921: he regarded him with something approaching contempt, to be compared unfavourably with the 'male and civilised' D'Annunzio;[134] his writing was a 'meticulous record of minor annoyance'.[135]

Yet Proust and Pound have the 'marble forest' of the palaces on the Grand Canal in common.

Proust began publishing his saga with *Du Coté de Chez Swann* (or *Swann's Way*) in 1913 and it was completed only in 1927, five years after his death.[136] Only then did the memories of Venice mesh: the uneven floor of the Baptistery and all the richness of building and decoration percolated through Ruskin, memories of his mother, absent and present, of the golden angel on the Campanile, the labyrinthine *calli*, Carpaccio's paintings and Fortuny's dresses, recorded in all their emblematic detail (Proust would not have known the dresses from Venice, but from Fortuny's couturier house in Paris in the Rue Pierre Charron, opened in 1920).[137]

Pound began *The Cantos*, a long series of verses that traffic across continents, languages and ages, in 1915.[138] 'That cryselephantine poem of immeasurable length which will occupy me for the next four decades' was how he described his project.[139] *A Draft of XVI Cantos* appeared in 1925, but the Venice cantos came after that, in *A Draft of XXX Cantos*, published in a limited edition in 1930, and in a larger edition in 1933.[140]

Although an assessment of historical Venice is clearly evident in his writing, Pound is never as negative as was his literary compatriot T. S. Eliot, poet of waste lands. Italy – Rappallo and Venice in particular – are important to Pound's life and writing, to his sense of world history, not to mention his approval of Fascist Italy and Mussolini. Eliot was but a tourist, and registered tourism's worst features in his poem 'Burbank with a Baedeker: Bleistein with a Cigar', a short sardonic poem about tourism in over-subscribed places.[141] Burbank is inadequate to the task of love, even images of gold horses and the golden Bucintoro are insufficient stimuli. Canaletto is sunk into 'protozoic slime', 'the rats are underneath the piles'. In echo of Shakespeare's Shylock: 'the jew is underneath the lot./ Money in fur'. Burbank but replicates the city's impotence – his perpetrator lacks Pound's sense of history. Venice is constrained by history and bathos:

> Who clipped the lion's wings
> And flea'd his rump and pared his claws?
> Thought Burbank, meditating on
> Time's ruins, and the seven Laws.[142]

In contrast, the Venice of Ezra Pound is exceedingly complex, both more contemporary and more historical than that of any other writer of his time. In canto XVII, one sails unerringly into Venice out of a Mediterranean seascape of caves and shells to 'the forest of marble', to a richness of stones fashioned into buildings, a man-made forest ornamented with leaves – 'the arbours of stone – marble leaf, over leaf'.

This Venice draws people – the proud *condottiere* Sigismondo Malatesta, the prince Cosimo de Medici, and the victims Borso and Carmagnola, who meet their death at the hands of the Serenissima. Carmagnola was strung up in the manner of public displays of punishment between the two columns, the columns where the young Ezra Pound idled away his days watching Venice, 'underneath the crocodile'. The ancient city is luxurious, both in the import of treasures and in those made by 'the men of craft' – the glassmakers, above all, *i vitrei*, in a city where the setting is competitively glass-like: 'the waters are richer than glass', and the brocades are 'Bronze gold, the blaze over the silver, dye-pots in the torch light'. The light is constantly redefined by the water and the movements of boats: 'The flash of waves under prows, And the silver beaks rising and crossing.'[143]

For in this city, appearing as if it has grown naturally from the water, the buildings seem so organic that they become like nature ('marble trunks out of stillness . . . the light now not of the sun . . . There, in the forest of marble/the stone trees . . .).[144] In canto XVI, Venice is emergent from the waves still, but it only just survives: 'the

Canal Grande has lasted at least until our time', in a wry answer to D'Annunzio, perhaps to his prophecy in the 1880s that the Grand Canal would be filled in – 'shops in the Piazza key up by/artificial respiration'.

But the beauty of Venice is undermined by the sordid aspects of its history. It is trapped in its cult of luxury – from Doge Selvo who 'mosaic'd' San Marco and whose wife introduced forks to the table, and with them, the vice of Luxuria, to Baron Franchetti, the then-owner of the Ca' d'Oro. Doge Lorenzo Tiepolo surrounded himself with fine skins, fine wines, silver and fabulous glass; he arranged jousts in the Piazza San Marco with the horses decked in gold, silver and jewels. But Venice will be crippled by Luxuria, by usury and unproductive moneylending. It is caught in contradictions, shining with light in the eye of God on the one hand, but no more than mud to the conqueror Napoleon on the other. Even the crafts are undermined: the weaver and the stonecutter are forestalled by usury. Venice inhabits its stage set, is deservedly betrayed by the League of Cambrai, sinks into its own mud.[145]

Much of the world is condemned by the practice of usury in Pound's mind. His fixation with monetary systems and governmental restraints is given Venetian treatment in canto XXV, which refers to the records of the Maggior Consiglio in 1255 with their restraints on gambling. Then, with the sharp cutting and dislocations that distinguish the *Cantos*, Pound invokes the birth of lion cubs in the doge's quarter of the Palazzo Ducale: they are living testimony to the beneficence of the lion of St Mark: 'all the Venetians and other folk who were in Venice that day that concurred all for this as it were miraculous sight.'[146]

This account is given the same weight of decree as mention of the constraints to be observed when the doge's daughter visits – she was not permitted to leave the palace. Epigrammatic lines follow, imaging the alterations to the Palazzo Ducale in compensation for the cramped quarters for the doge. The 'suspended facade' comes as a felicitous image:

> They built out over the arches
> and the palace hangs there in the dawn, the mist,
> in that dimness,
> Or as one rows in from past the murazzi.

Then to Titian, exacting his payments from the state, and the state exacting finished work from Titian. He is to be summoned to complete his commission in the Palazzo Ducale for the *Battle* started by Giovanni Bellini and left incomplete at the time of Bellini's death.[147] Titian is in danger of forfeiting his commission for the Fondaco dei Tedeschi. The patronage of artists is a constant theme: Carpaccio is in Jerusalem, then in Venice, decorating the Palazzo Ducale – decorations that would be lost in one of the great fires.[148]

In the huge orchestration of the *Cantos*, the beatific Venice of the earliest visit and *Night Litany* is recalled – as in canto LXXXV, with the carved mermaids on the altar of Santa Maria dei Miracoli – 'that jewel box', Pound called it. His response to the architecture and sculpture of Santa Maria dei Miracoli is closely linked to his enthusiasm for Sigismondo Malatesta and his Tempio at Rimini built by Alberti. Indeed, Pound is in some part responsible for the renewed attention given to Santa Maria dei Miracoli, which a few years before had represented a low point in taste for Ruskin.

In all, the Venice of the Ezra Pound *Cantos* is autobiographical, a powerful mind-montage of a scholar of literature, history and art, and one who has imaginative control of the immense sweep of time that constitutes Venetian culture. They are also the product of a mind obsessed with the 'sin' of usury and the state of the world. Pound's extremism and his support for the authoritarianism of Fascism led to his incarceration in Pisa after the Second World War. With quiet pathos, the caged poet of *The Pisan Cantos* asks: 'Will I ever see the Giudecca again? or the lights against it, Ca' Foscari, Ca' Giustinian, or the Ca' as they say of Desdemona.'[149] Benignly, Pound was led to a permanent home in Venice in the 1960s, and, indeed, to his death and burial there, rowed to San Michele on 3 November 1972.[150] More than others, Pound understood Venice to be both beatific, and exploiting.

Le Corbusier

In the 1920s and the 1930s historic Venice was still regarded as a classic example of urban planning. It was Le Corbusier who helped to further its reputation as an exemplary *urban* design by giving it a prominent role in his first focused study, *Urbanisme*, published in 1924. He had sought out Venice as a young architect, sketching the city, understanding the major buildings both as distinctive mass and in their sighting, activated by the sight lines imposed by canal, campo or Piazza. Venice offered Le Corbusier his most pungent model for the monumental and the picturesque.[151] In *Propos d'urbanisme* he declared that 'today Venice is still our teacher; classified circulation, supremacy of the pedestrian, the human scale. Natural conditions imposed by the element of water'.[152] He noted the civic pride evident in the marble paving; he applauded the uniformity of the Procuratie buildings on the Piazza; even the pigeons contributed to the modular format.[153]

Commendation was more substantial, if no more profound, in *La Ville radieuse*, published in 1934, at a time when Corbusier made an important personal appearance in Venice.[154] A decade later, addressing Americans in *When the Cathedrals were White*, he wrote about the League of Nations conference organised in the Palazzo Ducale on the subject 'Contemporary Arts and Reality, Art and the State'.[155] He declared that Venice 'because of its foundation on water, represents the most formal machinery, the most exact functioning, the most incontrovertible truth – a city which, in its unity, is unique in the world . . . made by the collaboration of everyone'. In the context of machine-age reforms popular in 1934, Venice was 'called to witness'.[156] Above all, Venice appeared exemplary in its history of transport. Its preservation of water and foot traffic was a great example for modern planning, a model of 'functional rigour', 'mechanistically impeccable', and a 'precise product of true human dimensions'.[157] The decision to keep the automobile out of Venice had been made only the previous year. In his pictorial presentation in *La Ville radieuse*, Le Corbusier, man of the Machine Age, persisted with traditional views of *calli*, bridges and gondolas, interspersed with photographs of San Giorgio Maggiore, the lion on the Piazzetta column and sculpted corners from the Palazzo Ducale. At the centre of the montage was Eugenio Miozzi's new garage, the Autorimessa at the Piazzale Roma (fig. 153).

Venice as an urban model showed itself to be capable of ingenious twentieth-century adaptations in the United State of America. The shaft and height of the Campanile, so prominent in the world press as it fell and rose again, was the inspiration for Gothic-style skyscrapers. In response to the interest in regulation of traffic by segregation, Venice became a precedent because of the very absence of the motor car in the city. A grand plan for Manhattan dreamed of separate transit systems, blending reality with dream. In an alarming adaptation, Harvey Wiley planned elevated walkways to evoke 'a city of arcades, plazas and bridges, with canals for streets . . . with all the loveliness of Venice . . . a very modernised Venice', with super-Gothic verticality and 'San Marco-like arcades'.[158] Venice anticipated 'the metropolis of tomorrow' and realised – if only on paper and in another continent – Nietzsche's prophecy of 'the city of the future' as a system of 'solitudes' in New York, the busiest city in the world, where, from the 1880s, there was a gondola on Central Park lake.

In Italy legislation was the route for urban planning. Amid deepening controversy, this situation continued throughout the twentieth century, with a sequence of Special

I CALL UPON VENICE AS A WITNESS

(PREAMBLE TO THE ANTWERP PLAN)

Two means of transportation: by foot on land, by gondola on the sea. Here: the network of waterways.

Venice is "shaped" by a lagoon.

Relative elevation + 0 is the basis of all measurements; there every measurement, even the crudest, is unquestionable; all disorder becomes order. So the plain of water – like the plain of land elsewhere – cannot be called a nuisance. Rather, a friend to architecture, one of its greatest props.

Here we see the thrust of multiple speeds, the big garage, terminus of overland roads. There is *not a single road* in Venice.

the garage is a blind alley.

153 Le Corbusier, Venice, *La Ville radieuse*, 1934.

Laws for Venice. The 1937 Provvidementi per la Salvaguardia del Caraterre Lagunare e Monumentale di Venezia was the first of the modern interventions that recognised the environmental expansion of the city into the lagoon territory. The word 'speciale' appeared for the first time in the Provisions: it has remained conspicuous in a vocabulary intent on special pleading for historic sites. In many ways the debate of the late 1930s anticipated the environmental argument of the 1970s and established the parameters of what has been called 'the problem of Venice'. Marghera was to be increasingly implicated, although in the late 1930s it was still the great achievement of Fascist Venice. An exceptional high tide in 1936 drew attention to the need to consider the larger picture.[159]

Over the next five years Duilio Torres was a constant critic of the 1937 law, tactfully reacting in the first instance with congratulations for the 'marvellous fervour and constancy' exhibited by the government in passing a law of double significance, one that both maintained a glorious past and encouraged 'the best actions of the future'.[160] He praised the funding for canal maintenance, the repair of buildings and their foundations, and the general provisions for *risanamento*; but he sounded a note of caution with respect to the real needs of the 'organism' that was Venice. The zones of greatest need were in the area of the station, at the head of the new bridge, and in the over-crowded Castello *sestiere*. Plans must now encompass Greater Venice, including Mestre and the lagoon islands.

The official Salvaguardia project of 1939 was the work of Eugenio Miozzi in his capacity as city engineer. By this time the traditional symbiosis of engineer and architect had been disrupted: Miozzi's plan was extensively criticised as the work of an engineer, lacking appropriate economic detailing and failing to address social and civil contingencies.[161] Voicing criticism in the new journal *Palladio*, Torres paid lip-service to Fascist involvement in urban planning, but then drew attention to the dangers of a plan based on indiscriminate statistics, bent on demolition without analysis of economic implementation or due regard for the environment.[162] The chief danger arose from the plan's zoning with respect to 'hygiene'. Failing to discriminate between monuments and vernacular areas, Miozzi's plan would have the effect of marooning San Marco like a desert and leaving only a few original houses in islands such as Burano. Sant'Elena's 'false style' would be preserved as the most intact area of vernacular housing. Torres anticipated the expanding interest in *Venezia minore* on the one hand, and the continuation of the nineteenth-century interest in the fabric of old 'historical' Venice on the other. The extensive historical fabric was insufficiently considered as were the Terraferma and the 'Babel' already created at Mestre.[163] Unnecessary demolition constituted a major danger when provision for replacement was not in place. As Torres stressed 'a *piano regolatore* is first of all political, then economic, then technical.'[164] It was a crucial insight. But the Piano, like so many after it, achieved few results.

Torres had identified a dilemma that remained constant: the quandary of intervention – how much, how little – *i disastri del fare*. [165] His position was later reinforced by Wladimiro Dorigo and the historians Giorgio Bellavitis and Giandomenico Romanelli, all unsparing in their criticism of Miozzi's plan. It was deemed no more adequate than the earlier attempts of 1867 and 1886, and additionally presumptuous in its citation of historical sources, being solely technical in nature, banal, superfluous and 'absolutely superficial with respect to the entrenched nature of the problems'. Urban matters and conservation were tragically separated.

The founding editor of *Palladio* and president of the Accademia d'Italia, Gustavo Giovannoni, replied in the next issue.[166] All the rhetoric of Fascist urban planning was brought to bear on Torres – and Venice. Giovannoni referred to the recent regulations as a demonstration of the 'fervent' interest that the Minister for Public Education, Giuseppe Bottai, and the Consiglio Superiore delle Scienze e delle Arte had for Venice. There was nothing but respect for the 'miraculous' city. Every bet was hedged: demolition would not be extensive, there would instead be *diradamento* – thinning out to ease congestion; development would be scheduled around the periphery, where new land areas could be created by infill. The work of filling in certain canals to facilitate pedestrian access would continue, notably in the area of Miozzi's new Rio di Noale in the vicinity of the station. Ground-floor inhabitants of inadequate housing would be re-housed. New housing would be evenly distributed amid green zones set up without undue geometrical planning and 'with lively colour and harmonic contrasts'. That Duilio Torres found the housing provisions inadequate for Venice is clear in an address he gave some five years later when he attacked the indiscriminate procedures and under-detailed studies that preceded demolition.[167]

The Biennale and the Casino

By the 1930 Count Volpi's position in Fascist Venice was unassailable: he took full credit for the invention of Marghera; with his control of business enterprises, he had moved without difficulty from supporting the Grimani administration to the heart of the Fascist regime, where he was eminent first as governor of Tripoli, then as Mussolini's Minister of Finance in 1925, then president of the Confinindustria.[168] He was vice-president of the chain of luxury hotels, the CIGA, and his cultural role was formidable (he was appointed president of the Biennale in 1930).[169] He was in a strong position to promote not only his native city, but also his own hotels. Rather than implementing Fascism's role for the Biennale, Volpi was able to identify the Biennale with particular Venetians interests, in line with the cultural pretensions of the regime, and assure its viability in a competitive national climate.[170] That the Biennale was a prestigious political platform was more than evident during the official visits of Hitler and Mussolini in 1934, when Volpi was prominent as host.

The Biennale consolidated its position and reputation between the wars. After the Grimani years, change was evident when Antonio Fradeletto was replaced by the vice-secretary Vittorio Pica in 1919.[171] Pica had followed the Biennale from its inception; he offered continuity after the cessation of exhibitions during the war. At the time of the appointment of the Fascist Mayor Davide Giordano, in 1920, he was able to function, but not without compromise and interference. Pica's interest in French art had been intense for two decades, and he continued that interest, exhibiting Cézanne in the Biennale of 1920 and Modigliani in 1922, soon after the young artist's death in Paris. Before the purge of the avant-garde in German and Soviet art in the 1930s, the Soviet pavilion showed Malevich and Rodchenko. The Expressionists and Neue Sachlichkeit painters were exhibited in the German pavilion.

Pica resigned in 1927. Antonio Maraini, a sculptor, appointed as general secretary in 1928, steered the Biennale through the Fascist years with zeal. He produced a forthright agenda for the sixteenth Biennale, adroitly managing a degree of separation between city government and the Biennale and taking full advantage of the prestige of the exhibition in a climate of nationalistic display.[172] Giulio Rosso designed the official poster with the complex of San Marco domes, the courtyard and façade of the Palazzo Ducale, the Molo, the Campanile seen in aerial view and the Italian flag high above the flags representing participant nations, proclaiming the pre-eminence of Italy in the most modern Cubist style. Maraini made much of the pre-eminence of the Venetian exhibit in the competitive climate of the Milan Esposizione del Novecento. He had emphasised the 'complex and delicate' mechanism of putting together a Biennale, and, most importantly perhaps, the obligation to show *contemporary* art, even while other nations were submitting their nineteenth-century masters. Aware of the history now accumulated by the Biennales, Maraini stressed the need for appropriate archives of Italian artists and full documentation. A library and archival collections destined to become the Biennale's archive were begun in some rooms in the Palazzo Ducale.

Of crucial importance for the Biennale's future was the national legislation passed to ensure the protection of the event, and Venice's pre-eminence as an art city. This was a considerable achievement at a time when there was competition among other cities to hold expositions.[173] In 1930 the Law of 1928 (n. 239), signed by Victor Emmanuel, established the Esposizione Biennale Internazionale d'Arte as a permanent institution and the leading art exhibition in Italy.[174] In 1932 further land across the Canale di Sant'Elena was added to the Giardini in order to accommodate a new pavilion devoted to the crafts. It was seen as another of Volpi's achievements.[175]

The Giardini established its characteristic appearance in the 1930s as more countries committed themselves to national pavilions.[176] Following the modernism of the Italian pavilion with Gio Ponti's new architecturally pure dome and the buildings by Brenno Del Guidice, the German and the United States pavilions rose in Neoclassical style. The architects of the American building, Aldrich and Delano, followed the Montecello model, which in effect returned Palladio to Italy from America. Denmark built its pavilion in 1932, again with a classical model. The Greek pavilion favoured a brick design with Byzantine reminiscences. In marked contrast to this classicism was Brenno Del Guidice's pavilion for Venice. Planned to house the crafts and decorative arts, it

154   Josef Hoffmann, Austrian Pavilion, Giardini di Biennale, 1934. Biennale di Venezia, Archivio Storico delle Arti Contemporanee.

dominated the adjacent land acquired in Sant'Elena. Del Guidice's pavilion was a further exercise in modernist Italianate classicism, with round-arched doorways opening on to an emphatic flat façade.

In 1934 a new Austrian pavilion was inaugurated: the creation of the prestigious Secessionist architect Josef Hoffmann, it was regarded as the most creative and elegant of the pavilions of the time (fig. 154). His first design for the Austrian pavilion was cancelled by the war: in 1912 he had envisaged an octagonal centralised building with a portico with fluted piers.[177] The 1934 pavilion was severely cubic, without columns or portico.[178] It was designed with a clerestory and tall internal arches, a high rectangular door and nothing to mar the exhibiting walls and the deliberate, clear fall of light. A glazed wall and paved courtyards for external sculpture further addressed the specific needs for exhibiting art. Vienna now sat peaceably beside Venice, some twenty years after the first design.

In his commentary on the Biennale between the years of 1920 and 1942, Lawrence Alloway has judged it a fundamental irony that an exhibition in support of international art took place in a period of increasing nationalism. But, from its inception in the nineteenth century, the history of the international exhibition, artistic or industrial, had as a fundamental aim the promotion of national goods in the applied and fine arts.[179] Whatever the distaste for aspects of Fascism, not least the symbiosis of art and war in Futurism, the official sanction of the Biennale ensured its survival and expansion, particularly in a time of economic depression. Unlike the National Socialists, no one retrospective style was linked to Fascism; however, totalitarian aspects of its arts patronage now began to appear. Following the generation of Tito and Milesi and other Venetian artists who had had conspicuous *sale* in earlier Biennales, a new generation of Novecento artists came to the fore in the 1920s and 1930s.

The 1920s were a period of European-wide 'return to order', often called the *rappel à l'ordre*, orchestrated in large part by Italian artists – the *valori plastici* of Carlo Carrà, and Giorgio de Chirico, for example – attempting to reassess classical sources, and to appreciate anew such Italian 'primitives' as Giotto, and those artists with strong formal and colourist qualities, such as Piero della Francesco. The work of Felice Casorati, shown in the first post-war Biennale, and earlier in the Ca' Pesaro exhibitions, exemplified the new clarity of form: it was the beginning of the style known as 'Novecento'. In 1924 Virgilio Guidi (Roman-born, but resident in Venice from

1927) took a leading position in the Novecento group when he exhibited *Tram*, in a group of six Novecento painters presented by Margherita Sarfatti, the mistress of Mussolini.[180]

The painting of Venice and the human figure within it by such artists as Guido Cadorin, Bortolo Sacchi, Ubaldo Oppi and Cagnaccio di San Pietro, took on a positive originality with New Realism, producing powerful alternatives to the picturesque view.[181] The New Realism retained something of the sharpness of certain Symbolist modes seen much earlier in the century and effectively cultivated by some of the Ca' Pesaro group. The continuity should not be underestimated, especially when the 'call to order' is interpreted as new in the 1920s. An example of the new figure-in-landscape is Guido Cadorin's modern girl beside a canal – *Canal* (Venice, private collection) – exhibited in 1921: is she hiding, or does she await a client, her arms covered with a net shawl that seems like a cage about her?[182]

The paintings of Bortolo Sacchi, who spent formative years in Munich before returning to Venice in 1919 and exhibiting with the Ca' Pesaro group, conjoins canal views of architecture and water with people, so that something strange and surrealistic is born, akin to the literary visions of Italo Calvino.[183] Sacchi's imagination appears fired by a grotesque tradition that he is able to locate in contemporary Venice, where faces might be masks, but equally might be exaggerated but natural features. The regions of air and water are disturbed in these paintings: figures issue out of the sea in *Venetian Fantasia* of 1920, in which a personification of the wind appears in front of a lagoon shipwreck.[184] Figures hurtle through space, falling from above canals, in an apparent reference to the city miracles painted by Gentile Bellini and Tintoretto – as in *A Dream (The Legend of the King)* which was shown at the Biennale of 1922.[185] *The Blind Man*, exhibited in 1924, is sharp to the point of compassionate cruelty in manner and subject: a blind man is led across a bridge (near the Fondamenta Nuove) by a cripple clutching his hurdy-gurdy; under the bridge, gondoliers strain at the oar, their urgency offset by the slow passage of the disadvantaged climbing above them. Sacchi's *The Foreigner*, exhibited in 1928, continues the disconcerting *Unheimlichkeit*, with his strange female figure swathed in white fur standing in a canal-scape, staring (fig. 155).[186]

A quality of melancholia, product of the lagoon's eerie stillness, its static waters and extensive sky, is also evident in Ubaldo Oppi's work: in his 1921 *Portrait of the Artist's Wife* the foreground is dominated by the three-quarter portrait of his wife, with hair in a fashionable bob and sharp manicured fingernails, against a close view of the island of San Giorgio Maggiore with ships' sails, a gondola and a strange bright horizon.[187]

Cagnaccio di San Pietro's paintings are similarly mysterious and sharp, denying any possibility of straight narrative, forcing dislocations between figures and their *mise-en-scène*.[188] An old fishermen sits with his catch on a *fondamenta* that is

155 Bortolo Sacchi, *The Foreigner*, 1928. Oil on canvas, 160 × 180 cm. Bassano, Museo Civico.

positioned well in front of Burano-like houses, too sharply focused for such great distance; beyond, strange clouds roll above the lagoon. In *Docking* two men are harnessed like horses and strain cruelly to pull a ship from the shores of a canal; on the ship's prow is a medallion of the Pietà, an image of male sacrifice (fig. 156). In the late 1920s Cagnaccio turned to landscape painting and religious themes. His views of the lagoon and Venice depict space to the point of provoking agoraphobia as they outline estuaries and *traghetti*, views of the Giudecca, or a water-shrine raised on piles in the lagoon.

In these years the Venetian *veduta* re-formed. There were two distinctive modes of presentation; crystal sharp with a metaphysical mark; or Baroque-expressionistic with free brush-stroke and swift colour, synthesising a speedy view. Carlo Carrà painted views of Venice, chunky and blunt, as in the 1926 *Canal in Venice* in which a lamp stretches out over the water and the lagoon horizon is touched with a strange light; everything is cubic and straight, undecorated, far from the characteristic Venice of the Gothic or the Baroque (fig. 157).[189] Negative space becomes dynamic in such pictures: the space above water, between buildings and across canals is charged.

Filippo de Pisis was resident in Venice in the late 1920s, where he painted a number of Venetian subjects.[190] Still lifes appear as if casually abandoned on the *barene* edge of the lagoon: celery, pomegranates and garfish inhabit the shore against water and sky in *Still Life: September in Venice*, 1930. A tragic undertow may be felt in some of his Venetian views. Such scenic painting, rapid and sure of view, far from the meditative, closely focused or carefully targeted, breaks through the saturation of Venetian landscape images inherited from the nineteenth century in painting, panorama and photography – and film.

The work of major figurative painters shifted to landscape painting in the later 1920s. Virgilio Guidi, whose career is one of the most significant in Venice in the first half of the twentieth century, virtually forsakes the human figure after 1927 in favour of new lagoonscapes, reduced and mysterious, on the very brink of abstraction.[191] The main focus is in the Giudecca area, with the Molino Stucky a favourite motif. De Pisis is a further example of artists' preference for the still life and the landscape in the later 1920s.

It is tempting to conclude that the shift from figurative subjects is also a shift from the overt values of Fascist figurative painting, although landscape painting as a record of *Italian* place was considered important. A form of abstraction was also acceptable because of the political stance of the Futurists: the second wave of Futurism, particularly the *aeropittura* – the air paintings – continued the programme

156   Cagnaccio di San Pietro, *Docking*. Oil on canvas, 200 × 173 cm. Venice, Cassa di Risparmio di Venezia Spa.

157 Carlo Carrà, *Canal in Venice*, 1926. Oil on canvas, 42.5 × 51.5 cm. Zurich, Kunsthaus.

158 Napoleone Martinuzzi, *Josephine Baker*. Glass. Destroyed.

of aggressive modernity into the 1930s.[192] Marinetti's group were shown regularly at the Biennales from 1934, thus maintaining a visible continuity of abstraction that was significant for the direction of at least one developing artist in Venice, Emilio Vedova.[193] In further evidence of the continuing interest in Futurism, Gino Severini was a close friend of the young painter Maria Deluigi.[194]

In the 1920s and 1930s the Biennales were also a showcase for Venetian glass and a stimulus for the progressive modernisation and creativity of the Murano glass industry.[195] The process of reinvention had begun in the Barovier workshop: with the Barovier family, Teodoro Wolf-Ferrari and Vittorio Zecchin as leading figures. After the war Zecchin continued his influential production, becoming art director of a new and propitious partnership between Giacomo Cappelin and Paolo Venini in 1921 – the new Venini company was to rival the Barovier.[196] One of the popular lines was the production of birds and animals, now debased, ubiquitous tourist items, but in the 1920s and 1930s inventive, sculptural and frequently witty. The 1928 Biennale showed animals and grotesques by the sculptor of the Murano war memorial, Napoleone Martinuzzi, favoured by D'Annunzio, who was recognised as 'a new phenomenon' in Muranese glass for his sculptural qualities and Art Deco style.[197] In 1925 he took over the directorship of the Venini company.[198]

Both Martinuzzi and Ercole Barovier produced a veritable menagerie of glass pigeons and tigers, fish and unicorns. Barovier's pigeon, shown in the 1930 Biennale, remains a favourite among many chic and witty pieces (fig. 159).[199] Martinuzzi created mushrooms and bunches of grapes, almost geometric, in the Deco manner. A sheer virtuosic feat must have been his life-size glass sculpture of Josephine Baker made for a glassmakers' festival at the Hotel Excelsior – a wonderfully stylised creation with bare breasts above an outré costume, beads suggestively draped between her legs (fig. 158).[200] Following the European taste for Art Deco, engraved glass became fashion-

1589 Ercole Barovier, *Pigeon*, 1930. Primavera glass, 30 cm. Venice, Collection Angelo Barovier.

able in the mid-1920s and solid glass in strong colours was produced by Ercole Barovier and others – very different from the filigree work and traditional forms of Murano glass.[201] For the 1926 Biennale the Venini firm produced an extravagant Deco fountain in blown glass with clear cups raised upon lobed stems, and a chandelier adorned with stems of tiny bells.[202]

The creation of the theatre and music festivals was a further aspect of the expansionist 1930s, in part to counter the success of the Quadrienniale in Rome.[203] In September 1930 the festival of music began. It rapidly gained momentum, involving the Benedetto Marcello Music Conservatory and the leading Venetian musician of the time, Gian Francesco Malipiero. He often worked with local themes, most notably in *Il Mistero di Venezia* (The Mystery of Venice) which included *Le Aquile di Aquileia* (The Acquileans of Acquilea), celebrating the founding of Venice by the exiles from Aquilea and the ceremony of the Sensa in which Venice is married to the sea.[204] Part of the suite included his 1925 *Il finto Arlecchino*, in the late eighteenth-century manner, from the time of the fall of the Republic, but certainly not in any spirit of decadence. As Malipiero described his plot, 'Donna Rossana offers her hand to the best singer of a madrigal she has composed'.[205] *I Corvi di San Marco* (The Ravens of San Marco) was a strange contemporary interpolation, with a masked parade and a public looking on at Venice's beauties.[206]

Malipiero was also responsible for consolidating a new historical musicology, with editions of Monteverdi and Vivaldi: in 1925 he had become president of the Istituto Italiano Antonio Vivaldi.[207] Like Ermanno Wolf-Ferrari, for whom Goldoni was a recurring inspiration, Malipiero invoked Goldoni in the *Tre commedie*, composed between 1920 and 1922, seeking, in his own simple words, 'a voyage of exploration among the narrow streets, canals, palaces and lagoons, made by a Venetian musician who has allowed Carlo Goldoni to take him by the hand'.[208] These 'symphonic fragments' are driven along by percussion which preserves a comedic up beat, while the diversity of instruments plays a dialogue; Sior Todero broods, the quarrels of Chioggia are *a brio*.[209] As Malipiero described his trio of comedies, *La bottega da caffè* represented the life of the street, *Sior Todero Brontolon* showed family life and *Le Baruffe chiozzotte*, Goldoni's play about a querulous character from Chioggia, the life of the lagoons.[210] Goldoni was never out of fashion in Venice: in 1936 Wolf-Ferrari premiered his *Il campaniello* suite, based on Goldoni, with lasting musical success. Studies of eighteenth-century music were not merely academic for these artists, but motivated their melodic treatments and orchestral verve. Thus, Malipiero's *La Cimarosiana* evokes Cimarosa's melodies and clarity of sound in another of the those exercises in revivifying the last years of the Republic.[211]

A theatre festival began in 1934; it was dedicated to the use of open-air venues – to *teatro all'aperto* – following the 1933 production of *Othello* in the courtyard of the Palazzo Ducale.[212] The new festival opened with Max Reinhardt's production of *The Merchant of Venice* played in the Campo San Trovaso, and Goldoni's *La bottega del caffè*, directed by Gino Rocco (himself a playwright in the Venetian dialect), in the Corte del Teatro at San Luca.[213] In 1905, well before his bizarre film, *Die venetianische Nacht*, Reinhardt had directed *The Merchant of Venice* in an acclaimed production that toured Europe after opening at the Deutsches Theater, Berlin.[214] In 1934 the bridge over the canal at San Trovaso became the stage, against a 'real backdrop'.[215] In 1938, the year of D'Annunzio's death, his *La Nave* was given a performance under the direction of Salvini in the garden area of Sant'Elena.[216] Its success was as much political as artistic, appealing in imperialist times.[217]

In the light of Venetian history of the previous century, the proposal to present Manzoni's *Il Conte di Carmagnola* in the 1941 festival is of considerable interest. Elio Zorzi, who was in charge of publicity, wrote to the secretary of the Biennale, Mariani, objecting that Manzoni's play 'was one of the most defamatory works against Venice ... among the large number of works affected by French propaganda against the Republic and the Council of Ten in order to justify Bonaparte's betrayal of Venice at Campoformio'.[218] Instead, and in line with the current zeal for Germany, Schiller's *I Masnadieri* (The Bandits) was produced, alongside Goldoni's *Il poeta fanatico*. Indeed it was Goldoni who formed the main staple of the theatre programmes. Foreign and avant-garde theatre was not important until the Biennales after the Second World War, after the nationalist cults of the 1930s had been halted.

The most lasting initiative was the creation of the Biennale of film.[219] Countries were invited to show their latest material and to bring their actors, directors and publicity machines to two weeks of screenings. Although Antonio Maraini claimed to have invented the idea of the cinema Biennale, so too did Volpi, whose control of industry, culture, tourism and the press was awesome.[220] The new venture was propitiously timed at the point when the 'talkies' were a novelty and the new star system was building. Cleverly scheduled for the height of summer, it was located not in old Venice or the Giardini, but in Volpe's territory on the Lido, at the Excelsior Hotel, which provided an outdoor screening area, grand accommodation and the showcase of the beach at the same time.[221] The Lido was an international meeting place for film stars in these glamour years, and has continued to be so.[222]

From the first Film Biennale, the international tourist package was firmly in place: the first poster announced reductions in air and train travel to the fourteen evenings of screening at the Excelsior. Posters brought together the full bill of attractions: a giant spool of film unravels in front of the column with the lion of St Mark, which looks out over to a silhouette of Palladio's Redentore, with a sickle moon in the sky (fig. 160). Old Venice was again revitalised by reference to the Lido, its modern style counterbalanced by the cultural authority of old Venice.

The 'Season' inspired the cinema, and the cinema inspired the 'season', coating it with glamour, galvanising it into spectacle with water performances in emulation of

Busby Berkeley, and offering endless plots involving grand hotels, honeymoons, vacations, brief encounters and choreographed swimming.[223] Maria Damerini wrote about these years between 1929 and 1940, which she called 'the last years of the lion', in which the cultural and social life of Venice appeared never to rest; she was confident that the city was in the avant-garde in many fields at that time.[224] Life turned around the 'season' and the Biennales, the visitors – musicians and actors, both local and inter-national – Stravinsky, Malipiero, Max Reinhardt. In 1932 Stravinsky conducted *Petrushka* and *Le Sacre du Printemps*.[225] It could be said of the music festival that it generated a musical arena that made Stravinsky one of the most important cultural visitors to Venice in the twentieth century, leading to the premiering of important works and the composition of works specifically for Venice.[226] Count Volpi gave entertainments at the Excelsior or his Palazzo San Beneto on the Grand Canal, where his ballroom had been frescoed by Ettore Tito in post-Tiepolo mode in celebration of the battles of Tripoli, the state Volpi had governed.[227] The Princess Edmond de Polignac and the Princess Maria von Thurn und Taxis were in town for the season; Marinetti was a visitor; and Alma Mahler was in residence. From 1930 the Società Adriatica di Navigazione motor launch left from the Zattere for Trieste, Brindisi, Corfu, Corinth and Piraeus on the luxury Mediteranean yacht circuit.[228]

A permanent cinema for the Biennale, a further initiative in cultural real estate, was on the drawing board

160 Poster for the first Biennale of Cinema, Esposizione Internazionale d'Arte Cinematographica, 1932. Biennale di Venezia, Archivio Storico delle Arti Contemporanee.

in 1936; sited near the Excelsior, it opened in 1937.[229] A complementary provision was the adjacent municipal casino, which opened in 1938. While the casino waited for its new premises, it used the dining room of the Excelsior Hotel, closely linked from the beginning with the new state project. The Excelsior had its own gaming rooms in the 1920s, fashionably hung with fabrics designed by Fortuny.[230] The Commune had considered such a casino for a long time, quite in line with the historic proclivity for gambling in the Republic and the lavish provisions for it. In 1892, the Englishman Bonnycastle who had been responsible for casinos at Nice and Monte Carlo, had put forward a proposal for a crystal palace in the Giardini, before the Biennale was located there.[231] In the later 1930s the Commune had acquired a number of distinctive buildings that were considered as possible venues: the list is interesting in its own right, including the Grand Hotel Gritti, the Palazzo Labia (celebrated for its frescoes by Tiepolo), the Palazzo Grassi (acquired from Giancarlo Stucky) and the Palazzo Guistinian.[232]

The Podestà had presented the case for a casino to the Minister of the Interior as a revenue issue, stressing the vulnerable economic situation in Venice, the number of poor and unemployed, the suppression of activity at the Arsenale for security reasons during the war and the non-Venetian workforce that manned Marghera who could be aided by casino taxes. In short, the heavy reliance of Venice on tourism represented its viable path to survival. Casino profits would be used to develop other cultural initiatives, including a budget for La Fenice to organise a concert season after refurbishment, and a budget for the revival of carnival and other attractions, including theatrical and musical events in the open air.[233] This concerted cultural thinking was of some importance for Venice. The Fenice renovations proceeded under the direction

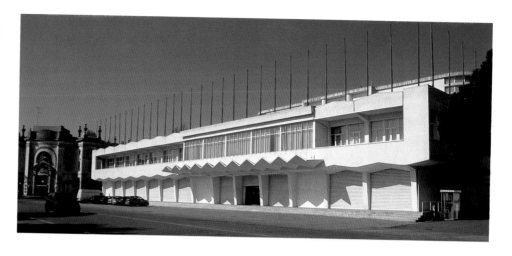

of the Eugenio Miozzi, with Nino Barbantini in charge of the decoration.[234] The atrium was enlarged in keeping with Giannantonio Selva's original Neoclassical design, which had been compromised during Meduna's rebuilding in the 1830s. New lighting and new stucco work refreshed the *salone*, and Meduna's narrow doors to the auditorium were widened. In the Fascist climate of classical revivals, Neoclassicism had renewed prestige: it was in 1956 that Elena Bassi published her monograph on Giannantonio Selva, and Gino Damerini wrote on Giuseppe Jappelli in 1933.[235]

Proposals for the casino's site were debated. Building on the site of Luna Park at Malamocco was rejected, and land was made available by demolishing the old fort at Quattro Fontane used by the Austrians – and by the Venetians in 1848–9. The fountains of drinkable water had historically provided the city of Venice with reserves, particularly in the time of blockades.[236] The Casino was eventually positioned as the central building in a large piazza fronting onto the sea, with the Palazzo del Cinema to the left and the open-air cinema to the right; a loggia linked the buildings. It effected further concentration of tourist facilities adjacent to the Excelsior and the CIGA chain of hotels. Once again Miozzi was the architect-engineer, working with Luigi Quagliata to produce a severe set of buildings in modern style, with a fashionably curved façade on the Palazzo del Cinema (fig. 161).[237] The over-scaled Piazza in front is terminated by a curvilinear terrace in front of the sand. The complex is contemporary with the renovated German pavilion in the Giardini designed in 1938 by Ernst Haiger with fashionable flat pilasters. The Casino, Duilio Torres's Italian pavilion from 1932, the Brenno Del Guidice Biennale buildings and Josef Hoffmann's Austrian pavilion: these constituted the modernist face of Venice in the 1930s.[238] Such buildings could be realised only in the designated modernist areas of the Giardini and the Lido.

The new Casino was advertised as 'open all the year round' in an endeavour to attract its clients beyond summer; but summer was *the* season for the Lido; and it was in its heyday in the 1930s. New sporting facilities had been developed in 1929: there was a golf course at Alberoni designed by a Scottish expert, Cruikshank, and tennis courts at the Excelsior.[239] Day and night life were perpetual spectacles, with not only guests, royalty, aristocracy and, increasingly, the new stars of film, but also Les Girls, who performed their acrobatics on the sand, and the night club Chez Vous.[240] And nearby, sick children were regimented in the sun at the Ospedale del Mare.[241]

While fashion was at the heart of Lido life, it also exemplified many of the Fascist ideals: the white-telephone-culture and the Grand Hotel, the cult of the body and the open air, and the leisure state of *dopolavoro*.[242] But rarely did the Lido fail to draw attention to its proximity to historic Venice. In one of the most telling advertisements for modern beach life, a modishly costumed figure in a new Jantzen-type wool swim-

162 M. Dudovich and M. Nizzoli, 'Bather in the Piazza', poster for the Lido and Venice, 1932.

suit wades into the Piazza San Marco as if she was about to confront, in all bravery and anticipation, the phallic form of the Campanile (fig. 162).[243]

Later, in the 1950s, the gambling seasons were divided between summer at the Lido and winter at the palace acquired by the Commune, the Vendramin-Calergi, famous as Wagner's last residence. In 1936 and 1937 the Commune tried to locate a winter casino in the Palazzo Guistinian, the historic *ridotto* leased by the Commune, but there was considerable religious opposition because of its proximity to the Basilica of San Marco and the church of the Salute.[244] The public *ridotto* in Calle Vallaresso had been one of the famous establishments of the Republic.[245]

New Museums

In the 1920s and 1930s cultural initiatives intensified and the major collections were consolidated. The Commune was active in the creation of new art collections and the provision of impressive venues to house them. The Museo Correr was relocated from the Fondaco dei Turchi to the Procuratie Nuove in 1922, with the important involvement of Pompeo Molmenti.[246] Teodoro Correr's collection had been much amplified since his bequest in 1836. Objects of all kinds were collected – paintings, architectural models, complete libraries fabulously housed in carved cabinets, puppets and toys from past, banners and armoury from great battles, and opulent chandeliers from patrician palaces. The upper floors of the Procuratie Nuove incorporated the Napoleonic wing with the grand staircase, ballroom and Neoclassical rooms in which Canova's sculptures and models were housed, *in situ* in rooms of their own period. The Procuratie buildings had been acquired by the city in 1920.

In these years Nino Barbantini demonstrated the breadth of his commitment to art by organising the Museo d'Arte Orientale from donated collections of material, notably the Di Borbone legacy, which was displayed on the upper floor of the Ca' Pesaro.[247] The collection opened in 1928. In the 1930s Barbantini turned his scholarship to older art, as he was prevented from commenting on contemporary art by an instruction from Rome.[248] He went on to organise commemorative exhibitions of Titian in 1935 in collaboration with the young scholar Rodolfo Pallucchini and, in 1937, Tintoretto. Both exhibitions were held at the Ca' Pesaro and had considerable prestige at a time when cultivation of the past determined many cultural initiatives. These exhibitions were the forerunners of the modern blockbuster.[249] The Titian exhibition brought together work from Venetian churches and galleries, the Louvre and collections in Great Britain, with catalogue contributions that were distinctive examples of new scholarship, discussing such issues as the relation of Titian to Giovanni Bellini and Giorgione.[250]

The coup of the 1930s was the purchase of Ca' Rezzonico, the Longhena palace on the Grand Canal, which had been bought in 1906 from Browning's son by Baron Lionello Hirschell de Minerbi.[251] An art and antiquarian dealer, the baron's reduced circumstances were doubtless owing to the extravagant life style he had conducted at the palace. The moment was propitious, since an exhibition devoted to the eighteenth century – Barbantini's *Settecento Italiano* showing art from the Republic's last century, so beloved by so many – had been notable at the Sale della Biennale in 1929. The Ca' Rezzonico was to show Settecento art in an appropriate setting – the palace ballroom was frescoed by Giambattista Tiepolo. Eighteenth-century material from the Correr collection, ceramics, tapestries, musical instruments and frescoes by Giandomenico Tiepolo detached from his villa in 1906, could be brought together in a new and fashionable period display.[252] Giulio Lorenzetti and Nino Barbantini were responsible for the installations, and Lorenzetti went on to publish on the lacquerwork and the majolica. The partnership also reorganised the Murano glass museum in 1932.[253] Once again St Mark's Day was chosen to celebrate a major event: this time in 1936 when the Ca' Rezzonico museum was opened. The ceremony was held in Count Volpi's ballroom.

In 1936 the Museo del Risorgimento was enlarged and reordered.[254] A museum devoted to patriotism and inaugurated in 1866 when Venice was joined with Italy, its collection documented the French and Austrian occupations from the late eighteenth century and, of course, the Revolution of 1848–9, with paintings, posters, documents and memorabilia such as Daniele Manin's desk and reading glasses. A part of the Correr museum, as it is again today, it became a distinctive entity in 1936, on the occasion of the twenty-fourth National Congress of the History of the Italian Risorgimento.

Hosting these cultural events from the centre of his hotel empire at the Lido, Volpi saw himself as an entrepreneurial twentieth-century doge heading the cultural renewal of Venice, as well as its post-war industrial might.[255] And that might was indeed considerable while Marghera prospered in the late 1930s, providing Mussolini's ever-expanding war effort with crucial industrial backing.[256] Volpi's development of the coking industry, Vetrocoke, has been described as the 'backbone' of industrial production in these years.[257]

Volpi's power appeared unassailable. He had villas and palaces in London and Rome, and he was the proprietor of the great Palladian villa at Maser.[258] In 1929 he had become the president of the body that cared for the fabric of San Marco, a position of importance for the physical conservation of the church. Vittorio Cini was

163 Ernst Haiger's
German Pavilion for the
Biennale di Venezia, 1938.

another citizen of importance to the industrial and cultural fate of Venice. He directed maritime industries in the Adriatic, held the directorship of the Credito Industriale and was substantially involved in the iron and steel industry.[259]

But it was Volpi who was likened to a doge. Amid the glamour of the Lido and the Villa Maser, the count was noted for his splendid appearances. Among the most reproduced photographs of the time – virtually an icon of compliance – was the 1934 visit to the Giardini by Mussolini and Hitler in the company of Count Volpi; the public affirmation of the 'brutal friendship'.[260] In 1993, some sixty years later, the German pavilion was given to the German artist Hans Haacke, who recreated the events of 1934, but transposed them to 1990, the year of the fall of the Berlin Wall (fig. 163). Haacke resurrected 'the battle cry of Venice: gondola! gondola!', the photographs of two thousand young fascists greeting the leaders, the adulation of the press, the welcome to the Führer as 'Meistersinger'.[261] Mercilessly he quoted the Italian press, *Il Lavoro Fascista*: 'The fact that Fascism and National Socialism let the seeds of a new culture sprout, is the best guarantee for the peaceful intentions of Fascist Italy and National Socialist Germany.'[262] This was the point at which the German pavilion was reinstated, after its years of secession to Austria, showing works that were politically supportive of the Reich: portraits of Hindenburg, of Hitler himself, Josef Wackerle's *National Emblem* and Werner Piene's *German Soil*, on loan from Hitler's personal collection.

The pavilion was renovated in 1938, and it was substantially unchanged in 1990, although divested of the swastika and the eagle; Haacke returned these insignia to the entrance portal. Over the central doorway was a photographic copy of a Deutschmark, dated 1990 – lest the link between the past and present be lost – and also the famous photograph of Hitler and Volpi at the Biennale. The floor of the empty pavilion was covered in rubble, the result of Haacke's jack-hammer demolition to create the work *Bodenlos* (Without a Floor) without foundations. The pavilion took on the aspect of the no-man's-land either side of the Berlin Wall, while the title recalled the blood and soil, *Blut und Boden*, invoked by the Nazis.[263] The bankruptcy of a cultural alliance was not permitted to be forgotten, nor the Biennale's alliance between art and politics.

The Accademia Gallery and Carlo Scarpa

Changes to the Accademia galleries followed the return of the artworks that had been removed from Venice during the First World War. From the time of Cicognara's presidency of the Academy, Titian's *Assunta* had been its centrepiece. In a reappreciation of its original siting, the painting was returned to Santa Maria dei Frari in 1918.[264] As director of the Accademia, Gino Fogolari endeavoured to restore the ecclesiastical character of the main hall of the Scuola della Carità to house the collection of Venetian Gothic altarpieces.[265] Carpaccio's St Ursula cycle was mounted on the walls of a small gallery behind a choir-stall, giving a contextual installation approximating to the original space.

In 1941 Vittorio Moschini was appointed director and began a long association with the Venetian architect Carlo Scarpa, which lead, after the war, to displays that were at once modern and classical. The installations have remained largely unchanged.[266] For Scarpa it was the beginning of a career that went beyond Venice and established him as a leading practitioner in the special area of museum display. Scarpa's career, an essentially *Venetian* career and among the most eminent, came to maturation in the 1930s. He was absorbed in a geometric mode of working, developed from such modernists as Frank Lloyd Wright and Adolf Loos. His designs were notable for the total absence of fascist rhetoric and retrospective classical references; thus, ornament was an aspect of structure rather than a trimming, part of the geometric clarity fundamental to building.[267] The quality of materials and their careful working were intrinsic to Scarpa's effects from the beginning. The immediate roots of this particular modernism lie in the work of Viennese artists such as Gustav Klimt, and in the craft orientation of the Wiener Werkstätte.[268] Scarpa's interest in furnishings, and in design overall, was evident in the work he produced with his close friend the painter Mario Deluigi.[269] Yet despite much modern material being available in exhibition and in reproduction over previous decades, Scarpa's architectural language must have appeared in the Venetian context as resolutely pared-down, ascetic – and aesthetic, particularly in his attention to the crafting of materials and his sympathy for placement. His entire practice can be seen as an elaboration of the principles at work at the beginning of his career, in the surety of the geometry, in the clarity of the light, and often, for the Venetian, in the inclusion of water. He had been attentive to the lesson of Palladio in the control of light as an active agent in his buildings, offsetting white walls, as in the surfaces of the Redentore. The principles of design and light, of ornament embedded in structure, still inform Scarpa's last work, built posthumously in 1978.[270] The door for the faculty of letters at the University of Venice adjoins the church of San Sebastiano, noted for its frescoes by Veronese, and delicately links a modern entrance to the old and revered. Such an achievement stands in defiance of those critics who uphold the separation of the contemporary and the traditional.

Scarpa's architectural work in the 1930s was in the area of interior design: the Caffè Lavena in the narrow street of the Frezzeria behind the Piazza in 1931, which (from surviving photographs) shows the influence of Adolf Loos; domestic contracts; the competition for the Accademia Bridge; and his major work from the 1930s, the new interior for offices and the main hall at the Ca' Foscari university from 1935 to 1937.[271] In the university's Aula Magna in the Ca' Foscari palace – an important example of Venetian Gothic – Scarpa created a modern version of a Gothic window behind the original windows of the outer façade. The original building was countered by intricate bands of wood and wooden grids in a renovation without imitation, yet profoundly in tune with the original building.[272]

In 1931, in a public letter to *Il Lavoro Fascista*, Scarpa announced that he was a Rationalist and thus in opposition to the Nationalist architect Marcello Piacentini.[273] As a member of a group of Venetian architects of like mind, he declared that, in effect, architecture had no alternative but to be rationalist: non-rational architecture failed to qualify as architecture.[274] Scarpa surely wrote a self-instruction when he claimed that: 'The great artist will be he [*sic*] who uses reinforced concrete and in adapting it to the rational purposes and functions of building is capable of including the spiritual and imaginative element, thus creating an artistic expression.'[275] In the 1930s pressure increased to exclude any foreign influence in the arts in favour of national models, which the Venetian Rationalists opposed. In defence of ideas prevalent elsewhere in Italy, Carlo Scarpa asked in his letter if 'the Gothic style [harmed] Venice when it gave us the Doge's palace?'[276]

The most significant aspect of Scarpa's work at this time was not architectural, but rather his glass, made for the Cappellin Venini glass company, and the design of their showrooms in Florence and Paris. In the 1930s he emerged as the modernist glass blower par excellence. His absorption in the tradition of the previous decade and a half is evident in his sensitivity to the lines of modernism reaching Venice from central Europe and the experiments of the Ca' Pesaro group. He was lastingly affected by the cubic and geometric patterns of the Wiener Werkstätte (and perhaps the Werkstätte's debt to Klimt, whose work he would have seen as a boy) and also Zecchin's work from the Ca' Pesaro years. Yet Scarpa's work has no residual Symbolism, nor is it Art Deco: it is modernist, and as such anticipates his architectural practice in the postwar period.

As with his later architecture, Scarpa's ornament in glassmaking is intrinsic: there are no excrescences such as handles, the decoration is born of the fused colour of the glass rods: indeed, this act of fusion, while keeping the cubes of colour distinct, is the *raison d'être* of the objects. Scarpa invented new textural effects. In his *sommerso* glass, shown at the 1934 Biennale, layers were superimposed so that they had depth and thickness, with bubbles captured deep within, and gold leaf glinting.[277] Bulges and sculpted leaf-like patterns protrude from heavy glass worked in the method he invented called *corroso*, which uses a mixture of sawdust and acid to give a glinting textural effect.[278] In his *battuto* works, he chiselled up the once fragile surface of glass with a grinding wheel. He favoured clean modest lines, as in the elegant high-necked vessels made as voluptuous as the fused rods of glass which swell at the vessel's broadest point, then contract at the neck, animating the glass with their bands of modern, solid colour.[279] These *tessuti velati* were presented at the 1940 Biennale. Colour was irregular, unexpected; stripes of blue and white on one side, black and blue on the other, with subtle changes in the interior. He also used the ancient murrhine process for bright ground bowls and plates often speckled in black, with a patch of some other dramatic colour (fig. 164).

In 1943 Scarpa adopted the Murano animal genre in a commission for table glass for the University of Padua.[280] The heraldic ox, the famous Bò, which has guarded the university since its medieval foundation, appears sleek, straining forward eagerly, horns aglow with gilt. It was in the company of the swan of philosophy, pharmacy's serpent and cup, the owl and sphere of science. All were dazzling miniature sculptures, virtuosic in their outlines and characterisation, their fluidity and luminosity, and the character of their detail.

However, it was the collaboration with Moschini and the Accademia galleries in 1941 that pointed the way to Scarpa's future and the beginning of his brilliant career in museum and Biennale design.

164 Carlo Scarpa, bowl, 1940. Murrhine glass, Venini & Co., Murano. Venice, Museo Vetrario.

Celluloid Venices and Francesco Pasinetti

In the 1930s the world danced on. The Lido was hosting the world's film stars: it was at the height of its glamour.[281] Not unexpectedly, Hollywood turned to Venice, finding it even more seductive during the Great Depression of the 1930s. With characteristic elan and superficiality, Hollywood cut through the darkness of Fritz Lang's *Destiny* to set up a Venice of robbery and intrigue, all in the nicest chic settings. In the opening Venetian sequence of Ernst Lubitsch's 1932 *Trouble in Paradise*, a gondolier garbage collector goes about his business while, in the tourist hotels, all is romantic dinners and leaping in and out of bedrooms in disguise.[282] Venice enters with the rubbish: a prophetic note of sordid realism opens a film about the triumph of double dealing. A 'countess' and a 'baron' dine in the aftermath of a robbery in their hotel: they mutually confess to their records as criminals. Venice facilitates both crime and love for them, and they move on to Paris – Paris is modern and Art Deco, in contrast to the history-laden scenes of the Venetian sets. *Trouble in Paradise* is an early example of the genre of films concerning hotel intrigue, which pick up in comic vein on the early prophetic scenario of Wilkie Collins's novel, *A Haunted Hotel*, and Max Reinhardt's *Eine venetianisches Nacht*.

The ultimate offering of life in the Grand Hotel was Mark Sandrich's 1935 *Top Hat*, a vehicle for the dance team of Fred Astaire and Ginger Rogers. The two are caught up in the inevitable comedy of mistaken identities in a courtship at an imitation Venice Hotel equipped with a swimming-pool Bacino, cut-out bridges and gondolas. Beside the water are coffee tables for the guests and dance floors for the troupe. The film proceeds with a *commedia dell'arte* line of courtship, falling in the water, love and romance, with reference to the quintessential tourist honeymoon Venice, moonlight and water. The scene for countless movies was set.

Anna Karenina, starring Greta Garbo, confirmed the agenda for the romantic tourist thereafter.[283] Through the hotel window can be seen a simulated Santa Maria della Salute, and the ill-fated lovers wonder if they will go to St Mark's and feed the pigeons, explore 'the little canals and murderous little alleyways where the doges used to dispose of their enemies . . . Shall we be really energetic and go out on the balcony . . .' History is again symbolised by wicked doges; the pigeons and St Mark's define the central space, but the nexus of the geography, the hotel room, is the real Venetian scenery.

In the same year, and in some contrast, the masterpiece of Venetian cinema appeared, Francesco Pasinetti's *Canale degli Angeli*, from a script by his brother, P. M. Pasinetti.[284] Francesco Pasinetti had been a leading film critic in Venice for a number of years: his formidable knowledge of world cinema is evident in his study of film from its origins until 1939.[285] He was well aware of the cinematic excursions already made to Venice, and reminded his readers that Venice was more than pigeons and the Bridge of Sighs, more than a city of tourists: it also had Porto Marghera and the new bridge, evidence of industrialisation. In writing about films made in Venice, he besought directors to look to authenticity rather than rely on cardboard settings and situations: he specifically noted *Trouble in Paradise* and Clarence Brown's *Anna Karenina* of 1936.[286]

Canale degli Angeli is a fiction, but it moves in an almost documentary manner following the life of a family in outer Venice (the Canale del Angeli in Murano), into the world of shipping and heavy industry, well away from the glamour and history of the old city, which is only occasionally glimpsed. Pasinetti himself described his film as 'a drama of psychological character set in the lagoon landscape around Venice'.[287] Industrial leitmotifs predominate, with close-up shots of cogs turning relentlessly, and chains performing the task of canal dredging. The taciturn husband, older than the wife, works for the office of the *vaporetti* on the Giudecca and is injured in an incident with the machines; he returns from hospital walking with a stick. The mother meets a young man, and Bruno, the child, falls ill, as if in response to the mother's betrayal. But family is confirmed: the lover takes a glamorous ship to America and the mother waves him farewell as the wake of the ship fills the screen.

Canale degli Angeli is a work of integrity and originality: the best of Venetian art in the 1930s. Although not well known, it surely anticipates the Neo-Realist films produced in Italy in the post-war years, such as Vittorio de Sica's 1948 *Bicycle Thieves*. In the context of international cinema and the Lido glamour of the early years of the Biennale that Pasinetti covered as a film critic, his own movie is set apart.[288] It is steadfast and serious to the point of polemic compared to the trivial honeymoon films of the time. Historic Venice is irrelevant to the family in Pasinetti's film; it is almost a foreign city, glimpsed only momentarily from afar. But in the international world of the movies Venice's fate was already sealed: it was a construction in cardboard for affluent hotel guests. *Top Hat* is truer to the common perception of Venice than is Pasinetti's beautiful, elegiac film about ordinary people outside the tourist industry. The last sequences of *Canale degli Angeli* are an allegory of the decline in the city's population after the arrival of Napoleon, and throughout the nineteenth and twentieth centuries. The wake of the steamer that carries the lover from Venice recalls the exodus of citizens in the so-called 'black years' of Fascism from 1931 to 1938, when forty thousand people left the Veneto.[289]

Chapter 9

THE IMPOSSIBLE REBUILDING:
AFTER THE WAR

Venice Endangered

As cities and countries were being invaded in 1940, the French writer Simone Weil exiled herself from Paris and began a version of the play *Venice Preserv'd – Venise sauvée*. In the first lines the peace of Venice is challenged by conspirators who predict that a few hours will see the last day of great Venice.[1] In the centre of the play, in act 2, Renaud looks at the city and sees a delicious place where the citizens have faith in its existence because of their families and possessions.[2] Jaffier's conspiracy has the potential to bring all that to shadows. Heritage and family security will be no more. For Violetta, who speaks with the voice of the author, it is beyond comprehension that Venice could one day be destroyed: God would not permit the destruction of such a beautiful thing; the most heinous enemy would not have the heart. She speaks as the conserving female, protectress of the beautiful and the civilised, knowing that 'the beauty of Venice defends it better than her soldiers' ('Sa beauté la défend mieux que les soldats').[3] In the final scene in which the conspirators die, she watches the sun light up the city of a thousand canals and light up the sea. Her vision is not only of Venice saved, but the impossibility of Venice lost.

In contrast, across enemy lines, the German writer Gerhard Nebel, a soldier in 1943, reacted to Venice adversely, ranking it as 'a centre that radiates the demonic'.[4] The city that is 'traced like seaweed in the sea' still registers the disturbing presence of Demeter and Pan, and contributes to European decay. Yet Nebel admits that Venice retains its erotic charge, its 'sweet slavery'.

The Resistance

Survival, and the reassessment of Fascism, came with the collapse of the Fascist regime in June 1943 (fig. 165). Venice, and nearby Padua, particularly its university, countered Fascism with a Resistance movement.[5] Anti-Fascists consolidated, as they did in other cities; Socialists regrouped; the Communists gained new prominence. After the national publication of the *Manifesto della Razza* on 14 July 1938, measures had been taken to restrict Jewish participation in public life – teaching in schools and at the university, and performing at La Fenice.[6] The leading citizen of the Jewish community, Dottore Giuseppe Jona, who had held various important civic posts, committed suicide on 17 September 1943, as the Fascists reactivated racial laws. Deportation began in December 1943.[7]

Yet Venice was compliant in the war years; there was no confrontation equivalent to the 'Four Days' of Naples or the siege of Florence.[8] Indeed, in the years of German occupation from 1943 until liberation in 1945 it was a haven for some.[9] There are testimonies to considerable vitality: Luigi Nono remembers 'a strange ambience', 'a kind of refuge that welcomed people like Massimo Bontempelli and Arturo Martini, Professor Arcangelo Vespignani, socialist and professor of Radiology, and Carlo

165 Gondolier and
passenger in gas-masks.

Cardazzo, who began the gallery Il Cavallino.[10] Venice became the temporary headquarters of the Ministry of Public Works, and the film industry moved from Rome to the Giardini for the duration of the war.[11] Attack by air was more dangerous for industrial Marghera than for the historic city. Marghera was bombed in May and June 1944, as were the Mestre railway and the aqueduct lines.[12]

The Partisan cause was activated by Armando Gavagnin in the 'forty-five days' between Mussolini's defeat on 24 July 1943 and the entry of the Germans on 8 September 1943.[13] As Manin had done before him, Gavagnin addressed the Venetians from the traditional rallying point, a table at Florian's in the Piazza.[14] A new Socialist party headed by Giovanni Tonetti was formed in August 1943.[15] In exile since 1926, Silvio Trentin returned from Paris where he had written important tracts against Fascism.[16] Following the Nazi occupation, he was arrested in Padua and died soon after, in March 1944.

During the 'forty-five days', newspapers were taken over by democrats: the writer Diego Valeri directed *Il Gazzettino*, but for a matter of days. A trial held by the Germans in 1944 condemned the staff of the *Il Gazzettino* to various terms of imprisonment and led to the so-called *Beffa del Goldoni* (The Mockery) at the Goldoni theatre on the evening of 12 March 1944, when three Partisans took over the stage.[17] On 26 July 1940 partisans exploded a bomb at the Nazi headquarters in Ca' Giustiniani, precipitating a large-scale deportation and the exile of Tonetti and Gavagnin.[18] There were reprisals in the city in retaliation for any German death – the Riva dell'Impero later became the Riva dei Sette Martiri in honour of seven men shot there in 1944.[19]

On 20 April 1944, after heavy fighting, the Partisan campaign achieved the freedom of Padua, followed, on 28 April, by the Venice Action, which took three thousand German prisoners.[20] Passing through the Veneto – from Monte Grappa to the Piave, to Belluno and Fruili – the liberation of northern Italy was effected by 8 May 1944. Venice was liberated by New Zealand troops under General Freyberg who, in an almost touristic spirit, 'captured' the Hotel Danieli where the general had spent his pre-war honeymoon. The British infantry completed the liberation for the Allies, turning the adjacent hotels into officers' clubs.[21]

In the water off the Sette Martiri, the tides now rise and fall on the bronze monument to the women of the Resistance sculpted by Augusto Murer, known as 'the sculptor of the Resistance', and set in place by architect Carlo Scarpa in 1968 (fig. 166).[22] A woman lies on an arrangement of concrete platforms designed by Scarpa: seaweed trails around her as she is covered and uncovered by the tides – now half-obscured, now in full view, in tribute to a frail Venetian Resistance.

Harry's Bar: Ernest Hemingway and Evelyn Waugh

There is no doubt of the scale and intensity of warfare and resistance in the Veneto district overall, and it echoes in Ernest Hemingway's novella *Across the River and Into the Trees*, published in 1950. Although not the greatest of Hemingway's writings, there is nevertheless undeniable poignancy in its account of the survival of a beautiful city after war.[23] An American colonel, Richard Cantwell, has led the Allies to the area and returns to Venice in the last hours of his life. Looking over the water from afar, like so many before him, he praises the Torcello 'boys' who first built the city; he identifies the campanile of Burano (recalling the island's association with lace), Murano (remembering its glass), and then Venice itself – 'Christ what a lovely town'. D'Annunzio is invoked as the colonel moves along the Grand Canal past the Casetta Rossa – 'with his lost eye, covered by the patch, and his white face, as white as the belly of a sole, new turned in the market, the brown side not showing . . .'[24] The colonel mistakes the Casetta Rossa as the venue for the love affair between D'Annunzio and Duse: 'the house where the poor beat-up bold boy had lived with the great, sad, and never properly loved actress', but, quite accurately, pays tribute to D'Annunzio as the 'great, lovely writer of *Notturno*'.[25] In the novella, the Second World War exists close to the memory of the First World War in which the colonel served as a lieutenant. The link with D'Annunzio reinforces the continuity of war and the literary association with *Notturno*, which is also the story of a fighting man and a *bon amant*.

Like most writing about Venice in the twentieth century, *Across the River and Into the Trees* is a visitor's novel, although not a tourist's novel. It is a tale of death *after* visiting Venice, of death occasioned not by Venice, but by war injuries from Allied service in the area. The love affair between the colonel and the young Contessa Renata is told without senti-mentality or undue indulgence, at the end of a military life. The obligatory lovers' gondola ride is taken with a bucket of champagne and a rug in winter. The warming presence of day-to-day Venice, a Venice of the 'cold hard light of morning' and of *acqua alta*, is felt throughout. There is a memorable visit to the Rialto market – 'the closest thing to a good museum' . . . 'to study the spread and high piled cheeses and sausages', and to buy supplies for the duck-shooting expedition on the lagoon. The colonel soon gravitates to Harry's Bar, as the author so often did: Hemingway is the bar's most famous visitor. As the colonel makes his way there from the nearby Hotel Gritti, he wishes he could walk around the city all his life.[26]

So, frequently, Venice provokes recollection, both of its own past, and the past of its visitors. It releases the level of the oneiric; it hovers in the collective memory. Evelyn Waugh succumbed to nostalgia in his wartime novel *Brideshead Revisited: The Sacred and Profane Memories of Captain Charles Ryder*, written in the first six months of 1944 when he was recovering from a parachuting injury.[27] The terrain is aristocratic England in the 1920s and 1930s, under threat at the time of writing. Waugh wrote with an appetite heightened by war and its deprivations, saturating his essay with gluttony for good things. In the company of the narrator, Sebastian Marchmain visits his father, Lord Marchmain, ensconced with his mistress in a Venetian palazzo, and so:

The fortnight at Venice passed quickly and sweetly – perhaps too sweetly; I was drowning in honey, stingless. On some days life kept pace with the gondola, as we nosed through the side-canals and the boatman uttered his plaintive musical bird-

166 Augusto Murer and Carlo Scarpa, monument to the Women of the Resistance, 1968. Giardini di Venezia.

cry of warning; on other days with the speed-boat bouncing over the lagoon in a stream of sun-lit foam; it left a confused memory of fiery sunlight on the sands and cool, marble interiors; or water everywhere, lapping on smooth stone . . . of melon and *prosciutto* on the balcony in the cool of the morning; of hot cheese sandwiches and champagne cocktails at Harry's bar.[28]

It is the inevitable, predictable visit, sweetened with the metaphor of honey, mildly modernised as the gondola gives way to the motor-boat and the still-novel Harry's Bar serves one of its famous toasted sandwiches. As the city's chic cocktail centre, Harry's Bar was the meeting point for the post-war influx of visitors, the place to be seen when crossing from the Lido, or from the closer new Hotel Gritti Palace.[29] It had opened modestly in May 1931 with one ground-floor room, four windows and no view. From the 1960s an upstairs dining room looked over the Bacino to San Giorgio Maggiore. Harry's Bar came into its own with the American influx after the war.

The New Painting

In the second half of the 1940s the Americans invaded in increasing numbers. Peggy Guggenheim, who became one of the city's most influential residents and a great bene-factor, made Venice her permanent home in 1947.[30] She brought her art collection, formed during the early 1940s from her New York gallery. *Art of Our Time*, was shown at the first post-war Biennale in 1948; 136 works were exhibited in the Greek Pavilion 'free because of the Greeks being at war'.[31] Peggy Guggenheim decided to live in Venice and did much to spearhead contemporary art activity after taking up residence in the Palazzo dei Venier Leoni on the Grand Canal, where she opened her collection to the public (see fig. 176).[32] Braque and Picasso, Jackson Pollock, the Surrealists – a whole range of Modernist artists were on permanent display in Venice for the first time.[33] It was the most decisive event for modern art in Venice since the creation of the Bevilacqua Foundation and the establishment of the Ca' Pesaro.

Peggy Guggenheim encountered determined painters in Venice, among the leaders of a new generation, in abstract painting in particular; she was, after all, a champion of Jackson Pollock. She befriended Giuseppe Santomaso and Emilio Vedova, whom she first met at the Caffè all'Angelo in 1946.[34] These artists joined together in 1945 in the Fronte Nuovo delle Arti, a politically activated art movement.[35] In 1946 a new manifesto had been signed in Venice in a 'sala di Palazzo Volpi'; the artists went on to exhibit in Milan, and then showed sixty-six works in one of the most important rooms in the 1948 Biennale. Their spokesman, the critic Giuseppe Marchiori, claimed them as the most representative artists of the generation coming after the Novecento.[36]

Santomaso and Vedova testify to a considerable Venetian vitality in the city, shattering the scenic dependence of earlier Modernists still tied to the picturesque. At the same time, their allegiance with artists elsewhere was indication of freedom from provincialism. Giuseppe Santomaso's early art had been affected by French modernism: he painted still lifes inspired by Braque in the early 1940s, but a commitment to social and politi-cal themes found expression in the series of cages and the abstract linear prisons that he painted in the 1940s. Santomaso's abstractions evoke the city and the lagoon and lead to the fluid geometries of the 1970s and the series *Lettere a Palladio*.[37] Emilio Vedova became one of the leaders of his generation in Italy, with an abstract expressionism as powerful as that of the American Franz Kline, with which it was often compared. In the 1930s his work was predominantly graphic, with energy and passion in its web of black lines. The early work has affinities with De Pisis and his melancholic, urgently drawn paintings of Venice, but in comparison De Pisis remains static, contemplative and scenic. Both De Pisis and Vedova drew the churches of Venice: in the 1930s Vedova was looking at the web of arches and upper spaces

167 Emilio Vedova, *San Moisè*, 1937–8. Oil on canvas, 50 × 23 cm. Venice, collection of the artist.

of San Moisè and San Salvatore, focusing on their roof zones where curves are set off against curves (fig. 167).[38] Alert to the complexity of art available in Italy in the 1930s, Vedova recognised the relevance of Futurism (in 1934 the *Aeropittura* had been shown at the Biennale): he registered 'Futurism as simultaneity'. It was a doctrine of movement, energy, change and modernity; all had their relevance, although the ideological base of the painting had decisively changed.

By his own admission Vedova was a *Venetian* artist, with a fervent adolescence spent as a *partigiano*.[39] He commented on a Venice in flux, destabilised and destabilising: these conditions observed many times, and often negatively, give his work an existentialist dimension. He asked:

> Do you know what it means to be born in Venice – emerged lands + suffered lands + watery air/light, sand banks, lagoon, suspended light . . . light reflected at once overcome deep inside us, drenched in light 'other' . . . interior . . . space, that goes to the indistinct, utopia, the sign.[40]

Such juxtapositions, drawn from the conditions of the lagoon, are gathered into the semantics of Modernism and the particular significations of abstract painting. The critic Germano Celant characterised Vedova as imprisoned in his soul, using his canvas as 'an arena of torments and fears, of sweetness and rage'.[41] To a marked extent, Vedova presents himself within the Venetian tradition, endorsing Baroque turmoil above Renaissance classicism. Tintoretto and Piranesi are cited as forebears, for, like Piranesi, Vedova dwells on the 'dark side of the brain', declaring that 'Piranesi is Venetian, his fantasy and polemicism is Venetian'.[42] As a young artist Vedova would have seen Pallucchini's 1937 exhibition of Tintoretto; he made variations on Tintoretto's work, but more important was the identification with Tintoretto's expres-

sive force and agitation. It is an agenda that begins in opposition to totalitarianism and the state of war, extended and renewed in the face of later events in Europe, such as the building of the Berlin Wall. An energy, a blackness that is not just of pigment, tears across Vedova's canvases from the 1940s to the 1990s (fig. 168). They were often irregularly shaped and free-standing, as if the rectangle and square of a normal canvas were too restricting. Works such as the *Plurimi* from the 1950s – shaped canvases free-standing on the floor – force abstraction into an allegorical mode, highlighting energy and anger, challenging constraints.

The eloquent Massimo Cacciari formulated 'Ten Points' in appreciation of Vedova. He remarked on the process of journeying, leaving tracks, being perpetually in flux, making marks that came out of silence, coaxed into speech by the artist's huge hands and finding stasis in the opposition between black and white. The works are meditations on dust and scraps, on laceration, inhabiting no place, mirroring and reflecting.[43] And finally, they carry a full weight of melancholy: 'It is the sign of Saturn, where the most sinister melancholy combines with the highest *speculative* force (and once again the mirror appears . . .).'[44]

168 (*above*) Emilio Vedova, *The Image of Time (Barricade)*, 1951. Egg tempera on canvas, 130.5 × 170.4 cm. Venice, The Peggy Guggenheim Collection, (The Solomon R. Guggenheim Foundation).

The associations arising from the Partisan years of the early 1940s and the immediate post-war years, together with the passionate need to create a new art committed to freedom, must have made the new artistic presence and cohesion strongly felt in Venice. In the Ristorante all'Angelo, host to the Ca' Pesaro painters some twenty years before, Vedova, with Santomaso and Pizzinato, collaborated on a triptych, a statement of Venetian solidarity in the years immediately after the war.[45]

Increasingly, these Venetian artists held their own in the post-war years. At the same time, in the influx that followed the war, Venice was host to the world's artists: Hemingway and Cocteau, Picasso, Dufy, Jean Arp came, and they posed – Hemingway with his hunting rifle in Torcello, Cocteau with pigeons in front of San Marco, Henry Moore beside the Tetrarchs at San Marco, Hans Hartung before the Bridge of Sighs, Stravinsky in a gondola. Salvador Dalí sported a miniature gondola in the famous moustache (fig. 169).[46] They came, like Sebastian Marchmain, to drown in Venetian honey after the deprivations of the war.

* * *

The Biennale Restored

The 1948 Biennale, the first after the war, brought together the avant-garde of post-Fascist Italy with comprehensive exhibitions of European Modernism suppressed during the reigns of Fascism and Nazism. Resurgent in spirit and ambitious to reconstitute the liberal history of twentieth-century Modernism, the 1948 exhibition has been called 'the most notable in the whole history of the Biennale'.[47] The catalogue underlined the difficulties that had been overcome, in particular the need to restore the unused pavilions, which had fallen into decay, and the obstacles to finance.[48] The symbolism of 1948 was not neglected: it was the 'glorious historical centenary of [Venice's] political reawakening and [its] civic risorgimento'.[49] Over four hundred artists were invited. There were exhibitions by Chagall, Kokoschka and Picasso, and a retrospective of Paul Klee, who had died in 1940. It was claimed that 'the 1948 Biennale was like opening a bottle of champagne. It was the explosion of modern art after the Nazis had tried to kill it.'[50]

The art historian Rudolf Pallucchini, who had collaborated with Nino Barbantini in the 1930s, became the new secretary to the Biennale. Pallucchini showed himself a notable custodian of European and Italian art, orchestrating comprehensive surveys of French art: in 1948 Impressionism, the Fauves and the Cubists; in 1950 the German Expressionists and the Blaue Reiter; Italian Futurist and Metaphysical art; the retrospectives of Kandinsky and Klee, and the Belgians, Ensor and Permeke.[51] The number of countries participating in the Biennales grew with the post-war recovery: from just fourteen in 1948 to twenty-six in 1952. In these years the Biennale assumed a confident position as a showcase for contemporary art. Subsidiary exhibitions were held in the Ala Napoleonica in the centre of the city: it was the beginning of the expansion that in later years would include almost all Venice – the islands and churches, the Riva, the Zattere and the Arsenale. Carla Scarpa's installations, both in the Giardini and city venues, gave a new appearance to the installations (fig. 170).[52]

It had often been claimed that Italy was ambivalent towards Modernism. The charge dates from the very first Biennales. Liberation, and efforts made to embrace the modern and the radical, ensured that the post-war Biennales became more determinedly avant-garde. Italian art continued to be acutely political, and was recognised as such. The allegorical state implied by the free brush-stroke had direct political import, which was pitted against figurative Social Realism. In these post-war years, inspiration for the humanist artist stemmed from the Partisan experience of the 1940s. It remained to underpin Vedova's entire oeuvre. In the work of his compatriot in music, Luigi Nono, that experience also kept its inspirational humanist power.

The Biennales were the highly visible stage on which the values of Europe, and Italy within it, were on parade. Debates over abstraction and realism and the prestige of American art were potent for the visual arts internationally, but the issue focused sharply on northern Italy – Milan as well as Venice – at the time of the 1948

169 (facing page bottom) Salvador Dalí, 1961.

170 (below) Carlo Scarpa, installation for Giacomo Manzù, 22nd Biennale di Venezia, Ala Napoleonica, 1964.

Biennale.[53] In that year the critic Giuseppe Marchiori championed the Nuovo Fronte delle Arte in their first exhibition in Milan. Within months the attack on abstract art by the leader of the Communist party, Palmiro Togliatti, led to a splintering of the group – and Vedova's passionate denunciation of strict Social Realism.

In the 1952 Biennale the Gruppo degli Otto, with Santomaso and Vedova as its Venetian members, exhibited together, championed by Lionello Venturi.[54] But Social Realism practised in Venice also registered its presence in the 1952 Biennale in the work of Armando Pizzinato. His *Insurrection in Venice* – a large-scale painting of Partisans holding up Nazi occupiers – demonstrated the enduring impact of the war years (fig. 171).[55]

Because the Biennale was arranged within national pavilions, presentations were exercises in foreign policy, no less. Issues current in the years 1948 to 1968 concerned the degree of French influence, the Biennale's alleged Francophilia – and the increasing competition from American art.[56] It is generally conceded that the great era of French dominance ended in 1956.[57] The United States, circumspect in the era of McCarthyism, showed Ben Shahn's Realist art in 1954 at the same time as the politically committed art of Renato Guttoso continued to concentrate the debate on Social Realism for Italian art.[58] Ten years later Robert Rauschenberg took first prize. In 1964 many commentators observed not only Rauschenberg's victory for American art over the school of Paris, but referred to 'an American imperialist campaign'.[59]

Rauschenberg's award became a major incident, which itself confirmed the role the Biennale now played in art politics. The American government was directly involved, appointing its own agent, Alan Solomon, and exerting pressure to have Sam Hunter as the first American on the international jury.[60] Because of the large consignment of American work, including work by Morris Louis and Kenneth Noland, Rauschenberg was not exhibited in the official American pavilion in the Giardini, so when the first prize was offered he was rejected on those grounds. The photograph of an open boat moored amid striped Venetian *pali* being loaded with Rauschenbergs to be transferred to the Giardini to legitimate the prize is a classic expression of the Biennale as a political art forum.[61]

As it has for many a foreign exhibitor at the Biennale, Venice exacted its tribute from Robert Rauschenberg. In late 1972 and 1973 he assembled sculptures known as *Venetians*, made in his 'combine' manner. They are among the first 'found' collages inspired by Venice.[62] Shown at the Leo Castelli Gallery in New York in 1973 was a picturesque assemblage of elements

172 (*below*) Robert Rauschenberg, *Franciscan, II* (*Venetian*), 1972. Fabric, resin-treated carboard, transparent tape on plywood support, string and stone, 221 × 294.6 × 120.7 cm. The Museum of Modern Art, New York. Kay Sage Tanguy Fund.

171 (facing page top)
Armando Pizzinato,
Insurrection in Venice,
1952. Oil on canvas,
200 × 140 cm. Rome,
Confederazione Generale
Italiana del Lavoro.

in post-surreal array, rich in textures and bizarre in conjunctions. An old tyre is held in place by a *palo* – one of the wooden lagoon markers. An unravelled piece of rubber threads up through wooden struts with subaqueous crumpled pieces of iron suspended on a trapeze affair over a bath tub filled with water. The saints are present: a white mosquito net, old white chairs and glass jars evoke Sant'Agnese; a tarpaper encrusted with barnacles and a coconut on a rope is San Pantalon. Ropes and stones from the canals and white cloth spread on the wall recall the gown of a Franciscan (fig. 172).

So Venice yielded up the rubbish of its canals and all its many hidden textures worked upon by age and water, to be ransacked by artists intent on combine and collage. In direct line of descent, in the 1997 Biennale Mark Dion crated up dredgings from canal beds for exhibition: a vat of sludge sat outside the pavilion, and inside fragments of china and glass were on display as in a *Wunderkammer*.[63]

The Transparent and the Opaque: Glass

Following the establishment of the Venezia pavilion at the Biennale and the regular display of glass, the art of Murano grew in vitality and prominence. Glass design in the post-war years revived in concert with the return of tourism and the growing fame of the firm of Venini.[64] The initiative of Egidio Costantini gave international status to the furnaces of Murano when he formed the Centro Studio Pittori nell'Arte del Vetro, inviting such famous painters as Picasso, Braque and Kokoschka to have a design realised in glass. In a famous Orphic phrase, Jean Cocteau described it as the 'Fucina degli Angeli' – the forge of the angels.[65] The currency of Spazialismo painting in Venice had its effect on glassmaking, giving it new freedom and colour, new shapes and daring asymmetrical forms.[66]

The experimental approach continued: on the one hand, glass was of breathtaking lightness, with vases and bowls shaped in traditional filigree forms; on the other, it was heavy and chunky in modernist colours and abstracted forms, distinctly up-to-date. One of the most noted glassmakers in the 1950s, Archimede Seguso, made both heavy sculptural pieces and the lightest filigree. The Venini workshops continued their notable output with inventions that were at once modern and traditional. The asymmetries of Modernism and the biomorphic shapes characteristic of a Venetian sculptor such as Alberto Viani had great potential for the molten forms of glass. In a climate of post-war abstraction, floreate and marine forms became fashionable – in Ercole Barovier's classic *Corinth* and *Damascus,* for example, shown at the 1948 Biennale. Made with rod and lattimo threads with gilding inside and out, Barovier's vessels seem like marine-dwelling objects perpetually washed by the sea.[67]

Fulvio Bianconi – a prolific and inventive glassmaker – became Venini's artistic director from 1947, following Carlo Scarpa. At the 1948 Biennale Bianconi presented his famous 'handkerchief', transparent and delicate with filigree work, fluid in shape with the 'handkerchief' folded out like a flower (fig. 173). His fan designs were of similar delicacy. Like the handkerchief, they were the finest filigree, but set on fluid, modern-looking bases.[68] Such pieces reinterpreted the accessories and the finesse of the eighteenth century, but other creations by Bianconi were entirely of his own time. The 'Vase with Vertical Stripes', exhibited in the twenty-sixth Biennale in 1952, was solidly coloured in teal, black and gold, unmistakably mid-twentieth century. The ubiquitous figurine tradition had an art application in Bianconi's *commedia dell'arte* figures, which appeared first at the 1948 Biennale. A troupe of quizzical beings in milk glass came to life, spotted and striped of costume, acrobatic in posture and in the turning of the glass itself (fig. 175).[69]

In 1959 the death of Paolo Venini, pre-eminent among Murano glassmakers, ended an era. Gio Ponti, who had reviewed Venetian glass in the pages of his journal *Domus* since the 1920s, was eloquent in praise of Venini's career.[70] The factory had hosted

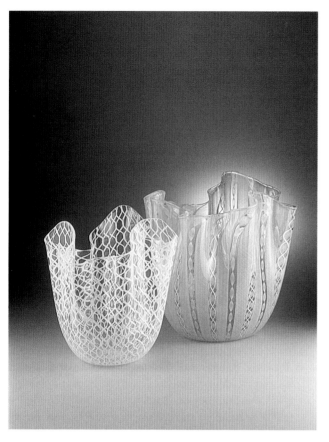

173 (*above left*) Fulvio
Bianconi, handkerchief vase,
1949–50. Glass, 27 × 27 cm.
Venini & Co., Murano.
Murano, Archivio Venini.

174 (*above right*) Dino
Martens, vase, Vetreria
Aureliano Toso, Murano,
*c.*1955. Glass, 21.3 cm.
Vaduz, Steinberg
Foundation for Art Glass of
the Twentieth Century.

175 Fulvio Bianconi,
Commedia dell'arte figures,
1948. Glass, Venini & Co.
Venice, Museo Vetrario.

many artists, including the distinguished Carlo Scarpa, who had worked with him from 1932 to 1947. Venini believed that Murano glass must be *modern*, and had been the foremost promoter of that commitment. International artists were invited to work at Venini's increasingly fruitful post-war practice. For the 1962 Biennale the American Thomas Stearn produced a memorable *Doge's Hat* – a vase in the shape of the dogal cornù, quite specific in its Venetian inspiration.[71]

Glass of the 1950s has been hailed as 'varied and wildly colourful'; and the period described as 'the most significant single decade in the history of glassmaking'.[72] Beside the bravura pieces created for Biennales, there were thousands of others in *zanfirico*: white, gold, multicoloured entrapped bundles and rods of colour, canes cut through to display colours like boiled sweets; vases swelling to the neck with pink stripes or trailing loops of glass on scallop handles; bottles with flared lips opening out in filigrees like flowers; bowls that are vortices of many colours spiralling out from their centre point; pinched bowls and vases with profiles rippling with filigree; murrhine vases obeying some cubic command then softened in the blowing; millefiori paperweights, every tourist's souvenir (fig. 174). The fashion for organic forms, diffused in the arts and design of the 1950s, gave life and new profiles to traditional vessels (fig. 176).

These creations in the contemporary vitalist mode seemed appropriate inhabitants of Venice for they suggested metaphors afloat in poetry, and renewed analogies with glass and fire dear to elemental Venetian symbolism. The visit to the glassmaker Seguso in D'Annunzio's *Il Fuoco* might come to mind, or the fictional Venetian glass nephew, a creation of the eighteenth-century glass-blower Alvise Luna and Casanova, no less, in his capacity as a conjurer.[73] Later, Joseph Losey's Veneto setting for the film

176 Peggy Guggenheim with a glass sculpture by Vinco Vianello, 1952.

of Mozart's *Don Giovanni* casts the Don as proprietor of a Murano glass furnace who takes his guests to witness the spectacle of glass redeemed by fire before being himself cast into the flames.[74] The aqueous metaphors of mirroring and reflecting, of shining mobile surfaces and underwater depths, the dramatic creation of glass through *movement*, in short, drove the creative production of Murano triumphantly in the 1950s.

Music and Painting: Luigi Nono and Emilio Vedova

The Biennales dedicated to music and theatre begun by Count Volpi in the 1930s continued to make Venice an important venue for new productions after the war. Plays by Sartre, Cocteau, Camus, Claudel and Pirandello were staged – as were regular performances of Goldoni.[75] In the International Festivals of Contemporary Music, compositions by the local musicians Luigi Nono (born in 1919) and the older Malipiero were regularly performed. Bruno Maderna, born in 1920 and one-time child prodigy in his city, was Nono's contemporary. Maderna was increasingly prominent as a conductor and, after performing a composition in the first post-war festival in 1946, as a composer.[76] The Viennese School was heard frequently; there were strong connections between Malipiero, Nono and Maderna, and Schoenberg and the Viennese School.[77] The Biedermeier Venice and Vienna of the past century were defunct: the pursuit of serial music and, increasingly, electronic music and the Darmstadt school, were the concerns of these musicians. In no sense was Venetian music provincial. Important premieres took place, among the most notable of which was Stravinsky's *The Rake's Progress* in 1951 at La Fenice, with a libretto by W. H. Auden.[78]

Not all commissions for the music festival, of course, resulted in Venice-specific works, but one example that did is Witold Lutoslawski's *Jeux vénitiens* for chamber orchestra, commissioned for 1961.[79] Its title conjures up the tradition of carnival suites in musical history, here enriched by being a work in an aleatory mode, allowing musicians to proceed individually through the score.

The major musical event of 1961 was the performance of Nono's opera *Intolleranza 1960* at La Fenice.[80] It was politically committed, artistically original and the finest fruit of a collaboration by artist and musician – Emilio Vedova and Luigi Nono. Bruno Maderna conducted the first performance. In the 1950s Vedova's art had been notable for a series of shaped canvases, charged with political intent. In gesture, energy and jagged black-based colour, they were anti-totalitarian in spirit. The paintings became characteristically cyclical, intended to be seen as ensembles: the first, in 1951, was the *Situations in Collision*. In a notable echo of Franz Kafka, Vedova wrote of the 'ice breaking' in him. The *Cycle of Protest* and the *Cycle of Nature* followed. As Pallucchini wrote in 1951, on the eve of Vedova's first exhibition in New York, 'I believe Vedova to be one of the most lively witnesses of this period in Europe'.[81]

Both Nono and Maderna were committed to Malipiero's programme to revive older Venetian music, and thus the full history of Venetian music, which had previously been unavailable.[82] Both Nono and Maderna commented upon the spatial quality of Venetian church music; both found the music of Gabrieli and the split choirs and orchestras of San Marco to be important for their multi-sited acoustics.[83] Like Malipiero, both were sensitive to the *visual* tradition in Venice, to the tradition of painting, and the physical presence of the lagoon and the cityscape.[84] Maderna has remarked of the Venetian sky:

> an unusual and, I would say, particularly majestic sky, perhaps because the line of the horizon often blends with the sea, so that it seems there is no horizon. I think that Gabrieli wanted to bring the sky and the colours of the piazza into the dark, mysterious Byzantine church. There is in Gabrieli, in fact, a real voluptuousness, almost a libido of sound, as there is of colour in Venetian painting.[85]

A renewed sense of tradition and the contemporary city fed a specific Venetian sense that travelled well beyond an eclectic *venezianità*.

The International Festival of Contemporary Music directed by Mario Labroca was Nono's 'provocation' for his 'musico-theatrical piece'.[86] Indeed *Intolleranza* is one of the most powerful Venetian works produced in this century. Nono's music was as 'engaged' as Vedova's painting, perhaps more specifically so through his explicit choice of texts. Like Vedova, Nono had been involved in Partisan activity in the early 1940s.[87] The initial conception of *Intolleranza* drew on the political theatre of Piscator and Meyerhold, especially the model of theatre in the round, which aimed to involve and activate the audience, and, in Italy, on Angelo Maria Ripellino's contemporary interest in Mayakovsky.[88] The libretto was a montage that created a 'Situations theatre' with specific allusions to actual events in 1960: in Belgium there were demonstrations in July; in Italy a Fascist restoration was predicted; there were struggles in Algiers with repercussions in Paris; and various forms of Neo-Fascism and Neo-Nazism, and a catastrophic flooding in the Po River region.[89]

Nono's narrative concerns an immigrant worker who is caught up in a demonstration, arrested, interrogated and tortured. Travelling later with a female worker, both are swept away when a river breaks its dams. *Intolleranza* is a collage of spoken and sung music and electronic sounds amplified spatially through the auditorium. Texts come from Ripellino, Eluard, Mayakovsky, Sartre and Brecht. In the beginning the emigrant sings with a chorus of miners, announcing his decision to return home, to emerge from the life in the pits where the miners come out 'in black masks with long smoky manes', and appear to the woman 'like a black statue', 'a black Eros'.[90] Arrested at a political demonstration, the immigrant is witness to torture and hears human cries; then the pleas of a population engulfed by the flood. This nerve-racking, exalted work admits the screams of tortured, human voices drawn to a point of agony. Yet there are moments of lyrical, gentle sound, as in the prelude to the song of the tortured prisoners. Vedova's setting for *Intolleranza* used projections of his characteristic gestural paintings combined with verbal slogans. He brought to the work his long-standing concern with humanitarian themes and his personal experience of conflict (fig. 177).[91]

177 Luigi Nono and Emilio Vedova, production of *Intolleranza 1960* at Teatro La Fenice, Venice, 1961. Venice, Archivio Luigi Nono.

In the same year Nono composed a tribute to Vedova, *Ommagio a Emilio Vedova*, his first electronic composition, of three minutes' duration.[92] Sounds are plucked out of space and are reciprocated across space; they are drawn out, and then cut short. Fluid and encircling, sounds sizzle and echo in homage to Vedova's spatial formats and his puncturing gestures. Pitch drops vertiginously from high to low, weighted and plopping like water, or sizzling like water in fire, ricocheting and rumbling, plumbing depths and then ascending again to the heights. The music responds to Vedova's spatial sense, to the way he showed his paintings – sometimes hung from the rafters, placed on the ground or spread around the vast spaces of the warehouse in Dorsorduro that he used for a studio. Creating visual resonances across space was at the heart of Vedova's way of working for which Nono found an aural equivalent. As he has memorably remarked, 'Venice is an acoustical multiuniverse'.[93] With Maderna as conductor, all three artists showed their responsiveness to the peculiarly Venetian spatial experience.

Nono's first electronic composition was a significant multi-dimensional moment for both painting and music, a further expansion into space and time. Vedova was compelled to take painting out of its static mode; Nono was committed to the difficult terrain of composing music that held itself on the edge of acoustic intolerance and disintegration. In work from the 1950s, such as *Il Canto Sospeso* (Suspended Song) of 1955–6 – Nono had used letters from resistance fighters written in 1942 as text – the words of a nineteen-year-old student, a twenty-two-year-old hairdresser . . .'[94] In 1954, aligning himself with Picasso, the primary example of the committed artist in those years, Nono wrote *La Victoire de Guernica* for chorus and orchestra. In 1953 Vedova painted a *Cycle of Protest (Contemporary Crucifixion)*, which might be thought of as a parallel to Nono's *Canto Sospeso*.

From 1961 to 1965 Vedova painted his *Plurimi* – a series of shaped canvases that stood on the floor, grouped like stage actors. They were, he claimed, 'born of a dynamic weapon, marked by an aggressive line which could no longer remain a static form'.[95] That form of presentation – assembling paintings almost as sculpture – was further developed during a residence in Berlin in 1964. The resulting work, the *Absurd Berlin Diary*, picked up on Dada and Expressionist traditions from Germany and Vedova's own commitment to gestural freedom and 'cycles of protest'; Vedova has maintained this method of grouping paintings like sculptures.[96] For the Montreal Expo in 1967 he produced an even more elaborate installation using fourteen simultaneous projectors and a suspended aluminium plate in combination with canvases and Murano glass.[97]

Explicit political comment was not the only priority for artists around 1960. For some the challenge was the exploration of new space and (having this in common with Vedova) an attack on the conventional boundaries between painting and sculpture. Spazialismo was founded by the Milanese artist Lucio Fontana, who in 1961 exhibited at the Palazzo Grazzi, a venue increasingly used for exhibitions.[98] The dealer Carlo Cardazzo was a creative bridge between Venice and Milan – with his gallery in Venice, the Cavallino and, in Milan, the Galleria del Naviglio.[99] Cardazzo launched Spazialismo across the two cities.[100]

Spazialismo has not yet been sufficiently recognised as an abstract movement nurtured in Venice. In follows lagoon space towards horizons, rather than the *calli* and canal systems of the city. It seeks the atmospherics

178   Lucio Fontana, *Spatial Concept*: *The Moon in Venice*, 1961. Oil on canvas, 150 × 150 cm. Turin, Istituto Bancario di San Paolo di Torino.

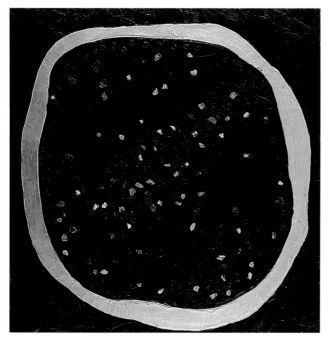

179 Virgilio Guidi,
The Lagoon at Burano,
1951. Oil on canvas,
90 × 120cm. Venice,
Galleria Internazionale
d'Arte Moderna,
Ca' Pesaro.

engendered by water and it appears to run counter to the strong movement of bi-par-
tisan art in Venice at the time. Yet Spazialismo's concern with liberation and with
spatial freedom make it a parallel rather than a counter movement.

Fontana's works were always 'spatial concepts', abstract participants in pure form,
but capable of allusions, as in the Venetian series that had an exotic Byzantine/
Romantic agenda evoking gold, silver dawns, marriage and nights of love (fig. 178).[101]
Formats were new and influential, offering surfaces that were almost sculpted, rich
tachist constructions glittering with fragments of Murano glass.

Virgilio Guidi's post-war painting, long associated with Venice, was also linked to
Spazialismo. Recognised for his magical realism in the Biennales of the early 1920s
(particularly *Tram*, shown at the 1924 Biennale), subsequent views of Venice favoured
the quasi-industrial landscape of the Giudecca.[102] But detail was forsaken as Guidi's
Spazialismo developed from a process of abstracting from the Venetian waterscape –
finding its utmost simplicity in the fluid horizon line between water and sky, the flat
terrains of air and lagoon set down in diaphanous bands of colour. A thin rectangle
of land, or the simple shape of a boat hull might be blocked in, but lightly (fig. 179).
Also part of the new Spazialismo, Mario Deluigi worked with a similar shift from the
figurative to abstraction, alluding to atomic structures and light.[103]

The range of the Biennale, and, importantly, its political orientation, was even more
in evidence in the 1960s. Many welcomed its capacity to scandalise, to dramatise
abstraction against figuration, to range the mythical entities of European art against
American, and so participate in the major re-orientation of art staged in the post-war
period. The questions for or against abstraction, or for realism, were not limited to
American art and its influence, for they ran deep in post-war Italian visual culture.
Italian critics such as Lionello Venturi, Carlo Ragghianti, Umberto Apollonio and
Giulio Carlo Argan fuelled debates on the political and intellectual orientation of the
arts.

In the volatile situation of 1968 the Biennale was accused of being 'bourgeois' and
nationalistic and became a focus for demonstration. Foreign students came to Venice

deliberately intending to disrupt the Biennale at a time when student movements were rife throughout Italy, not least in Venice itself, where the Accademia had been occupied for four months.[104] Nineteen Italian artists headed by Vedova withdrew their work from the Italian pavilion in the opening week and the police quelled riots in the Piazza (fig. 180). The influential critic Giulio Carlo Argan announced 'the death of the Biennale', now entrenched in conservative practices. However Pierre Restany insisted that Venice's had been a very minor 'revolution'.[105] Wladimiro Dorigo, an active voice from the left for reform, examined the situation in Venice and compared events in France, Germany, the USA and the student movement, referring to occupations and specific boycotts at such exhibitions as the Triennial in Milan and the Odéon in Paris.[106] The Venice Biennale was charged with being authoritarian, racist, impeding real communication, degrading the worker and manipulating the energy of workers.[107] In an echo of the Futurists, collusion with tourist activity was targeted, and the Biennale was accused of endorsing an art for the rich in an enslaving monoculture.[108] Similarly, the Venice section of the Italian Communist Party attacked the Festival of Contemporary Music for its privileged and specialist status and its irrelevance to the social economic and cultural life of the community.[109] Reform, which all sides agreed was necessary, came to be a semi-permanent part of subsequent Biennale agendas.

In the most poetic gesture of the fraught 1968 Biennale, the Argentinian painter Nicolas Uriburu painted the water of the Grand Canal a fluorescent green. One dawn, he took a boat and trailed pigment through the water, painting on Venice's most characteristic surface.[110]

Filmed on Location

The Americans continued their post-war invasion of the city. Venice became increasingly a city for foreign consumers, extolled as such in advertisements and film. *Three Coins in the Fountain* was the most famous of the mid-fifties travel films, splendid in new cinemascope, good-naturedly following three American girls in their *Italienische Reise*.[111] The girls were innocent, simultaneously assured and amazed, on the lookout for romance. Their adventure is located mainly in Rome, but Venice presented an opportunity for a swift and highly recognisable stop-over.

In some contrast, in 1952 the English film *Venetian Bird*, made by Ralph Thomas from the novel by Victor Canning, focused on an unglamorous, sleazy post-war city. *Venetian Bird* is an inside-Venice film. Even if the main character is an English visitor, the focus is on local counterfeiting and dissembling, which are presented as normal activities. The film follows the novel closely: Canning wrote the screenplay. Richard Todd played the disillusioned private detective, acutely aware of the squalor of his profession. He is Edward Mercer, raincoat slung over arm, who identifies the Venetian Uccello – the 'Bird' of the title – who was supposedly killed in a wartime bombing raid, but is still alive, married and actively planning the political assassination of a famous poet.[112] The murder is intended to engender unrest in the fragile state of Italy sufficient to facilitate an army and navy coup.

Venetian Bird does not seek to be exotic; Venice is its day-to-day self, but there is a dark density in its *calli* and *canale* that frustrates chase and suggests sites where evil is concealed and terrorism latent. The topography is predictable but not overplayed: the sweeping beauty of aerial views of the Piazza and San Marco is pushed away and elevated cameras follow roof chases and expose secret dwellings in the attics of the Procuratie left over from wartime Partisan days. The killer dies because he is beaten, not by a police gun, but at the hand of one of the best-known Venetian monuments. One of the Moors who strikes the hours on the Torre dell'Orologio finds the head of the terrorist Uccello beneath his hammer and the Bird plunges to his death in the Piazza.[113]

In tandem with the invention of the popular film in the 1950s came a spate of novels with Venice as setting.[114] It was the beginning of media voracity. There were quasi-historical plots – as in Dennis Wheatley's *The Rape of Venice*, set at the end of the days of the Republic and the time of the French invasion.[115] There was straightforward murder, in Patricia Highsmith's *The Talented Mr Ripley*, which sets up the hero in an apartment in Venice.[116] The multitudinous and deadly errands of the Cold War were well-suited to Venice as MI5 made a first dramatic appearance in John Hadley Chase's *Mission to Venice*. A wealthy Englishman, an ex-wartime fighter pilot, is intrigued to find out what has happened to an airforce colleague, and finds him being tortured in Venice for exposing a spy at the heart of London security.[117] Chase offered the first in a popular series of chases and getaways by water and land which have been so exploited by later novelists and film-makers. From New York to Paris to Venice: this was the Cold War itinerary for Helen McInnes's popular *The Venetian Affair*, published in 1963, in which the affair is a double matter of love and spying.[118]

BLACK AND WHITE

Hardly innocent, holding itself in perpetual readiness for both amateur and professional, Venice was swamped by photographers. At the turn of the century photographers engaged with the new Pictorialist photography in black and white, loving in its cultivation of tonal qualities and contrasts. Against the static images necessary in the first phase of photography's short history, the pictorialists were intent on the movement of light. They relished watery reflections. More mobile than their forerunners, they could approach their motif with their hand-held equipment from a range of angles.

In the first decade of the century the American photographer Alvin Langdon Coburn anticipated a whole aesthetic of back-canal photography when he photographed modest bridges at an angle, and the half circles reflected from arches of Istrian stone.[119] Walls close to the small canals added their drama of shadow and texture. When Coburn photographed the façade of a palazzo – as he did for the frontispiece of an

181 Federico Leiss, *Venice, Rio dell'Abbazia, c.1950.*

edition of Henry James's *The Wings of a Dove* – the recesses of darkness behind Gothic windows and doors share the velvety, liquid quality of the water.[120]

Around 1950 Venice was still a black-and-white subject par excellence. As early as 1941 Orson Wells let a lugubrious black gondola prow appear momentarily in the first sequence of *Citizen Kane*.[121] In 1954 his film of *Othello* inhabited a monochrome Venice, redolent of both power and poetry; the opening sequences show high and low angles, intent, sharp faces amid the shadows of the arcades of the Palazzo Ducale, before the action shifts to Cyprus.[122]

A post-war genre of poetical black-and-white photography blossomed when the photographic club, the Circolo La Gondola, was founded.[123] Ferruccio Leiss was among those practitioners who found new chiaroscuro effects within the city. He had come to Venice from Milan in 1933, and thereafter created photographs imbued with both realism and lyricism.[124] The subjects were fog-obscured distances, reflections of arched bridges and the peaked prows of boats taking the light or blackened into silhouettes. The views presume mobility, as the Piazzetta is seen from above, the domes of San Marco are photographed from the Torre dell'Orologio, and the Rialto Bridge curves up from beneath the arch (fig. 182). Smaller bridges turn away from the camera and nondescript *rii* angle and twist (fig. 181). These back views, which are both casual

182 Federico Leiss, *Venice,* c.1950.

and composed, exist apart from tourist Venice. They suggest the eye of the habitué, traversing the *fondamente*, climbing over the bridges, conscious at all times of the light and shadow.

This was also the terrain of the film-maker Francesco Pasinetti, limited by budget to short films during the 1940s, although no less devoted to a Venice other than the cardboard city of international movies.[125] His *Venezia minore* of 1942 is a view of the Venice that escapes visual cliché to inhabit quiet corners.[126] It belongs to children and keeps to their eyel-level and mobility. Although the opening shot is of the Campanile, it is not the famous buildings that dominate, but passages through Venice that gives glimpses of skylines, or the lower parts of buildings at child height, and their shadows and patches of sunshine, seldom their identifiable whole (fig. 183). The camera follows children up and down over bridges, in and out of the *calli*, stepping

down into boats, looking up at someone in an upper window. In pairs they cross a campo with their nun school-teacher. Thin little boys stand and row boats competently; the prow of a gondola is taller than they are. Shadows are sharp triangles across buildings, dramatising the *campi*. In the last sequences, a small girl is filmed from overhead as she goes into a church. Aerial sculptures are unseen above her, church music draws her in. Pasinetti's *Venezia minore* is the first short feature film about 'real' Venice.

TECHNICOLOUR

Pasinetti had observed in the 1930s that films starring Venice did little justice to reality, and this was increasingingly so in the years after the war, as the foreign feature film flourished. In Venice it was a time when demand for housing outstripped supply and a time of general strikes, many emanating from Marghera, but also those at the Cotonoficio and the Murano glassworks.[127] Local problems of survival and working life were remote from the tourist, but Venice was in technicolour for the visitor. In the film *Summertime* – also known as *Summer Madness* – based on a popular Broadway play of 1952,[128] Jane Hudson, a spinster from Ohio, played famously by Katherine Hepburn, is destined for a brief affair touched with melancholy.[129] A romantic gardenia floating on a canal out of reach, Hepburn's famous fall into the canal outside the antique shop in the Campo Santa Barbara where she has purchased a goblet of Murano glass: these are omens of the brevity of this love (fig. 184).

De Rossi, a dapper married man, pursues brief affairs, as a matter of course one imagines, in a Venice overly supplied with eager visitors. A shoe, recently bought in a flurry of excitement for an evening out, sits on a balcony perilously close to the water; the departure by train brings the adulterous lover too late to deliver his present and the train steams out. An urchin selling stolen goods – a professional operator from an early age – shows the face of Venice turned charmingly, but rapaciously, upon the tourist. The American guests at the *pensione* are caricatures of the relentless tourist. Not the first of the tourist films, but the most successful in the 1950s and among the first to present the modern city in colour, *Summertime* shows Venice and its residents oriented towards short-term visitors. In this respect, it is not unlike Mann's *Death in Venice*.

Dino Risi's *Venezia: la luna e tu*, made in 1958, also follows the tourist. It is the tale of a Venetian gondolier affianced to a lively Venetian girl, but attracted flirtatiously to all and sundry.[130] Replete with prime sites from the first frames, the gondolier Bepi is irritatingly Latin, full of gestures and mobile faces, in pursuit of American girls, who are likewise in pursuit of the pure Latin spirit assumed to be rampant in spirited Venice. High in vitality, packed with tourist moments – moonlight serenades on the water, wedding ceremonies as local colour – the film in fact shows the vacuity of a Venice given over to tourism. In this it was prophetic.

Films about tourists and films for tourists created a veritable genre in the 1950s, pandering to the taste for holiday romance, local colour and sights both exotic and familiar. It was in these years that the tourist began the take-over of the city. Two essayistic guidebooks, both of which have had many impressions, spoke to the new British and American tourists. Instead of travelling with a Baedeker, the tourist now read Mary McCarthy and James Morris.

In 1957 Mary McCarthy published *The Stones of Florence* and *Venice Observed*, the latter characterised by a phenomenal range and ease in the face of Venetian history, a lack of sentimentality and an unassailable conviction that 'the tourist Venice is Venice'.[131] The serious 'stones' are taken from Ruskin and transferred to Florence, altogether a more rational and responsible state. McCarthy's Venice is stylish, acerbic and perfectly pitched for tourist amusement and short concentration; it seeks a reader who wants a little of everything, able to glide over a millennium or so, then move on to the next place. It abounds with dismissals. The Republic is released from too great a burden of history, for that history is seen to consist of 'childish and twice told tales'; it is declared that 'no stones are as trite as those of Venice' and that San Marco is but 'a robber's den'.[132] Venetian literature is dismissed: 'Outside of Goldoni, there are no Venetian writers of any consequence.'[133]

McCarthy's account of art is the predictable tourist view of the mid-twentieth century: no artists after Tiepolo; Titian working more out of Venice than in it; Tintoretto over-prolific, but the true native son. The authorities on which the views are based are those historians fashionable at mid-century – Burckhardt and Berenson, with a dash of Horatio Brown, and the Elizabethan English ambassador Sir Henry Wotton for anecdotal colour. Burckhardt's *The Civilisation of the Renaissance in Italy*, freshly reprinted in 1955, perpetrated the view that Florence was the rational state and the cradle of the Renaissance while Venice was a practical state with enviable stability, but little intellectual weight. McCarthy reproduces Burckhardt's nineteenth-century view of the retardation of the

184   David Lean, *Summertime*, 1955. Film still. Lopert Film Productions, New York.

Renaissance in Venice exactly: and other opinions – for example, about the too-sharp tongue of Aretino, appropriately resident in Venice.[134]

In 1960 James Morris published a similar essay, called *Venice*, with the disclaimer that it was not a history book or a guidebook, 'not exactly a report . . . it was a highly subjective, romantic impressionistic picture less of a city than of an experience'.[135] More wide-ranging and quieter than McCarthy, Morris acknowledges art after the Renaissance (the Baroque is present) and history after the Republic. Early on he registers the melancholy of the Venetians who remain islanders, 'still a people apart, still tinged with the sadness of refugees'.[136] The recognition of Venice's amphibian status comes early; it is 'somewhere between freak and fairytale'.[137] It appears to follow that Venice is an outsider state, 'never loved', as if states make a habit of loving others.

Like Murray before him, many things are explained by comparison with the home country, Britain. Gondoliers are 'like undergraduates punting on the Cherwell', Doge Enrico Dandolo, 'stumps through the chronicles like a Venetian Churchill', and: 'Modern Venice is rich in conscientious craftsmen, people of strong and loyal simplicity, such as one imagines in the sea-ports of early Victorian England.'[138] And the English, apparently, were responsible for Venice's 'Romantic cult'.[139]

McCarthy and Morris give a new lease of life to the anecdotal and the trivial, finding any depth of history too devious. Both tell of blonde Venetian women bleaching their hair on the *altane*, gossipy and curious, keeping a close eye on the foreigners. Love of luxury comes from Byzantium, and so debauchery and licentiousness are ingrained in the historical Venetian character. 'Harlots and hedonists'; at least there is pleasure in the alliteration.[140]

Counting the lions and the churches, both writers subscribe wholeheartly to the view of the Republic's decline from the time of the League of Cambrai, then consummated – or finalised – by the advent of Napoleon. For Morris eighteenth-century Venice is nothing less than 'a paradigm of degradation'.[141] Both writers, in advance of many a film script, are fascinated by water-borne funerals, and Morris anticipates the prospect of a submerged Venice having a symmetry born of the waters, and returned to them. Modern Venetians are conditioned by a 'grisly heritage'.[142] In anticipation of many a film score, Morris writes of the sounds – echoing footsteps, ringing bells, water traffic; and of the winter, when 'all is dank, swirling, desolate'.[143] Throughout, the tourist city remains accommodating to its one million visitors (the statistic in the 1950s), treating them with 'unctuous sycophancy'.[144]

Nevertheless, the slower journey through Venice was still possible, following Lorenzetti and the new 'traditional' guides. Hugh Honour, erudite, urbane, companionable, takes the Moschini route, forming tours for a single morning or afternoon, or those needing an entire day.[145] The history of the Republic lives through its buildings and their decorations – in a Palladian morning, an excursion to the Lombard and Renaissance sculpture – at Santa Maria Miracoli, that church returned to the twentieth-century – to the Rialto market, to the Ca' Pesaro modern collection where Hayez, Favretto and Ciardi find rare commendation. Canova – 'the last of the great Venetians, he was the first of the international artists of the nineteenth century' – is as firmly in the Museo Correr as is Tintoretto in the Palazzo Ducale. In the Sala del Maggior Consiglio, Manin's last acts, closing the Republic, are recalled.[146]

VISCONTI'S *SENSO*

It is not surprising that the tourist is the star of so many of the films of the 1950s, that the visitor monopolises cinematic action. However, away from Hollywood the most equivocal – and powerful – face of Venice appears in Luigi Visconti's two films – *Senso* of 1954 and *Death in Venice* of 1973. No less powerful for being a retrospective and historical scrutiny of the city, *Senso* was at odds with the tourist film of the 1950s. Precisely because it shunned the comedy and bonhomie of such entertainments, *Senso* was the most significant evocation of Venice in its decade. In common with the other films, the very setting facilitates liaisons.

Senso was not Visconti's first essay in a film with a Venetian background. From quite early in his film-making career, in the mid-1940s, he had been interested in the early twentieth-century Russian countess, Maria Tarnowska, tried in Venice in 1910 for inciting a lover to murder her husband.[147] The clash of loyalties, the aristocratic presence and the milieu of Venice: these interests must have passed to *Senso*.

Boito's novella as the source of Visconti's film has been played down, but the film rings true to Boito's deeply ambivalent portraits of the city. Visconti might well have been imbued with Boito's insistent theme of Venetian entrapment, not just in *Senso*, but also in Boito's contemporary story *Il Collare di Buddha* (Buddha's Collar).[148] Venice hosts destructive and sordid affairs in both Boito's stories.

The first part of Visconti's *Senso* inhabits a historical Venice set in the troubled times of the Risorgimento. It opens with the historic clash in 1866 between Italians and Austrians at La Fenice during a performance of Verdi's *Il Trovatore*, and continues, as many have observed, in operatic vein. The reconstruction of the last moments of Austrian rule in Venice in the post-Fascist climate of the 1950s is significant, implicating the film in a reassessment of nationalism. Its reception showed it to be profoundly unsettling in the Italy of its time. The Italian censor and critics were not slow to recognise that Visconti was at work on a historical parable which made reference to the Resistance movements of 1943 to 1947 through its focus on the betrayals of the Risorgimento in the 1860s.[149]

The filmed city in *Senso* displays its eroticism of water and liquid shadows, its intense colour and its clandestine opportunities. Bodies may be discovered by the side of a canal. A well-head in the closely settled Ghetto is the place for a dawn kiss. As Angela dalle Vacche has put it in her study of Italian cinema:

> In *Senso*, the city of Venice becomes a character who witnesses the degradation of pure love into an erotic liaison. The reverberations of the water in the canals tell us that adultery, rather than romance is taking place in the putrid alleys . . . Venice is not just a silent accomplice, but also a condemning judge. In the ghetto, series of dark windows underline the theatricality of the affair. Like huge eyes, the windows subject private feelings to public scrutiny. This turning of passions into spectacle begins to increase our awareness, in a theatrical city like Venice, that what we consider private is always public, that the body erotic is a construct as social as the body politic.[150]

The style and the location make their own disclosure, for Visconti surely wants to expose the irrelevance of the mask that is so often associated with Venice. It is not a question of dramatising gestures in an operatic nineteenth-century manner: rather these histrionic characters *are* the roles they play. The countess and her love do not assume other roles; they *are* operatic, self-dramatising and so on: there is no other face, no hidden depths or other motives. The viewer sees that the mask *is* the character, and thus the customary fixation on Venice as what it is not is mimicked by the human actor. The relevance of Visconti's disclosure was made evident in the reaction to the film when it was shown at the Venice film Biennale, provoking charges that the character of Livia was scandalous and 'an insult to Venetian women'.[151]

Not for the first time, or the last, Venice is a seducer, and a trap. Visconti does not lay the charges directly, although they are compounded by his later *Death in Venice*. His central characters – whether Livia the 'wanton countess', or Aschenbach in *Death in Venice* – are both gullible and self-circumscribed: the city of Venice is a pertinent and seemingly inevitable backdrop to their foibles – to Lydia's betrayal in *Senso* and, in the case of Aschenbach, his death. Venice serves to bring its visitors to their full and vulnerable term.

Visconti's interest in 'decadence' as a moral concern is frankly expressed, clear evidence of a cultural continuity with Boito's time, and that of Thomas Mann in the generation following. As Visconti himself expressed it: 'I have a very high opinion of this decadence, as Thomas Mann had for example. I have drunk of his spirit: Mann was a decadent of the German culture; I of Italian formation. What has always interested me is the analysis of a sick society.'[152] Not only the characters are in a state fallen from grace and integrity, Venice itself is continuously targeted as a metaphorical expression of the Fall.

French Bad Faith: Jean-Paul Sartre

The French did not lose their fascination with Venice, although the Serenissima served increasingly as a testament to Bad Faith. Sartre was in Venice in 1951, making another visit to the city that served to dramatise the existentialist dilemma of doing or not-doing. He was a regular visitor to Italy, and in contact with members of the Communist Party in Rome.[153] His Venetian diagnosis was drafted in a novel never completed: *La Reine Albemarle ou le dernier touriste*, published in part in 1952.[154] Another section became 'Venice from My Window', published in 1957, invoking a Venice that is a massive presence, a heavy weight, a fine plumage painted on glass, but repellent to the viewer.[155]

Sartre made preliminary stops at Capri and Rome, but it is only Venice that has a sustained treatment in the remnant text. Marked by existentialist perversion, Sartre's self-tourist is an anti-tourist, borne in a gondola, experiencing the familiar impasse that the city conditions, floating on water that disorientates, cancelling reality. Sartre's unease is not too distant from Simmel's recalcitrant Venice, made increasingly anxious as the spirit, 'Being', becomes unanchored.[156]

At the centre of the Sartrean experience is *la nozione negative*, borne of the water experienced by the *flâneur* who is gondola-borne. Venice sets up a refraction that prompts personal analysis, testing the psyche and its orientation in the external world. It is late autumn, and dreary, in the off-season of 1951. The water is grey under a grey sky, the Piazza is deserted. With the literary precedents of Barrès and Mann in mind, Venice can be re-declared dead. The water has properties different to conventional water: it is not water, 'it is a hundred things at a time': a pustulous beast, a poisonous plant, a glass surface, disorder enclosed in order; it is the sweet slipping, the coming-into-Being between the cliffs of Being. Couched in negatives, water reflects the viewer-author. As a mobile element, it signifies a dangerous slippage of Being. Its reflective properties are narcissistic because self-returning, prompting the inevitable Sartrean discourse on Being in terms of desiring or repudiating. Sartre is in the grip of a dangerous castrating city; he sees it as effeminate; the powerful feminine power of the élite has castrated the doges, 'the roseate *tarantala* of the Adriatic has devoured the masculine'.[157]

Sartre, male student of Freud, is necessarily wary in the face of the oceanic feeling that Venice compels. Its disorder, its perpetual agitation make of it a 'no-man's-land' (Sartre's literal words), a neutral zone beyond responsibility. The water is a sorcerer, a contrary spirit; the sides of canals are separated, representing a state of Other, *l'autre*. Nor is the historical dimension lost as Sartre grapples with the water, which is seen as defence against ancient Rome and its anarchy; it reflects the decomposition of the Roman world and separates itself from it. A voyage to Torcello returns the water to barbaric times, to the early centuries of the Republic. More important than any defence from the Huns, difference is staked against Rome; the Venice of the water is a defence against the earth.[158]

Sartre's study of Tintoretto published in 1957, *Le Séquestre de Venise*, known in English as *The Prisoner of Venice* or *The Venetian Pariah* – is the most sustained work that Sartre actually published on Venice.[159] Fiercely anti-bourgeois, Tintoretto is taken to be the most characteristic and devoted of Venice's native sons, but one spurned by his city, which preferred to lavish attention and honour on Titian.[160] Tintoretto is a rebel, and 'the Doge's city reveals her contempt for the most celebrated of her sons'. A prophetic figure, Tintoretto is no less tragic in that he exists in an age of aristocracy that courts Titian as the painter of princes and can bestow little merit upon a member of the artisan class. Tintoretto is ejected from Titian's studio at the age of twelve; he becomes 'a blacklisted child' in a parable of rejection at a crisis point in Venetian history. Venice remains silent, and hypocritical. Tintoretto is frustrated, although never to the point of impotence:

> Left to himself, he would have covered every wall in the city with his paintings, no campo would have been too vast, no sotto portico too obscure for him to illuminate. He would have covered the ceilings, people would have walked across his most beautiful images, his brush would have spared neither the facades of the palaces nor the gondolas, or perhaps the gondoliers.[161]

Sartre insists on the fact that Tintoretto is of Venice, born there as Titian of Cadore was not. Tintoretto's art bears the imprint of his city.

In Sartre's interpretation, the decline of Venice is already predicted through Tintoretto; he carries the sour smell of the Republic's demise, reconstituted again in the decaying fabric of the 1950s as Sartre felt it. The true son of Venice has to bear the odour of rot, compelled by class – for he stands apart from the patricians at their festivals, from the 'charity' of the bourgeois, and the 'docility' of the people.[162] The Venice that Sartre has observed in his own visits is projected back to the time of Tintoretto: 'Pink houses with flooded cellars and walls criss-crossed with rats? . . . What odour is given off by stagnant canals with their urinous crosses and by grey mussels fastened with squalid cement to the underside of quays?[163]

Sartre's Venice is dead. Yet again it is the literary man's Venice, shaped by Barrès and Mann.[164] The morbidity and dankness of the city is pre-determined. Yielding to the certainties of tourism, some of the observations in 'Venice from my Window' do not move beyond the platitudinous – 'Venice is above all Venice'. But most importantly it is argued that the Venetians have disappeared; the tourists are now of such numbers it is impossible to register the indigenous residents; yet Sartre made this observation when the local population was at a high point, before the dramatic decline later in the century.[165] At the time when Visconti was filming *Senso*, Sartre registered the city's mid-century attraction and revulsion. It is at one and the same time the sweetest and the most perfidious, set in its water which embodies *la nozione negativa*.[166] In effect, the city undermines even the most narcissistic of visitors, outwits him with its own excessive narcissism, its reflecting nature that turns everything into a mirage.

Psycho-Geography

The foreigner in Venice was the token character of the 1950s, at the centre of many a scenario. Thus Situationist Ralph Rumney, 'sole member of the London psycho-geographical association', visited with his camera in 1957 in order to trace the zones of main psycho-geographical interest.[167] A trail is set up: this is an obsessive activity in modern Venice. A photo-essay scrapbook records the findings in the format of a continuous photo strip of black and white photographs with typed captions (fig. 185).[168] The city yields up its 'emotional zones', which are based on generalised collective views of areas such as the Arsenale, characterised as 'sinister', and the 'Gheto Vechio' [sic], 'beautiful' in its ambience. We trace the flight of 'A', at first 'depressing' in the area of the Arsenale, associated with the city's past glory, emanating a destruc-

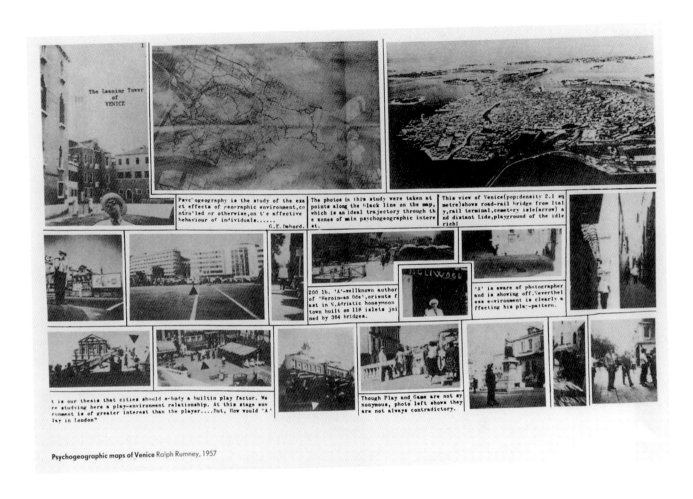

The Leaning Tower of VENICE

Psycogeography is the study of the exact effects of geographic environment, controlled or otherwise, on t'e affective behaviour of individuals......
G.E. Debord.

The photos in this study were taken at points along the black line on the map, which is an ideal trajectory through the zones of main psychogeographic interest.

This view of Venice(pop:density 2.1 sq metre)shows road-rail bridge from Italy,rail terminal,cemetery isle(arrow) and distant Lido,playground of the idle rich!

200 lb. 'A'-wellknown author of 'Heroin-an Ode',orients fast in N.Adriatic honeymoon town built on 118 islets joined by 364 bridges.

'A' is aware of photographer and is showing off.Nevertheless environment is clearly affecting his play-pattern.

t is our thesis that cities should embody a builtin play factor. We re studying here a play-environment relationship. At this stage environment is of greater interest than the player....But, How would 'A' lay in london?

Though Play and Game are not synonymous, photo left shows they are not always contradictory.

Psychogeographic maps of Venice Ralph Rumney, 1957

185 Ralph Rumney, psychogeographic map of Venice, 1957.

tive power capable of blotching the photographs; then we go by gondola to the island cemetery. In the first instance, a 'play factor' is set in place: 'A' plays for the camera; he climbs on to the back of a sculpted lion at the Arsenale gate; he notices the children playing in certain *campi* and they influence *his* play patterns. The old Ghetto, reached by ornamental Austrian iron bridges, is marked as the true centre of the city. The amateur camera records sharp angles, disappearing human backs inexpertly framed, and bridges that signify crossing. On the opposite island (crossing the Grand Canal in a *traghetto*), there are new opportunities to register Venetian pathology; re-crossing to the main island involves a steep descent down the Rialto bridgeway, which is 'a final unexplained sinister exercise'.[169]

In the Situationist register of the 'Sinister' and the 'Playful' we hear the echo of the French Surrealists journeying obsessively in their native Paris in the 1920s, creating their itineraries of *détournement*. There is no marked Surrealist presence in Venice, and it is a missing dimension, an absence not filled by the detective story or the murder chase. We miss the eroticism of Venice that might have been reignited by the Surrealists, anticipated in Apollinaire's dedicated reading of Venetian erotic literature and Baffo. We miss André Breton in Venice, although a disciple has insisted on his imaginary presence.[170] In 1932, in *Les Vases Communicants*, Breton evoked a distant isle which leads us, says Alain-Pierre Pillet who is looking for the Surrealists, to Venice, quoting Kafka's belief that Venice is 'the axe that breaks up the frozen sea in me'.[171] Pillet would like to transfer Breton's experience of Paris to Venice, to a city where one does not walk, but one is walked by a mysterious power . . . He would like to create a Venice beyond the closed centre of Paris, to include aquatic streets in anticipation of the architectural collages of Max Ernst. He sent out questionnaires desperately asking of the original Surrealists if Breton had ever mentioned Venice, and he learns of 'Marina', a painter who met Breton in 1946 in New York. She feels able to speak on Breton's behalf of Venice as *surrealiste*, as exaggerating nature in the indispensable condition that makes an artwork, of Venice as the tower of Babel, fusing the Orient and the Occident.[172] And Casanova's excesses, for he is 'surréaliste dans le libertinage'.[173]

The dedicated Alain-Pierre Pillet might well have looked to Raymond Roussel in the 1890s as he was a proto-Surrealist who actually knew Venice. But Roussel desired to forget it and created instead an independent topographical system that concealed the deep personal feeling he experienced there.[174] His need to do this was the result of psychological pressure. Visiting Venice in 1895 he met Ascanio, a sixteen-year-old boy who died soon after. As a consequence, Roussel suppressed the name of Venice in all later writings, but the city was invoked hermetically as the lost place of the beloved in all his subsequent geographies. Venice, always visited, is always present; it reconstitutes an *arcane* presence *in perpetuum*.

The Sounds of San Marco: Michel Butor and Stravinsky

Michel Butor came to Venice along the French path, in the footsteps of Proust and Ruskin, publishing in 1963 a *Description de San Marco*, in which San Marco is unveiled according to Fulcinelli's alchemical reading of cathedrals.[175] At the same time the building at the heart of Venice is recognised in its contemporary reality at the centre of the tourist trade – banal utterances, directions, explanations, comments on the pigeons, orders for coffee and Campari are slid between descriptions of the Basilica – comments in all languages, spoken within the direct vicinity of the theological programme expressed in the mosaics of San Marco to teach the people of all nations through word and image. Thus Butor makes his poetic excursion around the Basilica to the sound of the babble of tourist voices that cut through declarations of the city's divine origin, the centrality of the metaphor of water and (within San Marco) the concordances from the Old and New Testaments in the mosaics, which flow from a primary source in the waters of Paradise.[176]

Butor's prose poem also responds to Stravinsky and the musical dynamism of his Venetian-inspired music, which in turn is responsive to the acoustic complexity of San Marco and its tradition of multi-voiced choral works. In particular, Butor responds to Stravinsky's 1956 *Canticum sacrum ad honorem Sancti Marci Nominis*, which has been called 'a dark magnificent tribute to one of the most haunting churches in Christendom'.[177] Stravinsky's commission came from Alessandro Piovesan on behalf of the International Festival of Contemporary Music and was first performed in San Marco, with Stravinsky conducting, on 13 September 1956. Stravinsky had been a frequent visitor to Venice, bonded to it through the death in 1929 of his collaborator and friend Serge Diaghilev. He had frequently conducted works there in the contemporary festivals and premiered *The Rake's Progress* in 1951. The senior Venetian musician, Malipiero, had published a monograph on Stravinsky in 1945, the result of protracted meetings during international festivals and visits to Asolo during the 1930s.[178] As a young man Malipiero had heard that decisive performance of *The Rite of Spring* in Paris in 1913.[179]

It is immediately apparent that the structure of Stravinsky's *Canticum* is in five parts, which echo the five domes of San Marco, giving prominence to the central one, and that Stravinsky had considered the antiphonal principles of the church's historic music. As Robert Craft (Stravinsky's most devoted commentator) put it, 'he followed previous composers in the general method of sustaining rapid movement and then stopping it periodically in order to allow the sound to clear'.[180] Butor took up the architectural analogies and embellished Stravinsky's lineage within the musical tradition from the Gabrieli, Alessandro Raverri, Ludovico Grossi Viadana and Claudio

Monteverdi.[181] The inscriptions of the church are recorded, in line with the Babel-like nature given to tongues in both sacred and profane Venice, and in accordance with the theological virtues that are given voice (as the church inscribes the words of the virtues on its walls and arches), and the ultimate injunction to 'Go Forth and Preach'.

The elevated incantation of Stravinsky's music rises above the tourist voices, in a short space of time shifting in pace and texture in a constantly changing counterpoint of texts and sounds. Five parts echo the Basilica's five cupolas with the initial dedication: 'To the City of Venice in praise of its patron saint, the blessed Mark Apostle.' From above the choir celebratory notes sound from the trombone then the tenor sings poetic lines worked from the Song of Solomon, giving his invitation to the beloved to enter the garden that will be served by winds from both north and south. A flute in pastoral mode circles round the voice in what has been called 'perhaps the purest piece of lyric Stravinsky has written'.[182] In the central movement the Christian virtues are celebrated as the choir, preceded by the organ, sings of charity, hope and faith; the choirs divide and offer their different voices in the contrasting blocks of sound that were characteristic of the music of San Marco. Robert Craft has called this movement 'a cantata within a cantata'.[183] Trumpets again punctuate the human sound of the choir; in the song of Faith an oboe sounds; the word 'believe' (*credidi*) sounds out, together with dissonant trumpets. Then silence. The father of the deaf child takes up the challenge to believe and cries for acceptance: *credere* again emphasises belief, as the trumpets splutter almost jazz-like together with plucked notes from a double bass, a viola sounding and a falling Amen.

The many threads gathered up in Butor's 'description' return to a rich tradition, at odds with the demonstrations of bad faith in Sartre and *Senso*, and the trivialities of tourism in film. Stravinsky's association with Venice – consummated with his burial there in 1971 – re-confirmed the musical status of Venice.

The poet Peter Porter followed the funeral cortège in words as it left the church of Santi Giovanni e Paolo beside the equestrian monument to Colleoni, and was rowed to the cemetery of San Michele. In each death in Venice, the city's death is rehearsed:

> From Colleoni's shadow
> in a final purple,
> out of the grinner's black,
> an old man in a box
> is carried to a gondola
> and warped to the Isle
> of the Dead: the cypress dark
> must come to everyone
> or the refining fire.
> This is the death of Europe,
> this is the eclipse –
> an oar rises on the lagoon.[184]

The English Aesthetic: Adrian Stokes

Adrian Stokes exempted himself from the Bad Faith of the post-war years by virtue of inheriting the aesthetic tradition, still attentive to Walter Pater's musical inflections from the *fin de siècle*. Without struggle he could find 'the inner' expressed in Venice 'in terms of the outer'.[185] Stokes found an undefiled, still aesthetic Venice unaffected by contemporary politics. He was able to enter innocently, in a benign spirit of unchallenged conservatism, to admire the past, however outmoded such visits may have been in a period when it was becoming more customary to see cracks and sinking foundations. While he acknowledged a debt to Ezra Pound – both extolled Santa Maria dei Miracoli – it was Pound's lyricism, not his obsession with the economic malaise of the West, and Venice, that Stokes followed.[186]

In 'Venice: An Aspect of Art', written just before the end of the Second World War, the narrator floats along the canals observing 'sheerness and height' and 'blackness and whiteness' as principal characteristics of the architecture.[187] What is of interest (and it constitutes Stokes's individuality in the face of the city) is that it is *Renaissance* Venice that evokes his response, a Venice still in a time-warp, but it has moved onwards from Ruskin's Gothic. Venice-as-landscape is the response again, but in heightened form: buildings change into 'rock and cave' in answer to the English desire to weld place to parentage and to experience the city as feminine. For Stokes Venice 'is a potent symbol of the mother'; 'as we ride the canals we move within her circulation'; her architecture is experienced as 'precious apertures'.[188] Ruskin would have understood, even if he despised the Renaissance, and W. H. Auden for whom Venice was 'a city built by strong and passionate men in the image of their Mother'.[189]

Sartre and Stokes embody opposite positions with relation to the fluidity of Venice, the one wary of the wash of water, the other enchanted. In so far as cities can be gendered, then Venice is, by weight of history and association, female, giving rise to those qualities that Klaus Theweleit elicited in *Male Fantasies* – fluidity, malleability, close proximity to the unconscious, 'a life of emotion rather than intellect', in short, the dangerous state of the oceanic that Freud had described.[190]

It is hard to say for whom the reality principal is most in evidence: for those who would find an amniotic amnesia in the circulatory system of Mother Venice, or those who sense the imminence of death, and the urgent need to adjust to parental absence. Despite the self-projections in the name of psycho-analytic writing, no one could deny Stokes his insights, nor his felicitous project, which reconstitutes the Renaissance after nineteenth-century Gothic. Santa Maria dei Miracoli, curved on one side directly along the water, becomes 'the grandest of Venetian vessels'.[191] Its marble on the landed side is distant, yet it is as familiar as the paved street in which it is set: in this apparently simple observation is a view of Venetian paving in simultaneous harmony and in contrast with the architecture. Observing the paving underfoot (so admired by Nietzsche), we rediscover 'the immense toil of Venice' and its recovery (via Molmenti, an acknowledged source for Stokes) of Venetian *mud*, and the unpaved city where horses were once used.[192] The paving carries not only a poetical weight, but also an allegorical burden; it reveals a city ready for the incoming Renaissance.

Mapping the Old City: Domestic Venice

Contemporary needs were distant from the aesthetic brief that Stokes brought to Venice. In the first years of the war the city continued to wrestle with the Miozzi plan and the implementation of urgent housing. Duilio Torres was involved with designs for a complex for Sacca Fisola, the artificial island to the west of the Giudecca, but the crisis of Fascism and the German occupation terminated progress in state housing.[193]

In the post-war years 'the immense toil' that had made Venice was the subject of close urban studies. As ever, Venice strained after the modern but remained ambivalent, even fearful. This is particularly so in the commitment to contemporary architecture. The tragedy of the immediate post-war period was that the little that was actually built was disastrous. Venice still challenged the imagination of architects and they responded knowingly to the impositions of the past, the physical opportunities for siting on water, the social challenges, the urgent need for modern housing, but generally the designs remain on paper.

The historical fabric was discretely maintained over these years. The leading architect of the 1930s, Ferdinando Forlato, used reinforced cement and iron underpinnings to secure precious façades such as the Ca' d'Oro.[194] A new phase of historical cleansing took hold as buildings were divested of accretions and over-painting and returned to their presumed original state. A reaction against the interventions of the nineteenth century and the false historicist base of the nineteenth-century Gothic revival prompted much of this cleansing: for example Meduna's 1869 restorations in the Madonna del'Orto were removed, and painted decorations on columns were lifted to reveal decorations dating from 1399.[195]

In the 1950s the most conspicuous restoration project occurred on the island of San Giorgio Maggiore in the convent buildings, which had suffered abuse since the Napoleonic period when they were barracks for troops.[196] Appointed as principal restorer, Forlato removed nineteenth-century restorations in a process of 'liberation'. The cupola of the church of San Giorgio Maggiore was reinforced externally, as was the campanile. As a result of a great act of generosity, in one of the most important redeployments in the history of modern Venice, the monastic complex became the seat of the Fondazione Giorgio Cini, developed by Vittorio Cini as a memorial to his son, Giorgio, killed in an aircrash.[197] The Centre, dedicated to all aspects of Venetian culture, opened a new phase of international study and publication, through conferences and exhibitions. On the south side of the island, an outdoor amphitheatre, the Teatro Verde, was built by Angelo Scatollin.[198] Across the water on the adjacent Giudecca, the Albergo Cipriano, the new enterprise of Giuseppe Cipriani of Harry's Bar, was built by architects Brenno Del Guidice and Marino Meo, and became the new jewel in the CIGA crown of luxury hotels after its opening in 1958.[199]

A systematic investigation of historic *Venezia minore* occurred in the post-war years. A new phase in the description and analysis of the city had been inaugurated in 1926 with the publication of Giulio Lorenzetti's guide, *Venice and its Lagoon: Historical-Artistic Guide*.[200] It remained unsurpassed in the twentieth century as the most detailed guide to the fabric of the city, paying unusual attention to the simple house as well as the palace.

Lorenzetti's guide is midway between the itineraries developed for speed and comprehension in the previous century, and earlier guide formats attentive to areas (and *sestiere*) demanding more time. There are no asterisks to hurry the viewer to highlighted sites, although the 'key site approach' is evident from the book's First Itinerary, which is devoted to the centre of the city, the Piazza San Marco and its monuments. Its difference lies in the detailing and the tracking of lesser-known routes. Lorenzetti was a pioneer by virtue of the attention he paid to ordinary domestic architecture, to *Venezia minore*, cultivated by the exponents of *Venise rouge* in the last decades of the nineteenth century, but not previously the subject of close architectural study.

Take, as an example, Lorenzetti's presentation of the Campo di Santa Maria Mater Domini: 'a characteristic campo with old Venetian buildings', which are precisely and individually detailed:

> To l. no. 2174 XII cent. Houses of the Zane: three mullioned window with paterae and crosses, Venetian-byzantine style, XIII cent; opposite, no. 2179, Casa Barbaro with pointed-arch windows (XIV cent.), in the interior, courtyard with open-air staircase and fragments of sculpture, partly modern imitations – in the background no. 2123 Palazzetto Viario later Zane . . .[201]

Among the first ventures in post-war architectural writing was the 1947 publication *Venezia minore* by Egle Renata Trincanato. It stands at the beginning of a distinguished series of architectural studies produced in Venice.[202] Given the interest in *ambiente* and the preservation of tracts of the old city, such a study was a long time coming. The delay reflects the overriding fame of the major buildings and the concentration on churches and palaces. As pre-war exercises in urban planning were reactivated, there was an increasing need for fully inclusive studies.

Because of the modular nature of much domestic architecture, and its concentration and irregularities within available spaces, it was necessary to respond to buildings as contiguous and as specific responses to their sites.[203] Trincanato preserved a predominantly chronological approach, using characteristic examples from the medieval period onwards. The process of studying change and building superimposition could be revealing only if no one period was privileged: the method was one unlikely to have existed before the pluralism of the modern period. Such an emphasis was of fundamental importance for the urban description of Venice, its growth and change.

Trincanato's study followed the evolution of the first inner island settlement around the Rialto and the extreme points of Castello and Cannaregio after the exodus from Torcello, Malamocco and other settlements in the outer lagoon. The structure of continuous housing was analysed in its interdependent relationship with the arteries of canal and *calli*, and with the campo, the major open space in the configuration of joined houses. The physical configuration of land and water was shown to be fundamental to the evolutionary process. This was not a new observation: the appreciation of the campo as a breathing space had been emphasised by Camillo Sitte, although he was mainly interested in the Piazza San Marco. The minor *campi* were now of interest. Trincanato used line drawings as well as photographs to illustrate the study, showing not only façades, but plans of ground and upper floors. Of special interest is the insertion of a page of sketches by Le Corbusier suggesting his considerable influence on the perception of Venice as a human-scaled city.[204]

The examination of specific areas and the typologies developed from such studies have been a primary focus for academic study from the 1950s onwards, increasing the prestige of the Architectural Institute of the University of Venice. Saverio Muratori, appointed to the Institute in 1950, made a notable contribution to an 'operative' urban history focused on Venice (and later Rome). His *Studi per un operante storia urbana di Venezia* was published in 1960.[205] Both Lorenzetti and Trincanato suggest themselves as powerful influences for Muratori's student projects, which ran from 1954 until the later 1950s.

The remnants of domestic architecture constructed around the tenth century were Muratori's particular focus in the Campo di Santa Maria Mater Domini, which was chosen because it was 'a limited complex and relatively autonomous', yielding an understanding of types of building and local character, as well as the *difficulties* facing building projects. Investigation of the areas around San Giovanni Grisostomo and Calle di San Leo led to general observations on the appearance of the city in the tenth century.[206] The transition from Medieval-Byzantine to Gothic was presented not only in terms of continuity, but also of change, through the insertion of new elements.[207]

Manfredo Tafuri, Professor of Architectural History in the Architectural Institute of the University of Venice, noted of Muratori's contribution to urban studies:

> Urban analysis, as it has developed in Italy from the 1960s to the present, is undoubtedly indebted to Muratori's studies of Venice and Rome. These studies, moreover, have down played the interest in the *structure* of ancient fabrics, making the debate on 'existing conditions' anachronistic and lending a different dimension to the theme of historical centres.[208]

The method could be described as archaeological, exposing change and designating shifts in a building fabric over time. The focus on historical shift had clear lessons for the Venice of its time, which too often heard recommendations that that fabric was trapped in the past. The layers were now uncovered.

*   *   *

Urban Planning: Giuseppe Samonà and 'The School of Venice'

In the post-war years, the Architectural Institute became a major agent for change and, in its field, the most convincing example of intellectual leadership in Venice.[209] Giuseppe Samonà was responsible for the initial vitalisation. Born in Palermo, he came to Venice from Naples in 1936 and taught until 1973, making notable contributions to urban theory and practice from the 1950s. Bruno Zevi compared Venice in the years of Samonà's directorship, between 1948 and 1963, to the Bauhaus in Weimar and Dessau from 1919 to 1928.[210]

Samonà's importance was endorsed by his colleague Luciano Semerani:

> In 1936 a barbarian came to Venice. He was Giuseppe Samonà: an engineer, a Sicilian aristocrat, a provincial. In the long period of transition commonly known as the Decline of the Roman Empire, the barbarians were the only ones who could maintain security and keep power in their hands. Samonà became emperor. Slowly, but tenaciously and intelligently, he destroyed the legacy of Venice's Accademia delle Belle Arti . . .[211]

During the 1950s and 1960s the post-war agenda was set for the discussion of urban planning; these were also important training years at the Institute, and Samonà attracted distinguished non-Venetians to his faculty.[212] Franco Albini, from Milan, taught from 1955 to 1964 and directed the Institute from 1972 to 1974. Carlo Aymonino, Roman-born, was in Venice from 1964, and director from 1974 to 1979. Aldo Rossi, among the most famous of contemporary Italian architects, came from Milan in 1975. Valeriano Pastor, born in Trieste, graduated from the IVAV in 1955 and became director in 1979. Luciano Semerani, also from Trieste, became Professor of Topography and Street Construction in 1969. Trained in Milan, Vittorio Gregotti arrived in 1978, becoming one of the most influential figures in Italian architecture when he assumed the directorship of the architectural journal *Casabella* in 1982. Over the years *Casabella* has paid Venice considerable attention.[213] Manfredo Tafuri, one of the century's foremost architectural historians, came from Rome to be Professor of Architectural History in 1968.

The quest for a methodology was the preoccupation of the immediate post-war years, and here Muratori's typological studies of the 1950s were valuable in exposing the process of organic growth in historical areas. Muratori's project was a historical application of Samonà's contemporary practice. Typological analysis has subsequently been fundamental to the procedures of the School of Venice, perhaps obsessively so, but it was a methodology that sought to avoid the cul-de-sac of an over-privileged past opposed to intrusions or adaptations. It was recognised that analysis of architecture in Venice must be concerned with *re-founding*: Luciano Semerani explained that 'city, territory, type and figuration are the figures of the re-founding of architecture' and that re-founding takes account of the 'ashes' of the founder, but does not imitate them.[214] Samonà took the themes of city and territory, and type and figuration, as co-existent pairs, which had the effect of bringing the greater area of territory (and urban planning) to the forefront of practice and teaching.

His colleague Vittorio Gregotti credited Samonà with opening the Venice School to the protagonists of the modern movement in Italy while making understood the inseparable nature of urbanism and architecture.[215] The contact with 'modern masters' was crucial: in 1951, in a ceremony long remembered, Frank Lloyd Wright received an honorary degree in the Palazzo Ducale (he purchased a number of Scarpa's glass pieces at the time).[216] Under Samonà's aegis, the first session of CIAM, Centre International d'Architecture Moderne, was held in 1952 in the presence of Le Corbusier, who delivered his address *Apropos de Venise*.[217]

A milestone in the Institute's projects occurred in 1955 when Samonà published an analysis of the new Piano Regolatore in the prestigious journal *Urbanistica*.[218] Samonà noted that Venice's circumscribed form had curtailed the urban spread characteristic of other cities, and that modern construction had been comparatively limited. Some changes had taken place on the periphery with infill and other means, but these had been at the expense of attention to the centre. Congestion on the Grand Canal demonstrated the need to divert motor traffic away from it: Samonà considered the canal to be animated only in areas where there were no bridge crossings; it was more important for contemplation than for circulation. He recommended a policy that considered more than aesthetics, that recognised the reality of life on the periphery and the need for adequate transport. The area of the Piazzale Roma at the termination of the road bridge (to which Torres had already drawn attention) needed rationalisation and the removal of some functions to Marghera. Redeployment was recommended: the salt warehouses along the Zattere were an example. Such a Piano Regolatore would further aestheticise the city by resiting commercial interests elsewhere and restoring 'contemplation' in the centre. He called for urgent examination of *every* zone of the city, including Greater Venice, and Marghera and Mestre in particular.[219] Samonà anticipated many of the directives and concerns that were to be constant in urban discussion up to the 1990s.

Samonà had considerable sympathy for Marghera and Mestre, which had been urbanised in an abnormal way, artificially, and without apparent logical order. Marghera was seen as 'a perfect installation', a view that would *not* survive the 1950s.[220] Historic Venice had expelled industry, consequently it had become élitist, but impotent: stabilising Mestre could only benefit it. In order to encourage planned development away from Venice, Samonà insisted on the need for appropriate transport, particularly in the area of Piazzale Roma. He proposed an underwater tunnel to run from that area to the Fondamenta Nuove and the islands of Sant'Erasmo and Certosa, which would have a floating bridge to Cavallina. The old fantasy of bridges linking islands was revived in an endeavour, again prophetic, to move the concentration of mainland traffic away from the 'gangrenous' Piazzale Roma.

Samonà stressed the urban context rather than the single building in a method that was seen to focus on 'institutions and the struggle of class' according to one of his students. That approach is evident in his 1949 *L'Urbanistica e l'avvenire della città*.[221] The faculty has continued to interrogate the highly endowed Venetian past and the inheritance of an urban cul-de-sac: what can be done? Built architecture must be compelled to de-materialise; a heterodoxy dissolving the traditional linguistics of architecture must take its place.

Samonà's study of urbanism and the future of the city extended far beyond Venice. Manfredo Tafuri recognised the importance of this structural reading, noting that it favoured 'a historical reading stretched into space and time'.[222] The implication of such a position for Venice is that 'every part of the city has meaning'; and the consequence, a deflection away from the primacy accorded to the historic centre. The realisation of the importance of the periphery rather than of the central city, and the instruction to consider Mestre, doubtless reflected Samonà's partnership in the early 1950s with Luigi Piccinato, with whom Samonà had developed plans for the San Giuliano quarter on the outskirts of Mestre on the lagoon. The project originated in extensive plans for Mestre proposed in 1937. Considered a paradigm for residential organisation in the Italy of the 1950s, it aroused attention in international circles.[223]

In the early 1960s international attention also focused on the competition for an artificial island to receive traffic in the vicinity of the railway and the terminus of Piazzale Roma, to be known as the Tronchetto.[224] The creation of infill space was considered a viable contribution to enlivening the periphery. The plan was published with a three-dimensional model of the islands photographed from above, which gave the new areas apparent coherence and organic unity – as if the Barbari map were unchanged. But the new utility island, the Tronchetto, was back-door zoning and contributed to the degradation of the residential area nearby.

Aldo Rossi published an essay on the Tronchetto that was pointedly critical, intent on showing that the city's urban nature had been ignored in a number of the projects. He claimed the urbanistic theories were simplistic and their political implications insufficiently realised.[225] In Rossi's view only two projects – by Manfredo Nicoletti and Giuseppe Samonà – responded to the city's particular conditions. The project Ultima Parete alle Canal Grande (Last Wall on the Grand Canal) earned Rossi's particular scorn as a response to Venetian conditions at the end section of the Grand Canal. The Foscari group looked to the Zattere as a nearby area and showed some overall sense of the lagoon. The Manuso group had a sense of the city and an overall grasp of the potential division of traffic (pedestrian in the main city) and channel lines to the Lido, including a proposal, which was eventually realised, to link Marghera and Malamocco for heavy shipping. Rossi's response is evidence of the critical urban thinking that could be generated by architectural competitions.

One of the few actually to build in Venice was Ignazio Gardella, a graduate of the Institute. From 1953 to 1958 Gardella's house on the Zattere (Casa alle Zattere) was in process of planning and construction.[226] More imposing than its neighbours on that conspicuous waterfront, it raises its five stories and attic roof-top above them (fig. 186). Gardella respected the local vernacular in the irregular placement of windows and the prevalence of balconies, treating these in modern style, using traditional materials. Windows are framed in white stone, balconies are marble, the curve of the *fondamenta* is respected: in short, the past is balanced by a forthright avowal of modernism. But finally the insistent verticality of the motifs, in the treatment of the balconies, in the height of the building overall in the context of its neighbours, renders it out of sympathy with its neighbours. Gardella's house is an uneasy new dweller, even if precious as some demonstration of the acceptance of modern principles in its time.[227] Gardella certainly considered its accommodation in that particular city, stressing how it 'reflect[s] the pictorial values of Venetian architecture with their play of light and shadow reminiscent of the forms reflected in the water of the canals . . .'[228] Venice, more than most other places, begets intentionalism.

186 Ignazio Gardella, house on the Zattere, 1954.

Venice in the 1950s and 1960s raises the question not only of hostility to modernism, but also of disappointment with the quality of those contributions that have been allowed into the central city. Between 1955 and 1958 Samonà and Trincantato constructed offices and housing in the area opposite the station, adjacent to the church of San Simeone Piccolo. Maretto called the project 'one of the most interesting interpolations into the corpse of Venice'.[229] Tafuri responded with his characteristic complexity, describing the buildings as 'a text of fragments and oblique messages'.[230] Whatever the distinction of the architects, to an outsider these buildings appear bland, rigid, and heavy. Modernism was not impossible; the issue was, rather, the failure of contextualism, the failure to see that bland block-like buildings with heavy regular outlines were poor companions for the inflected and rich styles of existing architecture. The members of the School of Venice were not innocent in this regard.

* * *

Carlo Scarpa: The Venetian Architect

In his remarks on Venetian architecture in the Italian context, Manfredo Tafuri presented Giuseppe Samonà and Carlo Scarpa together as the 'two masters' (Italian architecture only has 'masters').[231] Indeed with Luigi Nono, Bruno Maderna and Emilio Vedova, Scarpa is one of the great Venetian artists of the century. In Tafuri's view, Scarpa was 'isolated' and 'unique', refusing to find 'decadence' in Venice: that refusal was his great strength.[232] Scarpa is regarded locally as *the* pre-eminent modernist master. Although controversial at first because of his lack of formal qualifications, and in early career noted more for his glass than his architecture, he held the position of professor at the faculty of architecture over a number of years. He became teaching assistant to Professor Cirilli in 1926 and was appointed professor in 1933. He was active in the faculty until 1976.

In Scarpa's formative years in the 1920s, Venice, weighted by a tradition still seen to be Gothic, was little affected by modernism. It was a museum city within Fascist Italy, ready to praise Marghera's industrial might, but wary of the entrance of the architecturally new. Modern architecture was compromised by virtue of being almost always 'solution' architecture, bearing the undue weight of a compromised site and the over-endowed setting with which it must contend. Yet Scarpa knew the Futurists, and continued to be close to other artists: his complex spatial treatments and his strong sense of surface design and detail are fed from sources other than architecture.[233] Coming gradually to architecture, in so far as he was given the opportunity, Scarpa demonstrated the potential of the modern within Venice, although only a small number of his projects have a home there. His architectural career was nurtured in the Venini glassworks, the galleries and the Biennales.

187 Carlo Scarpa, Olivetti showroom, Piazza San Marco, 1957–8.

Scarpa's use of the modern material concrete in conjunction with such rich, stable and historical materials as marble distinguished his practice from the outset. Materials that have a long association with Venice and its building tradition – marble, for example – were used to warm too stark a modernity. As many have observed, detail in Scarpa's work is distinctive, functional and beautiful: 'Each detail tells us the story of its making, of its placing, of its dimensioning.'[234] Although Scarpa worked knowingly with industrial materials and strong plain surfaces, he combined them with geometric ornament particularly suitable for parallel formations such as friezes, frames and perspective devices, ornamenting the surfaces and outlining the perpendiculars and horizontals that are fundamental to building. He built with angles and hovering planes, with strips of tesserae and with discreet brass outlining. It became possible for concrete to be opulent.

Scarpa's sense of asymmetry was powerful and (arguably) Venetian-born, for his buildings are seldom aligned on a central axis. Furthermore, he understood the asymmetry practised by the Viennese School in the early twentieth century and their sensuous use of materials in geometric configurations. Scarpa's period of building –

beyond design and small-scale renovation – began properly only after the war, in the 1950s. Conspicuous in the Piazza San Marco underneath the arches of the Procuratie Vecchie, is the Olivetti showroom of 1957–8, glowing quietly with its conjunction of squares and rectangles (fig. 187). The small space is animated by the geometries of its tiled floor and the floating marble staircase, itself like a sculpture stacking up to the mezzanine floor beside a small pool – that inevitable water accent – which reflects a sculpture by Alberto Viani.[235]

Scarpa's great talent as a museum architect, redesigning spaces and contextualizing paintings and sculpture in old buildings, is best known in the Museo di Palazzo Abatellis in Palermo, and in Verona at the Museo di Castelvecchio.[236] However, his initial installations were in Venice. He designed many temporary displays for special exhibitions and Biennales: he was responsible for the elegant arrangement of the Museo Correr in 1953, which still appears chaste and undated, and the room displaying Carpaccio's *Saint Ursula* series and the other *teleri* in the Accademia.[237] From 1948 into the 1970s, he was principal designer for the Italian pavilion at the Biennale, beginning with the seven rooms of the central pavilion, the Paul Klee retrospective and the installation of the Peggy Guggenheim collection in the Greek pavilion in 1948.[238] In 1950 the gallery owner Carlo Cardazzo commissioned a small book pavilion, which Scarpa designed with a daring off-centre pitched roof.[239] In 1952 he designed the entrance ticket office in the central pavilion, with a dramatic leaf-shaped roof, a pond and a rest area, and installed a Toulouse-Lautrec retrospective hung beneath draperies that diffused the light – a characteristic Scarpa technique. In 1954 he began work on the Venezuelan pavilion, keeping the existing trees and building around them in his favoured material, concrete.[240] The closest spiritual neighbour in the Giardini is the Hoffmann pavilion – in its rectilinear clarity, the roots of Scarpa's practice in the Viennese Secession is more than evident.[241] Horizontals and verticals appear particularly clear, offset by square latticed screens and geometric detail. A contemporary neighbour, who also extended the lineage of architecture from early modernism, was Gerrit Rietveld, who was constructing a new pavilion for the Netherlands in 1954 with a similar clarity.[242]

From 1961 to 1963 Scarpa remodelled the *piano terreno* of the Fondazione Querini-Stampalia at the request of its director Giuseppe Mazzariol, who wanted to implant modern architecture in Venice. Mazzariol was a figure of major cultural importance from the 1950s, when he took up the directorship of the Fondazione and of its historic collection of artworks, its library and its exhibition space.[243] Mazzariol's prominence in Venice was evident by his presidency of the Consorzio per lo Sviluppo Economico e Sociale della Provincia di Venezia (COSES) and his commitment to the idea of an international university of art.[244] He was the friend of artists and architects. This *magister venetiantatis*, as Massimo Cacciari styled him, had a perception of the contemporary accommodated in Venice that few could match.[245] He understood Venice as a site for experiment in architecture, rather than a terrain for conciliation of the past. He opposed the notion of the city bounded by a conservative programme that was alien to its inherent contradictory nature, contradictions that he himself would cherish and extend. It was an interpretation that became potent in Venice in the 1980s.

Housed in a sixteenth-century palazzo of no particular external distinction, on a small canal, the Fondazione Querini-Stampalia is approached over a small canal via a private bridge that Scarpa made in metal and teak raised on Istrian stone, suggesting traditional Venetian materials, but used in an indubitably modern style. Bolts and fasteners are conspicuous accents, an early instance of Scarpa's extraordinary detailing and joining. In the felicitous phrase of Scarpa's disciple Sergio Los, the bridge is 'shaped like a drawn bow'.[246] The flooding characteristic of the ground floor is used to full advantage as the water is channelled among stepping stones, which makes it seem sculpted (figs 188–9). The two gridded gates on the canal recall the traditional

188 and 189 Carlo Scarpa, ground-floor renovations at the Fondazione Querini-Stampalia, Rio di Santa Maria Formosa, 1961–3.

ironwork at the water level of great palaces on the Grand Canal, as well as the geometric modules of the School of Vienna. The low-ceilinged entry is relatively small in scale, but its spatial effect is complex because of the channelling and changes in floor level, the light through the water doors on one side and the different light through the glass to the garden on the other side, as well as the panelling beside the old brick and original features of the building, and the deep-coloured irregularly cut ceiling. The floor material changes in the small space from the entrance to the exhibition gallery, being Istrian stone in one section, and tesserae in another – the squared patterning recalls Paul Klee's abstracted paintings as well as traditional Venetian mosaics. It is possible to photograph the ground-floor interior in such a way as totally to belie external appearances.[247]

The small garden at the rear is raised up artificially, carefully bounded and paved, a tantalising green presence from inside. The garden receives a stream of water directed from the canal through the building into a geometric fountain. Istrian stone and concrete paving meet in another of Scarpa's exercises in formal abstraction, with modernist practices and traditional Venetian building side by side. On the wall is a mosaic designed by Scarpa's painter friend Mario Deluigi: another instance of the architect's productive friendship with practitioners across the arts.

Giuseppe Mazzariol, so appreciative of his commission (and his city) wrote of the bridge 'without doubt representing the lightest and swiftest joining arc realised in Venice in recent centuries'.[248] Scarpa has, in effect, made a sculpture of the ground floor, creating a complexity of floor levels, water channels and tiled areas in response to the feeling that the frequent *acque alte*, as Mazzariol put it, was 'an element that was not exceptional in the urban landscape'.[249] Mazzariol saw the water as 'a medium between inside and outside . . . becoming a luminous mirror', and a means of personalising the particular Venetian *spazio-ambiento*.[250]

Scarpa's work was both restoration and invention. In this way it proposed a radical new way of intervening in Venetian buildings, but one requiring the highest sensitivity and talent to create anew as well as to contextualise. The process has been likened to the practice of Viollet-le-Duc, which allowed a building to be changed in the process of restoration – but rarely has this been achieved with such mastery.[251]

From 1966 Scarpa worked on the creation of an entrance to the Institute of Architecture in Venice adjacent to the church of the Tolentini in Santa Croce (fig. 190). He

190   Carlo Scarpa, entrance to the University Institute of Architecture, (IUAV), Tolentino, 1966–72.

used an original doorway from the adjacent monastery, laying it on the ground, bordering it in concrete and covering it with water to form a reflective pool.[252] Ramps to each side of the entrance path are intricately bricked in sympathy with the exposed brick wall of the adjacent church, leaving its portico and high Corinthian columns just visible, as well as a tenement building losing its stucco – a typical Venetian montage.

Scarpa's architecture is characterised by Tafuri as 'hedonistic' (an epithet, surely, of a puritanical spirit).[253] The material of concrete with which Scarpa so often worked cannot readily be described as 'hedonistic', and yet undeniably Scarpa has aestheticised the material: in that respect Tafuri considers him 'hedonistic' and 'too expressive'.[254] But then the whole city is *too* emotional, too laden. The infiltrations of a rationalist architecture and theory are therefore particularly pungent: we think of Palladio, of course, but also the strength of the Neoclassical tradition, of Tommaso Temanza and Giannantonio Selva. When Manfredo Tafuri finds Carlo Scarpa's work *too* expressive, too magisterial in narration, these very excesses – if indeed they are so – save modernism from reductive blandness.[255]

Yet Tafuri's accounts of Scarpa's projects are masterly: he finds 'interrupted and "figured" angles, dislocated planes and water further diluting unstable forms . . . a true art of manipulation informs the fragments of words that seem "too rich"'.[256] It is a dialogue with history in which Scarpa demonstrates the persuasive contextualism of his architecture within Venice, proving that such a dialogue *is* possible.

Perhaps more than any other Venetian artist in the twentieth century, Scarpa has come to represent an expressiveness that is deeply Venetian. His play with water (to take just one element) is carried to the extent that he could submerge a vertical door in it, or make the lagoon itself the mobile setting for the monument to the Partisan women. The use of water is sweet evidence of his poetic *venezianità*. He is the exemplum of what Mazzariol and Barbieri have expressed with respect to Venice: that it is 'the great text of decomposition'.[257] Scarpa's glass was already forged in that intermediary zone of water and sand, a prelude to 'the great text of water and stone': his pieces described as 'like liquid made solid yet always on the point of melting away'.[258] Francesco Dal Co sees Scarpa's as work having a mythologising vein, particularly in its treatment of water.[259]

Even Tafuri, often sceptical of ties to place, compounds the Venetianness, if somewhat abstrusely, lauding Scarpa's abstraction, but also: 'his designs by figures, his "suspension of icons of the possible" in disassociated spaces, his use of masking facades, his work on materials and colours . . . and of course the multiple fluid references.'[260]

Imagining what might have been Carlo Scarpa's last dream, the Japanese architect, Arata Isozaki felt that the light of the Veneto region, must have appeared like that of Kyoto, where Scarpa died in 1978. That light was visionary in his architecture.[261]

Modernism Blocked

FRANK LLOYD WRIGHT

Scarpa's buildings in Venice are too few. Venetian prejudice against the new has been one of our constant themes: many dirges sound for lost opportunities in post-war Venice, most notably the exclusion of the 'Modern Masters' Frank Lloyd Wright, Le Corbusier and Louis Kahn.[262] From 1951 to 1953 Frank Lloyd Wright worked on a design for architectural student housing, intended as a memorial to the young architect Angelo Masieri, on a site adjacent to the Palazzo Balbi on the *volta* of the Grand Canal, opposite Ca' Foscari.[263] Masieri had worked with Carlo Scarpa and was on his way to visit Frank Lloyd Wright in the United States when he was killed. The family owned the small site at Ca' Foscari. It necessitated a triangular ground plan, to which Wright responded with a modern form of the typical palazzo, with strong vertical accents, balconies at two levels and corner pilasters designed in Murano glass (fig. 191).

In explanation of his building, Wright said that 'Venice does not float upon the water, but rests upon the silt at the bottom of the sea':

> In the little building that I have designed slender marble shafts, firmly fixed upon concrete piles (two to each) in the silt, rise from the water as do reeds or rice or any water plants. These marble piers carry the floor construction securely – the cantilever slab floors thus made safe to project between them into balconies overhanging the water – Venetian as Venetian can be. Not imitation but interpretation of Venice.[264]

191　Frank Lloyd Wright, design for student housing, (Masieri memorial), 1953. Ink, pencil, pastel on paper, 65 × 43 cm. Venice, Fondazione Querini Stampalia.

The plan had the strongest endorsement from local critics and architects, but not all. Opposition came from that one-time exponent of the avant-garde, Duilio Torres, who wrote an extraordinary essay rejecting the Wright proposal, largely on the grounds that Wright had reused a project of 1915 for the Emil Bach house.[265] Torres illustrated his rejection of Wright with Viennese, Dutch, American, English, Czechoslovakian and Italian examples of early twentieth-century architecture, demonstrating an inclusivist appreciation that was strangely at odds with his rejection of the late Wright design. Doubtless the real point was made by juxtaposing two villa designs by Giuseppe Torres and Duilio Torres executed in 1914, in advance of Wright's house of 1915.[266] The 'incomparable beauty of Venice' was again invoked to exclude a design that was seen not only as obsolete, but ignorant of tradition. Wright's project was, simply, 'an intrusion'.

In contrast, presenting Wright's Masieri memorial within the context of Venice, Sergio Bettini claimed that 'the figurative primacy, in contrast to the example of Florence, rests not with the single building but with the flow of its form in its entirety . . . Space in Venice is not felt as a closed form, but as a *continuum* which proceeds through time'.[267] It followed for Bettini that Wright understood the continuum of Venice and was sympathetic to its anticlassical nature. The triangular site would have been especially sympathetic.

Giuseppe Samonà had done much to promote Wright's hero status in the city. He responded to 'the poetical significance of the large balconies and the transparent corner pilasters giving extensive views of the Grand Canal'.[268] He evoked the coloured surfaces long recognised – particularly by Ruskin. To Samonà's eye and mind, Wright's merging façades dissolved the exterior in the interests of unity and reflective colour. Because the Masieri façade was not closed 'but open from inside and outside . . . one has the large windows of the ground floor which afford a view onto the inner spaces and also to part of the upper garden'.[269] He agreed that the piers would indeed 'rise like reeds from the water', and that the memorial status of the building would be manifest in the qualities of 'gentility' and of 'optimism', and the 'soft-speaking' of the architecture.

The Masieri project was rejected from timidity, and the failure of two Commune committees to bring themselves to commission a model or even to allow a façade mock-up on the site.[270] The elder Masieri died during the negotiations and the urgency of patronage lessened. Carlo Scarpa finally developed a students' union building for the site, which was approved only in 1983 and completed after Scarpa's death.[271]

LE CORBUSIER

In 1964 Le Corbusier was asked by the mayor of Venice to design a hospital at Cannaregio, in the western area, in the vicinity of San Giobbe.[272] Behind the request was the persuasive Venetian voice of Giuseppe Mazzariol, the chief commissioner of the project, and the fact that a competition had not produced an acceptable design.[273] Corbusier's association with Venice was of long standing and his association with the School of Venice reinforced over a decade earlier. He had been drawing in Venice since 1908. In 1962 he had made a plea for the special integrity of Venice in a letter to the mayor which asked that Venice should not be killed.[274] Yet Le Corbusier could appear unduly preservationist and even reactionary, since he wrote against the intrusion of industry in favour of Venice as a closed city, necessarily isolated by its water. The fact that it is without streets – and by that Corbusier obviously meant that it was free from road traffic – made it the most prodigious urban event on earth: yet again, a miracle. All inhabitants, including those tourists who were moved by Venice, fraternised and were made additionally human as they moved around a city admirable for its human scale.

Le Corbusier frankly endorsed a tourist city, recommending it as a place of hotels and a place for cultural and international discussion. His main point was to commend modern architecture, but only at a high level of excellence – not the American skyscraper, rather (and like an echo of Otto Wagner before the collapsed Campanile): 'when you must reconstruct, make it the most modern architecture possible. Don't seek to copy the old bricks and the old Venice made by hand.'[275]

The new hospital was intended to cover 70,000 metres and be three storeys high, with a church and a roof-top garden built on piles taking the structure out into the lagoon. Particular typologies were projected in the design: the horizontal spread of conventual hospitals such as the convent of San Zanipolo, and the small rectangular courtyards arranged on a cluster principle by building around them.[276] The corridors were seen to mirror Venetian *calli* – even though corridor configurations are usual in hospitals. Two particularly controversial aspects of the design were the windowless wards lit indirectly from the corridors, and the vehicular access intended to link the hospital with the Santa Lucia station across the water. Although Le Corbusier's prestige was considerable in Venice, the car access was viewed as dangerous: 'this smacks of some wild proposals recently advanced for incredible motor-car corridors leading to the heart of Venice'.[277] And yet the exclusion of motor traffic was one of the assets of Venice for Corbusier.

Nevertheless, Tafuri has commented on the *new* contribution Corbusier envisaged, knowingly inserted into the old fabric, but in a way that reactivated the entire city, not just the periphery of Cannaregio. Le Corbusier understood Venice as a city of *resistance* – Ruskin was his precursor in this respect, as was Tafuri himself, as a student of Sansovino. Tafuri concluded that Le Corbusier was pre-eminent in understanding the need to *resist* Venice.[278]

The hospital was almost Corbusier's last project: he died in 1965. It was never built and thus it became the second example of missed opportunities. However the design, and the presence of the master in the city have remained inspirational.

*   *   *

The third 'modern master', Louis Kahn, designed a conference hall – a Palazzo dei Congressi – for the public gardens in Castello – to be used for the Biennale, but to have a constant function as a congress centre accommodating 2,500 to 3,000 people. Once again Giuseppe Mazzariol was the active commissioner on behalf of the Venetian tourist body, the Azienda Autonoma di Soggiorno e Turismo.[279] Details were discussed with Mazzariol in Philadelphia in April 1968, and again in October. Kahn was in Venice in May 1968 to study the site.[280]

The palazzo was envisaged in reinforced concrete with marble details, with a longitudinal plan and an internal bridge-like structure that would link the function halls (fig. 192). It was to be surmounted by three lead-covered domes in frank homage to San Marco.[281] Again, Venetian correspondences were sought and found in reminiscences of the Palazzo Ducale in the rectangular structure, as well as in San Marco.[282] Studios and galleries were part of the complex. Views of Venice were available from the parapet windows, which appeared like three crescents. Kahn explained his project as 'a theatre in the round – where people look at people'.[283]

The project was then amplified to include two additional buildings for servicing the Biennale and for creating year-round art facilities in the area. Two extended buildings facing each other across a square were to contain studios, workshops and galleries for an academy. Another building near the water was to be a reception centre and restaurant.

Interruptions to Selva's park were at all times considered carefully, and resulted in the project being resited in the grounds of the Arsenale: one of the first of many pilot schemes to redevelop the Arsenale.[284] The idea of an extended academy and place for the arts and crafts was to evolve from Kahn's building.

The project was not approved. Students preferred to 'save the city from drowning' and the tourist agency was not successful in persuading the Commune of the project's worth.[285] Kahn was financially disadvantaged by the project, and yet he continued with new plans for the Arsenale site. 'Working on my project', Kahn declared, 'I was constantly thinking as if I was asking each building I love so much in Venice whether they would accept me in their company.'[286] The problem was not the consent of the buildings, but the prejudices of Venetians.

192 Louis Kahn, model of a design for a congress building, 1968. Philadelphia, University of Pennsylvania, Architectural Archives, George Pohl Collection.

The three projects by Wright, Le Corbusier and Kahn were seen to be intrusive, inappropriate to the hallowed fabric, even while it was acknowledged that they were not without sympathy to Venetian conditions. But a paralysis was evident in the face of new architecture from outside. Within Venice, extensions and rebuildings after the Second World War displayed a wanton lack of sympathy for adjacent edifices.

The worst crimes were the crimes for tourists, the extensions to hotels built on prime sites in the immediate post-war years. Virgilio Vallot's bland, over-regularised extension of the Daniele Hotel on the Riva degli Schiavoni remains particularly offensive in its crude Modernism, entirely misplaced beside the original Gothic palace.[287] Built between 1946 and 1948, it was an early indication of the revival of the tourist industry after the war. Still dominated by the pre-war Volpi monopoly CIGA, the hotel industry renewed its activity aided and abetted by the Christian Democrat mayor Giovanni Ponti, who had argued in the campaigns of 1949 that tourism was 'the bread' of Venice.[288] He stressed the importance of refurbishing hotels with 'decor, elegance, modernity'.[289] The upper zone of the Grand Canal rather than the pre-war Lido became the focus for post-war development. The Gritti Palace Hotel opened in 1948 with a waterside dining terrace looking across to Santa Maria della Salute – retaining the decorum of Andrea Gritti's palazzo after which it was named.[290] The Hotel Bauer-Grünwald was extended: Sardi's neo-Gothic treatment from the 1890s was an earlier essay in eclecticism. However, Marino Meo's modernist wing was arrogantly defiant of its context and brutally modernist in its plainness beside the church of San Moisè, the most extravagant façade in Venice (fig. 193).[291] Not architecturally intrusive, but not particularly distinguished, the Cipriani hotel on the Giudecca kept in touch with the golden centre of San Marco tourism – and Harry's Bar – with a motor launch service, and later became the much advertised destination of the Venice-Simplon-Orient Express.[292]

A cautious Modernism was evident at the railway station, which had been the subject of a competition in 1934: it was built finally between 1952 and 1955 by Paolo Perilli.[293] Set back from the canal and possessed of a certain emphatic horizontal dignity, it nevertheless makes little imaginative contribution to the water drama that unfolds after the train ride across the lagoon. In 1961 the Marco Polo airport opened on the outer reaches of the lagoon, serving Venice with a road link to the Piazzale Roma, or by water to the Lido and San Marco.

193 Marino Meo, Hotel Bauer-Grünwald extension, 1948.

On the Campo Manin, offices for the Casa di Risparmio, a large-scale development for inner Venice, jam clumsy modern quotations of Gothic windows into an obstructing, non-fluent space behind the statue of Daniele Manin. Angelo Scatollin's 1960s design, in consultation with Pier Luigi Nervi, produced a building of unyielding bulk, despite its vertical Venetian-type windows and ornamental Murano glass.

Increasingly, Venice favoured a neutral Modernism in the face of new ideas. But more urgent, and beyond aesthetics, was the physical threat from the elements: nemesis was at hand. The 'Problem of Venice' was debated increasingly in the late 1960s as various pressures on the city and its relationship with the industrial mainland came to international attention.

In 1959 came the first of a double-set of volumes on Venice written by Eugenio Miozzi, author of the 1939 plan, and the city engineer responsible for most of the modern bridges. His *Venezia nei secoli* (Venice through the Centuries) was an extended history of the city and lagoon (and of Miozzi's own projects) published in a de-luxe edition.[294] But the book was also an early and coherent statement about the potential death of the lagoon on the model of other swamp cities like Ravenna. In Miozzi's view in the past Venice's measures had always saved the city, but greater tidal movement and disturbances to the balance between lagoon and city were now serious.[295] He anticipated the need to arrest sedimentation, to restrict the wash from boats, particularly in the inner city (in diagrams, he analysed the wave's power of destruction), and the danger of fire and petrol leaks in the lagoon. But he still hoped for a viable commercial life and saw the need for deepening the canal from Malamocco to Marghera.

In 1969 UNESCO released its *Rapporto su Venezia*, the fruits of that international body's cogitations on the problems of Venice.[296] The report covered four areas: the land, air and water; the people (raising the question of Marghera in relation to Venice); the artistic and cultural patrimony; and 'Ideas', which concerned special legislation, science and technology in relation to Venice, and protection interests. The city's opposition to new architecture was among the issues addressed, including the rejected plans by Wright, Le Corbusier and Kahn.[297] The three had come to epitomise the equivocation surrounding the reception of modern architecture. But this was a relatively minor part of the report. The urgent address was to the major environmental threats facing the city and the lagoon, and, in particular, the consequences of the flood of 1966. It was claimed that Venice now faced a danger, in the form of corrosion and pollution, that was much greater than the one-time League of Cambrai.[298] The most dangerous day in the history of Venice had been 4 November 1966. The analysis of the causes of that exceptional *acqua alta*, the recovery from its consequences and, above all, the deliberations on future preventative measures were to be the major issues for Venice in the next decade – and beyond. In the 1970s deaths in Venice were to be re-enacted many times. And the city was to find itself arcane again, and even mysterious for there was renewed poetry in its doom. The flood confirmed the city's tenacity no less than its fragility. As Peggy Guggenheim remarked: 'When Venice is flooded it is even more truly beloved.'[299]

Chapter 10

DEAD OR DYING:
RESPONSES TO THE FLOOD

3 November 1966

Accounts of the days and nights of 3 and 4 November 1966 tell of the tempest conditions that prevailed through much of Italy, with torrential rain, a sirocco wind blowing at up to one hundred kilometres an hour and huge seas. Above all, for Venice, the high tide failed to turn at the appointed hour.[1] The sea was driven through the three openings to the lagoon. The island of Sant'Erasmo was submerged to the height of four metres; the narrowest point at Pellestrina was deluged as the huge blocks of Istrian stone in the Murazzi were dislodged; the Lido beaches were torn up and their cabins dispatched to the waves. Locked in the lagoon and driven by an onshore gale, the sea waters flooded the main city to a height of almost two metres and stayed there for twenty consecutive hours (fig. 194). All services were cut; there was total darkness and the real fear – *la grande paura* – that this time the sea would not recede (fig. 195). While the flood that devastated Florence was an extraordinary event, the flooding of Venice was but the extreme point in the long history of *acqua alta*.

The flood passed into legend. Its reek infuses the Venice episode of French novelist Michael Tournier's *Gemini*, published in 1975, which tells of identical twins, Jean and Paul Surin, the one searching for the other in Venice.[2] Jean observes that Venice itself is a pair of islands, like twins, which balance each other on each side of the Grand Canal. The image of reflection and distortion is characteristic of that most Venetian of products, the mirror. Reflection and duplication; a twin in a mirror image.

Within this unstable scenario of doubles the city is always mindful of death by water:

> As the rain persists, you sense the ever-increasing fear of floods growing in this city standing at water level. Perhaps the fearful, long-heralded coincidence between the quiet storm controlled by the astronomical sky and the meteorological storm is about to happen . . .[3]

Tournier's witness to the 1966 flood recalls:

> We had to wait until the evening of the next day for the water to flow back out of the lagoon into the sea through the three channels – the *bocche di porto* of the Lido, Malamocco and Chioggia. Then in the dusk, made still darker by a ceiling of leaden clouds, we saw all the streets and squares, and the ground floors of all the houses covered equally in a thick layer of oil and rotting seaweed and decomposing bodies . . .[4]

World consternation followed the flood. Concern at the possibility of a recurrence gave impetus to international, national and local bodies, not without tensions and disagreements in diagnoses and prognoses. More and more universally it was alleged that the cause was *not* the singular weather conditions, but the presence of Marghera and its industries, and, in particular, the destabilising of the lagoon by the excavation of a deep canal to Marghera for petrol tankers. In 1970 the Supino report specifically

linked the deep dredging of the canal between Malamocco on the Lido and Porto
Marghera to the 1966 flood.[5] Italia Nostra, its local chapter under the presidency of
Anna Maria Volpi, daughter of Count Volpi who had died in 1947, spearheaded the
criticism against Marghera's 'unnatural canal', excavated only some months before
the flood, in the spring of 1966.[6] The fact that the daughter disowned the developments of the father might be viewed with some irony. Yet Vittorio Cini, closely
involved with the foundation of Marghera and with Volpi, declared that the automobile bridge, which had been the result of Terraferma development, was 'a colossal
error' and he would be happy to destroy it with his own hands.[7]

The fishing industry was also attacked: 'soft' industry was pitted against 'hard'. It
was claimed that the artificial areas known as the *valle da pesca* contributed to the
unnatural tidal pattern, disturbing the lagoon's ecology.[8] The lagoon became the focus
of attention, which it has remained, aided and abetted by world interest in matters
ecological. The protection of the lagoon from undue pressure from the sea gave rise
to schemes for closing the three sea entrance points at the Lido. The need for legislating new protective laws was recognised at a national level.[9]

What emerged was the difficulty, or impossibility, of reaching a consensus on
the causes of the flood, and equally, a lack of agreement on preventative measures.
However, of great importance was the fact that Marghera was in process of further
development, with full support from principal politicians. Local government under
the Christian Democrat mayor, Favaretto Fisca, condoned the implementation of the
third zone of expansion.[10] Meetings of Italia Nostra proliferated. In 1969 a highly
critical film appeared, *Montanelli-Venezia*, scripted by the eminent *Corriere della Sera*
journalist and writer Indro Montanelli and the Venetian film-maker Giorgio Ponti.[11]
At the same time, there was firm support for Marghera at local government level.
When, in the elections of 1970, a *giunta* of Socialists, Republicans and Christian
Democrats took power with a Christian Democrat mayor, Giorgio Longo, there was

Quel giorno si infransero le regole che regolavano il rapporto tra laguna e mare: Adriatico forza otto
raffiche a cento km orari - Sedicimila persone persero ogni avere, danni per quattro miliardi di allora

Incredibile: marea a quasi 2 metri

Fuga in barca per quattromila, onde mai viste su Burano e Sant'Erasmo, litorale sommerso

Venezia

Al tramonto del 3 novembre, mentre continuava la pioggia torrenziale, la pioggia che da 24 ore frustava la città, lo scirocco colpiva con raffiche oltre i 70 km all'ora, la marea diede il primo, ancora debole, segnale dell'evento sconvolgente che stava per abbattersi su Venezia. Alle 18.15 la minima si fermò a 45 cm sul medio mare: erano ben 87 cm in più rispetto alla quota astronomica. Da quel «gradino» l'acqua riprese a salire: e poco dopo le 21, quando superò il metro - mentre sarebbe dovuta essere sotto lo zero - fu chiara a tutti la gravità della situazione.

La marea si fermò alle 1.30, ad un livello già ai limiti dell'emergenza - 127 cm. due spanne d'acqua in Piazza San Marco, due terzi della città allagati in anticipo di due ore sui ritmi astronomici.

Che «qualcosa» si fosse pauroso-amente rotto nelle regole dettate dalla natura sul rapporto tra la laguna e il mare, lo si capì poco prima dell'alba del 4 novembre - sempre sotto la pioggia - quando la marea, scesa di appena 10 cm e rimasta oltre un metro più alta della quota astronomica, riprese a crescere veloce e ancora in anticipo.

L'Adriatico forza otto e lo scirocco che uriava a 80 km all'ora con raffiche vicine ai 100 impedivano il deflusso in mare. Il sovvertimento delle regole ebbe un andamento parossistico: alle 12.20 la marea, giunta oltre il metro e mezzo, doveva scendere, e invece continuò a salire, fino a raggiungere alle 14.10 la quota mai registrata di un metro e 76 cm. Qui si fermò fino alle 17.30 e riprese poi a crescere ancora per lunghe angosciosanti ore (nelle quali invece sarebbe dovuta scendere) fino al livello impensabile di un metro e 94 cm. Alle 21, secondo i ritmi astronomici, la marea sarebbe dovuta ricrescere: quando ormai la paura attanagliava gli animi, con una nuova e ultima contraddizione, la marea scese a picco.

Venezia non aveva mai subito una marea così alta, né durata così a lungo (un assedio di 24 ore, il livello di «crisi» a 120 cm superato per 15 ore).

I numeri restituiscono le dimensioni del dramma, non l'angoscia e la disperazione: mancò l'energia elettrica in tutta la città, e i veneziani vissero al buio - impossibilitati ad uscire, spesso al freddo,

con i telefoni saltati, talora con pochi viveri - le ore più drammatiche; i 16 mila abitanti nei seimila pianterra persero ogni avere, e si dovettero ricoverare più di mille persone; oltre settemila tra negozi, esercizi pubblici, botteghe artigiane, officine, magazzini furono invasi dall'acqua e persero merci e macchinari: migliaia di tonnellate di rifiuti furono ammassate in strada (lo sgombero richiese uno sforzo immane e si concluse dopo nove giorni, quando in qualche buio l'aria già si ammorbava); libri e documenti andarono perduti a migliaia nelle biblioteche e negli archivi, centinaia di vasche di nafta si ruppero e un segno nero macchiò a lungo i muri; al Lido andarono distrutte le capanne della spiaggia, a Sant'Erasmo e a Cavallino i raccolti dell'orticoltura.

Per ripristinare l'energia elettrica e la rete telefonica occorsero sette giorni; i danni furono valutati in 40 miliardi («Il Gazzettino», per dare un'idea costava 50 lire).

Nella notte del 4 novembre i veneziani si riversarono a migliaia per le strade, alla luce delle candele e delle pile, come in un dolente pellegrinaggio collettivo nella città devastata.

Non avevano ancora saputo che si era accaduto sul litorale, ed era stato un bene: altrimenti un'ondata di panico li avrebbe travolti. I sottili cordone che protegge Venezia era stato squassato dal mare: a Pellestrina la violenza delle onde aveva aperto quattro grandi falle nei «murazzi», le colossali difese in massi di pietra d'Istria, vanto della Serenissima, e il mare era penetrato sulle case, costringendo alla fuga in barca tremila persone; al Lido la mareggiata aveva sommerso la spiaggia e danneggiato le dighe; sul litorale nord il mare era dilagato su un fronte di quattro chilometri, scavalcando la fascia costiera e sommergendola per 700 ettari, ed era esondato in laguna a colpire con onde mai viste le isole di Burano e di Sant'Erasmo. Venezia aveva corso il rischio di diventare preda del mare.

Qua e là, sui muri di Venezia, ci sono indicazioni del livello raggiunto dall'acqua il 4 novembre. I turisti si avvicinano, misurano sul proprio corpo, qualcuno si fa fotografare.

Il veneziano passa, guarda, e si sente ritornare addosso un lungo brivido.

Leopoldo Pietragnoli

Venezia fu «assediata» dalle acque con un livello di crisi a 120 centimetri superato per quindici ore.

QUELLA NOTTE AL GAZZETTINO

La rotativa sott'acqua, naufraghi in tipografia

Venezia

Anche dopo trent'anni è difficile dimenticare la notte di quel 4 novembre. Venezia per tutta la giornata si era trovata sotto un metro e mezzo abbondante d'acqua, ma anche il Lido era in buona parte sommerso, in particolare le piazze dei vaporetti, con le barche che tentavano il trasbordare i passeggeri sbarcati e rimasti prigionieri nell'imbarcadero, ma venivano rovesciate dalla forza dei flutti.

Scesa la notte, in qualche modo si trasbordo cominciò a riuscire, nei due sensi.

Il sottoscritto s'imbarcò (senso del dovere? curiosità? o semplice incoscienza?) alla volta di Rialto, per vedere di raggiungere in qualche modo Ca' Faccanon, sede del Gazzettino. Il viaggio fu un evento infernale: un imbarcadero dopo l'altro, sollevati ai massimi livelli dalla marea, tutti erano gremiti di folle urlanti, prigionieri dell'acqua e del buio più assoluto (tutte le linee elettriche erano saltate).

Per di più l'acqua del Canal Grande era stata invasa dalla nafta uscita dai serbatoi degli impianti di riscaldamento.

Anche a Rialto l'acqua era molto alta, ma il sottoscritto, tirati su al massimo i calzoni e levate calze e scarpe, riuscì a discendere e ad avviarsi, diguazzando, verso Ca' Faccanon. (Poi risultò che, camminando alla cieca, mi ero fatto un bel taglio sulla pianta di un piede calpestando un pezzo di vetro).

Il buio continuava ad essere assoluto, il mondo

sembrava popolato di fantasmi. Ca' Faccanon era anch'essa al buio, la rotativa al piano terra completamente sott'acqua. A tentoni, riuscii a trovare le scale e a salire fino al primo piano, dove si lavorava la tipografia. Un'impressione indicibile, il buio e il silenzio a un'ora in cui di solito il giornale ferveva di luci e di frastuono.

Qualche vaga ombra qua e là tra le linotype: qualche avventuroso tipografo che era anch'egli tentato d'avventura, per constatare cosa fosse successo al giornale. Ricordo che, nel buio, ci raggruppammo come naufraghi sperduti, in cerca di conforto. Qualche breve commento qua e là tanto: chi che era accaduto e ancora stava accadendo toglieva la voglia di parlare.

Non ricordo quanto tempo restammo là, intesa non si sa di che cosa. Da parte del sottoscritto, un penoso tentativo di far dello spirito: «Perché non andiamo su negli uffici e battiamo con le macchine da scrivere un numero speciale del Gazzettino e dopo prendiamo una barca e andiamo a venderlo in giro per la città?». Al che, una brusca risposta dal buio: «El ghe vaga lu, se proprio el vol...».

È strano, ma mentre ricordo ancora benissimo il viaggio d'andata e il palazzo del Gazzettino ridotto a una funerea catacomba, non ricordo come, poi, ho fatto a ritornare a casa.

Perché l'acqua alta e il buio durarono ancora parecchio, come durano indelebili nella nostra memoria di veneziani.

Sandro Sandrelli

L'INTERVISTA/ INDRO MONTANELLI

«Soltanto ciacole»

«È ciò che fanno i veneziani per questa città»

Milano

Trent'anni fa, la tremenda alluvione che colpì con tutti quel po' di Nordest anche Venezia, con tutto quel po' po' di danno che sappiamo.

Ma che cosa mise a nudo quell'evento straordinario e drammatico, della città lagunare, già sulla via della decadenza?

Lo abbiamo chiesto a Indro Montanelli, vecchio «innamorato deluso» della città.

Come si ricorderà, il «principe» del giornalismo «principe» del giornalismo riprende le famose immagini del motoscafo, dei tuffi. «Non avevo ancora la dimensione dell'evento - confessa - capii quanto l'acqua era salita solo quando cercai di tornare a casa. Allora abitavo a Santa Maria Formosa: per arrivarci camminai con l'acqua ben alta sul petto, la cinepresa ben alta sopra la testa». E a casa la sorpresa lia, ma del mondo, scegliendo come destino di vita soltanto la conservazione di se stessa - naturale gioiello di città - negligendo ogni legame con lo stato italiano. Deve diventare insomma una città intesa soltanto alla difesa della cultura del mondo, sotto l'egida dell'Onu?

Ma ciò è fattibile?

«È fattibile. L'Onu delegau un "Doge", che deve essere soprattutto un grande tecnico che si occupa delle acque; la città deve avere meno di centomila abitanti; deve diventare il luogo di elezione di grandi studi, di alto artigianato. E deve andare soprattutto contingentato il turismo... I barboni non devono andare a Venezia».

E sarebbe antidemocratico... Ti immagini le grida di lesa libertà?

«Sì, certo. Ma dicano pure che sono ingiusto; me ne strafotto... Ma per tutelare la città, certa gente non bisogna volerla».

Tu per lungo tempo hai condotto la battaglia per Venezia, poi hai smesso: come mai?

«Mi sono rotto le scatole, perché non ho trovato eco nei veneziani. I quali, mi dispiace dirlo, ma non hanno saputo, non sanno, non sanno, chi erano i loro antenati, che e poi sotto gli occhi di tutti! Tieni a mente che la decadenza non tocca mai soltanto le cose, ma entra anche nella spina dorsale degli uomini...».

Ergo?

«Venezia è una città senza spina dorsale; i veneziani ciacolano soltanto. Ecco quel che sanno fare, oggi. Scrivilo, scrivilo pure. La mia è un'invettiva».

E con questo, e una invettiva piena di amore-odio, ci pare, Indro Montanelli, con Venezia ha veramente chiuso.

Giovanni Lugaresi

Indro Montanelli lancia un'"invettiva" contro i veneziani.

LA TESTIMONIANZA/ SERGIO MANZONI E DUILIO STIGHER

«Filmammo il mare che era entrato in città»

«I pontiletti dei gondolieri galleggiavano, sbattevano sulle colonne della Basilica»

Venezia

Erano rimasti in città un po' per caso, richiamati dalla redazione della Rai a metà mattina, per riprendere un'acqua alta che si diceva eccezionale. L'eccezionalità che sarebbe entrata nella storia.

Fu così che Sergio Manzoni e Duilio Stigher filmarono le immagini più celebri dell'«acqua granda». Quelle che la sera stessa furono messe in onda dal telegiornale, sconvolgendo l'Italia e il mondo. Quelle che continuano a essere riproposte: un motoscafo enorme tra le Procuratie, dei ragazzi che si tuffano dal palco allestito per il 4 novembre.

Oggi i due cineoperatori sono in pensione, ma con servano un ricordo vivo. Per Stigher fu l'inizio della carriera in Rai: «Più assunto subito dopo». Per Manzoni l'ennesimo incontro con l'acqua: «Avevo iniziato a lavorare, nel '51, con l'alluvione del Polesine. E poi mi era sposato nel '60 con un'altra acqua alta eccezionale».

Un lavoro diverso, in quegli anni senza tecnologie avanzate, ancora legato ai treni per Roma e Milano dove il materiale doveva arrivare in tempo per essere mandato in onda. E anche quella mattina il due cineoperatori girano con l'incubo dell'ora, quando parte l'ultimo treno utile. «L'ac-

qua alta, allora come ora, si vendeva bene - ricorda Manzoni - anche all'estero. E naturalmente bisognava sempre avere lo sfondo della Basilica». Per quelque i due cineoperatori puntano a San Marco. Manzoni racconta: «Vedevo che l'acqua era piuttosto alta, ma non immaginavo quel che sarebbe successo». In Piazza riprende le famose immagini del motoscafo, dei tuffi. «Non avevo ancora la dimensione dell'evento - confessa - capii quanto l'acqua era salita solo quando cercai di tornare a casa. Allora abitavo a Santa Maria Formosa: per arrivarci camminai con l'acqua ben alta sul petto, la cinepresa ben alta sopra la testa». E a casa la sorpresa

definitiva: non c'è luce, né gas, soprattutto non funziona il telefono, impossibile contattare la Rai. «Le mie immagini arrivarono in redazione due giorni dopo».

Il termine dell'una lo rispetta invece Stigher. Solo sue le immagini che vanno in onda la sera. «Io mi mossi tardi, quando mi telefonò la redazione - racconta - L'acqua era già alta e chiesi un passaggio a due ragazzi che con un cofano giravano per il piazzale della Stazione. Non ricordo o che scalino arrivasse l'acqua». Con questo taxi d'eccezione Stigher raggiunge, anche lui, la Piazza. «I pontiletti dei gondolieri galleggiavano, sbattevano con-

tro le colonne della Basilica. Ricordo che ripresi dei piccioni morti che galleggiavano sull'acqua. Un'immagine cupa che dava il senso di quella giornata».

«La situazione nel pomeriggio era peggiorava: sempre più onde, sempre più buio - ricorda Stigher - Non c'erano più barche in giro, né gente che avesse voglia di divertirsi. I problemi arrivarono anche per noi quando tentammo di lasciare la Piazza perché si stavano incagliando. Le onde ci respingevano, andammo a cozzare con un fanale che per poco non ci cadde addosso. Era il mare con tutta la sua forza ad essere entrato in città».

Roberta Brunetti

no doubt of their endorsement of industry, and thus of the conflict of interest with the fate of the historic city.

In Venice, buildings both public and domestic had been affected by the flood and restorative measures were urgent. An editorial report signed by Indro Montanelli in *Corriera della Sera* in 1970 claimed corruption in funding allocated for Venetian restoration projects.[12] Not only the elements and the long history of its buildings made the city vulnerable; human management was at fault.

Nantas Salvalaggio, a Venetian-born journalist and novelist, gave a picture of the early 1970s in the wake of the flood that was fictional only in terms of its characters.[13] Published in 1974, *Il Campiello sommerso* (The Submerged *Campiello*) took a telling text from Goldoni's play *Il Campiello* in which the playwright chides those who pass the night in festival for on the morrow they will bid Venice farewell.[13] The novel foretells a further serious *acqua alta* in 1972; Marghera is once again implicated. Industrial interests have taken control of the lagoon and the historic city with the support of the Christian Democrats. At the same time 'Venice belongs to the world' and Venetians watched impassively as their city is taken over by world conservationists and the international set. Contemporary slogans reveal the clash of interests involved in saving Venice from 'the pirates of Marghera' and 'the Mafia of the Lagoon'. The finale is a treasure hunt organised by the Rotary Club and industry for the international set, who take off in gondolas from the Hotel Gritti to 'Save Venice' as low tide brings the stench of cats and dead fish, and mountains of rubbish. The Venetians protest weakly that while Venice is dying such a carnival is macabre. Goldoni's farewell was never more potential, and terminal.[14]

A musical reflection on an earlier turning point in Venetian history was composed in these post-flood years by Gian Francesco Malipiero – it is one of the composer's last works.[15] In a chamber opera called *Uno dei Dieci* (One of the Ten), composed in 1970, when the composer was eighty-eight years old, and performed in Siena the following year, Procurator Almorò da Mula is a survivor of the last Republican government – a Malipiero-like character – who cannot accept the end of the Republic and lives his domestic life in his senatorial gown, requiring his family and staff to live life as if the Republic still lived.[16] If Almorò da Mula has touches of Malipiero himself about him, he also recalls the ancient Venetian, the Marchese Gritti, a relic from the Republic, in Werfel's *Verdi: A Novel*.[17] Almorò da Mula expresses his disbelief that the Venetian Republic could fall: 'La Serenissima non cadra mai'. But his gondolier, who sings Tasso, has absorbed the new call for 'Fraternity, Equality and Liberty'.[18] A minuet opens the work, and their voices blend sadly together for, despite Mula's belief in an invincible Republic, Venice has fallen.

In Defence of Marghera

The plight of Venice was felt intensely by Malipiero, but it was also a social reality, a crisis in terms of future action and direction. The fullest analysis of the plight of the city in the second half of the twentieth century was offered in the writings of the Venetian Wladimiro Dorigo.[19] One of the most learned scholars of Venetian culture of his generation, he was the author of historical studies of the evolving city as well as being involved in local government as a member of the left wing of the Christian Democratic Party and Assessore all'Urbanistica from 1956 to 1959.[20] The title of his polemic, *Una Legge contro Venezia* (A Law against Venice), attacked the 'Special Law' passed in 1973, but, at the same time, Dorigo defiantly supported Marghera and its industrial activity in the face of charges from preservationists and Italia Nostra, who pinpointed Marghera as the principal cause of the flood.[21] Dorigo's appraisal, attentive to history, geography and the current political situation, took in the entire lagoon area, including the historic city of Venice, the satellite industrial cities of Mestre and

196 View of industrial Marghera.

Marghera and the area's industrial complex (fig. 196). This was a statement by a *resident*, not a body of international vigilantes.

Dorigo began his polemic well before the flood, in the climate of conferences and speculation on the fate of Venice. The matter of the book was rehearsed in a number of articles beginning as early as 1961.[22] Three articles reacting to the 1966 flood were published conspicuously in both Italian and English in the international journal *Casabella* in 1970.[23] Dorigo focused on the human element, depopulation and the redistribution of work and transport, asking whether it remained possible to live in Venice. The question was also asked of Marghera, and the viability of the relationship between the Venice of the historic islands and the Greater Venice of Marghera and Mestre was raised. Dorigo pointed out that housing posed yet another unresolvable question, one that had been a major contradiction in Venice since the late nineteenth century: is it the buildings or the inhabitants that need protection? This was the crucial question for Venetian urbanisation. Dorigo looked at the laws and the authorities responsible, to science and technology, and the measures taken to address the problems of the sea, the problems of population, and restoration. The UNESCO report had of necessity been restricted to matters cultural and ecological and had not engaged with local and national political systems.

Una Legge contro Venezia was published in the heightened emotional climate surrounding the threat to the architectural patrimony.[24] Dorigo declared that he was writing in patient rage in the face of Machiavellian absurdities, manoeuvres and clamorous errors.[25] Underpinning his argument is extensive statistical and technical data, but it is also an assessment in everyday terms of the state of Venice, both its physical and spiritual life: for this reason we must follow its arguments closely.

The city has an unusually large number of ancient structures, but Dorigo, despite his scholarship in the area, shows no sentimentality towards these when their preservation is set against the needs of residents; he was wary of its 'ersatz spirituality'.[26] He attacked the Italia Nostra organisation as well as restoration financed from the public purse that restored palaces (or their equivalent) and denied appropriate facilities to the working class. Dorigo puts people before buildings.

The central antithesis was familiar: the city is a monument pitted against the lagoon which is nature. Dorigo saw this as an externalisation of the plight of Venice and its cultivation as a museum by outsiders at the expense or expulsion of the local population.[27] The great Mother Venice appeared to be abandoning her children, forced to do so by the long years of oppression under foreign rule in the nineteenth century. Dorigo gives a strong account of the loss of Venetian self-sufficiency.[28] We can take this to be a complex phenomenon, involving not only self-rule, but also economics: the loss of trade routes to other areas of Europe and the Suez, to rail and shipping, the provision of goods to an island community, as well as the problems of the buildings and their high valuation. The historic analysis is positive in respect of Austrian contributions towards modernisation: the lagoon bridge and the Grand Canal bridges were the 'first steps' towards the abandonment of the traditional sea front; Marghera and Mestre were the 'decisive and irreversible' recent phases.[29] In terms of the continuities that made Venice a primary historic-artistic site, the maintenance of monuments, water transport and the development of a tourist infrastructure are significant, but in Dorigo's view they are over-emphasised.

Being island dwellers, Venetians partake of a special state of being, which Dorigo regards as a 'psychological' state. He claims Venetians have an 'aversion' to the Terraferma; but did they not take their *passeggiata* there as a matter of course, building their Palladian villas?[30] Significant numbers have emigrated to the Terraferma. Nevertheless, the question is intriguing: are there quintessential differences in being Venetian, in being a unique creature borne of a singular water life?

Dorigo was emphatic in his defence of modernisation and industrialisation: how else could a viable workforce be created from a population that would otherwise be completely in the service of the tourist industry, or have emigrated? The days of the pre-industrial Republic in which the *città industriale* could exist within the city had passed. Earlier in the century D'Annunzio and Rilke had expressed nostalgia for the one-time strength of Venice embodied in the Arsenale, but decades had intervened, and the schism between the *città industriale* at Marghera and the *città museo* in the islands now appeared irrevocable.[31] No doubt Dorigo was right to accuse the democratic ruling class of failing to take account of the range of vested interests in Greater Venice, both industrial *and* museological, in formulating any of the proposals for the city's salvation.

The idea of the 'death' of Venice, now a cliché, alludes to both the physical environment of the lagoon and the physical fabric of the historic city, as Miozzi had amply demonstrated in the last two volumes of his *Venezia negli secoli*, published in 1969.[32] But for Dorigo the decay of the city's civic heart was at risk because of the dire results of depopulation.[33] Beauty is not enough. The dramatic loss brought about by emigration was the result of poor quality housing and the lack of any intermediary zone of economic activity located between the tourist sector in Venice and industry in Marghera.[34] There had been improvements: the housing problem was not the same as that described by Raffaele Vivante in earlier years of the century when dire overcrowding and insanitary conditions bred cholera and tuberculosis. At the time that Dorigo wrote, the challenge to Venetian housing came from Terraferma housing, which offered the facilities of modern life and easy access to transport. It was also the affordability of such housing; in historic Venice only the foreign dollar could buy luxury accommodation. The stalemate was all too evident: restoration would enhance value; occupation and resale costs would rise; in short, Venice could not afford to improve its housing and the population was leaving as a consequence. Dorigo forecast that between 1971 and 1981 the population would fall to 80,000 inhabitants: it is the demographic tragedy of the historic city.[35] His estimates have been absolutely vindicated.

Few could dispute Dorigo's view that viable options for the residents of Venice have been drastically reduced. That the ideology of conservation is reactionary and class-inspired is less tenable. Is it not also élitist to suggest that works of art are of interest only to the upper classes and to deny the conservation of a beautiful city to 'lower' classes when it is evident that so many cherish their city? Dorigo pontificated:

> The laws for the reclamation of Venice and the system of subsidies for the work of restoration reflects the ideology of 'conservation' some would impose on Venice, at the cost of its historical and civil meaning and of the pitiless expulsion of lower classes, who are apparently less useful for the privileged and capitalistic ends to which some would like to direct the city.[36]

Historical meaning, it would seem, resides in the material fabric of the city: while the city is maintained, so too is its historical meaning. Dorigo's solution is the overhauling of all Venetian buildings, 'both aristocratic and common'. This might well create as much mystification as the other premises he would so earnestly expose and demystify. But one must ask what it means 'to overhaul' a building? What problems of modernisation and conservation are involved? For whom is the building overhauled? Will the local population have access to overhauled buildings? These questions have been current for well over one hundred years.

The physical environment of the lagoon and its hydraulics constituted the *querelle* of the lagoon. Dorigo claimed that the problem of *acqua alta* was not considered serious before the flood of 1966, but after the flood Marghera became the whipping-boy on grounds stated to be both geological and ecological.[37] Yet the process of tampering with the lagoon, its low-lying lands and the river tributary system was as old as Venice itself. Venetian history has been built on altering the lagoon. Dorigo argued that rising sea levels were neither the exclusive consequence of Marghera, nor the result of the alteration of the water table and subsequent subsidence.[38] The phenomenon of subsidence (everyone asks if Venice is sinking) was a recent phenomenon, linked to the global problem of sea levels in the ocean beyond the lagoon.

Dorigo marshalled evidence to answer the charge that Marghera has, by excavation and pollution, altered the subsoil water-table: 'The Experimental Geophysical Institute has demonstrated that the increased frequency of high tides is to be attributed to the double effect of local subsidence and glacial eustasism. These scientific events, then, look to natural events and not human works as causes of the flood.'[39]

Dorigo concluded that the problems of the lagoon were *not* the result of the creation of the industrial zone, but of inept and poorly planned political and managerial decisions. Marghera was the *salvation* of Venice and not the big bad industrial wolf. In short, the book rejected the view that Marghera was destroying the lagoon and the historic city. Dorigo certainly deepened the analysis of the complexities that faced the lagoon, the city of Venice, and the Marghera area, but he made the search for an effective answer to the problem of depopulation no easier. The reality of tourism, and even the city's moral duty with respect to tourism to allay the thirst for old Venice, and the responsibility of its world citizenship: these factors are not adequately addressed. Venice was beyond Venetian control.

However, it was not only the range of problems particular to Venice that was destroying it, but also national legislation. Bluntly, as Dorigo would have it (and his was not a lone voice), the national law approved on 16 April 1973, Law 171, opposed Venetian interests. It stood accused of 'mystification, sectarianism, provincialism and cultural dilettantism', of representing an 'incredible edifice of ignorance'.[40] The attitudes came from the 1950s, the decade that Dorigo saw as giving undue emphasis to the historical centre. In the 1960s the *querelle* became a *bagarre* – a riot, an uproar.[41] The savants claimed to have predicted the flood of 1966 in the international convention of 1962, when 'the problem of Venice' was identified. The opponents of Marghera had not joined ranks; indeed, one of the supporters of the navigation canal from Malamocco to Marghera was the national protective body, Italia Nostra. The legislative decision was made without consultation with the IV Gruppo (Idraulica) del

Comitato, who preferred a tactic that Dorigo called 'terrorismo idraulico'.[42] Atmospheric pollution was the new scandal, the new charge against Marghera. Dorigo held that the pollution problem was a seasonal profile and could not be blamed on Marghera.[43]

In the passage of Law 171 the opposition was summed up as reactionary and anti-rational in terms of effective planning. National bodies concerned with Venice were independent and there was no co-ordination between local government in the Veneto and the Commune of Venice. In effect, the law favoured centralism and autonomy, politically redefining the nature of planning by limiting local government. In fact the national responsibility for *la salvaguardia di Venezia*, the safeguarding of Venice, was equivocal.[44]

During the period from the flood of 1966 to the approval in May 1973 of Law 171, and the further protracted negotiations needed to plan the necessary *indirizzi* (the plans and regulations) every initiative was blocked and every proposal for building or infrastructure impeded.[45] A 'laboratory for the study of the dynamic of large landmasses' was to replace previous bodies. Scrutiny of the provision revealed major flaws – for example the scheme to lower the water level in the lagoon to prevent *acqua alta*, gave no thought to the implications of low tide – *acqua bassa*.

Dorigo concluded that the Special Law failed on almost every front: judicially, and in urban terms. It was authoritarian, superficial and without justification.[46] The Law's third section, devoted to active intervention, was unclear, confused in the delegation of authority, and without viable guarantees. It was biased towards larger operations, financially privileging only a small part of the built sector and leading, in the final analysis, to political confrontation.[47] Dorigo condemned the *Italian* handling of the problem of Venice, in short.

Dorigo was sued for defamation by Italia Nostra and its president Anna Maria Volpi.[48] He was, in the perception of many, misguided in his support of Marghera, but in fact he exemplified the Venetian quandary of the twentieth century: how to retain viable income and living standards by means other than tourism and how to maintain the vitality in the area. The ironies in the case of Venetian against Venetian were evident; but it was a dilemma common to all post-war conflicts between public ownership and community and environmental interests: indeed, they were not necessarily mutually antagonistic. Sources of employment were crucial for the survival of the citizens of historic Venice; they have remained so. Towards the end of the century, criticism of Marghera and the presence of heavy industry still raged and the confusion between national, regional and local levels of intervention and restoration remained.

Foreign Death Knells

In 1975 two journalists from the London *Observer*, Stephen Fay and Phillip Knightley, published *The Death of Venice*, claiming it was too late for the city to be saved.[49] Britain's zealous desire to intervene was long standing, going back to the involvement of Ruskin and William Morris, and actively continued by the Venice in Peril organisation of Lord Norwich and Sir Ashley Clarke. While Fay and Knightley's *Death of Venice* lacked the documentation and the historical depth of Dorigo's polemic, their conclusions were substantially the same, and represented a non-Italian and non-Venetian point of view. The authors refer to the Special Laws and especially the law of 1973, which divided the city into two zones. In Zone A, the central San Marco area, no alteration was to take place: as early as 1955 Samonà had drawn attention to the stalemate in the *sestiere* of San Marco. In Zone B, including such important areas as Castello and Cannaregio, alteration was permitted. Outer Venice, including Marghera, was left almost without controls.

It was not only the Italian measures that were held to be inadequate and impeding. The office of UNESCO, author of the 1968 *Rapporto su Venezia*, was obliged to withdraw in 1973, after opposition led by the socialist Gianni de Michelis, who was to become a conspicuous figure in Venetian politics over the next twenty years, until the defeat of his scheme for Venice as a convention centre in the year 2000.[50] In 1974, at the international consultative committee meeting held at the Cini centre on the Isola San Giorgio, De Michelis castigated UNESCO for its lack of diplomacy, accusing it of taking up the Venice scene 'only because it was finished at Abu Simbel, and now it would have us become a cross between a Nubian monument and Disneyland'.[51] The Venetians were growing accustomed to the designation of their city as Disneyland, a place of *ambiente* and monuments; it was infrequently remembered that it was a city where people lived.

Lack of continuity in national government, and the concomitant lack of national programmes for unemployment and inflation, thwarted an effective salvage programme. Problems beyond Venice restricted the flow of international funding.[52] Yet monuments were adopted for restoration by international groups: between 1976 and 1979, the British Sainsbury Fund undertook the restoration of the Porta della Carta, one of the prized entrances to the Palazzo Ducale; the French Comité Français pour la Sauvegarde de Venise worked on Santa Maria della Salute; and the British Venice in Peril fund on San Nicolo dei Mendicanti.[53]

For Dorigo the problem was basically political. Fay and Knightley reached the same conclusion in the mid-1970s. Like Ruskin before them, they brooded over the ancient decline of Torcello and saw it as the portent of a total exodus from historic Venice.

In 1983 Mario della Costa, a historian studying the city's restoration over two centuries, repeated the claim that the physical survival of Venice was in large part compromised by the inefficiencies of the 1973 law.[54] In his emphasis on the *unity* of the city over and above individual buildings, we hear again the nineteenth-century refrain of *Venezia ambiente*, of buildings absorbed into the texture of the city: this is *edilizio da tessuto*, the fabric that is the city, now impossible to administer overall because of the divisions of interest and zoning occasioned by the new law. The conflict is familiar from earlier ideologies of restoration, but little has been learned from historical precedent. The *action of maintenance* and the *action of transformation* are in continual conflict.

A much-reproduced photograph encapsulated the 'Venice in peril' of these years. The façade of Santa Maria della Salute appeared behind scaffolding with the warning, in Italian and English, 'Caduta angeli', 'Angels Dropping' (fig. 197).[55] The photographer, Giorgio Lotti, was the author of a collection of photographs assembled in 1970 with the title *Venezia muore* (Venice is Dying).[56] Publications such as *Difesa di Venice* (Defence of Venice) anthologised the official voices of Italian restoration headed by Italia Nostra and important Venetians such as Renato Padoan, Superintendent of Monuments, Anna Maria Volpi of Italia Nostra, and the architect and historian Giorgio Bellavitis, director of the Venetian chapter of Italia Nostra. The volume was obviously intended to reaffirm the Italian commitment to Venice. It was liberally interleaved with doom-laden photographs of *acqua alta*, crumbling masonry and heavy traffic on the Grand Canal, and it voiced the somewhat pathetic resolution that the world helps but we, the Italians, must also help.[57]

197   Giorgio Lotti, 'Basilica della Salute', from *Difesa di Venezia*, 1970.

Venezia caduta e salvezza (Venice Fallen
and Saved) included a photographic portfolio
by Aldo Durazzi exposing the crumbling
masonry and degraded stone of San Marco
and Santa Maria degli Miracoli, showing mercantile traffic and debris in the Grand Canal,
the abandoned cloisters of the convent of
Santa Teresa, Santi Cosma e Damiano and the
notorious basketball court in the Scuola della
Misericordia with fading frescoes vulnerable
behind spectator stalls.[58] Views of smoke
pouring out of Marghera were paired with
ocean-going liners and oil tankers passing the
historic buildings that line the basin of San
Marco. It was a new genre dedicated to
doomed Venice.

There was undeniable poetry in Venice's
demise: after all, it had been prophesied many
times. One of Lotti's night photographs captured a mysterious San Marco lapped by dark
water, casting its columnar reflections in anticipation of a permanently flooded city (fig.
198).[59] In another seminal view, which had the
full force of doom, an ocean-going vessel
ploughed past San Giorgio Maggiore through
the prime waters of the Bacino. This image
formed the cover of the widely circulated
edition of the English Architectural Review for
May 1971, edited by architectural historian
J. M. Richards and Professor Abraham
Rogatnick of the University of British Columbia. It was devoted to 'Venice: Problems and
Possibilities'.[60] A portfolio of illustrations
exposed the high water, pollution and industrialisation, and crumbling walls. The editors
tried to widen the understanding of the
network of problems facing Venice beyond the
saving of notable buildings: in other words,

198   Giorgio Lotti,
'Basilica di San Marco in
Acqua Alta', from Venice is
Dying, 1970.

this was an opportunity for the English-speaking world to move beyond the artistic
and archival preoccupations that had interested the English since Ruskin and Rawdon
Brown, to understand the larger topographical, technical, oceanographic, financial
and political issues at stake. 'The Humble House' featured, for example.[61] Yet that
issue may well have served as yet another death notice. In cavalier fashion, James
Morris wrote the prologue: 'My own solution for the problem of Venice is to let her
sink. She has died several deaths already.'[62]

Calvino's Invisible Cities and Palazzechi's Invisible Doge

The final days of Venice, submerged at last by vast waters, was the sobering if unex-
ceptional climax of Eugenio Trizio's L'ultima città, published in 1978.[63] But not all
accounts of Venice in the 1970s found the city a site of death, although it was vanquished or endangered in some way, or remembered because it was absent. In 1972

one of the most haunting accounts of its viability as a city of the mind was published by Italo Calvino, one of Italy's leading writers.[64] His *La città invisibile*, translated as *Invisible Cities*, evokes the many faces of Venice that are common to all cities. Through the travels of Venetian Marco Polo, Venice rediscovers its orientalism as, once more, it is turned from Europe towards the East and to fantasies of places conjured up by the traveller and told to Kubla Khan, insatiable for knowledge of foreign cities. All Marco Polo's travels refer to his home-city of Venice and its urban features, if only in details.

The book opens with two sections on 'Cities and Memory', which evoke the power of certain places in both individual and collective memory. The city is fiercely desired after Polo's passage through desert: desert which is not literally sand or the absence of water, but a want of imagination, which must be filled by abundant and precious features, such as silver domes or a crystal theatre. The cities rise up as urban conglomerates which exist as imprints of their past, beyond single buildings – recalling the urban studies of Muratori and Trincanato which uncovered the dense layers of the past as traces in the modern city. The Cities of Desire are posthumous, like Marco Polo himself: they suggest Nietzsche's posthumous city, which has travelled beyond death and become a place of traces so singular that they can never be eradicated. As Calvino put it, the city exists only as 'relationships between the measures of its space and the events of its past':

> As this wave from memories flows in, the city soaks up like a sponge and expands . . . [It] does not tell its past, but contains it like the lines of a hand, written in the corners of the streets, the gratings of the windows, the banisters of the steps, the antennae of the lightning rods, the poles, of the flags, every segment marked in turn with scratches, indentations, scrolls.[65]

Not surprisingly, many of Polo's remembered cities are water cities intercepted by canals, like Anastasia, 'a city with concentric canals watering it' or the city of Valdrada, looking on to water and becoming two cities, 'one erect above the lake, and the other reflected upside down'.[66] 'The inhabitants of such a mirror city know that each of their actions is both that action itself and its mirror image'.[67] Trading cities remember Venice; they are encrusted with jewels and loaded with the spices of the East, with pistachio nuts and poppy seeds.

Marco Polo is the collector of the ashes of all cities. The Khan is indefatigable in his quest for knowledge so that he can understand the ruin of his own empire before him. With Polo he visits Kin-sai in the imperial barge and discovers familiar attributes:

> bridges arching over the canals, the princely palaces whose marble doorsteps were immersed in the water, the bustle of light craft zigzagging, driven by long oars, the boats unloading baskets of vegetables at the market squares, the balconies, platforms, domes, campaniles, island gardens growing green in the lagoon's greyness.[68]

The Khan intuitively grasps the city's likeness to Venice and asks why Marco Polo has failed to describe his home city. In answer to the Khan's probing, Polo replies: 'Every time I describe a city I am saying something about Venice.' Absorbed into all other cities, Venice shares the headings of all the cities, which the book evokes and enumerates as Memories, Desire, Signs, Thin Cities (with scaffolding and spider-walks), Trading Cities, Cities and Eyes – the city of Valdrada is reflected in water; the City of Baucis is raised up on stilts like ancient Venice; the City and the Dead; Continuous Cities, Hidden Cities. Venice is all these.

But the name Venice cannot be spoken, nor can it be described. It is the ultimate palimpsest, its imprint is everywhere, carried far beyond its own terrain. Every city is analogous in some small part to Venice, but Kin-sai resembles it most closely. The very essence of cities is Calvino's subject, and Venice is the paradigm. If Venice is destroyed, or its citizens leave it and travel the earth, it must still exist, for its traces are everywhere.

At one point, in 1974, Calvino wrote directly on Venice in an article first published in German with the forthright title 'Ich glaube an das Venedig der Zukunft' (I believe in the Venice of the future). It was even more optimistically titled when it was included in Calvino's collected works as 'Venezia: Archetipo e utopia della città acquatica'.[69] Calvino gives the clue not only to the prominence of Venice in Marco Polo's tales told to the emperor, but also to the role of the city as both archetype in its historical dimension, and prototype in its potential life. There is no doubt of its singular status in Calvino's thought. He makes no mention of its fragility, or of residential frustration, only of its liberating geometry and its freedom from the confines of too much earth and human traffic. Untouched by straight lines, Venice is anti-Euclidean, and in this, most simply, it has a future as a prototype. Its modes of transportation are by foot or water; their separation is crucial, and beautiful. Venetian dwellings go back to the most archetypal, when men lived on houses raised up on stilts in the water: Calvino sees the food of the oceans being the sustenance of the future, and communities returning again to life lived in the ocean on the model of Venice.

Calvino's fictional realms – which inhabit specific elements and so often vacate the earth – are as much of the air as of the earth, with a baron who lives exclusively in trees (*Il Barone rampante*, written in 1957), and the air dwellings in *Invisible Cities*. Living in the elements of air and water is liberating to the imagination. The main doors of Venetian dwellings favour the water rather than the land, but the paths and squares of land are enriched, too; their nomenclature is unique, and the spatial sense valuable because it is discontinuous, enriched beyond the normal city in the passages along *fondamente* and the rising and falling that occurs as bridges are crossed. Human life can be lived with a sense of elements other than earth.

Another extraordinary fable was written in the 'unreal' period around the time of the flood. Aldo Palazzeschi's novel *Il Doge* was published in 1967, when the author, one-time Futurist with a period of study in Venice in economics and commerce at the University of Ca' Foscari, was eighty-two years old.[70] In 1913 he had performed at Marinetti's soirée at La Fenice. *Il Doge* draws on a strange mesh of historical and contemporary possibilities and fantasies by returning the memory of the doge. His leadership is bizarre in this city given over to mega-tourism. Visitors clog the city: 'At the entrance of the Piazza, as on the Riva and in front of the garden of the Palazzo Reale, one is barred by a high wall, unsurmountable, formed by an incalculable, unbelievable number of suitcases with the owners behind them and their porters . . .'[71]

The crowd gathers daily at midday in the Piazza in expectation of the doge's appearance on the loggia of the Palazzo Ducale. On the third day there is an official announcement of revolution and subsequently the doge appears with the dogaressa, a blonde – and a second female escort, a brunette. To the consternation of the population, bigamy appears sanctioned, but more dramatic events follow. Compounding the one-time collapse of the Campanile, the entire Basilica of San Marco disappears. The doge comes to the balcony of the Palazzo Ducale with the four golden horses whom he drives off into the sky. Not surprisingly, his subjects are disturbed and lose the capacity to sleep, for the doge has demonstrated his proximity to divine providence, confounding his mortal subjects. If all cities are ultimately invisible and exist only in the words of travellers, then so too, we might conclude, are systems of government, as Venice is not named by Marco Polo, and the Doge of Venice drives off into the sky.

* * *

P. M. Pasinetti: Expatriate Writer

At the time of the post-flood crisis, Calvino conceived of a city in terms of memory and other traces, absent rather than present. For Palazzeschi there are profound alterations, disappearances, irregularities, and a final abdication of government. Calvino's *La città invisibili* represents the most considerable and poetic *Italian* text on the subject of Venice in the twentieth century, but it is the novels of P. M. Pasinetti, written from 1960 onwards, which represent the most sustained reflection on the city's inhabitants – and the Veneto overall – by a *Venetian*. The brother of cinematographer Francesco, Pier Maria Pasinetti was closely involved in local film making with Francesco in the 1930s, before he himself went to pursue his academic career in the United States.[72] The Partibon family are the central figures in a saga that spreads across a number of volumes: the family has expanded from Venice, to the Veneto, to the world.[73] They represent the exodus and the journeying that takes Venetians away from Venice, yet they are forever returning. Exodus shapes the events and reactions in all Pasinetti's novels, which turn on the revelation of the entwined personal histories of Veneto families, their deep familiarity with the city and their identification with the political aspect of contemporary Italian-Venetian life. A member of the family – the charismatic Marco Partibon – has disappeared. He is in hiding because of political allegiances, or perhaps imprisoned. His absence haunts his descendants.

Both the past and the future of the city are understood through one-time residents who carry their own retrospectivity and that of their city, even in exile; they are not unlike Calvino's city, which is marked with 'scratches, indentations, scrolls'. The character Ersilia, for example, 'has embraced the notion of survival precisely because, deep down, she feels it's absurd . . . she finds analogies between her city and her family. We are longevous by mistake . . . survival is the curious accident, not death'.[74]

In *The Smile on the Face of the Lion*, first published in 1964, the theme of obduracy is uppermost. The novel centres on Bernardo Partibon, born in the Veneto countryside, but living in Venice from an early age before emigrating to California – duplicating the author's own experience. He returns to Italy and to scenes of his childhood; he smells the oil paint, varnish and turpentine in the studio of his painter-uncle, smells the food of the Veneto – the 'risotto with green peas, creamed stockfish, fried fish of a delicately golden hue'. He hears the bells and the gondoliers' voices.[75] The lions of the title smile at him with 'a formal, inaccessible, stubborn and desperate smile', which we can take to be the mark of Venice, of a character experienced as stubborn and longevous.[76]

Another character, Ovidio, takes up the status of Venice and the 'question of Venetian fibre', of

> that strong, terrible city badly sheltered against winter cold, frozen canals, fogs and humidity and atrocious discomforts, where you have to go on foot through the network of narrow streets, whose intricacy takes your breath away and dismays visitors. For centuries, with insufficient heating, on the mud, through extremely arduous architectural and structural organisations, they have created trade, galleys, arts, amusements. It's a hard, hard city, of stone, with floods every year, not in marshy lands, but in the most splendid centre of the city . . .[77]

But the obdurate city survives even the flood and its citizens are, in a sense, the palimpsest of the city.

For the characters in Pasinetti's novels the interrogation of the past is a Venetian characteristic they must work through: it is a compulsion for them. Long memories and ancestral lines drive further and further back into the modern city's ideological foundations – to the Fascism of the 1920s and 1930s – the period of the first novel, *Venetian Red* – to the brief period of Revolution and Republic under Daniele Manin, which forms both background and foreground to *Melodramma*, published in 1993. The longevity of memory traced through the line of the principal house of the Partibons is replayed and extended in *Melodramma*, in which Pasinetti explores mid-nineteenth-century Venice through his characters, while Verdi represents the Risorgimento spirit.[78] The city again plays an active role moulding the characters, stamping them with its history and its constraints.

Pasinetti, a literary historian as well as a writer of fiction, has commented on the role of historical events in novels, using episodes from Proust's *Remembrance of Things Past*, and the figure of Carlino Altoviti at the time of the fall of the Republic in Nievo's *Le Confessioni d'un Italiano*.[79] Indeed, he is the heir to Nievo. Pasinetti's saga of the Partibon family reaches back more than the eighty years of Nievo's octogenarian to a Venice under Manin's rule in *Melodramma*. As the fall of Venice and the aspirations towards unification form the events covering the lives and emotions of Nievo's characters, so too in Pasinetti, whose characters are actively affected by political events, 'we have always been part of the revolution and the republic', Giorgio declares in *Melodramma*.[80]

Pasinetti argues for the active contribution of exile from the homeland, as for the protagonist in *From the Academy Bridge*, who is shaped by Venice, but only realises the process of formation, like the author, from far away California.[81] Pasinetti is well aware of the problem of historical allusion for the Italian novel, exacerbated by 'political and intellectual confusion'.[82] He is aware of the limitations of Venice as a setting: it 'has more than the general disadvantages ... as a milieu it is actually too well known, and in the most doubtful ways'.[83] But, like Marco Polo in his incarnation by Calvino, Pasinetti takes it is as a given 'that a significant modern novel cannot be produced by a writer who has stuck to his native habitat'.[84]

Painted Letters to Palladio, and Serene Waves

If the death of Venice, and even the death-wish *for* Venice, and exodus from it are the primary themes of the 1960s and 1970s, that is not to say that beauty was not seen and preserved, that a lyrical mode was suspended, that Venice had become only traces of a past. Giuseppe Santomaso's suite of paintings from 1977, the *Letters to Palladio*, reassure us that the city's delicate geometries are still in place, and that ineluctable meeting of building, sky and water along the Giudecca – the stretch of Palladian water from the church of San Giorgio Maggiore, to the Redentore and to the Zitelle (fig. 199).[85] In Santomaso's paintings Palladio's buildings appear as envelopes – rectangular and pedimented. The geometry of the oblong is surmounted by a triangle that closes the shape: white, translucent, hanging against the sky, abutting the water.

These oils are washed so lightly that they have the translucence of watercolour. The envelopes float on the ground line which meets the canal, a horizontal slab sharing the lightness of the sky. Manfredo Tafuri has described this line of churches in another context: 'on the horizon, like over-concluded dreams, the shapes of the Redentore and San Giorgio Maggiore stand out, contrasting the impressionism of the urban *imagerie* with their calculated play of interpretations.'[86] In Santomaso's paintings, torn shapes, dark in tone, hover at the ground line, or float in the sky as the colours deepen. The weather that affects the fifth letter, we can suppose to be darker, more tenebrous of sky. Sometimes the day is very blue, as in the sixth letter. Or we suspect a sunset, discreet, not gaudy, as in the seventh epistle. *The Letters* are at once abstract and figurative, but never literal.

It may be that Santomaso's *Letters* are telling Palladio that his own buildings are already traces, receding, becoming phantom-like, now only the thinnest of membranes hanging between sky and lagoon, abstractions of a receding city. Perhaps after all they are memorials of a lost or flooded city.

199 Giuseppe Santomaso,
Letter to Palladio, 1977.
Oil on canvas,
123 × 89 cm. Venice,
The Peggy Guggenheim
Collection (The Solomon R.
Guggenheim Foundation).

The possibility of lyricism in the city of water also infuses Luigi Nono's 1976 work for piano and tape, *sofferte onde serene* (serene waves suffered) but there is, again, some element of ambivalence in the word *sofferte* (suffered/suffering).[87] Perhaps it could be said that the work sounds with the sweetness and ambiguities of Santomaso's churches hanging against sky and above water. The piano timbre is often diaphanous; it is vaporous, impressionistic, reminiscent of Debussy. Or more solid attacks drop to globular bass notes that are weighted like water, but then these depths are relinquished in favour of rippling passages and light treble. The collage is Venice-like, set quite literally, as it develops, with tolling bass bells that anchor and regulate the higher notes, sounding insistent, ancient and melancholy in this fragmented and disharmonious sound-world. Nono has described the very domestic context of this music for him, written in the Palladian stretches of the Giudecca:

> In my house on the Giudecca in Venice the sound of various bells rung in different ways and with different meanings reach our ears continuously, day and night, through the fog or in the sunshine.
> They are indications of life on the lagoon, on the sea.
> Calls to work and to meditation, warnings.
> And life continues there in the painful and calm necessity of the 'balance of the deep interior', as Kafka says.[88]

Without overt political import, without overt allegory, these Venetians sounds carry their meditation on the city and lagoon.

Comic-Strip Venice: Hugo Pratt

To these Venetian views, inevitably more intricate than those expressed by visitors, must be added with affection those of Hugo Pratt, comic-strip artist, who died in 1997.[89] Marco Polo finds an incarnation in the early twentieth century in the character Corto Maltese, who emerged in the 1960s in the French press, and then, still in the French language, in the Belgian *Pif*. Hugo Pratt lived in Venice as a child and returned there in 1942 to train at the Accademia di Belle Arti. He had himself experienced the world travels and residencies of his character, living in Ethiopia, Argentina and Brazil. His Corto Maltese is a comely creature, with his nautical uniform and handsome profile. That profile below the peaked hat, and the slant of the body, hands behind back, passing the domes of San Marco is one of his creator's most memorable images (figs 200–01). Maltese's sincere words uttered in *Le Fable de Venise* confirm his Venetianness: 'Venezia non mia lascia mai, è la mia vita e sarà la mia fine' (Venice will never leave me, it is my life and it will be my finish), words that could have been uttered by Calvino's Marco Polo.

Although he lives in the twentieth century, Corto Maltese still holds the key to the city's alchemy. The city is exotic, known to him by its Arabian name of Sirat al Bunjugiyyah – he is at home with all the traces of the East. Because of his travels and his education in the arcane arts, he can penetrate the wonders of Venice and its true exoticism. Like the Situationists, he relishes its psycho-geography. He can read the Greek inscriptions on the Corfù lions guarding the Arsenale.

Corto Maltese's Venice is that of his creator, whose maternal grandmother lived in the Vecchio Ghetto. Her knowledge of the Judeo-Greco-Venetian tradition yields the intimacy needed for following black magic and cabbalistic societies.[90] And there is a literary connection: Maltese's time in Venice is Baron Corvo's – around 1910, and the decade after Corvo's death. Corvo represents another exotic outsider, an adventurer; Corto follows a posthumous letter from him that he hopes will lead to a precious emerald. In *Le Fable de Venise*, the hunt for Solomon's seal entails cabbalistic encounters, roof-top chases, Arabian genii, an emerald and a beautiful princess (in accordance with the instructions from Baron Corvo), and, finally, the Revelation of St Mark.[91] The Venetian adventure culminates on 25 April, the day of St Mark, when Corto recovers Solomon's seal.

In another Venetian incident, Corto Maltese is travelling in the last years of the First World War. *Les Celtiques* is a strange and singular return to the period of war with Austria; Maltese visits Venice before going to Ireland and England.[92] The Venetian episode features an encounter with espionage, Franciscan monks, ancient Christian relief sculptures and characters in search of El Dorado. A crippled girl who lives alone in the lagoon – in a sinister house, with dark shadows and birds overhead – is really a spy for the Austrians. Maltese is involved in a Austrian air attack

200 and 201 Hugo Pratt, Corto Maltese, from *Le Fable de Venise*, 1981.

in the vicinity of her house which he enters, where he finds her intent upon the quest for El Dorado. She is revealed as a spy, but escapes. Ensnared by the city, Maltese declares he himself must leave Venice to escape its charms.

Hugo Pratt's Venice is a place of intrigue, a melting-pot for the Christian, Jewish and pagan. Corto Maltese makes it evident that adventure is still possible, that Venetians have an enviable natural relationship with their city: they can negotiate the roofs, walk in front of San Marco or San Pietro Castello, or talk to the myriad cats – as Corto does in one of the most memorable images in *Le Fable de Venise*, at night, beside a well-head. Corto's Venice is a night-time Venice: most often the sickle moon hangs in the sky, further evidence of a city still replete with magic.

Fictional Deaths

DON'T LOOK NOW

In the 1970s Venice was the setting for a number of films and novels, an ironic result of the focus on its fragility. Nicholas Roeg's *Don't Look Now*, starring Julie Christie and Donald Sutherland – the latter as an art restorer working in Venice – is an original variant on the theme of the mortality that the city impels, and an outstanding example of the horror film.[93] Its power lies in the disorienting presence of a small figure in a red raincoat that resembles one worn by the couple's recently drowned daughter. But the Venetian figure in a raincoat is a serial killer dwarf who appears as a flash of scarlet in dark alleys and whose footsteps echo in the acoustically sharpened silence of the city. The innocence of the child is inverted by the murderous dwarf, who reaches out to stab the child's father.

Early in the film, after the titles showing the daughter's death in England, the theme of grief at the loss of a child is compounded by an encounter in Venice with two sisters. One is a blind clairvoyant who can see the lost child. The child's father, John Baxter, is also clairvoyant, but he does not realise it, and he resists.[94] He foresees his own death: his wife and son and the two sisters appear in mourning in a funeral barge. Roeg's flashbacks and the sharp, swift editing parallel the speed with which the mind can be consumed by images that may or may not be actual and are caught up in the very morphology of Venice, its alleyways, iron gates, dark water and small *campi* confounding space. Flash-forwards point to foreknowledge through psychic vision. Mental disorientation meets topographical disarray.

Between Baxter and his wife, the sharing of their loss is poignantly considered, having its summation early in the film in a love scene, the first love-making, we are led to understand, since the daughter's death.[95] The city contributes to the regeneration of their love, although everything is precarious. Baxter nearly falls from the scaffold in the church he is restoring; glass is broken; mosaics are crushed, human certainty is undermined. From the outset, *Don't Look Now* is a winter film; the season is over and hotels are closing, dustsheets shroud furniture, the tourist sights play no role. Again Venice is the labyrinth that both conceals and begets evil, especially in slippery wet *calli* of wintertime where rats swim. The surfaces of water are pitted with rain; pigeons rise in clouds from empty squares.

Daphne du Maurier's short story 'Don't Look Now' provided the basis for Roeg's film: the bereaved Baxters, the clairvoyant blind sister, supernatural vision, the murdering dwarf. The story also registers the decline of Venice: John Baxter observes that the place is sinking, 'the whole city is slowly dying'.[96] In the film Laura Baxter quotes the words of one of the sisters: 'She says it's like a city in aspic left over from a dinner party and all the guests are dead and gone. It frightens her, too many shadows.'[97] The shadows are engendered by the mind, as well as the city.

The film develops an inexorable sense of tragedy initiated early on by the death of the daughter in England, followed by the various rehearsals of John Baxter's death,

202 Nicholas Roeg, *Don't Look Now*, 1973. Film still. Casey Productions, London/Eldorado Films, Rome.

which is almost sacrificial, as he tries to placate the dwarf. Roeg develops the character of Baxter in a topical way in the selection of his career as an art restorer in a period of international restoration projects. Baxter is at work, himself imperilled, in the climate of 'Venice in peril'. It is only in the last shocking sequences, when the dwarf lunges at Baxter with its knife that we realise it is not his daughter.

Other images, fraught with foreboding, underline the pull of Venice towards death – by water, in anticipation, when the daughter drowns, and later when a female body is crudely hoisted out of a canal. John Baxter's vision of his funeral procession takes place on the water (fig. 202). Venetian red is literally invoked in blood, the colour of which runs throughout the film, from the opening sequences with the raincoat that links daughter and murderer. Glass – associated with the city's liquidity, its industry at Murano, the mosaics that John Baxter is restoring – shatters on many occasions during the film. Not least, the theme of scopophilia, the 'looking' of the title which is both avowed and disavowed, links beauty and insight, as well as evil, permitting the passionate sex scene between Baxter and his wife and the vision of his funeral; and the gyrations as he dies after the stabbing.[98]

Anonimo Veneziano

Closer to sentimentality, yet touchingly intimate, the Italian film *Anonimo veneziano*, made in 1970, was developed from a script by the popular Veneto-born Giuseppe Berto, who then, in an inversion of the usual order, wrote a novel of the same name. In the film, director Enrico Maria Salerno is less explicit about the decay of Venice than Berto is in the book.[99] An estranged husband and wife spend a day together in Venice. The wife comes by train from Milan and immediately picks up the tensions that have strained the marriage. But she learns that her husband – handsome of course, and artistic – has an incurable disease and only five months to live. He is a musician, an oboist, who is that day recording a lost concerto by an 'anonymous Venetian'. The conjunction of death and music is once more played out in Venice, and in winter again. It is a village Venice, with rubbish in the water, sinking boats, *caffès* away from the tourist centre, a handful of passengers on the *vaporetto*. Light plays on the whiteness of Istrian stone on a grey day, and walks through the industrial quarter are a welcome respite from the relentlessly Mediterranean sunshine view of tourist Venice.

At one point in the film the wife tries on gold brocades from the house of Rubelli, characteristic luxury productions of Venice, for the husband wishes to make her a gift. The looms turn, and the workers at the looms watch intently as the gold cloth grows; but in the book the factory has closed, production has ceased, and in this way, Venice, too, is finished.[100] The finale signals the death of a man, and the death of a city.[101]

Does the Death in Venice theme reanimate the city in some way, or does it simply add to its topical condemnation and declare it posthumous? Opera and film persistently portray a site of disease, death and murder, of squalor and back-lane obscurity; they replay the themes both topographical and historical, part of the ancestry of thematics of plague, illness and compounding intrigue. Yet in Venice love and insight are reaffirmed – indeed the power of inter-personal relationships inaugurated or extended is as strong as the inevitability of death. Beauty is firmly in place, and the enchantment is effected by the city. The city liberates emotional and psychic tension – innocently, but with a hint of tragedy in Jane Hudson's summertime romance; more cruelly as John Baxter succumbs to the murderous dwarf; platonically, and fatally, as Gustav von Aschenbach yields to Tadzio. For those who come in from outside the characteristic disorientation has its effect in the labyrinth, but also some measure of love, eroticism, sexual freedom and insight.

VISCONTI

Luchino Visconti's two films with Venetian settings depict the city at times of historical crisis: in *Senso*, the years of Austrian rule in the 1860s, in *Death in Venice*, made in 1971, the years before the First World War.[102] Both films engage their protagonists in affairs that profoundly alter their lives in the erotic city in which the rational mind is challenged: the 'half fairy-tale, half-snare' as Thomas Mann had it; the sensual city named by Boito. All these implications are compounded in Visconti's handling of the Venetian setting: its claustrophobic, unhealthy rear view when Countess Serpieri comes upon a murdered Austrian soldier in *Senso*, or when Aschenbach trails Tadzio and finds cholera in *Death in Venice*. The chief protagonists have sensuality or a heightened appreciation in common: Aschenbach is exposed to the full fashions of the Lido salon recreated by Piero Tosi, and the androgynous figure of Tadzio, beguiling in sailor-suit or bathing costume, implicated in the seduction of the older man. In *Senso*, the uniform of the soldier is taut beside Serpieri's plunging necklines and reflecting satins. Sensuous characters are heightened in their sensuality in the sensuous city. Visconti adds the voluptuousness of music. Verdi's *Il Trovatore* is used with political intent in *Senso*, and also a Bruckner symphony composed at the time of Boito's novella in 1873; in *Death in Venice* music by Mahler compounds the time of Mann's story of 1911 with the death of Gustav Mahler in the same year.[103]

The view of Venice as a sensual city hardly needed reinforcement in the late twentieth century, but Visconti made it even more resonant in both aural and visual terms in the two historical periods he so trenchantly excavated. The undertow is in evidence: the weaknesses and corruption, the masquerade of both youth and age, indeed, the decay of western civilisation on the eve of the First World War.

203 Luchino Visconti, *Death in Venice*, 1971. Film still. Alfa Cinematografica, Rome/Production Editions Cinematographiques Française, Paris.

Visconti's deviations from the Thomas Mann novella are well known, especially the casting of Aschenbach not as a writer, but as a musician.[104] But the flavour of the crossing from Venice to the Lido remains true to the beauty and entrapment of which Mann wrote, and the glamour and international life of the Lido is explicit in early sequences at the Hotel des Bains – captured in fluent, voluptuous cinematography in the hotel dining-room scenes. The two Venices of Visconti's *Death in Venice* – the old *centro istorico* and the new Lido – are held in counterpoint throughout, the new working to condemn the old. The gondolier from the old city is dishonest, the old city is doused against infection; all its squalor is on show.[105]

Trailing the boy Tadzio in the city of Venice, the experience of cholera and disease in the city, the caricatured faces of troubadours and Aschenbach's own face made up by the barber in a parody of youth – hair dyed and lips rouged: these aspects follow the novella, but recreate it with visual brilliance, with the simultaneous pleasure and pain that the death theme elicits in the climate after the flood. The carnivalesque aspects of Visconti's film are a shrill indictment of the central character, with the young people on the arriving boat, and the grotesque cabaret of lewd figures offered to the hotel patrons on the Lido. Aschenbach, a parody of himself in both youth and age, is himself ready for the cabaret, or, more particularly for the Dance of Death. At the same time, Aschenbach's death on the beach (fig. 203), seated in a deck chair, is presented as something of an epiphany as he watches Tadzio pointing out to sea like the Angel of Death, indicating other horizons.

BENJAMIN BRITTEN'S OPERA

Benjamin Britten's *Death in Venice*, his last composition, first performed in 1973 with sets by John Piper, is valedictory, following Thomas Mann's focus on a writer in the last months of his life – not the Aschenbach musician created by Visconti.[106] Britten's Aschenbach re-engages with beauty, represented by the Polish boy Tadzio, who has the mythical quality of the Greek Eros, and the spirit of both Apollo and Dionysus. Myfanwy Piper's libretto is simple, sparse even, permitting the orchestral music to surround and even overtake the words. The city of Venice is stone and water, the aesthetic Venice of an Adrian Stokes:

> Ah Serenissima!
> Where should I come but you
> To soothe and revive me
> Where but to you
> To live that magical life
> Between the sea and the city.
> What lies in wait for me here,
> Ambiguous Venice
> Where water is married to stone
> And passion confuses the senses?

The city is repeatedly described as 'ambiguous'; 'the confusion' and the disorientation it inflicts on visitors is essential to Aschenbach's succumbing to Tadzio. That Venice is a caricature of itself and that life is a masquerade is suggested, of course, particularly in the various roles given to the counter-tenor, who is the gondolier, the porter, the tourist in the boat, the barber, and so on, playing a hectic range of shrill figures. Importantly, Tadzio and his friends and family are dancers accompanied by percussion, not singers. The orchestral music is their characterising device; the music pervades their whole bodies. The balletic quality of the opera bears it away from naturalism and specific history.

After first coming to Venice, making the crossing to the Lido with the unscrupulous gondolier, Aschenbach glimpses the boy and his family in the Lido hotel. It is clear from the words sung by Aschenbach upon entering the hotel that he explicitly understands the significance of the crossing. Britten's opera in general catches up the mythologies that are implicit in Mann's story, in particular Grecian myths of Thanatos and Eros with their strong Venetian location.[107] The premonition of death is already with him as he sings of the blackness of the gondola-hearse and the gondolier who rowed him across the Styx: 'I should have faded like echoes on the lagoon to nothingness.'

Although evil, foppery, masquerade and disease are experienced in Britten's opera, so too is consummate beauty. Commentators have seen a frankly homosexual desire expressed, in contrast to the ambivalence of Thomas Mann's story.[108] Aschenbach is transported by watching Tadzio dance on the beach in a Greek-style choral dance, 'The Games of Apollo' in act 1. He asks, 'How does such beauty come about?' This is one of many moments of frank contemplation of beauty, made poignant by the expectation of death. Aschenbach dreams of an ultimate meeting of Dionysius and Apollo through the intermediary of the Eros and the Ganymede, who is Tadzio. For the sense of Venice and its lagoon, the composer draws on the long-established rhythms of the barcarolle to follow Aschenbach on his gondola voyages and in this way the opera exudes a soothing, cradling feeling that protects its audience against too harsh a view of plague-infested Venice. Donald Mitchell writes of 'the spacious contours of the music that embodies Aschenbach's first view of the beach . . . It is an upsurge of lyricism, from a constricted heart, that plays a prominent role in the opera'.[109]

But the threat is there of course, declared by a clerk in the travel bureau: 'Death is at work, the plague is with us!' The multi-persons of the counter-tenor are other faces that leer out at Aschenbach as his sense of reality diminishes, and perhaps it is in this growing unreality that the music most powerfully suggests another dimension to Mann's classic tale. Visconti's collusion with Mann in exposing the secrecy of Venetian officials with respect to the plague is of little relevance in Britten's opera. Britten seeks an allegory of life, derived from a process of observation, introspection and a continuity of mythology expressed in the vain search for beauty and possession of the loved one, and the resolution – or the cancellation – of love by death. And yet again this revelation is wrought by a city and its surrounding waters.

KLUGE'S *MASS DEATH*

The glamorous pre-war Lido and its new hotels are the setting for Thomas Mann's *Death in Venice*, followed by Visconti and Britten, but there is one searing replay of Mann's theme that entirely subverts any lingering elements of pre-war grace. In 1973 Alexander Kluge published his *Mass Death in Venice*, based on an incident that occurred in 1969.[110] The story tells how, at the height of July, twenty-four inmates of the San Lorenzo old peoples' home died in the heat, and how 'those who remained' took revenge and killed the director of the institution, Dr Muratti. Kluge's horror story homes in on the political point of Mann's story, the official concealment of the plague, and gives it dire contemporary relevance. After Muratti's murder the survivors of the old peoples' home barricaded themselves in against the police, who occupied the kitchens. The police were provoked to shoot in self defence. Further carnage occurred. Two female cooks were attacked by the old people and their arteries slit; in response, the police shot blind into the room killing more residents and immobilised others with tear gas. The survivors were taken to a spa near the Alps, but 'they died there as a result of the sudden exposure to cold'.[111] The editor of the newspaper *Il Gazzettino* suggested that such events are 'negative' for the tourist traffic: 'People may get the idea that one travels to Venice to die here.'

In this terse novella of some three pages, events move with cruel speed. Only two sentences are needed to summon up Venice's miasmic history and its foul waters: 'In the summer of 1969 the sun weighed down for weeks on the city and waterways of Venice. The steamers and motorboats ploughed through the green waters of the lagoon which surrounded the houses like thick soup.'[112] The events of 1969 followed closely upon the great flood and the Biennale riots of 1968 in which the police were a conspicuous presence at the Giardini and the Piazza San Marco. Kluge himself witnessed confrontations on the Lido at the Cinema Biennale where his own film, *Artists under the Big Top*, was shown.[113]

The tradition of Aschenbach dying in Venice demanded a final epiphany, an affirmation of beauty recognised through the figure of Tadzio. This is only an echo beset with irony for Kluge who has the prefect of police ask, 'What do you think the last impressions of these old people were?' The criminal investigator could never know 'whether or not they saw something particularly beautiful in their minds while they were dying in this undignified manner'.

Escaping Venice: Aldo Rossi's Analogous City and Manfredo Tafuri's Histories

The vicious circles inscribing Venice are laid bare in Kluge's brief, cruel story set in the city of waterways, in the tourist city of tourism that neglects its older residents. The focus on an old peoples' home reflects the ageing population of a city more and more thoroughly old. From fictional fact to architecture: Aldo Rossi wrote in sombre vein on the city paralysed by the old. It should be abandoned. He would counter the extravagance of past Venetian architecture with the severity of a new rationalism.

Rossi joined the Institute of Architecture in 1975, after a period of four years in which he was banned from teaching because of his political activism. Semirani has identified Rossi's voice as 'tragic', 'sombre' and 'desperate', particularly in relation to Venice:

> The city is viewed synchronically, as a morphological fact; study and project, analysis and proposal are no longer separate – 'there is no jump in logic, but unity' as Aldo Rossi wrote in 1964; architectural composition becomes the *description* of precise choices – architecture as history, architecture as element in the city, architecture as construction; this description requires eloquence, so there is a monumental, *museum-like*, sombre and *desperate* intensification of the discourse.[114]

Rossi's essay on 'What Is To Be Done With Old Cities?' despairs at the very question.[115] The strategy is expressed bluntly: 'This old environment . . . is a reminder of old poverty and it is dear to us as evidence of a people's pain . . .'[116] He is aware of the paradox: that areas of scenographic appeal have accommodated the underprivileged – for example, the old ghettos of Prague and Venice. The act of conservation freezes monuments into immobility and old structures are inevitably surrounded by new contemporary configurations. This is in fact necessary, and in asking how to achieve it, Rossi rehabilitates Le Corbusier's *la ville radieuse*, which is still radical for him. Drastic action must be taken either to raze an old city, or step sideways from it. The example of Venice is spelled out: 'In Venice, it would be like taking San Giorgio, Santa Maria della Salute, the Doge's palace and St Mark's Square as fixed points of a triangulation around which to rebuild the city.'[117] Venice is not by any means the centre of Rossi's essay, but it figures as an example of a crisis of the past, and his remarks have added weight because of his residence there. Thus: 'The historic and picturesque parts should either be quickly destroyed to enable the monuments to play a direct part in the building up of the modern city or they should be retained in their entirety, wherever possible, as museums.' However, Venice is apparently beyond salvation for Rossi: 'I do not believe that the problem is how to make Venice habitable. Rather, I believe that the problem is how to abandon it immediately or transform its very function and reduce it completely into a monument city.'[118] At the same time Rossi is surely caught in a contradiction of his own making when, in his extensively translated publication of 1966, *The Architecture of the City*, he acknowledges the power of memory in cities. He accepts (and values) the reading of anthropologists and urban historians who give weight to the imagination and collective memory embodied in cities and this memory-bank affects his well-known concept of the 'analogous city'.[119]

Rossi has become particularly well known for his concept of the 'analogous city'.[120] His starting point is the Venetian tradition of the *capriccio*, in particular the nonexistent Palladian buildings and buildings that are inserted into an apparently realistic Venice in Canaletto's paintings. The memory-bank is crucial. As Rossi explains:

> I gave the example of Canaletto's fantasy view of Venice, a *capriccio* in which Palladio's project for the Ponte di Rialto, the Basilica of Vicenza and the Palazzo Chiericati are set next to each other and described as if the painter were rendering an urban scene he had actually observed. These three Palladian monuments, none of which are actually in Venice (one is a project; the other two are in Vicenza), nevertheless constitute an analogous Venice formed of specific elements associated with the history of both architecture and the city.[121]

Rossi's focus on the city's regional context transplants to Venice the character of Veneto cities which, like Venice, also have long histories.[122] Like his academic colleagues, Rossi takes typology as a starting point and, by so doing, participates in the Institute's structuralist persuasion, evident from Muratori onwards. It is a methodology that accommodates the layering of Venice from the Byzantine to the Gothic, from the Renaissance to the Baroque, and encourages the resolution of stylistic differences.[123] The analogous city might even recall Ruskin, since Rossi accepts Gothic as the most important point of reference for Venice and Veneto cities because it embodies a politically progressive rationale of the city state.[124] But the final point of reference lies with the interpreters of the Romanising mode in the Veneto, and Rossi's own progenitors, Palladio, Mantegna, Piranesi and Canova.[125] Palladio, for example, developed a rapport with the Veneto landscape and architecture and appears to have annulled the difference between civic and religious architecture. In this sense he forged a Neoclassical typology which, for Rossi, had emotional weight and authenticity.

Such an interpretation of the city extends and celebrates its diversity while paradoxically clinging to its totality: it is another version of heterodoxy, which has 'its echoes of the East and the North', orientations diverse enough to tear apart any homogeneity.[126] The city of Venice is a cultural artefact (again), and Rossi emphasises its construction as a man-made object, following Camillo Sitte to the heart of Venice, the Piazza San Marco. On the other hand, organic growth counter-balances deliberate creation and leads to the elimination or suppression of street networks that have evolved rather than been imposed.[127] While recognising a certain validity in the Gothic mode in his account of Venice, Rossi withstands Gothic's obvious influence and counters its charisma. His own work favours the Neoclassical tradition, which in turn feeds the Neo-rationalist position that is Rossi's political starting point, and the source of his aesthetic austerity.

In the face of a city that is not obviously rationalist, Rossi's voice is muffled. He seems to echo Calvino's Marco Polo recalling 'that primordial city built on the sea' when he writes:

> I try never to speak of Venice, even though it is one of the places where I have taught and hence lived for nearly twelve years. It is also strange that even though many events have been resolved for me in Venice, I still feel a relative stranger to the city more so certainly than I do to Trieste or New York or many other cities.[128]

The city as a locus of collective memory is now a popular concept and Rossi's interpretation has been seen to be seminal, for he suggests that an 'analogous city' is 'not quite a real city nor entirely a fictitious one' and he gives the city freedom.[129] (This mesh of fact and faction is the very attraction of Venice for architects – and writers such as Calvino and Palazzeschi). This ambivalence is productive, for it releases a kind of visual montage, capable of many reverberations. It moves outwards from the city to exude influence abroad, but also works inward, drawing other references, external expressions and echoes of itself to itself, enriching its own topography. Other members of the School of Venice have certainly indulged the play of the analogous emanating from Venice. In a study of modernist German architecture, Francesco Dal Co introduced Venetian bridges, both real and painted; he used an illustration of Bellini's *Miracle of the Holy Cross* and a map of 1373 that marked Venice as the centre of the world in order to declare that San Marco and its Piazza is the central space in a city that is a paradigm of the self-centred and the self-contained.[130]

Other members of the 'School of Architecture' have shown their interest in the Venetian past that is still represented in the present city so extensively.[131] Since 1968, under Manfredo Tafuri, architectural history has been active, particularly outstanding in the period of sixteenth-century studies in Venice and in the scrutiny of Modernism overall, in America as well as Europe.[132] Tafuri came to focus increasingly on Venetian history while underlining what he saw to be neurosis and unrest accompanying a fear of the new. That was his diagnosis of the sixteenth century, so often seen as 'The Golden Age'.[133] He uncovered the complexity of ideologies and the semblances of a Utopia desired by a declining patriciate. It may well be that Tafuri's sensitivity to the *Angst* of Venice is appropriate to a contemporary resident in the 1960s and 1970s, that he shares the city's pessimism in the 1970s with Aldo Rossi.

Tafuri's move from Rome to Venice marked a further stage in the consolidation of the intellectual life of Venetian academic architecture and the status and fame of the faculty. The place to which he came has been described as that 'passionate theatre of debate that then was Venice'.[134] In his 1969 monograph on Sansovino and the architecture of the sixteenth century, Tafuri might be seen replaying his own passage, making Sansovino's Roman experience crucial to his work in Venice. But Sansovino is also undermined by his new location, and by Venetian resistance to classical architecture and innovation.[135] Tafuri observed Sansovino 'becoming Venetian', as Tafuri himself was.[136] His subsequent focus on the church of San Francesco della Vigna carried the title *Harmony and Conflict*, making Tafuri's conflictual position evident from the outset.[137] The utopian theme still cherished by so many historians, and the still living myth of Contarini is undercut, and Renaissance certainty compromised.

Tafuri's probing studies in twentieth-century architecture have brought Modernism's ruined utopias to the surface. Beyond Venice he has been a major commentator on the architecture of his own time in global terms, and one of the most important. Both the sixteenth century and the twentieth have been well-traversed academically, but Tafuri has worked to unsettle and to expose the anxieties and conflicts at work in periods of apparent confidence. Existing in a state that had often been seen as utopic, he has also studied would-be Utopias in the USSR, Germany and the United States, exposing lost opportunities and compromised politics.

For other members of the Institute of Architecture, the considerations of ecological and technological history have been more limited, but nevertheless intense in focus. Studies of the management of the lagoon in the sixteenth-century, the period of Doge Gritti, and technological studies of the most prominent monuments, such as the Rialto Bridge and the Arsenale, have been published by Donatella Calabi, Paolo Morachiello and Ennio Concina.[138] In concert with Tafuri's position, the subject 'architecture' is seen as an *interrogation* of a monument and its urban and ideological context: the monument is almost necessarily a compromise between conflicting decisions. It is always in the process of formulation, affected by the exercise of power and the limitations of technologies. In the area of Venetian studies it becomes clear that the fabled wisdom of the Serenissima is constantly being eroded: in Tafuri's eyes, the insular policies constantly inhibited the full development of the Republic.

Architectural Fantasies: Designs for Cannaregio

Given the fraught nature of these readings of the past, which are ranged against prevalent notions of the Golden Age, what can we expect of architectural interpolations into the current city? The despair that attends modern Venice was once more in evidence, particularly in the 1970s. The largest schemes were, by necessity, for rehabilitation and redeployment. Exactly as in the early part of the century the pressure was to build 'as it was, where it was': *dov'era, com'era*. There have been concentrated projects, some obsessive, focused on certain areas of Venice: Cannaregio and the entrance to the city at the station, and in the following decade, the Giudecca, particularly for provision of housing. Building projects have multiplied for vacant buildings, notably the Arsenale in Castello and the empty shell of the Molino Stucky on the Giudecca. They continued to constitute student design projects for some decades, and to be the subjects of international competition and symposia.

Among the earliest was the 1978 project, *10 Immagini per Venezia*, which invited local and international architects to formulate designs for the Cannaregio area.[139] That project announced the recharging of Venice as *modern*, and the site of new initiatives. Such exercises in salvation were to persist into the next decades. Announcing the project, its convenor, Francesco Dal Co, invoked Ruskin, Simmel, Hofmannsthal's Andreas and Mann's Aschenbach to refer to the city's destabilising effect, no less accumulative in the 1960s and 1970s.[140] Among the first of a spate of similar polemics, *10 Immagini* willed Venice to be not merely old, but modern also, calling for it to host meditations on the modern, if only by reference to the spectacular absence of the new. For Dal Co, the Venetian modern was an expression of refounding and innovating: thus Palladio is the true architectural prototype of the Venetian adventurer.[141] Ennio Concino introduced Cannaregio as a dynamic urban area on the periphery, which included the vital terminal points from the mainland, as well as the area projected for Le Corbusier's hospital. By the 1970s Le Corbusier's unbuilt hospital had mythical status.[142] The focus on Cannaregio continued the interest in activating the outer areas of Venice in response to the zoning laws that made building in the San Marco area impossible.

Most of the architects' submissions were more given to poetic symbolism than to urban reality. However, in a typological response, the Spanish architect Rafael Moneo took up the basic configuration of narrow rectangular units of closely built land in the Cannaregio with designs for new cubic dwellings with long corridors imitating the characteristic *calli*.[143] Working with poetic analogies, the American John Hejduck

204 John Hejduk, *Thirteen Watchtowers for Cannaregio*, 1978. Pen and watercolour. Office of the architect.

proposed 'Thirteen Watchtowers for Cannaregio', a development from his earlier Venetian project devoted to 'The Cemetery of the Ashes of Thought' in 1974 (fig. 204).[144] He had at that time projected a necropolis of the mind, envisaging the defunct Molino Stucky building as a monument painted white inside, black outside, with walls inset with transparent cubes containing ashes of the works of those who had meditated on Venice: Proust, Gide, Melville, et al.[145] Hejduk declared that 'since 1974 Venice has preoccupied the nature of [my] work': 'It is the forum of my inner arguments . . . I suspect that in these past four years my architecture has moved from the "architecture of optimism" to the "architecture of pessimism".'[146] Venice works its melancholy again. In 1978 Hedjuck's 'Thirteen Towers of Cannaregio' were conceived in black and white, in simple geometries, each tower placed in a separate row. The exterior colour was described as 'basically Venetian pink, green, grey and white'. The architect required that:

> the city of Venice selects thirteen men, one for each tower for life-long residency. One man lives in one tower, and only he is permitted to inhabit and enter this tower. A fourteenth man is selected to inhabit the small house located in the campo. Each of the thirteen tower men is pledged not to reveal his interior decoration.[147]

On another campo was a 'House for an Inhabitant who refused to Participate', with a chamber in which there was a mirror in which the inhabitant could see only himself. Any citizen was permitted to climb the tower and observe him, but the observer ran the risk of being trapped by another observer. Extending this Nietzschean design to realise the exemplary solitudes of Venice, a house on a fabricated island was to be kept for temporary residencies in solitude.[148]

Another participant in the Cannaregio experiment made journeying and absence the motivation. Raimund Abraham's project for the area of the railway station and the termination point of the translagoon bridge created 'The Wall of Lost Journeys', to be made in blocks of marble with metallic revetments. He designed new squares named for The Workers, The People, Solitude, the House of Boats. A Hospital, recalling Corbusier's project contained houses of Hope, Birth, Non-Return (for the terminally ill), and a Tower of Wisdom.

The American architect Peter Eisenman, who was particularly close to members of the School of Venice and its urban project in these years, claimed that 'rather than trying to reproduce or simulate an existing Venice, whose historical authenticity cannot be replicated, [this project] acknowledges the limits of such an historicist project by constructing another, fictitious Venice in which the gridded structure of Le Corbusier's Venice hospital project . . . was imposed as a fictional past' (fig. 205).[149] Eisenman claimed he was turning towards memory rather than history, because memory permitted transformation.[150] In his 1980 'Three Texts for Venice', he wrote of the nostalgia bred of the loss of Corbusier's Venice hospital project, calling it 'one of the last anguishes of heroic modernism'.[151] Eisenman's design was sited in the same area and built on

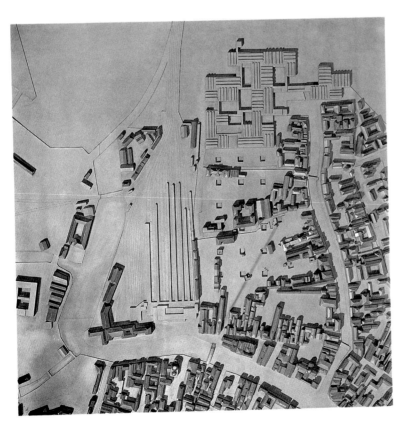

205 Office of Peter Eisenman, presentation model showing Cannaregio West and Le Corbusier's Venice hospital, 1978. Gold and pink paint over wood and cardboard, 8.5 × 100.5 × 100.5 cm. Peter Eisenman Archive. Canadian Centre for Architecture, Montréal.

Corbusier's grid proposal; it was painted gold and pink like some icon – or alchemical transformation.[152] His Cannaregio project has been seen to be a decisive direction for his later *Cities of Artificial Excavation* all of which worked with richly sedimented sites.[153]

The art writer Yve-Alain Bois called Eisenman's approach a 'discourse on memory and antimemory, decentering, displacement, absence, and reinvented history', designating it 'shrewd', but 'too metaphorical'.[154] But in terms of excess of metaphor it is Venice that is the primary guilty party, to be freshly exploited in the climate of Post-Modernism. Aldo Rossi appeared to go against it, but he also connived with history. He closed the city off with a wall; railway access ceased; the Piazzale Roma was redeveloped and a brick wall and a vast hotel arose on the Grand Canal.[155] Rossi returned Venice to its pre-industrial insularity and insisted on its tourist-only function. He sealed the city in again.

These 1978 projects for Cannaregio could all be seen as dreams couched in pessimism, lifting off into fantasy, but nevertheless concerned with some kind of melancholy residue that lingers in Cannaregio. In the years immediately after 1966 Venice had provoked extremes of representation, a flood of speculation on the city's death by drowning, decay, industrial and tourist exploitation, and depopulation. Once again it had unsettled its visitors, embroiled them in its snare, infected them with its plagues. For many it seemed choked by its past and offered little hope for sustainable modern life. The author P. M. Pasinetti's thesis of its resilience was sorely tested in the 1970s in a period when depopulation and emigration accelerated. Yet the city was still a paradigm of the beautiful; its utopias may have been challenged, but they were not effectively cancelled. That beauty may have been destabilised and overladen with memory for Aldo Rossi, it may have passed into invisibility for Italo Calvino, but it was nevertheless a perpetual point of reference – ever more so. The chameleon city could be an arcane background for Hugo Pratt's Corto Maltese. And its glamour was intact; it could also host James Bond.

The New Biennales

As the Cannaregio project demonstrated, architecture was an art of invention that could be exhibited and influential, even if not built. While exhibiting designs was international in the practice styled as Post-Modern, its manifestation in Venice was in large part due to the prominence of the Institute of Architecture, and of Vittorio Gregotti as director of the sector for the plastic arts in the Biennale. As a result of the pressures of 1968, the Biennale changed dramatically in the 1970s, the most eventful decade in its history. In 1973 the 'New Regulations of the Autonomous Body' were approved and the Socialist Carlo Ripa di Meana, president during the 1970s, announced that the Biennale was now a 'democratically organised cultural institute', that it guaranteed 'full freedom of ideas and forms of expression' and promoted the participation of every social class.[156] Ripa di Meana was eager to affirm that 'Venice was living'.[157] A revised committee included the Mayor of Venice, three members of the city council and representation from the province, the region and central government.[158] Prizes were abolished and commercial operations limited. The 1972 Biennale was the last to include decorative arts at the Giardini.[159]

The decade was one in which strenuous efforts were made to expand the types of exhibition and venues, and to publish activities as fully as possible.[160] In clamorous response to the criticisms of 1968 – Dorigo was almost as vocal as he had been with respect to Marghera – the Biennales were deliberately politicised, intended to work 'with a clear and distinct anti-fascist choice of direction' and to extend into the Veneto in an effort to engage a wider, less élite audience.[161] The 1974 Biennale was dedicated to the *coup d'etat* in Chile; that of 1976 to the democratic movement in Spain, thirty years after the beginning Civil War. In 1977, in the continued spirit of political commitment, an exhibition of dissenting artists from the Soviet Union caused an intervention against the Biennale by Carlo Argan, a noted Italian Communist and art historian, as well as provoking criticism from the Soviet Union.[162]

The first of the politically engaged Biennales, *B'74*, opened very publicly in the Palazzo Ducale with an international testimony against fascism in the presence of Ortensia Allende, widow of the assassinated Chilean president.[163] There were congresses, concerts of popular and experimental music, photographic murals and posters shown through the city, and projects responsive to Chile from European artists Matta, Vedova, Cascella and Giò Pomodoro.[164] Chilean posters were shown in the Piazza San Marco, in the Campo di Santa Marghera, traditionally a centre for political meetings, and throughout the Veneto. The cinema festival showed films about anti-fascism. Both cinema and stage productions registered the impact of feminism in the early 1970s.

In this climate of self-consciousness and self-scrutiny the Biennale's own history was researched, chronicled in various exhibitions and recorded in the documentary format of an *Annuario*. In 1976 a permanent archive was opened in the Ca' Corner della Regina, a handsome palazzo on the Grand Canal.[165] Wladimiro Dorigo was appointed as archivist, responsible for a project that aimed to make the archive not only a centre of history for the institution itself, but for contemporary art internationally. The historian Giandomenico Romanelli detailed the history of the Biennale's buildings and curated an extensive photographic exhibition on the arrangement and decorations of the Biennale from 1895.[166] The cinema Biennale replayed prize-winning films from the 1930s onwards. Ugo Mulas's photographs documenting the police clashes of 1968 (Mulas had died in 1973), were shown in the 1974 Biennale, exhibited in the newly opened salt warehouses – the Magazzini del Sale – a significant territorial expansion away from the Giardini, and an important act of conservation that, in effect, saved the nineteenth-century warehouses from demolition.[167] The Giudecca became a venue: the fate of the Molino Stucky, now deserted, became a question for debate – and continued to be so for the next twenty years.[168]

Installation and site-specific art, still controversial practices in the 1970s, were obviously well-suited to the new philosophy of exhibition beyond the art gallery: the expansion of venues in Venice was contemporary with the international critique of formal display and the authority of the gallery. It was not unusual for artists to respond specifically to Venice, of course; they had done so since the first Biennales. In 1972 an anthology of such painters curated by Toni Toniati – *Venezia: ieri, oggi, domani* (Venice: Yesterday, Today, Tomorrow) had shown the lengthy history and continued currency of reactions to the city. In the same year, *Four Projects for Venice* – an exhibition of the aborted designs by Frank Lloyd Wright, Le Corbusier and Louis Kahn as well as Carlo Scarpa – displayed unrealised architectural projects.[169]

Responses were geographically wide-ranging, and intrusions into the city and surrounding area were actively courted by the artists espousing installation art. In 1976 Christian Boltanski and Annette Messager assembled *Voyages de noces à Venise* (Honeymoons in Venice) consisting of ninety-six photographs and twenty-one drawings in coloured pencil – clichéd views and stock subjects were shared between the photographs, supposedly objective, and gauche amateur drawings.[170] In a heavy metal installation Jannis Kounellis used an old industrial barge, which he moored behind the Giudecca, to install a lighted lamp and a set of hanging deposits of coal dust – making a kind of shrine of the interior of the boat, which celebrated its metallic and industrial presence in its everyday setting.[171]

The music and drama Biennales, under the directorship of Luca Rankine, actively sought not only new venues, but new audiences, particularly of young people and people outside the formal theatre and concert hall. Moving outside Venice to the Terraferma at Marghera, *Othello* – now called *Cassio Governa a Cipro* (Cassio Gover-

nor of Cyprus) was played in a version 'revised' by Giorgio Manganelli and directed by Gianni Serra in a number of locations, including dockyards.[172] An effort was made to break out of the biannual format and co-ordinate cultural activities in the year in between, and in 1975 there was a determined effort in that respect, including the important exhibition curated by Harald Szeeman, *Le Macchine celibi* (The Bachelor Machines), dedicated to Marcel Duchamp and his followers.[173] The city was galvanised by the performances of the Living Theater from the United States, particularly their 'street theatre' *Six Public Acts*, performed in Piazza San Marco and surrounding *calli* (fig. 206). *The Money Tower* (*Torre del Denaro*) was played in the church of San

206 Performance by Living Theater in Piazza San Marco, Biennale di Venezia, 1975.

Lorenzo.[174] In the Giudecca boatyards Meredith Monk gave a silent performance called *Education of the Girlchild*.[175] The music Biennale paid tribute to Bruno Maderna, who had died prematurely in 1973.[176] Among his last compositions was *Venetian Journal*, which brought eighteenth-century Boswell back as a touring character among pre-recorded tapes of tourist babble, snatches of 'La Biondina in Gondoletta' and free passage for an oboist and singer to journey among the fragments.[177]

The Biennale's determined political involvement continued. A 'Committee for Information and the Means of Mass Communication', created in 1974, held workshops and seminars. A festival of dance, with related films and cinema was held, and at the Lido Cinema there was a colloquium on the Biennale as 'an institution for international cultural debate'.[178] Carlo Ripa di Meana maintained his idealism in the face of criticism, especially from lobbying groups and trade unions, who still considered the Biennale to be under-democratised. Thus the Biennale was a statement before it was a site:

> I think I can say that the new Biennale, while offering a free forum for people to express themselves, does not only stand for the pavilions of the Giardini, the palace of the Cinema, or other spaces which it disposes of, but especially, it has decided to guarantee a free forum where ideological alignments and purely ideological manifestations will be banished.[179]

It appears that the conventional homes of the Biennale in the Giardini and the Cinema Palace on the Lido were to be avoided if possible for they already had too great a residue of history. The cinema Biennale commemorated the centenary of the birth of D. W. Griffith with an important retrospective screened throughout the city, and in Mestre.[180]

It was resolved to maximise the Biennale organisation in the interval between the bi-annual Giardini exhibitions in order to keep the cultural activity alive and committed to a range of audiences in different venues. Harald Szeeman's *Bachelor Machines* opened with a happening orchestrated by James Lee Byars in the Piazza San Marco. Dressed characteristically in gold, Byars unfurled a sheet in the Piazza and, together with the crowd, carried his sail, a representation of the 'Holy Spirit', to the Magazzini del Sale.[181] In the spirit of redeployment, architects and artists were again invited to make proposals for the future use of the Molino Stucky, empty since 1956.[182] It was the occasion on which John Hejduck offered his *Cemetery for the Ashes of*

Thought and Italian sculptors Marco Ceroli and Gianfranco Fini installed a wooden box in Piazza San Marco to receive submissions, which they then burnt on the Giudecca. Some were unimpressed by this Neo-Dadaism.

A Veneto music group, the Canzoniere Veneto, responded to the problems of Venice with *El Miracolo roverso* (The Reversed Miracle), about the plague of 1630 and the inaction of authorities; the situation was transferred to the contemporary problem of pollution.[183] The Environmedia Group centred attention on the Giudecca, bringing audio-visual equipment to residents to enable them to record discussion of the problems on the island, such as the degradation of housing and lack of community facilities.[184]

The 1976 Biennale continued both the thematic focus, which was an important curatorial shift in the Biennale's organisation, and its political orientation. It followed with the opposition to Fascism in Spain from the Civil War of 1936 to 1976: the year before, in anticipation, a banner appeared on San Marco, hoisted from the balcony of the horses, denouncing capital punishment in Spain.[185] Germano Celant, as principal curator, nominated the theme *Ambiente arte* (Environment Art), timely for the contemporary interest in installation and land art. The choice of theme was vital and an issue in itself, since it had to respond to the cutting edge of visual practice. Celant, who was to have an ongoing relationship with the Biennale, had established a leading critical position with his presentations of Arte Povera, a first anthology of installation art in Italy. In *Ambiente arte*, Celant not only presented contemporary practitioners, but gathered up the modernist history of installation with a central exhibition *From Futurism to Body Art*, showing artists such as El Lissitzky and the Russian constructionists, Kandinsky's 1922 music room in Berlin and Sonia Delaunay's 'simultaneous' rooms. The practice of historicising the central contemporary theme passed on to future Biennales.

Although design and craft had been excluded from the Giardini, architecture and design were not neglected as a result of the participation of the architect Vittorio Gregotti. For the first time there was a detailed presentation of Rationalist architecture between the wars, and a focus on the German Werkbund of 1907 concentrated on early modernist design.

In 1976 individual countries responded with works that documented installations or theatrical performance through photographs: such as the British artist Richard Long's stone passages through various landscapes, or the performances of Czechoslovakia's Josef Svoboda. Joseph Beuys made a charismatic personal appearance accompanying his space-devouring *Tram Stop* in the main space of the German pavilion. Italian artists documented 'conflictual presences' in various cities. Frustrated by limited finances, the French 'Collective of Sociological Art' desired to bomb Venice – their Neo-Futurist project *Bombardando Venezia* was envisaged as a 'bludgeoning carried on respectable façades':

> a venture that will take place first and foremost in the open air. Every night, giant images and excerpts from cine-film material will be projected onto the façades of Venice's historical buildings by means of a photo canon, an exceptionally powerful movie projector. Set against the traditional architecture will be scenes coming on the one hand from the avant garde culture within the Biennale, and, on the other, from either the culture of the Venetian suburbs or that of cultural zones totally removed from Venice (Africa, America . . .) as revealed to us by the pictures provided by the mass-media. It will be a form of cultural short-circuiting . . .[186]

The thematic exhibition at the centre of the 1978 Biennale – *From Nature to Art: From Art to Nature* highlighted the artists' relation to nature, no longer in a purely landscape sense, but as a register of all living things.[187] The central exhibition was curated by a group headed by Achille Bonito Oliva, the eminent Italian curator who would continue to be involved with the Biennale. Natural forms included twigs and branches assembled by John Davis from Australia, the heavy stones of Ulrich Rückriem from Germany, the Englishman Mark Boyle's slabs of earth, sand and walls, and Olavi Lanu's figures grown into lichen in Finnish forests.

The 1978 Biennale was the last under Ripa di Meana's presidency. The forthright political themes in evidence from 1974 ceased, as he quietly acknowledged that the 1978 Biennale was an emergency in a year already blighted by the kidnapping of Aldo Moro and the activity of the Red Brigade. The *Annuario* for 1978 appeared only in 1982, as a much reduced document. The prize system suspended through the 1970s was reinstated in 1980: the Leone d'Oro reappeared. The architectural exhibitions, which were a major initiative of the 1970s, gained even more weight in 1980. The expansion of venues – the Magazzini del Sale, the church of San Lorenzo, the Archives at Ca' Regina, the Giudecca warehouses – these all remained for subsequent Biennales.

The orchestration of events in the 1970s was phenomenal, an effort to defeat the negativity that shrouded Venice in the early years of the decade. At the same time it might be observed that Venice now played the role of administrative host to a range of national curators and international visitors: the city was a city for others, a cultural venue given over to its guests.

Cinematic Adventurers: Don Giovanni, Casanova and James Bond

A fantasy Venice emerged forcibly in the late 1970s, anticipating the recovery of masques and carnival in the 1980s and the re-flaunting of a Venice of entertainment and gaiety in further defiance of its well-publicised 'death'. In the watery lands of Vicenza in the Veneto, at the Palladian villa La Rotonda and in the Teatro Olimpico, film-maker Joseph Losey depicted a Veneto version of Mozart's *Don Giovanni*.[188] Remembering the authorship of the libretto by the Venetian Lorenzo da Ponte, and the often-remarked likeness of Don Giovanni to Casanova, the shift of scene from Spain to the Veneto and to Palladio's La Rotonda was not too arbitrary. The venue was the choice of the administrator of the Théâtre Nationale Opéra de Paris, Rolf Liebermann, but Losey himself suggested that both the Palladian building in which the opera is staged and the costumes should have a mathematical quality appropriate to the music.[189] The move from Venice to its one-time possession Vicenza, and the flat, waterlogged lands of the Veneto releases a strange poetry, isolating characters as they are rowed slowly through the watery wastes, en route to glass furnaces or masked balls. This treatment of *Don Giovanni*, so well known an opera, released a strange wistfulness. It was Losey's return to the waters of the Veneto: in 1963 he had filmed *Eve* around Venice and Torcello, at Harry's Bar, San Michele and the Danieli.[190]

Water and fire dominate *Don Giovanni*, and in this it finds its resonance in those particularly Venetian elements. During the overture a masked party visits Don Giovanni's glassworks at Murano; coming by boat, they watch glass being made against the spectacular glow of a furnace; it anticipates the final fiery demise of the Don. Water, in close conjunction with fire, announces Losey's *Don Giovanni*, and closes it. Perhaps D'Annunzio's *Il Fuoco* is being echoed. Losey's is an analogous *Don Giovanni*, like the Rossi idea of displaced architecture transferred to opera. And it is another exercise in the pursuit of love – or lust – in the lands of the Serenissima.

Images of water also opened Fellini's film *Casanova*, released in 1978.[191] Like many of Fellini's creations, it revelled in masque and carnival, but the Venice of Casanova's early life was an obvious construction in cardboard. Venice's most licentious citizen is ferociously presented, unmasked and revealed as a sexual manikin deserving of his pathetic old age. He is a simulacrum in a city that is a simulacrum, a cardboard construction with the seams and joints knowingly displayed and a cardboard Rialto Bridge.[192]

207 Federico Fellini,
Casanova, 1977. Film still.
PEA produzioni Europee
Associate and FAST Films.

Fellini made no secret of his contempt for Casanova as Casanova presented himself in the famous *Memoirs*. He declared his intention to destroy the myth of the famed lover, whom he described as 'disgusting and supine: symbol of the *ancien régime* and the Counter-Reformation, an image of the frustrated, infantile, repressed Italian'.[193] A harsh diagnosis indeed, coming after the demolition already effected by Schnitzler and other foreign interpreters. Fellini brought Casanova back to Italy and made his failings specifically Italian – rather than Venetian. In Fellini's words, Casanova becomes 'a national phallic monument'.[194] Donald Sutherland was cast as Casanova; long and lugubrious of face, with a huge domed head, he appeared to Fellini as 'a big spermful waxwork with the eyes of a masturbator, as far removed as one could imagine from an adventurer and Don Juan-like Casanova' (fig. 207).[195] In answer to feminist critics, Fellini claimed he revealed how Casanova used women, how he contaminated his encounters, giving them 'fleeting, frustrating neurotic content'.[196]

In the film's first sequences, the titles appear superimposed on canal water at night agitated by reflections of fireworks as carnival takes place in front of a cardboard Rialto Bridge in the presence of the doge. Trumpeters on the bridge and incantations to Venus accompany the great work of hauling a huge-eyed head of Venus from the canal: the ropes slacken and it falls back into the water. The crowd gives itself over to the power of the spectacle: masks bob up in front of the camera and Casanova is revealed watching, masked, in the guise of a pierrot. The opening chants in Venetian dialect invoking 'Venus, our queen' were written by the Trevisan poet, Andrea Zanzotto.[197] In a letter to Zanzotto, Fellini described the head as 'the great Mediterranean mother, the mysterious feminine who lives in each one of us'; yet she is lost, lodged in the depths of the canal's mud.[198]

In accordance with his view of a regressive Casanova, Fellini asked Zanzotto to compose an 'infantile' song in Venetian dialect to be sung when Casanova meets a Venetian giantess in London: she is the living version of the giant female head lost in the lagoon. The London lover takes a bath and sings the 'Cantilena Londinese'. For Fellini, the iconography of his Casanova is sub-aquatic: the images are amniotic, of the placenta. At the same time Fellini's Venice is, to follow his words closely, decomposed and floating in algae, in mucous, mould and humidity.[199] It is, in fact, another post-flood Venice, given over to carnival in its first scenes, then exposing all the hollowness of one of its famous native sons. At the film's conclusion the exiled Casanova imagines himself returned to Venice, delivered in a carriage to the cardboard Rialto beside a frozen winter canal, waltzing with a mechanical woman, himself a clockwork marionette, perpetually winding himself up and performing his mechanical carnal acts, then running down, ticking towards death. In Casanova's last filmic minutes he breathes the word 'Venice', naming the city that has become invisible for him. In his love for Venice Fellini allows him to find his one integrity.

That quintessential invention of the 1960s, Ian Fleming's secret agent 007, James Bond, was no less a mechanical lover and international adventurer. Operating on the Cold War world stage of the 1960s and 1970s – the films following the books and extending the cult – fashionable Bond must necessarily spend some time in Venice which is, after all, between the East and the West. Ian Fleming kept Bond's exploits mainly in Britain, but the film-makers moved him around a dazzling international circuit appropriate to the hero's *savoir-faire*. In the 1963 *From Russia with Love*, directed by Terence Young with Sean Connery as the 'first' Bond, he is in Venice briefly to fight the organisation Spectre.[200] With the enemy vanquished, by the end of the movie he is free to indulge in a gondola ride with the inevitable female conquest, passing the Bridge of Sighs, that symbol, since Byron, of superficial romance.

In 1979 Lewis Gilbert's *Moonraker* starred Roger Moore as James Bond in more inventive and typically Venetian sequences of which Ian Fleming could hardly have dreamed.[201] Always well-provided with gadgetry, Bond has a motorised gondola that whips into action after an attack has been made on him from a passing funeral boat – the coffin opens and the 'body' leaps up to send daggers through the air. What follows is a high point in Venetian chase sequences – through back canals and under hazardous low bridges. The coup-de-grace is in line with Bond's personal arsenal: the gondola is amphibious and mounts the Piazzetta, then rounds the Piazza, scattering the pigeons, and amazing the clients at Quadri's and Florian's (fig. 208). The Venini glass company, well-sited in the Piazza next to the Torre dell'Orologio, is crucially placed for the disclosure of the crime: a sword fight with the enemy ensues in the Venini glass museum, with appropriate shattering of treasures – Bond, always the connoisseur, refrains from using a masterpiece as a missile. The enemy ends up ejected improbably through the glass zodiacal clock of the Torre dell'Orologio,

208 Lewis Gilbert, *Moonraker*, 1979. Film still. Eon Productions, London/Les Productions Artistes Associés, Paris.

landing in the grand piano of the Caffè Quadri, Bond muttering, 'Play it again Sam'. In the 1960 *Venetian Bird*, Venice was dingy, and agent Edward Mercer less than chic. In the late 1970s an impeccable James Bond visits technicolour Venice, knowing the best year for the Bollinger, and the best hotels.

The mood was changing: international chic was restored; Venice could inspire comedy again. After Bond, Venice could host Indiana Jones. It was once more perceived as international and glamorous: Cipriani's provided an episode in the 1979 *Who is Killing the Great Chefs of Europe?* – Fauso Zoppi, specialist chef, is drowned in the tank with his lobsters, murdered intimately amid his own speciality.[202]

Nevertheless, *Moonraker* still had a funeral boat, as did *Who is Killing the Great Chefs of Europe?* An ominous portent, it passes down the Grand Canal behind the diners on the balcony of the Hotel Gritti. But these funereal touches are light relief after Kluge, Visconti, Britten and Roeg, and the sombre legacy of the flood and the late 1960s. The solemnity of the famous funerals of 1971 and 1972, when first Igor Stravinsky, and then Ezra Pound were borne across the water to San Michele, might seem to have passed; the survival years from 1966 had been worked through; by the late 1970s there was a renewed audience for a fantastic Venice, further testimony to its powers of survival. New mythical Venices were on the architectural drawing board. In 1984 the pop star Madonna – in her Venetian exercise in the simulated *Like a Virgin* – reconfirmed the city's virginal state with a video seen more times around the world than any image of the flood. Carnival was ready to play again.

Chapter 11

THE CITY THAT WOULD BE MODERN:
THE 1980s

In the wake of the many deaths of the 1970s came renewed pleas for a modernised Venice in which the past would also be appropriately preserved and the ecology restored and balanced. Another *acqua alta* in 1979 and further depletion of the population gave urgency to preservation issues. The dead end reached with the Special Law of 1973 confirmed the failure of that legislation and the need to clarify operations at a regional level. It was not just Venice the city, but Venice in the Veneto. Special Law 798, passed in 1984, was a further endeavour at the national level to address the problem and rectify the constant criticisms accruing from the 1973 Special Law.[1] But the new law only compounded the situation by reconfirming the state government as principally responsible for the defence and maintenance of the hydraulic balance in the lagoon. Regional government was responsible for pollution control. The majority of funding was directed to projects for stabilising the lagoon – with *acqua alta* the priority. The most important measure to combat *acqua alta* was the barrier system to block high tides at the entrance points of the Lido. The scheme remains one of the most controversial proposals in Venetian history. A 'Consortium of New Venice' – the Consorzio Venezia Nuova – was proposed to implement the scheme, linking twenty-four firms in an operation to develop projects to 'save' Venice.[2] The consortium represented relevant regional interests, both public and private, giving them specific responsibility to introduce designs and plans. It had the appearance of meshing federal interests with the diverse regional interests.

The Consorzio has survived into the next century. It sees its responsibilities under the 1984 law as being to correct and maintain the equilibrium of the lagoon; to arrest the degradation of the lagoon basin by eliminating its causes; to attend to the sea level within the lagoon and protect inhabited areas from exceptional *acque alte* by developing mobile dikes to regulate the tides at the three openings to the Lido.[3] Written into it from inception, then, was the notion of the *bocche*, which were to control the entrance of the sea into the lagoon in dangerous (and extraordinary) conditions of 'storm surge'.

That the lagoon was now understood in a complex sense as a cultural entity was evident throughout the decade in the many conferences and publications (fig. 209).[4] In 1983 a UNESCO general study programme was implemented, with a highly detailed canal study and a study of the lagoon ecosystem.[5] Renewed enthusiasm was linked to the rise of green parties, a world-wide phenomenon, of course. The 1982 *Laguna tra fiumi e mare* – the title inscribing the delicate position of the lagoon 'between' water, river and sea – was polemical: it was introduced by Fulco Pratesis, president of the Italian chapter of the World Wildlife Fund.[6] The physical position of the lagoon was identified mid-way between the rivers feeding it and the sea entering it, thus challenging the efficacy of the *bocche* intended to limit the entrance of the sea at high tide. The environmentalists indicated that their priority was to control and cleanse the lagoon waters and those of the rivers entering it in order to allow the lagoon to cope more adequately with high tides. The historical data was re-examined, reaffirming that the lagoon had always been manipulated by the human populations living within it, diverting river waters, regulating and closing canals, infilling and joining islands. A multitude of interventions in the previous century had created the Malamocco port, closed off a significant number of canals, thus changing the natural flow of waters, and used steamships for aggressive dredging since 1842. The lagoon area had been reduced by fish farming, and industrial and urban infill. These changes have reduced the area of the lagoon and redirected the flow of tides.[7] The natural environment was in process of international re-evaluation, particularly as the lagoon was still rich in unsettled or deserted island areas and replete with birdlife, the value of which was enhanced beside such detrimental agents as fishing boats, the enclosure of fishing grounds (the *valli da pesca*) and heavy industry on the water's edge.

A focus on the history of sea levels in the lagoon and the changes in floor levels in buildings was a further consequence of the debate on the *bocche* and the international concern at global warming and rising sea levels. Paolo Antonio Pirazzoli, one of the scientists focusing on the geophysical nature of the lagoon, predicted that, given projections of heightened sea level in the future, a permanent separation of the sea from the lagoon would be necessary.[8] Study of sea levels led to new initiatives in archaeology, surprisingly late in its development in Venice: Boni was one of the pioneers in his investigations of the levels of the Piazza San Marco in 1885.[9] The history of the first Venetian settlements received new impetus, not just for its undoubted human interest, but because a geophysical history of the lagoon was in question.[10] In 1983 Wladimiro Dorigo was one of the first to publish on the origins of settlement in his *Venezia origini*, a project that was timely and original, even if criticism has been directed at some of his findings about sea levels.[11] Specialised archaeological methods developed to take readings well below sea level were initiated in the 1980s at four sites in Venice. The sites moved inwards from the early settlements in the outer lagoon, from the island of San Francesco del Deserto, where the oak rib of a boat was found; to San Pietro di Castello, where sixth-century construction was verified; to San Lorenzo, nearer to the heart of the city, where structures dating from the sixth century have been found beneath the ninth-century church; and finally, to the Piazza San Marco, where finds were verified from the seventh or eighth centuries.[12]

The Green Party, I Verdi, appeared officially for the first time in the 1985 local elections when a Socialist, Nereo Laroni, was elected mayor. I Verdi wanted the lagoon area recognised in cultural and ecological terms, designated a 'park' and protected as such. At the national level Bettino Craxi was in power and the 'Progetta Venezia' attracted new rhetoric, especially in 1986, twenty years after the flood of November 1966: Craxi pronounced the Progetta 'the first of a new generation of public works'.[13] At the same time, the first optimistic forecasts of a great Expo to be held in 1997 were made, and heralded as indication of a 'living' city determined not to live in its past.[14] A new phase of impact analysis was in the offing.

The Incomplete City

The paradox of tourism became quite evident in the 1980s. On the one hand tourism was the dominant industry, on the other it was the agent of the destruction of a fragile environment.[15] Its expansion was so dramatic that it had become an ecological hazard and an obstacle to daily life in the city. The one-day tourist was identified as the particular enemy – having time only for the central sites, crowding Piazza San Marco in particular, spending little money in the city, not using the hotels and clogging the *vaporetti*.[16] This new tourist was taken by bus in to the Piazzale Roma and then guided in intrusive groups around the city's major monuments. The economic return for the city was low; wear-and-tear was high. Planners met to devise alternative modes of tourism that were long-term and culturally less superficial; they spoke of a city of conferences and residencies, of summit meetings and other ways of demonstrating the city's less-than-superficial contemporary culture and relevance.

The mood was still buoyant after the 1970s. Planning zeal and a recharged futurism had surfaced in 1979, when an issue of the architectural journal *Rassegna* was devoted to the theme of 'Venezia città della moderna'.[17] Most of this special issue was written by the members of the Institute of Architecture, and it registered their will-to-modification and change. Vittorio Gregotti's essay, 'Venice and the New Modernism', endeavoured to turn Venice away from the burden of compromises, inhibitions and the criticisms of the Special Laws to something less negative.[18] Gregotti was to pursue and repeat this project over the next decades.[19] He tried to sidestep the paradox that saw modernity as being in conflict with Venice's homogeneity and a threat to the imaginary unity of the historic architectural fabric. Architectural practice had shifted in the new Post-Modernist age. Functionalism and avant-gardism were repudiated; the very notion of history had changed. Contextualism became the key to new practices, and here Venice could have an important role. Gregotti emphasised that building beside a rich residual past need *not* mean conservatism, but could inspire new and fruitful alignments. New 'intrusions' could become active agents in an active field, entering and transforming it. The rich context was a 'field of conflict', but the insertion of a new building could be a knowing intervention, taking full account of the past, but not succumbing to paralysis.

For the *Rassegna* writers, would-be architects of a Post-Modern Venice, the water was still regarded with ambiguity and treated as a constraint. Access from the mainland bridge – at the Tronchetto and in the area of the Piazzale Roma – had been a frequent target for architectural designs aimed at streamlining the entrance. For the majority of visitors and also for Venetians, entrance to and exit from the city is from the land, and necessarily by car or bus to Piazzale Roma or the Tronchetto, or by rail to Stazione Santa Lucia. Nico Ventura's essay on 'Water as Opportunity' recommended concentrating more water access and mooring around the peripheries of the islands in an attempt to counter the single point of entry via the road and railway bridge, which in turn caused overcrowding on the Grand Canal.[20] But Ventura also warned against the dangers of a 'super marina' culture that *over*-exploited the water element. The Grand Canal must retain its status; its preservation against undue traffic concerned many, not least because of the erosion of the foundations of buildings along the canal.

An article by Wladmiro Dorigo augmented Gregotti's point that Venice as a historical city had an urban diversity as important as its physical density.[21] He studied the naming of medieval streets and spaces to indicate the specialist evolution of certain areas. He looked at the public and private initiatives that had created communal spaces, particularly in areas of specific trading practice, and he mapped the ways in which public access to the water had been maintained since the agricultural and migratory periods of the first millennium, then subjected to fruitful innovation and redirection in the twelfth century. Historic Venice admitted the modern: that was the lesson.

In a designation that was to have future currency, Gianni Fabbri imaged Venice as an 'incomplete' city. It was a tautology, every city is, but it was useful for a history-locked centre. It was a way of condoning additions and accommodating the continuing reality of urban change. Fabbri used the example of a project by Samonà for the replanning of Piazza San Marco: it was an extraordinary exercise in nostalgia for vanished elements.[22] Samonà had wanted to reconstruct the old granary building, demolished during Napoleon's rule to make way for the royal garden. In place of the Piazza's present melange of buildings from different periods, so praised earlier in the century, Samonà wanted homogeneity with surrounding buildings. The uneven roofline of the Procuratie Vecchie, the Napoleonic wing, the Procuratie Nuove and the

Library should be adjusted so that the Library – the pre-eminent building – had clear prominence and governed the height of other buildings. The Procuratie Nuove should therefore have its upper floor removed; the demolished San Geminiano should be rebuilt; and the Procuratie Vecchie extended back to recreate the five arches destroyed to make way for the Napoleonic wing. Sansovino's plan would be 'finished' in an extraordinary return to some fixed point that 'completed' the Piazza according to aesthetics rather than historical evolution. It was another paper Venice of course, but provocative.

It was assumed by these architects that unbuilt or altered solutions might be superior because at the time of their design they were less conservative. Increasingly, Venice wished to be saved from the stultification implied by conservatism. What was *not* taken up in Fabbri's position, for instance, was the more realistic element implicit in the contribution by Gianugo Polesello: that the bond between modification and continuity could be as positive as it is negative.[23] Since the paradigm of modification/continuity was crude, Polesello preferred the more clumsy terminableness/indeterminableness. He wanted alternative solutions and creative intrusions, even in such a densely built city: 'Venice is a town which has been built upon itself (apart from a few exceptions) through processes of saturation of the free space and therefore with constant stratifications, replacements.'[24] As a consequence of the saturation, building must proceed within established boundaries with 'a geometry of assemblages, new places, new signs, new relationships'.[25]

Venice might well be seen as over-built and over-circumscribed for exactly those reasons. It has always preserved; increasingly so after the flood of 1966. For the international community the value of Venice lies in its past rather than in an architecturally brazen future. The lesson of the present has little relevance for foreign custodians. Meanwhile, in respect to history, Fabbri (and others, including Manfredo Tafuri) cites the sixteenth-century rebuilding of the Rialto Bridge as a 'missed opportunity', one that should have been given to Palladio's progressive classicising plan. Palladio's unbuilt bridge not only generated an immense nostalgia, it had also become the paradigm of fear of the progressive. The lesson remains.

Mapped from Above

The Venice *Rassegna* issue also marked the debut of a new cartographic project: a large-scale aerial photographic view of Venice: the *fotopiano*. Triumphantly entitled *Venezia forma urbis*, it was a new Barbari map, reinterpreting that particularly Venetian tradition of the bird's-eye view in new cibachrome technology.[26] The mapping flight took place on 25 May 1982, on behalf of the Commune of Venice and the town planning department.[27] Photography of the historic area was completed on one day, with subsequent days for the islands of the lagoon and the mainland. Photographs were taken at about one thousand metres altitude in a west-to-east move, making a total map of 358 sections, 196 of which were the historic centre. Ground-level and roof-level maps were among complementary surveys used to compensate for shadows or vegetation. The final outcome, the *Atlas of Venice*, published 186 photographs opposite geometric maps, directly equivalent in scale.[28] The map was proclaimed an essential contribution to planning. The result, reassuringly (in the optimistic mode of the 1980s), was a city of golden-red rooftops, water glistening in the sun, all manner of boats in aerial view, green trees in courtyards. A dense, harmonious fabric forms the city, opening out into the breathing spaces of *campielli* and campi and intercut by the canals. The city appeared felicitously again 'in the middle of salt water', its symbiosis evident in the clarity of the *fondamente* following the water's edge, and the puncuation of mooring spots and *pali*, the wooden markers, each in place in the water.[29] The extent of contiguous building shown from above in the Jacopo de' Barbari map of 1500 appeared at first glance unchanged: in the centre were the two twinned islands cut by the Grand Canal.[30] Each tree was in place, and the wake of each boat passing under the plane. *Venezia forma urbis* appeared remote from *acqua alta* and the wintry prognoses of the recent past.

Historians were also busy repositioning the historic city within the lagoon. The Barbari map was republished in large-scale by the house of Filippi, and understood as 'moralised geography', a proud statement of the Venice ruled auspiciously by friendly planets.[31] In 1982 the extensive collection of maps in the Museo Correr was the source of an exhibition and catalogue.[32] The rich cartographical tradition and the many historical panoramas issued over Republican centuries and afterwards were published by Giocondo Cassini in 1982: the material ranged from 1479 to 1855.[33] The last map is the Combatti map, prepared for the Scientific Congress of 1847, and updated in 1855. The central islands then breathed more freely around their peripheries, not yet so solidly built up. The gardens of the Giudecca and the Isola di San Giorgio Maggiore were still substantially in place, and indeed there were still a number of green plots throughout the main islands, particularly in the Cannaregio area and Santa Marta. The railway bridge and the station were shown, but the Marittima development had not begun. At the eastern end, the island of Sant'Elena was still an unbuilt area, except for its church. Over the map flew the double-head eagle of Habsbug Austria.

At the same time, maps from the nineteenth century, important for the interpretation of twentieth-century urban history, appeared in facsimile.[34] These historical studies went in tandem with the will-to-be-modern, putting sophisticated data at the service of town planning. They were also evidence of the concern to read the city in the lagoon and diffuse the privilege of the built-up area. They looked to all the islands and the surrounding waters in all their ecological richness, fragility and renewed impact for the historic centre.

The Return of Carnival

On the one hand a delicate ecology was at stake; on the other the economic viability of the city and its very vitality. To be merely old was to be mortal. Thus carnival came to the fore again in the 1980s. An early impetus came from the theatre division of the 1979 Biennale, organised by Maurizio Scaparro with a carnival theme.[35] Originally the farewell to pleasure before Lent, carnival gives expression to the desire to surmount death, to court glamour in the face of denial, to challenge constraints and, in then-contemporary terms, to defy the many valedictions visited upon Venice in the decade after the flood. For Venice it reactives a long and famous tradition.[36] In the 1980s glamour was actively courted, as were commercial initiatives. Mask shops burgeoned, as if the carnival imaged by Fellini in *Casanova* had stirred the populace to mimicry. The new carnival was a concerted bid for tourism, but to see it as that only is to deny the city's phoenix-like powers to renew itself. However artificial or commercialised, carnival expressed some sort of dynamism, and defied the prophets of Venetian doom.

It was the heyday of cibachrome photography, propitious for the photogenic pursuit of the harlequin after the sombre documentation of floods, decay and the evidence of *Venezia muore* in the 1970s. A million new versions of the *bautta* were moulded and painted, and a new photographic genre was born. The revised historical regatta spawned de-luxe photographic records and, after 1975, the Vogalonga – the local rowing regatta with a route that encircled the central islands – took on a calculated tourist dimension.[37]

In the 1980s Fulvio Roiter became the exponent of a new romantic and photogenic Venice, framing people and their surroundings in a sequence of best-selling books. He

210   Fulvio Roiter,
Venetian Nocturne, 1988.

had been a member of the La Gondola photographic circle in the 1950s, but he achieved prominence with *Essere Venezia* published in 1978, using the wide format of the photo-book. Most importantly, he affirmed that Venice was *living*.[38] Stylish, unafraid of sunsets in full colour or a full range of reflections in water, Roiter shot historic Venice, the lagoon and its islands.[39] Panoramic views unfolded beside close-ups rich in texture and play of light. Night scenes are silky in their darkness, illuminated with a scribble of time-exposure light (fig. 210). In daytime, the sun is full and the colour bright; rain is seductive, as are gondolas under snow. Waterbirds nest in the reeds in the lagoon islands; aerial views show the lagoon waters patterned like marbled silk. Not just the scenery, but the inhabitants also are depicted, and all are glamorous: children and old people, glass-workers and lacemakers. The city is revealed as vibrantly alive and nowhere in decline. Roiter shifted the international balance sheet from negative to positive, and reconciled Venice with its own, traditional beauty.

Essere Venezia is a visual narrative that begins with the far-off sighting of Venice emerging from the water, moving in from the Adriatic to the lagoon, showing sandbars in aerial view. Gradually towers emerge from the mist and the Palazzo Ducale, photographed from a speedboat, blurs above the waters. Andrea Zanzotto, who wrote for Fellini's *Casanova*, supplied the large-print text for *Essere Venezia*, taking reader-viewers from the primeval waters to 'the theme of the wooden pile', the markers in the lagoon: 'the stem, the

211   Fulvio Roiter,
Carnival, 1980s.

212 Emilio Vedova, *From the Carnival Cycle*, 1977–83. Mixed technique on cardboard, 100.5 × 76 cm. Venice, Collection of the artist.

measure and support, echoes everywhere in Venice, secure in its ingenuous and rough fragility, indicating an almost triangular movement. Those standing in clusters of three in the lagoon are dear to men, familiar as they are with winds and tides, points of reference in a wide choice of sea lanes . . .'[40] Following the journey into the heart of the city, the photographs open out to the Grand Canal, to the bridges and the islands, and record the carnivals, regattas and festivities, culminating in the fireworks for the feast of the Redentore. In the first of Roiter's books, *Living Venice*, the regatta was more colourful than the carnival, which was still mainly for children, but carnival images dominate in *Venice II* in 1984.[41] By then the genre was well established, and postcards and calendars of *carnevale* hung from every trader's stall (fig. 211).[42] There were monographs such as Alessandro Savella's glossy book with journalistic text by Nantas Salvalaggio, with shots of a thousand masked faces against a blur of famous backgrounds and exploding fireworks.[43]

Acknowledging film and photography as the media employed so zealously for re-depicting Venice, Zanotto referred to his recent experience with Fellini's *Casanova* and, it follows, Venetian narcissism. 'Venice is never sated with looking'; 'we are surrounded by narcissism of all kinds, not of the city itself but of all those great men [sic] who have looked at it'.[44] 'With the very opposite of commonsense', Zanotto declared, 'Fellini had to falsify Venice in order to plumb her depths.'[45] The city itself is innocent: it is the gaze of residents and tourists growing even more steadily in the 1980s that will not leave her alone. For Vedova, painting a carnival cycle over the years 1977–83, the face of carnival was prophetically scarred (fig. 212).

Aldo Rossi's Theatre of the World

Not only carnival, but the rich tradition of Venetian scenography was re-invented in the 1980s.[46] Venice and its scenic space was the theme of an exhibition proclaiming the 'truth' of the mask for the 1979 Biennale.[47] The theatre of the old Republic was reinvoked and the city, the Bacino in particular, celebrated as a site for spectacle: spectacle on the water, above all. This exercise was fully inclusive: *everything* about Venice and its history was construed as scenographic, beginning with Carpaccio's paintings of miracles in city settings, and including all the well-known monuments. To these 'fixed scenes' were added the gondola in daily and festive mode and images and myths that showed people within Venetian settings, including Fellini's *Casanova*. Catastrophes were scenographic: the first burning of Fenice and the Palazzo Ducale, the collapse of the Campanile, and the protective sandbags around San Marco during the First World War. Of course dogal ceremonies, religious festivals and state welcomes were included. The prisons were part of the scenographic tradition, represented by the lithographs of Francesco Gallimberti and Giovanni de Pian, dedicated to the dark side of the prison at the end of the Republic.[48]

Particularly emblematic for the 1979 Biennale, and to many its most memorable image, was Aldo Rossi's floating theatre in the manner of the sixteenth century Theatre of the World: the *theatrum mundi*.[49] Crafted in wood and topped by a ball and pennant, Rossi's boat was towed into Venice and moored conspicuously off the Punta della Dogana, near the church of the Salute (fig. 213). In form it was octagonal and turreted, floating on a square base. Across from its mooring place were the famous Palladian churches; it echoed their triangular pediments and shifting verticals. Above were the volutes on the dome of the Salute, and even closer, the golden ball on the Dogana (a rather neglected emblem), where the figure of Fortune turns at the bidding of the winds. Simple and child-like, Rossi's theatrical vessel was also solemn and ceremonial, with its pennant flying stiffly from the turret.

A latter-day participant in the water poetry of old Venice, this festive boat sailed into a well-documented tradition from its construction site at Fusina. After the Biennale it left Venice to travel across the Adriatic to Dubrovnik, remembering former Venetian territory beyond the sea. Such theatres, as Rossi was well aware, were no less than representations of the world: in the sixteenth century Guillo Camillo famously ascribed the training of memory to his theatre.[50] The temporary floating stage recalled that well-known worldly, flamboyant Venice, which welcomed distinguished visitors with floating machines famous for their splendour and ingenuity.

213 Aldo Rossi, Theatre of the World, Punta della Dogana, 1979–80.

Frequently eloquent in his castigation of old Venice, Rossi wrote about his 'happiness' in respect to this work:

> What pleases me above all is that the theatre is a veritable ship, and like a ship it is subject to the movements of the lagoon, the gentle oscillations, the rising and sinking; so that in the uppermost galleries a few people might experience a slight sea-sickness that proves distracting and is increased by the water line, which is visible beyond the windows. I cut these windows according to the level of the Lagoon, the Giudecca and the sky ... The magic is created by an unusual mixtures of typologies ...[51]

In his ambition to gather in sources outside Venice, and doubtless in pursuit of analogies, Rossi referred to the lighthouses of Maine, the wooden structures of the Po delta, the canals of Milan and Holland, and the early Venice made of wood, before marble and Istrian stone. Again he meditated on escape from a Venice that was too insular, finding a wider world in which the floating theatre could be divested of too-much Venice.

Intellectual discussion floated in with the theatre, for it was construed by the architectural world as an emblematic wonder. Certain formats of the past, such as the temporary floating theatres, were the very things to celebrate in an anti-monumental phase of architectural practice. Manfredo Tafuri declared that 'the ephemeral is eternal', if only through operation of memory.[52] According to Tafuri the temporary could be declared to be Rossi's valuable *anti-Venetian* quality. But the quality of Rossi's project also resided in the closed form of the theatre within the very 'fluidity' of Venetian scenic space. Here Palladio had built his 'over-concluded dreams' on the rim of St Mark's basin: the Redentore, the Zitelle and San Giorgio Maggiore. Many specifically

Venetian strands were joined together, and yet, as expected of Rossi, he disturbed the waters, challenging the insular tradition of the city by citing a world beyond.[53]

The architect Daniel Liebeskind enthused over Rossi's theatre, citing Kant and Newtonian physics. He argued for the objective space of architecture and for the theatre's particular 'inner locale', in which 'space subsequently unfolds itself'.[54] The theatre was a floating octagon of emptiness, drawing attention to the very *lack* of space in Venice, and so it registered spatial tensions within the city and, indeed, the tensions of all architecture in space. It was also a reminder of another great paradigm – 'The Ship of Fools'. The original floating theatres, Liebeskind continued, played to a privileged audience watching the reflection of their own privileges. Rossi's criticality was evident in this memory exercise, which interrogated the past as much as it represented it. In Liebeskind's view, Rossi's theatre was a 'construction of emptiness', and powerful for that reason.

The Biennale in the 1980s

Rossi's prominence was just one result of the new role given to architecture in the 1980s, a development of the exhibitions held in the Biennales of the 1970s and Vittorio Gregotti's direction of the visual arts sector. Following the interrogations of the 1970s the Biennales of the 1980s were solipsist, and determinedly divergent: 1980 saw *Chronographie* – Time and Memory in Contemporary Society – for artists and architects who presented installations in the deconsecrated church of San Lorenzo.[55] They arranged their itineraries of fragments for a viewer to gather up as he or she went through the space, intercercepting the place of the past amid the offerings of the present, a Post-Modern conjunction, perhaps. A complementary exhibition, *Il Tempo del Museo Venezia*, worked with a Venice that was yet again 'a place emblematic of a continuous opposition between past and present times'. But at the edge of the 1980s it was still 'a huge unburied corpse and the lagoon . . . the morgue for the city's corpses'.[56]

The Venice-in-contemplation-of-Venice solipsism recurred with the Biennale of mirrors in 1984. *Arte dello specchio* flattered the host city with one of its most overt metaphors. It could readily be yoked to avant-garde practices in the trans-avant-garde, to the 'intricate game of quoting, copying and mirror-images', as one critic spelled it out, for: 'the city of mirrors [was] the perfect site for an exhibition about our moment, a moment as fragile and as useful as glass.'[57] Many critics saw *Arte dello specchio* as reactionary, but then to others to be reactionary was to be Post-Modern.

The expansion of the Biennale's geography continued. *Aperto* exhibitions, 'open' only to younger artists, took place in the Sale del Magazzini at the Punta della Dogana. Four artists took over the Scuola Grande di San Giovanni Evangelista, one of Venice's quieter (and superlative) fifteenth-century buildings by Mauro Codussi. The lucid architecture, the clerestorey lighting and the strong tiling of the floors were supplemented and challenged by the American Bruce Naumann and the Italians Enzo Cucchi, who showed a specific time-angled 1984 painting, a triangle of fire set against an historic wall tomb, and Luciano Fabri, who placed his own column in the pilastered interior. The German artist Joseph Beuys, then at the height of his fame, parked a bicycle and his characteristic blackboards on the Codussian tiles.[58]

Adding to this varied range of events was a retrospective of Vedova's paintings at the Museo Correr, and a retrospective of *fin-de-siècle* Viennese art at the Palazzo Grazzi: one of the most comprehensive to date.[59] This was the moment, politically netural, to acknowledge the debt of Venice to Vienna.[60]

But it was architecture in the 1980s that seemed to offer the most spectacular and original displays. In 1980 the First International Exhibition of Architecture took place under the directorship of Paolo Portoghesi, the Roman architectural historian, who was particularly eloquent on the timely subject of Post-Modernism. The success of specific architecture Biennales was further evidence of the impact of the Institute of Architecture and its commanding reputation. With dramatic effect, the extensive space of the Corderie – the old rope-making factory of the Arsenale which was in process of restoration – was used for art display. It was significant as a spectacular space – a Piranesian space as Portoghesi saw it – but it also signalled the ending of military constraints associated with its occupation by the Italian navy. It was the beginning of the ceding of that space back to Venice.[61] It had been relinquished in 1797.

Portoghesi made the main axis of the Corderie into 'a new street', a Strada Novissima, lined with painted plywood façades designed by international architects and constructed by the set-makers of Cinecittà. Recalling the temporary structures that Venice made for its visitors and festivities, he noted the significant reuse of temporary spaces which both transformed the city and socialised it: 'Of all Italian cities, Venice is perhaps the one with the richest and most significant tradition of temporary space, seen in the floating machines and in the structures that can be reassembled in the fair of the 'SENSA' and which can be considered prefigurations of our street.'[62] He made the most of the Venetian tradition of façadism and scenography, which he eagerly connected to a renewed carnival aesthetic. It expressed the yearning for the imaginary in place of 'urban sterility', he claimed. Aldo Rossi's theatre moored in the Bacino was already a leitmotif for the new architecture, and the scenography.

The early 1980s, in large part under the aegis of the Biennales, was a period when representations of Venice were scrutinised. In cinema, for example, *L'Immagine e il mito di Venezia nel cinema* (The Image and Myth of Venice in Film) documented the extraordinary number of movies dedicated in whole or in part to Venice, from Albert Promio's gondola, pigeons and carnival in 1896, to the historical silent films of the first decade, to D'Annunzio and the many Casanovas, *Top Hat* and *Escape Me Never*, the post-war *Summertime*, James Bond, Visconti and Fellini, and, more recently, the Michelangelo Antonioni film *Identification of a Woman*, with sequences on the lagoon and in the Hotel Gritti.[63]

It was of no little importance that exhibitions in the 1980s began to demonstrate an interest in the art and culture from after the fall of the Republic. Scholarly interest in the nineteenth century was announced in Giandomenico Romanelli's fundamental 1977 publication *Venezia Ottocento: L'architettura e l'urbanistica*, which documented architecture from the fall of the Republic to the end of the nineteenth century.[64] The richness of nineteenth-century painting and architecture was evident in the exemplary exhibition *Venezia nell'Ottocento*, held in the Napoleonic wing of the Museo Correr.[65] Romanticism, the landscapes of Caffi and Ciardi, the history paintings inspired by Titian and Tintoretto, the architectural studies of Viollet-le-Duc and Ruskin, the many paintings of Marin Faliero and Doge Foscari, Favretto, and the Realists and Impressionists in the *fin de siècle*, came together for the first time. In the 1979 exhibition *Venezia e lo spazio scenico* the theatre and spectacle of the Municipality were displayed.[66]

In 1985 an exhibition of architecture was held, appropriately, in the Napolenic wing of the Museo Correr, uncovering possible Venices, *Le Venezie possibli*, following plans that had never been realised but were a significant part of the city's urban analysis and definition, attributions of an incomplete Venice.[67] The Palladian bridge intended for the Rialto was still the most famous case, but there were many speculations in the nineteenth century, including Selva's projects, bridges, underwater thoroughfares, possible railway lines and, of course, the later unrealised projects of Wright, Le Corbusier and Kahn. But, most significantly, the decades after the fall of Venice in 1797 were at last in place.

The presence of the Venetian past was particularly in evidence in the third 1985 architectural exhibition, in another tribute to the potency of the Architectural Institute and its efficacy in creating links with the School of New York. Moving from Berlin to Venice, the American Architect John Hejduk, who designed the 1978 towers of Cannaregio, created his architectural poem *The Slumber of Adam* – in the Piazza San Marco. A giant clock construction, a new Torre dell'Orologio, was constructed near the original landmark.[68] A vast machine on wheels, it was pulled into place by men literally dragging time, confronting the layers of the past that meet so famously in the Piazza.

Entirely current within this reinterpreted geography of Venice (the locus shifts, as we have seen, from the Giudecca, to Cannaregio, from the Lido to the basin of St Mark's), was the 1985 performance *The Course of the Knife*, by notable American artists Claes Oldenburg and Coosje van Bruggen, the American architect Frank Gehry and the well-known Italian curator and writer Germano Celant.[69] The ever-articulate Celant described it as a 'neo pop commedia dell'arte'.[70] The knife of the title was a giant Swiss army knife, red, bristling with corkscrews and subsidiary devices: it was made into a boat some fifteen metres long, capable of navigating canals (fig. 214). It had a corkscrew mask, and its appendages could be used as oars, in the best Venetian regatta tradition. The Knife was the central character, cutting its way through the performance. The scene of the action was the campo in front of the Arsenale gate, that richly decorated collage of sculptures dominated by the great eastern lions, the grand mementos of a maritime past. The space had been nominated by the Situationists as uncanny, but it was also somewhat banal, especially as the performance made much play with the rather ordinary outdoor *caffe* that faces the gate. It was already established that the navy was to vacate the Arsenale in the next decade, and the likelihood of the area's redevelopment for tourism was hardly surprising. The Oldenburg-Bruggen performance was the first exercise in its re-definition, and a wry comment on the increasing sea of mass tourism in the city.[71]

On land the Knife is powered by a human actor: it is Dr Coltello who sells souvenirs, but aspires to paint like Canaletto. As Germano Celant explained it: 'Set in Venice, the site of a dramatic encounter between former achievement and contemporary mass tourism, between past and present, between history and kitsch, it placed

214 Claes Oldenburg, Coosje van Bruggen, Frank O. Gehry and Germano Celant, *The Course of the Knife*, Campo di Arsenale, 1985.

itself – like all knives – halfway between the two sides of the historical wound; it worked on the local history's contradictions.'[72] Frankie P. Toronto (the architect Frank Gehry, born in Toronto) wanted to be an architect like Palladio. Van Bruggen played Georgio Sandbag who wanted to be like George Sand. Germano Celant was a billiard player with alchemical aspirations that likened him to Giordano Bruno. Objects added to the cutting-edge fun parlour set up in the Campo dell'Arsenale included a huge coffee cup for the modern tourist, an ancient temple and a column as architectural references, and a lion statue that mimicked the gate sculpture but was also capable of singing from Verdi's *Otello* (this was a character called the Chateaubriand Lion, who brought another celebrated guest back to Venice).

The actor-objects wandered around the campo, handing floating cutouts of Venice to the patrons of the *caffè*, sounds abounded: pigeons cooing, Venetian boat sounds, chatter of tourists. The end was appropriately apocalyptic, caused by the decision of the Niagara Falls and the Alps to honeymoon in Venice – Europe and America *à deux* – with cataclysmic result. The knife ship issued from the Arsenale as a projection of the Niagara Falls and appropriate sounds marked the last deluge.[73]

Yet again, time and memory were the preoccupations, the inscriptions upon the palimpsest of the city. It was evident that Biennale architecture could sidestep utility and extort the historical references that Venice could so abundantly provide. In 1985 the third architectural Biennale, under the directorship of Aldo Rossi, had a specific Venetian programme: architects were asked to respond to certain pre-eminent sites and re-design or complete them. They took the opportunity to challenge the celebrated Venetian resistance to modernism and participate in the bid for the 'completion' of the city.[74]

Venice was now a place of architectural carnival. A spate of imagined Venices, both provocative and serious, flowed off drawing boards. Eugenio Miozzi's Accademia Bridge, built as a temporary structure in 1934, was then under reconstruction. In a tautological exercise, the Biennale staged a competition for a new design: it capitalised on the weight of historical reference and the interest in the current rebuilding. The original Accademia Bridge, an economic and social response to conditions at the time of its building, had also been considered as a structure in confrontation with the Rialto, the first bridge across the Grand Canal.[75] The site at the Accademia gave a focus to the area below Santa Maria della Salute: there was never any challenge to the location of the crossing at that point. Miozzi's temporary wooden structure of 1934 had been in constant repair since 1948, but substitutes remained on paper. Predictable conservatism led to its rebuilding *com'era*.

Some participants in the 1985 competition approached the site with reticence, spanning the canal as unobtrusively and as elegantly as possible. Some wanted to respond to the history of the site, making reference to the Barbari map and the first Rialto drawbridge. Others wanted to command and dominate.[76] Of the first type, Francesco Cellini opened a circle in the centre of his bridge with the effect of shafting light through to the water underneath. Salvador Tarago Cid combined gently raked steps with a single tree.

The impact of Rossi's floating theatre was obvious in some fashionable reworkings with tower motifs. Frederic Schwartz used San Marco-like campaniles as suspension towers and, in a bid for historical profundity, superimposed his design on the Barbari map. Giancarlo Leoncello quoted circular motifs from the church of Il Redentore and the Palazzo Dario. Canella's project took up iron motifs reminiscent of Neville's first bridge, boldly swinging his structure off-centre to give a greater entrance area on the Accademia side. Designing an aggressive wooden structure, Dardi used references to hand machinery for suspension bridges with fanciful pulleys and wheels. Semirani proposed an escalator bridge with a crescent moon as the central motif, declaring it to be a 'Gateway to the East'. There were two designs in glass making reference to Venice as a crystalline city: most poetically by Izumi Oki, trained in Toyko but

215 Venturi, Rauch &
Scott Brown, project for the
Accademia Bridge, Terza
Mostra Internazionale di
Architettura, 1985.

practising in Milan, and Ludwig Thürmer. Vittorio de Feo's straight bridge with punched-out circles supported on the shores by massive seated caryatids was one of the few to use sculpture.

As the master-mind behind this carnival of bridges, Aldo Rossi favoured the American firm of architects, Venturi, Rauch and Scott-Brown (fig. 215). Their design was a traditional balustraded arch overlaid with faux-marble decorative motifs adapted from the Palazzo Dario (nearby on the Grand Canal) and Santa Maria dei Miracoli (at some distance). The pavements of San Marco were also quoted. Rossi described the design as 'discreetly fantastic . . . grafting a vision image of a Byzantine Venice seen through the eyes of English romanticism'.[77] It either strained these references or trivialised them.

In response to the exhibits, Paolo Portoghesi wrote of the bridge as object, ornament and gallery.[78] He commented on the interest of architects in Palladio, one of the challenging aspects that reasserts 'the presence of the past', but without mimicry. For him the primary example was Purini's design. Anselmi's flying carpet provoked designs that attempted to detach themselves from time. Scenographic plans responded to the scenery of the Grand Canal: Canella's bridge was 'a great theatrical design'. Pizzigoni offered what Portoghesi regarded as a 'symbolic' bridge, with 'great polygonal beams of glass that look as if they have escaped from a kaleidoscope'. Predag's cablewalk was hung with shapes of gondolas, and Semerani's bridge with a moon balcony was an oriental crescent, a 'porta orientale'.

The second Biennale project, for the Rialto market, did not capture the imagination of either architects or critics as did the Accademia Bridge. There was little scenographic appeal, the necessity for a new plan was not so clear, and the density of the existing building in the area was a formidable context to contend with. Any new plan had to embrace the fame of the Rialto Bridge with its unchangeable approaches, as well as the pathways through the markets and Sansovino's Fabbriche Nuove.

The third project considered the Guggenheim palace on the upper Grand Canal: the Ca' Venier dei Leone, Peggy Guggenheim's museum, which had become part of the American Guggenheim Foundation after her death in 1976. The palace remained unfinished, achieving only one storey of a possible three. Most of the architects increased the existing storey to two or three; some wished to dominate that area of the Grand Canal, to challenge even the church of the Salute.

The Cracow architect Witold Korski refused to alter the building, recording it in the format of a medal with the motto *Non plus ultra*. Locatelli refused to deviate from a classical stance, framing a Palladian-completed façade from across the canal, with Palladio's *Quattro Libri* open in front. Also flattering the Biennale director were the references to the 1980 Biennale floating tower. Dabac flanked his entrance with two pennanted towers. Mallwitz floated two cubes in the Grand Canal in front of the building. Giancarlo Leoncilli projected an enormous fluted column from the roof in an echo of the Campanile or the tower of the Chicago *Tribune* building.

Because they were only designs, architects in the Third Architectural Biennale could revel in fantasy, joining an international company delighted to invent projects for prime sites, exonerated from the realities of building. Yet again Venice demonstrated how thoroughly it was lodged in the international imagination, able to provoke an extraordinary range of inventions. But Manfredo Tafuri was unrelenting in his criticism of the event, while obviously deeming it to be of some importance, or at least symptomatic of its times.[79] According to Tafuri the projects failed to address such 'pressing problems' as 'the terminal on Piazzale Roma, the organisation of the Tronchetto, and the recovery of marginal areas'.[80] Architects were let loose in a Venice that became 'devoid of identity, or identified with the reign of the mask of frivolous discourse': those very marks, one might add, that so distinguish the culture of the 1980s. For Tafuri, the outcome (and we could wish his review to be more detailed) was 'paralysis, hypervenetianism, and uncontrolled hubris struggling to exorcise anxiety'; 'what was intended to be a "festival of architecture" was a kind of banquet around a city treated like a cadaver'.[81]

Beyond the Giardini and the glamour of so many international drawing boards, there were significant projects actually under construction, and they were in the fraught area of housing. In fact the 1980s was Venice's most significant and positive building period in the field of domestic architecture in the twentieth century.[82]

Housing

The *sestiere* of Cannaregio had been the focus for design projects in the 1970s: in the 1980s it was the Giudecca. With its Palladian churches and the annual Festa del Redentore, the island had long played a role in the scenography of St Mark's basin. The Giudecca was regarded as a garden island: the Eden Garden had been famous at the turn of the century, but retained only a vestige of its earlier extensive greenery in which D'Annunzio's Foscarina wandered in *Il Fuoco*. Stripped of many of its churches and monastic communities by Napoleon and the never-completed site of Selva's Campo di Marte in the early nineteenth century, the area had become the main centre of Venetian industrial activity in the ninteenth century, although, as we have seen, it had remained limited in its prosperity.[83] The industrial boom belonged to the days of the Molino Stucky, the Junghans factory, the Dreher brewery and Fortuny's workshop: in the 1950s they had fallen silent. On one tip of the island was the luxury Cipriani hotel, opened in 1958, but for the most part the Giudecca had modest housing densely packed into the narrow strip of the island, giving a sad sub-standard air to a one-time green zone.

Across the wide canal that had become the concourse for shipping on the way to Marghera via the notorious Canale di Petroli, the Giudecca has remained isolated, linked to the main islands only by *vaporetto* (fig. 216), but some changes and restoration were taking place. In an important invervention, the old Dreher brewery was converted to residential use.[84] Given the controversies, the polemics and the inaction in the face of endangered buildings, its conversion seems extraordinary. Giuseppe Cambriarsio, working within the factory's pre-built shell, opened its roof with a trio of bold skylights, and marked out the internal space under them with a central bricked walkway between new apartments rising to four storeys.[85] The apartments had maximum light and maximum protection, but externally the old building respected the industrial vernacular of the previous century.

On the south side of the island, in an area traditionally devoted to boat building, Vittorio Gregotti designed dockyards for the public company ACTV.[86] New designs for the empty shell of the Molino Stucky, by far the largest complex on the island, were regularly on student drawing boards.[87] In 1986 the Campo di Marte, located in

an inner area behind the Palladian church of the Zitelle, was a major focus for design projects. Ten European architects, most of whom had a connection with the Venice School or had participated in recent Biennales, showed plans for an area of community housing controlled by the IACP: the city planning department for 'popular housing'.[88]

Aldo Rossi's project was the most debated (he was the most conspicuous Venetian-based architect of the decade; fig. 217). Rossi followed the north–south orientation of buildings and *calli* already in existence, but his units were purposefully oriented to the church of the Zitelle and its orchard garden, maximising those green spaces still in place.[89] The church and its monastic buildings were intended to play the main role in developing a cultural centre for the island.

Rossi's complex was to be 'a small but beautiful city', having an outlook both to the Palladian Zitelle church and to the lagoon. There were to be three types of buildings: small brick houses of two storeys, four-storey edifices and a centre linked to other buildings by passageways. A long gallery formed a market and shops to serve the old residents of the island and the users of the nearby youth hostel. Different types of buildings were to be in different types of materials: traditional brick for the low buildings, *marmorino veneziano* for the four-storey ones, with traditional paving. The presentation drawings were among Rossi's most felicitous, emphasising the green belt and the proximity of the buildings to the Zitelle, and, in a bird's-eye presentation view, showing the prime location of the island near San Giorgio Maggiore with the background of the Campanile and the domes of San Marco.

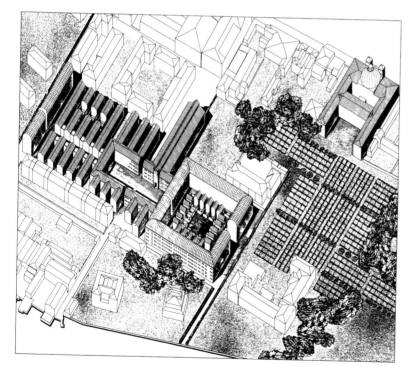

216 (*top*) Aerial view of the Giudecca.

217 (*above*) Aldo Rossi, design for housing for the Campo di Marte, Giudecca, 1985.

However, Giancarlo Caniggia was awarded the prize, and commended in particular for his knowledge of the city's construction. Caniggia was a student of Saverio Muratori, the pioneer of studies of Venetian typology, and clearly indebted to him. His presentation emphasised the typological path that led from the simple dwelling, the *domus elementare* developed from the simple reed huts to which Cassiodorus referred as the archetypal lagoon dwellings, to the *portego* and lateral courtyard fully formed in the twelfth century. These historic paths were foregrounded in Caniggia's presentation. He eagerly subscribed to the format of tradition and repetition that is, after all, the determinant of typology. The practice prompts the question: has Venice become too typological? Has the preoccupation been a restricting and conservative methodology for modern architecture?

In terms of actual building, not only in the Giudecca, but in Venice overall, it was Gino Valle who won laurels for a IACP complex on the Giudecca and the adjacent Sacca Fisola, constructed from 1980 to 1986 in the area to the rear of the Stucky mill (fig. 218). Valle was critical of the Sacca Fisola's existing housing, which he described as 'a piece of the suburbs of Mestre, cut out and stuck there on the lagoon'.[90] His new schemes did something to save that stark area. The complex of dwellings was sympathetic to the island's industrial past, echoing the Molino Stucky's emphatic brick construction by creating towers like small replicas of its industrial chimney.[91] The settlement has unity and intimacy by virtue of the apartments being paired so as to share a common peaked roof-line, but they are separated at the apex so they have privacy and light. The warmth of the brick, the unity that results from its extension to the paving and the patterning, with its precision and decorative interest, animate and integrate the ninety-four apartments. Each apartment preserves its autonomy and has its own staircase. Balconies with circles opened in them are like eyes that screen the space for inhabitants, but open up the inside to outside life. The *calli* – the corridors between buildings – and the *campi* – the communal squares in front – preserve a sense of traditional housing, but without undue typological reference. Valle has been absolved of the sin of picturesque 'hyper-venetian-ness'.[92]

Another distinguished initiative sympathetic to the scale and density of existing buildings was the apartments designed by Iginio Cappai, Pietro Mainardi and Valeriano Pastor on the Sacca Fisola in the Fregnan area (fig. 219). They maximised the site on the water's edge of two canals, building the residences over the canal at first-floor level, above small jetties.[93] Again brick was used, in sympathy with the dominant Molino Stucky. Like Valle's apartments, which are contiguous but still separate, this housing is in dramatic contrast to the 1960s tenement housing characteristic of Sacca Fisola.

218 (*below left*) Gino Valle, IACP housing complex, Giudecca, 1986.

219 (*below right*) Iginio Cappai, Pietro Mainardi and Valeriano Pastor, housing complex, Sacca Fisola, 1982–9.

220 (*above left*) Giancarlo de Carlo, housing, Mazzorbo, 1979–86.

221 (*above right*) Vittorio Gregotti, public housing, San Giobbe 1984–7.

Over the period from 1979 to 1987 Giancarlo de Carlo designed low-income houses on the island of Mazzorbo. Vittorio Gregotti developed public housing at San Giobbe, and nearby in San Girolamo, at the edge of Cannaregio facing the water. Bortuluzzi created a further area of public housing on behalf of the city urban planning office. Not only did these buildings relieve the problems of accommodation, they brought contemporary architecture into Venice and proved its efficacy, and its capacity for assimilation. Aware of the sanctioning of the past's presence and the hostility of public opinion to deviations from the Venetian type, most of the schemes of the 1980s made some reference to local practice.

Giancarlo de Carlo's housing for Mazzorbo affirmed the capacity of some Post-Modern architecture to make reference to traditional typologies, but also to be contemporary, creative and apparently uncompromised (fig. 220).[94] Traditional houses in the islands of Mazzorbo and Burano are brightly painted, in contrast to the *Venezia rossa* of the main islands. De Carlo followed the bright palette, although he inflected it away from primary to tertiary hues. The simple continuous block style of indigenous housing prevails, but in each block there are distinctive ovals housing the stair-wells. Windows are simple, outlined in white in the traditional Istrian stone, but placed in unconventional groupings, giving vitality to plain walls. Yet the complex appears as a unified block designed up to the water's edge, with its own *fondamenta*.

Two housing complexes built in Cannaregio during the 1980s appear more strained in their pursuit of the Post-Modern, and they lack the extravagant poetry that marked many of the designs in the 1978 competition. For the San Giobbe housing scheme, Vittorio Gregotti revived the traditional Venetian wooden roof terrace, the *altana*, in conjunction with a series of private outdoor spaces for each residence. 'Carpaccio chimneys' are a conspicuous feature on the skyline, and perhaps too easy a marker of Venetianness (fig. 221).[95] However, in this respect, the typological procedures dear to Venetian modern architecture are reasserted.[96] The structures give the roofline a kind of see-through geometry, and a sequence of bay windows in living areas counters the repetitive nature of much continuous housing. As with all architecture interpolated in Venice, the analysis of the pre-existing buildings was intensive, and markers on the original site – a tall tree and an old industrial chimney – designed into the new scheme.

A further housing project – Franco Bortoluzzi's at the Sacca San Girolomo, constructed between 1987 and 1990 – had an advantageous open site looking out over the lagoon.[97] Framing the view by arches, it presents a Venetian-articulated façade to passing *vaporetto* traffic. Again, the windows are not placed symmetrically, neither are the *campiello*-like spaces.

The most important building in the restricted field of public architecture was the hospital complex built as an extension to the civic hospital in the Scuola di San Marco in the 1980s. Like the Gregotti project, it is the work of a conspicuous member of the Architecture Institute, Lucio Semerani, in partnership with Gigetta Tamaro. Of course the history of Le Corbusier's rejected project surfaces to haunt all hospital projects, but lacking the spectactular extension out into the Cannaregio lagoon, additions had to be accommodated in an area already closely built. The new buildings fronting the the Fondamenta Nuove show sensitive regard for the existing lagoon view by using porthole windows. The architects described the site as 'the slightly sad edge of the city' (we recall Verdi in *Verdi: A Novel of the Opera*, succumbing to sadness on the Fondamenta Nuove), and described the placement of windows and elevations on the *fondamenta* as having 'a slow rhythm'.[98] That rhythm works across a set of distinctive four-storey units, one having a triangular gable beside flat-topped buildings, and the other three a row of attic windows. The façade is not rhetorical, but its detail activates space and captivates the spectator, particularly the porthole windows at ground level. On the rear façade, which is closer to the cloister idea of a traditional hospital, lunette formations bring to mind Codussi's façade for the Scuola di San Marco, still the hospital's principal entrance.

Bearing in mind earlier modern buildings in Venice – the Inail headquarters, the Cassa di Risparmio in the Campo Manin, even the Gardella House on the Zattere – the placement of windows unevenly, rhythmically, not merely away from obvious symmetry but in an irregular counter-balancing treatment, represents one of the major changes in building. The 'slow rhythm' animates a number of 1980s buildings – the Mazzorba houses, Gregotti's *altane* and courtyard formations, Gino Valle's turrets. They are all to some degree sympathetic to the variety and human scale of *Venezia minore*.

Politics and Redeployment

After the Stucky mill closed in 1956 designs for its reuse became a standard student exercise. It was to remain on the drawing board, but constantly under scrutiny, into the 1990s. The Arsenale also commanded attention; it became part of a grandiose scheme supposed to save Venice, and reanimate the Veneto. In 1987 Venice was nominated as the site of the European exposition for the year 2000. The recommendation was to be an continuing matter for planning, debate and speculation, local and international.

In the late 1980s issues of restoration and development of unusued and derelict warehouse and factory buildings were partially resolved. Productive new uses for old buildings became possible, providing their 'antiquity' – which was usually nineteenth century – was recognised and preserved as a legitimate part of a layered landscape. From the late 1970s to the 1980s buildings and equipment were gathered up and curated within the new field of industrial archaeology. Venice was to the forefront of this archaeology with the Arsenale and the ancient admixture of warehouses and palaces along the Grand Canal. In 1979 the Commune launched an 'itinerary' in catalogue and video form.[99] In 1980 the city exhibited itself with historical accompaniment as *Venezia città industriale*.[100] Fringe buildings were given a new focus: the warehouses along the Dogana, the old slaughterhouse by Salvadori and the industrial buildings on the Giudecca, with the Molino Stucky the most imposing. The Biennale had already sponsored a focus on the Molino in 1975; after so many projects and more analyses of its strange but familiar neo-Gothic appurtenances, it eventually became a development project.[101]

Nevertheless, the late 1980s, and the Expo proposal in particular, exposed the contradictory interests governing Venice, and all inappropriate interventions, sufficient to be called a crisis in politics. National and regional interests in the Veneto favoured Venice as the site of the exposition: the Socialist Gianni de Michelis, foreign minister in the Andreotti government, supported by the president of the Veneto, Carlo Bernini, was its leading advocate. De Michelis was the man of the decade. The Veneto, its cities and industrial centres – Marghera and Mestre, Treviso and Padua – stood to gain from the Expo in terms of new infrastructure and an influx of visitors drawn by the additional attraction of Venice as the ultimate tourist destination. But increasingly it became clear that Venice, and a majority of Venetians, found the pressure to be too great for the city to sustain. The issue was a wider one, involving the politics of the entire area, brought into focus by a referendum planned for 1989 asking whether historic Venice should be separated from Mestre and the Terraferma: in other words should the 1926 accord that grew from the foundation of Marghera be overturned? The referendum was to be one of the most important events of the late century.[102] Although separation was rejected, the referendum demonstrated that the Venetians of the historic islands were not unanimous: after all, tourism was the mainstay of the economy, and the issue of governance of the total lagoon had obviously not swayed voters. While Venice might be a tourist bonus for the Terraferma, it was also a burden.[103] In the larger arena it was clear that the Venetians themselves were not united on any of the issues crucial to their city – restoration, protection from high water and pollution – the inability to achieve results had a political base.

In the 1980s discussions increasingly emphasised that Venice must take the path of 'soft' development, and tourism rather than 'hard' industry was seen as preferable.[104] New cultural initiatives were visibly boosting figures for exhibition attendance: the Palazzo Grassi on the Grand Canal, owned by the Fiat company, had been extensively restored by the Milanese architect Gae Aulenti, who created a gallery for crowd-pulling exhibitions.[105] It opened in 1986 with an exhibition of Futurism, the most extensive to date. The 1988 exhibition on *I Fenici* attracted 75,000 visitors.[106] The Palazzo Grassi was a model of constructive private enterprise, developing and deepening the tourist experience, even though it has some of the most restrictive visitor controls in the international sector.

But in a few short years tourism had become 'hard'. On New Year's Eve of 1987 drunken crowds caused damage in the Piazza. That year the carnival was called the carnival of Ca' Farsetti, a reference to the Commune, which had permitted a rock band to perform in the Piazza San Marco.[107] As tourist figures increased, entrances to the city were under increasing pressure. The road bridge had to be closed at Easter 1987 because the Piazzale Roma car park was full. Publicity was given to Vittorio Cini's view, given just before his death, that the automobile bridge had been 'a colossal error' and that he would have liked to demolish it with his own hands; he had also wanted to transfer heavy industry from Marghera to the mouth of the Po.[108] The IUAV held a convention and exhibited studies of the projects for joining with the Terraferma over the last two hundred years – from the rail bridge to the road bridge and the schemes for the Tronchetta – the artificial island car park – in 1964.[109] In the next decade, a sub-lagoon metropolitan transit system would be debated.

In this climate, increasingly complicated by criticism of industry, the alarm at the prospect of the Veneto for Expo and new fears of mega-tourism, came recommendations that Venice host scientific and technological research and develop centres for environmental study and restoration. Many of the Expo ideas were stimulating and were not discarded. Gianni de Michelis's view that the 'epicentre of the expo must be the Arsenale' proved capable of a redirection that proposed the Arsenale as a centre for less obviously commercial schemes. It was possible to reject Expo, but to reconfirm a constructive unity with the mainland, with the development of the airport at Tessera, for example.

The Arsenale, that set of great spaces redolent of a long history, was already the framework for a great museum (fig. 222). The Biennale's use of the Corderie over

some years had amply demonstrated both its potential and its appeal (fig. 223).[110] Covering a valuable sixth of the area of the main island, the total fabric recalls the great naval strength of the Republic as well as its decline and still provokes emotion. Entrepeneurs and architects fascinated with its potential knew that the Italian navy were to vacate the area still in their use and return the site to the City of Venice.[111] In 1981–2 a report entitled 'Proposals for the Utilisation of the Arsenale' was prepared by national and local authorities, examining ownership, management and costs, and re-stating the responsibility for the patrimony in tandem with the urban transformation of the area.[112] Since state and regional resources would be inadequate to the giant task, private as well as public investment was necessary.

The Castello *sestiere*, which adjoins the Arsenale, also needed consideration, for projects for the area had been thwarted on many occasions. The Arsenale's immediate environs had traditionally housed the *arsenalotti* in modest dwellings. Selva's Giardini and the Strada Nuova were the most decisive reshapings of the area, followed in the Fascist years by Duilio Torres's extension of the promenade on the waterfront and his completion of the bridge planned by Selva. For the first time, the gardens had direct pedestrian access from San Marco. At the same time, Torres had despaired of the neglect of public housing in the area. A sequence of unrealised projects were ghosts in the area: Selva's full project for the Giardini and surrounding areas, Luigi Torelli's wild scheme

222 (*top*) The Arsenale, aerial view, *c.*1985.

223 (*above*) The Arsenale, view of the Corderie.

to develop the island of Sant'Elena as an aquatic area linked to the Riva degli Schiavoni by a raised carriageway, and Felice Martini's 1877 project for enlarging and reorganising areas of the Arsenale.[113]

By the 1980s most of the other workshops and dockyards were empty and revealed in all their haunting neglect to passengers on the *vaporetto* as it journeyed from St Mark's to the Fondamenta Nuove. Grandiose plans to develop the area as a convention centre accelerated in the climate of Expo: Gianni de Michelis, Assessore alla Pubblica Istruzione del Comune di Venezia, became increasingly prominent at the time of these debates, just before his bid to use the Arsenale as the centre of Expo 2000. The project was elaborated for the 1987 Triennale exhibition in Milan with the sponsorship of the Commune, the region and, among others, the CIGA hotel chain.[114] A range of interests joined in the project in a specifically Venetian compound that included not only political and business interests, but also academics and architects.

Both Luciano Semerani and De Michelis praised the potential of a vast exhibition site in the redeployed Arsenale to be opened up to science, technology and art. The available 'morphology' was of two types: single free-standing buildings, such as the Corderie, and sequences of buildings with shared walls and modular roofs. The internal docks offered regular bodies of water. The outer walls were another conspicuous element, originally cordoning off the complex to achieve the necessary autonomy of operations around the *darsene* to ensure military secrecy and protection. Semerani described the Arsenale in its current appearance as 'the product of Romantic engineers': 'a picturesque personage', 'a kind of scenographic crazy quilt of Gothic and Byzantine together, as if it was *this* Venice after all which prevailed over the magnificence of the sixteenth century and the Neoclassical modernisation'.[115] The inclusiveness of Post-Modernism was at work here.

In 1985 the Architecture Institute's *Progetto Arsenale*, an exhibition and catalogue co-ordinated by Professore Valeriano Pastor, documented and displayed the past, and called for creative interventions for the future.[116] Crucial to the emergent project was the orientation north across the lagoon to the airport at Tessera. The Arsenale City was only one part of the scheme, which depended on new development on the Terraferma in the vicinity of the Marco Polo airport with links to other islands.[117] Thus the periphery would be activated, in line with many recommendations. Also crucial was the link with such Veneto cities as Treviso and Padua, with the aim of generating regional activity throughout the area and reinvigorating the axis between Padua and Venice. The historic city was making its bid in relation to the wider Veneto region beyond Mestre and Marghera. The new project was promoted as a solution to problems of access, favouring air above road and rail. The Arsenale would be directly linked to the new centre by water, helping to decongest the clogged road-rail entrance at Piazzale Roma. International comparisons for new designs were eagerly offered: the Beaubourg in Paris, the Barbican Centre in London, the Experimental Centre in Freiburg and communication developments on Japanese models.

After the historical analysis, new designs for the 'reordered Arsenale' by architects of the IUAV at the Milan exhibition headed by Luciano Semerani were shown at the Milan Triennale in 1987.[118] Gianni de Michelis endorsed the 'patrimony of pure potential'. Venice would be reborn again; the new project was 'a symbol of [Venice's] perennial, matchless vitality'.[119] Luciano Sermerani ran to poetry: 'If the operation goes well, if it is not only a mask or face lift, if the Muse helps, then this hand [the the hand of time] will feel running along its palm the pure water of the future, assisted by the rustle of angel's wings at the window'.[120] The involvement in the new plans was presented against a background of intense years of historical study evident in the publications by Ugo Piazzarello, Vincenzo Fontana, Giorgio Bellavitis and Ennio Concini. The new future followed a carefully studied past.

The redevelopment emphasised exhibition potential, access, especially from the airport, and the 'creative' use of the water areas. Already existing areas were to be used for exhibitions and the water basins integrated as decorative and recreational spaces in proximity to workshops and factories. The Arsenale Nuovissima was envisaged as a production sector, with a new bridge and a new opening to the *darsene* of San Cristoforo, which would link the Bacino to the lagoon once more, as it had been before Napoleon. A navigable canal was to be opened on the north wall. The Corderie, the Artiligiera and the Magazzini Marittimi were to be pavilions. A scientific and technology area was to be focused around the Bacino delle Galeazze. The Squadratorium, built by Scalfarotto in the mid-eighteenth century, was glowingly described as 'an Enlightenment project' and the new designation was seen to follow Scalfarotto's rationalist example.[121] The Squadratorium was originally 147 metres in length, now drastically reduced and a mere shell, but it remained the most impressive building, evidence of the vitality of the late Republic.[122] It was to become the central convention centre. The Galeazze buildings were to be reconstructed and supplemented with new buildings along the Celestia wall. The Novissimetta would become a scientific and technological research centre. A 'memory sector' was be developed at the Arsenale Vecchi with a city museum, a restored Bucintoro block, and a maritime museum. The nineteenth-century offices were to become the Arsenale museum.

The buildings to be developed in the De Michelis project included the Squadratori, the Corderie, and a system of three small palazzi with 'analogous' piazzas for accommodation of jet-setting official guests. The water areas were to be adorned with bathing facilities, rafts, fountains and submerged piazzas.[123] High-class hotels would save visitors from what had become the 'melancholy' of the grand hotels of the Lido. In a reversal of the euphoria early in the century, it was accepted that the Lido would lose its hold on visitors and traffic be redirected back to the historic centre. The city was to play its greatest role: as cultural host to the world. Meanwhile, as if to confirm the potential range of visitors, an economic summit of world powers met, staying in the Hotel Gritti and ferrying to the Cini centre and, more modestly, international anarchists celebrated Orwell's '1984' in the traditionally socialist area of the Campo Santa Margherita.[124]

Many earnestly desired a modernised a city, a city that was not merely a museum, but had a viable function beyond tourism. The attitude has been traced in all its intermittence and uncertainty in this study; its adherents have been found less forceful than the proponents of a Venice as a city of the past.

Luigi Nono, Composer, and Massimo Cacciari, Philosopher

Gianni de Michelis was the most conspicuous citizen of the Venice of the 1980s; in 1993 Massimo Cacciari became mayor, and articulated different values. Cacciari's background as political activist and commentator, and his academic status as a philosopher and member of the Institute of Architecture, gave him a wide-ranging understanding of the city's problems. Beyond the academy, he did much to effect the intellectualisation of Venice from within, and to imbue the city with seriousness in a decade of masquerade and scenography. His inter-disciplinary work spanned philosophy, cultural analysis, architecture and urban criticism, and he also collaborated with Venetian artists.

Cacciari's varied interests and the acumen of his philosophy is evident in the libretto for Luigi Nono's work for voice and chamber instruments, *Prometeo, Tragedia dell' Ascolto* – *Prometheus, The Tragedy of Listening*.[125] The first version was premiered in Venice in 1984 with a setting built for the deconsecrated church of San Lorenzo by the Italian architect Renzo Piano (fig. 224). In preparation for *Prometeo*, Nono spoke of his intense researches into colour and music, his reading of colour theory and the colour plays of Schönberg, Scriabin and Kandinsky, and his many conversations with Vedova; but finally *Prometeo* needed a construction designed by an architect, rather than the imagery of a painter.[126] Piano's chamber for the production of *spatial* sound filled the church interior with huge curved timbers supporting steel platforms on which the singers could move above and around the audience. It appeared like an arch, or the hull of a boat, recalling D'Annunzio's *La Nave*.

For the libretto for *Prometeo*, Cacciari used Hesiod's *Theogony*, bringing together writings from the classical past with modern philosophers, bridging the past and the present. In the beginning passages from the *Theogony* are read by two speakers, then passages from Cacciari's philosophical mentors, particularly Hölderlin and Walter Benjamin, who provide the main inspiration for his text. Short passages make 'islands'; an angel comes forwards – Benjamin's angel after Paul Klee's painting *Angelus Novus*, and Rilke's angel from the *Duino Elegies* – to confirm, in the words of Hölderlin, that 'we are destined to find no resting place'.[127] The angelic mission in all its complexity is well understood by Cacciari, and detailed in his essay written at the time: *The Necessary Angel*.[128] Interceding between the realm of the gods and of man, Prometheus, the enemy of the god Zeus, brings fire to mankind. He is heroic in

the context of the sea (by virtue of his descent from parental sea gods, for he is the son of Clymene, the Oceanid). He sings of 'the richness of beautiful islands; 'On the sea my boat will be a thousand blue sails . . .'[129] Prometheus with his gift of fire is at the heart of the opera: who can avoid recalling the Venice of glass and fire sited at Murano, and that essential conjunction of elements remarked by D'Annunzio and Rilke? Or that Venice is a set of islands in water?

Prometeo sounds at times on the very edge of audibility, as if from an extra-terrestrial source, or Olympus perhaps. Instruments stab out sounds, or give out single attenuated notes, before silence. The sounds are islands in a realm more of angels than humans. The 'dream phantoms' of the text find their territory in Nono's music, now liberated from the human anguish that drove *Intolleranza*.

In the last years of his life (he died in 1990), Nono was still prepared to find the sources of his spatial music in San Marco and Giovanni Gabrieli, and recalled the placement of organ, choirs and soloists at different heights responding to the different geometries in San Marco.[130] He was still hearing the multi-universe of Venetian sounds, declaring that he listened to colour as he listened 'to the stones or the skies of Venice . . . with rapport between undulation and vibration'.[131] Cacciari added his own 'multisonority of space'.[132]

Prometeo's circle of sound, projected through and around space and, it seems, above and below it, had a corollary in a work composed at much the same time in another symbiosis of Venetian creative artists. In 1984 Nono wrote a musical elegy for Carlo Scarpa, who had died in 1978, dedicating an orchestral work to Scarpa's 'infinite possibilities'.[133] As in *Prometeo*, the spaces between sounds separate them, making them like distinct chambers that form into a total architecture. Sharp sounds are contrasted with long and drawn-out utterances, drum rolls sound beneath with sad sounds that might be voiced in mourning, ornamental plucked notes sound urgently before measured silences, like Scarpa's serene containments of space. Perhaps there is anger in *A Carlo Scarpa*, at opportunities withheld, or the termination of the work of a creative artist. Towards the end of *Prometeo*, the spirit had been affirmatory, but that affirmation was unsettled by a spirit of nihilism: as we have seen, deep uncertainties now attend the Venetian utopia.

Following the political articles of the 1960s and his activism in the factories of Marghera, Cacciari published wide-ranging academic essays, dwelling on the 'metropolis' as if to understand the nature of all cities, and (it might seem) the vestigial nature of his own, as well as its one-time master, Vienna.[134] He examined the exponents of the theory of the modern city, those creating its poetics, from Baudelaire to Simmel, Benjamin and the Viennese architect Adolf Loos. Nihilism and utopia appear together in apparent contradiction: nihilism undermines the utopic state, but at the same time, it re-confirms its very position as utopic (as it does in *Prometeo*). Cacciari's 'metropolis' broods upon the the lost status of Venice as a world centre. As Patrizia Lombardo put it in her fine introduction to the English translation of some of the essays, 'the philosophy of the city is . . . inevitably, impeccably, ineluctably – the philosophy, or a philosophy of Venice'.[135] She insists on the relevance of the modern as a result of the city's unique configuration: 'Venice, small and ancient as it is, with no cars, apparently so ideal as a refuge from the hustle and bustle of today's world, allows a *powerful intuition of modernity*.'[136]

The absence or presence of modernity, and the debate concerning its relevance, are crucial aspects of the city's recent history and character that are determined more by the absence of the modern than its presence. Cacciari's academic writings deliberate, if only by implication, on his own time even if he does not allude to the Venice of the flood, or revived carnival, or the city near the millennium threatened by Expo, but these were surely pressures upon his thought. As we have seen, the notion of Venice as 'unfinished' was current in the 1980s. The city was 'an essay' that could give rise only to fragmentary statements, but it was ready for change, rather than stasis.[137]

In his few crucial pages on Venice in *Architecture and Nihilism*, Cacciari dwells on turn-of-the-century texts: Nietzsche's is a leading voice, and a fundamental source of Cacciari's own philosophical position. Thus Cacciari can write that 'in the face of Venice, every value of the city . . . becomes useless, uncomprehending, silent'.[138] And, bluntly, Venice has no signification. Its being-as-game indicates that it is language only'.[139] The surfaces are those of a carnival of appearances; there is nothing behind the mask. So Cacciari claims of Venice (the Venice of the mind as much as the physical place) that 'All appearance exists in itself and for itself – a perfect mask that hides being, or rather, reveals the loss, the absence of being', with the consequence that 'Venice is a symbol of the loss of homeland', and 'an anti-city symbol'.[140] Such a reading re-endorses Georg Simmel's views in his essay on Venice written in 1907, and the Hofmannsthal of *Andreas oder die Vereinigten*, which Cacciari sees as an extension of Simmel's thought: thus Venice, the city of the adventurer, is a masked city.[141] And Cacciari notes that 'Aschenbach's "adventure" comes only four years after Simmel's "discovery" of Venice'.[142]

The mask (adopted by Andreas as soon as he reaches Venice) is the very emblem of concealed direction, and like many before him Cacciari takes it as a metaphor for his city and the human condition; he does not shy away from its reuse.[143] Perhaps his reading is restricted by being tied to now distant sources which expound an historically circumscribed point. Yet Cacciari cannot be unaware of the extent of the mask as a symbol of some complexity in the Symbolist period; it is not a single layer concealing a lack of identity, but has the chameleon-like potential to enhance mental life.

Proust is also among the turn-of-the-century voices to which Cacciari is attuned. It is claimed that Proust's idea of Venice was geological, but this is so only if one strand of Proust's more complex voyage to Venice is in focus. So Cacciari writes: 'Venice withdraws inside the Venetian house, with its charms and secrets . . . Proust saw Venice as a geological figure; he did not see houses, structures; Proust's idea of Venice was not at all a symbolical image, but nature.'[144] In one famous passage, Proust did indeed write of the palaces of the Grand Canal as cliffs of marble along the water, but he also experienced Venice as a constructed labyrinth. San Marco and its Baptistery which so fascinated him were replete with Ruskin's symbolism. But like Simmel, Nietzsche and Hofmannsthal, Proust is a *foreigner* in Venice, locked *outside* the Venetian house. To pursue the outsider metaphor, those writers do not have access to the smells of cooking and furniture polish that pervade the Venetian interiors of a writer such as Pasinetti. Nor does Cacciari, for he too appears like a guest locked outside.

This is the condition of the *unheimlich*: Cacciari's metaphor of the house from which he is excluded is telling.[145] What is disconcerting to Cacciari (and to Simmel before him) is the absence of firm meanings with respect to Venice. And yet it is the very richness of the idea of Venice which gives rise to this ambivalence, and the contradictory nature of meanings. Venice is a multitude of texts, as Calvino showed in *La città invisibili*. When Cacciari refers to Walter Benjamin and his study of Paris, he does not identify with Benjamin's fascination with the outré and relate Venice to Paris, and yet the city and lagoon may seem like an analogy to Benjamin's arcades, outmoded to be sure, but having their heightened surrealist appeal, claiming a citizenry across space and time.[146] Cacciari's harking back to Nietzsche and his solitudes releases the notion of Venice as a utopic self-contained island-state, severed from the Terraferma and having self-reference as its crux. It is a philosophy of neo-insularism, and, at the same time, a lament for the loss of island status: fragments that are contradictory and in ruin nevertheless journey towards the present.

In 1988, as if in preparation for political office, Cacciari led a convention on *The Idea of Venice*, sponsored by the Fondazione Istituto Gramsci.[147] The convention appears crucial alongside the project *Venezia 2000*, which endorsed the city's will-to-renewal in the Veneto region. Cacciari spoke then in broad terms of the history of Venice; one that was knowingly artificial, both as physical environment and as history – because of the unnatural rule of the Republic which turned against itself in the eighteenth century during its crisis of representation. Consequently, since 1797 Venice had succumbed to nostalgia, tourism and a succession of deaths, although the deaths are more anticipated than actual. Cacciari called for new forms that were not grounded in nostalgia: the mind set that has dominated for over two centuries must be challenged. Inevitably Venice is a museal city, but it must update and realise a role as host to scientific and technological research; the university must act as a locus of intellectual change.[148]

Cacciari projected contemporary strategies onto the Venetian past, disturbing history by way of ruminations on the present. Following Simmel's diagnos of the metropolis: 'its contradictions, its conflicts, its negativity, must be overcome.'[149] He wrote during a period of scrutiny directed at the so-called myth of Venice, not only by other Venetian academics such as Tafuri, but in international Venetian studies.[150] The myth held that the Venice of the Republic, the unviolated state, demonstrated an exceptional unity of ruled and ruler. But now, while the great Venetian artists were still celebrated in retrospectives, the utopia of the sixteenth century was increasingly exposed as political manipulation, as a patrician façade that subscribed to the view of the Serenissima as unassailable, and the very model of concerned government. At the very outset of the decade the historical utopia of the sixteenth century had been explored in an exhibition – *Architettura e utopia nella Venezia del Cinquecento* – curated by Lionello Puppi, and accompanied by an essay by Tafuri.[151] Cacciari's thoughts on 'the idea of Venice' must be taken within the larger scrutiny of the histories of the 1980s which left the Republic and the contemporary island city burdened by revisionism.

The present was tarnished; as for the past, Venice no longer had a Golden Age in the sixteenth century. Scholars, chief among them Manfredo Tafuri, deepened their analyses of the conservative means by which power was held against the interest of other parties. Tafuri's *Venice and the Renaissance*, first published in Italy in 1985, focused on the 'patrician mentality', which showed itself circumspect in regard to innovation, and thus brought 'renewal' constantly into crisis.[152] It was not a question merely of political threat such as the League of Cambrai posed, but a more comprehensive climate of anxiety that was religious as well as political. Realisation of what would now be called an ecological crisis related to the management of the lagoon;

the theories of Alvise Cornaro and others in conflict with him contributed to the disquiet.[153] Where these practices had been seen as utopian, they were now interpreted as symptoms of malaise. Advancement was countered by resistance.

The climate of anxiety and the crisis of renewal: these were also at issue in the 1980s. As the Master of the Game sang in *Prometeo*: 'Listen, does a breath of the air filled with the past not blow here still?'[154]

Popular Venice

Venetian scholars were muddying the waters of the past at a time of revived energy and ambitious schemes for the future. But for foreigners it was still a city of the imagination, arguably as potent a creation as the real city. Venice showed no diminution in its appeal to writers, film-makers and, now, pop stars. Perhaps Lewis Gilbert's *Moonraker* set the mood for the new decade by motorising gondolas and smashing up monuments – catapulting a criminal through the glass of the Torre dell'Orologio in a breathless moment of attack on the heritage. Muriel Spark turned an art historian into an accomplished gangster in *Territorial Rights*.[155] The new glamour of carnival effected a re-release of the Venetian libido. The city ran with its history, and especially its historical virginity. It re-routed its labyrinths for a whole sequence of chases. It trafficked with new ease between past and present.

Madonna Takes Venice

The ultimate expression of Venetian vitality – at least in its international exposure – was Madonna's 1984 video song *Like a Virgin*, which managed to scoop up a host of knowing references to traditional Venice.[156] With the lion of St Mark and the virginal city to the forefront, old sacrosanct Venice was propelled into a pop world of high energy gyration, and endless circulation.[157]

Madonna epitomised the 1980s carnavalesque, the new eroticism and, not least, the ease of historical reference possible in a post-modern world. 'Like a Vir-ir-ir-gin/Touched for the Ver-ry First Time', she shouted, many times, transferring from a boat in Manhattan – the Brooklyn bridge is behind, outlined with lights below a vast moon – to Venice. This is the travel trope of New York to Venice, the two island cities, favoured by New Yorkers in the 1920s when they applauded the circulatory system of Venice. New York was the city of the future with a waterfront that Peter Blake described as the 'New Venice'.[158] Madonna steps from her boat in New York to her boat in Venice and she is then propelled, bosom laden with Christian symbols, along canals, singing at full volume as she negotiates with equal ease the bridges and the lion of St Mark – a real lion, padding between the columns of the Piazzetta, strolling beneath his famous statue (fig. 225). In that pre-eminent area of Venetian display between the column of San Teodoro and the column of St Mark, sexual crime was punished, acts of rape, homosexuality and fornication incurred the loss of a nose, a hand, or life itself. Madonna comes to challenge the very boundaries of *eros*. It may be carnival, since a man wears the mask of the lion – indeed he may inhabit the lion's body. The lion man carries Madonna across the palazzo threshold, bedding her down in honeymoon city in an appropriate smothering of tulle. He sweeps her up, this insignia of St Mark, taking the simulated Virgin, the courtesan of Venice, symbolic of the Serenissima itself.

Madonna is thus overtly female, and cavorting by water in the essentially feminine water city, in the city of the Sensa where the doge – or the latter-day mayor – conducts Venice's most famous ceremony wedding Venice to the sea. Edward Muir reminds us that the *Sensa* was 'the most telling metaphor for Venetian domination

...a sexual one. A city so immersed in fertility ritual, so concerned with cosmetic appearances, was bound to take advantage of the most seductive imagery.'[159] This still pertains in the late twentieth century.

Thus an American outsider reactivates the role of the Virgin of Venice in the 1980s, restoring its energy and eroticism. Of course Madonna prostitutes Venice, but then this, too, is traditional, for prostitution was historically accommodated within the virginal image of the Serenissima. Venice and Venus in familiar elision. Madonna swings her multitude of crucifixes, wears black after shedding her electric blue Madonna top. 'It feels so good inside' she screams. She demonstrates her mastery of a city that has so often marked out its visitors as victims. She exploits its labyrinthine ways, riding easily beneath the Bridge of Sighs in her vessel, then, in her palazzo, she runs her hands across the bed sheets, unveils the chair from its dust-sheet, prepares to inhabit the present rather than the past. Like the ring that reweds Venice to the sea, Madonna's ditty circles endlessly, reconfirming the power of the erotic city. She made fatal play with the signs of the city at a time when the city itself was in pop mode.

Pursuit

The eroticism of the chase is long standing. Sophie Calle, the French photographer, set up a specifically Post-Modernist trail in her *Suite vénitienne*, published in 1983.[160] In the French tradition of the Situationists who wandered the city in the 1970s fixing it in casual, almost offhand snapshots, Calle decides to follow someone from Paris to Venice. Her narrator works with text and black and white photographs; she will follow 'Henri B' and record his Venetian visit (fig. 226). She boards the train, bringing her blonde disguise, hat, gloves, sunglasses and Leica camera fitted with a mirror lens that makes secret photography possible. She approaches hotels and *pensione* to find her subject, she recognises Venice as a labyrinth. *Calli* are photographed empty (she was surely aware of the symbolism of her own name) leading to closed doors. Henry B is located at last and his itinerary detailed carefully through the urban passageways, the *campi*, *ponte*, *calli* and *salizzade* – their names carefully recorded. He takes photographs and she imitates him. The trail is lost, picked up. 'So close to him, as if sharing an island, encircled by the waters of the lagoon.'[161]

It is the woman accompanying Henry B who poses the threat, which mounts with the pursuit. There are contacts, collaborations, various incidents in the tracking process. The chase turns up a moment of recognition through a meeting of eyes: he has found her ID card left on the desk at his *pensione*. Early on it was noted that carnival was about to begin: it does so, for this is a fable of the 1980s. Pursuer and pursued meet at Florian's: they part; another photograph of a back. The night of carnival is spent on a bench with a harlequin. Now that Henri B is aware of the chase, Venice becomes even more symbolically charged: the locus is familiar, metaphorical and yet the chase is banal. Necrophilia is abroad again. 'He likes cemeteries. I take the *vaporetto* and go to the Island of the Dead, Venice's main cemetery.'[162]

After six days of trailing, there is news of Henri B's return to Paris. Should she book his room, sleep in his bed, experience the futile substitution of one tourist for another? She takes a train in order to arrive at the Gare de Lyon in Paris an hour before him so that he can be photographed 'one last time'. A blank ensues; the episode is over – except for Jean Baudrillard's accompanying essay. It misses the exquisite pre-history of the chase located in Venice, but the 'cunning demon of seduction' is there: fol-

226 Sophie Calle, 'Please Follow Me,' from *Suite vénetienne*, 1983.

lowing and reflection are coupled, and 'nowhere more literally than in Venice'.[163] As Baudrillard sees it, the stakes are violent sexuality and the recognition of pursuit as seduction, as threat. Calle's project involves both, and is both sinister and banal. The trail is a job, an essay in post-modern futility perfectly located in Venice. Baudrillard's most salient observation concerns 'the mystery in the tactile closeness of the people circulating between the walls of the narrow streets of Venice. The mixture of promiscuity and discretion'.[164] Perhaps Baudrillard himself desperately desires to be followed.

Venice is the labyrinth in which the protagonists are constantly lost in the novella by Ian McEwan, *The Comfort of Strangers*, published in 1981. From the first pages it is evident that the tourist couple Colin and Mary are in a state of torpor – they are subject to bouts of sleeping and to bad dreams, and their relationship is fraught.[165] On one occasion, late at night, they meet the Venetian Robert, who insists on taking them to his nightclub, plying them with wine and telling the story of his cruel father manipulating his son against his daughters, handing out fear and corporal punishment, exposing Robert to his sisters' revenge. These are the cues for his behaviour. Later, dehydrated, imprisoned in the city, Colin and Mary are miraculously rescued by Robert and taken to his home. While they sleep, their clothes are stolen; Robert secretly photographs his Tadzio – Colin.

Sinister, sadistic, compelling: Venice is a destabilising locale in *The Comfort of Strangers*. Tiny details assault and unsettle, as when 'a cool, salty wind below along the street and stirred a cellophane wrapper against the step on which Colin and Mary were sitting'.[166] Venice is an outsider's Venice. San Marco is not named: it is 'a cele-

416

brated cathedral'; a baby's dress and drooling is described in more detail. Little snipes at feminism puncture the text as Robert explains – and his wife Caroline endorses – 'men must be men . . . must believe in themselves as men'. When Colin and Mary return, Mary has recognised a photograph of Colin from that first visit; he has been trailed and both Robert and Caroline are preparing the inevitable killing. Not surprisingly, their palazzo is in the vicinity of the hospital. On the balcony looking towards the cemetery, Caroline reveals to Mary the full extent of the crippling sadism and perversion she not only endured at the hands of Robert, but learned to relish. Their mutual involvement in Colin must lead to perversion: it is 'fantasy stepping into reality . . . like stepping a mirror'. Venice is at its traditional work, deceiving, cajoling, disorienting, working its cruelty, until Colin is calculatedly killed.

Virgins and Vampires

The historical past and the contemporary present run together in Barry Unsworth's novel *The Stone Virgin*, published in 1985. He too enters into a pact with the old-time virginal Venice.[167] The protagonists are fashionable indeed, especially after *Don't Look Now*, for Venice is invaded by English art restorers. Sir Hugo Templar leads the Venice Rescue team, and Simon Raikes, the central character, is responsible for the restoration of a Madonna dating from 1453. He has a new technique, using a quartz cutter. As he works it is revealed that this Madonna has magical powers. Everyone responds to the sensuality of the arm that guards the pudenda: indeed this Madonna is a statue in the service of adultery, and has been throughout her history. In the fifteenth century her Piedmontese maker was hanged for the alleged murder of the model Bianca, who inspired fornication as well as art.

The Stone Virgin has three historical layers; the period of the Quattrocento based on an account told by the sculptor; the memoirs of the last member of the Ziani clan in the days of the late Republic in 1743, which tells of the Madonna statue, celebrating the narrator's own adulterous relationship with a young patrician woman (together with gambling and sexual licence facilitated by the mask); and Simon Raikes, telling his story in the present. Raikes pieces the history together while he himself feels the power of the Virgin, succumbing at the same time to the living beauty of Venetian Chiara Litsov, of the ancient line of the Fornarini, who drowned the model for the stone virgin as an act of revenge. Chiara's husband, a sculptor, in turn meets death by drowning and we may well assume that Raikes, watching Chiara coming naked from a swim in the lagoon near where her late husband perished, might well feel foreboding. The lagoon is a dumping ground again. Death by drowning, the power of sculptor's art, the release occasioned by the mask, the decay of art and the industry of its restoration, and, not least, sexual potency in the lagoon: these are the themes of this melodrama. Some are current, some embedded in Venetian mythologies.

In the 1980s the history of the erotic was under academic investigation. Guido Ruggiero unlocked the historical situation in *The Boundaries of Eros* in 1985.[168] Focused largely on the sixteenth century, Ruggiero studied the constraints, freedoms, public demonstrations of justice in attitudes to rape, sodomy, adultery and prostitution, finding more intricacy and veracity than contemporaneous novels. Edward Muir's *Civic Ritual in Renaissance Venice*, published in 1981, extrapolated the 'myth' of Venice as the precondition for the famous rituals and festivals, religious in the first instance, and then turned to the service of the state.[169] The 'myth' is variously exposed by scholars through from the 1960s as they follow the persuasive mechanisms and projects about the inviolate virgin city, the Serenissima, like unto a Virgin, undefiled, ruled by a benevolent male patriciate, headed by the doge, who undertakes the symbolic rites on behalf of the Republic.[170] Thus, the view that the great ceremonies were spontaneous and natural celebrations of a unified city, or expressions of the Christian calendar, was questioned. The morality of the state was subjected to more complex readings, as was the Republic's fabled conjunction of liberty and justice.

A further determined contribution to the genre of the erotic, Erica Jong's *Serenissima: A Novel of Venice*, was published in 1982.[171] Jong unleashed the full repertoire of Venetian signifiers about the 'city of history', of mystery, doubleness, mirroring and deception. Here is, indeed, the city's overkill. American Jessica Pruitt, beautiful, of course, and sexy, is in Venice as a jury member of the film festival. She is later to star as Jessica in *The Merchant of Venice*. The present is traded for the past, when the present Rialto Bridge was newly built and high heels – *zoccoli* – were worn for protection against the damp. They clatter on the floor, and Jessica meets Shakespeare; they rescue a child born of a prostitute mother and eventually (after awakening, of course) the film *Serenissima* is confirmed with Jessica, already well-rehearsed in her role, as the star. In the fictive film, and in the novel, it is convincingly demonstrated that the Venetian signifiers are prey to over-use, glibness, phoney sexuality and cultural snobbism.

In the 1980s it appeared that female resolve in the climate of feminism deflected attention from a city of detectives and male murders. New forays into the past were proven possible, as Jeanette Winterson's *The Passion* of 1987 made clear.[172] Two young characters inhabit Napoleon's Europe and tell their stories marked by magic and madness. Henri is a soldier in Napoleon's army, a chef working long but devoted hours to satisfy the emperor's passion for chicken. He then trains as a soldier and serves in the Moscow campaign where he meets Venetian Vilanelle and they return to Venice. Vilanelle has webbed feet, quite normal for sons of Venetian boatmen, but unique for a female. She has the poise of a fabulist, an appetite for miracles and a vast capacity for passion. Before Moscow, she worked as a casino attendant in Venice and participates in masquerade: the central passion of the tale is her love for a Venetian lady whom she meets when disguised as a male. Henri returns with Vilanelle to Venice and is required to enter the palazzo of the female lover and retrieve Vilanelle's imprisoned heart, although in effect it is too late. Henri receives only the incestuous love of a brother. Pronounced mad after murdering Vilanelle's husband, Henri is incarcerated on the asylum island of San Servolo and eventually refuses to see Vilanelle, although she rows past and lets off fireworks for him. Henri will not leave the island. He cultivates a garden, growing roses whose perfume can be smelled across the water at San Marco.

Murder and madness, a coronet of rats with pink underbellies floating in the canals, Napoleon's destruction of churches and the creation of the public gardens, the hollow ceremonies performed by Venetians for Napoleon's birthday: *The Passion* creates a new and quirky historical Venice in which the city is again both setting and character, famed for its eroticism, infested with vermin, replete with masquerade and, not least, provocative of states of madness.

We know the uncanny is at home in Venice, and not least in evidence in the fabulist vein of *The Passion* with the heroine of the webbed feet. In the film *Vampires in Venice* of 1988, Augusto Camnito offered frissons that began with the mysterious disappearance of the vampire in Venice in 1786 at a time of plague and carnival.[173] Two hundred years later he returns to bring modern victims to their death.

Klaus Kinski is the vampire, glittering of eye, top lip curled back above fanged teeth, long grey locks and an undeniably sensual presence. Professor Paris, expert on vampires, has been asked to the Canin palace to explain Nosferatu's curse. Summoned up in a seance, Nosferatu restages his crimes against the women of the house with pursuits and killings in the *calli* (and the inevitable appearance of the water-borne hearse). Rats abound again. The virgin flings herself from the Campanile, but is saved by Nosferatu, bringing him love – and potential death. He manfully strides across the Molo at dawn carrying her naked body, while the huntsmen in the lagoon (who opened the film) replay the shooting, not of a duck, or a bat, but a vampire. The devil has been abroad again; death and life are again in combat with good and evil. Crucifixes sizzle in the presence of evil. Cazotte's devil is in Venice once more.

In the 1980s the revival of carnival, the popular novel, Madonna's *Like a Virgin*, the building of San Marco in Disneyland in Orlando, USA, Venetian displays in the Hotel Rio in Las Vegas: these are but some of the signs of the relentless commodification of the city. The tiniest Venetian detail in an advertisement signals the city's fame and prestige more exploited than any other. A gondola in front of San Giorgio and a hectic red sunset was used for some years by Alitalia, not just to advertise Venice, but all Italy. Carnival was a boon to advertising. Volvo motor boats had a carnivalesque couple in a water taxi, Santa Maria della Salute in mist behind: 'Even in the wet Volvo starts first time'. Sainsbury's UK advertised their imported *prosecco* with the same model, masked face, frilled cuff, hand holding glass. Advertisements play havoc with the water city: an Alfa Romeo is driven under the Bridge of Sighs on what looks like solid ice, and the canals are turned into wheatfields for a pasta advertisement.[174]

Every nation has used the sophistication of Venice to elevate its merchandise.[175] It is sufficient to place a box of Benson & Hedges cigarettes on the seat of a gondola, exotic to form the words Coca-Cola with pigeons eating well-placed corn on the Piazza San Marco; the distinctive bottle shape of Absolut Vodka fills the Piazzetta for the pigeons in a similar advertisement (figs 227–8), Helena Rubenstein 'Renaissance colours' take on resonance with Santa Maria della Salute in the background. Dunhill suitcases are piled on trolleys in front of the Bacino; Heinecken beer is to hand for an amateur painter at work on a bridge looking across to Santa Maria dei Miracoli; in the Piazza San Marco a young woman reads a letter from home, courtesy of Australia Post. Beck's beer is shipped in a water barge, 'Brewed in Germany, drunk all over the world'. Leisure, glamour, top sights: pieces of Venice ricocheted around the world while Venetians strained to inhabit an inhabitable city, or migrated.

227 (*below left*)
Advertisement for Benson & Hedges cigarettes, 1975.

228 (*below right*)
Advertisement for Absolut Vodka, c.1995.

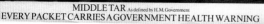

Gore Vidal, Pink Floyd and the Crisis of Tourism

In mid-decade the American Gore Vidal, claiming descent from the ancient Veneto Vidals, produced *Vidal in Venice* for world television, with the requisite accompanying book.[176] He was the voluble tourist travelling first class, ticking off the sights and the centuries, in every way a contrast to the discreet informed tourists of Susan Sontag's film of 1983, *Unguided Tour*.[177] Here we are to understand the equivocal position of the traveller, a position increasingly analysed by the sociologists of the 1980s in an ecology-conscious decade. The wear of millions of feet on fragile paving was seen to have an effect not dissimilar to storm surges.

Sontag's tourists, 'He' and 'She' are described as 'good tourists'.[178] The film appears as 'neither travelogue nor fully shaded fiction, but an extended contemplation of the irremediable. Part elegy, part comedic romance, *Unguided Tour* takes us through Venice during flood season while revealing episodes of an unnamed couples romantic finale.'[179] 'He' and 'She' visit a private room in La Fenice where Wagner and Diaghilev have been. The stone lions are still multitudinous, recalling the Orient and St Mark. Venice is unambiguously the paradigm of the world; it is also the capital of melancholy, the post-flood city, living under Sontag's Saturn. It is not straight-forward for the Sontag travellers.

In contrast Vidal charges through the city in his overly personalised documentaries, raving about the snow in winter, and likewise travelling with all speed through Venetian history, grabbing at Torcello here, a costume regatta there, ferried in a gondola, glancing at the Arsenale, at the Republic's far-flung empire, the Archives, the Palladian Villa Maser on the Terraferma. His accommodation was the Hotel Gritti where the air-conditioning was declared excellent. He quoted Coryatt, a sound authority on the courtesan industry in the sixteenth century, and covered the late eighteenth century as the customary period of carnival and decline. We are reminded that the Venetian Republic was drawing to its close as the American Republic was in the throes of birth. The 1784 document bearing the signatures of John Adams, Benjamin Franklin and Thomas Jefferson declares: 'The United States of America in Congress assembled, judging that an intercourse between the said United States and the Most Serene Republic of Venice, founded on the principles of equality, reciprocity and friendship, may be of mutual advantage. . . .' A brief sojourn quoting the Romantics and Henry James, a dash to the island cemetery to view the tomb of Diaghilev adorned with sculpted ballet shoes, a reflection on the high price of gondolas, admiration for Harry's Bar, reflections on magic and reflections in the water and, finally, the dawn – sweeping up the with mountains of garbage left by tourists in the Piazza San Marco.

Vidal's view may be taken as a typical view of Venice in the late twentieth century, informed by international circulation, with James Morris and Mary McCarthy as sources, giving more attention to foreigners in Venice than Venetians, having the requisite gondola journeys and water sequences, and paying lip service to the toll taken by tourism in which they are participants. Vidal gives a range of exotic and historical sites, a modicum of history concerning the one-time model of liberty, but mostly his Venice is the usual centre of sex, love, carnival and rubbish.

Vidal's closing sequences showing the rubbish being swept up in the Piazza San Marco at dawn were a portent. By 1989 the sheer number of visitors forced closure of the city 'for the sake of public order'. In 1984, the mayor, Mario Rigo, had already suggested that a ticket for entrance to the city be mandatory, and booked in advance as a control against numbers.[180] Attention was deflected from *acqua alta*; festivals, rock concerts and the attention of mega pop stars – Pink Floyd as well as Madonna – suggested that the city was making a bid for a youth audience. Pink Floyd's concert in 1989 was notorious, filling the centre city with a crowd of 200,000 on the night of the festival of Redentore in July 1989. For four centuries this had been Venice's traditional thansksgiving from the plague and had centred on the Palladian church of

229 Pink Floyd concert, 1989, photograph by Grazioni Arici.

Il Redentore to which the citizens came in religious process across a temporary bridge built on boats moored across the Giudecca canal. The bridge was not constructed in 1989.

In parodic echo of the *Theatrum mundi*, Pink Floyd performed on a floating stage moored opposite the Palazzo Ducale (fig. 229). Concentrated on the Piazza San Marco and the Piazzetta, the crowds were of such magnitude that a Venetian journalist claimed that Venice had been subjected to its most brutal aggression since the invasion of Napoleon.[181] It was this event above all that demonstrated the vulnerability of the city strained to the limit by the influx – and buried under so much debris afterwards that it needed the army to remove it. The piles of rubbish being swept up in the Piazza that were last shots of Gore Vidal's video were slight compared to the post Pink Floyd mountains.

The influx, the most extreme in Venice's history, served to demonstrate the fragility at the heart of Venice, and it sharpened debate. In power at the time of the proposal for Expo and the Pink Floyd concert, Mayor Antonio Casellati was under attack, with opposition headed by the Christian Democrats.[182] It was an opportunity to spell out that tourist groups ought to be limited in the central area, that permits should control the influx as for St Peter's in Rome, that museum initiatives should be redirected to Castello or Cannaregio to spread tourism evenly across the main island, that street vendors be prohibited in the central area, and bivouacing and casual eating outside forbidden in the interests of decorum.[183]

From mega-tourism to planned cultural tourism: this was the lesson of the decade. Politically precarious within the stronghold of their lagoon, the Venetians were now appearing as the displaced inhabitants of a famous city. Their architects and politicians were endeavouring to build out of the crisis of restrictive legislation and reactivate their city of the past and its buildings. Criticism of a mono-economy based only on tourism was increasingly heard. At the same time, the effort to turn the city towards a more complex economy coincided with Italian revelations of corruption no less evident in Venice and its local government than elsewhere. The 1990s were more sober times and there was a desperate attempt to make the city viable for the next millennium. At the end of the decade Sandro Meccoli wrote in *Il Gazzettino* that the exodus of Venetians was a demographic crisis, the gravest event in the history of Venice, unequalled in the past by pestilence or war.[184] The decade closed with two crucial question still unresolved: Expo or non Expo? Gates to close the Lido, or not?

The eventful and controversial years of the late 1980s also saw concrete results in research towards controlling *acqua alta*. Project Venice, Progetto Venezia, was launched in 1988, again after the protracted discussion by federal and regional powers as to which was responsible for the many stalemates in lagoon management.[185] The nominated focal points were (and not so surprisingly) urban pollution, farm pollution, silting and industrial pollution. In November 1988 MO.SE, the Modulo Sperimentale Elettro Meccanico – a prototype of the mechanism for locking the entrances to the Lido in the event of exceptionally high tide was launched in a strange latter-day Bucintoro campaign hosted by the mayor, Antonio Casellati.[186] MO.SE was a set of separately hinged gates to be positioned at the three openings of the Lido: in benign conditions the gates would rest on the seabed; when the lagoon mouths were threatened by high seas they would be raised above sea level by pumping in air, and would be deflated after the tidal swing.[187]

The MO.SE. protype was the primary evidence of the Venezia Consorzio Nuova at work. Opposition to the project was immediate, particularly from evironmental interests headed by Maurizio Calligari and Giuseppe Rosa Selva, who stressed the mounting danger of the petrol tankers' canal altering the waters of the lagoon.[188] Antonio Rusconi's analysis showed that had the Lido openings been sealed at the time of the great November flood of 1966, dire consequences would still have resulted from the influx of river water into the lagoon.[189] The importance of maintaining rather than blocking the tidal flow was repeatedly put forward in opposition to the gates. It was proposed that the ground level of the historic islands must be built up: this had been presented at a UNESCO meeting in April 1981. It was an elaborate enterprise only partly undertaken, earning increasing support.[190]

At the end of the decade debate was still raging. Venice appeared vulnerable from all sides: from the sea and the lagoon, the environmental and mechanical projects to control them, from its success as a leading world site of tourism and from its own citizens, particularly those in power.

Chapter 12

THE DOUBLE MILLENNIUM:
THE END OF THE CENTURY,
THE END OF VENICE

The Double Flood: Tourism and Acqua Alta

The 1980s closed in a spirit of reaction to *carnevale* and game-playing in films, novels and architectural design. The opposition to the Pink Floyd concert and Expo 2000 voiced in the editorials of art journals and by the world's 'Save Venice' organisations, was sufficient to shift the mood. Venice was yet again subject to the scrutiny of conservative international audiences. The decision on the site for Expo, to be taken by the European parliament, was the crucial event at the opening of the new decade. At the close of the 1990s two hundred years of post-Republican history were noted – rather than celebrated – and the question of the survival not only of the historic city, but of the lagoon faced with high waters, remained unresolved. The status of the historic city within the region and northern Italy was likewise unresolved.

In the first days of the 1990s Sandro Meccoli wrote in *Il Gazzettino* that a 'spiral of decadence . . . threatens to crush the city', and asked if, indeed, Venice could still be recognised as 'a city'.[1] The protection of the Lido was not in place: *acque alte* continued, and so did the housing crisis. Plans for a sub-lagoon metro were proposed – and defeated. The problem of keeping churches open was constant and their contents were in jeopardy from theft as well as neglect. The Biennales rolled onwards, but they were subject to bitter bureaucratic difficulties. Cultural tourism was well established, although tourism overall had accelerated into a threat as conspicuous as high tides and subsidence. Tourism was increasingly recognised as a form of pollution, profoundly destabilising for the local population.[2] It was the new flood, the Niagara Falls, the *acqua alta* that could not recede. New tourists were coming in busloads, with their *Eyewitness* guides showing everything in pictures, with shopping guides and a text modest enough not to spoil the glamour of full-colour photographs and seductive aerial-views.[3]

The Expo vote for Hanover rather than Venice was drawn in Strasbourg on 15 July 1990, with 195 'no' votes against 15 'yes' for Venice.[4] The result was construed as an implicit criticism of Italy's failure to manage Venice and Venetian politics decisively. Special pleading was *de rigueur*: if Europe wanted Venice to be free from the maltreatment of mass crowds it must assist in finding alternatives. Secession of Venice from Italy was mooted. Taking advantage of the Strasbourg result to raise the question of sovereignty, the journalist Meccoli attested that Venice had always been European, rather than Italian.[5] Perhaps Venice's late entry into united Italy in 1866 was still an issue. In demonstrating interest in Venice, particularly through the private 'Save Venice' organisations, Europe in effect committed itself to the rehabilitation of Venice in the late twentieth century.[6] According to Meccoli, France was especially implicated, as if Manin's hope that Venice would be saved by French intervention in 1848 was still alive. The adoption of Venice would be compensation for Napoleon's act in destroying the Republic.[7]

In the wake of widespread charges of corruption, which affected the government of Venice as much as the rest of Italy, there came a new sobriety, and calls for public accountability.[8] The then-president of the Consorzio Venezia Nuova, Luigi Zanda, pointed out that saving Venice was a moral issue.[9] Venice was one of a very few fully funded Italian programmes, and it was an acknowledged national priority. The key question was the ethics of spending those funds, allocated but not delivered. In order to effect the protection of the city in the lagoon, expenditure on public works and restoration was urgent.

A book published in 1991 by Gianfranco Bettin, *Dove volano i leoni: fine secolo a Venezia* (Where the Lions Fly: The Last Century in Venice) is yet another chronicle of the city's supposed ultimate years – and an indication of the views of governing Venetians.[10] Bettin reviewed the contradictions that beset his city, built so artificially on a vast raft, recalling the spaces painted by Guardi, which had become Nietzsche's solitudes and the silences in Luigi Nono's music. But in the early 1990s, as the Japanese architect Irata Isozaki was designing the gravestone for Luigi Nono's tomb on San Michele, the city of solitudes was threatened.[11]

Bettin's diagnosis was, fundamentally, political and sociological. In his view it was a lie, or at best an equivocation, that accused Venice of paralysis in the face of its problems, of being a state of non-doing, of *non-fare*.[12] Abstinence from action was not in fact the problem; it was rather that too much had been done too badly. Marghera was a prime example of destructive activity; the fishing industry was another.[13] At one time the self-contained territory of the Serenissima had been able to initiate a decisive line of action to build its Murazzi, and could draw on a unified philosophy that gave clear precedence to maintenance and control of the lagoon waters. The modern neglect of the Murazzi was evidence of a general shift in the nineteenth century away from valuing the water. Venice was a small city constantly affected by regional, national and international interests, without the autonomy to act for itself.

The problem of *acque alte* remained critical. Although the invading waters had never again reached the height of 4 November 1966, the consistency with which the city was inundated had increased. At the beginning of the century Piazza San Marco was flooded five to seven times a year; in the 1990s it was forty to sixty times.[14] Conferences, papers, prototypes had followed the new Special Law of 1984. The Consorzio Venezia Nuova had launched MO.SE, but the prototype gathered rust in the lagoon as environmental impact studies multiplied (fig. 230).[15] The problems remained, or were even exacerbated.[16] Closing the Lido openings was argued to be as hazardous as *acqua alta*. Further national legislation in February 1992, Law 139, committed national funding to the organisation, but it was regularly observed that these funds failed to reach their destination.[17]

230 Consorzio Venezia Nuova, MO.SE prototype, 1996.

Venice in the 1990s was concerned as much with the problems raised by tourism as with the MO.SE project and the condition of the lagoon. By the mid-1980s it was clear that the tourists' carnival was a success, however phoney the glamour. But it was incendiary for residents. Meccoli called the new commercial carnival 'a *danse macabre*' which reduced Venice to a shop window and its citizens to mere spectators.[18] Venice had become the opiate of the world, the most popular tourist destination. In 1986 the artist Krysztof Wodiczko had arranged a telling public project, on the model of his many exercises of photographic projection onto façades

of well-known public monuments, turning them into giant illuminations (fig. 231).[19] Tourists swamped the monuments and rendered them in their own base image. The Campanile wore a camera slung round its 'neck', the base of the equestrian statue of Colleoni was filled with gold coins; another attack on the Campanile San Marco rooted it at ground level in a pair of eighteenth-century boots; the illuminated campanile of Santa Maria Formosa held a camera at the ready in giant hands.

In advance of the Expo decision the international press focused on Venice with such headlines as 'Death Threat to Venice' and 'Nightmare in Venice'.[20] The Pink Floyd concert was regularly linked to the Expo proposal to demonstrate the danger of crowds: *Time* magazine called it 'The Battle of Venice'.[21] Ironically, the concert's long-term success has been that it halted the Expo by demonstrating the appalling consequences of convergence in the city centre. Although not on the same scale, the commercial carnival continued. In 1996 an audience of 124,000 packed the Piazza San Marco for Peter Gabriel's Womad concert.[22]

Brought to a head after the years of interchange following the flood of 1966, the Expo issue involved a clash of national, regional and local interests. Since Gianni de Michelis was the foremost advocate. But he was now in opposition to the city itself. After the concert the mayor, Antonio Casellati, in an about-face, spoke for a majority of Venetians when he claimed that the city itself had not endorsed Expo 2000 and that it would be 'an atomic bomb that would destroy our future. We would be a Disneyland, an empty museum'. Week after week in *Il Gazzettino* Sandro Meccoli made Venetian resistance and anger plain.[23] There were carnivalesque attacks on De Michelis – boats of protest on the Grand Canal and masked protesters. His head was carried on a platter in the 1989 carnival.[24] In April 1993 he left the Public Prosecutor's office in Venice after the first of his interrogations for corruption to the jeers of demonstrators; no longer endorsing him, they now shouted 'thief, buffoon, bandit, criminal, shame!'[25]

Programmed as big business, carnival reached a literal Disneyland height in 1992 under the direction of Davide Rampello, a member of Silvio Berlusconi's staff of Fininvest. It featured a clown covered with Swatch watches, a masked ball attended by a group flown in from Paris Club Med, a Greek ship for exotic accommodation moored near the Piazza and a Bugs Bunny cinema season played throughout the period on Berlusconi's television channels. With this overriding crassness, any connection with the historical carnival and its indigenous Venetian roots vanished.

Despite the largely negative issues that dominated the Venetian news in the 1990s and were reported internationally, Venice remained fascinating for film-makers and

231 Krystof Wodiczko, Venice Campanile illumination project, 1986.

writers in the 1990s; but a more realistic, even sadistic, spirit prevailed. A virtual Luna Park in the lagoon was projected in a novel by Gianni Riotta, *Ombra*, of 1995, commissioned by the Consorzio Venezia Nuova as part of the expansion of its patronage in the 1990s.[26] Riotto's scenario is outrageous, but not without foundation in fact. *Ombra* responded to the reinvention of carnival in the late 1970s and to the 'success' of such ventures as the Pink Floyd concert. It parodied the monocultural situation in which a city exists primarily for tourists, taking the entertainments to their logical conclusion.

Rats are everywhere in *Ombra*: they are no longer a feature of the history of plague or cholera. The fraudulent magnate Satori has the ultimate project to 'Save Venice' which is, in fact, a mockery of the external interests contributing to the city since 1966. His project, a *Chimera for San Marco*, required residents to assume the personalities of Venetian figures of the past and act them daily. As a result tourists and citizens would be 'integrated to perfection', the environment would be respected and jobs would multiply.[27] The lagoon would be sealed off from the sea, the canals drained and refilled (a comment on the discussion on dredging); some would have fresh water with fish, like an aquarium, and others were to be available for swimming.

A foundation – the Fondazione Chimera per San Marco – was to take charge of costuming, thus boosting the textile industry, and Burano. Casanova would escape from the leads; Byron would swim across the water from the Lido; there would be bull-fighting again, as there had been traditionally in the Campo San Stefano; and so on. Then, apocalyptically, the waters rise.

In not dissimilar vein, the Venetian artist Lodovico de Luigi predicted perpetual carnival and cataclysmic flood.[28] His paintings are a surrealist-derived genre, overstated, bordering on the banal, but dramatic enough nevertheless, and a symptom of his time. Grossly figurative, they present over-realised scenarios that envisage a Venice of the future under water. Most are variations on the ultimate *acqua alta*: buildings are submerged up to the second storey, the horses of San Marco have their heads only just above the surface, the two Moors on the Torre dell'Orologio mark the hours as waves crash around them. The Lido is no more, all submerged, Aschenbach's deck chair and boater hat are afloat. The Piazza San Marco appears in acute perspective that accentuates the crowd, thick as vermin, at play in a grotesque carnival. De Luigi had painted Santa Maria della Salute hoisted up on a drilling platform, dwarfed by an oil derrick behind it. In 1997 the prophecy that the lagoon would be taken over by oil-drilling appeared to be true as agitation mounted over plans for gas extraction in the Adriatic in the vicinity of the lagoon.[29]

Only some months after the publication of *Ombra*, a historical novel took the *acqua alta* of 1966 as its theme. *Acqua grande* was written by a Venetian journalist, Roberto Bianchin, and illustrated with documentary intent with high-water photographs by Gianfranco Tagliapietra.[30] The novel commemorates the thirty years from November 1966 until November 1996, recreating the nights of 3 and 4 November when the central characters, fishermen from the narrowest strip of Lido at San Pietro at Pellestrina, experience the full force of the flood. We witness the rising of the waters, the torrential rain and the huge seas, the sirocco blowing, the evacuation of houses and residents. And still the danger persists. The conclusion is unhesitating: there have been thirty subsequent years of debate, round tables, proposals, projects and studies. All has been useless chatter.[31]

Acqua grande tells a grim story of the historic past, but it is hardly less an indictment of its time of publication. The thirtieth anniversary was commemorated with a special issue of *Il Gazzettino*, which republished its leading pages of thirty years before, when the flood was *la grande paura*, the Great Fear, the Day of Horror.[32] Under the patronage of the President of the Republic, multi-media programmes were released by the Laboratorio Venezia 66–96, showing the measures taken to deal with the ecosystem, to recognise the elements of the crisis and present the researches for

232 'Trent'anni fa la
grande paura',
Il Gazzettino, 3 November,
1996.

232 'Trent'anni fa la grande paura', *Il Gazzettino*, 3 November, 1996.

intervention.[33] A film was released by a formidable consortium headed by the President of the Republic, including the Commune di Venezia, the Consorzio Venezia Nuova, the Soprintendenza per I Beni Ambientati, the two universities, UNESCO . . .[34] *Lagoon*, directed by Federico and Francesco De Melis, preferred the poetic to the apocalyptic. To the reassuring sound of pan pipes, it showed the restructuring of the Murazzi, the recreation of the *barene*: the positive measures taken since 1966, with only discreet editing-in of historic footage of the flood. Nevertheless the concluding words: 'in any game of cat and mouse one party will eventually lose', might well suggest that the forces of the sea must eliminate the lagoon and that, indeed, was the expectation.

Thus the anniversary of the flood was observed amid cries that the situation could still recur (fig. 232). A memorial concert given in San Marco, with music belonging to Mediterranean cultures, with Jewish music and Orthodox chant as well as Schubert, had water as its common theme. On that occasion the Venetian composer Claudio Ambrosini performed his *Frammenti d'Acque*, a 'drammaturgia' in Seven Stations: short pieces were played on glass instruments as well as traditional instruments, with sounds and noises originally recorded during the flood.[35] The 'Stations' followed the Introit: Marriage to the Water, to the Water Mother, the Cruel Mother (Acqua matrigna), to Tidal Waters, Huge Waters, Children of the Waters, and the Resurrection. Venetian waters being all these, are also the waters of a larger area: Ambrosini returned them to the eastern orientation of the one-time Republic.

In 1966 Venice had shared the front page of the international press with Florence, where the flood was more destructive in terms of lives lost; but in Florence the flood has not recurred.[36] Many left Venice as a direct result of the flood: in 1966 there were 121,000 residents; in 1996 only 70,000.[37] For the city it was a life-destroying exodus; nor was a solution in sight.

* * *

The State of the Lagoon: Pollution and Dredging

Since 1966, the lagoon – the waters that surround the islands of Venice and front the industrial sites of the Terraferma – had been as much in focus as the city. The issue of pollution vied with *acqua alta* as the most advertised problem; high tides were inevitably linked with pollution. The interest of the international media remained high, as witnessed by the 1995 British television programme for Channel 4 presented by David Munro, bluntly called *Death of Venice*.[38] It follows Giorgio Ferrari from the Anti-Pollution Office of the Magistrato delle Acque as he goes about his daily business inspecting the lagoon and the hundreds of outlets and pumping-stations that feed into it. Dr Ferrari and his team make surprise visits, monitor treatment plants, test the bubbles that are evidence of nitrogen, depleted oxygen and nitrogen-phosphate-based fertilisers. Not only is the heavy industry of Marghera implicated, but also the glass factories of Murano, which discharge arsenic and copper.

The programme showed the Consorzio Venezia Nuova testing a computerised system developed by Umberto Rosselli for assessing field data and determining pollution sources. A register was in effect. As well as measuring waterborne algae, an obvious threat to water quality, Channel 4 filmed a new problem: the plagues of midges that had accumulated around the rail track, swarming around lights and planes in quantities sufficient to close the airport. The film's music was lyrically funereal: Mahler's Adaggietto from the Fifth Symphony, with its obvious associations with Visconti's *Death in Venice*, and Bizet's *Pearl Fishers* followed footage of the constant daily monitoring of toxicity, airborne and waterborne, the plagues of the late twentieth century.

Pollution is a global problem, but the presence of oil tankers in the lagoon constituted a threat to the environment that many think had to be averted in advance of inevitable mishap. The demand for the exclusion of tankers from the lagoon was met with a proposal to establish an overland pipe supply to Marghera from Trieste and Ravenna, and a resolution was made in 1975. On 2 December 1994 a leak in the oil line between the port of San Leonardo and the refinery at Marghera reignited the debate on the presence of the petroleum industry in the lagoon.[39]

The state of the canals after decades of neglect was one of the principal dangers to the city.[40] In January 1996 the time taken to quench the fire at La Fenice was the result of a situation often forecast: fireboats could not negotiate canals that were insufficiently deep at times of low water as a result of the neglect of dredging.[41] The danger of fires in a city in which so much building is wood-lined constitutes one of Venice's greatest future hazards. There was insufficient water pressure to fight them.

The neglect of excavation of canals was a complaint raised by Conte Daniele Renier when the French took power in 1806. Zucchetta's 1985 study of *I Rii di Venezia* stressed the absolute priority of canal-dredging practices since the thirteenth century.[42] In 1996, 150 citizens from the Rio di Ca' Tron actively petitioned for their canal to be dredged. They described it as 'permanently dry, intolerably malodorant and always infested with huge rats'.[43]

The questions of pollution and water quality were closely linked. The deterioration of water quality is hardly exclusive to Venice, but it is compounded there by degeneration of the tidal system, proximity to Marghera's chemical activity, shifts in the composition of the sandbanks and channels in the lagoon, the dredging of the deep water canal for oil tankers – the Canale di Petroli – which has upset the equilibrium of the lagoon, and so on. The disposal of dredged waste is a further hazard. Debate on the disposal of lagoon mud in the Adriatic awaited an analysis in order to decide on the mud's degree of toxicity.

Suction-based dredges having the capacity to operate in canals either in water, or behind a temporary dam, were put into operation in 1992. The most effective procedure is to work on canals that have been dammed and pumped out, so that main-

tenance of foundations can be undertaken at the same time as the dredging. The failure of owners to comply frustrated such programmes. Owners deliberately neglected maintenance in order to reach a level of dilapidation that will give them recourse to a foundation subsidy from Special Law funds.

The Venetian press regularly carried reports of motor boats breaking speed limits and the constant erosion of foundations of buildings caused by the wash of the *vaporetti*, especially on the Grand Canal. The problem was indubitably linked to pollution in the Grand Canal and its 'bath of poison'.[44] In May 1996 the gondoliers threatened to withdraw from participation in the Festa della Sensa as a protest against motor traffic (*moti ondosi*). Strikes occurred regularly.[45] In a bid to curb these problems, a global monitoring system was to be set up in a traffic control office in the Arsenale in order to apprehend speedsters.[46]

The authorities have invested considerable resources in the effort to bring to public attention factual results in pollution control and the environmental recovery in the lagoon. In 1996 audiovisual and computer displays were opened – at Selva's church of San Maurizio, and at a special building in the Campo San Stefano.[47] The Consorzio was active in public education, making material available on the internet, in book form, in CD-ROM and videos in a *With Water and Against Water* pro-

233 (*top*) Conservation project, North Molo at Malamocco, Consorzio Venezia Nuova.

234 (*above*) Conservation project for the *barene*: Lagoon Management, Consorzio Venezia Nuova.

gramme.[48] They publicised significant restoration measures. Salt marshes, or *barene*, had been reconstructed to compensate for alteration in the terrain over the years: the dump that had taken over the Isola delle Tresse had been turned into arable land. Fish farms with appropriate tidal controls had been reopened. Some diversion of oil shipping had taken place. Embankments and lochs controlled specific areas against high water, notably at Malamocco (fig. 233). Jetties and coastlines had been artificially reinforced on the traditional principle of the Murazzi at Pellestrina and Chioggia (fig. 234). In 1996 it was proposed to raise some of the areas most vulnerable to *acqua alta*.[49]

Not many cities exist in such a singular marine and coastal terrain, between sea and swampland. As many have observed, the very singularity of the site is crucial to the 'myth' of a Venice wedded to the sea, and so on. To 'sustain' Venice, to use the terminology of the 1990s, is a special problem that addresses nature and extensive wetlands. To maintain them involves all aspects of management of a large and complex area, and every aspect of access for residents, tourists and industry. The number of the areas involved was recognised by the 1992 conference in Rio de Janiero on environment and development, which addressed Venice as a special case.[50] The terminology may have been new, but the problems had long been known and discussed.

Redevelopment

By the end of the century, the state of the lagoon and the canal system were still in debate as a consequence of the flood of 1966. The debate on certain buildings, especially those of considerable scale that had long stood empty in the context of accommodation crises, had stayed current for some decades. The Arsenale complex remains the most obvious, and also the Molino Stucky, empty since 1955. Closely connected with election promises to provide more housing, some progress was made – the old ice factory on the Giudecca was converted into housing, and in Castello 106 houses were inserted into an ex-convent. The Cacciari administration tackled the Teatro Malibran which was to be restored, and the tobacco factory.[51] The abattoirs were to be converted for use by the university. A plan for the Molino Stucky, the building that has most challenged the planners, was approved in January 1995. Restrictions were imposed in 1988 to conserve the buildings as a group, not the case with some earlier projects.[52] The financing of the project combined local government input with a private society linked to the bank San Paolo di Torino. The original Wullekopf structure will accommodate a hotel with four hundred rooms.[53] Housing is to be created in the buildings dating from 1895 to 1922 – in effect the renovation of the original mill – along the Giudecca. (The press had earlier campaigned for tenancy preference for Venetians.)[54] The old pasta factory and workshop was planned as a convention centre. In announcing the new scheme, the then mayor, Cacciari, claimed that the Stucky project, for some decades the very symbol of vacillation and decadence, would signal no less than the reversal of that decadence. On the Giudecca façade, a giant red and gold banner bearing the lion of St Mark effectively announced the end of speculation and the apparent decisiveness of the Commune in the mid-1990s (fig. 235).

235   Molino Stucky redevelopment project, 1996.

The university, and the IUAV in particular, have been primary clients in the quest for converted buildings. The Cottonificio complex was converted into IUAV premises, advertising Venice as the modern city with a huge wooden 'V' dominating the converted rooftop at Santa Marta. The rehabilitation of the lower Giudecca area continued with the conversion of the old refrigerated warehouses – the Magazzini Frigoferi – at San Basilio, in a further example of the productive change for derelict buildings.[55] The conversion of the old bead-making factory at Murano (the Conterie) into student accommodation was a similar initiative.[56] At issue in these conversions is the recognition of the needs of a community other than that of tourism, often proposed by critics of the monoculture, but so often frustrated.

On the Giudecca, the Junghans factory, recently closed, was planned for conversion into housing for three hundred students.[57] This was an effort to solve the local problem of the accommodation of the many foreign students who were seen as taking up vitally needed local housing. The vast tracts of unusable residential buildings constituted a pressing restoration need in the city: in August 1990 there were estimated to be 12,000 empty houses. Leonardo Benevolo some decades earlier had proclaimed that 'in the city, it is necessary to launch a large-scale restoration of the older houses, and abandon the idea of filling up empty areas with new houses'.[58]

The lagoon islands might seem romantic, but they suffered from isolation and decay. The Lido no longer entertained the world, and may well be the main victim of the veto on the sub-lagoon metro.[59] As special services diminish, the Lido has become known as the 'dormitory island', its beach was neglected and the Cinema Biennale was earmarked for the new Arsenale complex, if it takes place. But some of the lagoon islands became sites for development. For much of the twentieth century they have been forgotten outposts of the historic centre, but in the 1990s they have come into prominence as a result of the closure of medical and psychiatric services on the islands of San Servolo and San Clemente, and the interest in redeveloping buildings for commercial sale.[60]

Restoration of the island of San Servolo was one of the major projects in the 1990s. It was projected as an international campus for up to nine European and American institutions.[61] This activity must be seen as a product of the vitality of Venetian institutions, in this case, the university, formally based at Ca' Foscari, together with the Institute of Architecture, the indomitable IUAV.

In the private sphere, Edward de Bono, well-known 'lateral thinker', acquired the Isola di Tessera (its low lines, its balustrade on the water, and the vine-draped pergola are a familiar sight on the lagoon passage to the airport), which he wanted to transform into a 'centre for thought'.[62]

Access

Jobs were declining in central Venice; housing was problematic for residents even without the threat of flood. Access to Venice itself was one of the central problems, and particularly acute for residents. Transit to Venice from the mainland, and within it, had been recognised as a problem for decades. Tourist season statistics from 1998 recorded that 92,000 people entered Venice on working days; 104,000 on non-working days: 'every day the city receives the equivalent of a second population'.[63] The sheer time expended in moving around Venice, and moving from Venice to the mainland, has often been the subject of discussion.

It was a tourist problem, but it was also a workaday problem. Many Venetians work on the Terraferma – in Mestre and Padua. Workers come into Venice from those cities on a daily basis and everyone must pass either through the Piazzale Roma or the railway station. The link with the mainland had been a problem since the building of the road bridge. The bridge to the mainland is the means of linking the historic city with a variety of economic and housing possibilities beyond Venice which that flagship city of history could not provide. It is also a major route for the influx of some millions of tourists per annum without which the city could not survive. During carnival in 1991 it was neccesary to close the road entrance, so great was the tourist influx.

But the problems of access were not recent. Since the 1960s the western end of the city has been subject to many planning interrogations. The artificial island of the Tronchetto, given over to car parking, had been a further element in the concentration of motor traffic at the road terminus. The so-called 'road-rail-water system' dealt with the inflow of workers, visitors and residents across the lagoon bridge, whether by rail or car or bus, and their dispatch to quite distant terminals such as Lido, Murano, or Burano.[64] Avoiding the Grand Canal, and diverting more and more water traffic in a circular direction around the Giudecca Canal and the Fondamenta Nuove became a part solution in the 1990s.[65]

The port of Venice, the Marittima adjoining the railway station across from the Giudecca island, had also fallen into decay as merchant shipping declined and industrial freight moved to Marghera. But the withdrawal of port facilities from the Marittima had not relieved a problem exacerbated by growing tourist numbers.[66] Its tourist conversion was in process as, increasingly, luxury shipping berthed there. A passenger terminal was proposed, with berths for yachts and an 'arcade' nearby to link the Tronchetto decisively with the main island.[67]

Since 1985 the architecture faculty had addressed the range of problems relating to access to the islands, most comprehensively in the conference held in 1985 under the presidency of Valeriano Pastor.[68] Whether the planning measures ameliorated or exacerbated the problems remains to be seen. The early 1990s under Ugo Bergamo's Christian Democrat administration proposed a sub-lagoon metropolitan system, which (inevitably) became another ecological debate.[69] Opponents were no less vocal than at the time of Pompeo Molmenti and his *anti-pontisti* in the early part of the century.[70] Engineer Zollet proposed linking the Giudecca to the northern lagoon, as well as various islands, the Lido, and the Terraferma.[71] Three major lines were mooted: the Piazzale Roma with the Riva degli Schiavoni via the Giudecca and the Zattere; a line from the airport at Tessera to link the island of Murano with the Fondamenta Nuove to the Giardini, and a Mestre line from Piazzale Roma. The Piazza San Marco was deliberately kept from the centre of operations and the line was not to pass under it, in order to divert tourists away from the centre. Old ghosts of sub-lagoon bridges and railroads from the nineteenth century haunted the project. Italia Nostra voiced its opposition, and also I Verdi.[72] Sandro Meccoli wrote extensively on the issue in *Il Gazzettino*, declaring that the system would only contribute to depopulation.[73] Others saw a detrimental increase in short-term tourism.[74] In June 1993 the project was decisively vetoed by the Minister for Public Works, Francesco Merloni.[75]

For some, access to the islands of Venice other than by water was felt to be artificial – since the opening of the road bridge, and indeed the railbridge to the mainland – as had Ruskin. As motor traffic increased so too did the problem of accommodating it at the terminus at the Piazzale Roma, which had been criticised since its inception in the 1930s. With the huge increase in traffic, including tourist coaches – the mark of mass tourism – the area had proved grossly inadequate, and ugly. Journalists observed the chaos at midday in the Piazzale Roma.[76] For the fifth international Biennale of Architecture in 1991, two competitions were announced for a 'Gateway to Venice' in the Piazzale Roma.[77] Competitions in Venice are invariably diagnostic, their submissions are invariably mixed but creative, and the action that follows negligible.

Two integrated proposals were requested for two differently scaled projects in the Piazzale Roma area for the Gateway project. First, and most urgent, was the systematisation of the area as the terminal of public and private transport, with appropriate circulation and facilities. Secondly, the area on the Grand Canal on the Fondamenta di Santa Chiara was to be developed with appropriate accommodation for police, transport, first aid, refreshments and so on. The rear of the Rio Nuova in front of the Ponte Papadopoli and the park, and the area of the Rio di Sant'Andrea, were to be co-ordinated into a design with short-term parking for tourist coaches and taxi ranks. Some 126 submissions were received, with most responding with an amphitheatre-like construction that covered over the arrival and departure circuit. Many tried to link up with the water and take advantage of the access point to the Grand Canal. The winning proposal from the British architects Jeremy Dixon and Edward Jones proposed a rotunda 'in the form of a circus' with passengers circulating outside a central roofed area for the buses on the model of the Roman Colosseum and the Circus at Bath, England. Twenty departure bays (on the model of an air terminal) in a catherine-wheel formation gave access to the bus bays, and a loggia for terminal services was modelled on the customs house at the other of the city.

In June 1996 a bridge to link the Piazzale Roma with the station was presented in model by the Spanish architect Santiago Calatrava (fig. 236). 'The Fourth Bridge on the Grand Canal', announced the posters. Radical within the conservative context of Venetian bridge building, Calatrava's bridge recalled some of the proposals for the 1985 competition for the Accademia. In a plan of consummate elegance, Calatrava, whose reputation as a bridge designer was well established internationally, proposed a slender arc like an upturned gondola – wider at the centre, narrower at the ends – on a steel frame, but paved in the traditional Istrian stone with a parapet in glass surmounted by a brass handrail.[78]

A further bridge was mooted, proposed in glass by the Murano glassmaker Luciano Vistosi to replace the wooden bridge at the gateway of the Arsenale.[79] It was to be held in place by screws and bolts, with steps illuminated by optic fibres. Another essay in quintessential Venetian symbolism.

Employment, Population Decline and Regional Politics

As the influx of tourists grew, Venice simultaneously lost jobs in the non-tourist sector as business left the city for the mainland. In the 1990s Venice had the lowest per capita income in the Veneto. One third of the population was over sixty, and the birth rate had fallen below one quarter of the death rate per annum. The depletion of population was the saddest evidence of the diminution of Venice as a living city.[80]

The transfer of commercial offices from Venice to Mestre or Padua had been long established, making the declining economic status of Venice clear. The monoculture imposed by tourism had become even more evident. The closure of industry and offices in the 1990s suggested that only the direct services of the tourist infrastructure would remain a source of employment unless new strategies for the cultural and educational sector were implemented. In 1992–3 there were significant job losses in Murano, the closure of the Junghans factory on the Giudecca (one of the last survivors of the industrial Giudecca of the late nineteenth century), the transferral of the Adriatica shipping company's function from Venice to Naples, and the closure of the traditional insurance company, the Assicurazioni Generale, in March 1992 (vacating its offices in the upper storey of the Procuratie Vecchie). In January 1995 Alitalia announced the closure of its office in Venice.[81] In 1998 the director of the cinema club, the Pasinetti Videoteca, warned that by 2000 there might not be a commercial cinema in Venice.

The depletion of population in historic Venice encouraged political unions designed to strengthen strategies for the city's survival within the greater region: the one-time Serenissima now courts old vassals. Since 1926, when Greater Venice was formed with Mestre and Marghera, there has been unease and inequality in planning measures and only fitful efforts to create a genuine unity of interests from the mainland to the islands. In 1992 the twenty-six municipalities of Greater Venice sought a new status as a 'metropolitan city'.

There were also external political pressures. The Northern League led by Umberto Bossi from Milan had its impact on Veneto thinking. In defiance of a unified Italy, the mission of the Lega Nord was to declare the northern part of Italy independent of Rome and the south and establish Padania.[82] Bossi, as the founder of the new 'nation', took the initiative in destabilised times when the *mani pulite* trials for corruption were in play in the nation's courts.[83] In 1996 Bossi led his 'grand popular Festival' to Venice along the River Po for 652 kilometres, baptising Padania at the source of river using a 'precious flask' of Murano glass, playing Verdi, Puccini and Bellini in an apparent spirit of Risorgimento, and reaching Venice for a 'liturgical-mythical representation' which took place on the Riva delle Sette Martiri.[84] The culmination of the 'festival' in Venice was no doubt intended to symbolise the return of a notion of a Republic and the Serenissima, but attendance was low. As an Italian academic remarked, 'the Lega tried in September [1996] to conquer cosmopolitan Venice and thus crown itself with European power. But Venice, prestigious and cunning, remain unconquerable'.[85]

Even within Greater Venice allegiances continued to be unstable. All urban commentators have made some comment on the 'problem' of Marghera and Mestre with relation to Venice. Leonardo Benevolo called for an end to the squalor of the Terraferma cities; Mestre must become more beautiful than Venice.[86] But the issue of allegiance for residents remained tenuous. Referenda were held – inconclusively – to test the support for the administrative separation of Venice from Mestre and Cavallino-Treporti (one of the next most densely populated settlements on the lagoon).

More radical suggestions rehabilitated Venice within the European context: the European Community should take charge of Venice. This was the recommendation made by the European Community's Commissioner for the Environment, Carlo Ripa di Meana, in the post of Foreign Minister in the Italian Government (and the distinguished president of Biennales in the 1970s).[87] The idea of Venice as a separate state, on the model of the Vatican, was circulated in the French magazine *Le Pont* and the scheme put to the private committees for the preservation of Venice on 19 October 1991.[88] The bid for Europe was the background to local initiatives to promote Venice within an enhanced regional context. Massimo Cacciari began to work towards a metropolitan pact with Padua and Treviso – known as the PA-TRE-VE – which would develop the Tessera airport to serve a larger area of the Veneto.[89] The proposal was clearly in debt to Expo 2000 and its plans for the airport, as well as the Venetian interest in sharing the greater economic wealth and the trade viability of Padua and Treviso.

Venezia 2000 remained alive on the drawingboard; indeed, the project was published in 1995 with the proposals substantially unchanged.[90] The area around Tessera and the current Marco Polo airport was the primary nexus to be connected by *autostrada* to the cities of the north-east. The architect Renzo Piano designed an artificial mountain to be raised in the vicinity of the airport; its internal landscapes and waterways, convention centres and hotels, were linked by water in the vicinity of the airport to the Terraferma cities.[91] The 'Magnet', as it was called, would connect to Venice via water, in a direct line to a redeveloped Arsenale.[92] Other crucial axes would radiate out from the airport and the Magnet. Within Venice, the Piazzale Roma (and the Grand Canal) would benefit from the divergence of traffic, and the northern lagoon and the island of Murano (midway between the airport and the Arsenale), would be reactivated. The Magnet was an extraordinary invention, a transparent artificial mountain, rigorous in geometry, containing spaces of many different types.

The president of the Associazione Venezia 2000, Giuseppe de Rita, assumed an evangelical role in relation to the project.[93] De Rita's presentation was a frank criticism of the inertia within the ruling class in Venice.[94] A game was being played, he observed, a 'partita' against the internal fatigue of the city and the *rozzezza* – the 'coarse' nature of external interests (in reference to the De Michelis development that failed to secure Expo 2000).[95] In line with the development of the Consorzio Venezia Nuova, the Venezia 2000 project had been organised as a consortium of private interests favouring further privatisation: among the patrons were insurance companies, the publishing house of Marsilio and the Coin shopping chain. The allegiance should clearly continue so that the Venetian spirit could be militant again, no less.

The 2000 project was rerun with the conviction that Venice was still the *città speciale*, but De Rita warned that Venice was becoming a victim of itself, of 'being special', of being self-referential and excluded from the benefits of modern cities.[96] It was like a drama of Ibsen, trapped in the legacy of the past.[97] De Rita called again for a new citizen able to participate in a city geared towards research, but also capable of managing its inevitable tourism. While the Magnet and the new Arsenale remained on paper, the document *Venezia 2000* could only appear as a sad indictment of Venice by a Venetian.

A further 'New Plan', published in 1996 by Leonardo Benevolo, had emphatic regional recommendations. The reality for Venice, Benevolo claimed, was the industrial cities of the mainland, Mestre and Marghera. He renewed demands to supersede the nostalgia for old Venice and its obsolete planning and political centrality.[98] It was as if no master plan had ever spoken for the ring points of the lagoon from Cavallino to Chioggia, from the historic islands to Fusina, Mestre and Marghera, or as if Eugenio Miozzi's plans for spanning the lagoon with bridges had never been drafted. A review was published in *Domus* the following year, supportive in the main, but emphasising again the special water-based nature of central Venice and the need for restoring the 'lost independence' of Murano and Burano, and other islands.[99] At the same time the assessment was caught in the central contradiction: Benevolo's plan was 'the first praiseworthy masterplan drawn up for Venice. Unfortunately, it embraces the mainland . . .'[100]

The reality is that none of the symbolism, the civilisation, the tourist attractions and amenities of Venice is found in Mestre and Marghera; the Terraferma cities offer nothing to the tourist. Efforts to extend the Biennale to the Terraferma in 1997 – with an exhibition of industrial photography of Marghera and installations of the sculpture of Dennis Oppenheim – did not remove the irrelevance, or the repugnance, of the mainland cities for the tourist.[101] It is possible to visit Venice and remain unaware of the proximity of the mainland settlements.

Benevolo defended himself against any claim that his plan was not desirably 'amphibious'.[102] In reply to his critics he indicated that he was presenting 'a set of complementary situations', some on the mainland and others on the lagoon. The plan's novelty was that '*for the first time* [my italics] it is recognised that the independence of Venice as a water-based city is impossible or even destructive'.[103] This is tantamount to saying that Venice as a historic city is doomed, since its water-base has been the very condition of its creation and survival. By now the discussion was so clogged with alternatives any plan had to be compromised.

While the regional emphasis had political and planning adherents in the 1990s, it was clear that some Venetians saw themselves as neglected by Italy for over thirty years, in contrast to the European community's superior perception of the special nature of Venice, and its interest in the city's protection.[104] In 1992 Alvise Zorzi, well-known Venetian, secretary of private committees and author of *Venezia scomparsa*, floated the idea of appointing a foreign 'doge' to run the city, claiming that it was not the French or the Habsburg occupations that had destroyed so much, but the Venetians themselves. That diagnosis was being heard more often. According to Zorzi, Venice must negotiate a special status within Italy.[105] Whether a foreign doge, or a special state, the conclusion was recognition of impotence.

That the cultural heritage is located in the past rather than the present is an inevitable conclusion for Venice. Many have called for new cultural and technological initiatives, emphasising the need to develop cultural tourism rather than popular tourism. This stance has been regularly taken since the Pink Floyd concert in 1989, and the call is renewed every year at carnival.[106] Public funds should be spent not on carnival, but museums. In line with the philosophy of Venice 2000, cultural tourism extends to scientific and technological areas that have been annexed to the symbolic Arsenale and its excellence in pre-industrial technology and one-time commercial strength.[107] In a bid for relocation, the Architecture Institute proposed that it be sited within the Arsenale. It would be a non-commercial use of the prized site, but one that promoted and deepened the general cultural renaissance under discussion. The suggestion did not meet with universal approval.[108] Mayor Cacciari voiced his preference for the multi-use of such an extensive area, stating that 'the administration intended to confirm the presence of technological production, industrial, ship-building activities', and that the architecture project endorsed 'exhibitions, museums, university research departments'.[109]

The bid for leadership in technology was linked to the needs of Venice as a water city and the history of the city. The Arsenale became the centre for Thetis, an organisation with various responsibilities in water management and the firm Tecnomare was commissioned to develop technology specific to such urgent matters as dredging.[110] Beyond *acqua alta* and pollution, the Consorzio Venezia Nuova interested itself in publication and sponsorship of authors. Various agencies including IUAV and Tecnomare were incorporated. The Consorzio was linked beyond Venice to a group of eastern region countries monitoring pollution and investigating economic and environmental conditions in the Adriatic area.[111]

Another initiative connected to specific Venetian concerns was the foundation of an International Centre for Cities on Water in 1989. Water was to be reaffirmed as 'opportunity' rather than a liability, to cite the 1979 essay by Ventura. Sponsored, like so many operations in the 1990s, by a syndicate, Cities on Water linked the Commune, the University and the Consorzio Venezia Nuova. The Centre was briefed to address all matters connected with sea-based cities, such as the impact of sea levels, water quality, transport in the leisure and industrial areas, and the utilisation of waterfront structures. It began publishing a bi-monthly review, *Aquapolis*, and hosted international conferences with proceedings published each year. An exhibition held in 1991, *Waterfronts: A New Urban Frontier*, illustrated a range of planning options through the world, as well as focusing on Venice and Genoa.[112]

Yet even while the Venetians developed some initiatives and stalled others, the national situation, volatile and unstable as ever, impeded rather than facilitated. In 1992 it was claimed that the failure of state moneys to reach Venice was a matter of ethics.[113] The Senate had made its allocation and set up a special authority, but the continuing instability of the central government made follow-through and implementation virtually impossible.[114]

In 1993 Giuseppe de Rita pronounced on Venetian singularity again, claiming that 'without the bridges, trains, pedestrian access and Mestre, the city would today be abandoned, like a Pompeii of the lagoon lands'.[115] Venice, he claimed, had a vital place in the modern imagination, but it was limited by self-reference and the tourist mono-culture. The only sense in which Venice has capital city status was in tourism: for the very reason that it remained a place of nostalgia.[116] In creating its artificial spectacles, it offered itself as a simulacrum and must now be emancipated from its own imitations.[117] Its citizens must free themselves from the euphoria, apathy, anger and apocalyptic projections generated by tourism.[118] The transitory nature of tourism in the 1990s – its swift turnover – was destroying the city while having a negligible effect on the economy and making demands on the maintenance of the most conspicuous monuments against longer-term cultural attractions with professional and scholarly merit. An alternative must come from research centres, local expertise and international capital, including human capital.[119] A renewed citizen must participate in a city turned towards the hinterland where new networks of cultural and technological research could be brokered.[120] Salvation can come only through external forces, for in spite of the configuration of Greater Venice, the links with the region have been weakened rather than strengthened. Old ports and river links with Padua and Treviso should be reactivated.[121]

It may be that the self-referential Venice was being challenged on a number of fronts by some at least of its own citizens. Following the war in Bosnia Herzegovina, Gianfranco Bettin made a plea for peaceful intervention and awareness of neighbouring states in the face of the political myopia that had been ascendant in Venice for some decades.[122] Following a visit of Mayor Cacciari and Patriarch Cé to Sarajevo, Venice and Sarajevo became twin cities. Sympathy for the old territory of the Serenissima may yet acquire some meaning.

The Critique of the Tourist

Since 1973 and the passing of the Special Law, Venice itself has been given to special pleading, confident of the world's vigilance and appropriate intervention, moral and financial. Yet it appeared to have little perception that many of its visitors were highly critical of the tourist experience, well aware of exploitation, poor services and charges that were among the highest in the world. The misconception is that everyone wants to come to Venice regardless of the quality of the experience. The attack on the one-day tourist, known as the *pendolaro*, was constant in the Venetian press: they showed insufficient returns. The sociology of tourism regularly distinguishes between types of tourists: who is to say that a one-day visit is not significant.[123]

Venice colluded with consumer culture. It now had a Disney shop as well as a McDonald's (fig. 237).[124] And as recent carnivals made clear, it had colluded in making a spectacle of itself – as Saint-Didier pointed out, it did so in the seventeenth century. The substitution of mass tourism for high-quality study tourism was on paper only. Where an international reputation had been gained – as in the IUAV, the Institute of Architecture – the city appeared to have little sympathy for its appropriate housing, or indeed for the housing of students who were regularly accused of taking apartments from residents. Tourists are survival, but they are also the enemy. As one student of 'the international of the tourist' noted, 'Venice is perhaps the clearest example of a city that has been drained of local productivity through the success of international tourism . . . Disney, which has built a diminutive replica of Piazza San Marco at Disney World in Orlando, would have much to teach Venice in terms of the efficiency of consumption and maximisation of profit.'[125] Residents persistently espouse the Disneyland analogy, forgetting that they are custodians and not creators of their tourist attraction.[126] It is true that *vaporetti* and *calli*, churches and museums are over-crowded: but a restored city is not in fact a fabricated city, and to keep insisting that it has become cardboard makes mockery of the deep affection in which the city is held internationally, and the considerable financial backing received from international associations.

The hapless tourist remains without rights, although he or she may be well-prepared and sensitive to the city's past history and present fragility. Nor are museums, churches and exhibitions for tourists only; they surely enhance residential life, but in the case of Venice, not sufficiently to stem its population exodus. The 'power of place' exerts its pressures, beneficial or otherwise, on insiders, as well as outsiders.

237 Window of the Disney shop, Campo San Bartolommeo, 1997.

Patrimony and Survival

The patrimony on which tourism is based is forever fragile. Security of works in churches became an issue in 1992 after a sequence of thefts – a Bellini from the Madonna del'Orto in March, a sculpture by Vittorio from San Francesco della Vigna, three altar paintings from San Nicolò on the Lido in August, a lion from San Marco. These are more often local, or regional, crimes, of course. Proposals for security systems, surveillance and charges for entering churches were discussed together with schemes for regulated hours and entrance prices.[127]

It was evident that restoration of notable buildings was not a leading issue in the 1990s, for environmental problems took precedence. Vittorio Gregotti claimed in 1995 that the concentration on Venice's town planning in the past fifty years – from the first Piano Regolatore – had been the most passionate of any city in Europe.[128] He insisted on the old lines of thinking that offset Venice's 'palpable decadence' by 'the exceptional quality of its morphology', its intricate relationship between public and private space, and the variety of its urban routes and spaces.[129] Leonardo Benevolo bluntly claimed that Venice was a victim of municipal government which, at the same time, had to work with only part of the necessary means. Thus, decisions by local government were endlessly deferred. Venice was in crisis not only for lack of intervention, but because it had a long series of projects defined one by one, without interdisciplinary confrontation. The MO.SES project, which involved measuring the machinery against comprehensive environment effects, was the conspicuous example.

Still, international vigilance and the skills of restoration now concentrated in the city have combined in ongoing programmes: the intricate restoration of the crypt of San Marco, for example, and Santa Maria Miracoli.[130] The highly regarded Pietro Torto Prize for restoration, awarded annually since 1974, indicated the richness of international and local interventions in recent decades.[131] Venice has been restored since the nineteenth century largely by virtue of outside interest and finance.

The cultural deployment of old buildings, and the renegotiation of a dynamic cultural activity to deepen and legitimate the business of visiting Venice, is at issue at regular points. Bids to redevelop cultural life have included the greater use of the Biennale garden and pavilions. In the Dorsoduro, the Guggenheim Foundation took an active role in relation to its museum in the Palazzo Venier dei Leoni, expanding the rear of the palace into an abutting building to provide new facilities for exhibitions, a bookshop and a coffee house, as well as an enlargement of the sculpture garden.[132] The Dogana warehouses alongside Santa Maria della Salute had also been sought for redevelopment – in particular by the Solomon Guggenheim Foundation, which was granted a lease in 1992 to use the area as an extension of the Peggy Guggenheim Collection. In spite of opposition from the offices of the Guardia di Finanza, the Guggenheim initiative was eventually successful, and Vittorio Gregotti was commissioned to design it.[133]

The centre of Venice remains, of course, the Piazza of San Marco, which is regularly reviewed. Various efforts have been made to break down the concentration of tourism in the Piazza: new tourist routes have been devised and signposted in other areas of the city. There were headlines in the world's press when the famous pigeons contracted salmonella and bird-seed sellers were banned from the Piazza.[134] In the early 1990s souvenir stalls were prohibited, angering the displaced vendors who stormed the Palazzo Ducale on two occasions.

Everyone wants to be in the Piazza, and to see San Marco. The Patriarch has made a bid to increase the quality of reverence inside the Basilica, forbidding tour groups, limiting times of entrance, and banning photography and video cameras.[135] As well as the restoration of the crypt, a pavement of vinyl was laid in the Basilica in 1994 to protect the floor.[136] Ettore Vivo, Proto since 1981, was awarded the Pietro Torto

Prize for restoration in 1991 for promoting the photogramin relief method of determining the condition of the fabric. The Magistrato delle Acqua, the agency responsible for San Marco, tendered for a scientific model that would allow full appraisal of structural features.[137] The microclimate, which would necessarily include the impact of human traffic, was to be monitored.

Plans for rationalisation of the museums located around the Piazza sparked debate.[138] The fragility of the Palazzo Ducale led to the exclusion of temporary exhibitions from that site and their transferral to the Giudecca's salt warehouses or the Museo Correr. At the same time, greater circulation of tourists in other museums was set up with a linked entrance ticket, which would distribute visitors more evenly through the Museo Correr, the Archaeological Museum, certain areas of the Biblioteca Marciana and the Bevilacqua la Masa Foundation – all less visited than the Palazzo Ducale. This project, put forward by the Assessore alla Cultura, Gianfranco Mossetto, has had international attention, due in part to the formation of an international advisory committee representing such institutions as the National Gallery, London, and the Louvre, Paris. The vacated offices of the Assicurazioni in the Procuratie Vecchie led to a bid for that area to become a temporary exhibition area for foreign loans of material concerning Venice. Rooms of the Procuratie Nuove in the old palace were to be opened to the public.

Among the 'soft' options designed to consolidate Venice as the 'special city' of the future was the call to renew the arts and crafts for which it was traditionally famous. Mask shops flourished, lace designs are still turned out at Burano, wood turners, gilders and antique restorers were still tucked away in small streets, Fortuny products were made, and Rubelli fabrics kept the luxury tradition alive. However, Burano lace was in danger since the co-operative lacked funds.[139] And while the show-casing of glass from the great workshops had by no means ceased, and the showrooms of Venini and Seguso were still conspicuous, souvenir glass of frank vulgarity had the upper hand – lurid birds on vast glass branches, leaping fish, the ubiquitous glass animals. Venetian glass was no longer inevitably at the forefront of international design, although Lino Tagliapietra commanded a formidable reputation and was associated with specific individualised designs – such as his goblets encircled with 'Saturn's' planetary ring (fig. 238).[140] A bid to recover centrality in the world of glass occurred in 1996 with the first international 'Aperto' exhibition held at a number of venues, but principally in the Palazzo Ducale.[141]

In the days of the Republic in 1271, glass-blowers who left Venice to divulge its secrets elsewhere were under threat of execution: now glass-blowing belongs to the world. It was an American, Dale Chihuly, who has become the best-known glassmaker – but with obvious reference to Venice to which he came in 1968 as a Fulbright Scholar to observe the Venini workshop. He returned on a number of occasions, and collaborated with Lino Tagliapietra in Venice and in Seattle, Chihuly's base in America.[142] Chihuly exemplifies both the internationalism of art glass (he works in teams all over the world), and the conspicuous and primary inspiration of Venice – in his saturated colour and in the inevitable sense in his work of the metamorphosis of water and fire, of liquidity and the molten state. The American critic Donald Kuspit felt the need refer to Freud's oceanic feeling and to 'alchemic' material, the mystical substance that 'has the power to alter consciousness'. Chihuly's 1988 'Venetians' series, recognised as a central point in his oeuvre, resonates with 'uncanniness and shudder'.[143] Chihuly described how he had taken models of Venetian glass and 'branched out from there . . . They got more and more bizarre, and I liked that'.[144]

It was in 1996, however, in September, that he realised the full symbiosis in an installation known as *Chihuly over Venice*. The foreign artist returned to the nurturing point of his art and dazzled that audience with his extravagance, far in excess of their own, and his mastery. The chandelier, so powerfully identified with intricacy and decorativeness, particularly in the eighteenth-century creations of Giuseppe Briati,

238 Lino Tagliapietra, Saturn goblet, 1990. Venice, Murano, Museo Vetrario.

239 (*above left*) Dale Chihuly, chandelier, Isola di San Giacomo in Palude, 1996.

240 (*above right*) Dale Chihuly, chandelier, Palazzo Ducale, 1996.

exploded into the late twentieth century with vast scale and colour and a defiance of gravity in excess of any chandelier previously designed. Chihuly's creations challenged the air, were suspended over water, or hoisted above a bridge. They were sculptures – outdoor installations – shown beside water and under sky. Bluer than the sky, one creation is hoisted up on steel poles in front of the Palazzo Stern on the Grand Canal. Bulbous glass domes sprout below the stone domes of Santa Maria della Salute; a multi-tentacled creation in deep blue inhabits the cloister of Sant'Antonio and multi-coloured floats appear to have been hauled out of the water in front of the gondola boatyards at San Trovaso. On the deserted island of San Giacomo in Palude, waving fronds stood on the water's edge against the distant skyline of Venice (fig. 239).

Chihuly paid the ultimate compliment, but also posed the ultimate challenge from beyond the once exclusive centre of the glass-blower's art. The centrepiece of *Chihuly over Venice* was installed in the heart of the city, in the Palazzo Ducale, beneath an eighteenth-century chandelier by Briati (fig. 240). Chihuly's sprang up from the floor, crystal-clear, returning to the clarity and translucency of historic glass. A myriad of inverted twisting coils multiplied many times the already extravagant components of the original. Venice is a starting point for Chihuly's work, without question. But he is also part of the exodus from the city.

* * *

The Biennale

In 1995 the Biennale celebrated its centenary, after the usual vacillation and political debate. By then it was firmly established that the principal curator would be an international appointment, in this case, the French director of the Picasso Museum, Jean Clair. At the Palazzo Grassi an exhibition concentrated on the human body – *Body and Alterity* – showing works from across the period of the Biennale's history.[145] Giandomenico Romanelli organised a historic exhibition following the *Journeys of Taste* through the history of the Biennale, from its early Symbolist focus, including its early commitment to decorative art. A special exhibition followed the art of glass in its Biennale representations up to 1972.[146] Drawing together the history of one hundred years, Christian Boltanski orchestrated 'an event' that inscribed the names of all participating Biennale artists on the walls of the Italian pavilion and distributed leaflets in homage to the artists throughout the city.

In the last twenty to thirty years the Biennale had experienced the disruptions of 1968 and the political reorientation of Carlo Ripa di Meana's presidency, which led to the 1974 Biennale devoted to repression in Chile, and the 1977 Biennale hosting dissenting artists from the Soviet Union.[147] In the 1970s the field expanded to encompass the informality of political displays, installations and performances. The traditional site of the Biennale, the Giardini, became too small, and the repercussions of the international scene too extensive and environmentally oriented for the original site to contain everything. Gerzy Grotowski used the abandoned island of San Giacomo in Paludo for a theatre seminar in 1975. Vittorio Gregotti organised exhibitions at the salt warehouses on the Zattere, and it was the time of the projects for the Molino Stucky. In 1980 Paolo Portoghesi orchestrated the brilliant *Strada novissima* as the centrepiece of the first Architectural Biennale in the Corderie at the Arsenale, since then a regular venue.

In the late 1970s thematic exhibitions were introduced in the central Italian Pavilions. Under the presidency of Giuseppe Gallaso in the 1980s, exhibitions were anthologies such as *Art and Alchemy* and *Art and Biology*. Achille Bonito Oliva, whose fame as a critic rested on his support for the trans-avant-garde, was a conspicuous contributor, responsible for a new initiative, the special exhibition of young artists, *Aperto*, which ran for some years. Paolo Portoghesi took over the presidency in the late 1980s, and Gian Luigi Rondi in the 1990s. International representation expanded as the Berlin Wall fell; Berlin was in focus in 1990. Spawning Biennales from Sao Paolo to Sydney, challenged, from the 1970s, by the triennial Documenta at Kassel, the Venice *mostra* has nevertheless retained and even augmented its lead.[148]

The commitment of nations to their own pavilions guaranteed national attendances, even if the nations were no longer required to host from their own countries, but could choose those they wanted to represent. The central Italian Pavilion, now regularly guest-curated, could present wide-ranging international anthology exhibitions over and above national representation. The bid to utilise the Biennale facilities and the Italian Pavilion for regular contemporary art exhibitions was viewed as the logical extension of the Biennale's success in the eyes of Venetian political planners. That the Biennale was the linchpin of bids for increased and deepened cultural activity in historic Venice was evident in the *Venezia 2000* manifesto.[149] It had been closely linked to local government throughout its history, from its foundation under the patronage of the Commune and the first president, Mayor Riccardo Selvatico (whose descendent was the philosopher-mayor, Massimo Cacciari) and, in its opening ceremonies performed by the presidents and ministers of the Republic.[150] The close link with industry and tourism perpetuated Count Volpi's initiatives of the 1930s.

The Biennale has continued to provoke Venice-specific works, and to contribute to the city's many-layered iconography. Empathy and homage – and critique – are often enmeshed: for instance the Australian artist Narelle Jubelin exhibited *Trade Delivers*

241 Narelle Jubelin, assembled Venetian Burano lace gondola, from *Trade Delivers People*, Biennale di Venezia, 1990. Cotton petit-point ground, lace purchased Venice 1990, found Tramp Art frame, 30.5 × 30.5 cm. Melbourne, National Gallery of Victoria.

People in the 1990 *Aperto*.[151] Her characteristic medium is petit-point embroidery, readily associated with women and domesticity; for Venice she reworked her medium to include the lace-making women of Burano. Narelle Jubelin often uses highly recognisable, common motifs, or found elements – either objects or images – and articles deliberately purchased for a specific installation. The references are global, befitting a world city that is so instantly recognisable (as advertising with Venetian themes has proven so many times). Instantly associated with Venice is a Burano lace image of a gondola, which the artist set into her own petit-point background, absorbing and remaking that image (fig. 241). In an image that teased the northern hemisphere from a location in the south, an outline of Australia, recognisable to any reader of a world map, was worked into the cover of a domestic milk jug to protect the milk from insects – a kind of Antipodean alternative to Burano lace. The ancient trading prowess of Venice gave the *raison d'être* for the traffic in images and objects, of trading beads that mixed amber, silver and bone from Africa with glass beads from Venice, purchased by the artist.[152] Tribal masks from New Guinea counter those from Africa as the hemispheres of the north and the south mingled their treasures.

In 1990 the American artist Jenny Holzer showed her *Venice Project* in the American pavilion in the Giardini (fig. 242).[153] The floor was laid with marble tiles – black, red-brown, white – characteristic of local paving, interspersed with engraved Holzerian messages in French, Italian and English: 'Any Surplus is Immoral', 'Il Desiderio di Riproduzione e un Desiderio di Morte'. An LCD monitor ran further messages in two wings of the pavilion. This lapidary installation with its low lighting had the effect of turning the pavilion into a chapel. Holzer's 'truisms' and texts were spread beyond the Giardini, intruding into such public spaces as the airport, the station and the *vaporetti*, and printed on t-shirts. The Giardini installation, in the heart of the Biennale, was another exercise locating death somewhere in Venice.

In 1993 Hans Haacke's response to the anniversary of the visit of Hitler to the Biennale engaged directly and critically with the Biennale's internal history.[154] Haacke took the opportunity to expose the complicity between Fascist Italy and Nazi Germany at a time when a group of Venetian historians had published a *Political Travel Diary* for Venice, emphasising the political realities of a city that for the superficial tourist exists beyond politics.[155] For Haacke, in 1993, Count Volpi's luxury hotel culture was still

alive and linked with the Biennale, which early on had 'developed as an event to benefit the local restaurant and hotel industry and an asset in the development plans of the Venetian establishment'.[156] Perhaps nothing can survive without such links, and all culture is doomed, but culture is not only the literary thematics of death and love in the Serenissima, it is commerce and exploitation.

In the same year at the Biennale Nam June Paik produced *High Tech Gondolas* and *Rehabilitation of Ghenis Khan*, imitating the trans-continental voyages of the Venetian Marco Polo, now equipped with a bicycle, a diver's helmet and electronic equipment.[157]

Foreign Perceptions: Joseph Brodsky

Riotta's Venice in *Ombra* was a farcical carnival, threatened by flood. *Acqua grande*, the documentary novel of the November flood, was virtually a Venetian polemic for the double project of recalling the past and signalling the dangers still unresolved for the present. These were *Italian* perceptions of Venice in the 1990s. Foreign perceptions of Venice since the fall we know to have perpetuated its fallibility, dwelt on its mortality, and seen the beauty and the disease of the residual past.

The old fascination with the Venice of water still had its adherents in the 1990s. The spirit of conservatism had never run more strongly. Joseph Brodsky's *Watermark*, completed in November 1989, was eagerly embraced by Venetians – and Americans – as a late work from the pen of the 1987 Nobel Prize winner.[158] The book came about by a singular process of patronage from the president of the Consorzio Venezia Nuova, Luigi Zanda. The first edition of *Watermark* was not in English, the language it which it was written, but Italian: it was first published as *Fondamenta degli Incurabili*, referring to the ancient institution for the terminally ill behind the church of

Santa Maria della Salute.[159] Resident in the USA since 1972 and a high-profile USSR dissident, Brodzsky spent a month in Venice every winter. *Watermark* records his desultory, conventional views of the city with snatched references to other aspects of the author's life: when he arrives at the station Santa Lucia on a winter's night knowing only one person in Venice, the smell of frozen seaweed greets him, reminding him of his childhood by the Baltic.

The inevitable reflections in water abound, leading to a reflection on the special condition of Venice. Brodsky's Venice is resolutely that of an outsider and indeed he suggests that that is the only possibility; that the city belongs to outsiders. Taking the *vaporetto* on arrival 'the boat's slow progress through the night was like the passage of a coherent thought through the subconscious'.[160] The palaces to either side were 'enormous carved chests . . . filled with unfathomable treasures . . . the overall feeling was mythological, cyclopic'.[161] Here is the primordial again: Dickens's anonymous entrance at night, Proust's geology of palaces, Adrian's Stokes's amniotic voyages. Mirror themes almost always accompany those of water, with 'the mirror absorbing the body absorbing the city' and the passage through the deserted upper floors of a palazzo, visiting rooms full of mirrors that become more and more blackened. Finally the viewer is confronted with no self-reflection at all.

It is the city of the gaze yet again. The narcissism and display presumed to be created by the city issue from a notion of 'visual superiority' in 'the city of the eye'. The eye 'swims' in Venice. There are intimations of death, of the writer's cardiac condition, of friends living or dead who have introduced the writer into Venice. The city is a labyrinth again. Among early lures for Brodsky in his twenties in St Petersburg were cheap souvenirs, a poor print of Visconti's *Death in Venice*, and the experience of reading Henri de Régnier writing about Venice in winter: 'its atmosphere was twilit and dangerous, its topography aggravated with mirrors'. It was a setting for plots of 'love and betrayal'.

The Italian title, *Fondamenta degli Incurabili*, relates to a particular incident in the book: it cannot help but have symbolic resonance. The old hospice and *fondamenta* of the incurables is on the Zattere, behind Olga Rudge's house (the [Ezra] Pound woman' as Brodzsky ungraciously calls her), whom the writer had visited with Susan Sontag.[162] The 'Embankment of the Incurabili' unleashes essential speculations on the plague, and frissons not unlike those provoked by *Vampires in Venice* – 'the name conjures the hopeless cases, not so much strolling along as scattered about on the flagstones, literally expiring, shrouded, waiting to be carted – or rather, shipped away . . . gradually the funereal procession turns into a carnival, or indeed a promenade, where a mask would have to be worn'.[163] Does all this reflect a conversation with Susan Sontag concerning 'Illness as Metaphor', convincing Brodsky that 'the end of an illness is the end of its metaphors'? At the same time, in virtually the same breath, he can declare with all the banality of the instant tourist that in over-photographed Venice 'shares in Kodak are the best investment'.[164]

The labyrinth is in place again. Perhaps Sophie Calle could have guided Brodsky on a more rigorous passage and helped him muse on the confusion between hunter and prey that is always the dilemma of the labyrinth. Certainly the writer understands the links with Crete under the Old Republic that make the minotaur in the original labyrinth part of the antiquity of the Republic itself. Is he intending a variant on Henry James when he declares that 'the whole city, especially at night, resembles a gigantic orchestra, with dimly lit music stands of palazzi, with a restless chorus of waves, with the falsetto of a star in the winter sky', or is it Nietzsche: 'When I think of Venice I think of music'?[165]

If the echoes merely confirm that Venice *is* a place of echoes, Brodsksy's account is indubitably of his time, written in the late 1980s and recognising that the fate of Venice might be that of lost Atlantis and the need to 'install some sort of flap gate to stem the sea of humanity which has swelled in the last two decades by two billions and whose crest is its refuse'.[166] Recognising the urgency, Brodsky would have the military called in to dredge the canals. But mainly, and like many, he is in pursuit of beauty, not streamlined beauty, but the beauty of patina and confirmed canons of taste. The theme of plague is soon relinquished for further meditations on water, on feeling cat-like after a meal of fish, on finding beauty and *safety* to be synonymous. This last may be the crucial insight: that beauty is almost always conferred retro-spectively, canonically. It is of the past, enmeshed with self-preservation. In finding this past beauty Brodsky again risks bathos: observing that Carpaccio's poodle does not bite, for he belongs to the past tense, and is safe. In the present, the Peggy Guggen-heim collection can be written off, together with what seems to be all the visual art of the centre as 'cheap, self assertive, ungenerous, one dimensional': a sad turn against the present that has the effect yet again of condemning the city to its past, making it remain static. Brodsky's is yet another outsider's view that will not permit the city to move on.[167]

Crime in the Lagoon

Not surprisingly in view of the crises of flooding, silting, dredging, de-population and housing decay, a sordid Venice, definitively unromantic, made its entrance into liter-ature. Donna Leon's detective stories starring the quietly indefatigable Police Com-missioner Guido Brunetti feed on the crises of the 1990s in Venice and the Veneto: a poisoning at La Fenice (in advance of the fire), a beaten-up body at Marghera, chem-ical pollution, art theft and political bribery (no doubt based on the incident when the deputy major, Gianfranco Bettin, was intimidated by 'mafiosi' and, with a gun at his head, told not to meddle in drug-control matters), all compounded by the *acque alte* of the 1990s.[168]

Robert Girardi's novel *Vaporetto 13*, follows a brash American financier posted to Venice, where he has an affair with a mysterious woman bearing the ancient name of Vendramin. She is a ghost of the past, and eventually returns to the ossuary island Sant'Adriano, where the bones of doges and fishermen intermingle in another exemplum of multiple deaths. This is the Venice of the 1990s: 'Venice in January was deserted, a tomb. So quiet you could almost hear the sound of the palazzos crumbling into the black water, their pilings turning to mush after centuries embed-ded in the cold, salty mud of the lagoon . . .'[169]

Particularly soiled, even within the dour scenario characteristic of the decade, Michael Dibdin's *Dead Lagoon* takes its name from the backwater of the lagoon, the *laguna morta*, where the waters are beyond the reach of tides and are torpid, inert, and rubbish-catching.[170] Cats and seagulls scavenge for a bit of liver or fish. The dead lagoon and its inert waters casts their pall over the entire area of water and city. The very events of the 1990s imprint themselves in details. A local newspaper announces – falsely – the 'green light for the lagoon metro'. Umberto Bossi's bid for a Northern League makes local politics.

One of the most impressive of crime writers of the late twentieth century, Dibdin soon identifies the physical condition of the city and its waters with the conundrum of murder and contraband, as well as with troubling visions experienced by ancient residents. Ada Zulian, known locally as the Contessa, reports disturbances in her empty palazzo: somebody moves chairs and brings in fresh mud. She reports carni-val-like figures – a harlequin and a skeleton – rampaging at night. Detective Aurelio Zen is Venetian-born, but he is part of the Venetian exodus: he lives with his mother in Rome, where he has tackled various typical cases – murder in Calabria, an assisted suicide in St Peter's, kidnapping and fraud – and has returned on assignment to his home town. On previous assignments in Rome the memory of Venice is always strong. In Rome, Zen's mother refers to 'Old Umberto's boat', moored outside the Zen house in Cannaregio and disturbed every time the vaporetto passed; at another point Zen's girlfriend Tania reminds him of the 'Great Madonna in the apse of the cathedral on the island of Torcello'.[171] He is impervious to Venice's traditional beauty, although not to the tenacious hold that it has upon its natives – he and his mother – even when exiled to Rome.

It is the *bora* of winter that blows, and not the sirocco of summer. The refineries of Marghera immediately taint the scene under a 'bloated sun' and a 'dense bank of smog'. Venice is a place of small bars, more or less squalid: there is no Piazza San Marco, nothing of tourism but a squalid periphery through which, at one point, Zen follows his suspect, picking up an empty *vaporetto* here or there, finally reaching the Lido where the victim throws himself into the sea. Derangement is possible: not Brodsky's Fondamenta degli Incurabili, not Winterson's San Servolo: here San Clemente commands the mad. Rats infest an island – the islands of the lagoon are a telling part of the geography of the book – where a drug pusher goes to deposit contraband and finds a body half-consumed by rats, the remains of a victim, a former Bosnian wanted for war crimes who has been pushed from a helicopter. Local politics also affect Zen's case and his affair with an old friend Christine. The Nuova Repubblica Veneta is involved with Umberto Bossi's Northern League to separate Venice and Padua from Italy (and Rome in particular) in the middle 1990s.

Zen leaves Venice when the Contessa's case is withdrawn and the Durridge case taken out of his control. The 'affair' with Christine is exposed as a political manoeuvre, his father is reported alive after deserting from the army, living in Poland and unwilling to contact his family. Zen leaves a Venice that is sordid and run down, dubious in allegiances and both strident and impotent within the politics of Northern Italy. The troubled agenda in which Zen is enmeshed reaches back to the Second World War and to the 'cleansing' of Venetian Jews in the 1940s. Overall it is a harsh view presented by this fictional expatriate who is himself one of the statistics of the depopulated city.

More Deaths

In the 1970s the Italian film-makers Visconti and Fellini exposed the farcical in Venetian life, in *Casanova* and in the strident carnival sequence in *Death in Venice*. Farce was prominent in the writing of the 1990s – in *Ombra*, and in the novel that was the most sustained creation of the decade, Robert Coover's *Pinocchio in Venice*.

For writers in the 1990s winter has become *the* Venetian season. Two writers bring their protagonists to Santa Lucia in winter, not only Brodsky, but the eccentric star of Coover's novel, an aged professor who is yet another candidate for death in the city. The snow and the ice that greet him are but a projection of human winter as the last station of life. Yet *Pinocchio in Venice* proceeds in a tone of high comedy, taking on the disguises of carnival and the slippage of personality that Venice both provokes and avenges.[172] Professor Emeritus Pinenut, winner of two Nobel Prizes, arrives on a winter's night at the Stazione Santa Lucia without lodgings, carrying his computer with the last of his great works still needing one chapter to complete. The area of the station is imprinted instantly onto the city's geography as a kind of inversion of the Piazza San Marco and Bacino: at one end of the Grand Canal the church of San Simeone Piccolo mocks San Marco. Nearby the highly decorated church of the Scalzi appears like a carnival mask. Venice is perpetually in the act of mocking itself.

Robbed and led astray in the snow by a tourist clerk wearing the carnival mask of the Plague Doctor, the professor is arrested as a vagrant by the Carabinieri, but is recognised by police dog Alidoro as the original Pinocchio. He is returned to his one-time wooden state and his old circle of friends. The characters mouth the debased slogans – 'Ah, this thrice-renowned and illustrious city! This precious jewel, this voluptuous old Queen, this magical fairyland!' and so on.[173] But in a last elevation of carnivalesque spirit, it is also 'the original wet dream', sexually charged, but with excreta, blasphemy and sacrilege. Enfeebled, incontinent, bereft of his professional accoutrements, the professor emeritus, who has become Pinocchio finds himself in a rubbish bin filled up by tourists. But he is also like Petrarch: indeed Professor Pinenut is the Petrarch of his age, bringing his great gifts to the Serenissima.

In the context of this visit, familiar monuments take a nice turn. San Giorgio Maggiore has 'sagging cheeks' and a 'carbuncular dome' as the professor makes a last effort to understand Palladio.[174] The city's squalor and its manipulative management become an element in the comedy. Eugenio is a Gianni de Michelis character, masterminding the carnival; Eugenio aspires to a doge-like position with a penthouse in the Palazzo Ducale. He has frank plans to reconstitute the city as Disneyland and anticipates advertising on gondoliers' shirts and hats. *Acqua alta* is a certain tourist attraction – he watches it from his apartment overlooking the Piazza San Marco: 'Waves crash against the columns and resound in the arches below us, as if to loosen the palace from its very moorings and send us out to sea . . . wastebins bob in the Piazza like buoys . . .'[175]

There is no doubt that the traditional profile of the city is intact, but slanted midway between raucous distaste and fierce love, entirely typical of the 1990s. In the novel, a newly discovered Bellini – the improbably lewd *Madonna of the Organs* – is donated to the city. Count Agnello Ziani Orseolo, obviously a descendent of great doges, leads the ceremony of presentation to the Accademia. He is endowed with a phallus of such scale that it slaps the pavement as he walks, while he exclaims that Venice is the mother of all his pleasure and profit. On the return to the Palazzo Ducale, a communal urination ceremony is enacted from the Accademia bridge; it is 'a veritable downpour'.

The novel's highlight is a speedboat journey, well beyond legal limits – the unabashed voyage of a *moto ondoso*. Perhaps it is the last day of carnival, on which Pinocchio's supposed friend Eugenio has him encased in pizza dough in the shape of a donkey and baked in an oven. But his true friend, as with any honest soul in relation to Venice, is the lion of St Mark, now mangy and befuddled with grappa, remembering his sojourn in Paris, courtesy of Napoleon, as a taste of a real metropolis. The professor's exit, his obligatory death in Venice, is consummated in no less a setting than Santa Maria degli Miracoli, with 'the sheer marble walls, pale as old bone and glistening dewily', as if in anticipation. He is reconciled with the Blue-haired Fairy of his Pinocchio days and his Mamma, from his human life. They may be one and the same.

The sexuality unleashed by the Serenissima, traditionally indulgent of both male and female, was strident in the 1980s; in the 1990s undertones of sadism, cruelty and exploitation were never too distant. Paul Schrader's film version of *The Comfort of Strangers*, filmed in sickly orange in several sequences, follows the forlorn trail of the tourists Mary and Colin to the murderous outcome at the hands of the Venetian Robert and his crippled wife. It is Colin, rather than Mary, who is the object of ensnarement.[176]

Male beauty has always been on display in Venice, and it runs alluringly throughout Harold Brodkey's *Profane Friendship*, a book commissioned by the Consorzio Venezia Nuova as part of their rejuvenation project to attract intellectual and artistic capital.[177] It was Brodkey's last novel; he died in 1996.[178] The central figure, Nino, the son of an American writer who knows Hemingway, grows up in Venice in the 1930s, close to the beautiful Italian boy Onni. Brodkey's novel reaches towards corruption and heightened sexuality: it is inevitable, it would seem, for young Onni growing up as a Fascist youth. All the narrator's relationships are sexualised – with his brother Carlo, his mother, his nursemaid Zilda. After the war he picks up and consummates his relationship with Onni, a teenage male prostitute.

A real presence in the novel is the mutable Venetian light. As so often in the 1990s, it is winter light, obedient to something introspective and brooding. The spirit of Baron Corvo is abroad in the lagoon light – and in the male eroticism. As children, Onni and Nino run to school 'under a high, fleecy, gray morning sky, in dimmed winter light that was like airy tissue paper'.[179] When Nino returns to the city he finds 'a shrouded post-war Venice in the silver gloom emerged prow-like, looming with accumulated emotion and beauty, an ocean-liner-in-a-dream', and 'at noon a yellow stain with burnt rainbow veinings of brownish tint discoloured the fog over the glinting and shifting *Canalazzo*'.[180] The world still wants to find Aschenbach in Venice, and the undertow of death. In *Profane Friendship* Onni and Nino grow old, but Onni is still a famous film star, prattling on about the maintenance of beauty with talk of a little lipstick and reminiscences of Aschenbach's famous visit to a beautician.

Sex in Venice is possible, equally, and the erotic charge of sex and death never too distant from literature. Set in the 1990s the Australian novelist Rod Jones's *Night Pictures* is constantly in erotic mode, both heterosexual and homosexual, to the extent that the city becomes a charged 'map of the mind', with the 'the grand canal of desire' snaking through it.[181]

The world still wants to find Aschenbach in Venice, and the undertow of death. In *Profane Friendship*, Onni and Nino grow old, but Onni is still a famous film star, prattling on about the maintenance of beauty with talk of a little lipstick and reminiscences of Aschenbach's famous visit to a beautician.

Another candidate for ruminations on death in Venice is the Australian narrator 'R' of *Night Thoughts* by Robert Dessaix.[182] Diagnosed HIV positive, 'R' takes to travelling, writing home in the evenings about his encounters in Lake Maggiore, Bologna, Vicenza and Padua. He appears to find some sort of peace in Venice, although he can smell it 'rotting outside [his] window', but that is akin to his own self-perception: in other words, Venice acts as a metaphor of illness, being itself diseased. 'R' has many conversations with a Teutonic professor called Eschenbaum (*another* professor, Eschenbaum rather than Aschenbach), who tells long stories – about a sixteenth-century courtesan which keeps up the city's erotic dispensation – explaining the difference between Casanova and Marco Polo – Polo is conventionally sexed; Casanova is the true adventurer again, obsessed with time. Aschenbach's holiday in Venice is mentioned: 'apart from some difficulties with his luggage nothing really happened' – again like the narrator, who eventually gets a new suitcase with wheels. Reading Dante leads to a nightmare ride on the back of a leopard, but it becomes a more benign journey taken with the San Marco lion. Venice is also a palliative. And yet it is still wreaking revenge on its visitors, but in more modern form. *Comfort of Strangers* is a salient example of ensnarement and murder in the 1990s. *Night Thoughts* is not so extreme, but Professor Eschenbaum out on his evening prowl is trailed by 'R', who sees him mugged. When the professor has left town, 'R' sees various staff members at the hotel in the rapacious city wearing the professor's leather jacket, gold bracelet and Omega watch.

Ending the Cult: Too Much Venice

The Teutonic Aschenbach is the century's most famous visitor to Venice for it was he who so palpably demonstrated the city's destiny as a metaphor of illness. Suicide is attempted by visitors to Venice as a consequence of its association with death and dying,[183] but the French persist with their own self-defined tradition in the face of Venice and indeed, in 1995, a Frenchman visited the greatest insult upon the city since Chateaubriand. Régis Debray, journalist and political commentator, published his *Contre Venise*, declaring it was time to terminate the myth. In the buff-coloured Gallimard essay format, the work came branded with the ultimate message *Fin de culte*. Mayor Massimo Cacciari's anger was aroused; he responded in the local and international press.[184] But Debray's attack hardly varied from the long line of French criticisms of Venice, already in place in the days of the Republic. He simply re-endorsed one of the French traditions, exposing his own ambivalence towards Venice, and at the same time admitting to a deliberate exercise in provocation. His sole originality is that he uses the city of Naples as a comparison point: everything that is lively, spontaneous, marked by life, pertains to Naples; the opposite is the condition in Venice. In this new twist for detractors, the author declares the living reality of Naples above Venice.

Debray attacked what he saw as the 'phantom' that Venice had become, with its vulgar appeal to 'people of taste' – the author was provoked by an article in the popular press on President Mitterand as 'Venetian'. It is the special absurdity of his own compatriots, namely the good practitioner who goes to Venice annually more easily than the pilgrim to St James at Compostella, to be a celebrant at the Eucharist of Beauty.

Echoing Madame de Staël, Debray announces that Venice is a suffocating city, without greenery. It can only be effective if one understands the requirement to engage in play, the need to suspend time, to recognise the literal demands of theatre. The palaces are all pseudo-domiciles with no trace of life. The Ponte della Libertà might be so named because it offers the liberty to escape. Admittedly Venice has style, but that is its chief crime, since it endears itself to a *petite bourgeoisie* confirmed in its taste. Naples does not have taste, but then the comparison is so bland that any non-insular city would do. Any city that is industrialised, conventional in transport, moving quickly, having its quota of the modern and the functional would suffice for comparison. All Debray's negatives could be turned to positives, and indeed we recognise the attributes used regularly in previous decades to affirm the value of the artificial city as 'special'. Debray's response to the artificiality begins with the uncommon entrance by bridge or water to a city whose small scale makes it this snail city: *cette cité-escargot*.

Has the comparison with Naples been sustained to any point of value? Naples is said to call to the roving eye of the photographer, Venice to the painter, but in which century? Naples has its death ceremonies and exhibitions of corpses which excite pleasure, whereas Venice, Debray claims, is a carcass, an empty fossil. Trite indeed the injunction to 'see Naples and then die', for in order to see Venice death must come first.[185] Debray asks how to survive amid such overwhelming kitsch – all the versions of gondoliers' songs, for example, and the abounding process of fetishising fetishes?

Has Debray truly undermined the cult, exposed anything new? He takes his position at the teasing point between reality – artificial city, slow pace, the necessity for unorthodox entry and boat travel, etc. – and the Venice of the Imaginary, more a creation of writers than masons, more of painters than architects.[186] The problem is over-textualisation: we float on 'a platform of references'. Perhaps we meet again the diagnosis of no less than Cacciari himself: Venice is so saturated with meanings that it no longer signifies.

Debray's study is the continuation of two centuries of French texts reacting to Venice. Across the Channel, the English remained attached to the romantic legacy – witness the *version anglais* of *The Wings of a Dove*, filmed from the Henry James novel, in technicolour and postcard chic, at odds with its *memento mori* theme of consumption and betrayal.[187] Dying in Venice is kept alive, but beautifully.

The predominantly literary tradition beloved by the English, and the primary arena for their own contribution to the Imaginary of Venice, is encapsulated in Tony Tanner's 1992 study with its explicit title, *Venice Desired*.[188] While Tanner's preface mentions more contemporary works by Hemingway, Calvino, *The Comfort of Strangers* and *Pinocchio in Venice*, and he considers the early twentieth century of

Von Hofmannsthal, Proust and Pound, his work has a predominantly nineteenth-century focus. It re-endorses the traditional love-affair and the traditional voices. Fully produced as an English analysis of literary texts in contrast to Debray's speedy *essai*, Tanner's work stays with the canonical Byron, Ruskin and James. They are held at the centre of a study that preserves the Tristan and Isolde syndrome of excessive love leading to poison.

For Tanner, Venice is no mere collation of bricks, mortar and marble, it is an active personification.[189] Focusing in his introduction on Herman Melville's two poems on Venice, he writes that 'Venice has turned her sexual eye on the impressionable American'. The city is construed not merely as female, but as courtesan, actively involved in seduction. Tanner's conclusion might have been written by Ruskin, so sympathetic are its cadences:

> A Western city saturated with the East; a city of land and stone everywhere penetrated by water; a city of great piety and ruthless mercantilism; a city where enlightenment and licentiousness, reason and desire, indeed art and nature flow and flower together – Venice is indeed the surpassing-all-other embodiment of that 'absolute ambiguity' which is radiant life containing certain death . . .[190]

The pounding away at the theme of desire consumes each writer in each chapter, ensnared by the circularity of the syndrome. Thus Proust, who 'penetrates' Ruskin's description of Venice, is forbidden as a child to visit the beloved city. He is 'punished for his transgression – what one might call his premature ejaculation'.[191] We are captives of the 'desire flowing from Marcel to Venice' and 'from Venice to Marcel'.[192] 'For Marcel, to know about Venice was at once to desire it; and, inextricably, to know and experience desire was at once to desire Venice.'

The most ardent supporters of 'Venice in Peril', the English have not forsaken their own plenitudinous Venice of romance. Hugh Honour and John Fleming make that clear in an essay on Henry James, Whistler and Sargent, published with substantial readings from James's *Italian Hours*. Nor does John Pemble in *Venice Rediscovered*. He still seeks a salacious and anglophilic nineteenth century, a living, vivacious place albeit in ruin – culminating with Baron Corvo.[193]

In the 1990s Golden Ages were reclaimed and a bid made for the return of the great and familiar auras of the Venetian past. It was the Age of Titian, 'Prince of Painters', shown at the Palazzo Ducale and the National Gallery of Art in Washington in 1990.[194] The quatercentenary of Tintoretto was celebrated in 1993; the quatercentenary of Tiepolo in 1996. The bid for the revival of the venerable art of the Republic was evident in the exhibition of the art of the eighteenth century, the most comprehensive to date, billed as *The Glory of Venice*. It showed internationally in the global manner of the 1990s, beginning at the Royal Academy in London, moving to the National Gallery in Washington and ending in Venice at the Ca' Rezzonico.[195]

Much as photographing cities from the air was a fashion of the 1980s, photographing interiors became a genre in the 1990s. Venice was declared to be living again, and opulently so, behind its façades: indeed it proclaimed the very art of living as it revealed its 'hidden splendours'.[196] The Glorafilia needlework collection was the ultimate destiny of Venice's repertoire of the picturesque and the instantly recognisable at the turn of the century, trading off the fashion for the traditional interior.[197] A traycloth on a table at Florian's, a cushion, corded and embroidered, at the feet of a lion, scenes of carnival, mandolins and bridges, marbling and damasking, to be stitched around a nostalgic world.

* * *

The City and the Lagoon of the Past: From the Present

The telling of history is inevitably enmeshed in the values of its own age. Histories after the flood of 1966 are recommitted to diagnoses of the fragility of the Republic no less than Ruskin's history, written from the British Empire in the period of Austrian occupation. The century's most significant historian of Venice, Manfredo Tafuri, died in 1994, having effectively destabilised the Golden Age by exposing the tensions and insecurities that frustrated radical innovation and led the Republic into conservatism and impotence. In a critique of the 'boudoir architecture' of Post-Modernism, Tafuri used the metaphor of the mask again. Venice lingers as 'an allegory of a general condition', for the mask is obligatory, it must be worn to save one's soul.[198]

In his last book, *Ricerca del Rinascimento*, Tafuri returned to Sansovino's project to introduce the Roman Renaissance to Venice in certain patriciate palaces.[199] The cautious introduction of Roman and the Florentine influences constitutes the book's 'Epilogo lagunara'.[200] But the parameters of the question are about the present as well as the past, about 'the use of the new, on the one hand, and the 'jealous preservation of a sacred identity on the other': are they not the terms of debate in modern Venice?[201] Orthodoxy, the pressure towards preservation, timidity, even fear: Tafuri's Venetian of the Renaissance is the forerunner of the Venetian citizen of Tafuri's own time. Rafael Moneo goes even further in suggesting that the Sansovino of the *Ricerca* is Tafuri himself behind Sansovino's mask.[202] After Tafuri's death, Massimo Cacciari, delivering a funeral oration for him in the Tolentino cloister adjacent to the Institute of Architecture, reconfirmed Tafuri's belief in the need to mask.[203]

If Tafuri's Renaissance Venice was troubled, medieval Venice faced even greater challenges. The vulnerability of the Republic in this nascent period has been studied closely in recent years by the French historian Elizabeth Crouzot-Pavan. She brings the constant testings experienced by the Venetians of the past into focus in '*Sopra le acque salse*': *Espaces, pouvoir et société à Venise* ('Above the Salt Water': Space, Power and Society in Venice), published in 1992 by the French School in Rome.[204] Notable for its vast reading of archival material, the book sets out to show the physical survival of the city in the water, as well as the infrastructure and the social and political networks that were generated out of the physical reality of the city. This pre-Renaissance period was arguably more inventive, original – and provincial – than the Renaissance period in Venice, which looked to Florence and Rome.

The constant concern (across two centuries) is the process involved in winning dry land out of an always encroaching sea, consolidating the land frontiers, and negotiating public as well as private ownership of land. Crouzet-Pavan's book is no less a product of the great flood of 1966 than the many treatises, visual, vocal and musical, on dying Venice. The implication of the work is simple: the survival mentality was consciously wrought in the early centuries, and sheer physical survival – against the elements and against plague and illness fostered by physical conditions – has led to an unabated power struggle on the one hand, and the imposition of collective disciplines, on the other. The opposition of land and water has always been a determinant for the city and its settlements. Thus, a lugubrious quality spreads through this period; the city's inhabitants can never rest in physical certitude because of their continuing struggle against natural forces.

For Crouzet-Pavan Venice is a special 'conquest of space'. In the mid-thirteenth century this was revealed in the way in which the city was built in terms of group definition and ownership. The sheer labour involved is stressed: the notion of *travaux* (which might strike one as particularly French). Thus the conditions that determine and protect access ways along the water were crucial: the creation of *fondamenta*, the links between settlements taking up their irregular formats on emergent land, and the *calli* in reclaimed areas. The initial decentralisation of the city is a result of the first island settlement, which created 'the geography of the urban margins'. The centre,

San Marco, early in competition with the Rialto area, is only gradually consolidated and increasingly known from accounts of pilgrims in transit to the Holy Land.

The creation of public space, and the vigilance required to define and maintain it, is of obvious interest to the urban consciousness of late twentieth century. The medieval procedures for cleaning the city show the evolution of urban administration and reciprocal planning. The cleansing of canals was undertaken every three months, more often in summer.[205] The *podestà* made his inspection in July and August. Conflicts over the use of water were closely monitored – tanners and millers, for example, were subject to specific controls, as well as being relegated to specific areas. The singularity of Venice as acknowledged by its early chroniclers may be seen in part as a response to the strenuous measures necessary on a public and private level in order to sustain the most elementary maintenance of the site. Venetians constantly recalled the origins of their settlement in the mud and their common destiny in holding back the menace of the water. Time and time again Crouzot-Pavan deals with the fragility of the milieu and the instabilities that determined everyday life and administration.[206] The festivities for which the Republic was famed are but repetitions of ceremonies that defy death – the Sensa is the compelling example.

In the medieval period the lagoon was threatened by the silting up of the major rivers entering it: the Brenta, Sile and Piave. The evidence of physical shifts in the lagoon was recognised as causing the virtual demise of Torcello and the movement of key settlements from Malamocco to the Rialto. As Ruskin observed, the 'slow death' of Torcello is a *memento mori* for today's Venetians.[207] Having insufficient water, the port of Sant'Erasmo was closed by Senate decree in 1474, prompting fears that the city might run dry. Storms were particularly noticed in local history. (The conspiracy of Tiepolo-Querini in 1310, which was said to have provoked a great storm, was a seminal event in Giustina Renier Michiel's early nineteenth-century study of festivals). The vice of sodomy was regularly linked with the city's destruction, like Sodom and Gomorrah, long before Proust. In the simplest of inversions, or compensations, the instability of Venice gave rise to the myths of its very stability and of 'la durée de la République'.

Turning to texts generated by one's countrymen has comforted strangers for well over two centuries; Crouzot-Pavan is no exception in looking to French historian Amelot de la Houssaie. His history, published in 1677, compared the long duration of the Venetian Republic with Athens, Thebes, Rhodes and Rome.

Death appears always to have haunted the Republic. Crouzet-Pavan's eloquent 1981 essay: 'Venise et la mort à la fin du Moyen Age', makes the connection explicitly – and the concomitant preoccupation with *angoisse* – anguish, anxiety.[208] The emphasis recalls Tafuri's quest to expose its extent in the golden sixteenth century. Anxiety is always re-endorsed by the city's fragility; anxiety breeds an administration that accentuates duration, and, even more importantly, the myths and psychology of *la durée eternelle*. Thus the record of calamities must be kept alive: the immense flood of 1274, the cruel winter of 1494. This history was researched and written when modern Venice was coping with the consequences of the great flood and *la grande paura*, its own modern anguish.

The Fire at La Fenice, 1996

Fires are remembered in this closely settled city, so dependent in its internal structures on wood. The second burning of the opera house La Fenice in 1996 immediately entered the annals of the city's significant events (fig. 243). The theatre was near to the completion of its restoration programme when on 30 January fire gutted it completely, leaving only the front façade – and its phoenix. As if to demonstrate the often-voiced fear that low or empty canals posed a threat to essential services, the fire

243 La Fenice on fire,
29 January 1996,
photograph by Loris
Barbazza.

brigade could not approach by water because of the blocking of the canals behind the theatre and the difficulty of access to the small piazza through narrow *calli* to the front. The excavations, so long requested, blocked the small canals around the theatre: cruel local headlines affirmed that 'the most important initiative of the Cacciari administration, the excavation of the *rii*', had condemned the theatre to death. The shock that fire and not water could so endanger Venice occasioned concern for the city overall, accentuating its vulnerability. The world press revived their accounts of dying Venice, even while they pledged financial support.

That this was an internal crime, a sabotage by the workmen on the site, came as a stunning revelation after extensive investigation. That Venice could be threatened so entirely from within its own ranks heightened its danger, reinforced the extent of corruption. Doubtless many relished yet another demonstration of the inexorable power of the elements closely linked with Venetian history. The institution had not been happy in preceding years: difficulties of personnel and administration had been regular headlines on regional news. The November 1992 season had failed to open with Rossini's *Moses* as scheduled, and the audience was sent home; *Norma* was booed off the stage; and strikes by the musician's union left an orchestra of only three players on one occasion.[209] But the disappearance of such a symbol of musical continuity in Venice stirred singers and public alike.

International attention focused on the fire as one of the world's most destructive conflagrations.[210] The loss of Selva's building and the archives of a great operatic tradition were mourned internationally. As with the fall of the Campanile, the question of rebuilding *dov'era com'era* was immediately raised. Even as the embers were cooling, a world appeal was launched. The disaster appeared to be on the same scale as the collapse of the Campanile, bringing with it memories of the late Republic and the historic vitality of Venetian opera, a vitality too often regarded as lost in the 1990s.[211] Led by Luciano Pavarotti, famous voices sang their laments.

Cacciari, as mayor, announced the rebuilding with all speed, insisting it was a symbol of rebirth and, not least (and ironically), a boost to employment. Pilgrims, headed by President Scalfaro, came to the ruins to pay their respects. In the climate of scepticism surrounding the disbursal of funds, Cacciari found it necessary to indicate that international funds for La Fenice *would* reach their destination and that safeguards and co-ordinated policies for its restoration were in place.[212] As discussion took place to decide on the timetable for rebuilding, it might be well to recall the speedy construction of the first Fenice which took twenty-seven months, including demolition on the site and painting, and brought fame to its architect Giannantonio Selva.[213] Equally speedy was the rebuilding after the fire of 1836.

Paolo Portoghesi, president of Biennales and director of the first architectural Biennale, *The Presence of the Past*, called for a rebuilding of the original Selva theatre substantially altered in Meduna's rebuilding after 1836. A majority of architects opted for total renewal, and modernisation of equipment.[214] Some – like Portoghesi – wanted the ruins of the old theatre to be left intact. Even Aldo Rossi wanted the building 'exactly as it was before the fire'.[215]

A competition was held to appoint appropriate architects within given parameters: to rebuild *com'era*, but to modernise in the interests of an up-to-date theatre. The winners, Gae Aulenti and Antonio Foscari, were noted for their interventions within historic buildings, including the redevelopment of the Palazzo Grassi by Fiat in 1985.[216] For La Fenice, the date of completion was at first set for late 1999.[217] The project: to restore those parts still standing, the façade, mainly, and to overhaul and update scene-changing equipment, the accommodation of the orchestra, and so on.

The only clear voice of dissent was that of architectural historian Lionello Puppi, who saw the anomaly within the city's recent self-propaganda:

It is extraordinary and worrying that, just as everyone is talking about Venice and the Modern movement, and Modern art in Venice, the city should be faced with a highly meaningful disaster that provides an opportunity to demonstrate its capacity for renewal in word and deed. Now, when she could be opening herself at last to the modern world, Venice talks of nothing but a stale, reactionary return to the status quo . . . If we are of the opinion that Venice could and should have a significant role in the modern world then, for crying out loud. Where it was, yes, certainly, and bearing the scars of the catastrophe (the shell that has survived); but not as it was, even if simply to demonstrate clearly and convincingly that Venice intends to proceed creatively into the modern world rejecting mortality, mummification and decomposition.[218]

Thus Puppi espoused the 'incomplete city', but once again Venice endorsed the past. Puppi's logic was incontrovertible, entirely within the spirit of the guidelines of the advocates of Venice 2000. But in the face of fire and water, the impulse must be to conserve and defend a past that has proved so seductive, so lucrative. Even so, direct proceedings seem impossible in Venice. Difficulties over the tender thwarted the programme, stopping the contract for rebuilding.[219] Meanwhile the sale of souvenirs endorsed by Woody Allen (remarried in the Venice he loves), proceeded in a specially built boutique near the ruins. Postcards of the fire joined the carnival postcards. It is reconfirmed that any monument in Venice may be recreated, and, indeed, that the city can only benefit from such exercises well-funded from outside.

The smell of burning prompted a sad memoir on the city written by a resident, the psychiatrist Antonio Alberto Semi. Venice had been going up in smoke, *Venezia in fumo, 1797–1997*, over the two significant centuries after the Republic.[220] In Semo's diagnosis, in which Freud 'the Master of Vienna' is often invoked, Venice has become a city generating symbols, living on myth passed from a material to a spiritual plane, but on the material plane, frustrating administration, fostering bisexuality and causing the depletion of population.[221] The undredged canals hoard Venetian faeces. It has become a necropolis, served by devoted necrophiliacs; and yet its citizens, in the spirit of Goldoni, smile in the face of the calamities of the last two hundred years.

But Venetian necrophilia is no less than the expression of the neurosis of the Western world.[222] Obsession with Venice follows: it has relevance for the conditions that Freud observed, particularly bisexuality in the anal phase. The smell of the burning of Fenice was but the odour of universal necrophilia.

The Assault on the Campanile, 12 May 1997

It has been observed many times that Venice can act now only through symbol, and that those actions are inevitably cast in the roles of the past. A further demonstration, fuelled with symbolic intent, occurred with a siege on the Campanile on the occasion of the two hundredth anniversary of the fall of the Republic.[223] The event was staged with meticulous planning and technological skill by a group of eight ('Gli Otti di San Marco') mature men, headed by Luigi Faccia. Their intention – to reconstitute the Serenissima in the Veneto – was announced in advance, mysteriously by pirate transmission to public television at 8 p.m. on 17 March 1997: a 'Veneto Serenissimo Governo, founded in 1989, intended to liberate the area of the Veneto and reconstitute the Government of the Serenissima.'[224] As a one-time historic nation of Europe, Venice must reclaim that status: 'Arouse your ancient Veneto spirit and onwards, onwards, for San Marco.'[225]

Plans had been in formulation since 1992: taking over the Palazzo Ducale, the symbolic centre of the Serenissima, was rejected, for an army would be needed.[226]

244 The assault on the Campanile, 12 May 1997.

Another plan was to use a helicopter to drop propaganda over Venice in imitation of D'Annunzio's flight over Vienna in 1918.[227] Finally, a siege of the Campanile was planned – and accomplished. The tank for the operation was loaded at the Tronchetto – the car ferry for the Lido; the ferry staff were directed to ship the tank to a point in the Piazzetta between the columns where it could disembark and be driven the short distance to the Campanile. The siege took place three days before the anniversary of the fall of the Republic. Armed with machine guns, dressed in black and hooded, 'The Eight' arrived on Friday 9 May, and, at midnight, commanded the Campanile. Their tank, flying the standard of St Mark, soon impounded by police, stood symbolically in front of San Marco (fig. 244). Decisively controlled by the police from the morning of Saturday 10 May, fears of terrorism were soon dissipated, although the alarms made newspaper headlines. After the days of siege, the Eight were peaceably arrested. Analogies were drawn with the Futurist confrontation in 1910, but there was criticism of the threat of violence.

The formation of the Northern League and Umberto Bossi's object to establish the territory of Padania in secession from Rome is essential background to the exploits of the Eight. Bossi's Northern League expedition up the Po river to the Piazza San Marco to proclaim 'Padania', with Venice as its capital had taken place in September 1996.[228] That event was carefully defused, its impact negligible – except in the minds of *gli Otto*. Separatist ambitions were quickly attributed to 'the Eight', but Luigi Faccia declared that his group had proclaimed the independence of the Veneto before Bossi had proclaimed the independence of Padania.[229] It was Bossi's cue to renew his call for a Padania and a Lega Norda established by democratic means.

The siege of the Campanile involved no loss of life or damage, and only some hours of apprehension. In its futility, its careful planning, and its melange of absurdity and sincerity, it was a bizarre marker of the bicentennial occasion, no less poignant for being mounted by citizens from outside the historic city. It was an occasion that demonstrated to perfection Marx's view that history returns the second time as farce. Two hundred years after the fall, the eight bandits were captured and sentenced to between four and six years imprisonment.

AFTER TWO HUNDRED YEARS

On 20 April 1997 a poignant ceremony was held at the fort of Sant'Andrea, the scene of the firing of cannon against Napoleon's vessel entering the lagoon two hundred years earlier.[1] Now vacated by the military, the standard of St Mark flew again. Sanmichele's impressive rusticated building, which for some decades had been gradually sliding into the sea, could now be restored. Some three weeks later the arrival of Napoleonic rule was commemorated, on 12 May 1997.

The anniversary of the fall of the Republic was hardly to be celebrated with jubilation, but it was a shift of no little importance and under review in conferences and papers. The commemorations took place in a mood of acquiescence from Venetian contributors keen to highlight administrative excellence in the periods of French and Austrian rule. But after the spectacular history of independence in the Republic, Venice could only be weakened and compromised by foreign rule. Its verve had not been restored. The passing of two hundred years had seen the reduction of *Venetian* responsibility for the city – this has been observed many times.

Venice hosted conferences that examined the profit and loss of the past during the interregnum periods of French and Austrian rule, and its admission into the Italian state in 1866. The twentieth century was little examined. The Fondazione Cini hosted *Il 1797 e il metamorfosi di Venezia* with the optimistic subtitle: 'From state capital to city of the world.'[2] Papers pronounced on the decline of the aristocracy, the repercussions of the Enlightenment, Lorenzo da Ponte and Casanova, the Jewish community, Goethe and Wagner – the latter, a pre-eminent world citizen. In October a Fondazione Giorgio Cini conference focusing on Venice and Austria appeared to reflect only positively on the panorama of activity in the arts and politics during the Habsburg reign.[3] Exhibitions held during 1997 showed the years of transition from the aristocratic culture to the new order, from the doge to the Emperor Napoleon: *Dai dogi agli imperatori*.[4] *Venezia da stato a mito* took the iconography of Venice and its romantic and post-romantic activity in painting into the twentieth century.[5]

In November 1997 the Istituto di Scienze, Lettere ed Arti hosted a conference on the nineteenth century.[6] The *Memoirs* of the last doge, Lodovico Manin, were published, emphasising that he left office with honour.[7]

In the presence of their one-time captors around the conference table, the general tone of recall with relation to 1797 was polite. However Alvise Zorzi, author of the still-classic *Venezia scomparsa*, acknowledged in the press that the celebration of the fall of the Serenissima had aided the revaluation of rapport with the Terraferma, but took the opportunity to emphasise the 'artistic massacre' effected by Napoleon.[8] Further, the period of the Regno Italico from 1806 to 1814 had not empowered the Venetian bourgeoisie (and it might be argued that they have remained relatively impotent since that date). As well as experiencing the desecration of churches and their contents, Venice experienced the lowest economic and social point in its history as a result of the Napoleonic blockades. Some days earlier, in the context of the commemorations, a cultural officer, Gianfranco Mossetto, had stressed Napoleon's benefits and the positive nature of his transformation of the city's art and politics.[9]

Yet the aristocracy was destined to fall, and Venice was ill-prepared for convincing self-government. It could well be argued that this is still the case. Nevertheless, until now Venice *has* endured, fragile and vulnerable to the elements, corroded by water and atmospheric alteration, by tides high and low. That its intricate fabric in its many styles has been tolerated and conserved even to the degree it has is part of the marvel. That the international community has cared for Venice's restoration and survival is testimony not just to the power of its material past, but to the metaphysical symbolism embodied in the city. In spite of the decreasing number of Venetians and an economy contracted almost entirely to tourism, there is still residential life in Venice. But there is little agreement with regard to the city's future, only much discussion, resulting only in procrastination and obfuscation.

The very fact that Venice cannot accommodate the new is a consequence of its role as an allegory of ruin, actual to a marked degree, but also potential. Its stones crumble, sea threatens to submerge it. Yet its thrall cannot be broken, and indeed Venice is emblematic of the late twentieth century's preoccupation with ruin and traces. The dust accumulated in Walter Benjamin's Parisian arcades has its watery analogy in Venice. As a city, and as a system of government, Venice is the very embodiment of the abject, that quintessential post-modern state. The symptoms are melancholy, resignation, the simulacra transcending the real, the fascination with the fetish, which is the whole city and its history. Whatever the challenges mounted by architects with a belief in an unfinished Venice – the new bridges, a revamped Piazzale Roma, Renzo Piano's Magnet alongside the airport, the new Arsenale – they are but an impotent coda, postludes to a project thwarted and out of reach. A future cannot be comprehended, for survival itself is challenged. It is not the Gothic stones physically rotting in front of Ruskin in the nineteenth century, but the allegory of the city that represents all cities, and the impossible future. Venice is a victim of the Dionysian gaze, of Nietzsche's imposition that fills its one-time solitudes with both desire and death.[10]

Yet Venice *has* survived; the marble palaces are not yet level with the waters, but they have been more gravely threatened than ever before. The amount of restoration has been extensive, despite corruption and sabotage. In many parts of the city, although certainly not all, if the water rises, it laps against stone now freshly exposed. The main work has been the result of international programmes.

The city's reverberations in the imagination of that international world have persisted, even increased, and those reverberations have moved beyond the reactions of a Foscolo or a Canova to the events of 1797. The measure of creative thought provoked by the city must by now be in excess of any other place; the death of Venice has been one of the great tropes of modern times. It was *not* invented by Napoleon and reiterated by Lord Byron, Thomas Mann or Benjamin Britten, for it was already a perception in the seventeenth and eighteenth centuries, compounded, but not created by the fall of the Republic. Nor is *acqua alta*, or the continuing necessity for dredging anything new – these have always been challenges for the sea city. Venetians have always feared the vulnerability of their city and the lagoon, but they have also turned a beneficent face towards the waters, enhancing them, offering them compounding reflections, creating a scenography that is unique. If anxiety has been a prevalent condition in recent times, so it has been throughout the history of the Republic: recent historians have stressed that. They have worked to expose the anxiety in the past, but they have also confirmed the city's enduring utopic status.

Nor has the creativity of the city been the work only of foreign minds in recent times. For a small city, Venice has fostered considerable talents. In this century one need think only of Luigi Nono and Bruno Maderna in music, of Emilio Vedova, among the most powerful painters anywhere in the world (and winner of the Gold Lion at the 1997 Biennale) in the 1990s (fig. 245), of Carlo Scarpa – architect of infinite possibilities, as Luigi Nono described him – universally regarded as one of *the* modern masters, of P. M. Pasinetti's saga of the Partibon family. Many residencies have also been spectacular, particularly in the field of architecture and architectural

245 Emilio Vedova in his studio with the Disc 'Senza titolo 1996–7', preparing for his installation of the Vedova *sala*, Biennale d'Arte, 1997. Biennale di Venezia, Archivio Storico delle Arti Contemporanee.

history and theory: among them, Giuseppe Samonà, Manfredo Tafuri, Aldo Rossi. Massimo Cacciari is regarded as one of Italy's leading contemporary philosophers. Many centuries after Aldus Manutius, Venice still has a rich publishing industry. The house of Filippi is devoted to keeping historical material in print and has been responsible for many revivals of Ottocento work. The houses of Marsilio and Arsenale are exemplary in the publication of contemporary material.[11]

The end of the twentieth century appears but a compounding of the attitudes and actions already in place in the first decade. On the eve of the First World War the Futurists attacked Venetian moonlight, but the supply of electricity was already assured by entrepreneurial Venetians who were lighting the hotels and powering the trams on the Lido. Whatever the Futurists' opinion, tourism was seen as a viable industry; it expanded to applause in the 1920s and 1930s, and was fostered as a cultural initiative by Count Volpi. The dream of industrialisation was realised at the forefront of Italian activity: the creation of Marghera assured Venice's viability for at least the immediate future. No one foresaw that the tertiary development of Marghera would lead to gross pollution, or that the development of tourism would reach such a point that the city and residents would be intolerably affected – that Venetians would literally be driven out.

Venice has not fallen, but it is the victim of its very success. At the end of the century the advertisements flowed and the facsimile cities were under construction. A new hotel in Las Vegas rises above a Venetian complex built to scale to include the Palazzo Ducale, the Campanile, the Ca' d'Oro and the Rialto Bridge (fig. 250).[12]

246   Venice, Las Vegas, 1996.

The fragility of both the city and the lagoon have been a cause of local and international concern on a regular basis since 1797. It is hard to say whether the islands in the lagoon and their patrimony are any more at risk than they were in the time of Napoleon (it could be claimed that Napoleon's intervention assured the international protection of Venice), or that special problems affect Venice any more urgently than in other places in the world threatened by pollution, want of social services, and the general decline in quality of life for ordinary residents.

The weight of allegory lies heavily upon Venice. The result has been a resistance to change and the depletion of its population. The loss of the city for the Venetians is the result of too great a success for the rest of the world. It is, as one Venetian has claimed, 'the end of Venice as a city for Venetians'.[13]

Meanwhile the seas are rising.[14] In the city of the apocalypse the four golden horses are at the ready, pawing at the porch of San Marco, waiting to haul the city out of the waters and into the sky.

Notes

Introduction

1 Henri Lefebvre, *The Production of Space*, trans. Donald Nicholson-Smith, Basil Blackwell, Oxford, 1991.

2 Henry James, *Italian Hours*, William Heineman, London, 1909, p. 7.

3 Manfredo Tafuri, *Venice and the Renaissance* (1985), trans. Jessica Levine, MIT Press, Cambridge, Mass., and London, 1989.

4 Elizabeth Crouzet-Pavan, '*Sopra le acque salse*': *espaces, pouvoir et société à Venise à la fin du Moyen Age*, Ecole française de Rome, Pliniana, Perugia, 1992.

5 Guido Ruggiero, *The Boundaries of Eros: Sex, Crime and Sexuality in Renaissance Venice*, Oxford University Press, 1985. For the Casanova bicentenary, *Il mondo di Giacomo Casanova: un veneziano in Europa, 1725–1798*, Ca' Rezzonico, Venice. Marsilio, Venice, 1998.

6 Emmanuele Antonio Cicogna, *Saggio di bibliografia veneziana*, 2 vols (1847), Burt Franklin, New York, 1967. Cicogna was updated in 1885: *Bibliografia veneziana compilata da Girolamo Soranzo in aggiunta e continuazione del saggio di Emmanuele Antonio Cicogna*, Burt Franklin, New York, 1967.

7 Régis Debray, *Contre Venise*, Gallimard, Paris, 1995.

8 Tony Tanner, *Venice Desired*, Blackwell, Oxford, 1992.

9 Edward Said, 'Not all the Way to the Tigers: Britten's "Death in Venice"', *Critical Quarterly*, 41 (1999), p. 46.

10 Giovanni Distefano and Giannantonio Paladini, *Storia di Venezia, 1797–1997*, vol. 1, *Dai dogi agli imperatori*; vol. 2, *La dominante dominata*, Supernova-Grafiche Biesse, Venice, 1996; vol. 3, *Economia, politica, cultura, arte, religione, avvenimenti e protagonisti dall'inizio del secolo ai nostri giorni*, Supernova-Grafiche Biesse, Venice, 1997. Mario Isnenghi, 'Fine della storia', *Venezia itinerari per la storia della città*, Mulino, Bologna, 1997, pp. 405ff.

11 For example, Massimo Cacciari, *Architecture and Nihilism: On the Philosophy of Modern Architecture*, trans. Stephen Sartarelli, Yale University Press, New Haven and London, 1993; *Post-humous People: Vienna at the Turning Point* (1980), trans. Rodger Friedman, Stanford University Press, Ca., 1996.

Chapter 1

1 For the first historical accounts of the events terminating with the Republic and subsequent decades see Pietro Peverelli, *Storia di Venezia dal 1798 sino ai nostri tempi*, Castelazzo e De Gaudenzi, Turin, 1852; Girolamo Dandolo, *La Caduta della Repubblica di Venezia e i suoi ultimi cinquant'anni*, 2 vols, Studi Storichi, Naratovich, Venice, 1855–7. Samuele Romanin wrote the first comprehensive Italian history, closing with the entrance of the Austrians into the city on 18 January 1798, *Storia Documentata di Venezia* (1859), 10 vols, Filippi, Venice, 1975. Published 200 years after the fall of the Republic is Giovanni Distefano and Giannantonio Paladini, *Storia di Venezia, 1797–1997*, vol. 1, *Dai dogi agli imperatori*, Supernova-Grafiche Biesse, Venice, 1996. An accessible accounts of the Napoleonic conquest is given by Angus Herriot, *The French in Italy, 1796–1799*, Chatto & Windus, London, 1957. There is no detailed history of the Venetian eighteenth century and the close of the Republic in English, but see the valuable John Cushman Davis, *The Decline of the Venetian Nobility as a Ruling Class*, Johns Hopkins University Press, Baltimore, 1962. The standard modern work in English on the Republic, covering its many centuries, is John Julius Norwich, *A History of Venice*, Penguin, Harmondsworth, 1983, which treats 'The Fall' in the final chapter and the Epilogue, 'The Fall (1789–1797)', pp. 605–39. See also Christopher Hibberd, *Venice: The Biography of a City*, Grafton Books, London, 1988, ch. 12, 'Napoleonic Interlude, 1789–1814', pp. 185–96. Fundamental for the focus on architecture and urbanism from the late eighteenth century to the nineteenth century is Giandomenico Romanelli, *Venezia Ottocento: l'architettura l'urbanistica*, Albrizzi, Venice, 1988.

2 See Romanin, *Storia documentata di Venezia*, pp. 76–82. Norwich gives a succinct account, quoting Napoleon's dispatch, *History of Venice*, pp. 625–7.

3 For the documentation, and indication that Pizzamano now has the status of a minor hero, Andrea da Mosta, *Domenico Pizzamano: un uomo di mare veneziano contro Napoleone*, Editoria Universitaria, Venice, 1997.

4 *Letters and Documents of Napoleon*, vol. 1, *The Rise to Power*, selected and trans. John Eidred Howard, Cresset Press, London, 1961: letter 236, 30 April 1797, p. 184.

5 Ibid., pp. 184–5.

6 *An Accurate Account of the Republic of Venice and the True Character of Bonaparte*, translated from the manuscript of Vittorio Barzoni's *Rivoluzione della Repubblica Veneta*, published by John Hinckley, J. Hatchard, London, 1804, p. 77. This is a work of extreme rhetorical fervour, but it is accurate in terms of events and dispatches.

7 Ibid., p. 247.

8 Napoleon, 'Affaires de Venise', in *Recueils des pièces authentique sur le Captif de Saint-Hélène*, vol. 4, A. Corréard, Paris, 1822, p. 16: 'Ces imputations n'ayant point trouvé de contradicteurs contemporains, il est devenu important de le repousser, pour ne pas laisser plus longtemps l'erreur à la place de la vérité'.

9 Ibid., p. 241 and p. 255.

10 Ibid., pp. 275ff.

11 For the conspicuous presence of Venetian musicians in London see Frederick C. Petty, *Italian Opera in London, 1760–1800*, UMI Research Press, Ann Arbor, Mi., 1972, passim.

12 Joseph Rykwert, *The First Moderns: The Architects of the Eighteenth Century* (1980), MIT, Cambridge, Mass., and London, 1983, p. 288. On the Lodoli circle, pp. 288–337. Rykwert's account is exemplary, presenting the eighteenth-century Venetians as 'Moderns' as distinct from the 'last decadent flowering' treatment given in even such a magisterial study as Francis Haskell's *Patrons and Painters: Art and Society in Baroque Italy. A Study in the Relations between Italian Art and Society in the Age of the Baroque* (1963), Yale University Press, New Haven and London, 1980, see part II, 'Venice', pp. 245–383.

13 *Piranesi tra Venezia e l'Europa*, ed. Alessandro Bettagno, Leo S. Olschki, Florence, 1983. See especially Lionello Puppi, 'Appunti sulla educazione veneziana di Giambattista Piranesi', pp. 217–55. Rykwert regards Piranesi as 'Lodoli's most brilliant and most influential pupil', *The First Moderns*, p. 315.

14 Haskell gives an account in *Patrons and Painters*, pp. 249–67.

15 Massimo Gemin, 'Il Canal Grande di Venezia nel Settecento. La Teatralizzazione d'uno spazio vuoto', *Scritti in onore di Nicola Mangini*, Quaderni di Venezia Arti 2, Viella, Rome, 1994, p. 52, and subsequent discussion of the work of Massari, Temanza, Selva, et al. Paolo Polledri has argued for a dynamic as against a static notion of architecture and urbanism in the eighteenth century: 'Urbanism and Economics: Industrial Activities in Eighteenth Century Venice', *Journal of Architectural Education*, 41 (1988), pp. 15–19.

16 On the opus, Antonio Massari, *Giorgio Massari: architetto veneziano del Settecento*, Neri Pozza, Vicenza, 1971. On the decoration of the Pietà (noting the likely influence of Algarotti's Enlightenment views on Tiepolo), Deborah Howard, 'Giambattista Tiepolo's Frescoes for the Church of the Pietà in Venice', *Oxford Art Journal*, 9 (1986), pp. 11–28.

17 The decoration of the Ospedaletto music room was the collaborative work of Jacopo Guarana and perspective painter Agostino Mengozzi-Colonna: Michael Levey, *Painting in Eighteenth-Century Venice*, (1959) Phaidon, London, 1980, pp. 74–6. For the culture, architecture and decoration of the Ospedali: Bernard Aikema and Dulcia Meijers, *Nel regno dei poveri: arte e storia dei grandi ospedali veneziani in età moderna, 1474–1797*, Arsenale, Venice, 1989.

18 The Murazzi were under construction from 1744 until 1782, from plans by mathematician Bernardino Zendrini, following the concept of Vincenzo Coronelli. See S. Ciriacono: 'L'Idraulica Veneta; scienza, agricoltura e difesa del territorio, dalla prima alla seconda rivoluzione scientifica', *Storia della cultura Veneta: il Settecento*, vol. 5, part 2, ed. Girolamo Arnaldi and Manlio Pastore Stocchi, Neri Pozza, Vicenza, 1986, pp. 366–8.

19 J. W. von Goethe, *Italian Journey* (1816–29), trans. W. H. Auden and Elizabeth Mayer, Penguin, Harmondsworth, 1962, p. 99.

20 Peter Burke discusses the carnival over a wide-ranging period in 'Le Carnival de Venise, esquisse pour une histoire de longue durée', *Les Jeux à la Renaissance: études réunies par Philippe Ariés et Jean-Claude Margolis*, Librairie Philosophique, J. Vrin, Paris, 1982, pp. 55–64. See also L. Padoan Urban, 'Il carnevale veneziano',

Storia della cultura Veneta: il Settecento, vol. 5, part 1, ed. Girolamo Arnaldi and Manlio Pastore Stocchi, Neri Pozza, Vicenza, 1986, pp. 631–46.

21 Philippe Monnier, *Venice in the Eighteenth Century* (1907) trans. Philippe Monnier, Chatto & Windus, London, 1910, p. 19.

22 Stendhal, *Life of Rossini* (1824), trans. Richard N. Coe, Caldar & Boyars, London, 1970, p. 197.

23 Giacomo Casanova, *History of My Life*, trans. Willard R. Trask, Johns Hopkins University Press, Baltimore and London, 1997, vol. 1, p. 49.

24 Piero Del Negro considers Baffo's contemporary reputation and his political writings in exemplary detail in 'La "Poesia Barona" di Giorgio Baffo "Quarant'otto"', *Comunità*, 184 (1982), pp. 312–428.

25 Giorgio Baffo, *Poesie*, ed. Piero Chiari, Arnaldo Mondadori, Milan, 1974, p. 320.

26 *Nell'elezione del Papa Rezzonico*, ibid., p. 148; *Per la Soppression dei Gesuiti*, p. 318.

27 Ibid. p. 25, and for Del Negro's insights into the Querini sonnets, 'La "Poesia Barona" di Giorgio Baffo "Quarant'otto"', p. 408ff.

28 For a view that Lorenzo da Ponte 'lived his life with much the same adventurous opportunism that characterises his *buffa* creations', Andrew Steptoe, *The Mozart–Da Ponte Operas: The Cultural and Musical Background to Le Nozze di Figaro, Don Giovanni and Così fan Tutte*, Clarendon Press, Oxford, 1988, esp. p. 98ff.

29 See Tiziana Rizzo, *La Biondina in gondoleta: Marina Querini Benzon, una nobildonna a Venezia tra '700 e '800*, Neri Pozza, Vicenza, 1994. For a more salacious account, Claudio Dell'Orso, *Venezia Erotica: Illustrated Guide*, Glittering Images, Florence 1995, pp. 58–65, with translation.

30 The diffusion of the song is detailed in Kurt Adel, 'La Biondina in Gondoleta', *Osterreich in Geschichte und Literatur mit Geographie*, 11 (1974), pp. 86–102.

31 For Simon Mayr's career in Venice, John Stewart Allitt, *J. S. Mayr Father of Nineteenth-Century Italian Music*, Element Books, Shaftesbury, Dorset, 1989, pp. 40–51.

32 Stefania Bertelli gives an invaluable discussion of both foreign and Venetian reactions, finding the Venetians themselves quite cynical with regard to carnival: 'Il Carnevale nel mito del Settecento veneziano', *Studi Veneziani*, 10 (1986), pp. 137–70.

33 The well-developed tradition of the guidebook served as both a local record and a handbook for the *forestieri*: see Margaret Plant, '"No one enters Venice

as a Stranger", a History and Theory of (Venetian) Guidebooks', *Transition: Discourse on Architecture*, 34 (1991), pp. 56–80.

34 On the pictorial industry for tourists, Ilaria Bignamini and Giorgio Marini, 'Venice', *Grand Tour: The Lure of Italy in the Eighteenth Century*, ed. Andrew Wilton and Ilaria Bignamini, Tate Gallery, London, 1996, pp. 186–7. See also Bruce Redford, *Venice and the Grand Tour*, Yale University Press, New Haven and London, 1996.

35 *Forestiere illuminato intorno le cose più rare e curiose della città di Venezia e dell'isole circonvicine* (1740), Arnaldo Forni, Bologna, 1984, pp. 331–43.

36 William Barcham, 'Townscapes and Landscapes', *The Glory of Venice: Art in the Eighteenth Century*, ed. Jane Martineau and Andrew Robison, Yale University Press, New Haven and London, 1994, pp. 93–111.

37 For example, *Luca Carlevaris: le Fabriche e vedute di Venezia* (1703), ed. Isabella Reale, Marsilio, Venice, 1995.

38 In 1766, Canaletto represented the principal ceremonies that were engraved by Antonio Visentini. For Guardi's dogal festivities painted between 1766 and 1770 alluding to the election of Doge Alvise IV Mocenigo in 1763, see Arnauld Brejon de Lavergnée and Dominique Thiébaut, *Catalogue sommaire illustré des peintures du Musée du Louvre*, vol. 11, *Italie, Espagne, Allemagne, Grande-Bretagne et divers*, Editions de la Réunion des musées nationaux, Paris, 1981, pp. 185–6.

39 Canaletto and Antonio Visentini, *Le Prospettive di Venezia: urbis Venetiarum prospectus celebriorires* (J. B. Pasquali, 1842), Vianello Libri, Mestre, 1984.

40 The *Sensa* and other festivals are investigated in the now-classic study, Edwin Muir, *Civic Ritual in Renaissance Venice*, Princeton University Press, 1981. On the tradition of ceremonial welcomes, Patricia Fortini Brown, 'Measured Friendship, Calculated Pomp: The Ceremonial Welcomes of the Venetian Republic', *Triumphal Celebrations and the Rituals of Statecraft*, Papers in Art History from the Pennyslvania State University, 4, part 1, ed. Barbara Wisch and Susan Scott Munshower, Pennsylvania State University, University Park, 1990, pp. 136–86.

41 Casanova, *History of My Life*, vol. 3, pp. 235–6.

42 Ibid.

43 Goethe, *Italian Journey*, p. 88.

44 Haskell, chap. 10, 'Foreign Influences', *Patrons and Painters*, pp. 276–316.

45 For Algarotti's commission, ibid., p. 357.

46 André Corboz, in a fascinating essay, writes of Canaletto *negating* Venice. Corboz also catches up the reverberations

for the future, for the analogous architecture proposed by Aldo Rossi, for example (discussed in part 2 below). See 'Venezia negata', *Le Venezie possibili: da Palladio a Le Corbusier*, ed. Lionello Puppi and Giandomenico Romanelli, Electa, Milan, 1985, pp. 71-7.

47 Michael Levey, for example, regards Canaletto as almost 'prosaic': *Painting in Eighteenth-Century Venice*, p. 113. A sustained revisionist view is offered in Andre Corboz, *Canaletto: una Venezia immaginaria*, Alfieri, Venice, 1985. A further challenge to the notion of artistic decadence in Venice in the eighteenth century occurred with the 1994 exhibition (and catalogue), *The Glory of Venice*, op. cit.

48 Dario Succi, 'Gli inizi vedutistici di Francesco Guardi, con cenni sui Capricci', *Guardi: metamorfosi dell'immagine* (Problemi Critici per Antonio, Francesco e Giacomo), Stamperia di Venezia, Venice, 1987, pp. 57-82.

49 See Dario Succi on the period 1765-70, which he calls 'I periodo "Drammatico"', *Francesco Guardi: itinerario dell'avventura artistica*, Silvana, Milan, 1993, p. 47ff.

50 See the bicentenary volume *Tiepolo*, ed. Keith Christiansen, Ca' Rezzonico, Venice; Metropolitan Museum of Art, New York, Abrahms, New York, 1996.

51 The Palazzo Ducale decoration in 1745 still expresses, according to Haskell, the 'most perfect illustration' of the view that Venice was still one of the great powers: *Patrons and Painters*, p. 246.

52 Longhi and Goldoni have traditionally been linked together: Goldoni himself made the connection: see Philip L. Sohm, 'Pietro Longhi and Carlo Goldoni: Relations Between Painting and Theater', *Zeitschrift für Kunstgeschichte*, 45 (1982), pp. 256-73. For Longhi, Giorgio Busetto, *Pietro Longhi, Gabriel Bella: scena di vita veneziana*, Bompiani, Milan, 1995. On Longhi's *vedutismo domestico*, Romanelli, 'Spazio pubblico e luoghi privati', *Le Venezie possibili: da Palladio a Le Corbusier*, p. 120.

53 See the sumptuous presentation in Alvise Zorzi, *Venetia Felix: Gabriel Bella, Chronicler of the Republic*, F. M. Ricci, Milan, 1989.

54 For the barcarolle, see chap. 3 below.

55 Extracts from a range of Venetian journals from the eighteenth century are found in Marino Berengo, *Giornale veneziani del Settecento*, Feltrinelli, Milan, 1962. For an overview on journalism: Marco Cuza, 'Giornali e Gazzette', *Storia della cultura Veneta: il Settecento*, vol. 5, part 1, pp. 113-29. For a view of the journals as fundamental to the dissemination of Enlightenment ideas in the Veneto,

Paolo Preto, 'L'Illuminismo Veneto', ibid., pp. 1-23, passim, and Paola Zambelli, 'Dibattiti culturali nel Settecento a Venezia', *Rivista critica di storia della filosofia*, 20 (1965), pp. 414-47.

56 See the republished Gasparo Gozzi, *La Gazzetta Veneta*, ed. Antonio Zardo, Sansoni, Florence, 1978.

57 Zambelli refers to Griselini throughout her 'Dibattiti culturali nel Settecento a Venezia', noting him as 'L'animatore del periodico, autore di una apologia del Sarpi e di un'anonima commedia in difesa della massoneria, nemico tenace del "fanatismo" ecclesiastico, era senza dubbio una figura interessante e chiaramente rappresentativa dell'illuminismo veneto', p. 434. Griselini had published an 18-volume *Dizionario delle arti e de'mestiere*, Fenzo, Venice, 1768.

58 For extracts and comments on these journals and their writers, see again Berengo, *Giornale Veneziani del Settecento*.

59 Piero Del Negro, 'Gasparo Gozzi e la politica veneziana', *Gasparo Gozzi: il lavoro di un intellettuale nel Settecento veneziano*, ed. Ilaria Crotti and Ricciarda Ricorda, Antenore, Padua, 1989, p. 51.

60 See Canova's 'Abbozzo di biografia 1804-05', *Scritti: edizione nazionale delle opere di Antonio Canova*, ed. Hugh Honour, Istituto Poligrafico e Zecca dello Stato, Rome, 1994, pp. 296-319. For specific consideration of Canova in relation to Venice, Giuseppe Pavanello, 'The Venetian Canova', and Giandomenico Romanelli, 'A Yearning for Home', *Canova*, ed. Giuseppe Pavanello and Giandomenico Romanelli, Marsilio, Venice, 1992, pp. 45-50 and 53-9. In the same volume, Irene Favretto draws attention to the importance of Venetian collections of antiquities inspirational to Canova: 'Reflections on Canova and the Art of Antiquity', pp. 61-6.

61 See essays on these writers in *Studi Canoviani*, 1. *Le Fonti*, 2. *Canova e Venezia*, 2 vols, Bulzoni, Rome, 1973.

62 This is an abbreviated account of Venetian commissions and patronage: see Giuseppe Pavanello, 'The Venetian Canova', *Canova*, pp. 45-60, and Romanelli, 'A Yearning for Home', pp. 53-9.

63 Canova, 'Abbozzo di biografia, 1804-05', *Scritti: edizione nazionale delle opere di Antonio Canova*, p. 297. On these early sculptures, Pavanello, *Canova*, pp. 218-25, and for the Giovanni Falier stele which he worked on between 1805 and 1808, pp. 210-11.

64 For the Emo commission, Canova, 'Abbozzo di biografia, 1804-05', *Scritti: edizione nazionale delle opere di Antonio Canova*, p. 306.

65 The assertive central column of the final bust differs from the more diffuse

placements in early sketches, see *Venezia nell'età di Canova, 1780-1830*, ed. Elena Bassi et al., Alfieri, Venice, 1978, p. 65.

66 On Emo's floating batteries, Frederic C. Lane, *Venice: A Maritime Republic*, Johns Hopkins University Press, Baltimore, 1973, p. 421.

67 Cf. Giovanni Pindemonte, 'Sul momento del Cav. a proc. Emo, opera del celebre Canova', in Guy Dumas, *Echos de la chute de la République de Venise dans la littérature populaire* (Testes inédits ou rares), Bretonne, Rennes, 1961, p. 217.

68 Canova, 'Abozzo di biografia', *Scritti: edizione nazionale delle opere di Antonio Canova*, p. 306.

69 Giuseppe Pavanello, 'La Decorazione neoclassica nei palazzi veneziani', *Venezia nell'età di Canova, 1780-1830*, p. 281.

70 Cited by Elena Bassi, *Giannantonio Selva: architetto veneziano*, Leo S. Olschki, Florence, 1935, p. 5.

71 On the Cappello apartment and Selva, ibid., p. 285, and Riccardo Bratti, 'Appartamento del Procuratore Cappello', *Antonio Canova: nella vita artistica privata*, R. Deputazione, Venice, 1919, pp. 30-36. On the occasional of the opening of Cappello's apartment Saverio Bettinelli, scholar-writer from Mantua, gave a eulogy.

72 Fernando Mazzocca, 'Canova: A Myth in His Own Lifetime', *Canova*, p. 80.

73 See again Rykwert, *The First Moderns: The Architects of the Eighteenth Century*, and the significant exhibition and catalogue *Venezia nell'età di Canova, 1780-1830*.

74 For the diffusion of Masonic influence, Renata Targhetta, 'Ideologia Massonica e sensibilità artistica nel Veneto Settecentesco', *Studi Veneziani*, 16 (1988), pp. 171-211, in which Temanza's thought is specifically connected with Masonic interests in the circle of Consul Joseph Smith which he frequented: see pp. 199-203.

75 A valuable reassessment of Temanza is offered in Patrizia Valle, *Tommaso Temanza e l'architettura civile, Venezia e il Settecento: diffusione e funzionalizzazione dell'architettura*, Officina, Rome, 1989.

76 Ibid., p. 121. See again Targhetta, 'Ideologia massonica e sensibilità artistica nel Veneto Settecentesco', pp. 199-203.

77 Valle, 'L'Idraulica Veneta', *Tommaso Temanza e l'architettura civile*, pp. 54-62.

78 Tommaso Temanza, *Vite dei più celebri architetti e scultori veneziani che fiorirono nel Secolo Decimosesto* (1778), Labor, Milan, 1976.

79 For Temanza's *Antica Pianta dell'inclita città di Venezia*, 1781, Giocondo

Cassini, *Piante e vedute prospettiche di Venezia (1479–1855)*, Stamperia di Venezia, Venice, 1982, pp. 162–3.

80 David Kimbell takes this to be a formative event in the history of opera when *Andromeda* was performed with music by Francesco Manelli and Benedetto Ferrari's libretto: *Italian Opera*, Cambridge University Press, 1991, p. 112.

81 Ellen Rosand, *Opera in Seventeenth-Century Venice*, University of California, Berkeley, 1991.

82 The principal theatres were Sant'Angelo, San Bendetto (San Benedetto), San Moisè, San Samuele, San Giovanni Grisostomo, San Luca, San Cassiano. See Nicola Mangini, *I teatri a Venezia*, Murisa, Milan, 1974.

83 See the standard work: Eleanor Selfridge-Field, *Venetian Instrumental Music from Gabrieli to Vivaldi*, Praeger, New York, 1975. For a brief account, chap. 9, 'Vivaldi and the Eighteenth Century', H. G. Robbins Landon and John Julius Norwich, *Five Centuries of Music in Venice*, Thames & Hudson, London, 1991, pp. 109–38. See also *Antonio Vivaldi da Venezia all'Europa*, ed. Francesco Degrada and Maria Teresa Muraro, Electa, Milan, 1978.

84 Francesco Algarotti, 'Saggio sopra l'opera in musica', *Illuministi italiani*, vol. 11, *Opera di Francesco Algarotti e di Savverio Bettinelli*, *Stori e testi*, ed. Ettore Bonova, Riccardo Riccardi, Milan and Naples, 1969, pp. 435–80. David Kimbell discusses 'Algarotti and the Reform of Opera Seria', in *Italian Opera*, pp. 229–31. Kimbell says of Algarotti, he was 'a man one is tempted to describe as emblematic of eighteenth-century Italian cultural life'. Haskell considers Algarotti in *Patrons and Painters*, chap. 14, pp. 347–60.

85 Tom Laurenson discusses the box in terms of the social life of the times, and Milizia's objections in 'The Ideal Theatre in the Eighteenth Century: Paris and Venice', *Drama and Mimesis*, Cambridge University Press, 1980, pp. 58–61.

86 Goethe, *Italian Journey*, pp. 100–1, in which Goethe gives a sustained account of his experience of seeing *Le Baruffe chiozzotte* at the Teatro San Luca. From the vast bibliography of writings on Goldoni, perhaps most elegantly relevant in this context is Diego Valeri, 'Venezianità e universalità di Goldoni', *Sensibilità e razionalità nel Settecento*, vol. 2, ed. Vittore Branca, Sansoni, Florence, 1967, pp. 463–73.

87 Quoting *Mirandolina* in Carlo Goldoni, *The Venetian Twins, The Artful Widow, Mirandolina, The Superior Residence*, trans. Frederick Davies, Penguin, Harmondsworth, 1968, p. 233.

88 Manilio Brusatin and Giuseppe Pavanello, *Il Teatro La Fenice: i progetti,*

l'architettura, le decorazioni, Albrizzi, Venice, 1987. See also Loredano Olivato, 'Progetti di teatri', *Le Venezie possibili: da Palladio a Le Corbusier*, pp. 122–33. For a sumptuous presentation with short essays in English, Giandomenico Romanelli, Giuseppe Pugliese, José Sasportes, Patricia Veroli, photographs Graziano Arici, *Gran Teatro La Fenice*, Benedick Taschen, Cologne, 1999. The later fires will appear below.

89 See Olivato, 'Progetti di teatri', *Le Venezie possibili: da Palladio a Le Corbusier*, pp. 122–33 (including the later development of La Fenice).

90 For Temanza's designs, ibid., pp. 126–27.

91 Haskell regards Memmo as the most 'enlightened' member of the Venetian aristocracy. He was Provveditore at Padua where he created the Prà della Valle (or Prata della Valle) and, after ambassadorial service in Constantinople and Rome, became Procuratore di San Marco. See *Patrons and Painters*, pp. 364–68. Memmo's involvement in the subsequent project for La Fenice is made clear in his pamphlet of 1789, *Semplici lumi tendenti a render cauti i soli interessati nel Teatro da erigersi nella Parocchia di S. Fantino in Venezia*, extracted in Maria Teresa Muraro, *Gran teatro La Fenice*, Corbo e Fiore, Venice, 1996, pp. 106–7.

92 For Bianchi's designs, Olivato, 'Progetti di Teatri', *Le Venezie possibili: da Palladio a Le Corbusier*, pp. 128–9.

93 See Guardi's sketch, Antonio Morassi, *Guardi: tutti i disegni di Antonio, Francesco e Giacomo Guardi*, Alfieri, Venice, 1975, p. 409.

94 In general: John Rosselli, *The Opera Industry in Italy from Cimarosa to Verdi: The Role of the Impresario*, Cambridge University Press, 1984, pp. 84–94, with application to later years also.

95 For Selva, the seminal monograph remains Elena Bassi, *Giannantonio Selva: architetto veneziano*. Selva's description to accompany his model submitted to the competition is published in Muraro, *Gran teatro La Fenice*, pp. 88–93. For the Bianchi project, Olivato, 'Progetti di teatri', pp. 130–31. On the controversy between Bianchi and Selva: Thomas Bauman, 'The Society of La Fenice and its first Impresarios', *Journal of the American Musicological Society*, 39 (1986), p. 334.

96 For these works, Bassi, *Giannantonio Selva: architetto veneziano*, 'Le prime opere', p. 43ff.

97 Ibid., pp. 45–6.

98 Ibid., p. 47.

99 Kathleen Kuzmick Hansell, 'Pacchierotti [Paachiarotti], Gasparo [Gaspare]', *New Grove Dictionary of Opera*, vol. 3, ed. Stanley Sadie, Macmillan, London, 1992, pp. 807–8.

100 On *I Giuochi di Agrigento*, Dino Foresio, *Paisiello: nella vita, nell'arte, nella storia*, Mandese, Taranto, 1985, pp. 13–134; Bauman, 'The Society of La Fenice and its first Impresarios', pp. 337–40; Muraro, *Gran teatro La Fenice*, pp. 107–10. For the important representation of ballet in opera programmes, José Sasportes, 'Dance at the Teatro La Fenice, 1792–1900', *Gran teatro La Fenice*, ed. Romanelli et al., p. 277ff.

101 Bauman, 'The Society of La Fenice', p. 350. Valuable in studying the revolutionary history of *opera seria* in Venice in the 1790s is Thomas Bauman, 'Alessandro Pepoli's renewal of the Tragedia per Musica', *I vicini di Mozart: il teatro musicale tra Sette e Ottocento*, ed. Maria Teresa Muraro, Leo S. Olschki, Florence, 1989, pp. 211–20 (which also comments on Sografi).

102 Daniela Goldin, *La vera Fenice: librettisti e libretti tra Sette e Ottocento*, Einaudi, Turin, 1985, pp. 53–6.

103 Diderot and Voltaire in particular: see Nicola Mangini, 'Il Teatro francese in Italia nel Secolo XVIII', *Drammaturgia e spettacolo tra Settecento e Ottocento: studi e ricerche*, Livana, Padua, 1972, pp. 1–2.

104 For an overview of the diffusion of French culture in the Veneto, Paolo Preto, 'L'illuminismo Veneto', *Storia della cultura Veneta: il Settecento*, vol. 5, part 1, pp. 1–45. See also *Parigi/Venezia: cultura relazioni, influenze negli scambi intellettuali del Settecento*, ed. Carlo Ossola, Leo S. Olschki, Città di Castello, 1998.

105 Franco Venturi gives a brilliant, succinct coverage in his article taking its title from Voltaire: 'Venise et, par occasion, de la Liberté', *The Idea of Freedom: Essays in Honour of Isaiah Berlin*, ed. Alan Ryan, Oxford University Press, 1979, pp. 195–210.

106 Marc-Antoine Laugier, *Histoire de la République de Venise depuis sa fondation jusqu'à présent*, 12 vols, Paris, 1759–68; and *Observations sur l'architecture*, The Hague, 1765. Byron refers to Laugier's history in his notes to *Marino Faliero*, (see chap. 3 below). There is surprisingly limited discussion of Laugier's Venetian history, but see the valuable 'Costituzione e storia; Marc-Antoine Laugier', by Franco Venturi in his *Settecento riformatore*, vol. 2, *La Repubblica di Venezia, 1761–1797*, Einaudi, Turin, 1990, pp. 157–74. For comments on Laugier's interest in Lodoli and Venetian architecture, p. 159ff.

107 The connection between Laugier and Algarotti has been observed only in broad terms: see Rykwert, *The First Moderns: The Architects of the Eighteenth Century*, p. 298.

108 Amelot de la Houssaie, Secretary to the French Ambassador at Venice, *The*

History of the Government of Venice wherein the Policies, Councils and Laws of that State are fully related; and the use of the Ballotting Box exactly described. English trans. published by John Starkey, London, 1677, unpag. introduction. I have modernised the spelling. Casanova prepared a refutation hoping to win favour from Venice when he was exiled: Giacomo Casanova, *Confutazione della storia del Governo Veneto d'Amelot de la Houssaie*, 3 vols, Amsterdam and Lugano, 1769.

109 Casanova's defence of Venice is discussed by Annibale Bozzòla, *Casanova illuminista*, Società Tipografica Editrice Modenese, Modena, 1965, p. 57ff. Bozzòla is interested in a Casanova of the Enlightenment as well as the bedroom.

110 Houssaie's work (clearly in an abridgement) was advertised on the cover of *Il Patriotismo illuminato omaggio d'un cittadino alla patria*, Pietro Brandolese, Padua, 1797.

111 Houssaie, *The History of the Government of Venice*, p. 233, which begins with 'A Discourse concerning the Chief Causes of the Decay of the Venetian Commonwealth'.

112 Ibid., p. 154.

113 See below for discussion of the Municipality.

114 Houssaie, *The History of the Government of Venice*, unpag. introduction.

115 Umberto Corsini, *Pro e contro le idee di Francia: la pubblicistica minore del triennio rivoluzionario nello stato Veneto e limitrofi territori dell'Arciducato d'Austria*, Istituto per la Storia del Risorgimento Italiano, Rome, 1990, p. 92.

116 Jean-Jacques Rousseau, *The Social Contract* (1762), trans. Maurice Cranston, Penguin, Harmondsworth, 1968, p. 115, p. 132.

117 Jean-Jacques Rousseau, Book 7, *The Confessions of Jean-Jacques Rousseau* (1765), trans. J. M. Cohen, Penguin, Harmondsworth, 1985, p. 279ff. For a focus on the Venetian period: Madeleine B. Ellis, *Rousseau's Venetian Story: An Essay upon Art and Truth in Les Confessions*, Johns Hopkins University Press, Baltimore, 1966.

118 Jean-Jacques Rousseau, *Dictionnaire de musique* (1768), Johnson Reprint, New York, 1969, p. 40. Rousseau surmised that free entry to all the theatres contributed to the formation of the gondoliers' high standard of taste.

119 Goethe, *Italian Journey*, p. 93.

120 *Oeuvres complètes de Voltaire*, vol. 18, *Dictionnaire philosophique*, Hachette, Paris, 1876, pp. 461–3.

121 Voltaire, *Candide* (1759), trans. John Butt, Penguin, Harmondsworth, 1947, p. 117.

122 On *Il Re Teodoro in Venezia* (and its Venetian set designs) see Foresio,

Paisiello: nella vita, nell'arte, nella storia, pp. 96–9. Alfred Einstein has a pleasant essay pointing up the likeness to Da Ponte's Mozart libretti: 'A "King Theodore" Opera', *Essays on Music*, Faber & Faber, London, 1958, pp. 195–99. Musicologists today are eager to point out the connections between *Il Re Teodoro in Venezia* and Da Ponte's libretti for Mozart, especially *The Marriage of Figaro*, see Daniela Goldin, *La vera Fenice*, p. 35.

123 From the English production publication of 1797, *Il Re Teodoro in Venezia*, D. Stuart, London, 1797, p. 108.

124 Le Baron Albert de Montesquieu, *Voyages de Montesquieu*, G. Gounouilhou, Bourdeau, 1894–6, vol. 1, p. 23: 'le peuple de Venise est le meilleur peuple du monde', and p. 22: 'Le premier coup d'oeil de Venise est charmant, et je ne sache point de ville où l'on aime le [sic] mieux être, le premier jour, qu'à Venise, soit par la nouveauté du spectacle ou des plaisirs.'

125 Cited by Venturi, 'Venise, et par occasion de Liberté', p. 195.

126 Alexandre Limojohn de Saint-Didier, 'Du Carnival', *La Ville et la République de Venise*, Guillaume de Luyne, Paris, 1680, p. 367ff.

127 Quoted David W. Carrithers, 'Not so Virtuous Republics; Montesquieu, Venice and the theory of Aristocratic Republicanism', *Journal of the History of Ideas*, 52 (1991), p. 267.

128 For a profile on Angelo Querini (and his country house at Altichiero as an Enlightenment project), Haskell, *Patrons and Painters*, pp. 368–72.

129 For an account of this debate, Venturi, 'Venice, et, par occasion, de Liberté', p. 205, drawing on sources from Pietro Francheschi and Nicolò Balbi, from manuscripts in the Museo Correr and the Biblioteca Marciana respectively. For further discussion of the connections with French theorists, Gaetano Cozzi, 'La Repubblica di Venezia e il Regno di Francia tra Cinquecento e Seicento: fiducia e sfiducia', *Venezia e Parigi*, Electa, Milan, 1989, pp. 113–44. On Montesquieu, see the important article by Carrithers, 'Not so Virtuous Republics', pp. 245–68. It should be noted that Venice in the eighteenth century was construed universally as an oligarchy: in the sixteenth century it was widely held to be a mixed state: a *stato misto*. On this point, Franco Venturi is helpful: 'Venise et, par occasion, de la liberté', p. 199.

130 Pierre Darù, *Histoire de la République de Venise*, 7 vols, Didot, Paris, 1819.

131 For Darù's career, Bernard Bergerot, *Daru: Intendant Général de la Grand Armée*, Bibliothéque Napoléonienne Tallandier, Paris, 1991. Darù's controversial interpretation of Venetian history will be discussed in later chapters.

132 Rousseau, *The Confessions*, Book 7, 1743–4, p. 300ff.

133 Cited in Florence Pellae-Bougnol, 'I Francesi al carnevale di Venezia', *Venezia e Parigi*, pp. 169–96.

134 G. Tasini, *Cenni storici e leggi circa il libertinaggio in Venezia dal Secolo Decimoquarto alla caduta della Repubblica*, Filippi, Venice, 1969, p. 115.

135 *Johann Wolfgang von Goethe's Roman Elegies and Venetian Epigrams: A Bilingual Text*, trans., with introduction, notes and commentaries L. R. Lind, University Press of Kansas, Lawrence, 1974. I refer to Epigrams 67, 68 and 69.

136 Epigram 103 (paginated according to Epigram), ibid.

137 Giacomo Casanova, *Histoire de ma fuite des prisons de la République de Venise, qu'on appelle les Plombs*, Leipzig, 1787.

138 Giampiero Bozzolato looks at Casanova's reputation in Paris in 'Casanova e Parigi', *Venezia e Parigi*, pp. 197–210.

139 Casanova has been celebrated and castigated across two centuries. More recently celebration has been the order: cf. Lydia Flem, *Casanova or the Art of Happiness* (1995), trans. Catherine Temerson, Allen Lane, The Penguin Press, Harmondsworth, 1998.

140 Cesare Beccaria, *On Crime and Punishment and Other Writings*, ed. Richard Bellamy, trans Richard Davis et al., Cambridge University Press, 1995.

141 Foucault gives Beccaria's treatise a conspicuous place in part 2 of his *Discipline and Punish: The Birth of the Prison* (1975), trans. Ian Sheridan, Penguin, Harmondsworth, 1991, p. 73ff.

142 Beccaria, *On Crime and Punishment*, p. 37.

143 For a detailed account of reactions to Beccaria in Venice, Gianfranco Torcellan, 'Cesare Beccaria a Venezia', *Rivista Storica Italiana*, 76 (1964), pp. 720–48. It should be noted that Torcellan follows the later *positive* dissemination of Beccaria's views in the Veneto, and the writer's own visit to Venice in 1768.

144 Ibid., p. 726. See also Haskell's assessment of Pasquali, *Patrons and Painters*, p. 336ff.

145 Beccaria himself noted Facchinei's work as he told Andre Morellet, writing to him in Paris, *Crime and Punishment*, pp. 125–6: 'This man (Facchinei of Corfu) wanted to gain the favour of the Venetian Republic by attacking a book which had been very harshly proscribed, in the belief that the book came from the pen of a Venetian subject involved in the opposition to the state inquisition in the recent troubles which took place in Venice.'

146 As is clear in Carlo Grimaldo, 'Venezia e Veneziani nel carteggio Verri', *Archivio Veneto*, 71 (1962), pp. 49–60.

For Pietro Verri's regard for Goldoni see Sergio Romagnoli, 'Goldoni e gli Illuministi', *Carlo Goldoni, 1793–1993*, ed. Carmelo Alberti and Gilberto Pizzamiglio, Regione del Veneto, Venice, 1995, pp. 55–78.

147 The phrase refers to Marguerite Yourcenar, *The Dark Brain of Piranesi and other Essays* (1959–61), trans. Richard Howard, Farrar, Straus, Giroux, New York, 1985, p. 66ff.

148 William Beckford of Fonthill, *Dreams, Waking Thoughts and Incidents*, ed. Robert J. Gemmett, Fairleigh Dickinson University Press, Rutherford, NJ, 1972, p. 124.

149 For Joseph Balsamo, known as the Comte de Cagliostro, see the rather fanciful Barbara Zolezzi and Elisabetta De Pieri, *Cagliostro a Venezia: racconti tra realtà e finzione*, Todaro Editore, Lugano, 1998.

150 Jacques Cazotte, *Le Diable amoreux* (1772), trans. as *The Devil in Love* Judith Landry, Dedalus, London, 1991; Friedrich Schiller, *Der Geisterseher*, trans. as *The Ghost-Seer*, Henry G. Bohn with a critical introduction by Jeffrey L. Sammons, Camden House, Columbia, 1992. The work was begun in 1786.

151 Byron's letter to John Murray, 2 April 1817, '*So Late into the Night': Byron's Letters and Journals*, ed. Leslie A. Marchand, John Murray, London, 1976, vol. 5, p. 203.

152 Sammons discusses the impact of Cagliostro, *The Ghost-Seer*, p. viiff.

153 Goethe, 'Venezianische Epigrammen', 68 and 69, presented in German and English, pp. 122–3 in *Goethe*, introduced and ed. by David Luke, Penguin, Harmondsworth, 1964, pp. 127–8.

154 For a balancing view of the positive actions of the Venetian government in the later eighteenth century, Madeleine V. Constable, 'Tradition and Innovation: Venice from the Post Revolution to Napoleon', *History of European Ideas*, 6 (1985), pp. 325–39.

155 10 June 1796, to Citizen Lambert, Quartermaster General of the Army of Italy, *Letters and Documents of Napoleon*, p. 134.

156 Giovanni Distefano and Giannantonio Paladino, *Storia di Venezia, 1797–1997*, vol. 1, *Dai dogi agli imperatori*, p. 48 and n. 35.

157 Napoleon to Lallement from Palmanova, 30 April 1797, *Letters and Documents of Napoleon*, p. 186.

158 Lodovico Manin, *Io, L'Ultimo Doge di Venezia*, Canal, Venice, 1997, p. 5.

159 Ibid.

160 Ibid., p. 11.

161 Cf. Dandolo, *La Caduta della Repubblica di Venezia ed i suoi cinquant'anni*, p. 94.

162 A detailed account of the events from 2 May to the 17 May is given in *Esatto Diario di quanto é successo dalli 2 sino à 17 Maggio 1797 nella caduta della Veneta Aristocratia Repubblica*, Basilea, 1797.

163 Ibid., p. xxix, 'il tumulto in tuta la città'. For the arming of the Rialto Bridge, p. xxiii.

164 For a measured account written two hundred years later, Giovanni Pillinini, *1797: Venezia 'Giacobina'*, Editoria Universitaria, Venice, 1997.

165 Cf. the early decree (4 June), 'Bando e sentenza della democrazia control gli aristocratici veneti', cited ibid., pp. 130–35.

166 Cf. Pillinini, 'Il Passaggio dei poteri', ibid. p. 29ff.

167 *Istruzione del Popolo Libero*, cited Manlio Pastore Stocchi, '1792–1797: Ugo Foscolo a Venezia', *Storia di cultura veneta*, vol. 6, *Dall'età Napoleonica alla Prima Guerra Mondiale*, Neri Pozza, Vicenza, 1986, p. 47. My translation.

168 J. H. Lasalle and A. M. Mallet-du-Pan, *Sur la Révolution de Venise et les affaires d'Italie: marchands du nouveautés*, Paris, 1797, passim.

169 Vittorio Barzoni, *Rivoluzioni della Repubblica Veneta*, Venice, 1800, cited by A. Bozzolà, 'Vittorio Barzoni: un antigiacobino Veneto', *Archivio Veneto*, 110 (1959), p. 33.

170 Carlo Goldoni, *The Coffee House*, bilingual ed., trans. Jeremy Parzen, Marsilio, New York, 1998, p. 177.

171 A fascinating collection has been assembled by Guy Dumas in *Echos de la chute de la République de Venise dans la littérature populaire (textes inédits ou rares)*. See also his invaluable *La Fin de la République de Venise, aspects et reflects littéraires*, Presses Universitaires de France, Paris, 1964.

172 G. Occioni-Bonaffons, 'La Repubblica di Venezia alla vigilia della rivoluzione francese', *Rivista storica Italiana*, 6 (1889), pp. 699–724. For the Consul Smith circle, Targhetta, 'Ideologia Masonica e sensibilità', pp. 199–203.

173 *Discorso che venne pronunziato nel momento che s'innalzò in Venezia l'Albero della Libertà della Città del Cittadino Dandolo, Dalle Stampe del Cittadino Giovanni Zatta, Registrato al Comitato di Pubblica Istruzione il 2 Guigno 1797*. Dandolo was a pharmacist, son of a converted Jew. His Jacobin circle included Giuseppe Compagnoni, Alessandro Pepoli, Francesco Apostoli and Sografi, see Paolo Preto's detailed profile, 'Un "Uomo Nuovo" dell'età Napoleonica: Vincenzo Dandolo politico e imprenditore agricolo', *Rivista storica Italiana*, 144 (1982), pp. 46–8.

174 Alberto Rizzi, 'I leoni marciani', *Scultura esterna a Venezia: corpus delle sculture erratiche all'aperto di Venezia e della sua laguna*, Stamperia di Venezia, Venice, 1987, pp. 57–71.

175 Cf. Il Cittadino Maniago, *Al Popolo di Venezia*, Giustino Pasquali, Venice, 1797; *Istruzione d'un cittadino a suoi fratelli*, Pietro Brandolese, Padua 1797. For the new vocabulary: liberty, equality, etc., Corsini, *Pro e Contro l'Idee di Francia*, pp. 92–109.

176 Melchior Cesarotti, 'Il Patriotismo illuminato', *Opere selecte*, vol. 1, *Operette estetiche e politiche*, ed. Giuseppe Ortolani, Felice Le Monnier, Florence, 1945, pp. 407–28.

177 For the satirical works, Giandomenico Romanelli, 'Tamquam leo Rugien', in *The Lion of Venice: Studies and Research on the Bronze Statue in the Piazzetta*, ed. Bianca Maria Scarfi, Albrizzi, Venice, 1990, pp. 224–33. A detailed bibliography appears in Stefano Pillinini, *Il Veneto governo democratica in tipografia: opuscoli del periodio della municipalità provisoria de Venezia (1797), comune di Venezia assessorato alla pubblica istruzione sistema bibliotecario*, Arti Grafiche Gasparoni, Venice, 1990.

178 Details of organisation and committee structure are given in Distefano and Paladini, *Storia di Venezia, 1797–1997*, vol. 1, *Dai dogi agli imperatori*, pp. 132–6. For the presidents, p. 253, and the membership, pp. 253–4. See also Giuseppe Gullino, 'La Conguira del 12 Ottobre 1797 e la fine della Municipalità a Venezia', *Critica Storica*, 14 (1979), pp. 545–618. For an invaluable profile of Municipal members, pp. 607–18.

179 The study of the music of the Municipality by Riccardo Carnesecchi is valuable well beyond its focus on music, as it studies events month by month: 'Cerimonie, feste e canti: lo spettacolo della "Democrazia Veneziana" dal Maggio del 1797 al Gennaio del 1798', *Studi Veneziani*, 24 (1992), pp. 213–318.

180 Ibid., p. 231.

181 Francesco Gallimberti and Dioganni de Pian, *I Pozzi e i Piombi di Venezia*, Museo Correr, Venice, 1797: see *Venezia nel'età di Canova, 1780–1830*, p. 153, and Paolo Mariuz, 'Francesco Gallimberti, Dai "Fasti veneziani" alle "Carceri sotterracquee"', *L'Europa delle corte: alla fine dell'Antica Regime*, ed. Cesare Mozzarelli and Gianni Venturi, Bulzoni, Rome, 1991, pp. 221–32.

182 Francesco Zanotto attempted to challenge the prison myths in his *I Pozzi e i Piombi: antiche prigioni di stato della Repubblica di Venezia*, F. Brizeghel, Venice, 1876. (See chap. 5 below.)

183 'Le donne per natura sono eguali, anzi superiori agli huomini': 'Discorso della Cittadina Annetta Vadori pronunciata della Società di Pubblica Istruzione di Venezia in occasione che fu invitata a

prestare il giuramento: viver libero o morire', Dumas, *Echos de la chute de la république de Venise*, pp. 162ff. Corsini discusses the emancipation of women, *Pro e contro l'idee di Francia*, pp. 120–25.

184 On the Tree of Liberty festivities, Carnesechi, 'Cerimonie, feste e canti: lo spettacolo della "Democrazia veneziana" dal Maggio del 1797 al Gennaio del 1798', pp. 234–8.

185 Pillini, *1797: Venezia 'Giacobina'*, p. 54.

186 For an account of Marina Querini Benzon and the festivities, Rizzo, *La Biondina in Gondoleta: Marina Querini Benzon, una nobildonna a Venezia tra '700 e '800*, esp. ch. 14, pp. 135–41.

187 Carnesechi, 'Cerimonie, feste e canti: lo spettacolo della "Democrazia Veneziana" dal Maggio del 1797 al Gennaio del 1798', p. 238.

188 Ibid., pp. 239–40. Pillinini notes some caution by Municipalists who considered the elevation of Baiamonte Tiepolo to a 'democrat' was a historical distortion.

189 Alvise Zorzi, *Venezia scomparsa*, Electa, Milan, 1984, p. 35. Zorzi's source for the Grandenigo episode is Zanetti, *Guida di Murano*, 1866, and for other ceremonies, Zanetti, *Storia popolare di Venezia*, 1870–71.

190 Cited in Carnesecchi, 'Cerimonie, feste e canti: lo spettacolo della "Democrazia Venezia", dal Maggio del 1797 al Gennaio del 1798', p. 242ff. Carnesecchi quotes from the *Carte pubbliche stampate ed esposte ne'loughi più frequentari della Città di Venezia*.

191 Ibid., p. 243.

192 *Discorso del Cittadino Raffael Vivante tenuto a'suoi connazionali*, in Corsini, *Pro e contro l'idee di Francia*, pp. 303–6.

193 Giandomenico Romanelli, 'Urbanistica giacobina; "Una esatta divisione democratica, prudente e filosofica per Venezia"', *Psicon*, 4 (1975), pp. 47–55.

194 Ibid., p. 53.

195 The theatre is the aspect of the Municipality which is best covered. With specific reference to Venice see Dumas, ch. 5, 'Le Théatre Démocratique à Venise', *La Fin de la République de Venise*, pp. 353–87; Cesare De Michelis, 'Teatro e spettacolo durante la municipalità provvisoria di Venezia, Maggio–Novembre 1797', *Venezia e lo spazio scenico*, Biennale di Venezia, Venice, 1979, pp. 55–67, and Riccardo Carnesecchi, who discusses the theatre in his 'Cerimonie, festi e canti: lo spettacolo della "Democrazia Venezia", Dal Maggio del 1797 al Gennaio del 1798', pp. 213–318. Milena Montanile publishes Giovanni Pindemonte's *Orso Ipato* and Antonio Simeone Sografi's *La Rivoluzione di Venezia* in *I Giacobini a teatro: segni e strutture della propaganda rivoluzionaria in Italia*, Società Editrice

Napoletana, Naples 1984, and gives a detailed bibliography on Jacobin theatre in Italy.

196 On *Gli Orazi e i Curiazi* (and later interpretations in Milan), see the sustained article by Giovanni Morelli, 'L'Utopia roversa; Visioni melodrammatiche di Venezia da Milano', *Venezia Milano: storia civiltà e cultura nel rapporto tra due capitali*, Electa, Milan, 1984, p. 185ff. Carnesecchi notes the continuing performances to illustrate revolutionary battles, 'Cerimonie, festi e canti', p. 218.

197 Marita P. McClymonds, 'The Venetian Role in the Transformation of Italian Opera Seria during the 1790s', *I vicini di Mozart*, pp. 221–40. Note particularly, p. 237: 'In 1797, the number of tragic endings and the amount of stage carnage suddenly increased in Venice, all within the context of the newly-formed Citizens' Republic.'

198 For *Tieste* see Ugo Foscolo, *Opere*, vol. 1, ed. Franco Gavazzeni, Riccardo Ricciardi, Milan and Naples, 1974, p. 43ff. For the reception of *Tieste*, with some modification of its early reputation, Nicola Mangini, 'La vita teatrale nella Venezia del Foscolo (e la rappresentazione del *Tieste*)', *Drammaturgia e spettacolo tra Settecento e Ottocento: studi e richerche*, pp. 45–66. Carlo Dionsotti considers *Tieste* to be one of the worst things Foscolo wrote, but it had the polemical importance of being a tragedy, on a Greek theme with a structure derived from Alfieri rather than Greek models: 'Venezia e il noviziato di Foscolo', *Appunti sui moderni: Foscolo, Leopardi, Manzoni e altri*, Società editrice il Mulino, Bologna, 1988, p. 43.

199 Foscolo born 1778, Manzoni born 1785, Leopardi born 1798.

200 Manlio Pastore Stocchi, '1792–1797: Ugo Foscolo a Venezia', pp. 21–58.

201 Bruno Rosada, 'Foscolo scolaro a Venezia', *Atti dei convegni foscoliani*, Istituto Poligrafico e Zecca dello Stato Libereria dello Stato, Rome, 1988, pp. 107–25.

202 Gilberto Pizzamiglio, 'Ugo Foscolo nel salotto di Isabella Teotochi-Albrizzi', ibid., pp. 155–170.

203 See p. 73 below.

204 For a sustained examination of Barzoni's writings and activities, see again Bozzòla, 'Vittorio Barzoni, un anti-giacobino Veneto' pp. 13–71, especially p. 28ff: 'Il Barzoni attivo e animoso polemista durante il Regime Democratico a Venezia'. On the opposition to the Municipality in general, and Vittorio Barzoni in particular, Isabella Palumbo Fossati Casa, 'Il cielo è oscuro: Inquietudini, tensioni e contraddizioni in città nei mesi della Municipalità Provvisoria. Aspetti dell'opposizione al governo demo-

cratico', *Dai dogi agli imperatori: la fine della Repubblica tra storia e mito*, Electa, Milan, 1997, pp. 43–50.

205 In 1807 Isabella Teotochi Albrizzi published her 'Portraits' (*Ritratti*) dedicated to her son, profiling the distinguished friends in her circle. It ran to three editions. For Vivent De-Non [*sic*], see p. 11ff in *Ritratti scritti da Isabella Teotochi Albrizzi*, based on editions of 1807 and 1826, Libri Scheiwiller, Milan, 1987, p. 6ff. For detailed discussion and bibliographies, Cinzia Giorgetti, *Ritratto di Isabella: studi e documenti su Isabella Teotochi Albrizzi*, Le Lettere, Florence, 1992.

206 For Francesco Aglietti, from the edition of 1826 which also included Canova and Lord Byron, ibid. p. 37ff.

207 Ugo Foscolo, *Poesie*, ed. Guido Bezzola, Rizzoli, Milan, 1987, pp. 298–9: 'questo sonetto fu scritto, quando Venezia oligarchica si decise neutra.' See also Giorgio Luti, 'Foscolo e la Rivoluzione Francese', *Revue des etudes italiennes*, 38 (1992), pp. 59–69.

208 Foscolo, *Poesie*, p. 398.

209 See chap. 3 below.

210 For the 'Verbali' of the Municipality sessions relevant to Foscolo (and which make vigorous reading): Ugo Foscolo, *Scritti, letterari e politici dal 1796 al 1808*, ed. Giovanni Gambarin, Felice Le Monnier, Florence, 1972, p. 13.

211 Ibid., p. 14.

212 Quoted in De Michelis, 'Teatro e spettacolo durante la Municipalità Provvisoria di Venezia', p. 56. My translation.

213 Guy Dumas details reactions to the productions in 'La première Occupation française et le Théatre a Venise (1797)', *Bollettino Storico Livornese*, 4 (1954), pp. 176–82.

214 The prologue appears in Dumas, *Echos de la chute de la République de Venise*, pp. 159–61. Mattia Butturini was an active writer for the Venetian theatre and an admiring friend of Giovanni Pindemonte.

215 Note Stocchi's comments on the Alfierism of Foscolo's *Tieste* in '1792–97: Ugo Foscolo a Venezia', p. 35: 'L'alfierismo di Tieste e considerato in genere come la più acuta manifestazione indiretta di adesione all'ideologia democratica, e infatti la conformità mimetica al modello, ostentato quasi fino alla parodia in tratti come la scena III dell'atto IV, mira a mutuarne una valenza attuale di messaggio antioligarchico dell'ambiente veneziano.' See also Cesare de Michelis, 'Nicolò Ugo Foscolo e il Teatro Giacobino Veneziano', *Letterati e lettori nel Settecento veneziano*, Leo S. Olschki, Florence, 1979, pp. 225–55.

216 Foscolo, *Scritti letterari e politici dal 1796 al 1808*, p. 27.

217 Cf. Jean Henry, 'Antonio Canova and Early Italian Nationalism', *La scultura*

nel XIX Secolo, Comité International d'Histoire, 6, Libreria Universitaria, Bologna, 1979, pp. 17–31.

218 Cesare de Michelis, 'Antonio Simone Sografi e la tradizione Goldoniana', *Letterati e lettori nel Settecento veneziano*, pp. 203–24.

219 Bauman, 'The Society of La Fenice', p. 350. On democracy overstretched see Carnesecchi, 'Cerimonie, Festi e Canti', p. 265ff.

220 James Cushman Davis describes Pindemonte as 'a colourful figure, a poet with democratic ideas, who came to Venice after the family had been ennobled, was elected to the Senate, and served honourably as podestà in Vicenza', in *The Decline of the Venetian Nobility as a Ruling Class*, p. 143.

221 Dumas, *La Fin de la République de Venise*, p. 151.

222 Giovanni Pindemonte, Documento N. I (Appendice), *Poesie e lettere*, raccolte da Giuseppe Biadego, Zanichelli, Bologna, 1883, p. 327. Davis, in *The Decline of the Venetian Nobility as a Ruling Class* recommends caution in accepting the view of a 'new' family having difficulties with the government at the time of the French Revolution (p. 143). See also Piero del Negro, 'Venezia allo specchio: la crisi delle istituzioni repubblicane negli scritti del patrizio 1670–1797', *Transactions of the Fifth International Congress of the Enlightenment*, II, The Voltaire Foundation, Taylor Institution, Oxford, 1980, p. 926.

223 The play appears in Milena Montanile, *I giacobini a teatro: segni e strutture della propaganda rivoluzionaria in Italia*, Società Editrice Napoletana, Naples, 1984, pp. 31–93. Compare Giovanni Pindemonte's sonnet *Il giorno 16 maggio 1797*, cited in Stocchi, '1792–1797, Ugo Foscolo a Venezia', p. 47.

224 Sografi's *La Rivoluzione di Venezia* appears in Montanile, *I giacobini a teatro*, pp. 95–121.

225 De Michelis, 'Antonio Simone Sografi e la tradizione Goldoniana', ibid., p. 220.

226 For the synopsis of the plot, I follow De Michelis, ibid., p. 218. See the detailed treatment of the pertinent events in Giuseppe Gullino, 'La conguira del 12 Ottobre 1797 e la fine della Municipalità a Venezia', pp. 545–617.

227 Carnesecchi, 'Cerimonie, festi e canti: lo spettacolo della "Democrazia Veneziana", dal Maggio del 1797 al Gennaio del 1798', pp. 253–8.

228 Romanin, *Storia documentata di Venezia*, vol. 10, pp. 162–3.

229 Bembo's nostalgia is an emblematic case for the mood not just of Venetian life in the later Municipality, but its literature in the view of Manlio Pastore Stocchi,

'Tra "Paterno Governo" e parricidio: sentimento civile e inflessioni della letteratura del tramonto della Serenissima Repubblica', *Atti dell'Istituto Veneto di Scienze, Lettere ed Arti*, 154 (1995–6), pp. 773–4. The tears were provoked by the proposal for a Casa Patria to look after religious establishments and public assistance, to be chaired by the ex-doge Ludovico Manin.

230 For the Decreto della Municipalità with regard to the Viva San Marco, to publish material contrary to the authority of the government, etc. (24 July 1797), Pillinini, 1797: *Venezia 'Giacobina'*, pp. 138–9.

231 The list is published in Pillinini e Distefano, *Storia di Venezia 1797–1997*, vol. 1, *Dai dogi agli imperatori*, pp. 19–191.

232 For these intricate events, see again Gullino, 'La Conguira del 12 Ottobre 1797'.

233 For the preliminary Treaty of Leoben between Austria and France (18 April 1797; with 11 secret articles), which was the preliminary to Campoformio, see Romanin, *Storia documentata di Venezia*, vol. 10, pp. 252–60.

234 For Napoleon's reaction see Preto, 'Un "Uomo Nuovo" dell'età Napoleonica', p. 54.

235 Pillinini, *1797: Venezia 'Giacobina'*, p. 112.

236 For Foscolo's threat see Dumas, *La Fin de la République de Venise*, p. 455.

237 Bratti, *Antonio Canova nella vita artistica privata*, p. 360.

238 Pavanello and Romanelli, *Canova*, pp. 383–4.

239 The sketch for the work, which was also realised as a maquette, appears on the reverse side of a preliminary study for the *Pietà*. Ibid.

240 For the list of works (for the Veneto overall), Romanin, *Storia documentata di Venezia*, vol. 10, pp. 263–300.

241 For general remarks see Dorothy Mackay Quynn, 'The Art Confiscations of the Napoleonic Wars', *The American Historical Review*, 50 (1945), pp. 437–60. The situation after Waterloo is discussed in chap. 3 below. For the parade of sequestered work in Paris and their subsequent exhibition in the Louvre (Musée Napoleon) see Patricia Mainardi, 'Assuring the Empire of the Future: The 1798 Fête de la Liberté', *Art Journal*, 43 (1989), pp. 155–63.

242 For their vicissitudes and symbolism see Michael Jacoff, *The Horses of San Marco and the Quadriga of the Lord*, Princeton University Press, 1993.

243 Paul Fouché and Alboise, *Les Chevaux du Carrousel, Le Dernier Jour de Venise, Drama en cinq actes. Réprésenté pour la première fois sur le Théatre de la Gaité, le 14 Septembre, 1839*, probably published in Paris, 1839.

244 Anna Guidi Toniato, 'The Horses of San Marco from the Fall of the Republic to the Present Day', *The Horses of San Marco Venice*, trans. John and Valerie Wilton-Ely, Procuratoria di S. Marco and Olivetti, Milan, 1979, pp. 117–23. For the caption and other accounts from the French press see Massimiliano Pavan, 'Canova e il problema dei cavalli di San Marco', *Ateneo Veneto*, 12 (1974), p. 90.

245 Quoted in Bianca Maria Scarfì, 'The Bronze Lion of St Mark', *The Lion of Venice*, p. 35. Still substantially unpublished, the diary of Cicogna is in the Museo Correr, Venice. For an introduction, and citation of entries concerned with the visual arts in particular see Franco Bizzotto, 'I *Diari* di Emmanuele Antonio Cicogna', *Venezia Arti*, 2 (1988), pp. 75–83.

246 Scarfì, 'The Bronze Lion of St Mark', p. 34.

247 Distefano and Paladini, *Storia di Venezia, 1797–1997*, vol. 1, *Dai dogi agli imperatori*, p. 184.

248 Annibale Alberti, 'Pietro Edwards e le opere d'arte tolte da Napoleone a Venezia', *Nuova Antologia*, 5, ser. vii, 150 (1926), p. 334. The author has some reservations about Edwards, cf. p. 330: 'L'ottimo Edwards era certamente pieno di amore e di buona volontà, ma il guidizio critico e lo spirito profetico erano in lui piuttosto discutibili!' On Edwards see also Alessandro Conti, 'Vicende e cultura del restauro', *Storia dell'arte Italiana*, Einaudi, Turin, 1981, pp. 59–67, noting Conti's claim that 'Di governo in governo, fino alla sua scomparsa nel 1821, l'Edwards resta sempre uno dei protagonisti della tutela del patrimonio artistico di Venezia'.

249 On the spoliation of the treasury see Guido Perocco, 'Histoire du trésor de Sainte-Marc', *Le Trésor de Saint-Marc de Venise*, Olivetti, Milan, 1984, pp. 67–8.

250 For the despoliation of the Arsenale and the destruction of the Bucintoro see Mario Nani Mocenigo, 'L'Arsenale di Venezia durante la prima occupazione Francese', *Rivista di Venezia*, 6 (1927), pp. 247–53. The hull of the Bucintoro survived and was used as a floating prison until its demolition in 1824. A model preserved in the Museo Storico Navale was made prior to demolition, ibid., p. 253.

251 See Ennio Concina, 'La scienza nuova, l'Arsenale, le riforme (1690–1790), *L'Arsenale della Repubblica di Venezia: technice e istituzioni dal Medioevo all'età Moderna*, Electa, Milan, 1984, p. 203ff.

252 For an analysis of the building see Paolo Gennaro, 'The Squadratori: An Enlightenment Project', *L'Arsenale riordinato: nuovi progetti per Venezia*, Arsenale Editrice, Venice, 1987, p. 25ff.

253 Alvise Zorzi, *Venezia scomparsa*, pp. 43–7.

254 Mocenigo, 'L'Arsenale di Venezia durante la prima occupazione francese', pp. 247–53.

255 Maffioletti had intensive knowledge of the Arsenale. Cicogna cites his *Discorso nello aprirsi degli studii fiscico-matematici relativi alla navale architettura nell'Arsenale di Venezia*, in *Saggio di biografia veneziana* vol. 2, p. 541, and, in 1799, the *Discorso pei solenni esami del secondo biennio degli studii fisico-matematici nell'Arsenale di Venezia* (1800), p. 542.

256 Lawrence Sondhaus, 'Napoleon's Shipbuilding Program at Venice and the Struggle for Naval Mastery in the Adriatic, 1806–1814', *The Journal of Military History*, 43 (1989), pp. 349–62.

257 *Useless Memoirs of Carlo Gozzi* (1797), trans. John Addington Symonds, Oxford University Press, London, 1962, p. 284. For the context of Gozzi's last years (and the shifts in Venetian theatrical taste) see Piermario Vescovo, '"La più lunga lettera di Riposta che sia stata scritta", Riflessioni sull'ultimo Gozzi', *Carlo Gozzi: letteratura e musica*, ed. Bodo Guthmüller and Wolfgang Osthoff, Bulzoni, Rome, 1997, pp. 119–40.

258 *Memoirs of Lorenzo da Ponte* (1860), trans. Elisabeth Abott, ed. Arthur Livingston, J. B. Lippincott, Philadelphia and London, 1929, p. 247.

259 Ibid., p. 255.

260 Ippolito Nievo, *Opere*, ed. Sergio Romagnoli, La Letteratura Italiana, Storia e Testi, vol. 57, Riccardo Ricciardi, Milan and Naples, 1962, pp. 430–33. For discussion of Nievo within the Risorgimento context see chap. 4 below.

261 For Foscarini's *Della letteratura veneziana* and Gozzi's collaboration see Pietro del Negro, 'Gasparo Gozzi e la politica Veneziana', p. 7. On the *Della Perfezione*, Alessandro Chiribiri, 'L'Amor di patria nella Venezia del Settecento', in Daniela Bianchi and Giuseppe Rutto, *Idee e concezioni di patria nell'Europa del Settecento*, vol. 1, Il Segnalibro, Turin, 1989, p. 150ff.

262 Del Negro, 'Gasparo Gozzi e la politica veneziana', pp. 47–8.

263 For Francesco Gritti and Antonio Lamberti see Raffaelo Barbiera, *Poesie veneziane* (1886), Arnaldo Forni, Bologna, 1975, pp. 92–208.

264 George Knox, 'Domenico Tiepolo's Pulchinello Drawings: Satire, or a Labor of Love?', *Satire in the Eighteenth Century*, ed. J. D. Browning, Garland Publishing, New York and London, 1983, pp. 124–6.

265 Giandomenico Romanelli and Filippo Pedrocco date the frescoes from 1797, *Ca' Rezzonico*, Electa, Milan, 1986, pp. 57–81. For a view of the importance of the Pulcinello figure for Giambattista Tiepolo see Erika Esau, 'Tiepolo and Punchinello: Venice, Magic and Comme-dia Dell'Arte', *Australian Journal of Art*, 11 (1991), pp. 40–57.

266 For a treatment of literature in dialect see Giovanni Meli, 'Le letterature dialetti nel Settecento', *Storia della letteratura italiana*, vol. 4, *Il Settecento*, ed. Enrico Malata, Salerno and Rome, 1995, pp. 759–66.

267 On such matters see Florens Christian Rang, *Psicologia storica del carnevale*, Arsenale, Venice, 1983, and esp. the commentary by Venetian Massimo Cacciari, pp. 79–81.

268 Adelheid Geilt, *Domenico Tiepolo: The Pulchinello Drawings*, George Braziller, New York, 1986. For *The Prison Visit* and *The Release From Prison* (National Gallery of Art, Washington, DC), pp. 100–105.

269 Johann Gottfried Seume, *Spaziergang nach Syrakus*, cited in Giacomo Cacciapalgia, *Scrittori di lingua tedesca e Venezia/Deutschsprachige Schriftsteller und Venedig*, Stamperia di Venezia, Venice, 1985, pp. 121–7.

270 *The Poetical Works of William Wordsworth*, ed. Ernest de Selincourt and Helen Darbishire, vol. 3, Clarendon Press, Oxford, 1954, pp. 11–12.

271 For example: 'Advance – come forth from thy Tyrolean ground/ dear liberty!'

272 Bruce Redford is perhaps too swift to see Wordsworth as 'a brilliant encomiast' who 'falsifies her [Venice's] reputation in order to salvage it', *Venice and the Grand Tour*, p. 55. The sonnet begins with the word 'Once'.

Chapter 2

1 See the material based on French dispatches to Paris published by Ferdinand Boyer, 'Les Débuts du régime Napoléonien à Venise d'après les lettres inédites d'Eugène de Beauharnais (1806)', *Rassegna Storica del Risorgimento*, 64 (1957), p. 636. Boyer's article, based on the correspondence of Eugène de Beauharnais and dispatches from the Commissioner of Police, Lagarde, to Napoleon, remains a key interpretation of the first years of the French rule.

2 Other Municipalists who left Venice for various Cisalpine cities include Gaetano Benini, Antonio Collalto, Tommaso Gallino, Giuseppe Giuliani, Francesco Mengotti, Andrea Sordino, Giovanni Widmann and Tommaso Zorzi: from 'Note su Municipalisti', Giuseppe Gullino, 'La Congiura del 12 Ottobre 1797 e la fine della Municipalità veneziana', *Critica Storica*, 16 (1979), pp. 607–18.

3 Ugo Foscolo, *Ultime lettere di Jacopo Ortis, Opere* 4, Edizione Criticia, ed. Giovanni Gambarin, Felice Le Monnier, Florence, 1955, p. 295. The editions of 1798, 1802 and 1817 are discussed by Gambarin, Introduction, p. xiff.

4 Foscolo later claimed that Ortis 'may boast of having been the first book that induced the females and the mass of readers to interest themselves in public affairs': Ugo Foscolo, 'Essay on the Present Literature of Italy', *Saggi di letteratura italiana*, part 2, ed. Cesare Foligno, Felice Le Monnier, Florence, 1958, p. 469.

5 Ugo Foscolo, *Bonaparte liberatore (1797–99)* is dated 'Genova 26 Novembre, 1799'.

6 Michele Gottardi, *L'Austria a Venezia: società e istituzioni nella prima dominazione austriaca, 1798–1906*, Franco Angelo, Milan, 1993, is the most detailed study of the first period of Austrian rule. See also Alvise Zorzi, *Venezia austriaca*, Laterza, Rome and Bari, 1985.

7 Cristoph Becker, Axel Burkarth and August Bernhard Rave, 'The International Taste for Venetian Art, the Habsburg Empire', *The Glory of Venice: Art in the Eighteenth Century*, ed. Jane Martineau and Andrew Robison, Yale University Press, New Haven and London, 1994, pp. 45–52; Franca Zava Boccazzi, 'Episodi di pittura veneziana a Vienna nel Settecento', *Venezia/Vienna: il mito della cultura, veneziana nell'Europa asburgica*, ed. Giandomenico Romanelli, Electa, Milan, 1983, pp. 25–88.

8 Francis Haskell, *Patrons and Painters: Art and Society in the Age of the Baroque: A Study of the Relations between Italian Art and Society in the Age of the Baroque* (1963), Yale University Press, London and New Haven, 1980, p. 335.

9 David Kimbell considers Zeno's 'new libretto', *Italian Opera*, Cambridge University Press, 1991, p. 187ff.

10 Giovanni Morelli, 'Un Pomo d'Oro sull unverzehrlig Tisch: il lungo momento della connessione musicale di Venezia e Vienna', *Venezia/Vienna: il mito della cultura veneziana nell'Europa asburgica*, pp. 89–104. For Mozart in Venice see Paolo Cattelan, *Mozart, un mese a Venezia*, Marsilio, Venice, 2000.

11 On these speculations, Edward J. Dent, *Mozart's Operas* (1913), Oxford University Press, 1960, p. 44. See also Paul Nettl, 'Casanova and Don Giovanni', *The Saturday Review* (28 January 1956), p. 44ff. Dent also pursues the influnce of Goldoni on Da Ponte's libretto, p. 123ff.

12 See again *Memoirs of Lorenzo da Ponte, 1749–1838*, trans. Elizabeth Abbott, ed. Arthur Livingston, J. B. Lippincott, Philadelphia and London, 1929.

13 Noting the comment by Eleanor Selfridge-Field, *Venetian Instrumental Music from Gabrieli to Vivaldi*, Praeger, New York, 1975, p. 289, 'The place that drew the biggest repository of Venetian

musicians was consistently Vienna. So thorough was the Venetian permeation of Vienna in the years between Gabrieli and Vivaldi that it sometimes seem doubtful that there could have been an independent tradition of Viennese instrumental music.'

14 For example, Anna Giubertoni, 'Venezia nella letteratura austriaca moderna', *Venezia Vienna*, pp. 105–26. The theme is important in part 2 of this study.

15 Gottardi, *L'Austria a Venezia*, pp. 20–23.

16 With reference to Pesaro, the most eminent patrician to take up office under the new Austrian regime, Gottardi remarks, ibid., p. 33: 'Ma Pesaro fu solo la punta visibile dell'iceberg. Egli fu l'emblema di una parziale restaurazione patrizia, che troverà spazio anche doppo la sua morte, nelle persecuzione verso gli antichi oppositori democratici . . .'

17 Giandomenico Romanelli, *Venezia Ottocento: l'architettura, l'urbanistica*, Albrizzi, Venice, 1988, quotes extensively from the Principal Decrees of the 89 articles of the *Organizzazione di Venezia*, pp. 28–9. Romanelli emphasises the importance of the formulation of building regulations for the new era.

18 Gottardi, *L'Austria a Venezia*, p. 265.

19 Joseph Forsyth, *Remarks on Antiquities, Arts, and Letters in 1802 and 1803* (2nd edition), John Murray, London, 1816, p. 437. Forsyth was travelling after the peace of Amiens in 1801 and was seized by French police in Turin and detained in France throughout the period of the Napoleonic wars.

20 Gottardi, *L'Austria a Venezia*, p. 264.

21 Ibid., p. 265.

22 Ibid., p. 266.

23 For Canova's bust of Cimarosa see Giuseppe Pavanello and Giandomenico Romanelli, *Canova*, Marsilio, Venice, 1992, pp. 308–11.

24 See again Gilberto Pizzamiglio, 'Ugo Foscolo nel salotto di Isabella Teotochi-Albrizzi', *Atti dei convegni foscoliani*, Istituto Poligrafico e Zecca dello Stato Libreria dello Stato, Rome, 1988, pp. 155–70.

25 Ibid., p. 167.

26 Elena Bassi, *Giannantonio Selva: architetto veneziano*, Leo S. Olschki, Florence 1935, p. 50ff.

27 The Trieste theatre was opened on 21 April 1801. Ibid., pp. 66–9.

28 Giuseppe Pavanello, *L'Opera completa di Canova*, Rizzoli, Milan, 1976, entry 134.

29 Antonio Canova, 'Abbozzo di biografia 1804–05', *Scritti edizione nazionale delle Opere di Antonio Canova*, ed. Hugh Honour, Istituto Poligrafico e Zecca dello Stato, Rome, 1994, p. 310. The monument was installed in 1805.

30 For the early maquette for the Beneficence figure see Pavanello and Romanelli, *Canova*, pp. 172–3.

31 Quoted in Riccardo Bratti, *Antonio Canova nella sua artistica privata*, a Spese della R. Deputazione, Venice, 1919, p. 361 (my translation).

32 Canova, 'Abbozzo di biografia', *Scritti: edizione nazionale delle opere di Antonio Canova*, p. 312.

33 For a succinct biography of Molin: Gottardi, *L'Austria a Venezia*, pp. 105–6.

34 Cited by Girolamo Soranzo, *Biografia veneziana inaggiunta e continuazione nel 'Saggio' di Emanuele Antonio Cicogna*, Burt Franklin, New York, 1967, p. 232. The composer Bertoni was the successor of Galuppi at the Cappella di San Marco.

35 Gianfranco Folena, 'Cesarotti, Monti e il melodramma fra Sette e Ottocento', *Analecta Musicologica*, 22 (1982), pp. 245–6.

36 Gottardi, *L'Austria a Venezia*, p. 218. The confiscation was allegedly for anti-religious sentiments.

37 Alvise Zorzi, *Venezia scomparsa*, Electa, Milan, 1984, p. 51.

38 Gottardi, *L'Austria a Venezia*, p. 295.

39 Marino Zorzi, 'La Gestione del patrimonio librario', *Venezia e L'Austria*, ed. Gino Benzoni e Gaetano Cozzi, Marsilio, Venice, 1999, pp. 265–90.

40 On the Foscarini sale, ibid., pp. 267–8.

41 Haskell claimed that Farsetti was 'by far the most important figure behind the Neo-classical movement in Venice', *Patrons and Painters*, p. 362. For an important account of collecting in the Veneto, including antiquarians, see Kryszztof Pomian, 'Collectors, Naturalists and Antiquarians in the Venetian Republic of the Eighteenth Century', *Collectors and Curiosities: Paris and Venice, 1500–1800* (1978), trans. Elizabeth Wiles-Portier, Polity Press, Cambridge, 1990, pp. 185–257.

42 Romanelli, *Venezia Ottocento*, p. 20. The issue of Trieste was to fester in the second period of Austrian rule, see below.

43 An informative source for these decorations is Giuseppe Pavanello, 'La Decorazione Neoclassica nei palazzi veneziani', *Venezia nell'età di Canova, 1780–1830*, ed. Elena Bassi et al., Alfieri, Venice, 1978, p. 285.

44 Ibid., p. 281. For illustrations see Cesare M. Cunnacia with photography by Mark E. Smith, *Venice: Hidden Splendours*, Flammarion, Paris, 1994, pp. 93–4.

45 For the documents see M. G. Miggiani, 'Documenti sul bozzetto per il monumento a Francesco Pesaro di Antonio Canova', *Venezia Arti*, 4 (1990), pp. 176–85.

46 Cited, with contemporary sources, in Massimiliano Pavan, 'Canova e il problema dei cavalli di San Marco', *Ateneo Veneto*, 12 (1974), p. 93.

47 A.-F. Sergent-Marceau, *Coup-d'Oeil sentimental, critique et historique sur Venise* (1805), Slatkine, Geneva, 1981, p. 57: 'En vain j'ai cherché cette profondeur philosophique dans les pensées, qui caractérise le législateur; cette finesse dans le discours particulière à l'homme accoutumé aux discussions politiques . . .'

48 Ibid., p. 58.

49 The Napoleonic rule in Venice is not treated in any detail in the literature, with the exception of Giandomenico Romanelli, *Venezia Ottocento*, a crucial study of urban change during the French tenure – and afterwards. The only Venetian-based focus is Filippo Nani Mocenigo, *Del Dominio Napoleonica a Venezia (1806–1814, Note ed appunti)*, L. Nerlo, Venice, 1896, of historic importance since it was written 100 years from the effective close of the Republic, but it is inadequate as a modern treatment. In English (the area is also little treated), George B. McClellan, *Venice and Bonaparte*, Princeton University Press, 1931.

50 Ferdinand Boyer, 'Les débuts du Régime Napoléonien à Venise d'après les lettres inédites d'Eugène de Beauharnais (1806)', pp. 636–7.

51 Lawrence Sondhaus provides a crucial focus on Napoleon's naval ambitions and their consequences for Venice in 'Napoleon's Shipbuilding Program at Venice and the Struggle for Naval Mastery in the Adriatic, 1806–1814', *Journal of Military History*, 43 (1989), pp. 349–62.

52 Vincenzo Marchesi, 'La Guerra intorno a Venezia nel 1809', *Rivista del Risorgimento*, 1 (1895–96), pp. 712–20.

53 On the population see Gottardi, *L'Austria a Venezia*, p. 25.

54 Romanelli, *Venezia Ottocento*, chap. 2 passim.

55 But it would be a weakness in historical assessment if the provisions made in the previous century in the late days of the Republic were underestimated; regional works such as the hydraulic schemes for the Brenta, the Murazzi at Pellestrina, and the institutional provisions for orphans, the sick and the mentally ill, for example.

56 Boyer, 'Les débuts du régime Napoléonien à Venise', p. 637.

57 Paolo Favaro, 'Alvise e Francesco Pisani: due patrizi veneziani tra rivoluzione e restaurazione (1797–1815)', *Studi Veneziani*, 24 (1993), pp. 269–97. This is an invaluable study of the survival of one patrician family across the changes of administration from 1797.

58 Boyer, 'Les débuts du régime Napoléonien', p. 637.

59 Ibid., p. 643.

60 Ibid., pp. 642–3.

61 For the Consiglio Municipale dei Savi, 1806–14, see Sergio Barizza, *Il Comune di Venezia, 1806–1946. L'istituzione, il territorio: guida-inventario dell'Archivio Municipale*, Comune di Venezia, Venice, 1987, pp. 43–4.

62 Nani Mocenigo, *Dal Dominio Napoleonico*, p. 58.

63 Ibid.

64 Ibid., p. 68.

65 Ibid.

66 Boyer, 'Les débuts du régime Napoléonien', p. 639.

67 The Austrians were blamed for the decreases, ibid., p. 639.

68 For the circumstances of acquisition, by purchase and not confiscation see Ferdinand Boyer, 'Stendhal et l'acquisition par Napoléon de la Villa Pisani à Strà', *Le Divan* (1956), pp. 284–90.

69 Pavanello, 'La Decorazione Neoclassica nei palazzi veneziani', p. 287 and nn. 47 and 48, p. 297, with respect to realising the garden in French style.

70 For the appointments and structure of government see Barizza, *Il Comune di Venezia, 1806–1946*, pp. 11–12, 43–4. For a profile of Daniele Renier see p. 69. See also Filippo Nani Mocenigo, 'Persone', *Del Dominio Napoleonico a Venezia (1806–1814)*, p. 11ff. In 1806 Lagarde spoke frankly of the stagnation of all commerce, Boyer, 'Les débuts du régime Napoléonien', p. 639.

71 Romanelli states 'L'escavo dei canali si ebbe sotto il primo governo austriaco a Venezia, e diligente', a list follows, *Venezia Ottocento*, p. 109, n. 3.

72 Lagarde's letter is addressed to Général Savary, 19 June 1906, cited in Ferdinand Boyer, 'Pierre Lagarde policier de Napoléon a Venise en 1906', *Rassegna Storica del Risorgimento*, 66 (1957), p. 90.

73 Romanelli, *Venezia Ottocento*, p. 642. For biographies see Gullino's 'Note sui Municipalisti', in 'La Conguira del 12 Ottobre 1797 e la fine della Municipalità a Venezia', *Critica Storica*, 14 (1979), p. 607ff.

74 The document is given as the 'Rapporto del ministro segretario di Stato a S. M. I. e R. sulle rimostranze fattele dalla Deputazione Veneta in Parigi', Romanelli, *Venezia Ottocento*, p. 110, n. 8.

75 The first systematic index of the demolitions and altered uses was Giuseppe Tassini, *Edifici di Venezia distrutti o vôlti ad uso diverso da quello a cui furono in origine destinati* (1885), Filippi, Venice, n.d. Alvise Zorzi has detailed and documented the losses in *Venezia scomparsa*, Electa, Milan, 1984, passim.

76 Ibid., p. 52ff.

77 Ibid., p. 74.

78 Ibid., pp. 61–6.

79 Ibid., p. 87.

80 Boyer, 'Les débuts du régime Napoléonien à Venise', p. 640. The people involved are listed as Bernadin, Renier, Mani, Aldini and Correr – either Angelo or Nicoletto Correr.

81 Ibid., On connections between Milan and Venice see Susanna Biadene, 'Venezia e Milano unite sotto Napoleone: la cultura architettonica neoclassica', *Venezia Milano: storia, civiltà e cultura nel rapporto tra due capitali*, ed. Carlo Pirovano, Electa, Milan, 1984, pp. 201–32.

82 Lawrence Sondhaus, 'Napoleon's Shipbuilding Program at Venice', pp. 349, 352.

83 Paolo Morachiello, 'Note sul servizio dei Ponts et Chaussées sull'amministrazione napoleonica nell'Italia Settentrionale', *Atti dell'Istituto Veneto di Scienze, Lettere ed Arti*, 137 (1978–9), p. 167.

84 Nani Mocenigo, *Del Dominio napoleonico*, pp. 42–3.

85 Ibid., pp. 352–3.

86 Giorgio Bellavitis, *L'Arsenale di Venezia: storia di una grande struttura urbana*, Marsilio, Venice, 1983, p. 178.

87 'Il progetto delle dighe sul porto di Malamocco e la Torre di Porto Nuovo', ibid., p. 176ff.

88 Ibid.

89 See part 2 below, particularly in relation to the flood of 1966.

90 Salvini's career is detailed in Mario Marzari, *Progetti per L'imperatore: Andrea Salvini, ingegnere a l'Arsenale, 1802–1807*, Comune di Trieste, Trieste, 1990.

91 Ibid., p. 180.

92 The evidence that Selva was responsible for the Porta Nuova is hardly conclusive, but he is mentioned in connection with it in archives of the Accademia di Belle Arti, for 16 and 18 September and 9 October 1810: see Elena Bassi, *Giannantonio Selva: architetto veneziano*, pp. 120–21. For the engagement of the French engineers Prony and Sganzin, and for Salvini see Marzari, *Progetti per l'Imperatore*, pp. 106–21.

93 Sondhaus, 'Napoleon's Shipbuilding Program at Venice', p. 353, and, for conscription, p. 356.

94 Alexander Grab, 'The Kingdom of Italy and Napoleon's Continental Blockade', *Consortium on Revolutionary Europe, 1750–1850*, 18 (1988), p. 591. Gottardi gives a table of shipping, *L'Austria a Venezia*, pp. 104–6, giving ten English ships in 1805, but also noting thirty in 1803.

95 Romanelli, *Venezia Ottocento*, p. 53.

96 Ibid., pp. 106–8.

97 Ibid., p. 106.

98 Cf. John Pope-Hennessy on the exclusion of Verrocchio's statue of Colleoni from the Piazzetta, *Italian Renaissance Sculpture*, Phaidon, London, 1971, p. 298.

99 Pavanello, *Venezia nell'età di Canova*, p. 156.

100 The discussion on the statue in the Accademia di Belle Arti involving Selva is listed on 16 and 23 September and 9 October 1810, when the design for the pedestal was exhibited: Bassi, *Giannantonio Selva: architetto Veneziano*, pp. 120–21.

101 *Carta Topografica-Idrografica Militare della Laguna di Venezia e del litorale compreso tra l'Adige e il Piave*, cited in Marcello Zunica, 'Le carte della laguna di Venezia dall'inizio del IX di Venezia dall'inizio del XIX Secolo ai giorni nostri', in *Mostra storica della laguna di Venezia*, Stamperia di Venezia, Venice 1970, p. 307.

102 For these publications see Emmanuele Antonio Cicogna, *Saggio di bibliografia veneziana*, vol. 2, Burt Franklin, New York, 1967, p. 717.

103 For the continuing relevance of Zendrini's *Memorie storiche dello stato antico delle Lagune di Venezia* (published Seminario, Padua, 1811), see the many references in Piero Bevilacqua, *Venezia e le acque: una metafora planetaria*, Donzelli, Rome, 1995, p. 5, and passim. Giacomo Filiasi had published *Memoria delle procelle che annualmente sogliono regnare nelle maremme veneziana* in 1794.

104 Chateaubriand, *Correspondance générale*, vol. 1, 1797–1807, Gallimard, Paris, 1977, pp. 289, 639–40.

105 My paraphrase.

106 *Response à la lettre de M. Chateaubriand par M. Justine Renier Michiel en defense de Venise* was published anonymously in the *Giornale dell'Italiana Literatura*, Padua, 14 (1806), pp. 260–67.

107 [Renier Michiel], *Opere drammatiche di Shakespeare volgarizzate da una dama veneta*, vol. 1, *Otello*, Eredi Costantini, Venice, 1798.

108 On the reception of Renier's translation see Anna Busi, *Otello in Italia, (1777–1972)*, Adriatica, Bari, 1973, p. 20ff.

109 Renier Michiel, *Opere drammatiche di Shakespeare volgarizzate*, vol. 1, p. 5.

110 Ibid., p. 39.

111 See p. 44 in the introduction, ibid.

112 I follow the account in Vittorio Malamani, 'Giustina Renier Michiel: i suoi amici, il suo tempo', *Archivio Veneto*, 38 (1889), p. 59ff. See also *Risposta alla lettera del Signor Chateaubriand sopra Venezia*, Stamperia Rosa, Venice, 1806, and Emile Malakis, 'Another Feminine Answer to Chateaubriand's Slighting Remarks made about Venice in 1806', *Modern Language Notes* (April 1935), pp. 243–8.

113 Malamani, 'Giustina Renier Michiel, i suoi amici, il suo tempo', p. 59.

114 Ibid.

115 Ibid., p. 60.

116 Ibid., pp. 61–2.

117 Sacrati's pamphlet was entitled *Lettera di Fioriligi Taumanzioa Pastorella d'Arcadia all'ornatissimo signore Floriano Caldani Bolognese, P. Professore di anatomia nella Univerità di Padova*, Penada, Padua, 1807, see Emile Malakis, 'Another Feminine Answer', p. 244. Lavinia Dragoni's *A Mr Chateaubriand* is published in full, pp. 246–8.

118 Madame de Staël, *Correspondance générale*, vol. 5, part 2, *Le Léman et l'Italie*, 18 May 1804–9 November 1805, text edited and introduced by Béatrice W. Jasinsk, Hachette, Paris, 1885. p. 575. Note also the letter to Isabella Teotochi Albrizzi, making reference to Vivant Denon as a mutual friend: 14 June, 1805, pp. 592–3.

119 Madame de Staël, *Corinne, ou l'Italie*, ed Simone Balayé, Gallimard, Paris, 1985. The Venetian visit occurs in book 15, chap. 7, p. 420ff. Note Geneviève Gennari, *Le Premier Voyage de Madame de Staël en Italie et la genèse de Corinne*, Boivin, Paris, 1947, 'Venise et la Vénétie', pp. 102–12.

120 Cf. the letter, *Correspondance générale*, p. 574 (my translation): 'The situation in Venice is very singular: and when one is happy, all the mysterious customs excite poetic impressions. But for me they carry regrets: it is there that I place the goodbyes in my book . . .'

121 De Staël, *Corinne*, p. 281.

122 Jean-Jacques Rousseau, *Politics and Art: Letter to M. D. Alembert on the Theatre* (1758), trans. Allan Brown, Free Press of Glencoe, Ills., 1960, n. 126.

123 Ibid., see n. 113.

124 Madame de Krudener, *Valérie* (1801), introduction, notes and commentary by Michel Mercier, Klinckstek, Paris, 1974.

125 Letter 21, ibid., pp. 78–80.

126 Account by Antonio Pilot, *Napoleone a Venezia nel 1807*, G. Scarabellin, Venice, 1914.

127 And the triumphal arch for the visit of Pius VI in the same year, Bassi, *Giannantonio Selva: architetto veneziano*, pp. 45–7.

128 There are two accounts from the early twentieth century that looked back on the occasion: Antonio Santalena, 'Napoleone I. a Venezia', *L'Ateneo Veneto*, 30 (1907), pp. 213–41, and Antonio Pilot, *Napoleone a Venezia nel 1807*, in 1914.

129 Manilio Brusatin and Giuseppe Pavanello, chap. 3, '1807–1808, Una "nuova" Fenice per Napoleone', *Il Teatro La Fenice: i progetti, l'architettura, le decorazioni*, Albrizzi, Venice, 1987, pp. 152–63.

130 Sergio Barizza has called it the first special law of Venice, *Il Comune di Venezia, 1806–1946*, p. 11.

131 Francesca Zanella gives a singularly positive account of the Napoleonic interventions in 'I Progetti di grande et petite voyerie nella Venezia napoleonica', *Venezia Arti*, 1 (1987), pp. 54–61.

132 The decree is published in full in Romanelli, *Venezia Ottocento*, p. 114.

133 For the document see Romanelli, ibid., pp. 116–17, also Giandomenico Romanelli, 'La Commissione d'Ornato: da Napoleone al Lombardo Veneto', *Le macchine imperfette: architettura, programma, istituzioni nel XIX Secolo*, ed. P. Morachiello and G. Teyysot, Officina, Rome, 1980, pp. 129–43.

134 Romanelli, *Venezia Ottocento*, p. 114, n. 17.

135 Elena Bassi, 'L'Accademia', *Venezia nell'età di Canova, 1780–1830*, p. 313. See also Nani Mocenigo, *Del Dominio Napoleonico a Venezia*, pp. 98–9.

136 A. Bevilacqua, 'Diedo, Antonio', *Dizionario biografico degli italiani*, vol. 39, ed. Massimiliano Pavan, Istituto della Enciclopedia Italiana, Rome, 1991, pp. 766–9.

137 Francesca Cavazzana Romanelli, 'Restauri a Venezia nel Settecento: le "Licenze" dei Giudici del Piovego', *Restauro e Città*, 3/4 (1987), pp. 15–27. On p. 18 some comparisons are made with the Commissione all'Ornato.

138 Romanelli, *Venezia Ottocento*, p. 101.

139 Ibid., pp. 102, 103.

140 On Napoleon and the planning of Paris see Maurice Guerrini, *Napoleon and Paris: Thirty Years of History*, Cassell, London, 1967, esp. p. 81ff on the Rue de Rivoli and 'La Transformation de Paris'. Also H. N. Boon, *Rêve et réalité dans l'oeuvre économique et sociale de Napoléon III*, Martinus Nijhoff, The Hague, 1936, p. 100ff.

141 Guerrini, *Napoleon and Paris*, p. 81.

142 Jean-Louis Harouel, 'Les Fonctions de l'alignement dans l'organisme urbain', *Dix-huitième siècle*, 9 (1977), pp. 135–49, demonstrates the tenacity of this principle in French urban planning. See also H. Ballon, *The Paris of Henri IV: Architecture and Urbanism*, MIT, Cambridge, Mass., 1991.

143 A facsimile has been published: *Catasto napoleonico mappa della città di Venezia*, Ministero per I Beni Culturali e Ambientali, Archivio di Stato di Venezia, Realizzazione editoriale: Italo Novelli, Marsilio, Venice, 1988.

144 This is Ennio Concina's point: that the map is an 'exact' representation of the *forma urbis*, liberated from every contamination of allegory: 'La città dei catasti', ibid., p. 10.

145 Ferdinand Boyer, 'Napoléon I et les jardins publics en Italie', *Urbanisme et habitation: la Vie Urbaine*, 1 (1954), pp. 1–8, for remarks on similar provisions in Rome, Mantua, Milan, Turin, Genoa, Bologna and Venice.

146 Romanelli, *Venezia Ottocento*, pp. 101–2.

147 On the Republic's canal infill projects see 'Il Rio Terà', Gianpietro Zucchetta, *Un'altra Venezia: immagini e storia degli antichi canali scomparsi/ Another Venice: An Illustrated History of Concealed Venetian Canals*, Ericco, Venice, 1995, p. 38ff.

148 Zucchetta, an opponent of canal interment, is strongly critical of Selva in his coverage of 'The Via Garibaldi–Rio Terà de S. Anna', ibid., pp. 138–53.

149 Giulio Lorenzetti, *Venice and its Lagoon: Historical Artistic Guide* (1926), presentation by Nereo Vianello, trans. John Guthrie, Lint, Trieste, 1975, p. 305.

150 The Veneto interest in the English garden is studied in Margherita Azzi Visentini, *Il giardino veneto tra Sette e Ottocento, e le sue fonti*, Polifilo, Milan, 1988, passim. Selva was certainly interested in English gardens (such as Stowe), which he saw during his English tour of 1778–80, pp. 200–9: see Pierre de la Ruffinière du Prey, 'Giannantonio Selva in England', *Architectural History*, 25 (1982), pp. 20–34 (emphasising the singularity of Selva's travels). Visentini publishes the *Rapporti di G. Selva sui Giardini di Castello* in *Il giardino veneto*, pp. 252–9.

151 Giandomenico Romanelli, 'Per G. A. Selva urbanistica: inedita sui giardini di Castello', *Arte Veneta*, 26 (1972), pp. 263–2.

152 Romanelli details the response, ibid., p. 266. De Breme urged the demolition of two windmills on the *motta di San Antonio*, which he thought deformed the view, but they were still there in 1812.

153 Ibid., p. 267.

154 For its realisation by Salvadori see chap. 3 below.

155 Extract Diari, 1, Museo Correr, MS 2844, 14 July 1810, cited in Giuseppe Mazzariol, 'Regesto dei diari di Emmanuele Antonio Cicogna, 1798–1868', *Venezia Arti*, 1 (1987), p. 124.

156 Pinali's report *Sopra la decadenza di Venezia in fatto di lavori d'industria e d'opera di Belle Arte dalla caduta del Veneto* is published in full as Appendix 1 in Romanelli, *Venezia Ottocento*, pp. 464–75. It is an important document with regard to French rule, to be discussed further below.

157 Giannantonio Moschini, *Guida per la Città di Venezia all'Amico delle Belle Arte*, Alvisopoli, Venice, 1815, vol. 2, Frontispiece – see chap. 3 below, and Leopoldo Cicognara, Antonio Diedo and

Giannantonio Selva, the first edition: *Le Fabbriche più cospicue di Venezia, misurate, illustrate, ed intagliate dai membri, della Veneta reale Accademia di Belle Arti*, 2 vols, Alvisopoli, Venice, 1815, and subsequently *Le Fabbriche e i monumenti più cospicui di Venezia, misurate, illustrate ed intagliate dai membri della Veneta Reale Accademia di Belle Arti*, G. Antonelli, 2 vols, Venice, 1858.

158 *Lettere sul Giardini Pubblici di Venezia*, Portogruaro, Venice, 1826.

159 See, for example, George Sand's comments, chap. 3 below.

160 Franz Liszt, *An Artist's Journey: Lettres d'un Bacchelier Franz Liszt, 1835–1841*, trans. Charles Sutton, University of Chicago, Chicago and London, 1989, p. 116.

161 Romanelli on 'La Passeggiata alla Giudecca', *Venezia Ottocento*, pp. 61–3.

162 Lovisa gives a view of the churches of San Nicolò and San Giuseppe di Castello, reproduced in *Venezia 1717, Venezia 1993: immagini a confronti*, Silvana Editoriale, Milan, 1993, pp. 124–5.

163 On the loss of San Antonio see Cicogna in Mazzariol, 'Regesto dei diari di Emmanuele Antonio Cicogna', p. 124.

164 Giannantonio Moschini, *Della Letteratura veneziana del Secolo XVIII fino a'nostri giorni*, Palese, Venice, 1806.

165 Giannantonio Moschini, *Guida per l'Isola di Murano*, Stamperia Palese, Venice, 1808. For the 'arte de'vetri', p. 11ff.

166 *Memorie storiche de'Veneti primi e secondi del Conte Giacomo Filiasi*, 8 vols, Fenzo, Venice, 1796–8.

167 Emmanuele Antonio Cicogna, Cittadino Veneto, *Delle Inscrizioni veneziane raccolte ed illustrate*, 7 vols, Giuseppe Orlandelli, Picotti, Venice, 1824.

168 Ibid., vol. 1, p. 33.

169 Ibid., p. 62.

170 Nani Mocenigo, *Del Dominio Napoleonico*, p. 89; Zorzi, *Venezia scomparsa*, p. 68.

171 For a full transcript of Selva's letter of 1808, Romanelli, *Venezia Ottocento*, p. 119, n. 40.

172 Zorzi, *Venezia scomparsa*, p. 75.

173 Ibid., p. 79.

174 Ibid., p. 74.

175 Ibid., p. 78.

176 Francis Haskell, 'Some Collectors of English Art at the End of the Eighteenth Century', *Studies in Renaissance and Baroque Art Presented to Anthony Blunt on his Sixtieth Birthday*, ed. Michael Kitson and John Shearman, Phaidon, London, 1967, pp. 173–8.

177 Francis Haskell, 'La Dispersione e la conservazione del patrimonio artistico', *Storia dell'arte italiana*, Einaudi, Turin, 1981, p. 19. The first inspector was Anton Maria Zanetti il Giovane; Pietro Edwards

was the fourth appointment in 1778. By the time of the fall of the Republic Edwards claimed to have restored 450 paintings.

178 Romanelli, *Venezia Ottocento*, p. 104, n. 160.

179 Nani Mocenigo, *Del Dominio napoleonica a Venezia*, p. 91.

180 Cicognara's appointment followed the death of Almorò Pisani. For a biographical treatment and a valuable emphasis on the publications crucial to Cicognara's career as President of the Academy, see Giandomenico Romanelli, 'Leopoldo Cicognara e la politica delle belle arti', Giulio Argan, Giandomenico Romanelli and Giovanni Scarabello, *Canova, Cicognara, Foscolo*, Arsenale, Venice, 1979, pp. 34–47. See also the entry by G. D. Romanelli, 'Cicognara, Leopoldo', *Dizionario bibliografico degli Italiani*, vol. 15, ed. Alberto Ghisalberti, Istituto della Enciclopedia Italiana, Rome, 1981, pp. 421–8, with bibliography of Cicognara's writings.

181 Leopoldo Cicognara, *Del Bello, Raggionamenti*, Molini, Landi & Co., Florence, 1808.

182 A stinging criticism came from the new generation, from Niccolò Tommaseo: see Franco Bernabei's penetrating study of the shifts in taste involved, 'Lusinghe della grazia, corrucci del sublime: Cicognara e Tommaseo', *Arte Veneta*, 23 (1979), pp. 111–18. Cicognara's cusp-like position, politically and intellectually, is studied by Gianni Venturi, 'Leopoldo Cicognara: tracce di un intellettuale tra Antico Regime, Impero e Restaurazione', *L'Europe della corti alla fine dell'Antico Regime*, ed. Cesare Mozzarelli and Gianni Venturi, Bulzoni, Rome, 1991, pp. 171–89.

183 The only detailed study is Francesca Fedi, *L'ideologia del bello: Leopoldo Cicognara e il Classicismo tra Settecento e Ottocento*, Franco Angeli, Milan, 1990.

184 Cf. Rosario Assunto, 'Leopoldo Cicognara: teorico e storico dell'estetica', *Ateneo Veneto*, 10 (1972), pp. 3–17. For a view of Cicognara's critical stance and, indeed, the heresy of his views: Frances Haskell, 'Cicognaro eretico', *Jappelli e il suo tempo*, ed. G. Mazzi, Liviana, Padua, 1982, pp. 217–25.

185 *Elogio di Palladio: discorsi letto nella Reale Veneta Accademia di Belle Arti*, 1809, Venice, 1810, p. 42. See also the extract (which omits the final passages) in Paola Barocchi, *Storia moderna dell'arte in Italia: manifesti polemiche documenti*, vol. 1: *Dai Neoclassici ai Puristi, 1780–1861*, Giulio Einaudi, Turin, 1998, pp. 212–16. Cicogna gives an account of the eulogy and the displeasure occasioned by Cicognara's remarks, 15 August, 3 September and 21 December 1810, cited in

Franco Bizzotto, 'I Diari di Emmanuele Antonio Cicogna', *Venezia Arti*, 2 (1988), pp. 80–81.

186 Giuseppe Mazzariol, 'Spoglio sistematico del materiale archivistico presente nel Fondo Prefettura dell'Adriatico per il periodo compreso tra il 1806 e il 1814', *Venezia Arti*, 1 (1987), pp. 124–6. An important document specifies the concerns of the Commissione all'Ornato in 1812.

187 On the opposition to Selva's renovations to the Manin palace, headed by Padre Buratti, see the *Life of Selva* by Giovanni Poggi cited by Bassi, *Giannantonio Selva*, pp. 112–13.

188 Ibid., pp. 70–71. There is no convincing study of the replication of San Geminiano at San Maurizio.

189 For the design, *Venezia nell'età di Canova, 1780–1830*, pp. 206–97.

190 G. A. Selva, *Elogia di Michele Sanmicheli*, Venice, 1814; *Sulla Voluta ionica*, Padua, 1814.

191 Romanelli, *Venezia Ottocento*, p. 106.

192 A valuable overview of Venetian conservation is given in Gianfranco Pertot, *Venezia 'Restaurata': centosettanta anni di interventi di restauro sugli edifici veneziani*, Franco Angeli, Milan, 1988.

193 For these provisions see Richard Etlin, *The Architecture of Death: The Transformation of the Cemetery in Eighteenth-Century Paris*, MIT, Cambridge, Mass., 1984.

194 Romanelli, 'Progetti per il cimitero di Venezia', *Venezia nell'età di Canova*, p. 202.

195 Bassi, *Giannantonio Selva*, pp. 77–8.

196 Zorzi, *Venezia scomparsa*, p. 268. The adjacent concent of San Cristoforo was also rased.

197 For subsequent modifications, Barizza, *Il Comune di Venezia, L'Istituzione: il Territorio Guida-Inventario dell'Archivio Municipale*, p. 197.

198 Cicogna on 13 May 1814, cited in Franca Bizzotto, 'I Diari di Emmanuele Antonio Cicogna', p. 81.

199 On these regulations see Romanelli, *Venezia Ottocento*, pp. 53–4.

200 An accessible translation of Foscolo's *De'Sepolcri* is found in *The Penguin Book of Italian Verse*, ed. and trans. George Kay, Penguin, Harmondsworth, 1972, p. 244.

201 Agostino Sagredo, *San Cristoforo della Pace*, Alvisopoli, Venice, 1832, p. 4.

202 Ibid., p. 9.

203 Jules Lecomte, *L'Italie des Gens du Monde: Venise ou coup d'oeil, littérature, artistique, historique, sur les monuments et les curiosités de cette cité*, Hippolyte Souverain, Paris, 1844, p. 40. See chap. 4 below for further discussion of Lecomte.

204 Henry James, 'The Aspern Papers' (1888), in *The Aspern Papers and Other Stories*, Penguin, Harmondsworth, 1976, p. 43.

205 Romanelli, *Venezia Ottocento*, p. 109, n. 1.

206 This is one of Byron's earliest stanzas on Venice: [Venice. A Fragment], Lord Byron, *The Complete Poetical Works*, ed. Jerome J. McGann, vol. 4, Clarendon Press, Oxford, 1986, p. 47.

207 Giovanni Scirè Nepi et al., *Le Procuratie Nuove in Piazza San Marco*, Editalia, Rome, 1994.

208 Giuseppe Tassini, *Edifici di Venezia distrutti o vôlti ad diverso da quello a cui furono in origine destinati* (1885), p. 51. Zorzi, *Venezia scomparsa*, pp. 223–8 (his most sustained entry).

209 Antonio Quadri and Dionisio Moretti, *Il Canal Grande, La Piazza S. Marco, Venezia* (1828), facsimile, Viannello, Ponzano, Treviso, 1983, pl. VIII, 'Lato di S. Giminiano qual'era nel passato secolo'.

210 Cicognara, Diedo and Selva, *Le Fabbriche e i monumenti più cospicui di Venezia*, vol. 1, p. 127.

211 However, assessments of San Geminiano varied. While Antonio Ruggia saw its destruction as barbaric and asked for it to be reconstructed 'cosi com'era', Pietro Selvatico Estense (a successor to Cicognara as President of the Academy, and unsympathetic to classical art) was to claim that its elimination was no loss: see Zorzi, *Venezia scomparsa*, p. 71.

212 This is a virtual translation of Cicogna's account of Pinali's views cited by Romanelli, *Venezia Ottocento*, p. 85.

213 On the diary beginnings, 15 August 1810, Franco Bizzotto, 'I *Diari di Emmanuele Antonio Cicogna*', *Venezia Arti*, 2 (1988), p. 76.

214 Carroll William Westfall, 'Antolini's Foro Bonaparte in Milan', *Journal of the Warburg and Courtauld Institutes*, 32 (1969), pp. 366–85.

215 On this debate see Manfredo Tafuri, *Venice and the Renaissance* (1985), trans. Jessica Levine, MIT, Cambridge, Mass., and London, 1989, p. 166ff.

216 See the citations listed by Cicogna (who followed the controversy carefully as his diary entries show) in Emmanuele Cicogna, *Saggio di bibliografia veneziana*, vol. 2, Burt Franklin, New York, 1967, p. 651.

217 Bassi, *Venezia nell'età di Canova, 1780–1830*, p. 175.

218 Romanelli, *Venezia Ottocento*, p. 91.

219 To be discussed in chap. 3.

220 Giuseppe Pavanello, 'La Decorazione Neoclassica nei palazzi veneziani', *Venezia nell'età di Canova, 1780–1830*, p. 286.

221 See, in general, B. Paolo Torsello, 'Il Neoclassico della Piazza: l'Ala Napoleonica e il patriciata', *Piazza San Marco: l'architettura, la storia, le funzione*, Giuseppe Samonà et al., Marsilio, Venice, 1983 (3rd ed.), Umberto Franzoi, 'L'Ala Napoleonica', in Giovanni Scirè Nepri, *Treasures of Venetian Painting: The Gallerie dell'Accademia*, Thames & Hudson, London, 1991, pp. 119–16.

222 For the demolition of the Graneri di Terra Nova see Romanelli, *Venezia Ottocento*, p. 73. The Granary (and the adjacent Sanità) is represented by Lovisa in *Venezia 1717, 1993: immagini a confronto*, Silvana, Milan, 1993, pp. 56–7. On the warehouse and history see Michela Agazzi, 'I Granai della Repubblica', *Venezia Arti*, 7 (1993), pp. 52–4.

223 Gianpietro Zucchetta, *Venezia ponte per ponte*, vol. 2, Stamperia di Venezia, Venice, 1992, p. 94.

224 See Pavanello's fundamental essay 'La Decorazione Neoclassica nei palazzi veneziani', *Venezia nell'età di Canova, 1780–1830*, pp. 281–300, with crucial documentation on interior decoration from the late Settecento to the early Ottocento, and his focus on the Palazzo Reale, 'La decorazione del Palazzo Reale di Venezia', *Bollettino dei Musei Civici Veneziani*, 21 (1976), pp. 3–34.

225 Giuseppe Borsato was largely responsible, Pavanello, 'La Decorazione Neoclassica nei palazzi veneziani', p. 287.

226 As noted in a letter by Giacomo Albertolli cited by Susanna Biadene, 'Venezia e Milano unite sotto Napoleone: la cultura architettonica Neoclassica', *Venezia Milano: storia civiltà e cultura nel rapporto tra due capitali*, Electa, Milan, 1984, p. 224.

227 Given his historical importance, Borsato has been little studied, but see N. Ivanof, 'Borsato, Giuseppe', *Dizionario biografia degli italiani*, vol. 13, ed. Alberto Ghisalberti, Istituto della Enciclopedia Italiana, Rome, 1971, pp. 117–18.

228 *Venezia nell'età di Canova, 1780–1830*, p. 159, and for the *Descrizione*, pp. 158–9.

229 Ibid., p. 135. For the stage designs, Maria Ida Biggi, *Giuseppe Borsato: l'immagine e la scena, scenografo alla Fenice, 1809–1823*, Marsilio, Venice, 1995.

230 *Veduta della Sala del Maggior Consiglio in Palazzo Ducale*, ibid. p. 166.

231 Ibid., pp. 160–61.

232 Ibid., p. 138.

233 For the circumstances of the Napoleonic commission see Ferdinand Boyer, *Le Monde des arts en Italie et la France de la évolution et de l'Empire*, Società Editrice Internazionale, Turin, 1969, chap. 2, 'Canova, sculpteur de Napoléon', p. 131. See also Christopher M. S. Johns, 'Portrait Mythology: Antonio Canova's Portraits of the Bonapartes', *Eighteenth-Century Studies*, 28 (1994), p.

121. For a view of Canova's anti-French attitudes, see again Henry, 'Antonio Canova, the French Imperium and Emerging Nationalism in Italy', passim.

234 The 1802 conversation is noted in Canova's *Abbozzo di biografia 1804–1805, Scritti: edizione nazionale delle opere di Antonio Canova*, pp, 315–16.

235 Ibid.

236 For the vicissitudes see Johns, 'Portrait Mythology: Antonio Canova's Portraits of the Bonapartes', p. 124.

237 Boyer, *Le Monde des arts en Italie*, p. 135, n. 4.

238 Canova, 'Conversazione tra Antonio Canova e Napoleone', 1810, *Scritti: edizione nazionale delle opere di Antonio Canova*, p. 343ff.

239 Ibid.

240 Ibid., p. 351.

241 'I Veneziani . . . avendo fatto dipingere un S. Marco con la spada . . .', ibid.

242 Giandomenico Romanelli, 'Giannantonio Selva: studio di cultura per Canova alle Zattere', *Le Venezie possibili: da Palladio a Le Corbusier*, ed. Lionello Puppi and Giandomenico Romanelli, Electa, Milan, 1985, pp. 156–7.

243 For Romanelli's view of the high quality of the design, ibid., p. 156.

244 Bassi, *Giannantonio Selva*, pp. 83–5.

245 For the process of location and the design by Francesco Lazzari see Giuseppe Pavanello, 'The Gipsoteca', Pavanello and Romanelli, *Canova*, pp. 360–67.

246 *Opera di scultura e di plastica di Antonio Canova descritte di Isabella Albrizzi nata Teotochi* (1809), Milani-Landi, Florence, 1811. Cf. Francesco Romani Fratini, 'Opera di scultura e plastica di Antonio Canova di Isabella Teotochi Albrizzi', *Studi Canoviani*, vol. 1. *Le Fonte*, vol. 2. *Canova e Venezia*, pp. 43–70.

247 Guy Dumas, *Echos de la chute de la République de Venise dans le littérature populaire* (Testes inédits ou rares), Brettonne, Rennes, 1961, p. 48.

248 Hugh Honour, 'Canova's Three Graces', *The Three Graces: Antonio Canova*, Timothy Clifford et al., National Gallery of Scotland, Edinburgh, 1995, pp. 28, 44.

249 *Opera di scultura e di plastica di Antonio Canova descritte di Isabella Albrizzi nata Teotochi*, p. iii.

250 Ibid.

251 Ibid., p. v.

252 Ibid.

253 On the head of Helen see Pavanello and Romanelli, *Canova*, p. 316.

254 Lord Byron, *The Complete Poetical Works*, ed. Jerome J. McGann, vol. 4, Clarendon Press, Oxford, 1986, p. 46.

255 On the sculpture project see Francesco Fedi, 'La Genesis della storia

della Scultura e le correzioni di Pietro Giordani', chap. 4, *L'Ideologia del Bello: Leopoldo Cicognara e il Classicismo tra Settecento e Ottocento*, p. 133ff.

256 Leopoldo Cicognara, *Storia della scultura dal suo risorgimento fino al secolo di Napoleone per servire di continuazione alle Opere di Winckelmann e di Agincourt*, 3 vols, Picotti, Venice, 1813–19. On Cicognara's study of Canova see Alba Costamagna, 'Leopoldo Cicognara, L'Estetica', *Studi Canoviani*, vol. 1. *Le Fonti*, vol. 2. *Canova e Venezia*, pp. 71–88, and Michela di Macco, 'Cicognara e Canova', ibid., pp. 89–107. And in general Fernando Mazzocca, 'Canova: A Myth in His Own Lifetime', Pavanello and Romanelli, *Canova*, pp. 77–87.

257 Cicognara, *Storia della scultura dal suo risorgimento fino al secolo XIX*, vol. 1, p. 5.

258 Quoted by Hugh Honour from Cicognara's *Lettere ad Antonio Canova*, *The Three Graces: Antonio Canova*, p. 45.

259 Nani Mocenigo's gives a general account, *Del Dominio napoleonico a Venezia*, pp. 98–100.

260 The building complex comprised the Convent of the Lateran Canons, or Convento del Carità (Palladio 1561), the church of Santa Maria della Carità (1451–52) and the Scuola Grande della Carità, the first of the great confraternities.

261 For the range of designs, Susanna Biadene, 'L'Accademie di Belle Arti', *Le Venezie possibili: da Palladio a Le Corbusier*, pp. 160–68.

262 Elena Bassi, 'L'Accademia', *Venezia nell'età di Canova, 1780–1830*, p. 313.

263 On the collections and a concise history see Scirè Nepi, *Treaures of Venetian Painting: The Gallerie dell'Accademia*, passim.

264 See the entry on *Le Fabbriche* in *Venezia nell'età di Canova, 1780–1830*, pp. 246–7.

265 Nani Mocenigo, *Del Dominio napoleonico a Venezia*, p. 101.

266 On the painting see Pavanello, *Venezia nell'età di Canova, 1780–1830*, pp. 256–7, and for comments on Canova's bust of Cicognara see Pavanello and Romanelli, *Canova*, pp. 312–13.

267 For these early operas see Giuseppe Radiciotti, *Gioacchino Rossini: vita documentata, opere ed influenza su l'arte*, vol. 1, Arti Grafiche Majella di Aldo Chicca, Tivoli, 1927, pp. 58–62.

268 For these opera see Richard Osborne, *Rossini*, J. M. Dent, London, 1986, pp. 131ff.

269 On Gaetano Rossi see Daniela Goldin, *La vera Fenice: librettisti e libretti tra Sette e Ottocento*, Einaudi, Turin, 1985, p. 56ff.

270 Radiciotti, *Gioacchino Rossini*, 'La Celebrità', ibid., pp. 97–127.

271 Stendhal assumes an almost universal knowledge of *Tancredi* four years after its premiere, *Life of Rossini*, trans. Richard N. Coe, Calder & Boyars, London, 1970, p. 52.

272 For the sets see Biggi, *Giuseppe Borsato: l'immagine e la scena*, pp. 46–51.

273 For example *Maometto II* (1820) involved the defeat of the Venetians by the Turks in Negroponte.

274 The patriotic aspect of Verdi's operas with relation to Venice will be discussed below.

275 Osborne, *Rossini*, pp. 2–3.

276 Stendhal, *Life of Rossini*, p. 82.

277 Ibid., p. 87.

278 Ibid., p. 48.

279 Ibid., p. 69. See also Michele Girardi, 'A Venetian Masterpiece of the Absurd', *L'Italiana in Algeri*, The Royal Opera, London, 1993.

280 Vincenzo Marchesi, 'La Guerra intorno a Venezia nel 1809', *Rivista del Risorgimento*, 1, 1895–6, pp. 712–20.

281 Marchesi concludes (in the only study of the blockade): 'Venezia non dimostrarono in quei giorni apertamente la loro antipatia per Francesi', ibid., p. 720.

282 See the account by Enrico Castelnuovo (which remains the most detailed in these years in terms of both history and cultural activity, and which takes a clear and understanding view of the relative inertia of Venice during this period) *A Venezia, un secolo fa*, G. Ferrari, Venice, 1913, pp. 1–23. Diaries consulted: the *Giornale dell'assedio*, by Pompeo Mangiarotti, and Cicogna's *Scartabelli*. For the Cicogna diary see A. Pilot, 'Venezia nel blocco del 1813–14 da noterelle inedite del Cicogna', *Nuovo Archivio Veneto*, 93 (1914), pp. 191–227.

283 Ibid., pp. 199–200. On measures taken to prevent starvation from December 1813 see Reuben John Rath, *The Fall of the Napoleonic Kingdom of Italy (1814)* (1941), Octagon Books, New York, 1975, pp. 138–9.

284 Pilot, 'Venezia nel blocco', p. 204.

285 Ibid., p. 205.

286 The comment was made on 11 May, 1814, ibid. p. 217. For further comment on the rebirth of the Venetian Republic based on the despatches to Vienna from Baron Hager, president of the Viennese aulic police directory see Rath, *The Fall of the Napoleonic Kingdom of Italy (1814)*, pp. 178–9.

287 Buratti's poem, *Lamentazion al Prefeto de Venezia al tempo del Bloco del 1813*, appears in the classic collection of Venetian verse in dialect: Raffaello Barbiera, *Poesie Veneziane con uno studio sulla poesia vernacola e sul dialetto di Venezia* (G. Barbèra, Florence, 1886), Arnaldo Forni, Bologna, 1975, pp. 215–21. See also *Il Fiore della lirica veneziana*, vol. 3, *Ottocento e Novecento*, ed. Manlio Dazzi, Neri

Pozza, Venice, 1959, with introduction and selected poems, pp. 11ff. See comments by Castelnuovo, *A Venezia un secola fa*, pp. 4–5. For Stendhal's opinion (and a wider comment on Buratti's influence) see Manlio Dazzi, 'Buratti nel giudizio di Stendhal, con riferimenti a Manzoni, Porta, Pellico, Byron', *Nuova Rivista Storica*, 35 (1956), pp. 502–11.

288 For these events see Rath, *The Fall of the Napoleonic Kingdom in Italy (1814)*, p. 60, and passim.

289 Ibid., chap. 2, 'The stirring up of Liberal and National Sentiment', pp. 27–44.

290 See comments on the hatred of the French in Castelnuovo, *A Venezia un secola fa*, p. 11, and Cicogna's comments on the flood of invective and satire, 'Venezia nel Blocco del 1813–14', p. 214. Cicogna had a taste for satire and often recorded examples, see p. 222.

291 Rath, *The Fall of the Napoleonic Kingdom (1814)*, p. 211.

292 Making this point, Enrico Castelnuovo cites a letter from Foscolo to the Countess of Albany, 5 December 1814, in *A Venezia, un secolo fa*, p. 10.

293 Romanelli, *Venezia Ottocento*, p. 465: 'Il disastro dell'Arsenal di Venezia, quello da compiangersi amaramente, è la irreparabile demolizione di molti suoi cantieri di prima grandezza.'

294 Ibid., p. 509.

295 For the letter of 17 March see Foscolo, *Ultime lettere di Jacopo Ortis*, p. 331ff.

296 For Petrarch's view of 'the most marvellous city that I have ever seen', 'Petrarch and the Venetians', Patricia Fortini Brown, *Venice and Antiquity: The Venetian Sense of the Past*, Yale University Press, New Haven and London, 1996, pp. 65–6. For further connections see *Petrarca, Venezia e il Veneto*, Fondazione Giorgio Cini, L. S. Olschki, Florence, 1976. Foscolo was to publish a specific essay on Petrarch later in England, in 1823.

297 Foscolo: 'Terra senza abitatori può stare; popolo senza terra, non mai'.

298 Cited in R. Dollot, *Stendhal à Venise*, Editions du Stendhal-Club, P. Daupeley-Gouverneur, Paris, 1927, p. 35.

299 Stendhal, *Pages d'Italie: L'Italie en 1808, Moeurs romaines*, Paris, Le Divan, Kraus Reprint, New York, 1968, pp. 30–31.

300 Ibid., p. 29.

301 'Que j'abhorre Buonaparte de l'avoir sacrifiée à l'Autriche . . . Venise était plus sur le chemin de la civilisation que Londres et Paris. Aujourd'hui il y a cinquant milles pauvres': Stendhal, *Voyages en Italie*, Pléiade, Gallimard, Paris, 1973, p. 124.

Chapter 3

1 Carlo Pietrangeli, 'Ambassador Extraordinaire: Canova's Mission to Paris', *Canova*, ed. Giuseppe Pavanello and Giandomenico Romanelli, Marsilio, Venice, 1992, pp. 15–21.

2 Ibid., p. 17.

3 Ian Wardropper, 'Antonio Canova and Quatremère de Quincy: The Gift of Friendship', *Museum Studies*, 1 (1989), pp. 38–46.

4 Quatremère de Quincey, *Lettres sur le project d'enlever les monuments de l'Italie*, [n.p.] Rome, 1815.

5 Ibid., p. 55.

6 Ibid., p. 2.

7 Pietrangeli, 'Ambassador extraordinaire', p. 15. Canova was despatched to Paris in December 1814.

8 See Massimo Cesàreo, 'Gli Asburgo e l'arte nell'Italia della Restaurazione', *Ateneo Veneto*, 193 (1996), pp. 159–73. Cesàreo pays considerable attention to Cicognara's efforts, e.g. p. 166.

9 Massimiliano Pavan, 'Canova e il problema dei cavalli di San Marco', *Ateneo Veneto*, 12 (1974), p. 96, and his 'The Horses of San Marco in the Neoclassical and Romantic Epochs', *The Horses of San Marco, Venice*, trans. John and Valerie Wilton-Ely, Procuratoria di S. Marco and Olivetti, Milan, 1975, p. 113ff.

10 Ibid., pp. 97–8.

11 Scarfi, 'The Bronze Lion of St Mark', *The Lion of Venice: Studies and Research on the Bronze Statue in the Piazzetta*, ed Bianca Maria Scarfi, Albrizzi, Venice, 1990, p. 35. Ferrari's restoration is documented in the text.

12 Ibid., p. 49.

13 Quoted in Pavan, 'Canova e il problema dei cavalli di San Marco', p. 95. For the long-term controversy regarding the placement of the horses, see Michael Jacoff, *The Horses of San Marco and the Quadriga of the Lord*, Princeton University Press, 1993, chap. 6, 'The Problem of the Placement of the Horses of San Marco', p. 84ff.

14 Timothy Clifford, 'Canova in Context: The Sculptor, His Reputation, His British Patrons and His Visit to England', *The Three Graces: Antonio Canova*, ed. Hugh Honour and Aidan Weston-Lewis, National Gallery of Scotland, Edinburgh, 1995, pp. 9–18.

15 The various views are detailed in Pavan, 'Canova e il problema dei cavalli', p. 100ff. and Licia Borelli Vlad and Anna Guidi Toniati, 'The Origins and Documentary Sources of the Horses of San Marco', p. 130ff. Emmanuele Antonio Cicogna gives an extensive bibliography with relation to the discussion in *Saggio di bibliografia veneziana*, vol. 2 (1847), Burt Franklin, New York, 1967, pp. 681–2.

16 Giuseppe Pavanello, 'La decorazione dei palazzi veneziani negli anni del dominio austriaco (1814–1866)', *Il Veneto e l'Austria: vita e cultura artistica nelle città Venete, 1814–1866*, ed. Sergio Marinetti, Giuseppe Mazzariol and Fernando Mazzocca, Electa, Milan, 1989, pp. 259–60.

17 Adriani Augusti, 'Dal Palazzo dei Procuratori al Palazzo del Re: le vicende e la decorazione', *Le Procuratie Nuove in Piazza San Marco*, Editalia, Rome, 1994, pp. 159ff.

18 Pavanello, 'La decorazione Neoclassica nei palazzi veneziani', *Venezia nell'età di Canova, 1780–1830*, ed. Elena Bassi et al., Alfieri, Venice, 1978, p. 259.

19 Ibid., p. 262. Over the years there were further programmes, for example in 1825, and again in 1838 for the visit of Emperor Ferdinand.

20 See the section on the Giardino Reale in Eva Rita Rowedder Lehni, *Studien zu Lorenzo Santi (1783–1839)*, Centro Tedesco di Studi Veneziani, Venice, 1983, pp. 77–105.

21 Gianpietro Zucchetta, *Venezia ponte per ponte*, vol. 2, Stamperia di Venezia, Venice, 1992, pp. 88–9, and *Venezia nell'età di Canova, 1780–1830*, p. 186.

22 Lehni, *Studien zu Lorenzo Santi*, pp. 79–105; *Venezia nell'età di Canova*, p. 187.

23 It was intended that the coffee house should have marble statues in the central pavilion, and be a conservatory in winter. Representations of the four seasons were planned for the cupola.

24 Alvise Zorzi, *Venezia austriaca, 1798–1866*, Laterza, Rome and Bari, 1985, especially chap. 3, 'Lo stato di polizia', and 6, 'Il clero, le religioni'.

25 Cited in Antonio Pilot, *Echi della rivoluzione napoletana del 1820–21 in alcune note inedite del Cicogna*, Tipografia San Marco, Venice, 1922, pp. 3–4.

26 7 February 1829, Ibid., p. 5.

27 R. John Rath, 'The Habsburgs and the Great Depression in Lombardy-Venetia, 1814–18', *Journal of Modern History*, 13 (1941), pp. 305–20. Rath's argument for the positive intervention of Austria during a time of hardship has been endorsed by Paul Ginsborg, *Daniele Manin and the Venetian Revolution of 1848–49*, Cambridge University Press, 1979, 'The Venetian Countryside', p. 11ff. Ginsborg's study is one of the few dealing with the Austrian period.

28 Rath contests that 'The Austrian bureaucracy was almost surprisingly clumsy, slow and inefficient in establishing a new government in the recently acquired Italian provinces and did not succeed until 1815 and 1816 in substituting Austrian laws and institutions for the French ones': his documentation is drawn from the Staatsarchiv in Vienna: 'The Habsburgs and the Great Depression', p. 307.

29 Ibid.

30 For a demographic table comparing 1797 with 1824 see Romanelli, *Venezia Ottocento: l'architettura l'urbanistica*, Albrizzi, Venice, 1988, p. 47.

31 Ginsborg, *Daniele Manin and the Venetian Revolution of 1848–49*, p. 22.

32 For Shelley's *Julian and Maddalo: A Conversation*, *The Complete Poetical Works of Percy Bysshe Shelley*, ed. Thomas Hutchinson, Oxford University Press, 1912, pp. 185–99. And see William Christie, '"Despondency and Madness": Shelley in Conversation with Byron in *Julian and Maddalo*', *Byron Journal*, 21 (1993), pp. 43–60.

33 Giandomenico Romanelli, *Venezia Ottocento*, p. 155.

34 *Memoirs of Prince Metternich, 1773–1815*, ed. Prince Richard Metternich, trans. Mrs Alexander Napier, vol. 2, Richard Bentley & Son, London, 1880, p. 617. Metternich also reported that the courtiers were weary of Venice because there was nothing to do.

35 John Galiffe, *Italy and its Inhabitants: An Account of a Tour in that Country in 1816 and 1817*, John Murray, London, 1824, p. 129.

36 William Stewart Rose, *Letters from the North of Italy addressed to Henry Hallam Esq.*, 2 vols, John Murray, London, 1819, vol. 1, p. 278.

37 Romanelli publishes Pyrker's petition, August 1825, *Venezia Ottocento*, pp. 475–6.

38 Vittorio Malamani, 'L'Austria e i Bonapartisti (1815–1848)', *Rivista Storica Italiana*, 7 (1890), pp. 256–81.

39 For detailed documentation of Pellico's visit to Venice, subsequent trial and imprisonment see Giovanni Sforza, *Silvio Pellico a Venezia (1820–1822)*, R. Deputazione, Venice, 1917.

40 Silvio Pellico, *I miei prigioni* (1832), trans. *My Prisons: Memoirs of Silvio Pellico*, Robert Brothers, Boston, Mass., 1868. Note the comment by Franco Meregalli, in 'Venice in Romantic Literature', *Arcadia*, 18 (1983), p. 232: 'It was said that the publication of *Le miei prigioni* by Silvio Pellico (which came out in 1832 and which, all over Europe, contributed to reinforcing the myth of Venice groaning in her Austrian chains) cost the Austrians more than a lost battle.'

41 According to Paul Ginsborg, 'the educated Venetian found his world dominated by the police and censorship': *Daniele Manin and the Venetian Revolution of 1848–49*, p. 8, and indeed Ginsborg takes surveillance and the constriction of liberty to be the principal causes of the uprising in 1848. For an account of censorship, Giampietro Berti, 'Censura e cultura nella Venezia austriaca',

Il Veneto austriaco, 1814–1866, ed. Paolo Preto, Fondazione Cassamarca, Padua, 2000, pp. 194–209.

42 Romanelli, *Venezia Ottocento*, p. 150.

43 Alvise Zorzi, *Venezia scomparsa*, Electa, Milan, 1984, p. 151.

44 For an overview see Mario dalla Costa, 'Restauro, conservazione e manutenzione: i temi di una polemica ai restauri dell'Ottocento nella Basilica di San Marco', *Restauro e Città*, 3/4 (1986), pp. 40–49.

45 Zorzi, *Venezia scomparsa*, p. 121.

46 For the Canova work see Giuseppe Pavanello, *L'opera completa del Canova*, Rizzoli, Milan, 1976, pp. 123–4, and *Venezia nell'età di Canova, 1780–1830*, p. 251. For the presentation volume see Leopoldo Cicognara, *Omaggio delle Provincie Venete alla Maestà di Carolina Augusta Imperatrice d'Austria*, Alvisopoli, Venice, 1818 (Museo Correr), noted with illustrations and entries by Dorigato and Pavanello, *Venezia nell'età di Canova, 1780–1830*, pp. 246–50. Cicogna's diary entry on the work, 12 August 1817, is cited in Franco Bizzotto, 'I *Diari* di Emmanuele Antonio Cicogna', *Venezia Arti*, 2 (1988), p. 81.

47 *Venezia nell'età di Canova, 1780–1830*, pp. 246–50.

48 Melchior Missirini gives a contemporary account in *Della vita di Antonio Canova*, Nicolò Bettoni, Milan, 1824: 'Morte del Canova', p. 195ff; on the funeral, p. 203ff; and the ceremonies at Possagno, p. 207ff.

49 Giuseppe Borsato, *Leopoldo Cicognara giving his Funeral Oration in front of the Body of Canova at the Accademia of Venice*, signed 1824. Galleria d'Arte Moderna, Venice: *Venezia nell'età di Canova, 1780–1830*, p. 261.

50 For the Titian memorial decreed in 1838, see below.

51 Philipp P. Fehl, 'At Titian's Tomb', *Decorum and Wit: The Poetry of Venetian Painting. Essays in the History of the Classical Tradition*, Irsa, Vienna, 1992, pp. 306–12.

52 On the tomb in Possagno, Paolo Mariuz, 'A Tomb for Canova', *Canova*, ed. Pavanello and Romanelli, pp. 344–59.

53 Vittorio Malamani comments on Cicognara's popularity in his *Memorie del Conte Leopoldo Cicognara: tratte dai documenti originale*, Ancora, Merlo, Venice, 1888, p. 7.

54 Leopoldo Cicognara, *Biografia di Antonio Canova*, Alvisopoli, Venice, 1823.

55 For the Canova works see Giuseppe Pavanello, *L'Opera completa del Canova*, Rizzoli, Milan, 1976, p. 119. For the Borsato painting see *Venice Vienna: il mito della cultura Veneziana nell'Europa asburgica*, ed. Giandomenico Romanelli, Electa, Milan, 1983, p. 147. Jacopo Treves de'Bonfil has been described as 'una delle figure più rappresentative del mondo finanziario e imprenditoriale veneziano dell'Ottocento', in Alvise Zorzi's *Venezia austriaca, 1798–1866*, Laterza, Rome and Bari, 1984, p. 259.

56 On the introduction of Romanticism in Northern Italy at this point, William Spaggiari, *Il Ritorno di Astrea: civiltà letteraria della restaurazione*, Bulzoni, Rome, 1990, p. 9.

57 Pierre Darù, *Histoire de la République de Venise*, vol. 1, Didot, Paris, 1819: opening passage, my translation.

58 See entries in Cicogna, *Saggio di bibliografia veneziana*, vol. 1, pp. 88–9.

59 The poem appears in Guy Dumas, *Echos de la chute de la Republique de Venise dans la littérature populaire*, Brettone, Rennes, 1961, pp. 313–14.

60 G. Luciani, 'Un Complément inédit à "L'Histoire de la République de Venise" de Darù: La correspondance de P. Darù avec l'Abbé Moschini', *Revue de etudes italiennes*, 6 (1959), pp. 105–48.

61 For this charge see ibid., p. 127; and for one of his justifications of impartiality, p. 124.

62 *Discorsi sulla storia Veneta cioè Rettificazione di alcuni e equivoci riscontrati nella Storia di Venezia del sig. Darù del co. Domenico Tiepolo patrizio Veneto*, Mattiuzzi, Udine, 1828.

63 Of interest in this context is John D. Jump, 'A Comparison of *Marin Faliero* with Otway's *Venice Preserv'd*', *Byron Journal*, 5 (1977), pp. 20–33.

64 Darù, *Histore de la République de Venise*, vol. 7, pp. 431–557.

65 Ibid., p. 563. For comment on Tiepolo see Massimo Canella, 'Appunti e spunti sulla storiografia veneziana', *Archivio Veneto*, 107 (1976), pp. 81–2.

66 Pierre Darù, *Histoire de la République de Venise*, vol. 7, Didot, Paris, 1819, p. 568.

67 For a detailed coverage see John Lindon, 'Foscolo, Darù e la Storia di Venezia', *Revue des etudes italiennes*, 27 (1981), pp. 8–39, passim. For a biography of Foscolo's life in England (undocumented), Carlo Maria Franzero, *A Life in Exile: Ugo Foscolo in London, 1816–1827*, W. H. Allen, London, 1977.

68 For Roscoe's interest see introduction, Ugo Foscolo, *Scritti vari di critica storica e letteraria, 1817–1827*, ed. Uberto Limentani, with J. M. A. Lindon, Felice Le Monnier, Florence, 1978, p. lxxv, n. 3.

69 *Quarterly Review*, 21 (1825), p. 439. Note also Foscolo, *Scritti vari di critica storica e letteraria, 1817–1827*, p. 443, claiming that the Republic represented 'the horrors of the foulest system of assassination and tyranny, the most deliberate violation of the laws of God that obligation of morality that ever assumed the shape of human government'.

70 Foscolo, reviewing *Memorie Venete di Giovanni Gallicciolli, prete, per la nuova collezione di documenti per serviere alla Storia Venezia*, Venice, 1826, 'History of the Democratical Constitution of Venice', ibid., pp. 472–560.

71 Cited in the introduction, ibid., p. lxxv, n. 2.

72 Ibid., p. 538.

73 Foscolo, 'Memorie del Casanova', ibid., pp. 564–609.

74 Ibid., p. 609.

75 Thomas Moore, *Letters and Journals of Lord Byron with Notices of His Life*, John Murray, London, 1830, vol. 2, p. 52.

76 See Andrew Rutherford, 'The Influence of Hobhouse on *Childe Harold's Pilgrimage*, Canto IV', *Review of English Studies*, 12 (1961), pp. 391–7.

77 Canto 4 is *not* entirely devoted to Venice: in stanza 30, Byron moves to Arquà and writes of Petrarch (which may also reflect at least indirectly on Foscolo and his *Jacopo Ortis*), thence to Ferrara, etc.

78 Percy Bysshe Shelley, 'Lines Written Among the Euganean Hills', composed in 1818, only some months after *Childe Harold's* fourth canto: *The Complete Poetical Works of Percy Bysshe Shelley*, ed. Thomas Hutchinson, Oxford University Press, 1912, pp. 550–54. For the circumstances of Shelley's visit to Venice, see Michael Foot, *The Politics of Paradise: A Vindication of Byron*, Harper & Row, New York, 1988, p. 228ff.

79 William Beckford of Fonthill, *Dreams, Waking Thoughts, and Incidents*, ed. Robert J. Gemmett, Fairleight Dickinson University Press, Rutherford, NJ, 1972.

80 See the wide-ranging essay by Marie-Hélène Girard, 'Le Personnage de Marino Faliero dans le Romanticisme français', *Trois Figures de l'imaginaire littéraire*, Actes du XII Congrés de la Société Française de Littérature générale et Comparée recueillis et publiés par Edouard Gaède, La Faculté des Lettres et Sciences Humaines de Nice, Nice, 1982, pp. 125–44.

81 E. T. A. Hoffmann, *Doge und Dogaressa*, was written in 1817, and published the following year. The story takes as its starting point the painting of the doge by C. Kolbe, exhibited in 1816 in the Berlin Academy of the Arts. The painting is reproduced in Erik Forssman, *Venedig in der Kunst und im Kunsturteil des 19. Jahrhunderts*, Almquist & Wirksells, Stockholm, 1971, p. 32. For an English version see *Tales of Hoffmann*, trans. R. J. Hollingdale, Penguin, Harmondsworth, 1982, pp. 253–309.

82 For Manzoni's connection with Venice (and his later revisions with respect to Venice) see Vittore Branca, 'Manzoni

and Venice', *Italian Quarterly*, 17 (1963), pp. 63–70; also *Manzoni: il suo e il nostro tempo*, ed. Carlo Pirovano, Electa, Milan, 1985, pp. 206–7.

83 Francesco Lomonaco, *Vita degli eccelenti italiani*, 2 vols, Milan, 1802–1803.

84 An accessible account of the historical background is given in John Julian Norwich, *A History of Venice*, Penguin, Harmondsworth, 1983, chap. 22, 'Carmagnola', p. 300ff. For an analysis of the play and its Venetian context, with contemporary analogies, Gilberto Lonardi, 'Il Carmagnola, Venezia e il "Potere inguisto"', *Manzoni, Venezia e il Veneto*, ed. Vittore Branca, Ettore Caccia and Cesare Galimberti, Olschki, Florence, 1976, pp. 19–41; and the closely related essay by Gilberto Lonardi, 'Alle origini della scena manzoniana', *Revue des études italiennes*, 32 (1986), pp. 132–41.

85 Noting that Manzoni was the grandson of Cesare Beccaria.

86 Alessandro Manzoni, *Il Conte di Carmagnolo*, act 2, scene 6, Garzanti, Milan, 1991, pp. 64–5.

87 See Enrico Castelnuovo, *A Venezia un secolo fa*, G. Ferrari, Venice, 1913, p. 9, alleging a greater cultural vitality in Milan.

88 Ugo Foscolo, 'Dell nuova scuola dramattica italiana', *Saggi di letteratura italiana*, vol. 2, ed. Cesare Foligno, Felice Le Monnier, Florence, 1958, p. 559ff.

89 Ibid., p. 594.

90 Lord Byron, *Marino Faliero, Doge of Venice, An Historical Tragedy, in Five Acts, The Complete Poetical Works*, vol. 4, ed. Jerome J. McGann, Clarendon Press, Oxford, 1986, p. 298ff.

91 On 2 April 1817 Byron wrote to John Murray: 'There is still, in the Doge's palace the black veil painted over Falieri's picture & the staircase wheron he was first crowned Doge, & subsequently decapitated. This was the the thing that most struck my imagination in Venice . . .' *So Late into the Night', Byron's Letters and Journals*, vol. 5, *1816–1817*, ed. Leslie A. Marchand, John Murray, London, 1976, p. 203.

92 For the Faliero episode in Darù: *Histoire de la République de Venise*, vol. 5, p. 95ff. Byron appended transcriptions of his sources and published a sprightly preface assessing the historical material.

93 Byron, *Marino Faliero, Doge of Venice*, p. 543, citing *L'Ouvrage Historie Littéraire d'Italie, par P. L. Ginguené*, vol. 9, chap. 26, p. 144, Editions de Paris, 1819.

94 Girolamo Soranzo, *Bibliografia veneziana in aggiunta e continuazione del 'Saggio' di Emmanuele Antonio Cicogna* (1885), Burt Franklin, New York, 1967, p. 225. See again Girard, 'Marino Faliero dans le Romanticisme français', p. 133, n.

52; and pp. 133–138, on Delavigne's popular play.

95 *Oeuvres complètes de Casimir Delavigne*, Ch. Lahure, Paris, 1855, pp. 148–80. For the appendix, pp. 182–4.

96 Cicogna, *Saggio di bibliografia veneziana*, vol. 1, pp. 282–3.

97 William Ashbrook, *Donizetti*, Cassell, London, 1965, pp. 487–5. Donizetti's opera deals with the wife's adulterous relationship as well as a more complicated intrigue which involves Steno against the doge. For some comments see Philip Gossett, 'The Théâtre-Italien', *Music in Paris in the Eighteen-Thirties*, ed. Peter Bloom, Pendragon Press, Stuyvesant, NY, 1987, pp. 345–9.

98 Cicogna, *Saggio di bibliografia veneziana*, vol. 1, p. 282.

99 Soranzo, *Bibliografia veneziana in aggiunta e continuazione del 'Saggio' di Emmanuele Antonio Cicogna*, p. 225.

100 Ibid.

101 Lee Johnson, *The Paintings of Eugène Delacroix: A Critical Catalogue*, vol. 1, *1816–1831*, Clarendon Press, Oxford, 1981, pp. 97–102. Johnson points out that Delacroix departs from Byron by staging the execution on the landing, rather than the top of the staircase. Not only is the subject Venetian, but Delacroix's painterly focus on Venetian masters for their colouristic and glazing effects was fundamental for his inspiration as a painter.

102 *The Two Foscari, An Historical Tragedy, Lord Byron: The Complete Poetical Works*, vol. 6, ed. Jerome J. McGann, Clarendon Press, Oxford, 1986, p. 143.

103 Quoted sympathetically by Foot, *The Politics of Paradise: A Vindication of Byron*, p. 299.

104 *Finden's Landscapes and Portrait Illustrations to the Life and Works of Lord Byron*, John Murray, London, 1833. D. Harding, *Venice from the Entrance to the Grand Canal*; C. Stanfield, *Lido and Port St Nicholas*, ibid., no pagination.

105 On the French appetite for Byron see Lucien Cattan, 'La Venise de Byron et la Venise des Romantiques français', *Revue de littérature comparée*, 5 (1925), pp. 89–102. See also Michéle Maréchal-Trudel, *Chateaubriand, Byron et Venise: un mythe contexté*, A.-G. Nizet, Paris, 1978.

106 Moore, *Letters and Journals of Lord Byron*; vol. 2, pp. 51–2.

107 Le Comte de Forbin et Louis Dejuinne, *Un Mois à Venise ou Recueil de vues pittoresques*, Englemann, Paris, 1825. For selected plates see *Venezia nell'Ottocento: immagini e mito*, ed. Giuseppe Pavanello and Giandomenico Romanelli, Electa, Milan, 1983, pp. 15–16, pp. 79, 196.

108 'Venise contribua puissamment aux

progrès de la civilisation européene': Foreword Forbin and Dejuinne, *Un Mois à Venise*, p. 1.

109 Ibid., p. 38.

110 On allegorical representations at this time see *Venezia nell'Ottocento: immagini e mito*, pp. 13–20.

111 Forbin and Dejuinne, *Un Mois à Venise*, pp. 3, 5.

112 *Venezia nell'Ottocento: immagini e mito*, p. 79, in which the work is presented as among the earliest chronologically in the section on 'Notturno veneziano'.

113 Forbin and Dejuinne, *Un Mois à Venise*, p. 16.

114 J. R. Herbert and Thomas Roscoe, *Legends of Venice*, Longman's, London, 1840. See *Venezia nell'Ottocento*, p. 173.

115 See the stimulating treatment by David McPherson, *Shakespeare, Jonson and the Myth of Venice*, University of Delaware Press, Newark, NJ, 1991.

116 Bravos are everywhere in the novel by Mrs Catherine Smith, *Barozzi; or The Venetian Sorceress: A Romance in the Sixteenth Century*, A. K. Newman & Co., London, 1815.

117 M. G. [Monk] Lewis, *The Bravo of Venice: A Romance* (1804), Arno, McGrath, New York, 1972, chap. 8, p. 97. For the 'indolent and gossiping Venetians' see p. 76. On the bravo see Uberto Limentani, 'La presenza di Venezia nella cultura inglese, Preromantica e del primo Ottocento', *Ateneo Veneto*, 20 (1982), p. 13.

118 August Anicet Bourgeois, *La Vénitienne*, 1834. For Saverio Mercadante's opera see notes by Roberto di Perna for the recording, *Il Bravo*, conductor Bruno Aprea, Orchestra Internazionale d'Italia, Nuova Era, 6971/3, 1991.

119 James Fenimore Cooper, *The Bravo*, G. P. Putnam & Sons, The Knickerbocker Press, New York, n.d., Preface, p. iii: 'The author has endeavoured to give his countrymen in this book, a picture of the social system of one of the soi-disant republics of the other hemisphere. There has been no attempt to portray historical characters, only too fictitious in their graver dress, but simply to set the familiar operations of Venetian policy.'

120 Ibid., p. 145.

121 Ibid., p. 413.

122 Luigi Carrer, 'Osservazioni sul Bravo, storia veneziana di Fenimore Cooper, 1835', in *Opere scelte*, vol. 2, *Prose*, Florence, 1855, pp. 486–91.

123 Ibid., p. 486.

124 *Ruskin's Letters from Venice, 1851–1852*, ed. John Lewis Bradley, Yale University Press, New Haven, 1955, p. 207.

125 Victor Hugo, 'Lucrèce Borgia', *Théatre complet*, Pléiade, Gallimard, Paris, 1964, p. 293ff.

126 On the incisive influence of Piranesi on Hugo see Luzuis Keller, *Piranèse et les Romantiques français*, José Corti, Paris, 1966, chap. 3, p. 145ff.

127 For Victor Hugo and 'L'Angelo Tyran de Padou' see Ibid., 1894ff. For Italian criticism of these plays see G. Gambarin, 'Per la Fortuna di alcuni scrittori stranieri nel Veneto nella prima metà dell'Ottocento', *Nuovo Archivio Veneto*, 27 (1914), pp. 143–4.

128 For Donizetti's *Lucrezia Borgia* see Ashbrook, *Donizetti*, pp. 481–2. Ponchiello's *La Gioconda* is discussed in chapter 5 below.

129 David Blayney Brown, *Turner and Byron*, Tate Gallery, London, 1992. For Turner's Venetian opus see Lindsay Stainton, *Turner's Venice*, British Museum, London, 1985.

130 Jan Piggott, *Turner's Vignettes*, Tate Gallery, London, 1993. For the context of the first Venetian work see Cecilia Powell, 'Topography, Imagination and Travel: Turner's Relationship with James Hakewill', *Art History*, 5 (1982), pp. 408–25. For the work for Samuel Rogers see Adele M. Holcomb, 'A Neglected Classical Phase of Turner's Art: His Vignettes to Rogers' 'Italy', *Journal of the Warburg and Courtauld Institutes*, 32 (1969), pp, 405–10.

131 For further discussion see Margaret Plant, 'Venetian Journeys', *Turner*, ed. Michael Lloyd, National Gallery of Australia, Thames & Hudson, London, 1996, pp. 144–63.

132 Anne Lyles, *Turner: The Fifth Decade. Watercolours 1830–1840*, Tate Gallery, London, 1992.

133 *Venezia nell'Ottocento: immagini e mito*, pp. 160–61. For a broad coverage of English work see Timothy Wilcox, John Christian and J. G. Links, *Visions of Venice: Watercolours and Drawings from Turner to Procktor*, Bankside Gallery, London, 1990.

134 Piggott, *Turner's Vignettes*, no. 65, p. 108.

135 Vittore Benzon, *Nella, Poema*, Alvisopoli, Venice, 1830. In the poem, the origin of the Venetian citizens is Roman, come to Aquileia and from there to be the first settlers of the Venetian islands.

136 Cicogna gives extensive listings of description and guides to the city from the fifteenth century onwards, with the various editions of contemporary works: *Saggio di bibliografia veneziana*, vol. 2, pp. 597–607. Soranza gives the later material and additional titles: *Bibliografia veneziana*, p. 601. French and German guides are included, but only one in the English language, and that translated from the German (*Venice: Her Art, Treasures and Historical Associations*, A. Müller, 1864), p. 601.

137 On guidebooks in general up until that time, E. S. De Beer, 'The Development of the Guide-Book until the early Nineteenth Century', *Journal of the British Archaeological Association*, 15 (1952), pp. 35–46.

138 Giannantonio Moschini, *Guida per l'Isola di Murano*, Stamperia Palese, Venice, 1808.

139 Giannantonio Moschini, *Guida per la Città di Venezia all'amico delle belle arti*, Alvisopoli, Venice, 1815.

140 Ibid., pp. 76, 618, 394.

141 Giannantonio Moschini, *Itinéraire de Venise*, Alvisopoli, Venice, 1817.

142 Ibid., p. 389.

143 Antonio Quadri, *Otto Giorni a Venezia*, 2 vols., Francesco Andreola, Venice, 1821–2. Cicogna lists the various editions.

144 'L'osservatore troverà in essi il più chiaro monumento della possanza, e ricchezza della cessata Repubblica'.

145 Ibid., vol. 2, pp. xliv–xlv. Like Moschini, Quadri followed with a French version in 1837: *Huit Jours à Venise*, Antonie Bazzarini, Venice, 1838, which opened with a comprehensive portfolio of engravings of the principal monuments, figures and sights: Canova, the Colleoni, the four horses of St Mark, a gondola, the English dispensary and, in line with the clear bid to be useful to the foreign tourist, illustrations of the international hotels of Venice: the Grand Hotel Royal, Hotel de l'Europe, the Hotel Royal du Lion Blanc, and the Hotel de la Reine d'Angleterre.

146 Antonio Quadri and Dionisio Morelli, *Il Canale Grande di Venezia* (1828), fascimile reproduction, Viannello libri, Ponzano, Treviso, 1983.

147 Piero Buratti, *Elefanteide: storia Verissima dell'Elefante* (1817), intro. and notes by Tiziano Rizzo, Filippi, Venice 1988.

148 Cicogna, *Saggio di bibliografia veneziana*, vol. 1, p. 265.

149 Angelo Ventura, 'La formazione intellettuale di Daniele Manin', *Il Risorgimento*, 9 (1959), pp. 4–5.

150 Nereo Vianello, *La Tipografia di Alvisopoli e gli annali di sue publicazione*, Olschki, Florence, 1967.

151 Giustina Renier Michiel, *Origine delle feste veneziane*, Alvisopoli, Venice, 5 vols, 1817–27. For Cicogna's comment, 'Quest'opera per lo spirito patrio con cui è scritta si legge molto volontieri', see *Bibliographia veneziana*, vol. 1, p. 228.

152 Dedication to the 1817 edition cited by Vittorio Malamani, 'Giustina Renier Michiel, I suoi amici, il suo tempo', *Ateneo Veneto*, 38 (1889), p. 327.

153 *Venezia nell'età di Canova, 1780–1830*, p. 278.

154 Luigi Carrer, *Anello di sette gemme o Venezia e la sua storia considera-* *zioni e fantasie*, Co' Tipi del Gondoliere, Venice, 1838.

155 Castelnuovo notes its importance in *A Venezia un secolo fa*, p. 21.

156 *Delle Inscrizioni veneziane raccolte ed illustrate da E. A. Cicogna*, 6 vols, Presso Giuseppe Orlandelli, Venice, 1824–53.

157 See again Spina, 'La Biblioteca di Emmanuele Antonio Cicogna', *Studi Veneziani*, 29 (1985), passim, and Attilia Dorigato, 'Emmanuele Antonio Cicogna bibliofilo e cultore patrie memorie', *Una città e il suo museo: un secolo e mezzo di collezioni civiche veneziane*, Museo Correr, Venice, 1988, pp. 143–6.

158 There is little literature on the Campanile restoration. In *Saggio di bibliografia veneziana*, Cicogna cites *Narrazione storica del Campanile di S. Marco in Venezia dal tempo della sua fondazione fino al suo inalzamento, e dell'angelo che se collocherà nella sua estremità*, Molinari, Venice, 1822. Marcel Proust's writing on the angel in *Remembrance of Things Past* is discussed in chap. 6, below.

159 Ibid., p. 652: *Collezione de' più pregevoli monumenti sepolcrali della città di Venezia e sue isole con illustrazioni del n. uomo Antonio Diedo segretario dell'I. R. Accademia di Belle Arti di Venezia, e del professore di scultura sig. Luigi Zandomeneghi, Opera delineata da Antonio Mauro, Pietro Quarena, ed Angelo Soavi, e incisa da varii alunni della Accademia suddetta*, Picotti, Venice, 1831.

160 Cicogna, *Del Gobbo di Rialto*, *Saggio di biografia veneziana*, vol. 2, p. 642.

161 J. N. L. Durand, *Raccolta e Paralello delle fabbriche classiche di tutti i tempi: opera publicata per cura de' professori della I. R. Accademia di Belle Arti*, G. Antonelli, Venice, 1833.

162 Ibid., pp. 256–9.

163 The Archive's history is given in chap. 1, B. Cecchetti, *L'Archivio di Stato in Venezia negli anni, 1876–1880*, P. Naratovich, Venice, 1881, pp. 1–24. See also Francesca Cavazzana Romanelli, 'Gli archivi della Serenissima: concentrazioni e ordinamenti', *Venezia e l'Austria*, ed. Gino Benzoni e Gaetano Cozzi, Marsilio, Fondazione Giorgio Cini, Venice, 1999, pp. 291–308.

164 John Pemble gives a spirited account in 'A Window on the Past', *Venice Rediscovered*, Clarendon Press, Oxford, 1995, pp. 73–86.

165 Lehni, *Studien zu Lorenzo Santi*, p. 223. For the infill of the canal, Gianpietro Zucchetta, *Un'altra Venezia: immagini e storia degli antichi canali scomparsi. Another Venice: An Illustrated History of Concealed Venetian Canals*, Ericco, Venice, 1995, pp. 260–61.

166 Ugo Tucci, 'Ranke and the Venetian Document Market', *Leopold von*

Ranke and the Shaping of the Historical Discipline, ed. George G. Iggerans and James M. Powell, Syracuse University Press, 1990, p. 100.

167 Paul Kaufman, 'Rawdon Brown and his Adventures in Venetian Archives', *English Miscellany*, 18 (1967), pp. 282–302.

168 Giandomenico Romanelli, '"Vista cadere la patria . . .", Teodoro Correr tra "Pietas" civile e collezionismo erudito', *Una città e il suo museo*, pp. 13–28, and Attilia Dorigato, 'Il Collezionismo a Venezia e la nascita delle civiche raccolte', *Il Veneto e l'Austria*, pp. 309–13. Also Giandomenico Romanelli, *Correr Museum*, Electa, Milan, 1985. On other legacies to the state: Zorzi, *Venezia scomparsa*, p. 127. For a comprehensive account of the formation of Venetian museums: Krzysztof Pomian, *Collections and Curiosities: Paris and Venice, 1500–1800*, trans. Elizabeth Wiles-Portier, Polity Press, Cambridge, 1990, esp. chap. 8, 'Private Collections, Public Museums', pp. 258–75.

169 See again Dorigato, 'Emmanuele Antonio Cicogna bibliofilo e cultore di patrie memorie', *Una Città e il suo museo*, pp. 143–6.

170 Pompeo Molmenti, *La Storia di Venezia nella vita privata dalle origini alla caduta della Repubblica* (1880), Istituto Italiano d'Arte Grafiche, Bergamo 1928, discussed below. Parts of the Correr collection were later ceded to specialist collections, such as the Glass Museum at Murano and the Museum of the Eighteenth Century at Ca' Rezzonico. See part 2 below.

171 For paintings of Titian and Tintoretto see Pavanello, 'I Geni della pittura veneziana', *Venezia nell'Ottocento: immagini e mito*, pp. 128–41.

172 *Michelangelo Grigoletti e il suo tempo*, ed. Giuseppe Maria Pilo, Electa, Milan, 1971, p. 155.

173 Ibid.

174 *Il Veneto e l'Austria*, p. 41.

175 Ibid., pp. 174–5. Romanelli, *Venezia nell'Ottocento: l'architettura l'urbanistica*, pp. 138–9.

176 Alfred de Musset, *Le Fils du Titien*, *Oeuvres complètes en prose*, text verified and annotated by Maurice Allem and Paul Courant, Pléiade, Paris, 1962, pp. 412–53. Hugo von Hofmannsthal, *Der Tod des Tizians*, discussed in chap. 6.

177 For the iconography and development of the tomb see Zygmunt Wazbinski, 'Tiziano Vecellio e la "Tragedia della sepoltura"', *Tiziano e Venezia*, Convegno Internazionale di Studi, Venice, 1976, Neri Pozza, Vicenza, 1980, pp. 255–73, which includes Zandomeneghi's *Description of the Monument*, 1839.

178 Fehl's analysis, 'At Titian's Tomb', p. 329. On the political aspects see

179 Giovanni Pillini, 'Il Regime doganale austriaco', *Archivio Veneto*, 22 (1984), p. 68. The shipping movements are tabled on pp. 70–71. Kent Robert Greenfield in 'Commerce and New Enterprise at Venice, 1830–48', *Journal of Modern History*, 11 (1939), notes a 100 per cent increase in shipping between 1836 and 1844: pp. 317–18.

180 James Fenimore Cooper, *Gleanings in Europe: Italy*, State University of New York, Albany, 1981, pp. 284–5.

181 For the Corpo di Guardia, Romanelli, *Venezia Ottocento: l'architettura l'urbanistica*, p. 200, and Giovanni Casoni, *Guida per Arsenale di Venezia*, Venice, 1829, cited in Romanelli, *Venezia Ottocento*, p. 569. For the renovations, restorations and new warehouses see Giorgio Bellavitis, *L'Arsenale di Venezia: storia di una grande struttura urbana*, Marsilio, Venice, 1983, pp. 188–95.

182 See Alberto Noli, 'L'Attività del Paleocapa nel campo delle costruzioni marittime e la sistemazione del Porto di Malamocco', *Ingegneria e politica nell'Italia dell'Ottocento: Pietro Paleocapa*, Istituto Veneto di Scienze, Lettere ed Arti, Venice, 1990, pp. 139–52. See also Vincenzo Fontana, 'Il Destino della laguna e della città di Venezia nell'opera di Pietro Paleocapa', ibid., pp. 119–38.

183 Vincenzo Fontana, 'Pietro Paleocapa a Venezia 1817–1820 e 1830–1848', *Giuseppe Jappelli e il suo tempo*, p. 285. Paleocapa was Minister for Public Construction in Manin's republican government: Ginsborg, *Daniele Manin*, pp. 112–14.

184 Ibid., p. 286.

185 B. Paolo Torsello, 'Il Neoclassico nella Piazza', *Piazza San Marco: l'architettura, la storia, le funzioni*, Marsilio, Venice, 1982, pp. 196–7. Note that Romanelli finds Santi 'decisively minor', *Venezia Ottocento L'Architettura l'urbanistica*, p. 166.

186 For the range of designs see *Venezia nell'età di Canova, 1730–1830*, pp. 188–9.

187 Agostino Sagredo, 'Chiese ed altri luoghi sacri del culto cattolico' (including San Marco), in 'Note sugli ammiglioramenti di Venezia', *Annali universali di statistica economia pubblica: storia, viaggi e commercio*, 75, Società degli Editori degli Annali Universali delle Scienze e dell'Industria, 1843, pp. 187–201, also Alvise Zorzi, chap. 6, 'Il Clero, la religione, le regioni', *Venezia austriaca, 1798–1866*, Laterza, Rome and Bari, 1985, pp. 285–312.

188 Sagredo, 'Note sugli ammiglioramenti di Venezia', p. 189.

189 Ibid., p. 190.

190 Ibid., p. 192.

191 On San Silvestro, Lehni, *Studien zu Lorenzo Santi*, p. 225.

192 *Il Teatro La Fenice in Venezia edificato dall'architetto Antonio Selva nel 1792 e ricostruito in parte in 1836 dai Fratelli Tommaso e Giambattista Meduna*, Antonelli, Venice, 1849. For 'I pochi difetti', and the modifications, pp. 14ff. See also Manilio Brusatin and Giuseppe Pavanello, *Il Teatro La Fenice: i progetti, l'architettura, le decorazioni*, Albrizzi, Venice, 1987, chap. 5, '1837, La Fenice risorta', pp. 137ff., and Giandomenico Romanelli, Giuseppe Pugliese, José Sasportes and Patrizia Veroli, *Gran Teatro La Fenice*, trans. Jonathan Benison and Jeremy Scott, Benedikt Taschen, Cologne, 1997, pp. 166ff. Romanelli remarks, p. 175, that 'the Meduna brothers' theatre . . . could pride itself on being both a faithful reconstruction of Selva's masterpiece and a modern reappraisal of it'.

193 Sagredo, 'Note sugli ammiglioramenti di Venezia', p. 187.

194 Romanelli lists the principal works in 'Per Giuseppe Salvadori architetto', *Bollettino del Centro Internazionale di Studi di Architettura Andrea Palladio*, 15 (1973), pp. 437–53.

195 Gianpietro Zucchetta, *Venezia ponte per ponte*, vol. 2, Stamperia di Venezia, Venice, 1992, pp. 342–4.

196 The process of enlargement began in 1817. See Romanelli, *Venezia Ottocento L'Architettura l'urbanistica*, p. 152.

197 Two important studies focus on the industrial archaeology of the Veneto in the nineteenth century: *Venezia città industriale: gli insediamenti produttivi del 19 Secolo*, Marsilio, Venice, 1980, and *Archeologia industriale nel Veneto*, ed. Franco Mancus, Silvano, Milan, 1990.

198 Daniela Mazzotta, 'Il Macello Comunale di Venezia', *Archeologia Industriale nel Veneto*, pp. 175–6. For illustrations and designs see Romanelli, *Venezia Ottocento L'Architettura l'urbanistica*, pp. 222–3. For the French revisions of slaughtering practice see Ann F. La Berge, *Mission and Method: The Early Nineteenth-Century French Public Health Movement*, Cambridge University Press, 1992, p. 121.

199 Sergio Barizza, 'Il gas e Venezia: la prima volta del "nuovo", le contraddizioni di sempre', *Cheiron*, 7 (1989), pp. 147–58; Mazzotta, 'Le Officine del Gas di Venezia', *Archaeologia industriale nel Veneto*, pp. 169–70.

200 Sagredo, 'Note sugli ammiglioramenti di Venezia', p. 75.

201 Chateaubriand, 8 June 1845: 'Ne craigniez rien pour le pont. Il ne déparera point Venise. C'est une artère de plus pour

amener le sang au coeur', *Lettres à Madame Récamier*, Flammarion, Paris, 1951, p. 521.

202 To be discussed in chap. 6.

203 Giandomenico Romanelli, 'Vincenzo Coronelli: proposta di ponte tra San Marco e Giudecca', *Le Venezie possibili: da Palladio a Le Corbusier*, ed. Lionello Puppi and Giandomenico Romanelli, Electa, Milan, 1985, pp. 113–15.

204 Luigi Casarini, *Sulla Origine ingrandimento e decadenza del commercio di Venezia e sui mezzi che nella presente de lei situazione praticare pottrebbonsi per imperdirne la minacciata rovina. Memoria letta al Veneto Ateneo nella seduta XXV al Veneto Ateneo nella seduta a xxv Luglio MDCCXXII*, Venice, 1823. On the bridge and relevant railway development see Giancarlo Consoni and Graziella Tonon, 'Transporti e strategie di sviluppo nel Secolo XIX', *Venezia Milano: storia civilità e cultura nel rapporto tra due capitali*, Electa, Milan, 1984, pp. 233ff., and Carla Uberti, 'Il Ponte ferroviario e la stazione', *Le Venezie possibili: da Palladio a Le Corbusier*, p. 228. The later controversies are discussed below.

205 Consoni and Tonon, 'Transporti e strategie di sviluppo nel Secolo XIX', p. 235, and Romanelli, *Venezia Ottocento L'Architettura l'urbanistica*, pp. 147–9.

206 Ibid., p. 243.

207 Ibid., p. 240, n. 48.

208 Consoni and Tonon, 'Transporti e strategie', *Venezia Milano: storia civilità e cultura nel rapporto tra due capitali*, p. 280, n. 27.

209 Tommaso Meduna, *Veduta del ponte ferroviario da Campalto a Venezia secondo il progetto del 1836*, Romanelli, *Venezia Ottocento L'Architettura l'urbanistica*, pp. 202–3.

210 Ginsborg treats 'The Railroad Question' in *Daniele Manin and the Venetian Revolution 1848–49*, pp. 51–8. Manin is conspicuous in this context.

211 For instance, *Hand-book for Travellers in Northern Italy, comprising Turin, Milan, Pavia, Cremona, The Italian Lakes, . . . Venice, 14th edition, carefully revised, with a travelling map and 32 plans of towns, galleries, etc.*, John Murray, London, 1877, p. 340.

212 Adolfo Bernardello, 'L'Origine e la realizzazione della stazione ferroviaria di Venezia (1838–1866), *Storia Urbana*, 9 (1985), pp. 3–45.

213 Uberti dates the Crovato view as 1846, Romanelli as 1835.

214 Quoted in Antonio Pilot, 'Il ponte sulla laguna nel 1849', *Rassegna storica del Risorgimento Italiano*, 15 (1928), p. 3.

215 The 'real estate revolution' was initiated earlier in the century as patrician property changed hands and the bourgeois and Jewish citizens became property owners: see Renzo Derosas, 'Il mercato

fondiario nel Veneto del primo Ottocento', *Quaderni Storici*, 22 (1987), pp. 549–78.

216 On the residents of the palace (and its modernisations during the century), Giandomenico Romanelli, *Tra Gotico e Neogotico: Palazzo Cavalli Franchetti a San Vidal*, Albrizzi, Venice, 1990. For further French residencies see Romanelli, 'I Gigli in gondola: avventure e disavventure di Borboni in esilio sulle rive del Canal Grande', *Venezia e Parigi*, Electa, Milan, 1989, pp. 259–92.

217 Chateaubriand, *Mémoires d'Outre Tombe*, vol. 2, book 4, Pléiade, Gallimard, Monaco, 1958. On Chateaubriand and Venice see Maurice Levaillant, *Chateaubriand, Madame Récamier et les Mémoires d'Outre-Tombe, (1830–1850)*, from unpublished documents, Librairie Delagrave, Paris, 1936: Part 3, 'La Leçon de Venise ou la Beauté du Soir', pp. 109ff.

218 Voltaire, *Candide or Optimism* (1759), trans. John Butt, Penguin, Harmondsworth, 1947, p. 124.

219 Chateaubriand, *Mémoires d'Outre-Tombe*, vol. 2, book 4, chap. 4, p. 770.

220 'Neuf siècles de Venise vue de la Piazzetta', ibid., pp. 1023ff.

221 The accounts relevant to Venice are found in chap. 8, Silvio Pellico, *My Prisons: Memoirs*. Chateaubriand is accused of jealousy by Sforza, 'Il Visconte di Chateaubriand gelose delle Mie Prigione', Sforza, *Silvio Pellico a Venezia (1820–1822)*, pp. 267ff.

222 Jean-Jacques Rousseau, *The Confessions of Jean-Jacques Rousseau* (1765), trans. J. M. Cohen, Penguin, Harmondsworth, 1985, p. 298.

223 'Dans les cercles de belles Dames, or les dernières Vénitiennes', ibid., pp. 170–84.

224 M. Valèry, *Voyages historiques et littéraires en Italie pendant les années 1826, 1827 et 1828, ou l'indicateur Italien*, Louis Hauman & Cie., Brussels, 1835. For Venice, book 6, pp. 114–61. M. Valéry's *Historical, Literary and Artistical Travels in Italy*, trans. C. E. Clifton, Baudry's European Library, Paris, 1842. For Venice, pp. 144ff.

225 Ibid., p. 145.

226 Ibid., p. 144.

227 See chap. 6 below.

228 M. Valery's *Historical, Literary and Artistical Travels in Italy*, p. 148.

229 Ibid., p. 186.

230 The liaison is well-documented. See, for example, Raffaello Barbiera, *Nella Città dell'amore: passioni illustri a Venezia (1816–1861), con lettere inedite di Giorgio Sand . . .*, Fratelli Treves, Milan, 1923, and Jean Pommier, *Autour du drame de Venise, G. Sand et Musset au lendemain de Lorenzaccio*, Libraire Nizet, Paris, 1958. Paul Wiegler, 'The Chimera of Venice' (i.e.

Musset), *Genius in Love and Death*, trans. Carl Rauschenbuch, Albert & Charles Boni, New York, 1929, pp. 126–35.

231 For example August Brizeux (in the steps of Byron), 'Fragment d'un Livre de Voyage Venise', *Revue des Deux Mondes*, 16 (1833), pp. 54–62.

232 *Mémoires de J. Casanova de Seingalt, écrits par lui-même*, Paris, Ponthieu & Cie., 1826–38, 12 vols. See the bibliography in J. Rives Childs, *Casanova: A New Perspective*, Paragon House, New York, 1988, p. 319.

233 Such analogies are applied with determination in Grégoire Morgulis, 'Musset et Casanova', *Etudes italiennes*, 3 (1956), pp. 163–95. The cultivation of Byron is also relevant here, see Pommier, chap. 6, 'Byron et Musset', *Autour de drame de Venise*, pp. 102–25.

234 Alfred de Musset, 'La Nuit vénitienne ou Les Noces de Laurette', *Théatre complète*, text verified and annotated by Maurice Allem, Gallimard, Paris, 1958, pp. 389–418.

235 This is the version written in 1865 specifically for Gounod to set to music (compounding the theme of servitude), see Alfred de Musset, *Poésies complètes*, text verified and annotated by Maurice Allem, Pléiade, Paris, 1957, p, 628. For the original version, pp. 80–82.

236 James Harding describes Gounod's setting of *Venise* as 'a typical example of his method. A brief introduction sketches the quiet flow of water, and then a rhythmic accompaniment, slow and regular as the lapping waves, depicts evening in Venice, the clouded moon and the stillness of the lagoons. The words are discreetly supported by the music, no more, and at every turn the melodic line enhances the literary values of the poem': *Gounod*, Stein & Day, New York, 1973, p. 91.

237 See F. Feuillet de Conches, *Léopold Robert: Sa vie, ses oeuvres et sa correspondance*, Paris, Michel Lévy, 1854. Robert's interest in Venice, with emphasis on the picturesque, is described in letters, pp. 199–209.

238 George Sand, *Story of My Life*, ed. Thelma Jurgrau, State University of New York Press, Albany, 1991, p. 1135.

239 Robert abandoned his initial Venetian subject, *Carnevale de Venise*, and sought out picturesque characters in Pellestrina and Chioggia, in the vicinity of the Murazzi.

240 *Oeuvres de Alfred de Musset: Mélanges de littérature et de critique*, Alphonse Lemerre, Paris, 1951, pp. 195–200. See also Erik Forssman, *Venedig in der Kunst und im Kunsturteil des 19. Jahrhunderts*, p. 52. Note also the work by August Graf von Platen, *Das Fischermädchen von Burano*, which tells of a fisher-girl mending her nets as she awaits the

return of her beloved. As night falls over the lagoon, she dreams of their expeditions to Torcello: August Graf von Platen, *Sämtliche Werke Hist.-kristische, Ausgabe*, ed. M. Koch and E. Petzet (1910), Olms, Hildesheim, 1969, pp. 154–8.

241 George Sand, *Lettres d'un voyageur*, trans. Sacha Rabinovitch and Patricia Thomson, Penguin Books, Harmondsworth, 1987.

242 For an engaging feminist reading see Karyna Szmurlo, 'La Topographie du Désir: George Sand et Venise', *The Traveler in the Life and Works of George Sand*, ed. Tamara Alvarez-Detrell and Michael G. Paulson, Whitson Publishing Co., Troy, New York, 1994, pp. 66–78, and Anne E. McCall, 'On the Heels of Corinne: Venice, Sand's Traveller and a Case for Urban Renewal', *Romanic Review*, 89 (1998), pp. 219–30.

243 P. Mesrop Gianascian lists the Venice-related works in 'Venise dans l'oeuvre de George Sand', *Venezia nelle letterature moderne*, ed. Carlo Pellegrini, Istituto per la Collaborazione Culturale, Venice, 1961, p. 163: *Leone Leoni, Les Maîtres mosaïstes, Derniére Aldini*, all 1837; *L'Uscoque, L'Orco*, 1838; *Consuelo*, 1842; and *L'Historie de ma Vie*, 1847.

244 In chap. 1 of *Les Maîtres mosaïstes*, Tintoretto says: 'The mosaic art is not . . . a low vocation; it is a true art, brought from Greece by able masters, of whom we should speak only with deep respect . . . mosaic-work has preserved to us intact the traditions of color; and herein, so far from being inferior to painting, it has this advantage which cannot be denied: it resists the wear and tear of time, as well as the ravages of the atmosphere. . . .' George Sand, *The Master Mosaic-Workers*, trans. Charlotte C. Johnston, Little, Brown & Co., Boston, Mass., 1895, pp. 18–19.

245 George Sand, *Consuelo, A Romance of Venice*, Da Capo, New York, 1979, p. 5.

246 Ibid., p. 6.

247 Sand, *Story of My Life*, p. 955.

248 Ibid., pp. 954–5.

249 Ibid.

250 Ibid., p. 959.

251 Sand, *Lettres d'un Voyageur*, p. 107.

252 These two signifant losses are noted by John Rosselli in 'La vita musicale a Venezia dal 1815 al 1966', *Venezia e l'Austria*, pp. 37–51. At least two (salacious) novels explore the world of the Venetian castrati in the eighteenth century: Anne Rice, *Cry to Heaven* (1990), Penguin, Harmondsworth, 1991, and Jim Williams, *Scherzo: A Venetian Entertainment*, Simon & Schuster, London, 1999.

253 See Stendhal's comments in *Life of Rossini*, trans. Richard N. Coe, Caldar & Boyars, London, 1970, pp. 44ff.

254 Maria Teresa Muraro, *Gran Teatro La Fenice*, Corbo e Fiore, Venice, 1996, p. 14.

255 For succinct comment on these years, Ibid., p. 83. Julian Budden briefly notes Rossini's triumph in 1823 – 'wreaths flung into the water, a flotilla of gondolas escorting the maestro to his lodgings, and a water-borne band regaling him with a selection from his score'. *The Operas of Verdi*, vol. 1, *From Oberto to Rigoletto*, Cassell, London, 1973, p. 139.

256 On Sand's early musical education, Enid M. Sandring, 'Rossini and his Music in the Life and Works of George Sand', *Nineteenth-Century French Studies*, 10 (1981/82), pp. 17–26.

257 Sand, *Lettres d'un voyageur*, pp. 77–8.

258 Ibid., p. 85.

259 See the comprehensive article by Herbert Schneider, 'Die Barkarole und Venedig', *L'Opera tra Venezia e Parigi*, ed. Maria Teresa Muraro, Fondazione Giorgio Cini, Studi di Musica Veneta, 14, Leo S. Olschki, Florence, 1988, pp. 11–53. On Rousseau, p. 12.

260 The Barcarolle was not written in the first instance for *Les Contes d'Hoffmann*, but Offenbach's interest in Venice is affirmed in other works. See chap. 5 below.

261 See again Tiziana Rizzo, *La Biondina in Gondoleta: Maria Querini Benzon, una nobildonna a Venezia tra '700 e '800*, Neri Pozza, Vicenza, 1994, pp. 190–91.

262 Licia Sirch, 'Le Canzoni in dialetto Veneziano di Antonio Buzzolla', *Antonio Buzzolla: una vita musicale nella Venezia romantica*, ed. Francesco Passadore and Licia Sirch, Minelliana, Adria, 1994, pp. 327ff.

263 Rossana Dalmonte, 'Liszt and Venice: Between Poetics and "Rezeptionsgeschichte"', *Journal of the American Liszt Society*, 27 (1990), p. 20.

264 Raffaello Barbiera, *Poesie veneziane*, Arnaldo Forni, Bologna, 1975, pp. 221–2.

265 For Schubert's poems, see the interesting note by Graham Johnson for volume 15 of the Hyperion Schubert Edition (sung by Margaret Price), CDJ33015 (1991), pp. 20–22. For Schumann's settings of Thomas Moore: 'Row gently here, my gondolier' and 'When through the Piazzetta Night breathes her cool air', Eric Sams, *The Songs of Robert Schumann*, Eulenberg, London, 1969, pp. 67–9.

266 The first version of *Nuits d'été* in 1840 was for voice and piano; now well-known, the orchestral version was published in 1856. Plausible connections with Hoffmann's *Doge und Dogaressa* in its recent French translation, and with treatments of Marino Faliero by Byron, Delacroix, Delavigne and Donizetti, are made by Peter Bloom in 'In the Shadows of Les Nuits d'Eté', *Berlioz Studies*, ed. Peter Bloom, Cambridge University Press, 1992, pp. 106–9.

267 Kent Robert Greenfield, 'Commerce and New Enterprise at Venice, 1830–48', p. 313, observes: 'After 1830 Venice began to revive and in the years preceding the revolution of 1848 its prospects were viewed with optimism not only by visitors but by the leaders of business in the city. It should also be noted that there was a major cholera epidemic in 1835.'

268 Quoting Samuel Rogers, Palgrave declares minute description to be unnecessary in view of the coverage: 'The consequence is that no one enters Venice as a stranger; almost every feature of importance is already more or less known', *Hand-book for Travellers in Northern Italy: States of Sardinia, Lombardy and Venice, Parma and Piacenza . . . as far as the Val d'Arno. With a Travelling Map*, John Murray & Son, London, 1842, p. 342.

269 The set of sonnets by August Graf von Platen was written in 1825 following von Platen's visit to Venice in 1824. See (together with the *Epigramme*), *Scrittori di Lingua Tedesca e Venezia*, ed. Giacomo Caccipaglia, La Stamperia, Venice, 1984, pp. 132–6, For a broad interpretation see Louis Sauzin, 'August von Platen et ses sonnets vénitiens', *Venezia nelle Letterature Moderne*, pp. 150–61.

270 The first edition of Rogers's *Italy* was published anonymously in 1822. An authored *Italy Part One* was published in 1824; *Italy Part Two* in 1828. For Turner's illustrations and a chronology of Rogers's publications see Adele M. Holcomb, 'A Neglected Classical Phase of Turner's Art: His Vignettes to Rogers's *Italy*', *Journal of the Warburg and Courtauld Institutes*, 32 (1969), pp. 405–10.

271 Charles Dickens, 'An Italian Dream' (1846), *Pictures from Italy. American Notes for General Circulation and Pictures from Italy*, Mandarin, London, 1991, pp. 351–8.

272 Bruce Redford writes eloquently of the Eidophusikon and its influence on William Beckford, *Venice and the Grand Tour*, Yale University Press, New Haven and London, 1996, pp. 108–14.

273 The Barker brothers first introduced the panorama in Edinburgh in 1789; they included Venice at the Strand Panorama in 1819. Silvia Bordini, *Storia del panorama: la visione totale nella pittura nel XIX secolo*, Officina, Rome, 1984, p. 243.

274 *The Spectacular Career of Clarkson Stanfield, 1783–1867: Seaman, Scene-Painter, Royal Academician*, Tyne and Wear County Council Museums, Newcastle-upon-Tyne, 1979, p. 92. The diorama was 20 feet high, 300 feet long,

painted on cloth and took from 15 to 20 minutes to run.

275 For panoramic views, Giorgio Bellavitis and Giandomenico Romanelli, *Venezia*, Laterza, Rome and Bari, 1989, pp. 185–8.

276 Reproduced in Giocondo Cassini, *Piante e vedute prospettiche di Venezia (1479–1855)*, Stamperia di Venezia, Venice, 1982, pp. 186–8.

277 Ibid., pp. 180–81, and Mary Pittaluga, *Ippolito Caffi, 1809–1806*, Neri Pozza, Vicenza, 1971.

278 Giuseppe Pavanello, 'Notturno veneziano', *Venezia nell'Ottocento: immagini e mito*, p. 79.

279 Ibid., p. 47.

280 On these frescoes see Maria Luisa Frongia, 'Le Opere pittoriche delle Sale Superiori del Caffè Pedrocchi', *Jappelli e il suo tempo*, pp. 599–630.

281 For Borsato's painting (Pinacoteca Tosio Martinengo, Brescia) see *Venezia nell'Ottocento: immagini e mito*, p. 64.

282 Giandomenico Romanelli, 'Benghal Flares and Nocturnal Bombardments: The Nineteenth-Century Venice of Ippolito Caffi', also in Italian in *Italia al Chiaro di Luna, Italy by Moonlight: The Night in Italian Painting, 1550–1850*, Il Cigno Galileo Galilei, Rome, 1990, pp. 57–61.

283 Zorzi, *Venezia austriaca*, chap. 7, 'Feste, piaceri, spettacoli, conversazioni: i "Foresti"', pp. 343ff.

284 For example Ted Scapa, *Venice in November*, Bentli, Berne, 1979.

285 For the war panoramas see Bordini, *Storia del panorama*, pp. 213–30. For Caffi see Romanelli, 'Benghal Flares and Nocturnal Bombardments', and Pavanello and Romanelli, *Venezia nell'Ottocento: l'Architettura l'urbanista*, Electa, Milan, 1983, p. 180.

286 On alternatives, and continiuty in the class structure see Andrea Zannini, 'Vecchi poveri e nuovi borghesi', *Venezia e l'Austria*, pp. 169–94, noting that in the Settecento there were many that might be called 'bourgeois', but who were to be the professionals of the following century, p. 186.

287 Gianfranco Torcellan, 'Politica e cultura nella Venezia del '700', *Studi veneziani*, 8 (1966), p. 495: 'Venezia decrepita, cadavere vivente cui a Campoformio si firmò un atto di morto puramente formale'.

Chapter 4

1 For Daniele Manin, see Paul Ginsborg, *Daniele Manin and the Venetian Revolution of 1848–49*, Cambridge University Press, 1979, which remains the standard work, in Italian, as in English. See also more recently, Paul Ginsborg, 'Il Rivoluzionario Daniele Manin', in *Venezia Quarantotto: episodi, luoghi e protagonista di una Rivoluzione, 1848–49*, ed. Giandomenico Romanelli, Michele Gottardi, Franca Lugato and Camillo Tonini, Electa, Milan, 1998. The latter exhibition and catalogue represents a major re-evaluation of the Revolution. See also George Macaulay Trevelyan's classic *Manin and the Venetian Revolution of 1848*, Longmans, Green & Co, London, 1923. For a compact treatment of Tommaseo see Gido Bezzola, 'Niccolò Tommaseo e la cultura veneta', *Storia di cultura veneta*, vol. 6, *Dall'età napoleonica alla Prima Guerra Mondiale*, ed. Girolamo Arnaldi and Manlio Pastore Stocchi, Neri Pozza, Vicenza, 1986, pp. 143–63. Dalmatian-born, Tommaseo spent over-all only a dozen years resident in Venice.

2 Francesco Hayez, *Le mie memorie*, Reale Accademia di Belle Arti in Milano, Milan, 1865, chap. 1, pp. 1–13.

3 Ibid., pp. 4–5.

4 For a background essay on Milan and the visual arts, Fernando Mazzocco, 'Painting in Milan and Venice in the First Half of the Century', *Ottocento Romanticism and Revolution in Nineteenth-Century Italian Painting*, ed. Roberta J. M. Olsen, American Federation of Arts and Centro Di, Florence, 1992, pp. 51–8.

5 As Hayez reported it in his memoirs, Cicognara regarded Hayez's new painting as inferior to his early work, having 'un certo decadimento': *Le miei memorie*, pp. 45–6.

6 Ferdinando Mazzocca, *Francesco Hayez Catalogo ragionato*, Federico Motta, Milan, 1994, pp. 137–9; and for an account of the relevance of Milan to the context of the painting, Ferdinando Mazzocca, 'La Polemica Classico-Romantica dal Pietro Rossi al Carmagnola, 1818–1821', *Hayez*, ed. Maria Cristina Gozzoli and Fernando Mazzocca, Electa, Milan, 1983, pp. 76ff.

7 But this was hardly a new theme, remembering (for example) the prominence of family leave-taking in *Gli Orazi e i Curiazi*. Nevertheless Hayez's painting was interpreted as 'Romantic'.

8 Hayez, *Le mie memorie*, p. 46.

9 For his activity as a fresco painter, Giuseppe Pavanello, 'Hayez frescante Neoclassico', *Arte Veneta*, 33 (1979), pp. 273–83, and Giuseppe Pavanello, 'Hayez Decoratore a Venezia e a Padova', *Hayez*, ed. Maria Cristina Gozzoli and Ferdinando Mazzocca, Electa, Milan, 1983, pp. 45–9.

10 Niccolò Tommaseo, 'Bellezza e Civiltà' (1838), in Paola Barocchi, *Storia moderna dell'arte in Italia*, vol. 1, *Manifeste polemiche documenti: dai Neoclassici ai Puristi, 1780–1861*, Giulio Einaudi, Turin, 1998, p. 293.

11 For Hayez's volumes given to the Milan Accademia see *Le mie memorie*, 'La biblioteca di un pittore del periodo romantico nota dei libri donati dal Cav. Hayez alla Biblioteca academica', p. 196. Hayez's historical sources are succinctly treated in Gozzoli and Mazzocca, *Hayez*, especially, 'Il Mito di Venezia, 1832–1867', pp. 176–98.

12 Carlo Castellaneta and Sergio Coradeschi, *L'Opera completa di Hayez*, Rizzoli, Milan, 1971, figs 47, 1–7, including sketches and Mazzocca, *Francesco Hayez Catalogo ragionato*, pp. 137–9.

13 Girolamo Soranzo, *Bibliografia veneziana in aggiunta e continuazione del 'Saggio' di Emmanuele Antonio Cicogna* (1885), Burt Franklin, New York, 1967, p. 226.

14 In two versions, Mazzocca, *Ferdinando Hayez Catalogo ragionato*, figs 212 a–b.

15 For a historical account see Maria Luisa Mariotti Masi, *Bianca Cappello: una veneziana alla corte dei Medici*, Mursia, Milan, 1986.

16 Emmanuele Antonio Cicogna, *Saggio di bibliografia veneziana*, vol. 1, Burt Franklin, New York, 1967, pp. 284–5.

17 For an account of Foscarini's career see John Julius Norwich, *A History of Venice*, Penguin, Harmondsworth, 1983, pp. 525–9.

18 Soranzo, *Bibliografia veneziana*, p. 240.

19 Foscarini: 'città superba! il tuo crudel Lione /Disarmato dagli anni andrà deriso/ Privo del'ire, onde la morte e bella/ Egli cadrà senza mandai ruggito'; Giovan Battista Niccolini, 'Antonio Foscarini', in *Tragedie nazionali*, vol. 2, Corrado Gargiolli, Milan, 1880, p. 615.

20 Annotazioni, ibid., p. 623.

21 Malamani discusses the Foscarini issue in *Memorie del Conte Leopoldo Cicognara: tratte dai documenti originali*, Ancroa, Merlo, Venice, 1888, pp. 305–9.

22 Alvise Zorzi, 'La Caduta della Repubblica nelle lettere di Bernardino Renier', *Ateneo Veneto*, 34 (1996), p. 23.

23 For an interesting view on public and private interests in the family see Benjamin Arbel, 'The Reign of Caterina Cornaro (1473–1489) as a family affair', *Studi Veneziani*, 26 (1993), pp. 67–85.

24 For the Bellini see Howard Collins, 'Time, Space and Gentile Bellini's *The Miracle of the Cross at the Ponte San Lorenzo* (Portraits of Caterina Cornaro and Pietro Bembo)', *Gazette des beaux-arts*, 100 (1982), pp. 201–8.

25 Cicogna, *Saggio di bibliografia veneziana*, p. 284.

26 William Ashcroft, *Donizetti*, Cassell, London, 1965, pp. 495–6. The opera was first performed in Teatro San Carlo, Naples, in 1844.

27 Ibid., fig. 340. In 1844 Hayez had painted *Marino Faliero rebuking Stefano*

(Milan, private collection), Mazzocco, *Francesco Hayez Catalogo*, fig. 237 a/b.

28 See, for example, Anthony Arblaster, *Vive la Libertà: Politics in Opera*, Verso, New York and London, 1992, chap. 4, 'Verdi the Liberal Patriot', pp. 91-146.

29 John Rosselli, *The Opera Industry in Italy from Cimarosa to Verdi: The Role of the Impressario*, Cambridge University Press, 1984, p. 94. The families involved were the Loredan and Barbarigo.

30 The dream occurs at the beginning of act 2: 'Ah! lo ravviso!...è desso...è Carmagnola!'

31 Giuseppe Verdi, *I due Foscari*: the chorus introduction act 1, *I due Foscari*, quoted from p. 12, Phillips recording, conducted Lamberto Gardelli, Orf Symphony Orchestra and Chorus, 6700 105 (1977), p. 11.

32 Jacopo Foscarini's first aria, ibid., p. 12: 'There lies my Venice...there is her sea. Queen of the waves, I salute you! Though you have been cruel to me/yet I am the most loyal of your sons.'

33 See Alberto Cosulich, 'Alberghi – Locande – Osterie – Caffè', *Viaggi e turismo a Venezia dal 1500 al 1900*, 'I Sette', Venice 1990, pp. 103-24.

34 Giandomenico Romanelli, *Venezia Ottocento: l'architettura l'urbanistica*, Albrizzi, Venice, 1988, pp. 310-12.

35 For the refurbishment of Quadri's and Florian's see Lodovico Cadorin see Romanelli, *Venezia Ottocento*, pp. 318-23. On this eclectic style, sufficiently distinctive to be known as 'Lo stile Cardorino', see Pavanello, 'La Decorazione dei palazzi veneziana negli anni del dominio austriaco', *Il Veneto e l'Austria: vita e cultura artistica nelle città venete, 1818-16*, ed. Sergio Marinetti, Giuseppe Mazzariol and Ferdinando Mazzocca, Electa, Milan, 1989, p. 270ff.

36 Agostino Sagredo, 'Note sugli ammiglioramenti di Venezia', *Annali universali di statistica economia pubblica: storia, viaggi e commercio*, 75, Società degli Editori degli Annali Universali delle Scienze e dell'Industria, 1843, p. 78, also Adolfo Bernardello, 'La Ferrovia e i traghetti: gondolieri, barcaioli e remiganti nella Venezia di metà Ottocento', *Venetica: rivista di storia delle Venezie*, 3 (1985), p. 93, considering the controversy caused by the new service.

37 The figures are taken from Ginsborg, *Daniele Manin and the Venetian Revolution of 1848-49*, pp. 31-2.

38 On the baths, and the tourist industry in general, see Sagredo, 'Note sugli ammiglioramenti di Venezia', pp. 309-13. For a general historical account see Nelli-Elena Vanzan Marchini, *Venezia: i piaceri dell'acqua*, Arsenale, Venice, 1997.

39 Sagredo, 'Note sugli ammiglioramenti di Venezia', p. 313.

40 Romanelli, 'I gigli in gondola: avventure e disavventure di Borboni in esilio sulle rive del Canal Grande', *Venezia e Parigi*, Electa, Milan, 1989, p. 259.

41 Romanelli has studied the renovations in detail in *Tra Gotico e Neogotico: Palazzo Cavalli Franchetti a San Vidal*, Albrizzi, Venice, 1990.

42 Richard J. Goy, *The House of Gold: Building a Palace in Medieval Venice*, Cambridge University Press, 1992, p. 255.

43 Giandomenico Romanelli and Filippo Pedrocco, *Ca' Rezzonico*, Electa, Milan, 1986, p. 8.

44 Kent Roberts Greenfield, 'Commerce and New Enterprise at Venice, 1830-48', *The Journal of Modern History*, 2 (1939), where a range of products are listed: 'gold-beaters' work, silken fabrics, straw hats, wrought leather, colors, and medicines'. Those listed as most important were 'manufactories of fancy glass and enamel wares, glass, wax, woolen caps, gondola covers, coarse serges, clerical cloth, colours, the sugar refineries and the printing establishments' (p. 319).

45 Giovanni Mariacher, 'Le Arti del vetro, dell'oreficeria e del bronzo nella prima metà dell'Ottocento', *Il Veneto e l'Austria: vita e cultura artistica nelle città venete, 1814-1866*, ed. Sergio Marinelli, Giuseppe Mazzariol and Ferdando Mazzocca, Electa, Milan, 1989, p. 292.

46 Ibid.

47 Attila Dorigato, *Murano Glass Museum*, Electa, Milan, 1986, p. 56, with works from the museum collection, pp. 58-9. For Bigaglia see Giovanni Sarpellon, *Miniature Masterpieces: Mosaic Glass, 1838-1924*, Prestel, Munich, 1995, p. 63.

48 The names here are selected from a wide activity. For more detail see Paolo Costantini and Italo Zannier, *Venezia nella fotografia dell'Ottocento*, Arsenale, Böhm, Venice, 1986: p. 65 for L. P. Lerebours; for Alexander John Ellis, p. 67. Important articles by Paolo Costantini have some overlap: 'Dall'immagine elusiva all'immagine critica', *Fotologia*, 3 (1985), pp. 12-29; 'Un Rivoluzione nell'arte del disegno: L'ingresso della fotografia nella produzione d'immagine di Venezia', *Venezia Arti*, 2 (1988), pp. 84-93, gives prominence to the new 'paradigms' established by Lerebours and Ellis.

49 Illustrated in Costantini and Zannier, *Venezia nella fotografia dell'Ottocento*, pp. 70-71.

50 Ibid., p. 35.

51 See the wide-ranging illustrations (including paintings) in Dorothea Ritter, *Venedig in frühen Photographien von Domenico Bresolin, 'Pittore fotografo'*, Brauss, Heidelberg, 1996.

52 Italo Zannier, *The Naya Collection*, O. Böhm, Venice, 1981. See p. 19 for the disagreement between Ponti and Naya that led to a trial for forgery. Janet E. Buerger treats the confusion between the opus of Ponti and Naya in 'Carlo Naya: Venetian Photographer. The Archaeology of Photography', *Image*, 26 (1983), pp. 1-18.

53 Jules Lecomte, *L'Italie du gens du monde: Venise ou coup d'oeil littéraire, artistique, historique, poétique et pittoresque, sur les monuments et les curiosités de cette cité*, Hippolyte Souverain, Paris, 1844, p. 206.

54 Ibid., p. 67.

55 'La place Saint-Marc, c'est le coeur de Venise, tout y va, tout y vient, comme faut le sang pour le coeur', p. 73.

56 Ibid., p. 63.

57 Cf. ibid., p. 73: 'dans le but de se rendre la France favorable, le peuple proposait de plante, sur le milieu de la Place Saint-Marc l'arbre de la liberté, et de bruler aux pied les insignes de l'ancient gouvernement'.

58 Ibid., p. 8.

59 Ibid., pp. 615-48.

60 Ibid., chap. 12, 'Société biographie vénitiennes'; pp. 620-37.

61 Ibid., pp. 44-5.

62 *Hand-book for Travellers in Northern Italy: States of Sardinia, Lombardy and Venice, Parma and Piacenza...as far as the Val d'Arno. With a Travelling Map*, John Murray & Son, London, 1842. For Sir Francis Palgrave, *Dictionary of National Biography*, eds Sir Leslie Stephen and Sir Sidney Lee, Oxford University Press, vol. 15, 1917, pp. 107-9.

63 *Hand-book for Travellers in Northern Italy*, pp. 328, 345.

64 Ibid., p. 345

65 Ibid., p. 371.

66 Ibid., p. 328. Later Murray editions were to reduce the anti-French observations, but the contemporary state of Venice and the Napoleonic demolitions thirty years earlier still occasioned passion.

67 Ibid., p. 338.

68 Ibid.

69 Ibid., p. 328

70 This enthusiasm for Venetian colour is by no means isolated: cf. 'not even Canaletti's pencil, can convey an adequate idea of the delicate consolidation of a structure where colour also is as influential as form', ibid., p. 330.

71 Ibid., p. 329.

72 Ibid., p. 352.

73 *The Letters of Edward Gibbon*, vol. 1, *1750-1755*, ed. V. E. Norton, Cassell, London, 1956, p. 67; Granz Grillparzer, 'Tagebuch auf der Reise nach Italien 1819', *Scrittori di lingua tedesca e Venezia/Deutschsprachige Schriftsteller und Venedig*, ed. Giacomo Cacciapaglia, La Stamperia di Venezia, Venice, 1985, p. 130; *Ruskin in Italy: Letters to his Parents, 1845*, ed. Harold I. Shapiro, Clarendon Press, Oxford, p. 198.

74 John Ruskin, *St Mark's Rest: The History of Venice. Written for the Help of the Few Travellers who still care for her Monuments*, George Allen, London, 1884. Cf. p. 1: 'Go first into the Piazzetta, and stand anywhere in the shade, where you will see its two granite pillars. Your Murray tells you that they are "famous" . . .'

75 John Ruskin, *The Works of Ruskin*, vol. 10, *The Stones of Venice*, vol. 2, *The Sea Stories*, ed. Cook and Wedderburn, George Allen, London, 1904, p. 18.

76 *Ruskin in Italy*, p. 202.

77 However, in the preface to the second edition, Ruskin endeavours to correct the view that Venetian architecture is the 'most noble' of the school of Gothic, and commends Verona. Ruskin, *The Seven Lamps of Architecture*, Everyman, J. M. Dent, 1956, p. xxiii.

78 *Ruskin in Italy*, p. 199.

79 Mario Dalla Costa, *La Basilica di San Marco e i restauri dell'Ottocento: le idee di E. Viollet-le-Duc, J. Ruskin e le 'osservazioni' di A. P. Zorzi*, La Stamperia di Venezia, Venice, 1983, p. 10.

80 Writing in the authoritative volumes on the Basilica published later in the century, Pietro Saccardo declared the mosaics 'void of effect and [their] execution quite unworthy of the place, as it was carried out with materials of all kinds': 'Mosaics', *Basilica di San Marco in Venezia: illustra nella storia e nell'arte da scrittori Venezia sotto la direzione di C. Boito*, Ongania, Venice, 1880–93, p. 707.

81 Romanelli regards him highly: see 'Architettura Romantica nel Veneto; linguaggi e personaggi', *Il Veneto e l'Austria*, p. 385, and claims Ruskin was 'hysterical' with respect to Meduna's restoration.

82 To be discussed in the next chapter.

83 *Ruskin in Italy*, p. 201.

84 Ibid., p. 200.

85 'No book of mine has had so much influence on contemporary art as *The Stones of Venice*', preface to the third edition, 1874. For his influence on restoration, discursively discussed see Giuseppe Rocchi, 'John Ruskin e le origine della moderna teoria del restauro', *Restauro*, 13–14 (1974), pp. 13–73.

86 Ruskin, *The Works of Ruskin*, vol. 9, *The Stones of Venice*, vol. 1, p. 21.

87 Ibid., p. 4.

88 Paul Kaufmann, 'Rawdon Brown and his Adventures in Venetian Archives', *English Miscellany*, 18 (1967), noting the friendship with Effie, pp. 291–8.

89 Ruskin, *The Works of Ruskin, The Stones of Venice*, vol. 1, p. 4. Ruskin refers to the later edition of *Fabbriche di Venezia*, which is substantially the work of Cicognara (see citation earlier), with additional comments by Fontana.

90 Pietro Selvatico, *Sulla Architettura e sulla scultura in Venezia dal Medio Evo sino ai nostri giorni* (Paolo Ripamonti Carpano, Venice, 1847), Arnaldo Forni, Bologna, 1980. For Selvatico's critical thought overall see Franco Bernabei, *Pietro Selvatico nella critica e nella storia delle arti figurative dell'Ottocento*, Neri Pozza, Vicenza, 1974.

91 *Le Voyage d'Italie d'Eugene Viollet-le-Duc, 1836–7*, Ecole National Supérieure des Beaux Arts and Centro Di, Florence, 1980, p. 22.

92 Ibid., pp. 230–31.

93 An overview is given in Mario Dalla Costa, *La basilica di San Marco e i restauri dell'Ottocento*, La Stamperia di Venezia, Venice, 1983.

94 'Restaurer un édifice, ce n'est pas l'entretenir, le réparer ou le refaire, c'est le rétablir dans un état complet qui peut n'avoir jamais existé à un moment donné.' Eugene-Emmanuel Viollet-le-Duc, 'De la Restauration des anciens édifies en Italie', *Dictionnaire raisonné de française du XI et XVI Siècle*, vol. 8, A. Morel, Paris, 1868, pp. 114–16.

95 Ibid., p. 5.

96 *Ruskin in Italy*, pp. 207, 200.

97 Ibid., p. 209.

98 See comments on a visit to Torcello and 'the horrible marsh', ibid., p. 206.

99 Ibid., p. 218.

100 There were some signs of industrialisation, and the modernisation of existing activities such as sugar refining. In 1840 the Società Veneta Commerciale was formed to stimulate port trading. See Greenfield, 'Commerce and New Enterprise at Venice', p. 320.

101 Maria Teresa Muraro, *Gran Teatro La Fenice*, Corbo e Fiore, Venice, 1996, pp. 62–5. Both curtains appear in lithographs made by Giovanni Pividor to celebrate La Fenice's reopening, see ibid., pp. 64, 65.

102 For Verdi's association with the Venetian opera house see *Verdi e la Fenice*, Diego Valeri et al., Ente Autonomo del Teatro La Fenice nel Cinquantenario della Morte del Maestro, Venice, 1951.

103 *Attila* was based on the German play by Zacharias Werner, *Attila, König der Hunnen*, of 1808. Charles Osborne comments on Werner's *Schicksaldrama* in relation to the libretto in *The Complete Operas of Verdi: A Critical Guide*, Pan Books, London, 1969, pp. 135–7.

104 For a detailed coverage of the eight operas on which Bertoja worked with Verdi, and much history relating to La Fenice see Evan Barker, 'Verdi's Operas and Giuseppe Bertoja's Designs at the Gran Teatro la Fenice, Venice', in *Opera in Context: Essays on Historical Staging from the Late Renaissance to the Time of Puccini*, ed. Mark A. Radice, Amadeus Press, Portland, Or., 1998, pp. 209–356. For the *Attila* set see *Gran Teatro la Fenice* (Romanelli), pp. 220–21.

105 Letter from Cassiodorus, the praetorian prefect of King Theodoric the Ostrogoth, from Ravenna to 'the Maritime Tribues', AD 523, cited in John Julius Norwich, *Venice: A Travellers' Companion*, Constable, London, 1990, p. 68.

106 Quoted from the EMI recording, 7 49952 1/2/4 (1990), *Attila*, Teatro alla Scala, Milan, conductor Riccardo Muti, p. 58. 'Dear homeland, at once mother and queen / of powerful, generous sons, / now a ruin, a desert, a desolation / over which reign silence and gloom; / but from the seaweed of these billows, / like a new phoenix arisen, / thou shalt live again proud and more lovely, / the wonder of the land and sea.'

107 See below.

108 For an account of Foscarini's career see Raffaello Barbiera, *Poesie veneziane con uno studio sulla poesia vernacola e sul dialetto di Venezia* (1886), Arnaldo Forni, Bologna, 1975, p. 256.

109 Jacopo Vincenzo Foscarini, *Canti pel popolo veneziano illustrati con note da Giulio Pullè* (1844), Arnaldo Forni, Bologna, 1974.

110 Ibid., pp. 22–3.

111 Ibid., p. 65.

112 For Dall'Ongaro see W. D. Howells's sympathetic review, *North American Review*, 228 (1866), pp. 26–42, with translation of *The Ring of the Last Doge*, pp. 37–8. Also G. Monsagrati and G. Pulce, 'Dall'Ongaro, Francesco', *Dizionario biografico degli italiani*, vol. 36, Istituto della Enciclopedia Italiana, Rome, 1986, pp. 138–43.

113 For *Apollo's* gas lighting see Agostino Sagredo, 'Note sugli ammiglioramenti di Venezia', *Annali universali di statistica economia pubblica: storia, viaggi e commercio*, 75, Società degli Editori degli Annali Universali delle Scienze e dell'Industria, 1843, p. 187, n. 11.

114 Riccardo Carnesecchi, *Venezia sorgesti dal duro selvaggio: la musica patriottica negli anni della Repubblica di Manin*, Il Cardo, Venice, 1994, p. 26, and on the political role of the Venetian theatre at this time see Piermario Vescovo, '"La Patria tradita": la scena veneziana nel 1848–49', *Venezia Quarantotto: episodi, luoghi e protagonista di una rivoluzione, 1848–49*, pp. 64–9.

115 Beccaro, 'Carrer, Luigi', *Dizionario biografico degli italiani*, vol. 20, 1980, pp. 733–4, for this activity.

116 *Venezia e le sue lagune*, ed. Giovanni Correr, Antonelli, Venice, 1848.

117 Laura Lattes, *Luigi Carrer: la sua vita, la sua opera*, Miscellanea di Storia Veneta, vol. 10, R. Deputazione Veneta di Storia Patria, 1916: *Canto di Guerra*, p. 91ff.

118 Ginsborg, *Daniele Manin and the Venetian Revolution of 1848–49*, p. 68.

119 Franca Lugato, 'Il Nono Congresso degli Scienziati Italiani a Venezia', *Venezia Quarantotto: Episodi, luoghi e protagonista di una rivoluzione, 1848–49*, pp. 100–101.

120 Pavanello, 'La decorazione dei palazzi veneziani negli anni del dominio Austriaco 1814–1866': the section: 'L'avvio al gusto eclettico: Imprese decorative in occasione del nono congresso degli scienziati italiani', *Il Veneto e l'Austria*, p. 264ff., and *Venezia Quarantotto: episodi, luoghi e protagonista di una rivoluzione, 1848–49*, pp. 104–7. Jappelli's Caffè Petrocchi in Padua was inaugurated in 1842 for the fourth Italian Scientific Congress, ibid., p. 265.

121 Ibid., p. 266.

122 Fabrizio Magani, 'La storia scolpita: *Il Panteon Veneto*', *Venezia e l'Austria*, p. 371.

123 Ibid., passim, for the commissions. The scheme continued until 1931, with Carlo Gozzi the last commission (p. 372).

124 Samuele Romanin, *Storia documentata di Venezia*, 10 vols, 1853–61. Massimo Canella claims the work was commenced in 1847, 'Appunti e spunti sulla storiografia veneziana', *Archivio Veneto*, 107 (1976), p. 91 and Camillo Manfroni, 'Gli studi storici in Venezia dal Romanin ad oggi', *Nuovo Archivio Veneto*, 8 (1908), pp. 352–72.

125 Canella, 'Appunti e spunti sulla storiografia veneziana', p. 92.

126 Cicogna, *Saggio di bibliografia veneziana*.

127 Cicogna, Preface, Ibid., p. xiv.

128 Gianjacopo Fontana, *Venezia monumentale: i Palazzi* (1847), with 82 illustrations by Marco Moro, Filippi, Venice, 1967.

129 On some of these publications see Franco Bernabei, 'Critica, storia e tutela delle arte', *Storia della cultura veneta*, vol. 6, *Dall'età napoleonica alla Prima Guerra Mondiale*, pp. 397–428. Taking up with some precision the reactions of aristocracy and bourgeois to the fall of the Republic and the 'new history' (as it might be called), see Canella, 'Appunti e spunti sulla storiografia Veneziana', pp. 73–116. The activity of Venetian scholars is covered in the Cicogna and Soranza bibliographies. For an essay that gives some prominence to Manin's contribution on jurisprudence in the Veneto see Gaetano Cozzi, 'Venezia e le sue lagune', *Venezia e l'Austria*, pp. 323–41.

130 Ibid., p. ix.

131 In the introduction he writes against 'the cold reason of Milizia' and the reforms of Lodoli, ibid., p. xii.

132 Ibid., for the remarks on Canova, p. 485, and for Selva, p. 477.

133 See the facsimile edition, Bernardo and Gaetano Combatti, *Planimetria della Città di Venezia presentata dal Giandomenico Romanelli*, Vianello, Ponzano/Treviso, 1987. Romanelli regards the map as 'the perfect representation of Habsburg Venice'. Ibid. (no pagination).

134 As early as 1827 Manin had read a paper on the origins of the Venetian dialect to the Ateneo: Angelo Ventura, 'La Formazione intellettuale di Daniele Manin', *Il Risorgimento*, 9 (1957), p. 4.

135 Ginsborg, *Daniele Manin*, p. 67.

136 Ibid., p. 84.

137 Ibid.

138 Ibid., pp. 71–2. Tommaseo was born in the former Venetian territory of Sebenico, Dalmatia, in 1802, studied law at Padua and was involved in lexicography in Florence from 1827. He was in Venice from 1839 to 1849. He published *Relazione degli ambasciatori veneziani nel secolo XVI* in 1838. See again Bezzola, 'Niccolò Tommaseo e la cultura veneta'.

139 Ginsborg, *Daniele Manin*, p. 75.

140 Ibid., p. 50.

141 Ibid., p. 76.

142 Ibid., p. 72. Verdi's *I Lombardi*, played in Treviso, was also given a stirring reception, ibid., p. 76.

143 Ginsborg saw the Arsenale as *the* key to the city, ibid., p. 96.

144 Trevelyan, *Daniele Manin*, pp. 104–5.

145 In Ginsborg's account, the issue for the *arsenalotti* was their exclusion from the National Guard as well as their discontent at the hands of Austrians, *Daniele Manin*, pp. 98–100.

146 For a profile on members, etc., see Adolfo Bernardello, 'Per una storia della Guardia Civica a Venezia nel 1848–49', *Venezia e l'Austria*, ed. Gino Benzoni and Gaetano Cozzi, Marsilio, Venice, 1999, pp. 401–18.

147 Ibid., p. 101.

148 Ibid., p. 95.

149 For the provisional government see Sergio Barizza, *Il Comune di Venezia, 1806–1946: l'istituzione, il territorio, guida-inventario dell'Archivio Municipale*, Comune di Venezia, Venice, 1987, pp. 45–6.

150 Ibid., p. 229. Ginsborg stresses the sympathy that Manin had with the poor, indeed he saw it as the most striking feature of the new Republic, pp. 226–7.

151 Cited doc. 2124, 20 August 1848, Alberto Errera, *Daniele Manin e Venezia (1804–1853)*, Successor Le Monnier, Florence, 1875, p. 479. My translation.

152 Ibid., p. 121. For the *caffè* see Giuseppe Toffanin Jr., 'Il Caffè Pedrocchi periodico padovano', *Giuseppe Jappelli e il suo tempo*, ed. Giuliana Mazzi, Liviana, Padua, 1982, pp. 243–8.

153 Ginsborg, *Daniele Manin*, p. 121.

154 Manlio Brusatin and Giuseppe Pavanello, *Il Teatro La Fenice: i progetti, l'architettura, le decorazioni*, Albrizzi, Venice, 1987, p. 195.

155 Ginsborg, *Daniele Manin*, p. 71, p. 352.

156 Riccardo Carnesecchi, *Venezia sorgesti dal duro servaggio: la musica patriottica negli anni della Repubblica di Manin*, Il Cardo, Venice, 1994, p. 44.

157 Ibid., passim, with extraordinary documentation and musical examples.

158 Piermario Vescovo, '"La patria tradita": La scene veneziana nel 1848–1849', *Venezia Quarantotto: episodi, luoghi e protagonista di una rivoluzione, 1848–49*, pp. 64–9.

159 Ibid., p. 32. Carnesecchi gives the full programmes for the theatres through the period of the Revolution in *Venezia sorgesti dal duro servaggio: la musica patriottica negli anni della Repubblica di Manin*.

160 Ibid., p. 32.

161 Ibid., pp. 32–4.

162 Quoted in Frank Walker, *The Man Verdi*, Alfred A. Knopf, New York, 1972, p. 188.

163 *Narrative of Scenes and Events in Italy from 1847 to 1849 including the Siege of Venice by Lieutenant-General Pepe, Commander-in-Chief of the Army of Expedition of Naples and the Forces of the Venetian Republic*. Henry Colburn, London, 1850.

164 On the defence build-up see Greenfield, 'Commerce and New Enterprise in Venice', p. 323.

165 From the diary 30 July 1849 by Jacopo Zennari (Secretario), Rinaldo Fulin, 'Venezia e Daniele Manin, Ricordi', *Nuovo Archivio Veneto*, 9 (1895), p. CL. There are repeated comments on the tranquillity and goodwill of the populace (as well as the price and scarcity of food) in the anonymous diary: 'Venezia dal Maggio al 16 Agosto 1840 (Diario di un Anonimo)', *Miscellanea Venezia, 1848–1849*, Reggio Istituto per la Storia del Risorgimento Italiano, vol. 5, Rome, 1936, pp. 134–40.

166 Quoted in Ginsborg, *Daniele Manin*, p. 301.

167 Fulin, 'Venezia e Daniele Manin', pp. CXXI–CXXV.

168 Ibid.

169 Ginsborg, *Daniele Manin*, p. 271. Cited from Tommaseo, *Venezia*, vol. 1, p. 71.

170 'Relazione sui capi d'arte che Venezia avrebbe potuto costituire in pegno d'un pestito', in Fulin, 'Venezia e Daniele Manin': see particularly the statement with regard to the conservation of the paintings (p. CXXV): 'I nostri dipinti, da lunghissimi anni esposti in luoghi generalmente umide e poco ventilati, hanno tutti dal più al meno subito influenze, le quali se no si manifestano apertamente finché non sono

tocchi, si rivelerebbero al certo appena fossero posti in condizioni diverse.' For the list of works proposed, pp. CXXVIII–CXXXI.

171 Antonio Pilot, 'Venezia resisterà all'Austriaco ad ogni costo', G. Scarabellin, Venice, 1915.

172 Pier Maria Pasinetti, Melodramma, Marsilio, Venice, 1993. Pasinetti's novels will be discussed in Part 2.

173 Ginsborg, Daniele Manin, p. 271.

174 Pepe, Narrative of Scenes and Events in Italy, 1847 to 1849, p. 314.

175 Antonio Pilot, 'L'Assalto al palazzo del Patriarca Cardinale G. Monico a Venezia nell'Agosto 1849', Rassegna Storica del Risorgimento, 11 (1924), pp. 121–7. On the Church during the Revolution see Bruno Bertoli, 'Il 1848 e il dramma della chiesa veneziana', Venezia Quarantotto: episodi, luoghi e protagonista di una rivoluzione, 1848–49, pp. 58–63.

176 Ginsborg, Daniele Manin, p. 353. For a focus on the Church during the revolution, and this incident see Silvio Tramontin, 'Patiarca e clero veneziano nel 1848–49', La chiesa Veneziana dal tramonto della Serenissima al 1848, ed. Maria Leonardi, Edizioni Studium Cattolico Veneziano, Venice, 1986, pp. 111–35.

177 Ginsborg, Daniele Manin, p. 363.

178 Arnaldo Fusinato, 'A Venezia (19 Agosto 1849)', Poesie patriottiche inedite, P. Carrara, Milan, 1878, pp. 40ff. On the two brothers Fusinato see Carlo Dazzi, 'Due patrioti veneti: Arnaldo e Clemente Fusinato', Ateneo Veneto, 128 (1941), pp. 315–42.

179 Fusinato, 'A Venezia', Poesie Patriottiche Inedite, p. 42.

180 Pepe, Narrative of Scenes and Events, p. 318.

181 Christine Trivulce de' Belgiojoso, 'L'Italie et la Révolution italienne de 1848', Revue des Deux Mondes, 24 (October 1848), pp. 785–824.

182 Ibid., p. 823. My translation.

183 Ibid., p. 788.

184 Ibid. My translation.

185 Giuseppe Pavanello, 'L'epoca contemporanea', Venezia nell'Ottocento: immagini e mito, pp. 182–3. The range of Querena's war paintings appear in Venezia Quarantotto: episodi, luoghi e protagonista di una rivoluzione, 1848–49, pp. 42–159.

186 On Caffi's role as a militant patriot see Mary Pittaluga, Il Pittore Ippolito Caffi, 1808–1866, Neri Pozza, Vicenza, 1971, p. 63.

187 For Caffi's war paintings see Venezia Quarantotto: episodi, luoghi e protagonista di una rivoluzione, 1848–49, pp. 168–75.

188 Ibid., p. 76.

189 Venezia nell'Ottocento: immagini e mito, ed. Giuseppe Pavanello and Giandomenico Romanelli, Electa, Milan, 1983, pp. 184–5. The painting is now in the Museo del Risorgimento, Venice.

190 Ibid., pp. 186–7.

191 Niccolò Tommaseo, 'A Venezia', Opere, ed. A. Bottenghi, R. Ricciardi, Milan, 1958, pp. 41–3. See also the poem Le Nozze del Mare, 1869, which returns to imagery of the Bucintoro and the patrician, and expressions of sorrow at the debilitated city, pp. 147–9.

192 The most detailed account of the immediate post-Revolution measures is found in Giovanni Gambarin, 'La delegazione veneziana a Vienna nel Settembre 1849', Rassegna storica del Risorgimento, 64 (1957), pp. 725–33, but it is undocumented.

193 Mario Brunetti, 'A Venezia dopo la Capitolazione 1849: "L'Epurazione" di Luigi Carrer e di Jacopo Vincenzo Foscarini dalla direzione della Raccolta Correr', Archivio Veneto, 60/61 (1957), pp. 115–21.

194 For the documentation see ibid., pp. 118–21.

195 Priuli was President of the Commission for Benefactions (la Commissione di beneficenza). His letter, written in Vienna, addressed to Barone Fini, is cited in full in Giandomenico Romanelli, Venezia Ottocento: l'architettura l'urbanistica, Albrizzi, Venice, 1988, p. 346.

196 Ibid. My translation.

197 Gambarin, 'La delegazione veneziana a Vienna, nel Settembre 1849', p. 728.

198 Ibid., p. 728ff.

199 Effie in Venice: Unpublished Letters of Mrs John Ruskin Written from Venice Between 1849–1852, ed. Mary Lutyens, John Murray, London, 1965, p. 127. For John Ruskin's letters in this period, Ruskin's Letters from Venice, 1851–52, ed. John Lewis Bradley, Yale University Press, New Haven, 1955.

200 Ibid., pp. 92, 100.

201 Ibid., pp. 131–2.

202 Ibid., p. 66.

203 Effie in Venice, p. 196.

204 Ruskin, Letter to Revd W. L. Brown, 11 December 1849: The Works of John Ruskin, vol. 36, The Letters of Ruskin, 1827–1869, p. 105. See also Appendix 3, The Stones of Venice, vol. 3, 'Austrian Government in Italy', pp. 254–5.

205 David H. Pinkney, Napoleon III and the Rebuilding of Paris, Princeton University Press, NJ, 1972.

206 Sagredo, 'Note sugli ammiglioramenti di Venezia', pp. 69–72, for discussion relating to the need for the bridge.

207 Giuseppe Salvadori's project is illustrated, Le Venezie possibili: da Palladio a Le Corbusier, pp. 218–20.

208 For the modernisation of the Franchetti-Cavalli see Romanelli, Venezia Ottocento: l'architettura l'urbanistica, p. 301ff. and Tra Gotico e Neogotico: Palazzo Cavalli Franchetti a San Vidal, Albrizzi, Venice, 1990.

209 Romanelli, Venezia Ottocento, 'Una vicenda esemplare: il Ponte dell'Accademia', p. 204.

210 Ibid.

211 'New Bridge over the Grand Canal', Illustrated London News (29 January 1853), pp. 81–2, with illustration. See also J. G. James, 'The Evolution of Iron Bridge Trusses to 1850', The Newcomen Society for the Study of the History of Engineering and Technology Transactions, 52 (1980–81), p. 83. It is suggested that the firm of Neville, Nash & Co., an Anglo-Italian group, was active in Turin, applying for French patents in 1838 and 1840 for a system of framing long-span bridges and roofs.

212 Romanelli, Venezia Ottocento, p. 232ff. Gianpietro Zucchetta, Venezia ponte per ponte, vol. 2, Stamperia di Venezia, Venice, 1992, pp. 24–31.

213 Romanelli, Venezia Ottocento, p. 219.

214 This will be discussed in part 2.

215 Giulio Lorenzetti, Venice and its Lagoon: Historical-Artistic Guide, Lint, Trieste, 1975, p. 282; Alvise Zorzi, Venezia scomparsa, Electa, Milan, 1984, p. 178, and Gianpietro Zucchetti, Venezia ponte per ponte, vol. 2, pp. 42–51.

216 Ponte dei Conzalfelzi, ibid., p. 259; Ponte dell'Acquavita, pp. 420–21; Ponte della Malvasia Vecchia, p. 136; Ponte dei Ragusei, p. 727. For designs of some of these bridges, see Venezia nell' Ottocento: immagini e mito, pp. 229–33.

217 Le Venezie possibili: da Palladio a Le Corbusier, section 6, 'Tra Ottocento e Novecento; gli ingegneri e i loro problemi', p. 170ff.

218 For example Ennio Concina, L'Arsenale della Repubblica di Venezia: techniche e istituzioni dal Medioevo all'Età Moderna, preface by Manfredo Tafuri, Electa, Milan, 1984; Manfredo Tafuri, Humanism, Technical Knowledge and Rhetoric: The Debate in Renaissance Venice, Walter Gropius Lecture, Harvard University Graduate School of Design, 1986.

219 See again Patrizia Valle, Tommaso Temanza e l'architettura civile: Venezia e il Settecento, Officina, Rome, 1989.

220 Zucchetta documents the interments and castigates them: 'The Nineteenth Century Closures', Un'altra Venezia: immagini e storia degli antichi canali scomparsa, Silvano, Milan, 1995, p. 53ff.

221 According to Eugenio Miozzi, in Venezia nei secoli. La città, 1, Libeccio, Venice, 1957, p. 219, Meduna also opposed the 'mania to fill in the rii', favouring, rather, the straightening of calli, p. 219.

222 Zucchetta, *Un'altra Venezia: immagini e storia degli antichi canali scomparsa*, p. 64.

223 See the valuable article, Alberto Magrini, 'Piani regolatori di Venezia nel passato e nell'avvenire', *Ateneo Veneto*, 117 (1934), pp. 54–9.

224 On the widening of the Ponte della Paglia see Gianpietro Zucchetta, *Venezia ponte per ponte*, vol. 2, pp. 164–9.

225 See the listing in Alberto Magrini, 'Piani regolatori di Venezia nel passato e nell'avvenire', p. 55.

226 Mario Universo, 'Il progetto di Giuseppe Jappelli per un entrepôt alle Zattere e per una nuova stazione per viaggiatori presso la Punta della Dogana', *Le Venezie possibili: da Palladio a Le Corbusier*, pp. 174–1811. Romanelli, *Venezia Ottocento*, pp. 264–73.

227 G. B. Meduna, 'Planimetria progetto di un entrepôt da erigersi in prossimità della Stazione dell'I. R. Strade Ferrata a S. Lucia, 1850', ibid., p. 307.

228 Ibid., p. 328.

229 C. Damerini, 'Le Pitture di Luigi Querena per un progetto di riforma della Riva degli Schiavoni', *Ateneo Veneto*, 122 (1939), p. 300.

230 Ibid., p. 189.

231 For the report see Romanelli, *Venezia Ottocento*, pp. 346–467.

232 Francesco da Camino, *Venezia e i suoi bagni*, Tipografia del Commercio, Venice, 1858.

233 Alberto Cosulich, *Viaggi e turismo a Venezia dal 1500 al 1900*, Edizione 'I Sette', Venice, 1990, p. 145.

234 Camillo Boito was born in Rome in 1836; his father was from the Veneto, his mother was a Polish countess. The family, with Arrigo, the younger brother born in 1842 and destined to be a distinguished writer and librettist for Verdi, moved to Venice where their father fought in the Revolution of 1848–9. The marriage was dissolved in 1851. Camillo Boito's formative years were spent in Venice, studying at the Accademia under Pietro Selvatico: see Pier Luigi Ciapparelli, 'Agli anni all'Accademia di Venezia', *Camillo Boito: un'architettura per l'Italia Unita*, Marsilio, Venice, 2000, pp. 9–30. He assumed the chair in architecture before he left in 1886 for Milan. *Senso* appeared in the second collection of 'Vain Tales' – *Senso: nuova storielle vane*, in 1883. See Camillo Boito, *Gite di un artista*, ed. Maria Cecilia Mazzi, De Luca Edizione d'Arte, Rome, 1990.

235 Camillo Boito, *Senso and other Stories*, trans. Christine Donougher, Dedalus, Sawtry, Cambridgeshire, 1993, pp. 23–4.

236 Ibid., p. 25.

237 Camillo Boito, 'Quattr'ore al Lido. Schizzo dal vero', *Storielle Vane, Tutti Racconti*, ed. Roberto Bigazzi, Valec-chi, Florence, 1970, pp. 337–44. The story was originally published in *La Nuova Antologia*, 11 (August 1876).

238 'Gli stabilimento balneari nell'800 a Venezia', *Lido di oggi: Lido di allora*, ed. G. Pecorai, vol. 1, 1987, pp. 9ff.

239 Percy Bysshe Shelley, *Julian and Maddalo, A Conversation*, 1818, *The Complete Poetical Works of Percy Bysshe Shelley*, ed. Thomas Hutchinson, Oxford, 1912, p. 185.

240 Charles Nodier, *Jean Sbogar* (1818), Librarie Honoré Champion, Paris, 1987, pp. 136ff.

241 William Dean Howells, *Venetian Life* (1866) Archibald Constable, London, and Houghton Mifflin & Co, Boston and New York, 1907, p. 160. Howells was among the earliest American residents, publishing letters in the *Boston Advertiser* from 1863 which formed the basis for the later *Venetian Life*. For a discussion of his period of residence in Venice, his interest in Italian literature and his novels with Venetian themes see James L. Woodress, Jr, *Howells and Italy*, Greenwood Press, New York, 1952.

242 Ibid., p. 161.

243 To be discussed in part 2, chap. 7.

244 A. Pilot, 'Venezia dal 1851 al 1866 dei diari inediti del Cicogna', *Nuovo Archivio Veneto*, 32 (1916), p. 400ff. Cicogna was a close witness during the Risorgimento until unification. His observations have not appeared in the English literature on Venice at this time, hence the prominence of his account in what follows.

245 September 1855, ibid., p. 413.

246 Ibid., p. 414.

247 16 June, 1859: 'Sembra, in fatti, che gli Austriaci adoperino ogni mezzo per farsi odiare malcontente', ibid., p. 426.

248 Ibid., p. 432.

249 For a discussion of the reasons why Austria did not cede Venetia see Nancy Nichols Barker, 'Austria, France, and the Venetian Question, 1861–1866', *Journal of Modern History*, 36 (1964), pp. 145–55, and Richard B. Elrod, 'Austria and the Venetian Question, 1860–1866', *Central European History*, 4 (1971), pp. 149–70.

250 For these proposals and the document from Metternich's missives see Barker, 'Austria, France and the Venetian Question', p. 145.

251 Elrod, 'Austria and the Venetian Question', p. 157.

252 Cicogna in Pilot, 'Venezia dal 1851 al 1866 dei diari inediti del Cicogna', pp. 434–5.

253 John W. Bush, *Venetia Redeemed: Franco-Italian Relations*, Syracuse University Press, 1967.

254 Ibid., p. 8.

255 *Illustrated London News* (18 September 1847), p. 177. Note the later *The Urgency of the Venetian Question*, trans. Count Charles Arrivabene with a dedication to Lord Houghton, William Ridgway, Picadilly, London, 1864.

256 'Il passeggio della piazza, allorquando si cominciò la band tedesca, si transferì al giardinetto or sulle zattere', Cicogna in Pilot, 'Venezia dal 1851 al 1866 dei diari inediti del Cicogna', p. 437.

257 Richard Wagner, *My Life*, trans. Andrew Gray, ed. Mary Whittall, Cambridge University Press, 1983, p. 577.

258 Ibid.

259 Ibid., p. 583.

260 Théophile Gautier, *Journeys in Italy*, trans. Daniel B. Vermilye, Hutchinson, London, 1903, pp. 250–51.

261 Cicogna in Pilot, 'Venezia dal 1851'.

262 Ibid., p. 441.

263 Ibid., p. 477 (May 1866).

264 Ibid.

265 Ippolito Nievo, 'Venezia e la libertà', *Opere*, ed. Sergio Romagnoli, La Letteratura Italiana, Storia e Testi, 57, Riccardo Ricciardi, Milan and Naples, 1952, pp. 1033–52. The paraphrase is drawn from the document overall.

266 For an general account of Nievo's life and activity see Sergio Romagnoli, 'Ippolito Nievo', *Storia di cultura veneta*, vol. 6, *Dall'età napoleonica alla Prima Guerra Mondiale*, pp. 165–87.

267 Giovanni Verga, *I Carbonari della montagna: sulle lagune*, Edizione Nazionale delle Opere di Giovanni Verga, vol. 1, Felice Le Monnier, Florence, 1988.

268 For this work and other examples of the iconography see *Venezia nell'Ottocento: immagini e mito*, pp. 13–20.

269 For the political overtones of the Exposition see Albert Boime, 'The First Italian National Exposition of 1861', *The Art of the Macchia and the Risorgimento: Representing Culture and Nationalism in Nineteenth-Century Italy*, University of Chicago, Chicago and London, 1993, p. 165ff.

270 Antonio Zona, *Venezia in lacrime fra le braccia della liberata Milano* (private collection), ibid., p. 13.

271 For Andrea Appiani, *Venezia che spera* see *Venezia nell'Ottocento: immagini e mito*, pp. 15–16.

272 These were, chronologically: *Allocuzione di Antonio Paoletti recitata il giorno 17 Febraio 1861 . . . rappresentate La Entrata di Enrico III Re di Francia nel Nostro Canal Grande*, Tipografia del Commercio, Venice, 1861; *Orazione di Antonio Paoletti Pittore Storico . . . rappresentante una Visita di Enrico III a Veronica Franco*, Tipografia del Commercio, Venice, 1862; *Orazione di Antonio Paoletti . . . L'Arrivo di Antonio Grimani a Venezia dopo l'Esilio*, Tipografia del Commercio, Venice, 1865.

273 See again Romanelli, *Tra Gotico e Neo Gotico: Palazzo Cavalli Franchetti a*

San Vidal, Albrizzi, Venice, 1990, p. 139ff. Also his 'Palazzo Cavalli-Franchetti a S. Vidal; da Giambattista Meduna a Camillo Boito', *Restauro e Città*, 3/4 (1986), pp. 71–83.

274 See Bartolomeo Cecchetti, *Una Passeggiata nel giardino dei Conti Papadopoli in Venezia*, Fratelli Vistentini, Venice, 1887.

275 For the Molmenti painting see *Venezia nell'Ottocento: immagini e mito*, pp. 178–9.

276 Ibid., p. 183.

277 Pietro Giordani, *Di sei statuette d'illustri italiani fatte da Bartolomeo Ferrari Al Nob. Antonio Papadopoli*, G. Antonelli, Venice, 1862.

278 For *Gli Amori garibaldini*, *Opere*, pp. 990–1008.

279 Cited Marcello Gorra Cecconi, *Nievo e Venezia*, La Stamperia di Venezia Editrice, Venice, n. d. p. 20.

280 *I Confessioni d'un Italiano* was first published as *Le Confessioni di un Ottagenario*, Le Monnier, Florence, 1867. For an abridged English translation see *The Castle of Fratta*, trans. Lovett F. Edwards, Oxford University Press, London, 1957.

281 On the connections between Manzoni and Nievo see Iginio de Luca, 'L'Addio di Lucia nei *Promessi Sposi* e l'addio di Carlo Altoviti nelle *Confessioni d'un Italiano*', *Manzoni: Venezia e il Veneto*, ed. Vittore Branca, Ettore Caccia and Cesare Galimberti, Olschki, Florence, 1976, pp. 161–99.

282 Ippolito Nievo, 'Venezia nel 1797', *Nuova Antologia Scienze, Lettere ed Arti*, 1866, pp. 139–66. This was the first part of *I Confessioni* to be published – in the early months after Venetian liberation.

283 Cited in chap. 1 above.

284 On the relation between Nievo and Foscolo, only partially explored, see Riccardo Scarpa, 'Da Ugo Foscolo a Ippolito Nievo: il risorgere della libertà Italiana dalle Ceneri del Cessato Stato Veneto', *Rassegna Storica del Risorgimento*, 72 (1985), pp. 171–7.

285 Marcella Gorra, 'Nievo e Venezia', *Ateneo Veneto*, 5, n. s. (1967), pp. 68–9.

286 Ippolito Nievo, *Angelo di Bontà* (1856), Lucarini, Rome, 1988.

287 Ibid., p. 254.

288 For an account see again Bush, *Venetia Redeemed: Franco-Italian Relations, 1864–1866*.

289 *Il Comune di Venezia negli ultimi mesi della dominazione austriaca: relazione e documenti*, Tipografia del Commercio, Venice, 1867, p. xi.

290 Pilot, 'Venezia dal 1851 al 1866', p. 480. My translation.

291 Two poems are cited here from *Poesie politiche a Venezia*, Giovanni Cecchini, Venice, 1866: *ode scritta in occasione della partenza degli austriaca da Venezia*, and *Il Canto del gondoliere a Venezia*, no pagination.

Chapter 5

1 Camillo Boito, *Senso and Other Stories*, trans. Christine Donougher, Dedalus, Sawfry, Cambs, 1993, p. 22.

2 Giandomenico Romanelli, in *Venezia Ottocento: l'architettura l'urbanistica*, Albrizzi, Venice, 1988, cites Mack Smith on Garibaldi's negative reaction, p. 367. On the unification, giving a wide-ranging coverage up to 1875 and the visit of Franz Josef (a reconciliation with Austria, at least officially), *Venezia*, ed. Emilio Franzina, Laterza, Rome and Bari, 1986, pp. 3–113.

3 Gino Damerino, 'L'Anno 1867 a Venezia', *Ateneo Veneto*, 121 (1937), p. 5.

4 Girolamo Induno, *Ingresso di Vittorio Emanuele II a Venezia (7 November 1886)*, Milan, Museo del Risorgimento. See also popular press illustrations in Alberto Cosulich, *Viaggi e turismo a Venezia: dal 1500 al 1900*, 'I Sette', Venice 1990, pp. 62–7. Like his brother Domenico, Girolamo was a Risorgimento artist who had fought in Garibaldi's army.

5 For the Buzzola work see Girolamo Soranzo, *Bibliografia veneziana in aggiunta e continuazione del 'Saggio' di Emmanuele Antonio Cicogna*, Burt Franklin, New York, 1967, p. 698. For Buzzola's music see *Antonio Buzzolla: una vita musicale nella Venezia romantica*, ed. Francesco Passadora and Licia Sirch, Adria, Minelliana, 1994. For Boito's appearance at Fenice see Piero Nardi, *Vita di Arrigo Boito*, A. Mondadori, Verona, 1942, p. 227.

6 Dalla Libera's suite of paintings, now in the Museo Correr, Venice, are illustrated in *Venezia Quarantotto: episodi, luoghi, protagonisti di una rivoluzione, 1848–49*, Electa, Milan, 1998, pp. 192–4.

7 Alvise Zorzi *Venezia scomparsa*, Electa, Milan, 1984, pp. 136–7. On the controversy that surrounded the siting of the tomb (in relation to a painting that places it within San Marco) see *Venezia Quarantotto*, p. 195.

8 Luigi Borro was also responsible for the Manin tomb. For an assessment of the Manin statue see Giorgio Nonveiller, 'Aspetti della scultura a Venezia dal 1860 al 1960', *Modernità allo specchio: arte e Venezia (1860–1960)*, ed. Toni Toniato, Supernova, Venice, 1995, pp. 150–51, and for the monuments to Manin, Tommaseo, Paleocapa and Garibaldi see Luisa Alban, 'Venezia Italiana mette in *campo*, l'epopea del 1848–1849', *Venezia Quarantotto*, pp. 76–83.

9 Zorzi, *Venezia scomparsa*, p. 135.

10 The Tommaseo sculpture was the work of Francesco Barzaghi (1882).

11 The monument to Garibaldi was the work of Augusto Benevito: Renzo Salvadori, *Duemila anni scultura a Venezia*, Canal, Venice, 1986, p. 143.

12 For illustrations see *Venezia Quarantotto*, pp. 199–201.

13 Zorzi, *Venezia scomparsa*, p. 130.

14 Ibid., p. 130.

15 Ibid., pp. 110–12.

16 Victor Cérésole, *La Vérité sur les déprédations austrichiennes à Venise: Trois lettres à M. Armand Baschet*, 2nd ed., corrected and augmented, H. F. et M. Münster, Venice, 1866.

17 Girolamo Dandolo died that year. He was author of the important contemporary history, *La Caduta di Venezia e i suoi ultimi cinquant'anni*, Naratovich, Venice, 1855–7.

18 P. Preto, 'Cecchetti, Bartolomeo', *Dizionario biografico degli italiani*, vol. 24, ed. Alberto M. Ghisalberti, Istituto della Enciclopedia Italiano, Rome, 1980, pp. 227–30.

19 See Anna Giubertoni emphasising Viennese nostalgia, 'Venezia nella letteratura austriaca moderna', and Massimo Cacciari, 'Viaggio estivo', both in *Venezia Vienna: il mito della cultura Veneziana nell'Europa asburgica*, ed. Giandomenico Romanelli, Electa, Milan, 1983, pp. 105–6, and ibid., pp. 127–40.

20 Heinrich Benedikt: 'Uno dei meriti maggiori dell'amministrazione austriaca fu la cura costante per Venezia marittima', in 'L'Austria e il Lombardo-Veneto', *La civiltà Veneziana nell'età romantica*, Sansoni, Florence, 1961, p. 43. For the claim with regard to Trieste, p. 44.

21 Ibid., p. 43.

22 Ibid., p. 52.

23 Ibid., p. 56.

24 Paul Ginsborg, *Daniele Manin and the Venetian Revolution of 1848–49*, Cambridge University Press, 1979, p. 45.

25 Giandomenico Romanelli, 'Architettura Romantica nel Veneto: linguaggio e personaggi', *Il Veneto e l'Austria: vita e cultura artistica nelle città Venete, 1814–1866*, ed. Sergio Marinetti and Giuseppe Mazzariol, Fernando Mazzocca, Electa, Milan, 1989, pp. 383–8.

26 Cf. Donald J. Olsen, 'The Vienna of Franz Joseph', in *The City as a Work of Art: London, Paris, Vienna*, Yale University Press, New Haven and London, 1986, p. 58ff.

27 George R. Collins and Christiane Crasemann Collins, *Camillo Sitte: The Birth of Modern City Planning*, with a translation of the 1889 Austrian edition of his *City Planning According to Artistic Principles*, Rizzoli, New York, 1986, p. 258. Sitte was Director of the Staatsgewerbeschule in Vienna from 1883,

during the time of major building activity in Vienna. For an account of his background see ibid., p. 21ff. For an assessment of Sitte and his international influence (record of a conference held at the Istituto Veneto di Scienze, Lettere ed Arti, Venice, in 1990) see *Camillo Sitte e i suoi interpreti*, Franco Angeli, Milan, 1992.

28 Ibid., pp. 163, 165.

29 Ibid., p. 196.

30 Cf. ibid., p. 229: 'In our discussions so far street networks have not been mentioned . . . neither those of ancient Athens, of Rome, of Nuremberg, nor of Venice. They are of no concern artistically, because they are inapprehensible in their entirety.'

31 Ibid., p. 304.

32 The impact of Venice on twentieth-century urban thought will be discussed in part 2.

33 *The Letters of Franz Liszt to Olga von Meyendorff, 1871–1886, in the Mildred Bliss Collection at Dumbarton Oaks*, trans. William R. Tyler, Dumbarton Oaks, Washington, DC, 1979, p. 557.

34 To engage with Manet's reworking of Venetian art is beyond the scope of this book, but on the modernity of his treatment see, for example, T. J. Clark, *The Painting of Modern Life: Paris in the Art of Manet and His Followers*, Alfred A. Knopf, New York, 1984, chap. 2, 'Olympia's Choice', p. 79ff.

35 See, in general, Carl E. Schorke, *Fin-de-Siècle Vienna: Politics and Culture*, Vintage, New York, 1981.

36 'The Ringstrasse, its Critics, and the Birth of Urban Modernism', ibid., p. 24ff.

37 'Gustav Klimt: Painting and the Crisis of the Liberal Ego', ibid., p. 208ff.

38 Fritz Novotny and Johannes Dobai, *Gustav Klimt: With a Catalogue Raisonné of his Drawing*, Thames & Hudson, London, 1968, commenting on Klimt as the heir of Hans Makart, p. 381.

39 See Dobai's catalogue, ibid. p. 295, noting that Klimt underlined the importance of the Kunsthistorisches Museum decorations for his later style.

40 See part 2, chap. 1 below.

41 For Venice and Vienna in the eighteenth century see Franca Zava Boccazzi, 'Episodi di pittura veneziana a Vienna nel Settecento', *Venezia Vienna*, p. 25; and on music see Giovanni Morelli, 'Un pomo d'oro sull'unverzehrlich Tisch: il lungo momento della connessione musicale di Venezia e Vienna', ibid., pp. 89–104.

42 For the vicissitudes of the poorly received libretto by F. Zell and Richard Genée (and the accusation of plagiarism) see Andrew Lamb, 'Nights in Venice', *Musical Times* (December 1976), pp. 989–91. See also *Eine Nacht in Venedig*, Anna Giubertoni, 'Venezia nella letteratura moderna', *Venezia Vienna*, pp. 109–10.

43 On the hectic nature of the Viennese waltz see Henry Schnitzler, 'Gay Vienna: Myth and Reality', *Journal of the History of Ideas*, 15 (1954), esp. pp. 110–11, and comments generally on late nineteenth-century Vienna, p. 103: 'the "gaiety of Vienna", it has been suggested, is a gaiety of escape, frequently born of anguish, even of despair; it is invariably a gaiety with, deep down, a bad conscience or a least an awareness of its dubious character.'

44 Richard Traubner, *Operetta: A Theatrical History*, Oxford Unversity Press, New York, 1983, p. 14.

45 Strauss's *An der shönen blauen Donau (The Blue Danube)* was prepared for chorus and piano version in 1867: Peter Kemp, *The Strauss Family: Portrait of a Musical Dynasty*, Baton Press, Kent, 1985, pp. 60–71, for the *Geschichten aus dem Wienerwald (Tales from the Vienna Woods)*, 1868, p. 76.

46 Francesco Zanotto, *I Pozzi ed i piombi: antichi prigioni di stato della Repubblica di Venezia*, G. Brizeghel, Venice, 1876, p. 128.

47 [Lady Eastlake], 'Venice Defended', *Edinburgh Review*, 166 (July 1877), p. 192. For her assessment of Darù see p. 192.

48 Edmond Bonnal, *La Chute d'une république: Venise d'après les archives secrètes de la République*, Libraire de Firmin-Didot, Paris, 1885.

49 Edmondo Bonnal, *Caduta d'una Repubblica Venezia*, trans. Giuseppe Ughi, Pietro Naratovich, Venice, 1888.

50 Deidre O'Grady, 'The Devil's Advocate: Evil in the Works of Arrigo Boito', *The Last Troubadours: Poetic Drama in Italian Opera, 1597–1887*, Routledge, London and New York, 1991, pp. 180–201. Also Giovanni Morelli, 'L'Utopia roversa: Visioni melodrammatiche di Venezia da Milano', *Venezia Milano: storia civiltà e cultura nel rapporto tra due capitali*, Electa, Milan, 1984, p. 200.

51 Cf. Raeffaelo Barbiera, *Poesie veneziane* (1886) Arnaldo Forni, Bologna, 1975, p. 299: 'Se deve solo accennar al Boito poeta veneziano, che del dialetto del Goldoni conosce e maneggia bene la varietà e la leggiandrie.' Barbiera anthologises Boito's 'La Canzon de La Spatola', and 'La Presa de Tabaco', ibid., pp. 300–304).

52 For the circumstances of the completed composition, and the work overall, Alexander Faris, *Jacques Offenbach*, Faber & Faber, London and Boston, 1980, p. 196ff.

53 J. Offenbach, *Le Pont des Soupirs*, opera buffa, libretto by Hector Crémiux and Ludovic Halevy, E. Gerard, Paris, 1868.

54 Faris, *Jacques Offenbach*, p. 83.

55 J. Offenbach, P. Siraudin and Jules Moinaux, *Le Voyage MM. Dunanan Père et Fils*, Théâtre Bouffes Parisiens, Paris, 1862.

56 Ibid., p. 95.

57 For Hoffmann's original story in translation, 'The Story of the Lost Reflection', in *The Best Tales of Hoffmann*, ed. with an intro. by E. F. Bleiler, Dover Books, New York, 1967, p. 116ff.

58 Robert Browning, 'A Toccata of Galuppi's (from *Dramatic Lyrics*), *The Poetical Works of Robert Browning*, vol. 1, Smith, Elder & Co, London, 1897, p. 266. For Browning's visits to Venice see *Browning e Venezia*, ed. Sergio Perosa, Leo S. Olschki, Florence, 1971: Jacob Korg, *Browning and Italy*, Ohio University Press, Athens, Oh., and London, 1983.

59 Browning, 'In a Gondola' (from *Dramatic Romances*), *The Poetical Works of Robert Browning*, vol. 1, pp. 399–400.

60 Browning, 'Fifine at the Fair' (1872), ibid. vol. 2, p. 354.

61 Ibid., p. 359.

62 Ibid., p. 360.

63 Rosella Mamoli Zorzi, 'Palazzi e personaggi del mondo veneziano di Browning', *Browning e Venezia*, pp. 117–24.

64 On the readings see Michael Meredith, 'Speaking Out in Venice and London', ibid., pp. 85–94. On reading to Mrs Bronson see p. 87.

65 Colin Partridge, *Senso: Visconti's Film and Boito's Novella. A Case Study of the Relation Between Literature and Film*, Edwin Mellen Press, New York, 1991. Partridge gives one of the rare accounts of Boito's literature in English. Anthony Trollope published a story on the subject of love between a Venetian and an Austrian: 'The Last Austrian to Leave Venice' (1867), *Anthony Trollope: The Complete Stories*, vol. 5, ed. Betty Sane Stemp Breyer, Texas Christian University Press, Fort Worth, 1983, pp. 109–29.

66 Boito's 'Buddha's Collar' is translated in Camillo Boito, *Senso and Other Stories*, 1993, pp. 189–207. For the quotation see p. 189.

67 Romanelli, *Venezia Ottocento: l'architettura l'urbanistica*, p. 365.

68 Ibid.

69 Giorgio and Maurizio Crovate, *Regate e regatanti*, Comune di Venice, Venice, 1982, p. 31.

70 Ibid., p. 33.

71 *Commissione per lo studio d'un piano di riformo delle vie e canale della città di Venezia*, ibid., p. 373.

72 For Giuseppe Bianco's project see Romanelli, *Venezia Ottocento*, pp. 380–82. Also Alberto Magrini, 'Piano regolatori di Venezia nel passato e nel avvenire', *Ateneo Veneto*, 117 (1934), pp. 56–7.

73 Cf. Ann F. La Berge, *Mission and Method: The Early Nineteenth-Century French Public Health Movement*, Cambridge University Press, 1992, for public health measures in Paris.

74 For Les Halles see David H. Pinkney, *Napoleon III and the Rebuilding of Paris*, Princeton University Press, NJ, 1972, p. 79.

75 See Carl E. Schorske, 'The Ringstrasse, Its Critics, and the Birth of Urban Modernism', *Fin-de-Siècle Vienna: Politics and Culture*, Vintage Books, New York, 1981, pp. 24–115.

76 Romanelli attends to the projects of Grubissich, Bianco, Fornoni, Trevisanato, G. B. Meduna (the latter, according to Romanelli, 'certamente la più relevante e razionale proposta per la viabilità in Venezia', p. 385), A. De Reali, the plan for embankments and canals by Romano-Lavezzari-Petich, Marsich, Biondetti-Crovato, Conte Martinengo; Vulten, A de Marco, B. Foratti and Andrea X (anonymous), in *Venezia Ottocento*, pp. 379–402.

77 For the Trevisanato plan see ibid. pp. 382–3; for the Provvidimenti proposed by Gaspare Biondetti-Crovato see ibid. pp. 394–5.

78 Alvise Pietro Zorzi, *Sulla demolizione della Chiesa di S. Moisè*, Tempo, Venice, 1877, p. 24 (this important tract will be discussed below). For demolition projects in Paris see the maps in Howard Saalman, *Haussmann: Paris Transformed*, George Braziller, New York, 1977.

79 Pietro Marsich, *Sul Riordinamento della Città di Venezia*, Studio Primo, Tipografia del Commercio, Venice, 1867. For the areas and their extension see p. 4.

80 'Giova però qui ammettere un fatto generale: che tutti i miglioramenti da farsi nelle vie di terra non devona le importantissime vie di acqua, le quali, specialità di Venezia, sono e saranno sempre le più brevi, le più naturali, le più ricercate. E a questo proposito insisto sulla mia idea esternata altrove d'introdurre la piccola navigazione a vapore', ibid., p. 18.

81 'Tutta la vita cittadina qui si concentra, la borghesia e la nobiltà predominano sulle altre classi,' ibid., p. 5.

82 Ibid., pp. 13–14.

83 *10 Immagini per Venezia*, ed. Francesco Dal Co, Mostra dei Progetti per Cannaregio Ovest, Officina, Venice, 1980. The competition will be discussed in part 2, chap. 4 below.

84 'Il proletariato veneziano è refugiato in questo asilo di miseria e di abbandono. Strano contrasto! Attorno alla gran mole dantesca dell'arsenale pullalano i vermi!', Marsich, *Sul Riordinamento della Città di Venezia*, p. 15.

85 Cf. the account of the formation of the then-current sewerage project in Paris, Pinkey, *Napoleon III and the Rebuilding of Paris*, pp. 127ff.

86 Nelli-Elena Vanazan Marchini, *Venezia da laguna a città*, Arsenale, Venice, 1985, citing submissions from 1842, p. 130, also Daniele Mazzotta, 'L'Acquedotto di Venezia', *Archeologia industriale nel Veneto*, pp. 171–2.

87 Ibid., p. 125.

88 Vanazan Marchini, 'L'igiene dei pozzi', *Venezia da laguna a città*, p. 120ff.

89 For Marsich's project and plans see Sergio Barizza, 'Strade e canali', *Le Venezie possibili: da Palladio a Le Corbusier*, ed. Lionello Puppi and Giandomenico Romanelli, Electa, Milan, 1985, p. 208.

90 For the sequence of proposals see Romanelli, 'Mercato del pesce a Rialto', *Venezia nell'Ottocento*, p. 231; also Sergio Barozza, 'Mercato', *Le Venezie possibili: da Palladio a Le Corbusier*, p. 196ff; Zorzi, *Venezia scomparsa*, pp. 141–2.

91 Ibid., p. 142.

92 Torelli's publication ran to a total of 104 pages in large format: *Progetto di conguinzione della Piazzetta di S. Marco e l'Isola di S. Elena mediante una Via Pensile lungo la Riva degli Schiavoni la formazione di una grande arena naturica fra i giardini pubblici de l'isola suddetta prosposto. Prefetto Senatore L. Torelli al Cittadini di Venezia nel 1871*, Marco Visenti, Venice, 1872. Also *Le Venezie possibili: da Palladio a Le Corbusier*, p. 208.

93 Quoted in G. Damerini, 'L'anno 1867 a Venezia', p. 10.

94 Romanelli, *Venezia Ottocento*, p. 412.

95 On Fano see ibid., p. 415.

96 Ibid., p. 422.

97 Meduna, 'Le Proposte di miglioramenti di G. B. Meduna', ibid. pp. 383–6. He calls Meduna's document 'the most relevant and rational proposal for the viability of Venice'.

98 Paolo Maretto treats the Neo-Lombard 'between Revival and Mannerism', in *La casa veneziana: nella storia della città dalle origini all'Ottocento*, Marsilio, Venice, 1986, pp. 499–505.

99 Ibid., p. 212, and Donatello Calabi and Paolo Morachiello, 'Rialto: "Sacrario" da conservare or rinnovare?', *Le Venezie possibili: da Palladio a Le Corbusier*, pp. 69–70.

100 Ibid., pp. 69–70, and Romanelli, *Venezia Ottocento*, p. 212.

101 Ibid.

102 For Neville's Ponte del Ghetto Nuovo see Gianpietro Zucchetta, *Venezia ponte per ponte*, vol. 2, Stamperia di Venezia, Venice 1992, pp. 483–4.

103 Antonio Foscari, 'La reforma pedonale attuata in Venezia nel Secolo XIX', *La rivista Veneta*, 10 (1969), pp. 24–8, and Alberto Cosulich, *Venezia nell'800: vita economia costume*, Edizioni Colomiti, San Vito di Cadore, 1988, 'Servizi in Città', p. 203ff.

104 Adolfo Bernardello, 'La ferrovia e i traghetti: gondolieri, barcaioli e remignanti nella Venezia di metà dell'Ottocento', *Venetica: rivista di storia delle Venezie*, 3 (1985), pp. 93–9.

105 Nicolo Randolfi, 'Trasformazione urbana e produzione industriale nella Venezia dell'Ottocento', *Venezia, città industriale: gli insediamenti prodottivi del 19 Secolo*, Marsilio, Venice, 1980, p. 26.

106 Giacinto Gallina, *Serenissima* (1891), Filippi, Venice, 1975.

107 For this important generation of artists who dominated Venetian painting and the Biennales for some twenty years see *La pittura in Italia: l'Ottocento*, ed. Enrico Castelnuovo, Electa, Milan, 1991, p. 189ff. For Milesi see Clauco Benito Tiozzo, *Alessandro Milesi*, Pittori, Helvetia, Venice, 1989, and *Venezia nell'Ottocento*, p. 206.

108 For Luigi Nono and the paintings here see ibid., pp. 201–40.

109 Ibid., pp. 203–4.

110 On the industrial aspects of the nineteenth century see *Venezia città industriale*, esp. Nicolo Randolfi, 'Trasformazione urbana e produzione industriale del 19 Secolo', pp. 11–28, and Giandomenico Romanelli, 'Alla ricerca di un linguaggio', pp. 29–32; the well-illustrated *Archeologia industriale nel Veneto*, ed. Franco Mancuso, Silvano, Milan, 1990, with individual coverage of remaining buildings; *Itinerari di archeologia industriale a Venezia: comune di Venezia*, with video, directed by Hans Wieser, Treviso, 1979; and *Le Venezie possibili: da Palladio a Le Corbusier*, esp. 'Tra Ottocento e Novecento: gli ingegneri e i loro problemi', p. 170ff.

111 For the Eden Garden, Christiana Moldi-Ravenna and Tudy Sammartini, *Secret Gardens of Venice*, photographs by Gianni Berengo Gardin, Arsenale, Venice, 1992, p. 17.

112 For the industries on the Giudecca see Sicinio Bonfanti, *La Giudecca nella storia nell'arte e nella vita*, Libreria Emiliano, Venice, 1930, section 4, 'La vita delle industrie e dei commerci', pp. 243–53. Also Francesco Basaldella, *Giudecca: cenni storici*, Basaldella, Venice, 1983.

113 V. Manzini, 'La Stazione Marittima', cites Randolfi, 'Riformazione urbane', *Venezia, città industriale*, p. 20.

114 See Giovanni Distefano and Giannantonio Paladini, *Storia di Venezia, 1797–1997*, vol. 2, *La dominante dominata*, Supernova-Grafiche Biesse, Venice, 1996, n. 225, p. 336. For the Ca' Farsetti restoration at this time see Romanelli, *Venezia Ottocento*, p. 437.

115 Ibid., pp. 430–31. See also Vincenzo Fontana, 'Pietro Paleocapa a Venezia (1817–1820 e 1830–1848). L'ingegneria come politica del territorio', *Giuseppe Jappelli e il suo tempo*, ed.

Guliana Mazzi, Livana, Padua, 1982, pp. 277–94. Carla Uberti, 'La Stazione Marittimma', *Le Venezie possibili: da Palladio a Le Corbusier*, pp. 238–42.

116 For a detailed account see Walter Bigatton, Maurizio Bordugo and Guido Lutman, *Il Storio del cotonificio veneziano: l'industria Pordonese Amman-Wepfer tra Ottocento e Novecento*, Biblioteca dell'Immagine, Pordenone, 1994.

117 Daniele Mazzotta, 'Il cotonificio veneziana', *Archeologia industriale nel Veneto: gli insediamenti produttivi del 19 Secolo*, pp. 198–9.

118 The fundamental research was established by Jürgen Julier, *Il Molino Stucky a Venezia*, Centro Tedesco di Studi Veneziani, Venice, 1978. See more recently Francesco Amenolagine, ed., *Molino Stucky: ricerche storiche e ipotesi di restauro*, Il Cardo, Treviso, 1995, and Daniele Mazzotta, 'Il Molino Stucky', *Archeologia industriale nel Veneto*, pp. 200–202.

119 Wullekopf and his lineage in Hanover are treated in detail in Ute Angeringer, Sasa Dubrici and Alessandro Marchi, 'Wullekopf e l'architettura Neogotica della scuola di Hannova', *Molino Stucky, Ricerche Storiche*, pp. 37–43.

120 Julier, *Molino Stucky*, pp. 15–22. Also Daniele Mazzotta, 'Il Molino Stucky', *Archeologia industriale nel Veneto: gli insediamenti produttivi del 19 Secolo*, pp. 200–202. and p. 39.

121 Barizza, 'Collegamento stabile Venezia-Giudecca', *Le Venezie possibili: da Palladio a Le Corbusier*, p. 210, and 'Strade e Canale', ibid., p. 207ff.

122 Julier, *Il Molino Stucky*, p. 10.

123 The restoration project will be considered in part 2.

124 Giorgio Bellavitis, *L'Arsenale di Venezia: storia di una grande struttura urbana*, Marsilio, Venice, 1983, p. 227.

125 As in the *Officina delle Armi*. See photograph 14 (and indeed the photographic folio overall) in Ugo Pizzarello and Vincenzo Fontana, *Pietre e legni dell'Arsenale di Venezia*, L'Altra Riva, Venice, 1983, p. 51ff.

126 Paolo Costantini and Italo Zannier, *Venezia nella fotografia dell'Ottocento*, Arsenale and O. Böhm, Venice, 1986, p. 119.

127 Bellavitis, *L'Arsenale di Venezia: storia di una grande struttura urbana*, p. 228.

128 Guido Perocco and Renzo Trevisan, *Giacomo Favretto*, Umberto Allemandi & Co., Turin, 1986, pp. 94–5.

129 The curtain dated from 1878, Maria Teresa Muraro, *Gran teatro la Fenice*, Corbo & Fiore, Venice, 1996, p. 72.

130 Mario de Biasi, 'Vincenzo Zanetti e la sua opera', Vincenzo Zanetti, *Guida di Murano e delle celebri sue fornaci vetrarie*, (1866, correzzione rettifiche e guinte, 1890) Arnaldo Forni, Venice, 1985, pp. 13–21.

131 For a guide to the collection see Attilia Dorigato, *Murano Glass Museum*, Electa, Milan, 1986.

132 Cf. Karlis Karklins, *Glass Beads: The Nineteenth-Century Levin Catalogue and Venetian Bead Book and Guide to Descriptions of Glass Beads*, Minister of Supply and Services, Quebec, Canada, 1985. The Levin catalogue is comprised of two collections of glass and stone beads assembled by Moses Lewin Levin, a London bead merchant whose business operated from 1830 to 1915. For an important focus on the bead and paper-weight art and industry: Giovanni Sarpellon, *Miniature Masterpieces: Mosaic Glass, 1838–1924*, Prestel, Munich, 1995.

133 Ibid., p. 66. For an evocative technical and aesthetic background on colour in earlier glass see Paul Hills, 'Transparency, *Lucidezza* and the Colours of Glass', *Venetian Colour: Marble, Mosaic, Painting and Glass, 1250–1550*, Yale University Press, New Haven and London, 1999, pp. 109ff. For a rich collection emphasing the colour range of Murano glass at the time: *I colori di Murano nell'800: The Colours of Murano in the Nineteenth Century*, ed. Aldo Bova, Rossella Junck and Puccio Migliaccio, Arsenale, Venice, 1999.

134 Sarpellon, *Miniature Masterpieces: Mosaic Glass, 1838–1924*, p. 19ff.

135 Francesca Trevellato analyses the implications of bead-threading for Venetian women and society in 'Out of Women's Hands: Notes on Venetian Glass Beads, Female Labour and International Trade', *Beads and Bead Makers: Gender, Material Culture and Meaning*, ed. Lidia D. Sciama and Joanne B. Eicha, Berg, Oxford, 1998, pp. 47–83.

136 For a discussion of the trading of the conterie, ibid. p. 64ff.

137 Cf. Patricia Mainardi, *Art and Politics of the Second Empire: The Universal Expositions of 1855 and 1867*, Yale University Press, New Haven and London, 1987.

138 Dorigato, *Murano Glass Museum*, p. 14.

139 Giandomenico Romanelli, *Correr Museum*, Electa, Milan, 1985, p. 236. Romanelli does state that the chandelier is *probably* by Giuseppe Briati. There are notable examples of Briati's chandeliers in the Museo Ca' Rezzonico.

140 Sarpellon, *Miniature Masterpieces: Mosaic Glass, 1838–1924*, p. 33.

141 Vincenzo Zanetti, 'Fabrica di soffiati e di vetri a filigrana ad uso antico della ditta Antonio Dr Salviati', *Guida da Murano e delle celebri sue fornaci vetrarie*, pp. 91–4. See also Giovanni Mariacher, 'Le arti del vetro, dell'oreficeria e del bronzo nella prima metà dell'Ottocento', *Il Veneto e l'Austria: vita e cultura artistica nelle città venete, 1814–1866*, ed. Sergio Marinelli, Giuseppe Mazzariol and Ferdinando Mazzocca, Electa, Milan, 1989, p. 293; Reimo Liefkes, 'Antonio Salviati and the Nineteenth-Century Renaissance of Venetian Glass', *Burlington Magazine*, 136 (1994), pp. 283–90; Sheldon Barr and John Bigelow Taylor, *Venetian Glass: Confections in Glass, 1855–1914*, Harry N. Abrams, New York, 1998.

142 Liefkes, 'Antonio Salviati and the Nineteenth-Century Renaissance of Venetian Glass', p. 283.

143 Ibid., p. 285.

144 See the papers of the symposium *Austen Henry Layard tra l'Oriente e Venezia*, ed. F. M. Fales and B. J. Hickey, L'Erma di Bretschneider, Rome, 1987.

145 Barr, *Venetian Glass: Confections in Glass, 1855–1914*, p. 33.

146 Vincenzo Zanetto, *Delle attuali condizione dell'industria vetraria nelle venete lagune: discorso letto in Murano*, 1869.

147 Ibid., p. 34.

148 Illustrated in Dorigato, *Murano Glass Museum*, pp. 66, 67, 69.

149 Illustrated in Doretta Davanzo Poli, photographs Mark E. Smith, *Arts and Crafts in Venice*, Könemann, Cologne, 1999, p. 182.

150 Barr, *Venetian Glass*, p. 30.

151 Marina Barovier, ed., *Art of the Barovier Glassmakers in Murano, 1866–1872*, Arsenale, Verona, 1993, p. 14.

152 Illustrated, ibid., p. 28.

153 See the many examples in Barr, *Venetian Glass*.

154 Ibid., p. 93.

155 Guillermo de Osmo, *Mariano Fortuny: His Life and Work*, Aurum Press, London, 1980, esp. chap. 4, 'Fashion and Textiles', pp. 80–119. For Proust and the house of Fortuny, see below, chap. 6, and part 2, chap. 1. More generally see Silvio Fusoe and Sandro Mescolo, *Mercato e travestimento: l'artigianate d'arte a Venezia fine '800 inizi '900*, Marsilio, Venice, 1984.

156 Elizabeth Vedrenne, *Living in Venice*, Thames & Hudson, London, 1990, p. 14.

157 Romanelli gives considerable emphasis to Guggenheim (together with Selvatico and Boito, similarly interested in the arts and crafts) in 'Architetti e architetture a Venezia tra Otto e Novecento', *Antichità Viva*, 4 (1972), pp. 26–9.

158 Stefano Moronato, 'La collezione di tessuti Michelangelo Guggenheim', *Una città e il suo museo: un secolo e mezzo di collezioni civiche veneziane*, Museo Correr, Venice, 1988, pp. 205–12.

159 Camillo Boito, 'Le industrie artistiche all'Esposizione di Milano', *Nuovo*

Antologia, 59 (1881), pp. 493-509, repr. Camillo Boito, *Il nuovo e l'antico in architettura*, ed. Maria Antonietta Crippa, Jaca Books, Milan, 1988, p. 199ff.

160 Ibid., p. 199

161 Ibid., p. 200

162 G. M. Urbani de Gheltof, *A Technical History of the Manufacture of Venetian Laces (Venice–Burano)*, trans. by Lady Layard, Ongania, Venice, 1882. The laces described are *punto tagliato, punto areticello, punto in aria, punto tagliato a fogliami, merletto a fuselli, punto di Burano, punto di Venezia*.

163 Appendix, ibid., pp. 53–7.

164 See the sociological analysis by Lidia D. Sciama, 'Lacemaking in Venetian Culture', *Dress and Gender: Making and Meaning in Cultural Contexts*, pp. 121–44.

165 Michelangelo Jesurum, *Cenni sull'industria dei merletti: storici e statistici*, Marco Visentini, Venice, 1873. For Jesurum see Doretto Davanazo Poli, 'Il Tessile a Venezia tra '800 e '900', *Mercato e travestimento: l'artigianato d'arte a Venezia, fine '800 inizi '900*, ed. Silvio Fuso and Sandro Mesola, Marsilio, Venice, 1984, pp. 13–14.

166 See again Gallina, *Serenissima*.

167 Ciardi also painted views of the Piazza San Marco etc. His subject matter also included the Terraferma, with the Sile canal and the foothills of Mt Grappa, but at all times he felt the weight of a low horizon and would seem to be forever recalling the geometry and space of the lagoon.

168 Pietro Selvatico, *L'Arte insegnata nelle Academie secondo le norme scientifiche, Atti dell' I. R. Accademia di Belle Arti in Venezia*, Venice, 1852, pp. 28–9. See also Paolo Costantini, 'Pietro Selvatico: fotografia e cultura artistica alla metà dell'Ottocento', *Fotologia*, 4 (1986), pp. 54–67.

169 Elena Bassi, 'Grigoletti e l'Accademia', *Michelangelo Grigoletti e il suo tempo*, ed. Giuseppe Maria Pilo, Electa, Milan, 1971, pp. 21–3.

170 In order of date of birth: Federico Zandomeneghi, 1841–1917; Napoleoni Nani, 1841–1900; Guglielmo Ciardi, 1842–1917; Giacomo Favretto, 1849–77; Luigi Nono, 1850–1918.

171 Enrico Piene, *Zandomeneghi: l'uomo e l'opera*, Bramante, Busto Arisizio, 1979.

172 Clauco Benito Tiozzo, *Alessandro Milesi: pittore*, Edizioni Helvetia, Venice, 1989, p. 10, for details on antagonism between Grigoletti and Milesi.

173 On the Macchiaioli and Venetian contacts, and an overview of the generation of painters see Giuseppe Pavanello et al., 'La pittura dell'Ottocento a Venezia e nel Veneto', *La pittura in Italia. L'Ottocento*, pp. 169–218. Also Roberta J. M.

Olson, *Ottocento Romanticism and Revolution in Nineteenth-Century Italian Painting*, The American Federation of Arts, Florence, 1992, pp. 28–9.

174 Italo Zannier, *Venice: The Naya Collection*, O. Böhm, Venice, 1981, p. 23.

175 See plates reproduced in ibid., pp. 33–9.

176 For example the *Kerbside Toilette*, 1865, pl. 14, ibid., or the *Cortile ai Tolentini*, ibid., pl. 61.

177 The fourth remodelled edition, Baedeker, *Italy: Handbook for Travellers*, Karl Baedeker, Leipzig, 1877. On Baedeker see James F. Muirhead (publisher of the later Blue Guides), 'Baedeker in the Making', *Atlantic Monthly* (1966), p. 648, acknowledging the debt to Murray.

178 Ibid., p. 213.

179 Ibid., p. 223.

180 Wilkie Collins, *The Haunted Hotel: A Mystery of Modern Venice* (1879), Dover Publications, New York, 1982.

181 Ibid., pp. 60–61.

182 Ibid., p. 109.

183 For a focus on James in Venice see *Henry James e Venezia*, ed. Sergio Perosa, Leo S. Olschki, Florence, 1987.

184 Henry James, 'Venice' (1882), *Italian Hours*, William Heinemann, London, 1909, p. 1.

185 Ibid., p. 2. Mr Ruskin is roundly attacked in the writings on Florence, see 'Italy revisited', ibid., pp. 127–30. For Tony Tanner's comments on James and Ruskin see *Venice Desired*, Blackwell, Oxford, 1992, pp. 169–70.

186 James, 'Venice', *Italian Hours*, p. 3.

187 Ibid., pp. 7–10.

188 Ibid., p. 13.

189 'Venice, An early Impression' (1772), ibid., p. 54.

190 Ibid.

191 For Manet's Venice pictures see François Cahin, Charles S. Moffett and Michel Melot, *Manet, 1823–83*, Metropolitan Museum of Art, Harry N. Abrams, New York, 1983, pp. 373–7. For the French Impressionists and some comment on their relationship to traditional Venetian painting see Erik Forsmann, *Venedig in der Kunst und im Kunsturteil des 19. Jahrhunderts*, Almquist & Wirksells, Stockholm, 1971, pp. 168–96, and Francesca Castellani, 'L'Eclat de la lumière et le luxe de la couleur. Un itinerario nel mito dei maestri Veneti attraverso le copie francesi dell'Ottocento', *Venezia da stato a mito*, Fondazione Giorgio Cini, Venice, Marsilio, Venice, 1997, pp. 134–45.

192 Barbara Ehrlich White, 'Renoir's Trip to Italy', *Art Bulletin*, 51 (1969), pp. 333–51. The catalogue of Italian paintings lists eight Venetian works.

193 Robert Harold Getscher, *Whistler and Venice*, Ann Arbor, Mich., 1981, and

Hugh Honour and John Fleming, *The Venetian Hours of Henry James, Whistler and Sargent*, Little Brown & Co., Boston, Mass., 1991.

194 Linda Ayres, 'Sargent in Venice', in *John Singer Sargent*, ed. Patricia Hills, Whitney Museum of American Art, Harry N. Abrams, New York, 1986, pp. 49–71, and Margaretta M. Lovell, *Venice: The American View, 1860–1920*, The Fine Arts Museums of San Francisco, San Francisco, 1985, esp. pp. 95–107 for the paintings discussed here. See also Margaretta M. Lovell, *A Visitable Past. Views of Venice by American Artists, 1860–1915*, University of Chicago, Chicago and London, 1989.

195 For the Royal Academy view of Venice see Julian Halsby, *Venice, The Artist's Vision: A Guide to British and American Painters*, chap. 4, 'City of Palaces, Pigeons, Poodles and Pumpkins. The Victorians in Venice, 1840–80', B. T. Batsford, London, 1990, pp. 60–78.

196 Forsmann, *Venedig in der Kunst und im Kunsturteil des 19. Jahrhunderts*, p. 174 (for Dill and Björck), and p. 176 (for Skånberg).

197 For Frank Duveneck see Lovell, *Venice: The American View, 1860–1920*, pp. 37–8; Robert Blum, pp. 36–9; Charles Coleman, pp. 34–5.

198 Ruskin, in discussion of Byzantine palaces, *The Works of Ruskin*, vol. 9, *The Stones of Venice*, vol. 2, ed. Cook and Wedderburn, George Allen, London, 1904, p. 132.

199 Ibid., p. 131.

200 The restoration is described in detail, 'Sui Restauri del Fondaco dei Turchi', *L'ingegneria a Venezia nell'ultima ventennio*, Naratovich, Venice, 1887, pp. 1–5.

201 Ibid., and more recently, Peter Lauritzen, *Venice Restored*, Michael Joseph, London, 1986, pp. 48–9.

202 Camillo Boito, in an important article to be discussed below, 'Rassegna artistica, Venezia ne' suoi vecchi edifici', *Nuova Antologia*, 20 (1872), p. 925.

203 For an indication of Boito's ongoing role in Italian conservation, and his significance for Gustavo Giovannoni and Massimo Piacentini (see part 2, chap. 8 below) see Richard A. Etlin, *Modernism in Italian Architecture, 1890–1940*, MIT, Cambridge, Mass., 1991, pp. 124ff. See also Alberto Grimoldi, 'A ciascuno il proprio Boito interpretazioni passate e recenti di un protagonista dell'Ottocento', Marco Maderna, *Camillo Boito: pensiero sull'architettura e dibattito coevo*, Guerini & Associati, Milan, 1995, pp. 11–34; and *Camillo Boito: un architettura per l'Italia unita*, ed. Guido Zucconi and Francesca Castellani, Marsilio, Venice, 2000.

204 Pietro Selvatico, *Sulla Architettura e sulla scultura in Venezia dal Medio*

Evo sino ai nostri giorni (1857), Arnaldo Forni, Bologna, 1980, pp. 32–3. For discussion of Selvatico's views, together with Ruskin's see Vincenzo Fontana, 'Camillo Boito e il restauro a Venezia', *Casabella*, 472 (1981), pp. 48–53.

205 On the organic analogies, not unusual at the time see ibid., p. 48. For some detail on the nature of his restoration see Vincenzo Fontana, 'Restauro e storia dell'architettura nell'Ottocento italiano', *Restauro e Città*, vol. 1, 1985, pp. 19ff.

206 Boito refers to Ruskin's reaction to the *Cattedrale di Murano* described in part 2 of *The Stones of Venice*, in 'I Restauri di San Marco', *Nuova Antologia*, 28 (1879), p. 710.

207 Alvise Piero Zorzi, *Osservazioni intorno ai ristauri interni ed esterni della Basilica di San Marco con tavole illustrative di alcune iscrizioni Armene*, Ongania, Venice, 1877; repr. Filippi, Venice, n.d. For an overall focus see Mario dalla Costa, *La Basilica di San Marco e i restauri dell'Ottocento, Le idee de E. Viollet-le-Duc, J. Ruskin e le 'Osservazioni' di A. P. Zorzi*, Stamperia di Venezia, Venice, 1983 (noting that Boito merits no attention). With respect to Ruskin see John Unrau, *Ruskin and St Mark's*, Thames & Hudson, London, 1984.

208 Zorzi, *Osservazioni intorno ai ristauri interni ed esterni della Basilica di San Marco con tavole illustrative di alcune iscrizioni Armene*, p. 17. On the colour in the stones see Zorzi's section on pumice cleaning and scraping (*pomiciatura e raschiamenti*), pp. 61ff.

209 Ibid., pp. 161ff. citing 'De la Restauration des anciens édifices en Italie'.

210 Ibid., p. 41.

211 William Morris to the editors of the *Daily News*, 31 October 1879, in *The Collected Letters of William Morris*, ed. Norman Kelvin, vol. 1, *1848–1880*, Princeton University Press, 1984, p. 529.

212 The letters cited run in chronological sequence, ibid., from p. 528. On behalf of the Society, Morris wrote a letter to the editors of various Italian newspapers pleading that he was no less critical of the English procedures (27 November 1879), pp. 544–5. See also the letter of 1880, pp. 594–5.

213 Ibid., p. 543.

214 Boito, 'I Restauri di San Marco', pp. 702–21.

215 Gio. Battista Meduna, 'The Restoration of St Mark's, Venice', *Building News* (13 February 1880), p. 203.

216 *Valore dei monumenti: l'Avvenire dei monumenti in Venezia*, Fontana, Venice, 1882, pp. 5–21. The writer refers to Ruskin's *Fors Clavigera*, p. 7.

217 Alvise Zorzi, *Sulla Demolizione della Chiesa di S. Moisè*, Dalla Tipografia del Tempo, Venice, 1877. Meduna appears to be implicated adversely, as Zorzi notes

that he had had the job of restoring the façade and roof in 1864: p. 15.

218 Selvatico, *Sulla Architettura e sulla scultura in Venezia*, p. 430.

219 *Ruskin's Venice*, ed. Arnold Whittick, George Godwin, London, 1976, p. 185.

220 Zorzi, *Sulla Demolizione della Chiesa di San Moisè*, p. 7.

221 Ibid., p. 10. On the destroyed buildings see 'Tavella descrittiva delle distruzioni de'palazzi e chiese operate in Venezia dalla caduta della Repubblica a'di nostri', p. 27ff.

222 Gianfranco Pertot, *Venezia 'Restaurata': centosettanta anni di interventi di restauro sugli edifici Veneziani*, Franco Angeli, Milan, 1988, pp. 44–5.

223 *Ruskin's Letters from Venice, 1851–1852*, ed. John Lewis Bradley, Yale University Press, New Haven, 1955, p. 128.

224 Boito, 'Il Palazzo Ducale' (1882), *Gite di un artista*, ed. Maria Cecilia Mazzi, De Luca Edizioni d'Arte, Rome, 1990, pp. 41–55.

225 Franco Lugato, 'Dai restauri di fine Ottocento all'inaugurazione del museo', in Antonio Manno, *Palazzo Ducale: guida al Museo dell'Opera*, Canal e Stamperia, Venice, 1996, pp. 17–20. On the different reactions to the restoration of the Palazzo Ducale and San Marco, see Luca Beltrami, 'La Conservazione dei monumenti nell'ultimo ventennio', *Nuova Antologia*, 38 (1892), p. 456.

226 For the detail of the restoration see Vincenzo Fontana, 'I Palazzo Ducale di Venezia alla fine dell'Ottocento', *Restauro e Città*, 3–4 (1996), pp. 50–57.

227 Since 1996 the columns and machinery Forcellini used have been on display in the Palazzo Ducale. See illustrations in Manno, *Palazzo Ducale Guida al Museo dell'Opera*.

228 Forcellini's report of 1884, cited ibid., p. 51.

229 Pertot, *Venezia 'Restaurata'*, p. 52.

230 Camillo Boito, 'Le Trifore del Palazzo Ducale a Venezia', *Nuovo Antologia*, (December 1899), p. 547. The Barbari map, dated 1500, recognised then as the work of 'Alberto Duro' and Gentile Bellini's *Procession of the Cross in the Piazza San Marco*, dated 1496, were both consulted for the accuracy of their depiction of the architecture.

231 See the discussion in Vincenzo Fontana, 'Restauro e storia dell'architettura nell'Ottocento Italiano', *Restauro e Città*, 1 (1985), pp. 9–20. This article is valuable in contextualising Venetian practices in Italy overall.

232 Beltrami, 'La Conservazione dei monumenti', p. 451.

233 Fontana, 'Restauro e storia dell'architettura nell'Ottocento italiano', p. 10.

234 Camillo Boito, 'I Nostri Vecchi Monumenti, Necessità di una legge per conservarli. Prima parte', and 'Seconda Parte', repr. Camillo Boito, *Il Nuovo e l'antico in architettura*, ed. Maria Antonietta Crippa, Jaca Books, Milan, 1988, pp. 73–106.

235 Costantino, 'Pietro Selvatico; Fotografia e cultura artistica alla metà dell'Ottocento', pp. 64–6.

236 For example, J. W. Bunney, *The West Front of St Mark's, 1877–82*, in John Unrau, *Ruskin and St. Mark's*, pl. xi; Alberto Proscocimi, *Views of the Façade and Interior of the Basilica San Marco, 1885–1887*, for Ferdinando Ongania, see Jeffrey Spier and Gordon Morrison, *San Marco and Venice*, National Gallery of Victoria, Melbourne, 1997, p. 24.

237 Paolo Fambri, 'L'Avvenire di Venezia', *Nuova Antologia di Scienze, Lettere ed Arti*, 9 (1878), pp. 132–62. Fambri was to be president of the Grande Esposizione Nazionale d'Arte in 1887. For his important political career see N. Labanca, 'Fambri, Paolo', *Dizionario biografico degli italiani*, vol. 44, Istituto della Enciclopedia Italiana, Rome, 1994, pp. 510–15.

238 Fambri, 'L'Avvenire di Venezia', p. 136.

239 Ibid., p. 151. Fambri was responding to ideas broached by Manfrin: see Zorzi, *Venezia scomparsa*, p. 148.

240 Ibid., p. 152.

241 Sitte, *The Birth of Modern City Planning*, p. 304.

242 *Basilica di San Marco in Venezia, illustra nella storia e nell'arte da scrittori Venezia sotto la direzione di C. Boito*, 8 vols, Ongania, Venice, 1880–93; *La Basilique de St Marc à Venise au double point de vue de l'art et de l'histoire sous la direction da prof. Camillo Boito*. F. Ongania, 1889–90; *The Basilica of San Marco in Venice illustrated from the points of view of Art and History by Venetian Writers under the direction of Prof. Camillo Boito*. F. Ongania, 1880–1888.

243 P. Costantini, 'Ferdinando Ongania and the Golden Basilica: A Documentation Programme in Nineteenth-Century Venice', *History of Photography*, 8 (1984), pp. 314–28.

244 Federico Berchet, 'Modern Restorations from 1797 to 1893', *The Basilica of Saint Mark*, part 3, vol. 6, trans. Frederick Home Rosenberg of Venice, 1893, pp. 925ff.

245 Pietro Saccardo, 'Mosaics', ibid., p. 707.

246 Ibid., p. 929.

247 Ibid.

248 Alvise Zorzi, *Venezia scomparsa*, Electa, Milan, 1984, pp. 136. For the ongoing debate through the nineteenth century, with the various projects, including a monument to the Risorgimento and

Manin see Susanna Biadene, 'Le botteghe alla base del Campanile', Il *Campanile di San Marco: Il crollo e la recostruzione*, Palazzo Ducale, 1992, Silvana, Venice, 1992, pp. 31–4.

249 Much of this background, essential for the orientation of the young Molmenti, is given in Antonio Fradeletto, 'Commemorazione del M. E. Pompeo Molmenti', *Atti del Reale Istituto Veneto di Scienze Lettere ed Arti*, 88 (1928–9), pp. 57–84.

250 Marin Sanudo, *Diarii*, ed. Rinaldo Fulin, F. Stefani and Nicolò Barozzi, F. Visentini, Venice, 58 vols, 1879–1902.

251 Il *Conservatorio di Musica Benedetto Marcello di Venezia*, 1876–1976, ed. Pietro Verardo, Stamperia di Venezia, Venice, 1977. For the institutions in general see Giovanni Distefano and Giannantonio Paladini, *Storia di Venezia, 1797–1997*, vol. 2, *La dominante dominata*, Supernova, Grafiche Biesse, Venice, 1997, p. 299.

252 Pompeo Molmenti, *La Storia nella vita privata dalle origini alla caduta della Repubblica*, 3 vols, (Roux and Favale, Turin 1880), Istituto Italiano d'Arte Grafiche, Bergamo, 1928. The English translation is by Horatio F. Brown, *Venice: Its Individual Growth from the Earliest Beginnings to the Fall of the Republic*, 6 vols, George Allen, London, 1906–8.

253 See *In Attesa degli sposi*, Galleria Nazionale d'Arte Moderna, Rome, illus. 65, in Guido Perocco and Renzo Trevisan, *Giacomo Favretto*, Umberto Allemandi & Co., Turin 1986.

254 Pompeo Molmenti, *Tiepolo: la Villa Valmarana*, Ferd. Ongania, Venice, 1880.

255 Francis Haskell cites Selvatico, *Rediscoveries in Art: Some aspects of Taste, Fashion and Collecting in England and France*, Cornell University Press, Ithaca, 1976, p. 130. In the discussion of the 'rediscovery' of Tiepolo in France and England, Delacroix is given an important role, p. 112.

256 Camillo Boito, *Gite di un artista*, p. 32, 'sua insolenza di fantasia'; p. 34, 'è piena di febbrile curiosità'. Boito mentions Carpaccio and Tiepolo as being 'in gran voga', p. 29.

257 Giorgio Pullini on 'La commedia post-Goldoniana, veneta e italiana', in 'Il teatro fra scena e Società', *Storia di Cultura Veneta*, vol. 6, *Dall'età napoleonica alla Prima Guerra Mondiale*, ed. Girolamo Arnaldi and Manlio Pastore Stocchi, Neri Pozza, Vicenza, 1986, pp. 266ff.

258 For Eleanora Duse, see next chapter.

259 Richard Wagner, *My Life*, trans. Andrew Gray, ed. Mary Whitall, Cambridge University Press, 1983, p. 576. For Wagner's death in Venice, see next chapter.

260 *Venezia nell'Ottocento: Immagini e mito*, ed. Giuseppe Pavanello and Giandomenico Romanelli, Electa, Milan, 1983, p. 256. See also Enrico Gamba's 1872 painting, *Goldoni studiando dal vero*, p. 215.

261 Pompeo Molmenti, *Carlo Goldoni Ssudi di Pompeo Molmenti*, Ongania, Venice, 1880, p. 126 (my translation).

262 Giosué Carducci, *Rime e ritmi*, ed. Manara Valgimigli and Giambattista Salinari, Zanichelli, Bologna, 1964, pp. 99–112.

263 In 1887 Perocco and Trevisan, *Giacomo Favretto*, p. 189.

264 For the expositions, see ibid., p. 194.

265 Pompeo Molmenti is still incredulous at the death ten years after, see his 'La Vita e l'opera di Giacomo Favretto', *Venezia nuovi studi di storia e d'arte*, G. Barberà, Florence 1897, pp. 360–407.

266 For an account of Molmenti's politics (and his increasing conservatism) see M. Donaglio, 'Il difensore di Venezia: Pompeo Molmenti fra idolatria del passato e pragmatismo politico', *Venetica*, 13 (1996), pp. 45–72.

267 Camillo Boito, 'Rassegna artistica: Venezia ne'suoi vecchi edifici', *Nuova Antologia*, 20 (1872), pp. 916–27.

268 The writing on painting has had much less emphasis, but see Franco Bernabei, 'Boito critico dell'arte veneta', *Camillo Boito: un'architettura per l'Italia unita*, ed. Guido Zucconi and Francesca Castellani, Marsilio, Venice, 2000, pp. 146–53.

269 For example, the Public Library of Victoria in Melbourne, Australia.

270 Fontana cites the *Carta del Restaura* with discussion in 'Restauro e storia dell'architettura nell'Ottocento italiano', p. 10ff.

271 Ibid.

272 Giuseppe Rocchi, 'Camillo Boito e le prime proposte normative del restauro', *Restauro*, 3 (1974), pp. 46–57; Alberto Grimoldi, *Omaggio a Camillo Boito*, Franco Angeli, Milan, 1991. A number of papers treat Boito's restoration projects in Milan and his original architecture.

273 Giandomenico Romanelli, 'Lo scalone del Boito', *Tra Gotico e Neogotico: Palazzo Cavalli-Franchetti a San Vidal*, Albrizzi, Venice, 1990, pp. 181–93.

274 Boito had ample opportunity to see central European architecture: see Massimiliano Savorra on 'I Viaggi', *Camillo Boito: un'architettura per l'Italia unita*, pp. 24–9; and through his knowledge of the work of his Viennese predecessor at the Brera Academy, Baron Schmidt: see Maria Grazia Sandri, 'Federico Schmidt, predecessore di Boito alla Scuola di Architettura dell'Accademia

di Belle Arti di Brera', *Omaggio a Camillo Boito*, ed. Alberto Grimoldi, Franco Angeli, Milan, 1991, pp. 57–66. Boito was particularly known in Padua for the staircase of the Museo Civico, the Scuole Elementari alla Reggia Carrerese, and his reconstruction of the Donatello altarpiece in the Church of Il Santo: see Tiziana Serena, 'Boito, Selvatico e i grandi nodi urbani', and Francesco Castelanni, 'La Basilica del Santo e le arti decorative', *Camillo Boito: un'architettura per l'Italia unita*, pp. 80ff. His teaching at the Brera Academy in Milan, and his editorship of the journal devoted to industrial design, *Arte Italiana Decorativa e Industriale*, are further evidence of his spectacular range of interests.

275 Boito, 'Venezia e suoi'vecchi edifici', p. 918.

276 Ibid., p. 921.

277 On the new bridge and its demolition (replaced by a bridge in traditional masonry) see Gianpietro Zucchetta, *Venezia ponte per ponte*, vol. 2, Stamperia di Venezia, Venice, 1992, pp. 239–41.

278 Camillo Boito, 'Venezia che scompare Sant'Elena e Santa Marta', *Nuova Antologia*, 61 (1893), pp. 629–45.

Chapter 6

1 As one of the characters puts it in Gabriele d'Annunzio's *The Flame* (1900), trans. Susan Bassnett, Quartet Books, London, 1991, p. 154.

2 Material relating to Wagner in Venice has been collected in Richard Wagner, *Diario veneziano*, ed. Giuseppe Pugliesse, Corvo & Fiori, Venice, 1983. It brings together extracts from Wagner's diary and biography, the letters of Matilde Wesendonk from 1858, the diary of Cosimo Wagner from 1876 to 1882 and from 1882 to 1883, with relevant letters.

3 For an introduction to this lineage see Giuliana Giobbi, 'Gabriele d'Annunzio and Thomas Mann: Venice, Art and Death', *European Studies*, 19 (1989), pp. 55–68. Thomas Mann's *Death in Venice* is discussed in the next chapter, part 2, below.

4 Friedrich Nietzsche, *Ecco Homo: How One Becomes What One Is*, trans. R. J. Hollingdale, Penguin, Harmondsworth, 1986, p. 99.

5 *Correspondence of Wagner and Liszt*, trans. with preface by Francis Hueffer, revised W. Ashton Ellis, Vienna House, New York, 1973, originally Charles Scribner's Sons, New York, 1897, vol. 2, pp. 243, 250. In fact Liszt advised Wagner against Venice because of the uncertainty of the Austrian government.

6 Richard Wagner, *My Life*, trans. Andrew Gray, ed. Mary Whittall, Cambridge University Press, 1983, p. 572.

7 Ibid., p. 578.

8 *Cosima Wagner's Diaries*, vol. 2, *1878–1883*, ed. and annotated Martin Gregor-Dellin and Dietrich Mack, trans. Geoffrey Skelton, Harcourt, Brace & Jovanovich, New York, 1980, p. 845.

9 For that visit see Dalmonte, 'Liszt and Venice: Between Poetics and Rezeptionsgeschichte', *Journal of the American Liszt Society*, 27 (1990), pp. 22–4.

10 For a discussion of the 'experimental' aspects of these late works, for example 'chromatic voice-leading' and tonal stability, see David Butler Cannata, 'Perception and Apperception in Liszt's Late Piano Music', *Journal of Musicology*, 15 (1997), pp. 178–207.

11 For example Hellmuth Petriconi, 'La Mort de Venise & Der Tod in Venedig', *Das Reich des Untergangs: Bemerkungen über ein mythologisches Thema*, Hoffmann & Campe, Hamburg, 1958, pp. 67–95. Werner Vortriede, 'Richard Wagners Tod in Venedig', *Euphorion*, 19 (1955), pp. 334–59; W. Pabst, 'Satan die alten Götter in Venedig', *Euphorion*, 52 (1958), pp. 378–95; Erwin Koppen, *Dekadenter Wagnerismus: Studien zur europäischen Literatur des Fin de Siècle*, Walter der Gruyter, Berlin, 1973, esp. chap. 3, 'Tödliches Venedig', pp. 214–396; Erwin Koppen, 'Wagner und Venedig', *Zu Richard Wagner*, ed. H. J. Loos and G. Massenkeil, Bouvier, Bonn, 1984, pp. 101–2.

12 Decadence in its literary manifestation is well-worked in Christiane Schenk, *Venedig im Spiegel der Décadence: Literatur des Fin de Siècle*, Peter Lang, Frankfurt, 1987.

13 D'Annunzio, *The Flame*, p. 302.

14 Maurice Barrès, *La Mort de Venise* (1903) *La Mort de Venise suivie de carnets de voyage inédits et de documents*, ed. Marie Odile Germain, Christian Pirot, Paris, 1990, p. 79.

15 Ibid.

16 Cf. Christiane Schenk, *Venedig im Spiegel der Décadence-Literatur des Fin de Siècle*, passim. Also Giandomenico Romanelli, 'Venezia nell'Ottocento: ritorno alla vita e nascita del mito della morte', *Storia di cultura veneta*, vol. 6, *Dall'età Napoleonica alla Prima Guerra Mondiale*, ed. Girolamo Arnaldi and Manlio Pastore Stocchi, Neri Pozza, Vicenza, 1986, pp. 749–66.

17 Pietro Gasti and Peter Gast were pseudonyms of Johann Heinrich Köselitz. See Alfred Lowenberg and David Charlton, 'Gast, Peter', *The New Grove Dictionary of Music and Musicians*, vol. 7, ed. Stanley Sadie, Macmillan, London, 1980, p. 180. For an account of the relationship see Frederick R. Love, 'Prelude to a Desperate Friendship: Nietzsche and Peter Gast in Basel', *Nietzschen-Studien*, 1 (1972), pp. 261–85. During Nietzsche's

1884 visit, Peter Gast went through his opera *Der Löwe von Venedig* with Nietzsche, who endeavoured on a number of occasions to have it performed. For letters from Nietzsche addressed to Gast see *Nietzsche Lettres à Peter Gast*, André Schaeffner Rocher, Monaco, 1957.

18 Nietzsche was in Venice in 1880, April 1884, April 1885 and September 1887. For a keen estimate of his importance see Massimo Cacciari, 'Viaggio estivo', in *Venezia Vienna: il mito della cultura veneziana nell Europa asburgica*, ed. Giandomenico Romanelli, Electa, Milan, 1983, pp. 127–40. The sustained nature of Cacciari's study of Viennese culture will be explored below, in part 2.

19 For example Friedrich Nietzsche, 'The Case of Wagner: Turinese Letter of May 1888', trans. Walter Kaufmann, in *The Birth of Tragedy and the Case of Wagner*, Vintage, New York, 1967, pp. 155ff.

20 *Ecce Homo: How One Becomes What One Is*, p. 62. Compare the letter to Franz Overbeck, May 1884: 'Hier bin ich im Hause Köselitzens, in der stille Venedigs, und höre Musik, die vielfach selber eine Art idealisches Venedig ist', Friedrich Nietzsche, *Werke in drei Bände*, vol. 3, K. Slechta, Carl Hanser, Munich, 1956, p. 1219

21 Nietzsche to Franz Overbeck, and to Franziska Nietzsche, *Friedrich Nietzsche Briefwechsel*, ed. Giorgio Colli und Mazzino Montinari, Walter de Gruyter, Berlin, New York, 1981, pp. 14, 16.

22 Nietzsche, '"Mein Glück", Lieder des Prinzen Vogelfrie, Die fröhliche Wissenschaft', 1882, *Nietzsche Werke*, ed. Giorgio Colli und Mazzino Montinari, Berlin, New York, 1973, vol. 2, p. 322. The reference to the study of San Marco occurs in *The Genealogy of Morals*; I have used the translation by Francis Golffin, *The Birth of Tragedy and the Genealogy of Morals*, Doubleday & Co., New York, 1956, p. 244.

23 For the history of the composition and its publication, see Roger Hollinrake, 'A note on Nietzsche's Gondellied', *Nietzschen-Studien*, 4 (1975), pp. 139–45, noting the comments on Nietzsche and Wagner.

24 Nietzsche, *Ecce Homo*, pp. 62–3.

25 Nietzsche an Franz Overbeck: 'Auch Delacroix wollte Rom nicht, es machte ihm Furcht. Er schwärmte für Venedig, wie Shakespeare, wie Byron, wie George Sand. Die Abneigung gegen Rom auch bei Theoph. Gautier – und bei Rich. Wagner.' Friedrich Nietzsche, *Nachgelassene Fragmente, Herbst 1860 bis Herbst 1872, Nietzsche Werke*, III, 3, ed. Giorgio Colli and Mazzino Montinari, Walter de Gruyter, Berlin, New York, 1978, p. 910.

26 Friedrich Nietzsche, *Daybreak:*

Thoughts on the Prejudices of Morality, trans. R. J. Hollingdale, Cambridge University Press, 1982, p. 494.

27 Nietzsche, '100 tiefe Einsamkeiten bilden zusammen die Stadt Venedig – dies ihr Zauber. Ein Bild für die Menschen der Zukunft', *Morgenröthe, Nachgelassene Fragmente, Nietzsche Werke V/1 Angang 1880 bis Frühjahr 1881*, ed. Giorgio Colli and Mazzino Montinari, Walter de Gruyter, Berlin, New York, 1978, p. 368.

28 Ibid.

29 'Eine einsame glückselige Insel', Nietzsche to Gast, 3 August 1883, *Nietzsche Briefwechsel III, 1, Friedrich Nietzsche Briefe, Januar 1880–Dezember 1884*, ed. Giorgio Colli and Mazzino Montinari, Walter de Gruyter, Berlin, New York, 1981, p. 418.

30 Friedrich Nietzsche, *Beyond Good and Evil: Prelude to the Philosophy of the Future*, trans. R. J. Hollingdale, Penguin, Harmondsworth, 1990, pp. 199–200.

31 These comments are made in Massimo Cacciari, Francesco Dal Co and Manfredo Tafuri, 'Il Mito di Venezia', *Venezia città del moderno: Venice City of the Modern, Rassegna*, 22 (1985), p. 8. See also Cacciari, 'Viaggio estivo', p. 27, and 'Venezia postuma', *Venezia nell'Ottocento: Immagini e mito*, ed. Giuseppe Pavanello and Giandomenico Romanelli, Electa, Milan, 1983, p. 265.

32 There is a specific literature with relation to Barrès and Venice. See Pierre Jourda, 'La Venise de Maurice Barrès', *Venezia nelle letterature moderne*, ed. Carlo Pellegrini, Istituto per la Collaborazione Culturale, Venice, 1961, pp. 192–201; Enzo Caramaschi, 'Maurice Barrès et Venise', *Maurice Barrès*, Actes du colloque organisé par la Faculté des lettres et des sciences humaines de l'Université de Nancy, 1962, pp. 265–84; Enzo Caramaschi, 'Maurice Barrès et Venise', *Etudes de littérature française*, Adriatica, Bari & A. G. Nicet, Paris, 1967, pp. 257ff; Emmanuel Godo, *La Legende de Venise: Barrès et la tentation de l'ecriture*, Presses Universitaires du Septentrion, Paris, 1996.

33 Relevant passages from *Un Homme libre* are republished in Marice Barrès, *La Mort de Venise*, pp. 111–27. For the triumph over Venice, see p. 118.

34 The 'Pantheon' forms the material of chap. 3, 'Les ombres qui flottent sur les couchants de l'adriatique', ibid., pp. 51–84.

35 Marcel Proust, *Against Sainte-Beuve and Other Essays*, trans. John Sturrock, Penguin, Harmondsworth, 1994.

36 'Une Soirée dans le silence et le vent de la Mort', pp. 39–51; 'Le Chant d'une Beauté qui s'en va vers la Mort', Barrès, *La Mort de Venise*, pp. 85–91.

37 Explored by Godo, *La Legende de Venise: Barrès et la tentation de l'ecriture*, pp. 209ff.

38 Frank Walker, *The Man Verdi*, Alfred A. Knopf, New York, 1972, p. 449.

39 George Martin, 'Verdi and the Risorgimento', *Aspects of Verdi*, Robson Books, London, 1988, p. 27.

40 The Verdi opera has been interpreted in the light of post-Risorgimento difficulties in the Italian nation and expansion in Africa by Jeremy Tambling in his compelling *Opera and the Culture of Fascism*, Clarendon Press, Oxford, 1996, 'Verdi and Imperialism: *Otello*', pp. 73ff.

41 On the mixed reception see Gary Schmidgall, 'Incredible Credo', *Shakespeare and Opera*, Oxford University Press, New York, 1990, pp. 240–50.

42 *The Verdi–Boito Correspondence*, ed. Marcello Conati and Mario Medici, with a new introduction by Marcello Conati, English language edition prepared by William Weaver, University of Chicago Press, Chicago and London, 1996, p. 117.

43 Stendhal, *Life of Rossini*, trans. Richard N. Coe, Calder & Boyars, London, 1970, p. 235.

44 For the criticisms of Rossini's *Otello* (ineffective as a tragic opera, inadequate in the treatment of Iago, but meritricious in the third act, particularly in the treatment of Desdemona), and comparisons with Verdi and Boito's treatment, see John W. Klein, 'Verdi's *Otello* and Rossini's', *Music and Letters*, 45 (1964), pp. 130–40.

45 *Nietzsche Lettres à Peter Gast*, 13 June 1987, p. 266.

46 Camillo Boito, 'Il Maestro di setticlavio: novella veneziana' (1891), *Senso e altri racconti*, ed. Matilde Dillon Wanke, Arnoldo Mondadori, Milan, 1994, pp. 247ff. Wanke provides a provocative interpretation of the story's connection with Arrigo, see pp. XLIIff.

47 Vernon Lee, 'A Wicked Voice', in *Hauntings, Fantastic Stories*, Heinemann, London, 1890. Erwin Koppen writes of Vernon Lee's story in a Wagnerian context of decadence: 'Ein englisher Tod in Venedig', *Dekadenter Wagnerismus: Studien zur europäischen Literatur des Fin de Siècle*, pp. 233–7.

48 The image of Venice as Virgin/Venus is central to discussions of 'the myth' of Venice. See again Edward Muir, *Civic Ritual in Renaissance Venice*, Princeton University Press, 1981, passim.

49 Henry James, 'Venice', *Italian Hours*, William Heinemann, London, 1909, p. 73.

50 'Venice', ibid., pp. 7, 8, and 'Grand Canal', p. 32.

51 Henry James, *The Wings of a Dove*, (1902), Hardmondsworth, Penguin, 1965.

52 Cf. Michela Rusi, 'Una Foscarina del Cinquecento: Gaspara Stampa', *D'Annunzio e Venezia*, pp. 209–18.

53 Letters are cited and various references made in Claudine Brécourt-Villars, *D'Annunzio et la Duse: Les Amants de Venise*, Stock, Paris, 1994.

54 For Gustave Moreau's *Venise* see *Venezia nell'Ottocento: Immagini e mito*, ed. Giuseppe Pavanello and Giandomenico Romanelli, Electa, Milan, 1983, pp. 19–20.

55 On Ruskin's sexual imaginings (as writers see them) see Denis Cosgrove, 'The Myth and the Stones of Venice: A Historical Geography of a Symbolic Landscape', *Journal of Historical Geography*, 8 (1982), pp. 163–4, and cf. Jay Fellows in 'Capricious Sinuosities: Venice and the City as Mind' *John Ruskin*, ed. Harold Bloom, Chelsea House, New York, New Haven, Edgemont, 1986, p. 35, and, in full flight, J. B. Bullen, 'Ruskin, Venice, and the Construction of Femininity', *Review of English Studies*, 66 (1995), pp. 502–20. Writing *The Stones of Venice* shortly after his marriage to Effie Gray, Ruskin might well be said to be married more to Venice, which is like his New Jerusalem, 'prepared as a bride', than to Effie. And again (the point is a fascinating one), Tony Tanner, *Venice Desired*, Blackwell, Oxford, 1992, p. 68: 'It would be too easy and not particularly illuminating to talk of a massive displacement of the activities of the marriage bed into the exploration of the city. But . . . there can be no doubt that Ruskin's most intense love affair was with Venice.'

56 For this last visit, Jan Akin Burd, *Christmas Story: John Ruskin's Venetian Letters of 1876–1877*, University of Delaware Press, Newark and London, 1990.

57 Tanner, *Venice Desired*, has chapters on Byron, Ruskin, James, Hofmannsthal, Proust and, from the twentieth century, Ezra Pound.

58 *The Memoirs of Jacques Casanova Written by Himself, Now for the First Time Translated into English* (by Arthur Machen), privately printed, London, 1894, 12 vols, Paul Mariéton, *Une Histoire d'Amour: George Sand et A. de Musset. Documents inédits, Lettres de Musset*, G. Havard Fils, Paris, 1897.

59 See below.

60 G. B. Lorenzi, *Legge e memorie Venete sulla prostituzione fino alla caduta della Repubblica*, Tipografia del Commercio di Marco Visentini, Venice, 1870–72, by the Count of Oxford.

61 For *La Tariffa delle puttane di Venegia* (1535) see Antonio Barzaghi, *Donne or cortigiane? La Prostituzione a Venezia documenti di costume dal XVI al XVIII secolo*, Bertani, Verona, 1980, pp. 168–91.

62 Charles Le Brosses, *L'Italie galante et familière en XVIII siécle*, Paris, 1885; M. E. de Montaigne, *L'Italia alla fine del Secolo XVI: giornale di Viaggio in Italia nel 1580–1581*, Città di Castello, S. Lapi, 1895; C. L. de Montesquieu, *Voyages de Montesquieu*, publiès par le baron Albert de Montesquieu G. Gounouilho, 2 vols, Bordeaux, 1894–96.

63 Giuseppe Tassini, *Cenni storici e leggi circa il libertinaggio in Venezia dal secolo XIV alla caduta della Repubblica*, (*c*.1889), Filippi, Venice, 1968.

64 For Didier see ibid., p. 73, and De Brosses, p. 103.

65 Edgar Allan Poe, 'The Assignation', first published as 'The Visionary', *Godey's Lady's Book*, 1844, in *Tales of Mystery and Imagination*, ed. Graham Clarke, Everyman, London and Vermont, 1993, pp. 155–66.

66 Ibid., p. 161.

67 For a historical account see Guido Ruggiero, *The Boundaries of Eros: Sex Crime Sexuality in Renaissance Venice*, Oxford University Press, New York, 1985.

68 *Venice: A Documentary History, 1450–1630*, ed. David Chambers and Brian Pullan, Blackwell, Oxford, 1992, p. 124.

69 Beckford's self-description is cited from a letter of 1780 in Elinor Shaffer, 'William Beckford in Venice, Liminal City', *Venetian Views, Venetian Blinds, English Fantasies of Venice*, ed. Manfred Pfister and Barbara Schaff, Rodopi, Amsterdam, 1999, p. 80; for Byron see Louis Crompton, *Byron and Greek Love: Homophobia in Nineteenth-Century England*, University of California, Berkeley, 1985, also writes of William Beckford.

70 *The Memoirs of John Addington Symonds*, ed. Phyllis Grosskurth, Hutchinson, London, 1984, p. 272. See, in general, chap. 17, 'Angelo Fusato'.

71 One example is John Addington Symonds, 'Theme', *New and Old: A Volume of Verse*, Smith, Elder & Co., London, 1880, p. 174.

72 Note the comment on the first version of the five painted by the artist: 'Carlo Böcklin (1910) has mentioned the castle of Alfonso of Aragon on the island of Ischia as the model for this work, which shows how irrelevant the original locations are with Böcklin, and how fruitless it is to try and track them down'. *Arnold Böcklin, 1827–1910*, Arts Council Pro Helvetia, London, 1971, p. 31

73 Maurice Barrès, *Le Mort de Venise*, p. 40.

74 Manlio Brusatin, *Arte dell'oblio*, Einaudi, Turin, 2000, pp. 70–73.

75 Giandomenico Romanelli, *Venezia Ottocento: l'Architettura l'urbanistica*, Albrizzi, Venice, 1988, p. 395.

76 Ibid., p. 395 and 402.

77 Italico Brass painted a series of works depicting the bridge processions, see Maria Masau Dan, *Italico Brass*, Electa, Milan, 1991, pp. 116ff. (the earliest appears to be 1909).

78 Friedrich Nietzsche, *Thus Spake Zarathustra: A Book for Everyone and No One*, trans. R. J. Hollingdale, Penguin, Harmondsworth, 1961, p. 133. Nietzsche describes the view to the *Toteninsel* from his window to Franz Overbeck, March, 1880, see *Nietzsche Briefwechsel Friedrich Nietzsche Briefe, Januar 1880–Dezember 1884*, p. 14.

79 The literature on Fortuny remains general. The basic monograph is Guillermo de Osma, *Mariano Fortuny: His Life and Work*, Rizzoli, New York, 1980. For illustrations see A. M. Deschodt, *Mariano Fortuny: un Magicien de Venise*, Flammarion, Paris, 1979. For a further essay see Silvio Fuso and Sandro Mescola, *Immagini e materiali del Laboratorio Fortuny*, Marsilio, Venice, 1978, pp. 11–30; on the occasion of the fiftieth anniversary of Fortuny's death, the exhibition/catalogue *Mariano Fortuny*, ed. Maurizio Barberis, Claudio Franzini, Silvio Fuso and Marco Tosa, Marsilio, Venice, 1999.

80 De Osma, chap. 1, 'The Formative Years', *Mariano Fortuny: His Life and Work*, pp. 14ff.

81 Cristina Nuzzi, 'Fortuny artista wagneriano', *Fortuny nella Belle Epoque*, Palazzo Strozzi, Florence, 1984, pp. 25–35.

82 De Osma, *Mariano Fortuny: His Life and Work*, p. 148.

83 On the photography see Italo Zannier, 'Mariano Fortuny fotografo', *Immagini e materiali del laboratorio Fortuny*, pp. 31–6,

84 For a photograph of the Grand Canal *c.*1889 in this format see De Osma, *Mariano Fortuny: His Life and Work*, p. 32, and 'A view of Venice in the 1890s', pp. 28–9.

85 'Stage-Lighting and Theatre Design', ibid. pp. 58ff.

86 Maurizio Barberis, 'La Luce di Fortuny', *Mariano Fortuny* (1999), pp. 41–7.

87 Ibid., pp. 72–3. For Duse and D'Annunzio see Emilio Mariano, 'Eleonora Duse e Gabriele d'Annunzio a Venezia', *D'Annunzio e Venezia*, Convegno di Studio, ed. Emilio Mariano, Lucarini, Rome, 1991, pp. 29–44.

88 For the Francesco da Rimini designs see De Osma, *Mariano Fortuny: His Life and Work*, pp. 73–4.

89 Wagner, *My Life*, p. 573.

90 On the senior Fortuny's Rome studio I have followed the note in Susanna Scotoni, *D'Annunzio e l'arte contemporanea*, SPES, Florence, 1981, p. 78, n. 138.

91 The visit to Madame de Fortuny's palace is described by Henri de Régnier in 'Veduta di Venezia' (1906), *La Vie vénetienne*, Mercure de France, Paris, 1963, pp. 80–81.

92 Doretta Davanzo Poli and Stefania Moronato, *Le Stoffe dei veneziani*, Albrizzi, Venice, 1994.

93 On the fabrics see Jean-Michel Tuchscherer, 'La Création d'etoffes', in *Mariano Fortuny, Venise*, Musée Historique de Tissus de Lyon, Lyon, 1980, particularly the section on 'Le chromatisme de Fortuny', p. 22.

94 Doretta Davanzo Poli, 'The Art and Craft of Weaving in Venice', *Mestieri della moda Venezia: The Crafts of the Venetian Fashion Industry*, Ala Napoleonica and Museo Correr, Edizioni del Cavallini, Venice, 1988, pp. 39–55, and silk-weaving examples in colour, pp. 182–6. For a monographic treatment see Doretta Davanzo Poli, *Seta e ora: la collezione tessile di Mariano Fortuny*, Arsenale, Venice, 1997. Fortuny's materials have been beguilingly photographed in Deschodt, *Fortuny, Magicien de Venise*. Also De Osma, *Mariano Fortuny: His Life and Work*, passim.

95 On Guggenheim's collection, which included lace, see Ileana Chiappini di Sorio, 'Un'antologia di antichi tessuti', *Una città e il suo museo, Un secolo e mezzo di collezioni civiche veneziane*, Museo Correr, Venice, 1988, pp. 213–47.

96 Gabriel Vial and Odile Valansot, 'Procéedés et techniques', *Mariano Fortuny, Venise*, pp. 25–7, and for the garments, Delphine Desveaux, *Fortuny*, Thames & Hudson, London, 1998.

97 See part 2, chap. 7 below.

98 The central study remains Gino Damerini, *D'Annunzio e Venezia* (1943), postfazione di Giannantonio Paladini, Marsilio, Venice, 1992. See also *D'Annunzio e Venezia*. The article by Guido di Pino, 'Venezia nell'opera di Gabriele d'Annunzio', *Venezia nella letterature moderne*, pp. 291–9 is largely superceded. An important article by Mario Isnenghi, 'D'Annunzio e l'ideologia della Venezianità', *Rivista di Storia Contemporanea*, 3 (1990), pp. 419–31, and republished, *D'Annunzio e Venezia*, pp. 229–44, (the latter citation is retained below) is more relevant to the later discussion of D'Annunzio in the twentieth century in part 2.

99 D'Annunzio, *Il Fuoco*, pp. 307ff.

100 For D'Annunzio's long relationship with Michetti, and his interest in contemporary art, see Scotoni, *D'Annunzio e l'arte contemporanea*, with appendixes (concerning the Biennale and his positive reaction to Selvatico), Damerini, *D'Annunzio e Venezia*, pp. 269–70.

101 Gabriele D'Annunzio, 'Sogno d'un tramonto d'autunno' (tragic poem) (1899), *Tragedie, sogni e misteri*, vol. 1, Arnaldo Mondadori, Verona, 1946, pp. 49–90.

102 D'Annunzio, *The Flame*, p. 7.

103 Ibid., p. 296.

104 Ibid., p. 201.

105 See part 2, chap. 2 below.

106 D'Annunzio, *The Flame*, p. 90.

107 Ibid., pp. 62ff. Benedetto Marcello is less well known now than his contemporary Vivaldi: that his name was given to the Venice Conservatorium is a measure of his considerable importance in the nineteenth century. For some comments on D'Annunzio's interest in Italian Baroque music see Pietro Buscaroli, '*Il Fuoco* svolta di gusto musicale D'Annunziano', *D'Annunzio e Venezia*, pp. 77–191. The notebooks kept at the time of writing show D'Annunzio's growing interest in Italian musicians: see Patrizia Cantini, 'Venezia nei *Taccuini* del *Fuoco* (1896–1899)', ibid., pp. 121–42.

108 Michael Talbot notes Marcello's *Arianna*, categorised as an *intreccio scenico musicale* given in Florence in 1727. *The New Grove Dictionary of Music and Musicians*, vol. 11, ed. Stanley Sadie, Macmillan, London, 1980, p. 649.

109 Oscar Wilde, *The Picture of Dorian Gray* (1891), Penguin, Harmondsworth, 1984, p. 182.

110 Camillo Boito writes of 'La somma virtù, l'unica virtù, la quale importi all'artista, quella di essere pittoreschi', 'Il colore a Venezia', *Storielle vane: tutti i racconti*, p. 431.

111 *Venezia e la peste, 1348–1797*, ed. Comune di Venezia, Marsilio, Venice, 1980.

112 For an overview see *La memoria della salute: Venezia e il suo ospedale dal XVI al XX secolo*, ed. Nelli-Elena Vanzan Marchini, Arsenale, Venice, 1985.

113 Sergio Barizza, *Il Comune di Venezia, 1806–1946: l'istituzione, il territorio, guida-inventario dell'Archivio Municipale*, Commune di Venezia, Venice, 1987, p. 191.

114 Cf Giandomenico Romanelli see 'La casa dei poveri', *Venezia Ottocento: l'architettura l'urbanistica*, Albrizzi, Venice, 1988, pp. 402–10. For the miasmatic theory of disease and the Italian tradition see Carlo M. Cipolla, *Miasma and Disease: Public Health and the Environment in the Pre-Industrial Age*, trans. Elizabeth Potter, Yale University Press, New Haven and London, 1992.

115 'Atti di rilevazione dello stato di salubrità delle case', 1874, Barizza, *Il Comune di Venezia, 1806–1946: l'istituzione, il territorio, guida-inventario dell'Archivio Municipale*, pp. 193–194.

116 The 'Progetti della Giunta Municipale' (1886), in *Lo Sventramento di Venezia. Polemica: progetti della Giunta Municipale. Delendae venetiae di P. G. Molmenti. Arti-coli del Bacchighione, della difesa e della riforma, deliberazioni del Consiglio Accademico. Lettera di P. G. Molmenti. Rimonstranze delgi artisti italiani*, Giovanni Alzetta, Venice, 1887, pp. 7ff.

117 For the demolition programmes see ibid., pp. 17–19.

118 Pompeo Molmenti, 'Delendae venetiae', *Nuova Antologia*, 9 (1883), pp. 413–28, and ibid., pp. 9–25 (pagination refers to the republished paper).

119 *Lo Sventramento di Venezia* (pagination for Molmenti's article refers to this edition).

120 'Venezia artistica', ibid., pp. 45–57.

121 Ibid., p. 54.

122 Eva Tea, *Giacomo Boni nella vita e nel suo tempo*, Ceschina, Milan, 1932.

123 Giacomo Boni, *Il cosidetto Sventramento: appunti di un veneziano*, Stabilimento Tipografico Italiano, Rome, 1887.

124 Giacomo Boni, *Venezia imbellettata*, Stabilimento Tipografico Italiano, Rome, 1887.

125 For the Fondaco dei Turchi see ibid., pp. 13–24; for the Palazzo Ducale, pp. 29–37; for the exodus of works of art, pp. 25–8.

126 Dammerini, *D'Annunzio e Venezia*, p. 266.

127 See part 2, chap. 1.

128 See Paolo Somma, *Venezia nuova: la politica della casa, 1893–1941*, Comune di Venezia, Marsilio, Venice, 1983, p. 8. See also Romano Chirivi's discussion of *Il piano di Risanamento del 1891* in 'Eventi urbanistici dal 1846 al 1962', *Urbanistica*, 52 (1968), pp. 87–8, with maps detailing demolitions between 1866 and 1905. See also Gianfranco Pertot, *Venezia 'restaurata': centosettanta anni di interventi di restauro sugli edifici Veneziani*, Franco Angeli, Milan, 1988, pp. 47–49.

129 Somma, *Venezia nuova: la politica della casa, 1893–1941*, pp. 15–16.

130 The proposals commenced in 1889 with A. Cadel, *A Proposito di una nuovo ponte sulla Laguna*. For the history of negotiations and building see Carlo Uberti, 'Il Ponte automobilistico', *Le Venezie possibili: da Palladio a Le Corbusier*, ed. Lionello Puppi and Giandomenico Romanelli, Electa, Milan, 1985, pp. 243–51.

131 Pompeo Molmenti, 'Venezia calunniata' (1894). Molmenti's polemical articles from 1886 to 1923 are collected in *I nemici di Venezia*, Polemiche raccolte e annotate da Elio Zorzi, Zanichelli, Bologna, 1923.

132 Pompeo Molmenti, 'Un nuovo ponte sulla Laguna di Venezia', *La Nuova Antologia* (16 March 1898), p. 278. A substantial part of this argument is reported in Gertrude Slaughter, *Heirs of Old Venice*, Yale University Press, New Haven, 1927, pp. 171–83.

133 Pompeo Molmenti, 'Per Venezia e per l'arte', *Emporium*, 70 (1900), pp. 313–22.

134 Ibid., p. 313.

135 On the 'terribile pericolo per l'igiene', ibid., p. 321.

136 Ian Littlewood situates the Palazzo Cappello near San Simeone Grande in the *sestiere* of San Polo: *Venice: A Literary Companion*, John Murray, London, 1991, p. 63.

137 Henry James, *The Aspern Papers and Other Stories*, Penguin, Harmondsworth, 1976, p. 25.

138 Cited in Katherine A. Lochnar, *The Etchings of James McNeill Whistler*, Yale University Press, New Haven and London, 1984, p. 184.

139 Molmenti, *I Nemici di Venezia*, 1890, p. 38.

140 *Calli e canali di Venezia* (Ongania, 1893), Filippi, Venice, 1976, p. xv.

141 English edition, *Calli e canali di Venezia*, Ongania, Venice, 1890–91, p. 3.

142 The report, the work of Carlo Emo, was published as *L'Edilizia Venezia: atti della Società per l'Arte Pubblica in Venezia, Domande al Sindaco di Venezia per l'edilizia veneziana*, Tipografia della Gazzetta, Venice, 1899.

143 Prince Fréderic de Hohenlohe-Waldembourg, *Notes vénetiennes*, Renaudie, Paris, 1899, pp. 5, 7.

144 Emo, *L'Edilizia Venezia*, p. 6.

145 See part 2, chap. 1.

146 Girolamo Levi was responsible for the external renovations, including a new wing and a garden; Michelangelo Guggenheim for the interior decor. See Grigore Arbore Popescu and Sergio Zoppi, *Palazzo Papadopoli a Venezia*, Consiglio Nazionale delle Ricerche, Rome, 1993.

147 On his life and range of initiatives overall see Stefania Moronato, 'La Collezione di tessuti Michelangelo Guggenheim', *Una città e il suo museo*, pp. 205–12.

148 For illustrations drawn from a publication of 1899, ibid.

149 See Richard J. Goy: *The House of Gold, Building a Palace in Medieval Venice*, Cambridge University Press, 1992, p. 255.

150 For the Franchetti restorations see ibid. Goy suggests that 'Franchetti's positive achievement perhaps outweighs his less sensitive attempts at "improvement"'.

151 Gabriele D'Annunzio, 'Apparizione di San Sebastiano', *Prose di romanzi e prose di ricerca*, vol. 2, Arnaldo Mondadori, Milan, 1978, pp. 1030–34. This translation cited in Francesco Valcanover, *Ca' d'Oro: The Giorgio Franchetti Gallery*, Electa, Milan, 1986, p. 84.

152 Notably *La Bozzeta de l'ogio*, 1871, and *I Recini da Festa*, 1876. On these years and the contacts with Gallina and painter Favretto see Antonio Fradeletto, 'Un Sindaco poeta', *La lettura: revista mensile del Corriere della Sera*, 8 (1908), pp. 1–11. For the poetry, including the celebrated sonnet 'A Venezia,' *Il fiore della lirica Veneziana*, vol. 3, ed. Manlio Dazzi, Neri Pozza, Venice, 1959, pp. 223–33.

153 Giorgio Pullini, 'Il teatro fra scena e società', *Storia di cultura veneta*, vol. 6, *Dall'età napoleonica alla Prima Guerra Mondiale*, ed. Girolamo Arnaldi and Manlio Pastore Stocchi, Neri Pozza, Vicenza, 1986, pp. 271–2.

154 Sardi is inadequately studied. Virtually the only coverage is Giandomenico Romanelli, 'Architetti e architetture a Venezia tra Otto e Novecento', *Antichità Viva*, 5 (1972), pp. 35–8.

155 Illustrated in ibid., p. 32. Romanelli makes a point of comparison with the Palazzo Cavalli-Franchetti and other palaces in the immediate vicinity.

156 For an account one hundred years afterwards see Giandomenico Romanelli, 'Biennale 1895: The Birth, Infancy and First Acts of a Creature of Genius', *Venice and the Biennale: Itineraries of Taste*, Fabbri, Monza, 1995, pp. 21–47.

157 Lawrence Alloway claims the regulations for the 1895 exhibition were modelled on the Munich Glaspalast exhibitions of 1886 and 1888. See *The Venice Biennale 1895–1968: From Salon to Goldfish Bowl*, Faber & Faber, London, 1969, p. 33.

158 Camillo Boito, 'La Mostra nazionale di belle arti in Venezia', *Nuova Antologia*, 12 (1887), p. 48ff. For illustrations of the plan of the Esposizione and pavilions, Marco Mulazzani, *I Padiglioni della Biennale a Venezia, 1887–1993*, p. 25.

159 Ibid., pp. 53ff.

160 On the versions of this painting and Tito's *Immagini di Venezia* see *Ettore Tito, 1859–1941: archivi della pittura veneziana*, ed. Alessandro Bettagno, Electa, Milan, 1998, pp. 200–202.

161 P. G. Molmenti, 'Is Venice to Disappear?', *The Graphic* (5 March 1898); A. P. Zorzi, 'Vandalisme', *L'Art*, 25 (1881), pp. 93, 284–5.

162 Paolo Rizzi and Enzo di Martino, *Storia della Biennale, 1895–1982*, Electa, Milan, 1987, p. 16.

163 A succinct account of the history is found in Enzo di Martino, *La Biennale di Venezia, 1895–1995: cento anni di arte e cultura*, Giorgio Mondadori, Milan, 1995: see p. 13. The Commission comprised Bartolomeo Bezzi, Marius de Maria, Antonio Fradeletto, Giuseppe Minio, Emilio Marsili and Augusto Sezanne.

164 On Fradeletto and the history of the early Biennales see Giuliana Donzello, 'Le Biennale veneziane di Antonio Fradeletto', *Arte e collezionismo, Fradeletto e Pica: primi segretari alle Biennale Veneziane, 1895–1926*, Firenze Libri, Florence, 1987.

165 This observation, and many others of relevance, are discussed in Shearer West, 'National Desires and Regional Realities in the Venice Biennale, 1895–1914', *Art History*, 18 (1995), pp.

404–34 (the writer does seem unduly surprised that nationalism is a leading issue of the time).

166 Antonio Fradeletto, 'Riccardo Selvatico e la sua generazione', *Commedie e poesie veneziane di Riccardo Selvatico*, Fratelli Treves, Milan, 1919, pp. L–XXXVI.

167 Romanelli gives an account of the attendant political skirmishes in 'Biennale 1895: The Birth, Infancy and First Acts of a Creature of Genius', *Venice and the Biennale: Itineraries of Taste*, pp. 20–25.

168 On the façade see Flavia Scotton, *Mario de Maria: nell'atelier del pittore delle lune*, Electa, Milan, 1983, p. 42. See the illustration, Marco Mulazzani, *I padiglioni della Biennale a Venezia, 1887–1993*, p. 26.

169 For a wide-ranging coverage of the criticism of the first Biennales see Maria Mimeta Lamberti, 'The Contexts of the Early Exhibits, from the End of the Century to the First World War: Artists and the Public in the Giardini', *Venice and the Biennale: Itineraries of Taste*, pp. 39ff.

170 Di Martino, *La Biennale di venezia, 1895–1995: cento anni di arte e cultura*, p. 20.

171 Paolo Zatti, 'Le Prime Biennali Veneziane (1895–1912). Il contributo di Vittorio Pica', *Venezia Arti*, 7 (1993), pp. 111–16.

172 Vittorio Pica, 'Arte aristocratica' (originally a lecture delivered in Naples 1892), in Paola Barocchi, *Testimonianze e polemiche figurative in Italia dal Divisionismo al Novecento*, G. D. Anna, Messina, 1974, pp. 46–56.

173 Pica, 'Impressionista e Sintesi assenti alla I Biennale' (*L'Arte Europeo a Venezia*, Naples, Pierro, 1895), ibid., pp. 89–96,

174 Zatti, 'Le Prime Biennali veneziane', ibid., pp. 112–13.

175 Enzo di Martino, *La Biennale di Venezia, 1895–1995: cento anni di arte e cultura*, p. 21.

176 Attilia Dorigato, '1895–1930: Anni difficili del vetro alle Biennale', Marino Barovier, Rosa Barovier Mentasi and Attilia Dorigato, *Il vetro di Murano alle Biennale, 1895–1930*, Leonardo Arte, Milan, 1995, p. 13.

177 Flavia Scotton, 'Applied Art: From the Foundation to the Venezia Pavilion', *Venice and the Biennale: Itinaries of Taste*, p. 123.

178 Giovanni Sarpellon, 'Art Glass and the Biennale', ibid., p. 139.

179 For illustrations of works held in the Museo d'Arte Moderna, Ca' Pesaro, see ibid., pp. 336–7.

180 Scotton, 'Applied Art: From the Foundation to the Venezia Pavilion', ibid., p. 124.

181 For the history of the collection see Giandomenico Romanelli, *Ca' Pesaro: la Galleria d'Arte Moderna: introduzione alle raccolte* (with English text), Electa, Milan, 1991.

182 To be taken up in part 2.

183 *Venice nell'Ottocento: Immagine e mito*, p. 205. For Tito's international reputation see Ludwig Brosch, 'The Paintings of Ettore Tito', *The Studio*, 36 (1912), pp. 307–9, and Selwyn Brinton, 'The Recent Work of Ettore Tito', *The Studio*, 80 (1920), pp. 3–8,

184 De Osma, *Mariano Fortuny: His Life and Work*, p. 39.

185 See the poster in Di Martino, *La Biennale di Venezia*, p. 14.

186 See the sociologically oriented analysis by Lidia D. Sciama, 'The Venice Regatta: From Ritual to Sport', *Sport, Identity and Ethnicity*, ed. Jeremy MacClancy, Berg, Oxford, 1996, pp. 137–65.

187 *La Biennale di Venezia: archivio storico delle arti contemporanea*, ed. Giandomenico Romanelli, Venice, 1977.

188 D'Annunzio, 'Ommagio a Venezia', Barocchi, *Testimonianze e polemiche figurative in Italia*, pp. 73–80. See the essay by Ernesto Guidorizzi, 'Colori di Venezia nell'*Orazione* a Palazzo Ducale', *D'Annunzio e Venezia* (Atti del Convegni di Studi), pp. 143–69. For Giorgione in the nineteenth century see Jaynie Anderson, 'Giorgione's Critical Fortunes and Misfortunes', *Giorgione: The Painter of 'Poetic Brevity'*, Flammarion, Paris and New York, 1997, pp. 235–63.

189 Barocchi, *Testimonianze e polemiche figurative in Italia*, pp. 77ff. See also D'Annunzio's 'Venezia e Giorgione', originally published in *Il Convito*, 1 (1895), ibid. pp. 80–82.

190 D'Annunzio, *The Flame*, p. 54.

191 With later works such as *La Nave* and *Notturno*, and the wartime activity in Venice, to be covered in part 2.

192 On the Accademia changes under curator Giulio Cantalamessa see Giovanna Sciré Nepi and Francesco Valcanover, *Accademia Galleries of Venice*, Electa, Milan, 1985, pp. 9–11.

193 Paul Bourget, *Cosmopolis* (1892), Librarie Artheme Fayard, Paris, 1947.

194 Gino Damerini, *D'Annunzio e Venezia*, p. 52, and De Osma, *Mariano Fortuny: His Life and Work*, pp. 31–3, based on Damerini.

195 William Weaver, *Duse: A Biography*, Thames & Hudson, London, 1984, pp. 108ff.

196 Michael de Cossart, *The Food of Love: Princesse Edmond de Polignac (1865–1943) and her Salon*, Hamish Hamilton, London, 1978, p. 79.

197 See, for example, Julian Halsby's chapter, 'Fontaine de Jouvence: John Singer Sargent and his Circle at the Palazzo Barbaro', *Venice, The Artist's Vision: A Guide to British and American Painters*, B. T. Batsford, London, 1990, pp. 113–22. For the Curtis paintings see *Venezia: da stato a mito*, ed. Alessandro Bettagno, Fondazione Giorgio Cini, Venice, Marsilio, Venice, 1997, pp. 387–8.

198 On Hohenlohe see Damerini, *D'Annunzio e Venezia*, pp. 52ff.

199 See the sympathetic article by Brian Pullan, 'Horatio Brown, John Addington Symonds and the History of Venice', *War, Culture and Society in Renaissance Venice: Essays in Honour of John Hale*, ed. David S. Chambers, Cecil H. Clough and Michael E. Mallett, Hambledon Press, London & Rio Grande, 1993, pp. 213–35,

200 Henry James, *Letters from the Palazzo Barbaro*, ed. Rosella Mamoli Zorzi, Pushkin Press, London, 1998, p. 179.

201 Sargent, *An Interior in Venice, Venezia nell'Ottocento: Immagini e mito*, pp. 208–209.

202 James, *Letters from the Palazzo Barbaro*, is richly annotated and includes letters by the Curtises and Isabella Stewart Gardner. For Isabella Stewart Gardner see Morris Carter, *Isabella Stewart Gardner and Fenway Court* (1925), Riverside Press, Cambridge, Mass., 1963, p. 109.

203 James, 'Casa'Alvisi', *Italian Hours*, pp. 77–82.

204 See the correspondence *More than Friend: The Letters of Robert Browning to Katherine de Kay Bronson*, ed. Michael Meredith, Wedgestone Press, Winfield, 1985, especially pp. lxiii–lxvi, 'Death in Venice'. Katharine Bronson's reminiscences appear in 'Browning in Venice', published in 1902, as Appendix B, pp. 147–65. Browning's *Asolando: Fancies and Facts* was published in 1890.

205 Jacob Korg, *Browning and Italy*, Ohio University Press, Athens, Oh., 1983, p. 213.

206 Hugo von Hofmannsthal, 'Der Tod des Tizians, Bruchstück', *Gedichte und Lyrische Dramen, Gesammelte Werke*, Erste Band, S. Fisher, Berlin (1952), pp. 181ff.

207 Cf. the speeches: 'Ich war in halben Traum bis dort gegangen', then Desiderio, 'Siehst du die Stadt', ibid., pp. 66–7.

208 Hugo von Hofmannsthal, 'Der Abenteuer und die Singerin oder Die Geschenke des Lebens', *Sämtliche Werke V, Dramen 3*, ed. Manfred Hoppe, S. Fisher, Frankfurt am Main, 1992, pp. 95–249. On this work and later references to Casanova in Hofmannstahl's opus see Friedrich Schröder, 'Materialien zu Hofmannstahl's Casanova-Lektüre', *Modern Austrian Literature*, 21 (1991), pp. 13–21, and Martha Bowditch Alden, 'The Distillation of an Episode: Casanova's Memoirs, a Source for Hofmannstahl's *Der Abenteuer und die Sängerin*', *German Quarterly*, 53 (1980), pp. 189–98, citing the source in Casanova's memoirs.

209 The classic study is Claudio Magris, *Habsburgische Mythos in die Oesterreichischen Literatur*, Otto Müller Verlag, Salzburg, 1966. See also Anna Giubertoni, 'Venezia nella letteratura austriaca moderna', *Venezia Vienna: Il mito della cultura veneziana nell'Europa asburgica*, ed. Giandomenico Romanelli, Electa, Milan, 1983, esp. pp. 112ff.

210 Hugo von Hofmannsthal, *Das gerettete Venedig* (1904), *Dramen 11*, S. Fischer Verlag, Berlin, 1954, pp. 78ff.

211 The remark is made in *Senso*.

212 See part 2 for further discussion of the works introduced in this paragraph.

213 Peter Collier gives a conscientious account in *Proust and Venice*, Cambridge University Press, 1989.

214 George D. Painter, *Marcel Proust*, Penguin, Harmondsworth, 1977, vol. 1, p. 310.

215 Marcel Proust, *Jean Santeuil*, trans. Gerard Hopkins, Penguin, Harmondsworth, 1985.

216 For this circle, see again De Cossart, *The Food of Love: Princesse Edmond de Polignac*, passim.

217 Ibid., p. 31. For Fauré's Venetian songs see Jean-Michel Nectoux, *Gabriel Fauré: A Musical Life*, trans. Roger Nichols, Cambridge University Press, 1991, pp. 178–80.

218 Jay Fellows, in 'Capricious Sinuosities: Venice and the City as Mind', p. 37.

219 For the work on Ruskin: Marcel Proust, *On Reading Ruskin: Preface to La Bible D'Amiens and Sésame de les Lys*, Yale University Press, New Haven and London, 1987. For the visit, Painter, *Marcel Proust*, vol. 1, p. 257. Julia Kristeva has remarked on the significance of Ruskin and his work on Amiens as it transfers to Venice: *Time and Sense: Proust and the Experience of Literature* (1994) trans. Ross Guberman, Columbia University Press, New York and Chichester, 1996, p. 102: 'Proust's preface to *La Bible d'Amiens* contains a dramatisation of the sense of metaphor operating between Venice–Amiens–Venice. The reader is invited to go to Ameins "which was once the Venice of France".'

220 Marcel Proust, *Against Saint-Beuve and Other Essays* (1971), trans. John Sturrock, Penguin, Harmondsworth, 1994, pp. 191–92.

221 'On Reading', ibid., p. 226.

222 Reynaldo Hahn, *Chansons en dialecte vénitien*, 1901. For the evidence of the friendship and affection of Proust for Hahn, *Lettres de Marcel Proust à Reynaldo Hahn*, ed. Philippe Kolb, Gallimard, Paris, 1956.

223 Painter, *Marcel Proust*, p. 267. The most recent biography adds nothing to Painter's account with respect to Venice: Cf. William C. Carter, *Marcel Proust*, Yale University Press, New Haven and London, 2000, p. 298.

224 Kristeva, *Time and Sense: Proust and the Experience of Literature*, pp. 109–10.

225 Proust engages with the effects of Ruskin's theology in 'John Ruskin', *Against Sainte-Beuve and Other Essays*, pp. 161ff.

226 Carter, *Isabella Stewart Gardner and Fenway Court*, p. 103.

227 Ibid.

228 Cf. Maria Cristina Buscioni, *Esposizione e 'Stile Nazionale', 1861–1925: Il linguaggio dell'architettura nei padiglioni italiani delle grandi kermesse nazionali ed internazionali*, Alinea, Florence, 1990, pp. 167–9.

229 See Childe Hassam, *The Agriculture Building*; Lawrence Carmichael Earle, *The World's Columbian Exposition of 1893*; Charles Caryl Coleman, *The Afterglow in the Lagoon: World's Columbian Exposition*, 1893; Charles Graham, *The Electricity Building, World's Columbian Exposition*; Harris Neil, Wim de Wit, James Gilbert and Robert W. Rydell, *Grand Illusions: Chicago's World's Fair of 1893*, Chicago Historical Society, Chicago, 1893, pp. 33, 34, 39.

230 The 'Grand Canal' was established by Louis XIV in the Lake of Versailles between 1669 and 1672. See J. K. Fennebresque, *La Petite Venise: Histoire d'une corporation nautique*, Picard, Paris and Bernard, Versailles, 1899.

231 Irme Kiralfy, *Venice, the Bride of the Sea*, Olympia 1891–2, Geo. Newnes, The Strand, London, 1891.

232 Cf. *Illustrated London News* (26 October 1866).

233 See the substantial coverage in Norbert Rubey and Peter Schoenwald, *Venedig in Wien: Theater-und Vergnügungsstadt der Jahrhundertwende*, Ueberreuter, Vienna, 1990. I am grateful to Monica Lausch for bringing the importance of the *Venedig im Wien* to my attention in her unpublished dissertation 'Image and Impact: Venice in Austrian Art and Architecture', Department of Visual Arts, Monash University, 1993, pp. 14–20.

234 On the pavilion by the architect Ceppi see Buscioni, *Esposizioni e 'Stile Nazionali' (1861–1925)*, pp. 167–9.

235 Rem Koolhaas, *Delirious New York: A Retroactive Manifesto for Manhattan*, Oxford University Press, New York, 1978, p. 45.

236 Koolhaas makes much of the apocalyptic fire, ibid., p. 63.

237 Filippo Nani-Mocenigo, *Sulla caduta della Repubblica di Venezia*, Atti della R. Deputazione Veneta di Storia Patria, Venice, 1896–7. Note the earlier address: Vincenzo D. Marchesi, *La Decadenza della Repubblica veneta, Discorso tenuto presso il Veneto Ateneo nella Chiusa Degli Esami di Storia Patria il 6 Giugno, 1886*, Stabilimento Tipo-Lit. M. Fontana, Venice, 1886.

238 Pompeo Molmenti, *Venice: Its Individual Growth from the Earliest Beginnings to the Fall of the Republic*, vol. 6, George Allen, London, 1908, p. 179.

239 Sandro Simionato, 'La politica dell'amministrazione comunale Veneziano e lo sviluppo del Lido, 1895–1914', *Storia Urbana*, 8 (1984), pp. 83–4.

240 For the Tiepolo administration from 1888 until 1890 see Giovanni Distefano and Giannantonio Paladini, *Storia di Venezia, 1797–1992*, vol. 2, *La dominante dominata*, Supernova, Venice, 1996, pp. 306–9; for the Selvatico administration, 1890–95, see pp. 308–13; for the Grimani administration from 1895 see pp. 306–9.

241 Edmond and Jules de Goncourt, *French Eighteenth-Century Painters* (1856–75), trans. Robin Ironside, Phaidon, Oxford, 1948, p. 8. For an ingenious later treatment of Watteau in fiction see Philippe Sollers, *Watteau in Venice (Le Fête à Venise*, 1991), trans. Alberto Manguel, Charles Scribner's Sons, New York, 1994.

242 'Let not melancholy thoughts distress you; come with me, let us climb into our gondola and make for the open sea. We will go past harbours and islands which surround the city, and the sun will sink in a cloudless sky and the moon will rise.' Trans. Laura Sarti, *The Songmakers Almanac: Souvenirs de Venise*, Hyperion Records, A66112, 1983. For the circumstances in which Hahn probably composed and performed these songs as a guest of the Princesse de Polignac see De Cossart, *The Song of Love: Princesse Edmond de Polignac*, p. 72. The poem appears in Raffaello Barbiera, *Poesie veneziane* (1886), Arnaldo Forni, Bologna, 1975, pp. 284–5.

Chapter 7

1 Venice, California, was founded by Abbott Kinney in 1905: 'it created a dream city of gondolas, bridges, and lagoons out of the squaggy sands and marshes south of Santa Monica. The overall layout was the work of Norman and Ronbert Marsh, who also designed public structures like the ornate canal-bridges, and some uninhabited private houses': Reyner Banham, *Los Angeles: The Architecture of Four Ecologies*, Penguin, Harmondsworth, 1973, pp. 158–9. For historic photographs and a detailed account of the construction see Jeffrey Stanton, *Venice California, 1904–1930*, based on a historic photo exhibition by Annette del Zoppo, Venice, California, 1978.

2 Sergio Romano, *Giuseppe Volpi:*

Industria e finanza tra Giolitti e Mussolini, Bompiani, Milan, 1979, early chapters.

3   See M. Donaglio, 'Il Difensore di Venezia: Pompeo Molmenti fra idolatria del passato e pragmatismo politico', *Venetica*, 13 (1996), pp. 45–72.

4   See again Pompeo Molmenti, 'Il ponte carrozzabile tra Venezia e la Terraferma', 1898, pp. 87ff; and, in the new century, 'Ancor il ponte tra Venezia e la Terraferma', 1903, *I nemici di Venezia*, polemical writings collected and edited by Elio Zorzi, Zanichelli, Bologna, 1924, pp. 237–49.

5   See chap. 8 below.

6   For ACNIL (Azienda Comunale per la Navigazione Interna Lagunare) see Giovanni Distefano and Giannantonio Paladini, *Storia di Venezia, 1797–1997*, vol. 3, *Dalla monarchia alla Repubblica*, Supernova-Grafiche Biesse, Venice, 1997, pp. 21–2.

7   Wladimiro Dorigo, *Una Legge contro Venezia: natura storia interessi nella questione della città e della laguna*, Officina Edizioni, Rome, 1973, p. 61. The basic account of the port's foundation is Cesco Chinello, *Porto Marghera, 1902–1926: alle origini del 'Problema di Venezia'*, Marsilio, Venice, 1979.

8   On Foscari, Romani, *Giuseppe Volpi: Industria e finanza tra Giolitti e Mussolini*, pp. 14ff., and Giovanni Distefano and Giannantonio Paladini, *Storia di Venezia, 1797–1997*, vol. 3, *Dalla monarchia alla repubblica*, pp. 22–4.

9   An official publication documents the fall and rebuilding: *Il Campanile di San Marco riedificato: studi, ricerche, relazioni*, with writings by P. Molmenti, A. Fradeletto, L. Beltrami, G. Boni, Comune di Venezia, Venice, 1912. The most recent treatment is *Il Campanile di San Marco: Il crollo e la ricostruzione 14 Luglio 1902–25 Aprile, 1912*, Palazzo Ducale, Sala dello Scrutinio, Venice, Silvana Editoriale, Venice, 1992.

10   See the report on the faults by A. Robertson, 'Why the Campanile Collapsed', *The Architect and Contract Reporter* (25 July 1902), pp. 57–9.

11   Ibid., pp. 57–8.

12   For Giacomo Boni's report on the ruins and the preliminaries of reconstruction, 'Sostruzioni e macerie', *Il Campanile di San Marco riedificato*, pp. 28–65, which includes some of his archaeological findings.

13   Boni's archaeological project had been an important initiative in conjunction with the repaving of the Piazza San Marco. The opportunity was taken to determine the Piazza's original format, to locate the canal that had been filled in, and to study the foundations of the medieval hospice, the Orseolo Ospizio, and the ancient well that once stood in the centre of the Piazza: Maurizio Fenzo, 'Il sottosuolo della Piazza

San Marco', *Il Campanile di San Marco: Il crollo e la ricostruzione*, pp. 69–82.

14   See the photograph, ibid., p. 55.

15   'Più che la Basilica, più che la dimora dogale, era esso la immagine visibile del vigor maschio di Venezia, della dominazione e della gloria', P. Molmenti, 'La Vita del Campanile', *Il Campanile di San Marco riedificato*, p. 17.

16   For D'Annunzio's reaction see Gino Damerini, *D'Annunzio e Venezia*, Albrizzi, Venice, 1992, p. 268. For Carducci's comment, generally endorsed by those of socialist persuasion who saw other priorities such as housing, see Enrio Corradini, 'Un solo "no" e molti "si" (per il campanile di San Marco)', *La Rassegna Scolastica*, 7 (31 July 1902), pp. 527–9.

17   The story is told in Richard Buckle, *Diaghilev*, Atheneum, New York, 1979, p. 541.

18   'Le stramberie d'un ingegnere Viennese', *L'Adriatico* (17 July 1902), p. 2. In Seccessionist Vienna, Otto Wagner had effectively challenged the historicism of the Ringstrasse project. See, for example, Schorske's treatment of Wagner and 'The Ringstrasse and the Birth of Urban Modernism', *Fin-de-Siècle Vienna: Politics and Culture*, Random House, New York, 1981, pp. 83ff.

19   Romanelli, 'Com'era e dov'era?', *Il Campanile di San Marco*, p. 13.

20   For these suggestions, Giandomenico Romanelli, 'Il Campanile di San Marco', *Le Venezie possibili: da Palladio a Le Corbusier*, ed. Lionello Puppi and Giandomenico Romanelli, Electa, Milan, 1985, pp. 252–9.

21   Otto Wagner, 'Laienurteile in der Kunst' (1911), republished in *Protokolle: Wiener Halbjahresschrift für Literatur, Bildende Kunst und Musik*, ed. Otto Breicha, Vienna and Munich, 1974, pp. 195–9.

22   Ibid., p. 196.

23   Ibid., p. 198.

24   Alois Riegl, 'The Modern Cult of Monuments; Its Character and its Origins' (originally *Gesammelte Aufsätze*, Filser, Augsburg and Vienna, 1912), trans Kurt W. Foster and Diane Ghirardo, *Oppositions*, 26 (1984), pp. 21–51.

25   Ibid., p. 29.

26   Ibid., p. 37.

27   One example: 'Venezia e il Campanile di San Marco', *Emporium*, 16 (August 1902), pp. 144–68.

28   *Il Campanile di San Marco riedificato*.

29   Giacomo Boni, *Venezia imbellettata*, Stabilmento Tipografico Italiano, Rome, 1887.

30   Giandomenico Romanelli, 'La Loggetta e la sua ricomposizione', *Il Campanile di San Marco: Il crollo e la ricostruzione*, pp. 138–52.

31   *Italico Brass*, ed. Maria Masau

Dan, Electa, Milan, 1991, pls. 72, 73, 74, 75.

32   Alessandro Bettagno, *Ettore Tito, 1859–1941*, Fondazione Giorgio Cini, Electa, Milan, 1998, pp. 210–11. By this time Tito was virtually an official painter in Venice.

33   The 1905 poster depicted a girl gesturing across the Bacino towards the tower; in 1909 a pair of maidens gesture towards the rising edifice crowned with scaffold: plates in *Ottant'anni di allestimenti alla Biennale*, ed. Giandomenico Romanelli, La Biennale di Venezia, Archivio Storico delle Arti Contemporanee, 1977, LXV and CXXVII, p. 101. Nico Stringa notes that in 1912 specific work dedicated to Venice appeared in the Biennale (by Augusto Sezanne, Carlo Lorenzetti and Toso Borella), 'The Grand Decorative Cycles, 1903–1920', *Venice and the Biennale: Itineraries of Taste*, Fabbri, Monza, 1995, pp. 134–5.

34   Massimiliano Ongaro, *I monumenti ed il restauro*, lecture to the Ateneo Veneto (5 March, 1906), C. Ferrari, Venice, 1906. For an overview of Ongaro's position and his restoration of the abbey of San Gregorio in particular see Gianfranco Pertot, *Venezia 'restaurata': centosettanta anni di interventi di restauro sugli edifici veneziani*, Franco Angeli, Milan, 1988, pp. 59ff.

35   Ongaro, 'Certo è che la sostituzione del nuovo al'antico accompagnò quasi sempre la esuberanza della concezione artistica', *I Monumenti ed il restauro*, p. 7.

36   Ibid., p. 24.

37   Massimiliano Ongaro, *L'Architettura moderna a Venezia*, lecture to the Ateneo Veneto (9 February 1912), Venezia Istituto Veneto di Arti Grafiche, Venice, 1912.

38   Ibid., p. 10.

39   Ibid., p. 11.

40   Ibid., p. 21.

41   Carlo Emo, *L'Edilizia veneta: atti della Società per l'Arte Pubblica in Venezia, Domande al Sindaco di Venezia per l'edilizia veneziana*, tipografia della Gazzetta, Venice, 1899.

42   G. Lavini, 'Venezia', *L'Architettura Italiana*, 5, no. 2, (November 1909), pp. 13–14.

43   For the demolition of the market see Alvise Zorzi, *Venezia scomparsa*, Electa, Milan, 1984, p. 141.

44   Gianfranco Pertot, *Venezia 'restaurata': centosettanta anni di interventi di restauro sugli edifici veneziani*, Franco Angeli, Milan, 1988, p. 61.

45   Ibid.

46   Giuseppe Torres was born in Venice in 1872 and trained at the Accademia di Belle Arti. He died prematurely in 1935. For a succinct biography and list of principal works, writings and bibliography see *Progetti per la città Veneta, 1926–1981*

(Comune di Vicenza, Teatro Olimpico), Neri Pozza, Vicenza, 1982.

47 The new garage was illustrated in *L'Architettura Italiana*, Turin (September, 1908), 3, no. 12, p. 51, pl. XCVI.

48 Giandomenico Romanelli, 'Il sogno Secessionista di Giuseppe Torres', *Le Venezie possibili: da Palladio al Le Corbusier*, pp. 260–65.

49 For example Richard A. Etlin, *Modernism in Italian Architecture, 1890–1940*, MIT, Cambridge, Mass., and London, 1991, p. 37, esp. p. 44: 'The Venetian architects Giuseppe Torres and Guido Sullam created several works that rank among the most notable achievements of Arte Nuova'.

50 Duilio Torres assumes major importance as an urbanist in the years between the wars. For a profile see *Progetti per la città Veneta, 1926–1981*, pp. 46–48 and discussion below.

51 See again the eloquent essay by Cacciari, 'Viaggio estivo', *Venezia Vienna. Il mito della cultura veneziana nell'Europa asburgica*, ed. Giandomenico Romanelli, Electa, Milano, 1983, pp. 127–40.

52 Carlo Scarpa, 'Può l'architettura essere poesia', an address to the Academy of Vienna, 16 November 1976, cited in Francesco Dal Co and Giuseppe Mazzariol, *Carlo Scarpa, 1906–1978*, Electa, Milan, 1989, p. 283.

53 Massimo Cacciari, *Posthumous People: Vienna at the Turning Point*, trans. Rodger Friedman, Stanford University Press, 1996.

54 See chap. 11 below for further discussion of the influence of the Viennese School.

55 Aldo Rossi, 'Adolf Loos, 1870–1933', *Casabella*, 222 (1958).

56 For example Manfredo Tafuri, *The Sphere and the Labyrinth: Avant-Gardes and Architecture from Piranesi to the 1970s* (1980) trans. Pellegrino d'Acierno and Robert Connolly, MIT, Cambridge, Mass., and London, 1987.

57 Alfredo Melani, 'Architettura conservatrice a Venezia', *Italia*, 1, no. 2 (1912), pp. 28–34.

58 Etlin presents Melani as 'the most radical critic' of his time: *Modernism in Italian Architecture, 1890–1940*, p. 10. Giandomenico Romanelli details views of Melani within the conservative climate in 'Nuova edilizia veneziana all'inizio del XX Secolo', *Venezia Città del moderno/Venice: City of the Modern*, *Rassegna*, 7 (1985), pp. 10–17 (with English translation).

59 Ibid., p. 29.

60 The design was published in *L'Architettura Italiana*, 3, no. 12 (1908), p. 50, with (high-quality illustrations), pls XCIII and XCIV. This article is of singular importance as it profiled new Venetian architecture in the national press. For project drawings for the house, *Progetti per la città Veneta, 1926–1981*, pp. 38–9.

61 The icons and other Ravennate details were used by Torres in his votive chapel for the Bettioli in the cemetery of San Michele: see *L'Architettura Italiana*, 1908, p. 49, and pls LXXXX, XC and XCI.

62 Etlin, *Modernism in Italy: Architecture, 1890–1940*, p. 10.

63 Giovanni Sardi was not illustrated, possibly because his self-conscious, almost parodying eclecticism was not limited to Gothic, but incorporated Lombard, Byzantine and other Eastern elements, as in the Hotel Excelsior then under construction.

64 For the stages of the design see Carlo Pirovano, *Mario de Maria: nell'atelier del pittore delle lune*, Electa, Milan, 1983, pp. 40–41.

65 Ibid., pp. 26–7.

66 Ibid., pp. 32–3.

67 For the Berti houses see Guido Zucconi, *Venice: An Architectural Guide*, with an essay by Donatella Calabi, Arsenale Editrice, Venice, 1993, p. 123.

68 On Fortuny's fabrics and costumes in their time and in the French context in particular see Paolo Peri, 'La Trama della sua vita', *Fortuny nella Belle Epoque* (Florence, Palazzo Strozzi), Milan, Electa, 1984, pp. 61–72.

69 Guillermo de Osma, *Mario Fortuny: His Life and Work*, Rizzoli, New York, 1980, pp. 32–3. Delphine Desveaux, in *Fortuny*, Thames & Hudson, London, 1998, emphasises the role played by Fortuny's wife, Henriette, in the production of motifs for his fabrics, see p. 9.

70 Ibid., p. 80.

71 Ibid., pp. 106–107 and part 1 above. See Peter Collier, chap. 6, 'Fortuny (I): A Phoenix too Frequent', and chap. 7, 'Fortuny (II): Carpaccio's Material', in *Proust and Venice*, Cambridge University Press, 1989, pp. 79–115; Mary Lydon, 'Pli Selon: Proust and Fortuny', *Romanic Review*, 82 (1990), pp. 438–46.

72 Marcel Proust, *Remembrance of Things Past*, 'The Captive', trans. C. K. Scott Moncrieff and Terence Kilmartin; and by Andreas Mayor, Chatto & Windus, London, 1981, p. 401.

73 Ibid.

74 Ibid., p. 401. On Fortuny's colour see Jean-Michel Tuchscherer, 'Le chromaticisme de Fortuny', in *La Création d'Etoffes: Fortuny*, Musée Historique des Tissus de Lyon, Lyon, 1980, p. 27. On colour in traditional Venetian fabrics see Paul Hills, 8, 'Silks, Dyes and the Discrimination of Colours, 1470–1530', *Venetian Colour: Marble, Mosaic, Painting and Glass, 1250–1550*, Yale University Press, New Haven and London, 1999, pp. 173ff.

75 Peggy Guggenheim, *Out of This Century: Confessions of an Art Addict*, Universe Books, New York, 1979, p. 354.

76 Beyond the arts 'the politics of nostalgia' (and D'Annunzio in this context) have been studied with authority in Richard Drake, *Byzantium for Rome; The Politics of Nostalgia in Umbertian Italy, 1878–1900*, University of Carolina University Press, Chapel Hill, NC, 1980.

77 Maria Mimita Lamberti deals with the question of the representation of Impressionism (and a range of other issues) in 'The Contexts of the Early Exhibits, from the End of the Century to the First World War: Arts and the Public in the Giardini', *Venice and the Biennale: Itineraries of Taste*, pp. 39–47. Published in the year of the Biennale's centennial, this is the most comprehensive history of the Biennales to date.

78 Marco Mulanzzani, *I Padiglioni della Biennale a Venezia*, Electa, Milan, 1996, pp. 37–40. The Venetian architect Virgilio Vallot altered the building in 1948.

79 The British pavilion was a readaptation of an existing pavilion under the direction of Edwin Alfred Rickards, with internal decoration by Frank Brangwyn; ibid., pp. 50–52. The first German pavilion for Bavarian art was built by the Venetian academic architect Daniele Donghi. It was demolished in 1938; ibid., pp. 46–9.

80 Ibid., pp. 41–5. The architect was Géza Maróti.

81 Ibid., p. 53.

82 Ibid., p. 55.

83 Lamberti, 'The Contexts of the Early Exhibits from the End of the Century to the First World War: Arts and the Public in the Giardini', p. 45.

84 Mulanzzani, *I Padiglioni della Biennale*, pp. 94–100.

85 Romanelli, *Ottant'anni di allestimenti alla Biennale*, pls CXC and CXCIII.

86 Ester Coen, Licisco Magagnato and Guido Perocco, *Boccioni a Venezia: dagli anni romani alla mostra d'estate a Ca' Pesaro*, Mazzotta, Milan, 1985, p. 65.

87 Chiara Alessandri, Giandomenico Romanelli and Flavia Scotton, *Venezia: gli anni di Ca' Pesaro, 1908–1920*, Mazzotta, Milan, 1987, pp. 225–26.

88 Nico Stringa, 'The Great Decorative Cycles, 1903–1920', *Venice and Its Biennale: Itineraries of Taste*, pp. 129–38.

89 The artists commissioned were Walter Crane, Alfred East and George Frampton, with decoration and furniture by Frank Brangwyn, executed by T. S. Henry: *Ottant'anni di allestimenti alla Biennale*, p. 27.

90 Sophie Bowness and Clive Phillpot, 'Frank Brangwyn at the Biennale: Decorative Schemes for the Sala Inglese', *Britain at the Venice Biennale*, The British Council, London, 1995, pp. 29ff.

91 Luigina Bortolatto, 'On the Cupola "Given Back to the Light" just as Galileo Chini "Gave it to Venice in 1909", and

"The Imaginary of Galileo Chini"', *XLII Esposizione Internazionale d'Arte: la Biennale di Venezia XLII*, La Biennale di Venezia, 1986, pp. 18–35.

92 Ibid., p. 22.

93 See *Galileo Chini e l'Oriente: Venezia, Bangkok, Salsomaggiore*, ed. Maurizia Bonatti Bacchini, PPS, Parma, 1995.

94 Stringa, 'The Great Decorative Cycles', *Venice and its Biennale: Itineraries of Taste*, pp. 133–5.

95 Ibid., pp. 135–6.

96 For a reconstruction of this seminal exhibition see Rossana Bossaglia, Enzio Godoli and Marco Rosci, eds, *Torino 1902: le Arti decorative, internazionale d'arte decorative moderno*, Fabbri, Milan, 1902.

97 For the displays of decorative arts see Scotton, 'Applied Art: From the Foundation to the Venice Pavilion', *Venice and the Biennale: Itineraries of Taste*, pp. 123ff.

98 Romanelli, *Ottant'anni di allestimenti alla Biennale*, p. 27.

99 Illustrated ibid., pp. 100–102.

100 Guido Perocco, 'Italico Brass e la pittura veneziana', *Italico Brass*, pp. 23–30.

101 For the portraits see *Alessandro Milesi Pittore*, ed. Clauco Benito Tiozzo, Edizioni Helvetia, Venice, 1989.

102 Ibid., p. 7. Giandomenico Romanelli, *Ca' Pesaro: la Galleria d'Arte Moderna: Introduzione alle raccolte*, Electa, Milan, 1991, p. 7. On the purchases and donations see Giuliana Donzello, *Arte e collezionismo: Fradeletto e Pica primi segretari alle Biennali veneziane, 1895–1926*, Firenze Libri, Florence, 1987.

103 Enzo di Martino, 'La Fondazione dei ribelli', *Venezia: gli anni di Ca' Pesaro, 1908/1920*, p. 76,

104 Many aspects of Barbantini's career are considered in the papers in *Atti del Convegno Nino Barbantini a Venezia* (Palazzo Ducale, Venice, 1992), Canova, Treviso, 1995. For his early career in Venice in particular see Flavia Scotton, 'Barbantini a Ca' Pesaro: la Galleria d'Arte Moderna', pp. 15–39.

105 Guido Perocco publishes many letters, *Origini dell'arte moderna a Venezia*, Canova, Treviso, 1984, passim.

106 In 1911. Ibid., p. 181.

107 Damerini's review of the Summer Exhibition at Palazzo Pesaro, *Gazzetta di Venezia*, (16 July 1910) is reprinted in Ester Coen, Licisco Magagnato and Guido Perocco, *Boccioni a Venezia: dagli anni Romani alla mostra d'estate a Ca' Pesaro*, Mazzotta, Milan, 1985, pp. 84–7. For a profile on Damerini see Giannantonio Paladini, 'Damerini e Venezia', Gino Damerini, *D'Annunzio a Venezia* (1943), postfazione di Giannantonio Paladini, Marsilio, Padua, pp. 301–18.

108 Perocco, *Origini dell'arte moderna a Venezia (1908–1920)*, p. 97.

109 Alessandri, Romanetti and Scotton, *Venezia: gli anni di Ca' Pesaro, 1908/1920*, p. 44.

110 Ibid.

111 Massimo di Carlo, 'Amedeo Modigliani', ibid., pp. 164–7.

112 Massimo di Carlo and Massimo Simonetti, 'Boccioni: vita, opere e incontri', *Boccioni a Venezia: dagli anni romani alla mostra d'Estate a Ca' Pesaro*, pp. 140ff.

113 For Gino Rossi, *Venezia: gli anni di Ca' Pesaro*, pp. 182–90; for Umberto Moggioli, pp. 168–73; Pio Semeghini, pp. 194–201; Luigi Scopinich pp. 191–93.

114 These years are covered in some detail in Coen, Magagnato and Perocco, *Boccioni a Venezia: dagli anni romani alla mostra d'estate a Ca'Pesaro*. See in particular Ester Coen, 'La Mostra di Ca' Pesaro', pp. 81–2. For contemporary reviews see pp. 83ff.

115 Perocco, *Origini dell'arte moderna a Venezia (1908–1920)*, p. 101.

116 Coen, Magagnato and Perocco, *Boccioni a Venezia: dagli anni Romani alla mostra d'estate a Ca' Pesaro*, pp. 74, 76.

117 Perocco, *Origini dell'arte moderna a Venezia (1908–1920)*, p. 113.

118 Sarpellon finds this tendency constitutes an 'ambiguity' in the art of glassmaking, see 'Art Glass and the Biennale', *Venice and the Biennale: Itineraries of Taste*, p. 141.

119 For the advent of Zecchin and Wolf-Ferrari in the Barovier firm see Barovier, *Art of the Barovier Glass Makers in Murano, 1866–1972*, ed. Marina Barovier, Arsenale, Venice, 1993, pp. 52ff.

120 Quoted in Perocco, *Origini dell'arte moderna a Venezia (1908–1920)*, pp. 316–21.

121 Guido Perocco, *Opere giovanili di Teodoro Wolf-Ferrari*, Azienda Autonoma di Soggiorno e Turismo di Venezia, Venice, 1968.

122 See again Barovier, *Art of the Barovier Glass Makers in Murano, 1866–1972*, figs. 32–3; 48; 51–2.

123 John Pemble describes the foreign set with panache in his chapter on 'The New Patricians', *Venice Rediscovered*, Clarendon Press, Oxford, 1995, pp. 30ff.

124 Annie Vivant travelled to Trani where Tarnowska was serving her prison sentence. See A. Vivanti Chartres, *Marie Tarnowska*, with an introductory letter by L. M. Bossi, William Heinemann, London, 1915. She later published a 'novel' in Italian (as Annie Vivanti), *Circe Romanzo*, A. Mondadori, Milan, 1927.

125 'The Trial All the World is Watching', *Illustrated London News* (19 March 1910), p. 432. Professor Bossi, who attended Marie Tarnowska, made an eloquent plea for compassion, and for the case to be viewed as an instance of 'criminal impulse determined by morbid physical condition': preface, Vivanti Chartres, *Marie Tarnowska*.

126 For these circles, see the previous chapter.

127 Bernard Hickey, 'Lady Layard's Venice Circle', *Austen Henry Layard tra l'Oriente e Venezia*, ed. F. M. Fales and B. J. Hickey, L'Erma di Bretschneider, Rome, 1987, pp. 159–65, is a richly detailed account of the hospital activities, the guests (Lady Augusta Gregory is of particularly interest), the art collection, and so on. See also Dr Felix Arnott, 'Layard, the Anglican Layman and His Contribution to Venice', ibid. pp. 149–57.

128 Pemble, *Venice Rediscovered*, p. 52.

129 Leon Edel, *Henry James: A Life*, Harper & Row, New York, 1985, p. 633. For the writing of *The Wings of the Dove* (1902) see p. 547ff.

130 Margaretta M. Lovell, *Venice, the American View: 1860–1920*, The Fine Arts Museums of San Francisco, San Francisco, 1984, p. 109ff.

131 Wendy Baron and Richard Stone, *Sickert Paintings*, Yale University Press, New Haven and London, 1992: see pp. 106–8, 120–23, 132–5.

132 Boldini's first Venetian paintings date from 1885. Other Venetian paintings date from 1890, 1895, 1897, 1905, 1907: see *Boldini*, Società le Belle Arti ed Esposizione Permanente, Milan, Mazzotta, Milan, 1989.

133 The Venetian context, including the role of the *Gazzetta di Venezia* directed by Luciano Zuccoli, is discussed in Isenenghi, 'D'Annunzio e l'ideologia della venezianità', *D'Annunzio e Venezia*, ed. Emilio Mariano, Lucarini, Rome, 1991, pp. 229–44.

134 Gabriele D'Annunzio, 'La Nave', *Tragedie, sogni e misteri*, vol. 11, Arnoldo Mondadori, Milan, 1966, pp. 3–210. For an English version: *La Nave, 'The Ship'*, adapted by R. H. Elkin, G. Ricordi & Co, New York, 1919. See also Paolo Puppa, 'La Nave a Venezia', *D'Annunzio e Venezia* (Convegno di Studio), pp. 353–70.

135 Cited in Franco Mancini, 'La Scene e Bella: Objectivity and Transfiguration in Gabriele d'Annunzio's Set Designs', *Italian Art, 1900–1945*, ed. Pontus Hulten and Germano Celant, Rizzoli, New York, 1989, p. 157.

136 See the next chapter.

137 Damerini, *D'Annunzio e Venezia*, p. 101.

138 Ibid., p. 102. For remarks on the clerical opposition see Isenenghi, 'D'Annunzio e l'ideologia della venezianità', pp. 234–5.

139 Damerini, *D'Annunzio e Venezia*, p. 109.

140 Henri de Régnier, *La Peur*

d'Amour, Calmann-Lévy, Paris, 1912, and the collection of essays which has remained in print, *La Vie vénitienne* (with *L'Atlanta ou La Vie vénitienne*), Mercure de France, Paris, 1986.

141 *Letters of Rainer Maria Rilke, 1892–1910*, trans. Jane Bannard Greene and M. D. Herter Norton, W. W. Norton & Co, New York, 1945, p. 329.

142 Ibid., p. 397.

143 Rainer Maria Rilke, *Selected Letters, 1902–26*, trans. R. F. C. Hull, Macmillan, London, 1946, p. 381.

144 Rainer Maria Rilke, *New Poems: The Other Part*, trans. Edward Snow, North Point Press, San Francisco, 1987, pp. 134–5 (with the original German).

145 Rainer Maria Rilke, *The Notebooks of Malte Laurids Brigge*, trans. H. D. Herter Norton, Norton, New York, 1949.

146 Ibid., p. 203.

147 Ibid., p. 204.

148 Ibid.

149 Rilke, *New Poems: The Other Part*, pp. 138–9.

150 *Mallarmé*, trans. Anthony Hartley, The Penguin Poets, Harmondsworth, 1965, p. 121.

151 Rainer Maria Rilke, 'Eine Szene aus dem Ghetto von Venedig', *Geschichten vom lieben Gott* (1900), *Sämtliche Werke*, vol. 4, *Frühe Erzählungen und Dramen*, Insel-Verlag, Munich, 1969, pp. 337–45.

152 Ibid., p. 344.

153 Donald Prater, *A Ringing Glass: The Life of Rainer Maria Rilke*, Clarendon Press, Oxford, 1986, pp. 176–7.

154 Rainer Maria Rilke, *New Poems: The Other Part*, p. 307.

155 A. J. A. Symons, *The Quest for Corvo* (1934) Penguin, Harmondsworth, 1966. Baron Corvo, *The Venice Letters*, ed. Cecil Woolf, Cecil & Amelia Woolf, London, 1974.

156 Ibid., p. 68.

157 *The Venice Letters*, p. 68.

158 Nevertheless, Symons sees Rolfe as 'a lost Englishman in Venice', *The Quest for Corvo*, p. 28.

159 Frederick Rolfe, Baron Corvo, *The Desire and Pursuit of the Whole: A Romance of Modern Venice*, with an introduction by A. J. A. Symons and foreword by W. H. Auden, Cassell, London, 1934.

160 See Symons, *The Quest for Corvo*, for an account of the period of critical ill health after 1910, p. 250ff.

161 Ibid., notably in chaps 25, 26.

162 Quoted in Symons, ibid., p. 26.

163 Corvo, *The Desire and Pursuit of the Whole*, p. ix.

164 Ibid., p. 270; p. 281.

165 Symons, *The Quest for Corvo*, pp. 33–4.

166 The most sustained treatment is Carlo Montanaro's 'Appunti per una storia del cinema muto a Venezia', *L'Im-magine e il mito di Venezia nel cinema*, Biennale de Venezia, Venice, 1983, pp. 181–99.

167 Fiorello Zangrando, 'Quando il cinema si chiamava Venezia (1906–1945)', *Ateneo Veneto*, 19 (1981), p. 89.

168 Montanaro, 'Appunti per una storia del cinema muto a Venezia', p. 193.

169 Ibid.

170 'Vecchio cinema a Venezia', *Giornale economico della Camera di Commercio*, 6 (1971), p. 753.

171 For a filmography see the invaluable compilation by Piero Zanotto and C. C. Shulte in *L'Immagine e il mito di Venezia nel cinema*, p. 68ff.

172 Zangredo, 'Quando il cinema si chiamava Venezia (1906–1945)', p. 91.

173 Montanaro, 'Appunti per una storia del cinema muto a Venezia', p. 193.

174 Max Reinhardt director, *Eine venetianische Nacht*, from the play by Karl Vollmüller: Maria Carmi, Joseph Klein, Alfred Abel, Ernest Matray. Union-Film, Berlin, 1913.

175 S. L. Styan describes the play, which clearly varies from the film, and lacks the film's scope of location: *Max Reinhardt*, Cambridge University Press, 1982, p. 30.

176 Montanaro, 'Appunti per una storia del cinema muto a Venezia', p. 188.

177 Mario Verdone, 'I film di D'Annunzio e da D'Annunzio', *Quarderni del Vittoriale*, 1977, p. 16.

178 *La Nave*, directed Arrigo Frusta, Ambrosio Film, Turin, 1911.

179 Giandomenico Romanelli gives an account of 'La Casa dei Poveri', *Venezia Ottocento: l'architettura l'urbanistica*, Albrizzi, Venice, 1988, pp. 402–10.

180 The chronology follows Paola Somma, *Venezia nuova: la politica della casa, 1893–1941*, Comune di Venezia, Marsilio, Venice, 1983, p. 15. This is an essential study on the subject of Venetian housing. See also Paola Somma, 'L'Edilizia residenziale pubblica dall'inizio del secolo alla Seconda Guerra Mondiale', *Edilizia Popolare*, 175 (1983), pp. 21–31. Also invaluable: Elia Barbiani, *Edilizia popolare a Venezia: storia, politiche, realizzazioni dell'Istituto Autonomo per le Case Popolari della Provincia di Venezia*, Electa, Milan, 1983.

181 Most of these projects were by Marisch: Somma, *Venezia nuova: la Politica della casa*, pp. 16–25.

182 Cf. Riciotti Bratti, *Venezia comparsa*, G. Scarabellin, Venice, 1911. Bratti claimed that demolition rarely took place for reasons of sanitation.

183 Angelo Fano, *Sul problema delle abitazione a Venezia*, Tipografia Economica, Venice, 1910.

184 Dott. Prof. R. Vivante, Medico Capo dell'Ufficio d. Igiene, *L'Igiene stradale in Venezia*, Municipio di Venezia, Venice, 1900. For an appreciation of Vivante see Paola Somma, 'L'Attività al Comune di Venezia nella prima metà del secolo', *Storia Urbana*, 14 (1981), pp. 213–31.

185 Raffaele Vivante, *Il Problema delle abitazioni in Venezia*, Ferrari, Venice, 1910.

186 Ibid., p. 15.

187 Sandro Simionato, 'La Politica dell'amministrazione comunale veneziana e lo sviluppo del Lido, 1895–1914', *Storia Urbana*, 8 (1984), esp. section 2, 'Rapporti fra Amministrazione Comunale e Società dei Bagni', pp. 84ff.

188 Ibid., p. 82.

189 See the illustrations in the folio volume by Giovanni Sicher, *Le Ville moderne in Italia: Ville del Lido a Venezia*, C. Crudo & Co, Turin, 1913.

190 For the Torres project see Somma, *Venezia nuova: la Politica della casa, 1893–1941*, p. 30.

191 Ibid., p. 96.

192 Giorgio Moscarda, *Venezia nel 1930*, Società Ms. Fra Compositori, Venice, 1898.

193 Ferruccio Farina, 'Colore di mare: Immagine e propaganda balneare del Lido di Venezia e della riviera di Romagna', *Lido e lidi: società, moda, architettura e cultura balneare tra passato e futuro*, Marsilio, Venice, 1989, pp. 80ff.

194 Maria Cristina Buscioni, 'Torino 1902: esposizione internazionale d'arte decorativa moderna', *Esposizione e 'Stile Nazionale', 1861–1925: Il linguaggio dell'architettura nei padiglioni italiani delle grandi kermesse nazionali ed internazionali*, Alinea, Florence, 1990, pp. 174–85.

195 Eliana Brotto, 'Il Villino Monplaisir: Guido Costante Sullam', *Lido di oggi, Lido di allora*, 1987, pp. 85–91.

196 Burkhard Rukschio and Roland Schachel, 'Project for Moissi House: The Lido of Venice', *Adolf Loos: Leben und Werk*, Risenz Verlag, Salzburg and Vienna, 1982, pp. 182–4. Loos was photographed in swimming costume on the Lido during his visit in 1913, see p. 183.

197 The unbuilt projects of Le Corbusier, Frank Lloyd Wright and Louis Kahn are discussed in chap. 9 below.

198 Thomas Mann, 'Der Tod in Venedig', *Erzählung, Fiorenza, Dichtungen Gesammelte Werke*, vol. 7, Fischer, Frankfurt-am-Main, 1970, pp. 444–525; *Death in Venice*, trans. H. T. Lowe-Porter, Penguin, Harmondsworth, 1955. Visconti and Britten will be discussed below.

199 Thomas Mann, 'Enttäuschung', ibid., pp. 43–61; 'Disillusionment', trans. H. T. Lowe-Porter, *Stories of Three Decades*, Secker & Warburg, London, 1936, pp. 23–7.

200 Hugo von Hofmannsthal, 'The Letter of Lord Chandos', *Selected Prose*, trans. Mary Hottingen and Tania and

James Stein, intr. Hermann Broch, Pantheon Books, New York, 1952, p. 130. Tony Tanner discusses the letter in some detail in the context of Hofmannsthal's Venetian-based work, *Venice Desired*, Blackwell, Oxford, 1992, p. 211.

201 Mann, *Death in Venice*, p. 16.

202 Cf. James D. Steakley, *The Homosexual Emancipation Movement in Germany*, Arno, New York, 1974, pp. 21ff.

203 Ibid., p. 37.

204 Cf., for example, Robert Aldrich, *The Seduction of the Mediterranean: Writing, Art and Homosexual Fantasy*, Routledge, London, 1993: 'The Mediterranean Obsession, Death in Venice', pp. 1–12.

205 For the circumstances, personal and literary, at the time of writing, Herbert Lehnert, 'Thomas Mann's Interpretations of *Der Tod in Venedig* and Their Reliability', *Rice University Studies*, 50 (1964), pp. 41–60.

206 Ilsedore B. Jonas cites *Gesang von Kindchen*, *Song of the Little Child* of 1919, *Thomas Mann and Italy*, trans. Betty Crouse, University of Alabama Press, 1979, pp. 41–2.

207 Ibid., p. 42.

208 The connection with Wagner's death is constantly drawn in the literature: see Werner Vordtried, 'Richard Wagner's Tod in Venedig', *Euphorion*, 52 (1958), esp. pp. 383ff; Erwin Koppen's focus on 'Aschenbach und Wagner' in *Dekadenter Wagnerismus: Studien zur Europäischen Literatur des Fin de siècle*, Walter der Gruyter, Berlin, 1973, pp. 225–33. The poet Von Platen has also been taken as a progenitor: for a wide-ranging view of the sources of *Death in Venice* as much for Mann as for Benjamin Britten (see below, chap. 10) see Christopher Palmer, 'Towards a Genealogy of Death in Venice', *The Britten Companion*, ed. Christopher Palmer, Faber & Faber, London, 1984, pp. 250–67.

209 The essay was written on Hotel des Bains notepaper: Thomas Mann, *Pro and Contra Wagner*, trans. Allan Blunden, with an introduction by Erich Heller, Faber & Faber, London, 1985.

210 Cited from *Briefe an Paul Amann*, in Jonas, *Thomas Mann and Italy*, p. 42.

211 Lida Kirchberger, 'Death in Venice and the Eighteenth Century', *Monhatshefte*, 58 (1966), pp. 327–8.

212 Ibid.

213 Peter Franklin, 'Distant Sounds – Fallen Music: "Der ferne Klang" as "Woman's Opera"?', *Cambridge Opera Journal*, 3 (1991), p. 168, for discussion of the second 'Venetian' act.

214 Ibid., p. 26.

215 Thomas Mann, 'Lebensabriss', *Neue Rundschaus*, vol. 61 (June 1930), pp. 732ff. Wolfgang Leppmann, in 'Time and

Place in Death in Venice', *German Quarterly*, 48 (1975), pp. 66–75, claims that Mann neglects to mention the great heatwave of 1911, the death of Mahler etc. and is at pains in fact to be *imprecise* in chronological treatment. However, the conditions giving rise to the epidemic appear quite specific.

216 Ibid., p. 37.

217 Achile Talenti, *Il Lido di Venezia: storia dalle sue origini ad oggi. Come si crea una città*, Angelo Draghi, Padua, 1922, 126–30.

218 Ibid., p. 128.

219 Visconti's film version will be discussed below in the context of the 1960s.

220 Laura Lepri gives an invaluable focus on Futurist activities in Venice in 'La Parabola del Futurismo veneziano: 1910–1925', *Studi Novecenteschi*, 14 (1987), pp. 167–93.

221 'Contra Venezia passatista', Maria Drudi Gambillo and Teresa Fiori, *Archivi del Futurisme*, De Luca, Rome, 1957, pp. 19–20. English trans. in *Futurismo e Futurismi*, Bompiani, Milan, 1986, p. 596.

222 My remarks here owe much to the lucid exposition of R. A. Webster, *Industrial Imperialism in Italy, 1908–1915*, University of California, Berkeley and Los Angeles, 1975, esp. pp. 204ff. The *Sade* was preceded by the Cellina Società Italiana per le Forze Idrauliche del Veneto, founded in 1900.

223 Ibid., p. 121.

224 F. T. Marinetti, 'D'Annunzio, son fils et la Mer Adriatique', *Scritti francesci*, intro. and ed. Pasquale A. Jannini, Arnoldo Mondadori, Milan, 1983, p. 419. For a view of the relationship between D'Annunzio and Marinetti see Jared M. Becker, *Nationalism and Culture: Gabriele D'Annunzio and Italy After the Risorgimento*, Peter Lang, New York, 1994, esp. ch. 7, 'Aestheticizing the Industrial Age: D'Annunzio, Marinetti and Modernity', pp. 183ff.

225 Quoted in *Marinetti: Selected Writings*, edited with an introduction by R. W. Flint, Farrar, Straus & Giroux, New York, 1972, p. 13.

226 'Ruskin aurait certainement applaudi a ses passéistes vénitiens, qui ont voulu reconstruire cet absurde Campanile di San Marco, comme s'il agissait d'offrir à une fillette qui a perdu sa grand'mère une poupée en carton et en étoffe qui resemble à la défunte', F. T. Marinetti, *Le Futurisme*, Bibliothèque Internationale d'Edition, E. Sansot, Paris, 1911, p. 35.

227 Ibid., p. 34.

228 Reproduced in Giovanni Lista, *Marinetti e le Futurisme: Etudes, documents, iconographie rénus*, L'Age d'Homme, Lausanne, 1977, n.p.

229 *Archivi del Futurismo*, pp. 21–2. 'Marinetti's Futurist Speech to the

Venetians' appears in Flint, *Marinetti: Selected Writings*, pp. 56–8.

230 Ibid., p. 58.

231 Ibid.

232 Corrado Govoni, *Poesie*, 1903–1959, ed. Giuseppe Ravegnani, Mondadori, Milan, 1961, pp. 149–51.

233 In Italian, with English trans. in Zgibniew Folejewski, *Futurism and Its Place in the Development of Modern Poetry: A Comparative Study and Anthology*, University of Ottawa, 1980, pp. 158–63.

234 *I Quattro Rusteghi* is known in English as *The School for Fathers*, see 'I Quattro Rusteghi', *Kobbé's Complete Opera Book*, ed. Earl of Harewood, Bodley Head, London, 1987, pp. 999ff.

235 Philippe Monnier, *Venise au dix-huitième siècle*, Perrin, Paris, 1907; *Venice in the Eighteenth Century*, trans. from the French of Philippe Monnier, Chatto & Windus, London, 1910.

236 Ibid., p. 19.

237 Ibid., p. 239.

238 Hugo von Hofmannsthal, *Andreas*, trans. Marie D. Hottinger (1936), Pushkin Press, London, 1998. Monnier's influence is explored in David H. Miles, *Hofmannsthal's Novel Andreas: Memory and Self*, Princeton University Press, New Jersey, 1972, chap. 10, 'Venice: Dream-Theater of the Inner Self', pp. 174ff.

239 This comment by Hofmannsthal, *Andreas*, p. 115, is made in his commentary notes towards finished the project – which was, however, left incomplete.

240 Hugo von Hofmannsthal, *Venice Preserved: Tragedy*, authorised trs. from the German, Elisabeth Walter, Richard G. Badger, Boston, 1915, pp. 575–6.

241 Ibid., pp. 584–5.

242 Ibid., p. 639.

243 Lewis Lockward, in 'The Element of Time in Der Rosenkavalier', in *Richard Strauss: New Perspectives on the Composer and His Works*, ed. Bryan Gilliam, Duke University Press, Durham and London, 1992, notes the 'paradox and anachronism' in the use of the waltz, p. 245.

244 Friedrich Schröder, 'Materialien zu Hofmannsthals Casanova-Lektüre', *Modern Austrian Literature*, 24 (1991), pp. 13–21. Schröder sees the years between 1907 and 1909 as those in which Hofmannsthal was most intensively in pursuit of Casanova. In Munich at the beginning of October 1909 Hofmannsthal planned an essay on Casanova.

245 Ibid. Schnitzler's *Casanova's Homecoming* is discussed in the next chapter.

246 Hugo von Hofmannsthal, *Selected Prose*, pp. 198–206. For a heavily allegorical interpretation of this work which takes the narrator on a symbolic journey to the

underworld see Donald Flanell-Friedman, 'Rebirth in Venice: Hofmannsthal's *Errinerung schöner Tage*', *Studies in Short Fiction*, 26 (1989), pp. 17–22.

247 Georg Simmel, 'Venedig', *Zur Philosophie der Kunst: Philosophische und Kunstphilosophische Aufsätze*, Gustav Kiepenheurer, Potsdam, 1922, pp. 67–73.

248 Massimo Cacciari considers that 'Simmel's image of Venice is identical to that of *Andreas oder die Vereinigten*. They present literally the same impressions. The city is masked – there can be no interlacement, no interrelations of signification: 'The City as Essay', in 'The Dialectics of the Negative and the Metropolis', *Architecture and Nihilism: On the Philosophy of Modern Architecture*, trans. Stephen Sartarelli, Yale University Press, New Haven and London, 1993, p. 95.

249 Simmel, 'Venedig', p. 71: 'Denn dies ist das Tragische an Venedig, wodurch es zum Symbol einer ganz einzigen Ordnung unserer Formen der Weltauffassung wird: dass die Oberfläche, die ihr Grund verlassen hat, der Schein, in dem kein Sein mehr lebt, sich dennoch als ein Vollständiges und Substanzielles gibt, als der Inhalt eines wirklich zu erlebenden Lebens.'

250 Ibid., p. 73.

251 *L'Oeuvre de Giorgio Baffo*, in Guillaume Apollinaire, *Oeuvres en prose complètes*, NRF, Gallimard, 1993, pp. 688–99. See again Paolo del Negro, '"La Poesia Barona" di Giorgio Baffo Quarant'otto', *Comunità*, 184 (1982), for Apollinaire, p. 325.

252 Apollinaire, *Oeuvres en prose complètes*, p. 698.

253 Letter from Alice Monet cited in Philippe Piguet, *Monet et Venise*, Herschler, Paris, 1986, p. 34.

254 The itinerary is described in maps and photographs, ibid., pp. 63–5. See also Sylkie Patin, 'La Venezia di Monet', *Venezia da stato a mito*, ed. Alessandro Bettagno, Fondazione Giorgio Cini, Marsilio, Venice, 1997, pp. 146–53.

255 Octave Mirbeau, *Combats esthétiques*, vol. 2, *1893–1914*, ed. Pierre Michel and Jean-Francois Nivet, Séquier, Paris, 1993.

256 Gustave Geffroy, cited ibid., pp. 116 (my translation).

257 'Venise vue par le regard à la fois le plus ingénu et le plus savant', cited ibid., p. 117.

258 For Pound's first visit to Venice see Humphrey Carpenter, *A Serious Character: The Life of Ezra Pound*, Delta, New York, 1988, pp. 89–96. Pound's Venetian visits are detailed in A. Walton Litz, 'Pound in Venice, 1913', *Ezra Pound a Venezia*, ed. Rosella Mamoli Zorzi, Leo S. Olschki, Florence, 1985, pp. 31–44. The Venetian aspects of *The Cantos* will be discussed in the next chapter.

259 Walter L. Adamson has written extensively on the Florentine circles, see, for instance, 'The Language of Opposition in Early Twentieth-Century Italy: Rhetorical Continuities Between Prewar Florentine Avant-Gardism and Mussolini's Fascism', *Journal of Modern History*, 64 (1992), pp. 22–51, and *Avant-Garde Florence: From Modernism To Fascism*, Harvard University Press, Cambridge, Mass., 1993.

260 Buckley reports this from the reminiscences of Vera Stravinsky, *Diaghilev*, p. 237.

261 'Il Lido nella guerra', *Lido di oggi, Lido di allora*, vol. 2, 1987, p. 50.

262 For an account of Diaghilev's death in Venice, Buckle, *Diaghilev*, pp. 538ff.

Chapter 8

1 Corrado Ricci was Direttore Generale alle Antichità e Belle Arti.

2 Gino Damerini gives an account of the war years in 'Venezia di guerra', chap. 4 of *D'Annunzio e Venezia*, Albrizzi, Venice, 1992, pp. 129–48. See also Paul Savi-Lopes, 'La Défense de Venise', *Venise avant et pendant la guerre*, special issue *L'Art et les artistes*, 5 (1918), pp. 13–21.

3 Laura M. Ragg, *Crises in Venetian History*, Methuen, London, 1928, pp. 268–92. For the use of seaweed see p. 228.

4 For details on the protection of monuments and the naval missions organised from the area see Giovanni Scarabello, *Il Martirio di Venezia durante la Grand Guerre e l'opera di difesa della marina italiana*, 2 vols, Stab. Gazzettino Illustrato, Venice, 1933, pp. 55ff.

5 Andrea Moschetti, *I Danni ai monumenti e alle opere d'arte delle Venezie nella guerra mondiale 1915–1918*, C. Ferrari, Venice, 1932.

6 Note Anthony Rhodes, 'The Warrior', *The Poet as Superman: A Life of Gabriele D'Annunzio*, Weidenfeld & Nicholson, London, 1959, pp. 150ff.

7 'Venezia di guerra', Damerini, *D'Annunzio a Venezia*, pp. 129–48.

8 Gabriele D'Annunzio, *Nocturne and Five Tales of Love and Death*, trans. Raymond Rosenthal, Marlboro, Vermont, 1978, pp. 217ff.

9 *Gian Francesco Malipiero: Piano Music*, played by Sandro Ivo Bartoli, notes by John C. G. Waterhouse, DCA 929 (1995). For the war period (Malipiero experienced the war in Asolo) see John C. G. Waterhouse, *Gian Francesco Malipiero: The Life, Times and Music of a Wayward Genius, 1882–1973*, Harwood Academic Publishers, Amsterdam, 1999, pp. 23ff.

10 For Debussy and Malipiero, consider the 1920 *A Claudio Debussy, Gian*

Francesco Malipiero: Piano Music, played by Sandro Ivo Bartoli. ASV CD DCA 929 (1994).

11 For Malipiero's setting of *Il Sogno d'Autunno* (unpublished, and not recorded) see *Gian Francesco Malipiero: The Life, Times and Music of a Wayward Genius, 1882–1983*, pp. 110ff.

12 The *Sinfonie del silenzio e de la morte* has been recorded by the Moscow Symphony Orchestra, conducted by Antonio de Almeida, Marco Polo, 8.223603 (1993).

13 Camillo Alberto Sebellin, *Venezia nel conflitto europeo*, Giuso Fuga, Venice, 1916, p. 12.

14 Antonio Pilot, *Napoleone a Venezia nel 1807*, G. Scarabellin, Venice, 1914; 'Venezia nel blocco del 1813–1814 da noterelle inedite del Cicogna', *Nuovo Archivio Veneto*, 93 (1914), pp. 191–227; Nani Mocenigo, 'Dell'ultimo dominio Austriaco in Venezia, 1849–1866' (1915), Venice, 1916.

15 Antonio Fradeletto, *La Storia di Venezia e l'ora presente d'Italia*, STEN, Turin, 1916.

16 This is the rhetorical view of Roberto Michels, 'La Sociologie de Venise dans l'après-guerre', *Revue Internationale de Sociologie* (1920), pp. 124ff.

17 Giandomenico Romanelli, 'Il Sogno Seccessionista di Giuseppe Torres', *Le Venezie possibli: da Palladio a Le Corbusier*, ed. Lionello Puppi and Giandomenico Romanelli, Electa, Milan, 1985, p. 261.

18 On the monument see Giorgio Nonveiller, 'Aspetti della scultura a Venezia dal 1860 al 1960', *Modernità allo specchio: Arte a Venezia (1860–1960)*, ed. Toni Toniato, Supernova, Venice, 1995, pp. 164–7.

19 For a focus on the episode see Michael A. Ledeen, *The First Doge: D'Annunzio at Fiume*, Johns Hopkins University Press, Baltimore, 1977.

20 Ibid., p. 212.

21 Guido Marussig exhibited with the Ca' Pesaro artists. He moved to Milan in 1916. Victor Emmanuel III acquired *Prue dentate* from the Esposizione Internazionale d'Arte in 1920. Gabriela Belli, 'Guido Marussig', *Venezia: gli anni di Ca' Pesaro, 1908–1920*, Mazzotta, Milan, 1987, pp. 162–3.

22 Ibid., p. 247.

23 For the speech see *Scritti politici di Gabriele d'Annunzio*, ed. Paolo Alatri, Feltrinelli, Milan, 1980, pp. 186–7, and for comment see Ledeen, *The First Doge: D'Annunzio at Fiume*, p. 16; Damerini, *D'Annunzio e Venezia*, pp. 247–8.

24 'Non a me gli evviva ma a Colleoni', ibid., p. 250.

25 Ibid., p. 259.

26 See the monograph, Annamaria Andreoli, *The Vittoriale*, Electa, Milan,

1996, copiously illustrated, including glass and sculpture by Martinuzzi. For the interior decorations see Valerio Terraroli, 'Cadorin, D'Annunzio e la Stanza dei "Sogni Puri"', *Guido Cadorin*, Electa, Milan, 1987, pp. 102–10; Giovanni dalla Pozza, 'D'Annunzio e Guido Cadorin nella Stanza del Lebbroso', *D'Annunzio e Venezia*, Convegno di Studio ed. Emilio Mariano, Lucarini, Rome, 1991, pp. 371–8, Rossana Bossaglia, 'D'Annunzio e gli artisti delle Venezie', ibid., pp. 303–14.

27 For the portrait see cat. no. 2, pl. 30 in Giuseppina dal Canton, *Astolfo de Maria, 1891–1946*, Electa, Milan, 1996. See also Anna Chiara Tommasi, 'Divagazioni intorno a quattro dipinti Veneziani al Vittoriale', *D'Annunzio e Venezia*, pp. 359–69.

28 Piero Foscari, *Per il più largo dominio di Venezia, la città e il porto*, cited in Santo Peli, 'Le Concentrazioni finanziarie industriali nell'economia di guerra; Il caso di Porto Marghera', *Studi Storici*, 16 (1975), p. 193.

29 Cesco Chinello is the principal historian of Marghera: *Porto Marghera, 1902–1926. Alle origini del 'Problem di Venezia'*, Marsilio, Venice, 1979. See also the short, illustrated account by Alessandro Filippo Nappi, *Storia di Marghera da periferia a città*, Cetid, Mestre and Venice, 1994.

30 Peli, 'Le Concentrazioni finanziarie industriali nell'economia di guerra; Il caso di Porto Marghera', p. 193.

31 Ibid.

32 Ibid., p. 203. See also the details of the syndicate formed on 1 February 1917 to study the port in Luigi Scano, *Venezia Terra e acqua* (postfazione di Edoardo Salzano), Edizioni delle Autonomie, Rome, 1985, p. 49. Scano's study is fundamental for twentieth-century Venetian studies.

33 Ibid., pp. 182–3. For an account of Volpi's business dealings before Marghera see R. A. Webster, *Industrial Imperialism in Italy, 1908–1915*, University of California, Berkeley and Los Angeles, 1975, pp. 206ff. The significance of the Electrical Society in the negotiations for Marghera is made clear in Peli, 'Le Concentrazioni finanziarie industriali nell'economia di guerra; il caso di Porto Marghera', pp. 183ff.

34 Sergio Romano, *Giuseppe Volpi: Industria e finanza tra Giolitti e Mussolini*, Bompiani, Milan, 1979, chap. 6, 'Guerra e Dopoguerra', pp. 63ff.

35 Ibid., p. 189.

36 For those involved see Scano, *Venezia terra e acqua*, p. 52, and Romano, *Giuseppe Volpi: Industria e finanza tra Giolitti e Mussolini*, pp. 196–9. Peli concludes in 'Le Concentrazioni finanziarie industriali nell'economia di guerra' (p. 204): 'It is difficult to imagine that the Marghera project would have seen the light without big profits, the euphoria of investment, the tendency towards industrial concentration and the collusion between political classes and the industrial world which the economy of war produced and exalted.'

37 Coen detailed the history of location and initial development in E. Coen, *Il Porto di Venezia*, La Poligrafica Italiana, Venice, 1925.

38 Piero Foscari, *Il piano regolatore per l'ampliamento del porto e della città di Venezia: la nuova stazione marittima e la nuova zona edilizia a Marghera*, cited in Romano, *Giuseppe Volpi: Industria e finanzia tra Giolitti e Mussolini*, p. 11.

39 Quoted in Chinello, *Porto Marghera, 1902–1926*, p. 206.

40 On attitudes to Fiume and the emphasis on nationalism as an accompaniment to Fascism see Luca Pes, 'Il Fascismo urbano a Venezia: origine e primi sviluppi, 1895–1922', *Italia Contemporanea*, 169 (1987), p. 76.

41 The key article by Pes, ibid., pp. 63–84.

42 In compliance with the Fascist regime, the position of Sindaco became Podestà in 1926 when Pietro Orsi was appointed.

43 Pes, 'Il Fascismo urbano a Venezia', p. 77. The chronology of headlines from *La Gazzetta di Venezia*, cited in Paula Somma, *Venezia nuova: la politica della casa, 1893–1941*, Comune di Venezia, Marsilio, Venice, 1983, pp. 513ff., makes the violence clear – as well as the strikes leading to the general strike. Via Garibaldi was the scene of a number of clashes between the Fascists and Socialists.

44 Giovanni Venni, *Venezia nuova: I grandi lavori per il Porto di Marghera*, Bortoli, Venice, 1924.

45 Gino Piva, 'Un altra Venezia', *Emporium*, 305 (1920), pp. 235–42.

46 Giuseppe Volpi, Conte di Misurata, *Venezia antica e moderna*, Atena, Rome, 1939, p. 32. See again Sergio Romano, *Giuseppe Volpi: Industria e finanza tra Giolitti e Mussolini*.

47 Ibid., p. 28.

48 Paul Somma, 'Il Quartiere Giuseppe Volpi a Porto Marghera', *Venezia nuova: la politica della casa, 1893–1941*, pp. 101–6.

49 'Il Problema dell'abitazione a Mestre a l'attività del locale Istituto Autonomo per le Case Popolari', ibid., pp. 106–9.

50 The discussion had in fact been protracted over some decades: 'Il Territorio', Sergio Barizza, *Il Comune di Venezia, 1806–1946: l'istituzione, il territorio, guida-inventario dell'Archivio Municipale*, Comune di Venezia, Venice, 1987, pp. 113ff.

51 'Dove è porto di Venezia, è territorio di Venezia', ibid., p. 128.

52 For further discussion of the difficulties in Mestre at this time see Giandomenico Romanelli, 'Sotto l'ala del leone, Venezia e Mestre: alle origini di un problema', *COSES Informazione*, 19, 12 (1980), pp. 17–27.

53 A. Salvadori, *Per una 'più grande' Venezia protesta verso il mare e contro il Porto di Mestre*, Venice, 1917.

54 Giacomo Trevissoi, *Di alcuni problemi Veneziani*, C. Ferrari, Venice (1925), 1929.

55 See again the overview studies of planning Elia Barbiani and Giorgio Conti, 'Venezia: dalla città speciale al modello di sviluppo speciale', *Urbanistica*, 68/69 (1978), esp. pp. 124–6.

56 Richard A. Etlin, in *Modernism in Italian Architecture, 1890–1940*, Cambridge, Mass., and London, 1991, mentions Torres only in relation to this building, the Istituto Elioterapico ed Ortopedico, calling it 'the most famous "rationalist" building before the advent of the Italian rationalist movement', p. 237.

57 Duilio Torres, *Contributo agli studi sul Piano Regolatore di ritocco e di ampliamento della città di Venezia*, Venice (May 1941), pp. 329–42, citing *Gazzetta di Venezia* (18 December 1923; 8 February 1924; 24 February 1924).

58 *Piano Regolatore* for the Frezzeria area, 1927, illustrated *Progetti per la città veneta, 1926–1981* (Comune di Vicenza, Teatro Olimpico, 1982), Neri Pozza, Vicenza, 1982, p. 48.

59 Duilio Torres, 'La nuova architettura e Venezia', *Ateneo Veneto* 1 (1933), pp. 161–81.

60 Illustrated *Progetti per la città veneta, 1926–1981*, p. 31.

61 Ugo Nebbia, 'Una Dimora di caccia e pesca nell'Isoletta di Valle Zappa nella Laguna di Venezia', *Architettura e Arti Decorative*, fasc. VII (1924–5), pp. 566–70.

62 Torres, 'La nuova architettura', p. 173.

63 Ibid., p. 165.

64 Alberto Magrini, 'Piani Regolatori di Venezia nel passato e nell'avvenire', *Ateneo Veneto*, 117, 1 (1934), p. 66: 'conserviamo così Venezia, senza tradirla con i vani bigottismi e sentimentalismi di decadenti, ma dandole il volto nuovissimo, che sarà sempre funzionalmente e esteticamente, il più con-sono alla sua tradizione alla sua fisionomia inimitabile e alla sua eterna grandezza.'

65 Contingencies between Fascism and Rationalism are studied in Diana Yvonne Ghirado, 'Italian Architects and Fascist Politics: An Evaluation of the Rationalist's Role in Regime Building', *Journal of the Society of Architectural Historians*, 39 (1980), pp. 109–27.

66 Gustavo Giovannoni, 'Vecchie città

ed edilizia nuova', *Nuova Antologia*, n. 47 (June 1913), pp. 449–72.

67 Torres, 'La nuova architettura', p. 177. Paolo Maretto, *Architettura del XX Secolo in Italia: Venezia*, Vitali & Ghianda, Genoa, 1969, p. 88.

68 Giuseppe Torres provides a well-illustrated account of Del Guidice's early work in the Veneto, 'Recenti opere di architetti Lombardi e delle Venezie', 'Veneti', *Architettura e Arti Decorative*, fasc. v (1922–3), pp. 304–17.

69 For a curriculum vitae of Del Guidice see *Progetti per la città, 1926–1981*, pp. 43–5. For early years see Romanelli, 'La cifra di Ca' Pesaro: spezzoni d'avanguardia, brandelli d'accademia', *Venezia: gli anni di Ca' Pesaro, 1908–1920*, p. 21.

70 A profile appears in Marco Mulazzani, *I Padiglioni della Biennale a Venezia*, Electa, Milan, 1996, pp. 73–6.

71 Antonio Maraini, 'L'Architettura e le arti decorative alla XVI Biennale Veneziana', *Architettura e Arti Decorative*, fasc. II (1928/29), pp. 49–65. For these pavilions see Mulazzani, *I Padiglioni della Biennale a Venezia*, pp. 73–6.

72 Nico Stringa, 'The Great Decorative Cycles, 1903–1920', ibid., pp. 332–5.

73 The formal garden in front with clipped lawns and trees represented a late adaptation of Viennese style.

74 See the political interpretation in Marla Stone, 'The State as Patron: Making Official Culture in Fascist Italy', *Fascist Visions: Art and Ideology in France and Italy*, ed. Matthew Affron and Mark Antliff, Princeton University Press, 1997, pp. 229–31.

75 Mulazzani, *I Padiglioni della Biennale a Venezia*, pp. 84–5.

76 Maretto, *Architettura del XX Secolo in Italia: Venezia*, p. 91. Maretto objects to the building introduced into a Gothic area.

77 Somma, 'La colonizzazione di S. Elena e il Quartiere Vittorio Emanuele III', *Venezia nuova: la Politica della casa, 1893–1941*, pp. 79–81.

78 The 1911 competition with D. Torres, F. Finzi and G. Allesandri, *Progetti per la città veneta*, p. 37.

79 Duilio Torres, 'Colonizzazione della Sacca di S. Elena in Venezia', *Architettura e Arti Decorative*, fasc. III (March 1926–7), pp. 118–27.

80 Cf. 'Appartamenti nuovi per diecimila abitanti a per oltre 80 milioni di lire', in 'Il nuovo volto di Venezia dopo dieci anni di Fascismo', *Rivista di Venezia a cura del Comune*, II, n. 10 (October 1932), pp. 445–8. For Torres's comments see 'Colonizzazione della Sacca di S. Elena in Venezia', p. 126.

81 Ibid., p. 36.

82 Gustavo Giovannoni, 'Il Risana-

mento urbanistico di Venezia', *Palladio*, III (1939), p. 274.

83 Somma, 'L'Attività del Comune e delle opere pie fra le due Guerre Mondiale', *Venezia Nuova: la Politica della casa, 1893–1941*, pp. 25–6.

84 Alberto Magrini, 'Gruppi urbanistici e Piano Regolatori: studio per un Piano Regolatore di Venezia e Mestre', *Le Tre Venezie* (August 1931), p. 505. The figure is cited in Elia Barbiani, *Edilizia popolare a Venezia: storia, politiche, realizzazioni dell'Istituto Autonomo per le Case Popolari della Pro-vincia di Venezia*, Electa, Milan, 1983, p. 19.

85 Raffaele Vivante, *Nuovo contributo allo studio del problema delle abitazioni*, Garzia, Venice, 1935.

86 Pompeo Molmenti, *I Nemici di Venezia*, polemical writings collected and ed. by Elio Zorzi, Zanichelli, Bologna, 1924.

87 Romano, *Giuseppe Volpi: Industria e finanza tra Giolitti e Mussolini*, p. 202.

88 Elio Zorzi, 'Il Ponte del Littorio sulla Laguna', *Nuova Antologia*, I (1933), p. 408.

89 Alberto Zajotti gives the history of negotiations with a photographic documentation of the construction in 'Cento anni di progetti, di studi e di tentativi spolti', *Rivista di Venezia*, 4 (1933), p. 165.

90 Romano Chirivi gives a succinct account of the negotiations leading to the bridge, including the competition of 1919, in 'Eventi urbanistici dal 1846 al 1962', *Urbanistica*, 52 (1968), 'Il Collagamento di Venezia con la Terraferma', pp. 84–6; 'Il ponte automobilistico translagunare', pp. 90–91. See also Gianpietro Zucchetta, 'Ponte della Libertà', *Venezia ponte per ponte*, vol. 2, Stamperia di Venezia, Venice, 1992, pp. 18–22, with photographs of construction.

91 Nevertheless there was little commentary on Miozzi before Francesco Indovina, 'Eugenio Miozzi e il nuovo volto della città nel'900', Giovanni Distefano and Giannantonio Paladini, *Storia di Venezia, 1797–1997*, vol. 3, *Dalla monarchia alla repubblica*, Supernova-Grafiche Biesse, Venice, 1997, pp. 380–5. And see now Valeria Farinati in *Profili veneziani del Novecento*, vol. 2, *Virgilio Guidi, Eugenio Miozzi, Francesco Pasinetti, Teresa Sensi*, ed. Giovanni Distefano and Leopoldo Pietragnoli, Supernova, Venice, 1999, pp. 26–47.

92 Miozzi's four-volume history of Venice is interleaved with photographs and pen and ink drawings of his designs: *Venezia nei secoli*, 4 vols, Libeccio, Venice, 1957–69.

93 'Hier ist eine Stadt ohne Auto, ohne Droschken, ohne Pferde, ohne Esel, ohne

Bäume, mit wenig Hunden, vielen Katzen ...' Paul Klee, *Briefe an die Familie*, vol. 2, *1907–1940*, ed. Felix Klee, Du Mont, Cologne, 1979, Letter of October 1932, p. 1190.

94 Zorzi, 'Il Ponte del Littorio sulla Laguna', p. 427: 'Il Fascismo veneziano respinge ogni fantasia su progetti di penetrazione in Venezia di mezzi di trasporto terreste oltre i limiti insuperabili già segnati con la costruzione del nuovo ponte sulla laguna'.

95 Ernst Bloch, 'Venedigs italienische Nacht' (1934), *Literarische Aufsätze*, Suhrkampverlag, Frankfurt am Main, 1965, p. 401.

96 Ibid.

97 For Torres's comment see 'Contributo agli studi sul piano regolatore', p. 267. For the latter description see Piazzale Roma ... si sono trasformati in una vastissima e ancora avanzante necrosi', Giorgio Bellavitis and Giandomenico Romanello, *Venezia*, Laterza, Rome and Bari, 1989, p. 235. See also Alvise Zorzi, *Venezia scomparsa*, Electa, Milan, 1984, pp. 172–3.

98 Gino Damerini, *Giardini di Venezia*, Zanicelli, Bologna, 1931.

99 Alfredo Zajotti, 'Nuovi ponti a Venezia', *Le Tre Venezie*, 1933, pp. 268–9.

100 M. Ballarin, 'Perché dovrebbero essere demoliti i ponti in ferro sul Canal Grande a Venezia', *Ingegneria*, 4, n. 10 (1926), pp. 372–6.

101 Sergio Barizza, 'Ponte dell'Accademica', *Le Venezie possibili: da Palladio a Le Corbusier*, pp. 216–27; Gianpietro Zucchetta, *Venezia ponte per ponte*, vol. 2, Stamperia di Venezia, Venice, 1992, pp. 42–51.

102 Ibid., and Eugenio Miozzi, 'Il ponte di legno sul Canal Grande a Venezia', *Annali dei Lavori Pubblici*, 1933, pp. 431–42, and Alfredo Zajotti, 'Nuovi ponti a Venezia', *Le Tre Venezie*, 1933, pp. 267–9.

103 Zajotti, 'Nuovi ponti a Venezia', pp. 267–8.

104 Zucchetta, *Venezia ponte per ponte*, vol. 2, p. 31.

105 Barizzi, 'Ponte dell'Accademia', *Le Venezie possibili: da Palladio a Le Corbusier*, pp. 216–27.

106 Dennis P. Doordan, *Building Modern Italy: Italian Architecture, 1914–1936*, Princeton Architectural Press, New York, 1988, p. 105.

107 Carla Uberti, 'Il Ponte ferroviario e la stazione', *Le Venezie possibli: da Palladio a Le Corbusier*, pp. 229–37.

108 For 'The Value Vacuum of German Art', pp. 51ff. Hermann Broch, *Hugo von Hofmannsthal and his Time*, trans. Michael P. Steinberg, Chicago University Press, 1984, p. 81.

109 See again the fine essay by Anna Giubertoni implicating Boito in *Senso* and

Strauss in *Eine Nacht in Venedig*, 'Venezia nella letteratura austriaca moderna', *Venezia Vienna: Il mito della cultura veneziana nell'Europa asburgica*, ed. Giandomenico Romanelli, Electa, Milan, 1983, pp. 105–26.

110 Michael Müller, *Franz Kafka Der Process*, Philipp Reclam, Stuttgart, 1993, p. 8.

111 Erich Wolfgang Korngold, *Violanta*, Libretto Hans Müller, CBS records, 01-79229-10,1980 (1980). With Walter Berry, Eva Marton, Bavarian Radio Chorus, Munich Radio Orchestra, Marek Janowski; essay by Christopher Palmer.

112 'Aus den Gräbern selbst die Toten/Tanzen heute Brust an Brust', ibid., p. 34.

113 Arthur Schnitzler, *Casanova's Homecoming* (1918), Brentano's, London, 1922, p. 13.

114 Stefan Zweig, *Drei Dichter Ihres Lebens: Adepts in Self-Portraiture: Casanova, Stendhal, Tolstoy*, trans. Eden and Cedar Paul, George Allen & Unwin, London, 1929.

115 Ibid., p. 79.

116 Ibid., p. 34, p. 38.

117 The original *Le Bordel de Venise* is elusive, but see plates in Claudio dell'Orso, *Venezia libertina: I luoghi della memoria erotica*, Arsenale, Venice, 1999, pp. 34–5.

118 Guillaume Apollinaire, 'Casanova Comédie parodique', *Oeuvres poétiques*, Gallimard, Paris, 1959, pp. 964–1024. Monograph essays are found in *Guillaume Apollinaire 18, le Casanova' d'Apollinaire 'comédie parodique'*, textes rénus par Michel Décaudin, Lettres Modernes, Minard, Paris, 1991, in particular, Jacqueline Bellas, 'Apollinaire Librettiste Casanova et l'Ecriture Parodique', pp. 67–102. The introductory pages sketch the literary reception.

119 Jean-Jacques Heude, 'Le Casanova de Henry Defosse', ibid., pp. 41–65. Defosse is best known for his orchestration of *La Boutique Fantasque*.

120 Michel Décaudin, 'Historie d'un texte', ibid., p. 13.

121 Casanova has made many appearances in cinema, see *Il Cinema ai tempi di Casanova*, ed. Roberto Ellero, Marsilio, Venice, 1998.

122 Stills in Richard Abel, *French Cinema: The First Wave, 1915–1929*, Princeton University Press, 1984, pp. 187–9. Fellini's *Casanova* is discussed in chap. 10 below.

123 'Casanova', *Cinéa-Ciné pour-tous* 88 (1 July 1927), p. 23, quoted, ibid., p. 189.

124 Henri de Régnier, *Casanova chez Voltaire: Les Conversations*, Libraire Plon, Paris, 1929. The volume includes the original material from the *Memoirs*: see

Casanova, *History of My Life*, vol. 6, chap. 10, pp. 223ff.

125 On the Verdi revival which Werfel fostered see George Martin, 'Franz Werfel and the "Verdi Renaissance"', *Aspects of Verdi*, pp. 61–77.

126 For a discussion of the factual background see Donald Gresch, 'The Fact of Fiction: Franz Werfel's Verdi: Roman der Oper', *Current Musicology*, 28 (1979), pp. 30–40.

127 Franz Werfel, *Verdi: A Novel of the Opera*, trans. Helen Jessiman, Allen, Towne & Heath, New York, 1947, p. 3.

128 Ibid., chap. 8, 'The Fires of Carnival', pp. 269ff.

129 Ibid., p. 284.

130 Ibid., p. 379.

131 Ibid., p. 411.

132 Frederick W. Ott, *The Films of Fritz Lang*, Citadel Press, Secaucus, New Jersey, 1979, p. 89.

133 Siegfried Kracauer, *From Caligari to Hitler: A Psychological Study of the German Film*, Noonday, New York, 1959, p. 90.

134 Humphrey Carpenter, *A Serious: Character: The Life of Ezra Pound*, Delta, New York, 1990, p. 426.

135 Ibid.

136 See again George D. Painter, *Marcel Proust: A Biography* (1959) Penguin, Harmondsworth, 1977.

137 Guillermo de Osma, *Mariano Fortuny: His Life and Work*, Rizzoli, New York, 1980, p. 147. Fortuny opened a factory for production of his fabrics on the Giudecca in 1922, p. 148.

138 Ezra Pound, *The Cantos*, Faber & Faber, London, fourth impression, 1994. A full (or fulsome) discussion of the references to Venice in the *Cantos* is given by Tony Tanner, chap. 7, 'Ezra Pound: The White Forest of Marble', in *Venice Desired*, pp. 269ff. (The discussion of Robert Browning is apposite.) Tanner makes much of the comparison with Ruskin. It is difficult to agree with Robert Casillo's confident assertion that Ruskin and Pound 'held similar values, examined the same artefacts and issues, and often reached the same conclusion': 'The Meaning of Venetian History in Ruskin and Pound', *University of Toronto Quarterly*, 55 (1986), p. 235. Accepting the basic moralistic reading of both authors, one might note the likeness to the Municipality reading of Venetian history and its crisis points: note, p. 243, Casillo quoting from *Canto* 67: 'Venice at first democratical . . .'

139 Carpenter, *A Serious Character: The Life of Ezra Pound*, p. 287.

140 Ibid., p. 476.

141 T. S. Eliot, *Selected Poems*, Faber & Faber, London, 1964, pp. 34–5.

142 Ibid.

143 Pound, *The Cantos*, p. 78.

144 *Canto* XVII, ibid., p. 76,

145 References here are to *Canto* LI, ibid., pp. 250ff.

146 *Canto* XXV, ibid., p. 116.

147 For Bellini's cycle see Wolfgang Wolters, *Der Bilderschmuck des Dogenpalastes*, Franz Steiner, Wiesbaden, 1983, pp. 169–70.

148 For Carpaccio's cycle see ibid.

149 Pound, *The Cantos*, p. 546.

150 For the final Venice years see Humphrey Carpenter, *A Serious Character: The Life of Ezra Pound*, pp. 893ff.

151 See the sketches made *circa* 1915 in *Le Corbusier: pittore e sculptore*, Museo Correr, Arnoldo Mondadori, Milan, 1986, p. 174, with the motto (p. 174), 'Je prends Venise parcequ'elle offre le monument et le pittoresque'.

152 Le Corbusier, *Propos d'urbanisme* (1929) *Concerning Town Planning*, trans. Clive Entwistle, Architectural Press, London, 1947, p. 32.

153 Le Corbusier, *L'Urbanisme* (1924), translated as *The City of Tomorrow and Its Planning*, Architectural Press, London, 1971, p. 71.

154 Le Corbusier, *La Ville radieuse: Elements d'une doctrine d'urbanisme pour l'équipment de la civilisation machiniste*, Vincent, Fréal & Cie, Paris, 1964, pp. 268–9. It was at this point that Le Corbusier's relationship with Fascist Italy brought him into contact with Giuseppe Bottai and Mussolini, see Giorgio Ciucci, 'A Roma con Bottai', *Rassegna*, 2 (1980), pp. 66–71.

155 Le Corbusier, *When the Cathedrals Were White: A Journey to the Country of Timid People*, Routledge, London, 1948, pp. 7–8.

156 Le Corbusier, *La Ville Radieuse*, p. 268.

157 Ibid.

158 Rem Koolhaus, *Delirious New York: A Retroactive Manifesto for Manhattan*, Oxford University Press, New York, 1978, pp. 101–3.

159 Alvise Zorzi, *Venezia scomparsa*, Electa, Milan, 1984, p. 182.

160 Duilio Torres, 'La Legge per Venezia del 21 Agosto, 1937, n. 1901', *Urbanistica*, n. 1 (Jan.–Feb. 1938), pp. 19–22.

161 Zorzi, *Venezia scomparsa*, p. 178.

162 Duilio Torres, 'Il Piano di Sistemazione Edilizia di Venezia e i suoi pericoli', *Palladio*, III, n. 4 (1939), pp. 175–9.

163 Ibid., p. 177.

164 Ibid., p. 178.

165 Cf. Gianfranco Bellin, *Dove volano il leone: fine secolo a Venezia*, Garzanti, Milan, 1991, 'I disastri del "fare"', pp. 61ff. Gustavo Giavannoni, 'Il Risanamento urbanistico di Venezia',

Palladio: rivista Bimestrale del Centro di Studi per la Storia dell'Architettura, 3 (1939), pp. 273–4.

167 Duilio Torres, 'Precisazioni sul "Diradamento" in Tema di Urbanistica', *Ateneo Veneto*, 131 (1944), pp. 68–71.

168 Cf. Roland Sarti, 'Giuseppe Volpi', *Uomini e volti del Fascismo*, Bulzoni, Rome, 1980, pp. 523–46, for a gentle assessment of Volpi in the Fascist period.

169 The requirement was an eminent person resident in Venice, Rabitti, 'The Events and the People: The Brief History of an Institution', *Venice and the Biennale: Itineraries of Taste*, Fabbri, Monza, 1995, p. 35.

170 This point is at variance with the view expressed in Marla Stone's 'Challenging Cultural Categories: The Transformation of the Biennale under Fascism', *Journal of Modern Italian Studies*, 4 (1999), pp. 184–208, affirming that Venice was the recipient of the Fascist programme: many of the aspects mentioned were in place with Selvatico's first Biennale in 1895 (for example the use of Venetian images for promotion, and discounted fares).

171 See Zalti, 'Le Prime Biennale Veneziane, 1895–1912: Il Contributo di Vittorio Pica', and Rabitti, 'The Events and the People: The Brief History of an Institution', *Venice and the Biennale: Itineraries of Taste*, pp. 31ff.

172 Antonio Maraini, 'L'Architettura e le arti decorative alla XIV Biennale veneziana', *Architettura e Arti Decorative*, 2 (February 1928–9), pp. 49–65, with excellent illustrations of the new buildings.

173 See Mario Isenenghi, 'La Politica dei Festival', in 'Cultura', *Venezia*, ed. Emilio Franzina, Laterza, Rome and Bari, 1986, pp. 454–6.

174 Lawrence Alloway, *The Venice Biennale, 1895–1968: From Salon to Goldfish Bowl*, Faber & Faber, London, 1969, p. 113. For many years this undetailed account was the only available history of the Biennale.

175 Pietro Chiesa comments: 'questo padiglione fu voluto dalla attiva genialità del Conte Volpi, e realizzata dalla passione di Beppe Ravà per valorizzare la produzione artistico-industriale a Venezia', 'Il Vetro alla Biennale veneziana', *Domus*, 55 (1932), p. 416.

176 Marco Mulazzani, *I Padiglioni della Biennale a Venezia*, Electa, Milan, 1996, pp. 68–9.

177 For the façade plan, and floor plan of the 1912 building see Edoard F. Sekler, *Josef Hoffmann: The Architectural Work, Monograph and Catalogue of Works*, Princeton, NJ, 1985, pp. 146–7, and cat. 157, pp. 347–8.

178 For the 1934 pavilion see ibid., pp. 210–11, cat. 359, pp. 430.

179 Mulazzani, *I Padiglioni della Biennale a Venezia*, p. 95.

180 See the three-volume monograph by Franca Bizzotto, Dino Marangon and Toni Toniato, *Virgilio Guidi: catalogo generale dei dipinti*, Electa, Milan, 1998: Bizzotto, 'Il primo periodo veneziano (1927–1935)', also Toni Toniato, 'Virgilio Guidi e la pittura veneziana del suo tempo', *Modernità allo specchio: arte a Venezia, 1860–1960*, Supernova, Venice, 1995, p. 121. See also Margherita Sarfatti, 'Exposition de six peintres du Novecento', reprinted *Les Realismes, 1919–1939*, Centre Georges Pompidou, Paris, 1980, pp. 92–3. For the Biennale in these years see Sileno Salvagnini, 'Art as Vocation and Art as Non-Vocation', *Venice and the Biennale: Itineraries of Taste*, pp. 57–68, and for Venice paintings see Dal Canton, 'Artists from the Veneto at the Biennale', pp. 116–19.

181 *Realismo Magico: pittura e scultura in Italia, 1919–1925*, ed. Maurizio Fagiolo dell'Arc, Mazzotta, Milan, 1988, esp. Sergio Marinelli, 'L'Area Veneta, Il Realismo non abita in Bisanzio', pp. 87ff. The cohesion and authority of works by Venetian artists in this manner suggest they are deserving of more sustained scrutiny.

182 *Les Realismes, 1919–1939*, p. 64.

183 The main monograph by Carlo Munari, *Bortolo Sacchi*, Edizioni Galleria S. Marco, Bassano del Grappa, 1972, gives only basic information. Sacchi was born in Venice in 1892, painted with the landscapist Francesco Sartorelli, and in Munich attended the academy of Hugo von Habermann (he was president of the Munich Secession), returning to Venice in 1919 and exhibiting regularly in Biennales until 1942. A recent study accompanied an exhibition in 2000: *Bortolo Sacchi, 1892–1978: dipinti, disegni, ceramiche*, ed. Giuseppina Dal Canton and Nico Stringa, Marsilio, Venice, 2000.

184 *Fantasia veneziana*, 1920, pl. v, p. 14; *La Canzone del Veneto*, 1920, pl. vii, p. 18, Munari, *Bortolo Sacchi* (Cassiano).

185 Illustrated in *Realismo magico*, p. 94. Marinelli identifies the source of the sky-borne figure as Tintoretto's San Cassiano angel.

186 Ibid., p. 90.

187 Ibid., p. 167.

188 Renato Barilli, Giuseppina dal Canton and Toni Toniato, *Cagnaccio di San Pietro*, Electa, Milan, 1991.

189 Ibid., p. 104.

190 Maria Cristina Bandera, 'De Pisis e Venezia', *Modernità allo specchio: arte a Venezia*, pp. 96–115. De Pisis pays homage to Venice in *Ore Veneziane*, ed. Bona de Pisis and Sandro Zanotto, Longanesi, Milan, 1974.

191 See again Bizzotto, 'Il Primo Periodo veneziano (1927–1935), Toni Toniato, 'Virgilio Guidi e la pittura veneziana del suo tempo', *Modernità allo specchio: arte a Venezia*, pp. 116–47.

192 For a concise treatment see Enrico Crispolti, 'Second Futurism', *Italian Art in the Twentieth Century: Painting and Sculpture, 1900–1988*, ed. Emily Braun, Royal Academy of Arts, London, Prestel-Verlag, Munich, 1989, pp. 165–71.

193 See chap. 10 below.

194 Caterina de Luigi, 'Mario Deluigi', *Profili veneziani del Novecento*, ed. Giovanni Distefano and Leopoldo Pietragnoli, Supernova, Venice, 1999, p. 9.

195 Micalla Martegani Luini, 'The Revival of Glass and Ceramics', *The Italian Metamorphosis, 1943–1968*, Solomon R. Guggenheim, New York, 1994, pp. 220–28, and Giovanni Sarpellon, 'Art, Glass and the Biennale', *Venice and the Biennale: Itineraries of Taste*, pp. 141–2.

196 For the cirumstances see Franco Deboni, *Venini Glass*, with a preface by Dan Klein, Umberto Allemandi & Co, Turin, 1996. For the glass industry in the 1920s and 1930s and the main shifts in personnel see Dorigato, *Murano Glass Museum*, Electa, Milan, 1986, pp. 71–87.

197 See 'DIR', 'Nuovi vetri muranesi, *Domus*, 143 (February 1929), pp. 31–2.

198 Deboni, *Venini Glass*, p. 17.

199 *Art of the Barovier: Glassmakers in Murano, 1866–1972*, ed. Marina Barovier, Arsenale, Venice, 1993, p. 112.

200 Deboni, *Venini Glass*, p. 19. The original work is lost.

201 Ibid., pp. 110ff.

202 Ibid., pp. 16–17.

203 On this point see Sileno Salvagnini, 'L'Arte in azione: Fascismo e organizzazione della cultura artistica in Italia', *Italia Contemporanea*, 173 (1988), with comments on the decline of the Biennale di Venezia, circa 1930, pp. 12ff.

204 Gian Francesco Malipiero, *L'armonioso labirinto: teatro da musica, 1913–1970*, ed. Marzio Pieri, Marsilio, Venice, 1992, pp. 166–75. The work was composed in 1928 and premiered in 1932: *Malipiero scrittura e critica*, ed. Maria Teresa Muraro, Leo S. Olschki, Florence, 1984, p. 149, and Waterhouse, *Gian Pietro Malipiero*, pp. 163ff. Waterhouse considers *Le Aquile di Aquileia* to be one of Malipiero's most resplendent scores' (p. 163), but *I Corvi di San Marco*, representing a degenerate contemporary tourist state, 'seems puny' (p. 165).

205 Malipiero, *L'Armonioso labirinto: Teatro da musica, 1913–1970*, p. 148.

206 Ibid., p. 166.

207 Malipiero, 'Per un Istituto di Studi Monteverdiani', ibid. pp. 158–9; 'L'Ora Vivaldiana', ibid., pp. 168–9.

208 Malipiero, ibid., pp. 133–4.

209 Gian Francesco Malipiero, *Symphonic Fragments from Three Goldoni Comedies (1925)*, Orchestra della Svizzera Italiana, conductor, Christian Benda, Marco Polo, 8.225118, 1997.

210 Malipiero, 'Memorie Utili ovvero: Come nasce nei musicisti il desiderio di scrivere per il teatro', *Malipiero: strittura e critica*, pp. 147–8.

211 Gian Francesco Malipiero, *La Cimarosiana for Orchestra (1921)*, Orchestra della Svizzera Italiana, Christian Benda, Marco Polo 8.225118 (1997).

212 Carmelo Alberti, 'Panorami di Sentimento, di favole. Le Rappresentazioni all'aperto nei primi anni della Biennale-Teatro (1931–1941)', *Venezia Arti*, 2 (1988), pp. 115–28, and see again Isnenghi, 'Festival del Teatro', *Venezia*, pp. 460–63. As Alberti notes, open-air theatre was certainly not exclusive to Venice.

213 For the performances see Enzo Di Martini, *La Biennale di Venezia, 1895–1995, Cento anni di arte e cultura*, Giorgio Mondadori, Milan, 1995, pp. 147ff.

214 For Reinhardt's long-standing interest in the play see Erika Fischer-Lichte, 'Theatre as Festive Play: Max Reinhardt's Production of The Merchant of Venice in Venice', *Venetian Views, Venetian Blinds, English Fantasies of Venice*, ed. Manfred Pfister and Barbara Schaff, Rodopi, Amsterdam, 1999, pp. 169–80.

215 S. L. Styan, *Max Reinhardt*, Cambridge University Press, 1982, p. 61. Living close by in San Trovaso, Maria Damerini describes the rehearsals in *Gli ultimi anni del leone, Venezia 1929–1940*, preface Mario Isnenghi, Mario Isnenghi, Il Poligrafo, Padua, 1988, p. 150. Gino Damerini was the supervisor of the Festival del Teatro.

216 Damerini, *D'Annunzio e Venezia*, p. 72. In 1938 the commemorative tablet celebrating the composition of *Notturno* was put in place at the Casetta Rossa. Ibid. p. 272–3.

217 For a brief comment on the political implications see Alberti, 'Panorama di sentimento, di favole', p. 123.

218 Letter from Zorzi to Maraini, 20 May 1941, cited ibid., p. 128.

219 For a historical analysis (following the increasing input of the Fascist administration), and primary material see Francesco Bono, 'La Mostra del cinema di Venezia; nascita e sviluppo nell'anteguerra (1932–1939)', *Storia Contemporanea*, 12 (1991), pp. 513–49. Also *Twenty Years of Cinema in Venice*, edited by the management, The Venice Biennial International Exhibition of Cinematographic Art, Edizione dell'Ateneo, Rome, 1952.

220 On Volpi's presidency see Romolo Bazzoni, *60 Anni della Biennale di Venezia*, Lombroso, Venice, 1962, pp. 129–85.

221 Giandomenico Romanelli, 'La Stagione d'oro della balnearità al Lido: una funzione della "Grande Venezia"', *Lido e lidi: società, moda, architettura e cultura balneare tra passato e futuro*, Marsilio, Venice, 1989, pp. 110–17.

222 Giuseppe Qhigi, 'Il Cinema in bikini: una via Italiana', ibid., pp. 118–26.

223 Ibid.

224 Damerini, *Gli ultimi anni del leone, Venezia 1929–1940*, p. 77: 'La città era, in quel tempo, all'avanguardia in molti campi.'

225 Ibid., pp. 98–101.

226 See below, chap. 10.

227 Romano, *Giuseppe Volpi*, p. 195, and illus. in Bettagno, *Ettore Tito, 1859–1941*, Fondazione Giorgio Cini, Venice, Electa, Milan, 1998, p. 20.

228 Damerini, *Gli ultimi anni del leone, Venezia 1929–1940*, p. 78.

229 *Lido di oggi, Lido di allora: The Lido Then and Now* (August 1987), pp. 50–51.

230 Guillermo de Osma, *Mariano Fortuny: His Life and Work*, Rizzoli, New York, 1980, pp. 150–51.

231 Sergio Barizza, *Il Casino Municipale di Venezia: una storia degli anni 30*, Arsenale, Venice, 1988, pp. 10–13.

232 Ibid., p. 13.

233 See the correspondence of the minister of the interior, ibid., pp. 58ff.

234 For the renovations see Manlio Bursatin and Giuseppe Pavanello, *Il Teatro La Fenice: I progetti, l'architettura, le decorazioni*, Albrizzi, Venice, 1987, pp. 228–34.

235 Elena Bassi, *Giannantonio Selva: architetto veneziano*, L. Olschki, Florence, 1935. For Damerini's 1933 *Un Architetto veneziano dell'800. Giuseppe Jappelli* see Damerini, *D'Annunzio e Venezia*, p. 133.

236 Barizza, *Il Casino Municipale: una storia degli anni'30*, p. 18.

237 On the project see Giandomenico Romanelli, 'Il Palazzo del Cinema al Lido', *Annuario 1975, Eventi del 1974*, Biennale di Venizia, Venice, 1975, pp. 669–71.

238 For the changes to the German pavilion see Mulazanni, *I Padiglioni della Biennale a Venezia*, pp. 46–8. Torres had been responsible for some alterations to the German pavilion *circa* 1935, ibid., p. 46. Del Giudice's fire station was an exception to the Lido and Giardini siting.

239 For the tennis club see *Lido di oggi, Lido di allora* (August 1987), p. 43; the golf club, p. 51.

240 See photographs in 'Gli anni ruggenti del Lido', in Alvise Zorzi, *Venezia ritrovata, 1895–1939*, Arnoldo Mondadori, Milan, 1995, pp. 77–89.

241 See the number of photographs by Giacomelli devoted to 'Sanità e assistenza tra cerimonie e parate', in *Venezia Novecento: reale fotografia Giacomelli*, Skira, Milan, 1998, pp. 60ff.

242 There are many studies, see for example Victoria de Grazia, *The Culture of Consent: Mass Organization of Leisure in Fascist Italy*, Cambridge University Press, 1981.

243 Poster by Dudovich and Nizzoli, 1932. Gerruccio Farina, 'Colore di Mare. Immagine e propaganda del Lido di Venezia e delle Riviera di Romagna', *Lido e lidi: società, moda, architettura e cultura balneare tra passato e futuro*, pp. 90–91.

244 Ibid., p. 22.

245 Emanuela Zucchetta, *Antica ridotti veneziani*, Fratelli Palombi, Rome, 1978, pp. 96ff. Marco Dandolo had been given permission to opening a gaming house in 1639, but it was suppressed in 1774 in an endeavour to restrict public gambling. Dandolo's *ridotto* was a classic building of its type with stucco work and frescoes representing the Triumph of Bacchus and Prosperity and, in all fairness, Adverse Fortune.

246 Sergio Barizza, 'Le Sedi del museo: da Casa Correr al Fontego dei Turchi, alle Procuratie', *Una Città e il suo museo: Un secolo e mezzo di collezioni civiche veneziane*, Museo Correr, Venice, 1988, pp. 291–8.

247 Fiorella Spadavecchia, 'Nino Barbantini e il Museo d'Arte Orientale di Venezia', *Nino Barbantini a Venezia*, ed. Sileno Salvagnini and Nico Stringa, Canova, Treviso, 1995, pp. 97–107.

248 Nico Stringa, 'Notizie biografiche', ibid., p. 142.

249 Francesco Valcanover, 'Nino Barbantini e la Mostra di Tiziano del 1935', ibid., pp. 89–97.

250 Ibid., p. 90.

251 Giandomenico Romanelli and Filippo Pedrocco, *Ca' Rezzonico*, Milan, Electa, 1986.

252 Filippo Pedrocco, 'Un Museo "Ambientale": Ca' Rezzonico', *Una Città e il suo museo: un secolo e mezzo di collezioni civiche veneziane*, pp. 271–90.

253 Dorigato, 'Murano Glass Museum: The Building and the History of the Collections', *Murano Glass Museum*, pp. 7ff.

254 Maurizio Fenzo, 'Memorie pattriottiche, gli allestimenti del Museo del Risorgimento', *Una Città e il suo museo: un secolo e mezzo di collezioni civiche veneziane*, pp. 193–204.

255 Romano, *Giuseppe Volpi*, p. 196.

256 For the figures showing the increase between 1928 and 1939 see Rolf Petri, 'Strategie monopolistiche e Veneto industriale', *Venetica: rivista di storia delle veneziane*, 2 (1984), p. 7.

257 Ibid., p. 9.

258 Damerini, *Gli ultimi anni del leoni*, p. 209.

259 M. Rebershak, 'Cini, Vittorio', *Dizionario biografico degli italiani*, vol. 25, dir. Alberto M. Ghisalberto, Società Grafica Romana, Rome, 1981, pp. 626ff.

260 The allusion is to F. W. Deakin, *The Brutal Friendship: Mussolini, Hitler and the Fall of Italian Fascism*, Anchor Books, New York, 1966.

261 Hans Haacke, 'Gondola! Gondola!', in Hans Haacke, *Bodenlos*, ed. Klaus Bussmann and Florian Matzner, Biennale Venedig, 1993, Deutscher Pavilion, Edition Cantz, Stuttgart, 1993, p. 27.

262 Quoted from the *Frankfurter Zeitung* (16 June 1934), ibid., p. 28.

263 Walter Grasskamp, 'No-Man's Land', ibid., p. 62. Grasskamp's essay details Haacke's other site-responsive works.

264 On the Accademia in these years see Scirè Nepi, *Treasures of Venetian Painting: The Gallerie dell'Accademia*, pp. 19ff. For Scarpa and the Accademia specifically see Giovanna Scirè Nepi, 'The Gallerie dell'Architettura Carlo Scarpa, 1906–1978', in Francesco Dal Co and Giuseppe Mazzariol, *Carlo Scarpa, 1906–1978* (1984), Electa, Milan, 1987, pp. 154–8.

265 Gino Fogolari was director from 1906 until 1941.

266 Albertini and Gangoli, *Scarpa: musei ed esposizioni*, Jaca Book, Milan, 1992, pp. 28–9.

267 Sergio Los (a student and associate), writes about the heritage of Wright and also, generally, of Japanese architecture, in *Carlo Scarpa: An Architectural Guide*, Arsenale, Verona, 1995, pp. 23ff.

268 To run together these influences is to gloss over the critique between them, particularly in respect to the role of ornament. See here the essay by Massimo Cacciari, 'Loos and His Contemporaries', *Architecture and Nihilism: On the Philosophy of Modern Architecture*, Yale University Press, New Haven and London, 1983, pp. 101ff.

269 Note the comment of Deluigi's daughter: 'Trai I suoi compagni, Carlo Scarpa, che sara per lui l'amico di tutta la vita', in 'Maria Deluigi', *Profili veneziani del Novecento*, p. 8.

270 'Il corragio di Scarpa' is invoked by Giuseppe Mazzariol with relation to this project: 'Da Carlo Scarpa: due porte, l'ombra, la luce', *Venezia Arti*, 1 (1987), pp. 80–81.

271 Dal Co and Mazzariol, *Carlo Scarpa, 1906–1978, Le Opere*, pp. 98–103.

272 Los, *Carlo Scarpa*, pp. 24–5. Later modifications were carried out with Valeriano Pastor, 1954–6.

273 The letter is cited in Dal Co and Mazzariol *Carlo Scarpa*, pp. 279–80.

274 The other signatories were Aldo Folin, Guido Pellizar, Renato Penosto and Angelo Scattolin. Ibid.

275 Ibid., p. 279.

276 Ibid., p. 280.

277 Deboni, *Venini Glass*, p. 210.

278 Ibid., p. 211. This technique was seen at the 1936 Biennale.

279 Marina Barovier, *Carlo Scarpa: I Vetri di Murano, 1927–1947*, Il Cardo, Venice, 1991, pp. 116–23.

280 Ibid., pp. 29–36.

281 Giannantonio Paladini, 'La stagione d'oro della balnerità al Lido: una funzione della 'Grande Venezia', *Il Lido e lidi*, pp. 110–17.

282 For a plot synopsis see Robert Carringer and Barry Sabath, *Ernst Lubitsch: A Guide to References and Resources*, G. K. Hall, Boston, Mass., 1978, no. 68.

283 Clarence Brown, *Anna Karenina*, with Greta Garbo and Frederick March, Metro Godwyn Mayer, 1936.

284 The shooting script has been published in *Venezia nel cinema di Francesco Pasinetti*, Quaderni Videoteca Pasinetti, Comune di Venezia, Venice, 1997, pp. 24–84. The literary opus of P. M. Pasinetti will be discussed below. For a profile on Francesco Pasinetti see Carlo Montanaro, *Profili veneziani del Novecento*, vol. 2, pp. 48–77.

285 Francesco Pasinetti, *Storia del cinema dalle origini a oggi*, Edizioni di Bianco e Nero, Rome, 1939. It might be noted that Lang's *Die Müde Tod* and Reinhardt's *Eine venetianisches Nacht* are not included in Pasinetti's history.

286 Francesco Pasinetti, 'Venezia nel film e nella realtà', *Cinema*, 2, no. 26 (1937), pp. 50–51, republished in *L'Arte del cinematografo*, Marsilio, Venice, 1980, which brings together the film criticism, essays on Pasinetti, and his film bibliography.

287 Pasinetti, *Storia del cinema*, p. 262.

288 As it was within the Fascist film industry. For a discussion that refers to such themes as 'the myth of the Grand Hotel' see James Hay, *Popular Film Culture in Fascist Italy: The Passing of the Rex*, Indiana University Press, Bloomington and Indianapolis, 1987.

289 Giovanni Distefano and Giannantonio Paladini, *Storia di Venezia, 1797–1997*, vol. 3, *Dal monarchia alla Repubblica*, Supernova – Grafiche Biesse, Venice, 1997, p. 116, citing the migration figure from 'the years of the great migration 1931 to 1938'.

Chapter 9

1 Simone Weil, Act 1, *Venise sauvée*: 'Nous allons donc voir se lever dans quelques heures le dernier jour de cette grande Venise', *Poèmes suivis de Venise sauvée: Lettre de Paul Valèry*, Gallimard, Paris, 1986, p. 43. A rare performance, only the second, was given at the Teatro Carignano, Turin, in 1994; directed by Luca Roncini, it incorporated Weil's notes and comments on the unfinished work and made the allegorical implications plain. See Maria Nadotti, 'My City Was Gone', *Artforum*, 32 (1994), p. 11 and p. 117.

2 In Roncini's production 'Water dripped from exposed pipes over the actors' heads, then stagnated in large puddles on the floor . . . [the actors] prisoners of some malarial underground that seemed an inversion of the airy Venice canals, perhaps a prophecy on their future'. Ibid., p. 11.

3 For Violetta's speech see Weil, *Poèmes suivis de Venise sauvée*, pp. 88–9.

4 Gerhard Nebel, *Unter Partisanen und Kreuzfahrern* [Memoirs of the Campaign in Italy, 1944–1945], Ernst Klett, Stuttgart, 1950, pp. 110–14.

5 For Egidio Meneghelli and the Resistence from the University of Padua see *1943–1945: Venezia nella Resistenza Testimonianze*, ed. Giuseppe Turcato and Agostino dal Bo, Comune di Venice, Tipografia Commerciale, Venice, 1976, p. 19ff.

6 For an account of the treatment of the Jewish community see *Gli Ebrei a Venezia, 1938–1945*, ed. Renata Segre, Querini Stampalia, Venice, 1995.

7 Ibid., p. 148, and 'La Prima Deportazione', p. 151ff.

8 Umberto Dinelli, *La Guerra Partigiana nel Veneto*, Marsilio, Venice, 1976. For the period analysed politically, economically and socially see *Venezia nel Secondo Dopoguerra*, ed. Maurizio Rebershak, Poligrafo, Padua, 1993.

9 Giovanni Distefano and Giannantonio Paladini, 'La Seconda Guerra Mondiale, Venezia, l'isola come rifugio', *Storia di Venezia, 1797–1997*, vol. 3, *Dalla monarchia alla Repubblica*, Supernova-Grafiche Biesse, Venice, 1997, pp. 121ff.

10 Luigi Nono, 'Un'Autogiografia dell'autore racconta da Enzo Restagno', *Nono*, ed. Enzo Restagno, Edizioni di Torino, Turin, 1996, p. 3 and p. 7.

11 On Cine Città in September 1943 see Romolo Bazzoni, *60 Anni della Biennale di Venezia*, Lombroso, Venice, 1962, pp. 137–8, and Giuseppe Ghigi, 'Il Sogno di "Cinevillagio". Le attività produttive dal 1942 al 1952', *L'Immagine e il mito di Venezia nel cinema*, Biennale di Venezia, Venice, 1983, pp. 203–4.

12 Cesco Chinello, 'Sindacato e industria a Marghera', *Venezia nel secondo dopoguerra*, p. 77. Also Cesco Chinello, *Classe, movimento, organizzazione: le lotte operaie a Marghera/Venezia, I percorsi di una crisi, 1945–1955*, Franco Angeli, Milan, 1984.

13 See 'Un combattente democratica

Armando Gavagnin', *1943–1945: Venezia nella Resistenza*, p. 397. The '45 days' are studied in the Venetian press in M. Reberschak, 'Stampa periodica e opinione pubblica a Venezia', *Archivio Veneto*, 64 (1971), pp. 95–134.

14 Dinelli, *La guerra partigiana nel Veneto*, p. 133.

15 Distefano and Paladini, *Storia di Venezia*, vol. 3, *Dalla monarchia alla repubblica*, p. 140.

16 Moreno Guerrato, *Silvio Trentin: un democratico all'opposizione*, Vangelista, Milan, 1981, p. 9 and passim. Guerrato states that 'the figure of Silvio Trentin is among the most vigorous and fascinating of Italian antifascism', (p. 7). See Egidio Meneghetti, 'Ricordo di Trentin', *1943–1945: Venezia nella Resistenza*, pp. 39–41.

17 Distefano and Paladini, *Storia di Venezia*, vol. 3, *Dalla monarchia alla repubblica*, p. 147.

18 Ibid., p. 145.

19 Ibid., p. 146.

20 'The Battle of the Veneto', Roberto Battaglia, *The Story of the Italian Resistance*, trans. P. D. Cummins, Odhams Press, London, 1957, pp. 278–81.

21 James Morris, *Venice*, Faber & Faber, London, 1960, p. 260.

22 Raffaele de Grada notes the sculptor's range of resistance momuments beyond Venice, in *Augusto Murer*, Arti Grafiche Tamarre, Bologna, 1972. For Scarpa's contribution see Francesco Dal Co and Giuseppe Mazzariol, *Carlo Scarpa, 1906–1978*, Electa, Milan, 1989, cat. 168, p. 132. See also Sergio Los, *Carlo Scarpa*, with photographs by Klaus Frahm, Benedit & Taschen, Cologne, 1993, p. 32; and Sergio Los, *Carlo Scarpa: An Architectural Guide*, Arsenale, Verona, 1985, pp. 86–7. For drawings related to the project see *Carlo Scarpa: Selected Drawings*, GA Document 21, Tokyo, 1988, p. 65.

23 The adverse criticism, in both Hemingway's personal circle and in the literary reception of *Across the River and Into the Trees*, is covered by James R. Mellow, *Hemingway: A Life without Consequences*, Hodder & Stoughton, London, 1994, pp. 552ff.

24 Ernest Hemingway, *Across the Rivers and Into the Trees* (1950), Granada, St Albans, 1982, p. 40.

25 Ibid., p. 41.

26 Ibid.

27 Evelyn Waugh, *Brideshead Revisited: The Sacred and Profane Memories of Cap-tain Charles Ryder* (1945), Penguin, Harmondsworth, 1951.

28 Ibid., pp. 98–9.

29 See the account of its foundation by Arrigo Cipriani, *The Harry's Bar Cookbook*, Smith Gryphon, London, 1991.

30 Peggy Guggenheim, *Out of This Century: Confessions of an Art Addict*

Universe Books, New York, 1979. See also Philip Rylands, 'Peggy Guggenheim a Venezia', *Spazialismo: arte astratta Venezia, 1950–1960*, ed. Luca Massimo Barbero, Il Cardo, Venice, 1996, pp. 108–115.

31 Ibid., p. 326, and 'La Collezione Peggy Guggenheim', *XXIV Biennale di Venezia Catalogo*, Edizioni Serenissima, Venice, 1948, pp. 319–33.

32 See chap. 19, 'Palazzo Venier dei Leoni', ibid., pp. 333ff.

33 Modern artists were represented in the Ca' Pesaro collection, of course.

34 For her first meetings with Vedova and Santomaso see Guggenheim, *Out of This Century: Confessions of an Art Addict*, pp. 325–6.

35 Marcia E. Vetrocq, 'Painting and Beyond: Recovery and Regeneration, 1943–1952', *The Italian Metamorphosis, 1943–1968*, organised by Germano Celant, Solomon R. Guggenheim Museum, New York, 1994, pp. 20–31; and Franco Miracco, 'Dalle Avanguardie: storiche al Fronte Nuovo delle Arti', *Modernità allo specchio: arte a Venezia (1860–1960)*, ed. Toni Toniato, Supernova, Venice, 1995, pp. 195–209.

36 Rooms XXXIX and XL, *XXIV Biennale di Venezia Catalogo*, pp. 163–8.

37 Loretta Daminato, *Santomaso: opere, 1939–1986*, Electa, Milan, 1986. For the *Lettere a Palladio*, see the following chapter.

38 Germano Celant, *Vedova, 1935–1984*, Electa, Milan, 1984, for 1936 pen and ink drawings of Venetian churches and Vedova's own comment, 'Un pittore guidica l'architettura 1956', see pp. 48–9.

39 Vedova, 'Dal diario di un pittore partigiano', *Venezia nella Resistenza, 1943–1945*, pp. 477–82.

40 Quoted from studio notebooks, *XLVII Esposizione Internazionale d'Arte Future, Present, Past*, La Biennale di Venezia, Venice, 1997, p. 638.

41 Germano Celant, 'In Total Freedom: Italian Art, 1943–1968', *The Italian Metamorphosis, 1943–1968*, p. 5.

42 Letter to Rudy Fuchs cited in Eccher, *Emilio Vedova*, p. 79.

43 I compress and interpret Cacciari's 'Per Vedova; Dieci pensieri' (with parallel English translation) in Danilo Eccher, *Emilio Vedova*, Hopefulmonster, Turin, 1996, pp. 109–22.

44 Ibid., p. 122.

45 Miracco, 'Dalle Avanguardie Storiche al Fronte Nuove delle Arti', p. 206.

46 See the many illustrations from the period in *L'Officina del contemporaneo Venezia 50'–'60*, ed. Luca Massimo Barbaro, Charta, Milan, 1997.

47 Enzo di Martini, *La Biennale di Venezia, 1895–1995: cento anni di arte e cultura*, Giorgio Mondadori, Milan, 1995,

p. 54; Gabriella Belli, 'Nineteen-Forty-Eight and the Surrounding Years', *Venice and the Biennale: Itineraries of Taste*, Fabbri, Monza, 1995, pp. 139–43.

48 Giovanni Ponte, 'Prefazione', *XXIV Biennale di Venezia catalogo*, Five artists – Carrà, Casorati, Marini, Morandi and Semeghini – and five critics – Barbantini, Longhi, Palluchini, Ragghianti and Venturi, met in August/September 1947 and January 1948 to define the plan of the Biennale.

49 'Glorioso centenario storico del nostro risveglio politico e del nostro risorgimento civile', Ibid.

50 Vittorio Carrain, *Peggy Guggenheim and Her Friends*, ed. Virginia M. Dort, Berenice, Milan, 1994, p. 150.

51 Pallucchini had previously been responsible for major historical exhibitions in Venice, Pascale Budillon Puma, *La Biennale di Venezia dalla guerra alla crisi, 1948–1968*, Palomar, Bari, 1995, p. 29.

52 For the *Mostre storiche e speciale* see Enzo di Martini, *La Biennale di Venezia, 1895–1995: cento anni di arte e cultura*, p. 113ff.

53 Marcia E. Vetrocq gives a lucid exposition of the cultural, political and critical state of post-war Italian art in 'National Style and the Agenda for Abstract Painting in Post-War Italy', *Art History*, 12 (1989), pp. 448–71.

54 De Micheli, 'Realism and the Post-War Debate', *Italian Art in the Twentieth Century: Painting and Sculpture, 1900–1988*, ed. Emily Braun, Royal Academy of Arts, London, Presel-Verlag, Munich, 1985, p. 287.

55 Cf. *Pizzinato: l'arte come bisogno di libertà*, saggio di Giovanni Carandente, Marsilio, Venice, 1981.

56 Puma, *La Biennale di Venezia dalla guerra alla crisi, 1948–1968*; also Maurizio Calvesi, 'The Avant-Garde Biennales', *Venice and the Biennale: Itineraries of Taste*, pp. 95–102.

57 Ibid., p. 102.

58 Frances K. Pohl, 'An American in Venice: Ben Shahn and United States Foreign Policy at the 1954 Venice Biennale', *Art History*, 4 (1981), pp. 80–113.

59 Cf. Lawrence Alloway, 'The award of the prize to Robert Rauschenberg in 1964 confirmed the shift away from post-war abstract art. Inevitably it was also treated as a combat of American art against European, as well as a political drama': *The Venice Biennale, 1895–1968: From Salon to Goldfish Bowl*, Faber & Faber, London, 1969, p. 149. See the detailed discussion of the political involvement of the USA in the 1964 Biennale in Laurie J. Monahan, 'Cultural Cartography: American Designs at the 1964 Venice Biennale', *Reconstructing Modernism: Art in New York, Paris, and Montreal, 1945–1964*, MIT, Cambridge, Mass.,

1990, pp. 369–416, and Annette Michelson's sane overview, 'The 1964 Biennale', *Art International*, 8 (1964), p. 38.

60 Monahan, 'Cultural Cartography: American Designs at the 1964 Biennale', details the American 'marvel of cultural engineering' and the campaign.

61 Ibid., p. 374.

62 For the Untitled 'Venetians', *Robert Rauschenberg: a Retrospective*, ed. Walter Hopps and Susan Davidson, Guggenheim Museum New York, 1997, pp. 342–7. Note. too, Rauschenberg's 1952 photograph of gondola prows, dark water against dark wood, in a quasi-abstract composition, p. 73.

63 *BV97*. *La Biennale di Venezia. XLVI Esposizione Internazionale d'Arte*, p. 467.

64 Franco Deboni, *Venini Glass*, Umberto Allemandi & Co, Turin, 1996. In the preface, Dan Klein lists the following firms active in Murano: Seguso, Barovier & Toso, Aureliano Toso, Fratelli Toso, Barbin, Avem, Cenedese, Galliano, Ferro (p. 12). Rosa Barovier Mentasti implies the importance of the context of Spazialismo, in 'Fermenti spaziali a Murano', *Spazialismo: arte astratta Venezia, 1950–1960*, ed. Luca Massimo Barbero, Il Cardo, Venice, 1996, pp. 122–9.

65 'Fucina degli angeli', *Domus*, 326 (1957), p. 35.

66 For glassmaking in the context of Spazialismo see Rosa Barovier Mentasti, 'Fermenti Spaziali a Murano', *Spazialismo: arte astratta Venezia, 1950–1960*, pp. 122–9.

67 *Art of the Barovier: Glassmakers in Murano, 1866–1972*, ed. Marina Barovier, Arsenale, Venice, 1993, p. 124. Maurizio Cocchi, *50 Vetri di Murano del 900 Capolavori*, In. Arte, Milan, 1991, pp. 62–3.

68 Ibid., pp. 94–5.

69 Deboni, *Venini Glass*, pp. 27–8, and figs 95–6.

70 Gio Ponti, 'La Scomparsa di Paolo Venini', *Domus*, 359 (October 1959), p. 6, pp. 34–5, and Giovanni Sarpellon, 'Art, Glass and the Biennale', *Venice and the Biennale: Itineraries of Taste*, pp. 139–43.

71 Illus. ibid., p. 431, and Deboni, *Venini Glass*, fig. 170.

72 Leslie Pina, *Fifties Glass*, Schiffer, Pennyslvania, 1995, p. 10.

73 Elinor Wylie, *The Venetian Glass Nephew* (1925), Academy Chicago, Chicago, 1984.

74 For Losey's film and its Venetian setting, see chap. 10 below.

75 For *Il Festival del Teatro* see Enzo di Martino, *La Biennale di Venezia, 1895–1995: cento anni di arte e cultura*, Giorgio Mondadori, Milan, 1995, p. 147ff.

76 Raymond Fearn, *Bruno Maderna*, Harwood Academic Publishers, Chur,

1990, Appendix 11, 'Towards a Biography', p. 332.

77 For *Il Festival della Musica* see ibid., p. 151ff. Nono also worked closely with the Darmstadt school.

78 For the commission and chronology of composition from 1947 see Vera Stravinsky and Robert Craft, *Stravinsky in Pictures and Documents*, Simon & Schuster, New York, 1978, pp. 386ff.

79 Cf. Steven Stucky, *Lutoslawski and His Music*, Cambridge University Press, 1981, pp. 133–41. The work was not fully completed for the festival.

80 Wladimiro Dorigo, in his role as director of the theatre section of the Biennale, had an influence on the work in its initial stages: see 'Un'autobiografia dell'autore raccontata da Enzo Restagno', *Nono*, pp. 53–4.

81 Rodolfo Pallucchini, 'Lettera a Catherine Vivano', cited in Eccher, *Emilio Vedova*, n.p.

82 For the impact of Malipiero's historical and theatrical projects, and the explorations with Maderna in the Marciana library, see 'Un autobiografia dell'autore raccontata da Enzo Restagno', *Nono*, ed. Enzo Restagno, Edizioni di Torino, Turin, 1987, pp. 3–4.

83 'An autobiografia dell'autore raccontata da Enzo Restagno', ibid., p. 3.

84 For Malipiero's sense of Venice, 'In difesa dell'arte musicale: Venezia città polare', *Malipiero: scrittura e critica*, pp. 164–7. Nono remarks on the 'classic resonances of the School of San Marco and the Lagoon reverberating with light and the colour of the sky', Restagno, *Nono*, p. 57.

85 'Bruno Maderna and a conversation with Christoph Bitter, 31.10.1971', Fearn, *Bruno Maderna*, p. 314. For Nono's Venetian reactions see the interview Restagno, *Nono*, p. 6.

86 Luigi Nono, 'Intolleranza 1960, a detailed overview' accompanies the Teldec recording (in German) Staatsoper Stuttgart, conductor Bernhard Kontarsky, Teldec, 4509-97304-2, 1995, pp 11–24.

87 Friedrich Spangemacher, *Luigi Nono; Die elektronische Musik, Historischer Kontext – Entwicklung – Kompositionstechnik*, Gustav Bosse, Regensburg, 1983, p. 42.

88 David Osmond-Smith, 'Intolleranza', *New Grove Dictionary of Opera*, vol. 2, ed. Stanley Sadie, Macmillan, London, 1992, p. 812.

89 For an extended discussion see Luigi Pestalozza, 'Intolleranza 1960' (1960/61), in *Luigi Nono: Texte Studien zu Seiner Musik*, ed. Jürg Stenzl, Atlantis, Zurich, 1973, pp. 348–79.

90 Citing the libretto of *Intolleranza*, trans. Hugh Graham, Teldec, p. 119.

91 Nono had first approached the Czechoslovakian director Josef Svoboda

for the designs, which were censored. See Wilcox Dearn, '*Intolleranza*: Political Allegory or Multimedia Extravagance', *Theatre Survey*, 37 (1996), pp. 116–34.

92 Luigi Nono, *Canti di Vita e d'Amore: per Bastiana, Omaggio a Vedova*, CD Wergo Music of Our Century, WER 286229-2 (1993).

93 Quoted by Gianfranco Bettin, *Laguna Mondo: conversazione con Fenzo Franzin*, Edicolo, Portogruaro, 1997, p. 7.

94 Luigi Nono, *Il Canto Sospeso*, Berliner Philharmoniker, Claudio Abbado, Sony, SK53360 (1993).

95 Vedova, 'From Sketchbooks of Preparatory Drawings to The Plurimi, 1961–1965', in Eccer, *Emilio Vedova*, p. 40.

96 *XLVII Esposizione Internazionale d'Arte*, 1997, pp. 638ff.

97 Vedova, 'Technical notes on Percorso/Plurimo/Luce', Eccer, *Emilio Vedova*, pp. 186ff.

98 For a detailed account of his 'Venetian' works see Enrico Crispolti, 'Fontana versus Venezia', *Spazialismo: arte astratta Venezia, 1950–1960*, pp. 12–23.

99 For Carlo Cardazzo see *L'Officina del contemporaneo Venezia '50–'60*, pp. 114–30.

100 See the detailed monograph *Spazialismo: arte astratta Venezia, 1950–1960*, For the First and Second Manifestos of Spazialismo, signed in Milan in 1947 and 1948, and 1951 see *The Italian Metamorphosis, 1943–1968*, p. 713, p. 716.

101 Fontana signed the First and Second manifestos of Spazialismo in Milan in 1947 and 1948, Ibid.

102 Toni Toniato, 'Virgilio Guidi e la pittura veneziana del suo tempo', *Modernità allo specchio: arte a Venezia (1860–1960)*, ed. Toni Toniato, Supernova, Venice, 1995, pp. 117–47.

103 Giorgio Coventova, 'Marco de Luigi e lo Spazialismo veneziano', ibid., pp. 210–23.

104 Pierre Restany, 'A Failure in Attempted Suicide', *Domus*, 466 (September 1968), English trans., p. 54.

105 Ibid.

106 Wladimiro Dorigo, 'La contestazione delle manifestazioni artistiche e il problema della trasformazione della Biennale', *Quest'Italia: periodico di politica e di cultura*, 125–6 (1968), pp. 69ff.

107 Ibid., p. 72.

108 Ibid.

109 Ibid., p. 74.

110 Restany, 'A Failure in Attempted Suicide', p. 54.

111 *Three Coins in the Fountain*, directed Jean Gegulesco, 1954, with Clifton Webb, Dorothy McGuire, Jean Peters, Louis Jourdan, Maggie McNamara, Rossano Brazzi.

112 *Venetian Bird*, directed Ralph Thomas, Betty E. Box Productions, 1952, with Richard Todd, Eva Bartok.

113 In the book he simply falls to his death from the rooftop.

114 For a focus on the popular novel, always a telling area for study of contemporary life, Peter Sarter, *Venedigbilder: Der Venedigmythos und die zeitgenössischen Venedigbilder in der Literatur*, Materealis Verlag, Frankfurt, 1992, and Angelika Corbineau-Hoffmann, *Paradoxie der Fiction: Literarische Venedig-Bilder, 1797–1984*, Walter de Bruyter, Berlin, 1993.

115 Dennis Wheatley, *The Rape of Venice*, Hutchinson, London, 1959 (which would seem to owe something to the Victorian novelist Max Pemberton, whose *Beatrice: A Romance of the Last Days of the Venetian Republic and of Napoleon's Campaigns in Italy*, Georges Newnes, London, c.1900, traverses the same period and some of the same historical charcters).

116 Patricia Highsmith, *The Talented Mr Ripley* (1955), Vintage, New York, 1999.

117 James Hadley Chase, *Mission to Venice* (1954), Grafton, London, 1967.

118 Helen McInnes, *The Venetian Affair*, The Companion Book Club, Watford, Herts, 1963.

119 For a succinct discussion of Coburn's Venetian photographs see Mark Evans, *Impressions of Venice from Turner to Monet*, National Museum of Wales, Cardiff, Lund Humphries, London, 1992, pp. 62–6.

120 On the photographic project for James see Hugh Honour and John Fleming, *The Venetian Hours of Henry James, Whistler and Sargent*, Little, Brown & Co., Boston, Toronto and London, 1991, pp. 160–63.

121 *Citizen Kane*, directed Orson Welles, 1941, with Joseph Cotten, Everett Sloane.

122 *Othello*, directed Orson Welles, 1952, with Orson Welles, Michael Machliammoir, Suzanne Clouttie.

123 On the Circolo, Italo Zannier, *30 Anni di fotografia a Venezia: Il circolo 'La Gondola', 1948–1978*, Marsilio, Venice, 1980. For photographs in quality reproduction with brief commentary on associations and practitioners see Italo Zannier, *Sublime fotografia: una breve storia*, Corbo & Fiore, Venice, 1992, pp. 20ff.

124 Italo Zannier, *Ferruccio Leiss: fotografo a Venezia*, Electa, Milan, 1979.

125 Giovanna Grignaffini, 'Pasinetti minore', *Pasinetti: l'arte del cinematografo, articoli e saggi teorici*, ed. Ilario Ierace and Giovanni Grigraffini, Marsilio, Venice, 1980, pp. 23–5, and Miriam Botter, 'I documentari Veneziani: sceneggiature desunte e note critiche', *Venezia nel cinema di Francesco Pasinetti*, Quaderni Videoteca Pasinetti, Comune di Venezia, Venice, 1997, pp. 143–225.

126 Ibid., pp. 23–5.

127 See, in general, Cesco Chinello, *Classe, movemento, organizzazione, Le Lotte operaie a Marghera/Venezia: I percorsi di una crisi, 1945–55*, Franco Angeli, Milan, 1984.

128 The play was Arthur Laurents's *The Time of the Cuckoo*, 1952.

129 *Summertime (Summer Madness)*, directed David Lean, 1955, with Katharine Hepburn, Rossano Brazzi.

130 *Venezia, la luna e tu*, director Dino Risi, with Alberto Sordi, Marisa Allasio, Inge Schoener, 1958, Mondadori Video, Milan.

131 Mary McCarthy, *The Stones of Florence and Venice Observed* (1956), Penguin, Harmondsworth, 1974, p. 177.

132 Ibid., p. 176, p. 193.

133 Ibid., p. 219.

134 Jacob Burckhardt, *The Civilisation of the Renaissance in Italy: An Essay* (1868), Phaidon, London, 1955, pp. 100–03. Middlemore's translation dates from 1878.

135 James Morris, *Venice* (1960), Faber & Faber, London, 1974 (revised). Foreword to new edition, p. 11.

136 Ibid., p. 31. Morris has a full chapter on melancholia, see pp. 115ff.

137 Ibid.

138 Ibid., pp. 49, 39, 48.

139 Ibid., p. 113.

140 Ibid., p. 71.

141 Ibid., p. 117.

142 Ibid., p. 184.

143 Ibid., p. 204.

144 Ibid., p. 216.

145 Hugh Honour, *The Companion Guide to Venice* (1965), Fontana, London, 1970. There have been many editions. J. G. Links, the noted Canaletto scholar, published *Venice for Pleasure*, Bodley Head, London, 1966, using the route-following format, and in the same year a translation of Diego Valeri, *A Sentimental Guide to Venice*, Aldo Martello, Milan, 1966 appeared.

146 Ibid., pp. 111, 53.

147 The film reached full script stage, in collaboration with Michelangelo Antonioni, Guido Piovene and Antonio Angeli. See Gianni Rondolino, *Luchino Visconti*, Utet, Turin, 1981, p. 157ff. Visconti directed Goldoni's *Locandiera* on stage in the 1950s, ibid., pp. 383–4.

148 Dalle Vacche plays down the relevance of Boito, remarking unjustly that 'Verdi was the primary source of *Senso*. Visconti's secondary source was a minor writer, Boito . . .', Angela dalle Vacche, *The Body in the Mirror: Shapes of History in Italian Cinema*, Princeton University Press, 1992, p. 146. For the story see Camillo Boito, 'Buddha's Collar' (1883), *Senso (and other Stories)*, trans. Christine Donougher, Dedalus, Sawtry, Cambs, 1993, pp. 189–207.

149 For a discussion of the censorship see Dalle Vacche, *The Body in the Mirror: Shapes of History in Italian Cinema*, pp. 127ff. See also Nowell-Smith, *Luchino Visconti*, p. 90, and Teresa de Lauretis, 'Visconti's *Senso*, Cinema and Opera', *The Italian Metamorphosis*, pp. 450–57.

150 Dalle Vacche, *The Body in the Mirror*, pp. 144–5.

151 For the Biennale reaction see De Lauretis, 'Visconti's *Senso*: Cinema and Opera', p. 457.

152 Quoted in Giorgio Padoan, '"Senso" da Camillo Boito a Luchino Visconti', *Letteratura italiana e arti figurative III*, ed. Antonio Franceschetti, Leo S. Olschki, Florence, 1988, p. 1269. My translation.

153 For the works discussed below and Sartre's contact with Italy see Annie Cohen-Solal, *Sartre: A Life*, Heinemann, London, 1987, pp. 319ff.

154 Jean-Paul Sartre, *La Reine Albemarle ou le dernier touriste, fragments*, Gallimard, Paris, 1991. For an Italian version underlining the relevance to Venice: *l'ultimo turista, frammenti*, text established and ed. Arlette Elkaïm Sartre, Il Saggiatore, Milan, 1993.

155 Jean-Paul Sartre, 'Venice from my Window', *Verve*, 7 (1952), pp. 87–90.

156 Sartre, *La Reine Albemarle ou le dernier touriste, fragments*, p. 73.

157 Ibid., p. 8.

158 Ibid., p. 74–5.

159 For the writing see Cohan-Solal, *Sartre: A Life*, pp. 379–81.

160 Jean-Paul Sartre, 'Le Séquestre de Venise' (1957), translated as 'The Venetian Pariah', *Essays in Aesthetics*, selected and trans. by Wade Baskin, Peter Owen, London, 1964.

161 Ibid., p. 11.

162 Ibid., p. 55.

163 Ibid.

164 Sartre begins *La Reine Albemarle ou le dernier touriste, fragments*, with 'La Morte a Venezia, for it is the foreigner's over-riding perception . . .', p. 61.

165 Discussed below.

166 Sartre, *L'Ultima turistica, frammenti*, p. 103.

167 I follow A. Bonnet, 'Art Ideology, and Everyday Space: Subversive Tendencies from Dada to Postmodernism', *Environment and Planning D: Society and Space*, 10 (1992), p. 7.

168 Ralph Rumney, 'Psychogeographic Maps of Venice' (1957), *Endless Passion . . . An Endless Banquet, A Situationist Scrapbook*, ed. Iwona Blazwick in consultation with Mark Frances, Peter Wollen and Malcolm Imrie, Verso, Institute of Contemporary Art, London, 1989, pp. 45–9.

169 Ibid., p. 49.

170 Alain-Pierre Pillet, 'André Breton à Venise: Le Plaisir d'une enquête', *Du Sur-*

réalisme et du plaisir: Champs des activités surréalistes, ed. Jacqueline Chénieux-Gendrin, Librarie José Corti, Paris, 1987.

171 Ibid., p. 154.

172 Ibid., p. 259.

173 Ibid., p. 257.

174 I follow Harry Mathews and George Perec, 'Roussel and Venice. Outline of a Melancholy Geography'; *Atlas Anthology 111*, ed. Alastair Brotchie and Malcolm Green, Atlas Press, London, 1985, pp. 69–86.

175 Michel Butor, *Description de San Marco*, Gallimard, Paris, 1963. Barbara Marson discusses the alchemical reading in 'An Interpretation through Pattern and Analogy of Michel Butor's Description de San Marco', *Forum for Modern Language Studies*, 14 (1978), pp. 72–8.

176 J. Walti-Walters, 'The Architectural and Musical Influences on the Structure of Michel Butor's *Description de San Marco*', *Revue de Littérature Comparée*, 53 (1979), pp. 65–78; Bodo Guthmüller, *Libro e Basilica su description de San Marco di Michel Butor*, Centro Tedesco di Studi Veneziani, Quaderni 23, Venice, 1982.

177 H. C. Robbins Landon and John Julius Norwich, *Five Centuries of Music in Venice*, Thames & Hudson, London, 1991, p. 185. The work is composed for tenor and baritone with chorus and orchestra. CD version: Igor Stravinsky (with Poulenc Motets) *Symphony of Psalms, Cantecum Sacrum*, Christ Church Cathedral Choir, Oxford, Simon Preston conductor, notes by Veronica Slater, Decca, 430 346–2 (1991). For a sustained analysis see Eric Walter White, *Stravinsky: The Composer and His Works*, Faber & Faber, London, 1979, pp. 481–9.

178 Gian Francesco Malipiero, *Stravinsky*, Cavallino, Venice, 1945.

179 For the impact of *The Rite of Spring* see John C. G. Waterhouse, *Gian Francesco Malipiero: The Life, Times and Music of a Wayward Genius, 1882–1973*, Harwood Academic Publishers, Amsterdam, 1999, pp. 18–19.

180 Robert Craft, 'A Concert for Saint Mark', *The Score*, 18 (1956), p. 35. The analysis is valuably detailed.

181 Ibid., p. 77.

182 Eric Stein, 'Igor Stravinsky Canticum Sacrum Ad Honorem Sancti Marci Nominis', *Tempo*, 40 (1956), pp. 3–4.

183 Craft, 'A Concert for Saint Mark', p. 41.

184 Peter Porter, 'La Déportation sur la Mort d'Igor Stravinsky', *Preaching to the Converted*, Oxford University Press, London, 1972, p. 56.

185 Adrian Stokes, 'Giorgione's Tempesta', 'Venice An Aspect of Art', first published 1945, *The Critical Writings of Adrian Stokes*, vol. 2, *1937–1958*, Thames & Hudson, London, 1978. p. 129.

186 Tony Tanner considers the impact of Pound on Stokes, in particular in *The Stones of Rimini* with its opening focus on Venice and 'stone and water', *Venice Desired*, Blackwell, Oxford, 1992, pp. 316–19.

187 Cf. Stokes, 'Venice An Aspect of Art', p. 113: 'I hope I have made it clear how more precious the apertures of Venice became with the onset of the fifteenth century'.

188 Ibid., p. 93.

189 For discussion of the role of Melanie Klein's psychoanalytic theory for Stokes see Geoffrey Newman, 'Adrian Stokes and Venice', *The British Journal of Aesthetics*, 35 (1995), p. 256.

190 Klaus Theweleit, *Male Fantasies*, vol. 1, *Women, Floods, Bodies, Histories* (1977), trans. Stephen Conway, University of Minnesota, Minneapolis, 1987, p. 380, with notes to Freud, *Civilisation and its Discontents*.

191 Ibid., p. 100.

192 Ibid., p. 116.

193 For the development of Sacca Fisola see Riccardo Vianello, *Sacca Fisola: origini, storia e toponomastica*, Helvetia, Venice, 1987, pp. 17ff. For the Torres project see Valeriano Pastor, 'Progetti e costruzioni a Venezia nel Dopoguerra. Il contributo dell'esperienza Veneziana alla soluzione dei problemi della casa', *Costruire a Venezia: trent'anni di edilizia residenziale pubblica*, ed. Tullio Campostrini, Il Cardo, Venice, 1993, pp. 32–7.

194 Gianfranco Pertot, *Venezia 'restaurata': centosettanta anni di interventi di restauro sugli edifici veneziani*, Franco Angeli, Milan, 1988, p. 76.

195 Ibid., pp. 73–5. The Fenice Theatre was also freed of Meduna's interventions.

196 Ibid., pp. 82ff.

197 For the Centre, *Venti anni di attività della Fondazione Giorgio Cini*, Fondazione Giorgio Cini, Venice, 1971.

198 Paolo Maretto, *Architettura del XX Secolo in Italia: Venezia*, Vitali & Ghianda, Genoa, 1969, pp. 110–11.

199 For the Cipriano see ibid., p. 124.

200 Guilio Lorenzetti, *Venice and its Lagoon: Historical-Artistic Guide*, trans. John Guthrie, Lint, Trieste, 1975.

201 Ibid., p. 475.

202 Egle Renata Trincanato, *Venezia minore*, Esperia, Milan, 1948. See also the pocket version: *A Guide to Venetian Domestic Architecture*, ed. Renzo Salvadori, Canal Books, Venice, 1980.

203 Trincanato, *Venezia minore*, chap. 1, 'Urbanistica Veneziana', p. 35ff.

204 Ibid., p. 50.

205 Saverio Muratori, *Studi per un operante storia urbana di Venezia*, Istituto Poligrafico dello Stato, Libreria dello Stato, Rome, 1960.

206 Ibid., 'La città del X secolo', p. 19.

207 Ibid., 'Sviluppi tecnici del Gotico'; 'Caratteri estetici del Gotico', p. 25.

208 Manfredo Tafuri, *History of Italian Architecture, 1944–1985* (1982), trans. Jessica Levine, MIT Press, Cambridge, Mass., 1989, p. 60.

209 *The School of Venice, Architectural Design*, 55 (1985); Luciano Semerani, 'La Scuola di Venezia', *Progetti per la città di veneta, 1926–1981*, Comune di Vicenza, Teatro Olimpico, 1982, pp. 11–19; chap. 7, 'The School of Venice', *Theorizing a New Agenda for Architecture: An Anthology of Architectural Theory, 1965–1995*, ed. Kate Nesbitt, Princeton Architectural Press, New York, 1996, pp. 338–68.

210 Bruno Zevi, in *Giuseppe Samonà, 1923–1975: cinquant'anni di architettura*, Officina, Rome, 1975, p. 150.

211 Luciano Semerani, 'Why not?', *The School of Venice, Architectural Design*, p. 4.

212 Manfredo Tafuri considered the appointment of Samonà and his choice of staff in this way: 'Giuseppe Samonà brought to Venice a few of the liveliest protagonists of the Italian debate: Zevi, Albini, Gardella, Giancarlo De Carlo, Belgiojosa, Scarpa, Luigi Piccinato and Giovanni Astengo. These men helped turn Samonà's school into a stronghold of progressive activity.' *History of Italian Architecture, 1944–1985*, trans. Jessica Levine, MIT Press, Cambridge, Mass., and London, 1990, p. 22.

213 Biographies and bibliographies of this architects appear in *Progetti per la città veneta, 1926–1981*.

214 Semerani, 'Why not?', *The School of Venice*, p. 5.

215 Vittorio Gregotti, 'Reconstructing a History', *The Italian Metamorphosis*, p. 561.

216 Francesco Tentori, *Imparare da Venezia: Il ruolo futuribile di alcuni progetti architettonici veneziani dei primi anni '60*, Officina, Rome, 1994, an important study for staking the continuity of the 1960s with the 1990s.

217 Ibid., and Leonardo Fiori, 'Il corso estivo del Ciam a Venezia', *Domus*, 276/77 (December 1952), pp. 31–2. For the text see *L'Officina del contemporaneo Venezia '50–'60*, pp. 240–43.

218 Giuseppe Samonà, 'Per un Piano Regolatore di Venezia', *Urbanistica*, 26 (1955), pp. 71–80.

219 Ibid., p. 72, which calls for 'excursions into every zone of the city'.

220 Ibid., p. 77.

221 Tentori in *Giuseppe Samonà*, p. 155.

222 Manfredo Tafuri, *Theories and History of Architecture* (1976), trans. Giorgio Verrechia, Granada, Norwich, 1980, p. 59.

223 Donatella Calabi, 'Venezia: Il piano della sua periferia in Terraferma, 1934–1959', *Costruire a Venezia: trent'anni di edilizia residenziale pubblica*, ed. Tullio Campostrini, Il Cardo, Venice, 1993, p. 70. See also Giorgio Ciucci, 'Progetti per quartieri residenziali in terraferma. Il Quartiere San Giuliano, il Concorso del Quartiere CEP alle Barene di San Giuliano, il Quartiere CEP di Campalto', ibid., pp. 107–26. Samonà has written on the subject: 'Nuovo unità residenziale a Marghera–Mestre', *Urbanistica*, 7 (1951); and 'Problemi urbanistici sul Quartiere di San Giuliano', *Casabella-Continuatà*, 218 (1968).

224 See the report of the jury: 'Concorso internazionale per il Piano Particolareggiato della nuova Sacca del Tronchetto', *Urbanistica*, 42–3 (1965), pp. 101–10. The jury results were also published in *Casabella*, together with Aldo Rossi's critical essay, 'Considerazioni sul Concorso', *Casabella*, 293 (1964), pp. 2–17. Tentori uses the Tronchetto as one of his focal examples in *Imparare da Venezia*, pp. 143–6 and passim.

225 Rossi, 'Considerazioni sul Concorso', pp. 2ff.

226 Ignazio Gardella, exhibition and catalogue curated by Fabio Nonis, Sergio Boidi, Harvard University Graduate School of Design, Electa, Milan, 1986, pp. 54–9. Gardella's practice was largely in Milan: for his career see *Progetti per la città veneta*, pp. 57–60.

227 Cf. Tafuri: 'the languages are there, already configured: what is left is to play at their edges, to slightly erode them, to test their resistance', quoted in *Casabella: il progetto storico di Manfredo Tafuri/The Historical Project of Manfredo Tafuri*, 619–20 (1995), p. 85.

228 Gardella, cited *Ignazio Gardella*, p. 14.

229 'La Nuova Sede', *Casabella*, 244 (October 1960), pp. 4–13.

230 Manfredo Tafuri, *History of Italian Architecture, 1944–1985*, p. 66.

231 See chap. 6, 'Two "Masters": Carlo Scarpa and Giuseppe Samonà', ibid., pp. 111–16.

232 Ibid., p. 112.

233 On this point see Ellen Soroka, 'Restauro in Venezia', *Journal of Architectural Education*, 47 (1994), p. 224 and n. 5, p. 239. (In general an important article discussing the history of restoration back to the nineteenth century and Viollet-le-Duc, Ruskin and Boito in relation to Scarpa and his intervention in old buildings.)

234 Marco Frascari, 'The Tell-the-Tale Detail', *Theorizing a New Agenda for Architectural Theory: An Anthology of Architectural Theory, 1965–1995*, p. 506.

235 See the photographs by Klaus Frahm in Sergio Los, *Carlo Scarpa*, Benedikt Taschen, Cologne, 1993. For contemporary photographs see 'Il nuovo negozio Olivetti a Venezia', *Domus*, 362 (1960), pp. 9–14.

236 Bianca Albertini and Sandro Bagnoli, *Scarpa: musei ed esposizioni*, Jaca Book, Milan, 1992. See also Giovanna Scirè Nepi, 'The Gallerie dell'Accademia', *Carlo Scarpa: The Complete Works*, pp. 154–7.

237 For the Biennale installations and special exhibitions see Albertini and Bagnoli, *Scarpa: musei ed esposizione*, chap. 7, 'La Biennale', pp. 186–92 (including the Venezuelan pavilion), pp. 196–7 (Mostra del Palazzo Ducale), and photographs pp. 201ff. For the Correr see pp. 29–31, 35–8, figs 58–62, 70, 91, 116–26. For the Accademia see pp. 28–9, 34–5, 93–104, figs 27–8, 47–58.

238 For these installations and Biennale buildings see *Carlo Scarpa: The Complete Works*, pp. 11ff.

239 The pavilion was destroyed by fire in the 1980s.

240 Marco Mulazzani, *I Padiglioni della Biennale a Venezia*, Electa, Milan, 1996, pp. 94–100.

241 For Hoffmann's pavilion, ibid., pp. 86–8.

242 Rob Docter, *The Most Beautiful Space I Know: The Netherlands Biennale Pavilion in Venice by Gerrit Rietveld*, Uitgeverij 010 Publishers, Rotterdam, 1995.

243 Giorgio Busello, 'Mazzariol alla Querini', *Giuseppe Mazzariol 50 artisti a Venezia*, ed. Chiara Bertola, Electa, Milan, 1992, pp. 15–22.

244 Paolo Costa, 'Asterischi d'outsider', ibid., pp. 23–4; Vincenza Fontana, 'L'Università Internazionale dell'Arte', pp. 27–9.

245 Massimo Cacciari, 'Mazzariol "magister venetianitatis"', ibid., pp. 53–5.

246 Los, *Carlo Scarpa*, p. 104.

247 See the photographs in Giuseppe Mazzariol, 'Un'Opera di Carlo Scarpa; Il riordino di un antico palazzo veneziano', *Zodiac*, 13 (1964), pp. 26–9.

248 'Varcato il ponte – che rappresenta senza alcun dubbio il più leggero e rapido arco di conguinzione che sia stato realizzato a Venezia negli ultimi secoli . . .', ibid., p. 40.

249 Ibid.

250 Ibid., p. 27.

251 Soroko, 'Restauro in Venezia', pp. 225ff, and for the specific restoration project for the building see pp. 229ff.

252 On the doorway see Giuseppe Mazzariol, 'Da Carlo Scarpa: due porte, l'ombre, la luce', *Venezia Arti*, 1 (1987), pp. 73–81, which also treats the entrance to San Sebastiano for the Facoltà di Lettere e Filosofia di Venezia.

253 Tafuri, *History of Italian Architecture*, p. 112.

254 Ibid., p. 51.

255 Ibid. Scarpa is compared with Albini and 'the quiet murmur of [his] apodictic signs', in 'Aufklärung II: The Museum, History and Metaphor (1951–1967)', ibid.

256 Ibid., p. 112

257 Dal Co and Mazzariol, *Carlo Scarpa: The Complete Works*, p. 20.

258 Ibid., p. 13.

259 Ibid., p. 69.

260 Ibid., p. 90.

261 Arata Isozaki, 'L'ultimo sogno', ibid., p. 220.

262 Luisi Querci della Rovere, 'Tre progetti per Venezia rifiutati: Wright, Le Corbusier, Kahn', *Le Venezie possibili: da Palladio a Le Corbusier*, pp. 270–71.

263 Rovere, 'Il Masieri Memorial di Frank Lloyd Wright', ibid., pp. 272–5.

264 Quoted in *L'Officina del contemporaneo: Venezia '50–'60*, p. 238.

265 Duilio Torres, 'Secessione, Liberty e architetti italiani dell'epoca', *Rivista di Ingegneria* (December 1956), pp. 2–18. For the Emil Bach house see p. 10, fig. 30.

266 Ibid.

267 Sergio Bettini, 'Venice and Wright', *Metron-architettura: Frank Lloyd Wright: Masieri Memorial, Venezia*, n. 49–59, 1969, p. 29.

268 Giuseppe Samonà, 'Ricordo di Masieri', p. 30.

269 Ibid.

270 Initially the plan was rejected by the Commissione Igienico-Edilizia del Comune di Venezia (16 April 1954) and the same board augmented on 21 April 1954, confirming objects against irregularities. It went before the Consiglio Comunale on 2 July 1954: Rovere, 'Il Masieri Memorial di Frank Lloyd Wright', pp. 272–4.

271 A succinct account of the long negotiations is given in Sergio Los, *Carlo Scarpa: An Architectural Guide*, pp. 96–9.

272 There is an extensive literature. For a succinct account see Luisa Querci della Robera, 'L'ospedale di Le Corbusier a San Giobbe', *Le Venezie possibili: da Palladio a Le Corbusier*, ed. Lionello Puppi and Giandomenico Romanelli, Electa, Milan, 1985, pp. 229–85. For a coverage fully illustrated with the plans and models see Wolfram Fuchs, Robert Wisher, *Le Corbusiers Krankenhausprojekt für Venedig*, Dietrich Reimer Verlag, Berlin, 1985.

273 Valeriano Pastor, 'Per un'etica dell'architettura', *Giuseppe Mazzariol 50 artisti a Venezia*, pp. 57–67.

274 Pietro Zampetti, *Il problema di Venezia*, Sansoni, Florence 1976 pp. 87–9.

275 Ibid.

276 Agnoldomenico Pica, 'Il progetto di Le Corbusier per l'ospedale di Venezia', *Domus*, 427 (1965), p. 7.

277 Ibid.

278 Manfredo Tafuri, *Theories and History of Architecture*, Granada, London, 1980, p. 61. Jélène Lipstadt and Harvey Mendelsohn read Le Corbusier as central to Tafuri's thought, particularly in *Theories and History of Architecture*, in 'Philosophy, History, and Autobiography: Manfredo Tafuri and the 'Unsurpassed Lesson' of Le Corbusier', *Assemblage*, 22 (1994), pp. 58–103.

279 David B. Brownlee and David G. De Long, *Louis I. Kahn: In the Realm of Architecture*, Museum of Contemporary Art, Los Angeles, Rizzoli, New York, 1991, p. 405. The account of the project draws upon the Kahn archive.

280 Ibid.

281 Giuseppe Mazzariol, 'Un progetto per Venezia', *Lotus*, 6 (1969). Also Luisa Querci della Rovere, 'Il Palazzo dei Congressi di Louis Kahn ai Giardini', *Le Venezie possibili: da Palladio a Le Corbusier*, pp. 286–91.

282 Kahn's descriptions are cited from the Mazzariol essay, 'Un progetto per Venezia'.

283 Quoted in *Officina del contemporaneo Venezia '50–'60*, p. 245.

284 Brownlee, *Louis I. Kahn: In the Realm of Architecture*, p. 406.

285 Ibid., p. 406.

286 *Officina del contemporaneo Venezia '50–'60*, p. 245.

287 Mazzariol, 'Un progetto per Venezia', pp. 114–15.

288 Marcia Gabriella Diri, 'La Società veneziana', Reberschak, *Venezia nel Secondo Dopoguerra*, p. 26.

289 Ibid.

290 The Gritti publicity flaunts its Libro d'Oro, with distinguished guests from Somerset Maugham and Ernest Hemingway onwards, and, retrospectively, Ruskin's residence at the palace when it was the Casa Wetzlar.

291 Similar blandness marks Marino Meo's construction of the Palazzetto Foscari on the Grand Canal.

292 For the Cipriani see the work of Del Guidice and Meo between 1956 and 1958, Paolo Maretto, *Architettura del XX Secolo in Italia Venezia*, Vitali & Ghianda, Genoa, 1969, p. 124. In 1976 the Cipriani was acquired by the American-born shipping magnate, James B. Sherwood. For the association with the Orient Express, see Shirley Sherwood, *Venice Simplon–Orient Express: The World's Most Celebrated Train*, Weidenfeld & Nicolson, London, fourth rev. ed. 1996.

293 Carlo Uberti, 'Il Ponte Ferroviario e la Stazione', *Le Venezie possibili: da Palladio a Le Corbusier*, pp. 228–37.

294 Eugenio Miozzi, *Venezia nei secoli: la città*, 2 vols, Libeccio, Venice, 1959.

295 Prefazione, vol. 1, n.p.

296 *UNESCO Rapporto su Venezia*,

Edizioni Scientifiche e Techniche, Mondadori, Milan, 1969.

297 Ibid., pp. 205ff.

298 Ibid., p. 122.

299 Peggy Guggenheim, *Out of This Century: Confessions of an Art Addict*, Universe Books, New York, 1979, p. 379.

Chapter 10

1 My account is based on Giulio Obici, *Venezia fino a quando?*, Preface by Teresa Foscari Foscolo, historical notes by Cesare de Michelis, Marsilio, Padua, 1967; Roberto Bianchin, *Acqua granda: Il romanzo dell'alluvione*, photographs by Gianfranco Taglia-pietra, Filippi, Venice, 1996, and the commemorative edition of *Il Gazzettino*, 'Trent'anni fa la Grande Paura' (3 November 1996). For a politically oriented account which follows the chronology of relevant publications see Luigi Scano, *Venezia: terra e acqua*, Edizioni delle Autonomie, Rome, 1985, 'La Contestazione', pp. 137ff. For a document covering various aspects of legislation and projections see Agenzia ANSA, *Venice, 1966–1996: Thirty Years of Protection as Covered by the Press*, Rome, 1996, distributed by Consorzio Venezia Nuova.

2 Michel Tournier, *Gemini*, trans. Anne Carter, Editions Gallimard, 1975, Minerva, London, 1989.

3 Ibid., p. 329.

4 Ibid.

5 See Sandro Meccoli, *La Battaglia per Venezia*, preface by Bruno Visentini, Sugaro, Milan, 1977. 'Il Corriere rivela i resultati di Supino: il canale dei petroli aumenta le acque alte' (December 1969), pp. 52–4.

6 Giannandrea Mencini, *Venezia acqua e fuoco: la politica dell'Salvaguardia' dall'alluvione del 1966 al rogo della Fenice*, Il Cardo, Venice, 1996, chap. 1, 'Dalla catastrofe alla salvaguardia: L'alluvione e la prima Legge Speciale (1966–1973)', pp. 3–21, for the background this important volume is retrospective, written thirty years after the flood. For Anna Maria Volpi's intervention, pp. 8–9.

7 'Dialogo con Vittorio Cini', November 1966, Meccoli, *La Battaglia per Venezia*, pp. 55–7.

8 Mencini, *Venezia acqua e fuoco*, p. 7.

9 Ibid., p. 10, and 'A Problem of "preeminent national interest"', *Venice, 1966–1996: Thirty Years of Protection as Covered by the Press*, pp. 23–34.

10 For Marghera's expansion in these years see Cesco Chinello, *Storia di uno sviluppo capitalistico: Porto Marghera e Venezia, 1951–1973*, Editori Riuniti, Rome, 1975.

11 Meccoli, 'Al cinema Rossini

Montanelli presenta il suo documentario e propone per Venezia un'alta autorità', (December 1969), *La Battaglia per Venezia*, pp. 55–7.

12 Mencini, *Venezia acqua e fuoco*, p. 16.

13 Nantas Salvalaggio, *Il Campiello sommerso* (1974), Biblioteca Universale Rizzoli, Milan, 1983.

14 The Goldoni lines preface the last chapter: 'Chi si passi la notte in festa, in brio; Poi diremo diman: Venezia, addio', p. 173.

15 See Meccoli, 'Gian Francesco Malipiero', *La Battaglia per Venezia*, pp. 125ff.

16 G. Francesco Malipiero, *Uno dei Dieci*, Ricordi, Milan, 1972. Performed Teatro dei Rinnuovati, Siena, 28 August 1971.

17 John C. G. Waterhouse notes that 'in Italy it has beome almost a commonplace to identify the opera's protagonist ... with Malipiero himself', *Gian Francesco Malipiero: The Life, Times and Music of a Wayward Genius, 1882–1973*, Harwood Academic Publishers, Amsterdam, 1999, p. 369. He includes a photograph taken in Vienna in 1932 that shows Werfel with Malipiero, Alfredo Casella and Alban Berg (no pagination).

18 Malipiero, *Uno dei Dieci*, pp. 24–5.

19 Wladimiro Dorigo, *Una Legge contro Venezia: natura storia interessi nella questione della città e della laguna*, Officina, Rome, 1973.

20 Wladimiro Dorigo, *Venezia origini: fondamenti, ipostesi, metodi*, Electa, Milan, 1983. For Dorigo's involvement with government see Lesco Chinello, *Forze politiche e sviluppo capitalistico: Porto Marghera e Venezia, 1951–1973*, Riuniti, Rome, 1975, pp. 39–43, and Scano, *Venezia: terra e acqua*, pp. 87ff. for Dorigo's involvement with draft planning from 1954 to 1957.

21 On the confrontation between Dorigo and Italia Nostra see Meccoli, *La Battaglia di Venezia*, pp. 73–7.

22 Wladimiro Dorigo, 'La Salvezza di Venezia: mito e realtà', *Humanitas*, 6 (1961), pp. 886–916, which followed urban shifts form the Piano Regolatore of 1891, to Marghera, to the plan of 1939.

23 Wladimiro Dorigo, 'Marghera e Venezia: appunti per una demistificazione', *Casabella*, 349 (1979), pp. 22–9; 'Venezia perde i Veneziani'; *Casabella*, n. 350–51 (1970), pp. 58–66; 'Alternative per Venezia?', *Casabella*, n. 352 (1970), pp. 20–27.

24 Cf. Indro Montanelli, Giuseppe Samonà and Francesco Valcanover, *Venezia caduta e salvezza*, photographic text by Aldo Durazzi, Sansoni, Florence, 1972.

25 Dorigo, *Una Legge contro Venezia*, p. 19.

26 Ibid., p. 23.

27 Ibid., p. 50: 'Questa città antica e ancora, relativamente, una città completa, anche se non è più una città autosufficiente.'

28 'I settant'anni di depressione fra Bonaparte e l'Austria', ibid., p. 55.

29 'I miti ottocenteschi', ibid., p. 57.

30 'Contro la Terraferma', ibid., p. 61

31 On the *querelle* 'città-industria o città-museo', ibid., p. 73.

32 Eugenio Miozzi, *Venezia nei secoli*, vols 3 and 4, Libeccio, Venice, 1969. Miozzi's volumes should be considered as a response to the floods of the 1960s.

33 Dorigo, *Una Legge contro Venezia*, p. 89.

34 Exodus from Venice is the matter of chap. 3, 'La communità veneziana fra esodo e risanamento', ibid., pp. 89–100.

35 Ibid., p. 95. For further discussion of depopulation and its relation to housing see *Materiali Veneti 4: abitare a Venezia: esodo e sfratti*, 1976. Chinello discusses the 'esodo' further in the appendix, 'Brevi cenni critici sulla 'Legge Speciale' per Venezia', *Storia di uno sviluppo capitalistico: Porto Marghera e Venezia*, pp. 282–91.

36 Quoted from the English synopsis, Dorigo, 'Venezia perde i Veneziani', p. 59.

37 Dorigo, 'La Questione idraulica lagunare', *Una Legge contro Venezia*, p. 232.

38 'Caratteri recenti e antichi della subsidenza', ibid., p. 241.

39 Quoted from the English synopsis, Dorigo, 'Venezia perde i Veneziani', p. 59.

40 Dorigo, *Una Legge contro Venezia*, p. 408.

41 Ibid., p. 409.

42 Ibid., p. 413.

43 Ibid., p. 414.

44 'La legge . . .', ibid., p. 423.

45 Ibid., p. 443.

46 Ibid., p. 475.

47 Ibid., p. 478.

48 The case against Dorigo in 1969 is reported in Meccoli, *La Battaglia per Venezia*, pp. 73–7.

49 Stephen Fay and Philip Knightley, *The Death of Venice*, André Deutsch, London, 1976.

50 UNESCO *Rapporto su Venezia*, ed. Edgardo Marcouni, preface René Maheu, Mondadori, Milan, 1969. The relationship of Venice and UNESCO is a complex one. Compare, for example, the conflicting programmes of Leonardo Benevolo and UNESCO, the city council and Edoardo Salzano, and Prof. Giovanni Astengo with relation to the housing, restoration and the cost/rent ration in the 1970s as discussed in Luigi Bussadori, 'Venezia: piano particolareggiata. I termini della contesta', *Casabella*, 419 (1976), pp. 34–5.

51 Ibid., p. 99.

52 Ibid., chap. 9, 'The International Crusade', pp. 107ff.

53 The international restoration programmes from 1965 to 1983 are itemised in Gianfranco Pertot, *Venezia 'restaurata': centosettanta anni di interventi di restauro sugli edifici veneziani*, Franco Angeli, Milan, 1988, pp. 140–46. See also, *Twenty Years of Restoration in Venice*, Soprintendenza di Ben Ambientali e Architettonici di Venezia, Venice, 1986.

54 Mario dalla Costa, 'Il recupero del patrimonio architettonico ed edilizio veneziano oggi', *Storia Architettura*, 62 (1983), pp. 77–88.

55 *Difesa di Venezia: contributi per una azione di conoscenza e di difesa di Venezia e della sua Laguna di: Italia Nostra, Renato Padoan, Francesco Valcanover, Anna Maria Cicogna Volpi, Giorgio Bellavitis, Mario Rinaldo, Nani Valle, Antonio Casellati*, ed. Giorgio Bellavitis, Centro Culturale Pirelli, Milan, Alfieri, Venice, 1970.

56 Italo Zannier, *Sublime fotografia Il Veneto: una breve storia*, Corbo e Fiore, Venice, 1992, pp. 21, 79.

57 Ibid., p. 37.

58 Indro Montanelli, Giuseppe Samonà and Francesco Valcanover, *Venezia caduta e salvezza*, photographs by Aldo Durazzi, Sansoni, Florence, 1972.

59 Ibid., p. 21.

60 *The Architectural Review*, 169 (1971).

61 John Gaitanakis, 'Housing Study', ibid., pp. 275–80; Egle Renata Trincanato, 'The Humble Venetian House', ibid., pp. 285–92.

62 James Morris, prologue, ibid., p. 259.

63 Eugenio Trizio, *L'Ultima città*, Vallecchi, Florence, 1978.

64 Italo Calvino, *La Città invisibili*, Einaudi, Turin 1972, trans. William Weaver, as *Invisible Cities*, Picador, London, 1974.

65 Ibid., p. 13.

66 Ibid., pp. 14, 44.

67 Ibid.

68 Ibid., p. 68.

69 Italo Calvino, 'Ich glaube an das Venedig der Zukunft', *Merian*, 27 (1974); pp. 87–90; 'Venezia: archetipo e utopia della città aquatica', *Italo Calvino: saggi, 1945–1985*, vol. 2, Arnoldo Mondadori, Milan, 1995, pp. 2688–92.

70 Aldo Palazzeschi, *Il Doge* (1967), ed. Marco Marchi con un scritto di Luciano de Maria, Arnaldo Mondadori, Milan, 1994.

71 Ibid., p. 51 (my translation).

72 For a profile written at the time of the television series based on the novel *Rosso Veneziano* see Meccoli, *La Battaglia per Venezia*, pp. 131–5.

73 The early sequence of the novels as written, though not as published: *Red Venetian* (*Rosso veneziano* published in 1959, first in English), *La Confusione* (1964) with revised title *Il Sorriso del leone*, *Il Ponte dell'Accademia*, 1968.

74 P. M. Pasinetti, *From the Academy Bridge*, Random House, New York, 1970 (*Il Ponte dell'Accademia*, Bompiani, Milan, 1968), p. 290.

75 P. M. Pasinetti, *The Smile on the Face of the Lion*, Random House, New York, 1965 (*La Confusione*, Bompiani, Milan, 1964), pp. 114, 190.

76 Ibid., p. 331.

77 Ibid., p. 339.

78 P. M. Pasinetti, *Melodramma*, Marsilio, Venice, 1993.

79 Pier Maria Pasinetti, 'Historical Events as Structuring Elements in Non-Historical Novels', *Yearbook of Italian Studies* (1973–5), pp. 161–82.

80 Cited in Cristina della Coletta, 'Historiographic metafiction: P. M. Pasinetti's *Melodramma*', *Quaderni d'Italianistica*, 15 (1994), pp. 121–36. The article offers an analysis of the ideological frames within *Melodramma*.

81 Ibid., p. 182.

82 Pasinetti, 'Historical Events as Structuring Elements in Non-Historical Novels', p. 180.

83 Ibid., p. 181.

84 Ibid.

85 Giuseppe Santomaso, *Lettere a Palladio*, curated Fred Licht, Peggy Guggenheim Collection, Venice (December 1992–March 1993).

86 Manfredo Tafuri, 'L'Ephemere est eternel: Aldo Rossi a Venezia', *Domus*, 602 (1980), p. 7.

87 Luigi Nono, *Como una ola de fuerza y luz . . . sofferte onde serene . . . Contrappunto dialettico alla mente*, Nino Antonellini, director, *sofferte onde serene* played by Maurizio Pollini, essay by Doris Döpke, Deutsche Grammophon, 423 248–2 (1988).

88 Cited without source by Doris Döpke, ibid., p. 5.

89 See the catalogue published for the commemorative exhibition after Pratt's death: Hugo Pratt, *Viaggiatore incantato*, Electa, Milan, 1996, and for an account of his life see Piero Zanotto, 'Hugo Pratt', *Profili veneziani del Novecento 1*, ed. Giovanni Distefano and Leopoldo Pietragnoli, Supernova, Venice, 1999, pp. 60ff. See also, *World Encyclopedia of Comics*, vol. 2, ed. Maurice Horn, Chelsea House, New York, p. 564.

90 For Maltese's life history and his other travels see *Corto Maltese memorie*, Rizzoli, Milan, 1989.

91 Hugo Pratt, *Fable de Venise (SIRAT al BUNDUQYYIATT)*, Casterman, Tournai, 1981.

92 Hugo Pratt, *The Celts* (1975), Harvill Press, London, 1996.

93 *Don't Look Now*, Director Nicholas Roeg, with Julie Christie and Donald Sutherland, Casey Productions, London, Eldorado Films, Rome, 1973. See the monograph: Mark Sanderson, *Don't Look Now*, BFI Modern Film Classics, British Film Institute, London, 1996.

94 Sabine Schülting is especially attentive to the 'crystalline regime' of the film in her treatment of 'A Cinema of the Seer', in 'Dream Factories: Hollywood and Venice in Nicolas Roeg's *Don't Look Now*', *Venetian Views, Venetian Blinds: English Fantasies of Venice*, ed. Manfred Pfister and Barbara Schaff, Rodopi, Amsterdam, 1999, pp. 203ff.

95 As Mark Sanderson remarks, 'If [Roeg's] masterpiece does chill the blood, it also warms the heart in its anatomy of love and loss'. Ibid., p. 15.

96 Daphne du Maurier, *Don't Look Now and Other Stories* (1970), Penguin, Harmondsworth, 1973, p. 26. For a Venice-based interpretation of the story, Virginia Richter, 'Tourists Lost in Venice: Daphne du Maurier's "Don't Look Now" and Ian McEwan's *The Comfort of Strangers*', *Venetian Views, Venetian Blinds: English Fantasies of Venice*, pp. 181–94.

97 Quoted, Sanderson, *Don't Look Now*, p. 28.

98 As Donald Sutherland himself remarked of the final convulsive scene, 'dying began to feel almost like a sexual rite', ibid., p. 31.

99 *Anonimo veneziano*, directed by Enrico Maria Salerno, with Florinda Bolkan and Tony Musante, 1970. On Berto's considerable activity in cinema see Mino Giarda, 'Giuseppe Berto e il cinema', *Giuseppe Berto: la sua opera, il suo tempo*, ed. Ebardo Artico and Laura Lepri, Marsilio, Leo S. Olschki, Venice, 1989, pp. 269–71.

100 Giuseppe Berto, *Anonimo veneziano*, Rizzoli, Milan, 1976, p. 107.

101 Ibid., p. 117.

102 *Death in Venice*, directed by Luchino Visconti, with Dirk Bogarde, Mark Burns, Bjorn Andresen, Marisa Berenson, Silvana Mangano, 1971.

103 See Sandro Naglia, *Mann, Mahler, Visconti: 'Morte a Venezia'*, Tracce, Pescara, 1995, and the discussion of the music by Henry Bacon, *Visconti: Explorations of Beauty and Decay*, Cambridge University Press, 1998, pp. 165ff.

104 For observations on the relationship of the film to the novel and departures from it see John France Fetier, 'Visconti's Cinematic Version of *Death in Venice*', *Approaches to Teaching Mann's 'Death in Venice' and other Short Fiction*, ed. Jeffrey B. Berlin, The Modern Language Association of America, New York, 1992, pp. 146–52.

105 Cf. Carolyn Galerstein, 'Images of Decadence in Visconti's *Death in Venice*', *Literary Film Quarterly*, 34 (1985), pp. 29–34.

106 Benjamin Britten, *Death in Venice*, in two acts, libretto by Myfanwy Piper after the story by Thomas Mann. First performance 1973. There are many accounts drawing connections between Thomas Mann, Britten and Visconti: Christopher Palmer, 'Towards a Genealogy of *Death in Venice*', *The Britten Companion*, ed. Christopher Palmer, Faber & Faber, London, 1984, pp. 250–67'; Roger Hillman, 'Deaths in Venice', *European Studies*, 12 (1992), pp. 291–311.

107 Donald Mitchell beautifully contextualises *Death in Venice* in Britten's larger oeuvre, referring to the church parables and the choral dances in *Gloriana*, etc., '*Death in Venice*: The Dark Side of Reflection', *The Britten Companion*, pp. 238–49.

108 For example Daniel Fischlin in the over-entitled '"Eros is in the Word": Music, Homoerotic Desire, and the Psychopathologies of Fascism, or the "Strangely Fruitful Intercourse" of Thomas Mann and Benjamin Britten', *The Work of Opera: Genre, Nationhood, and Sexual Difference*, ed. Richard Dellamora and Daniel Fischlin, Columbia University Press, New York, 1997, pp. 209–33.

109 Mitchell, 'Death in Venice, The Dark Side of Reflection', p. 244.

110 Kluge, 'Mass Death in Venice', p. 63.

111 Alexander Kluge, 'Mass Death in Venice', trans. Jeffrey S. Librett, *New German Critique*, 30 (Fall 1983), pp. 61–3. See also the essay following, which takes the form of an ironical academic investigation of the co-ordinates at work in Kluge's story: Rainer Stollman, 'Reading Kluge's Mass Death in Venice', ibid., pp. 65–95.

112 Ibid., p. 61.

113 Stollman, 'Reading Kluge's Mass Death in Venice', p. 67, details co-ordinate events, but does not mention the flood.

114 Semerani, 'Why Not?', *The School of Venice: Architectural Design*, 55, 5/6 (1985), guest-edited Luciano Semerani, p. 10.

115 Aldo Rossi, 'What is to be done with Old Cities', ibid., pp. 19ff.

116 Ibid., p. 19.

117 Ibid., p. 22.

118 Ibid., p. 23.

119 Aldo Rossi, *The Architecture of the City* (1966), introduction Peter Eisenman, trans. Diane Ghirardo and Joan Ockman, MIT Press, Cambridge, Mass., and London, 1982, pp. 21, 33.

120 Ibid., p. 168, and 'An Analogical Architecture', *Theorizing a New Agenda for Architecture*, pp. 348–52.

121 Rossi, *The Architecture of the City*, p. 168.

122 Rossi, 'Caratteri urbani delle città Venete', *Progetti per la città veneta, 1926–1981*, Neri Pozza, Vicenza, 1982, pp. 102–10. As Peter Eisenman has written in 'The House of the Dead as the City of Survival', *Aldo Rossi in America; 1976 to 1979*, Institute for Architecture and Urban Studies, New York, 1976, p. 8: 'For Rossi, the analogical method is an attempt to force us away from our cultural disposition to see the reality of a city as a narrative in a continuous time and fixed place, to encounter a city which is constituted or elements from different places and different times.'

123 Carlo Aymonino, 'Type and typology', ibid., p. 49. Aymonino developed his typological research during the 1960s, publishing his Venice lectures in 1964 and 1965. For Rossi's reference see p. 182.

124 Ibid., p. 106.

125 Ibid.

126 Rossi, *The Architecture of the City*, p. 18.

127 Ibid., p. 35.

128 Aldo Rossi, *A Scientific Autobiography*, MIT Press, Cambridge, Mass., and London, 1981, p. 65.

129 M. Christine Boyer, *The City of Collective Memory: Its Historical Imagery and Architectural Entertainments*, MIT Press, Cambridge, Mass., and London, 1994: 'The Analogous City' is an important treatment of the School of Venice in the fourth chapter, 'The Art of Collective Memory'. See esp. pp. 173ff. Yet Venice, the city known to visitors before they visit it, plays a slight role in this book overall.

130 Francesco Dal Col, *Figures of Architecture and Thought: German Architecture Culture, 1880–1920*, Rizzoli, New York, 1990, figs 53–6.

131 Rossi, *A Scientific Autobiography*, p. 65.

132 Paolo Morachiello, 'The Department of Architectural History: A Detailed Description', *The School of Venice*, pp. 70–71. On the writing on the twentieth century see Margaret Plant, 'The Nostalgia of Manfredo Tafuri', *Transition, Discourse on Architecture*, nos 27/28 (1989), pp. 105–11.

133 For example 'Sapienza di Stato' e 'Atti Manciati', Architettura e tecnica urbana nella Venezia del '500', Manfredo Tafuri, *Architettura e Utopia nella Venezia del Cinquecento*, Electa, Milan, 1980, pp. 16–39; and with Antonio Foscari, *Armonio e conflitti: la chiesa di S. Francesco della Vigna nella Venezia del '500*, Einaudi, Turin, 1983.

134 Jean-Louis Cohen, 'Ceci n'est pas une histoire', *The Historical Project of Manfredo Tafuri, Casabella*, 619–20 (1995), p. 49. The author goes on to say that 'Venice in the early seventies was virgin terrain where historical teaching could be completely redesigned' (p. 50).

135 Manfredo Tafuri, *Jacopo Sansovino e l'architettura del '500 a Venezia*, Marsilio, Venice, 1969.

136 Francesco Paolo Fiore, 'The Autonomy of History', *Casabella, The Historical Project of Manfredo Tafuri*, pp. 103–10.

137 Tafuri, *Armonia e conflitti: la chiesa di San Francesco della Vigna nella Venezia del '500 e l'architettura del 500 a Venezia*.

138 Donatella Calabi and Paolo Morachiello, *Rialto: le Fabbriche e il ponte*, Einaudi, Turin, 1987. Ennio Concina, *L'Arsenale della Repubblica di Venezia: tecniche e istituzioni dal medioevo all'età moderna*, Electa, Milan, 1988.

139 The projects were shown at the Ala Napoleonica in April 1980: *10 Immagini per Venezia: Raimund Abraham, Rafael Moneo, Carlo Aymonino, Valeriano Pastor, Peter Eisenman, John Hejduk, Bernhard Hoeseli, Rafael Moneo, Valeriano Pastor, Giangugo Polesello, Aldo Rossi, Luciano Semerani*, ed. Raimund Abraham Francesco Dal Co, Officina, Rome, 1980. On the project and the links of the School of Venice with New York architectural circles see Joan Ockman, 'Venice and New York', *Casabella, The Historical Project of Manfredo Tafuri*, p. 65.

140 Francesco Dal Co, 'Venezia e il moderno', ibid., pp. 9–11, passim.

141 Ibid., p. 10.

142 Ennio Concina, 'Dinamiche urbane di una periferia: nota su Cannaregio', *10 Immagini per Venezia*, p. 12

143 Rafael Moneo, ibid., pp. 93–104. For Moneo's sympathy for the School of Venice see 'The "Ricerca" as Legacy', *The Historical Project of Manfredo Tafuri*, pp. 133–41.

144 John Hejduk, *10 Immagini per Venezia*, pp. 66–76.

145 John Hejduk, *Mask of Medusa: Works, 1947–1983*, ed. Kim Shkapich, Rizzoli, New York, 1985, p. 83.

146 Ibid., p. 80.

147 Ibid., p. 82.

148 Ibid., p. 345.

149 Peter Eisenman, *a + u 1988*, Tokyo, Japan, p. 14. For Eisenman's sympathy for the School of Venice see his introduction to Aldo Rossi, *The Architecture of the City*, pp. 3ff., and Joan Ackman, 'Venice and New York', *The Historical Project of Manfredo Tafuri*, p. 56.

150 The Cannaregio project is fully covered in *Cities of Artificial Excavation: The Work of Peter Eisenman, 1978–1988*, ed. Jean-François Rédard, Centre Canadien d'Architecture/Canadian Centre for Architecture, Montreal, Rizzoli International Publications, 1994, pp. 46–71. It includes the 'Three Texts for Venice'.

151 Ibid., p. 47.

152 Eisenman's linked his alchemy with Giordano Bruno.

153 See *Cities of Artificial Excavation*, passim. The other sites were Berlin, Long Beach, California, and La Villette in Paris.

154 Yve-Alain Bois, 'Surfaces', ibid., p. 39.

155 Aldo Rossi, *10 Immagini per Venezia*, pp. 138–52.

156 *La Biennale di Venezia: annuario 1975, Eventi del 1974*, ed. Archivio Storico delle Arti Contemporanee, Venice, 1975, p. 31.

157 Carlo Ripa di Meana, 'Venezia è Viva', ibid., pp. 621–4.

158 'Law No 438, July 26 1973. New regulations of the autonomous Body "La Biennale di Venezia", including the composition and role of the Steering Committees', *Annuario 1975*, pp. 31–7.

159 Sarpellon, 'Art, Glass and the Biennale', *Venice and the Biennale: Itineraries of Taste*, Fabbri, Monza, 1995, p. 142.

160 The *Annuario* was produced three times, each volume running to well over a thousand pages.

161 Ibid., p. 72.

162 For brief comment see Enzo Di Martino, *La Biennale di Venezia, 1895–1995: cento anni di arte e cultura*, Giorgio Mondadori, Milan, 1995, p. 66.

163 For the speeches see *Annuario 1975*, pp. 802–13.

164 Ibid., pp. 201ff.

165 Wladimiro Dorigo, 'L'Archivio Storico delle Arti Contemporanee: storia, situazione, prospettive' (with bibliography), ibid., pp. 698–717.

166 *Ottanti'anni di allestimenti alla Biennale*, ed. Giandomenico Romanelli, La Biennale di Venezia, Archivio Storico delle Arti Contemporanee, Venice, 1977.

167 Romanelli, 'Scheda sui Saloni alle Zattere', *Annuario 1975*, pp. 848–55.

168 Romanelli (with Jürgen Julier), 'Scheda sul Molino Stucky', ibid., pp. 866–75.

169 *La Biennale di Venezia*, 1972.

170 Lynn Gumpert, *Christian Boltanski*, Flammarion, Paris, 1996, p. 60.

171 Mary Jane Jacob, *Jannis Kounellis*, Museum of Contemporary Art, Chicago, 1986, pp. 112–13.

172 *Annuario 1974*, p. 227.

173 *Le Macchine celibi: The Bachelor Machines*, exh. curated by Harald Szeeman, Magazzini del Sale, Alfieri, Civitanova Marche, 1975.

174 *Annuario 1975*, pp. 431ff. Giuseppe Bartolucci and Lorenzo Capellini, *Il Segno teatrale: avanguardie alla Biennale di Venezia 1974/76*, Electa, Milan, 1978, pp. 16–23.

175 'Il Movimento ed il Silenzio di Meredith Monk', ibid., pp. 44–51.

176 For tributes to Maderna see *Annuario 1975*, pp. 828–47, including Luigi Nono's 'Ricordi'.

177 Bruno Maderna, *Venetian Journal da Boswell* (1972), for tenor, orchestra and magnetic tape, Ricordi, Milan, 1974.

178 For the Committee for Information see *La Biennale Annuario 1976: eventi del 1975*, Archivio Storico delle Arti Contemporanee, Venice, 1976, pp. 147–51; for the festival of dance see p. 199; and the Colloqiuum, p. 243.

179 Ibid., p. 249.

180 Ibid., pp. 280–81.

181 *Annuario 1976: eventi 1975*, p. 173, and Maria Ramos, *James Lee Byars: The Palace of Perfect*, Fundação de Serralves, Oporto, 1997, p. 257. This event begins Byars's long association with Venice, see p. 263.

182 *Annuario 1976: eventi 1975*, pp. 175–6.

183 Ibid., p. 205. Words and music by Luisa Ronchini and Alberto d'Amico.

184 Ibid., p. 147.

185 *Annuario 1976: eventi 1975*, p. 470.

186 Manifesto of Hervè, Fischer, Fred Forest and Jean-Paul Thénot, *B76, La Biennale di Venezia, Section of Visual Arts and Architecture, General Catalogue*, vol. 1, Venice, 1976, p. 68.

187 *La Biennale di Venezia. From Nature to Art. From Art to Nature. Section of Visual Arts and Architecture. General Catalogue*, Venice, 1978.

188 Joseph Losey director, *Don Giovanni*, 1979: Ruggero Raimondi, John Macurdy, Edda Moser, Kiri Te Kanawa.

189 Michel Ciment, *Conversations with Losey*, Methuen, London & New York, 1995, p. 366. For the choice of venue involving Rolf Libermann see David Caute, *Joseph Losey: A Revenge on Life*, Faber & Faber, London, 1994, p. 424.

190 Losey's *Eve*, which starred Jeanne Moreau, is virtually impossible to view now. See Caute, chap. 18, 'Eve', ibid., pp. 155ff.

191 Federico Fellini, director, *Casanova*, 1976: Donald Sutherland, Tina Aumont, Cicely Brown, Carmen Scarpitta.

192 A tendentious article pursues this theme; see Dale Bradley, 'History to Hysteria: Fellini's Casanova Meets Baudrillard', *Canadian Journal of Political and Social Theory*, 13 (1989), pp. 129–39.

193 *Fellini on Fellini*, ed. Costanzo Costantini, trans. Sobhrab Sorosshian, Faber & Faber, London and Boston, 1994, p. 90.

194 Ibid., p. 93.

195 Ibid., p. 89.

196 Ibid., p. 96.

197 Andrea Zanzotto, *Filò: per il Casanova di Fellini*, Arnoldo Mondadori, Milan, 1988.

198 Federico Fellini, 'Caro Andrea', ibid.

199 'Di iconografia subacquea del film, l'immagine placentaria, amniotica, di una Venezia de composta e fluttuante di alghe, di muscosità, di buio muffito e umido': Fellini, quoted in Andrea Zanzotto, ibid., p. 5.

200 Ian Fleming, *From Russia with Love*, Jonathan Cape, London, 1957. Film directed by Terence Young with Sean Connery as James Bond, Richard Maibaum, Johanna Harwood, United Artists Corporation, 1963.

201 Ian Fleming *Moonraker*, Jonathan Cape, London, 1955. Film directed by Lewis Gilbert, with Roger Moore as James Bond, screenplay by Christopher Wood, United Artists Corporation, 1979.

202 *Who is Killing the Great Chefs of Europe?* directed by Ted Kotcheff, with George Segal and Jaqueline Bisset, co-starring Robert Morley, screenplay by Peter Stone, Lorimar Distribution, 1978.

Chapter 11

1 Giannandrea Mencini, *Venezia acqua e fuoco: 'Salvaguardia' dall'alluvione del 1966 al rogo della Fenice*, Il Cardo, Venice, 1996, pp. 43ff. For the special legislation relating to Venice see the Appendix, pp. 119–21.

2 Ibid., p. 143.

3 The objectives were publicised retrospectively in the Consorzio publication, *Quaderni Trimestrali Consorzio Venezia Nuova*, 1, no. 1 (1993), p. 2, and all subsequent issues.

4 For the 'initiatives' taken in the 1970s see Scano, 'La Recostituzione del sistema lagunare', Luigi Scano, *Venezia Terra e acqua*, Edizioni delle Autonomie, Rome, 1985, pp. 333ff. See the wide-ranging article on the lagoon's changes during the nineteenth and twentieth centuries: Paolo Rosa Salva, 'Trasformazioni ambientali ed alterazioni nella laguna Veneta', *Urbanistica*, 62 (1974), pp. 6–44, with an extensive range of historical maps. For a comprehensive presentation (in the next decade) of the lagoon as eco-system, history, place or agriculture, festivals, hunting, marine and bird life, etc., *La laguna di Venezia*, ed. Giovanni Caniato, Eugenio Turri and Michele Zanetti, UNESCO, Cierre Edizioni, Verona, 1995.

5 Agenzia ANSA, *Venice, 1966–1996: Thirty Years of Protection as Covered by the Press*, Rome, 1996, distributed by Consorzio Venezia Nuova, p. 131.

6 Cristina Nasci et al., *Laguna tra fiumi e mare*, Filippi, Venice, 1982.

7 Ibid., pp. 15–18.

8 Paolo Antonio Pirazzoli, 'Possible Defenses Against a Sea-Level Rise in the Venice Area, Italy', *Journal of Coastal Research*, 7 (1991), pp. 231–48. Since the 1970s Pirazzoli has published on extreme tides in Venice as well as rising sea levels in general. See his literature cited in ibid., p. 246.

9 The interest of Boni's initiatives have been acknowledged by archaeologists, see A. J. Ammerman, Maurizia de Min, Rupert Housely and C. E. McClennen, 'More on the Origins of Venice', *Antiquity*, 69 (1995), p. 505.

10 A. J. Ammerman, Maurizia de Min and Rupert Housely, 'New Evidence on the Origins of Venice', *Antiquity*, 66 (1992), pp. 13–916; 'More on the Origins of Venice', and A. J. Ammerman, C. E. McClennen, M. de Min and R. Housely, 'Sea-level Change and the Archaeology of Early Venice', *Antiquity*, 73 (1999), pp. 303–12.

11 Wladimiro Dorigo, *Venezia origini: fondamenti, ipotesi, metodi*, Electa, Milan, 1983.

12 In particular Ammerman, de Min, Housley and McClennen, 'More on the Origins of Venice', pp. 501–10.

13 Agenzia ANSA, *Venice, 1966–1996*, p. 42.

14 Mencini, *Venezia acqua e fuoco: 'Salvaguardia' dall'alluvione del 1966 al rogo della Fenice*, p. 55.

15 For a valuable study of tourism within the twentieth-century history of Venice see Franco Lombardi, *Città storiche urbanistica e turismo: Venezia e Firenze*, Mercury, Florence, 1992.

16 Ibid.; and see, for example, comments by Gabriel Zanetto, 'Une Ville turistique et ses habitants: le cas de Venise', *Loisir et societé/Society and Leisure*, 9 (1986), p. 119.

17 *Venezia: città del moderno/Venice: City of the Modern*, Rassegna, 7 (1985): special issue.

18 Vittorio Gregotti, 'Venezia Città della nuova modernità', ibid., pp. 74–7; a further translation appeared as 'Venice and the New Modernism', trans. Judith Landry, *AA files*, 10 (1985), pp. 13–17.

19 Notably in a volume sponsored by Consorzio Venezia Nuova, Vittorio Gregotti, *Venezia: città della nuova modernità*, Consorzio Venezia Nuova, Venice, 1998.

20 Nico Ventura, 'L'Acqua come opportunità', *Venezia: città del nuova moderno/Venice: City of the Modern*, Rassegna, pp. 62–5. The 'rediscovery' of the perimeters of the lagoon was an important emphasis: it was contended that Mestre had turned its back on the lagoon, while Marghera had 'enhanced' the waterland. For Ventura's later comments in his capacity as Professor of Transport Infrastructures, at the Polytechnic in Milan, see 'Historical Perspectives and Present Problems', *Cities on Water and Transport*, ed. Rinio Bruttomesso, International Centre Cites on Water, Venice, 1995, pp. 92–7.

21 Wladimiro Dorigo, 'Toponomastica urbana nella formazione della città', ibid., pp. 46–55. English translation by Carey Bernitz.

22 For Samonà's scheme see 'Caratteri morfologici del sistema architettonico di Piazza San Marco', Giuseppe Samonà et al., *Piazza San Marco: l'architettura, la storia, le funzioni*, Marsilio, Venice, 1982, pp. 9–38.

23 Gianugo Polesello, 'Venice and the Project', *Venezia: città del moderno/Venice: City of the Modern*, Rassegna, p. 29.

24 Ibid.

25 Gianni Fabbri, 'Venezia, città non compiuta', trans. Lidia Zanardi, ibid., p. 24.

26 'Il Fotopiano di Venezia', ibid., pp. 84–8.

27 *Venezia Forma Urbis*, Marsilio, Venice, 1985. Scano discusses the project in *Venezia, Terra e acqua*, pp. 392–4. There was an international trend towards aerial views of cities in the 1980s, collections of which formed a new, fashionable type of coffee-table book and Venice was not immune: see Guido Rossi and Franco Masiero, *Venice from the Air*, Weidenfeld & Nicolson, London, 1988.

28 *Atlante di Venezia della città in scale: 1:1000 nel fotopiano e nella carta numerica; Atlas of Venice*, Comune di Venezia, Marsilio, Venice, 1989. The technical procedures are well detailed. See Mario Fondelli, 'Technical Procedures for the New Map of Venice', pp. 37–46.

29 Donatella Calabi contributes a wide-ranging essay on the historical cartography with readings of the new map: 'Images of a City "in the Middle" of Salt Water', ibid., pp. 405–12.

30 For the Barbari map see Giocondo Cassini, *Piante e vedute prospettiche di Venezia, 1479–1855*, with an urban introduction by Egle R. Trincanato, La Stamperia, Venice, 1982, pp. 40–45.

31 See Jürgen Schultz, 'Jacopo de' Barbari's View of Venice: Map Making, City Views, and Moralized Geography before the Year 1500, *Art Bulletin*, 61 (1978), pp. 425–78.

32 Giandomenico Romanelli and Susanna Biadene, *Venezia, piante e vedute*, Museo Correr, Venice, 1982.

33 Cassini, *Piante e vedute prospettiche di Venezia, 1479–1855*.

34 *Planimetria della città di Venezia*, from the 1846 edition of Bernardo e Gaetano Combatti, presented by Giandomenico Romanelli, Vianello, Treviso, 1987.

35 Paolo Rizzi and Enzo di Martino speak of 'la clamorosa riscoperta del Carnevale in chiave teatrale', *Storia della Biennale, 1895–1982*, Electa, Milan, 1982, p. 71. The *Carnevale-teatro* included G. Scabia, *Il giro del diavolo e del*

suo angelo per la città di Venezia all'inizio del carnevale.

36 On the history and the revival, but *not* the commercial exploitation see D. K. Feil, 'How Venetians Think about Carnival and History', *Australian Journal of Anthropology*, vol. 8 (1998), pp. 141–62.

37 Adriana Favaro and Cecilia Casaril, *Regata storica*, photography by Oreste Cagnate, Arcani, Treviso, 1994. And for the increasingly conspicuous role of the regatta see again, Lidia Sciama, 'The Venice Regatta: From Ritual to Sport', *Sport, Identity and Ethnicity*, ed. Jeremy MacClancy, Berg, Oxford, 1996, pp. 127–65, which explores the history of rowing in the lagoon, preparations for major races and the celebration of rowers.

38 Fulvio Roiter, *Essere Venezia: Living Venice*, text by Andrea Zanzotto, Magnuzi edizioni, Udine, 1978.

39 Fulvio Roiter, *Islands and Lagoons of Venice*, text by Peter Lauritzen (1978), Vendome Press, New York, 1980.

40 Andrea Zanzotto, *Essere Venezia: Living Venice*, n.p.

41 Fulvio Roiter, *Venice 11* (1984), text by Olivier Bernier, New York, 1985, *Venezia in maschera*, Vianello, Treviso, 1995.

42 See, for example, 'Looking Behind the Mask, Hans H. Siwik: Photography Before the Surface', *Leica Fotografie*, 1 (1985), pp. 18–23; 'Portraits with 120–1000 Film: Karl Jürgen Freund', ibid., pp. 26–30. (I am grateful to Anne Marsh for these references)

43 Alessandro Savella, *The Carnival of Venice*, text Nantas Salvalaggio, Silvana, Milan, 1984. A further example in the ubiquitous genre: the folio-scaled Shirley and David Rowan, *Carnival in Venice*, Harry N. Abrams, New York, 1989.

44 Zanotto, *Essere Venezia: Living Venice*, n.p.

45 Ibid.

46 *Venezia e lo spazio scenico*, Palazzo Grassi, La Biennale di Venezia, Venice, 1979.

47 Alessandro Fontana, 'La Verità delle maschere', ibid., pp. 21–36.

48 See part 1, chap. 1 above.

49 The theatre opened on 11 November 1979.

50 For the history of the temporary theatre see Manlio Brusatin, 'Theatrum mundi novissimi', *Aldo Rossi: Teatro del Mondo*, ed. Manlio Brusatin and Alberto Prandi, Cluva Libreria, Venice, 1982, pp. 17–47.

51 Aldo Rossi, *A Scientific Autobiography*, MIT, Cambridge, Mass., and London, 1981, pp. 67–8.

52 Manfredo Tafuri, 'L'Ephémère est eternel: Aldo Rossi à Venezia', *Aldo Rossi Teatro del Mondo*, pp. 145–9.

53 Manfredo Tafuri, 'L'Ephémère est eternel', ibid., p. 46.

54 Daniel Liebeskind, 'Deus ex Machina. Machina ex Deo. Aldo Rossi's Theater of the World', ibid. p. 9.

55 See the illustrated review by Pierre Restany, 'Il Tempo del museo Venezia', *Domus*, 614 (1981), pp. 33–41, and Arturo Quintavalle, 'Chronografie, Memory and Time', pp. 35–41.

56 *Il tempo del museo Venezia: tema cronografico per architetti e artistici*, La Biennale Progetto Speciale 1980, Venezia, quotation from Gianfranco Bettetini, p. 7, and Alessandro Mendini, p. 9.

57 Ingrid Sischy, 'La Biennale', *Domus*, 652 (1984), p. 68. For the mixed critical reaction in 1984 see ibid., p. 69ff.

58 See the illustrated report by Corinna Ferrari, 'Quartetto: Dream Passage in Venice', *Domus*, 652 (1984), p. 73. The painting by Enzo Cucchi, *In 1984 a Millenarian Transport Begins to Move Through Prehistory*, is reproduced *in situ* in the Scuola Grande di San Giovanni Battista in Diane Waldmann, *Enzo Cucchi*, Solomon R. Guggenheim Museum, New York, 1986, pp. 78–9.

59 Vedova was shown in 1984 at the Ala Napoleonica and the Magazzini del Sale in a presentation by Pontus Hulten, catalogue essay by German Celant (*Arcipelago Vedova*). For the Vienna exhibition at the Palazzo Grassi: *Le arti a Vienna: dalla Secessione alla caduta dell'Impero asburgico*, Edizioni La Biennale, Mazzotta, Milan, 1984.

60 Paolo Portoghesi, 'Venezia–Vienna', ibid., pp. 11–118.

61 Manlio Brusalin, 'The Tana Reopened: Machines and Workshops for the Arsenale of Venice', *The Presence of the Past: First International Exhibition of Architecture*, La Biennale di Venezia, Venice, 1980, pp. 342–8.

62 Paolo Portoghesi, 'The End of Prohibitionism', ibid., p. 13. On the tradition to which Portoghesi refers see Jennifer M. Fletcher, 'Fine Art and Festivity in Renaissance Venice: The Artist's Part', *Sight and Insight: Essays on Art and Culture in Honour of E. H. Gombrich at Eighty-five*, ed. John Onions, Phaidon, London, 1994, pp. 129–51, and *Venezia e lo spazio scenico*, passim.

63 *L'Immagine e il mito di Venezia nel cinema*, Biennale di Venezia, Venice, 1983.

64 Romanelli, *Venezia Ottocento*, has been cited many times in part 1.

65 *Venezia nell'Ottocento: Immagini e mito*, ed. Giuseppe Pavanello and Giandomenico Romanelli, Electa, Milan, 1983, has also been cited many times.

66 Cesare de Michelis, 'Teatro e spettacolo durante la Municipalità Provvisoria di Venezia, Maggio Novembre 1797', *Venezia e lo spazio scenico*, pp. 57–68.

67 *Le Venezie possibili: da Palladio a Le Corbusier*.

68 John Hejduk, *The Collapse of Time: And Other Diary Constructions*, Architectural Association, London, 1987.

69 The event is described and documented by Germano Celant, Claaes Oldenburg, Coosje van Bruggen and Frank O. Gehry, *Il Corso del Coltello: The Course of the Knife*, Rizzoli, New York, 1987. The project was presented by Il Gruppo Finanziario Tessile and the Commune of Venice, curated and produced by Germano Celant.

70 'San Marco sul Niagara', *Domus*, 665 (1985), p. 74.

71 That the actors were aware of the new status of the Arsenale is clear from comments, *Il Corso del Coltello: The Course of the Knife*, p. 52.

72 Ibid., p. 21.

73 'San Marco sul Niagara', ibid., p. 75.

74 *Terza Mostra Internazionale di Architettura: progetto Venezia*. 2 vols, La Biennale di Venezia, Venice, Electa, Milan, 1985.

75 Francesco Dal Co contributed a history of the bridge with lengthy quotation from Romanelli's study of its gestation in the previous century: 'Ponte dell'Accademia', ibid., pp. 318–25.

76 For the designs see ibid., pp. 326–429.

77 Aldo Rossi, 'I progetti per il Ponte dell'Accademia alla Biennale Architecttura/Designs for the Accademia Bridge at the Biennale Architetture', *Lotus*, 47 (1985), pp. 50–51.

78 Paolo Portoghesi, 'Per il nuovo Ponte dell'Accademia: note sul Concorso della Biennale di Venezia/Briefs on the Venice Biennale Competition', ibid., pp. 27–51.

79 Manfredo Tafuri, 'Venice 1985: The Architecture Biennale', *History of Italian Architecture, 1944–1985*, trans. Jessica Levine, MIT, Cambridge, Mass., and London, 1990, pp. 185–7.

80 Ibid., p. 185.

81 Ibid., p. 186. Tafuri held that the Biennale was not worthy of Rossi, but was in keeping with Paolo Portoghesi's strategies (earlier criticised). However, the Rossi Biennale did not stimulate architectural imagination to the degree that Portoghesi's *Strada Novissima* had done in 1980.

82 A number of detailed articles in the journal *Edilizia Popolare* document the concern with public housing in the 1980s: Nereo Laroni asks whether to preserve or develop in 'Salvaguardia e/o sviluppo', *Edilizia Popolare*, 175 (1983), pp. 50–51; Edoardo Salzano asks to go beyond the Special Laws in 'Oltre la Legge Speciale', ibid., pp. 42–5; Tullio Campostrini, 'Gli interventi di recupero nel patrimonio dello IACP di Venezia nel centro storico', *Edilizia Popolare*, 176 (1984), pp. 90–97, focuses largely on the Sacca San Girolamo

in Cannaragio; Edgarda Feletti, 'La Politica del recupero nel Comune di Venezia: l'emergenza e la strategia', ibid., pp. 98–105, studying the measures following the Special Laws from its 'first phase of recovery' in 1978; 'I progetti per gli anni Ottanta', ibid., pp. 86–9, again with reference to San Girolamo. The historical study edited by Elia Barbiani, *Edilizia popolare a Venezia* was published in 1983, and the exhibition *Venezia nuova: la Politica della casa, 1893–1941*, with catalogue by Paolo Somma, took place in the same year.

83 For an overview of the Giudecca in the context of the new housing developments see Marco de Michelis, 'Nuovi progetti all Giudecca: tipi di edificazione e morfologia dell'isola. New Projects at the Giudecca: Building Types and Morphology of the Island', *Lotus International*, 51 (1986), pp. 79–107.

84 Ibid., pp. 98–9, and 'Programma di sperimentazione ex Legge 94/1982', *Edilizia Popolare*, n. 176 (1984), pp. 139–40.

85 See plans, section and axonometry, Valeriano Pastor, 'Progetti e costruzione a Venezia nel Dopoguerra', *Costruire a Venezia: trent'anni di edilizia residenziale pubblica*, ed. Tullio Campostrini, Il Cardo, Venice, 1993, pp. 50–51.

86 Giandomenico Romanelli, 'Cantieri Veneziani l'isola della Giudecca come area industriale', *Lotus* 28 (1980), pp. 56–8.

87 For the new dockyards see De Michelis, 'New Projects at the Giudecca', ibid., p. 95.

88 *Dieci progetti di concorso per la ricostruzione di Campo di Marte alla Giudecca*, ed. Tiziana Quaglia and Giorgio Polli, Marsilio, Venice, 1986. The architects were Carlo Aymonino, Mario Botta, Gianfranco Caniggia, James Goan, Tomasz Mankowski, Josè Rafael Moneo Valles, Boris Podrecca, Aldo Rossi, Alvaro Siza Vieira, Aldo and Hannie Van Eyck.

89 For Rossi's project see ibid., pp. 92–9.

90 Valle quoted in Crozet, 'On Gino Valle's Project at the Giudecca', p. 109. The Sacca Fisola was the site for a scheme by Duilio Torres and engineer Bertanza in 1943: illustrated in *Costruire a Venezia: trent'anni di edilizia residenziale pubblica*, pp. 133–4.

91 For a tribute to Valle's use of brick see Alfonso Acocella, *An Architecture of Place*, Laierconsult, Rome, 1992, pp. 311–28.

92 See the complimentary account by Pierre Alain Croset, 'On Gino Valle's Project at the Giudecca', *Lotus International*, 51 (1986), pp. 109–28.

93 For plan and elevation see De Michelis, 'New Projects at the Giudecca', p. 97.

94 Pastor, 'Progetti e construzione a Venezia nel Dopoguerra', *Costruire a Venezia: trent'anni di edilizia residenziale pubblica*, pp. 46–52.

95 Carpaccio's *Miracle of the Cross*, the well-known depiction of these historical chimneys is deliberately reproduced in the context of the design in *Venezia: città del moderno/Venice: City of the Modern*, *Rassegna*, 7 (1985), p. 35.

96 On the scheme see Ermanno Ranzani, 'Gregotti Associati, Quartiere Residenziale Area ex-Saffa, Venezia', *Domus*, 704 (April 1989), pp. 25–35.

97 Valeriano Pastor, 'Progetti e costruzioni a Venezia nel Dopoguerra', *Costruire a Venezia: trent'anni di edilizia residenziale pubblica*, p. 57.

98 'Luciano Semerani e Gigetta Tamaro: ospedale a Venezia', *Domus*, 688 (1987), p. 2.

99 *Archeologia industriale a Venezia*, directed Hans Wieser, photography Wolfgang Thomaseth, Production, Comune di Venezia, Venice, 1979.

100 *Venezia città industriale: gli insediamenti produttivi del XIX secolo*, Marsilio, Venice, 1980. See also the later study, Giorgio Bellavitis and Franco Mancuso, *Archaeologia industriale nel Veneto*, Silvana, Venice, 1990.

101 The Biennale-sponsored focus in 1975 was presented as *A proposito del Mulino Stucky*. In 1978 Jürgen Julier wrote the first historical study. *Il Mulino Stucky: ricerche storiche e epotesi di restauro*, ed. Francesco Amendolagine, Il Cardo, Treviso, 1995, presents the history and reclamation-in-progress. See also Raffaela Giuseppetti, *Un castello in laguna: storia di Molino Stucky*, Il Cardo, Venice, 1995. For the development, see below.

102 According to Sandro Meccoli, *Ponte della Libertà, e altri scritti veneziani*, Arsenale, Verona, 1990, p. 126.

103 Meccoli analyses the referendum results, ibid., p. 129.

104 In April 1988 the minister of the environment Gingio Ruffero, used the hard/soft analogy, ibid., p. 39.

105 Giandomenico Romanelli, *Palazzo Grassi: storia, architettura, decorationi dell'ultimo palazzo veneziano*, Albrizzi, Venice, 1986. For Gae Aulenti's museum conversion see Gilberto Botti, 'Gae Aulenti: Architecture and Museography', *Lotus International*, 53 (1987), p. 65.

106 Ibid., pp. 67–8.

107 Ibid., p. 94.

108 Ibid., p. 40.

109 *Accessibilità a Venezia: atti del convegno*, ed. Patrizia Montini and Piero Antonio, Cluva Università, Venice, 1985. See also Guglielmo Zambrini, 'Alcuni questioni di accessibilità', *Idea di Venezia: atti del convegno 17/18 June, 1988*, ed. Umberto Curi, Quaderni della Fondazione Istituto Gramsci Veneto 3/4, Arsenale, Venice, 1988, pp. 113–18.

110 Eugenio Vassallo, 'The "Corderie" in the Venice Arsenal', *Twenty Years of Restoration in Venice*, Soprintendenza ai Beni Ambientali e Architettonici di Venezia, Venice, 1987, pp. 75–82.

111 For example in *Progetto Arsenale: studi e ricerche per l'Arsenale di Venezia*, ed. Paolo Gennaro and Giovanni Testi, Cluva, Università, Venice, 1985. The buildings are documented in photographs with built models and diagrams. For an account of new deployment see Carlo Mannani with Maurizio Sabini, 'L'Assedio dell'Arsenale', *Casabella*, 485 (1982), pp. 14–24.

112 Ibid., p. 15.

113 Ibid.

114 *L'Arsenale reordinato: nuovi progetti per Venezia*, Arsenale, Venice, 1987.

115 Ibid., p. 31.

116 *Progetto Arsenale: studi e ricerche per l'Arsenale di Venezia*.

117 See 'Il Sistema dell'accessibilità come uno degli elementi fondativi del progetto di recupero per l'Arsenale', ibid., pp. 152–7.

118 *L'Arsenale riordinato: nuovi progetti per Venezia*.

119 Gianni de Michelis, ibid., Preface in English and Italian, pp. 9–11.

120 Luciano Semerani, ibid., 'La trasformazione dell'Arsenale', p. 41.

121 See again Gennaro, 'The Squadratori: An Enlightenment Project', *L'Arsenale reordinato*, pp. 25–8.

122 Ibid.

123 Ibid., p. 39.

124 Agnaldo S. Maciel, *Another Venice: Images of an International Anarchist Meeting, Venezia 1984*, Black Rose Books, Montreal, 1986.

125 Luigi Nono, *Prometeo, tragedia dell'ascolto*, 1984/1985, libretto Massimo Cacciari. Recorded with libretto in translation, Ensemble Modern, conductor Ingo Metzmacher, EMI, 5 55209 2 (1985).

126 Nono in discussion in 'Un'Autobiografia dell'autore raccontata da Enzo Restagno', *Nono*, ed. Enzo Restagno, Edizioni di Torino, Turin, 1996, pp. 70–71. Vedova was, however, involved with the lighting for the first performance.

127 Hölderlin's *Hyperions Schicksalslied* provides the central words for the 'Second Island', setting up the long perspective from classical to modern times, the unchanging message of doom and the allegorical buffeting of the waters: 'But we are destined to find no resting-place; and suffering mortals dwindle and fall blindly from one hour to the next, hurled like water from ledge to ledge, downwards for years to the vague abyss,' quoted in the translation by Michael Hamburger, *Hölderlin*, Penguin, Harmondsworth, 1961, p. 26.

128 Massimo Cacciari, *The Necessary*

Angel (1987), trans. Miguel E. Vatter, State University of New York Press, Albany, 1994, and 'Loos and His Angel', in *Architecture and Nihilism: On the Philosophy of Modern Architecture*, introduction Patrizia Lombardo; trans. Stephen Sartarelli, Yale University Press, New Haven and London, 1993, pp. 143ff.

129 Nono, *Prometeo*, Third/Fourth/Fifth Island, libretto, pp. 68ff.

130 'Verso *Prometeo*. Conversazione tra Luigi Nono e Massimo Cacciari raccolta da Michele Bertaggia', *Nono*, p. 255.

131 'Io stesso mi sforzo di *ascoltare i colori*, così come ascolto le pietre o i cieli di Venezia: come rapporti tra undulazioni, vibrazioni . . .', ibid., p. 257.

132 Ibid., p. 258.

133 Luigi Nono, *Varizioni canoniche: a Carlo Scarpa, architetto, ai suoi inifiniti possibili*, *No hay caminos, hay que caminar*, Michael Gielen, Sinfonieorchester des Sudwestfunks, Baden-Baden, Astrée CD, E 8741 (1990).

134 In particular: Massimo Cacciari, *Architecture and Nihilism: On the Philosophy of Modern Architecture* (the material is revised from earlier essays), and *Posthumous People: Vienna at the Turning Point*, trans. Rodger Friedman, Stanford University Press, Stanford, 1996. For an account of the political writings and Cacciari's activism after 1968, see Lombardo's introduction to *Architecture and Nihilism*, passim. For the political writings, n. 7, p. 214.

135 Cacciari, *Architecture and Nihilism: On the Philosophy of Modern Architecture*, p. xiv.

136 Ibid., p. xx.

137 Massimo Cacciari, 'Il mito di Venezia/The Myth of Venice' (with Francesco Dal Co, Manfredo Tafuri), *Venezia: città del moderno/Venice: City of the Modern*, *Rassegna*, 7, 1985, p. 9, trans. Andrea Janowski.

138 Cacciari, 'The City as Essay', in *Architecture and Nihilism*, ibid., p. 87ff.

139 Ibid., p. 94.

140 Ibid., p. 95.

141 Ibid.

142 Ibid.

143 For a general reflection on the mask see Massimo Cacciari, 'Memoria sul carnevale', in Florens Christian Rang, *Psicologia storica del carnevale* (1927), Arsenale, Venice, 1983, pp. 83ff. I have studied the allusions to the mask in such writers as Hugo von Hofmannsthal and Rilke in 'The Mask Face', in Margaret Plant, *Paul Klee, Figures and Faces*, Thames & Hudson, London, 1978, pp. 30ff.

144 Cacciari, *Architecture and Nihilism*, p. 95.

145 On the *unheimlich* and architecture see the rich interpretative essay, Anthony Vidler, *The Architectural Uncanny: Essays in the Modern*

Unhomely, MIT, Cambridge, Mass., and London, 1994.

146 Cf. Margaret Cohen, *Profane Illumination: Walter Benjamin and the Paris of Surrealist Revolution*, University of California Press, Berkeley and Los Angeles, 1993.

147 *Idea di Venezia*, Atti del convegno 17/18 June 1988, ed. Umberto Curi, Quaderni della Fondazione Istituto Gramsci Veneto 3/4, Arsenale, Venezia 1988. Cacciari's contribution also appeared in *Casabella*, n. 557 (1989), pp. 42–58.

148 Others, and especially academics, of course, endorsed this view. See, for example, the contribution of Giandomenico Romanelli, 'Memoria e museo', *Idea di Venezia*, pp. 23–43; Paolo Perulli, 'Venezia città della scienza? Necessaria ma improbabile', pp. 77–84; Innocenzo Cervelli, 'Il dibattito sull'università', pp. 85–90.

149 Cacciari, 'The City as Essay', in *Architecture and Nihilism*, p. 90.

150 See n. 170 below.

151 Manfredo Tafuri, '"Sapienza di stato" e "Atti manciati": architettura e tecnica urbana nella Venezia del '500', *Architettura e utopia nella Venezia del Cinquecento*, Electa, Milan, 1980, pp. 16–39.

152 Manfredo Tafuri, *Venice and the Renaissance* (1985), trans. Jessica Levine, MIT, Cambridge, Mass., 1989. For a focus on Tafuri's Renaissance studies see Howard Burns, 'Tafuri and the Renaissance', *Casabella* 619–20 (1995), pp. 114–33.

153 See Tafuri, 'A Theater, a "Fountain of Sil", and "A Shapeless Little Island with a Hill": Project by Alvise Cornaro for the Restructuring of the Bacino of San Marco', *Venice and the Renaissance*, pp. 139ff.

154 Nono, *Prometeo*, libretto, p. 62.

155 Muriel Spark, *Territorial Rights* (1979), Penguin, Harmondsworth, 1991.

156 Madonna was born of second-generation Italian immigrants to the United States of America, and had a Catholic upbringing. See the biography by Douglas Thompson, *Like a Virgin: Madonna Revealed*, Smith Gryphon, London, 1991.

157 In what follows I draw upon my article 'Madonna in Venice', *Art & Text*, 30 (September–November 1988), pp. 20–29.

158 Manfredo Tafuri mentions Blake in *The Sphere and the Labyrinth: Avant-Gardes and Architecture from Piranesi to the 1970s* (1980) trans. Pellegrini d'Acierno and Robert Connolly, MIT Press, Cambridge, Mass., 1987, p. 291.

159 Edward Muir, *Civic Ritual in Renaissance Venice*, Princeton University Press, 1981, p. 119.

160 Sophie Calle and Jean Baudrillard,

Suite Vénitienne: Please Follow Me, original Editions de l'Etoile, Paris, 1983, trans. Dany Barash and Danny Hatfield, Bay Press, Seattle, 1988.

161 Ibid., p. 40.

162 Ibid., p. 56.

163 Ibid., p. 77.

164 Ibid., p. 85. In 1984 Sophie Calle returned to Venice as a chambermaid and photographed selected residents' bedrooms over the short periods of their stay: see *Ecrit sur l'image: L'Hôtel*, Editions de l'Etoile, Paris, 1984.

165 Ian McEwan, *The Comfort of Strangers*, Jonathan Cape, London, 1981. The film version will be discussed in the next chapter. For some comment on McEwan's novel owing 'much to Mann and Du Maurier' etc. see George B. von der Lippe, 'Death in Venice in Literature and Film: Six Twentieth-Century Versions', *Mosaic*, 32 (1999), pp. 43ff.

166 McEwan, *The Comfort of Strangers*, p. 43.

167 Barry Unsworth, *The Stone Virgin* (1985), Penguin, Harmondsworth, 1986.

168 Guido Ruggiero, *The Boundaries of Eros: Sex Crime and Sexuality in Renaissance Venice*, Oxford University Press, New York, 1985.

169 Edward Muir, *Civic Ritual in Renaissance Venice*. Muir discusses the 'historiography of the myth' and 'The myth abroad', pp. 23ff.

170 The literature exposing the 'myth' in fact gears up in the 1960s with G. Fasoli, 'Nascita di un mito', in *Studi in onore di Gioacchino Volpe nel centenario della nascita*, G. Volpe, Rome, 1978, pp. 544–78, and gains further momentum with F. Gaeta, 'Alcune considerazione sul mito di Venezia', *Bibliothèque d'Umanisme et Renaissance*, 23 (1961), pp. 58–75. A magisterial study in English was a product of the mid-1980s: James S. Grubb, 'When Myths Lose Power: Four Decades of Venetian Historiography', *Journal of Modern History*, 58 (1986), pp. 43–94.

171 Erica Jong, *Serenissima: A Novel of Venice*, Bantam, London, 1982.

172 Jeanette Winterson, *The Passion* (1987), Penguin, Harmondsworth, 1988. For an interpretative essay see Judith Seaboyer, 'Second Death in Venice: Romanticism and the Compulsion to Repeat in Jeanette Winterson's *The Passion*', *Contemporary Literature*, 38 (1997), pp. 483–509.

173 *Vampires in Venice*, Italy, 1988, directed by Augusto Caminito with Klaus Kinsky, Donald Pleasence, Cristopher Plummer, Barbara de Rossi, Yorgo Voyagis, Anne Knecht.

174 Scott Hughes reported these advertisements critically in *The Independent* (30 March 1998).

175 Robert Casillo, 'Dirty Gondola: The Image of Italy in Amercian Advertise-

ments', *Word & Image*, 1 (1985), pp. 330–50.

176 Gore Vidal, *Vidal in Venice*, ed. George Armstrong, photographs by Tore Gill, Weidenfeld & Nicholson, London, in association with Channel Four Television, Antelope, 1985.

177 *Unguided Tour*, written and directed by Susan Sontag, 1983. Prod. Giovannella Zannoni for Lunga Gittata Cooperative, RAI rete 3. Colour, 72 min. Sontag's brief story 'Unguided Tour', which appears in *I, Etcetera* (it precedes the film), is about tourism, but is not centred in Venice: Susan Sontag, *I, Etcetera*, Vintage Books, New York, 1979, pp. 233–46.

178 Gary Indiana, 'Susan Sontag's "Unguided Tour"', *Artforum*, 23 (1983), p. 67.

179 Vidal, *Vidal in Venice*, p. 120.

180 Alberto Francesconi, 'Venezia: città a numero chiuso', *Il Gazzettino* (12 November 1996), p. 1.

181 Meccoli, 17 July 1989, *Ponte della Libertà e altri scritti veneziani*, p. 134.

182 For an account of the political implications see Mencini, *Venezia acqua e fuoco: 'Salvaguardia' dall'alluvione del 1966 al rogo della Fenice*, p. 72–6.

183 Meccoli, *Ponte della Libertà e altri scritti veneziani*, p. 137.

184 Ibid., pp. 139, 144.

185 Agenzia ANSA, *Venice 1966–1996: Thirty Years of Protection as Covered by the Press*, p. 103.

186 Mencini, *Venezia acqua e fuoco: 'Salvaguardia' dall'alluvione del 1966 al rogo della Fenice*, p. 63, and *Venice 1966–1996: Thirty Years of Protection as Covered by the Press*, pp. 42ff.

187 For a background see 'Fixed or Mobile Barriers?', ibid., pp. 78ff.

188 'The Oil-spill Threat', ibid., p. 106.

189 Ibid., pp. 65, 80.

190 Ibid., p. 8.

Chapter 12

1 Sandro Meccoli, *Ponte della Libertà e altri scritti veneziani*, Arsenale, Verona, 1990, p. 191.

2 Interview with Gianfranco Mossetto, 'Turismo e cultura nel nostro futuro', *Nexus*, 11 (July–August 1994), pp. 1, 4. For the effect on the local population see Gabriel Zanetto, 'Une Ville turistique et ses habitants: Le Cas de Venise', *Loisir et société*, 9 (1986), pp. 117–24.

3 Susie Boulton and Christopher Catling, *Venice and the Veneto* (1995), Eyewitness Travel Guides, Dorling Kindersley, London, 1997. It should be noted that Lorenzetti's guide remains in print.

4 Meccoli analyses the results 15 June 1990, *Ponte della Libertà e altri scritti veneziani*, p. 22.

5 Meccoli's 1988 paper, 'Venezia capitale d'Europa', ibid., pp. 255–63.

6 Ibid., p. 261.

7 21 July 1990, ibid., p. 231.

8 Giannandrea Mencini, *Venezia acqua e fuoco: 'Salvaguardia' dall'alluvione del 1966 al rogo della Fenice*, Il Cardo, Venice, 1996, p. 91.

9 Luigi Zanda, 'Morality and Venice', *Art Newspaper* (December 1992), p. 1, noting that 'This year not one lira of government funds has been spent on restoration', Ibid. The chronicle of the year 1994 presented by "Theophanes Brittanicus" details many instances of corruption and deferred funds: 'A Chronicle of Venice', *The Art Newspaper*, 34 (January 1994), pp. 20–3.

10 Gianfranco Bettin, *Dove volano i leoni: fine secolo a Venezia*, Garzanti, Milan, 1991. Bettin was deputy mayor in the Massimo Cacciari Giunta Comunale di Venezia.

11 'Luigi Nono's Gravestone', *Japan Architecture* (1993), pp. 153–4: 'Basalt stone symbolizes the hardened spirit of a composer who has devoted himself to the reform of this world through music'. Note also the inauguration of the Luigi Nono archive, 'Nicola Cisternino, 'L'Archivio Luigi Nono', *Nexus*, 21 (1996), p. 13.

12 Bettin, *Dove volano i leone: fine secolo a Venezia*, p. 9.

13 Ibid., pp. 65–7.

14 Alberto Scotti, 'Progettazione delle opere di difesa dalla acque alte', *Quaderni Trimestrali, Consorzio Venezia Nuova*, 1, n. 3 (1993), p. 13.

15 On the ongoing enquiries into the impact of MO.SE see Mencini, *Venezia acqua e fuoco: 'Salvaguardia' dall'alluvione del 1966 al rogo della Fenice*, pp. 94ff.

16 On funding problems, in particular in 1991, see *Agenzia ANSA, Venice 1966–1996: Thirty Years of Protection as Covered by the Press*, Rome, 1996, pp. 95ff.

17 'La Legislazione per la Salvaguardia di Venezia e il riequilibrio della Laguna dal 1973 al 1994', *Quaderni Trimestrali Consorzio Venezia Nuova*, n. 4 (1994), n. 1 (1995), pp. 9–12.

18 Meccoli, *La Ponte della Libertà e altri scritti veneziani*, pp. 199, 219.

19 Krzystof Wodiczko, 'Public Projects', *October*, 38 (1986), pp. 3–22, and Douglas Crimp, Rosalyn Deutsche and Ewa Lajer-Burcharth, 'A Conservation with Krzystof Wodiczko', ibid., pp. 3–52.

20 Brian James, 'Nightmare Venice', *The Australian* (2–3 December 1989). Michele Nayman, 'Death Threat to Venice', *The Age* (Melbourne; 1 June, 1990).

21 Cathy Booth, 'The Battle of Venice', *Time* (28 May 1990), p. 63.

22 Roberto Ballarin, 'Assalto a Venezia: 125 mila per il carnevale della musica', *Il Gazzettino* (19 February 1996), p. 119.

23 Meccoli, *Ponte della Libertà e altri scritti veneziani*, passim.

24 James, 'Nighmare Venice'.

25 Walter Little and Edouardo Posada-Carbo, *Political Corruption in Europe and Latin America*, Macmillan, London, 1996, p. 1.

26 Gianni Riotti, *Ombra: un capriccio veneziano*, Rizzoli, Milan, 1995. For further details of the literary patronage of the Consorzio see the discussion of Joseph Brodsky below.

27 Ibid., p. 43. Chapter 4 announces Satori's project.

28 Lodovico de Luigi was born in 1933 in Venice. For a biography see Giuseppe M. Pilo and Simone Viani, *Venezia: quale immagine?* Istituto di Storia dell'Università degli Studi di Udine, Grafiche Editoriali Artistiche Pordenonesi, 1980, p. 70.

29 GAM, 'Venice, Agip Gas Attack', *The Art Newspaper*, 71 (June 1997), p. 3.

30 Roberto Bianchin, *Acqua Grande*, Filippi, Venice, 1996.

31 I follow remarks on p. 103, ibid.

32 *Il Gazzettino* (3 November 1996), p. 1.

33 66–96 *Laboratorio Venezia: la Laguna, i fiumi, la città e il mare*. Centro Internazionale Città d'Acqua, 1997 (2 CD-ROM).

34 *Lagoon*, directed by Federico and Francesco de Melis, produced by Livio Negri, narrated by Nicholas Farrell, photographed by Giuesppe Baresi, International Centre Cities on Water, Venice, 1997.

35 Letter to the author from Claudio Ambrosini, 31 October 1999.

36 'Venice, Thirty Years from November 4, 1996', Agenzia ANSA, *Venice, 1966–1996*, pp. 139ff.

37 *Il Gazzettino* (Sunday, 3 November 1996).

38 *Death of Venice*, written and directed by David Munro, Goldhawk for Channel Four Television, 1995.

39 Mencini follows these negotiations in *Venezia acqua e fuoco: 'Salvaguardia' dall'alluvione del 1966 al rogo della Fenice*, pp. 100–101. See also 'The Oil-spill Threat', Agenzia ANSA, *Venice, 1966–1996*, p. 106.

40 For instance 'Incontro con Paolo Parisatti, Prima emergenza: escavo canali', *Nexus*, 19 (1996), p. 2.

41 For the Fenice fire, see below.

42 Gianpietro Zucchetta, *I Rii di Venezia: la storia degli ultimi tre secoli*, Helvetia, Venice, 1985, p. 40.

43 'Una petizione per il Rio di Ca' Tron', *Il Gazzettino* (12 December 1996).

44 Silvio Testa, 'Canal Grande, un

bacino di veleni: bisogna vietare i motori fuoribordo e ridurre le potenze di tutti gli altri', *Il Gazzettino* (31 August 1995), p. 1.

45 S.T., 'Motorizziamo le Gondole!', *Il Gazzettino* (Sunday, 11 June 1995), p. 11.

46 May Gaskin, 'High Tec Saves Venice', *Sunday Times* (24 March 1996), p. 10.

47 A publication was made available: *le attività per la salvaguardia di Venezia e della sua laguna*, Trimestrali Consorzio Venezia Nuova, Ministero dei Lavori Pubblici, Magistrato alle Acque di Venezia, 1997.

48 For example CD-ROM, *With Water and Against Water: Measures for the Safeguarding of Venice and its Lagoon*, Ministry of Public Works, Venice Water Authority, Concessionary Consorzio Venezia Nuova, 1996.

49 According to Agenzia ANSA, 'the idea of combatting "high water" by raising up the historic centre of Venice was presented at a UNESCO meeting in April 1981. An Italian company had already tried this type of operation on the island of Poveglia about ten years previously', p. 82. See also A.P. 'Considerazioni dopo un 1996 di Acque Alte. Il medio mareè crescuito di cinque centimetre', *Il Gazzettino* (20 January 1997). See also Roberto Brunetti, 'Solleviamo Venezia', *Il Gazzettino* (30 November 1996).

50 *Venezia sostenibile: suggestioni dal futuro*, ed. Ignazio Musu, Società Editrice Il Mulino, Bologna, 1998.

51 'L'ex Macello a San Giobbe potrà ospitare l'Università', *Il Gazzettino* (10 April 1996).

52 Francesco Amendolagine, Sasa Dobrocici and Alessandro Marchi, 'The Project for the Restoration of the Molino Stucky, Venice', *Water and the Industrial Heritage: The Reuse of the Industrial and Port Structures in Cities on Water*, ed. Rinio Bruttomesso, Marsilio, Venice, 1999, pp. 116–19; Francesco Amendolagine (ed.), *Molino Stucky: ricerche storiche e ipotesi di restauro*, Il Cardo, Treviso, 1995.

53 Amendolagine et al., 'The Project for the Restoration of the Molino Stucky, Venice', ibid., p. 118.

54 Silvio Testa, 'Il Molino Stucky al decollo', *Il Gazzettino* (13 January 1995), p. 1; Paolo Barbaro, 'Il Molino della Giudecca', *La Stampa* (27 January 1995), p. 21.

55 Marino Folin, 'L'Istituto Universitario di Architettura di Venezia come committente', *Venezia, La nuova architettura*, ed. Marco de Michelis, Skira, Geneva and Milan, 1999, pp. 22–4.

56 Under construction by Carlo Cappai, cf. 'Concorso per il restauro delle Conterie nell'isola di Murano: residenze per studenti', ibid., pp. 72–7.

57 'Zucchi architetti: Trasformazione dell'area ex Junghans alla Giudecca', *Casabella*, 629 (1995), pp. 50–1.

58 The comment appears to be made in 1979, cited in Agenzia ANSA, *Venice 1966–1996*, p. 87.

59 Giuseppe Tedesco, 'Lido, un'isola lasciata allo sbando', *Il Gazzettino* (10 June 1992).

60 On the degradation of the islands see De Rita, *Venezia: una città speciale*, p. 36.

61 Paul Bombard, 'A Venetian Venture', *Times Higher Educational Supplement* (June 1995). Felici 'Cino' Casson, 'San Servolo: Isola de genii', *Nexus*, 3 (February–March 1995), p. 6.

62 Roberto Miracapillo, 'Una Venezia capitale delle idee', *Il Gazzettino* (2 June 1996).

63 Cited from Maria Rosa Vittadini, 'The Urban Transport System: Transport via Water and Land', *Cities on Water and Transport*, p. 98.

64 Nico Ventura, 'Historical Perspectives and Present Problems', *Cities on Water and Transport*, ed. Rino Bruttomesso, International Centre Cities on Water, Venice, 1995, p. 97.

65 Ibid.

66 Valeria Giannella and Maurizio Gambuzza, 'Marittima e Arsenale nel contesto delle trasformazione urbane a Venezia, *Urbanistica*, 98 (1990), pp. 42ff.

67 V. Giannella and M. Gambuzza, 'La Marittima e il porto a Venezia', *Urbanistica*, 98 (1990), pp. 142–53. See also Alfreco Baroncino (Venice Port Authority), 'Port and Urban Transport: Developments in Venice', *Cities on Water and Transport*, p. 113. For the Studio Gregotti plan to develop the Marittima as a tourist berth see *Domus*, 727 (1991), pp. 46–55.

68 *Accessibilità a Venezia*, ed. Patrizia Montini and Pier Antonio Val, Cluva, Venice, 1985, followed by the publication, *Venezia tra innovazione funzionale e architettura della città: quattro progetti per l'area ovest*, ed. Rinato Bocchi and Claudio Lamanna, Marsilio, Venice, 1986.

69 For an account of the lines see Roberto Piccoli, 'An Underwater Transportation Network in the Venice Lagoon', *Cities on Water and Transport*, pp. 137–42.

70 Cf. Gian Antonio Stella, 'Il futuro di Venezia: Il metrò in una laguna di polemiche', *Corriere della Sera* (22 April 1992), p. 14. Writing on the 'oxymoron' of the metro in a brief, but bracing essay, Sandy McCreery suggests: 'What is so oxymoronic about the Venice Metro, is its juxtaposition of the double texture identified as the subjective characteristic of all urban space by theorists like De Certeau and practioners like Debord: the labyrinthine, on the one hand and the rational, on the other.' 'Venice Metro', *Strangely Familiar: Narratives of Architecture in the City*, ed. Iain Borden et al., Routledge, London and New York, 1996, p. 45. For a further insistent view of a viable underwater system see Roberto Piccoli, 'Underwater Transportation Network in the Venice Lagoon', *Cities on Water and Transport*, pp. 137–42.

71 Mencini, *Venezia acqua e fuoco: 'Salvaguardia' dall'alluvione del 1966 al rogo della Fenice*, pp. 90–91.

72 For example, Leopolo Pietragnoli, 'I Verdi annunciano guerra dura al progretto della sublugunare', *Il Gazzettino* (28 April 1992).

73 Meccoli, *Ponte della Libertà e altri scritti veneziani*, p. 205.

74 Mencini, *Venezia acqua e fuoco: 'Salvaguardia' dall'alluvione del 1966 al rogo della Fenice*, p. 90.

75 Paolo Coltro, 'A sogno veneziano della metropolitana muore sulla laguna', *Corriere della Sera* (13 June 1993).

76 Meccoli, *Ponte della Libertà e altri scritti veneziani*, 7 April 1990, p. 210. Paolo Pennisi, 'Che brutta confusione al Tronchetto e a Piazzale Roma', *Nexus*, 10 (1994), pp. 1–2.

77 *Quinta Nostra Internazionale di Architettura Concorso Internazionale: 'Una Porta per Venezia'*, La Biennale di Venezia, Electa, Venice, 1991. On the cinema, Nicola di Battista, 'Biennale di Venezia: 10 Architetti per il Nuovo Palazzo del Cinema al Lido', *Domus*, 730 (September 1991), pp. 54–77. Further projects announced were an Italian pavilion and bookshop in the Biennale garden complex and a new design for the Palazzo del Cinema on the Lido, long held to be inadequate.

78 Sergio Polano, 'Santiago Calatrava: Il quarto ponte sul Canal Grande', *Casabella*, 637 (1996), pp. 2–8. The political point was emphasised: 'a fourth bridge for the Grand Canal at Piazzale Roma will be a tangible, concrete sign for the community and for architectural culture of a profound renewal so fundamental for the policies of urban management in an amphibious city like Venice' (p. 3). See also 'Quarto ponte sul Canal Grande', *Venezia: la nuova architettura*, pp. 44–51.

79 'World's First Glass Bridge to be Built in Venice', *Art Newspaper*, 62 (1996), p. 8.

80 Roberto Brugnoli, 'Continua la "Grande Fuga". La Città ha perso in quattro mesi altri 838 abitanti, 352 dei quali in centro storico', *Il Gazzettino* (15 May 1996).

81 *Il Gazzettino* (Friday, 13 January 1995), p. 1.

82 See the analysis by Adriana Destro, 'A New Era and New Themes in Italian Politics: The Case of Padania', *Journal of Italian Studies*, 2 (1997), pp. 358–77.

83 For an overview see David Nelken,

'A Legal Revolution? The Judges and Tangentopoli', *The New Italian Republic: From the Fall of the Berlin Wall to Berlusconi*, ed. Stephen Gundle and Simon Parker, Routledge, London, 1996, pp. 191–205.

84 Ibid., pp. 362ff.

85 Ibid., p. 372.

86 Leonardo Benevolo, 'La nuova gronda lagunare', *Venezia: la nuova architettura*, p. 186.

87 Carlo Ripa di Meana and Alvise Zorzi, *Idea Europee per Venezia*, Quaderni della Associazione Carlo Cattaneo, Consulato Generale d'Italia in Lugano, 1992.

88 'Are the Italians Fit to Look after Venice?', *The Art Newspaper* (15 February 1992), pp. 1, 2.

89 Riccardo Chiaberge, 'E Venezia non sarà più isola', *Corriere della Sera* (26 January 1995), p. 12.

90 *Venezia 2000: Idee e progetti*, ed. Antonio Preiti and Gia Marotto, Marsilio, Venice, 1995.

91 Ibid., pp. 24–6, with full illustrations of the Magnet, in which project architects Ugo Camerino and Gian Paolo Mar were also involved. Piano's reputation for grandiose designs is particularly associated with the Beaubourg centre in Paris.

92 As *Venezia 2000: Idee e progetti*.

93 Giuseppe de Rita, in *Venezia 2000: Idee e progetti*, ed. Antonio Preiti and Gia Marotto, Marsilio, Venice (1995), and in *Una Città speciale: rapporto su Venezia*, Marsilio, Venice, 1993. The publishing house Marsilio is a member of the Consorzio Venezia Nuova.

94 Ibid., pp. 12, 13.

95 The word 'partita' is used throughout.

96 'La Città speciale', ibid., pp. 35–47.

97 Ibid., p. 356.

98 *Venezia: Il nuovo Piano Urbanistico*, ed. Leonardo Benevolo, Laterza, Bari, 1996.

99 Pierluigi Cervellati, 'Venezia: Il nuovo Piano Urbanistico', *Domus*, 790 (1997), p. 116.

100 Ibid.

101 For the relevant catalogues see Germano Celant, *Dennis Oppenheim*, Ente Zona Industriale di Porta Marghera, Charta, Milan, 1997; Paolo Costantini and Gianfranco Mossello, *Venezia-Marghera: fotografie e trasformazioni*, Ente Zona Industriale di Porto Marghera, Charta, Milan, 1997.

102 Leonardo Benevolo, *Domus*, 795 (1998), p. 126.

103 Ibid., p. 126.

104 Meccoli, *Ponte della Libertà e altri scritti veneziani*, p. 229.

105 Alvise Zorzi, 'Italians, Fight Parliament Yourselves', *Art Newspaper* (February 1992). See also Zorzi's views with Meana, n. 45 above.

106 Roberto Balbaran, 'Carnevale, tra concensi e critichi', *Il Gazzettino* (22 February 1996).

107 See the 1998 International Laboratory of Architecture and Urban design focus: *The Edge of the Arsenal: L'intorno dell'Arsenale*, Editore Maggioli, Santarcangelo di Romagno, 1999.

108 'Architettura all'Arsenale: Cacciari scrive alla Marina', *Il Gazzettino* (15 July 1995).

109 Massimo Cacciari, 'Venice', ibid., pp. 10–11.

110 Rosanna Mavian, 'Alta technologia a Venezia', *Nexus*, n. xvii (January—February 1996), p. 2. Interview with director of Tecnomare, Domenico Lalli.

111 The countries include Slovenia, Croatia, Bosnia Herzegovina, Montenegro, Albania and Greece.

112 *Waterfronts: A New Urban Frontier*, ed. Centro Internazionale, Città d'Acqua, Venice, 1991.

113 *Art Newspaper* (December 1992), p. 1.

114 'Italian Senate votes 1.4 billion for Venice', *Art Newspaper* (17 April 1992).

115 Giuseppe de Rita, *Venezia: città speciale rapporto su Venezia*, Marsilio, Venice, 1993, pp. 22–3.

116 Ibid., pp. 41–2.

117 Ibid., p. 101.

118 Ibid.

119 'Venezia come polo della ricerca', pp. 56ff. Meccoli writes about the *pendolari* who make short-term use of the city.

120 De Rita, *Venezia: una Città speciale*, p. 101.

121 Ibid., p. 336.

122 Gianfranco Bettin, *Laguna Mondo: conversazione con Renzo Franzin*, Edicolo Editore, Portogruaro, 1997.

123 For example, Erik Cohen, 'A Phenomenology of Tourist Experiences', *Sociology*, 13 (1979), pp. 179–201.

124 Roberto Ballarin, 'Topolino, Mionni e Pippi arrivano in gondola', *Il Gazzettino* (31 May 1997). Roberta Brunetti, 'McDonald's si "mangia" la città', *Il Gazzetttino* (24 April 1997).

125 Richard Ingersoll, 'The International of the Tourist', *Casabella*, 631 (1996), p. 118. In this intelligent article, Venice is compared with Paris, with the latter's productive environment and development of tourist venues, but the cities are surely different, for Paris is after all a capital centre of magnitude within its own country, and Europe.

126 Consider Rolf Petri, 'Disneyland in der Lagune: Tourismus als Selbstentfremdung', *Venedig ein politisches Reisebuch*, ed. Rolf Petri, VSA, Hamburg, 1986, pp. 212–21.

127 'Italian Senate votes 1.4 billion for Venice while churches may close for lack of $40,000', *Art Newspaper* (17 April 1992).

128 Gregotti in preface to Leonardo Benevolo, 'Primi riflessioni sul Piano Regolatore', *Casabella*, 624 (1995), p. 43.

129 Ibid., and Vittorio Gregotti, *Venezia: città della nuova modernità*, Consorzio Venezia Nuova, 1998, p. 18.

130 Anna Somers Cockes, 'Sta Maria Miracoli Celebrates its Rebirth on Lepanto Day', *Art Newspaper*, 75 (November 1997), p. 4. See the list 'no longer in restauro', in Lidia Panzeri, 'How They Built in Venice Over 1000 Years', *Art Newspaper*, 69 (April 1997).

131 See *XXI Premio Pietro Torta per il Restauro di Venezia 1994*, Ateneo Veneto, 1994. In the 1980s see the comprehensive listing in *Twenty Years of Restoration in Venice*, Soprintendenza ai Beni Ambientali e Architettonici di Venezia, Venice, 1987, and the general account by Peter Lauritzen, *Venice Preserved*, Michael Joseph, London, 1986.

132 Roger Bevan, 'Guggenheim Expands with a New $1.3 Million Wing', *Art Newspaper*, 38 (May 1994), p. 15.

133 See 'Uno spazio espositivo museale alla Punta della Dogana (Museo Guggenheim)', *Venezia: la nuova architettura*, pp. 90–93.

134 FF. 'Sterilizziamo I piccioni', *Il Gazzettino* (1 July 1996).

135 Glaudio Pasgnaletto, 'Nella Basilica di San Marco, niente guide, visite limitate', *Il Gazzettino* (13 July 1995). Paolo Navarro, 'In Basilica di San Marco piccoli gruppi e silenziosi', *Il Gazzettino* (12 July 1995); 'Go Ahead for Super Museum around St Mark's Square', *Art Newspaper*, 59 (May 1996), p. 22. Fiorella Minervino, 'Rivoluzione di fine millennio in Piazza San Marco: dal Ducale al Correr un nuovo grande spazio d'arte', *Corriere della Sera* (11 May 1996).

136 Lidia Panzieri, 'Pavimento di vinile da ieri a S. Marco', *Il Gazzettino* (May 1994).

137 L.P. 'No Haste over Restoring St Mark Basilica', *Art Newspaper* (16 March 1992).

138 Targata Parigi, 'Supermuseum San Marco', *Corriere della Sera* (5 July 1995), p. 29.

139 'Burano. Difficoltà finanziarie. merletto, morta la cooperativa', *Il Gazzettino* (10 March 1996).

140 Giovanni Sarpellon, *Lino Tagliapietra*, Arsenale, Venice, 1994.

141 Attilia Dorigato and Dan Klein, *International New Glass*, Venezia Aperto Vetro, Arsenale, Venice, 1996.

142 See the biographical outline in *Chihuly*, essay by Donald Kuspit, Portland Press, Seattle, and Harry N. Abrams, New York, 1997.

143 Cf. Kuspit, 'The Venetians are decisive in our recognition of Chihuly as a fine artist', ibid., p. 32. Not surprisingly

Venice is Chihuly's 'favourite city on earth', see n. 33, p. 50.

144 Ibid., p. 47, n. 145.

145 46 Esposizione Internazionale d'Arte. La Biennale di Venezia: Jean Clair, Identity and Alterity, Figures of the Body, 1895–1995, Marsilio, Venice, 1995.

146 Giandomenico Romanelli, Venice and the Biennale, Itineraries of Taste, Fabbri, Monza, 1995, Barovier, Mentasi, Dorigato, Il Vetro di Murano alle Biennale, 1895–1972, Leonardo Arte, Milan, 1995. Romanelli's historical reconstructions of the Biennales go back to the 1970s and his history of installations. See also the substantial investigation that accompanied the 1988 competition for the Padiglione Italia: 'From the 'Pro Arte' Palazzo to the Italian Pavilion', Padiglione Italia 12 Progetti per la Biennale di Venezia, Electa, Milan, 1988.

147 See Enzo di Martini, La Biennale di Venezia, 1895–1995: cento anni di arte e cultura, Giorgio Mondadori, Milan, 1995, pp. 63ff.

148 Even if procedings were fraught; see Meccoli, 'Progetto della Fondazione "Biennale di Venezia"', Ponte della Libertà e altri scritti veneziani, pp. 265–9.

149 'La Biennale: una nuovo legge cent'anni dopo', Venezia 2000, pp. 127–37.

150 Giuseppe Tedesco, 'Biennale, occasione di rinascita', Il Gazzettino (11 June 1995), p. 1.

151 Narelle Jubelin, Trade Delivers People, with essay by Vivian Johnson, Aperto, La Biennale di Venezia, 1990.

152 See again Lidia Sciama, 'Lace-making in Venetian Culture', and on bead-trading, Trivellato, 'Out of Women's Hands: Notes on Venetian Glass Beads, Female Labour and International Trades', Dress and Gender: Making and Meaning in Cultural Contexts, ed. Ruth Barnes and Joanne B. Eicher, Berg, New York, Oxford, 1992, esp. pp. 65ff.

153 La Biennale di Venezia XLIV Esposizione Internazionale d'Arte, Fabbri, La Biennale, Venice, 1990, pp. 220–27, and Jennifer Holzer, The Venice Project, Albright Knox, Buffalo, 1991.

154 See Chapter 9 above.

155 Hans Haacke, 'Gondola! Gondola!', Bodenlos, Biennale Venedig, 1993, Cantz, Stuttgart, 1993, p. 27.

156 Ibid., p. 33.

157 XLV Esposizione Internazionale d'Arte, Punti Cardinale dell'Arte, Edizioni la Biennale, Marsilio, Venice, 1993, pp. 176–7.

158 Joseph Brodsky, Watermark, Hamish Hamilton, London, 1992.

159 Meccoli writes of the patronage in Ponte della Libertà e altri scritti veneziani, pp. 169–72.

160 Ibid., p. 12.

161 Ibid., p. 13.

162 Meccoli took exception to Brodsky's treatment of Ezra Pound, regarded as a foreigner assimilated into Venice, Il Ponte della Libertà e altri scritti veneziani, pp. 237–8. He refers to 'the stupendous' Night Litany.

163 Ibid., p. 75.

164 Ibid., p. 80.

165 Ibid., p. 97.

166 Ibid., p. 99.

167 His views are further expressed in La Corriere della Serra (1 March 1996): 'Venezia muore, l'ultima accusa di Brodskij'.

168 Donna Leon, Death at La Fenice, Harper Collins, New York, 1992; The Anonymous Venetian, Macmillan, London, 1994; Acqua Alta, Macmillan, London, 1996.

169 Robert Girardi, Vaporetto 13, Hodder & Stoughton, London, 1997. Indira Ghose deals well with 'The Mean Streets of Venice' (and Donna Leon), in 'Venice Confidential', Venetian Views: Venetian Blinds, English Fantasies of Venice, ed. Manfred Pfister and Barbara Shaff, Rodopi, Amsterdam, 1999, pp. 213–24.

170 Michael Dibdin, Dead Lagoon, Faber & Faber, London, 1994.

171 Michael Dibdin, Vendetta, Faber & Faber, London, 1990, and Cabal, Faber & Faber, London, 1992.

172 Robert Coover, Pinocchio in Venice, Heinemann, London, 1991. For an essay on the novel's intertextuality and Bakhtin's carnevalesque see Judith Seaboyer, 'Robert Coover's Pinocchio in Venice: An Anatomy of a Talking Book', Venetian Views: Venetian Blinds, English Fantasies of Venice, pp. 237–55.

173 Coover, Pinocchio in Venice, p. 202.

174 Ibid., p. 177.

175 Ibid., p. 185.

176 The Comfort of Strangers, directed by Paul Schrader with Christopher Walken, Rupert Everett, Helen Mirren, Manfredi Aliquo, 1990.

177 Harold Brodkey, Profane Friendship, Jonathan Cape, London, 1994.

178 Harold Brodkey, My Venice, gathers draft material for Profane Friendship, and other writings about Venice: Henry Holt, New York, 1998.

179 Ibid., p. 41.

180 Ibid., pp. 82–3.

181 Rod James, Night Pictures, Random House, Sydney, 1997.

182 Robert Dessaix, Night Thoughts: A Journey Through Switzerland and Italy, Pan MacMillan Australia, Sydney, 1996.

183 John Phillips, 'Death in Venice Inspires Trail of Tourist Suicides', The Times (October 1996).

184 Régis Debray, Contre Venise, Gallimard, Paris, 1995.

185 Ibid., p. 40.

186 Ibid., p. 52.

187 The Wings of a Dove, director Iain Softely, with Helena Bonham Carter, Linus Roach, Alison Elliot, 1997.

188 Tony Tanner, Venice Desired, Blackwell, Oxford, 1992.

189 Ibid., p. 9.

190 Ibid., p. 368.

191 Ibid., p. 245.

192 Ibid., p. 243.

193 Hugh Honour and John Fleming, The Venetian Hours of Henry James, Whistler and Sargent, Little, Brown & Company, Boston, Toronto and London, 1991, and John Pemble, Venice Rediscovered, Clarendon Press, Oxford, 1995.

194 Titian Prince of Painters, Marsilio, Venice, 1990.

195 The Glory of Venice: Art in the Eighteenth Century, ed. Jane Martineau and Andrew Robison, Yale University Press, New Haven and London, 1994. On the exhibition at Ca' Rezzonico see Art Newspaper, 44 (January 1994).

196 Elizabeth Vedrenne, photographs Andre Martin, Living in Venice, Thames & Hudson, London, 1990; Frédéric Vitous; Photography Jérôme Darblay, Venice: The Art of Living, Stewart, Tabori & Chang, New York, 1991 (originally Flammarion, Paris, 1990); Cesare M. Cunaccia, photography Mark E. Smith, Venice: Hidden Splendours, Flammarion, Paris, 1994.

197 Carole Lazarus and Jennifer Berman, Glorafilia: The Venice Collection, Twenty-five Original Projects in Needlepoint and Embroidery, Conran, Octopus, London, 1991.

198 Manfredo Tafuri, The Sphere and the Labyrinth: Avant-Gardes and Architecture from Piranesi to the 1970s, trans. Pellegrino d'Acierno and Robert Connolly, MIT, Cambridge, Mass., and London, 1978, p. 299.

199 Manfredo Tafuri, Ricerca del Rinascimento: principi, città, architetti, Einaudi, Turin, 1992.

200 'Capitolo Settimo, Epilogo lagunare. Jacopo Sansovino dall'inventio alla consuetudo', ibid., pp. 305ff.

201 Thus Tafuri describes Sansovino's task in Venice, introducing the new into the conservative, ibid., p. 305.

202 Jose Rafael Moneo, 'The Ricerca Legacy', Casabella, 619–20 (1995), Il progetto storico di Manfredo Tafuri/The Historical Project of Manfredo Tafuri, p. 141.

203 Massimo Cacciari, 'Quid tum'. Funeral oration delivered 25 February 1994 in the Tolentini cloister at the Istituto Universitario di Architettura in Venice', ibid., p. 169.

204 Elizabeth Crouzet-Pavan, Sopra le acque salse: Espaces, pouvoir et société à Venise, Ecole française de Rome, 2 vols, Rome, 1992.

205 Ibid., p. 293.

206 Cf. 'La tentative de défense d'un milieu fragile', ibid. vol. 1, pp. 307ff. 'L'eau menaçante', pp. 313ff.

207 Cf. Elisabeth Crouzet-Pavan, *La Morte lente de Torcello: Histoire d'une cité disparu*, Fayard, Paris, 1995. See also 'Venice and Torcello: History and Oblivion', *Society for Renaissance Studies*, 8 (1994), pp. 416–27.

208 Elizabeth Pavan, 'Imaginaire et politique: Venise et la mort à la fin du Moyen Age', *Espaces Urbains, société et religion*, 93 (1981), pp. 467–93.

209 Reported by 'Theophannes Brittanicus', for 20 November 1993, 'A Chronicle of Venice', *Art Newspaper*, 34 (January 1994), p. 23.

210 Mencini, 'La Fenice in cenere', *Venezia, acqua e fuoco*, pp. 107–9. Assessment of the causes of fire is beyond this study. Electrical problems unresolved in the last stages of the restoration have been discounted, since there appears to be more than one source of the fire, and the evidence of inflammable liquids. An act of terrorism was an early suspicion.

211 Silvio Testa, 'A una voce "Com'era e dov'era"', *Il Gazzettino* (Tuesday 30 January 1996), p. 2.

212 'A letter to The Art Newspaper from the Mayor of Venice over the Fenice', *Art Newspaper*, no. 57 (March 1996), p. 5.

213 Elena Bassi, *Giannantonio Selva: Architetto veneziano*, Leo S. Olschki, Florence, 1935, p. 57.

214 Maria Ida Biggi, 'It's Official: It Will Be an Old-style Fenice', *Art Newspaper*, no. 62 (September 1966). Survey of reactions compiled by Alessandro Allemandi and Benedetto Camerani.

215 Ibid.

216 On the conversion see 'Gae Aulenti, Antonio Foscari, Palazzo Grassi Venezia', *Domus*, 674 (1986), pp. 48–61.

217 Lidia Panzeri, 'La Fenice Theatre, Venice. In 823 days as it was, where it was', *Art Newspaper*, 73 (September 1997), p. 2.

218 Lionello Puppi, 'Venice, Forgery as Usual', *Art Newspaper*, no. 62 (September 1996), p. 28.

219 'Venice, Fenice Shambles', *Art Newspaper*, 79 (March 1998), p. 1.

220 Antonio Alberto Semi, *Venezia in fumo: 1797–1997*, Raffaello Cortina, Milan, 1996.

221 On the cult of bisexuality see ibid., p. 78; on the smiling, pp. 81ff., on the necropolis, pp. 92, and 97ff; for the demographic observations, p. 101.

222 Ibid., p. 98.

223 My account is based substantially on reports from *Il Gazzettino*, *La Corriere della Sera*, and Alvise Fontanella, *1997 Il Ritorno della Serenissima*, Editoria Universitaria, Venice, 1997. Giovanni Distefano and Giannantonio Paladini close their history of modern Venice with an account of the double catastrophe: 'Il rogo della Fenice e l'assalto al Campanile di S. Marco', *Storia del Venezia: 1797–1997*, vol. 3, *Dalla monarchia alla Repubblica*, Supernova-Grafiche Biesse, Venice, 1997, pp. 419–28.

224 Fontanella, *1997: il ritorno della Serenissima*, p. 17.

225 Ibid., p. 26.

226 Ibid., p. 47.

227 Ibid., p. 47.

228 Richard Owen, 'Padania Mania Ebbs', *The Times* (21 September 1996).

229 Fontanella, *1997: Il ritorno della Serenissima*, p. 185.

After Two Hundred Years

1 A. P. 'Ceremonia sull'isola di Sant'Andrea a 200 Anni dalla caduta della Serenissima', Raniero da Mosto. 'Duecento anni fa Venezia affrontò Napoleone', *Il Gazzettino* (20 April 1997).

2 *Il 1797 e il metamorfosi di Venezia, Da Capitale di Stato a Città del Mondo*, XXXVII Corso Internazionale di Alta Cultura, Fondazione Giorgio Cini, 2–14 Settembre 1996.

3 *Venezia e l'Austria*, Convegno Internazionale di Studi Storici, Fondazione Giorgio Cini, 28–31 October 1997.

4 *Dai Dogi agli Imperatori: la fine della Repubblica tra storia e mito*, Palazzo Ducale and Museo Correr, Electa, Milan, 1997.

5 *Venezia: da stato a mito*, Fondazione Giorgio Cini, Marsilio, Venice, 1997.

6 *Dopo la Serenissima*, Palazzo Loredano, Campo Santo Stefano, 27–27 November 1997.

7 *Lodovico Manin: io, l'ultimo Doge di Venezia*, Canal, Venice, 1997. Giuseppe Campolieti, 'Lodovico Manin, caduta con onore', *Il Gazzettino* (21 August 1997).

8 Alvise Zorzi, 'Venezia: Dominatrice cara al popolo', *Il Gazzettino* (26 November 1997), p. 23.

9 Gianfranco Mossetto, 'Benemerenze di Napoleone', *Il Gazzettino* (1 October 1997).

10 Cf. Hal Foster's remarks on the gaze – and indeed on the avant-garde at the end of the century – in *The Return of the Real: The Avantgarde at the End of the Century*, MIT, Cambridge, Mass., and London, 1996, p. 140.

11 Nicoletta Gazzoli, 'Librerie Filippi', *Nexus*, 19 (1996), p. 13.

12 Giles Whittell, 'The Strip Gambles on Fine Art', *The Times* (6 June 1998), p. 15.

13 Meccoli, *Ponte della Libertà e altri scritti veneziani*, p. 193.

14 There is little disagreement with the principle of sea-level rises, but estimates over the next one hundred years vary from 20cm to 50cm, according to the UN Intergovernmental Panel on Climate Change. Professor Edmund Penning-Rowsell of Middlesex University observes that on the latter estimate Venice would be flooded on average every day in 2050. Edmund Penning-Rowsell, 'Bearding the Lion in its Den: A New Proposal to Save Venice', *The Times* (25 April 1998), p. 22.

Photograph Credits

Index

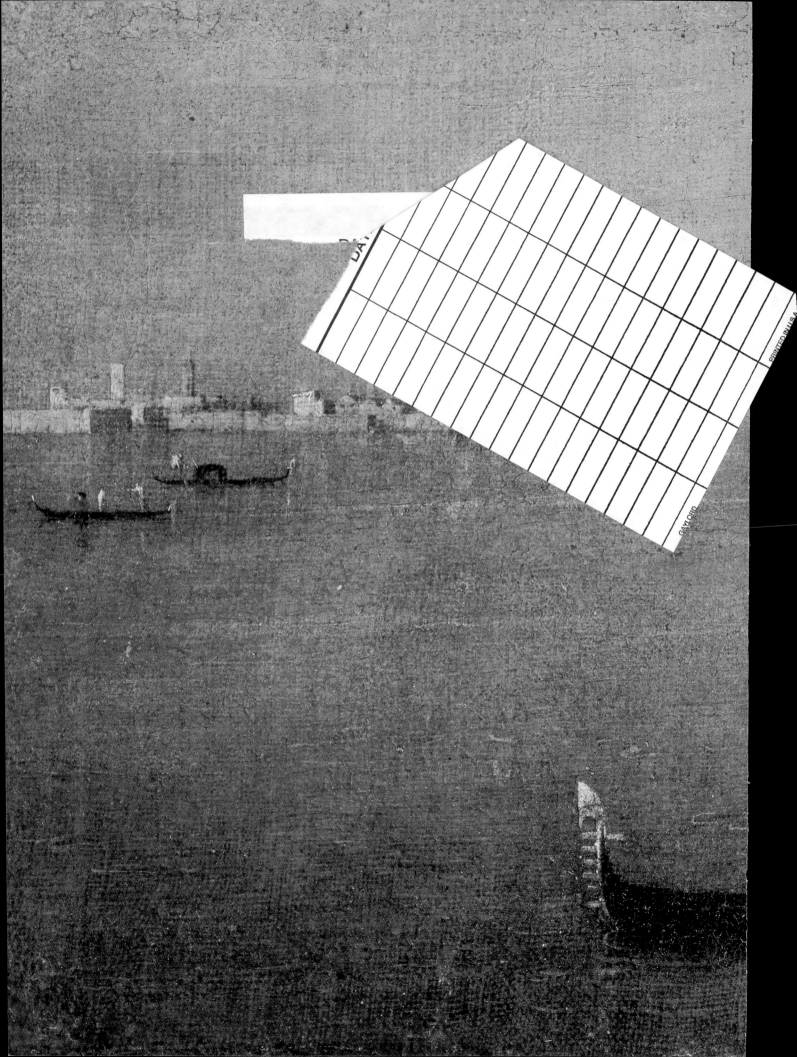